ENCYCLOPEDIA OF BRITISH FOOTBALL

PHIL SOAR

WILLOW BOOKS
Collins
8 Grafton Street, London W1

Editor: Peter Arnold
Art Editor: Gordon Robertson
Production: Richard Churchill

Artwork by Paul Buckle

Willow Books
William Collins Sons & Co Ltd London, Glasgow . Sydney . Auckland . Toronto . Johannesburg

First published 1974
This edition published 1987

British Library Cataloguing In Publications Data
Soar, Phil
  Encyclopaedia of British Football——
  5th ed.
  1. Soccer——Great Britain——Records
  1. Title
  796.334′0941   GV944.G7
  ISBN 0-00-218290-4

Typeset by MS Filmsetting Limited, Frome, Somerset
Printed and Bound in Italy by LEGO spA

Endpapers *Jan Molby, Liverpool's Great Dane, breaking through against Merseyside rivals Everton in the 1986 FA Cup final at Wembley.*
These pages *The 1986 Milk Cup final, with John Aldridge of winners Oxford United evading a tackle from Queen's Park Rangers' Steve Wicks. The following season Aldridge was with Liverpool, Wicks with Chelsea and the Cup had become the Littlewoods Cup.*

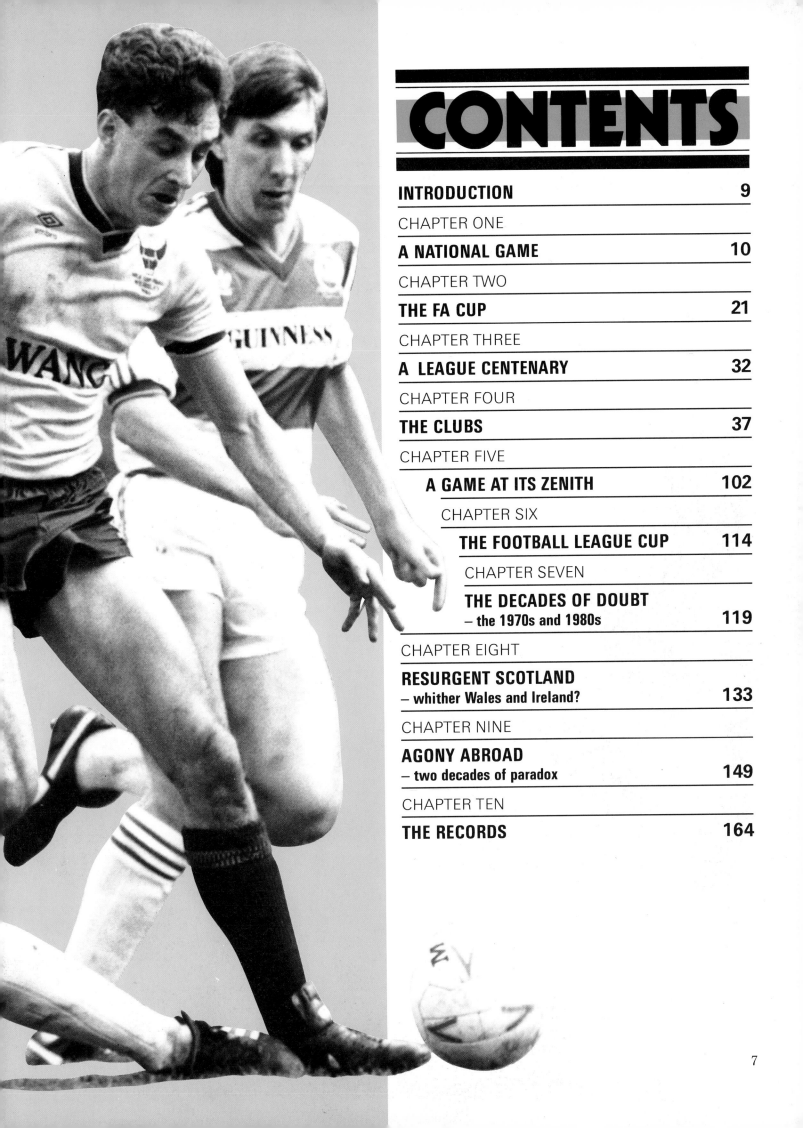

CONTENTS

Alex McLeish of Aberdeen with the Scottish FA Cup in 1986, after the 3–0 defeat of Hearts.

INTRODUCTION

As British football approaches the 1990s, the game is threatened from many sides, and is changing more rapidly than at any time since the 1890s when its pattern was largely established.

It is sad for football enthusiasts that two of the most important pictures in the new edition of this encyclopedia are of events off the field: the tragic fire at Valley Parade, the ground of Bradford City, and the terrible scenes on the terraces at the Heysel Stadium in Brussels, when British hooliganism achieved its ultimate depravity.

Both events, horrific in themselves, have a continuing impact on the very existence of the game, affecting attendances and, by extension, finances. Even before Bradford, the safety and facilities at football stadiums were under scrutiny, and many clubs had been forced to close sections of their grounds in order to comply with newly passed or enforced legislation. The days when spectators could be packed in, as in the great days of the late 1940s, could never return.

Of course in those days crowds were good-humoured, and the kind of organized hooliganism which is almost standard in parts of the crowd nowadays was completely absent. British football has had its tragedies before – 66 died at Ibrox Park as recently as 1971 – but there was a sinister difference at the Heysel. While the fact that people eventually died might have been accidental, the deaths were the consequence of the far from accidental behaviour of the hooligan element. It was the worst act of football vandalism so far. However, mini versions of the same sort of thing had become almost normal on many British grounds over the preceding years, and had had the effect of helping to reduce football's band of regular supporters. The half-committed fan found many more satisfying ways of spending Saturday afternoon than in the company of louts like these.

The effect of Heysel on the field was the banning of English clubs from European competition. This has helped to promote the traffic of players away from the Football League – not only the likes of Gary Lineker and Ian Rush to the Continent, but also players like Terry Butcher and Chris Woods to Scotland, where European football is still part of the season.

Yes – it is a changing time for British football. It is not all gloom. Everton supporters are among those who have seen their team play their best football for years. That millions watch the best games on television proves that the basic appeal remains. It will be many years before Wembley is big enough to hold all who want to watch the FA Cup final.

The glorious history of the British game and its facts and figures are more fascinating than ever in the light of the present developments. This encyclopedia, completely revised and updated, reflects it all, and we hope that it will add to the readers' enjoyment of the greatest of all sports.

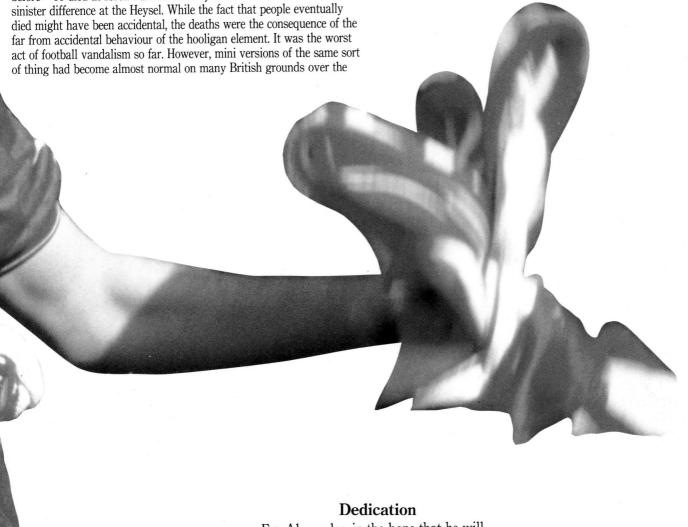

Dedication

For Alexander, in the hope that he will
one day see Nottingham Forest win the FA Cup.

CHAPTER ONE

A NATIONAL GAME

Football was invented in Britain, but then so were most other games which are played worldwide. Whether football is *the* national game is open to dispute; in Scotland it certainly is, in Wales certainly not. The claims of cricket are promoted by many in England, though few of those many ever go to watch a game. Cricket's claims are surely lessened by the peculiar, presumably unique, way that the national championship (called the county championship) is played out week after week in literally empty grounds. What other country supports a supposedly national game with such indifference? And what other game would nonetheless happily continue unabashed year after year?

Soccer's claims are greater; on a good weekend half a million will watch, and perhaps another million play. For a national game, nonetheless, it is ill-served by its literature, whereas cricket, baseball and even golf and rugby can easily fill a bookshelf. The real pre-eminence of soccer can be traced to the introduction of the Saturday half-day in the late 19th century. That created the opportunity for groups of working men to watch and play the games they cared about. And they chose soccer over all alternatives.

But, coming to the end of the 1980s, a full century after that seminal time, there were serious doubts about the future. Those doubts could best be illustrated in the simplest ways. In the September, October or November of 1986 a trip to Stamford Bridge would suffice. Theoretically second only to West Ham in London the previous season, Chelsea were now holding court to few more than 12,000 fans in that sombre, cavernous mausoleum of theirs.

The football tended to be poor, but that was not particularly significant. The ground was ringed by fences, making viewing difficult for anyone in the first eight or nine rows. A decade before there would have been advertising hoardings and no fences. Now there was much of the latter (but not electrified, as the club chairman had wished) but little of the former. Twenty years before, what hoardings there were on League grounds were charmingly local—garages, newspapers and the like. In two decades that small delight of the game had moved full circle, throwing out the parochial, encouraging the national, and fading back into what little was available. Few seemed to want to advertise anymore. The organisations which had been set up to promote such exposure and make money for the clubs had gone bankrupt. After all the fuss over shirt advertising four years before (whether it was to be allowed or not), a casual visitor to Stamford Bridge might be surprised to see the home side's shirts totally unadorned. Since the dramas of a night game against Sunderland eighteen months earlier there had been a distinct lack of enthusiasm for being quite so closely associated with Chelsea.

And, if you had decided you wanted to watch a different game on television that night, or on Sunday afternoon, you would probably have been unlucky. After two decades during which *Match of the Day* and *Sunday Soccer* had become institutions, part of every man's timetable and the bane of wives throughout the land, the screens had gone blank. An occasional live game (almost invariably and tediously featuring either Liverpool or Manchester United) might pop up, but mostly the screens took little notice of the national game. When there were just two channels, football was on both. Now there were four, broadcasting up to 18 hours a day each, there seemed no room at the inn. The Sunday live TV games (the only ones available to the public) had their own ironies. Only a decade before there had been two issues on which the football authorities seemed certain to stand firm—football was never played on a Sunday and live football was never to be shown, whatever day of the week. In 1987 Sunday was fine, live was fine and the League was even happy to change its kick-off times (to such oddities as 2.35 and 3.05) to accommodate the all-seeing eye.

Two years before the guess would have been that a shortage of football was because the clubs had denied the

The presence of the television cameras and numerous photographers, commentators and reporters for the final match of Bradford City's successful 1984–85 season meant that England's worst-ever football disaster was fully recorded for posterity. Fifty-six died and many more were injured as this tremendous fire enveloped the stand within seconds of its starting. It was the first of two great tragedies to colour British football in the mid-1980s.

television companies access. Indeed, they did so, led by Robert Maxwell in a particularly bad-tempered and staggeringly ill-timed way in 1985. But the eventual truth was that television had rejected football. It no longer attracted enough viewers or, more importantly to the independent companies, the right advertisers. It was no longer a guaranteed spot on any advertiser's schedule. Snooker, depressingly, was a far bigger draw, an entirely contrived televisual event. Even American Football could regularly draw three million viewers on a Sunday night, of whom only one in a thousand could ever have seen a game live. And if you had wanted to watch a European soccer game, the real quality? Then highlights from Barcelona versus Juventus were available, or even Rangers and Celtic matches. But of the mere English, nothing at all on a Wednesday night until the later stages of the cup competitions.

Soccer was tired, unappealing and no longer entirely acceptable. What had happened in less than ten years, arguably less than five? Various strands had to come together to induce the remarkable sight of the football authorities begging the television companies for exposure (when three years before the usual line had been that television was destroying football) but they can be summarised, at the end, in the names of two cities—Bradford and Brussels.

In May 1985 those two places, in their own very different ways, hosted spectacles that were effectively to bring to an end the post-war history of English football. Their ripples would be felt to the end of the century, probably beyond. It was an absurd understatement to say they caused football history to be rewritten. They *were* football history, key events that would dominate the game for decades. After May 1985, it could never again be the same sport, nor did it desire to be.

Bradford came first. An attractive Yorkshire woollen town, once the home of the merchants and money makers when the north of England was the richest place on earth, it had seen little football success in sixty years. Its second club, Park Avenue, had folded with a crash in 1970. But in May 1985 Bradford City were celebrating their promotion, under manager Trevor Cherry, to the Second Division. Their final home game of the season was against Lincoln City. It was a fine occasion, almost out of the history books. A cheerful crowd of 11,076, absolutely no trouble, a well behaved opposition in Lincoln City. Because of Bradford's promotion, there were even television cameras present, the first time in years they had appeared at Valley Parade. It was perhaps the sheer chance of the presence of the cameras which, more than anything else, was to give the event the significance it attained. 'Fifty dead in soccer fire' is a terrible headline. But seeing it happen, people literally on fire, time after time in your own front room is much more searing.

Just before half-time it is likely that an entirely innocent event, one which is duplicated ten thousand times a week, started the chain reaction. A cigarette was stubbed into a plastic cup. They dropped down a hole between the old

Right The culmination of many years of loutish behaviour by British football supporters on the continent: the emergency services beginning to deal with catastrophe sparked off by so-called Liverpool fans who could not resist attacking Juventus fans at the Heysel Stadium, Brussels, before the European Cup Final of 1985. The appeal on the notice board would mean nothing to the instigators of such brutality.

Above A new trend in British football in the 1980s, forced on certain clubs by the hooligan element. Luton Town fans at the 'members' turnstiles, requiring a member's card to get in.

wooden floorboards; the cigarette was not quite out. Beneath the stand was an accumulation of rubbish. It caught fire. Within sixty seconds the whole stand was alight. Fifty-six died. It was the worst soccer disaster ever in England. Only the Ibrox disaster of 1971 surpassed it in the United Kingdom. The club had been warned that the old wooden stand was a fire risk. But because Bradford were still in the Third Division they did not yet come under the stringent safety rules that applied to First and Second Division clubs. Within three months, of course, they would have done so.

There was much beating of chests, the searching out of scapegoats. The government immediately imposed further safety measures which, combined with attempts to completely segregate opposing fans, made it almost impossible to get into some grounds at all, short of SAS training or pre-booked season tickets. Clubs like Crystal Palace, Luton and Blackpool to all intents and purposes kept casual visitors away altogether.

Government policy, in a particularly remote way, was by no means blameless in the affair in the first place. There was no doubt at all that many grounds had decayed beyond the point that they should have been regarded as public stadia. Despite the building of impressive new structures on a few grounds (notably Chelsea, Wolves, Forest, Rangers, Ipswich and Spurs) most clubs had little hope of really significant improvements. And, of the ones mentioned above, Chelsea,

Wolves and Ipswich were all to suffer major problems in absorbing the cost of what they had done. In Chelsea's case, their magnificent but desperately ill-timed West Stand (still, in real terms, the most expensive stand ever built on an English ground) effectively bankrupted the club and the Londoners were the first of many to feel the eager breath of the receiver.

One major reason for these problems was simply the tax structure. The cost of a new player could be deducted from profits for tax purposes, a new stand could not. When corporation tax was at 50 per cent this meant, very simply, that a million-pound player really cost £500,000 to a profitable club, but a million pounds spent on a stand really did amount to a million pounds. It was one strong reason for buying a player at the end of a successful season, and not improving the ground. One could blame the men who made those decisions, but the government's sudden interest smacked of hypocrisy on this score alone.

It was just three weeks after Bradford that the second, even more shocking, of the two disasters was to occur. Liverpool were the holders of the European Cup. They were unquestionably the best club side in Europe, probably the world, now dominating the competition like no other side since Real Madrid in the less competitive heyday of the 1950s.

In the eight years since their first final appearance in 1977, Liverpool had won the trophy on four occasions, had never lost a final, and were now in their fifth European Cup final in nine seasons. Only their home-based compatriots, Forest and Villa, plus SV Hamburg in 1983, had managed to keep the competition at all open.

Liverpool's opponents on 29 May 1985, in the Heysel Stadium, Brussels, were mighty Juventus of Turin. A year before they had won the Cup Winners Cup; in 1983 they had lost 1–0 to Hamburg in the European Cup final. These two were clearly the best teams of their age.

But nothing that happened on the field that night (Juventus won 1–0 with an erroneously awarded penalty) was of any relevance. Fans in the Heysel had not been particularly well segregated. At the Liverpool end were large numbers of Italian supporters who had bought their tickets in Brussels (Belgium has a large Italian community). The police were notable for their absence and the usual taunting began. It spilled over, initially, into the sort of violence that had become all too familiar to British clubs over the years. Even on the day of the Bradford disaster, an innocent fan had been killed at St Andrews when Leeds fans had pushed over a wall. His was not the first death—there had been others at Huddersfield, Coventry, Middlesbrough and in South London. It was not even front page news anymore. British fans abroad, starting really with the Leeds riot in Paris in 1974, followed by Spurs fans in Rotterdam and going on to the disgraces of Turin in 1980, Basel in 1981 and then simply everywhere England travelled, were equally culpable, but police forces in Europe were generally less geared to dealing with the problem.

That was certainly true in Brussels, though there should have been more than enough warning. The taunting turned into fighting at the fringes; then, as the fans were not segregated and the fences were flimsy, Liverpool fans brust through into the Juventus areas. In England that would probably have been that. A certain amount of skirmishing, perhaps a few minor injuries, and the police quickly on the scene. But here in Brussels, the generally law-abiding Italians, who had largely been blameless, were not expecting this assault, nor knew how to deal with it. So they moved away, some ran from the Liverpudlians, and the result was that those furthest from the trouble suffered worst. They were crushed into a corner, a wall collapsed, and thirty-nine were dead in an instant.

It was the culmination of two decades of rapidly declining standards. When Spurs won the Double in 1961 there were no fences, no fighting, no obscene chanting, barely any swearing to speak of. In twenty years football had become home from home for armed camps and animals. The first question was why? The reasons cannot possibly be simple, but they are available. Firstly the problem is not football's. Football just happens to provide a very convenient and anonymous means of expressing the downward trends of an increasingly depressed society. In 1961 a seventeen-year-old youth identified with his team or country but had no apparent need to fight publicly for it; in 1987 a significant section of British youth appears to feel the need to make a public statement which involves violence. Perhaps the most interesting aspect of the violence which follows England trips abroad is that the guilty literally still do not understand the nature of, nor the reactions to, their excesses. There is still a belief that they are somehow 'doing their bit for England', fighting where others don't. The moral debates of *News at Ten* or the *Daily Telegraph* are really not relevant or heard by the underclass of the terraces of Stamford Bridge and Elland Road.

Television has had a critical part to play (not of itself as a medium, nor as a reflection of those working there) in the way that British society has swung round somehow to believe in the pre-eminence of the television eye, to acknowledge this as the only apparent significance, to, in Clive James's words: 'Become a society where the ultimate goal of everyone seems to be no more and no less than simply to appear on television.'

Crowd invasions of the pitch in England were virtually unknown until a famous fifth round tie between Leeds and Sunderland in 1967. The match was televised, the invasion was shown and, while they were not weekly affairs, suddenly imitative crowd invasions were no longer that unusual. On a different level, the almost comical way in which television disseminated chants (so that, within two weeks of Liverpool never walking alone, teams from Plymouth to Carlisle were also happily strolling among thousands) was a depressing sign of the decline of real provincialism and independence. One of the glories of the game had been that the Pompey Chimes, Norwich's 'On the Ball, City' or even 'Glory, Glory Hallelujah' had been unique.

Television glorified all aspects of football, the good and the bad. There was simply no way that television commentators, government ministers, social workers or football club chairmen, all middle-ground, middle-class figures, could place themselves in the position of a seventeen-year-old unemployed gas fitter with no O-levels from a council estate in Ilford, Kirkby or Moss Side. The cultures didn't meet, didn't even touch; what seemed important to the denizens of the terraces was totally incomprehensible to the people purporting to try and solve the problem.

After Brussels, UEFA had little choice. It seemed a little unfair on Liverpool, who were a well-run club and who had rightly enjoyed an excellent record of behaviour in the first ten years of their great era (1964–74), but they were understandably banned from all European competition for at least one footballing generation. All English clubs were banned until further notice, and Liverpool were to be banned for three years beyond that date. Effectively all fixtures involving English sides against non-English opposition (including the Scots) were eliminated, with the sole exception of the national side, which was allowed to continue though under intense scrutiny. It was the very least UEFA could do, and it was a great pity that it had not been done much earlier. The ban did not apply to Welsh, Irish or Scots clubs.

In England the debate raged, not helped by uninformed interventions from the government, almost entirely composed of men (and women) who admitted to never having been near a soccer match in their lives (and, hence, a very good cameo illustration of the nature of the problem). Why Liverpool should spark the disaster was a good question, though in truth it was a disaster waiting for somewhere to happen. The Ulster question, relevant to Liverpool, was obviously a factor. The constant repetition, night after night, on British television screens of violent scenes in Ulster, of petrol bombs, rubber bullets, another soldier shot, a firebombing here, a cold-blooded massacre there, had affected the psyche of the mainland, not just Ireland. When 'Fire on the Mersey' became a national issue after the 1981 Toxteth riots (again, why Liverpool first?) it should have been clear that so much of the violence, its style and its development, was imitative of what had been seen nightly on television for a dozen years from Belfast. It was easy to forget that, by 1985, a whole generation had grown up, and was breeding its own children, and had

A 1980s sign of good marketing of the game, or a sell-out of its dignity? After much discussion on shirt advertising, the League itself was 'sold'—first to Canon, and then, for the 1986–87 season, to the Today newspaper. The League president, Philip Carter (left) and Today managing director, Terry Cassidy, signing the contract which they hoped, foolishly, would lead the fans to think of something called 'The Today League'.

13

never seen anything of Northern Ireland but nightly violence. And to whom that very violence had been a constant feature of their nightly television diet.

The Falklands War, 'The Empire Strikes Back', probably exacerbated this in 1982. It was an excuse for much macho nonsense which was a consolation in a society slowly but surely slipping away—in its wealth, its standards, its own beliefs. It encouraged a sort of glorification of nationalistic violence which was to be seen only too clearly on England's journeying abroad. It was almost Brechtian in its ironies.

A large number of strands came together in 1985 and 1986, though they did not lead to any obviously coherent philosophy or set of solutions. These strands involved a long-awaited reduction in the number of fixtures, a recognition that the League was too large, the loss of television support, the effects of the loss of European competition, the debate about hooliganism and the continuing decline in attendances. In a sense it was the latter that was the biggest trigger, because it meant money. In 1949–50 over 40 million people watched Football League matches, in 1985–86 that figure was down to a mere 16 million and still falling precipitously off a cliff. Since 1976–77 attendances had fallen dramatically from 26 million to 16 million. Looking back, it is clear that 1980 was the great break point, with Bradford and Brussels offering a mighty push to a stone already rolling downhill fast in 1985. For nearly twenty years, football had been declining into the marginality associated with other Victorian products.

As *ICC Business Ratios* said in a recent book about football club finances: '... clubs continue to behave like corner shops threatened by supermarkets, who continue to believe that they can run a viable service and tinker with their products, only to turn round and discover that their customers have deserted them, their shops are empty.'

The customers have gone to television, to snooker, to DIY centres, to American Football, even to play with the kids. Many do not care anymore and it is absurd to suggest that there can possibly be a first-class structure supporting 92 clubs in the year 2000. By 1985 the big clubs, bluffing a Super League and worse, persuaded their smaller brothers that the game was up. They demanded, and got, a larger slice of the cake. Unfortunately, the cake was so fast in decline that they would only end up with the same, if not less, in real pound coins. In the space of 24 months, Bristol City, Wolves, Charlton, Middlesbrough, Swansea and Halifax all found themselves in various forms of bankruptcy or receivership, and many more came close.

At long last moves were made to reduce the ridiculous number of games the top clubs play each season—in 1979–80 Arsenal, who reached the FA Cup final and the European Cup Winners Cup final, played no less than 70 first-class fixtures. The First Division was to be gradually reduced to 20 clubs over three years (via a complex system of play-offs at season's end) and, with the lack of European fixtures, this would afford considerable and long-awaited relief as well as add interest at the end of the season.

Sadly, several chairmen immediately began to undo much of the good by trying to invent even more utterly pointless, irrelevant and embarrassing competitions to fill the holes. The ScreenSport Super Cup, sponsored by a cable sports programme, was created for those teams who were not allowed to enter European competition (one or two of whom, led by Manchester United, foolishly tried to take legal action against the FA and UEFA for excluding them) and, even more embarrassing, the ludicrously named Full Members Cup was created for First and Second Division clubs. Though attendances at some games struggled to reach four figures, the first

May 1985 was a terrible month for football. There was a death at St Andrews, Birmingham, when fans rioted during the Birmingham City versus Leeds United match. One target of the fans, as seen here, is the police, suggesting that a broad antagonism to 'law and order' drives the hooligans rather than any purely footballing motives.

final (between Chelsea and Manchester City) was attended by nearly 60,000 trophy-starved supporters and the event was deemed a 'success'. Chelsea won 5–4, having been 5–1 ahead five minutes from time. The competition remained the Full Members Cup in the absence, understandably, of anyone wishing to sponsor it. Attendances at most games were literally comical. They could not have covered the cost of the turnstile staff. When Charlton, a First Division club, played Birmingham on 4 November 1986, they did so before exactly 821 persons. By 1987 there was some reason to hope that these nonsensical events, created solely to promote extra cash for the clubs, would die a rapid and natural death.

The football calendar had still not really absorbed the arrival of the Football League, later Milk, now Littlewoods, Cup, the main effect of which, in the long term, seemed simply to detract from the real, FA Cup, final at Wembley. The Football League seemed addicted to changing the name of its competitions, presumably not stopping to think by how much they were thus devalued. While the League Cup went from Milk to Littlewoods, the League itself changed from Football League to Canon League to Today League. Tomorrow is anyone's guess. The League's sponsorship with Canon was at least credible because the product had been attempting to establish its name and because it meant the League was associated with a quality brand. The case with Today— which supposedly committed £5 million to the League over three years—was different. A newspaper which had suffered a disastrous launch, the sponsor was already something of a commercial embarrassment, selling no more than 300,000 per day. The question had to be: would it survive the full three-year period? In many ways, the League had found a sponsor which perfectly mirrored its own problems.

Happily few took these names seriously, except the sponsors, and presumably they had some idea why they were spending their money so strangely. The League also tried to introduce a British Cup, involving the top Scottish clubs and (presumably) the likes of mighty Coleraine and Newport County. The timing was poor. The Scots had increased their fixture list to 44 games for two seasons and had little to gain by playing English sides. They still had Europe.

The effects of the European ban were soon to take serious and clinical effect. The most obvious were the loss of cash and players. The cash was particularly large to the likes of Liverpool and Spurs, but the loss of players was probably more serious. In the World Cup summer of 1986, the three most exciting strikers in the English game were all purchased by European clubs. Ian Rush, the golden boy and best of them all, went for £3 million to Juventus (though he played with Liverpool on loan for another season), Mark Hughes went to Barcelona from Manchester United for £2 million and Gary Lineker, scorer of 40 goals the season before, and top scorer in the World Cup, also went to Barcelona from Everton for £2.75 million. The country's three leading clubs had each lost their main draw. This could not have anything but a negative effect on the game, the crowds, the atmosphere. It was exactly what the Scots had been complaining about for decades.

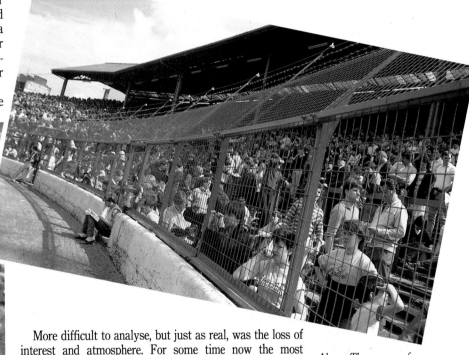

More difficult to analyse, but just as real, was the loss of interest and atmosphere. For some time now the most significant thing about winning the League was that it gave entry to Europe. Winning the European Cup was the great prize—as Liverpool, Forest, Villa and United had so dramatically shown. Now that excitement was lost. In an era when football was rapidly eliminating borders, the Football League was forced back inside its own domestic confines, and these confines were found sorely wanting.

For clubs like Norwich or Southampton, who could not realistically hope to win the League, the loss of the UEFA Cup places was particularly tragic. That was much of the justification for striving to finish fourth or fifth in the League. Without that incentive, and, following, let's say for example, a third round defeat at Highbury in the FA Cup, there had to be question marks about what they were playing for or why their fans should turn up. The ban seemed unfair on clubs of that size, as well as Nottingham Forest, Leicester, Newcastle and the like, for they bore little if any of the blame of the past

Above *The answer of Chelsea chairman Ken Bates to the mid-1980s wave of terrace violence was to instal electric fencing at Stamford Bridge, but it was ruled unlawful.*

twenty years and yet they suffered just as much as the guilty: Liverpool, Chelsea, Manchester United, Millwall, Spurs and, above all others, Leeds United.

The internal reaction of the League and FA to the whole question of violence and hooliganism was, at best, confused. It came to a head in the Luton Town affair of October 1986.

Luton are and were a small club which had done well, under David Pleat, to dip in and out of the First Division in the previous decade. They had never won anything, nor looked likely to do so, since an FA Cup final appearance in 1959.

Theirs was a small, cramped ground, holding only 16,000 at most. It was particularly peculiar in being almost completely surrounded by tight, terraced housing, which tended to suffer on the odd occasions that other clubs brought their hooligan element. Luton had no apparent homegrown violence of their own. On 13 March 1985 Luton had played Millwall in an FA Cup quarter-final and won 1–0. At the end of the game, a few hundred Millwall fans had effectively started a riot. They did not seem to be attacking the Luton fans, but rather the police, who were bombarded with seats ripped from the stands. It was a vicious, unprovoked attack, though one which should not have surprised anyone who had followed the disgraceful track record at The Den, a ground closed more often for misbehaviour than any other in the country.

The scenes were televised and provoked great disquiet, though Luton were basically regarded as blameless. This was the first of the four incidents which created a growing sense of unease through the Spring of 1985, and which culminated in Brussels. The second incident was certainly more serious than that at Luton, but because it did not happen in front of network television cameras (and because Chelsea refused to release their own film of the various incidents) it did not enter folklore in the same way. The occasion was the second leg of a Milk Cup semi-final between Chelsea and Sunderland at Stamford Bridge. Chelsea had lost the first leg at Roker 2–0 but their fans were still strangely confident of their going through to Wembley. They had experienced a roller coaster ride to this stage, at one point coming back from a 0–3 deficit at Hillsborough to draw 4–4, and many at the Bridge had convinced themselves that their day had come at last.

Sunderland felt otherwise. They went into a deserved 2–1 lead through goals from Clive Walker, who had previously been a Chelsea player. The rumbling from the stands became ominous. Stamford Bridge already boasted seven foot high fences but it was less well protected on the Main Stand side, where trouble could hardly have been predicted to begin. But begin there it did. Dozens of seats were ripped out and thrown onto the pitch. An intense frustration gripped the ground. Chelsea were to be denied their trip to Wembley. A small number of fans invaded the pitch. Several policemen ran on to arrest them. The Chelsea players understandably stopped. Sunderland half-heartedly knocked the ball downfield to Colin West, unguarded in a Chelsea penalty area shared by one goalkeeper, three policemen and a fleeing fan. West casually put the ball in the net and, to the amazement of all, the referee allowed the goal. Chelsea were 1–3 down, and out (the final result was 2–3). Pandemonium ensued.

The incident was more serious than that at Luton because the ground was packed and more people were involved. It was a clear instance of fans trying to intimidate and trying to get a game stopped because their team was losing, whereas at Luton the violence had been far more random. It was not the first time fans had tried to stop a game because their team was behind—it had happened at Old Trafford in 1974 when Denis Law and Manchester City put United into the Second Division

(Law had been a United player), and it had happened at least twice at Leeds. The game at Chelsea was the one which should really have set the alarm bells ringing.

Soon afterwards came the death at St Andrews and, finally, Brussels. But, returning to Luton, that small club had decided to try something specific rather than keep mouthing the usual platitudes. Taking a line from the government, they introduced a .membership card scheme and banned away supporters. Only local, card-carrying members would forthwith be admitted to home games. The FA, and in particular Ted Croker, were commendably relaxed about the scheme and approved it. The League Management Committee mumbled but did nothing until Luton were drawn to play Cardiff in the League/Milk/Littlewoods Cup. The rules of that competition allow for the visiting club to receive 25 per cent of the seats. Though the FA had said they probably would not apply any similar rule in the FA Cup, the League insisted that Luton comply this time. Luton refused, the League put the matter to a vote of the clubs and Luton lost by 81 to 6 with five abstentions. Luton refused to play the game elsewhere (as a somewhat peculiar matter of principle) and were ejected from the competition.

There were numerous side issues. The Luton chairman was a prospective parliamentary candidate for the Tories and it would be naive to pretend the matter did not have political undertones. The government went over the top and demanded that all clubs draw up proposals for membership schemes within six weeks. It was not clear whether this edict had the force of law.

Nonetheless, it was difficult to see why the League had reacted quite so crassly. Luton were clearly an exceptional case—a small club, with a particularly difficult ground loca-

The early forerunners of modern-day matches were timeless brawls between neighbouring parishes or villages; this is a representation of one around the 15th century. The term 'Derby' comes from an annual match played in that town between the parishes of St Peter's and All Saints and last contested on Shrove Tuesday 1846.

television still showed little interest in highlights and barely any more in Sunday afternoon fare. The fans continued to vote with their feet, generally left comfortably at home in carpet slippers. A welcome four per cent increase in gates in 1987 was hailed as a turning point; it wasn't, of course, just a slight adjustment to the massive falls in 1985 and 1986.

It was a situation that could never have been envisaged twenty years before as Spurs won the Double, Ipswich surprised the League and Manchester United and Celtic took the European Cup in consecutive seasons. It was a situation that would have seemed even odder to the public schoolboys of Charterhouse, Harrow, Rugby and Winchester who founded the game one hundred years before that.

Initially, each school had its own rules. While boys were still at school, the fact that they played to a strange set of rules hardly mattered. When, however, they left for the universities or for business in the provinces, it became clear that if they were to continue playing football they were going to need a universal set of rules, acceptable to all teams. Up until the 1850s, two teams at, say, Oxford, would only be playing on familiar ground if every player had been to the same school; as things turned out, a major game was often preceded by a long correspondence and lengthy argument about the conventions. Was handling to be allowed? How many players on each side? How long should the pitch be? How wide the goals? Would carrying the ball be permitted? ('Yes', would say all the Old Rugbeians; 'No', would say almost everyone else.) And even when the game got under way, confusion and protests would necessitate long midfield conferences between the two captains.

In time it became usual for the Rugby men, and their small but growing company of followers from other schools, to play on their own, and for the others, from Westminster, Charterhouse, Shrewsbury, Harrow and so on, to come to some compromise over the rules of the 'dribbling' game.

Few of these early codes of rules have come down to us intact, but snatches from them give a clear idea of the patterns of the early game, and in particular how boring it must have been to stand in the cold and watch.

In almost every case the game was won or lost (if indeed any goals at all were scored in the one, or two, or three afternoons laid aside for it) in the interminable, seething scrimmage. The aim of the game was, by dint of skilful footwork, to dribble the ball solo through the opposing team, who would all gang up in a scrum to defend. If one man was tackled (and tackling was usually unceremonious and often brutal), another would gather the ball and perform his own solo run until possession was lost and the opposition forwards started the same process in reverse.

The first serious attempts at laying down the rules of football went some way to improving it as a spectacle. In 1848, at Cambridge, 14 men representing Eton, Harrow, Winchester, Rugby and various other public schools, after a seven-hour session, produced the so-called 'Cambridge Rules'—rules that were adapted and tightened up twice in the 1850s.

Goals were awarded for balls kicked between the flag posts and under the string; goal kicks and throw-ins were given much as today (though throw-ins, taken with one hand only, might travel as far as a kick); catching the ball direct from the foot was allowed, provided the catcher kicked it immediately (no running with the ball, despite that delegate from Rugby); and there was a much more workable offside law—a man could play a ball passed to him from behind, so long as there were *three* opponents between him and the goal.

The game was now established on a common foundation. Competition was possible, and winning became important. By

tion which had suffered from one of the worst incidents in recent years. Their taking this step had no obvious longer term implications. It did not imply that everyone should do the same, just as QPR's installation of a plastic pitch suited their circumstances. Indeed, by letting the matter go quietly, the League could have avoided the outside pressure that subsequently grew. Surely in a League of 92 clubs, there was room for one like Luton to try such an experiment.

Many other clubs, particularly in London, were worried about the principle. The received wisdom, correct or otherwise, was that if only card-holders could get into grounds there would be a dramatic effect on casual and away support. The top London clubs would probably lose a quarter of their gates, and a higher percentage for the big games. But the action they had taken seemed more likely than not to bring about the very thing they claimed to want to avoid. At some point the clubs would be forced into some step which they still considered too extreme. Why had the simple expulsion of the likes of Millwall and Leeds United not been considered? Would the world really be a much worse place without Leeds, arch-cynics of the 1960s and their followers, arch-thugs of the 1980s. It was they, in the Revie era, who introduced so much of the cynicism into the English game. The hooligans would go elsewhere, we are told. Well, would they? And does not something have to be tried—or perhaps there will not be much left to salvage? Gates of 12,000 at Stamford Bridge, 20,000 at White Hart Lane, 15,000 at the City Ground when Forest are top of the First Division do not exactly leave a lot of fat on the calf.

So the 1987–88 season could be described, at best, as a time of uncertainty. The English clubs were still not back in Europe (though Wrexham, of the Fourth Division, were),

1855 rules like these were the basis of inter-university matches, and the legendary inter-school matches of public school fiction had begun to blossom.

Amid all this activity in the leisurely atmosphere of the universities and the public schools there emerged, almost out of the blue, the first recognizable 'football club'.

The old, hard, ruthless town football had been played in Sheffield for many years, but sometime in 1854 or 1855 (though the oldest existing rulebook is dated 1857), after Sheffield Cricket Club had inaugurated a new ground at Bramall Lane, one of the cricketers—William Prest—and some friends from the Collegiate School in Sheffield formed the Sheffield Football Club.

They wrote a constitution and a set of rules (not unlike the Cambridge Rules, though a bit rougher—pushing with the hands was allowed) and specified that every member should have two caps—one red, one dark blue—to distinguish the teams in games played among themselves.

This small band of old school acquaintances, with no apparent encouragement from the gentlemanly scholars from 'down South', had laid the foundations of football in the North of England. Within five years there were 15 different clubs in the Sheffield area, and an 1861 match between the great local rivals, Sheffield and Hallam, drew a gate of 600 spectators. (Seventy-five years later, at the same Bramall Lane, Sheffield United crammed in 68,000-plus for a Cup-tie.)

Meanwhile, back among the law-makers, rules and regulations were being hammered out, published, revised, re-negotiated and re-published in a thoroughly confusing burst of activity. At Uppingham School in Rutland, where football was distinguished by an enormously wide goal (with, incidentally, a cross-bar rather than tapes between the posts), another great Victorian educationalist, J. C. Thring, issued the rules for what he called *The Simplest Game*. They were indeed very simple, and provided a very straightforward game—no violence, no kicking at the ball in the air, nobody allowed in front of the ball, etc. They were unadventurous, but they provoked great interest, and a number of schools agreed to adopt them.

And at Cambridge, things were moving again. The rules

for a match between Cambridge Old Etonians and Cambridge Old Harrovians, in November 1862, specified 11-a-side, an umpire from each side plus a neutral referee, goals 12ft across and up to 20ft high, an hour and a quarter's play only, and the three-man offside rule. These rules were said to have worked well; in the following year they formed a vital part of the revised Cambridge Rules and, in the following months, those of the newly formed Football Association.

In the month of October 1863 football, in the South at least, came of age. The eager young gentlemen of Cambridge University issued their definitive set of rules, but almost at once the control of the game passed from the scholars to the clubs, where it has remained ever since.

The formation of the Football Association was bitter and often ill-tempered, and a certain stubbornness on both sides ensured that the split between the Rugby code and the dribbling code became too wide ever to be mended. The real divergence was not over running with the ball, but over 'hacking'. Rugby men felt it was manly and courageous to tackle an opponent by kicking him on the shin; the dribbling men did not, and voted it out. The Rugby men called the dribbling men cowards, and walked out of the Football Association for ever.

In 1863, football was still far from the game we know today. Every player was still allowed to handle the ball, and when he caught it he could 'make a mark' and so win a free kick; there was, in the first FA laws, a 'touch-down' rule, allowing a free kick at goal after a ball had been kicked over the opposing goal line and touched down (the Rugby 'try', in fact); there was still disagreement over offside, and the FA started off with the Rugby-style 'no one interfering with play in front of the ball' rule.

By 1863, enough clubs and individuals had become enthusiastic about the game for some of them to arrange a meeting to discuss the possibility of a single set of rules. They eventually came together on 26 October 1863.

In a sense, the most interesting thing about that meeting in the Freemasons' Tavern, Great Queen Street, Holborn, was not the teams that were represented but those that were not. There was, for instance, no one from the main provincial

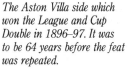

The Aston Villa side which won the League and Cup Double in 1896–97. It was to be 64 years before the feat was repeated.

centres of the game—Sheffield, Glasgow and Nottingham—nor, more surprisingly, from Cambridge, where the first formal laws had been drawn up in 1848. As a result it was 20 years before the whole country accepted uniform procedures.

The thirteen laws that were eventually approved are indicative of the origins of the men who drew them up. They were, basically, the laws of the game as played at Harrow and by the teams of Harrovian Old Boys—particularly No Names (of Kilburn) and Forest School, who became the famous Wanderers in 1864.

The Blackheath Club, which played to the rules of the game at Rugby, had broken away by the end of 1863, though that alternative game did leave behind it one significant innovation—the more precise name for its competitor. The story may not be true, but one Charles Wreford-Brown, who later became a notable official of the FA, was asked by some friends at Oxford whether he would join them for a game of 'rugger'. He refused, claiming that he was going to play 'soccer'—evidently a play on the word association. The name caught on.

There was no immediate attempt by the new Football Association to integrate all the various other codes around the country. Not until Charles Alcock, who had been at Harrow from 1855 to 1859, joined the committee did some sort of impetus build up. The rigorous offside law, basically that still employed in rugby, was revised when Westminster and Charterhouse schools joined, but the most important step was the arrival of Yorkshire representatives in 1867.

Yorkshire is the home of the oldest of all football clubs—Sheffield FC. The first written evidence of the club's existence dates from 1857—though it may have been founded as early as 1854. By the later date, however, it had its own rules and its secretary approached the newly formed FA in 1863 with a view to integration. The FA did not even bother to reply.

The north Midlands generally was to the provinces what Harrow was to the Home Counties. It was here that the first of the present League clubs originated—Notts County (often referred to as Nottingham before 1882) in 1862, Nottingham Forest in 1865 and Chesterfield in 1866. There have been suggestions that a Stoke club was established by a group of Old Carthusians in 1863—but 19th century records give the date as no earlier than 1867.

The first hint of a game that the modern supporter might be able to identify with was the Notts County–Nottingham Forest clash of 1866. The only score of the day came at the end of a 'negative scoreless afternoon' (shades of the present day) when 'there was a sort of steeplechase across the goal-line and over the grandstand railings ... where W R Revis, of the Forest, touched down. The place-kick, 15 yards at right angles from the goal-line was taken by the same player.' The ball had merely to go between the posts as there was no cross-bar.

As can be deduced, the Nottingham game was a hybrid, relying on a mixture of Rugby, Sheffield and London rules, but with the expansion of the FA to accommodate Sheffield uniformity was not far away. As Alcock himself wrote, '... the objects of the Association are to still further remove the barrier which prevent the accomplishment of one universal game.'

By 1870 Alcock, now secretary of the FA, had established unofficial internationals between England and Scotland (or rather a team of Scots resident in London) and a regular London-Sheffield encounter. The growing competitiveness of the game encouraged him to add another suggestion in 1871—a challenge cup 'for which all clubs belonging to the Football Association should be invited to compete'. The idea was unashamedly based on the interhouse knock-out competition at Harrow—the winners being referred to as the 'Cock House'.

The holders of the new trophy, known as the FA Challenge Cup, were to enjoy two invaluable advantages—they were exempt until the Final and they could choose where it was played. Fifteen clubs entered in the first year, though only twelve competed. Of these, two, Maidenhead and Marlow, have entered in each and every subsequent year. The real attraction was the appearance of Queen's Park, the Glasgow side that had been formed in 1867 and had still not had a single goal scored against them. They drew with the Wanderers, at the Oval, in the semi-final but could not afford to return for a replay and the Wanderers went on to beat Royal Engineers in the Final at the same venue. The only goal of the match was scored by Matthew Betts, playing under the assumed name of A H Chequer—meaning that he was a member of the Old Harrovian side Harrow Chequers—and 2,000 people paid the not insubstantial sum of one shilling to watch. Captain of the Wanderers was one Charles W Alcock.

Football came late to the major industrial conurbations. Aston Villa came into being in 1874 with neighbours Small Heath (to be renamed Birmingham) following a year later. In Lancashire Blackburn and Bolton both saw the light of day in 1874 and the Newton Heath side (later Manchester United)

The major problem facing the embryonic Football Association in the 1860s and 1870s was the vast divergence of rules still operating. At Uppingham, where J. C. Thring had drawn up 'The Simplest Rules' in 1862 (around when this picture was taken), teams numbered 15-a-side and attacked a goal stretched right across the pitch. Uppingham's was probably the first code to employ a crossbar, but did not allow the ball to go above waist height.

SUNDERLAND
F.C.
1901-2

was founded at the Lancashire and Yorkshire Railway Company's engine depot of that name in 1878.

It was a time of hope for Lancashire. After the near starvation of the 1860s—when cotton supplies were cut off during the American Civil War—and the economic depression of the early 1870s, an industrial boom was absorbing all who needed work. Immigrants flocked in from the agricultural areas and the Celtic fringes and football turned this to its advantage. Advertisements in the Glasgow papers attracted the Scottish 'professors' who taught the English the 'passing' as opposed to 'dribbling' game. Some teams, notably Preston, took on so many Scots that English players felt positively lonely and it is to this era and not the reign of Shankly at Liverpool that we owe the oft-repeated cry of the overlooked, 'you need to wear a kilt to get into that team.'

There were, of course, inducements. A Scot named J J Lang claimed he was the first ever professional when Sheffield Wednesday paid him to move from Glasgow in 1876. By 1880, while most of the players had other jobs, they received substantial remuneration from playing the game—not unlike the 'shamateurs' of the 1960s—and, in consequence, football was taken much more seriously than in the south. The days of the gentleman amateur were almost over.

The 1881 Cup Final—between Old Etonians and Old Carthusians—was the last of the all-amateur finals and, indeed, the last all-southern Final until Spurs met Chelsea in 1967. Old Carthusians later went on to become the first club to win both the FA Cup (1881) and the Amateur Cup (1894 and 1897).

While Etonians managed to defeat Blackburn Rovers the following year, the inevitable happened in 1883 when Blackburn Olympic became the first club to take the trophy out of the Home Counties. It would have been difficult to devise a better pair of teams to illustrate the differences between the game, and the life, in the South and the North. The Old Etonians speak for themselves—representatives of all that was privileged in the South of England; gentlemen amateurs with the time and income to allow their devotion to the game when they thought fit. Blackburn Olympic came from the most industrialized area in the world—the dingy terraces that crawl like centipedes up and down the valleys of

the mid-Lancashire weaving towns breeding many of the players that were not imported from Scotland.

From then on the South had very little say on the field for a long time. The Cup stayed in Blackburn for a record four years—Blackburn Rovers following up the short-lived Olympic's success and equalling Wanderers' three successive wins. The Old Etonian success in 1882 was the last by a southern club until Spurs' dramatic intervention in 1901. In fact, between Etonians' last win and Spurs' Double in 1961, the Cup returned south on only seven occasions.

As far as the Cup was concerned, the centre of gravity certainly moved south after 1961. In the next 25 years no less than 19 finalists were southern sides, almost all from London. But the League, after Arsenal's strange Double in 1971, was really to be the story of Liverpool. They came to dominate that competition to such an extent that their very success was surely one of the causes of the declining interest in the game. Between 1973 and 1986 (14 seasons) Liverpool won the trophy nine times, came second on four occasions and only once finished lower (fifth in 1981). In 1984 they completed only the third championship hat-trick ever, fifty years after Arsenal and sixty after Huddersfield. And in 1986 they finally won the coveted Double, the fifth in history, by beating neighbours Everton to both trophies.

But the whole was less than the sum of the parts. It was actually rather less interesting than it sounds. Though Liverpool certainly dominated the game more than Villa in the 1890s or Arsenal in the 1930s (who did not have European Cups to add to the trophy room either), the Merseysiders singularly failed to elicit the intense emotional responses of their predecessors. Perhaps it was because their city was in decline (unlike 19th century Birmingham or London in the 1930s), perhaps it was because the game was in decline and they were not riding a wave of interest. Perhaps it was their style, perhaps their willingness to give tough players like Smith, Case and Souness their heads. Only when Liverpool were in the later stages of European tournaments did they receive the ungrudging support of the nation.

Though Arsenal were never popular in the 1930s, grounds were packed week after week with fans at least wanting to see them beaten. Liverpool never even evoked that intensity of response. They were efficient, clever, good, well managed and well run, but they never went to the heart. Even in the early 1980s Manchester United or Spurs could attract more fans away. And Liverpool's dominance inevitably made the championship less interesting. Fewer clubs competed, there was less reason to go to the local ground each Saturday. The memorable seasons were the ones when there was real opposition—Everton's rise in 1984 and 1985, Derby's dramatic final pushes in 1972 and 1975, above all others probably Forest's excellent championship of 1977–78 after they had finished only third in the Second Division the season before.

Football, nonetheless, remains the national game, though the centre of enthusiasm in the late 1980s is probably north of the border rather than south of it. Liverpool will not be there for ever, nor will the European ban. Meanwhile Arsenal's Centenary season of 1986–87 saw a revival in their fortunes, capped by a long-awaited trophy in the Littlewoods Cup, and with their North London neighbours Spurs also playing well, a London challenge to Merseyside's supremacy at last looked promisingly substantial. There are still massive problems to solve. It is almost certain that attendances will decline further before these are sorted out. But if the game can emerge with a League of sensible size playing in well constructed stadiums and with the hooligan element eliminated, then it clearly has a future and it can recover just as the game in Scotland has recovered. We will wait for the 1990s with high hopes.

CHAPTER TWO

THE FA CUP

The FA Cup final of 1986 was a throwback. It was a game of great significance not just because Liverpool played Everton in the first Merseyside FA Cup final, and not just because Everton were desperately trying to prevent Liverpool win a Double that the Toffees had let slip from their grasp a year before. No, what made the FA Cup final of 1986 so unusual was that it was the first time in a quarter-century that the event had regained its place as the season's highlight. Since English clubs began to make a showing in Europe in the early 1960s, the FA Cup final had slowly lost its earlier pre-eminent place. It was a rare season in which it was now seen as the highlight—1970 and 1971 were perhaps exceptions, so were Manchester United's denials of Liverpool's Double in 1977 and Everton's in 1985.

But in 1986 there were no European competitions as far as the English were concerned, so the FA Cup final acquired a new significance for that reason alone. It was, at long last, the moment when Liverpool's Double finally came to pass. Two years earlier they had completed a hat-trick of Championships, but in two decades of almost constant success they had failed so often at the FA Cup hurdle. They had, indeed, won the trophy only twice—in 1965 and 1974. Twelve years later Liverpool made no mistake. Though Gary Lineker had put Everton ahead, the inevitable Ian Rush scored twice and Liverpool won 3–1.

For Everton it was a bitter, double Double blow. They had chased Liverpool through the season and were to end up runners-up in both competitions, only the fifth team in history to so finish. Far worse, they had come so close to their own Double the season before and had seen it slip away in the most unlikely circumstances. Their opponents in 1985 had been

Manchester United. Everton, going in as Champions and Cup holders (having beaten Watford 2–0 the year before) were clear favourites. They became far more so after Kevin Moran was sent off by referee P Willis. The United centre-back had upended Peter Reid in an illegal but over-enthusiastic rather than vicious tackle. Sadly his and Reid's protests did not convince the referee and Moran became the first man ever to be sent off in an FA Cup final. Manchester United responded well. The game went to extra time and Norman Whiteside scored the only goal with a stunningly skilful left-footed curler which crept from behind the marking defender inside Neville Southall's far post. It was the only sort of goal which could have deprived Everton of their prize, the chance of which would perhaps never come their way again.

At least most of their team had the consolation of having won the Cup a year before, in 1984. Everton's victims that year had been Watford, who had only entered the First Division in 1982. It was a deeply moving occasion for many Watford fans, including Elton John, who was not ashamed to cry at the end. Perhaps he was giving thanks for his good luck—Watford had met Charlton, Brighton, a relegated Birmingham and Plymouth, semi-finalists while nineteenth in the Third Division, on their way to Wembley. The final was notable for Everton's second goal, which was credited to Andy Gray despite the forward not having touched the ball. He actually headed the back of Steve Sherwood's hand and Sherwood allowed the ball to escape his grasp into the net. As Gray did not touch the ball, it was hardly his goal, but nor was it Sherwood's. Perhaps the correct decision was to award it to them jointly.

Sherwood never got his Cup winners medal, but no doubt

Ian Rush, Liverpool's goal-scoring machine of the 1980s, sets his seal on the 1986 Cup Final by driving his second goal past Everton captain Kevin Ratcliffe and goalkeeper Bobby Mimms. Liverpool won 3–1 to achieve the double and relegate neighbours Everton into second place in Cup and Championship.

The FA Cup Final of 1985, and a lucky moment for Manchester United. There is no Everton player in the picture, but Peter Reid's shot was on its way to the net when this lunge by John Gidman diverted the ball onto the post. Gary Bailey and Norman Whiteside (who was to score the winner) watch.

FA CUP SUCCESS 1872–1987

	Cup Final wins	Cup Final appearances	Semi-final appearances
*Tottenham Hotspur	7	8	12
Aston Villa	7	9	17
Newcastle United	6	11	13
Manchester United	6	10	17
Blackburn Rovers	6	8	16
West Bromwich Albion	5	10	18
*Wanderers	5	5	3
Arsenal	5	11	16
Everton	4	10	21
Wolverhampton Wanderers	4	8	13
Manchester City	4	8	10
Bolton Wanderers	4	7	12
Sheffield United	4	6	10
Liverpool	3	6	15
Sheffield Wednesday	3	5	15
West Ham United	3	4	5
Preston North End	2	7	10
Old Etonians	2	6	6
Sunderland	2	3	10
*Nottingham Forest	2	2	9
*Bury	2	2	2
Huddersfield Town	1	5	7
Derby County	1	4	13
Leeds United	1	4	7
Oxford University	1	4	6
Royal Engineers	1	4	4
Chelsea	1	3	10
Burnley	1	3	8
Portsmouth	1	3	4
Blackpool	1	3	3
Southampton	1	2	10
Notts County	1	2	4
Cardiff City	1	2	3
Clapham Rovers	1	2	3
Barnsley	1	2	2
Charlton Athletic	1	2	2
*Ipswich Town	1	1	3
*Old Carthusians	1	1	3
*Blackburn Olympic	1	1	2
*Bradford City	1	1	1
*Coventry City	1	1	1
Leicester City	—	4	7
Birmingham City	—	2	9
Queens Park (Glasgow)	—	2	4
Brighton	—	1	1
Fulham	—	1	5
Bristol City	—	1	2
Luton Town	—	1	2
Watford	—	1	3
Queens Park Rangers	—	1	1
Millwall	—	—	3
Stoke City	—	—	3
Swifts	—	—	3
Crystal Palace	—	—	2
Darwen	—	—	2
Grimsby Town	—	—	2
Swansea City	—	—	2
Swindon Town	—	—	2
Cambridge University	—	—	1
Crewe Alexandra	—	—	1
Derby Junction	—	—	1
Glasgow Rangers	—	—	1
Hull City	—	—	1
Marlow	—	—	1
Norwich City	—	—	1
Old Harrovians	—	—	1
Oldham Athletic	—	—	1
Port Vale	—	—	1
Reading	—	—	1
Shropshire Wanderers	—	—	1
Plymouth Argyle	—	—	1
York City	—	—	1

*Undefeated in final.

he would echo these sentiments: 'I've got a League Championship medal, a Fairs Cup medal, a League Cup medal and dozens of caps—but sometimes I think I'd swap the lot for a place in a Cup winning side.' The words were actually those of Billy Bremner before Leeds United's long-awaited success at Wembley in 1972, but they could have come from any of a large number of professionals, that enormous group who have never been lucky enough to carry the Cup around the arena after the highlight of the English season.

The FA Cup has an undeniable aura about it. Not only is it the oldest football competition in the world, not only is its Final watched by hundreds of millions of people *outside* Britain, not only is it the annual showpiece for Britain's national sport, but it has been elevated far beyond that. It is now a ritual, different from a royal wedding or a moon-landing only in that it occurs at more predictable intervals.

In 1971 the BBC published a list of the biggest audiences for single programmes in the history of British television. Four of the top ten were Cup Finals and the statistics have not changed since. And despite all the protestations about the League Championship being the ultimate test of professional ability, there is the sneaking suspicion that no-one would sacrifice an FA Cup winners medal for a Championship.

For, in the last resort, football must be a game about eleven men against eleven, about one team leaving the field victorious and the other vanquished, about a packed stadium saluting just one team—just one winner.

In its ultimate simplicity the FA Cup is the forerunner of competitions all over the world. But in a sense it is a lot more than that, for the hundred-year history of the FA Cup is also the history of English football.

It was in the offices of *The Sportsman*, a London newspaper, on 20 July 1871, that seven men took a hesitant step and made football history. The central figure was 29-year-old Charles Alcock, secretary of the FA and the man who suggested that: '...it is desirable that a Challenge Cup shall be established in connection with the Association...' Among the other six present were Matthew Betts, who scored the first ever Cup Final goal, and Captain Francis Marindin, later president of the FA, who appeared in two Finals and refereed another eight.

Alcock had pinched the idea for his competition from his old school, Harrow, where there was a simple knock-out tournament among the houses, the winner being known as the 'Cock House'. The FA ordered a Cup from Martin, Hall and Company; it cost a mere £20 and stood just 18 inches high.

Fifteen clubs entered the first year—all but Donington School, Spalding, and the great Queen's Park of Glasgow coming from the home counties. In fact Donington scratched without playing a game and never entered again, thus establishing some kind of record.

The strict knock-out principle was not yet in operation; four clubs played in the third round and four in the next, in part through byes and in part through a rule which allowed both teams which drew to go through to the next round.

The Cup's beginnings were undoubtedly humble. Just 2,000 people turned out for the Final to see men dressed in trousers and caps (Royal Engineers wore 'dark blue serge knickerbockers'), who changed ends every time a goal was scored and who won throw-ins by touching the ball down in rugby fashion if it went out of play. The Kennington Oval pitch would have hardly been recognizable to present-day supporters—there was no centre circle, no half-way line, no penalty area and a tape instead of a cross-bar. Alcock's team, the Wanderers, beat the Engineers 1–0.

The century that followed can be roughly divided into four phases—largely determined by the geographical location of the Final. Firstly there was the amateur era, then the Northern takeover, the Crystal Palace period and, finally, the post-1923 Wembley era.

Ten years after that first Final the Old Etonians beat Blackburn Rovers at the Oval. When the final whistle blew, the victorious captain, Arthur Kinnaird, of the red beard and long white trousers, stood on his head in front of the pavilion. It was appropriate that his should be the final gesture of an age ready to be confined to the history books; he appeared in nine of the first twelve Finals, five times on the winning side. Only James Forrest of Blackburn Rovers and C H R Wollaston of the Wanderers received so many winners medals.

Kinnaird's winning appearances were with Old Etonians in 1879 and 1882, and Wanderers, in 1873, 1877 and 1878. His first for the Wanderers was the only occasion on which the Final was contested on the challenge basis that was written into both the competition's title and its original rules. The Wanderers, being the holders, not only had the solitary game to play—the Challenge Final in which they beat Oxford University 2–0—but they were also allowed to choose the venue of that match, which is the reason for Lillie Bridge's one moment of sporting significance.

The Wanderers also entered the records in a unique way in 1878—they won the Cup for the third consecutive time and thus, according to the rules, outright. It was, however, returned with the proviso that it should never again be handed to one team in perpetuity. In fact the scene was a little more comical than that. Charles Alcock, as secretary of the Wanderers, handed back the Cup and asked that it should never be won outright. Charles Alcock, now in his role as secretary of the FA, was only too happy to agree.

In the years that followed only one club—Blackburn Rovers between 1884 and 1886—has repeated the feat, and they were presented with a special shield which still hangs in their boardroom.

It was to Blackburn, in fact, that the Cup fled when it left the gentlemen amateurs of the South. That Lancastrian cotton-weaving town had two fine clubs in the 1880s— Olympic, who became the first side from outside the home counties to win the trophy, in 1883, and Rovers, who won it in the subsequent three seasons.

But the Blackburn clubs were not the first 'outsiders' to make their mark on the competition. In 1879 Nottingham Forest became the first of England's northern sides to reach the semi-finals—and at their first attempt—but more significant was the performance of Darwen, a neighbour of Blackburn, the same year. In the previous round they had held Old Etonians to two draws, the first by scoring four times in the last 15 minutes, but had gone down 6–2 on their third visit to the capital.

Darwen were unlucky that the rule under which all ties after the second round had to be played at the Oval was still in force. No semi-final was contested outside London until 1882, when Blackburn Rovers drew with Sheffield's The Wednesday at Huddersfield and beat them in Manchester, but for the next few years—before the Irish and Scottish FAs banned their clubs from entering—ties were played all over the United Kingdom. As a result Linfield captured the unique record of never having lost a Cup tie. They drew 2–2 with Nottingham Forest in 1889, and then withdrew before the replay, never to enter again.

Forest had actually arrived in Ireland and played a friendly instead, but it helped create an odd record for them as well, for they are the only club to have been drawn to play FA Cup ties in all four home countries. In 1885, after a drawn game at Derby, Forest had replayed a semi-final with Glasgow's Queen's Park at Merchiston Castle School, Edinburgh, the

Everton's resurgence in the mid-1980s was one of the features of English football. They won the FA Cup in 1984 with a victory over Watford.
Above *Player of the year Neville Southall and centre-forward Graeme Sharp parade the trophy, with Trevor Steven behind. They won caps for Wales, Scotland and England respectively.*
Left *Everton lost the finals of 1985 and 1986, the first being notable for the first sending-off in a Wembley final. Despite the appeals of Manchester United's Kevin Moran, referee Peter Willis sent him off for a foul on Peter Reid. Ten-man United won 1–0.*

only FA Cup semi-final ever contested outside England.

But to return to Darwen, whose performance was in no small way due to the presence of two Scots, Fergus Suter and James Love, both of whom had been 'mislaid' by Partick Thistle on a tour of England. They were, of course, among the first of the professionals that were soon to take over the competition and football south of the border.

The issue of payment did not actually come to a head until January 1884, when Preston North End drew with mighty Upton Park, one of the original entrants in 1872 and still staunch supporters of the lily-white amateur game. The Londoners protested that Preston had included professionals, North End admitted as much, and were disqualified.

Just over a year later the FA sensibly bowed to the inevitable and professionals were allowed provided, among other clauses, they were: '... annually registered in a book to be kept by the committee of the FA ...'

At least Preston had the satisfaction of seeing Upton Park humbled in the next round by neighbours Blackburn Rovers, on their triumphant march to the first of a hat-trick of wins. At the time Blackburn were also midway through a record of 24 Cup games without defeat, which lasted from a 1–0 setback at the hands of Darwen in the second round of the 1882–83 competition to the December of 1886.

But it was not Rovers who first brought the Cup to Lancashire, rather a long since defunct outfit called Blackburn Olympic. When their captain, Warburton, got back to a deserved civic reception in 1883, he declared to the crowd: 'The Cup is very welcome to Lancashire. It'll have a good home and it'll never go back to London.' He was quite right. In the next twelve years it went no further south than Birmingham where, in 1895, it was stolen from the window of a football-boot manufacturer, William Shillcock.

In an edition of the *Sunday Pictorial* in February 1958 one

Tension in the tunnel before the 1956 Final. Birmingham skipper Len Boyd bounces the ball against a wall while the Manchester City players huddle round the man with the plan—number 9 Don Revie.

Harry Burge, at the age of 83, admitted to having stolen the Cup and melted it down for counterfeit half-crowns. If that is true it is a sad commentary on the economics of the times—the Cup contained less than £20 worth of silver and could hardly have justified the effort.

Fortunately for the FA the chairman of Wolverhampton Wanderers had presented his players with scaled-down replicas when they won the trophy in 1893, and it was therefore possible to create a reproduction of the original.

That same Wolves victory was on the occasion of the first Final to be contested outside the capital. Surrey CCC, alarmed at the size of the crowd for the 1892 Final, withdrew the Oval as a venue and, in recognition of Lancashire's supremacy, the game's premier event switched to the country's second city, Manchester. There the Fallowfield ground was besieged by a crowd which broke down the barriers and fell through the wooden terracing in a remarkable harbinger of both the first Wembley Final, 30 years later, and the Ibrox disaster, then less than ten years away.

A week earlier Everton's reserve team had thrashed Wolves 4–2 in a First Division game but this time it was a different story with the Midlanders' captain Allen scoring the only goal of the match. The next season saw an equally surprising result. Second Division Notts County beat Bolton 4–1 at Goodison Park, after reasonably protesting that it was virtually a home game for Bolton, and their centre-forward Jimmy Logan scored a hat-trick to equal William Townley's 1890 feat for Blackburn Rovers.

After the 1894 Final the FA must have concluded that London was the only rightful place for the showpiece of the season, and it has been played there with only one exception ever since (1915), although five replays have been played elsewhere. The obvious choice was Crystal Palace—though the FA's decision to move the game to London can be viewed a little cynically in the light of the fact that only one of the finalists who ever played at the Palace was a London club—Spurs, in 1901—and only two others, Southampton and Bristol City, came from south of Birmingham.

Crystal Palace in 1895 was already a Victorian weekend playground—something like a cross between Battersea Fun Fair and Brighton beach—and it had a huge natural bowl which was used for sporting events. Terracing as it is known today was never built there; most of the 80 or so thousand at Finals stood on the steep grassy slopes of the east side.

The first Final at the Palace (not, incidentally, the present home of Crystal Palace) was the third clash between Birmingham rivals West Bromwich and Aston Villa—they are still the only clubs to have met each other three times in a Final. At kick-off both had won once each, but Villa went on to take the Cup this time, promptly lost it to Mr Burge, but were back again two years later to carry off the new trophy after a Final which ranks with 1948 and 1953 as one of the greatest.

It was also a particularly significant game for it gave Villa a League-Cup Double which looked, for 64 years, like being the last of all time. Villa had won the League by the massive margin of eleven points (there were only 16 clubs in the division) and at the Palace defeated Everton 3–2, all the goals coming in the 25 minutes before half-time.

The club that took Villa's mantle of 'the team of all the talents' was Newcastle United—possessors of what is surely the oddest of all Cup Final records. In five Finals at the Crystal Palace they did not win one game, yet they did not lose at Wembley until their sixth match there!

The Geordies' record between 1905 and 1911 is startling in its consistency. They reached the Final in 1905, 1906, 1908, 1910 and 1911. In 1910 they admittedly managed to draw with Second Division Barnsley, and beat them in the replay at

Goodison to record their only pre-First World War win. In 1909 they lost a semi-final by the game's only goal to Manchester United, so the only year in the seven between 1905 and 1911 that they did not reach the last four was 1907.

That season—one in which they won the League—Newcastle suffered a first round knock-out at St James' Park to a club then languishing at the bottom of the Southern League. And the name of the club whose feat must rank alongside the giant-killing exploits of Walsall and Colchester? Irony of ironies . . . Crystal Palace. It was almost as if the very name made the Northumbrians go weak at the knees.

When the two great sides of the era—Villa and Newcastle—met in 1905 they drew a crowd of 101,117 to a game that seemed to have little appeal for the Londoner—but even this figure had been surpassed four years earlier for a game that will surely remain unique for all time.

Since the Final returned in 1895 Londoners had regarded it, more than a little disdainfully, as an affair for provincials—rather like an Agricultural Exhibition at Earls Court is regarded today. In fact London had only one League club—Arsenal—at the turn of the century and had never had a professional interest in the Final.

Then, in the first year of the new century, came a record-breaking Final. 1901 saw Tottenham become the only non-League club to win the Cup since the Football League was founded, though they needed a replay against Sheffield United—winners two years before—to do it. The attendance printed in the following day's papers—114,815—was the largest ever at a football match and has been surpassed in England only twice since—at the 1913 and 1923 Finals.

Sandy Brown, who scored twice at Crystal Palace and once in the replay at Bolton, became the first man to score in every round of the Cup (a feat not equalled until 1935) and his total of 15 Cup goals has yet to be surpassed.

And on top of all this was a violently disputed goal which only the referee and the Sheffield United team of the hundred thousand present thought was justified. The incident was no doubt quite comical to non-partisan spectators. Clawley, the Spurs goalkeeper, clashed with Bennett, a Sheffield forward, and the ball ran behind. Clawley appealed for a goal-kick, Bennett for a corner and the referee silenced them both by awarding a goal. He apparently judged Clawley to have been *behind* his own goal-line before carrying the ball out and being challenged by Bennett.

London's star fell as quickly as it had risen and the capital did not have another representative in the Final until 1915, when Chelsea lost in the muted atmosphere of a wartime Old Trafford, to the side their fellow Londoners had defeated—Sheffield United.

The Yorkshiremen, however, did not carry off the same trophy Spurs had deprived them of. The design of the latter had been pirated for another competition in Manchester and so the second of the three FA Cups was presented to Lord Kinnaird—whose nine Final appearances is still a record—to mark his 21 years as President of the Football Association.

The present trophy, weighing 175oz and standing 19in high, was ordered from Fattorini and Sons of Bradford and, appropriately if strangely, Bradford City were its first holders. Strangely, because neither Bradford club had been near a Final before and neither has been near one since.

As remarkable as the ability of some clubs to keep coming back and taking the Cup is the inability of others to get near it. Take Sunderland for instance. By the time they finally took the trophy back to Wearside in 1937, they had won the League Championship six times. But near neighbours and rivals Newcastle already had seven Final appearances to their credit—and another three soon to follow. Sunderland's only

previous Final was another of the classics— the 1913 game that attracted a crowd even bigger than at the 1901 Final. They assembled for a decisive game, for it was the only Final in the first hundred years of the Cup to be contested by the clubs that finished first and second in the League. In the end Sunderland won the League and Villa the Cup.

Seven years later several Villa players provided an illusion of continuity when they again collected winners medals. In the interim Europe had been at war for four years and the Crystal Palace had been requisitioned as a service depot. There was no prospect of it being available before 1923 and the FA had to look elsewhere for a venue.

Having decided that London was still the only possible home for the Cup Final—a contentious conclusion that was not particularly well received in Manchester, Birmingham or Liverpool—the FA were left with only one choice. The White

Top *The programme for the second of the Cup Final meetings between West Bromwich Albion and Aston Villa in 1892. This was the last final to be played at The Oval.*

Above *An overenthusiastic Everton fan at Wembley in 1966 annoys Brian Labone but gives Brian Harris (far left) a chance to see if the cap fits.*

25

Year	Venue	Winners		Scorers	Runners-up		Scorers	Attendance
1872	Kennington Oval	Wanderers	1	Betts	Royal Engineers	0		2,000
1873[1]	Lillie Bridge	Wanderers	2	Kinnaird, Wollaston	Oxford University	0		3,000
1874	Kennington Oval	Oxford University	2	Mackarness, Patton	Royal Engineers	0		2,000
1875*	Kennington Oval	Royal Engineers	1	Scorer not known	Old Etonians	1	Bonsor	3,000
Replay	Kennington Oval	Royal Engineers	2	Renny-Tailyour, Stafford	Old Etonians	0		3,000
1876	Kennington Oval	Wanderers	1	Edwards	Old Etonians	1	Bonsor	3,000
Replay	Kennington Oval	Wanderers	3	Hughes (2), Wollaston	Old Etonians	0		3,500
1877*	Kennington Oval	Wanderers	2	Heron, Kenrick	Oxford University	1	Kinnaird (o.g.)	3,000
1878[2]	Kennington Oval	Wanderers	3	Kenrick (2), Wace	Royal Engineers	1	'From a Rush'	4,500
1879	Kennington Oval	Old Etonians	1	Clarke	Clapham Rovers	0		5,000
1880	Kennington Oval	Clapham Rovers	1	Lloyd-Jones	Oxford University	0		6,000
1881	Kennington Oval	Old Carthusians	3	Page, Wynyard, Parry	Old Etonians	0		4,500
1882	Kennington Oval	Old Etonians	1	Anderson	Blackburn Rovers	0		6,500
1883*	Kennington Oval	Blackburn Olympic	2	Matthews, Costley	Old Etonians	1	Goodhart	8,000
1884	Kennington Oval	Blackburn Rovers	2	Brown, Forrest	Queen's Park (Glasgow)	1	Christie	4,000
1885	Kennington Oval	Blackburn Rovers	2	Brown, Forrest	Queen's Park (Glasgow)	0		12,500
1886	Kennington Oval	Blackburn Rovers	0		West Bromwich Albion	0		15,000
Replay[3]	The Racecourse, Derby	Blackburn Rovers	2	Brown, Sowerbutts	West Bromwich Albion	0		12,000
1887	Kennington Oval	Aston Villa	2	Hunter, Hodgetts	West Bromwich Albion	0		15,500
1888	Kennington Oval	West Bromwich Albion	2	Woodhall, Bayliss	Preston North End	1	Dewhurst	19,000
1889	Kennington Oval	Preston North End	3	Gordon, Goodall, Thompson	Wolverhampton Wanderers	0		22,000
1890	Kennington Oval	Blackburn Rovers	6	Townley (3), Lofthouse, Southworth, Walton	The Wednesday	1	Bennett	20,000
1891	Kennington Oval	Blackburn Rovers	3	Southworth, Townley, Dewar	Notts County	1	Oswald	23,000
1892	Kennington Oval	West Bromwich Albion	3	Nicholls, Geddes, Reynolds	Aston Villa	0		25,000
1893	Fallowfield, Manchester	Wolverhampton Wanderers	1	Allen	Everton	0		45,000
1894	Goodison Park	Notts County	4	Logan (3), Watson	Bolton Wanderers	1	Cassidy	37,000
1895	Crystal Palace	Aston Villa	1	Devey	West Bromwich Albion	0		42,560
1896[4]	Crystal Palace	The Wednesday	2	Spiksley (2)	Wolverhampton Wanderers	1	Black	48,836
1897	Crystal Palace	Aston Villa	3	Campbell, Devey, Crabtree	Everton	2	Bell, Hartley	65,891
1898	Crystal Palace	Nottingham Forest	3	Capes (2), McPherson	Derby County	1	Bloomer	62,017
1899	Crystal Palace	Sheffield United	4	Bennett, Beers, Priest, Almond	Derby County	1	Boag	78,833
1900	Crystal Palace	Bury	4	McLuckie (2), Wood, Plant	Southampton	0		68,945
1901	Crystal Palace	Tottenham Hotspur	2	Brown (2)	Sheffield United	2	Bennett, Priest	114,815
Replay	Burnden Park, Bolton	Tottenham Hotspur	3	Cameron, Smith, Brown	Sheffield United	1	Priest	20,740
1902	Crystal Palace	Sheffield United	1	Common	Southampton	1	Wood	76,914
Replay	Crystal Palace	Sheffield United	2	Hedley, Barnes	Southampton	1	Brown	33,068
1903	Crystal Palace	Bury	6	Leeming (2), Ross, Sagar, Plant, Wood	Derby County	0		63,102
1904	Crystal Palace	Manchester City	1	Meredith	Bolton Wanderers	0		61,374
1905	Crystal Palace	Aston Villa	2	Hampton (2)	Newcastle United	0		101,117
1906	Crystal Palace	Everton	1	Young	Newcastle United	0		75,609
1907	Crystal Palace	The Wednesday	2	Stewart, Simpson	Everton	1	Sharp	84,584
1908	Crystal Palace	Wolverhampton Wanderers	3	Hunt, Hedley, Harrison	Newcastle United	1	Howie	74,967
1909	Crystal Palace	Manchester United	1	Turnbull A	Bristol City	0		71,401
1910	Crystal Palace	Newcastle United	1	Rutherford	Barnsley	1	Tufnell	77,747
Replay	Goodison Park	Newcastle United	2	Shepherd (2 inc a penalty)	Barnsley	0		69,000
1911[5]	Crystal Palace	Bradford City	0		Newcastle United	0		69,098
Replay	Old Trafford	Bradford City	1	Spiers	Newcastle United	0		58,000
1912	Crystal Palace	Barnsley	0		West Bromwich Albion	0		54,556
Replay*	Bramall Lane	Barnsley	1	Tufnell	West Bromwich Albion	0		38,555
1913	Crystal Palace	Aston Villa	1	Barber	Sunderland	0		120,081
1914	Crystal Palace	Burnley	1	Freeman	Liverpool	0		72,778
1915	Old Trafford	Sheffield United	3	Simmons, Kitchen, Fazackerley	Chelsea	0		49,557
1916–19		Competition suspended						
1920	Stamford Bridge	Aston Villa	1	Kirton	Huddersfield Town	0		50,018
1921	Stamford Bridge	Tottenham Hotspur	1	Dimmock	Wolverhampton Wanderers	0		72,805
1922	Stamford Bridge	Huddersfield Town	1	Smith (penalty)	Preston North End	0		53,000
1923[6]	Wembley	Bolton Wanderers	2	Jack, Smith J R	West Ham United	0		126,047
1924	Wembley	Newcastle United	2	Harris, Seymour	Aston Villa	0		91,695
1925	Wembley	Sheffield United	1	Tunstall	Cardiff City	0		91,763
1926	Wembley	Bolton Wanderers	1	Jack	Manchester City	0		91,447
1927	Wembley	Cardiff City	1	Ferguson	Arsenal	0		91,206
1928	Wembley	Blackburn Rovers	3	Roscamp (2), McLean	Huddersfield Town	1	Jackson	92,041
1929	Wembley	Bolton Wanderers	2	Butler, Blackmore	Portsmouth	0		92,576
1930	Wembley	Arsenal	2	James, Lambert	Huddersfield Town	0		92,448
1931	Wembley	West Bromwich Albion	2	Richardson W G (2)	Birmingham	1	Bradford	92,406
1932	Wembley	Newcastle United	2	Allen (2)	Arsenal	1	John	92,298

Hart Lane and Highbury of 1919 were not like they are today, and only Stamford Bridge was large enough.

So Chelsea's impersonal arena it was—a decision that nearly caused the FA a lot more criticism. By the semi-final stage the arrangements for the Final itself were far too advanced for the venue to be changed—but the Chelsea side that had reached the last pre-War Final were alive and well, third in the League, and favourites to reach the first post-War Final as well. The Pensioners went to Bramall Lane for their semi-final against Aston Villa with the prospect of a home tie in the Final—though it was technically against the rules of the competition. It was Billy Walker who saved the FA's face. He scored two goals, Villa won 3–1 and went on to beat Huddersfield at Stamford Bridge.

The three Stamford Bridge Finals were among the most anonymous ever. All three were won by the only goal of the match, and the attendances in 1920 and 1922 were among the lowest of the century, coming nowhere near to filling the ground.

The 1922 game was called the most forgettable of all time, but suddenly acquired a new significance after a sequel 16 years later. The earlier game was a lamentable affair—even the FA minutes commented on the conduct of the players. It was appropriate that it should be decided by a disputed penalty when Preston's right-back Hamilton brought down Huddersfield's winger Billy Smith on the edge of the area, though many said outside it. After a lengthy and heated discussion between the Preston players and the referee, Smith himself took it and scored.

The 1938 game was equally drab, and the contestants were—Huddersfield and Preston. At least it was better tempered and had reached the last minute of extra-time without a goal when Huddersfield's centre-half Young tripped George Mutch and Mutch himself converted the penalty. The story goes that Bill Shankly—then playing for Preston—told Mutch to 'shut your eyes and hit it'. He had obviously been coached in something like that vein, for the ball hit the bar on its way in.

But back in 1923 no doubt everyone was glad to get away from Stamford Bridge to Wembley, where the FA had co-operated in a scheme to incorporate a vast new stadium in the British Empire Exhibition, scheduled to open in 1924. The Empire Stadium was ready a year earlier and public enthusiasm was enormous. Unfortunately the FA were lulled by the below capacity crowds at Stamford Bridge and thought that Wembley—capable of holding 127,000 according to the Exhibition authorities—would be adequate.

They were perhaps unlucky in that one of the contestants was West Ham, then leading the Second Division and the darlings of East London. In the end the FA publicly thanked a

Year	Venue	Winners		Scorers	Runners-up		Scorers	Attendance
1933	Wembley	Everton	3	Stein, Dean, Dunn	Manchester City	0		92,950
1934	Wembley	Manchester City	2	Tilson (2)	Portsmouth	1	Rutherford	93,258
1935	Wembley	Sheffield Wednesday	4	Rimmer (2), Palethorpe, Hooper	West Bromwich Albion	2	Boyes, Sandford	93,204
1936	Wembley	Arsenal	1	Drake	Sheffield United	0		93,384
1937	Wembley	Sunderland	3	Gurney, Carter, Burbanks	Preson North End	1	O'Donnell	93,495
1938*	Wembley	Preston North End	1	Mutch (penalty)	Huddersfield Town	0		93,497
1939	Wembley	Portsmouth	4	Parker (2), Barlow, Anderson	Wolverhampton Wanderers	1	Dorsett	99,370
1940–45		Competition suspended						
1946*	Wembley	Derby County	4	Turner H (og), Doherty, Stamps (2)	Charlton Athletic	1	Turner H	98,000
1947*	Wembley	Charlton Athletic	1	Duffy	Burnley	0		99,000
1948	Wembley	Manchester United	4	Rowley (2), Pearson, Anderson	Blackpool	2	Shimwell (penalty), Mortensen	99,000
1949	Wembley	Wolverhampton Wanderers	3	Pye (2), Smyth	Leicester City	1	Griffiths	99,500
1950	Wembley	Arsenal	2	Lewis (2)	Liverpool	0		100,000
1951	Wembley	Newcastle United	2	Milburn (2)	Blackpool	0		100,000
1952	Wembley	Newcastle United	1	Robledo G	Arsenal	0		100,000
1953	Wembley	Blackpool	4	Mortensen (3), Perry	Bolton Wanderers	3	Lofthouse, Moir, Bell	100,000
1954	Wembley	West Bromwich Albion	3	Allen (2 inc a penalty), Griffin	Preston North End	2	Morrison, Wayman	100,000
1955	Wembley	Newcastle United	3	Milburn, Mitchell, Hannah	Manchester City	1	Johnstone	100,000
1956	Wembley	Manchester City	3	Hayes, Dyson, Johnstone	Birmingham City	1	Kinsey	100,000
1957	Wembley	Aston Villa	2	McParland (2)	Manchester United	1	Taylor	100,000
1958	Wembley	Bolton Wanderers	2	Lofthouse (2)	Manchester United	0		100,000
1959	Wembley	Nottingham Forest	2	Dwight, Wilson	Luton Town	1	Pacey	100,000
1960	Wembley	Wolverhampton Wanderers	3	McGrath (og), Deeley (2)	Blackburn Rovers	0		100,000
1961	Wembley	Tottenham Hotspur	2	Smith, Dyson	Leicester City	0		100,000
1962	Wembley	Tottenham Hotspur	3	Greaves, Smith, Blanchflower (penalty)	Burnley	1	Robson	100,000
1963	Wembley	Manchester United	3	Law, Herd (2)	Leicester City	1	Keyworth	100,000
1964	Wembley	West Ham United	3	Sissons, Hurst, Boyce	Preston North End	2	Holden, Dawson	100,000
1965*	Wembley	Liverpool	2	Hunt, St John	Leeds United	1	Bremner	100,000
1966	Wembley	Everton	3	Trebilcock (2), Temple	Sheffield Wednesday	2	McCalliog, Ford	100,000
1967[7]	Wembley	Tottenham Hotspur	2	Robertson, Saul	Chelsea	1	Tambling	100,000
1968*	Wembley	West Bromwich Albion	1	Astle	Everton	0		100,000
1969	Wembley	Manchester City	1	Young	Leicester City	0		100,000
1970*	Wembley	Chelsea	2	Houseman, Hutchinson	Leeds United	2	Charlton, Jones	100,000
Replay*	Old Trafford	Chelsea	2	Osgood, Webb	Leeds United	1	Jones	62,000
1971*	Wembley	Arsenal	2	Kelly, George	Liverpool	1	Heighway	100,000
1972	Wembley	Leeds United	1	Clarke	Arsenal	0		100,000
1973	Wembley	Sunderland	1	Porterfield	Leeds United	0		100,000
1974	Wembley	Liverpool	3	Keegan (2), Heighway	Newcastle United	0		100,000
1975	Wembley	West Ham United	2	Taylor A (2)	Fulham	0		100,000
1976	Wembley	Southampton	1	Stokes	Manchester United	0		100,000
1977	Wembley	Manchester United	2	Pearson, Greenhoff J	Liverpool	1	Case	100,000
1978	Wembley	Ipswich	1	Osborne	Arsenal	0		100,000
1979	Wembley	Arsenal	3	Talbot, Stapleton, Sunderland	Manchester United	2	McQueen, McIlroy	100,000
1980	Wembley	West Ham United	1	Brooking	Arsenal	0		100,000
1981*	Wembley	Tottenham Hotspur	1	Hutchison (o.g.)	Manchester City	1	Hutchison	100,000
Replay	Wembley	Tottenham Hotspur	3	Villa 2, Crooks	Manchester City	2	Mackenzie, Reeves (pen)	92,000
1982*	Wembley	Tottenham Hotspur	1	Hoddle	Queen's Park Rangers	1	Fenwick	100,000
Replay	Wembley	Tottenham Hotspur	1	Hoddle (pen)	Queen's Park Rangers	0		90,000
1983*	Wembley	Manchester United	2	Stapleton, Wilkins	Brighton & Hove Albion	2	Smith, Stevens	100,000
Replay*	Wembley	Manchester United	4	Robson 2, Whiteside, Muhren (pen)	Brighton & Hove Albion	0		92,000
1984	Wembley	Everton	2	Sharp, Gray	Watford	0		100,000
1985	Wembley	Manchester United	1	Whiteside	Everton	0		100,000
1986	Wembley	Liverpool	3	Rush 2, Johnston	Everton	1	Lineker	98,000
1987	Wembley	Coventry City	3	Bennett, Houchen, Mabbutt o.g.	Tottenham Hotspur	2	Allen C, Kilcline o.g.	98,000

*After half-an-hour's extra time. Extra time became compulsory in 1913. [1]Challenge system. The holders, Wanderers, were exempt until the Final.
[2]Wanderers won the trophy outright but restored it to the Association. [3]Blackburn Rovers were also awarded a special shield to mark their third consecutive win.
[4]After the Cup had been stolen in 1895, the FA ordered a replica. The 1896 Final was the first time it was awarded.
[5]After the Cup's design had been duplicated for another competition it was withdrawn and presented to Lord Kinnaird on his completing 21 years as President of the Football Association. The present trophy was first awarded in 1911. [6] Official attendance figure. Actual attendance was probably in excess of 200,000. [7]Substitutes allowed for the first time.

policeman called George Scorey and his white horse Billy that the game took place at all. West Ham were less pleased with the behaviour of the FA's equine saviour. Their game relied on the use of fast-running wingers Richards and Ruffell and, as trainer Charlie Paynter said afterwards: 'It was that white horse thumping its big feet into the pitch that made it hopeless. Our wingers were tumbling all over the place, tripping up in great ruts and holes.' Maybe, but it did not stop Ted Vizard having an excellent game on the left-wing for Bolton. The FA were more generous to PC Scorey, regularly sending him tickets for later Finals—but he was not much interested in football and never went to another match.

When Arsenal returned to Wembley for the Centenary Cup Final in 1972 they at least had statistics on their side. Newcastle had won in 1951 and 1952, Spurs in 1961 and 1962 and Arsenal had taken the trophy in 1971. But the portents were to be overcome by Leeds in their third FA Cup Final, for Allan Clarke scored the only goal of the match and Arsenal became the very first holders to return to Wembley and lose.

It was a defeat which reminded their followers of the inter-War period. Mighty Arsenal were the giants who strode across the thirties, winning the League five times but having a strangely chequered history in the Cup. True, they did win it twice, but far better remembered are the two occasions when they lost. The first of these was in 1927, when Cardiff with eight internationals and only one Englishman in their side took the Cup out of England for the first and only time. The solitary goal of the game came from a speculative shot by Cardiff's centre-forward Ferguson. The ball seemed to be easily gathered by Arsenal's Welsh international goalkeeper Dan Lewis, but he seemed to indulge in a grotesque parody of his trade, the ball slipping away from his fumblings and rolling slowly over the line.

Lewis blamed the incident on his new jersey, and to this day Arsenal always wash goalkeepers' jerseys before they are used, to get rid of any surplus grease. It was a pity that they could not wash away their Cup luck as easily.

Still, there was nothing contentious about Arsenal's 2–0 win over Huddersfield in the 1930 Final, a game remembered for the moment when the *Graf Zeppelin* appeared over the Stadium. The airship—pride of a re-emergent Germany—dipped in salute and passed on sedately.

Two years later Arsenal were back to suffer the greatest of all Cup Final controversies. Their opponents were eternal Cup runners-up Newcastle, and the losers medals seemed destined to make their familiar trek to the North East as early as the fifteenth minute when John put Arsenal ahead. But it was not to be.

Davidson, the Newcastle centre-half, sent a long ball along the right, Richardson went for it but it appeared to be hit too

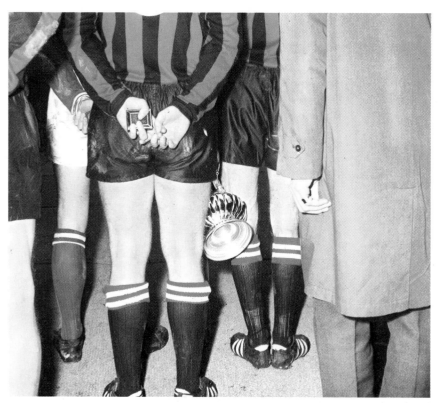

amateur Blyth Spartans defeated both Crewe and Stockport in successive rounds of the 1971–72 competition, the managers of both the Fourth Division clubs lost their jobs.

Victories by non-League clubs over their League brothers are common enough of course—in 1956–57 it happened as many as eleven times. But since the League added a Third Division in 1920 there have been only six instances of a non-League club beating a First Division side, only two away from home. Hereford did well in the third round of 1972, drawing at Newcastle and winning the replay. *Old Moore's Almanac* for the year had predicted that a non-League side would win the Cup and Hereford certainly did their best to oblige—drawing with West Ham in the next round before going down 3–1.

Superstition seems to play a big part in the Cup, where Portsmouth were the arch-adherents. In 1934 they employed manager Jack Tinn's lucky spats to bring them fortune and comedian Bud Flanagan to tell them jokes in the dressing room before the game with Manchester City. It did no good, City coming back to win 2–1 after losing the 1933 Final. City did the same thing in 1956, beating Birmingham with the 'Revie plan' after losing to Newcastle in 1955.

The 1934 Final was the occasion on which Frank Swift fainted. He said that the tension of the last few minutes, when he spent his time between the posts musing on how difficult it would be to clean the Cup and listening to the photographers counting down the seconds, was simply too much and he collapsed as the final whistle went.

Portsmouth's rituals proved luckier five years later. Their opponents Wolves arrived at Wembley as the hottest favourites of the century and full of a publicity seeking course of 'monkey glands'. Portsmouth preferred to rely on the spats again and, when the signature book came round, were heartened to see that Wolves players were so nervous that their signatures were barely legible.

Portsmouth won the Cup easily and proceeded to hold it for the longest period ever—seven years. This, however, was less due to their prowess than the Second World War.

After that lengthy intermission the Cup re-appeared in unfamiliar form. Because of the lack of a League programme, the FA decided to hold the Cup on a home-and-away basis—for the first and only time. It was not really a success, but it created its talking points.

Bradford PA lost 3–1 at home to Manchester City in the fourth round and then went on to win 8–2 at Maine Road, while Charlton became only the second team to *lose* a Cup game and still reach the Final. Fulham beat them 2–1 in the third round at Craven Cottage but Charlton had already won the first leg 3–1 and went through. One previous occasion when this had happened was the second part of a three-match quarter-final fiasco in 1890. Wednesday beat Notts County 5–0 in the first part. County protested to the FA, the game was replayed and County won 3–2. This time it was Sheffield's turn to protest and the eventual result was a 2–1 win for Wednesday—who went on to lose the Final rather ignominiously 6–1 to Blackburn Rovers.

The 1946 Final was almost as high scoring a game—Derby winning 4–1. That surprised no one for it took Derby's tally for the competition to 37, the highest aggregate since 1887–88 when Preston beat Hyde 26–0. Charlton's Bert Turner was the central figure of the game, scoring an own goal for Derby and within a minute equalizing with a free-kick which went in off Doherty's legs.

There followed two years later one of a pair of great Finals that have to be regarded in tandem. In the first the League runners-up, Manchester United, beat Blackpool 4–2 in what has always been regarded as the 'purest' of the Wembley games. Blackpool reached Wembley twice more in the next

Above After the party's over: Manchester City have beaten Leicester City 1–0 in the 'after the gold rush' final of 1969 and Tony Book holds the Cup while Glyn Pardoe clings onto his medal. *Right* 'Happy' Harry Hampton scores one of the two goals with which Villa beat Newcastle in the 1905 Final. It was the first year of a disastrous spell for the Geordies: between 1905 and 1911, they appeared in five Finals at Crystal Palace and did not win there once.

hard for him and looked to have bounced out of play before he hooked it back across the goal. The Arsenal defence stopped and Allen was left free to flick the ball into the net.

The referee, a Mr Harper, carved himself an everlasting niche in soccer history by allowing the goal and Newcastle went on to win via another by Allen. That particular incident—and the photographs of the day tended to support the view of the Arsenal defence rather than that of the referee—ranks as the most arguable Cup Final goal ever.

For a time it was quite impossible to keep Arsenal out of the Cup headlines. In the third round the following season they went to Walsall, a club of no great pretensions, and lost 2–0 in a game that still ranks above Yeovil–Sunderland and Colchester–Leeds as the greatest of all the giant-killing acts. The reasons are emotional rather than analytical. What more needs to be said than that Arsenal spent more on their boots in 1933 than Walsall had paid in transfer fees for their team?

The little clubs can indeed add drama, and one of the most appealing things about the Cup is the periodic appearance of the giantkillers. On occasions it has even gained a club admission to the League—Peterborough after their successes in the 1950s and Hereford and Wimbledon after their exploits in the 1970s are perhaps the best examples. Often enough it has cost managers of League clubs their positions. When

five years, losing to Newcastle in 1951 and facing Bolton in 1953, a game consigned to legend as 'the Matthews Final'. Blackpool came back from 3–1 down 20 minutes from time and 3–2 down with just three minutes of normal time left to win 4–3 in the game which will probably always rank—whatever its merits—as *the* Cup Final.

It was a game in keeping with the heady atmosphere of 1953, of the Coronation, of Everest, of Gordon Richards' Derby win, of the Hungarians' visit to Wembley. Yet tacticians point to Bolton's strange response to left-half Eric Bell's injury in the first half. Bell moved to the left-wing. Inside-left Harry Hassall, no great tackler, moved to left-half and, when left-back Ralph Banks went down with cramp twenty minutes from the end, he was left marking Matthews. As a result, Matthews' right-wing was left as open as the proverbial barn door and Bolton paid the price.

Bell's injury was a portent for the next decade. Between 1952 and 1961 only two Finals—1954 and 1958—were not marred by some vital injury. And, significantly, only two of the teams that suffered—Manchester City in 1956 and Nottingham Forest in 1959—eventually won the Cup. The phenomenon, dubbed 'the Wembley hoodoo', was generally attributed to the turf.

Danny Blanchflower explained after the 1961 Final: 'It was a lush trap; the ideal pitch should have a little give in it. But Wembley is too soft. It pulls at the lower muscles of the leg, braking some efforts and ruining the natural timing.' After that particular game—in which Len Chalmers of Leicester suffered torn ligaments—the hoodoo seemed to die away. Substitutes were first introduced in 1967 and it was never an issue again. Perhaps cutting the grass a little shorter made the difference.

Wolverhampton were the great team of the fifties, winning three Championships, yet their two Cup wins were in the last year of the previous decade and the first of the next. And they were against, perhaps, the two worst post-War finalists. In 1949 Leicester arrived at Wembley with the sole distinction of being the worst placed League club (they finished nineteenth in the Second Division) ever to reach the Final. In fact with one point less they would have been playing Third Division football in the August of the same year. Leicester's 3–1 defeat was the prelude to three more in the next 20 years—leaving them with the undisputed position of chief bridesmaid.

Wolves' 1960 opponents were in some ways even more ragged. Blackburn Rovers received a transfer request from centre-forward Derek Dougan on the morning of the match, left-back Dave Whelan broke a leg and right-half McGrath scored an own goal. It was the most one-sided of all the Wembley Finals and, while promising to herald in an even more successful decade than the one before for the Mid-landers, it was in fact manager Cullis's swansong. Five years later Wolves were playing Second Division football.

Manchester United's post-war record is far sadder. Despite their wins in 1948, 1963 and 1977, it is the games of 1957 and 1958 that they must be remembered by. Not only did United become the first club to lose successive finals at Wembley, but they did so in tragic circumstances.

United approached Wembley in 1957 as League Champions, having reached the semi-final of the European Cup, and on the verge of becoming perhaps the best British club side ever. Real Madrid had beaten them in the European Cup, but it had disheartened nobody, and Busby had said: '... the only difference between the teams was in their experience, and we shall soon acquire that ...' To add spice to the Cup Final their opponents were Aston Villa, the last club to do the Double that United seemed to have so firmly in their grasp.

But within minutes Villa's outside-left McParland had crashed into the United keeper Ray Wood and fractured his cheekbone. Wood went off, Jackie Blanchflower had to take over, and the machine was disturbed. McParland scored two goals to give Villa a record seventh win. As one journalist put it the next day: 'McParland was the man of the match—bagging two goals and one goalkeeper.'

But if 1957 could be called tragic for United, then 1958 was cataclysmic. That was, of course, the year of Munich. Six of the 1957 Wembley side—Byrne, Colman, Edwards, Whelan, Taylor and Pegg—were dead. Two—Johnny Berry and Jackie Blanchflower—survived but never kicked a ball again. And what happened next has become a legend.

The FA waived its rules to allow Stan Crowther, a member of the Villa side that had beaten United in 1957, to play for United after having turned out for Villa already in the competition. Ernie Taylor, already a successful Cup Finalist with Blackpool and Newcastle, was brought to hold the team together. And as if partaking in some medieval ritual, the crowd support bordered on religious fanaticism. Wherever the new United appeared gates were closed. In the Cup Sheffield Wednesday were the first to fall before this uncanny force, then the favourites West Bromwich, then Second Division Fulham after two semi-final games which ended as 2–2 and 5–3.

And so they arrived at the gates of Wembley, where their opponents were to be Bolton. Poor Bolton. Five years earlier every uncommitted observer had wanted them to lose so that Stanley Matthews could get his winners medal. This time they must have had a sneaking suspicion that even their own fans would not have minded too much if the Cup had ended up just five miles down the road at Old Trafford.

But the fates had let things go far enough. Within three minutes a very unghostly Nat Lofthouse put Bolton one up and, early in the second half, made it two with a charge that bundled ball and goalkeeper Gregg into the back of the net.

The myth has grown up that it was Lofthouse's charge that lost United the game. That is unlikely. In many ways they had looked what they were—a team carried along on a wave of fantacism that could not, in the end, disguise the makeshift nature of the effort. After all, only Foulkes and Charlton had played in both Finals. In the space of six years and three Finals in the 1920s Bolton had used just 17 players. United had been forced to use 20 in successive appearances.

Ricky George's extra-time shot flies past Newcastle United keeper Ian McFaul and Hereford thus becomes the first non-League side to defeat First Division opposition for nearly a quarter of a century. It was this win which effectively gained Hereford a place in the Fourth Division in the same year, 1972.

Manchester's Yorkshire counterpart—Leeds—have a record almost as sad. The team that Don Revie brought from the shadows became the first to take second place in both major competitions on two separate occasions, 1965 and 1970. What was sadder was the universal opinion that, in the latter Final, Leeds were the better of the two sides. But then the best side is surely the one that scores most goals and Chelsea did precisely that in the first replay since the Final moved to Wembley.

One club with a very satisfactory post-War Cup record is Tottenham. They have won five Finals, to bring their total to seven appearances and a record seven wins. The third, fourth and fifth of these came within the space of six years—1961, 1962 and 1967—and the first, a 2–0 win against Leicester, earned Spurs the first double for 64 years.

The first season of the decade seems to have a fascination for White Hart Lane. Spurs won the Cup first in 1901, next in 1921, the League for the first time in 1951, the Double in 1961, the League Cup in 1971 and the FA Cup again in 1981.

Newcastle have been almost as successful at Wembley. In seven appearances they have won five times and they share with the North Londoners the distinction of being the only club to win in consecutive seasons there. The Magpies were successful in 1924, 1932, 1951, 1952 and 1955, and were not beaten until Liverpool and Manchester City overcame them in the 1974 FA Cup and 1976 League Cup. The fact that they beat Arsenal twice—1932 and 1952—only serves to stress how poor London's record has been in an event that the FA have always insisted should be held there.

But Spurs' Double in 1961 was the precursor of a remarkable run of success for the capital—the more so in comparison with what had gone before. Between 1961 and 1982 London clubs won eleven of the 22 finals. In the previous 60 years they had won just six.

Arsenal's Double was the more remarkable of the two if only for its unpredictability. With Spurs in 1961 the possibility had been discussed from very early on in the season. Arsenal came through at the last moment in both competitions—overhauling Leeds after being six points behind with just six weeks to go, taking 27 points from their last 16 matches, and scoring a last-minute penalty to draw with Stoke in the semi-final.

On the Monday of Cup Final week they beat Spurs—appropriately as their North London neighbours were then the only 20th-century Double winners—to take the League, and five days later squeezed past Liverpool at Wembley to deprive Spurs of their uniqueness. It was Arsenal's 64th game of the season.

Strangely it was left to Arsenal to try and prevent yet another Double the following season. They failed, after a dour game which, if nothing else, epitomized the football of the early seventies and ended in its most familiar score: 1–0. Leeds were in no way dispirited by the manner of their victory—it was third time lucky for both the club and for Allan Clarke, the man who scored the only goal of the Final.

Having won the one that had eluded them for so long however, Leeds went to Wolverhampton just two days later needing a single point for the elusive Double. But they lost 2–1.

Leeds defeat the following year, 1973, by Sunderland was the most emotional of the post-War finals (excluding perhaps 1953) and was the first of several Second Division successes. Fulham were beaten by West Ham in 1975, Southampton beat Manchester United in 1976, Arsenal went down to West Ham in 1980 and QPR took Spurs to a replay in 1982. West Ham have the odd distinction that all their finals have featured Second Division clubs—they were in that League in 1923 and 1980, as were their opponents in 1964 and 1975. Certainly the

GIANT-KILLING BY NON-LEAGUE CLUBS 1919–86

Victories over First Division sides

*Cardiff City	2	Oldham Athletic	0	1919–20
*Sheffield Wednesday	0	Darlington	2 (after 0–0 draw)	1919–20
†Corinthians	1	Blackburn Rovers	0	1923–24
Colchester United	1	Huddersfield Town	0	1947–48
Yeovil Town	2	Sunderland	1	1948–49
Hereford United	2	Newcastle United	1 (after 2–2 draw)	1971–72
Burnley	0	Wimbledon	1	1974–75
Birmingham City	1	Altrincham	2	1985–86

Victories over Second Division sides

*Coventry City	0	Luton Town	1 (after 2–2 draw)	1919–20
*Fulham	1	Swindon Town	2	1919–20
*Plymouth Argyle	4	Barnsley	1	1919–20
*Wolverhampton W	1	Cardiff City	2	1919–20
Wolverhampton W	0	Mansfield Town	1	1928–29
Chelmsford City	4	Southampton	1	1938–39
Colchester United	3	Bradford PA	2	1947–48
Yeovil Town	3	Bury	1	1948–49
†Bishop Auckland	3	Ipswich Town	2 (after 2–2 draw)	1954–55
Lincoln City	4	Peterborough United	5 (after 2–2 draw)	1956–57
Notts County	1	Rhyl	3	1956–57
Worcester City	2	Liverpool	1	1958–59
Ipswich Town	2	Peterborough United	3	1959–60
Newcastle United	1	Bedford Town	2	1963–64
Blyth Spartans	3	Stoke City	2	1977–78
Harlow Town	1	Leicester City	0 (after 1–1 draw)	1979–80

Biggest victories over League sides

Carlisle United	1	Wigan Athletic	6	1934–35
†Walthamstow Avenue	6	Northampton Town	1	1936–37
Derby County	1	Boston United	6	1955–56
Hereford United	6	Queen's Park Rangers	1	1957–58
Barnet	6	Newport County	1	1970–71

Progress to last sixteen (present fifth round)

*1919–20 Cardiff City
*1919–20 Plymouth Argyle
1947–48 Colchester United
1948–49 Yeovil Town
1977–78 Blyth Spartans

*The Third Division did not come into being until 1920. In the 1919–20 season the best Southern League clubs were of a comparable standard with Second Division sides. †Amateur club.

appearance of five non-First Division sides in the space of ten finals suggests a convergence of standards, though perhaps those of elaborate defensive tactics rather than forward skill. Sunderland, Southampton and West Ham all won their finals 1–0, conclusions which mirror the increasing ability of teams throughout the game to score a single goal and hold onto that lead against apparently superior opponents. It was a trend that hopefully reached its peak in the European Cup with Nottingham Forest's defeat of SV Hamburg and Aston Villa's conquest of Bayern Munich.

As the 1970s went on, the most surprising feature of the Cup was the way the South came to dominate it. Between 1975 and 1982, only one northern club, Manchester United in 1977, actually took the trophy back to its traditional home. Even worse, only 5 of the 16 finalists in that period were from Lancashire and none at all came from the Midlands, North East or Yorkshire. Strangely, this was not mirrored in the League or League Cup—competitions then dominated by Liverpool, Nottingham Forest and Aston Villa with scarcely anyone else getting a look in.

Though Manchester United's denial of Liverpool's treble in 1977 was surely the most unexpected of results, the finals of 1978 and 1981 were the ones that appealed to the public. Ipswich had long been seeking a Cup final win to go with their lone League Championship, and when it came against Arsenal it had to be worked for. The woodwork kept Ipswich at bay for so long that it seemed certain Wembley was watching another 'lucky Arsenal' display, with the Gunners sneaking a last minute winner. In the end it was not to be, Roger Osborne scoring the only goal and going off straight afterwards with mental rather than physical exhaustion.

Spurs virtually made Wembley their home ground in 1981 and 1982, appearing there seven times in 18 months. Both the 1981 final against Manchester City and the 1982 version

against QPR had to be replayed, the first occasions replays had taken place at Wembley. Spurs were lucky to draw with Manchester City at all, Glenn Hoddle's 81st minute free-kick going in off Tommy Hutchison's shoulder and giving Hutchison the distinction of scoring for both sides, only the second time this had happened. The replay of this, the Centenary final, lived up to its billing, with one of the best games in the competition's history. Spurs won 3–2 in the end, the final goal coming from Ricky Villa's memorable dribble, the best individual Cup Final goal in living memory.

Hoddle scored again the following year—twice. His was Spurs' only goal of a 1–1 draw, then he converted a sixth minute penalty to win the replay 1–0. QPR were the better team and unlucky to go away with the losers medals, but Spurs were clearly exhausted at the end of a terrible season for them. After bravely contesting four trophies, the Cup Final was their final hope and was preceded by the loss of their two Argentinians—Ardiles and Villa—because of the Falklands War.

A less publicized aspect of the 1982 Cup Final replay was its similarity to the 1923 'White Horse' Final. This was not so much because a Second Division London side was playing, but because it was the only other time that it had been possible to turn up and buy a ticket at the gate. The attendance was only 90,000 and the unheard of had happened—empty seats at the Cup final. It was a sign that not even the game's premier event was immune from the cold winds of recession blowing over the nation's soccer fields. But while the recession was certainly felt at the top, football at other levels had never been healthier. That was fortunate for the FA Cup, for in many ways it is a competition for the 600 or so little clubs who set off in the 36 first qualifying rounds well before summer turns to autumn.

A club like Boden Colliery Welfare, playing in the North-Eastern Geographical Division in September 1987 is faced with 15 rounds before reaching Wembley. Of course, hardly any of the clubs which start at this early stage even reach the First Round proper. Twenty-four of the best non-League sides are exempt until the Fourth (the last) Qualifying Round, and the winners from that round go on to the First Round proper where they are joined by the Third and Fourth Division clubs and the previous season's FA Challenge Trophy finalists. After two rounds this number has been cut to twenty, who are joined by the 44 big boys of the First and Second Division.

The Cup, however, has a place for the likes of Abergavenny Thursdays and Irthlingborough Diamonds. It started, and remains, a competition for all the clubs affiliated to the Football Association—and it is a place they guard manfully.

Really it is a competition—and most certainly a Final—for the fan. It is the fan who pays £100 for black market tickets, who turns mortals into immortals simply because they scored a goal, who talks about it, dreams about it and relives it for months, who would not give away a Final ticket for a fortune, because the most valuable thing a fortune can buy is a Cup Final ticket.

Danny Blanchflower puts it the players' way: 'In truth we are brainwashed about the Cup Final. A player hears so much about it before he gets there ... the "majestic" twin towers ... the "hallowed" green turf ... the "royal" greeting ... the crowd singing "Abide With Me" ... It all sounds like some distant religious ceremony that takes place at the end of the season in the promised land. The reality of it can never live up to the dream. The dream is not for the player, it is for the fan ... the lover of the game who doesn't really know what it is like out there and never *will* know. It is the fan's day, which is why some 400 million of them all over the world tune in on Cup Final day.'

Spurs' Glenn Hoddle beats QPR's Peter Hucker easily with a 6th minute penalty in the 1982 Cup Final replay. It was the only goal of the game. Hoddle had three scoring shots in the four games which made up the 1981 and 1982 finals. In the first 1981 game his free-kick was deflected by Tommy Hutchison, in the first 1982 game his shot was deflected by Tony Currie (but Hoddle was awarded the goal), and this penalty won the replay.

CHAPTER THREE

A LEAGUE CENTENARY

The season 1987–88, was, without question, a red letter one. It was the centenary season (though not the hundredth) of the oldest League competition in the world. That famous institution, the Football League (never mind the Canons and Todays) had been created on 23 March 1888, at Anderton's Hotel in London. William McGregor had gathered several of the major Northern and Midland sides together on the eve of the Cup final. They were worried about falling gate receipts when they could not fulfil their fixtures because of Cup replays and the like, and they resolved to solve the problem with a guaranteed fixture list among the top dozen or so clubs. McGregor didn't like the name Football League, because for some reason he thought it would be confused with the politically extreme Irish Land League, but his objections were overruled and Football League it became. Exactly 100 years later the most striking thing about the whole affair is how little it has really changed.

Certainly the centenary season saw some elements of flux. Several Third and Fourth Division clubs remained under a real threat of bankruptcy. The First Division was in process (via a complicated set of play-offs) of being reduced from 22 to 20 clubs, the first time for nearly 70 years that there had been

Watford rose from the Fourth to the First Division in the space of five years (1978–82) and their off-field publicity was almost as good as that on the park. Chairman Elton John added some undreamed-of glamour, here handing out gold discs to his principal strikers Luther Blissett and Ross Jenkins. Both had been with the club since the Fourth Division days and Blissett even managed to score a hat-trick on his first full England appearance, late in 1982 against Luxembourg.

any fundamental change to its structure. And back in 1982 the League had controversially introduced three points for a win.

This latter change had been interesting because, excepting at the margin of a third promotion or relegation place, it had made little difference to where clubs finished. It did, nonetheless, genuinely appear to have encouraged a slightly more positive attitude to goalscoring after the death of the mid-1970s. What does remain true is that, unlike the FA Cup or European Cup, what matters is not just what you do—but what your contemporaries do. Take the example of the great Nottingham Forest side of 1978–79.

On 7 October 1978 Nottingham Forest established a new record of 35 League games without defeat by beating Wolves 3–1. Their last League defeat had been on 19 November 1977 at Leeds, the supplanted record holders. A month later, on 4 November 1978, their goalless draw with Everton established another record—that of 36 consecutive first-class competitive games without defeat. The beaten record, held by Blackburn Rovers, had been established all of 96 years previously, in 1881–82. Since that defeat by Leeds, Forest had played 59 first-class games (six FA Cup, nine League Cup, four European Cup, the FA Charity Shield and 39 First

Division) and had been beaten just once (on 11 March 1978) by West Bromwich Albion in an FA Cup quarter-final. Their next game, a 3–2 victory at Everton in the League Cup on 7 November 1978, was also their 18th consecutive *away* first-class game (excluding matches on neutral grounds such as Wembley) without defeat—also a record. The following Saturday, their 3–1 win at Tottenham was their 21st consecutive away League game without defeat—and another record.

Forest had broken virtually every record in the book—longest undefeated run, longest undefeated League run, longest run of away matches without defeat, most away League matches without defeat—and they went on to win the European Cup undefeated at the first attempt. And yet they did not win the Championship at the end of that season, Liverpool finishing eight points clear with a record of 68, the highest ever achieved by the Champions during the two points for a win era. Forest finished with 60 points, a total surpassed by only 12 of the League Champions in the 35 seasons between the War and the introduction of three points for a win, and the equivalent only by three since that date.

It was a perfect illustration of the unfortunate truth about the League Championship—that it is as much what your contemporaries do as what you achieve yourself that deter-mines the difference between success and failure. And, apart from the twice a year you play them, you cannot control those opponents, or *their* opponents. On 30 March 1960, Wolves beat Burnley 6–0 at Molineux. One month later Burnley won their very last game of the season to sneak into first place in the First Division for the only time in the whole season. Wolves had led the table throughout, had just hit Burnley for six, but lost the Championship to them by one point on the very last day of the season. Wolves had a better goal average—a point would have done it. They had won the Championship in 1958 and 1959 and won the Cup in 1960. With just one more point, they would have won the Double *and* taken a hat-trick of Championships in one fell swoop. It can be a bitter game.

Hence Leeds could win the Championship in 1969 by scoring 66 times (one fewer than the number of points they got), while forty years earlier Manchester City mustered 23 goals more and were relegated! Leeds' 66-goal tally—one less than the record 67 points they amassed—was perfectly respectable in a climate of defensive football. City's 1926 total of 89, however, was not—unfortunately for them—as extra-ordinary then as it would have been forty years on.

For those years saw the decline and fall of positive attacking football. Preventing goals is easier than scoring them, and the 'smash-and-grab' type of football, with goals on the quick break out of defence as introduced by Herbert Chapman at Arsenal, rapidly became the favoured tactic.

That style of play was perhaps best seen at its peak when the Gunners themselves played against Aston Villa in 1935. Territorially outplayed, Arsenal were restricted to just nine shots at goal, eight of them from their England centre-forward, Ted Drake. The score? Aston Villa 1 Arsenal 7. Drake scored all seven Arsenal goals.

In the early days of the League, Sunderland, for example, won the 1893 title with 100 goals—and 48 points—from just 30 matches. But defences quickly became more sophisticated and the offside trap, brought to a fine art by Bill McCracken of Newcastle in the middle twenties, showed itself as early as 1909. In that year, Newcastle won the title with only 65 goals.

It is interesting to speculate what might have happened if the Football League's original intention to award points only for wins had been carried through. The mind boggles at the

Watford's Steve Sims dominates the Coventry attack during a 1984 First Division game. Watford finished their debut season in Division 1 (1982–83) in second place, the highest position ever for a debutant excepting only Ipswich's one-off championship in 1962. In 1983–84, Watford's exciting football took them to the FA Cup Final.

goals there might have been had a drawn game remained valueless in terms of points! However, it was not to be, for after 10 weeks of the first season it was decided that drawn games should be worth a point to each side.

At the end of the first season, Preston North End were champions. That inaugural season, 1888–89, when Preston also won the FA Cup without conceding a goal, their League record was so outstanding that it remains an imperishable landmark in soccer history.

In their 22 League matches, they won 18 times and drew four, scoring 74 goals against 15. They are the only British club ever to have gone through a season without a defeat in either League or Cup.

Preston were champions again in the League's second season, though they were beaten four times. In 1890–91, however, they finished second. It was Everton who took the title away from them, and who were to become the most consistent League club, spending all but five of the next 84 seasons in the top division. The record for unbroken membership now belongs to Arsenal, who have been members since 1919 through to the present day.

Considering that the North East has produced only three major clubs, Sunderland, Newcastle and Middlesbrough, the area has done well in terms of First Division membership—at least one of the three was there until 1962—especially as none was an original League member.

There were twelve of those: Wolves, Everton, Preston, Burnley, Derby, Notts County, Blackburn Rovers, Bolton, Stoke, Accrington, Aston Villa and West Bromwich Albion. The North East was not the only region with no representative in the first League. Not one of that dozen came from London or the South.

By 1983, the story was different. The Home Counties had five clubs in the First Division, the Midlands as many as seven, Lancashire was down to four and Yorkshire and the once mighty North East had only Sunderland. The five remaining clubs—Ipswich, Brighton, Norwich, Swansea and Southampton—came, needless to say, from elsewhere, though Luton and Watford might be added to the list of the relatively unfamiliar. But that fact is important. Very few First Division teams have come from elsewhere. In the League's first 100 years, just twelve clubs have been situated outside the traditional areas of football power—London, the Midlands, Lancashire, Yorkshire and the North East—areas which contain some 80 percent of the country's population.

They are Grimsby (who joined the First Division in 1901), Bristol City (1906), Cardiff (1921), Portsmouth (1927), Luton (1955), Ipswich (1961), Southampton (1966), Norwich (1972), Carlisle (1974), Brighton (1979), Swansea (1981) and Watford (1982).

This is not because the industrial areas produce the best players, but because they provide more spectators. Crowds paying money at the gate means money to spend on new players. It is a harsh fact of football life that the clubs with the best support tend to get the best players. There are exceptions—Aston Villa and Newcastle since the War.

It was different in 1888 when the League started. Professionalism had been legal for only three years; money was not yet all important. Then, the best players came from those parts of the country where there were most young men. And with Lancashire and the Midlands centres of heavy industry, they were able to attract young men from Scotland, Ireland and Wales, where jobs were few. Many a skilful footballer emerged from kickabouts with his workmates.

But as industry began to spread, so did the quality and scope of the game. It is no coincidence that the first team from the South to join the League was a works team—Woolwich Arsenal. The Crimea had made a munitions factory on the bank of the Thames important to the country's war effort. More was to come from that factory than shells.

Not that Arsenal were the first 'outside' club to penetrate the monopoly of the Midlands and Lancashire. Arsenal did not really emerge until the League was 16 years old.

The first 'newcomers' were Sunderland, in 1890, and who won the Championship in 1891 and 1892, when Sheffield's The Wednesday joined the First Division, a year ahead of the other Sheffield club, United.

The arrival of these three was no surprise. Sunderland had a fine team drawn from a mixture of local Northerners and Scotsmen who had been tempted over the border, while Sheffield was one of the first towns in which organized football was played. Indeed, the Sheffield amateur club, formed in 1857, is the oldest in the world.

Sunderland had been champions six times when they were relegated in 1958, which, when added to Newcastle's four, gives the North East an impressive record considering its

population. Lancashire, of course, boasting the Liverpool and Manchester clubs in addition to earlier giants of the League such as Blackburn, Preston and Burnley, have easily the best record with 39 of the first 87 Championships.

There have been few discernable patterns with regard to the winning of the League, except perhaps for the years 1963–70. Then the title seemed to be the preserve of the North. Champions in those years were Everton, Liverpool, Manchester United, Liverpool, United again, Manchester City, Leeds and Everton. Eight Championships, and seven of them won by Lancashire's two major cities.

Leeds' 1968–69 success was their first. Yorkshire neighbours Huddersfield, however, collected three in consecutive seasons during the twenties, under the guidance of the famous Herbert Chapman, later to build the Arsenal team that became the first club to emulate Huddersfield's feat.

Huddersfield's first Championship they won dramatically. For at the end of the 1923–24 season Cardiff City also had 57 points, and the two clubs' goal averages were remarkably similar. Huddersfield had scored 60 goals against 33, Cardiff 61 against 34. Huddersfield had a microscopic advantage: under goal difference Cardiff would have been top.

And that was tragic for Cardiff. For in their last game of the season, the Welshmen had been awarded a penalty in the last minute at Birmingham. No one wanted to take it, but eventually Len Davies stepped up. He missed it, the game ended in a goalless draw and Huddersfield were champions.

If Huddersfield's climb to the top had been dramatic, Cardiff's rise—and their subsequent decline—was even more spectacular. Admitted to the Second Division in 1920, they won promotion in their first season. Curiously, they were then only a 200th part of a goal behind Birmingham in first place.

Within seven years, Cardiff had been Championship runners-up, beaten FA Cup Finalists, and Cup winners in 1927. Within another seven, they were seeking re-election after finishing bottom of the Third Division South.

That same season, 1933–34, Huddersfield scored more goals than any of their First Division rivals. Perhaps that was some atonement for their poor tally that had deprived Cardiff of what would have been their first and only Championship success. For those 60 goals Huddersfield scored in 1923–24 comprised the lowest aggregate since the War.

The War seemed momentarily to have arrested the trend of fewer and fewer goals, and even the advent of the 'policeman'

LEAGUE CHAMPIONSHIP

	Winners	Runners-up		Winners	Runners-up		Winners	Runners-up
1888–89	Preston North End	Aston Villa	1924–25	Huddersfield Town	West Bromwich Albion	1963–64	Liverpool	Manchester United
1889–90	Preston North End	Everton	1925–26	Huddersfield Town	Arsenal	1964–65	**Manchester United	Leeds United
1890–91	Everton	Preston North End	1926–27	Newcastle United	Huddersfield Town	1965–66	Liverpool	Leeds United
1891–92	Sunderland	Preston North End	1927–28	Everton	Huddersfield Town	1966–67	Manchester United	Nottingham Forest
1892–93	Sunderland	Preston North End	1928–29	Sheffield Wednesday	Leicester City	1967–68	Manchester City	Manchester United
1893–94	Aston Villa	Sunderland	1929–30	Sheffield Wednesday	Derby County	1968–69	Leeds United	Liverpool
1894–95	Sunderland	Everton	1930–31	Arsenal	Aston Villa	1969–70	Everton	Leeds United
1895–96	Aston Villa	Derby County	1931–32	Everton	Arsenal	1970–71	Arsenal	Leeds United
1896–97	Aston Villa	Sheffield United	1932–33	Arsenal	Aston Villa	1971–72	Derby County	Leeds United
1897–98	Sheffield United	Sunderland	1933–34	Arsenal	Huddersfield Town	1972–73	Liverpool	Arsenal
1898–99	Aston Villa	Liverpool	1934–35	Arsenal	Sunderland	1973–74	Leeds United	Liverpool
1988–1900	Aston Villa	Sheffield United	1935–36	Sunderland	Derby County	1974–75	Derby County	Liverpool
1900–01	Liverpool	Sunderland	1936–37	Manchester City	Charlton Athletic	1975–76	Liverpool	Queen's Park Rangers
1901–02	Sunderland	Everton	1937–38	Arsenal	Wolverhampton Wanderers	1976–77	Liverpool	Manchester City
1902–03	The Wednesday	Aston Villa	1938–39	Everton	Wolverhampton Wanderers	1977–78	Nottingham Forest	Liverpool
1903–04	The Wednesday	Manchester City	1939–46	No competition		1978–79	Liverpool	Nottingham Forest
1904–05	Newcastle United	Everton	1946–47	Liverpool	Manchester United	1979–80	Liverpool	Manchester United
1905–06	Liverpool	Preston North End	1947–48	Arsenal	Manchester United	1980–81	Aston Villa	Ipswich Town
1906–07	Newcastle United	Bristol City	1948–49	Portsmouth	Manchester United	1981–82	Liverpool	Ipswich Town
1907–08	Manchester United	Aston Villa	1949–50	**Portsmouth	Wolverhampton Wanderers	1982–83	Liverpool	Watford
1908–09	Newcastle United	Everton	1950–51	Tottenham Hotspur	Manchester United	1983–84	Liverpool	Southampton
1909–10	Aston Villa	Liverpool	1951–52	Manchester United	Tottenham Hotspur	1984–85	Everton	Liverpool
1910–11	Manchester United	Aston Villa	1952–53	**Arsenal	Preston North End	1985–86	Liverpool	Everton
1911–12	Blackburn Rovers	Everton	1953–54	Wolverhampton Wanderers	West Bromwich Albion	1986–87	Everton	Liverpool
1912–13	Sunderland	Aston Villa	1954–55	Chelsea	Wolverhampton Wanderers			
1913–14	Blackburn Rovers	Aston Villa	1955–56	Manchester United	Blackpool			
1914–15	Everton	Oldham Athletic	1956–57	Manchester United	Tottenham Hotspur			
1915–19	No competition		1957–58	Wolverhampton Wanderers	Preston North End			
1919–20	West Bromwich Albion	Burnley	1958–59	Wolverhampton Wanderers	Manchester United			
1920–21	Burnley	Manchester City	1959–60	Burnley	Wolverhampton Wanderers			
1921–22	Liverpool	Tottenham Hotspur	1960–61	Tottenham Hotspur	Sheffield Wednesday			
1922–23	Liverpool	Sunderland	1961–62	Ipswich Town	Burnley			
1923–24	**Huddersfield Town	Cardiff City	1962–63	Everton	Tottenham Hotspur			

**League title won on goal average.

centre-half, the result of the offside law change in 1925 and exemplified by Arsenal's Herbie Roberts, could do little to stop the surge of goalscoring. In 1931, when the Championship was Arsenal's they scored 127 goals, while Aston Villa, runners-up that season, themselves scored a record 128.

After the Second World War, football boomed but goals, like everything else, were in short supply. That was until the great young Manchester United side of the mid-fifties. In 1957, just before the Munich disaster, they scored 103 goals, as did Wolves the next year. In 1959, Wolves surpassed themselves with 110.

But with the Spurs team that won the double in 1960–61 came one of the last centuries before the massed defences took over. Though Tottenham scored a conspicuous 111 goals in 1962–63, Everton's 84 gave them six more points and thus the title. No club has scored 100 First Division goals since.

The fall-off in goalscoring can be clearly seen at the other end of the table. While Spurs won the Double, Newcastle went down with 86 goals to their credit. Compared with the miserable 27 Huddersfield scraped together when they were relegated just over a decade later, Newcastle might well curse their misfortune.

In the 1970s goals were even tighter. From 1960 and 1965 Spurs scored 115, 88, 111, 97 and 87 League goals in the five seasons. A decade later, in a period when they reached four

Cup finals, their goal scoring figures went 54 (3rd), 63 (6th), 58 (8th), 45 (11th) and 52 (19th). Their League positions and Cup finals show that they were by no means an unsuccessful team. The margins had, however, become much tighter with fewer goals being scored. A draw when you are 1–0 down is a lot easier to achieve than when the deficit is 4–1. Fewer goals lead, inevitably, to more low scoring draws and the possibility, if not likelihood, of the poorer teams sneaking an undeserved win. At the most extreme, teams could still survive and barely score at all. The most absurd example of this came from Second Division Orient in 1974–75. They finished 12th with a point a game record of 42 points. And yet they scored only 28 goals—an average of $1\frac{1}{2}$ points per goal!

The First Division in recent years has suffered from the dominance of Liverpool. The Merseysiders won 9 of the 14 Championships that followed Derby's surprise success of 1972. In that year Liverpool should have won the trophy as well. They went to Arsenal for the last game of the season needing a win to clinch it, but only drew 0–0. On the same evening Leeds needed just a draw at Wolves and they, in their turn, would have been champions. The result of a game destined to feature in future lawsuits was 2–1 to Wolves, so Derby, who had completed their fixtures and gone off to Majorca sure they would be caught, were unexpectedly declared Champions for the first time.

Derby's manager was, of course, Brian Clough and the only real challenge the city of Liverpool have had in the last 14 years has come from Clough and his East Midland clubs Derby and Forest, plus Aston Villa. Though Clough had left, Derby won another Championship in 1975 (albeit with only 53 points) and the East Midlands connection had been cemented after ex-Derby captain Dave Mackay moved from Nottingham Forest as manager. Clough took the vacant chair at the City Ground, gradually built his squad, and, between April 1977 and May 1979 Forest moved from a team on the fringe of promotion in the Second Division, through the First Division Championship to becoming worthy, and by no means lucky, European Champions. It was the fastest rise in football history. Promoted only third behind Wolves and Chelsea, they became the only club to win the First Division Championship immediately after being promoted other than as Second Division champions.

Liverpool were, of course, second that year. In fifteen seasons, Liverpool have finished other than first or second only once—fifth behind Aston Villa in 1981. And they won the European Cup that season to compensate! The Liverpool phenomenon is a remarkable one, but it has made the League less interesting. To maximize national involvement, and to motivate the fans, the honours have to be shared around. Even in Liverpool in 1984 football fans were bored. It had happened too often. They had even won the European Cup three times—what else was there to achieve? And, after all this, attendances at Anfield were dropping fast. Minor sides were scrapped, the full-time staff was cut to just enough for two teams. It made little difference to the club's consistency in the League. For the 8th time in 12 years the Merseysiders walked away with the Championship, having seen off a determined but never entirely convincing challenge from Manchester United. It was Joe Fagan's first Championship as manager and it simply sustained Liverpool's norm since the days of Shankly. But in one way it was new—it gave Liverpool their first hat-trick in the League. Two years later, in 1986, Kenny Dalglish added the other ultimate prize—the Double—when Liverpool beat Everton into second place in both competitions. All that remained was the glittering treble they had come so close to in 1977—the FA Cup, League and European Cup. Sadly, that would be a long time coming.

CHAPTER FOUR

THE CLUBS

Club information is correct at 1 June 1987. In some cases the strips featured are the traditional club colours and do not incorporate such fashions as thin vertical lines, which, like the rash of manufacturers' symbols which appeared on shirts around 1980, are unlikely to be permanent features.

KEY

q	— qualifying rounds/competition
P	— promoted (also, for Scottish clubs, Premier League)
R	— relegated
IIIS	— Third Division South
IIIN	— Third Division North
C	— Football/Scottish League champions
p	— preliminary round
L	— failed to gain re-election

A typical Brian Robson power header as he gets in front of his marker John Bumstead in the 1986–87 League match between Manchester United and Chelsea at Old Trafford.

37

Founded: 1926
Address: Recreation Ground, High Street, Aldershot
Telephone: Aldershot 20211
Ground capacity: 16,000
Playing area: 117 by 76 yards
Record attendance: 19,138 v Carlisle United, FA Cup 4th round replay, 28.1.70
Record victory: 8–1 v Gateshead, Division IV, 1958–59
Record defeat: 0–9 v Bristol City, Division III(S), 28.12.46
Most League points (3 for win): 75, Division IV, 1983–84
Most League points (2 for win): 57, Division IV, 1978–79
Most League goals: 83, Division IV, 1963–64
League scoring record: 26, John Dungworth, Division IV, 1978–79
Record League aggregate: 171, Jack Howarth, 1965–71 and 1972–77
Most League appearances: 461, Murray Brodie, 1964–83
Most capped player: 1 (10 in all), Peter Scott, Northern Ireland.

THE ALDERSHOT RECORD

	Division and place		Cup round reached		Division and place		Cup round reached
1933	SIII	17	5	1963	IV	11	2
1934	SIII	14	5	1964	IV	9	4
1935	SIII	18	3	1965	IV	18	2
1936	SIII	11	1	1966	IV	17	2
1937	SIII	22	1	1967	IV	10	3
1938	SIII	18	3	1968	IV	9	1
1939	SIII	10	2	1969	IV	15	1
1946			4	1970	IV	6	4
1947	SIII	20	2	1971	IV	13	3
1948	SIII	19	2	1972	IV	17	2
1949	SIII	21	3	1973	IV	4P	2
1950	SIII	20	1	1974	III	8	2
1951	SIII	18	3	1975	III	20	1
1952	SIII	12	2	1976	III	21R	3
1953	SIII	19	1	1977	IV	17	1
1954	SIII	17	2	1978	IV	5	1
1955	SIII	14	2	1979	IV	5	5
1956	SIII	15	3	1980	IV	10	3
1957	SIII	19	1	1981	IV	6	1
1958	SIII	18	3	1982	IV	16	2
1959	IV	22	1	1983	IV	18	3
1960	IV	13	1	1984	IV	5	1
1961	IV	10	4	1985	IV	13	2
1962	IV	7	2	1986	IV	16	1
				1987	IV	6P	4

Founded: 1886
Address: Arsenal Stadium, Highbury, London N.5
Telephone: (01) 226 0304
Ground capacity: 60,000
Playing area: 110 by 71 yards
Record attendance: 73,295 v Sunderland, Division I, 9.3.35
Record victory: 12–0 v Loughborough Town, Division II, 12.3.1900
Record defeat: 0–8 v Loughborough Town, Division II, 12.12.96
Most League points (3 for win): 71, Division I, 1981–82
Most League points (2 for win): 66, Division I, 1930–31
Most League goals: 127, Division I, 1930–31
League scoring record: 42, Ted Drake, Division I, 1934–35
Record League aggregate: 150, Cliff Bastin, 1930–1947
Most League appearances: 500, George Armstrong, 1960–1977
Most capped player: 49, Pat Rice, Northern Ireland

FA Cup	Year	Opponents	Score	Scorers
Winners	1930	Huddersfield Town	2–0	James, Lambert
	1936	Sheffield United	1–0	Drake
	1950	Liverpool	2–0	Lewis 2
	1971	Liverpool	*2–1	Kelly, George
	1979	Manchester United	3–2	Talbot, Stapleton, Sunderland
Runners-up	1927	Cardiff City	0–1	
	1932	Newcastle United	1–2	John
	1952	Newcastle United	0–1	
	1972	Leeds United	0–1	
	1978	Ipswich Town	0–1	
	1980	West Ham	0–1	
League Cup				
Winners	1987	Liverpool	2–1	Nicholas 2
Runners-up	1968	Leeds United	0–1	
	1969	Swindon Town	*1–3	Gould

* after extra time

THE ARSENAL RECORD

	Division and place		Cup round reached		Division and place		Cup round reached
1890			q	1938	I	1C	5
1891			1	1939	I	5	3
1892			1	1946			3
1893			1	1947	I	13	3
1894	II	9	1	1948	I	1C	3
1895	II	8	1	1949	I	5	4
1896	II	7	1	1950	I	6	Winners
1897	II	10	q	1951	I	5	5
1898	II	5	1	1952	I	3	Final
1899	II	7	1	1953	I	1C	q-f
1900	II	8	q	1954	I	12	4
1901	II	7	2	1955	I	9	4
1902	II	4	1	1956	I	5	q-f
1903	II	3	1	1957	I	5	q-f
1904	II	2P	2	1958	I	12	3
1905	I	10	1	1959	I	3	5
1906	I	12	s-f	1960	I	13	3
1907	I	7	s-f	1961	I	11	3
1908	I	14	1	1962	I	10	4
1909	I	6	2	1963	I	7	5
1910	I	18	2	1964	I	8	4
1911	I	10	2	1965	I	13	4
1912	I	10	1	1966	I	14	3
1913	I	20R	2	1967	I	7	5
1914	II	3	1	1968	I	9	5
1915	II	5P	2	1969	I	4	5
1920	I	11	2	1970	I	12	3
1921	I	9	1	1971	I	1C	Winners
1922	I	17	q-f	1972	I	5	Final
1923	I	11	1	1973	I	2	s-f
1924	I	19	2	1974	I	10	4
1925	I	20	1	1975	I	16	q-f
1926	I	2	q-f	1976	I	17	3
1927	I	11	Final	1977	I	8	5
1928	I	10	s-f	1978	I	5	Final
1929	I	9	q-f	1979	I	7	Winners
1930	I	14	Winners	1980	I	4	Final
1931	I	1C	4	1981	I	5	3
1932	I	2	Final	1982	I	5	4
1933	I	1C	3	1983	I	10	s-f
1934	I	1C	q-f	1984	I	6	3
1935	I	1C	q-f	1985	I	7	4
1936	I	6	Winners	1986	I	7	5
1937	I	3	q-f	1987	I	4	q-f

ASTON VILLA

Founded: 1874
Address: Villa Park, Trinity Road, Birmingham 6
Telephone: (021) 327 6604
Ground capacity: 48,000
Playing area: 115 by 75 yards
Record attendance: 76,588 v Derby County, FA Cup quarter-final, 2.3.46
Record victory: 13–0 v Wednesday Old Alliance, FA Cup 1st round, 30.10.86
Record defeat: 1–8 v Blackburn Rovers, FA Cup 3rd round, 1888–89
Most League points (3 for win): 68, Division I, 1982–83
Most League points (2 for win): 70, Division III, 1971–72
Most League goals: 128, Division I, 1930–31
League scoring record: 49, Pongo Waring, Division I, 1930–31
Record League aggregate: 213, Harry Hampton, 1904–1920 and Billy Walker, 1919–1934
Most League appearances: 560, Charlie Aitken, 1961–76
Most capped player: 33 (34 in all), Peter McParland, Northern Ireland

FA Cup	Year	Opponents	Score	Scorers
Winners	1887	West Bromwich Albion	2–0	Hodgetts, Hunter
	1895	West Bromwich Albion	1–0	Chatt
	1897	Everton	3–2	Campbell, Wheldon, Crabtree
	1905	Newcastle United	2–0	Hampton 2
	1913	Sunderland	1–0	Barber
	1920	Huddersfield Town	1–0	Kirton
	1957	Manchester United	2–1	McParland 2
Runners-up	1892	West Bromwich Albion	0–3	
	1924	Newcastle United	0–2	
League Cup				
Winners	1961	Rotherham United	A0–2	
			H3–0	O'Neill, Burrows, McParland
	1975	Norwich City	1–0	Graydon
	1977	Everton	0–0	
		Replay	*1–1	Kenyon og
		Replay	*3–2	Nicholl, Little 2
Runners-up	1963	Birmingham City	A1–3	Thomson
			H0–0	
	1971	Tottenham Hotspur	0–2	

* after extra time

THE VILLA RECORD

Year	Division and place		Cup round reached	Year	Division and place		Cup round reached
1880			3	1933	I	2	4
1881			4	1934	I	13	s-f
1882			4	1935	I	13	3
1883			q-f	1936	I	21R	3
1884			4	1937	II	9	3
1885			3	1938	II	1P	s-f
1886			2	1939	I	12	4
1887			Winners	1946	I		q-f
1888			1	1947	I	8	3
1889	I	2	q-f	1948	I	6	3
1890	I	8	2	1949	I	10	4
1891	I	9	2	1950	I	12	3
1892	I	4	final	1951	I	15	4
1893	I	4	1	1952	I	6	3
1894	I	1C	q-f	1953	I	11	q-f
1895	I	3	Winners	1954	I	13	3
1896	I	1C	1	1955	I	6	4
1897	I	1C	Winners	1956	I	20	4
1898	I	6	1	1957	I	10	Winners
1899	I	1C	1	1958	I	14	3
1900	I	1C	q-f	1959	I	21R	s-f
1901	I	15	s-f	1960	II	1P	s-f
1902	I	8	1	1961	I	9	5
1903	I	2	s-f	1962	I	7	q-f
1904	I	5	2	1963	I	15	4
1905	I	4	Winners	1964	I	19	3
1906	I	8	3	1965	I	16	5
1907	I	5	2	1966	I	16	3
1908	I	2	3	1967	I	21R	4
1909	I	7	1	1968	II	16	4
1910	I	1C	3	1969	II	18	5
1911	I	2	2	1970	II	21R	3
1912	I	6	2	1971	III	4	1
1913	I	2	Winners	1972	III	1P	1
1914	I	2	s-f	1973	II	3	3
1915	I	13	2	1974	II	14	5
1920	I	9	Winners	1975	II	2P	5
1921	I	10	q-f	1976	I	16	3
1922	I	5	q-f	1977	I	4	q-f
1923	I	6	1	1978	I	8	3
1924	I	6	Final	1979	I	8	3
1925	I	15	3	1980	I	7	q-f
1926	I	6	5	1981	I	1C	3
1927	I	10	3	1982	I	11	5
1928	I	8	5	1983	I	6	6*
1929	I	3	s-f	1984	I	10	3
1930	I	4	q-f	1985	I	10	3
1931	I	2	3	1986	I	16	4
1932	I	5	4	1987	I	22R	3

BARNSLEY

Formed: 1887 (as Barnsley St Peter's)
Address: Oakwell Ground, Grove Street, Barnsley, Yorkshire
Telephone: 0226 295353
Ground capacity: 35,500
Playing area: 111 by 75 yards
Record attendance: 40,255 v Stoke City, FA Cup 5th round, 15.2.36
Record victory: 9–0 v Loughborough Town, Division II, 28.1.1899; 9–0 v Accrington Stanley, Division III(N), 3.2.34
Record defeat: 0–9 v Notts County, Division II, 19.11.27
Most League points (3 for win): 67, Division II, 1981–82
Most League points (2 for win): 67, Division III(N), 1938–39
Most League goals: 118, Division III(N), 1933–34
League scoring record: 33, Cecil McCormack, Division II, 1950–51
Record League aggregate: 123, Ernest Hine, 1921–26 and 1934–38
Most League appearances: 514, Barry Murphy, 1962–78
Most capped player: 9 (15 in all). Eddie McMorran, Ireland

FA Cup	Year	Opponents	Score	Scorers
Winners	1912	West Bromwich Albion	0–0	
		Replay	1–0	Tufnell
Runners-up	1910	Newcastle United	1–1	Tufnell
		Replay	0–2	

THE BARNSLEY RECORD

Year	Division and place		Cup round reached	Year	Division and place		Cup round reached
1895			1	1946			5
1896			p	1947	II	10	4
1897			1	1948	II	12	3
1898			p	1949	II	9	3
1899	II	11	1	1950	II	13	3
1900	II	16	p	1951	II	15	3
1901	II	15	p	1952	II	20	4
1902	II	11	p	1953	II	22R	4
1903	II	8	2	1954	NIII	2	2
1904	II	8	1	1955	NIII	1P	2
1905	II	7	1	1956	II	18	4
1906	II	12	2	1957	II	19	5
1907	II	8	q-f	1958	II	14	3
1908	II	16	1	1959	II	22R	3
1909	II	17	1	1960	III	17	1
1910	II	9	Final	1961	III	8	q-f
1911	II	9	2	1962	III	20	2
1912	II	6	Winners	1963	III	18	3
1913	II	4	2	1964	III	20	5
1914	II	5	1	1965	III	24R	2
1915	II	3	1	1966	IV	16	2
1920	II	12	2	1967	IV	16	3
1921	II	16	1	1968	IV	2P	1
1922	II	3	3	1969	III	10	3
1923	II	9	2	1970	III	7	3
1924	II	11	1	1971	III	12	2
1925	II	15	2	1972	III	22R	2
1926	II	18	1	1973	IV	14	1
1927	II	11	4	1974	IV	13	2
1928	II	14	3	1975	IV	15	1
1929	II	16	3	1976	IV	12	1
1930	II	17	3	1977	IV	6	2
1931	II	19	5	1978	IV	7	2
1932	II	21R	3	1979	IV	4P	2
1933	NIII	8	3	1980	III	11	2
1934	NIII	1P	1	1981	III	2P	5
1935	II	16	3	1982	II	6	3
1936	II	20	q-f	1983	II	10	4
1937	II	14	3	1984	II	14	3
1938	II	21R	4	1985	II	11	6
1939	NIII	1P	3	1986	II	12	3
				1987	II	11	5

BIRMINGHAM CITY

Founded: 1875
Address: St Andrew's, Birmingham 9
Telephone: (021) 772 0101
Ground capacity: 44,500 (9,000 seated)
Playing area: 115 by 75 yards
Record attendance: 66,844 v Everton, FA Cup 5th round, 11.2.39
Record victory: 12–0 v Walsall Town Swifts, Division II, 17.12.1892; 12–0 v Doncaster Rovers, Division II, 11.4.03
Record defeat: 1–9 v Blackburn Rovers, Division I, 5.1.1895; 1–9 v Sheffield Wednesday, Division I, 13.12.30
Most League points (3 for win): 82, Division II, 1984–85
Most League points (2 for win): 59, Division II, 1947–48
Most League goals: 103, Division II, 1893–94
League scoring record: 33, Walter Abbott, Division II, 1898–99
Record League aggregate: 249, Joe Bradford, Division I, 1920–35
Most League appearances: 486, Gil Merrick, 1946–60
Most capped player: 28, Malcolm Page, Wales

FA Cup	Year	Opponents	Score	Scorers
Runners-up	1931	West Bromwich Albion	1–2	Bradford
	1956	Manchester City	1–3	Kinsey
League Cup				
Winners	1963	Aston Villa	H3–1 A0–0	Leek 2, Bloomfield

THE BIRMINGHAM RECORD

Year	Division and place		Cup round reached		Year	Division and place		Cup round reached
1889*			1		1948	II	1P	3
1890			2		1949	I	17	3
1891			d		1950	I	22R	3
1892			2		1951	II	4	s-f
1893	II	1	1		1952	II	3	4
1894	II	2P	1		1953	II	6	q-f
1895	II	12	1		1954	II	7	4
1896	I	15R	1		1955	II	1P	q-f
1897	II	4	1		1956	I	6	Final
1898	II	6	q		1957	I	12	s-f
1899	II	8	2		1958	I	13	3
1900	II	3	q		1959	I	9	5
1901	II	2P	3		1960	I	19	3
1902	I	17R	p		1961	I	19	5
1903	II	2P	1		1962	I	17	3
1904	I	11	p		1963	I	20	3
1905	I	7	1		1964	I	20	3
1906†	I	7	4		1965	I	22R	3
1907	I	9	1		1966	II	10	4
1908	I	20R	1		1967	II	10	q-f
1909	II	11	1		1968	II	4	s-f
1910	II	20	1		1969	II	7	5
1911	II	16	1		1970	II	18	3
1912	II	12	1		1971	II	9	3
1913	II	3	3		1972	II	2P	s-f
1914	II	14	3		1973	I	10	3
1915	II	6	3		1974	I	19	4
1920	II	5	3		1975	I	17	s-f
1921	II	1P	1		1976	I	19	3
1922	II	18	§		1977	I	13	4
1923	I	17	1		1978	I	11	3
1924	I	14	2		1979	I	21R	3
1925	I	8	3		1980	II	3P	5
1926	I	14	4		1981	I	13	4
1927	I	17	4		1982	I	16	3
1928	I	11	5		1983	I	17	4
1929	I	15	4		1984	I	20R	6
1930	I	11	4		1985	II	2P	3
1931	I	19	Final		1986	I	21R	3
1932	I	9	4		1987	II	19	4
1933	I	13	6					
1934	I	20	5					
1935	I	19	6					
1936	I	12	3					
1937	I	11	3					
1938	I	18	3					
1939	I	21R	5					
1946††			s-f					
1947	II	3	q-f					

*–as Small Heath until 1905
†–as Birmingham until 1945
††–as Birmingham City
§–did not enter
d–disqualified for fielding an ineligible player

BLACKBURN ROVERS

Founded: 1875
Address: Ewood Park, Blackburn
Telephone: Blackburn 55432
Ground capacity: 25,000
Playing area: 116 by 72 yards
Record attendance: 61,783 v Bolton Wanderers, FA Cup quarter-final, 2.3.29
Record victory: 11–0 v Rossendale United, FA Cup, 1st round, 25.10.1884
Record defeat: 0–8 v Arsenal, Division I, 25.2.33
Most League points (3 for win): 73, Division II, 1984–85
Most League points (2 for win): 60, Division III, 1974–75
Most League goals: 114, Division II, 1954–55
League scoring record: 43, Ted Harper, Division I, 1925–26
Record League aggregate: 140, Tom Briggs, 1952–1958
Most League appearances: 589, Derek Fazackerley, 1970–86
Most capped player: 41, Bob Crompton, England

FA Cup	Year	Opponents	Score	Scorers
Winners	1884	Queen's Park	2–1	Brown, Forrest
	1885	Queen's Park	2–0	Forrest, Brown
	1886	West Bromwich Albion	0–0	
			2–0	Sowerbutts, Brown
	1890	Sheffield Wednesday	6–1	Dewar, Southworth, Lofthouse, Townley 3
	1891	Notts County	3–1	Dewar, Southworth, Townley
	1928	Huddersfield Town	3–1	Roscamp 2, McLean
Runners-up	1882	Old Etonians	0–1	
	1960	Wolverhampton Wanderers	0–3	

THE BLACKBURN RECORD

Year	Division and place		Cup round reached		Year	Division and place		Cup round reached
1880			3		1933	I	15	4
1881			2		1934	I	8	3
1882			Final		1935	I	15	5
1883			2		1936	I	15	5
1884			Winners		1936	I	22R	4
1885			Winners		1937	II	12	3
1886			Winners		1938	II	16	3
1887			2		1939	II	1P	q-f
1888			2		1946			3
1889	I	4	s-f		1947	I	17	5
1890	I	3	Winners		1948	I	22R	4
1891	I	6	Winners		1949	II	14	3
1892	I	9	2		1950	II	16	3
1893	I	9	s-f		1951	II	6	3
1894	I	4	s-f		1952	II	14	s-f
1895	I	5	2		1953	II	9	3
1896	I	8	1		1954	II	6	4
1897	I	14	3		1955	II	6	3
1898	I	15	1		1956	II	4	5
1899	I	6	1		1957	II	4	3
1900	I	4	2		1958	II	2P	s-f
1901	I	9	1		1959	I	10	4
1902	I	4	1		1960	I	17	Final
1903	I	16	2		1961	I	18	5
1904	I	15	3		1962	I	16	q-f
1905	I	13	1		1963	I	11	3
1906	I	9	1		1964	I	7	5
1907	I	12	2		1965	I	10	3
1908	I	14	1		1966	I	22R	q-f
1909	I	4	3		1967	II	4	3
1910	I	3	3		1968	II	9	3
1911	I	12	s-f		1969	II	19	5
1912	I	1C	s-f		1970	II	8	3
1913	I	5	q-f		1971	II	21R	3
1914	I	1C	3		1972	III	10	1
1915	I	3	1		1973	III	3	2
1920	I	20	1		1974	III	13	3
1921	I	11	1		1975	III	1P	3
1922	I	15	3		1976	II	15	3
1923	I	14	2		1977	II	12	5
1924	I	8	1		1978	II	5	4
1925	I	16	s-f		1979	II	22R	4
1926	I	12	4		1980	III	2P	4
1927	I	18	3		1981	II	4	3
1928	I	12	Winners		1982	II	10	3
1929	I	7	q-f		1983	II	11	3
1930	I	6	5		1984	II	6	5
1931	I	10	5		1985	II	5	5
1932	I	16	4		1986	II	19	4
					1987	II	12	3

BLACKPOOL

Founded: 1887
Address: Bloomfield Road, Blackpool
Telephone: Blackpool 404331
Ground capacity: 12,696
Playing area: 111 by 73 yards
Record attendance: 39,118 v Manchester United, Division I, 19.4.32
Record victory: 10–0 v Lanerossi Vincenza, Anglo-Italian tournament, 10.6.72
Record defeat: 1–10 v Huddersfield Town, Division I, 13.12.30; 1–10 v Small Heath Division II, 2.3.01
Most League points (3 for win): 86, Division IV, 1984–85
Most League points (2 for win): 58, Division II, 1929–30 & 1967–68
Most League goals: 98, Division II, 1929–30
League scoring record: 45, Jimmy Hampson, Division II, 1929–30
Record League aggregate: 247, Jimmy Hampson, 1927–38
Most League appearances: 568, Jimmy Armfield, 1952–1971
Most capped player: 43, Jimmy Armfield, England

FA Cup	Year	Opponents	Score	Scorers
Winners	1953	Bolton Wanderers	4–3	Mortensen 3, Perry
Runners-up	1948	Manchester United	2–4	Shimwell (pen), Mortensen
	1951	Newcastle United	0–2	

THE BLACKPOOL RECORD

	Division and place	Cup round reached		Division and place	Cup round reached
1892		1	1946		4
1893		1	1947	I 5	3
1894	p		1948	I 9	Final
1895	p		1949	I 16	4
1896		1	1950	I 7	q-f
1897	II 8	1	1951	I 3	Final
1898	II 11	p	1952	I 9	3
1899	II 16	2	1953	I 7	Winners
1900*	p		1954	I 6	5
1901	II 12	p	1955	I 19	3
1902	II 12	p	1956	I 2	3
1903	II 14	q	1957	I 4	5
1904	II 15	p	1958	I 7	3
1905	II 15	1	1959	I 8	q-f
1906	II 14	3	1960	I 11	4
1907	II 13	1	1961	I 20	3
1908	II 15	1	1962	I 13	3
1909	II 20	2	1963	I 13	3
1910	II 12	1	1964	I 18	3
1911	II 9	1	1965	I 17	3
1912	II 14	2	1966	I 13	3
1913	II 20	1	1967	I 22R	3
1914	II 16	1	1968	II 3	4
1915	II 10	1	1969	II 8	3
1920	II 4	2	1970	II 2P	4
1921	II 4	2	1971	I 22R	4
1922	II 19	1	1972	II 6	3
1923	II 5	1	1973	II 7	3
1924	II 4	2	1974	II 5	3
1925	II 17	q-f	1975	II 7	3
1926	II 6	3	1976	II 10	4
1927	II 9	3	1977	II 5	3
1928	II 19	3	1978	II 20R	3
1929	II 8	3	1979	III 12	2
1930	II 1P	4	1980	III 18	1
1931	I 20	4	1981	III 23R	2
1932	I 20	3	1982	IV 12	4
1933	I 33R	5	1983	IV 21	2
1934	II 11	4	1984	IV 6	4
1935	II 4	3	1985	IV 2P	1
1936	II 3	4	1986	II 12	2
1937	II 2P	3	1987	III 9	1
1938	I 12	4			
1939	I 15	3			

*–failed to obtain re-election in 1899

BOLTON WANDERERS

Founded: 1874
Address: Burnden Park, Bolton, BL3 2QR
Telephone: Bolton 389200
Ground capacity: 43,200
Playing area: 113 by 76 yards
Record attendance: 69,912 v Manchester City, FA Cup 5th round, 18.2.33
Record victory: 13–0 v Sheffield United, FA Cup 2nd round, 1.2.1890
Record defeat: 0–7 v Manchester City, Division I, 21.3.36
Most League points (3 for win): 64, Division III, 1983–84
Most League points (2 for win): 61, Division III, 1972–73
Most League goals: 96, Division II, 1934–35
League scoring record: 38, Joe Smith, Division I, 1920–21
Record League aggregate: 255, Nat Lofthouse, 1946–1961
Most League appearances: 519, Eddie Hopkinson, 1956-1970
Most capped player: 33, Nat Lofthouse, England

FA Cup	Year	Opponents	Score	Scorers
Winners	1923	West Ham United	2–0	Jack, J R Smith
	1926	Manchester City	1–0	Jack
	1929	Portsmouth	2–0	Butler, Blackmore
	1958	Manchester United	2–0	Lofthouse (2)
Runners-up	1894	Notts County	1–4	Cassidy
	1904	Manchester City	0–1	
	1953	Blackpool	3–4	Lofthouse, Moir, Bell

THE BOLTON WANDERERS RECORD

	Division and place	Cup round reached		Division and place	Cup round reached
1882		2	1934	II 3	q-f
1883		3	1935	II 2P	s-f
1884		4	1936	I 13	3
1885		q	1937	I 20	5
1886		3	1938	I 7	3
1887		q	1939	I 8	3
1888		q	1946		s-f
1889	I 5	q	1947	I 18	4
1890	I 9	s-f	1948	I 17	3
1891	I 5	1	1949	I 14	3
1892	I 3	1	1950	I 16	4
1893	I 5	1	1951	I 8	4
1894	I 13	Final	1952	I 5	3
1895	I 10	q-f	1953	I 14	Final
1896	I 4	s-f	1954	I 5	q-f
1897	I 8	2	1955	I 18	4
1898	I 11	q-f	1956	I 8	4
1899	I 17R	1	1957	I 9	3
1900	II 2P	1	1958	I 15	Winners
1901	I 10	2	1959	I 4	q-f
1902	I 12	2	1960	I 6	4
1903	I 18R	1	1961	I 18	4
1904	II 7	Final	1962	I 11	3
1905	II 2P	q-f	1963	I 18	3
1906	I 6	1	1964	I 21R	4
1907	I 6	3	1965	II 3	5
1908	I 19R	3	1966	II 9	4
1909	II 1P	1	1967	II 9	4
1910	I 20R	1	1968	II 12	3
1911	II 2P	1	1969	II 17	4
1912	I 4	3	1970	II 16	3
1913	I 8	1	1971	II 22R	4
1914	I 6	3	1972	III 8	4
1915	I 17	s-f	1973	III 1P	5
1920	I 6	1	1974	II 11	4
1921	I 3	1	1975	II 10	3
1922	I 6	2	1976	II 4	5
1923	I 13	Winners	1977	II 4	3
1924	I 4	2	1978	II 1P	5
1925	I 3	2	1979	I 17	3
1926	I 8	Winners	1980	I 22R	5
1927	I 4	5	1981	II 18	3
1928	I 7	4	1982	II 19	4
1929	I 14	Winners	1983	II 22R	3
1930	I 15	3	1984	III 10	3
1931	I 14	4	1985	III 17	1
1932	I 17	3	1986	III 18	1
1933	I 21R	5	1987	III 21R	3

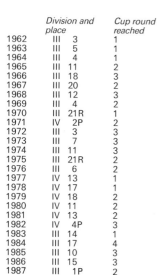

Founded: 1899 (as Boscombe)
Address: Dean Court, Bournemouth, Hampshire
Telephone: Bournemouth 35381
Ground capacity: 12,130
Playing area: 112 by 75 yards
Record attendance: 28,799 v Manchester United, FA Cup quarter-final, 2.3.57
Record victory: 11–0 v Margate, FA Cup 1st round, 20.11.71
Record defeat: 0–9 v Lincoln City, Division III, 18.12.82
Most League points (3 for win): 88, Division IV, 1981–82
Most League points (2 for win): 62, Division III, 1971–72
Most League goals: 88, Division III(S), 1956–57
League scoring record: 42, Ted Macdougall, 1970–71
Record League aggregate: 202, Ron Eyre, 1924–1933
Most League appearances: 412, Ray Bumstead, 1958–1970
Most capped player: Colin Clarke, 6, N. Ireland

Founded: 1903
Address: Valley Parade Ground, Bradford BD8 7DY
Telephone: Bradford 306062
Ground capacity: 16,000
Playing area: 110 by 76 yards
Record attendance: 39,146 v Burnley, FA Cup 4th round, 11.3.11
Record victory: 11–1 v Rotherham United, Division III(N), 25.8.28
Record defeat: 1–9 v Colchester United, Division IV, 30.12.61
Most League points (3 for win): 94, Division III, 1984–85
Most League points (2 for win): 63, Division III(N), 1928–29
Most League goals: 128, Division III(N), 1928–29
League scoring record: 34, David Layne, Division IV, 1961–62
Record League aggregate: 118, Bobby Campbell, 1981–84, 1984–86
Most League appearances: 502, Cec Podd, 1970–84
Most capped player: 9, H. Hampton, Ireland

FA Cup	Year	Opponents	Score	Scorers
Winners	1911	Newcastle United	0–0	
	Replay		1–0	Spiers

THE BOURNEMOUTH RECORD

	Division and place	Cup round reached		Division and place	Cup round reached
1924	SIII 21	*	1962	III 3	1
1925	SIII 20	q	1963	III 5	1
1926	SIII 8	4	1964	III 4	1
1927	SIII 7	3	1965	III 11	2
1928	SIII 14	3	1966	III 18	3
1929	SIII 9	5	1967	III 20	2
1930	SIII 10	3	1968	III 12	3
1931	SIII 10	1	1969	III 4	2
1932	SIII 15	4	1970	III 21R	1
1933	SIII 18	1	1971	IV 2P	2
1934	SIII 21	2	1972	III 3	3
1935	SIII 17	1	1973	III 7	3
1936	SIII 8	3	1974	III 11	3
1937	SIII 6	3	1975	III 21R	2
1938	SIII 13	2	1976	III 6	2
1939	SIII 15	3	1977	IV 13	1
1946		1	1978	IV 17	1
1947	SIII 7	3	1979	IV 18	2
1948	SIII 2	3	1980	IV 11	2
1949	SIII 3	3	1981	IV 13	2
1950	SIII 12	4	1982	IV 4P	3
1951	SIII 9	2	1983	III 14	1
1952	SIII 14	1	1984	III 17	4
1953	SIII 9	1	1985	III 10	3
1954	SIII 19	2	1986	III 15	3
1955	SIII 17	3	1987	III 1P	2
1956	SIII 9	1			
1957	SIII 5	q-f			
1958	SIII 9	2			
1959	III 12	1			
1960	III 10	4			
1961	III 19	3			

*–did not enter

THE BRADFORD CITY RECORD

	Division and place	Cup round reached		Division and place	Cup round reached
1904	II 10	p	1951	NIII 7	1
1905	II 8	p	1952	NIII 15	2
1906	II 11	3	1953	NIII 16	2
1907	II 5	3	1954	NIII 5	1
1908	II 1P	1	1955	NIII 21	3
1909	I 18	3	1956	NIII 28	
1910	I 7	2	1957	NIII 9	1
1911	I 5	Winners	1958	NIII 3	3
1912	I 11	q-f	1959	III 11	4
1913	I 13	1	1960	III 19	5
1914	I 9	2	1961	III 22R	2
1915	I 10	q-f	1962	IV 5	3
1920	I 15	q-f	1963	IV 23	3
1921	I 15	2	1964	IV 5	1
1922	I 21R	2	1965	IV 19	1
1923	II 15	1	1966	IV 23	1
1924	II 18	1	1967	IV 11	1
1925	II 16	3	1968	IV 5	2
1926	II 16	3	1969	IV 4P	1
1927	II 22R	3	1970	III 10	3
1928	NIII 6	2	1971	III 19	2
1929	NIII 1P	4	1972	III 24R	1
1930	II 18	5	1973	IV 16	4
1931	II 10	4	1974	IV 8	4
1932	II 7	3	1975	IV 10	1
1933	II 11	3	1976	IV 17	q-f
1934	II 6	3	1977	IV 4P	1
1935	II 20	4	1978	III 22R	1
1936	II 12	5	1979	IV 15	2
1937	II 21R	3	1980	IV 5	3
1938	NIII 14	3	1981	IV 14	1
1939	NIII 3	1	1982	IV 2P	1
1946		1	1983	III 12	3
1947	NIII 5	1	1984	III 7	1
1948	NIII 14	2	1985	III 1P	3
1949	NIII 22	2	1986	II 13	3
1950	NIII 19	2	1987	II 10	4

Founded: 1889
Address: Griffin Park, Braemar Road, Brentford, Middlesex TW8 ONT
Telephone: (01) 560 2021
Ground capacity: 10,000
Playing area: 114 by 75 yards
Record attendance: 39,626 v Preston North End, FA Cup quarter-final, 5.3.38
Record victory: 9–0 v Wrexham, Division III, 15.10.63
Record defeat: 0–7 v Swansea Town, Division III(S), 8.11.24; 0–7 v Walsall, Division III(S), 19.1.57
Most League points (3 for win): 68, Division III, 1981–82
Most League points (2 for win): 62, Division III(S), 1932–33; Division IV, 1962–63
Most League goals: 98, Division IV, 1962–63
League scoring record: 38, John Holliday, Division III(S), 1932–33
Record League aggregate: 153, Jim Towers, 1954–1961
Most League appearances: 514, Ken Coote, 1949–1964
Most capped player: 12, Idris Hopkins, Wales

THE BRENTFORD RECORD

	Division and place	Cup round reached		Division and place	Cup round reached
1920		1	1957	SIII 8	2
1921	III 21	1	1958	SIII 2	1
1922	SIII 9	1	1959	III 3	4
1923	SIII 14	p	1960	III 6	2
1924	SIII 17	p	1961	III 17	1
1925	SIII 21	p	1962	III 23R	3
1926	SIII 18	2	1963	IV 1P	1
1927	SIII 11	5	1964	III 16	4
1928	SIII 12	3	1965	III 5	3
1929	SIII 13	2	1966	III 23R	2
1930	SIII 2	1	1967	IV 9	3
1931	SIII 3	4	1968	IV 14	1
1932	SIII 5	4	1969	IV 11	2
1933	SIII 1P	1	1970	IV 5	1
1934	II 4	3	1971	IV 14	5
1935	II 1P	3	1972	IV 3	1
1936	I 5	3	1973	III 22R	1
1937	I 6	4	1974	IV 19	1
1938	I 6	q-f	1975	IV 8	2
1939	I 18	3	1976	IV 18	3
1946		q-f	1977	IV 15	2
1947	I 21R	4	1978	IV 4P	2
1948	II 15	4	1979	III 10	1
1949	II 18	q-f	1980	III 19	1
1950	II 9	3	1981	III 9	2
1951	II 9	3	1982	III 8	2
1952	II 10	4	1983	III 9	2
1953	II 17	4	1984	III 20	3
1954	II 21R	3	1985	III 13	3
1955	SIII 11	4	1986	III 10	1
1956	SIII 6	2	1987	III 11	2

Founded: 1900
Address: Goldstone Ground, Old Shoreham Road, Hove, Sussex
Telephone: Brighton 739535
Ground capacity: 29,000
Playing area: 112 by 75 yards
Record attendance: 36,747 v Fulham, Division II, 27.12.58
Record victory: 10–1 v Wisbech, FA Cup 1st round, 13.11.65
Record defeat: 0–9 v Middlesborough, Division II. 23.8.58 -
Most League points (3 for win): 72, Division II, 1984–85
Most League points (2 for win): 65, Division III(S), 1955–56, Division III, 1971–72
Most League goals: 112, Division III(S), 1955–56
League scoring record: 32, Peter Ward, Division III, 1976–77
Record League aggregate: 113, Tommy Cook, 1922–29
Most League appearances: 509, Tug Wilson, 1922–36
Most capped player: 15 (16 in all), Gerry Ryan, Eire

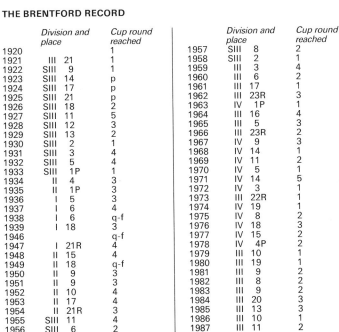

FA Cup	Year	Opponents		Score	Scorers
Runners-up	1983	Manchester United		*2–2	Smith, Stevens
	Replay			0–4	

* after extra time

THE BRIGHTON RECORD

	Division and place	Cup round reached		Division and place	Cup round reached
1906		2	1952	SIII 5	1
1907		1	1953	SIII 7	3
1908		2	1954	SIII 2	2
1909		1	1955	SIII 6	3
1910		1	1956	SIII 2	2
1911		2	1957	SIII 6	1
1912		1	1958	SIII 1P	2
1913		2	1959	II 12	3
1914		3	1960	II 14	5
1915		2	1961	II 16	4
1920		p	1962	II 22R	3
1921	III 18	2	1963	III 22R	1
1922	SIII 19	2	1964	IV 8	1
1923	SIII 4	2	1965	IV 1P	1
1924	SIII 5	3	1966	III 15	2
1925	SIII 8	2	1967	III 19	4
1926	SIII 5	1	1968	III 10	2
1927	SIII 4	3	1969	III 12	2
1928	SIII 4	2	1970	III 5	2
1929	SIII 15	1	1971	III 14	3
1930	SIII 5	5	1972	III 2P	2
1931	SIII 4	4	1973	II 22R	3
1932	SIII 8	3	1974	III 19	1
1933	SIII 12	5	1975	III 19	3
1934	SIII 10	4	1976	III 4	3
1935	SIII 9	3	1977	III 2P	1
1936	SIII 7	3	1978	II 4	4
1937	SIII 3	1	1979	II 2P	3
1938	SIII 5	3	1980	I 15	4
1939	SIII 3	1	1981	I 19	3
1946		5	1982	I 13	4
1947	SIII 17	1	1983	I 22R	Final
1948	SIII 22	3	1984	II 9	5
1949	SIII 6	1	1985	II 6	4
1950	SIII 8	1	1986	II 11	6
1951	SIII 13	4	1987	II 22R	3

Founded: 1894
Address: Ashton Gate, Bristol BS3 2EJ
Telephone: Bristol 632812
Ground capacity: 30,868
Playing area: 115 by 75 yards
Record attendance: 43,335 v Preston North End, FA Cup 5th round, 16.2.35
Record victory: 11–0 v Chichester, FA Cup 1st round, 5.11.60
Record defeat: 0–9 v Coventry City, Division III(S), 28.4.34
Most League points (3 for win): 82, Division IV, 1983–84
Most League points (2 for win): 70, Division III(S), 1954–55
Most League goals: 104, Division III(S), 1926–27
League scoring record: 36, Don Clark, Division III(S), 1946–47
Record League aggregate: 315, John Atyeo, 1951–1966
Most League appearances: 597, John Atyeo, 1951–1966
Most capped player: 26, Billy Wedlock, England

FA Cup	Year	Opponents	Score
Runners-up	1909	Manchester United	0–1

THE BRISTOL CITY RECORD

	Division and place	Cup round reached		Division and place	Cup round reached
1899		1	1948	SIII 7	2
1900		2	1949	SIII 16	3
1901		q	1950	SIII 15	1
1902	II 6	4q	1951	SIII 10	5
1903	II 4	2	1952	SIII 15	2
1904	II 4	1	1953	SIII 5	1
1905	II 4	2	1954	SIII 3	3
1906	II 1P	1	1955	SIII 1P	1
1907	I 2	2	1956	II 11	3
1908	I 10	1	1957	II 13	5
1909	I 8	Final	1958	II 17	5
1910	I 16	2	1959	II 10	4
1911	I 19R	1	1960	II 22R	3
1912	II 13	1	1961	III 14	4
1913	II 16	1	1962	III 6	3
1914	II 8	1	1963	III 14	3
1915	II 13	2	1964	III 5	4
1920	II 8	s-f	1965	III 2P	3
1921	II 3	1	1966	II 5	3
1922	II 22R	1	1967	II 15	5
1923	SIII 1P	2	1968	II 19	5
1924	II 22R	3	1969	II 16	3
1925	SIII 3	2	1970	II 14	3
1926	SIII 4	3	1971	II 19	3
1927	SIII 1P	2	1972	II 8	3
1928	II 12	3	1973	II 5	4
1929	II 20	3	1974	II 16	q-f
1930	II 20	3	1975	II 5	3
1931	II 16	3	1976	II 2P	3
1932	II 22R	4	1977	I 18	3
1933	SIII 15	2	1978	I 17	3
1934	SIII 19	3	1979	I 13	4
1935	SIII 15	5	1980	I 20R	3
1936	SIII 13	1	1981	II 21R	5
1937	SIII 16	1	1982	III 23R	4
1938	SIII 2	2	1983	IV 14	1
1939	SIII 8	1	1984	IV 4P	3
1946		4	1985	III 5	2
1947	SIII 3	2	1986	III 9	2
			1987	III 6	3

Founded: 1883
Address: Twerton Park, Bath
Telephone: 0272-510 363
Ground capacity: 20,000
Playing area: 114 by 78 yards
Record attendance: 38,472 v Preston North End, FA Cup 4th round, 30.1.60
Record victory: 15–1 v Weymouth, FA Cup preliminary round, 17.11.1900
Record defeat: 0–12 v Luton Town, Division III(S) 13.4.36
Most League points (3 for win): 79, Division III, 1983–84
Most League points (2 for win): 64, Division III(S), 1952–53
Most League goals: 92, Division III(S), 1952–53
League scoring record: 33, Geoff Bradford, Division III(S), 1952–53
Record League aggregate: 245, Geoff Bradford, 1949–64
Most League appearances: 545, Stuart Taylor, 1966–80
Most capped player: 10 (14 in all), Neil Slatter, Wales

THE BRISTOL ROVERS RECORD

	Division and place	Cup round reached		Division and place	Cup round reached
1921	III 10	1	1957	II 9	4
1922	SIII 14	q	1958	II 10	6
1923	SIII 13	q	1959	II 6	3
1924	SIII 9	q	1960	II 9	4
1925	SIII 17	1	1961	II 17	3
1926	SIII 19	1	1962	II 21R	3
1927	SIII 10	3	1963	III 19	1
1928	SIII 19	2	1964	III 12	4
1929	SIII 19	2	1965	III 6	3
1930	SIII 20	3	1966	III 16	1
1931	SIII 15	4	1967	III 5	3
1932	SIII 18	2	1968	III 15	3
1933	SIII 9	3	1969	III 16	5
1934	SIII 7	2	1970	III 3	2
1935	SIII 8	3	1971	III 6	2
1936	SIII 17	3	1972	III 6	3
1937	SIII 15	3	1973	III 5	1
1938	SIII 15	1	1974	II 2P	3
1939	SIII 22	2	1975	II 19	4
1946		2	1976	II 18	3
1947	SIII 14	1	1977	II 15	3
1948	SIII 20	4	1978	II 18	5
1949	SIII 5	1	1979	II 16	5
1950	SIII 9	1	1980	II 19	3
1951	SIII 6	6	1981	II 22R	4
1952	SIII 7	4	1982	III 15	1
1953	SIII 1P	3	1983	III 7	2
1954	II 9	3	1984	III 5	2
1955	II 9	4	1985	III 6	3
1956	II 6	4	1986	III 16	4
			1987	III 19	1

Founded: 1882
Address: Turf Moor, Burnley, Lancashire
Telephone: Burnley 27777
Ground capacity: 23,000
Playing area: 115 by 73 yards
Record attendance: 54,755 v Huddersfield Town, FA Cup 3rd round, 23.2.24
Record victory: 9–0 v Darwen, Division I, 9.1.1892; 9–0 v Crystal Palace, FA Cup 2nd round replay, 1908–09; 9–0 v New Brighton, FA Cup 4th round, 26.1.57; 9–0 v Penrith, FA Cup 1st round, 17.11.84
Record defeat: 0–10 v Aston Villa, Division I, 29.8.25; 0–1 v Sheffield United, Division I, 19.1.29
Most League points (3 for win): 80, Division III, 1981–82
Most League points (2 for win): 62, Division II, 1972–73
Most League goals: 102, Division I, 1960–61
League scoring record: 35, George Beel, Division I, 1927–28
Record League aggregate: 178, George Beel, 1923–1932
Most League appearances: 530, Jerry Dawson, 1906–1929
Most capped player: 51 (55 in all), Jimmy McIlroy, Northern Ireland

Founded: 1885
Address: Gigg Lane, Bury, Lancs
Telephone: (061) 764 4881/2
Ground capacity: 8,000
Playing area: 112 by 72 yards
Record attendance: 35,000 v Bolton, FA Cup 3rd round, 9.1.60
Record victory: 12–1 v Stockton, FA Cup 1st round replay, 1896–97
Record defeat: 0–10 v Blackburn Rovers, FA Cup preliminary round, 1.10.1887; 0–10 v West Ham United, Milk Cup 2nd round, 2nd leg, 25.10.84
Most League points (3 for win): 84, Division IV, 1984–85
Most League points (2 for win): 68, Division III, 1960–61
Most League goals: 108, Division III, 1960–61
League scoring record: 35, Craig Madden, Division IV, 1981–82
Record League aggregate: 129, Craig Madden, 1978–86
Most League appearances: 506, Norman Bullock, 1920–1935
Most capped player: 11 (14 in all), W Gorman, Republic of Ireland and 4, Northern Ireland

FA Cup	Year	Opponents	Score	Scorers
Winners	1914	Liverpool	1–0	Freeman
Runners-up	1947	Charlton Athletic	0–1	
	1962	Tottenham Hotspur	1–3	Robson

THE BURNLEY RECORD

	Division and place	Cup round reached		Division and place	Cup round reached
1889	I 9	2	1937	II 13	5
1890	I 11	1	1938	II 6	4
1891	I 8	2	1939	II 14	3
1892	I 7	2	1946		3
1893	I 6	2	1947	II 2P	Final
1894	I 5	1	1948	I 3	3
1895	I 9	1	1949	I 15	5
1896	I 10	2	1950	I 10	5
1897	I 16R	1	1951	I 10	3
1898	II 1P	3	1952	I 14	q-f
1899	I 3	1	1953	I 6	5
1900	I 17R	1	1954	I 7	4
1901	II 3	2	1955	I 10	3
1902	II 9	1	1956	I 7	4
1903	II 18	q	1957	i 7	q-f
1904	II 5	q	1958	I 6	4
1905	II 11	q	1959	I 7	q-f
1906	II 9	1	1960	I 1C	q-f
1907	II 7	1	1961	I 4	s-f
1908	II 7	1	1962	I 2	Final
1909	II 14	q-f	1963	I 3	4
1910	II 14	2	1964	I 9	q(f
1911	II 8	q-f	1965	I 12	5
1912	II 3	1	1966	I 3	4
1913	II 2P	s-f	1967	I 14	3
1914	I 12	Winners	1968	I 13	3
1915	I 4	3	1969	I 14	4
1920	I 2	2	1970	I 14	4
1921	I 1C	3	1971	I 21R	3
1922	I 3	1	1972	II 7	3
1923	I 15	1	1973	II 1P	3
1924	I 17	s-f	1974	I 6	s-f
1925	I 19	1	1975	I 10	3
1926	I 20	3	1976	I 21R	3
1927	I 5	5	1977	II 16	4
1928	I 18	3	1978	II 11	4
1929	I 19	4	1979	II 13	5
1930	I 21R	3	1980	II 21R	4
1931	II 8	4	1981	III 8	2
1932	II 19	3	1982	III 1P	4
1933	II 19	q-f	1983	II 21R	6
1934	II 13	3	1984	III 12	3
1935	II 12	s-f	1985	III 21R	3
1936	II 15	3	1986	IV 14	2
			1987	IV 22	1

FA Cup	Year	Opponents	Score	Scorers
Winners	1900	Southampton	4–0	McLuckie 2, Wood, Plant
	1903	Derby County	6–0	Ross, Sagar, Leeming 2, Wood, Plant

THE BURY RECORD

	Division and place	Cup round reached		Division and place	Cup round reached
1895	II 1P	2	1946		4
1896	I 11	q-f	1947	II 17	3
1897	I 9	2	1948	II 20	3
1898	I 14	1	1949	II 12	3
1899	I 10	2	1950	II 18	4
1900	I 12	Winners	1951	II 20	3
1901	I 5	2	1952	II 17	3
1902	I 7	q-f	1953	II 20	4
1903	I 8	Winners	1954	II 17	3
1904	I 12	2	1955	II 13	3
1905	I 17	2	1956	II 16	3
1906	I 17	1	1957	II 21R	3
1907	I 16	3	1958	NIII 4	2
1908	I 7	2	1959	III 10	3
1909	I 17	2	1960	III 7	3
1910	I 13	2	1961	III 1P	1
1911	I 18	1	1962	II 18	3
1912	I 20R	2	1963	II 8	4
1913	II 11	2	1964	II 18	4
1914	II 10	2	1965	II 16	3
1915	II 11	2	1966	II 19	3
1920	II 5	2	1967	II 22R	4
1921	II 11	1	1968	III 2P	3
1922	II 11	1	1969	II 21R	3
1923	II 6	3	1970	III 19	1
1924	II 2P	1	1971	III 22R	3
1925	I 5	1	1972	IV 8	3
1926	I 4	4	1973	IV 13	1
1927	I 19	3	1974	IV 4P	1
1928	I 5	4	1975	III 14	4
1929	I 21R	5	1976	III 13	4
1930	II 5	3	1977	III 7	2
1931	II 13	4	1978	III 15	1
1932	II 5	q-f	1979	III 19	3
1933	II 4	4	1980	III 21R	5
1934	II 12	4	1981	IV 12	3
1935	II 10	3	1982	IV 9	2
1936	II 14	4	1983	IV 5	2
1937	II 3	4	1984	IV 14	2
1938	II 10	4	1985	IV 4P	1
1939	II 16	3	1986	III 20	2
			1987	III 16	1

CAMBRIDGE UNITED

Founded: 1919*
Address: Abbey Stadium, Newmarket Road, Cambridge
Telephone: Teversham 2170/3555
Ground capacity: 12,000 (1,200 seated)
Playing area: 115 by 75 yards
Record attendance: †8,691 v Grimsby Town, Division IV, 27.12.71
Record victory: 6–0 v Darlington, Division IV, 18.9.71
Record defeat: 0–6 v Aldershot, Division III, 13.4.74; 0–6 v Darlington, Division IV, 28.9.74; 0–6 v Chelsea, Division II, 15.1.83
Most League points (3 for win): 51, Division II, 1982–83
Most League points (2 for win): 65, Division IV, 1976–77
Most League goals: 87, Division IV, 1976–77
League scoring record: 24, David Crown, Division IV, 1985–86
Record League aggregate: 74, Alan Biley, 1975–80
Most League appearances: 410, Steve Fallon, 1974–86
Most capped player: 7 (15 in all), Tom Finney, Northern Ireland.
* as Abbey United. Changed name to Cambridge United in 1949
† ground record: 14,000 v Chelsea, Friendly, 1.5.70

THE CAMBRIDGE RECORD

	Division and place		Cup round reached		Division and place		Cup round reached
1971	IV	20	2	1979	II	12	3
1972	IV	10	2	1980	II	8	4
1973	IV	3P	1	1981	II	13	3
1974	III	21R	3	1982	II	14	3
1975	IV	6	3	1983	II	12	5
1976	IV	13	1	1984	II	22R	3
1977	IV	1P	1	1985	III	24R	1
1978	III	2P	2	1986	IV	22	1
				1987	IV	11	2

CARDIFF CITY

Founded: 1899
Address: Ninian Park, Cardiff, CF1 8SX
Telephone: 0222 398636/7/8
Ground capacity: 43,000
Playing area: 114 by 78 yards
Record attendance: *57,800 v Arsenal, Division I, 22.4.53
(*Ground record: 61,566, Wales v England, 14.10.61)
Record victory: 9–2 v Thames, Division III(S), 6.2.32
Record defeat: 2–11 v Sheffield United, Division I, 1.1.26
Most League points (3 for win): 86, Division III, 1982–83
Most League points (2 for win): 66, Division III(S), 1946–47
Most League goals: 93, Division III(S), 1046–47
League scoring record: 31, Stan Richards, Division III(S), 1946–47
Record League aggregate: 128, Len Davies, 1920–31
Most League appearances: 471, Phil Dwyer, 1972–85
Most capped player: 39 (41 in all), Alf Sherwood, Wales

FA Cup	Year	Opponents	Score	Scorers
Winners	1927	Arsenal	1–0	Ferguson
Runners-up	1925	Sheffield United	0–1	

THE CARDIFF RECORD

	Division and place		Cup round reached		Division and place		Cup round reached
1920			3	1957	I	21R	4
1921	II	2P	s-f	1958	II	15	5
1922	I	4	q-f	1959	II	9	4
1923	I	9	3	1960	II	2P	3
1924	I	2	q-f	1961	I	15	3
1925	I	11	Final	1962	I	21R	3
1926	I	16	4	1963	I	10	3
1927	I	14	Winners	1964	II	15	3
1928	I	6	5	1965	II	13	3
1929	I	22R	3	1966	II	20	4
1930	II	8	4	1967	II	20	4
1931	II	22R	3	1968	II	13	3
1932	SIII	9	3	1969	II	5	3
1933	SIII	19	1	1970	II	7	3
1934	SIII	22	2	1971	II	3	4
1935	SIII	19	1	1972	II	19	5
1936	SIII	20	1	1973	II	20	4
1937	SIII	18	3	1974	II	17	3
1938	SIII	10	3	1975	II	21R	3
1939	SIII	13	4	1976	III	2P	4
1946			3	1977	II	18	5
1947	SIII	1P	3	1978	II	19	3
1948	II	5	3	1979	II	9	3
1949	II	4	5	1980	II	15	3
1950	II	10	5	1981	II	19	3
1951	II	3	3	1982	II	20R	3
1952	II	2P	3	1983	III	2P	2
1953	I	12	3	1984	II	15	3
1954	I	10	4	1985	II	21R	3
1955	I	20	3	1986	III	22R	1
1956	I	17	4	1987	IV	13	4

CARLISLE UNITED

Founded: 1904
Address: Brunton Park, Carlisle
Telephone: Carlisle 26237
Ground capacity: 18,158
Playing area: 117 by 78 yards
Record attendance: 27,500 v Birmingham City, FA Cup 3rd round, 5.1.57; 27,500 v Middlesbrough, FA Cup 5th round, 7.2.70
Record victory: 8–0 v Hartlepool United, Division III(N), 1.9.28; 8–0 v Scunthorpe United, Division III(N), 25.12.52
Record defeat: 1–11 v Hull City, Divisior III(N), 14.1.39
Most League points (3 for win): 80, Division III, 1981–82
Most League points (2 for win): 62, Division III(N), 1950–51
Most League goals: 113, Division IV, 1963–64
League scoring record: 42, Jimmy McConnell, Division III(N), 1928–29
Record League aggregate: 126, Jimmy McConnell, 1928–32
Most League appearances: 466, Alan Ross, 1963–79
Most capped player: 4, Eric Welsh, Northern Ireland

THE CARLISLE RECORD

	Division and place		Cup round reached			Division and place		Cup round reached
1929	NIII	8	2		1961	IV	19	2
1930	NIII	15	3		1962	IV	4P	3
1931	NIII	8	3		1963	III	23R	3
1932	NIII	18	2		1964	IV	2P	5
1933	NIII	19	2		1965	III	1P	1
1934	NIII	13	2		1966	II	14	4
1935	NIII	22	1		1967	II	3	4
1936	NIII	13	1		1968	II	10	4
1937	NIII	10	3		1969	II	12	3
1938	NIII	12	1		1970	II	12	5
1939	NIII	19	1		1971	II	4	4
1946			2		1972	II	10	3
1947	NIII	16	3		1973	II	18	5
1948	NIII	9	1		1974	II	3P	4
1949	NIII	15	1		1975	I	22R	q-f
1950	NIII	9	3		1976	II	19	3
1951	NIII	3	3		1977	II	20R	4
1952	NIII	7	1		1978	III	13	3
1953	NIII	9	1		1979	III	6	3
1954	NIII	13	1		1980	III	6	4
1955	NIII	20	2		1981	III	19	4
1956	NIII	21	1		1982	III	2P	3
1957	NIII	15	3		1983	II	14	3
1958	NIII	10	2		1984	II	7	3
1959	IV	10	2		1985	II	16	4
1960	IV	19	1		1986	II	20R	4
					1987	III	22R	1

CHARLTON ATHLETIC

Founded: 1905
Address: Selhurst Park, London SE25 6PH
Telephone: (01) 771 6321
Ground capacity: 36,000
Playing area: 114 by 78 yards
Record attendance: 75,031 v Aston Villa, FA Cup 5th round, 12.2.38 (at the Valley)
Record victory: 8–1 v Middlesborough, Division I, 12.9.53
Record defeat: 1–11 v Aston Villa, Division II, 14.11.59
Most League points (3 for win): 77, Division II, 1985–86
Most League points (2 for win): 61, Division III(S), 1934–35
Most League goals: 107, Division II, 1957–58
League scoring record: 32, Ralph Allen, Division III(S), 1934-35
Record League aggregate: 153, Stuart Leary, 1953–62
Most League appearances: 583, Sam Bartram, 1934–56
Most capped player: 19, John Hewie, Scotland

FA Cup	Year	Opponents		Score	Scorers
Winners	1947	Burnley		1–0	Duffy
Runners-up	1946	Derby County		1–4	Turner H

THE CHARLTON RECORD

	Division and place		Cup round reached			Division and place		Cup round reached
1922	SIII	16	q		1958	II	3	4
1923	SIII	12	4		1959	II	8	4
1924	SIII	14	2		1960	II	7	4
1925	SIII	15	p		1961	II	10	3
1926	SIII	21	3		1962	II	15	4
1927	SIII	13	2		1963	II	20	4
1928	SIII	11	3		1964	II	4	3
1929	SIII	1P	3		1965	II	18	4
1930	II	13	4		1966	II	16	3
1931	II	15	3		1967	II	19	3
1932	II	10	3		1968	II	15	3
1933	II	22R	3		1969	II	3	4
1934	SIII	5	4		1970	II	20	4
1935	SIII	1P	1		1971	II	20	3
1936	II	2P	3		1972	II	21R	3
1937	I	2	3		1973	III	11	3
1938	I	4	5		1974	III	14	1
1939	I	3	3		1975	III	3P	2
1946			Final		1976	II	9	5
1947	I	19	Winners		1977	II	7	3
1948	I	13	5		1978	II	17	3
1949	I	9	3		1979	II	19	4
1950	I	20	4		1980	II	22R	3
1951	I	17	3		1981	III	3P	5
1952	I	10	3		1982	II	13	3
1953	I	5	3		1983	II	17	3
1954	I	9	3		1984	II	13	4
1955	I	15	3		1985	II	17	3
1956	I	14	5		1986	II	2P	3
1957	I	22R	3		1987	I	19	3

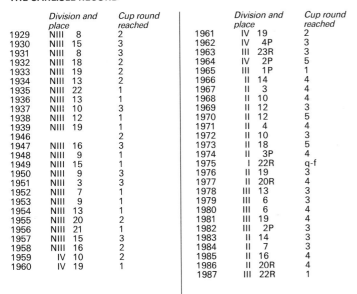

Founded: 1905
Address: Stamford Bridge, London SW6
Telephone: (01) 385 5545/6
Ground capacity: 45,000
Playing area: 114 by 71 yards
Record attendance: 82,905 v Arsenal, Division I, 12.10.35
Record victory: 13–0 v Jeunesse Hautcharage, 1st Rd European Cup Winners Cup 29.9.71
Record defeat: 1–8 v Wolverhampton Wanderers, Division I, 26.9. 53
Most League points (3 for win): 88, Division II, 1983–84
Most League points (2 for win): 57, Division II, 1906–07
Most League goals: 98, Division I, 1960–61
League scoring record: 41, Jimmmy Greaves, 1960–61
Record League aggregate: 164, Bobby Tambling, 1958–1970
Most League appearances: 655, Ron Harris, 1962–80
Most capped player: 24 (82 in all), Ray Wilkins, England

FA Cup	Year	Opponents	Score	Scorers
Winners	1970	Leeds United	*2–2	Houseman, Hutchinson
			*2–1	Osgood, Webb
Runners-up	1915	Sheffield United	0–3	
	1967	Tottenham Hotspur	1–2	Tambling
League Cup				
Winners	1965	Leicester City	H3–2	Tambling, Venables (pen) McCreadie
			A0–0	
Runners-up	1972	Stoke City	1–2	Osgood

* after extra time

THE CHELSEA RECORD

	Division and place	Cup round reached		Division and place	Cup round reached
1906	II 3	3q	1952	I 19	s-f
1907	II 2P	1	1953	I 19	5
1908	I 13	2	1954	I 8	3
1909	I 11	2	1955	I 1C	5
1910	I 19R	2	1956	I 16	5
1911	II 3	s-f	1957	I 12	4
1912	II 2P	2	1958	I 11	4
1913	I 18	2	1959	I 14	4
1914	I 8	1	1960	I 18	4
1915	I 19	Final	1961	I 12	3
1920	I 3	s-f	1962	I 22R	3
1921	I 18	q-f	1963	II 2P	5
1922	I 9	1	1964	I 5	4
1923	I 19	2	1965	I 3	s-f
1924	I 21R	1	1966	I 5	s-f
1925	II 5	1	1967	I 9	Final
1926	II 3	4	1968	I 6	q-f
1927	II 4	q-f	1969	I 5	q-f
1928	II 3	3	1970	I 3	Winners
1929	II 9	5	1971	I 6	4
1930	II 2P	3	1972	I 7	5
1931	I 12	q-f	1973	I 12	6
1932	I 12	s-f	1974	I 17	3
1933	I 18	3	1975	I 21R	4
1934	I 19	5	1976	II 11	5
1935	I 12	3	1977	II 2P	3
1936	I 8	5	1978	I 16	5
1937	I 13	4	1979	I 22R	3
1938	I 10	3	1980	II 4	3
1939	I 20	q-f	1981	II 12	3
1946		5	1982	II 12	q-f
1947	I 15	4	1983	II 18	4
1948	I 18	4	1984	II 1P	3
1949	I 13	5	1985	I 6	4
1950	I 13	s-f	1986	I 6	4
1951	I 20	5	1987	I 14	4

Founded: 1884
Address: Sealand Road, Chester, CH1 4LW
Telephone: Chester 371376
Ground capacity: 20,500 (2,100 seated)
Playing area: 114 by 76 yards
Record attendance: 20,500 v Chelsea, FA Cup 3rd round replay, 16.1.52
Record victory: 12–0 v York City, Division III(N), 1.2.36
Record defeat: 2–11 v Oldham Athletic, Division III(N) 19.1.52
Most League points (3 for win): 84, Division IV, 1985–86
Most League points (2 for win): 56, Division III(N), 1946–47; Division IV, 1964–65
Most League goals: 119, Division IV, 1964–65
League scoring record: 36, Dick Yates, Division III(N), 1946–47
Record League aggregate: 83, Gary Talbot, 1963–1967 and 1968–1970
Most League appearances: 408, Ray Gill, 1951–1962
Most capped player: 7 (30 in all), W Lewis, Wales

THE CHESTER RECORD

	Division and place	Cup round reached		Division and place	Cup round reached
1932	NIII 3	2	1963	IV 21	1
1933	NIII 4	4	1964	IV 12	2
1934	NIII 10	2	1965	IV 8	3
1935	NIII 3	3	1966	IV 7	3
1936	NIII 2	2	1967	IV 19	1
1937	NIII 3	4	1968	IV 22	2
1938	NIII 9	3	1969	IV 14	2
1939	NIII 6	4	1970	IV 11	4
1946		3	1971	IV 5	3
1947	NIII 3	4	1972	IV 20	1
1948	NIII 20	4	1973	IV 15	1
1949	NIII 18	2	1974	IV 7	3
1950	NIII 12	2	1975	IV 4P	1
1951	NIII 13	1	1976	III 17	2
1952	NIII 19	3	1977	III 13	5
1953	NIII 20	1	1978	III 5	2
1954	NIII 24	1	1979	III 16	2
1955	NIII 24	1	1980	III 9	5
1956	NIII 17	1	1981	III 18	1
1957	NIII 21	1	1982	III 24R	I
1958	NIII 21	2	1983	IV 13	1
1959	IV 13	2	1984	IV 24	1
1960	IV 20	2	1985	IV 16	1
1961	IV 24	1	1986	IV 2P	1
1962	IV 23	2	1987	III 15	4

CHESTERFIELD

Founded: 1866
Address: Recreation Ground, Saltergate, Chesterfield, Derbyshire
Telephone: Chesterfield 32318
Ground capacity: 11,200
Playing area: 114 by 72 yards
Record attendance: 30,968 v Newcastle United, Division II, 7.4.39
Record victory: 10–0 v Glossop North End, Division II, 17.1.03
Record defeat: 1–9 v Port Vale, Division II, 24.9.32
Most League points (3 for win): 91, Division IV, 1984–85
Most League points (2 for win): 64, Division IV, 1969–70
Most League goals: 102, Division III(N), 1930–31
League scoring record: 44, Jimmy Cookson, Division III(N), 1925–26
Record League aggregate: 153, Ernie Moss, 1969–76; 1979–81; 1984–86
Most League appearances: 613, Dave Blakey, 1948–1967
Most capped player: 4 (7 in all), Walter McMillen, Northern Ireland

THE CHESTERFIELD RECORD

	Division and place	Cup round reached		Division and place	Cup round reached
1900	II 7	p	1951	II 21R	3
1901	II 14	1	1952	NIII 13	2
1902	II 16	p	1953	NIII 12	2
1903	II 6	p	1954	NIII 6	4
1904	II 11	p	1955	NIII 6	1
1905*	II 5	p	1956	NIII 6	2
1906*	II 18	2	1957	NIII 6	3
1907*	II 18	1	1958	NIII 8	1
1908*	II 19	2	1959	III 16	3
1909*	II 19L	1	1960	III 18	1
1910		1	1961	III 24R	3
1911		p	1962	IV 19	2
1912		p	1963	IV 15	2
1913		1	1964	IV 16	3
1914		1	1965	IV 12	3
1915		p	1966	IV 20	1
1920		p	1967	IV 15	1
1921		p	1968	IV 7	3
1922	NIII 13	p	1969	IV 20	3
1923	NIII 4	p	1970	IV 1P	1
1924	NIII 3	p	1971	III 5	2
1925	NIII 7	p	1972	III 13	3
1926	NIII 4	3	1973	III 16	2
1927	NIII 7	3	1974	III 5	1
1928	NIII 16	1	1975	III 15	3
1929	NIII 11	3	1976	III 15	1
1930	NIII 4	3	1977	III 18	2
1931	NIII 1P	1	1978	III 9	2
1932	II 17	4	1979	III 20	1
1933	II 21R	5	1980	III 4	1
1934	NIII 2	3	1981	III 5	3
1935	NIII 10	3	1982	III 11	2
1936	NIII 1P	2	1983	III 24R	1
1937	II 15	3	1984	IV 13	2
1938	II 11	5	1985	IV 1P	2
1939	II 6	3	1986	III 17	1
1946		3	1987	III 17	1
1947	II 4	4			
1948	II 16	3			
1949	II 6	3			
1950	II 14	5			

* – as Chesterfield Town

COLCHESTER UNITED

Founded: 1937
Address: Layer Road, Colchester, Essex
Telephone: Colchester 74042
Ground capacity: 4,999
Playing area: 110 by 71 yards
Record attendance: 19,072 v Reading, FA Cup lst round, 27.11.48
Record victory: 9–1 v Bradford City, Division IV, 30.9.61
Record defeat: 0–7 v Leyton Orient, Division III(S), 5.1.52; 0–7 v Reading, Division III(S), 18.9.57
Most League points (3 for win): 81, Division IV, 1982–83
Most League points (2 for win): 60, Division IV, 1973–74
Most League goals: 104, Division IV, 1961–62
League scoring record: 37, Bobby Hunt, Division IV, 1961–62
Record League aggregate: 131, Martyn King, 1959–65
Most League appearances: 613, Mickey Cook, 1969–84
Most capped player: None

THE COLCHESTER RECORD

	Division and place	Cup round reached		Division and place	Cup round reached
1946		p	1967	III 13	2
1947		1	1968	III 22R	3
1948		5	1969	IV 6	2
1949		1	1970	IV 10	1
1950		p	1971	IV 6	q-f
1951	SIII 16	1	1972	IV 11	1
1952	SIII 10	3	1973	IV 22	2
1953	SIII 22	3	1974	IV 3P	1
1954	SIII 23	1	1975	III 11	2
1955	SIII 24	1	1976	III 22R	1
1956	SIII 12	1	1977	IV 3P	4
1957	SIII 3	1	1978	III 8	2
1958	SIII 12	1	1979	III 7	5
1959	III 5	4	1980	III 5	3
1960	III 9	1	1981	III 22R	3
1961	III 23R	2	1982	IV 6	3
1962	IV 2P	1	1983	IV 6	1
1963	III 12	1	1984	IV 8	3
1964	III 17	2	1985	IV 7	2
1965	III 23R	2	1986	IV 6	1
1966	IV 4P	1	1987	IV 5	2

COVENTRY CITY

Founded: 1883
Address: Highfield Road, Coventry
Telephone: Coventry 57171
Ground capacity: 20,000 (all seated)
Playing area: 110 by 75 yards
Record attendance: 51,457 v Wolverhampton Wanderers, Division II, 29.4.67
Record victory: 9–0 v Bristol City, Division III(S), 28.4.34
Record defeat: 2–10 v Norwich City, Division III(S), 15.3.30
Most League points (3 for win): 50, Division I, 1981–82, 1983–84, 1984–85
Most League points (2 for win): 60, Division IV, 1958–59 & Division III, 1963–64
Most League goals: 108, Division III(S), 1931–32
League scoring record: 49, Clarrie Bourton, Division III(S), 1931–32
Record League aggregate: 171, Clarrie Bourton, 1931–37
Most League appearances: 486, George Curtis, 1956–1970
Most capped player: 21 (48 in all), Dave Clements, Northern Ireland

FA Cup	Year	Opponents	Score	Scorers
Winners	1987	Tottenham Hotspur	*3-2	Bennett, Houchen, Mabbutt o.g.

* after extra time

THE COVENTRY RECORD

Year	Division and place		Cup round reached
1908			1
1909			q
1910			q-f
1911			3
1912			2
1913			1
1914			4q
1915			6q
1920	II	20	1
1921	II	21	6q
1922	II	20	2
1923	II	18	5q
1924	II	19	1
1925	II	22R	1
1926	NIII	16	1
1927	SIII	15	2
1928	SIII	20	1
1929	SIII	11	1
1930	SIII	6	3
1931	SIII	14	2
1932	SIII	12	1
1933	SIII	6	2
1934	SIII	2	2
1935	SIII	3	3
1936	SIII	1P	1
1937	II	8	5
1938	II	4	3
1939	II	4	3
1946			3
1947	II	8	4
1948	II	10	4
1949	II	16	3
1950	II	12	3
1951	II	7	3
1952	II	21R	4
1953	SIII	6	3
1954	SIII	14	1
1955	SIII	9	3
1956	SIII	8	1
1957	SIII	16	1
1958	SIII	19	2
1959	IV	2P	2
1960	III	5	1
1961	III	15	3
1962	III	14	2
1963	III	4	q-f
1964	III	1P	2
1965	II	10	3
1966	II	3	5
1967	II	1P	3
1968	I	20	4
1969	I	20	4
1970	I	6	3
1971	I	10	3
1972	I	18	4
1973	I	18	6
1974	I	16	5
1975	I	14	4
1976	I	14	4
1977	I	19	4
1978	I	7	3
1979	I	10	3
1980	I	15	4
1981	I	16	5
1982	I	14	q-f
1983	I	19	4
1984	I	19	4
1985	I	18	4
1986	I	17	3
1987	I	10	Winners

CREWE ALEXANDRA

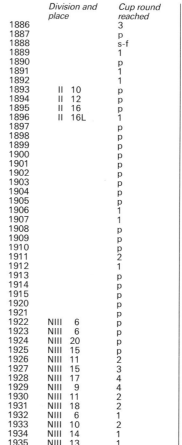

Founded: 1877
Address: Gresty Road, Crewe, Cheshire
Telephone: Crewe 213014
Ground capacity: 17,000
Playing area: 112 by 74 yards
Record attendance: 20,000 v Tottenham Hotspur, FA Cup 4th round, 30.1.60
Record victory: 8–0 v Rotherham United, Division III(N), 1.10.32
Record defeat: 2–13 v Tottenham Hotspur, FA Cup 4th round replay, 3.2.60
Most League points (3 for win): 66, Division IV, 1984–85
Most League points (2 for win): 59, Division IV, 1962–63
Most League goals: 95, Division III(N), 1931–32
League scoring record: 34, Terry Harkin, Division IV, 1964–65
Record League aggregate: 126, Bert Swindells, 1928–1937
Most League appearances: 436, Tommy Lowry, 1966–1977
Most capped player: 12 (30 in all), William Lewis, Wales

THE CREWE RECORD

Year	Division and place		Cup round reached
1886			3
1887			p
1888			s-f
1889			1
1890			p
1891			1
1892			1
1893	II	10	p
1894	II	12	p
1895	II	16	p
1896	II	16L	1
1897			p
1898			p
1899			p
1900			p
1901			p
1902			p
1903			p
1904			p
1905			p
1906			1
1907			1
1908			p
1909			p
1910			p
1911			2
1912			1
1913			p
1914			p
1915			p
1920			p
1921			p
1922	NIII	6	p
1923	NIII	6	p
1924	NIII	20	p
1925	NIII	15	p
1926	NIII	11	2
1927	NIII	15	3
1928	NIII	17	4
1929	NIII	9	4
1930	NIII	11	2
1931	NIII	18	2
1932	NIII	6	1
1933	NIII	10	2
1934	NIII	14	1
1935	NIII	13	1
1936	NIII	6	3
1937	NIII	20	3
1938	NIII	8	2
1939	NIII	8	2
1946			1
1947	NIII	8	1
1948	NIII	10	4
1949	NIII	12	3
1950	NIII	7	2
1951	NIII	9	2
1952	NIII	16	1
1953	NIII	10	1
1954	NIII	16	2
1955	NIII	22	1
1956	NIII	24	1
1957	NIII	24	1
1958	NIII	24	1
1959	IV	18	1
1960	IV	14	4
1961	IV	9	4
1962	IV	10	2
1963	IV	3P	2
1964	III	22R	1
1965	IV	10	1
1966	IV	14	4
1967	IV	5	3
1968	IV	4P	1
1969	III	23R	2
1970	IV	15	1
1971	IV	15	2
1972	IV	24	1
1973	IV	21	3
1974	IV	21	1
1975	IV	18	1
1976	IV	16	1
1977	IV	12	1
1978	IV	15	2
1979	IV	24	2
1980	IV	23	1
1981	IV	18	1
1982	IV	24	2
1983	IV	23	1
1984	IV	17	1
1985	IV	10	1
1986	IV	12	1
1987	IV	17	1

Founded: 1905
Address: Selhurst Park, SE25 6PH
Telephone: (01) 653 4462
Ground capacity: 36,000
Playing area: 112 by 74 yards
Record attendance: 51,482 v Burnley, Division II, 11.5.79
Record victory: 9–0 v Barrow, Division IV, 10.10.59
Record defeat: 4–11 v Manchester City, FA Cup 5th round, 20.2.26
Most League points (3 for win): 66, Division II, 1985–86
Most League points (2 for win): 64, Division IV, 1960–61
Most League goals: 110, Division IV, 1960–61
League scoring record: 46, Peter Simpson, Division III(S), 1930–31
Record League aggregate: 154, Peter Simpson, 1930–1936
Most League appearances: 489, Jim Cannon, 1973–86
Most capped player: 14 (out of 51) Paddy Mulligan, Eire; 14 (out of 18) Ian Walsh, Wales; 14 (out of 38), Peter Nicholas, Wales

THE PALACE RECORD

	Division and place	Cup round reached		Division and place	Cup round reached
1921	III 1P	2	1957	SIII 20	3
1922	II 14	2	1958	SIII 14	3
1923	II 16	1	1959	IV 7	3
1924	II 15	3	1960	IV 8	3
1925	II 21R	2	1961	IV 2P	2
1926	SIII 13	5	1962	III 15	3
1927	SIII 6	1	1963	III 11	2
1928	SIII 5	2	1964	III 2P	2
1929	SIII 2	5	1965	II 7	q-f
1930	SIII 9	3	1966	II 11	3
1931	SIII 2	4	1967	II 7	3
1932	SIII 4	2	1968	II 11	3
1933	SIII 5	1	1969	II 2P	3
1934	SIII 12	4	1970	I 20	5
1935	SIII 5	1	1971	I 18	3
1936	SIII 6	2	1972	I 20	3
1937	SIII 14	1	1973	I 21R	4
1938	SIII 7	3	1974	II 20R	3
1939	SIII 2	1	1975	III 5	2
1946		3	1976	III 5	s-f
1947	SIII 18	3	1977	III 3P	3
1948	SIII 13	3	1978	II 9	3
1949	SIII 22	1	1979	II 1P	5
1950	SIII 7	1	1980	I 13	3
1951	SIII 24	1	1981	I 22R	3
1952	SIII 19	1	1982	II 15	q-f
1953	SIII 13	2	1983	II 15	5
1954	SIII 22	1	1984	II 18	4
1955	SIII 20	2	1985	II 15	3
1956	SIII 23	1	1986	II 5	3
			1987	II 6	4

Founded: 1883
Address: Feethams Ground Darlington, County Durham
Telephone: Darlington 65097
Ground capacity: 20,000
Playing area: 110 by 74 yards
Record attendance: 21,023 v Bolton Wanderers, League cup 3rd round, 14.11.60
Record victory: 9–2 v Lincoln City, Division III(N), 7.1.28
Record defeat: 0–10 v Doncaster Rovers, Division IV, 25.1.64
Most League points (3 for win): 85, Division IV, 1985–85
Most League points (2 for win): 59, Division IV, 1965–66
Most League goals: 108, Division III(N), 1929–30
League scoring record: 39, David Brown, Division III(N), 1924–5
Record League aggregate: 90, Alan Walsh, 1978–84
Most League appearances: 442, Ron Greener, 1955–1967
Most capped player: None

THE DARLINGTON RECORD

	Division and place	Cup round reached		Division and place	Cup round reached
1911		3	1954	NIII 21	1
1912		2	1955	NIII 15	3
1913		p	1956	NIII 15	2
1914		p	1957	NIII 18	2
1915		1	1958	NIII 20	5
1920		2	1959	IV 16	3
1921		1	1960	IV 15	2
1922	NIII 2	1	1961	IV 7	2
1923	NIII 9	p	1962	IV 13	1
1924	NIII 6	1	1963	IV 12	1
1925	NIII 1P	1	1964	IV 19	1
1926	II 15	2	1965	IV 17	3
1927	II 21R	4	1966	VI 2P	2
1928	NIII 7	3	1967	III 22R	2
1929	NIII 19	3	1968	IV 16	1
1930	NIII 3	1	1969	IV 5	2
1931	NIII 11	1	1970	IV 22	1
1932	NIII 11	3	1971	IV 12	2
1933	NIII 22	4	1972	IV 19	2
1934	NIII 16	1	1973	IV 24	1
1935	NIII 5	2	1974	IV 20	1
1936	NIII 12	3	1975	IV 21	2
1937	NIII 22	4	1976	IV 20	1
1938	NIII 19	1	1977	IV 11	3
1939	NIII 18	2	1978	IV 19	1
1946		2	1979	IV 21	3
1947	NIII 17	2	1980	IV 22	2
1948	NIII 16	1	1981	IV 8	1
1949	NIII 4	3	1982	IV 13	1
1950	NIII 17	1	1983	IV 17	1
1951	NIII 18	1	1984	IV 16	4
1952	NIII 23	1	1985	IV 3P	4
1953	NIII 21	1	1986	III 13	1
			1987	III 23R	2

DERBY COUNTY

Founded: 1884
Address: Baseball Ground, Shaftesbury Crescent, Derby DE3 8NB
Telephone: 0332 40105
Ground capacity: 26,500
Playing area: 110 by 71 yards
Record attendance: 41,826 v Tottenham Hotspur, Division I, 20.9.69
Record victory: 12–0 v Finn Harps, UEFA Cup 3rd round, 15.9.76
Record defeat: 2–11 v Everton, FA Cup 1st round, 18.1.90
Most League points (3 for win): 84, Division III, 1985–86
Most League points (2 for win): 63, Division II, 1968–69, Division III(N), 1955–56, 1956–57
Most League goals: 111, Division III(N), 1956–57
League scoring record: 37, Jack Bowers, Division I, 1930–31 and Ray Straw, Division III(N), 1956–57
Record League aggregate: 291, Steve Bloomer, 1892–1906 and 1910–1914
Most League appearances: 486, Kevin Hector, 1966–78; 1980–82
Most capped player: 28, Roy McFarland, England

FA Cup	Year	Opponents	Score	Scorers
Winners	1946	Charlton Athletic	*4–1	Stamps 2, Doherty, o.g.
Runners-up	1898	Nottingham Forest	1–3	Bloomer
	1899	Sheffield United	1–4	Boag
	1903	Bury	0–6	

* after extra time

THE DERBY RECORD

	Division and place		Cup round reached		Division and place		Cup round reached
1885			1	1935	I	6	5
1886			3	1936	I	2	q-f
1887			2	1937	I	4	5
1888			2	1938	I	13	3
1889	I	10	2	1939	I	6	3
1890	I	7	1	1946			Winners
1891	I	11	2	1947	I	14	5
1892	I	10	1	1948	I	4	s-f
1893	I	13	1	1949	I	3	q-f
1894	I	3	q-f	1950	I	11	q-f
1895	I	15	1	1951	I	11	4
1896	I	2	s-f	1952	I	17	3
1897	I	3	s-f	1953	I	22R	3
1898	I	10	Final	1954	II	18	3
1899	I	9	Final	1955	II	22R	3
1900	I	6	1	1956	NIII	2	2
1901	I	12	1	1957	NIII	1P	2
1902	I	6	s-f	1958	II	16	3
1903	I	9	Final	1959	II	7	3
1904	I	14	s-f	1960	II	18	3
1905	I	11	1	1961	II	12	3
1906	I	15	2	1962	II	16	4
1907	I	19R	3	1963	II	18	4
1908	II	6	1	1964	II	13	3
1909	II	5	s-f	1965	II	9	3
1910	II	4	2	1966	II	8	3
1911	II	6	q-f	1967	II	17	3
1912	II	1P	2	1968	II	18	3
1913	I	7	1	1969	II	1P	3
1914	I	20R	2	1970	I	4	5
1915	II	1P	1	1971	I	9	5
1920	I	18	1	1972	I	1C	5
1921	I	21R	2	1973	I	7	6
1922	II	12	1	1974	I	3	4
1923	II	14	s-f	1975	I	1C	5
1924	II	3	2	1976	I	4	s-f
1925	II	3	1	1977	I	15	q-f
1926	II	2P	4	1978	I	12	5
1927	I	12	4	1979	I	19	3
1928	I	4	4	1980	I	21R	3
1929	I	6	4	1981	II	6	3
1930	I	2	4	1982	II	16	3
1931	I	6	3	1983	II	13	5
1932	I	15	5	1984	II	20R	6
1933	I	7	s-f	1985	III	7	1
1934	I	4	5	1986	III	3P	1
				1987	II	1P	3

DONCASTER ROVERS

Founded: 1879
Address: Belle Vue Ground, Doncaster
Telephone: Doncaster 535281
Ground capacity: 10,500
Playing area: 110 by 77 yards
Record attendance: 37,149 v Hull City, Division III(N), 2.10.48
Record victory: 10–0 v Darlington, Division IV, 25.1.64
Record defeat: 0–12 v Small Heath, Division II, 11.4.03
Most League points (3 for win): 85, Division IV, 1983–84
Most League points (2 for win): 72, Division III(N), 1946–47
Most League goals: 123, Division III(N), 1946–47
League scoring record: 42, Clarrie Jordan, Division III(N), 1946–47
Record League aggregate: 180, Tom Kettley, 1923–29
Most League appearances: 406, Fred Emery, 1925–36
Most capped player: 14, Len Graham, Northern Ireland

THE DONCASTER ROVERS RECORD

	Division and place		Cup round reached		Division and place		Cup round reached
1902	II	7	p	1961	IV	11	1
1903*	II	16	q	1962	IV	21	1
1905*	II	18	q	1963	IV	16	2
1924	NIII	9	q	1964	IV	14	3
1925	NIII	18	1	1965	IV	9	3
1926	NIII	10	2	1966	IV	1P	1
1927	NIII	8	2	1967	III	23R	1
1928	NIII	4	1	1968	IV	10	3
1929	NIII	5	1	1969	IV	1P	3
1930	NIII	14	4	1970	III	11	2
1931	NIII	15	2	1971	III	23R	1
1932	NIII	15	2	1972	IV	12	1
1933	NIII	6	3	1973	IV	17	3
1934	NIII	5	1	1974	IV	22	3
1935	NIII	1P	1	1975	IV	17	2
1936	II	18	3	1976	IV	10	1
1937	II	22R	3	1977	IV	8	1
1938	NIII	2	3	1978	IV	12	1
1939	NIII	2	4	1979	IV	22	2
1946			1	1980	IV	12	2
1947	NIII	1P	3	1981	IV	3P	3
1948	II	21R	3	1982	III	19	2
1949	NIII	3	1	1983	III	23R	1
1950	NIII	1P	4	1984	IV	2P	1
1951	II	11	3	1985	III	14	4
1952	II	16	5	1986	III	11	1
1953	II	13	3	1987	III	13	2
1954	II	12	5				
1955	II	18	5				
1956	II	17	5				
1957	II	14	3				
1958	II	22R	3				
1959	III	22R	3				
1960	IV	17	3				

*–Doncaster failed to gain re-election. Elected in 1904 and 1923.

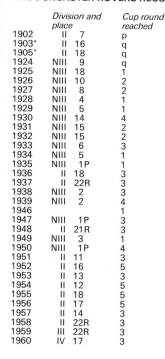

EVERTON

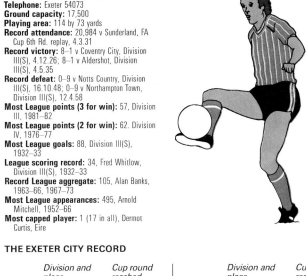

Founded: 1878
Address: Goodison Park, Liverpool L4 4EL
Telephone: (051) 521 2020
Ground capacity: 53,091 (25,000 seated)
Playing area: 112 by 78 yards
Record attendance: 78,299 v Liverpool, Division I, 18.8.48
Record victory: 11–2 v Derby County, FA Cup 1st round, 18.1.1890
Record defeat: 4–10 v Tottenham Hotspur, Division I, 11.10.58
Most League points (3 for win): 90, Division I, 1984–85
Most League points (2 for win): 66, Division II, 1930–31
Most League goals: 121, Division II, 1930–31
League scoring record: 60, Dixie Dean, Division I, 1927–28
Record League aggregate: 349, Dixie Dean, 1925–1937
Most League appearances: 465, Ted Sagar, 1929–53
Most capped player: 37 (72 in all), Alan Ball, England

FA Cup	Year	Opponents	Score	Scorers
Winners	1906	Newcastle United	1–0	Young
	1933	Manchester City	3–0	Stein, Dean, Dunn
	1966	Sheffield Wednesday	3–2	Trebilcock 2, Temple
	1984	Watford	2–0	Sharp, Gray
Runners-up	1893	Wolverhampton Wanderers	0–1	
	1897	Aston Villa	2–3	Bell, Boyle
	1907	Sheffield Wednesday	1–2	Sharp
	1968	West Bromwich Albion	*0–1	
	1985	Manchester United	0–1	
	1986	Liverpool	1–3	Lineker
League Cup				
Runners-up	1977	Aston Villa	0–0	
		Replay	*1–1	Latchford
		Replay	*2–3	Latchford, Lyons
	1984	Liverpool	*0–0	
		Replay	0–1	

* after extra time

THE EVERTON RECORD

	Division and place	Cup round reached			Division and place	Cup round reached
1887		1		1936	I 16	3
1888		2		1937	I 17	5
1889	I 8	q		1938	I 14	4
1890	I 2	2		1939	I 1C	q-f
1891	I 1C	1		1946		3
1892	I 5	1		1947	I 10	4
1893	I 3	Final		1948	I 14	5
1894	I 6	1		1949	I 18	4
1895	I 2	q-f		1950	I 18	s-f
1896	I 3	q-f		1951	I 22R	3
1897	I 7	Final		1952	II 7	3
1898	I 4	s-f		1953	II 16	s-f
1899	I 4	2		1954	II 2P	5
1900	I 11	1		1955	I 11	4
1901	I 7	2		1956	I 15	q-f
1902	I 2	1		1957	I 15	5
1903	I 12	q-f		1958	I 16	4
1904	I 3	1		1959	I 16	5
1905	I 2	s-f		1960	I 15	3
1906	I 11	Winners		1961	I 5	3
1907	I 3	Final		1962	I 4	5
1908	I 11	q-f		1963	I 1C	5
1909	I 2	2		1964	I 3	5
1910	I 10	s-f		1965	I 4	4
1911	I 4	3		1966	I 11	Winners
1912	I 2	q-f		1967	I 6	q-f
1913	I 11	q-f		1968	I 5	Final
1914	I 15	1		1969	I 3	s-f
1915	I 1C	s-f		1970	I 1C	3
1920	I 16	1		1971	I 14	s-f
1921	I 7	q-f		1972	I 15	5
1922	I 20	1		1973	I 17	4
1923	I 5	1		1974	I 7	4
1924	I 7	2		1975	I 4	5
1925	I 17	3		1976	I 11	3
1926	I 11	3		1977	I 9	s-f
1927	I 20	4		1978	I 3	4
1928	I 1C	4		1979	I 4	3
1929	I 18	3		1980	I 19	s-f
1930	I 22R	4		1981	I 15	q-f
1931	II 1P	s-f		1982	I 8	3
1932	I 1C	3		1983	I 7	3
1933	I 11	Winners		1984	I 7	Final
1934	I 14	3		1985	I 1C	Final
1935	I 8	q-f		1986	I 2	Final
				1987	I 1C	5

EXETER CITY

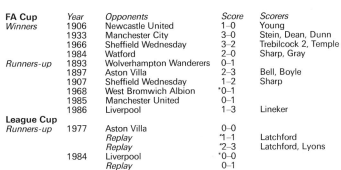

Founded: 1904
Address: St. James' Park, Exeter
Telephone: Exeter 54073
Ground capacity: 17,500
Playing area: 114 by 73 yards
Record attendance: 20,984 v Sunderland, FA Cup 6th Rd. replay, 4.3.31
Record victory: 8–1 v Coventry City, Division III(S), 4.12.26; 8–1 v Aldershot, Division III(S), 4.5.35
Record defeat: 0–9 v Notts County, Division III(S), 16.10.48; 0–9 v Northampton Town, Division III(S), 12.4.58
Most League points (3 for win): 57, Division III, 1981–82
Most League points (2 for win): 62, Division IV, 1976–77
Most League goals: 88, Division III(S), 1932–33
League scoring record: 34, Fred Whitlow, Division III(S), 1932–33
Record League aggregate: 105, Alan Banks, 1963–66, 1967–73
Most League appearances: 495, Arnold Mitchell, 1952–66
Most capped player: 1 (17 in all), Dermot Curtis, Eire

THE EXETER CITY RECORD

	Division and place	Cup round reached			Division and place	Cup round reached
1909		2		1953	SIII 17	1
1910		5q		1954	SIII 9	1
1911		1		1955	SIII 22	1
1912		4q		1956	SIII 16	3
1913		4q		1957	SIII 21	1
1914		2		1958	SIII 24	1
1915		1		1959	IV 5	1
1920		6q		1960	IV 9	3
1921	SIII 19	1		1961	IV 21	1
1922	SIII 21	5q		1962	IV 18	1
1923	SIII 20	5q		1963	IV 17	1
1924	SIII 16	2		1964	IV 4P	2
1925	SIII 7	1		1965	III 17	2
1926	SIII 20	1		1966	III 22R	1
1927	SIII 12	3		1967	IV 14	1
1928	SIII 8	4		1968	IV 20	2
1929	SIII 21	3		1969	IV 17	3
1930	SIII 16	1		1970	IV 18	2
1931	SIII 13	6		1971	IV 9	1
1932	SIII 7	3		1972	IV 15	2
1933	SIII 2	1		1973	IV 8	1
1934	SIII 9	1		1974	IV 10	1
1935	SIII 11	2		1975	IV 9	1
1936	SIII 22	1		1976	IV 7	1
1937	SIII 21	5		1977	IV 2P	1
1938	SIII 17	2		1978	III 17	3
1939	SIII 14	1		1979	III 9	2
1946		2		1980	III 8	1
1947	SIII 15	1		1981	III 11	q-f
1948	SIII 11	1		1982	III 18	1
1949	SIII 12	3		1983	III 19	1
1950	SIII 16	4		1984	III 24R	1
1951	SIII 14	4		1985	IV 18	1
1952	SIII 23	2		1986	IV 21	3
				1987	IV 14	1

FULHAM

Founded: 1880
Address: Craven Cottage, Stevenage Road, London SW6
Telephone: (01) 736 5621/6561/2/3
Ground capacity: 25,680
Playing area: 110 by 75 yards
Record attendance: 49,335 v Millwall, Division II, 8.10.38
Record victory: 10–1 v Ipswich Town, Division I, 26.12.63
Record defeat: 0–9 v Wolverhampton Wanderers, Division I, 16.9.59
Most League points (3 for win): 78, Division III, 1981–82
Most League points (2 for win): 60, Division II, 1958–59 & Division III, 1970–71
Most League goals: 111, Division III(S), 1931–32
League scoring record: 41, Frank Newton, Division III(S), 1931–32
Record League aggregate: 159, Johnny Haynes, 1952–70
Most League appearances: 598, Johnny Haynes, 1952–70
Most capped player: 56, Johnny Haynes, England

FA Cup	Year	Opponents	Score
Runners-up	1975	West Ham United	0–2

THE FULHAM RECORD

Year	Division and place		Cup round reached		Year	Division and place		Cup round reached
1904			1		1950	I	17	3
1905			q-f		1951	I	18	q-f
1906			2		1952	I	22R	3
1907			2		1953	II	8	3
1908	II	4	s-f		1954	II	8	4
1909	II	10	2		1955	II	14	3
1910	II	7			1956	II	9	4
1911	II	10	1		1957	II	11	4
1912	II	8	q-f		1958	II	5	s-f
1913	II	9	1		1959	II	2P	4
1914	II	11	1		1960	I	10	4
1915	II	12	2		1961	I	17	3
1920	II	6	1		1962	I	20	s-f
1921	II	9	3		1963	I	16	3
1922	II	7	2		1964	I	15	4
1923	II	10	1		1965	I	20	3
1924	II	20	2		1966	I	20	3
1925	II	12	2		1967	I	19	4
1926	II	19	q-f		1968	I	22R	4
1927	II	18	4		1969	II	22R	4
1928	II	21R	3		1970	III	4	1
1929	SIII	5	2		1971	III	2P	1
1930	SIII	7	4		1972	II	20	4
1931	SIII	9	3		1973	II	9	3
1932	SIII	1P	3		1974	II	13	4
1933	II	3	3		1975	II	9	Final
1934	II	16	3		1976	II	12	3
1935	II	7	3		1977	II	17	3
1936	II	9	s-f		1978	II	10	3
1937	II	11	3		1979	II	10	4
1938	II	8	3		1980	II	20R	3
1939	II	12	4		1981	III	13	4
1946			3		1982	III	3P	2
1947	I	15	3		1983	II	4	4
1948	II	11	q-f		1984	II	11	3
1949	II	1P	3		1985	II	9	3
					1986	II	22R	3
					1987	III	18	3

GILLINGHAM

Founded: 1893
Address: Priestfield Stadium, Gillingham, Kent
Telephone: Medway 51854
Ground capacity: 22,000
Playing area: 114 by 75 yards
Record attendance: 23,002 v Queen's Park Rangers, FA Cup 3rd round, 10.1.48
Record victory: 10–1 v Gorleston, FA Cup 1st round, 16.11.57
Record defeat: 2–9 v Nottingham Forest, Division III(S), 18.11.50
Most League points (3 for win): 83, Division III, 1984–85
Most League points (2 for win): 62, Division IV, 1973–74
Most League goals: 90, Division IV, 1973–4
League scoring record: 31, Ernie Morgan, Division III(S), 1954–55; Brian Yeo, Division IV, 1973–74
Record League aggregate: 135, Brian Yeo, 1963–75
Most League appearances: 571, John Simpson, 1957–72
Most capped player: 3, Tony Cascarino, Eire

THE GILLINGHAM RECORD

Year	Division and place		Cup round reached		Year	Division and place		Cup round reached
1899*			1		1952	SIII	22	2
1900			p		1953	SIII	20	2
1901			p		1954	SIII	10	1
1902			p		1955	SIII	4	2
1903			p		1956	SIII	10	1
1904			p		1957	SIII	22	2
1905			p		1958	SIII	22	3
1906			1		1959	IV	11	1
1907			2		1960	IV	7	3
1908			2		1961	IV	15	1
1909			p		1962	IV	20	1
1910			p		1963	IV	5	3
1911			1		1964	IV	1P	1
1912			p		1965	III	7	2
1913			p		1966	III	6	1
1914			2		1967	III	11	2
1915			1		1968	III	11	1
1920			1		1969	III	20	2
1921	III	22	p		1970	III	20	5
1922	SIII	18	1		1971	III	24R	1
1923	SIII	16	p		1972	IV	13	3
1924	SIII	15	1		1973	IV	9	1
1925	SIII	13	p		1974	IV	2P	1
1926	SIII	10	2		1975	III	10	1
1927	SIII	20	2		1976	III	14	2
1928	SIII	16	3		1977	III	12	1
1929	SIII	22	1		1978	III	7	2
1930	SIII	21	1		1979	III	4	1
1931	SIII	16	2		1980	III	16	1
1932	SIII	21	1		1981	III	15	2
1933	SIII	7	2		1982	III	6	4
1934	SIII	17	2		1983	III	13	2
1935	SIII	20	1		1984	III	8	4
1936	SIII	16	2		1985	III	4	4
1937	SIII	11	2		1986	III	5	3
1938†	SIII	22	1		1987	III	5	3
1939			q					
1946			q					
1947			3					
1948			3					
1949			q					
1950			2					
1951	SIII	22	2					

*–New Brompton Excelsior until 1913
†–Not re-elected   Re-elected 1950

GRIMSBY TOWN

Founded: 1878 (as Grimsby Pelham)
Address: Blundell Park, Cleethorpes, Lincolnshire
Telephone: 0472 691420
Ground capacity: 22,000
Playing area: 114 by 74 yards
Record attendance: 31, 657 v Wolves FA Cup 5th round 20.2.37
Record victory: 9–2 v Darwen, Division II 15.4.1899
Record defeat: 1–9 v Arsenal, Division I 28.1.31
Most League points (3 for win): 70, Division II, 1983–84
Most League points (2 for win): 68, Division III(N), 1955–56
Most League goals: 103, Division II, 1933–34
League scoring record: 42, Pat Glover, Division II, 1933–34
Record League aggregate: 182, Pat Glover, 1930–39
Most League appearances: 448, Keith Jobling, 1953–69
Most capped player: 7, Pat Glover, Wales

THE GRIMSBY RECORD

	Division and place	Cup round reached		Division and place	Cup round reached
1893	II 4	2	1948	I 22R	3
1894	II 5	1	1949	II 11	4
1895	II 5	p	1950	II 11	4
1896	II 3	2	1951	II 22R	3
1897	II 3	1	1952	NIII 2	2
1898	II 12	1	1953	NIII 5	3
1899	II 10	1	1954	NIII 17	3
1900	II 6	1	1955	NIII 23	3
1901	II 1P	p	1956	NIII 1P	3
1902	I 15	1	1957	II 16	3
1903	I 17R	2	1958	II 13	3
1904	II 6	1	1959	II 21R	4
1905	II 13	1	1960	III 4	2
1906	II 8	1	1961	III 6	1
1907	II 11	1	1962	III 2P	1
1908	II 18	q-f	1963	II 19	3
1909	II 13	1	1964	II 21R	3
1910	II 19L	1	1965	III 10	2
1911		3	1966	III 11	4
1912	II 9	p	1967	III 17	1
1913	II 7	1	1968	III 21R	1
1914	II 15	1	1969	IV 23	1
1915	II 17	1	1970	IV 16	1
1920	II 22M	1	1971	IV 19	1
1921	III 13	2	1972	IV 1P	1
1922	NIII 3	1	1973	III 9	4
1923	NIII 14	p	1974	III 6	3
1924	NIII 11	1	1975	III 16	2
1925	NIII 12	p	1976	III 18	1
1926	NIII 1P	3	1977	III 23R	2
1927	II 17	3	1978	IV 6	3
1928	II 11	3	1979	IV 2P	1
1929	II 2P	3	1980	III 1P	3
1930	I 18	3	1981	II 7	3
1931	I 13	5	1982	II 17	5
1932	I 21R	5	1983	II 19	4
1933	II 13	4	1984	II 5	3
1934	II 1P	4	1985	II 10	4
1935	II 5	3	1986	II 15	3
1936	I 17	s-f	1987	II 21R	3
1937	I 11	5			
1938	I 20	3			
1939	I 10	s-f			
1946		3			
1947	I 16	4			

M – not re-elected in Second Division but invited to join newly formed Third Division.

HALIFAX TOWN

Founded: 1911
Address: Shay Ground, Halifax HX1 2YS
Telephone: Halifax 53423
Ground capacity: 16,500
Playing area: 110 by 75 yards
Record attendance: 36,885 v Tottenham Hotspur, FA Cup 5th round, 14.2.53
Record victory: 7–0 v Bishop Auckland, FA Cup 2nd round replay, 10.1.67
Record defeat: 0–13 v Stockport County, Division III(N), 6.1.34
Most League points (3 for win): 60, Division IV, 1982–83
Most League points (2 for win): 57, Division IV, 1968–69
Most League goals: 83, Division III(N), 1957–58
League scoring record: 34, Albert Valentine, Division III(N), 1934–35
Record League aggregate: 129, Ernest Dixon, 1922–1930
Most League appearances: 367, John Pickering, 1965–74
Most capped player: 1, Mick Meagan, Eire

THE HALIFAX RECORD

	Division and place	Cup round reached		Division and place	Cup round reached
1922	NIII 19	p	1958	NIII 7	1
1923	NIII 7	1	1959	III 9	2
1924	NIII 14	2	1960	III 15	2
1925	NIII 9	p	1961	III 9	2
1926	NIII 5	1	1962	III 18	1
1927	NIII 4	1	1963	III 24R	2
1928	NIII 12	2	1964	IV 10	1
1929	NIII 13	1	1965	IV 23	1
1930	NIII 21	1	1966	IV 15	1
1931	NIII 17	2	1967	IV 12	3
1932	NIII 17	3	1968	IV 11	3
1933	NIII 15	5	1969	IV 2P	4
1934	NIII 9	3	1970	III 18	1
1935	NIII 2	1	1971	III 3	1
1936	NIII 17	2	1972	III 16	1
1937	NIII 7	1	1973	III 20	2
1938	NIII 18	1	1974	III 9	2
1939	NIII 12	3	1975	III 17	2
1946		1	1976	III 24R	3
1947	NIII 22	2	1977	IV 21	3
1948	NIII 21	1	1978	IV 20	1
1949	NIII 19	1	1979	IV 23	1
1950	NIII 21	1	1980	IV 18	4
1951	NIII 22	1	1981	IV 23	1
1952	NIII 20	1	1982	IV 19	1
1953	NIII 14	5	1983	IV 11	1
1954	NIII 23	1	1984	IV 21	1
1955	NIII 14	1	1985	IV 21	2
1956	NIII 19	2	1986	IV 20	1
1957	NIII 11	1	1987	IV 15	1

HARTLEPOOL UNITED

Founded: 1908
Address: The Victoria Ground, Clarence Road, Hartlepool
Telephone: Hartlepool 72584
Ground capacity: 3,300
Playing area: 113 by 77 yards
Record attendance: 17,426 v Manchester United, FA Cup 3rd round, 5.1.57
Record victory: 10–1 v Barrow, Division IV, 4.4.59
Record defeat: 1–10 v Wrexham, Division IV, 3.3.62
Most League points (3 for win): 70, Division IV, 1985–86
Most League points (2 for win): 60, Division IV, 1967–68
Most League goals: 90, Division III(N), 1956–57
League scoring record: 28, Bill Robinson, Division III(N), 1927–28
Record League aggregate: 98, Ken Johnson, 1949–1964
Most League appearances: 448, Watty Moore, 1948–1964
Most capped player: 1 (11 in all), Ambrose Fogarty, Eire

THE HARTLEPOOL RECORD

	Division and place	Cup round reached		Division and place	Cup round reached
1922	NIII 4	p	1958	NIII 17	2
1923	NIII 15	p	1959	IV 19	2
1924	NIII 21	p	1960	IV 24	1
1925	NIII 20	1	1961	IV 23	1
1926	NIII 6	p	1962	IV 22	3
1927	NIII 17	1	1963	IV 24	1
1928	NIII 15	1	1964	IV 23	1
1929	NIII 21	1	1965	IV 15	2
1930	NIII 8	1	1966	IV 18	3
1931	NIII 20	1	1967	IV 8	1
1932	NIII 13	1	1968	IV 3P	1
1933	NIII 14	2	1969	III 22R	1
1934	NIII 11	2	1970	IV 23	2
1935	NIII 12	2	1971	IV 23	1
1936	NIII 8	3	1972	IV 18	2
1937	NIII 6	2	1973	IV 20	1
1938	NIII 20	2	1974	IV 11	1
1939	NIII 21	2	1975	IV 13	2
1946		1	1976	IV 14	3
1947	NIII 13	2	1977	IV 22	1
1948	NIII 19	2	1978	IV 21	4
1949	NIII 16	1	1979	IV 13	3
1950	NIII 18	2	1980	IV 19	1
1951	NIII 16	2	1981	IV 9	1
1952	NIII 9	3	1982	IV 14	2
1953	NIII 17	2	1983	IV 22	2
1954	NIII 18	1	1984	IV 23	1
1955	NIII 5	4	1985	IV 19	2
1956	NIII 4	3	1986	IV 7	2
1957	NIII 2	3	1987	IV 18	1

HEREFORD UNITED

Founded: 1924
Address: Edgar Street, Hereford
Telephone: 0432 276666
Ground capacity: 17,500
Playing area: 111 by 80 yards
Record attendance: 18,114 v Sheffield Wednesday, FA Cup 3rd round, 4.1.58
Record victory: 11–0 v Thynnes, FA Cup qualifying rounds, 13.9.47
Record defeat: 1–6 (home) v Wolves, Division II, 2.10.76; 0–5 v Wrexham, Division III, 22.12.73; 1–6 v Tranmere, Division III, 29.11.75; 2–7 v Arsenal, FA Cup 3rd round replay, 22.1.85
Most League points (3 for win): 77, Division IV, 1984–85
Most League points (2 for win): 63, Division III, 1975–76
Most League goals: 86, Division III, 1975–76
League scoring record: 35, Dixie McNeil, Division III, 1975–76
Record League aggregate: 85, Dixie McNeil, 1974–77
Most League appearances: 330, Chris Price, 1976–86
Most capped player: 1 (7 in all), Brian Evans, Wales

THE HEREFORD RECORD

	Division and place	Cup round reached		Division and place	Cup round reached
1973	IV 2p	1	1980	IV 21	2
1974	III 18	4	1981	IV 22	2
1975	III 12	2	1982	IV 10	4
1976	III 1P	3	1983	IV 24	1
1977	II 22R	4	1984	IV 11	1
1978	III 23R	1	1985	IV 5	3
1979	IV 14	1	1986	IV 10	2
			1987	IV 16	1

Founded: 1908
Address: Leeds Road, Huddersfield HD1 6PE
Telephone: Huddersfield 20445/6
Ground capacity: 32,000
Playing area: 115 by 75 yards
Record attendance: 67,037 v Arsenal, FA Cup quarter-final, 27.2.32
Record victory: 10–1 v Blackpool, Division I, 13.12.30
Record defeat: 0–8 v Middlesbrough, Division I, 3.9.50
Most League points (3 for win): 82, Division III, 1982–83
Most League points (2 for win): 66, Division IV, 1978–80
Most League goals: 101, Division IV, 1979–80
League scoring record: 35, George Brown, Division I, 1925–26, Sam Taylor, Division II, 1919–20
Record League aggregate: 142, George Brown, Division I, 1921–1929; 142, Jim Glazzard, 1946–56
Most League appearances: 520, Billy Smith, 1914–1934
Most capped player: 31 (41 in all), Jimmy Nicholson, Northern Ireland

FA Cup	Year	Opponents	Score	Scorers
Winners	1922	Preston North End	1–0	Smith (pen)
Runners-up	1920	Aston Villa	*0–1	
	1928	Blackburn Rovers	1–3	Jackson
	1930	Arsenal	0–2	
	1938	Preston North End	*0–1	

* after extra time

THE HUDDERSFIELD RECORD

	Division and place	Cup round reached		Division and place	Cup round reached
1911	II 13		1954	I 3	3
1912	II 17	1	1955	I 12	q-f
1913	II 5	2	1956	I 21R	3
1914	II 13	2	1957	II 12	5
1915	II 8	1	1958	II 9	3
1920	II 2P	Final	1959	II 14	3
1921	I 17	3	1960	II 6	4
1922	I 14	Winners	1961	II 20	4
1923	I 3	3	1962	II 7	4
1924	I 1C	3	1963	II 6	3
1925	I 1C	1	1964	II 12	5
1926	I 1C	4	1965	II 8	4
1927	I 2	3	1966	II 4	5
1928	I 2	Final	1967	II 6	3
1929	I 16	s-f	1968	II 14	3
1930	I 10	Final	1969	II 6	4
1931	I 5	3	1970	II 1P	3
1932	I 4	q-f	1971	I 15	4
1933	I 6	4	1972	I 22R	q-f
1934	I 2	4	1973	II 21R	3
1935	I 16	3	1974	III 10	2
1936	I 3	4	1975	III 24R	1
1937	I 15	3	1976	IV 5	4
1938	I 15	Final	1977	IV 9	1
1939	I 19	s-f	1978	IV 11	1
1946		3	1979	IV 9	1
1947	I 20	3	1980	IV 1P	1
1948	I 19	3	1981	III 4	3
1949	I 20	4	1982	III 17	4
1950	I 15	3	1983	III 3P	3
1951	I 19	5	1984	II 12	4
1952	I 21R	3	1985	II 13	4
1953	II 2P	4	1986	II 16	3
			1987	II 17	3

Founded: 1904
Address: Boothferry Park, Hull HU4 6EU
Telephone: 0482 52195/6
Ground capacity: 28,000
Playing area: 112 by 75 yards
Record attendance: 55,019 v Manchester United, FA Cup quarter-final, 16.2.49
Record victory: 11–1 v Carlisle United, Division III(N), 14.1.39
Record defeat: 0–8 v Wolverhampton Wanderers, Division II, 4.11.11
Most League points (3 for win): 90, Division IV, 1982–83
Most League points (2 for win): 69, Division III, 1965–66
Most League goals: 109, Division III, 1965–66
League scoring record: 39, Bill McNaughton, Division III(N), 1932–33
Record League aggregate: 195, Chris Chilton, 1960–1971
Most League appearances: 511, Andy Davidson, 1947–67
Most capped player: 15 (59 in all), Terry Neill, Northern Ireland

THE HULL RECORD

	Division and place	Cup round reached		Division and place	Cup round reached
1906	II 5	1	1952	II 18	5
1907	II 9	1	1953	II 18	4
1908	II 8	2	1954	II 15	5
1909	II 4	1	1955	II 19	3
1910	II 3	1	1956	II 22R	3
1911	II 5	3	1957	NIII 8	3
1912	II 7	1	1958	NIII 5	4
1913	II 12	2	1959	III 2P	1
1914	II 7	1	1960	II 21R	3
1915	II 7	q-f	1961	III 11	3
1920	II 11	1	1962	III 10	2
1921	II 13	q-f	1963	III 10	3
1922	II 5	2	1964	III 8	3
1923	II 12	1	1965	III 4	2
1924	II 17	1	1966	III 1P	q-f
1925	II 10	3	1967	II 12	3
1926	II 13	3	1968	II 17	3
1927	II 7	5	1969	II 11	3
1928	II 14	3	1970	II 13	3
1929	II 12	3	1971	II 5	q-f
1930	II 21R	s-f	1972	II 12	5
1931	NIII 6	3	1973	II 13	5
1932	NIII 8	3	1974	II 9	3
1933	NIII 1P	3	1975	II 8	3
1934	II 15	4	1976	II 14	4
1935	II 13	3	1977	II 14	3
1936	II 22R	3	1978	II 22R	3
1937	NIII 5	1	1979	III 8	2
1938	NIII 3	3	1980	III 20	1
1939	NIII 7	2	1981	III 24R	4
1947	NIII 11	3	1982	IV 8	3
1948	NIII 5	3	1983	IV 2P	1
1949	NIII 1P	q-f	1984	III 4	2
1950	II 7	4	1985	III 3P	3
1951	II 10	5	1986	II 6	4
			1987	II 14	5

IPSWICH TOWN

Founded: 1887
Address: Portman Road, Ipswich, Suffolk IP1 2DA
Telephone: Ipswich 219211
Ground capacity: 38,000
Playing area: 112 by 72 yards
Record attendance: 38,010 v Leeds United, FA Cup 6th round, 8.3.75
Record victory: 10–0 v Floriana, Malta, European Cup, 25.9.62
Record defeat: 1–10 v Fulham, Division I, 26.12.63
Most League points (3 for win): 83, Division I, 1981–82
Most League points (2 for win): 64, Division III(S), 1953–54 & 1955–56
Most League goals: 106, Division III(S), 1955–56
League scoring record: 41, Ted, Phillips, Division III(S), 1956–57
Record League aggregate: 203, Ray Crawford, 1958–1963 & 1966–1969
Most League appearances: 591, Mick Mills, 1966–82
Most capped player: 47 (53 in all), Allan Hunter, Northern Ireland

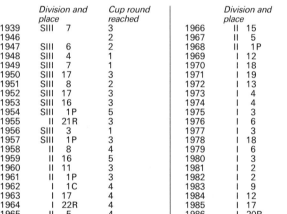

FA Cup	Year	Opponents		Score	Scorers
Winners	1978	Arsenal		1–0	Osborne

THE IPSWICH RECORD

	Division and place		Cup round reached			Division and place		Cup round reached
1939	SIII	7	3		1966	II	15	3
1946			2		1967	II	5	5
1947	SIII	6	2		1968	II	1P	3
1948	SIII	4	1		1969	I	12	3
1949	SIII	7	1		1970	I	18	3
1950	SIII	17	3		1971	I	19	5
1951	SIII	8	2		1972	I	13	4
1952	SIII	17	3		1973	I	4	4
1953	SIII	16	3		1974	I	4	5
1954	SIII	1P	5		1975	I	3	s-f
1955	II	21R	3		1976	I	6	4
1956	SIII	3	1		1977	I	3	4
1957	SIII	1P	3		1978	I	18	Winners
1958	II	8	4		1979	I	6	q-f
1959	II	16	5		1980	I	3	q-f
1960	II	11	3		1981	I	2	s-f
1961	II	1P	3		1982	I	2	5
1962	I	1C	4		1983	I	9	5
1963	I	17	4		1984	I	12	4
1964	I	22R	4		1985	I	17	6
1965	II	5	4		1986	I	20R	4
					1987	II	5	3

LEEDS UNITED

Founded: 1904 †
Address: Elland Road, Leeds LS11 OES
Telephone: 0532 716037
Ground capacity: 39,423
Playing area: 117 by 76 yards
Record attendance: 57,892 v Sunderland, FA Cup 5th round, 15.3.67
Record victory: 10–0 v Lyn Oslo, European Cup, 1st Rd, 17.9.69
Record defeat: 1–8 v Stoke City, Division I, 27.8.34
Most League points (3 for win): 69, Division II, 1985–85
Most League points (2 for win): 67, Division I, 1968–69
Most League goals: 98, Division II, 1927–28
League scoring record: 42, John Charles, 1953–54
Record League aggregate: Peter Lorimer, 168, 1965–79, 1983–86
Most League appearances: 629, Jack Charlton, 1953–1973
Most capped player: 54, Billy Bremner, Scotland

FA Cup	Year	Opponents		Score	Scorers
Winners	1972	Arsenal		1–0	Clarke
Runners-up	1965	Liverpool		*1–2	Bremner
	1970	Chelsea		*2–2	Charlton, Jones
				*1–2	Jones
	1973	Sunderland		0–1	
League Cup					
Winners	1968	Arsenal		1–0	Cooper

† as Leeds City. Reconstituted as Leeds United 1920   * after extra time

THE LEEDS RECORD

	Division and place		Cup round reached			Division and place		Cup round reached
1906 †	II	6			1956	II	2P	3
1907 †	II	10	1		1957	I	8	3
1908;	II	12	1		1958	I	17	3
1909 †	II	12	2		1959	I	15	3
1910 †	II	17	1		1960	I	21R	3
1911 †	II	11	1		1961	II	14	3
1912 †	II	19	2		1962	II	19	3
1913 †	II	6	1		1963	II	5	5
1914 †	II	4	2		1964	II	1P	4
1915 †	II	15	2		1965	I	2	Final
1920‡	II				1966	I	2	4
1921	II	14	1q		1967	I	4	s-f
1922	II	8	1		1968	I	4	s-f
1923	II	7	2		1969	I	1C	3
1924	II	1P	3		1970	I	2	Final
1925	I	18	1		1971	I	2	5
1926	I	19	3		1972	I	2	Winners
1927	I	21R	4		1973	I	3	Final
1928	II	2P	3		1974	I	1C	5
1929	I	13	4		1975	I	9	q-f
1930	I	5	4		1976	I	5	4
1931	I	21R	5		1977	I	10	s-f
1932	II	2P	3		1978	I	9	3
1933	I	8	5		1979	I	5	3
1934	I	9	3		1980	I	11	3
1935	I	18	4		1981	I	9	3
1936	I	11	5		1982	I	20R	4
1937	I	19	3		1983	II	8	4
1938	I	9	4		1984	II	13	3
1939	I	13	4		1985	II	7	3
1946			3		1986	II	14	3
1947	I	22R	3		1987	II	4	s-f
1948	II	18	3					
1949	II	15	3					
1950	II	5	q-f					
1951	II	5	4					
1952	II	6	5					
1953	II	10	3					
1954	II	10	3					
1955	II	4	3					

† – as Leeds City
‡ – Leeds expelled from the League after 8 matches. Fixtures transferred to Port Vale, who finished 13th

Founded: 1884
Address: Filbert Street, Leicester
Telephone: Leicester 555000
Ground capacity: 32,000
Playing area: 112 by 75 yards
Record attendance: 47,298 v Tottenham Hotspur, FA Cup 5th round, 18.2.28
Record victory: 10–0 v Portsmouth, Division I, 20.10.28
Record defeat: 0–12 v Nottingham Forest, Division I, 21.4.09
Most League points (3 for win): 70, Division II, 1982–83
Most League points (2 for win): 51, Division II, 1956–57
Most League goals: 109, Division II, 1956–57
League scoring record: 44, Arthur Rowley, Division II, 1956–57
Record League aggregate: 262, Arthur Chandler, 1923–1935
Most League appearances: 530, Adam Black, 1919–1935
Most capped player: 37 (73 in all) Gordon Banks, England

FA Cup	Year	Opponents	Score	Scorers
Runners-up	1949	Wolverhampton Wanderers	1–3	Griffiths
	1961	Tottenham Hotspur	0–2	
	1963	Manchester United	1–3	Keyworth
	1969	Manchester City	0–1	
League Cup				
Winners	1964	Stoke City	H1–1	Gibson
			A3–2	Stringfellow, Gibson, Riley
Runners-up	1965	Chelsea	A2–3	Appleton, Goodfellow
			H0–0	

THE LEICESTER RECORD

	Division and place	Cup round reached		Division and place	Cup round reached
1894		2	1946		3
1895	II 4	1	1947	II 9	5
1896	II 8	4q	1948	II 9	5
1897	II 9	4q	1949	II 19	Final
1898	II 7	1	1950	II 15	3
1899	II 3	4q	1951	II 14	3
1900	II 5	1	1952	II 5	3
1901	II 11	1	1953	II 5	3
1902	II 14	p	1954	II 1P	q-f
1903	II 15	2q	1955	I 21R	3
1904	II 18	4q	1956	II 5	4
1905	II 14	1	1957	II 1P	3
1906	II 7	1	1958	I 18	3
1907	II 3	1	1959	I 19	4
1908	II 2P	2	1960	I 12	q-f
1909	I 20R	2	1961	I 6	Final
1910	II 5	q-f	1962	I 14	3
1911	II 15	2	1963	I 4	Final
1912	II 10	2	1964	I 11	3
1913	II 15	1	1965	I 18	q-f
1914	II 18	1	1966	I 7	5
1915	II 19	6q	1967	I 8	3
1920	II 14	3	1968	I 13	q-f
1921	II 12	1	1969	I 21R	Final
1922	II 9	3	1970	II 3	5
1923	II 3	2	1971	II 1P	q-f
1924	II 12	1	1972	I 12	4
1925	II 1P	q-f	1973	I 16	3
1926	I 17	3	1974	I 9	s-f
1927	I 7	1	1975	I 18	5
1928	I 3	5	1976	I 7	5
1929	I 2	5	1977	I 11	3
1930	I 8	3	1978	I 22R	4
1931	I 16	3	1979	II 17	4
1932	I 19	5	1980	II 1P	3
1933	I 19	3	1981	I 21R	4
1934	I 17	s-f	1982	II 8	s-f
1935	I 21R	4	1983	II 3P	3
1936	II 6	5	1984	I 15	3
1937	II 1P	4	1985	I 15	5
1938	I 16	4	1986	I 19	3
1939	I 22R	4	1987	I 20R	3

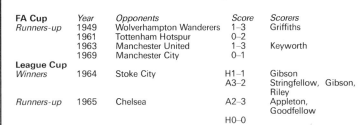

Founded: 1883
Address: Sincil Bank, Lincoln
Telephone: Lincoln 22224
Ground capacity: 16,225
Playing area: 110 by 75 yards
Record attendance: 23,196 v Derby County, League Cup 4th Rd, 15.11.67
Record victory: 11–1 v Crewe Alexandra, Division III(N), 29.9.51
Record defeat: 3–11 v Manchester City, Division II, 23.3.1895
Most League points (3 for win): 77, Division III, 1981–82
Most League points (2 for win): 74, Division IV, 1975–76
Most League goals: 121, Division III(N), 1951–52
League scoring record: 42, Allan Hall, Division III(N), 1931–32
Record League aggregate: 144, Andy Graver, 1950–1954, 1958–1961
Most League appearances: 402, Tony Emery, 1946–1959
Most capped player: 3 (7 in all), David Pugh, Wales; 3 (6 in all), George Moulson, Eire

THE LINCOLN RECORD

	Division and place	Cup round reached		Division and place	Cup round reached
1885		3	1935	NIII 4	2
1886		1	1936	NIII 4	1
1887		1	1937	NIII 2	2
1888		p	1938	NIII 7	2
1889		p	1939	NIII 17	3
1890		2	1946		2
1891		1	1947	NIII 12	3
1892		p	1948	NIII 1P	1
1893	II 9	p	1949	II 22R	3
1894	II 8	p	1950	NIII 4	1
1895	II 13	q	1951	NIII 5	1
1896	II 13	p	1952	NIII 1P	3
1897	II 16	p	1953	II 15	3
1898	II 14	p	1954	II 16	4
1899	II 12	p	1955	II 16	3
1900	II 9	p	1956	II 8	3
1901	II 8	p	1957	II 18	3
1902	II 5	2	1958	II 20	3
1903	II 10	1	1959	II 19	3
1904	II 12	q	1960	II 13	3
1905	II 9	1	1961	II 22R	4
1906	II 13	2	1962	III 22R	1
1907	II 19	2	1963	IV 22	3
1908	II 20L	1	1964	IV 11	3
1909		1	1965	IV 22	3
1910	II 15	p	1966	IV 22	1
1911	II 21L	p	1967	IV 24	1
1912		2	1968	IV 13	1
1913	II 8	p	1969	IV 8	3
1914	II 19	1	1970	IV 8	2
1915	II 16	1	1971	IV 21	3
1920	II 21L	1	1972	IV 5	1
1921		2	1973	IV 10	1
1922	NIII 14	p	1974	IV 12	1
1923	NIII 13	q	1975	IV 5	3
1924	NIII 19	p	1976	IV 1P	4
1925	NIII 8	p	1977	III 9	3
1926	NIII 15	1	1978	III 16	1
1927	NIII 11	3	1979	III 24R	1
1928	NIII 2	3	1980	IV 7	1
1929	NIII 6	3	1981	IV 2P	2
1930	NIII 5	2	1982	III 4	1
1931	NIII 2	2	1983	III 6	1
1932	NIII 1P	2	1984	III 14	2
1933	II 18	3	1985	III 19	1
1934	II 22R	3	1986	III 21R	1
			1987	IV 24R	1

Lincoln City were replaced by Scarborough in May 1987

59

LIVERPOOL

Founded: 1892
Address: Anfield Road, Liverpool 4
Telephone: (051) 263 2361
Ground capacity: 45,000
Playing area: 110 by 75 yards
Record attendance: 61,905 v Wolverhampton Wanderers, FA Cup 4th Rd, 2.2.52
Record victory: 11–0 v Strömgodset, European Cup Winners Cup, 17.9.74
Record defeat: 1–9 v Birmingham City, Division II, 11.12.54
Most League points (3 for win): 88, Division I, 1985–86
Most League points (2 for win): 68, Division I, 1978–79 †
Most League goals: 106, Division II, 1895–96
League scoring record: 41, Roger Hunt, Division II, 1961–62
Record League aggregate: 245, Roger Hunt, 1959–1969
Most League appearances: 640, Ian Callaghan, 1960–1978
Most capped player: 59 (62 in all), Emlyn Hughes, England

FA Cup	Year	Opponents	Score	Scorers
Winners	1965	Leeds United	*2–1	Hunt, St John
	1974	Newcastle United	3–0	Keegan 2, Heighway
	1986	Everton	3–1	Rush 2, Johnson
Runners-up	1914	Burnley	0–1	
	1950	Arsenal	0–2	
	1971	Arsenal	*1–2	Heighway
	1977	Manchester United	1–2	Case
League Cup				
Winners	1981	West Ham	1–1*	A. Kennedy
		Replay	2–1	Dalglish, Hansen
	1982	Tottenham	3–1*	Whelan 2, Rush
	1983	Manchester United	2–1	Kennedy, Whelan
	1984	Everton	0–0	
		Replay	1–0	Souness
Runners-up	1978	Nottingham Forest	0–0	
		Replay	0–1	
	1987	Arsenal	1–2	Rush

* after extra time † record under two-points-for-a-win system.

THE LIVERPOOL RECORD

	Division and place	Cup round reached		Division and place	Cup round reached
1894	II 1P	q-f	1946		4
1895	I 16R	2	1947	I 1C	s-f
1896	II 1P	2	1948	I 11	4
1897	I 5	s-f	1949	I 12	5
1898	I 9	q-f	1950	I 8	Final
1899	I 2	s-f	1951	I 9	3
1900	I 19	2	1952	I 11	5
1901	I 1C	1	1953	I 17	3
1902	I 11	2	1954	I 22R	3
1903	I 5	1	1955	II 11	5
1904	I 17R	1	1956	II 3	5
1905	II 1P	1	1957	II 3	3
1906	I 1C	s-f	1958	II 4	q-f
1907	I 15	q-f	1959	II 4	3
1908	I 8	3	1960	II 3	4
1909	I 16	2	1961	II 3	4
1910	I 2	1	1962	II 1P	5
1911	I 13	2	1963	I 8	s-f
1912	I 17	2	1964	I 1C	q-f
1913	I 12	3	1965	I 7	Winners
1914	I 16	Final	1966	I 1C	3
1915	I 14	2	1967	I 5	5
1920	I 4	q-f	1968	I 3	q-f
1921	I 4	2	1969	I 2	5
1922	I 1C	2	1970	I 5	q-f
1923	I 1C	3	1971	I 5	Final
1924	I 12	q-f	1972	I 3	4
1925	I 4	q-f	1973	I 1C	q-f
1926	I 7	4	1974	I 2	Winners
1927	I 9	5	1975	I 2	4
1928	I 16	4	1976	I 1C	4
1929	I 5	4	1977	I 1C	Final
1930	I 12	3	1978	I 2	3
1931	I 9	3	1979	I 1C	s-f
1932	I 10	q-f	1980	I 1C	s-f
1933	I 14	3	1981	I 5	4
1934	I 18	5	1982	I 1C	s-f
1935	I 7	4	1983	I 1C	5
1936	I 19	4	1984	I 1C	4
1937	I 18	3	1985	I 2	s-f
1938	I 11	5	1986	I 1C	Winners
1939	I 11	5	1987	I 2	3

LUTON TOWN

Founded: 1885
Address: 70 Kenilworth Road, Luton
Telephone: Luton 411622
Ground capacity: 16,500
Playing area: 112 by 72 yards
Record attendance: 30,069 v Blackpool, FA Cup 6th round replay, 4.3.59
Record victory: 12–0 v Bristol Rovers, Division III(S), 13.4.36
Record defeat: 0–9 v Small Heath, Division II, 12.11. 1898
Most League points (3 for win): 88, Division II, 1981–82
Most League points (2 for win): 66, Division IV, 1967–68
Most League goals: 103, Division III(S), 1936–37
League scoring record: 55, Joe Payne, Division III(S), 1936–37
Record League aggregate: 243, Gordon Turner, 1949–1964
Most League appearances: 494, Bob Morton, 1949–1964
Most capped player: 45, Mal Donaghy, N. Ireland

FA Cup	Year	Opponents	Score	Scorers
Runners-up	1959	Nottingham Forest	1–2	Pacey

* after extra time

THE LUTON TOWN RECORD

	Division and place	Cup round reached		Division and place	Cup round reached
1898	II 8	1	1956	I 10	3
1899	II 15	p	1957	I 16	3
1900	II 17L	p	1958	I 8	3
1921	SIII 9	3	1959	I 17	Final
1922	SIII 4	2	1960	I 22R	5
1923	SIII 5	1	1961	II 13	5
1924	SIII 7	1	1962	II 13	3
1925	SIII 16	1	1963	II 22R	3
1926	SIII 7	2	1964	III 18	3
1927	SIII 8	3	1965	III 21R	3
1928	SIII 13	3	1966	IV 6	2
1929	SIII 7	3	1967	IV 17	2
1930	SIII 13	1	1968	IV 1P	2
1931	SIII 7	2	1969	III 3	3
1932	SIII 6	3	1970	III 2P	2
1933	SIII 14	q-f	1971	II 6	3
1934	SIII 6	3	1972	II 13	3
1935	SIII 4	4	1973	II 12	q-f
1936	SIII 2	4	1974	II 2P	5
1937	SIII 1P	4	1975	I 20R	3
1938	II 12	5	1976	II 7	4
1939	II 7	3	1977	II 6	4
1946		3	1978	II 13	4
1947	II 13	5	1979	II 18	3
1948	II 13	5	1980	II 6	3
1949	II 10	5	1981	II 5	4
1950	II 17	3	1982	II 1P	4
1951	II 19	4	1983	I 18	4
1952	II 8	q-f	1984	I 16	3
1953	II 3	5	1985	I 13	s-f
1954	II 6	3	1986	I 9	6
1955	II 2P	5	1987	I 7	4

MANCHESTER CITY

Founded: 1887
Address: Maine Road, Moss Side, Manchester M14 7WN
Telephone: (061) 226 1191/2
Ground capacity: 52,500
Playing area: 117 by 79 yards
Record attendance: 84,569 v Stoke City, FA Cup quarter-final, 3.3.34
Record victory: 11–3 v Lincoln City, Division II, 23.3.95
Record defeat: 1–9 v Everton, Division I, 3.9.06
Most League points (3 for win): 74, Division II, 1984–85
Most League points (2 for win): 62, Division II, 1946–47
Most League goals: 108, Division II, 1926–27
League scoring record: 38, Tom Johnson, Division I, 1928–29
Record League aggregate: 158, Tom Johnson, 1919–1930
Most League appearances: 565, Alan Oakes
Most capped player: 48, Colin Bell, England

FA Cup	Year	Opponents	Score	Scorers
Winners	1904	Bolton Wanderers	1–0	Meredith
	1934	Portsmouth 2–1	2–1	Tilson, 2
	1956	Birmingham City	3–1	Hayes, Dyson, Johnstone
	1969	Leicester City	1–0	Young
Runners-up	1926	Bolton Wanderers	0–1	
	1933	Everton	0–3	
	1955	Newcastle United	1–3	Johnstone
	1981	Tottenham	*1–1	Hutchison
	Replay		2–3	Mackenzie, Reeves pen.
League Cup				
Winners	1970	West Bromwich Albion	2–1	Doyle, Pardoe
	1976	Newcastle United	2–1	Barnes, Tueart
Runners-up	1974	Wolverhampton Wanderers	1–2	Bell

* after extra time

THE MANCHESTER CITY RECORD

	Division and place	Cup round reached		Division and place	Cup round reached
1893 †	II 5		1948	I 10	5
1894 †	II 13		1949	I 7	3
1895	II 9		1950	I 21R	3
1896	II 2		1951	II 2P	3
1897	II 6	1	1952	I 15	3
1898	II 3	2	1953	I 20	4
1899	II 1P	2	1954	I 17	4
1900	I 7	1	1955	I 7	Final
1901	I 11	1	1956	I 4	Winners
1902	I 18R	2	1957	I 18	3
1903	II 1P	1	1958	I 5	3
1904	I 2	Winners	1959	I 20	3
1905	I 3	2	1960	I 16	3
1906	I 5	1	1961	I 13	4
1907	I 17	1	1962	I 12	4
1908	I 3	3	1963	I 21R	5
1909	I 19R	1	1964	II 6	3
1910	II 1P	q-f	1965	II 11	3
1911	I 17	2	1966	II 1P	q-f
1912	I 15	2	1967	I 15	q-f
1913	I 6	2	1968	I 1C	4
1914	I 13	q-f	1969	I 13	Winners
1915	I 5	3	1970	I 9	4
1920	I 7	2	1971	I 11	5
1921	I 2	1	1972	I 4	3
1922	I 10	3	1973	I 11	5
1923	I 8	1	1974	I 14	4
1924	I 11	s-f	1975	I 8	3
1925	I 10	1	1976	I 8	4
1926	I 21R	Final	1977	I 2	5
1927	II 3	3	1978	I 4	4
1928	II 1P	5	1979	I 15	4
1929	I 8	3	1980	I 17	3
1930	I 3	5	1981	I 12	Final
1931	I 8	3	1982	I 10	4
1932	I 14	s-f	1983	I 20R	4
1933	I 16	Final	1984	II 4	3
1934	I 5	Winners	1985	II 3P	3
1935	I 4	3	1986	I 15	4
1936	I 9	5	1987	I 21R	3
1937	I 1C	q-f			
1938	I 21R	q-f			
1939	II 5	4			
1946		4			
1947	II 1P	5	† – as Ardwick		

MANCHESTER UNITED

Founded: 1878
Address: Old Trafford, Manchester M16 0RA
Telephone: (061) 872 1661/2
Ground capacity: 58,500
Playing area: 116 by 76 yards
Record attendance: * 70,504 v Aston Villa, Division I, 27.12.20
Record victory: 10–0 v Anderlecht, European Cup 1956–57
Record defeat: 0–7 v Aston Villa, Division I, 27.12.30; 0–7 v Blackburn Rovers, Division I, 10.4.26; 0–7 v Wolverhampton Wanderers, Division II, 26.12.31
Most League points (3 for win): 78, Division I, 1981–82
Most League points (2 for win): 64, Division I, 1955–57
Most League goals: 103, Division I, 1956–57 & Division I, 1958–59
League scoring record: 32, Dennis Viollet, Division I, 1959–60
Record League aggregate: 198, Bobby Charlton, 1956–73
Most League appearances: 606, Bobby Charlton, 1956–73
Most capped player: 106, Bobby Charlton, England

FA Cup	Year	Opponents	Score	Scorers
Winners	1909	Bristol City	1–0	Turnbull (A)
	1948	Blackpool	4–2	Rowley 2, Pearson, Anderson
	1963	Leicester City	3–1	Herd 2, Law
	1977	Liverpool	2–1	Pearson, Greenhoff, J.
	1983	Brighton	2–2	Stapleton, Wilkins
	Replay		4–0	Robson 2, Whiteside, Muhren
	1985	Everton	1–0	Whiteside
League Cup				
Runners-up	1957	Aston Villa	1–2	Taylor
	1958	Bolton Wanderers	0–2	
	1976	Southampton	0–1	
	1979	Arsenal	2–3	McQueen, McIlroy
	1983	Liverpool	1–2	Whiteside

* Ground record: 76,962 for Wolverhampton Wanderers v Grimsby Town, FA Cup semi-final, 25.3.39

THE MANCHESTER UNITED RECORD

	Division and place	Cup round reached		Division and place	Cup round reached
1890 †		1	1946		4
1891 †			1947	I 2	4
1892 †			1948	I 2	Winners
1893 †	I 16	1	1949	I 2	s-f
1894 †	I 16R	2	1950	I 4	q-f
1895 †	II 3	1	1951	I 2	q-f
1896 †	II 6	2	1952	I 1C	3
1897 †	II 2	q-f	1953	I 8	5
1898 †	II 4	2	1954	I 4	3
1899 †	II 4	1	1955	I 5	4
1900 †	II 4		1956	I 1C	3
1901 †	II 10	1	1957	I 1C	Final
1902 †	II 15		1958	I 9	Final
1903	II 5	2	1959	I 2	3
1904	II 3	2	1960	I 7	5
1905	II 3		1961	I 7	4
1906	II 2P	q-f	1962	I 15	s-f
1907	I 8	1	1963	I 19	Winners
1908	I 1C	q-f	1964	I 2	s-f
1909	I 13	Winners	1965	I 1C	s-f
1910	I 5	1	1966	I 4	s-f
1911	I 1C	3	1967	I 1C	4
1912	I 13	q-f	1968	I 2	3
1913	I 4	3	1969	I 11	q-f
1914	I 14	1	1970	I 8	s-f
1915	I 18	1	1971	I 8	3
1920	I 12	2	1972	I 8	4
1921	I 13	1	1973	I 18	3
1922	I 22R	1	1974	I 21R	4
1923	II 4	2	1975	II 1P	3
1924	II 14	2	1976	I 3	Final
1925	II 2P	1	1977	I 6	Winners
1926	I 9	s-f	1978	I 10	4
1927	I 15	3	1979	I 9	Final
1928	I 19	q-f	1980	I 2	3
1929	I 12	4	1981	I 8	4
1930	I 17	3	1982	I 3	3
1931	I 22R	4	1983	I 3	Winners
1932	II 12	3	1984	I 4	3
1933	II 6	3	1985	I 4	Winners
1934	II 20	3	1986	I 4	5
1935	II 5	4	1987	I 11	4
1936	II 1P	4			
1937	I 21R	4			
1938	II 2P	5			
1939	I 14	3	† – as Newton Heath		

MANSFIELD TOWN

Founded: 1891 (as Mansfield Wesleyans)
Address: Field Mill Ground, Quarry Lane, Mansfield, Notts
Telephone: Mansfield 23567
Ground capacity: 23,500
Playing area: 115 by 72 yards
Record attendance: 24,467 v Nottingham Forest, FA Cup 3rd round, 10.1.53
Record victory: 9–2 v Rotherham United, Division III(N), 27.12.32; 9–2 v Hounslow Town, FA Cup 1st round replay, 5.11.62
Record defeat: 1–8 v Walsall, Division III(N), 19.1.33
Most League points (3 for win): 81, Division IV, 1985–86
Most League points (2 for win): 68, Division IV, 1974–75
Most League goals: 108, Division IV, 1962–63
League scoring record: 55, Ted Harston, Division III(N), 1936–37
Record League aggregate: 104, Harry Johnson, 1931–1936
Most League appearances: 417, Don Bradley, 1949–1962
Most capped player: 6 (38 in all), John McClelland, Northern Ireland

THE MANSFIELD RECORD

	Division and place		Cup round reached			Division and place		Cup round reached
1932	SIII	20	1		1963	IV	4P	3
1933	NIII	16	1		1964	III	7	3
1934	NIII	17	1		1965	III	3	2
1935	NIII	8	3		1966	III	19	1
1936	NIII	19	1		1967	III	9	4
1937	NIII	9	2		1968	III	20	1
1938	SIII	14	3		1969	III	15	q-f
1939	SIII	16	2		1970	III	6	5
1946			3		1971	III	7	2
1947	SIII	22	1		1972	III	21R	2
1948	NIII	8	3		1973	IV	6	1
1949	NIII	10	3		1974	IV	17	2
1950	NIII	8	2		1975	IV	1P	5
1951	NIII	2	5		1976	III	11	2
1952	NIII	6	1		1977	III	1P	1
1953	NIII	18	3		1978	II	21R	3
1954	NIII	7	1		1979	III	18	1
1955	NIII	13	1		1980	III	23R	3
1956	NIII	18	2		1981	IV	7	3
1957	NIII	16	1		1982	IV	20	1
1958	NIII	6	3		1983	IV	10	2
1959	NIII	20	1		1984	IV	19	2
1960	III	22R	3		1985	IV	14	2
1961	IV	20	2		1986	IV	3P	1
1962	IV	14	2		1987	III	10	1

MIDDLESBROUGH

Founded: 1876
Address: Ayresome Park, Middlesbrough
Telephone: Middlesbrough 819659/815996
Ground capacity: 42,000 (10,200 seated)
Playing area: 115 by 75 yards
Record attendance: 53,596 v Newcastle United, Division I, 27.12.49
Record victory: 9–0 v Brighton, Division II, 23.8.58
Record defeat: 0–9 v Blackburn Rovers, Division II, 6.11.54
Most League points (3 for win): 49, Division II, 1983–84
Most League points (2 for win): 65, Division II, 1973–74
Most League goals: 122, Division II, 1926–27
League scoring record: 59, George Camsell, Division II, 1926–27
Record League aggregate: 326, George Camsell, 1925–1939
Most League appearances: 563, Tim Williamson, 1902–1923
Most capped player: 26, Wilf Mannion, England

FA Cup	Amateur	Year	Opponents	Score	Scorers
Winners		1895	Old Carthusians	2–1	Mullen, Nelmes
		1898	Uxbridge	2–1	Bishop, Kempley

THE MIDDLESBROUGH RECORD

	Division and place		Cup round reached			Division and place		Cup round reached
1888			q-f		1936	I	14	q-f
1889			q		1937	I	7	3
1890			q		1938	I	5	5
1891			q		1939	I	4	4
1892			2		1946			5
1893			2		1947	I	11	q-f
1894			1		1948	I	16	5
1895			2		1949	I	19	3
1896			2q		1950	I	9	4
1897			1q		1951	I	6	3
1898			5q		1952	I	18	4
1899			2q		1953	I	13	3
1900	II	14	p		1954	I	21R	3
1901	II	6	q-f		1955	II	12	3
1902	II	2P	1		1956	II	14	4
1903	I	13	p		1957	II	6	4
1904	I	10	q-f		1958	II	7	4
1905	I	15	1		1959	III	13	3
1906	I	18	3		1960	II	5	3
1907	I	11	2		1961	II	5	3
1908	I	6	1		1962	II	12	5
1909	I	9	1		1963	II	4	4
1910	I	17	1		1964	II	10	3
1911	I	16	3		1965	II	17	5
1912	I	7	2		1966	II	21R	3
1913	I	16	3		1967	III	2P	3
1914	I	4	1		1968	II	6	4
1915	I	12	2		1969	II	4	3
1920	I	13	2		1970	II	4	q-f
1921	I	8	1		1971	II	7	4
1922	I	8	1		1972	II	9	5
1923	I	18	2		1973	II	4	3
1924	I	22R	1		1974	II	1P	4
1925	II	13	1		1975	I	7	q-f
1926	II	10	4		1976	I	13	3
1927	II	1P	5		1977	I	12	q-f
1928	I	22R	5		1978	I	14	q-f
1929	II	1P	4		1979	I	12	3
1930	I	16	5		1980	I	9	4
1931	I	7	3		1981	I	14	q-f
1932	I	18	3		1982	I	22R	3
1933	I	17	5		1983	II	16	5
1934	I	16	3		1984	II	17	5
1935	I	20	3		1985	II	19	3
					1986	II	21R	3
					1987	III	2P	3

Founded: 1885
Address: The Den, Cold Blow Lane, New Cross, London SE14 5RH
Telephone: (01) 639 3143
Ground capacity: 16,000
Playing area: 112 by 74 yards
Record attendance: 48,672 v Derby County, FA Cup 5th round, 20.2.37
Record victory: 9–1 v Torquay United, Division III(S). 29.8.27; 9–1 v Coventry City, Division III(S), 19.11.27
Record defeat: 1–9 v Aston Villa, FA Cup 4th round, 28.1.46
Most League points (3 for win): 90, Division III, 1984–85
Most League points (2 for win): 65, Division III(S), 1927–28; Division III, 1965–66
Most League goals: 127, Division III(S), 1927–28
League scoring record: 37, Dick Parker, Division III(S), 1926–27
Record League aggregate: 79, Derek Possee, 1967–1973
Most League appearances: 523, Barry Kitchener, 1967–1982
Most capped player: 22 (23 in all), Eamonn Dunphy, Eire

THE MILLWALL RECORD

	Division and place	Cup round reached		Division and place	Cup round reached
1895		1	1946		4
1896		1	1947	II 18	3
1897		1	1948	II 22R	3
1898		q	1949	SIII 8	2
1899		q	1950	SIII 22	1
1900		s-f	1951	SIII 5	4
1901		1	1952	SIII 4	2
1902		p	1953	SIII 2	3
1903		s-f	1954	SIII 12	2
1904		1	1955	SIII 5	3
1905		1	1956	SIII 22	1
1906		2	1957	SIII 17	5
1907		2	1958	SIII 23	2
1908		1	1959	IV 9	2
1909		3	1960	IV 5	1
1910		1	1961	IV 6	1
1911		1	1962	IV 1P	1
1912		1	1963	III 16	2
1913		1	1964	III 21R	1
1914		3	1965	IV 2P	4
1915		2	1966	III 2P	2
1920		1	1967	II 8	3
1921	III 7	1	1968	II 7	3
1922	SIII 12	q-f	1969	II 10	4
1923	SIII 6	2	1970	II 10	3
1924	SIII 3	1	1971	II 8	3
1925	SIII 5	1	1972	II 3	4
1926	SIII 3	5	1973	II 11	5
1927	SIII 3	q-f	1974	II 12	3
1928	SIII 1P	3	1975	II 20R	3
1929	II 14	4	1976	III 3P	2
1930	II 14	5	1977	II 10	3
1931	II 14	3	1978	II 16	q-f
1932	II 9	3	1979	II 21R	3
1933	II 7	4	1980	III 14	4
1934	II 21R	4	1981	III 16	2
1935	SIII 12	4	1982	III 9	3
1936	SIII 12	3	1983	III 17	1
1937	SIII 8	s-f	1984	III 9	2
1938	SIII 1P	3	1985	III 2P	6
1939	II 13	4	1986	II 9	5
			1987	II 16	3

Founded: 1882
Address: St James' Park, Newcastle-on-Tyne NE1 4ST
Telephone: (0632) 328361
Ground capacity: 38,000
Playing area: 115 by 75 yards
Record attendance: 68,386 v Chelsea, Division I, 3.9.30
Record victory: 13–0 v Newport County, Division II, 5.10.46
Record defeat: 0–9 v Burton Wanderers, Division II, 15.4.95
Most League points (3 for win): 80, Division II, 1983–84
Most League points (2 for win): 57, Division II, 1964–65
Most League goals: 98, Division I, 1951–52
League scoring record: 36, Hughie Gallacher, Division I, 1926–27
Record League aggregate: 178, Jackie Milburn, 1946–1957
Most League appearances: 432, Jim Lawrence, 1904–1922
Most capped player: 40, Alf McMichael, Northern Ireland

FA Cup	Year	Opponents	Score	Scorers
Winners	1910	Barnsley	*1–1	Rutherford
		Replay	2–0	Shepherd 2 (1pen)
	1924	Aston Villa	2–0	Harris, Seymour
	1932	Arsenal	2–1	Allen 2
	1951	Blackpool	2–0	Milburn 2
	1952	Arsenal	1–0	Robledo (G)
	1955	Manchester City	3–1	Milburn, Mitchell, Hannah
Runners-up	1905	Aston Villa	0–2	
	1906	Everton	0–1	
	1908	Wolverhampton Wanderers	1–3	Howie
	1911	Bradford City	*0–0	
		Replay	0–1	
	1974	Liverpool	0–3	
League Cup				
Runners-up	1976	Manchester City	1–2	Gowling

* after extra time

THE NEWCASTLE RECORD

	Division and place	Cup round reached		Division and place	Cup round reached
1893		1	1939	II 9	5
1894	II 4	2	1946		3
1895	II 10	2	1947	II 5	s-f
1896	II 5	2	1948	II 2P	3
1897	II 5	1	1949	I 4	3
1898	II 2P	2	1950	I 5	4
1899	I 13	2	1951	I 4	Winners
1900	I 5	2	1952	I 8	Winners
1901	I 6	1	1953	I 16	4
1902	I 3	q-f	1954	I 15	5
1903	I 14	1	1955	I 8	Winners
1904	I 4	1	1956	I 11	q-f
1905	I 1C	Final	1957	I 17	4
1906	I 4	Final	1958	I 19	4
1907	I 1C	1	1959	I 11	3
1908	I 4	Final	1960	I 8	3
1909	I 1C	s-f	1961	I 21R	q-f
1910	I 4	Winners	1962	II 11	3
1911	I 8	Final	1963	II 7	4
1912	I 3	1	1964	II 8	3
1913	I 14	q-f	1965	II 1P	3
1914	I 11	1	1966	I 15	4
1915	I 15	q-f	1967	I 20	4
1920	I 8	2	1968	I 10	3
1921	I 5	3	1969	I 9	4
1922	I 7	2	1970	I 7	3
1923	I 4	1	1971	I 12	3
1924	I 9	Winners	1972	I 11	3
1925	I 6	2	1973	I 9	4
1926	I 10	5	1974	I 15	Final
1927	I 1C	5	1975	I 15	4
1928	I 9	3	1976	I 15	q-f
1929	I 10	3	1977	I 5	4
1930	I 19	q-f	1978	I 21R	4
1931	I 17	4	1979	II 8	4
1932	I 11	Winners	1980	II 9	3
1933	I 5	3	1981	II 11	5
1934	I 21R	3	1982	II 9	4
1935	II 6	4	1983	II 5	3
1936	II 8	5	1984	II 3P	3
1937	II 4	3	1985	I 14	3
1938	II 19	3	1986	I 11	3
			1987	I 17	5

NEWPORT COUNTY

Founded: 1912
Address: Somerton Park, Newport, Monmouthshire
Telephone: Newport 277543
Ground capacity: 8,000
Playing area: 110 by 75 yards
Record attendance: 24,268 v Cardiff City, Division III(S), 16.10.37
Record victory: 10–0 v Merthyr Town, Division III(S), 10.4.30
Record defeat: 0–13 v Newcastle United, Division II, 5.10.46
Most League points (3 for win): 78, Division III, 1982–83
Most League points (2 for win): 61, Division IV, 1979–80
Most League goals: 85, Division IV, 1964–65
League scoring record: 34, Tudor Martin, Division III(S), 1929–30
Record League aggregate: 99, Reg Parker, 1948–1954
Most League appearances: 530, Ray Wilcox, 1946–1960
Most capped player: 3 (10 in all), Nigel Vaughan, Wales

THE NEWPORT RECORD

	Division and place		Cup round reached
1920			1
1921	III	15	q
1922	SIII	20	1
1923	SIII	22	p
1924	SIII	10	q
1925	SIII	6	p
1926	SIII	17	2
1927	SIII	9	1
1928	SIII	9	1
1929	SIII	16	2
1930	SIII	18	2
1931	SIII	22	2
1932*			
1933	SIII	21	2
1934	SIII	18	2
1935	SIII	22	1
1936	SIII	21	1
1937	SIII	19	2
1938	SIII	16	3
1939	SIII	1P	3
1946			3
1947	II	22R	3
1948	SIII	12	2
1949	SIII	15	5
1950	SIII	21	3
1951	SIII	11	4
1952	SIII	6	3
1953	SIII	15	3
1954	SIII	15	1
1955	SIII	19	1
1956	SIII	19	1
1957	SIII	12	4
1958	SIII	11	1
1959	III	17	4
1960	III	13	3
1961	III	13	1
1962	III	24R	2
1963	IV	20	1
1964	IV	15	4
1965	IV	16	3
1966	IV	9	1
1967	IV	18	1
1968	IV	12	3
1969	IV	22	1
1970	IV	21	3
1971	IV	22	1
1972	IV	14	1
1973	IV	5	2
1974	IV	9	1
1975	IV	12	2
1976	IV	22	1
1977	IV	19	2
1978	IV	16	1
1979	IV	8	4
1980	IV	3P	1
1981	III	12	1
1982	III	16	1
1983	III	4	3
1984	III	13	3
1985	III	18	1
1986	III	19	3
1987	III	24R	2

* Newport were not re-elected in 1931, and took Thames' place in 1932. Did not enter Cup 1931–32.

NORTHAMPTON TOWN

Founded: 1897
Address: County Ground, Abingdon Avenue, Northampton NN1 4PS
Telephone: Northampton 31553
Ground capacity: 11,150
Playing area: 120 by 75 yards
Record attendance: 24,523 v Fulham, Division I, 23.4.66
Record victory: 11–1 v Southend United, Southern League, 30.13.09; 10–0 v Walsall, Division III(S), 5.11.27
Record defeat: 0–11 v Southampton, Southern League, 28.12.01
Most League points (3 for win): 64, Division IV, 1985–86
Most League points (2 for win): 68, Division IV, 1975–76
Most League goals: 109, Division III(S), 1952–53 & Division III, 1962–63
League scoring record: 36, Cliff Holton, Division III, 1961–62
Record League aggregate: 135, Jack English, 1947–1960
Most League appearances: 521, Tommy Fowler, 1946–61
Most capped player: 12 (16 in all), E Lloyd Davies, Wales

THE NORTHAMPTON RECORD

	Division and place		Cup round reached
1906			1
1907			1
1908			1
1909			1
1910			2
1911			2
1912			3
1913			1
1914			p
1915			2
1920			p
1921	III	14	1
1922	SIII	17	2
1923	SIII	8	p
1924	SIII	8	1
1925	SIII	9	1
1926	SIII	12	3
1927	SIII	18	2
1928	SIII	2	3
1929	SIII	3	3
1930	SIII	4	3
1931	SIII	6	1
1932	SIII	14	4
1933	SIII	8	2
1934	SIII	13	5
1935	SIII	7	3
1936	SIII	15	1
1937	SIII	7	1
1938	SIII	9	1
1939	SIII	17	1
1946			3
1947	SIII	13	3
1948	SIII	14	2
1949	SIII	20	2
1950	SIII	2	5
1951	SIII	21	4
1952	SIII	8	1
1953	SIII	3	2
1954	SIII	5	2
1955	SIII	13	1
1956	SIII	11	3
1957	SIII	14	1
1958	SIII	13	4
1959	IV	8	2
1960	IV	6	1
1961	IV	3P	3
1962	III	8	3
1963	III	1P	1
1964	II	11	3
1965	II	2P	3
1966	I	21R	3
1967	II	21R	3
1968	III	17	1
1969	III	21R	3
1970	IV	14	5
1971	IV	7	1
1972	IV	21	2
1973	IV	23	1
1974	IV	5	2
1975	IV	16	2
1976	IV	2P	1
1977	III	22R	1
1978	IV	10	2
1979	IV	19	1
1980	IV	13	1
1981	IV	10	1
1982	IV	22	2
1983	IV	15	3
1984	IV	18	2
1985	IV	23	2
1986	IV	8	1
1987	IV	1P	3

Founded: 1905
Address: Carrow Road, Norwich NOR 22
Telephone: 0603 612131
Ground capacity: 25,500
Playing area: 114 by 74 yards
Record attendance: 43,984 v Leicester City, FA Cup quarter-final, 30.3.63
Record victory: 10–2 v Coventry City, Division III(S), 15.3.30
Record defeat: 2–10 v Swindon Town, Southern League, 5.9.08
Most League points (3 for win): 84, Division II, 1985–86
Most League points (2 for win): 64, Division III(S), 1950–51
Most League goals: 99, Division III(S), 1952–53
League scoring record: 31, Ralph Hunt, Division III(S), 1955–56
Record League aggregate: 122, Johnny Gavin, 1945–1954 & 1955–1958
Most League appearances: 590, Ron Ashman, 1947–1964
Most capped player: 18 (64 in all) Martin O'Neill, Northern Ireland

League Cup	Year	Opponents	Score	Scorers
Winners	1962	Rochdale	A3–0	Lythgoe 2, Punton
			H1–0	Hill
	1985	Sunderland	1–0	Chisholm o.g.
Runners-up	1973	Tottenham Hotspur	0–1	
	1975	Aston Villa	0–1	

THE NORWICH RECORD

	Division and place	Cup round reached		Division and place	Cup round reached
1906		2	1952	SIII 3	3
1907		2	1953	SIII 4	2
1908		2	1954	SIII 7	5
1909		3	1955	SIII 11	2
1910		1	1956	SIII 7	3
1911		2	1957	SIII 24	1
1912		1	1958	SIII 8	3
1913		2	1959	III 4	s-f
1914		1	1960	III 2P	1
1915		3	1961	II 4	5
1920		q-f	1962	II 17	5
1921	III 16	1	1963	II 11	q-f
1922	SIII 15	1	1964	II 17	3
1923	SIII 18	1	1965	II 6	3
1924	SIII 11	1	1966	II 13	5
1925	SIII 12	2	1967	II 11	5
1926	SIII 16	1	1968	II 9	4
1927	SIII 16	3	1969	II 13	3
1928	SIII 17	2	1970	II 11	3
1929	SIII 17	3	1971	II 10	3
1930	SIII 8	1	1972	II 1P	3
1931	SIII 21	2	1973	I 20	3
1932	SIII 10	2	1974	I 22R	3
1933	SIII 3	1	1975	II 3P	3
1934	SIII 1P	1	1976	I 10	5
1935	II 14	5	1977	I 16	3
1936	II 11	3	1978	I 13	3
1937	II 17	4	1979	I 16	3
1938	II 14	3	1980	I 12	3
1939	II 21R	3	1981	I 20R	4
1946		3	1982	II 3P	5
1947	SIII 21	2	1983	I 14	6
1948	SIII 21	2	1984	I 14	5
1949	SIII 9	2	1985	I 20R	4
1950	SIII 11	3	1986	II 1P	3
1951	SIII 2	5	1987	I 5	4

Founded: 1865
Address: City Ground, Nottingham NG2 5FJ
Telephone: Nottingham 868236
Ground capacity: 35,000 (14,200 seated)
Playing area: 115 by 78 yards
Record attendance: 49,946 v Manchester United, Division I, 28.10.67
Record victory: 14–0 v Clapton, FA Cup 1st round, 17.1.1891
Record defeat: 1–9 v Blackburn Rovers, Division II, 10.4.37
Most League points (3 for win): 74, Division I, 1983–84
Most League points (2 for win): 70, Division III(S), 1950–51
Most League goals: 110, Division III(S), 1950–51
League scoring record: 36, Wally Ardron, Division III(S), 1950–51
Record League aggregate: 199, Grenville Morris, 1898–1913
Most League appearances: 614, Bob McKinlay, 1951–1970
Most capped player: 36 (64 in all), Martin O'Neill, Northern Ireland

FA Cup	Year	Opponents	Score	Scorers
Winners	1898	Derby County	3–1	Capes 2, McPherson
	1959	Luton Town	2–1	Dwight, Wilson
League Cup				
Winners	1978	Liverpool	0–0	
	Replay		1–0	Robertson (pen)
	1979	Southampton	3–2	Birtles 2, Woodcock
Runners-up	1980	Wolverampton Wanderers	0–1	

THE FOREST RECORD

	Division and place	Cup round reached		Division and place	Cup round reached
1879		s-f	1934	II 17	4
1880		s-f	1935	II 9	5
1881		2	1936	II 19	4
1882		1	1937	II 19	3
1883		3	1938	II 20	4
1884		2	1939	II 20	3
1885		s-f	1946		3
1886		3	1947	II 11	5
1887		3	1948	II 19	3
1888		5	1949	II 21R	3
1889		2	1950	SIII 4	2
1890		1	1951	SIII 1P	2
1891		q-f	1952	II 4	3
1892		s-f	1953	II 7	4
1893	I 10	2	1954	II 4	3
1894	I 7	q-f	1955	II 15	5
1895	I 7	q-f	1956	II 7	3
1896	I 13	1	1957	II 2P	q-f
1897	I 11	q-f	1958	I 10	4
1898	I 8	Winners	1959	I 13	Winners
1899	I 11	q-f	1960	I 20	4
1900	I 8	s-f	1961	I 14	3
1901	I 4	2	1962	I 19	4
1902	I 5	s-f	1963	I 9	q-f
1903	I 10	2	1964	I 13	3
1904	I 9	2	1965	I 5	5
1905	I 16	2	1966	I 18	4
1906	I 19R	3	1967	I 2	s-f
1907	II 1P	1	1968	I 11	4
1908	I 9	1	1969	I 18	3
1909	I 14	q-f	1970	I 15	3
1910	I 14	3	1971	I 16	5
1911	I 20R	1	1972	I 21R	3
1912	II 15	1	1973	II 14	3
1913	II 17	2	1974	II 7	q-f
1914	II 20	1	1975	II 16	4
1915	II 18	1	1976	II 8	3
1920	II 18	1	1977	II 3P	4
1921	II 18	1	1978	I 1C	q-f
1922	II 1P	3	1979	I 2	5
1923	I 20	1	1980	I 5	4
1924	I 20	1	1981	I 7	q-f
1925	I 22R	2	1982	I 12	3
1926	II 17	q-f	1983	I 3	3
1927	II 5	4	1984	I 3	2
1931	II 17	3	1985	I 9	4
1932	II 11	3	1986	I 8	3
1933	II 5	3	1987	I 8	3

NOTTS COUNTY

Founded: 1862
Address: Meadow Lane, Nottingham NG2 3HS
Telephone: Nottingham 861155
Ground capacity: 24,045
Playing area: 117 by 76 yards
Record attendance: 47,301 v York City, FA Cup quarter-final, 12.3.55
Record victory: 15–0 v Rotherham United, 1st round FA Cup, 24.10.1885
Record defeat: 1–9 v Aston Villa, Division I, 16.11.1888; 1–9 v Blackburn Rovers, Division I, 16.11.1889; 1–9 v Portsmouth, Division II, 9.4.27
Most League points (3 for win): 71, Division III, 1985–86
Most League points (2 for win): 69, Division IV, 1970–71
Most League goals: 107, Division IV, 1959–60
League scoring record: 39, Tom Keetley, Division III(S), 1930–31
Record League aggregate: 125, Les Bradd, 1967–78
Most League appearances: 564, Albert Iremonger, 1904–1926
Most capped player: 8, Harry Cursham, England

FA Cup	Year	Opponents	Score	Scorers
Winners	1894	Bolton Wanderers	4–1	Watson, Logan 3
Runners-up	1891	Blackburn Rovers	1–3	Oswald

THE COUNTY RECORD

	Division and place	Cup round reached		Division and place	Cup round reached
1878		1	1932	II 16	3
1879		1	1933	II 15	3
1880		1	1934	II 18	3
1881		3	1935	II 22R	3
1882		3	1936	SIII 9	3
1883		s-f	1937	SIII 2	1
1884		s-f	1938	SIII 11	4
1885		q-f	1939	SIII 11	4
1886		5	1946		2
1887		q-f	1947	SIII 12	3
1888		q	1948	SIII 6	4
1889	I 11	2	1949	SIII 11	4
1890	I 10	3	1950	SIII 1P	4
1891	I 3	Final	1951	II 17	3
1892	I 8	q	1952	II 15	4
1893	I 14R	2	1953	II 19	4
1894	II 3	Winners	1954	II 14	3
1895	II 2	1	1955	II 7	q-f
1896	II 10	1	1956	II 20	3
1897	II 1P	2	1957	II 20	3
1898	I 13	1	1958	II 21R	4
1899	I 5	2	1959	III 23R	1
1900	I 15	2	1960	IV 2P	2
1901	I 3	2	1961	III 5	1
1902	I 13	1	1962	III 13	2
1903	I 15	3	1963	III 7	1
1904	I 13	1	1964	III 24R	2
1905	I 18	1	1965	IV 13	2
1906	I 16	1	1966	IV 8	1
1907	I 18	q-f	1967	IV 20	1
1908	I 18	2	1968	IV 17	1
1909	I 15	1	1969	IV 19	1
1910	I 19	1	1970	IV 7	1
1911	I 11	1	1971	IV 1P	3
1912	I 16	2	1972	III 4	4
1913	I 19R	1	1973	III 2P	3
1914	II 1P	1	1974	II 10	3
1915	I 16		1975	II 14	4
1920	I 21R	3	1976	II 5	3
1921	II 6	2	1977	II 8	3
1922	II 13	s-f	1978	II 15	5
1923	II 1P	1	1979	II 6	4
1924	I 10	2	1980	II 17	3
1925	I 9	3	1981	II 2P	4
1926	I 22R	5	1982	I 15	3
1927	II 16	3	1983	I 15	4
1928	II 15	3	1984	I 21R	6
1929	II 5	3	1985	II 20R	4
1930	II 22R	3	1986	III 8	4
1931	SIII 1P	4	1987	III 7	2

OLDHAM ATHLETIC

Founded: 1894*
Address: Boundary Park, Oldham
Telephone: 061 624 4972
Ground capacity: 26,324
Playing area: 110 by 74 yards
Record attendance: 47,671 v Sheffield Wednesday, FA Cup 4th round, 25.1.30
Record victory: 11–0 v Southport, Division IV, 26.12.62
Record defeat: 4–13 v Tranmere Rovers, Division III(N), 26.12.35
Most League points (3 for win): 61, Division II, 1982–83
Most League points (2 for win): 62, Division III, 1973–74
Most League goals: 95, Division IV, 1962–63
League scoring record: 33, Tommy Davis, Division III(N), 1936–37
Record League aggregate: 110, Eric Gemmell, 1947–54
Most League appearances: 525, Ian Wood, 1966–80
Most capped player: 9 (24 in all), Albert Gray, Wales
*as Pine Villa, name changed to Oldham Athletic in 1899

THE OLDHAM RECORD

	Division and place	Cup round reached		Division and place	Cup round reached
1907		2	1952	NIII 4	2
1908	II 3	2	1953	NIII 1P	3
1909	II 6	1	1954	II 22R	3
1910	II 2P	1	1955	NIII 10	2
1911	I 7	2	1956	NIII 20	1
1912	I 18	3	1957	NIII 19	2
1913	I 9	s-f	1958	NIII 15	2
1914	I 3	1	1959	IV 21	3
1915	I 2	q-f	1960	IV 23	2
1920	I 17	1	1961	IV 12	2
1921	I 19	1	1962	IV 11	4
1922	I 19	2	1963	IV 2P	1
1923	I 22r	1	1964	III 9	3
1924	II 7	2	1965	III 20	3
1925	II 18	1	1966	III 20	3
1926	II 7	3	1967	III 10	3
1927	II 10	3	1968	III 16	1
1928	II 7	4	1969	III 24R	1
1929	II 18	3	1970	IV 19	2
1930	II 3	4	1971	IV 3P	1
1931	II 12	3	1972	III 11	1
1932	II 18	3	1973	III 4	1
1933	II 16	3	1974	III 1P	4
1934	II 9	4	1975	II 18	3
1935	II 21R	3	1976	II 17	3
1936	NIII 7	2	1977	II 13	5
1937	NIII 4	3	1978	II 8	3
1938	NIII 4	1	1979	II 14	5
1939	NIII 5	1	1980	II 11	3
1946		2	1981	II 15	3
1947	NIII 19	2	1982	II 11	3
1948	NIII 11	2	1983	II 7	3
1949	NIII 6	3	1984	II 19	3
1950	NIII 11	3	1985	II 14	4
1951	NIII 15	3	1986	II 8	3
			1987	II 3	3

ORIENT

Founded: 1881
Address: Leyton Stadium, Brisbane Road, Leyton, London E10 5NE
Telephone: (01) 539 2223/4
Ground capacity: 26,500 (7,171 seated)
Playing area: 110 by 75 yards
Record attendance: 34,345 v West Ham United, FA Cup 4th round, 25.1.64
Record victory: 9–2 v Aldershot, Division III(S), 10.2.34; 9–2 v Chester, League Cup 3rd round, 15.10.62
Record defeat: 0–8 v Aston Villa, FA Cup 4th round, 30.1.29
Most League points (3 for win): 72, Division II, 1984–85
Most League points (2 for win): 66, Division III(S), 1955–56
Most League goals: 106, Division III(S), 1955–56
League scoring record: 35, Tommy Johnston, Division II, 1957–58
Record League aggregate: 121, Tommy Johnston, 1956–1962
Most League appearances: 430, Peter Allen, 1965–1978
Most capped player: 8 (30 in all), Tony Grealish, Eire

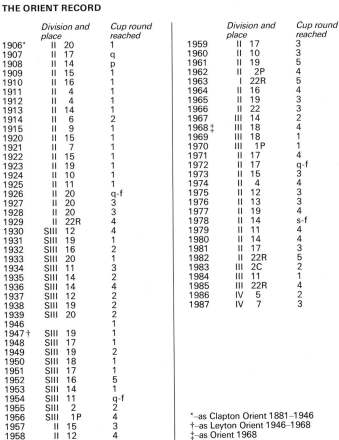

THE ORIENT RECORD

	Division and place	Cup round reached		Division and place	Cup round reached
1906*	II 20	1	1959	II 17	3
1907	II 17	q	1960	II 10	3
1908	II 14	p	1961	II 19	5
1909	II 15	1	1962	II 2P	4
1910	II 16	1	1963	I 22R	5
1911	II 4	1	1964	II 16	4
1912	II 4	1	1965	II 19	3
1913	II 14	1	1966	II 22	3
1914	II 6	2	1967	III 14	2
1915	II 9	1	1968 ‡	III 18	4
1920	II 15	1	1969	III 18	1
1921	II 7	1	1970	III 1P	1
1922	II 15	1	1971	II 17	4
1923	II 19	1	1972	II 17	q-f
1924	II 10	1	1973	II 15	3
1925	II 11	1	1974	II 4	4
1926	II 20	q-f	1975	II 12	3
1927	II 20	3	1976	II 13	3
1928	II 20	3	1977	II 19	4
1929	II 22R	4	1978	II 14	s-f
1930	SIII 12	4	1979	II 11	4
1931	SIII 19	1	1980	II 14	4
1932	SIII 16	2	1981	II 17	3
1933	SIII 20	1	1982	II 22R	5
1934	SIII 11	3	1983	III 2C	2
1935	SIII 14	2	1984	III 11	1
1936	SIII 14	4	1985	III 22R	4
1937	SIII 12	2	1986	IV 5	2
1938	SIII 19	2	1987	IV 7	3
1939	SIII 20	2			
1946		1			
1947 †	SIII 19	1			
1948	SIII 17	1			
1949	SIII 19	2			
1950	SIII 18	1			
1951	SIII 17	1			
1952	SIII 16	5			
1953	SIII 14	1			
1954	SIII 11	q-f			
1955	SIII 2	2			
1956	SIII 1P	4	*—as Clapton Orient 1881–1946		
1957	II 15	3	†—as Leyton Orient 1946–1968		
1958	II 12	4	‡—as Orient 1968		

Orient reverted to Leyton Orient in 1987

OXFORD UNITED

Founded: 1896*
Address: Manor Ground, Beech Road, Headington, Oxford
Telephone: Oxford 61503
Ground capacity: 14,232
Playing area: 112 by 78 yards
Record attendance: 22,730 v Preston North End, FA Cup quarter-final, 29.2.64
Record victory: 7–0 v Barrow, Division IV, 19.12.64
Record defeat: 0–5 (home) v Nottingham Forest, League Cup 3rd round, 4.10.78; 0–5 v Cardiff City, Division II, 8.2.69; 0–5 v Cardiff City, Division II, 12.9.73
Most League points (3 for win): 95, Division III, 1983–84
Most League points (2 for win): 61, Division IV, 1964–65
Most League goals: 91, Division III, 1983–84
League scoring record: 30, John Aldridge, Division II, 1984–85
Record League aggregate: 73, Graham Atkinson, 1962–1973
Most League appearances: 480, John Shuker, 1962–1977
Most capped player: 6 (17 in all) Dave Roberts, Wales; 6 (41 in all) Billy Hamilton N. Ireland
* as Headington United. Name changed to Oxford United 25.6.60

Milk Cup Winners	Year	Opponents		Score	Scorers
	1986	QPR		3–0	Hebberd, Charles, Houghton

THE OXFORD RECORD

	Division and place	Cup round reached		Division and place	Cup round reached
1961		3	1974	II 18	3
1962		1	1975	II 11	3
1963	IV 18	3	1976	II 20R	3
1964	IV 18	q-f	1977	III 17	1
1965	IV 4P	1	1978	III 18	1
1966	III 14	1	1979	III 11	1
1967	III 15	1	1980	III 17	1
1968	III 1P	1	1981	III 14	2
1969	II 20	3	1982	III 5	5
1970	II 15	3	1983	III 5	3
1971	II 14	5	1984	III 1P	5
1972	II 15	3	1985	II 1P	4
1973	II 8	4	1986	I 18	3
			1987	I 18	3

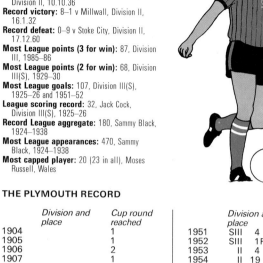

Founded: 1934
Address: London Road, Peterborough, PE2 8AL
Telephone: 0733 63947
Ground capacity: 28,000
Playing area: 112 by 76 yards
Record attendance: 30,096 v Swansea Town, FA Cup 5th round, 20.2.65
Record victory: 8–1 v Oldham Athletic, Division IV, 26.11.69
Record defeat: 1–8 v Northampton Town, 'Fa Cup 2nd round, replay, 18.12.46
Most League points (3 for win): 82, Division IV, 1981–82
Most League points (2 for win): 66, Division IV, 1960–61
Most League goals: 134, Division IV, 1960–61
League scoring record: 52, Terry Bly, Division IV, 1960–61
Record League aggregate: 122, Jim Hall, 1967–75
Most League appearances: 482, Tommy Robson, 1968–81
Most capped player: 8 (21 in all), Tony Millington, Wales

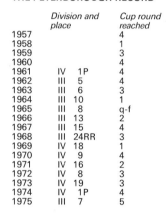

THE PETERBOROUGH RECORD

	Division and place		Cup round reached
1957			4
1958			1
1959			3
1960			4
1961	IV	1P	4
1962	III	5	4
1963	III	6	3
1964	III	10	1
1965	III	8	q-f
1966	III	13	2
1967	III	15	4
1968	III	24RR	3
1969	IV	18	1
1970	IV	9	4
1971	IV	16	2
1972	IV	8	3
1973	IV	19	3
1974	IV	1P	4
1975	III	7	5

	Division and place		Cup round reached
1976	III	10	4
1977	III	16	2
1978	III	4	3
1979	III	21R	2
1980	IV	8	1
1981	IV	5	5
1982	IV	5	3
1983	IV	9	3
1984	IV	7	1
1985	IV	11	2
1986	IV	17	5
1987	IV	10	1

RR   relegated (for illegal payments)
Actually finished ninth

Founded: 1886
Address: Home Park, Plymouth, Devon
Telephone: Plymouth 52561/2/3
Ground capacity: 38,000
Playing area: 112 by 75 yards
Record attendance: 43,596 v Aston Villa, Division II, 10.10.36
Record victory: 8–1 v Millwall, Division II, 16.1.32
Record defeat: 0–9 v Stoke City, Division II, 17.12.60
Most League points (3 for win): 87, Division III, 1985–86
Most League points (2 for win): 68, Division III(S), 1929–30
Most League goals: 107, Division III(S), 1925–26 and 1951–52
League scoring record: 32, Jack Cock, Division III(S), 1925–26
Record League aggregate: 180, Sammy Black, 1924–1938
Most League appearances: 470, Sammy Black, 1924–1938
Most capped player: 20 (23 in all), Moses Russell, Wales

THE PLYMOUTH RECORD

	Division and place		Cup round reached
1904			1
1905			1
1906			2
1907			1
1908			2
1909			3
1910			1
1911			1
1912			1
1913			2
1914			2
1915			1
1920			3
1921	III	11	3
1922	SIII	2	1
1923	SIII	2	3
1924	SIII	2	1
1925	SIII	2	1
1926	SIII	2	3
1927	SIII	2	3
1928	SIII	3	1
1929	SIII	4	4
1930	SIII	1P	3
1931	II	18	3
1932	II	4	4
1933	II	14	3
1934	II	10	3
1935	II	8	4
1936	II	7	4
1937	II	5	4
1938	II	13	3
1939	II	15	3
1946			3
1947	II	19	3
1948	II	17	3
1949	II	20	3
1950	II	21R	3

	Division and place		Cup round reached
1951	SIII	4	3
1952	SIII	1P	1
1953	II	4	5
1954	II	19	4
1955	II	20	3
1956	II	21R	3
1957	SIII	18	2
1958	SIII	3	3
1959	III	1P	3
1960	II	19	3
1961	II	11	3
1962	II	5	4
1963	II	12	3
1964	II	20	3
1965	II	15	4
1966	II	18	4
1967	II	16	3
1968	II	22R	3
1969	III	5	1
1970	III	17	2
1971	III	15	1
1972	III	8	1
1973	III	8	4
1974	III	17	3
1975	III	2P	4
1976	II	16	3
1977	II	21R	3
1978	III	19	3
1979	III	15	1
1980	III	15	1
1981	III	7	3
1982	III	10	1
1983	III	8	3
1984	III	19	2
1985	III	15	2
1986	III	2P	3
1987	II	7	4

PORTSMOUTH

Founded: 1898
Address: Fratton Park, Frogmore Road, Portsmouth
Telephone: Portsmouth 731204/5
Ground capacity: 36,000
Playing area: 116 by 73 yards
Record attendance: 51,385 v Derby County, FA Cup quarter-final, 26.2.49
Record victory: 9–1 v Notts County, Division II, 9.4.27
Record defeat: 0–10 v Leicester City, Division I, 20.10.28
Most League points (3 for win): 91, Division III, 1982–83
Most League points (2 for win): 65, Division III, 1961–62
Most League goals: 91, Division IV, 1979–80
League scoring record: 40, Billy Haines, Division II, 1926–27
Record League aggregate: 194, Peter Harris, 1946–1960
Most League appearances: 764, Jimmy Dickinson, 1946–1965
Most capped player: 48, Jimmy Dickinson, England

FA Cup	Year	Opponents	Score	Scorers
Winners	1939	Wolverhampton Wanderers	4–1	Parker 2, Barlow, Anderson
Runners-up	1929	Bolton Wanderers	0–2	
	1934	Manchester City	1–2	Rutherford

THE PORTSMOUTH RECORD

	Division and place	Cup round reached		Division and place	Cup round reached
1900		1	1949	I 1C	s-f
1901		q-f	1950	I 1C	5
1902		q-f	1951	I 7	3
1903		1	1952	I 4	q-f
1904		1	1953	I 15	3
1905		2	1954	I 14	5
1906		1	1955	I 3	3
1907		2	1956	I 12	4
1908		3	1957	I 19	4
1909		2	1958	I 20	4
1910		2	1959	I 22R	5
1911		1	1960	II 20	3
1912		2	1961	II 21R	3
1913		1	1962	III 1P	1
1914		1	1963	II 16	4
1915		1	1964	II 9	3
1920		1	1965	II 20	3
1921	SIII 12	1	1966	II 12	3
1922	SIII 3	1	1967	II 14	4
1923	SIII 6	1	1968	II 5	5
1924	SIII 1P	1	1969	II 15	4
1925	II 4	2	1970	II 17	3
1926	II 11	3	1971	II 16	4
1927	II 2P	4	1972	II 16	5
1928	I 20	3	1973	II 17	3
1929	I 20	Final	1974	II 15	5
1930	I 13	4	1975	II 17	3
1931	I 4	5	1976	II 22R	4
1932	I 8	5	1977	III 20	3
1933	I 9	3	1978	III 24R	2
1934	I 10	Final	1979	IV 7	2
1935	I 14	4	1980	IV 4P	3
1936	I 10	3	1981	III 6	1
1937	I 9	3	1982	III 13	1
1938	I 19	4	1983	III 1P	2
1939	I 17	Winners	1984	II 16	4
1946		3	1985	II 4	3
1947	I 12	4	1986	II 4	3
1948	I 8	4	1987	II 2P	4

PORT VALE

Founded: 1876
Address: Vale Park, Hamil Road, Burslem, Stoke-on-Trent
Telephone: Stoke-on-Trent 814134
Ground capacity: 16,500
Playing area: 116 by 76 yards
Record attendance: 50,000 v Aston Villa, FA Cup 5th round, 20.2.60
Record victory: 9–1 v Chesterfield, Division II, 24.8.32
Record defeat: 0–10 v Sheffield United, Division II, 10.12.1892 (home); 0–10 v Notts County, Division II, 26.2.1895
Most League points (3 for win): 88, Division IV, 1982–83
Most League points (2 for win): 69, Division III(N), 1953–54
Most League goals: 110, Division IV, 1958–59
League scoring record: 38, Wilf Kirkham, Division II, 1926–27
Record League aggregate: 154, Wilf Kirkham, 1923–29, 1931–33
Most League appearances: 761, Roy Sproson, 1950–1972
Most capped player: 7 (18 in all), Sammy Morgan, Northern Ireland

THE PORT VALE RECORD

	Division and place	Cup round reached		Division and place	Cup round reached
1893*	II 11	q	1955	II 17	4
1894*	II 7	q	1956	II 12	4
1895*	II 15	q	1957	II 22R	3
1896*	II 14L	p	1958	SIII 15	2
1897*		p	1959	IV 1P	1
1898*		2	1960	III 14	5
1899*	II 9	1	1961	III 7	3
1900*	II 11	1	1962	III 12	5
1901*	II 9	1	1963	III 3	4
1902*	II 13	1	1964	III 13	4
1903*	II 9	p	1965	III 22R	2
1904*	II 13	p	1966	IV 19	3
1905*	II 16	2	1967	IV 13	2
1906*	II 17	1	1968	‡II 18	1
1907*	†II 16	2	1969	IV 13	3
1908*		p	1970	IV 4P	2
1909*		p	1971	III 17	1
1910*		p	1972	III 15	3
1911*		p	1973	III 6	3
1912*		p	1974	III 20	3
1913*		p	1975	III 6	1
1914		1	1976	III 12	2
1915		q	1977	III 19	5
1920	§II 13	1	1978	III 21R	2
1921	II 17	p	1979	IV 16	1
1922	II 18	1	1980	IV 20	1
1923	II 17	p	1981	IV 19	3
1924	II 16	p	1982	IV 7	3
1925	II 8	1	1983	IV 3P	1
1926	II 8	3	1984	III 23R	1
1927	II 8	4	1985	IV 12	3
1928	II 9	5	1986	IV 4P	2
1929	II 21R	3	1987	III 12	2
1930	NIII 1P	2			
1931	II 5	4			
1932	II 20	4			
1933	II 17	3			
1934	II 8	3			
1935	II 18	3			
1936	II 21R	4			
1937	NIII 11	3			
1938	NIII 15	1			
1939	SIII 18	2			
1946		3			
1947	SIII 10	4			
1948	SIII 8	1			
1949	SIII 13	1			
1950	SIII 13	4			
1951	SIII 12	3			
1952	SIII 13	1			
1953	NIII 2	2			
1954	NIII 1P	s-f			

* – As Burslem Port Vale. Name changed in 1913
L – failed to obtain re-election
† – Burslem Port Vale resigned from the League
§ – Port Vale returned to the League, taking over the fixtures and records of Leeds City on 9 October 1919
‡ – Expelled from the League for financial irregularities and therefore technically finished 24th. Obtained re-election immediately

Founded: 1881
Address: Deepdale, Preston PR1 6RU
Telephone: Preston 795919
Ground capacity: 19,500
Playing area: 112 by 78 yards
Record attendance: 42,684 v Arsenal, Division I, 23.4.38
Record victory: 26–0 v Hyde, FA Cup 1st series 1st round, 15.10.1887
Record defeat: 0–7 v Blackpool, Division I, 1.5.48
Most League points (3 for win): 61, Division III, 1981–82
Most League points (2 for win): 61, Division III, 1970–71
Most League goals: 100, Division II, 1927–28 & Division I, 1957–58
League scoring record: 37, Ted Harper, Division II, 1932–33
Record League aggregate: 187, Tom Finney, 1946–1960
Most League appearances: 447, Allan Kelly, 1961–75
Most capped player: 76, Tom Finney, England

FA Cup	Year	Opponents	Score	Scorers
Winners	1889	Wolverhampton Wanderers	3–0	Dewhurst, Ross, Thompson
	1938	Huddersfield Town	*1–0	Mutch (pen)
Runners-up	1888	West Bromwich Albion	1–2	Goodall
	1922	Huddersfield Town	0–1	
	1937	Sunderland	1–3	O'Donnell (F)
	1954	West Bromwich Albion	2–3	Morrison, Wayman
	1964	West Ham United	2–3	Holden, Dawson

* after extra time

THE PRESTON RECORD

	Division and place		Cup round reached		Division and place		Cup round reached
1884			4	1938	I	3	Winners
1885			†	1939	I	9	q-f
1886			3	1946			5
1887			s-f	1947	I	7	q-f
1888			Final	1948	I	7	q-f
1889	I	1C	Winners	1949	I	21R	4
1890	I	1C	q-f	1950	II	6	3
1891	I	2	1	1951	II	1P	4
1892	I	2	q-f	1952	I	7	3
1893	I	2	s-f	1953	I	2	4
1894	I	14	2	1954	I	11	Final
1895	I	4	2	1955	I	14	4
1896	I	9	1	1956	I	19	3
1897	I	4	q-f	1957	I	3	5
1898	I	12	1	1958	I	2	3
1899	I	15	2	1959	I	12	5
1900	I	16	q-f	1960	I	9	q-f
1901	I	17R	1	1961	I	22R	4
1902	II	3	1	1962	II	10	q-f
1903	II	7	2	1963	II	17	3
1904	II	1P	2	1964	II	3	Final
1905	I	8	q-f	1965	II	12	4
1906	I	2	1	1966	II	17	q-f
1907	I	14	1	1967	II	13	3
1908	I	12	1	1968	II	20	4
1909	I	10	2	1969	II	14	4
1910	I	12	1	1970	II	22R	3
1911	I	14	2	1971	III	1P	4
1912	I	19R	1	1972	II	18	4
1913	II	1P	1	1973	II	19	3
1914	I	19R	3	1974	II	21R	3
1915	II	2P	1	1975	III	9	3
1920	I	19	3	1976	III	8	2
1921	I	16	s-f	1977	III	6	2
1922	I	16	Final	1978	III	3P	2
1923	I	16	2	1979	II	7	4
1924	I	18	1	1980	II	10	3
1925	I	21R	2	1981	II	20R	3
1926	II	12	3	1982	III	14	1
1927	II	6	4	1983	III	16	3
1928	II	4	3	1984	III	16	1
1929	II	13	3	1985	III	23R	2
1930	II	16	3	1986	IV	23	1
1931	II	7	3	1987	IV	2P	4
1932	II	13	5				
1933	II	9	3				
1934	II	2P	q-f				
1935	I	11	q-f				
1936	I	7	4				
1937	I	14	Final				

†—Preston expelled by FA

Founded: 1885
Address: South Africa Road, London W12 7PA
Telephone: (01) 743 0262/3/4/5
Ground capacity: 27,500
Playing area: 112 by 72 yards
Record attendance: 35,353 v Leeds United, Division I, 28.4.74
Record victory: 9–2 v Tranmere Rovers, Division III, 3.12.60
Record defeat: 1–8 v Mansfield Town, Division III, 15.3.65; 1–8 v Manchester United, Division I, 12.2.69
Most League points (3 for win): 85, Division II, 1982–83
Most League points (2 for win): 67, Division III, 1966–67
Most League goals: 111, Division III, 1961–62
League scoring record: 37, George Goddard, Division III(S), 1929–30
Record League aggregate: 172, George Goddard, 1926–1934
Most League appearances: 519, Tony Ingham, 1950–1963
Most capped player: 26 (56 in all), Don Givens, Eire

FA Cup	Year	Opponents	Score	Scorers
Runners-up	1982	Tottenham	*1–1	Fenwick
		Replay	0–1	
League Cup				
Winners	1967	West Bromwich Albion	3–2	Morgan (R), Marsh, Lazarus
Runners-up	1986	Oxford United	0–3	

* after extra time

THE QPR RECORD

	Division and place		Cup round reached		Division and place		Cup round reached
1900			2	1953	SIII	21	1
1901			q	1954	SIII	18	3
1902			q	1955	SIII	15	1
1903			q	1956	SIII	18	1
1904			q	1957	SIII	10	3
1905			q	1958	SIII	10	2
1906			1	1959	III	13	2
1907			1	1960	III	8	2
1908			2	1961	III	3	2
1909			1	1962	III	4	3
1910			q-f	1963	III	13	3
1911			1	1964	III	15	3
1912			1	1965	III	14	2
1913			2	1966	III	3	3
1914			q-f	1967	III	1P	3
1915			3	1968	III	2P	3
1920			1	1969	I	22R	3
1921	SIII	3	2	1970	II	9	q-f
1922	SIII	5	1	1971	II	10	3
1923	SIII	11	q-f	1972	II	4	3
1924	SIII	22	1	1973	II	2P	5
1925	SIII	19	1	1974	I	8	q-f
1926	SIII	22	2	1975	I	11	5
1927	SIII	14	*	1976	I	2	3
1928	SIII	10	1	1977	I	14	4
1929	SIII	6	1	1978	I	19	5
1930	SIII	3	3	1979	I	20R	3
1931	SIII	8	3	1980	II	5	3
1932	SIII	13	4	1981	II	8	3
1933	SIII	16	3	1982	II	5	Final
1934	SIII	4	3	1983	II	1P	3
1935	SIII	13	2	1984	I	5	3
1936	SIII	4	1	1985	I	19	3
1937	SIII	9	3	1986	I	13	3
1938	SIII	3	2	1987	I	16	5
1939	SIII	6	3				
1946			5				
1947	SIII	2	3				
1948	SIII	1P	q-f				
1949	II	13	3				
1950	II	20	3				
1951	II	16	3				
1952	II	22R	3				

* – did not enter

Founded: 1871
Address: Elm Park, Norfolk Road, Reading
Telephone: Reading 57878/9/0
Ground capacity: 27,000 (3,200 seated)
Playing area: 112 by 77 yards
Record attendance: 33,042 v Brentford, FA Cup 5th round, 19.2.27
Record victory: 10–2 v Crystal Palace, Division III(S), 4.9.46
Record defeat: 0–18 v Preston North End, FA Cup, 1st round, 27.1.1894
Most League points (3 for win): 94, Division III, 1985–86
Most League points (2 for win): 65, Division IV, 1978–79
Most League goals: 112, Division III(S), 1951–52
League scoring record: 39, Ronnie Blackman, Division III(S), 1951–52
Record League aggregate: 156, Ronnie Blackman, 1947–1954
Most League appearances: 471, Steve Death, 1969–82
Most capped player: 8, Pat McConnell, Northern Ireland

THE READING RECORD

	Division and place		Cup round reached		Division and place		Cup round reached
1900			1	1949	SIII	2	2
1901			3	1950	SIII	10	3
1902			2	1951	SIII	3	3
1903			1	1952	SIII	2	3
1904			1	1953	SIII	11	1
1905			1	1954	SIII	8	1
1906			1	1955	SIII	18	3
1907			1	1956	SIII	17	2
1908			1	1957	SIII	13	3
1909			1	1958	SIII	5	3
1910			1	1959	III	6	1
1911			q	1960	III	11	3
1912			3	1961	III	18	3
1913			3	1962	III	7	1
1914			1	1963	III	20	1
1915			1	1964	III	6	2
1920			1	1965	III	13	4
1921	III	20	1	1966	III	8	3
1922	SIII	13	1	1967	III	4	2
1923	SIII	19	1	1968	III	5	3
1924	SIII	18	1	1969	III	14	3
1925	SIII	14	2	1970	III	8	1
1926	SIII	1P	3	1971	III	21R	3
1927	II	14	s-f	1972	IV	16	4
1928	II	18	4	1973	IV	7	4
1929	II	15	5	1974	IV	6	2
1930	II	19	3	1975	IV	7	1
1931	II	21R	3	1976	IV	3P	1
1932	SIII	2	1	1977	III	21R	3
1933	SIII	4	3	1978	IV	8	2
1934	SIII	3	3	1979	IV	1P	3
1935	SIII	2	5	1980	III	7	4
1936	SIII	3	3	1981	III	10	1
1937	SIII	5	3	1982	III	12	1
1938	SIII	6	1	1983	III	21R	1
1939	SIII	5	1	1984	IV	3P	2
1946			1	1985	III	9	3
1947	SIII	9	3	1986	III	1P	4
1948	SIII	10	3	1987	II	13	3

Founded: 1907
Address: Spotland, Willbutts Lane, Rochdale, Lancashire
Telephone: 0706 44648
Ground capacity: 12,000
Playing area: 113 by 75 yards
Record attendance: 24,231 v Notts County, FA Cup 2nd round, 10.12.49
Record victory: 8–1 v Chesterfield, Division III(N), 18.12.26
Record defeat: 0–8 v Wrexham, Division III(N), 28.12.29; 1–9 v Tranmere, Division III(N), 25.12.31
Most League points (3 for win): 55, Division IV, 1985–86
Most League points (2 for win): 65, Division IV, 1978–79
Most League goals: 105, Division III(N), 1926–27
League scoring record: 44, Albert Whitehurst, Division III(N), 1926–27
Record League aggregate: 119, Reg Jenkins, 1964–73
Most League appearances: 317, Graham Smith, 1966–74
Most capped player: None

League Cup	Year	Opponents	Score
Runners-up	1962	Norwich City	H0–3
			A0–1

THE ROCHDALE RECORD

	Division and place		Cup round reached		Division and place		Cup round reached
1913			1	1955	NIII	12	3
1914			p	1956	NIII	12	1
1915			2	1957	NIII	13	1
1920			1	1958	NIII	10	1
1921			1	1959	III	24R	1
1922	NIII	20	p	1960	IV	12	2
1923	NIII	12	p	1961	IV	17	1
1924	NIII	2	p	1962	IV	12	2
1925	NIII	6	p	1963	IV	7	1
1926	NIIII	3	2	1964	IV	20	2
1927	NIII	2	1	1965	IV	6	1
1928	NIII	13	2	1966	IV	21	2
1929	NIII	17	1	1967	IV	21	1
1930	NIII	10	1	1968	IV	19	1
1931	NIII	21	1	1969	IV	3P	1
1932	NIII	21	1	1970	III	9	1
1933	NIII	18	1	1971	III	16	4
1934	NIII	22	1	1972	III	18	1
1935	NIII	20	1	1973	III	13	1
1936	NIII	20	1	1974	III	24R	2
1937	NIII	18	1	1975	IV	19	2
1938	NIII	17	1	1976	IV	15	3
1939	NIII	15	1	1977	IV	18	1
1946			3	1978	IV	24	1
1947	NIII	6	3	1979	IV	20	1
1948	NIII	12	2	1980	IV	24	3
1949	NIII	7	1	1981	IV	15	1
1950	NIII	3	2	1982	IV	21	1
1951	NIII	11	3	1983	IV	20	1
1952	NIII	21	3	1984	IV	22	3
1953	NIII	22	1	1985	IV	18	1
1954	NIII	19	1	1986	IV	18	3
				1987	IV	21	2

Founded: 1884
Address: Millmoor Ground, Rotherham, Yorkshire
Telephone: Rotherham 562434
Ground capacity: 18,500
Playing area: 115 by 76 yards
Record attendance: 25,000 v Sheffield United, Division II, 26.1.52; 25,000 v Sheffield Wednesday, Division II, 13.12.52
Record victory: 8–0 v Oldham Athletic, Division III(N), 26.5.47
Record defeat: 1–11 v Bradford City, Division III(N), 25.8.28
Most League points (3 for win): 67, Division III, 1981–82
Most League points (2 for win): 71, Division III(N), 1950–51
Most League goals: 114, Division III(N), 1946–47
League scoring record: 38, Wally Ardron, Division III(N), 1946–47
Record League aggregate: 130, Gladstone Guest, 1946–1956
Most League appearances: 459, Danny Williams, 1946–1962
Most capped player: 6, Harry Millership, Wales

League Cup	Year	Opponents	Score	Scorers
Winners	1960–61	Aston Villa	H2–0 A0–3	Webster, Kirkman

THE ROTHERHAM RECORD

	Division and place	Cup round reached		Division and place	Cup round reached
1894*	II 14	q	1961	II 15	4
1895*	II 12	q	1962	II 9	3
1896*	II 15	1	1963	II 14	3
1920†	II 17	q	1964	II 7	3
1921†	II 19	q	1965	II 14	4
1922†	II 16	q	1966	II 7	4
1923†	II 21R	1	1967	II 18	4
1924†	NIII 4	q	1968	II 21R	5
1925†	NIII 22	q	1969	III 11	2
1926‡	NIII 14	3	1970	III 14	3
1927	NIII 19	1	1971	III 8	3
1928	NIII 14	3	1972	III 5	4
1929	NIII 16	1	1973	III 21R	2
1930	NIII 20	3	1974	IV 15	2
1931	NIII 14	1	1975	IV 3P	3
1932	NIII 19	1	1976	III 16	2
1933	NIII 17	1	1977	III 4	3
1934	NIII 21	3	1978	III 20	3
1935	NIII 9	2	1979	III 17	3
1936	NIII 11	2	1980	III 13	2
1937	NIII 17	1	1981	III 1P	2
1938	NIII 6	2	1982	II 7	3
1939	NIII 11	1	1983	II 20	3
1946		4	1984	II 18	3
1947	NIII 2	3	1985	II 12	1
1948	NIII 2	3	1986	II 14	4
1949	NIII 2	4	1987	III 14	1
1950	NIII 6	3			
1951	NIII 1P	4			
1952	II 9	4			
1953	II 12	5			
1954	II 5	4			
1955	II 3	4			
1956	II 19	3			
1957	II 17	3			
1958	II 18	3			
1959	II 20	3			
1960	II 8	4			

* – Rotherham Town, who resigned from the League in 1896
† – Rotherham County elected to the League in 1919
‡ – Rotherham County and Rotherham Town amalgamated to form Rotherham United at the start of the 1925–26 season

---

Founded: 1904
Address: Old Show Ground, Scunthorpe, South Humerside
Telephone: Scunthorpe 842954/848077
Ground capacity: 27,000
Playing area: 112 by 78 yards
Record attendance: 23,935 v Portsmouth, FA Cup 4th round, 30.1.54
Record victory: 9–0 v Boston United, FA Cup 1st round, 21.11.53
Record defeat: 0–8 v Carlisle United, Division III(N), 25.12.52
Most League points (3 for win): 83, Division IV, 1982–83
Most League points (2 for win): 66, Division III(N), 1957–58
Most League goals: 88, Division III(N), 1957–58
League scoring record: 31, Barry Thomas, Division II, 1961–62
Record League aggregate: 109, Steve Cammack, 1979–81, 1981–86
Most League appearances: 600, Jack Brownsword, 1950–1965
Most capped player: None

THE SCUNTHORPE RECORD

	Division and place	Cup round reached		Division and place	Cup round reached
1951	NIII 12	q	1972	IV 4P	1
1952	NIII 14	3	1973	III 24R	3
1953	NIII 15	3	1974	IV 18	4
1954	NIII 3	4	1975	IV 24	1
1955	NIII 3	2	1976	IV 19	1
1956	NIII 9	4	1977	IV 20	1
1957	NIII 14	2	1978	IV 14	1
1958	NIII 1P	5	1979	IV 12	1
1959	II 18	3	1980	IV 14	1
1960	II 15	4	1981	IV 16	2
1961	II 9	4	1982	IV 23	3
1962	II 4	3	1983	IV 4P	3
1963	II 9	3	1984	III 21R	4
1964	II 22R	3	1985	IV 9	2
1965	III 18	1	1986	IV 15	2
1966	III 4	1	1987	IV 8	3
1967	III 18	2			
1968	III 23R	2			
1969	IV 16	1			
1970	IV 12	5			
1971	IV 17	3			

SHEFFIELD UNITED

Founded: 1889
Address: Bramall Lane, Sheffield S2 4SU
Telephone: 738955/6/7
Ground capacity: 49,000 (15,300 seated)
Playing area: 117 by 75 yards
Record attendance: 68,287 v Leeds United, FA Cup 5th round, 15.2.36
Record victory: 10–0 v Port Vale, Division II, 10.12.18; 10–0 v Burnley, Division I, 19.1.29
Record defeat: 0–13 v Bolton Wanderers, FA Cup 2nd round, 1.2.90
Most League points (3 for win): 96, Division IV, 1981–82
Most League points (2 for win): 60, Division II, 1952–53
Most League goals: 102, Division I, 1925–26
League scoring record: 41, Jimmy Dunne, Division I, 1930–31
Record League aggregate: 205, Harry Johnson, 1919–1930
Most League appearances: 629, Joe Shaw, 1948–1966
Most capped player: 25, Billy Gillespie, Northern Ireland

FA Cup	Year	Opponents	Score	Scorers
Winners	1899	Derby County	4–1	Bennett, Beers, Almond, Priest
	1902	Southampton	1–1	Hedley, Barnes
	1915	Chelsea	3–0	Simmons, Fazackerley, Kitchen
	1925	Cardiff City	1–0	Tunstall
Runners-up	1901	Tottenham Hotspur	2–2	Bennett, Priest
	Replay		1–3	Priest
	1936	Arsenal	0–1	

THE UNITED RECORD

	Division and place		Cup round reached		Division and place		Cup round reached
1890			2	1938	II	3	4
1891			1	1939	II	2P	5
1892			2	1946			4
1893	II	2P	2	1947	I	6	q-f
1894	I	10	1	1948	I	12	3
1895	I	6	2	1949	I	22R	4
1896	I	12	2	1950	II	3	4
1897	I	2	1	1951	II	8	4
1898	I	1C	1	1952	II	11	q-f
1899	I	16	Winners	1953	II	1P	4
1900	I	2	q-f	1954	I	20	3
1901	I	14	Final	1955	I	13	3
1902	I	10	Winners	1956	I	22R	5
1903	I	4	2	1957	II	7	3
1904	I	7	q-f	1958	II	6	5
1905	I	6	1	1959	II	3	q-f
1906	I	13	2	1960	II	4	q-f
1907	I	4	1	1961	II	2P	s-f
1908	I	17	1	1962	I	5	q-f
1909	I	12	1	1963	I	10	5
1910	I	6	1	1964	I	12	4
1911	I	9	1	1965	I	19	4
1912	I	14	1	1966	I	9	4
1913	I	15	1	1967	I	10	5
1914	I	10	s-f	1968	I	21R	q-f
1915	I	6	Winners	1969	II	9	3
1920	I	14	2	1970	II	6	4
1921	I	20	1	1971	II	2P	3
1922	I	11	1	1972	I	10	3
1923	I	10	s-f	1973	I	14	4
1924	I	5	1	1974	I	13	3
1925	I	14	Winners	1975	I	6	4
1926	I	5	4	1976	I	22R	4
1927	I	8	3	1977	II	11	3
1928	I	13	s-f	1978	II	12	3
1929	I	11	3	1979	III	20R	3
1930	I	20	4	1980	III	12	2
1931	I	15	5	1981	III	21R	3
1932	I	7	4	1982	IV	1P	1
1933	I	10	4	1983	III	11	3
1934	I	22R	3	1984	III	3P	3
1935	II	11	4	1985	II	18	3
1936	II	3	Final	1986	II	7	4
1937	II	7	4	1987	II	9	4

SHEFFIELD WEDNESDAY

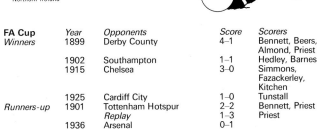

Founded: 1867
Address: Hillsborough, Sheffield S6 1SW
Telephone: Sheffield 343123
Ground capacity: 50,174
Playing area: 115 by 75 yards
Record attendance: 72,841 v Manchester City, FA Cup 5th round, 17.2.34
Record victory: 12–0 v Halliwell, FA Cup 1st round, 17.1.1891
Record defeat: 0–10 v Aston Villa, Division I, 5.10.1912
Most League points (3 for win): 88, Division II, 1983–84
Most League points (2 for win): 62, Division II, 1958–59
Most League goals: 106, Division II, 1958–59
League scoring record: 46, Derek Dooley, Division II, 1951–52
Record League aggregate: 200, Andy Wilson, 1900–20
Most League appearances: 502, Andy Wilson, 1900–20
Most capped player: 33, Ron Springett, England

FA Cup	Year	Opponents	Score	Scorers
Winners	1896	Wolverhampton Wanderers	2–1	Spiksley 2
	1907	Everton	2–1	Stewart, Simpson
	1935	West Bromwich Albion	4–2	Rimmer 2, Palethorpe, Hooper
Runners-up	1890	Blackburn Rovers	1–6	Bennett
	1966	Everton	2–3	McCalliog, Ford

THE WEDNESDAY RECORD

	Division and place		Cup round reached		Division and place		Cup round reached
1881			4	1938	II	17	3
1882			s-f	1939	II	3	5
1883			4	1946			5
1884			2	1947	II	20	5
1885			3	1948	II	4	4
1886			†	1949	II	8	4
1887			†	1950	II	2P	3
1888			q-f	1951	I	21R	3
1889			q-f	1952	II	1P	3
1890	I		Final	1953	I	18	3
1891	I		q-f	1954	I	19	s-f
1892	I		q-f	1955	I	22R	4
1893	I	12	q-f	1956	II	1P	3
1894	I	12	s-f	1957	I	14	3
1895	I	8	s-f	1958	II	22R	5
1896	I	7	Winners	1959	II	1P	3
1897	I	6	1	1960	I	5	s-f
1898	I	5	2	1961	I	2	q-f
1899	I	18R	1	1962	I	6	5
1900	II	1P	2	1963	I	6	4
1901	I	8	1	1964	I	6	3
1902	I	9	1	1965	I	8	3
1903	I	1C	1	1966	I	17	Final
1904	I	1C	s-f	1967	I	11	q-f
1905	I	9	s-f	1968	I	19	5
1906	I	3	q-f	1969	I	15	4
1907	I	13	Winners	1970	I	22R	4
1908	I	5	1	1971	II	15	3
1909	I	5	3	1972	II	14	3
1910	I	11	1	1973	II	10	5
1911	I	6	1	1974	II	19	3
1912	I	5	1	1975	II	22R	3
1913	I	3	3	1976	III	20	3
1914	I	18	q-f	1977	III	8	1
1915	I	7	3	1978	III	14	2
1920	I	22R	1	1979	III	14	3
1921	II	10	2	1980	III	3P	2
1922	II	10	1	1981	II	10	3
1923	II	8	3	1982	II	4	3
1924	II	8	2	1983	II	6	s-f
1925	II	14	2	1984	II	2P	6
1926	II	1P	3	1985	I	8	5
1927	I	16	4	1986	I	5	s-f
1928	I	14	5	1987	I	13	q-f
1929*	I	1C	4				
1930	I	1C	s-f				
1931	I	3	4				
1932	I	3	5				
1933	I	3	3				
1934	I	11	5				
1935	I	3	Winners				
1936	I	20	4				
1937	I	22R	4				

* – The club officially changed their name to Sheffield Wednesday in the summer of 1929. Before then they were known as The Wednesday.
† – Did not enter

SHREWSBURY TOWN

Founded: 1886
Address: Gay Meadow, Shrewsbury, Shropshire
Telephone: Shrewsbury 60111
Ground capacity: 18,000
Playing area: 116 by 76 yards
Record attendance: 18,917 v Walsall, Division III, 26.4.61
Record victory: 7–0 v Swindon Town, Division III(S), 6.5.55
Record defeat: 1–8 v Norwich City, Division III(S), 13.9.52 (home); 1–8 v Coventry City, Division III 22.10.63
Most League points (3 for win): 70, division II, 1981–82
Most League points (2 for win): 62, Division IV, 1974–75
Most League goals: 101, Division IV, 1958–59
League scoring record: 38, Arthur Rowley, 1958–59
Record League aggregate: 152, Arthur Rowley, 1958–1965
Most League appearances: 370, Ken Mulhearn, 1971–80
Most capped player: 5 (12 in all), Jimmy McLaughlin, Northern Ireland

THE SHREWSBURY RECORD

	Division and place		Cup round reached		Division and place		Cup round reached
1951	NIII	20	*	1976	III	9	3
1952	SIII	20	1	1977	III	10	3
1953	SIII	23	4	1978	III	11	3
1954	SIII	21	1	1979	III	1P	q-f
1955	SIII	16	1	1980	II	13	3
1956	SIII	13	2	1981	II	14	4
1957	SIII	9	1	1982	II	18	q-f
1958	SIII	17	1	1983	II	9	4
1959	IV	4P	2	1984	II	8	5
1960	III	3	1	1985	II	8	3
1961	III	10	3	1986	II	17	3
1962	III	19	4	1987	II	18	3
1963	III	15	3				
1964	III	11	1				
1965	III	16	5				
1966	III	10	5				
1967	III	6	3				
1968	III	3	3				
1969	III	17	1				
1970	III	15	2				
1971	III	13	2				
1972	III	12	3	* – Shrewsbury withdrew,			
1973	III	15	2	refusing to play in the qualifying			
1974	III	22R	1	rounds after being elected to the			
1975	IV	2P	1	Football League			

SOUTHAMPTON

Founded: 1885
Address: The Dell, Milton Road, Southampton SO9 4XX
Telephone: Southampton 39445/39633
Ground capacity: 25,000
Playing area: 110 by 72 yards
Record attendance: 31,044 v Manchester United, Division I, 8.10.69
Record victory: 11–0 v Northampton, Southern League, 28.12.01
Record defeat: 0–8 v Tottenham Hotspur, Division II, 28.3.36; 0–8 v Everton Division I, 20.11.71
Most League points (3 for win): 77, Division I, 1983–84
Most League points (2 for win): 61, Division III(S), 1921–22 & Division III, 1959–60
Most League goals: 112, Division III(S), 1957–58
League scoring record: 39, Derek Reeves, Division III, 1959–60
Record League aggregate: 182, Mick Channon, 1966–77, 1979–82
Most League appearances: 713, Terry Paine, 1956–74
Most capped player: 45 (46 in all), Mick Channon, England

FA Cup	Year	Opponents	Score	Scorers
Winners	1976	Manchester United	1–0	Stokes
Runners-up	1900	Bury	0–4	
	1902	Sheffield United	1–1	Wood
	Replay		1–2	Brown
League Cup				
Runners-up	1979	Nottingham Forest	2–3	Peach, Holmes

THE SOUTHAMPTON RECORD

	Division and place		Cup round reached		Division and place		Cup round reached
1895			1	1946			4
1896			1	1947	II	14	4
1897			2	1948	II	3	q-f
1898			s-f	1949	II	3	3
1899			q-f	1950	II	4	3
1900			Final	1951	II	12	3
1901			1	1952	II	13	3
1902			Final	1953	II	21R	5
1903			1	1954	SIII	6	1
1904			2	1955	SIII	3	2
1905			q-f	1956	SIII	14	2
1906			q-f	1957	SIII	4	3
1907			2	1958	SIII	6	2
1908			s-f	1959	III	14	3
1909			1	1960	III	1P	4
1910			2	1961	II	8	4
1911			1	1962	II	6	3
1912			1	1963	II	13	s-f
1913			1	1964	II	5	3
1914			1	1965	II	4	4
1915			3	1966	II	2P	3
1920			1	1967	I	19	4
1921	III	2	3	1968	I	15	4
1922	SIII	1P	2	1969	I	7	4
1923	II	11	q-f	1970	I	11	4
1924	II	5	3	1971	I	7	5
1925	II	7	s-f	1972	I	19	3
1926	II	14	3	1973	I	13	3
1927	II	13	s-f	1974	I	20R	5
1928	II	17	3	1975	II	13	3
1929	II	4	3	1976	II	6	Winners
1930	II	7	3	1977	II	9	5
1931	II	9	3	1978	II	2P	4
1932	II	14	3	1979	I	14	q-f
1933	II	12	3	1980	I	8	3
1934	II	14	3	1981	I	6	5
1935	II	19	4	1982	I	7	3
1936	II	17	3	1983	I	12	3
1937	II	18	3	1984	I	2	s-f
1938	II	15	3	1985	I	5	5
1939	II	18	3	1986	I	14	s-f
				1987	I	12	3

Founded: 1906
Address: Roots Hall Ground, Victoria Avenue, Southend-on-Sea, Essex
Telephone: Southend 40707
Ground capacity: 13,500
Playing area: 110 by 74 yards
Record attendance: 31,033 v Liverpool, FA Cup 3rd round, 10.1.79
Record victory: 10–1 v Golders Green, FA Cup 1st round, 24.11.34; 10–1 v Brentwood, FA Cup 2nd round, 2.12.68
Record defeat: 1–11 v Northampton, Southern League, 30.12.09
Most League points (3 for win): 69, Division III, 1981–82
Most League points (2 for win): 67, Division IV, 1980–81
Most League goals: 92, Division III(S), 1950–51
League scoring record: 31, Jim Shankly, Division III(S), 1928–29 & Sammy McCrory, Division III(S), 1957–58
Record League aggregate: 122, Roy Hollis, 1953–1960
Most League appearances: 451, Sandy Anderson, 1950–1963
Most capped player: 9, George Mackenzie, Republic of Ireland

THE SOUTHEND RECORD

	Division and place		Cup round reached		Division and place		Cup round reached
1910			2	1954	SIII	16	2
1911			1	1955	SIII	10	3
1912			q	1956	SIII	4	4
1913			1	1957	SIII	7	4
1914			1	1958	SIII	7	3
1915			2	1959	III	8	1
1920			1	1960	III	12	2
1921	III	17	3	1961	III	20	2
1922	SIII	22	2	1962	III	16	1
1923	SIII	15	q	1963	III	8	2
1924	SIII	19	2	1964	III	14	1
1925	SIII	10	q	1965	III	12	1
1926	SIII	11	5	1966	III	21R	3
1927	SIII	19	2	1967	IV	6	1
1928	SIII	7	2	1968	IV	6	1
1929	SIII	12	1	1969	IV	7	4
1930	SIII	11	2	1970	IV	17	1
1931	SIII	5	1	1971	IV	18	3
1932	SIII	3	2	1972	IV	2P	2
1933	SIII	13	4	1973	III	14	1
1934	SIII	16	3	1974	III	12	3
1935	SIII	21	3	1975	III	18	3
1936	SIII	18	3	1976	III	23R	5
1937	SIII	10	2	1977	IV	10	3
1938	SIII	12	3	1978	IV	2P	3
1939	SIII	12	4	1979	III	13	3
1946			1	1980	III	22R	2
1947	SIII	8	3	1981	IV	1P	1
1948	SIII	9	1	1982	III	7	1
1949	SIII	18	1	1983	III	15	3
1950	SIII	3	3	1984	III	22R	1
1951	SIII	7	1	1985	IV	20	1
1952	SIII	9	5	1986	IV	9	1
1953	SIII	8	1	1987	IV	3P	2

Founded: 1883
Address: Edgeley Park, Stockport, Cheshire
Telephone: 061 480 8888
Ground capacity: 6,000
Playing area: 110 by 75 yards
Record attendance: 27,833 v Liverpool, FA Cup 5th round, 11.2.50
Record victory: 13–0 v Halifax Town, Division III(N), 6.1.34
Record defeat: 1–8 v Chesterfield, Division II, 19.4.02
Most League points (3 for win): 64, Division IV, 1985–86
Most League points (2 for win): 64, Division IV, 1966–67
Most League goals: 115, Division III(N), 1933–34
League scoring record: 46, Alf Lythgoe, Division III(N), 1933–34
Record League aggregate: 132, Jack Connor, 1951–1956
Most League appearances: 465, Robert Murray, 1952–1963
Most capped player: 1, Harry Hardy, England

THE STOCKPORT RECORD

	Division and place		Cup round reached		Division and place		Cup round reached
1901	II	17	q	1954	NIII	10	3
1902	II	17	p	1955	NIII	9	1
1903	II	17	q	1956	NIII	7	1
1904	II	16	p	1957	NIII	5	1
1905*			p	1958	NIII	9	4
1906	II	10	1	1959	III	21R	3
1907	II	12	1	1960	IV	10	2
1908	II	13	1	1961	IV	13	4
1909	II	18	2	1962	IV	16	1
1910	II	13	2	1963	IV	19	1
1911	II	17	p	1964	IV	17	1
1912	II	16	1	1965	IV	24	4
1913	II	19	1	1966	IV	13	2
1914	II	12	p	1967	IV	1P	1
1915	II	14	1	1968	III	13	1
1920	II	16	1	1969	III	9	3
1921	II	20R	1	1970	III	24R	2
1922	NIII	1P	p	1971	IV	11	1
1923	II	20	p	1972	IV	23	2
1924	II	13	p	1973	IV	11	3
1925	II	19	2	1974	IV	24	1
1926	II	22R	3	1975	IV	20	1
1927	NIII	6	1	1976	IV	21	1
1928	NIII	3	2	1977	IV	14	1
1929	NIII	2	3	1978	IV	18	2
1930	NIII	2	3	1979	IV	17	3
1931	NIII	7	2	1980	IV	16	1
1932	NIII	12	1	1981	IV	20	1
1933	NIII	3	2	1982	IV	18	2
1934	NIII	3	2	1983	IV	16	1
1935	NIII	7	5	1984	IV	22	1
1936	NIII	5	1	1985	IV	22	1
1937	NIII	1P	1	1986	IV	11	1
1938	II	22R	3	1987	IV	19	1
1939	NIII	9	4				
1946			1				
1947	NIII	4	3				
1948	NIII	17	4				
1949	NIII	8	3				
1950	NIII	10	5				
1951	NIII	10	4				
1952	NIII	3	1				
1953	NIII	11	3				

* – failed to gain re-election in 1904. Returned when Division II increased from 19 to 20 clubs in 1905

Founded: 1863 (though no recorded reference before 1867)
Address: Victoria Ground, Stoke-on-Trent, Staffordshire
Telephone: 0782 413511
Ground capacity: 31,700
Playing area: 116 by 75 yards
Record attendance: 51,380 v Arsenal, Division I, 29.3.37
Record victory: 10–3 v West Bromwich Albion, Division I, 4.2.37
Record defeat: 0–10 v Preston North End, Division I, 14.9.1889
Most League points (3 for win): 57, Division I, 1982–83, 1985–86
Most League points (2 for win): 63, Division III(N), 1925–27
Most League goals: 92, Division III(N), 1926–27
League scoring record: 33, Freddie Steele, Division I, 1936–37
Record League aggregate: 142, Freddie Steele, 1934–1939
Most League appearances: 506, Eric Skeels, 1958–76
Most capped player: 36 (73 in all), Gordon Banks, England

League Cup	Year	Opponents	Score	Scorers
Winners	1972	Chelsea	2–1	Conroy, Eastham
Runners-up	1964	Leicester City (aggregate)	1–1	Bebbington
			2–3	Viollet, Kinnell

THE STOKE CITY RECORD

Year	Division and place		Cup round reached	Year	Division and place		Cup round reached
1889	I	12	p	1949	I	11	5
1890	I	12L	q-f	1950	I	19	3
1891			q-f	1951	I	13	5
1892	I	13	q-f	1952	I	20	4
1893	I	7	1	1953	I	21R	4
1894	I	11	2	1954	II	11	4
1895	I	14	2	1955	II	5	4
1896	I	6	q-f	1956	II	13	5
1897	I	13	2	1957	II	5	3
1898	I	16	2	1958	II	11	5
1899	I	12	s-f	1959	II	5	4
1900	I	9	1	1960	II	17	3
1901	I	16	1	1961	II	18	5
1902	I	16	q-f	1962	II	8	4
1903	I	6	q-f	1963	II	1P	3
1904	I	16	1	1964	I	17	5
1905	I	12	2	1965	I	11	4
1906	I	10	2	1966	I	10	3
1907	I	20R	1	1967	I	12	3
1908*	II	10	q-f	1968	I	18	4
1909			1	1969	I	19	5
1910			1	1970	I	9	4
1911			1	1971	I	13	s-f
1912			p	1972	I	17	s-f
1913			1	1973	I	15	3
1914			1	1974	I	5	3
1915			p	1975	I	5	3
1920	II	10	1	1976	I	12	5
1921	II	20	1	1977	I	21R	3
1922	II	2P	3	1978	II	7	3
1923	I	21R	2	1979	II	3P	3
1924	II	6	1	1980	I	18	3
1925†	II	20	1	1981	I	11	3
1926	II	21R	4	1982	I	18	3
1927	NIII	1P	1	1983	I	13	4
1928	II	5	q-f	1984	I	18	3
1929	II	6	3	1985	I	22R	3
1930	II	11	3	1986	II	10	3
1931	II	11	3	1987	II	8	5
1932	II	3	5				
1933	II	1P	4				
1934	I	12	q-f				
1935	I	10	3				
1936	I	4	5				
1937	I	10	4				
1938	I	17	4				
1939	I	7	3				
1946			q-f				
1947	I	4	5				
1948	I	15	4				

* – resigned from League
† – name changed to Stoke City in 1925

Founded: 1879
Address: Roker Park Ground, Sunderland, Co. Durham
Telephone: Sunderland 40332
Ground capacity: 37,875
Playing area: 113 by 74 yards
Record attendance: 75,118 v Derby County, FA Cup quarter-final replay, 8.3.33.
Record victory: 11–1 v Fairfield, FA Cup 1st round, 2.2.1895
Record defeat: 0–8 v West Ham United, Division I, 19.10.68; 0–8 v Watford, Division I, 25.9.82
Most League points (3 for win): 52, Division I, 1983–84
Most League points (2 for win): 63, Division III(N), 1926–27
Most League goals: 109, Division I, 1935–36
League scoring record: 43, David Halliday, Division I, 1928–29
Record League aggregate: 209, Charlie Buchan, 1911–1925
Most League appearances: 537, Jim Montgomery, 1962–1977
Most capped player: 34, Martin Harvey, N. Ireland

FA Cup	Year	Opponents	Score	Scorers
Winners	1937	Preston North End	3–1	Gurney, Carter, Burbanks
	1973	Leeds United	1–0	Porterfield
Runners-up	1913	Aston Villa	0–1	
League Cup				
Runners-up	1985	Norwich City	0–1	

THE SUNDERLAND RECORD

Year	Division and place		Cup round reached	Year	Division and place		Cup round reached
1890			1	1938	I	8	s-f
1891	I	7	q-f	1939	I	16	5
1892	I	1C	s-f	1946			5
1893	I	1C	s-f	1947	I	9	3
1894	I	2	2	1948	I	20	3
1895	I	1C	s-f	1949	I	8	4
1896	I	5	2	1950	I	3	4
1897	I	15	2	1951	I	12	q-f
1898	I	2	1	1952	I	12	3
1899	I	7	2	1953	I	9	4
1900	I	3	2	1954	I	18	3
1901	I	2	1	1955	I	4	s-f
1902	I	1C	2	1956	I	9	s-f
1903	I	3	1	1957	I	20	4
1904	I	6	1	1958	I	21R	3
1905	I	5	1	1959	II	15	3
1906	I	14	3	1960	II	16	3
1907	I	10	3	1961	II	6	q-f
1908	I	16	1	1962	II	3	4
1909	I	3	q-f	1963	II	3	5
1910	I	8	3	1964	II	2P	q-f
1911	I	3	1	1965	I	15	4
1912	I	8	3	1966	I	19	3
1913	I	1C	Final	1967	I	17	5
1914	I	7	q-f	1968	I	16	3
1915	I	8	1	1969	I	17	3
1920	I	5	3	1970	I	21R	3
1921	I	12	1	1971	II	13	3
1922	I	12	1	1972	II	5	4
1923	I	2	2	1973	II	6	Winners
1924	I	3	1	1974	II	6	3
1925	I	7	2	1975	III	4	4
1926	I	3	5	1976	II	1P	q-f
1927	I	3	3	1977	I	20R	3
1928	I	15	4	1978	II	6	3
1929	I	4	3	1979	II	4	3
1930	I	9	5	1980	II	2P	3
1931	I	11	s-f	1981	I	17	3
1932	I	13	4	1982	I	19	4
1933	I	12	q-f	1983	I	16	3
1934	I	6	4	1984	I	13	4
1935	I	2	4	1985	I	21R	3
1936	I	1C	3	1986	II	18	4
1937	I	8	Winners	1987	II	20R	3

SWANSEA CITY

Founded: 1900 (as Swansea Town)
Address: Vetch Field, Swansea
Telephone: Swansea 474114
Ground capacity: 26,496
Playing area: 110 by 70 yards
Record attendance: 32,796 v Arsenal, FA Cup 4th round, 17.2.68
Record victory: 12–0 v Sliema Wanderers, E.C.W.C., 15.9.82
Record defeat: 1–8 v Fulham, Division II, 22.1.38
Most League points (3 for win): 69, Division I, 1981–82
Most League points (2 for win): 62, Division III(S), 1948–49
Most League goals: 90, Division II, 1956–57
League scoring record: 35, Cyril Pearce, Division II, 1931–32
Record League aggregate: 166, Ivor Allchurch, 1949–1958, 1965–1968
Most League appearances: 585, Wilfred Milne, 1919–1937
Most capped player: 42 (68 in all), Ivor Allchurch, Wales

THE SWANSEA RECORD

	Division and place		Cup round reached		Division and place		Cup round reached
1921	III	5	2	1968	IV	15	4
1922	SIII	10	3	1969	IV	10	3
1923	SIII	3	p	1970*	IV	3P	3
1924	SIII	4	2	1971	III	11	4
1925	SIII	1P	2	1972	III	13	4
1926	II	5	s-f	1973	III	23R	1
1927	II	12	q-f	1974	IV	14	1
1928	II	6	3	1975	IV	22	1
1929	II	19	4	1976	IV	11	1
1930	II	15	3	1977	IV	5	1
1931	II	20	3	1978	IV	3P	3
1932	II	15	3	1979	III	3P	3
1933	II	10	3	1980	II	12	5
1934	II	19	5	1981	II	3P	3
1935	II	17	4	1982	I	6	3
1936	II	13	3	1983	I	21R	3
1937	II	16	5	1984	II	21R	3
1938	II	18	3	1985	III	20	3
1939	II	19	3	1986	III	24R	2
1946			3	1987	IV	12	4
1947	II	21R	4				
1948	SIII	5	3				
1949	SIII	1P	2				
1950	II	8	4				
1951	II	18	3				
1952	II	19	5				
1953	II	11	3				
1954	II	20	4				
1955	II	10	5				
1956	II	10	3				
1957	II	10	3				
1958	II	19	3				
1959	II	11	3				
1960	II	12	4				
1961	II	7	5				
1962	II	20	3				
1963	II	15	4				
1964	II	19	s-f				
1965	II	22R	5				
1966	III	17	1				
1967	III	21R	2				

* – Name changed to Swansea City during 1969–70 season

SWINDON TOWN

Founded: 1881
Address: County Ground, Swindon, Wiltshire
Telephone: Swindon 22118
Ground capacity: 25,000 (6,500 seated)
Playing area: 114 by 72 yards
Record attendance: 32,000 v Arsenal, FA Cup 3rd round, 15.1.72
Record victory: 10–1 v Farnham United Brewery, FA Cup 1st round, 28.11.25
Record defeat: 1–10 v Manchester City, FA Cup 4th round replay, 29.1.30
Most League points (3 for win): 102, Division IV, 1985–86
Most League points (2 for win): 64, Division III, 1968–69
Most League goals: 100, Division III(S), 1926–27
League scoring record: 47, Harry Morris, Division III(S), 1926–27
Record League aggregate: 216, Harry Morris, 1926–1933
Most League appearances: 770, John Trollope, 1960–80
Most capped player: 30 (50 in all), Rod Thomas, Wales

League Cup Winners	Year	Opponents	Score	Scorers
	1969	Arsenal	3–1	Smart, Rogers 2

* after extra time

THE SWINDON RECORD

	Division and place		Cup round reached		Division and place		Cup round reached
1906			1	1952	SIII	16	5
1907			q	1953	SIII	18	3
1908			3	1954	SIII	19	2
1909			1	1955	SIII	21	1
1910			s-f	1956	SIII	24	4
1911			q-f	1957	SIII	23	2
1912			s-f	1958	SIII	4	1
1913			3	1959	III	15	2
1914			2	1960	III	16	1
1915			1	1961	III	16	2
1920			2	1962	III	9	1
1921	III	4	2	1963	III	2P	4
1922	SIII	6	2	1964	II	14	5
1923	SIII	9	1	1965	II	21R	3
1924	SIII	6	q-f	1966	III	7	3
1925	SIII	4	1	1967	III	8	5
1926	SIII	6	4	1968	III	9	4
1927	SIII	5	1	1969	III	2P	3
1928	SIII	6	4	1970	II	5	q-f
1929	SIII	10	5	1971	II	12	4
1930	SIII	14	4	1972	II	11	3
1931	SIII	12	1	1973	II	16	4
1932	SIII	17	1	1974	II	22R	3
1933	SIII	22	3	1975	III	4	4
1934	SIII	8	3	1976	III	19	3
1935	SIII	16	4	1977	III	11	4
1936	SIII	19	1	1978	III	10	3
1937	SIII	13	2	1979	III	5	4
1938	SIII	8	4	1980	III	10	4
1939	SIII	9	2	1981	III	17	2
1946			1	1982	III	22R	3
1947	SIII	4	2	1983	IV	8	4
1948	SIII	16	5	1984	IV	15	4
1949	SIII	4	3	1985	IV	8	1
1950	SIII	14	2	1986	IV	1P	1
1951	SIII	17	2	1987	III	3P	4

Founded: 1898
Address: Plainmoor, Torquay, Devon
Telephone: Torquay 38666/7
Ground capacity: 4,999
Playing area: 112 by 74 yards
Record attendance: 21,908 v Huddersfield Town, FA Cup 4th round, 29.1.55
Record victory: 9–0 v Swindon Town, Division III(S), 8.3.52
Record defeat: 2–10 v Fulham, Division III(S), 7.9.31; 2–10 v Luton Town, Division III(S), 2.9.33
Most League points (3 for win): 67, Division IV, 1983–84
Most League points (2 for win): 60, Division IV, 1959–60
Most League goals: 89, Division III(S), 1956–57
League scoring record: 40, 'Sammy' Collins, Division III(S), 1955–56
Record League aggregate: 204, 'Sammy' Collins, 1948–1958
Most League appearances: 443, Dennis Lewis, 1947–1959
Most capped player: None

THE TORQUAY RECORD

	Division and place		Cup round reached		Division and place		Cup round reached
1928	SIII	22	Sc	1964	IV	6	2
1929	SIII	18	2	1965	IV	11	3
1930	SIII	19	1	1966	IV	3P	1
1931	SIII	11	3	1967	III	7	1
1932	SIII	19	1	1968	III	4	1
1933	SIII	10	2	1969	III	6	2
1934	SIII	20	2	1970	III	13	1
1935	SIII	10	2	1971	III	10	4
1936	SIII	10	2	1972	III	23R	3
1937	SIII	20	1	1973	IV	18	2
1938	SIII	20	1	1974	IV	16	1
1939	SIII	19	2	1975	IV	14	1
1946			1	1976	IV	9	1
1947	SIII	11	1	1977	IV	16	1
1948	SIII	18	3	1978	IV	9	1
1949	SIII	9	4	1979	IV	11	3
1950	SIII	5	2	1980	IV	9	2
1951	SIII	20	1	1981	IV	17	3
1952	SIII	11	2	1982	IV	15	1
1953	SIII	12	1	1983	IV	12	4
1954	SIII	13	1	1984	IV	9	1
1955	SIII	8	4	1985	IV	24	2
1956	SIII	5	3	1986	IV	24	2
1957	SIII	2	3	1987	IV	23	1
1958	SIII	21	2				
1959	IV	12	3				
1960	IV	3P	2				
1961	III	12	2				
1962	III	21R	2				
1963	IV	6	2				

Sc – scratched

Founded: 1882
Address: 748 High Road, Tottenham, London N17
Telephone: (01) 801–3411
Ground capacity: 48,200
Playing area: 110 by 73 yards
Record attendance: 75,038 v Sunderland, FA Cup quarter-final, 5.3.38
Record victory: 13–2 v Crewe Alexandra, FA Cup 4th round, 3.2.60
Record defeat: 0–7 v Liverpool, Division I, 2.9.78
Most League points (3 for win): 77, Division I, 1984–85
Most League points (2 for win): 70, Division II, 1919–20
Most League goals: 115, Division I, 1960–61
League scoring record: 37, Jimmy Greaves, Division I, 1962–63
Record League aggregate: 220, Jimmy Greaves, 1961–1970
Most League appearances: 655, Steve Perryman, 1969–1986
Most capped player: 75 (119 in all), Pat Jennings, Northern Ireland

FA Cup	Year	Opponents	Score	Scorers
Winners	1901	Sheffield United	2–2	Brown 2
			3–1	Cameron, Smith, Brown
	1921	Wolverhampton W	1–0	Dimmock
	1961	Leicester City	2–0	Smith, Dyson
	1962	Burnley	3–1	Greaves, Smith, Blanchflower (pen)
	1967	Chelsea	2–1	Robertson, Saul
	1981	Manchester City	*1–1	Hutchison o.g.
		Replay	3–2	Villa 2, Crooks
	1982	Queen's Park Rangers	*1–1	Hoddle
		Replay	1–0	Hoddle (pen)
Runners-up	1987	Coventry City	* 2–3	Allen C, Kilcline o.g.

* after extra time

League Cup				
Winners	1971	Aston Villa	2–0	Chivers 2
	1973	Norwich City	1–0	Coates
Runners-up	1982	Liverpool	1–3	Archibald

* after extra time

THE SPURS RECORD

	Division and place		Cup round reached		Division and place		Cup round reached
1895			4q	1946			3
1896			1	1947	II	6	3
1897			3q	1948	II	8	s-f
1898			2q	1949	II	5	3
1899			q-f	1950	II	1P	5
1900			1	1951	I	1C	3
1901			Winners	1952	I	2	4
1902			1	1953	I	10	s-f
1903			q-f	1954	I	16	q-f
1904			q-f	1955	I	16	5
1905			2	1956	I	18	s-f
1906			3	1957	I	2	5
1907			3	1958	I	3	4
1908			1	1959	I	18	5
1909	II	2P	3	1960	I	3	5
1910	I	15	3	1961	I	1C	Winners
1911	I	15	2	1962	I	3	Winners
1912	I	12	1	1963	I	2	3
1913	I	17	2	1964	I	4	3
1914	I	17	2	1965	I	6	5
1915	I	20R	2	1966	I	8	5
1920	II	1P	q-f	1967	I	3	Winners
1921	I	6	Winners	1968	I	7	5
1922	I	2	s-f	1969	I	6	q-f
1923	I	12	q-f	1970	I	11	4
1924	I	15	1	1971	I	3	q-f
1925	I	12	3	1972	I	6	q-f
1926	I	15	4	1973	I	8	4
1927	I	13	3	1974	I	11	3
1928	I	21R	5	1975	I	19	3
1929	II	10	3	1976	I	9	3
1930	II	12	3	1977	I	22R	3
1931	II	3	4	1978	II	3P	3
1932	II	8	3	1979	I	11	q-f
1933	II	2P	4	1980	I	14	q-f
1934	I	3	5	1981	I	10	Winners
1935	I	22R	5	1982	I	4	Winners
1936	II	5	q-f	1983	I	4	5
1937	II	10	q-f	1984	I	8	4
1938	II	5	q-f	1985	I	3	4
1939	II	8	4	1986	I	10	5
				1987	I	3	Final

TRANMERE ROVERS

Founded: 1883
Address: Prenton Park, 14 Prenton Road West, Birkenhead
Telephone: 051 608 3677/4194
Ground capacity: 18,000
Playing area: 112 by 74 yards
Record attendance: 24,424 v Stoke City, FA Cup 4th round, 5.2.72
Record victory: 13–4 v Oldham Athletic, Division III(N), 26.12.35
Record defeat: 1–9 v Tottenham Hotspur, FA Cup 3rd round replay, 14.1.53
Most League points (3 for win): 75, Division IV, 1984–85
Most League points (2 for win): 60, Division IV, 1964–65
Most League goals: 111, Division III(N), 1930–31
League scoring record: 35, Robert 'Bunny' Bell, Division III(N), 1933–34
Record League aggregate: 104, Robert 'Bunny' Bell, 1931–36
Most League appearances: 595, Harold Bell, 1946–64
Most capped player: 3 (24 in all), Bert Gray, Wales

THE TRANMERE RECORD

Year	Division and place		Cup round reached	Year	Division and place		Cup round reached
1922	NIII	18	q	1958	NIII	11	3
1923	NIII	16	q	1959	III	7	2
1924	NIII	12	p	1960	III	20	1
1925	NIII	21	p	1961	III	21R	2
1926	NIII	7	p	1962	IV	15	1
1927	NIII	9	1	1963	IV	8	3
1928	NIII	5	3	1964	IV	7	1
1929	NIII	7	2	1965	IV	5	1
1930	NIII	12	1	1966	IV	5	1
1931	NIII	3	1	1967	IV	4P	2
1932	NIII	4	3	1968	III	19	5
1933	NIII	11	4	1969	III	7	1
1934	NIII	7	4	1970	III	16	4
1935	NIII	6	2	1971	III	18	1
1936	NIII	3	4	1972	III	19	4
1937	NIII	19	1	1973	III	10	2
1938	NIII	1P	3	1974	III	16	2
1939	II	22R	3	1975	III	22R	3
1946			2	1976	IV	4P	1
1947	NIII	10	1	1977	III	14	1
1948	NIII	18	2	1978	III	12	1
1949	NIII	11	1	1979	III	23R	2
1950	NIII	5	2	1980	IV	15	2
1951	NIII	4	2	1981	IV	21	2
1952	NIII	11	4	1982	IV	11	1
1953	NIII	12	3	1983	IV	19	3
1954	NIII	14	3	1984	IV	10	1
1955	NIII	19	1	1985	IV	6	2
1956	NIII	16	2	1986	IV	19	2
1957	NIII	23	1	1987	IV	20	2

WALSALL

Founded: 1888 (as Walsall Town Swifts)
Address: Fellows Park, Walsall, Staffordshire
Telephone: Walsall 22791
Ground capacity: 24,100
Playing area: 113 by 73 yards
Record attendance: 25,453 v Newcastle United, Division II, 29.8.61
Record victory: 10–0 v Darwen, Division II, 4.3.1899
Record defeat: 0–12 v Small Heath, Division II, 17.12.1892; 0–12 v Darwen, Division II, 26.12.1896
Most League points (3 for win): 75, Division III, 1983–84; 1985–86
Most League points (2 for win): 65, Division IV, 1958–60
Most League goals: 102, Division IV, 1959–60
League scoring record: 40, Gilbert Alsop, Division III(N), 1933–34 & 1934–35
Record League aggregate: 184, Tony Richards, 1954–63; 184, Colin Taylor, 1958–63, 1964–68, 1969–73
Most League appearances: 467, Colin Harrison, 1964–82
Most capped player: 15 (18 in all), Mick Kearns, Eire

THE WALSALL RECORD

Year	Division and place		Cup round reached	Year	Division and place		Cup round reached
1893*	II	12	p	1960	IV	1P	2
1894*	II	10	p	1961	III	2P	1
1895*	II	14L	q	1962	II	14	4
1896			p	1963	II	21R	3
1897	II	12	p	1964	III	19	1
1898	II	10	1	1965	III	19	1
1899	II	6	p	1966	III	9	4
1900	II	12	1	1967	III	12	3
1901	II	16L	p	1968	III	7	4
1922	NIII	8	1	1969	III	13	3
1923	NIII	3	p	1970	III	12	3
1924	NIII	17	p	1971	III	20	2
1925	NIII	19	p	1972	III	9	4
1926	NIII	21	1	1973	III	17	2
1927	NIII	14	3	1974	III	15	2
1928	SIII	18	1	1975	III	8	5
1929	SIII	14	3	1976	III	7	1
1930	SIII	17	4	1977	III	15	3
1931	SIII	17	3	1978	III	6	5
1932	NIII	16	1	1979	III	22R	1
1933	NIII	5	4	1980	IV	2P	2
1934	NIII	4	2	1981	III	20	2
1935	NIII	14	3	1982	III	20	2
1936	NIII	10	3	1983	III	10	3
1937	SIII	17	4	1984	III	6	1
1938	SIII	21	2	1985	III	11	3
1939	SIII	21	5	1986	III	6	3
1946			1	1987	III	8	5
1947	SIII	5	3				
1948	SIII	3	3				
1949	SIII	14	4				
1950	SIII	19	1				
1951	SIII	15	1				
1952	SIII	24	1				
1953	SIII	24	1				
1954	SIII	24	3				
1955	SIII	23	3				
1956	SIII	20	3				
1957	SIII	15	1				
1958	SIII	20	1				
1959	IV	6	1				

* – as Walsall Town Swifts

WATFORD

Founded: 1891
Address: Vicarage Road, Watford WD1 8ER
Telephone: Watford 49747/8/9
Ground capacity: 28,462
Playing area: 113 by 73 yards
Record attendance: 34,099 v Manchester United, FA Cup 4th round, 3.2.69
Record victory: 10–1 v Lowestoft, FA Cup, 1st round, 27.11.26
Record defeat: 0–10 v Wolverhampton Wanderers, FA Cup 1st round replay, 13.1.12
Most League points (3 for win): 80, Division II, 1981–82
Most League points (2 for win): 71, Division IV, 1977–78
Most League goals: 92, Division IV, 1959–60
League scoring record: 42, Cliff Holton, Division IV, 1959–60
Record League aggregate: 144, Tommy Barnett, 1928–1939
Most League appearances: 411, Duncan Welbourne, 1963–74
Most capped player: 28, John Barnes, England

FA Cup	Year	Opponents	Score
Runners-up	1984	Everton	0–2

THE WATFORD RECORD

	Division and place		Cup round reached		Division and place		Cup round reached
1906			2	1952	SIII	21	2
1907			1	1953	SIII	10	2
1908			1	1954	SIII	4	1
1909			1	1955	SIII	7	3
1910			1	1956	SIII	20	2
1911			1	1957	SIII	11	2
1912			1	1958	SIII	16	1
1913			p	1959	IV	15	2
1914			p	1960	IV	4P	5
1915			p	1961	III	4	3
1920			p	1962	III	17	3
1921	III	6	2	1963	III	17	4
1922	SIII	7	2	1964	III	3	2
1923	SIII	10	1	1965	III	9	1
1924	SIII	20	3	1966	III	12	2
1925	SIII	11	1	1967	III	3	3
1926	SIII	15	2	1968	III	6	3
1927	SIII	21	2	1969	III	1P	4
1928	SIII	15	1	1970	II	19	s-f
1929	SIII	8	4	1971	II	18	4
1930	SIII	15	2	1972	II	22R	3
1931	SIII	18	5	1973	III	19	3
1932	SIII	11	q-f	1974	III	7	2
1933	SIII	11	3	1975	III	23R	1
1934	SIII	15	1	1976	IV	8	1
1935	SIII	6	2	1977	IV	7	3
1936	SIII	5	4	1978	IV	1P	3
1937	SIII	4	1	1979	III	2P	2
1938	SIII	4	3	1980	II	18	q-f
1939	SIII	4	3	1981	II	9	4
1946			4	1982	II	2P	5
1947	SIII	16	2	1983	I	2	5
1948	SIII	15	1	1984	I	11	Final
1949	SIII	17	1	1985	I	11	5
1950	SIII	6	4	1986	I	12	6
1951	SIII	23	1	1987	I	9	s-f

WEST BROMWICH ALBION

Founded: 1879
Address: The Hawthorns, West Bromwich B71 4LF
Telephone: (021) 525 8888
Ground capacity: 39,129 (12,500 seated)
Playing area: 115 by 75 yards
Record attendance: 64,815 v Arsenal, FA Cup quarter-final, 6.3.37
Record victory: 12–0 v Darwen, Division I, 4.4.1892
Record defeat: 3–10 v Stoke City, Division I, 4.2.37
Most League points (3 for win): 57, Division I, 1982–83
Most League points (2 for win): 60, Division I, 1919–20
Most League goals: 105, Division II, 1929–30
League scoring record: 39, William G Robinson, Division I, 1935–36
Record League aggregate: 218, Tony Brown, 1963–79
Most League appearances: 574, Tony Brown, 1963–80
Most capped player: 33 (43 in all), Stuart Williams, Wales

FA Cup	Year	Opponents	Score	Scorers
Winners	1888	Preston North End	2–1	Bayliss, Woodhall
	1892	Aston Villa	3–0	Geddes, Nicholls, Reynolds
	1931	Birmingham City	2–1	W G Richardson 2
	1954	Preston North End	3–2	Allen 2, Griffin
	1968	Everton	1–0	Astle
Runners-up	1886	Blackburn	0–0	
		Replay	0–2	
	1887	Aston Villa	0–2	
	1895	Aston Villa	0–1	
	1912	Barnsley	0–0	
		Replay	0–1	
	1935	Sheffield Wednesday	2–4	Boyes, Sandford
League Cup				
Winners	1966	West Ham United	A1–2	Astle
			H4–1	Kaye, Brown, Clark (C), Williams
Runners-up	1967	Queen's Park Rangers	2–3	Clark (C) 2
	1970	Manchester City	1–2	Astle

THE ALBION RECORD

	Division and place		Cup round reached		Division and place		Cup round reached
1885			q-f	1935	I	9	Final
1886			.Final	1936	I	18	4
1887			Final	1937	I	16	s-f
1888			Winners	1938	I	22R	4
1889	I	6	s-f	1939	II	10	4
1890	I	5	1	1946			4
1891	I	12	s-f	1947	II	7	4
1892	I	12	Winners	1948	II	7	4
1893	I	8	1	1949	II	2P	q-f
1894	I	8	1	1950	I	14	3
1895	I	13	Final	1951	I	16	3
1896	I	16	q-f	1952	I	13	5
1897	I	12	2	1953	I	4	4
1898	I	7	q-f	1954	I	2	Winners
1899	I	14	q-f	1955	I	17	4
1900	I	13	q-f	1956	I	13	5
1901	I	18R	s-f	1957	I	11	s-f
1902	II	1P	1	1958	I	4	q-f
1903	I	7	1	1959	I	5	5
1904	I	18R	1	1960	I	4	5
1905	II	10	p	1961	I	10	3
1906	II	4	1	1962	I	9	5
1907	II	4	s-f	1963	I	14	4
1908	II	5	2	1964	I	10	4
1909	II	3	2	1965	I	14	3
1910	II	11	3	1966	I	6	3
1911	II	1P	2	1967	I	13	4
1912	I	9	Final	1968	I	8	Winners
1913	I	10	1	1969	I	10	s-f
1914	I	5	3	1970	I	16	3
1915	I	11	1	1971	I	17	4
1920	I	1C	1	1972	I	16	3
1921	I	14	1	1973	I	22R	5
1922	I	13	3	1974	II	8	5
1923	I	17	3	1975	II	6	4
1924	I	16	q-f	1976	II	3P	5
1925	I	2	q-f	1977	I	7	3
1926	I	13	3	1978	I	6	s-f
1927	I	22R	3	1979	I	3	5
1928	II	8	3	1980	I	10	3
1929	II	7	q-f	1981	I	4	4
1930	II	6	3	1982	I	17	s-f
1931	II	2P	Winners	1983	I	11	4
1932	I	6	3	1984	I	17	5
1933	I	4	4	1985	I	12	3
1934	I	7	3	1986	I	22R	3
				1987	II	15	3

WEST HAM UNITED

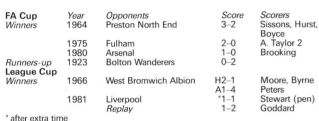

Founded: 1900
Address: Boleyn Ground, Green Street, Upton Park, London E13
Telephone: (01) 472 2740
Ground capacity: 35,500
Playing area: 110 by 72 yards
Record attendance: 42,322 v Tottenham Hotspur, Division I, 17.10.70
Record victory: 10–0 v Bury, League (Milk) Cup 2nd round 2nd leg, 25.10.83
Record defeat: 2–8 v Blackburn Rovers, Division I, 26.12.63
Most League points (3 for win): 84, Division I, 1985–86
Most League points (2 for win): 66, Division II, 1980–81
Most League goals: 101, Division II, 1957–58
League scoring record: 41, Vic Watson, Division I, 1929–30
Record League aggregate: 306, Vic Watson, 1920–1935
Most League appearances: 624, Billy Bonds, 1967–85
Most capped player: 108, Bobby Moore, England

FA Cup	Year	Opponents	Score	Scorers
Winners	1964	Preston North End	3–2	Sissons, Hurst, Boyce
	1975	Fulham	2–0	A. Taylor 2
	1980	Arsenal	1–0	Brooking
Runners-up	1923	Bolton Wanderers	0–2	
League Cup				
Winners	1966	West Bromwich Albion	H2–1	Moore, Byrne
			A1–4	Peters
	1981	Liverpool	*1–1	Stewart (pen)
		Replay	1–2	Goddard

* after extra time

THE HAMMERS RECORD

	Division and place		Cup round reached		Division and place		Cup round reached
1913			2	1955	II	8	3
1914			2	1956	II	16	q-f
1915			1	1957	II	8	4
1920	II	7	3	1958	II	1P	5
1921	II	5	1	1959	I	6	3
1922	II	4	1	1960	I	14	3
1923	II	2P	Final	1961	I	16	3
1924	I	13	2	1962	I	8	3
1925	I	13	3	1963	I	12	q-f
1926	I	18	3	1964	I	14	Winners
1927	I	6	4	1965	I	9	4
1928	I	17	4	1966	I	12	4
1929	I	17	q-f	1967	I	16	3
1930	I	7	q-f	1968	I	12	5
1931	I	18	3	1969	I	8	5
1932	I	22R	4	1970	I	17	3
1933	II	20	s-f	1971	I	20	3
1934	II	7	4	1972	I	14	5
1935	II	3	3	1973	I	6	4
1936	II	4	3	1974	I	18	3
1937	II	6	3	1975	I	13	Winners
1938	II	9	3	1976	I	18	3
1939	II	11	5	1977	I	17	3
1946			4	1978	I	20R	4
1947	II	11	3	1979	II	5	3
1948	II	6	3	1980	II	7	Winners
1949	II	7	3	1981	II	1P	3
1950	II	19	4	1982	I	9	4
1951	II	13	4	1983	I	8	3
1952	II	12	4	1984	I	9	5
1953	II	14	3	1985	I	16	6
1954	II	13	4	1986	I	3	6
				1987	I	15	5

WIGAN ATHLETIC

Founded: 1932
Address: Springfield Park, Wigan
Telephone: Wigan 44433
Ground capacity: 25,000
Playing area: 117 by 73 yards
Record attendance: 27,500 v Hereford, FA Cup 2nd round, 12.12.53
Record victory: 7–2 v Scunthorpe, Division IV, 12.3.82 (away)
Record defeat: 0–5 v Bristol Rovers, Division III, 26.2.83; 0–5 v Chelsea, FA Cup 3rd round replay 26.1.85
Most League points (3 for win): 91, Division IV, 1981–82
Most League points (2 for win): 55, Division IV, 1978–79 and 1979–80
Most League goals: 80, Division IV, 1981–82
League scoring record: 19, Les Bradd, Division IV, 1981–82
Record League aggregate: 62, Peter Houghton, 1978–84
Most League appearances: 296, Colin Methven, 1979–86
Most capped player: None
* Following the disbanding of Wigan Borough in 1931, the first club to resign from the League mid-season. Wigan Athletic were elected to the League at the end of the 1977–78 season.

THE WIGAN RECORD

	Division and place		Cup round reached		Division and place		Cup round reached
1979	IV	6	1	1983	III	18	1
1980	IV	6	4	1984	III	15	3
1981	IV	11	1	1985	III	16	3
1982	IV	3P	1	1986	III	4	4
				1987	III	4	q-f

WIMBLEDON

Founded: 1889
Address: Plough Lane, Durensford Road, Wimbledon, London SW19
Telephone: (01) 946 6311
Ground capacity: 13,500
Playing area: 110 by 85 yards
Record attendance: 18,000 v H.M.S. Victory, FA Amateur Cup, 23.2.35
Record victory: 15–2 v Polytechnic, FA Cup preliminary round, 7.2.29
Record defeat: 0–8 v Everton, League Cup 2nd round, 29.8.78
Most League points (3 for win): 98, Division IV, 1982–93
Most League points (2 for win): 61, Division IV, 1978–79
Most League goals: 97, Division III, 1983–84
League scoring record: 29, Alan Cork, 1983–84
Record League aggregate: 117, Alan Cork, 1977–86
Most League appearances: 266, Alan Cork, 1977–86
Most capped player: None

THE WIMBLEDON RECORD

	Division and place		Cup round reached		Division and place		Cup round reached
1978	IV	13	1	1983	IV	1P	1
1979	IV	3P	3	1984	III	2P	2
1980	III	24R	2	1985	II	12	5
1981	IV	4P	4	1986	II	3P	3
1982	III	21R	2	1987	I	6	q-f

WOLVERHAMPTON WANDERERS

Founded: 1876 (as St Luke's School, Blakenhall)
Address: Molineux, Wolverhampton, WV1 4QR
Telephone: Wolverhampton 712181
Ground capacity: 25,000
Playing area: 115 by 72 yards
Record attendance: 61,315 v Liverpool, FA Cup 5th round, 11.2.39
Record victory: 14–0 v Crosswell's Brewery, FA Cup qualifying rounds, 13.11.1886
Record defeat: 1–10 v Newton Heath, Division I, 15.10.1892
Most League points (3 for win): 75, Division II, 1982–83
Most League points (2 for win): 64, Division I, 1957–58
Most League goals: 115, Division II, 1931–32
League scoring record: 37, Dennis Westcott, Division I, 1946–47
Record League aggregate: 164, Billy Hartill, 1928–1935
Most League appearances: 501, Derek Parkin, 1967–82
Most capped player: 105, Billy Wright, England

FA Cup	Year	Opponents	Score	Scorers
Winners	1893	Everton	1–0	Allen
	1908	Newcastle United	3–1	Hunt, Hedley Harrison
	1949	Leicester City	3–1	Pye 2, Smyth
	1960	Blackburn Rovers	3–0	McGrath (og), Deeley 2
Runners-up	1889	Preston North End	0–3	
	1896	Sheffield Wednesday	1–2	Black
	1921	Tottenham Hotspur	0–1	
	1939	Portsmouth	1–4	Dorsett
League Cup				
Winners	1974	Manchester City	2–1	Hibbit, Richards
	1980	Nottingham Forest	1–0	Gray

THE WOLVES RECORD

Year	Division and place		Cup round reached	Year	Division and place		Cup round reached
1884			2	1935	I	17	4
1885			1	1936	I	15	3
1886			4	1937	I	5	q-f
1887			3	1938	I	2	4
1888			3	1939	I	2	Final
1889	I	3	Final	1946			4
1890	I	4	s-f	1947	I	3	4
1891	I	4	q-f	1948	I	5	4
1892	I	6	q-f	1949	I	6	Winners
1893	I	11	Winners	1950	I	2	5
1894	I	9	1	1951	I	14	s-f
1895	I	11	q-f	1952	I	16	4
1896	I	14	Final	1953	I	3	3
1897	I	10	2	1954	I	1C	3
1898	I	3	2	1955	I	2	q-f
1899	I	8	2	1956	I	3	3
1900	I	4	2	1957	I	6	4
1901	I	13	q-f	1958	I	1C	q-f
1902	I	14	1	1959	I	1C	4
1903	I	11	1	1960	I	2	Winners
1904	I	8	2	1961	I	3	3
1905	I	14	2	1962	I	18	4
1906	I	20R	2	1963	I	5	3
1907	II	6	1	1964	I	16	3
1908	II	9	Winners	1965	I	21R	q-f
1909	II	7	1	1966	II	6	5
1910	II	8	2	1967	II	2P	4
1911	II	9	3	1968	I	17	3
1912	II	5	3	1969	I	16	4
1913	II	10	2	1970	I	13	4
1914	II	9	2	1971	I	4	4
1915	II	4	2	1972	I	9	3
1920	II	19	2	1973	I	5	s-f
1921	II	15	Final	1974	I	12	3
1922	II	17	1	1975	I	12	3
1923	II	22R	2	1976	I	20R	q-f
1924	NIII	1P	3	1977	II	1P	q-f
1925	II	6	1	1978	I	15	4
1926	II	4	3	1979	I	18	s-f
1927	II	15	q-f	1980	I	6	5
1928	II	16	4	1981	I	18	s-f
1929	II	17	3	1982	I	21R	3
1930	II	9	3	1983	II	2P	4
1931	II	4	q-f	1984	I	22R	3
1932	II	1P	4	1985	II	22R	3
1933	I	20	3	1986	III	23R	1
1934	I	15	4	1987	IV	4	1

WREXHAM

Founded: 1873
Address: Racecourse Ground, Mold Road, Wrexham
Telephone: Wrexham (0978) 262129
Ground capacity: 28,500
Playing area: 117 by 75 yards
Record attendance: 34,445 v Manchester United, FA Cup 4th round, 26.1.57
Record victory: 10–1 v Hartlepool
Record defeat: 0–9 v Brentford, Division IV, 3.3.62
Most League points (3 for win): 60, Division IV, 1985–86
Most League points (2 for win): 61, Division IV, 1969–70; 61, Division III, 1977–78
Most League goals: 106, Division III(N), 1932–33
League scoring record: 44, Tom Bamford, Division III(N), 1933–34
Record League aggregate: 175, Tom Bamford, 1928–34
Most League appearances: 592, Arfon Griffiths, 1959–61, 1962–79
Most capped player: 28 (51 in all), Dai Davies, Wales

THE WREXHAM RECORD

Year	Division and place		Cup round reached	Year	Division and place		Cup round reached
1922	NIII	12	2	1958	NIII	12	1
1923	NIII	10	3	1959	III	18	1
1924	NIII	16	2	1960	III	23R	3
1925	NIII	16	q-f	1961	III	16	1
1926	NIII	19	1	1962	IV	3P	3
1927	NIII	13	2	1963	III	9	3
1928	NIII	11	4	1964	III	23R	2
1929	NIII	3	1	1965	IV	14	2
1930	NIII	17	4	1966	IV	24	2
1931	NIII	4	3	1967	IV	7	2
1932	NIII	10	1	1968	IV	8	1
1933	NIII	2	2	1969	IV	9	2
1934	NIII	6	1	1970	IV	2P	4
1935	NIII	18	2	1971	III	9	1
1936	NIII	18	1	1972	III	16	3
1937	NIII	8	3	1973	III	12	2
1938	NIII	10	2	1974	III	4	q-f
1939	NIII	14	1	1975	III	13	1
1946			3	1976	III	6	1
1947	NIII	7	2	1977	III	5	4
1948	NIII	3	2	1978	III	1P	q-f
1949	NIII	9	1	1979	II	15	4
1950	NIII	20	2	1980	II	16	5
1951	NIII	14	2	1981	II	16	5
1952	NIII	18	2	1982	II	21R	4
1953	NIII	3	3	1983	III	22R	2
1954	NIII	8	3	1984	IV	20	1
1955	NIII	18	2	1985	IV	15	1
1956	NIII	14	1	1986	IV	13	2
1957	NIII	12	4	1987	IV	9	3

YORK CITY

Founded: 1922
Address: Bootham Crescent
Telephone: York 24447
Ground capacity: 13,158
Playing area: 115 by 75 yards
Record attendance: 28,123 v Huddersfield Town, FA Cup 5th round, 5.3.38
Record victory: 9–1 v Southport, Division III(N), 2.2.57
Record defeat: 0–12 v Chester, Division III(N), 1.2.36
Most League points (3 for win): 101, Division IV, 1983–84
Most League points (2 for win): 62, Division IV, 1964–65
Most League goals: 96, Division IV, 1983–84
League scoring record: 31, Bill Fenton, Division III(N), 1951–52
31, Alf Bottom, Division III(N), 1955–56
Record League aggregate: 125, Norman Wilkinson, 1954–66
Most League appearances: 481, Barry Jackson, 1958–70
Most capped player: 7 (10 in all), Peter Scott, Northern Ireland

THE YORK RECORD

	Division and place	Cup round reached		Division and place	Cup round reached
1930	NIII 6	3	1962	IV 6	1
1931	NIII 12	3	1963	IV 14	3
1932	NIII 10	1	1964	IV 22	1
1933	NIII 20	1	1965	IV 3P	2
1934	NIII 12	1	1966	III 24R	1
1935	NIII 15	3	1967	IV 22	2
1936	NIII 16	1	1968	IV 21	1
1937	NIII 12	4	1969	IV 21	3
1938	NIII 11	q-f	1970	IV 13	4
1939	NIII 20	3	1971	IV 4	P
1946		4	1972	III 19	2
1947	NIII 15	1	1973	III 18	3
1948	NIII 13	1	1974	III 3P	1
1949	NIII 14	2	1975	II 15	3
1950	NIII 22	1	1976	II 21R	4
1951	NIII 17	3	1977	III 24R	2
1952	NIII 10	1	1978	IV 22	1
1953	NIII 4	1	1979	IV 10	4
1954	NIII 22	1	1980	IV 17	2
1955	NIII 4	s-f	1981	IV 24	1
1956	NIII 11	4	1982	IV 17	2
1957	NIII 7	2	1983	IV 7	3
1958	NIII 13	4	1984	IV 1P	2
1959	IV 3P	1	1985	III 8	5
1960	III 21R	3	1986	III 7	2
1961	IV 5	3	1987	III 20	2

ABERDEEN

Founded: 1903
Address: Pittodrie Stadium, Aberdeen AB2 1QH
Telephone: (0224) 632328/633497
Ground capacity: 22,600 (all seated)
Playing area: 110 by 71 yards
Record attendance: 45,061 v Heart of Midlothian, Scottish Cup 4th round, 13.3.54
Record victory: 13–0 v Peterhead, Scottish Cup 3rd round, 10.2.23
Record defeat: 0–8 v Celtic, Division I, 30.1.65
Most League points: 61, Division I, 1935–36
Most League goals: 96, Division I, 1935–36
League scoring record: 38, Benny Yorston, Division I, 1929–30
Record League aggregate: 160, Harry Yorston, 1950–57
Most capped player: 51, Willie Miller, Scotland

Scottish Cup	Year	Opponents	Score	Scorers
Winners	1947	Hibernian	2–1	Hamilton, Williams
	1970	Celtic	3–1	Harper, McKay 2
	1982	Rangers	*4–1	McLeish, McGhee, Strachan, Cooper
	1983	Rangers	*1–0	Black
	1984	Celtic	2–1	Black, McGhee
	1986	Hearts	3–0	Hewitt 2, Stark
Runners-up	1937	Celtic	1–2	Armstrong
	1953	Rangers	1–1	Yorston
			0–1	
	1954	Celtic	1–2	Buckley
	1959	St Mirren	1–3	Baird
	1967	Celtic	0–2	
	1978	Rangers	1–2	Ritchie
League Cup				
Winners	1946	Rangers	3–2	Baird, Williams, Taylor
	1956	St Mirren	2–1	og, Leggat
	1977	Celtic	2–1	Jarvie, Robb
	1986	Hibernian	3–0	Black 2, Stark
Runners-up	1947	Rangers	0–4	
	1979	Rangers	1–2	Davidson
	1980	Dundee Utd	0–0	
		Replay	0–3	

* after extra time

THE ABERDEEN RECORD

	Division and place	Cup round reached		Division and place	Cup round reached
1906	I 12	2	1954	I 9	Final
1907	I 11	2	1955	I 1C	s-f
1908	I 8	s-f	1956	I 2	5
1909	I 8	2	1957	I 6	6
1910	I 4	3	1958	I 12	q-f
1911	I 2	s-f	1959	I 13	Final
1912	I 9	3	1960	I 15	2
1913	I 8	2	1961	I 6	3
1914	I 14	3	1962	I 12	3
1915	I 14		1963	I 6	q-f
1916	I 11		1964	I 9	3
1917	I 20		1965	I 12	1
1918	†		1966	I 8	s-f
1919	†		1967	I 4	Final
1920	I 17	4	1968	I 5	2
1921	I 11	3	1969	I 15	s-f
1922	I 15	s-f	1970	I 8	Winners
1923	I 5	4	1971	I 2	s-f
1924	I 13	s-f	1972	I 2	q-f
1925	I 15	4	1973	I 4	q-f
1926	I 11	s-f	1974	I 4	3
1927	I 8	2	1975	I 5	q-f
1928	I 7	4	1976	P 7	4
1929	I 7	4	1977	P 3	4
1930	I 3	3	1978	P 2	Final
1931	I 6	q-f	1979	P 4	s-f
1932	I 7	1	1980	P 1C	s-f
1933	I 5	2	1981	P 2	4
1934	I 5	q-f	1982	P 2	Winners
1935	I 6	s-f	1983	P 3	Winners
1936	I 3	q-f	1984	P 1C	Winners
1937	I 2	Final	1985	P 1C	s-f
1938	I 6	3	1986	P 4	Winners
1939	I 3	s-f	1987	P 4	3
1947	I 3	Winners			
1948	I 10	3			
1949	I 13	1			
1950	I 8	q-f			
1951	I 5	q-f			
1952	I 11	q-f			
1953	I 11	Final			

† Aberdeen did not compete

AIRDRIEONIANS

Founded: 1878
Address: Broomfield Park, Airdrie, Lanarkshire
Telephone: Airdrie 62067
Ground capacity: 18,000 (2,000 seated)
Playing area: 112 by 68 yards
Record attendance: 24,000 v Hearts, Scottish Cup 4th round, 8.3.52
Record victory: 15–1 v Dundee Wanderers, Division II, 1.12.1894
Record defeat: 1–11 v Hibernian, Division I, 24.10.59
Most League points: 60, Division II, 1973–74
Most League goals: 107, Division II, 1965–66
League scoring record: 45, H. G. Yarnell, Division I, 1916–17
Most capped player: 9, Jimmy Crapnell, Scotland

Scottish Cup	Year	Opponents		Score	Scorers
Winners	1924	Hibernian		2–0	Russell 2
Runners-up	1975	Celtic		1–3	McCann

THE AIRDRIEONIANS RECORD

	Division and place	Cup round reached		Division and place	Cup round reached
1895	II 6	1	1938	II 3	1
1896	II 5	p	1939	II 4	2
1897	II 4	p	1947	II 2P	1
1898	II 8	p	1948	I 15R	q-f
1899	II 6	1	1949	II 3	1
1900	II 9	1	1950	II 2P	1
1901	II 2	1	1951	I 14	q-f
1902	II 4	1	1952	I 13	q-f
1903	II 1P	1	1953	I 14	3
1904	I 12	1	1954	I 15R	1
1905	I 4	s-f	1955	II 1P	s-f
1906	I 3	3	1956	I 5	q-f
1907	I 4	1	1957	I 11	q-f
1908	I 6	1	1958	I 16	1
1909	I 5	3	1959	I 5	2
1910	I 9	2	1960	I 16	3
1911	I 11	2	1961	I 13	s-f
1912	I 10	2	1962	I 15	1
1913	I 4	3	1963	I 11	2
1914	I 6	3	1964	I 15	3
1915	I 10		1965	I 17R	2
1916	I 15		1966	II 2P	1
1917	I 4		1967	I 13	2
1918	I 15		1968	I 13	q-f
1919	I 13		1969	I 7	q-f
1920	I 7	1	1970	I 12	2
1921	I 10	1	1971	I 10	s-f
1922	I 16	3	1972	I 15	4
1923	I 2	2	1973	I 18R	q-f
1924	I 2	Winners	1974	II 1P	3
1925	I 2	3	1975	I 11	Final
1926	I 2	q-f	1976	I 7	3
1927	I 4	2	1977	I 6	3
1928	I 13	3	1978	I 10	3
1929	I 15	3	1979	I 6	4
1930	I 12	3	1980	I 2P	4
1931	I 9	2	1981	P 7	3
1932	I 14	s-f	1982	P 10R	3
1933	I 18	2	1983	I 5	q-f
1934	I 18	1	1984	I 10	4
1935	I 14	q-f	1985	I 5	3
1936	I 19R	2	1986	I 9	4
1937	II 4	2	1987	I 5	3

ALBION ROVERS

Founded: 1881
Address: Cliftonhill Park, Coatbridge, Lanarkshire
Telephone: Coatbridge 32350
Ground capacity: 9,000 (580 seated)
Record attendance: 27,381 v Rangers, Scottish Cup 2nd round, 8.2.36
Record victory: 12–0 v Airdriehill, Scottish Cup 1st round, 3.9.1887
Record defeat: 1–9 v Motherwell, Division I, 2.1.37
Most League points: 54, Division II, 1929–30
Most League goals: 101, Division II, 1929–30
League scoring record: 41, Jim Renwick, Division II, 1932–33
Most capped player: 1 (2 in all), Jock White, Scotland

Scottish Cup	Year	Opponents		Score	Scorers
Runners-up	1920	Kilmarnock		2–3	Watson, Hillhouse

THE ALBION ROVERS RECORD

	Division and place	Cup round reached		Division and place	Cup round reached
1904	II 9	2	1954	II 7	2
1905	II 8	p	1955	II 11	5
1906	II 3	p	1956	II 17	4
1907	II 6	p	1957	II 5	4
1908	II 9	1	1958	II 17	2
1909	II 10	1	1959	II 10	1
1910	II 9	p	1960	II 10	2
1911	II 3	p	1961	II 17	1
1912	II 11	p	1962	II 18	2
1913	II 9	p	1963	II 7	1
1914	II 2	1	1964	II 9	3
1915	II 9		1965	II 11	p
1916			1966	II 7	1
1917			1967	II 8	p
1918			1968	II 8	p
1919			1969	II 7	3
1920	*I 22	Final	1970	II 11	1
1921	I 17	s-f	1971	II 7	3
1922	I 11	2	1972	II 18	3
1923	I 19R	1	1973	II 18	1
1924	II 5	1	1974	II 17	2
1925	II 15	1	1975	II 12	4
1926	II 9	3	1976	II 9	3
1927	II 16	1	1977	II 6	4
1928	II 8	4	1978	II 8	3
1929	II 4	3	1979	II 7	1
1930	II 3	3	1980	II 4	1
1931	II 9	2	1981	II 12	2
1932	II 16	2	1982	II 11	3
1933	II 5	q-f	1983	II 10	4
1934	II 1P	q-f	1984	II 14	1
1935	I 16	2	1985	II 9	1
1936	I 5	q-f	1986	II 13	2
1937	I 20R	2	1987	II 8	3
1938	II 2P	3			
1939	I 16R	1			
1947	II 4	3			
1948	II 2P	1			
1949	II 16R	2			
1950	II 11	2			
1951	II 8	2			
1952	II 14	3			
1953	II 16	3			

* Elected to First Division in 1919

ALLOA ATHLETIC

Founded: 1878
Address: Recreation Ground, Alloa, Clackmannanshire
Telephone: Alloa 722695
Ground capacity: 8,600
Playing area: 110 by 75 yards
Record attendance: 12,800 v Dunfermline, Scottish Cup 3rd round replay, 22.2.39
Record victory: 9–2 v Forfar Athletic, Division II, 18.3.33
Record defeat: 0–10 v Dundee, Division II, 8.3.47; 0–10 v Third Lanark, League Cup, 8.8.53
Most League points: 60, Division II, 1921–22
Most League goals: 92, Division II, 1961–62
League scoring record: 49, Wee Crilley, Division II, 1921–22
Most capped player: 1, Jock Hepburn, Scotland

THE ALLOA RECORD

	Division and place		Cup round reached		Division and place		Cup round reached
1920			2	1958	II	8	1
1921			3	1959	II	13	3
1922	II	1P	3	1960	II	13	2
1923	I	20R	1	1961	II	11	q-f
1924	II	16	2	1962	II	4	2
1925	II	4	2	1963	II	9	2
1926	II	16	2	1964	II	16	2
1927	II	15	3	1965	II	10	p
1928	II	15	3	1966	II	8	1
1929	II	13	1	1967	II	13	1
1930	II	19	1	1968	II	17	1
1931	II	13	2	1969	II	18	p
1932	II	13	1	1970	II	6	p
1933	II	11	1	1971	II	16	3
1934	II	15	2	1972	II	16	3
1935	II	10	1	1973	II	12	2
1936	II	4	1	1974	II	12	2
1937	II	9	1	1975	II	15	2
1938	II	11	1	1976	II	3	3
1939	II	2	q-f	1977	II	2P	4
1947	II	5	1	1978	I	13R	3
1948	II	12	2	1979	II	6	3
1949	II	14	2	1980	II	14	3
1950	II	16	1	1981	II	6	1
1951	II	16	1	1982	II	2P	4
1952	II	7	2	1983	I	6	3
1953	II	9	2	1984	I	14R	3
1954	II	11	1	1985	II	2P	3
1955	II	15	5	1986	I	14R	4
1956	II	13	5	1987	II	6	1
1957	II	15	5				

ARBROATH

Founded: 1878
Address: Gayfield Park
Telephone: (02414) 72157
Ground capacity: 10,000
Record attendance: 13,510 v Rangers, Scottish Cup 3rd round, 23.2.52
Record victory: 36–0 v Bon Accord, Scottish Cup 1st round, 12.9.85
Record defeat: 0–8 v Kilmarnock, Division II, 3.1.49
Most League points: 57, Division II, 1966–67
Most League goals: 87, Division II, 1967–68
League scoring record: 45, Dave Easson, Division II, 1958–59
Record League aggregate: 120, Jimmy Jack, 1966–71
Most League appearances: 319, Ian Stirling, 1960–71
Most capped player: 2 (5 in all), Ned Doig, Scotland

THE ARBROATH RECORD

	Division and place		Cup round reached		Division and place		Cup round reached
1922	II	16	1	1958	II	3	2
1923	II	20	1	1959	II	2P	2
1924	II	17	2	1960	I	18R	2
1925	II	5	3	1961	II	12	2
1926	II	10	2	1962	II	6	2
1927	II	19	1	1963	II	6	2
1928	II	10	1	1964	II	3	2
1929	II	3	3	1965	II	7	1
1930	II	9	2	1966	II	6	p
1931	II	15	3	1967	II	3	1
1932	II	11	2	1968	II	2P	2
1933	II	10	1	1969	I	18R	1
1934	II	3	2	1970	II	5	1
1935	II	2P	1	1971	II	3	3
1936	I	12	1	1972	II	2P	3
1937	I	14	2	1973	I	15	3
1938	I	11	1	1974	I	13	4
1939	I	17R	1	1975	I	18	q-f
1947	II	12	s-f	1976	I	5	3
1948	II	13	2	1977	I	8	q-f
1949	II	7	1	1978	I	9	3
1950	II	14	1	1979	I	10	3
1951	II	13	1	1980	I	13R	3
1952	II	16	3	1981	II	9	3
1953	II	7	1	1982	II	3	1
1954	II	14	2	1983	II	3	2
1955	II	12	5	1984	II	5	2
1956	II	18	5	1985	II	14	1
1957	II	10	5	1986	II	8	4
				1987	II	11	1

AYR UNITED

Founded: 1910
Address: Somerset Park, Ayr
Telephone: (0292) 263435
Ground capacity: 18,500 (1,500 seated)
Playing area: 111 by 75 yards
Record attendance: 25,225 v Rangers, Division I, 13.9.69
Record victory: 11–1 v Dumbarton, League Cup, 13.8.52
Record defeat: 0–9 v Rangers, Division I, 16.11.29; 0–9 v Hearts, Division I, Division I, 28.2.31
Most League points: 60, Division II, 1959–60
Most League goals: 122, Division II, 1936–37
League scoring record: 66, J. Smith, Division II, 1927–28
Most capped player: 3, Jim Nisbet, Scotland

THE AYR RECORD

	Division and place	Cup round reached		Division and place	Cup round reached
1899*	II 8	p	1952	II 3	1
1900*	II 8	p	1953	II 5	3
1901*	II 6	2	1954	II 9	2
1902*	II 8	1	1955	II 8	5
1903*	II 3	2	1956	II 2P	6
1904*	II 3	1	1957	I 18R	2
1905*	II 5	1	1958	II 5	1
1906*	II 7	p	1959	II 1P	3
1907*	II 8	2	1960	I 8	q-f
1908*	II 3	p	1961	I 18R	2
1909*	II 5	1	1962	II 9	1
1910*	II 7	2	1963	II 13	2
1911	II 2	p	1964	II 14	q-f
1912	II 1	1	1965	II 18	1
1913	II 1P	2	1966	II 1P	1
1914	I 10	1	1967	I 18R	1
1915	I 5		1968	II 5	1
1916	I 4		1969	II 2P	2
1917	I 15		1970	I 14	1
1918	I 18		1971	I 14	3
1919	I 7		1972	I 12	4
1920	I 10	3	1973	I 6	s-f
1921	I 14	3	1974	I 7	q-f
1922	I 14	2	1975	I 7	3
1923	I 10	3	1976	P 6	4
1924	I 14	q-f	1977	P 8	4
1925	I 19R	2	1978	P 9R	3
1926	II 3	1	1979	I 4	4
1927	II 8	1	1980	I 3	4
1928	II 1P	2	1981	I 6	3
1929	I 16	2	1982	I 6	3
1930	I 9	2	1983	I 12	3
1931	I 18	3	1984	I 12	3
1932	I 17	1	1985	I 7	4
1933	I 16	2	1986	I 13R	4
1934	I 8	2	1987	II 4	3
1935	I 18	2			
1936	I 20R	1			
1937	II 1P	1			
1938	I 17	q-f			
1939	I 14	1			
1947	II 11	2			
1948	II 10	1			
1949	II 9	2			
1950	II 13	1			
1951	II 3	q-f			

* Ayr FC (combined with Ayr Parkhouse in 1910)

BERWICK RANGERS

Founded: 1881
Address: Shielfield Park, Tweedmouth, Berwick-on-Tweed, Northumberland, England
Telephone: (0289) 7424/2554
Ground capacity: 10,673 (1,473 seated)
Playing area: 112 by 76 yards
Record attendance: 13,365 v Rangers, Scottish Cup 1st round, 28.1.67
Record victory: 8–1 v Forfar, Division II, 25.12.65; 8–1 v Vale of Leithen, Scottish Cup Preliminary round, 30.9.67
Record defeat: 1–9 v Dundee Utd, Division II, 21.4.56; 1–9 v Hamilton, Division I, 2.8.80
Most League points: 54, Division II, 1978–79
Most League goals: 83, Division II, 1961–62
League scoring record: 38, Ken Bowron, Division II, 1963–64
Record League aggregate: 106, Eric Tait, 1970–85
Most League appearances: 393, Eric Tait, 1970–86

THE BERWICK RECORD

	Division and place	Cup round reached		Division and place	Cup round reached
1956	II 14	1	1972	II 13	2
1957	II 18	1	1973	II 9	3
1958	II 19	1	1974	II 6	1
1959	II 10	1	1975	II 10	3
1960	II 9	1	1976	II 11	1
1961	II 11	1	1977	II 8	1
1962	II 8	1	1978	II 4	3
1963	II 17	1	1979	II 1P	q-f
1964	II 12	1	1980	I 12	q-f
1965	II 8	1	1981	I 14R	3
1966	II 11	1	1982	II 4	2
1967	II 10	2	1983	II 9	3
1968	II 14	1	1984	II 3	3
1969	II 16	1	1985	II 13	2
1970	II 9	1	1986	II 12	3
1971	II 13	2	1987	II 14	3

BRECHIN CITY

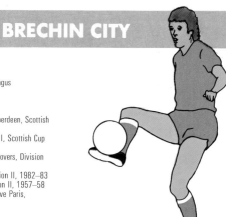

Founded: 1906
Address: Glebe Park, Brechin, Angus
Telephone: Brechin 2856
Ground capacity: 7,291
Playing area: 110 by 67 yards
Record attendance: 8,123 v Aberdeen, Scottish Cup 3rd round, 3.2.73
Record victory: 12–1 v Thornhill, Scottish Cup 1st round, 28.1.26
Record defeat: 0–10 v Albion Rovers, Division II, 25.1.38
Most League points: 55, Division II, 1982–83
Most League goals: 80, Division II, 1957–58
League scoring record: 51, Dave Paris, 1948–49
Most capped player: None

THE BRECHIN RECORD

	Division and place	Cup round reached		Division and place	Cup round reached
1924		1	1960	II 12	1
1925		1	1961	II 14	3
1926		3	1962	II 19	2
1927		2	1963	II 19	2
1928		2	1964	II 15	2
1929		2	1965	II 19	p
1930	II 20	1	1966	II 16	p
1931	II 16	1	1967	II 20	1
1932	II 19	1	1968	II 16	1
1933	II 15	1	1969	II 17	p
1934	II 14	2	1970	II 14	p
1935	II 15	3	1971	II 19	3
1936	II 16	1	1972	II 15	2
1937	II 16	1	1973	II 19	3
1938	II 18	1	1974	II 19	3
1939	II 10	1	1975	II 17	1
1947	*	p	1976	II 13	2
1948	*	p	1977	II 13	3
1949	*	p	1978	II 14	3
1950	*	1	1979	II 11	2
1951	*	2	1980	II 7	3
1952	*	1	1981	II 4	3
1953	*	1	1982	II 5	3
1954	*	2	1983	II 1P	2
1955	II 16	4	1984	I 5	3
1956	II 6	6	1985	I 9	4
1957	II 6	5	1986	I 10	3
1958	II 7	1	1987	I 11R	4
1959	II 5	2			

* Brechin competed in Division C

CELTIC

Founded: 1888
Address: Celtic Park (Parkhead), Glasgow SE
Telephone: (041) 554 2710
Ground capacity: 67,500 (9,000 seated)
Playing area: 115 by 75 yards
Record attendance: 92,000 v Rangers, Division I, 1.1.38
Record victory: 11–0 v Dundee, Division I, 26.10.1895
Record defeat: 0–8 v Motherwell, Division I, 30.4.37
Most League points: 67, Division I, 1915–16 & 1921–22
Most League goals: 116, Division I, 1935–36
League scoring record: 50, Jimmy McGrory, Division I, 1935–36
Record League aggregate: 397, Jimmy McGrory, 1922–23 & 1924–1938
Most League appearances: 486, Billy McNeill, 1958–75
Most capped player: 62, Danny McGrain, Scotland

Scottish Cup

	Year	Opponents	Score	Scorers
Winners	1892	Queen's Park	†5–1	Campbell 2, McMahon 2, og
	1899	Rangers	2–0	Hodge, McMahon
	1900	Queen's Park	4–3	Divers 3, McMahon
	1904	Rangers	3–2	Quinn 3
	1907	Heart of Midlothian	3–0	Orr (pen), Somers 2
	1908	St Mirren	5–1	Bennett 2, Quinn, Hamilton, Somers
	1911	Hamilton Athletic	0–0	
			2–0	Quinn, McAtee
	1912	Clyde	2–0	McMenemy, Gallagher
	1914	Hibernian	0–0	
			4–1	McColl 2, Browning, McAtee
	1923	Hibernian	1–0	Cassidy
	1925	Dundee	2–1	Gallagher, McGrory
	1927	East Fife	3–1	McLean, Connelly, og
	1931	Motherwell	2–2	McGrory, Craig
			4–2	Thomson 2, McGrory 2
	1933	Motherwell	1–0	McGrory
	1937	Aberdeen	2–1	Crum, Buchan
	1951	Motherwell	1–0	McPhail
	1954	Aberdeen	2–1	Fallon, og
	1965	Dunfermline Athletic	3–2	Auld 2, McNeill
	1967	Aberdeen	2–0	Wallace 2
	1969	Rangers	4–0	McNeill, Lennox, Connelly, Chalmers
	1971	Rangers	1–1	Lennox
			2–1	Macari, Hood (pen)
	1972	Hibernian	6–1	McNeill, Deans 3, Macari 2
	1974	Dundee United	3–0	Hood, Murray, Deans
	1975	Airdrieonians	3–1	Wilson 2, McCluskey (pen)
	1977	Rangers	1–0	Lynch (pen)
	1980	Rangers	1–0	McCluskey
	1985	Dundee United	2–1	Provan, McGarvey
Runners-up	1889	Third Lanark	1–2	McCallum
	1893	Queen's Park	1–2	Blessington
	1894	Rangers	1–3	Maley
	1901	Heart of Midlothian	3–4	McOustra 2, McMahon
	1902	Hibernian	0–1	
	1909	Rangers	2–2	
			1–1	
	1926	St Mirren	0–2	
	1928	Rangers	0–4	
	1955	Clyde	1–1	Walsh
			0–1	
	1956	Heart of Midlothian	1–3	Haughney
	1961	Dunfermline Athletic	0–0	
			0–2	
	1963	Rangers	1–1	Murdoch
			0–3	
	1966	Rangers	0–0	
			0–1	
	1970	Aberdeen	1–3	Lennox
	1973	Rangers	2–3	Dalglish, Connelly (pen)
	1984	Aberdeen	1–2	P. McStay

League Cup

Winners	1957	Partick Thistle	0–0	
			3–0	McPhail 2, Collins
	1958	Rangers	7–1	Wilson, Mochan 2, McPhail 3, Fernie
	1966	Rangers	2–1	Hughes (2 pen)
	1967	Rangers	1–0	Lennox
	1968	Dundee	5–3	Chalmers 2, Wallace, Lennox, Hughes
	1969	Hibernian	6–2	Wallace, Auld, Lennox 3, Craig
	1970	St Johnstone	1–0	Auld
	1975	Hibernian	6–3	Deans 3, Johnstone, Wilson, Murray
	1983	Rangers	2–1	Nicholas, McLeod
Runners-up	1965	Rangers	1–2	Johnstone
	1971	Rangers	0–1	
	1972	Partick Thistle	1–4	Dalglish
	1973	Hibernian	1–2	Dalglish
	1974	Dundee	0–1	
	1976	Rangers	0–1	
	1977	Aberdeen	1–2	Dalglish
	1978	Rangers	1–2	Edvaldsson
	1984	Rangers	*2–3	McClair, Reid (pen)

* after extra time
† replay after first game disrupted by crowd with Celtic leading 1–0

THE CELTIC RECORD

Year	Division and place	Cup round reached	Year	Division and place	Cup round reached
1889		Final	1936	I 1C	2
1890		1	1937	I 3	Winners
1891	I 3	s-f	1938	I 1C	3
1892	I 2	Winners	1939	I 2	4
1893	I 1C	Final	1947	I 7	1
1894	I 1C	Final	1948	I 12	s-f
1895	I 3	3	1949	I 6	1
1896	I 1C	1	1950	I 4	3
1897	I 4	1	1951	I 7	Winners
1898	I 1C	2	1952	I 9	1
1899	I 2	Winners	1953	I 8	4
1900	I 2	Winners	1954	I 1C	Winners
1901	I 2	Final	1955	I 2	Final
1902	I 2	Final	1956	I 5	Final
1903	I 5	3	1957	I 5	s-f
1904	I 3	Winners	1958	I 3	3
1905	I 1C	4	1959	I 6	s-f
1906	I 1C	3	1960	I 9	s-f
1907	I 1C	Winners	1961	I 4	Final
1908	I 1C	Winners	1962	I 3	s-f
1909	I 1C	Final	1963	I 4	Final
1910	I 1C	4	1964	I 3	4
1911	I 5	Winners	1965	I 8	Winners
1912	I 2	Winners	1966	I 1C	Final
1913	I 2	3	1967	I 1C	Winners
1914	I 1C	Winners	1968	I 1C	1
1915	I 1C		1969	I 1C	Winners
1916	I 1C		1970	I 1C	Final
1917	I 1C		1971	I 1C	Winners
1918	I 2		1972	I 1C	Winners
1919	I 1C		1973	I 1C	Final
1920	I 2	3	1974	I 1C	Winners
1921	I 2	3	1975	I 3	Winners
1922	I 1C	3	1976	P 2	3
1923	I 3	Winners	1977	P 1C	Winners
1924	I 3	1	1978	P 5	4
1925	I 4	Winners	1979	P 1C	q-f
1926	I 1C	Final	1980	P 2	Winners
1927	I 3	Winners	1981	P 1C	s-f
1928	I 2	Final	1982	P 1C	4
1929	I 2	s-f	1983	P 2	s-f
1930	I 4	3	1984	P 2	Final
1931	I 2	Winners	1985	P 2	Winners
1932	I 3	3	1986	P 1C	q-f
1933	I 4	Winners	1987	P 2	4
1934	I 3	4			
1935	I 2	4			

CLYDE

Founded: 1878
Address: Shawfield Park, Glasgow C5
Telephone: (041) 647 6329
Ground capacity: 22,000 (3,500 seated)
Playing area: 110 by 70 yards
Record attendance: 52,000 v Rangers, Division I, 21.11.08
Record victory: 11–1 v Cowdenbeath, Division II, 6.10.51
Record defeat: 0–11 v Rangers, Scottish Cup 4th round, 13.11.1880; 0–11 v Dumbarton, Scottish Cup 4th round, 22.11.1879
Most League points: 64, Division II, 1956–57
Most League goals: 122, Division II, 1956–57
League scoring record: 32, Bill Boyd, Division I, 1932–33
Most capped player: 12, Tommy Ring, Scotland

Scottish Cup	Year	Opponents	Score	Scorers
Winners	1939	Motherwell	4–0	Martin 2, Wallace, Noble
	1955	Celtic	1–1	Robertson
		Replay	1–0	Ring
	1958	Hibernian	1–0	Coyle
Runners-up	1910	Dundee	2–2	Chalmers, Booth
		First replay	0–0	
		Second replay	1–2	Chalmers
	1912	Celtic	0–2	
	1949	Rangers	1–4	Galletly

THE CLYDE RECORD

	Division and place	Cup round reached		Division and place	Cup round reached
1892	I 7	p	1936	I 18	s-f
1893	I 10	1	1937	I 10	s-f
1894	II 3P	3	1938	I 15	1
1895	I 7	3	1939	I 9	Winners
1896	I 9	2	1947	I 10	1
1897	I 9	1	1948	I 6	3
1898	I 10	1	1949	I 14	Final
1899	I 8	3	1950	I 13	2
1900	I 10R	2	1951	I 15R	3
1901	II 4	2	1952	II 1P	2
1902	II 12	p	1953	I 5	q-f
1903	II 12	1	1954	I 8	2
1904	II 2	1	1955	I 7	Winners
1905	II 1	1	1956	I 17R	s-f
1906	II 2P	1	1957	II 1P	q-f
1907	I 8	1	1958	I 4	Winners
1908	I 17	p	1959	I 15	2
1909	I 3	s-f	1960	I 6	s-f
1910	I 5	Final	1961	I 17R	1
1911	I 7	q-f	1962	II 1P	2
1912	I 3	Final	1963	I 17R	2
1913	I 9	s-f	1964	II 2P	2
1914	I 9	2	1965	I 7	1
1915	I 17		1966	I 11	1
1916	I 16		1967	I 3	s-f
1917	I 13		1968	I 8	2
1918	I 17		1969	I 13	2
1919	I 17		1970	I 16	1
1920	I 16	1	1971	I 15	4
1921	I 7	2	1972	I 17R	3
1922	I 10	3	1973	II 1P	3
1923	I 16	1	1974	I 15	3
1924	I 19R	3	1975	I 16	3
1925	II 3	2	1976	I 14R	3
1926	II 2P	3	1977	II 7	3
1927	I 17	3	1978	II 1P	1
1928	I 15	1	1979	I 9	3
1929	I 17	3	1980	I 14R	3
1930	I 11	2	1981	II 8	3
1931	I 12	2	1982	II 1P	3
1932	I 13	q-f	1983	I 10	4
1933	I 12	s-f	1984	I 8	4
1934	I 14	1	1985	I 8	3
1935	I 10	2	1986	I 11	3
			1987	I 9	3

CLYDEBANK

Founded: 1965 (new club)
Address: New Kilbowie Park, Clydebank
Telephone: (041) 952 2887
Ground capacity: 9,000 (all seated)
Playing area: 110 by 68 yards
Record attendance: 14,900 v Hibernian, Scottish Cup 1st round, 10.2.65
Record victory: 8–1 v Arbroath, Division I, 3.1.77
Record defeat: 1–9 v Galafairydean, Scottish Cup, qualifying round, 15.9.65
Most League points: 58, Division I, 1976–77
Most League goals: 78, Division I, 1978–79
League scoring record: 28, Blair Miller, Division I, 1978–79

THE CLYDEBANK RECORD

	Division and place	Cup round reached		Division and place	Cup round reached
1918	I 9		1980	I 9	3
1919	I 10		1981	I 10	q-f
1920	I 5		1982	I 4	4
1921	I 20		1983	I 3	3
1922	I 22R		1984	I 4	4
1923	II 2P		1985	I 2P	3
1924	I 20R		1986	P 10	3
1925	II 2P		1987	P 11R	q-f
1926	I 20R				
1927	II 3				
1928	II 14				
1929	II 16				
1930	II 18				
1931*	II 15				
1965†	II 5	1			
1966‡		p			
1967§	II 18	p			
1968	II 9	p			
1969	II 13	p			
1970	II 13	2			
1971	II 5	3			
1972	II 9	4			
1973	II 17	1			
1974	II 10	3			
1975	II 7	4			
1976	II 1P	2			
1977	I 2P	4			
1978	P 10R	3			
1979	I 3	4			

* Old Clydebank disbanded
† East Stirlingshire Clydebank
‡ Clydebank juniors
§ Clydebank

Founded: 1881
Address: Central Park, Cowdenbeath, Fife
Telephone: Cowdenbeath 511205
Ground capacity: 10,000
Playing area: 110 by 75 yards
Record attendance: 25,586 v Rangers, League Cup quarter-final, 21.9.49
Record victory: 12–0 v St Johnstone, Scottish Cup 1st round, 21.1.28
Record defeat: 1–11 v Clyde, Division II, 6.10.51
Most League points: 60, Division II, 1938–39
Most League goals: 120, Division II, 1938–39
League scoring record: 40, Willie Devlin, 1925–26
Most capped player: 3, Jim Paterson, Scotland

THE COWDENBEATH RECORD

Year	Division and place	Cup round reached	Year	Division and place	Cup round reached
1906	II 9	p	1950	II 5	2
1907	II 7	1	1951	II 11	1
1908	II 12	p	1952	II 8	2
1909	II 11	p	1953	II 13	2
1910	II 11	p	1954	II 13	2
1911	II 5	p	1955	II 14	2
1912	II 4	p	1956	II 7	5
1913	II 5	p	1957	II 3	4
1914	II 1	p	1958	II 6	1
1915	II 1		1959	II 14	1
1916			1960	II 19	3
1917			1961	II 8	2
1918			1962	II 14	1
1919			1963	II 8	2
1920		1	1964	II 17	1
1921		p	1965	II 12	1
1922	II 2	2	1966	II 10	2
1923	II 11	2	1967	II 6	1
1924	II 2P	2	1968	II 12	1
1925	I 5	1	1969	II 12	1
1926	I 7	1	1970	II 2P	p
1927	I 7	2	1971	I 18R	4
1928	I 9	2	1972	II 5	3
1929	I 13	2	1973	II 7	3
1930	I 16	2	1974	II 13	3
1931	I 7	q-f	1975	II 19	2
1932	I 12	2	1976	II 5	4
1933	I 17	1	1977	II 12	1
1934	I 20R	3	1978	II 10	3
1935	II 12	1	1979	II 5	2
1936	II 10	3	1980	II 8	3
1937	II 6	3	1981	II 3	4
1938	II 6	2	1982	II 9	2
1939	II 1	2	1983	II 8	1
1947	II 14	3	1984	II 13	3
1948	II 5	2	1985	II 4	3
1949	II 13	2	1986	II 10	1
			1987	II 7	1

Founded: 1872 (as Dumbarton Athletic)
Address: Boghead Park, Dumbarton, Strathclyde
Telephone: Dumbarton 62569
Ground capacity: 18,000
Record attendance: 18,000 v Raith Rovers, Scottish Cup quarter-final, 2.3.57
Record victory: 13–1 v Kirkintilloch Central, Scottish Cup 1st round, 1.9.1888
Record defeat: 1–11 v Albion Rover, Division II, 30.1.26; 1–11 v Ayr United, League Cup, 13.8.52
Most League points: 52, Division II, 1971–72
Most League goals: 101, Division II, 1056–57
League scoring record: 38, Kenny Wilson, Division II, 1971–72
Most capped player: 8, John Lindsay, Scotland; 8, James McAulay, Scotland

Scottish Cup	Year	Opponents	Score	Scorers
Winners	1883	Vale of Leven	2–2	
		Replay	2–1	
Runners-up	1881	Queen's Park	1–3	
	1882	Queen's Park	2–2	
		Replay	1–4	
	1887	Hibernian	1–2	
	1891	Hearts	0–1	
	1897	Rangers	1–5	

THE DUMBARTON RECORD

Year	Division and place	Cup round reached	Year	Division and place	Cup round reached
1891	I 1C†	Final	1950	II 15	2
1892	I 1C	3	1951	II 9	1
1893	I 7	2	1952	II 10	3
1894	I 5	2	1953	II 10	1
1895	I 10	2	1954	II 16L	1
1896	I 10R	1	1955	*	4
1897	II 10	Final	1956	II 4	4
1898	*	1	1957	II 9	q-f
1899	*	1	1958	II 4	1
1900	*	p	1959	II 4	2
1901	*	p	1960	II 6	1
1902	*	p	1961	II 10	2
1903	*	p	1962	II 17	1
1904	*	p	1963	II 12	1
1905	*	p	1964	II 6	2
1906	*	p	1965	II 14	1
1907	II 4	p	1966	II 12	q-f
1908	II 2	p	1967	II 14	1
1909	II 4	p	1968	II 10	p
1910	II 4	1	1969	II 14	1
1911	II 1	p	1970	II 7	1
1912	II 3	1	1971	II 4	2
1913	II 6E	q-f	1972	II 1P	4
1914	I 19	2	1973	I 16	4
1915	I 13		1974	I 10	3
1916	I 9		1975	I 14	q-f
1917	I 10		1976	I 4	s-f
1918	I 8		1977	I 7	3
1919	I 15		1978	I 4	q-f
1920	I 11	1	1979	I 7	q-f
1921	I 21	4	1980	I 4	3
1922	I 20R	1	1981	I 8	4
1923	II 4	1	1982	I 11	4
1924	II 10	1	1983	I 7	3
1925	II 8	2	1984	I 2P	4
1926	II 11	q-f	1985	P 9R	3
1927	II 18	2	1986	I 6	3
1928	II 11	1	1987	I 3	3
1929	II 14	3			
1930	II 16	1			
1931	II 10	1			
1932	II 12	1			
1933	II 9	2			
1934	II 6	1			
1935	II 16	2			
1936	II 18	3			
1937	II 15	2			
1938	II 7	1			
1939	II 11	1			
1947	II 13	q-f			
1948	II 11	3			
1949	II 15	3			

†shared jointly with Rangers
* not members of League
E – elected to First Division

Founded: 1893
Address: Dens Park, Dundee, Angus
Telephone: Dundee 826104
Ground capacity: 22,381 (12,130 seated)
Playing area: 110 by 75 yards
Record attendance: 43,024 v Rangers, Scottish Cup 2nd round, 7.2.53
Record victory: 10–0 v Alloa Athletic, Division II, 8.3.47; 10–0 v Dunfermline Athletic, Division II, 22.3.47
Record defeat: 0–11 v Celtic, Division I, 26.10.1895
Most League points: 55, Division I, 1978–79
Most League goals: 113, Division II, 1946–47
League scoring record: 38, David Halliday, Division I, 1923–24
Record League aggregate: 111, Alan Gilzean, 1960–64
Most League appearances: 341, Doug Cowie, 1947–61
Most capped player: 24, Alex Hamilton, Scotland

Scottish Cup	Year	Opponents	Score	Scorers
Winners	1910	Clyde	2–2	Hunter, Langlands
		First replay	0–0	
		Second replay	2–1	Bellamy, Hunter
Runners-up	1925	Celtic	1–2	McLean (D)
	1952	Motherwell	0–4	
	1964	Rangers	1–3	Cameron
League Cup				
Winners	1952	Rangers	3–2	Flavell, Pattillo, Boyd
	1953	Kilmarnock	2–0	Flavell 2
	1974	Celtic	1–0	Wallace
Runners-up	1968	Celtic	3–5	McLean (G) 2, McLean (J)
	1981	Dundee United	0–3	

THE DUNDEE RECORD

	Division and place		Cup round reached
1894	I	8	p
1895	I	8	s-f
1896	I	5	2
1897	I	5	q-f
1898	I	7	s-f
1899	I	10	1
1900	I	6	q-f
1901	I	7	q-f
1902	I	9	2
1903	I	2	s-f
1904	I	5	s-f
1905	I	7	1
1906	I	7	1
1907	I	2	2
1908	I	4	2
1909	I	2	2
1910	I	6	Winners
1911	I	6	s-f
1912	I	8	2
1913	I	14	q-f
1914	I	7	2
1915	I	15	
1916	I	8	
1917	I	16R	
1918†			
1919†			
1920	I	4	2
1921	I	4	q-f
1922	I	4	3
1923	I	7	1-f
1924	I	5	2
1925	I	8	Final
1926	I	10	2
1927	I	5	3
1928	I	14	3
1929	I	18	3
1930	I	14	q-f
1931	I	8	3
1932	I	11	2
1933	I	15	3
1934	I	12	2
1935	I	8	1
1936	I	13	3
1937	I	9	3
1938	I	19R	1
1939	II	6	2
1947	II	1P	q-f
1948	I	4	1
1949	I	2	s-f
1950	I	6	1
1951	I	3	q-f
1952	I	8	Final
1953	I	7	2
1954	I	7	3
1955	I	8	5
1956	I	13	6
1957	I	10	5
1958	I	11	3
1959	I	4	1
1960	I	4	2
1961	I	10	2
1962	I	1C	1
1963	I	9	q-f
1964	I	6	Final
1965	I	6	1
1966	I	9	2
1967	I	6	1
1968	I	9	2
1969	I	9	1
1970	I	6	s-f
1971	I	5	q-f
1972	I	5	4
1973	I	5	s-f
1974	I	5	s-f
1975	I	6	s-f
1976	P	9R	3
1977	I	3	s-f
1978	I	3	3
1979	I	1P	q-f
1980	P	9R	3
1981	I	2P	3
1982	P	8	q-f
1983	P	6	4
1984	P	8	s-f
1985	P	6	q-f
1986	P	6	q-f
1987	P	6	s-f

† No Second Division

Founded: 1910*
Address: Tannadice Park, Dundee, Angus
Telephone: Dundee 86289
Ground capacity: 22,250 (2,263 seated)
Playing area: 110 by 74 yards
Record attendance: 28,000 v Barcelona, Fairs Cup 2nd round, 16.11.66
Record victory: 14–0 v Nithsdale Wanderers, Scottish Cup 1st round, 17.1.31
Record defeat: 1–12 v Motherwell, Division II, 23.1.54
Most League points: 56, Premier Division, 1982–83
Most League goals: 108, Division II, 1935–36
League scoring record: 41, John Coyle, Division II, 1955–56
Record League aggregate: 202, Peter McKay, 1947–48
Most League appearances: 624, Hamish McAlpine, 1969–86
Most capped player: 25, David Narey, Scotland
* As Dundee Hibernians. Name changed to Dundee United in 1923

Scottish Cup	Year	Opponents	Score	Scorers
Runners-up	1974	Celtic	0–3	
	1981	Rangers	0–0	
		Replay	1–4	Dodds
	1985	Celtic	1–2	Beedie
Runners-up	1987	St Mirren	*0–1	
League Cup				
Winners	1980	Aberdeen	0–0	
		Replay	3–0	Pettigrew 2, Sturrock
	1981	Dundee	3–0	Dodds, Sturrock 2
Runners-up	1982	Rangers	1–2	Milne
	1985	Rangers	0–1	

* after extra time

THE DUNDEE UNITED RECORD

	Division and place		Cup round reached
1911*	II	8	p
1912*	II	10	p
1913*	II	10	2
1914*	II	4	1
1915*	II	11	
1920*	†		p
1921*	†		p
1922*	II	19	1
1923‡			2
1924	II	9	1
1925	II	1P	2
1926	I	17	1
1927	I	20R	q-f
1928	II	6	2
1929	II	1P	q-f
1930	I	19R	2
1931	II	2P	2
1932	I	19R	3
1933	II	13	2
1934	II	17	1
1935	II	4	3
1936	II	7	2
1937	II	14	1
1938	II	14	2
1939	II	9	2
1947	II	10	1
1948	II	15	2
1949	II	8	2
1950	II	8	2
1951	II	4	1
1952	II	4	3
1953	II	8	1
1954	II	15	1
1955	II	13	4
1956	II	8	5
1957	II	13	6
1958	II	9	2
1959	II	17	2
1960	II	2P	2
1961	I	9	2
1962	I	10	2
1963	I	7	s-f
1964	I	8	1
1965	I	9	2
1966	I	5	2
1967	I	9	s-f
1968	I	11	2
1969	I	5	q-f
1970	I	5	2
1971	I	6	4
1972	I	9	3
1973	I	7	3
1974	I	8	Final
1975	I	4	4
1976	P	8	4
1977	P	4	3
1978	P	3	s-f
1979	P	3	3
1980	P	4	4
1981	P	5	Final
1982	P	4	q-f
1983	P	1C	3
1984	P	3	5
1985	P	3	Final
1986	P	3	s-f
1987	P	3	Final

* as Dundee Hibernians
† Scottish Second Division not reformed until 1921
‡ Name changed to Dundee United. Dundee Hibernians did not compete in the League 1922–23.

DUNFERMLINE ATHLETIC

Founded: 1885
Address: East End Park, Dunfermline
Telephone: Dunfermline 24295
Ground capacity: 27,000 (3,100 seated)
Playing area: 114 by 72 yards
Record attendance: 27,816 v Celtic, Division I, 30.4.68
Record victory: 11–2 v Stenhousemuir, Division II, 27.9.30
Record defeat: 0–10 v Dundee, Division II, 22.3.47
Most League points: 59, Division II, 1925–26
Most League goals: 120, Division II, 1957–58
League scoring record: 55, Bobby Skinner, Division II, 1925–26
Record League aggregate: 154, Charlie Dickson, 1955–64
Most League appearances: 301, George Peebles, 1956–66
Most capped player: 6 (12 in all), Andy Wilson, Scotland

Scottish Cup	Year	Opponents	Score	Scorers
Winners	1961	Celtic	0–0	
		Replay	2–0	Thomson, Dickson
	1968	Heart of Midlothian	3–1	Gardner 2, Lister (pen)
Runners-up	1965	Celtic	2–3	Melrose, McLaughlin
League Cup				
Runners-up	1950	East Fife	0–3	

THE DUNFERMLINE RECORD

	Division and place	Cup round reached		Division and place	Cup round reached
1922	II 8	2	1958	II 2P	3
1923	II 13	3	1959	I 16	q-f
1924	II 7	1	1960	I 13	2
1925	II 13	1	1961	I 12	Winners
1926	II 1P	1	1962	I 4	q-f
1927	I 18	3	1963	I 8	3
1928	I 20R	4	1964	I 5	s-f
1929	II 11	1	1965	I 3	Final
1930	II 10	1	1966	I 4	s-f
1931	II 3	1	1967	I 8	q-f
1932	II 10	q-f	1968	I 4	Winners
1933	II 3	1	1969	I 3	2
1934	II 2P	1	1970	I 9	1
1935	I 15	q-f	1971	I 16	4
1936	I 10	1	1972	I 18R	3
1937	I 19R	1	1973	I 2P	4
1938	II 9	1	1974	I 16	q-f
1939	II 5	3	1975	I 15	3
1947	II 8	1	1976	I 13R	3
1948	II 7	2	1977	II 3	3
1949	II 4	1	1978	II 3	2
1950	II 4	3	1979	II 2P	3
1951	II 10	1	1980	I 10	4
1952	II 6	3	1981	I 12	3
1953	II 11	1	1982	I 10	3
1954	II 8	2	1983	I 13R	4
1955	II 2P	6	1984	I 9	3
1956	II 16	5	1985	I 3	1
1957	I 17R	6	1986	I 1P	3
			1987	I 2P	3

EAST FIFE

Founded: 1903
Address: Bayview Park, Methil, Fife
Telephone: Leven 26323
Ground capacity: 15,000
Playing area: 110 by 71 yards
Record attendance: 22,515 v Raith Rovers, Division I, 2.1.50
Record victory: 13–2 v Edinburgh City, Division II, 11.12.37
Record defeat: 0–9 v Hearts, Division I, 5.10.57
Most League points: 57, Division II, 1929–30
Most League goals: 114, Division II, 1929–30
League scoring record: 42, J. Wood, Division II, 1926–27
Most capped player: 5 (8 in all), George Aitken, Scotland

Scottish Cup	Year	Opponents	Score	Scorers
Winners	1938	Kilmarnock	1–1	McLeod
		Replay	4–2	McKerrall 2, McLeod, Miller
Runners-up	1927	Celtic	1–3	Wood
	1950	Rangers	0–3	
League Cup				
Winners	1948	Falkirk	0–0	
		Replay	4–1	Duncan 3, Adams
	1950	Dunfermline Athletic	3–0	Fleming, Duncan, Morris
	1954	Partick Thistle	3–2	Gardiner, Fleming, Christie

THE EAST FIFE RECORD

	Division and place	Cup round reached		Division and place	Cup round reached
1921	II	3	1960	II 18	1
1922	II 12	1	1961	II 13	2
1923	II 9	3	1962	II 10	3
1924	II 13	2	1963	II 11	2
1925	II 9	1	1964	II 4	2
1926	II 4	1	1965	II 9	2
1927	II 6	Final	1966	II 4	1
1928	II 4	1	1967	II 5	2
1929	II 8	1	1968	II 3	2
1930	II 2P	1	1969	II 3	1
1931	I 20R	1	1970	II 10	q-f
1932	II 8	1	1971	II 2P	3
1933	II 7		1972	I 16	3
1934	II 13	1	1973	I 9	3
1935	II 9	1	1974	I 17R	3
1936	II 6	1	1975	II 5	3
1937	II 5	3	1976	I 12	3
1938	II 5	Winners	1977	I 12	q-f
1939	II 3	1	1978	I 14R	3
1947	II 3	q-f	1979	II 4	3
1948	II 1P	q-f	1980	II 10	3
1949	I 4	s-f	1981	II 11	3
1950	I 4	Final	1982	II 7	2
1951	I 10	1	1983	II 6	4
1952	I 3	2	1984	II 2P	4
1953	I 3	2	1985	II 10	3
1954	I 6	1	1986	II 5	3
1955	I 11	5	1987	I 4	3
1956	I 12	5			
1957	I 15	6			
1958	I 17R	1			
1959	II 8	1			

EAST STIRLINGSHIRE

Founded: 1881
Address: Firs Park, Falkirk, Stirlingshire
Telephone: Falkirk 23583
Ground capacity: 11,500
Playing area: 112 by 72 yards
Record attendance: 11,500 v Hibernian, Scottish Cup, 10.2.69
Record victory: 10–1 v Stenhousmuir, Scottish Cup 1st round, 1.9.1888
Record defeat: 1–12 v Dundee United, Division II, 13.4.36
Most League points: 55, Division II, 1931–32
Most League goals: 111, Division II, 1931–32
League scoring record: 36, Malcolm Morrison, Division II, 1938–39
Most capped player: 5, Humphrey Jones, Wales

THE EAST STIRLINGSHIRE RECORD

	Division and place	Cup round reached		Division and place	Cup round reached
1902	II 9	p	1960	II 15	3
1903	II 8	p	1961	II 16	1
1904	II 6	p	1962	II 11	2
1905	II 9	p	1963	II 2P	3
1906	II 12	p	1964	I 18R	3
1907	II 11	p	1965§	II 5	p
1908	II 5	p	1966	II 17	1
1909	II 9	p	1967	II 19	p
1910	II 8	p	1968	II 15	1
1911	II 7	1	1969	II 9	2
1912	II 9	2	1970	II 12	p
1913	II 3	2	1971	II 17	2
1914	II 8	2	1972	II 8	1
1915	II 4		1973	II 13	2
1920	†	2	1974	II 16	1
1921	†	3	1975	II 9	3
1922	II 15	3	1976	II 8	1
1923	II 19	1	1977	II 10	3
1924	*	3	1978	II 9	2
1925	II 18	2	1979	II 12	2
1926	II 18	1	1980	II 2P	1
1927	II 5	1	1981	I 11	q-f
1928	II 9	1	1982	I 13R	3
1929	II 12	2	1983	II 13	1
1930	II 12	1	1984	II 11	3
1931	II 7	1	1985	II 12	2
1932	II 1P	1	1986	II 11	1
1933	I 20R	1	1987	II 13	1
1934	II 9	3			
1935	II 14	1			
1936	II 8	1			
1937	II 7	1			
1938	II 13	1			
1939	II 17	1			
1947	‡	2			
1948	‡	2			
1949	‡	1			
1950	‡	1			
1951	‡	2			
1952	‡	1			
1953	‡	2			
1954	‡	1			
1955	‡	4			
1956	II 16	4			
1957	II 19	4			
1958	II 15	1			
1959	II 15	1			

* Did not compete
† No Second Division
‡ Competed in Division 'C'
§ as East Stirlingshire Clydebank

FALKIRK

Founded: 1876
Address: Brockville Park, Falkirk
Telephone: Falkirk 24121
Ground capacity: 22,000 (2,750 seated)
Playing area: 100 by 70 yards
Record attendance: 23,100 v Celtic, Scottish Cup 3rd round, 21.2.53
Record victory: 12–1 v Laurieston, Scottish Cup 2nd round, 23.3.1893
Record defeat: 1–11 v Airdrieonians, Division I, 28.4.51
Most League points: 59, Division II, 1935–36
Most League goals: 132, Division II, 1935–36
League scoring record: 43, Evelyn Morrison, Division I, 1928–29
Most capped player: 14 (15 in all), Alec Parker, Scotland

Scottish Cup	Year	Opponents	Score	Scorers
Winners	1913	Raith Rovers	2–0	Robertson, Logan
	1957	Kilmarnock	1–1	Prentice
		Replay	2–1	Merchant, Moran
League Cup				
Runners-up	1948	East Fife	0–0	
		Replay	1–4	Aikman

THE FALKIRK RECORD

	Division and place	Cup round reached		Division and place	Cup round reached
1902		q-f	1948	I 7	2
1903	II 7	q	1949	I 5	1
1904	II 4	q	1950	I 14	2
1905	II 2P	q	1951	I 16R	1
1906	I 13	1	1952	II 2P	q-f
1907	I 5	1	1953	I 13	3
1908	I 2	1	1954	I 13	2
1909	I 9	s-f	1955	I 12	7
1910	I 2	2	1956	I 14	5
1911	I 3	2	1957	I 14	Winners
1912	I 7	2	1958	I 10	q-f
1913	I 5	Winners	1959	I 17R	2
1914	I 5	1	1960	II 8	2
1915	I 6		1961	II 2P	1
1916	I 12		1962	I 14	1
1917	I 12		1963	I 13	1
1918	I 14		1964	I 14	q-f
1919	I 16		1965	I 16	1
1920	I 20	2	1966	I 10	1
1921	I 18	1	1967	I 14	2
1922	I 5	2	1968	I 15	1
1923	I 4	3	1969	I 17R	1
1924	I 15	s-f	1970	I 1P	q-f
1925	I 16	3	1971	I 7	3
1926	I 8	3	1972	I 14	3
1927	I 6	s-f	1973	I 14	4
1928	I 10	3	1974	I 18R	3
1929	I 11	3	1975	II 1	4
1930	I 7	q-f	1976	I 8	4
1931	I 14	3	1977	I 14R	3
1932	I 18	1	1978	II 5	1
1933	I 11	2	1979	II 3	3
1934	I 10	3	1980	II 1P	4
1935	I 20R	1	1981	I 9	4
1936	II 1P	s-f	1982	I 9	3
1937	I 7	2	1983	I 8	3
1938	I 4	q-f	1984	I 7	3
1939	I 5	3	1985	I 3	4
1947	I 11	3	1986	I 2P	4
			1987	P 10	3

FORFAR ATHLETIC

Founded: 1884
Address: Station park, Forfar, Angus
Telephone: Forfar 63576/62817
Ground capacity: 8,800 (850 seated)
Playing area: 115 by 69 yards
Record attendance: 10,800 v Rangers, Scottish Cup 2nd round, 2.2.70
Record victory: 14–1 v Lindertis, Scottish Cup 1st round, 1.9.1888
Record defeat: 2–12 v Kings Park, Division II, 2.1.30
Most League points: 63, Division II, 1983–84
Most League goals: 90, Division II, 1931–32
League scoring record: 45, Davie Kilgour, Division II, 1929–30

THE FORFAR RECORD

	Division and place	Cup round reached		Division and place	Cup round reached
1922	II 14	1	1966	II 19	p
1923	II 15	1	1967	II 16	p
1924	II 14	2	1968	II 7	1
1925	II 20	1	1969	II 6	p
1926	*	2	1970	II 18	2
1927	II 9	2	1971	II 15	3
1928	II 5	2	1972	II 17	3
1929	II 7	1	1973	II 16	2
1930	II 8	2	1974	II 18	3
1931	II 12	1	1975	II 20	2
1932	II 6	1	1976	II 12	3
1933	II 6	1	1977	II 14	2
1934	II 14	1	1978	II 6	2
1935	II 11	2	1979	II 8	2
1936	II 13	1	1980	II 3	2
1937	II 12	1	1981	II 5	2
1938	II 15	2	1982	II 6	s-f
1939	II 15	1	1983	II 4	4
1947	*	1	1984	II 1P	2
1948	*	1	1985	I 6	q-f
1949	*	1	1986	I 4	3
1950	II 10	1	1987	I 7	q-f
1951	II 14	1			
1952	II 12	1			
1953	II 15	2			
1954	II 12	2			
1955	II 10	5			
1956	II 15	5			
1957	II 16	4			
1958	II 12	2			
1959	II 12	1			
1960	II 16	2			
1961	II 18	3			
1962	II 16	1			
1963	II 18	1			
1964	II 18	3			
1965	II 17	1			

* Competed in Division 'C'

HAMILTON ACADEMICALS

Founded: 1875
Address: Douglas Park, Hamilton, Lanarkshire
Telephone: Hamilton 23108
Ground capacity: 14,065 (1,065 seated)
Playing area: 104 by 72 yards
Record attendance: 28,281 v Heart of Midlothian, Scottish Cup 3rd round, 3.3.37
Record victory: 10–2 v Cowdenbeath, Division I, 15.10.32
Record defeat: 1–11 v Hibernian, Division I, 6.11.65
Most League points: 56, Division I, 1985–86
Most League goals: 92, Division I, 1932–33
League scoring record: 34, Dave Wilson, Division I, 1936–37
Record League aggregate: 246, David Wilson, 1928–39
Most capped player: 2, Jimmy King, Scotland; 2, Bobby Howe, Scotland

Scottish Cup	Year	Opponents	Score	Scorers
Runners-up	1911	Celtic	0–0	
		Replay	0–2	
	1935	Rangers	1–2	Harrison

THE HAMILTON RECORD

	Division and place	Cup round reached		Division and place	Cup round reached
1899	II 5	p	1947	I 16R	1
1900	II 7	1	1948	II 3	1
1901	II 9	p	1949	II 10	1
1902	II 5	p	1950	II 6	1
1903	II 6	2	1951	II 7	2
1904	II 1	p	1952	II 9	2
1905	II 3	p	1953	II 2P	3
1906	II 4P	2	1954	I 16R	q-f
1907	I 16	p	1955	II 3	q-f
1908	I 11	1	1956	II 11	5
1909	I 16	1	1957	II 11	6
1910	I 15	p	1958	II 10	1
1911	I 16	Final	1959	II 7	3
1912	I 12	1	1960	II 4	1
1913	I 10	2	1961	II 6	2
1914	I 18	2	1962	II 13	2
1915	I 7		1963	II 4	3
1916	I 7		1964	II 13	2
1917	I 11		1965	II 4	3
1918	I 12		1966	I 18R	1
1919	I 14		1967	II 4	q-f
1920	I 21	1	1968	II 11	1
1921	I 15	3	1969	II 15	p
1922	I 18	4	1970	II 19	1
1923	I 18	3	1971	II 18	2
1924	I 12	3	1972	II 19	3
1925	I 13	s-f	1973	II 8	4
1926	I 12	2	1974	II 3	1
1927	I 15	3	1975	II 4	4
1928	I 18	2	1976	I 9	3
1929	I 12	2	1977	I 10	3
1930	I 13	s-f	1978	I 7	3
1931	I 10	2	1979	I 5	3
1932	I 10	s-f	1980	I 7	3
1933	I 8	1	1981	I 7	3
1934	I 11	2	1982	I 7	3
1935	I 4	Final	1983	I 11	3
1936	I 6	1	1984	I 9	4
1937	I 8	q-f	1985	I 4	3
1938	I 13	3	1986	I 1P	4
1939	I 7	2	1987	P 12R	4

HEART OF MIDLOTHIAN

Founded: 1874
Address: Tynecastle Park, Gorgie Road, Edinburgh 11
Telephone: (031) 337 6132
Ground capacity: 27,000 (7,000 seated)
Record attendance: 53,496 v Rangers, Scottish Cup 2nd round, 13.2.32
Record victory: 18–0 v Vale of Lothian, Edinburgh Shield, 17.9.1887
Record defeat: 1–8 v Vale of Leven, Scottish Cup 3rd round, 1882–83; 0–7 v Hibernian, Division I, 1.1.73
Most League points: 62, Division I, 1957–58
Most League goals: 132, Division I, 1957–58
League scoring record: 44, Barney Battles, Division I, 1930–31
Record League aggregate: 206, Jimmy Wardhaugh, 1946–59
Most capped player: 29, Bobby Walker, Scotland

Scottish Cup	Year	Opponents	Score	Scorers
Winners	1891	Dumbarton	1–0	Mason
	1896	Hibernian	3–1	Baird (pen), King, Michael
	1901	Celtic	4–3	Walker (R), Bell 2, Thomson
	1906	Third Lanark	1–0	Wilson
	1956	Celtic	3–1	Crawford 2, Conn
Runners-up	1903	Rangers	1–1	Walker (R)
	First Replay		0–0	
	Second replay		0–2	
	1907	Celtic	0–3	
	1968	Dunfermline Athletic	1–3	Lunn og
	1976	Rangers	1–3	Shaw
	1986	Aberdeen	0–3	
League Cup				
Winners	1955	Motherwell	4–2	Bauld 3, Wardhaugh
	1959	Partick Thistle	5–1	Bauld 2, Murray 2, Hamilton
	1960	Third Lanark	2–1	Hamilton, Young
	1963	Kilmarnock	1–0	Davidson
Runners-up	1962	Rangers	1–1	Cumming
	Replay		1–3	Davidson

THE HEARTS RECORD

Year	Division and place	Cup round reached		Year	Division and place	Cup round reached
1876	I	2		1928	I 4	3
1877	I	1		1929	I 4	1
1878		1		1930	I 10	s-f
1879		4		1931	I 5	2
1880		3		1932	I 8	3
1881		5		1933	I 3	s-f
1882		1		1934	I 6	3
1883		3		1935	I 3	s-f
1884		3		1936	I 5	1
1885		2		1937	I 5	3
1886		2		1938	I 2	1
1887		3		1939	I 4	3
1888		4		1947	I 4	q-f
1889		4		1948	I 9	2
1890		5		1949	I 8	q-f
1891	I 6	Winners		1950	I 3	2
1892	I 3	3		1951	I 4	3
1893	I 5	3		1952	I 4	s-f
1894	I 2	1		1953	I 4	s-f
1895	I 1C	s-f		1954	I 2	q-f
1896	I 4	Winners		1955	I 4	q-f
1897	I 1C	2		1956	I 3	Winners
1898	I 3	3		1957	I 2	5
1899	I 2	1		1958	I 1C	3
1900	I 4	s-f		1959	I 2	2
1901	I 10	Winners		1960	I 1C	2
1902	I 3	3		1961	I 8	q-f
1903	I 4	Final		1962	I 6	3
1904	I 2	1		1963	I 5	2
1905	I 8	2		1964	I 4	3
1906	I 2	Winners		1965	I 2	q-f
1907	I 9	Final		1966	I 7	q-f
1908	I 12	3		1967	I 11	1
1909	I 12	2		1968	I 12	Final
1910	I 12	3		1969	I 8	2
1911	I 14	1		1970	I 4	2
1912	I 4	s-f		1971	I 11	4
1913	I 3	s-f		1972	I 6	q-f
1914	I 3	2		1973	I 10	3
1915	I 2			1974	I 6	s-f
1916	I 6			1975	I 8	q-f
1917	I 14			1976	P 5	Final
1918	I 10			1977	P 9R	s-f
1919	I 6			1978	I 2P	4
1920	I 15	3		1979	P 9R	q-f
1921	I 3	s-f		1980	I 1P	q-f
1922	I 19	3		1981	P 10R	3
1923	I 12	2		1982	I 3	4
1924	I 9	4		1983	I 2P	q-f
1925	I 10	2		1984	P 5	4
1926	I 3	3		1985	P 7	q-f
1927	I 13	1		1986	P 2	Final
				1987	P 5	s-f

HIBERNIAN

Founded: 1875
Address: Easter Road, Edinburgh
Telephone: (031) 661 2159
Ground capacity: 29,316 (5,886 seated)
Playing area: 112 by 74 yards
Record attendance: 65,850 v Heart of Midlothian, Division I, 2.1.50
Record victory: 20–0 v Edinburgh Emmet, 10.1.1885
Record defeat: 0–10 v Rangers, Division I, 24.12.1898
Most League points: 57, Division I, 1980–81
Most League goals: 106, Division I, 1959–60
League scoring record: 42, Joe Baker, Division I, 1959–60
Record League aggregate: 185, Lawrie Reilly, 1946–58
Most League appearances: 348, Eddie Turnbull, 1946–59
Most capped player: 38, Lawrie Reilly, Scotland

Scottish Cup	Year	Opponents	Score	Scorers
Winners	1887	Dumbarton	2–1	Not known
	1902	Celtic	1–0	McGeachan
Runners-up	1896	Heart of Midlothian	1–3	O'Neill
	1914	Celtic	0–0	
	Replay		1–4	Smith
	1923	Celtic	0–1	
	1924	Airdrieonians	0–2	
	1947	Aberdeen	1–2	Cuthbertson
	1958	Clyde	0–1	
	1972	Celtic	1–6	Gordon
	1979	Rangers	0–0	
	First replay		0–0	
	Second replay		2–3	Higgins, MacLeod (pen)
League Cup				
Winners	1973	Celtic	2–1	Stanton, O'Rourke
Runners-up	1951	Motherwell	0–3	
	1969	Celtic	2–6	O'Rourke, Stevenson
	1975	Celtic	3–6	Harper 3
	1986	Aberdeen	0–3	

THE HIBERNIAN RECORD

Year	Division and place	Cup round reached		Year	Division and place	Cup round reached
1894	II 1	p		1937	I 17	2
1895	II 1P	2		1938	I 10	1
1896	I 3	Final		1939	I 13	s-f
1897	I 2	2		1947	I 2	Final
1898	I 3	q-f		1948	I 1C	s-f
1899	I 4	2		1949	I 3	q-f
1900	I 3	2		1950	I 2	1
1901	I 3	s-f		1951	I 1C	s-f
1902	I 6	Winners		1952	I 1C	1
1903	I 1C	q-f		1953	I 2	q-f
1904	I 10	2		1954	I 5	3
1905	I 5	1		1955	I 5	5
1906	I 11	q-f		1956	I 4	5
1907	I 12	s-f		1957	I 9	5
1908	I 5	q-f		1958	I 9	Final
1909	I 6	1		1959	I 10	q-f
1910	I 8	s-f		1960	I 7	q-f
1911	I 9	1		1961	I 7	q-f
1912	I 13	1		1962	I 8	1
1913	I 6	3		1963	I 16	3
1914	I 13	Final		1964	I 10	1
1915	I 11			1965	I 4	s-f
1916	I 19			1966	I 6	2
1917	I 17			1967	I 5	q-f
1918	I 16			1968	I 3	2
1919	I 18			1969	I 12	1
1920	I 18	2		1970	I 3	1
1921	I 13	1		1971	I 12	s-f
1922	I 7	2		1972	I 4	Final
1923	I 8	Final		1973	I 3	4
1924	I 7	Final		1974	I 2	q-f
1925	I 3	1		1975	I 2	3
1926	I 16	2		1976	P 3	q-f
1927	I 9	1		1977	P 6	4
1928	I 12	s-f		1978	P 4	4
1929	I 14	1		1979	P 5	Final
1930	I 17	3		1980	P 10R	s-f
1931	I 19R	3		1981	P 1P	q-f
1932	II 7	1		1982	P 6	4
1933	II 1P	q-f		1983	P 7	3
1934	I 16	3		1984	P 7	3
1935	I 11	3		1985	P 8	3
1936	I 17	2		1986	P 8	s-f
				1987	P 9	4

KILMARNOCK

Founded: 1869
Address: Rugby Park, Kilmarnock
Telephone: Kilmarnock 25184
Ground capacity: 17,600 (4,090 seated)
Playing area: 115 by 75 yards
Record attendance: 34,246 v Rangers, League Cup
Record victory: 12–0 v Girvan Amateurs, Ayrshire Cup Final, 8.12.82
Record defeat: 0–8 v Queen's Park, Division II, 1892–93; 0–8 v Hibernian, Division I, 22.8.25; 0–8 v Rangers, Division I, 27.2.37; 1–9 v Celtic, Division I, 13.8.38
Most League points: 58, Division II, 1973–74
Most League goals: 92, Division I, 1962–63
League scoring record: 35, Peerie Cunningham, Division I, 1927–28
Record League aggregate: 102, Jimmy Maxwell, 1931–34
Most League appearances: 424, Frank Beattie, 1954–71
Most capped player: 11, Joe Nibloe, Scotland

Scottish Cup	Year	Opponents	Score	Scorers
Winners	1920	Albion Rovers	3–2	Culley, Smith (J R), Shortt
	1929	Rangers	2–0	Aitken, Williamson
Runners-up	1898	Rangers	0–2	
	1932	Rangers	1–1	Maxwell
	Replay		0–3	
	1938	East Fife	1–1	McAvoy
	Replay		2–4	Thomson (pen), McGrogan
	1957	Falkirk	1–1	Curlett
	Replay		1–2	Curlett
	1960	Rangers	0–2	
League Cup				
Runners-up	1953	Dundee	0–2	
	1961	Rangers	0–2	
	1963	Heart of Midlothian	0–1	

THE KILMARNOCK RECORD

	Division and place	Cup round reached		Division and place	Cup round reached
1896	II 4	1	1947	I 15R	1
1897	II 3	s-f	1948	II 6	1
1898	II 1	Final	1949	II 11	1
1899	II 1P	q-f	1950	II 7	1
1900	I 5	q-f	1951	II 12	1
1901	I 5	2	1952	II 5	2
1902	I 7	3	1953	II 4	2
1903	I 9	2	1954	II 2P	2
1904	I 14	q-f	1955	I 10	6
1905	I 9	1	1956	I 8	6
1906	I 14	2	1957	I 3	Final
1907	I 17	2	1958	I 5	3
1908	I 14	s-f	1959	I 8	q-f
1909	I 10	1	1960	I 2	Final
1910	I 11	1	1961	I 2	2
1911	I 10	1	1962	I 5	q-f
1912	I 16	2	1963	I 2	2
1913	I 11	3	1964	I 2	s-f
1914	I 12	3	1965	I 1C	q-f
1915	I 12		1966	I 3	q-f
1916	I 10		1967	I 7	1
1917	I 6		1968	I 7	1
1918	I 3		1969	I 4	q-f
1919	I 9		1970	I 7	s-f
1920	I 9	Winners	1971	I 13	q-f
1921	I 12	2	1972	I 11	s-f
1922	I 17	2	1973	I 17R	4
1923	I 15	2	1974	II 2P	3
1924	I 16	2	1975	I 12	3
1925	I 12	q-f	1976	I 2P	q-f
1926	I 9	1	1977	P 10R	3
1927	I 16	2	1978	I 6	q-f
1928	I 8	4	1979	I 2P	4
1929	I 10	Winners	1980	P 8	3
1930	I 8	2	1981	P 9R	4
1931	I 11	s-f	1982	I 2P	q-f
1932	I 9	Final	1983	P 10R	3
1933	I 14	q-f	1984	I 6	3
1934	I 7	2	1985	I 12	3
1935	I 9	2	1986	I 3	4
1936	I 8	2	1987	I 6	3
1937	I 11	1			
1938	I 18	Final			
1939	I 10	2			

MEADOWBANK

Founded: 1974 (formerly Ferranti Thistle)
Address: Meadowbank Stadium, Edinburgh
Telephone: (031) 337 2442
Ground capacity: 16,500 (all seated)
Playing area: 105 by 72 yards
Record attendance: 4,000 v Albion Rovers, Scottish League Cup, 9.8.74
Record victory: 6–1 v Stenhousemuir, Division II, 6.2.82; 5–0 v Montrose, Division II, 5.2.83; 5–0 v Berwick Rangers, Division II, 19.2.83; 5–0 v Whitehill Welfare, City Cup semi-final, 17.3.85
Record defeat: 0–8 v Hamilton Academicals, Division II, 14.12.74
Most League points: 54, Division II, 1982–83
Most League goals: 43, Division II, 1977–78
League scoring record: 17, John Jobson, Division II, 1979–80

THE MEADOWBANK RECORD

	Division and place	Cup round reached		Division and place	Cup round reached
1975	II 18		1982	II 12	4
1976	II 14	2	1983	II 2P	1
1977	II 11	2	1984	II 11	3
1978	II 13	4	1985	I 13R	4
1979	II 14	4	1986	II 3	2
1980	II 12	3	1987	II 1P	4
1981	II 13	1			

MONTROSE

Founded: 1879
Address: Links Park, Montrose
Telephone: Montrose 3200
Ground capacity: 9,000
Playing area: 114 by 66 yards
Record attendance: 8,983 v Dundee, Scottish Cup 3rd round, 17.3.73
Record victory: 12–0 v Vale of Leithen, Scottish Cup 2nd round, 4.1.75
Record defeat: 0–13 v Aberdeen Reserves, Division C, 17.3.51
Most League points: 53, Division II, 1974–75
Most League goals: 78, Division II, 1970–71
Most capped player: 2 (6 in all), A. Keillor, Scotland

THE MONTROSE RECORD

	Division and place	Cup round reached		Division and place	Cup round reached
1930	II 11	q-f	1966	II 9	1
1931	II 8	3	1967	II 12	p
1932	II 17	1	1968	II 13	p
1933	II 17	2	1969	II 10	2
1934	II 16	1	1970	II 8	1
1935	II 17	1	1971	II 6	2
1936	II 12	1	1972	II 10	3
1937	II 13	1	1973	II 6	q-f
1938	II 16	1	1974	II 8	3
1939	II 14	2	1975	II 3	3
1947	*	p	1976	I 3	q-f
1948	*	q-f	1977	I 5	3
1949	*	1	1978	I 11	3
1950	*	1	1979	I 13R	3
1951	*	1	1980	II 9	2
1952	*	1	1981	II 7	2
1953	*	3	1982	II 10	3
1954	*	1	1983	II 14	2
1955	*	4	1984	II 12	2
1956	II 19	4	1985	II 1P	2
1957	II 17	5	1986	I 17	3
1958	II 14	2	1987	I 12R	3
1959	II 19	2			
1960	II 7	2			
1961	II 7	2			
1962	II 5	2			
1963	II 15	2			
1964	II 5	1			
1965	II 16	1			

* Montrose competed in C Division

Founded: 1874
Address: Cappielow Park, Greenock
Telephone: Greenock 23571
Ground capacity: 16,400 (6,400 seated)
Playing area: 110 by 71 yards
Record attendance: 23,500 v Rangers, Scottish Cup 3rd round, 21.2.53
Record victory: 11–0 v Carfin Shamrock, Acottish Cup, 13.11.1886
Record defeat: 1–10 v Port Glasgow Athletic, Division II, 5.5.1894; 1–10 v St Bernards, Division II, 14.10.33
Most League points: 69, Division II, 1966–67
Most League goals: 135, Division II, 1963–64
League scoring record: 41, Allan McGraw, Division II, 1963–64
Most capped player: 25, Jimmy Cowan, Scotland

Scottish Cup	Year	Opponents		Score	Scorers
Winners	1922	Rangers		1–0	Gourlay
Runners-up	1948	Rangers		1–1	Whyte
		Replay			
League Cup					
Runners-up	1964	Rangers		0–5	

THE MORTON RECORD

Year	Division and place		Cup round reached	Year	Division and place		Cup round reached
1894	II	8	p	1950	II	1P	2
1895	II	5	p	1951	I	12	2
1896	II	9	1	1952	I	15R	3
1897	II	5	s-f	1953	II	6	3
1898	II	3	2	1954	II	5	3
1899	II	7	2	1955	II	9	5
1900	II	2E	1	1956	II	9	5
1901	I	4	q-f	1957	II	4	5
1902	I	10	1	1958	II	13	2
1903	I	12	1	1959	II	11	3
1904	I	11	s-f	1960	II	14	1
1905	I	13	2	1961	II	19	2
1906	I	10	2	1962	II	3	2
1907	I	13	2	1963	II	3	1
1908	I	13	2	1964	II	1P	2
1909	I	17	1	1965	I	10	2
1910	I	17	2	1966	I	17R	1
1911	I	13	2	1967	II	1P	1
1912	I	6	q-f	1968	I	6	s-f
1913	I	13	2	1969	I	10	s-f
1914	I	4	2	1970	I	10	2
1915	I	4		1971	I	8	4
1916	I	3		1972	I	13	4
1917	I	2		1973	I	12	3
1918	I	4		1974	I	14	4
1919	I	3		1975	I	17	3
1920	I	6	s-f	1976	I	11	3
1921	I	9	2	1977	I	4	3
1922	I	12	Winners	1978	I	1P	q-f
1923	I	14	1	1979	P	7	4
1924	I	11	1	1980	P	6	q-f
1925	I	14	1	1981	P	8	s-f
1926	I	15	q-f	1982	P	7	3
1927	I	19R	1	1983	P	9R	4
1928	II	18	2	1984	I	1P	5
1929	II	2P	1	1985	P	10R	3
1930	I	18	1	1986	I	7	3
1931	I	16	3	1987	I	1P	4
1932	I	15	1				
1933	I	19R	1				
1934	II	5	1				
1935	II	6	2				
1936	II	3	q-f				
1937	II	2P	s-f				
1938	I	20R	3				
1939	II	12E	1				
1947	I	6	3				
1948	I	14	Final				
1949	I	15R	3				

E – elected to First Division

Founded: 1885*
Address: Fir Park, Motherwell, Lanarkshire
Telephone: Motherwell 63229
Ground capacity: 22,600 (3,200 seated)
Playing area: 110 by 72 yards
Record attendance: 35,632 v Rangers, Scottish Cup 4th round replay, 12.3.52
Record victory: 12–1 v Dundee United, Division II, 23.1.54
Record defeat: 0–8 v Aberdeen, Division I, 26.3.79
Most League points: 66, Division I, 1931–32
Most League goals: 119, Division I, 1931–32
League scoring record: 52, Bill McFadyen, Division I, 1931–32
Record League aggregate: 283, Hugh Ferguson, 1916–25
Most League appearances: 626, Bob Ferrier, 1918–37
Most capped player: 12, George Stevenson, Scotland
*As Wee Alpha. Changed name to Motherwell in 1886.

Scottish Cup	Year	Opponents		Score	Scorers
Winners	1952	Dundee		4–0	Watson, Redpath, Humphries, Kelly
Runners-up	1931	Celtic		2–2	Stevenson, McMenemy
		Replay		2–4	Murdoch, Stevenson
	1933	Celtic		0–1	
	1939	Clyde		0–4	
	1951	Celtic		0–1	
League Cup					
Winners	1951	Hibernian		3–0	Kelly, Forrest, Watters
Runners-up	1955	Heart of Midlothian		2–4	Redpath (pen), Bain

THE MOTHERWELL RECORD

Year	Division and place		Cup round reached	Year	Division and place		Cup round reached
1904	I	13	2	1949	I	12	2
1905	I	14	2	1950	I	10	1
1906	I	9	1	1951	I	9	Final
1907	I	10	1	1952	I	7	Winners
1908	I	10	2	1953	I	15R	3
1909	I	14	2	1954	II	1P	s-f
1910	I	10	3	1955	I	15	q-f
1911	I	17	3	1956	I	10	5
1912	I	14	3	1957	I	7	6
1913	I	7	2	1958	I	8	s-f
1914	I	17	4	1959	I	3	3
1915	I	18		1960	I	5	3
1916	I	14		1961	I	5	s-f
1917	I	8		1962	I	9	s-f
1918	I	5		1963	I	10	2
1919	I	5		1964	I	11	q-f
1920	I	3	1	1965	I	14	s-f
1921	I	5	q-f	1966	I	13	2
1922	I	13	3	1967	I	10	1
1923	I	13	s-f	1968	I	17R	1
1924	I	10	3	1969	II	1P	1
1925	I	18	3	1970	I	11	q-f
1926	I	5	1	1971	I	9	3
1927	I	2	1	1972	I	10	q-f
1928	I	3	q-f	1973	I	8	4
1929	I	3	q-f	1974	I	9	q-f
1930	I	2	3	1975	I	10	s-f
1931	I	3	Final	1976	P	4	s-f
1932	I	1C	q-f	1977	P	7	q-f
1933	I	2	Final	1978	P	6	4
1934	I	2	s-f	1979	P	10R	3
1935	I	7	q-f	1980	I	6	3
1936	I	4	q-f	1981	I	5	q-f
1937	I	4	q-f	1982	I	1P	3
1938	I	5	q-f	1983	P	8	3
1939	I	12	Final	1984	P	10R	5
1947	I	8	s-f	1985	I	1P	s-f
1948	I	8	3	1986	P	9	q-f
				1987	P	8	q-f

PARTICK THISTLE

Founded: 1876
Address: Firhill Park, Glasgow
Telephone: (041) 946 2673
Ground capacity: 22,000 (3,500 seated)
Playing area: 110 by 71 yards
Record attendance: 49, 838 v Rangers, Division I, 18.2.22
Record victory: 16–0 v Royal Albert, Scottish Cup 1 round, 17.1.31
Record defeat: 0–10 v Queens Park, Scottish Cup 5th round, 3.12.1881
Most League points: 56, Division II, 1970–71
Most League goals: 91, Division I, 1928–29
League scoring record: 41, Alec Hair, Division I, 1926–27
Most capped player: 51 (53 in all), Alan Rough, Scotland

Scottish Cup	Year	Opponents	Score	Scorers
Winners	1921	Rangers	1–0	Blair
Runners-up	1930	Rangers	0–0	
		Replay	1–2	Torbet
League Cup				
Winners	1972	Celtic	4–1	Rae, Lawrie, McQuade, Bone
Runners-up	1954	East Fife	2–3	Walker, McKenzie
	1957	Celtic	0–0	
		Replay	0–3	
	1959	Heart of Midlothian	1–5	Smith

THE PARTICK RECORD

Year	Division and place		Cup round reached		Year	Division and place		Cup round reached
1894	II	5	p		1937	I	13	3
1895	II	7	p		1938	I	7	3
1896	II	6	p		1939	I	11	1
1897	II	1P	1		1947	I	5	1
1898	I	8	1		1948	I	3	3
1899	I	9R	q-f		1949	I	11	q-f
1900	II	1P	q-f		1950	I	7	s-f
1901	I	11R	1		1951	I	6	1
1902	II	2P	1		1952	I	6	1
1903	I	8	q-f		1953	I	9	2
1904	I	7	1		1954	I	3	q-f
1905	I	6	q-f		1955	I	9	5
1906	I	5	2		1956	I	9	q-f
1907	I	14	1		1957	I	8	5
1908	I	15	2		1958	I	6	2
1909	I	18	2		1959	I	9	3
1910	I	16	2		1960	I	10	q-f
1911	I	4	2		1961	I	11	3
1912	I	5	1		1962	I	7	2
1913	I	17	3		1963	I	3	3
1914	I	15	q-f		1964	I	7	3
1915	I	8			1965	I	11	2
1916	I	5			1966	I	12	1
1917	I	9			1967	I	12	2
1918	I	6			1968	I	10	q-f
1919	I	4			1969	I	14	1
1920	I	13	3		1970	I	18R	1
1921	I	6	Winners		1971	I	1P	3
1922	I	6	s-f		1972	I	7	3
1923	I	11	1		1973	I	13	q-f
1924	I	8	q-f		1974	I	11	4
1925	I	7	3		1975	I	13	3
1926	I	14	3		1976	I	1P	4
1927	I	11	s-f		1977	P	5	3
1928	I	6	q-f		1978	P	7	s-f
1929	I	6	2		1979	P	8	s-f
1930	I	6	Final		1980	P	7	q-f
1931	I	4	2		1981	P	6	4
1932	I	6	q-f		1982	P	9R	3
1933	I	10	3		1983	I	4	q-f
1934	I	13	2		1984	I	3	3
1935	I	13	2		1985	I	11	3
1936	I	9	1		1986	I	8	3
					1987	I	8	3

QUEEN OF THE SOUTH

Founded: 1919
Address: Palmerston Park, Dumfries
Telephone: Dumfries 4853
Ground capacity: 20,850
Playing area: 111 by 73 yards
Record attendance: 24,500 v Hearts, Scottish Cup 3rd round, 23.2.52
Record victory: 11–1 v Stranraer, Scottish Cup 1st round, 16.1.32
Record defeat: 2–10 v Dundee, Division I, 1.12.62
Most League points: 55, Division II, 1985–86
Most League goals: 94, Division II, 1959–60
League scoring record: 33, Jimmy Gray, Division II, 1927–28
Most capped player: 3, Billy Houston, Scotland

THE QUEEN OF THE SOUTH RECORD

Year	Division and place		Cup round reached		Year	Division and place		Cup round reached
1926	II	17	1		1960	II	3	3
1927	II	11	1		1961	II	5	2
1928	II	12	1		1962	II	2P	2
1929	II	9	2		1963	I	15	q-f
1930	II	7	2		1964	I	17R	2
1931	II	5	1		1965	II	3	1
1932	II	9	2		1966	II	3	2
1933	II	2P	1		1967	II	9	1
1934	I	4	q-f		1968	II	6	2
1935	I	17	1		1969	II	5	1
1936	I	15	3		1970	II	3	1
1937	I	18	q-f		1971	II	11	3
1938	I	16	2		1972	II	7	3
1939	I	6	q-f		1973	II	11	3
1947	I	12	1		1974	II	4	4
1948	I	13	3		1975	II	2	4
1949	I	10	2		1976	I	10	q-f
1950	I	15R	s-f		1977	I	9	q-f
1951	II	1P	1		1978	I	12	4
1952	I	10	3		1979	I	14R	3
1953	I	10	q-f		1980	II	13	4
1954	I	10	3		1981	II	2P	2
1955	I	13	5		1982	I	14R	3
1956	I	6	q-f		1983	II	7	3
1957	I	16	5		1984	II	6	2
1958	I	15	q-f		1985	II	8	4
1959	I	18R	1		1986	II	2P	1
					1987	I	10	3

Founded: 1867
Address: Hampden Park, Glasgow
Telephone: (041) 632 1275/4090
Ground capacity: 74,730 (10,000 seated)
Playing area: 115 by 75 yards
Record attendance: 97,000 v Rangers, Scottish Cup 2nd round, 18.2.33 (*Ground record:* 149,547, Scotland v England, 17.4.37)
Record victory: 16–0 v St Peter's, Scottish Cup 1st round, 1885–86
Record defeat: 0–9 v Motherwell, Division I, 26.4.30
Most League points: 57, Division II, 1922–23
Most League goals: 100, Division I, 1928–29
League scoring record: 32, Peter Buchanan, Division II, 1962–63
Most capped player: 14, Watty Arnott, Scotland

Scottish Cup	Year	Opponents	Score	Scorers
Winners	1874	Clydesdale	2–0	
	1875	Renton	3–0	
	1876	Third Lanark	1–1	
		Replay	2–0	
	1880	Thornliebank	3–0	
	*1881	Dumbarton	3–1	
	1882	Dumbarton	2–2	
		Replay	4–1	
	†1884	Vale of Leven		
	1886	Renton	3–1	
	1890	Vale of Leven	1–1	
		Replay	2–1	
	1893	Celtic	2–1	
Runners-up	‡1892	Celtic	1–5	
	1900	Celtic	3–4	

* After a protested game which Queen's Park won 2–1
† Queen's Park awarded the cup after Vale of Leven failed to appear
‡ After protested game which Celtic won 1–0

FA Cup

	Year	Opponents	Score	
Runners-up	1884	Blackburn Rovers	1–2	Christie
	1885	Blackburn Rovers	0–2	

THE QUEEN'S PARK RECORD

	Division and place	Cup round reached		Division and place	Cup round reached
1872		(s-f†)	1927	I 12	2
1873		(s-f†)	1928	I 16	s-f
1874		Winners	1929	I 5	2
1875		Winners	1930	I 15	1
1876		Winners	1931	I 13	2
1877		q-f (3†)	1932	I 16	2
1878		3 (1†)	1933	I 9	2
1879		q-f	1934	I 15	2
1880		Winners	1935	I 12	2
1881		Winners	1936	I 14	1
1882		Winners	1937	I 15	2
1883		q-f	1938	I 12	2
1884		Winners	1939	I 19	2
		(Final†)	1947	I 13	3
1885		3 (Final†)	1948	I 16R	3
1886		Winners	1949	II 5	1
1887		s-f	1950	II 9	1
1888		s-f	1951	I 6	2
1889		3	1952	II 15	2
1890		Winners	1953	II 3	2
1891		q-f	1954	II 10	1
1892		Final	1955	II 4	4
1893		Winners	1956	II 1P	6
1894		s-f	1957	I 13	6
1895		1	1958	I 18R	3
1896		q-f	1959	II 18	2
1897		1	1960	II 11	3
1898		q-f	1961	II 15	1
1899		q-f	1962	II 12	1
1900		Final	1963	II 14	3
1901	I 8	2	1964	II 7	2
1902	I 8	q-f	1965	II 4	2
1903	I 10	1	1966	II 13	1
1904	I 8	1	1967	II 7	q-f
1905	I 12	1	1968	II 4	p
1906	I 16	2	1969	II 11	1
1907	I 15	s-f	1970	II 15	p
1908	I 16	q-f	1971	II 14	3
1909	I 15	q-f	1972	II 12	2
1910	I 14	q-f	1973	II 14	2
1911	I 18	2	1974	II 14	3
1912	I 17	p	1975	II 16	4
1913	I 18	3	1976	II 4	1
1914	I 16	q-f	1977	II 5	3
1915	I 29		1978	II 7	q-f
1916	I 18		1979	II 13	3
1917	I 18		1980	II 5	1
1918	I 7		1981	II 1P	1
1919	I 8		1982	I 8	q-f
1920	I 12	3	1983	I 14R	q-f
1921	I 19	1	1984	II 10	3
1922	I 21R	2	1985	II 10	2
1923	II 1P	3	1986	II 4	4
1924	I 17	3	1987	II 9	2
1925	I 17	2			
1926	I 13	2			

(†) progress in the FA Cup

Founded: 1893
Address: Stark's Park, Pratt Street, Kirkcaldy, Fife
Telephone: Kirkcaldy 263515
Ground capacity: 22,150 (3,150 seated)
Playing area: 113 by 67 yards
Record attendance: 31,306 v Heart of Midlothian, Scottish Cup 2nd round, 7.2.53
Record victory: 10–1 v Coldstream, Scottish Cup 2nd round, 13.2.54
Record defeat: 2–11 v Morton, Division II, 18.3.36
Most League points: 59, Division II, 1937–38
Most League goals: 142, Division II, 1937–38
League scoring record: 38, Norman Haywood, Division II, 1937–38
Most capped player: 6, Dave Morris, Scotland

Scottish Cup	Year	Opponents	Score
Runners-up	1913	Falkirk	0–2
League Cup			
Runners-up	1949	Rangers	0–2

THE RAITH ROVERS RECORD

	Division and place	Cup round reached		Division and place	Cup round reached
1903	II 11	p	1953	I 12	2
1904	II 5	p	1954	I 12	3
1905	II 10	p	1955	I 14	6
1906	II 8	p	1956	I 11	s-f
1907	II 10	q-f	1957	I 4	s-f
1908	II 1	q-f	1958	I 7	2
1909	II 2	p	1959	I 14	1
1910	II 2P	p	1960	I 11	1
1911	I 15	p	1961	I 16	3
1912	I 15	1	1962	I 13	3
1913	I 16	Final	1963	I 18R	s-f
1914	I 11	3	1964	II 10	1
1915	I 19		1965	II 13	p
1916	I 20		1966	II 5	p
1917	I 19		1967	II 2P	1
1918	*		1968	I 16	1
1919	*		1969	I 16	1
1920	I 19	3	1970	I 17R	1
1921	I 16	1	1971	II 8	5
1922	I 3	1	1972	II 11	5
1923	I 9	q-f	1973	II 3	3
1924	I 4	3	1974	II 5	3
1925	I 9	3	1975	II 13	3
1926	I 19R	2	1976	II 2P	4
1927	II 2P	1	1977	I 13R	2
1928	I 17	2	1978	II 2P	2
1929	I 20R	q-f	1979	I 11	3
1930	II 5	1	1980	I 5	3
1931	II 4	1	1981	I 4	3
1932	II 3	2	1982	I 12	3
1933	II 6	1	1983	I 9	3
1934	II 8	1	1984	I 13R	3
1935	II 13	2	1985	II 7	4
1936	II 17	1	1986	II 9	1
1937	II 8	1	1987	II 2P	q-f
1938	II 1P	q-f			
1939	I 20R	1			
1947	II 6	3			
1948	II 1P	2			
1949	II 1P	2			
1950	I 9	2			
1951	I 8	s-f			
1952	I 5	2			

* Raith Rovers did not compete

Founded: 1873
Address: Ibrox Stadium, Glasgow
Telephone: (041) 427 0159
Ground capacity: 44,000 (19,500 seated)
Playing area: 115 by 75 yards
Record attendance: 118,567 v Celtic, Division I, 2.1.39
Record victory: 14–2 v Blairgowrie, Scottish Cup 1st round, 20.1.34
Record defeat: 2–10 v Airdrieonians, 1886
Most League points: 76, Division I, 1920–21
Most League goals: 118, Division I, 1931–32 & 1933–34
League scoring record: 44, Sam English, Division I, 1931–32
Record League aggregate: 233, Bob McPhail, 1927–39
Most League appearances: 496, John Greig, 1962–78
Most capped player: 53, George Young, Scotland

Scottish Cup

	Year	Opponents	Score	Scorers
Winners	1894	Celtic	3–1	McCreadie, Barker, McPherson
	1897	Dumbarton	5–1	Miller, Hyslop, McPherson 2, Smith
	1898	Kilmarnock	2–0	Smith, Hamilton
	1903	Heart of Midlothian	1–1	
		First replay	0–0	
		Second replay	2–0	Mackie, Campbell
	1928	Celtic	4–0	Meiklejohn (pen), McPhail, Archibald 2
	1930	Partick Thistle	0–0	
		Replay	2–1	Marshall, Craig
	1932	Kilmarnock	1–1	McPhail
		Replay	3–0	Fleming, McPhail, English
	1934	St Mirren	5–0	Nicholson 2, McPhail, Smith, Main
	1935	Hamilton	2–1	Smith 2
	1936	Third Lanark	1–0	McPhail
	1948	Morton	1–1	Gillick
		Replay	1–0	Williamson
	1949	Clyde	4–1	Young (2 pens), Williamson, Duncanson
	1950	East Fife	3–0	Findlay, Thornton 2
	1953	Aberdeen	1–1	Prentice
		Replay	1–0	Simpson
	1960	Kilmarnock	2–0	Millar 2
	1962	St Mirren	2–0	Brand, Wilson
	1963	Celtic	1–1	Brand
		Replay	1–0	Johansen
	1973	Celtic	3–2	Parlane, Conn, Forsyth
	1976	Heart of Midlothian	3–1	Johnstone 2, MacDonald
	1978	Aberdeen	2–1	MacDonald, Johnstone
	1979	Hibernian	0–0	
		First replay	0–0	
		Second replay	3–2	Johnstone, Duncan, og
	1981	Dundee United	0–0	
		Replay	4–1	Cooper, Russell, MacDonald 2
Runners-up	1877	Vale of Leven	0–0	
		First replay	1–1	
		Second replay	2–3	Campbell, McNeil
	1879	Vale of Leven	1–1	Struthers
	1899	Celtic	0–2	
	1904	Celtic	2–3	Speedie 2
	1905	Third Lanark	0–0	
		Replay	1–3	
	1909	Celtic	2–2	Gilchrist, Bennett
		Replay	1–1	Gordon
	1921	Partick Thistle	0–1	
	1922	Morton	0–1	
	1929	Kilmarnock	0–2	
	1969	Celtic	0–4	
	1971	Celtic	1–1	Johnstone
		Replay	1–2	og
	1977	Celtic	0–1	
	1980	Celtic	0–1	
	1982	Aberdeen	*1–4	MacDonald
	1983	Aberdeen	*0–1	

League Cup

	Year	Opponents	Score	Scorers
Winners	1947	Aberdeen	4–0	Duncanson 2, Williamson, Gillick
	1949	Raith Rovers	2–0	Gillick, Paton
	1961	Kilmarnock	2–0	Brand, Scott
	1962	Heart of Midlothian	1–1	Millar
		Replay	3–1	Millar, Brand, McMillan
	1964	Morton	5–0	Forrest 4, Willoughby
	1965	Celtic	2–1	Forrest 2
	1971	Celtic	1–0	Johnstone
	1976	Celtic	1–0	MacDonald
	1978	Celtic	2–1	Cooper, Smith
	1979	Aberdeen	2–1	McMaster og, Jackson
	1982	Dundee United	2–1	Cooper, Redford
	1984	Celtic	*3–2	McCoist 3 (2 pens)
	1985	Dundee United	1–0	Ferguson
Runners-up	1952	Dundee	2–3	Findlay, Thornton
	1958	Celtic	1–7	Simpson
	1966	Celtic	1–2	og
	1967	Celtic	0–1	
	1983	Celtic	1–2	Bett

* after extra time

THE RANGERS RECORD

	Division and place		Cup round reached		Division and place		Cup round reached
1875			2	1928	I	1C	Winners
1876			2	1929	I	1C	Final
1877			Final	1930	I	1C	Winners
1878			4	1931	I	1C	2
1879			Final	1932	I	2	Winners
1880			1	1933	I	1C	3
1881			q-f	1934	I	1C	Winners
1882			q-f	1935	I	1C	Winners
1883			2	1936	I	2	Winners
1884			s-f	1937	I	1C	1
1885			q-f	1938	I	3	s-f
1886			1	1939	I	1C	3
1887			3	1947	I	1C	3
1888			2	1948	I	2	Winners
1889			2	1949	I	1C	Winners
1890			3	1950	I	1C	Winners
1891	I	1†	1	1951	I	2	2
1892	I	4	4	1952	I	2	q-f
1893	I	2	3	1953	I	1C	Winners
1894	I	4	Winners	1954	I	4	s-f
1895	I	3	1	1955	I	3	6
1896	I	2	3	1956	I	1C	q-f
1897	I	3	Winners	1957	I	1C	6
1898	I	2	Winners	1958	I	2	s-f
1899	I	1C	Final	1959	I	1C	3
1900	I	1C	s-f	1960	I	3	Winners
1901	I	1C	1	1961	I	1C	3
1902	I	1C	s-f	1962	I	2	Winners
1903	I	3	Winners	1963	I	1C	Winners
1904	I	4	Final	1964	I	1C	Winners
1905	I	2	Final	1965	I	5	q-f
1906	I	4	3	1966	I	2	Winners
1907	I	3	3	1967	I	2	1
1908	I	3	2	1968	I	2	q-f
1909	I	4	Final	1969	I	2	Final
1910	I	3	2	1970	I	2	q-f
1911	I	1C	3	1971	I	4	Final
1912	I	1C	2	1972	I	3	s-f
1913	I	1C	3	1973	I	2	Winners
1914	I	2	3	1974	I	3	4
1915	I	3		1975	I	1C	3
1916	I	2		1976	P	1C	Winners
1917	I	3		1977	P	2	Final
1918	I	1C		1978	P	1C	Winners
1919	I	2		1979	P	2	Winners
1920	I	1C	s-f	1980	P	5	Final
1921	I	1C	Final	1981	P	3	Winners
1922	I	2	Final	1982	P	3	Final
1923	I	1C	2	1983	P	4	Final
1924	I	1C	3	1984	P	4	5
1925	I	1C	s-f	1985	P	4	4
1926	I	6	s-f	1986	P	5	3
1927	I	1C	q-f	1987	P	1C	3

Founded: 1884
Address: Muirton Park, Perth
Telephone: Perth 26961
Ground capacity: 24,950 (2,415 seated)
Playing area: 115 by 74 yards
Record attendance: 29,972 v Dundee, Scottish Cup 2nd round, 10.2.52
Record victory: 8–1 v Partick Thistle, Scottish League Cup, 16.8.69
Record defeat: 1–10 v Third Lanark, Scottish Cup 1st round, 24.1.03
Most League points: 56, Division II, 1923–24
Most League goals: 102, Division II, 1931–32
League scoring record: 36, Jimmy Benson, Division II, 1931–32
Most capped player: 5, Sandy McLaren, Scotland

League Cup

	Year	Opponents	Score
Runners-up	1970	Celtic	0–1

THE ST JOHNSTONE RECORD

	Division and place		Cup round reached		Division and place		Cup round reached
1912	II	5	1	1953	II	14	2
1913	II	11	3	1954	II	6	1
1914	II	5	1	1955	II	7	6
1915	II	8		1956	II	3	5
1916				1957	II	12	5
1917				1958	II	11	2
1918				1959	II	6	3
1919				1960	II	1P	1
1920			2	1961	I	15	1
1921			p	1962	I	17R	2
1922	II	13	1	1963	II	1P	2
1923	II	3	1	1964	I	13	2
1924	II	1P	2	1965	I	13	2
1925	I	11	1	1966	I	16	q-f
1926	I	18	3	1967	I	15	2
1927	I	14	1	1968	I	14	s-f
1928	I	11	1	1969	I	6	s-f
1929	I	9	2	1970	I	13	1
1930	I	20R	2	1971	I	3	3
1931	II	6	2	1972	I	8	3
1932	II	2P	2	1973	I	11	3
1933	I	5	3	1974	I	12	4
1934	I	9	s-f	1975	I	9	4
1935	I	5	q-f	1976	P	10R	3
1936	I	7	3	1977	I	11	3
1937	I	12	2	1978	I	8	4
1938	I	8	2	1979	I	12	3
1939	I	8	1	1980	I	11	3
1947	II	9	1	1981	I	3	4
1948	II	9	2	1982	I	5	4
1949	II	6	1	1983	I	1P	4
1950	II	3	2	1984	P	9R	3
1951	II	5	2	1985	I	14R	3
1952	II	11	2	1986	II	6	3
				1987	II	5	4

Founded: 1876
Address: St Mirren Park, Love Street, Paisley, Renfrewshire
Telephone: (041) 840 1337
Ground capacity: 20,344
Playing area: 115 by 74 yards
Record attendance: 47,428 v Celtic, Scottish Cup 4th round, 7.3.25
Record victory: 15–0 v Glasgow University, Scottish Cup 1st round, 30.1.60
Record defeat: 0–9 v Rangers, Division I, 4.12.1897
Most League points: 62, Division II, 1967–68
Most League goals: 114, Division II, 1935–36
League scoring record: 45, Dunky Walker, Division I, 1921–22
Most capped player: 7, Iain Munro, Scotland; 7 Bob Thomson, Scotland

Scottish Cup

	Year	Opponents	Score	Scorers
Winners	1926	Celtic	2–0	McCrae, Howieson
	1959	Aberdeen	3–1	Bryceland, Miller, Baker
	1987	Dundee United	*1-0	Ferguson
Runners-up	1908	Celtic	1–5	Cunningham
	1934	Rangers	0–5	
	1962	Rangers	0–2	

League Cup

	Year	Opponents	Score	Scorers
Runners-up	1956	Aberdeen	1–2	Holmes

* after extra time

THE ST MIRREN RECORD

	Division and place		Cup round reached		Division and place		Cup round reached
1891	I	8	3	1936	II	2P	3
1892	I	10	1	1937	I	16	q-f
1893	I	3	q-f	1938	I	14	2
1894	I	6	2	1939	I	18	3
1895	I	5	2	1947	I	14	1
1896	I	8	2	1948	I	5	q-f
1897	I	6	2	1949	I	9	2
1898	I	6	2	1950	I	11	1
1899	I	5	2	1951	I	11	1
1900	I	8	1	1952	I	14	2
1901	I	9	s-f	1953	I	6	2
1902	I	5	s-f	1954	I	11	1
1903	I	6	s-f	1955	I	6	5
1904	I	6	q-f	1956	I	15	6
1905	I	10	s-f	1957	I	12	q-f
1906	I	8	s-f	1958	I	13	2
1907	I	7	q-f	1959	I	7	Winners
1908	I	7	Final	1960	I	14	2
1909	I	7	q-f	1961	I	14	s-f
1910	I	13	2	1962	I	16	Final
1911	I	12	1	1963	I	12	q-f
1912	I	18	1	1964	I	12	3
1913	I	12	q-f	1965	I	15	1
1914	I	20	s-f	1966	I	16	1
1915	I	9		1967	I	17R	2
1916	I	13		1968	II	1P	1
1917	I	7		1969	I	11	2
1918	I	11		1970	I	15	2
1919	I	11		1971	I	17R	4
1920	I	14	2	1972	II	4	4
1921	I	22	1	1973	II	5	2
1922	I	8	q-f	1974	II	11	3
1923	I	6	q-f	1975	II	6	2
1924	I	6	2	1976	I	6	3
1925	I	6	q-f	1977	I	1P	4
1926	I	4	Winners	1978	P	8	3
1927	I	10	2	1979	P	6	4
1928	I	5	3	1980	P	3	4
1929	I	8	s-f	1981	P	4	3
1930	I	5	q-f	1982	P	5	s-f
1931	I	15	s-f	1983	P	5	s-f
1932	I	5	1	1984	P	6	s-f
1933	I	7	2	1985	P	5	q-f
1934	I	17	Final	1986	P	7	q-f
1935	I	19R	3	1987	P	7	Winners

Founded: 1884
Address: Ochilview Park, Stenhousemuir
Telephone: Larbert (0324) 562992
Ground capacity: 10,450 (450 seated)
Record attendance: 13,000 v East Fife, Scottish Cup 4th round, 11.3.50
Record victory: 9–2 v Dundee United, Division II, 17.4.37
Record defeat: 2–11 v Dunfermline Athletic, Division II, 27.9.30
Most League points: 50, Division II, 1960–61
Most League goals: 99, Division II, 1960–61
League scoring record: 31, Evelyn Morrison, Division II, 1927–28; Robert Murray, Division II, 1936–37

THE STENHOUSEMUIR RECORD

Year	Division and place	Cup round reached	Year	Division and place	Cup round reached
1922	II 10	1	1958	II 16	2
1923	II 14	1	1959	II 3	2
1924	II 4	2	1960	II 5	3
1925	II 11	1	1961	II 3	1
1926	II 5	2	1962	II 15	3
1927	II 10	1	1963	II 16	1
1928	II 16	2	1964	II 11	1
1929	II 18	2	1965	II 15	1
1930	II 17	1	1966	II 18	p
1931	II 17	1	1967	II 17	p
1932	II 4	1	1968	II 18	p
1933	II 4	q-f	1969	II 19	1
1934	II 4	1	1970	II 16	p
1935	II 5	1	1971	II 10	2
1936	II 11	2	1972	II 14	1
1937	II 10	1	1973	II 10	2
1938	II 8	2	1974	II 15	2
1939	II 8	1	1975	II 11	1
1947	II 7	1	1976	II 10	3
1948	II 14	1	1977	II 9	1
1949	II 12	q-f	1978	II 12	1
1950	II 12	q-f	1979	II 10	2
1951	II 15	1	1980	II 6	2
1952	II 13	1	1981	II 10	3
1953	II 12	1	1982	II 13	1
1954	II 4	1	1983	II 11	3
1955	II 6	5	1984	II 7	1
1956	II 5	q-f	1985	II 5	2
1957	II 14	5	1986	II 7	3
			1987	II 12	2

Founded: 1945
Address: Annfield Park, Stirling
Telephone: Stirling 3584
Ground capacity: 19,000 (300 seated)
Record attendance: 26,400 v Celtic, Scottish Cup 4th round, 14.3.59
Record victory: 20–0 v Selkirk, Scottish Cup ?th round 8.12.84
Record defeat: 0–9 v Dundee United, Division I, 30.12.67
Most League points: 59, Division II, 1964–65
Most League goals: 105, Division II, 1957–58
League scoring record: 29, Joe Hughes, Division II, 1969–70
Most capped player: None

THE STIRLING ALBION RECORD

Year	Division and place	Cup round reached	Year	Division and place	Cup round reached
1947		p	1967	I 16	1
1948	II 8	2	1968	I 18R	1
1949	II 2P	1	1969	II 4	1
1950	I 16R	q-f	1970	II 4	1
1951	II 2P	1	1971	II 12	4
1952	I 16R	2	1972	II 3	2
1953	II 1P	2	1973	II 4	4
1954	I 14	3	1974	II 7	4
1955	I 16	5	1975	II 8	2
1956	I 18R	6	1976	II 6	4
1957	II 8	5	1977	II 1P	3
1958	II 1P	2	1978	I 5	4
1959	I 12	q-f	1979	I 8	3
1960	I 17R	2	1980	I 8	4
1961	II 1P	1	1981	I 13R	4
1962	I 18R	q-f	1982	II 8	1
1963	II 10	1	1983	II 5	2
1964	II 19	1	1984	II 4	3
1965	II 1P	q-f	1985	II 6	2
1966	I 15	2	1986	II 5	3
			1987	II 3	2

Founded: 1870
Address: Stair Park, Strnaraer, Wigtownshire
Telephone: Stranraer 3271
Ground capacity: 5,500
Record attendance: 6,500 v Rangers, Scottish Cup 1st round, 24.1.48
Record victory: 7–0 v Brechin City, Division II, 6.2.65
Record defeat: 1–11 v Queen of the South, Scottish Cup 1st round, 16.1.32
Most League points: 44, Division II, 1960–61 and 1971–72
Most League goals: 83, Division II, 1960–61
League scoring record: 27, Derek Frye, Division II, 1977–78
Most capped player: None

THE STRANRAER RECORD

Year	Division and place	Cup round reached	Year	Division and place	Cup round reached
1956	II 12	4	1972	II 6	2
1957	II 7	5	1973	II 15	4
1958	II 18	2	1974	II 9	2
1959	II 16	2	1975	II 14	2
1960	II 17	1	1976	II 7	2
1961	II 4	2	1977	II 4	2
1962	II 7	3	1978	II 11	2
1963	II 5	1	1979	II 9	2
1964	II 8	2	1980	II 11	2
1965	II 6	p	1981	II 14	2
1966	II 15	1	1982	II 14	1
1967	II 15	p	1983	II 12	2
1968	II 19	p	1984	II 8	2
1969	II 8	2	1985	II 11	3
1970	II 17	1	1986	II 14	2
1971	II 9	3	1987	II 10	2

CHAPTER FIVE

A GAME AT ITS ZENITH

Herbert Chapman's new approach to the whole field of club football prompted the Daily Mail *cartoonist Tom Webster to produce this strip in 1930. The famous south-bank clock is still a feature of the ground.*

The First World War saw the loss of nearly one million young British men, and a fair number of these had been professional footballers. There had been no serious football for five years and most clubs initially found it difficult to put new sides together. But it soon became clear that the game of football was no longer an infant. By 1921 the game had clearly entered its adolescence, even its maturity. In both England and Scotland the major leagues were expanded to reach what has effectively remained their current size and status. Indeed, nearly 70 years later, it is remarkable how little this structure has been disturbed since.

What was also true was that the game was entering the period when it was at its most significant in the life of the nation, a significance suitably symbolized by the opening of the Empire Stadium in 1923. When Wembley was built it was the grandest stadium on earth, a Mecca for football all over the world. Arsenal playing at Wembley in a Cup final, such as

happened in 1932 or 1936, was the pinnacle of the game.

Even a quarter of a century later, Wembley was deemed suitable to stage the Olympics. But, sixty years on, it equally perfectly symbolises what has happened to the game in that interval. As anyone who goes to a Cup final or an international knows, it is a tired, shabby monument, difficult to get to, impossible to park next to and depressingly situated in a tedious London suburb. Not for England the soaring excitement of an Azteca, the architecture of Munich, or the comfort of a Shea or Astrodome.

But in the 1920s we saw a gradual growth of interest in the game, which spilled over into the gigantic post-war attendances of the 1940s (reaching a peak of over 40 million in 1949–50). Interest was sustained through the 1950s, though not at the artificially high spectator levels of the 1940s, and the Spurs Double side of 1961, the introduction of European football and the almost religious reverence for Manchester United ensured there was no deep decline even in the 1960s.

The World Cup win of 1966 was not so much a peak, as a culmination. It summed up a glorious era for a glorious game and it concluded that period perfectly. But the signs were misread. It was really the conclusion of that period, and it was very soon afterwards that growing leisure time, colour television, the motorways and football's own lethargy combined to present football with a downward path it seemed to embrace with little thought for the consequences, the future or what place it should really strive for in late twentieth century Britain. How different from those heady days after the First World War, when the game was on the threshold of a glorious era.

The twenty years between the First and Second World Wars has been called the era of the manager. That is not quite accurate. In truth it was the era of one manager; just one man, whose achievements found an appropriate setting halfway through two turbulent decades in the 1930 FA Cup Final. Those ninety minutes were, quite simply, a microcosm of the whole period.

The combatants were Huddersfield Town and Arsenal. Just eleven years earlier the Yorkshire club's directors had recommended that the organization move, lock, stock and barrel, to Leeds, support and success being sadly elusive in a Huddersfield obsessed with rugby league. The same year Arsenal crept into the First Division by means which could only be described as devious, being elected after finishing only fifth in the immediate pre-War Second Division.

Four years before the 1930 Final Huddersfield had become the first club ever to win three consecutive League Championships and, five years after it, Arsenal did precisely the same thing. During their great years both were managed by the same man, Herbert Chapman, and, appropriately enough, the game in question was won by the club he then managed, Arsenal, over the club he had left, Huddersfield.

Herbert Chapman was born in the very far south of Yorkshire, at Kiveton Park, in 1873. His professional career in midfield with Spurs was distinguished largely by the lemon coloured boots he wore. In 1907 he became manager of the

Southern League side Northampton Town and later moved to Second Division Leeds City, who were ignominiously thrown out of the League in 1919 for making illegal payments to players. Their place was taken by Port Vale—who were to suffer exactly the same fate half a century later. Vale, however, were re-elected. Leeds were not and Chapman—suspended though his only involvement was an alleged timely incineration of the club's books—took a partnership in an engineering firm.

Not for long though. Huddersfield, rather than move to Leeds as their directors were then threatening, managed to raise some cash and sign a number of players. When his suspension was lifted, Chapman joined Huddersfield as manager in September 1920. Here the story really begins. Chapman's first success was the FA Cup of 1922, albeit via a disputed Billy Smith penalty, and two years later Huddersfield won the League Championship on goal average from Cardiff. The next season they retained the title with a new defensive record—only 28 goals conceded—and went on to make it a hat-trick in 1926.

By that time, however, Chapman had gone. His success at Huddersfield was remarkable, for he had no great financial resources and the Yorkshiremen, facing the fierce competition of rugby league, had never drawn large crowds. His team had few outstanding players—most notable was Alex Jackson, one of the Scottish 'Wembley Wizards' that crushed England 5–1 in 1928. Jackson was technically a right-winger, though he actually wandered all over the park. England captains

Clem Stephenson and Sam Wadsworth were valuable signings, while Sam Barkas was an excellent full-back partner for Wadsworth. Barkas, in fact, was one of Alf Ramsey's first boyhood idols.

Chapman's ability lay in choosing and moulding his players as parts of a whole—not just allowing them to function as individuals in the well-defined grooves laid down when 'positional' play was strict. He chose well at Huddersfield, but he was perhaps lucky in that his formation came right immediately. When he moved to Arsenal in 1925 it took rather longer to build a Championship side.

In a sense it was an appropriate time to move, for 1925 was also the year of the most significant tactical development since the 'passing' game had superseded the 'dribbling' game in the 1870s.

The immediate cause was the change in the offside law on 12 June 1925, when the '... fewer than three players between the attacker and the goal' clause was changed to '... fewer than two ...' The change had become desirable because so many teams were employing a very simple offside trap, bringing their defenders upfield to render lethargic forwards offside and sometimes confining play to a strip covering no more than 40 yards of the middle of the field.

The Notts County full-backs Morley and Montgomery had been guilty of this before the First World War, but it took their Newcastle counterparts McCracken and Hudspeth to elevate the 'offside game' to a fine art in the early 1920s. The pair became so identified with the ploy that when one side arrived at Newcastle Central station and a guard blew his whistle the centre-forward was heard to remark 'Blimey, offside already!'

When the trend became unacceptable the International Board—the law making body—finally acted; and the results were startling. In the 1924–25 season 1192 goals were scored in the First Division. In the next season that figure read 1703—an increase of almost 50 per cent, or, more graphically, an extra goal for every match played.

But while the immediate result was to move the advantage from defence to attack, the long term effect was probably negative, for the tactical result was, at its simplest, that one attacker became a defender.

Credit for devising the 'third-back game', as it became known, has never been adequately apportioned. Bob Gillespie of Queen's Park quickly made it his job to blot out the opposing centre-forward but folklore has it—with some concrete support—that the man behind the innovation was Herbert Chapman.

Chapman's first action on joining Arsenal had been to acquire a scheming inside-forward. His choice was Charlie Buchan from Sunderland, the man selectors said was 'too

clever to play for England'. The fee was an imaginative £2,000 down and £100 for every goal he scored in the subsequent season. Buchan scored 21. But it was a transfer significant beyond its immediate impact and strange terms.

In 1929 Henry Norris, Arsenal's chairman, sued the FA for libel after he had been suspended for making illegal payments. The Buchan case was particularly mentioned and it was shown that Buchan had been offered other inducements to join the club. Norris lost his case and far more for, when he died in 1934, he was an exile from football and the club that he had dragged from obscurity.

Charlie Buchan's return to Arsenal, the club he had actually walked out on before the War over eleven shillings expenses, was not a very happy one. One of his, and Chapman's, earliest matches for the club was a humiliating 7–0 defeat at Newcastle on 3 October 1925. Buchan was so upset at such a return to his old home that he and Chapman organized an immediate tactical discussion. One or the other (accounts vary as to who it was) proposed that Arsenal's

centre-half, Jack Butler, should adopt a purely defensive role and that one of the inside-forwards should drop back to supply the creative link between defence and attack that the centre-half could no longer provide.

Oddly enough Newcastle's centre-half, Charlie Spencer, claimed he had played just such a defensive role in that vital match, and the Arsenal plan may have come from observing Newcastle's success. Before 1925 the centre-half performed exactly the functions his title implied—he had played in the middle of the field helping indefence and instigating attacks.

Buchan expected to be given the creative inside-forward's job himself, but Chapman valued his goalscoring abilities too highly and detailed a reserve inside-forward, Andy Neil, to perform the midfield role at Upton Park the following week on Monday 5 October 1925. Arsenal won 4–0, with Buchan scoring twice.

Chapman gradually revised his team by pushing the full-backs out to mark the wingers, and using both his wing-halves (now free of their close-marking duties) to perform the midfield duties along with the withdrawn inside-forward. The scheme worked well enough, but was not perfected until Chapman purchased the vital creative link, Alex James, from Preston in 1929. Thus the team played in a formation which could loosely be described as 3–4–3 or 3–3–4, rather than the 2–3–5 of the pre-First World War era. Though most teams quickly copied Chapman's system, club programmes 45 years later were still putting down teams in the out-dated 2–3–5 pattern.

Between 1925 and 1930 Champan's team and tactics developed in step. Butler's successor as the 'policeman' centre-half was Herbie Roberts, acquired from Oswestry in 1926. His two full-backs were George Male and Eddie Hapgood, often partners for England. David Jack came from Bolton to replace Buchan for the first ever five figure fee (£10,370) in 1928 and, a year later, the key to the whole side arrived from Preston. Alex James was finally persuaded to adopt the midfield general role—spraying out long passes to the flying wingers Hulme and Bastin and to the unrefined but effective Jack Lambert at centre-forward.

That was essentially Chapman's great side of the early 1930s. Having lost the Cup Final of 1927, when Dan Lewis let the ball slide underneath his shiny new jumper and allowed Cardiff to take the Cup out of England for the first time, Arsenal returned to defeat Huddersfield 2–0 three years later.

The League was won for the first time in 1931 with 66 points (which remained a record until Leeds bettered it by one in 1969) and the following year Arsenal were at Wembley to lose by the famous 'over the line' goal to Newcastle: Allen's equalizing goal came from a cross which seemed well over the goal-line when Richardson made it. Between 1933 and 1935 Arsenal completed a hat-trick of League Championships, then beat Sheffield United in the Cup Final of 1936 and were champions again in 1938.

As Chapman died in 1934 he was neither with Huddersfield nor Arsenal when they completed their hat-tricks of Championships. He was succeeded at Highbury by George Allison, a radio commentator.

A simple recitation of Arsenal's successes in the 1930s, impressive though it is, tells only a part of the story. In a way that no other team, before or since, has ever approached, Arsenal somehow *were* football for a decade. In almost every way the Gunners' influence on the game was all-pervasive and Chapman's remarkable success on the field should never be allowed to conceal some remarkable achievements off it.

His skill as a public relations officer was certainly equal to his skill as a tactician. He claimed that as much energy had been expended getting the name of Gillespie Road tube station changed to Arsenal as had been exerted winning the Cup in 1930. He changed the name of the club from 'The Arsenal' to plain 'Arsenal' because, he explained, 'it will always be first on a list of clubs as well as on the field.' Appreciating the publicity value of the titled, he persuaded the board to accept Lord Lonsdale as one of the number and persuaded the Prince of Wales to open a new stand in 1932. He changed from the original Nottingham Forest colours to a red shirt with white sleeves because it was more distinctive, and later the red socks became blue and white hooped. This was so that the players could recognize each other without looking up in a melee and not, as Chapman had kidded, because 'red runs in the wash'.

Chapman was one of the first to experiment with numbering players—the FA finally accepted the idea for the 1933 Cup Final, five years after Chapman—and was in the forefront of schoolboy and youth training schemes.

In his trainer, Tom Whittaker, he appointed the first of the modern day physiotherapist coaches. Modern medical equipment, training routines and individual treatment all arrived at Highbury long before they had been considered elsewhere.

All in all, Arsenal were the very first of the wholly professional football clubs in the British Isles. Herein, perhaps, lies the key to the antipathy that followed, and still follows, the Gunners around the country. No story of the 1930s can be complete without considering this remarkable antagonism.

'Lucky Arsenal' was the cry that flitted across a decade. Time after time, Arsenal seemed happy to absorb the pressure of less talented attacks and win games by the simple expedient of the breakaway goal. It was difficult to convince the unsophisticated terraces or the ageing boardrooms of the 1930s that 80 minutes of unrewarded pressure was less valuable than one goal from a few sudden breaks by Hulme and Bastin. Indeed, it was to be another 30 years before British fans fully appreciated that the best of two teams is, by definition, the one that scores more goals.

It is, of course, impossible to view Arsenal out of historical perspective. The thirties were, for most of provincial Britain, arguably the worst decade for almost a century. In many of the textile towns unemployment reached a third of the workforce; in some places, like Jarrow, literally the whole

Dixie Dean scores the second of Everton's goals in their 3–0 win over Manchester City in a 1933 FA Cup Final, unique in the game's history. Not only was it the first time players were numbered but the only occasion on which they were numbered from 1 to 22. Numbering on shirts for League matches didn't come until 1939.

town was on the dole for years on end. To these towns Arsenal came to represent the wealth, the affluence, and the unfair advantage that London seemed to have stolen from the rest of the country. It was not too unrealistic to see Arsenal as a symbol of the wealth earned in the North but spent and enjoyed in the South.

With the football ground being almost the only entertainment outlet available to the working classes, it is not surprising that Arsenal became a subject of fierce emotional commitment—one way or the other. Walsall's defeat of Arsenal in the third round of the Cup in 1933 was a cause of widespread celebration all over the country, and the economic conditions of the times go no small way to explaining the peculiar position that one match still holds in the game's folklore—it was the perfect example of the poor, underfed weakling rising to humiliate a Goliath which had all the advantages.

On reflection Arsenal gained their reputation not by winning everything going—though they won a lot—but by always being the team to beat. They disturbed the cosy unthinking mood of the time where even the leading clubs were happy to meander along, appointing an old player as manager, reaching the odd semi-final here, the top five of the League there. This was success, this was football. Arsenal were simply of another generation. Instead of putting down men in chess-board formation—centre-forwards with iron foreheads and no feet, wingers on the touchline where they belonged—Arsenal experimented.

But Chapman's two great teams—Huddersfield and Arsenal—should not be allowed to disguise the fact that there were other sides of note in the inter-War period. Bolton, for instance, won the Cup in 1923, 1926 and again in 1929, the first being the occasion of the inaugural Wembley Final and the highest attendance ever at a British football match. West Bromwich won promotion from the Second Division and the FA Cup in 1931—a unique double—and the next year their promotion partners, Everton, went on to become only the second club to win the Second and First Division in consecutive seasons. With a Cup win in 1933, Everton were probably the closest rivals to Arsenal in the period. Dixie Dean had completed his remarkable 60-goal feat with a hat-trick in the last game of the 1927–28 season—against Arsenal—and went on to become a major attraction of the following decade.

On a wider front Britain was barely aware. While Cuba and the Dutch East Indies battled for the World Cup the Home Countries stood aloof from FIFA. England did not enter until 1950, when a traumatic game against the United States showed how 20 years of isolation could take their toll. Chapman may have built the strongest club side in the world, but that was far removed from the true international success that was so long coming. The in-bred British game had grown effete while foreigners flourished.

For the English, then, the era meant Arsenal and in the end that must be Chapman's epitaph. Mention the club in any soccer conscious country in the world and it will produce

106

instant recognition. The word no longer means a place where arms are kept, but rather the club that Herbert Chapman built. The name is a permanent memorial to the achievements of one man—and the club that had the good sense to appoint him.

Chapman's Arsenal team had faded by the time the Second World War began in 1939, but for many players their careers were ruined by the seven year suspension of football coinciding with their late twenties and early thirties. In 1939 Wolves appeared to have a team with a future—by 1946 they were all seven years older and Stan Cullis had to look for (and, as he did, find) new players to fit. That being said, the War also provided little opportunity for younger players to obtain the requisite experience, so the fixtures and the players on the first day of the season in 1946 bore an uncanny resemblance to that of the quickly aborted 1939–40 equivalent, which had lasted just three matches.

Of course, many names would appear no more, overtaken by age and tiring muscles. Others had been killed during the war, men like Tommy Cooper, the great Liverpool full-back who met his end as a despatch rider, Albert Clarke, Blackburn Rovers' gifted inside-forward killed in Normandy on D-Day, Harry Goslin, pre-War captain of Bolton Wanderers, killed in action in Italy, Coen, that fine Luton goalkeeper shot down in a raid over the Ruhr Valley on a RAF bombing raid, or youngsters just making their way in the game in 1939 like Reynolds, transferred from Charlton to Torquay United a few days before war began, called up and killed in action before he

had ever had the chance to kick a ball for his new club.

Others again were scattered all over the country, indeed all over the world, retained in the Forces and in essential industries. Consequently clubs gave League changes to men who before the war and again today would not have been allowed to lace a boot in a League dressing room.

In 1946–47 in the frantic bid to find and mould a decent combination clubs called on more men than ever before or since. Arsenal had 31 men on first team duty during the season, Huddersfield Town 32. In the Second Division Newport County's League roll call reached the astonishing figure of 41 and Bury, Leicester City, Manchester City, Millwall, Nottingham Forest and Sheffield Wednesday all topped the 30 mark. Beating them all were Hull City, in the Third North. They fielded 42 men.

Yet Saturday 31 August 1946 was a symbol to the British people that life was nearly back to normal. On that day a full programme of first class League fixtures was played in the British Isles for the first time since 2 September 1939. In fact the 1945–46 FA Cup competition had been completed under unique rules which required the games to be contested on a home-and-away basis. One resulting oddity was that Charlton became the first side to reach the Final after undisputably *losing* an earlier game. Fulham beat them 2–1 in one of the third round matches but Charlton won on aggregate by taking the other match 3–1.

At the time hundreds of thousands of men were already demobbed with their gratuities burning a hole in their pockets

Stamford Bridge again, but this time 25 years later. The first day of League football for seven long years and a symbol to the British public that life was nearly back to normal. Spectators cheerfully queue in the rain on 31 August 1946. Hundreds of men were demob happy with money to spend and some years to make up.

The 1930 Cup Final and Huddersfield are hit by an
Alex James free kick—the first of Arsenal's two goals.
This match cast its shadow in more ways than one.
First of all the German airship the Graf Zeppelin flew
over the ground, signifying German might and
aspirations that were to lead to bloody combat in nine
years' time. More immediately, and so far as football
was concerned, the great Huddersfield Town side under
which Herbert Chapman had dominated the League in
the late 1920s, was about to sink into obscurity from
which it has not yet risen, and Arsenal, Chapman's new
team, which had not won anything before, were about to
dominate football as no team had ever done. The
transfer of power could be said to date from this match.

and five or six years of their young lives to make up. Millions
in factories and industry had been earning more money than
ever before but as the war dragged on found less and less to
spend it on. Now, with football back, there would be
something exciting to help use up some of that cash, trips to
be made by train and coach with meals to buy in towns not
visited for many years, and wayside inns to dally at.

Rationing still blanketed all the civilizing amenities of life,
cars and television sets for all were still a dream, you could
not have a house built because of a word called licence.

Small wonder then that on 31 August 1946, when clubs
opened their grounds to the public shortly after noon, there
were long queues outside practically all of them. Small gates
were the exceptions, not the rule. In the Third Division South,
for example, only two clubs reported attendances of under
10,000. Crowds of 20,000 and 25,000 at this level were
commonplace.

This was to be a unique season in many ways. The fixtures
were a complete replica of those which had made for the
1939–40 campaign—a season which died after just seven
days. This heightened the illusion that life had been taken up
where it had left off. Ahead lay the terrible winter of 1946–47,

by far the worst of the century and at a time when food and
fuel were still heavily restricted. The winter struck late, and
with floodlighting still another future dream, clubs could not
get the alarming backlog of fixtures cleared. The season
became the longest in history, lasting from 31 August to the
following 14 June. The 1947–48 season began only 70 days
later.

Both sides of the freeze-up, however, the crowds poured in.
This was the time when a Jimmy Hill should have risen and
forced through the no-maximum wage for footballers still 15
years or more in the future. Instead, after arbitration, the
wage for the best First Division players was increased for the
1947–48 season to £12 a week maximum and £10 a week
during the close season.

When the balance sheets of 1946–47 were presented all but
half a dozen clubs reported profits, many of them substantial.
Stoke City led the way with £32,207, Burnley made £18,000,
Liverpool over £17,000, Middlesbrough £15,000 and Wolves
nearly £11,000. In Scotland, Rangers made £12,500; Queen of
the South, whose home town Dumfries has a population of
only 26,000, topped £11,000.

The 1946–47 season attracted some 35,000,000 spectators

but this record was left far behind in the second post-War campaign. When all the figures were in, the attendance total in first-class football alone topped 40,000,000. This was five million more than ever before and it represented the taking of £4,000,000 at the turnstiles. England won the Home International Championship and against foreign opposition were invincible. This made it possible for Lord Athlone, President of the Football Association, to deliver a speech at the annual meeting which smacked faintly of 'showing the flag'.

'At a time when exports are of paramount importance,' he said, 'football is far from being insignificant. A successful English referee in the Argentine or our international team in Italy is a way of speaking to other nations in a language ordinary people can understand.' For the first time the magic word 'television' came upon the scene. The FA was all for it, the Football League dead against it.

Two clubs dominated the English scene—Arsenal and Manchester United. United, for the first occasion in modern times, rose to a national eminence which has surrounded Old Trafford ever since. Colchester United, then members of the Southern League, had their first glorious hour when they knocked First Division Huddersfield Town out of the FA Cup.

In Scotland Hibernian took the Championship to Edinburgh for the first time since 1903. The team included Gordon Smith, Alec Linwood, Willie Ormond, Eddie Turnbull and an Englishman, Bobby Coombe. The most sensational transfer of the season came when Tommy Lawton, England's centre-forward, moved down to the Third Division, joining Notts County for a record £20,000 fee.

Surely 1948–49 could not see a new attendance record? In the event it did—easily. Leaving aside FA Cup games, internationals and the 30 major professional and amateur competitions outside the first class aegis, the number of people who attended League matches reached the never surpassed total of 41,271,424.

As the 20th century came up to its half way mark football reached a watershed. The boom was a long way from over but 1949–50 was to be the last season in which total League attendances for a season topped 40,000,000. This, too, was the last season of the League in the form of 88 clubs equally divided into four sections, for at the annual meeting four new clubs—Colchester United, Gillingham, Scunthorpe and Lindsey United and Shrewsbury Town—were admitted, two each to both sections of Division Three. The election of Scunthorpe to the Northern group was one of the strangest quirks of post-War football. On the first ballot Shrewsbury were elected easily but Workington and Wigan Athletic tied for second place. Rather than just a straightforward vote between the two tied clubs, the League took it into its head to organize another open ballot—the result being that Scunthorpe defeated both of their seemingly stronger opponents. Workington replaced New Brighton the following year but it took Wigan 30 more years to achieve their goal and by that time their opponents Workington had come and gone, finally voted out.

The fifth post-War season, although it was not realized at the time, marked the real beginning in a change in public tastes and habits. At long last the all round austerity and drabness was disappearing. People could now think in terms of cars, clothes, furniture, new fabrics, new colours, television sets, holidays abroad. No longer did sport, and soccer in particular, represent one of the few worthwhile things on which to spend spare money and time.

Tottenham were perhaps the first club to perceive the need to meet the new challenge from outside Britain which was about to engulf the national elevens of the four home countries. Arthur Rowe, Spurs manager, a silver haired Cockney, had instituted a style called 'push and run'. Briefly it meant doing the simple things quickly and accurately and it showed the benefits of a higher work rate than previously thought necessary from all eleven members of a side. Newly promoted from Division Two they cast a shadow of the worldwide greatness they were to earn a decade later by storming straight on to take the First Division title.

From that season the honeymoon between football and the fans was over. The game is still a crowd puller without parallel in any form of activity known to 20th-century man but it is unlikely ever to know again such a golden age at the turnstiles when in six years it was patronised by 236 million fans, a figure equivalent to the entire population of the United States or Russia. They were, indeed, the Golden Years.

An Englishman looking at football since those days of boom attendances will inevitably focus on one of two moments in time. One is the evening of 6 February 1958 when the plane carrying Manchester United, indisputably Britain's best club side, crashed on take-off from Munich airport. The other comes eight years later, the afternoon of 30 July 1966, when the country that gave the world the game finally took its place as more than an also ran. After two decades of

DAILY EXPRESS

No. 17,949

FRIDAY FEBRUARY 7 1958

3 a.m. forecast: Cold; snow or sleet likely

Price 2½

ALIVE Blanchflower, Edwards, Berry, Scanlon, Morgans, Gregg, Wood, Charlton, Viollet, Foulkes; Busby

DEAD Byrne, Bent, Jones, Whelan, Colman, Pegg, and Tommy Taylor

SURVIVORS SPEAK

THREE TAKE-OFF ATTEMPTS—AND THEN DISASTER

EXPRESS Photo News

SEE PAGES 2, 5, 6, 7 AND 16

Matt Busby called out: It's my legs, my legs...

Express Staff Reporters

MANCHESTER United footballers told last night the stark, dramatic story of how the airliner bringing them home from Yugoslavia had

February 1958 and the story that stunned a nation. Though the Daily Express *correctly reports Duncan Edwards as being alive he was to die later, the eighth player victim of the Munich air crash which created a legend around Manchester United.*

international mediocrity, a reputation had been re-established.

The World Cup win came at the midpoint of a decade which saw a complete change in the British game. The vital point was the abolition of the maximum wage in 1961. George Eastham had brought the whole question of players' conditions and contracts into the open and into the courts when Newcastle refused to give him a transfer. Victory for Eastham meant that men who had been restricted to a niggardly maximum wage of £20 a week could command three or four times that amount. Within a year Johnny Haynes, then captain of England, had become the first home footballer earning £100 a week.

It was perhaps unfortunate that this players' revolution should have occurred just as two other forces were changing the fabric of the game, a little more slowly to be sure, but just as vitally. One was the growth of private transport and an effective road system, allowing anyone within 40 miles of Manchester, say, to regard United as their local club.

The other factor was the introduction of regular televised games. This affected the game more subtly than the administrators had originally feared. Rather than simply staying at home to watch Spurs rather than going out to see Brentford—a matter of laziness—the really vital change was one of attitude. For spectators were persuaded that the football they wanted to see was that played by the major clubs and, in many cases, that alone.

And so the eventual effect of these changes was to strengthen those already strong and to weaken those already weak. Great old clubs like Bolton and Blackburn found that their reputations meant nothing beside the pull of George Best at Old Trafford. In 1971 Manchester United took a quite unprecedented step by making several of their League matches all-ticket. That was the result of 25 consecutive years

as the greatest draw in Britian. Three times Sir Matt Busby built great sides—the 1948 combination that won the Cup, the 1958 'Babes' who died at Munich and the 1968 European Cup winning side. But it was not so much the success and hours of incomparable entertainment that has tied United to the hearts of the British people, rather it was a single incident at a German airfield when the team that has been called the greatest English club side ever was destroyed.

Three decades later people who do not see a football match from one year to the next religiously go along to their local ground when United play—simply because of the legend of Munich. It made United more than a football team—it made them an article of football faith.

There were other good club sides—the orthodox fast-running Wolves of the 1950s who first introduced the British to European competition; the two North London 'double' sides of 1961 and 1971, so close geographically yet so far apart in style; Ipswich Town, the most unexpected winners in the history of the League and perfect proof that the age of method had arrived; Leeds United, 'the professionals', never giving anything away, never letting opponents relax, the worship-pers of workrate yet destined to become seemingly eternal runners-up; Celtic, so utterly dominant under Stein's command in the 1960s that Scottish football became as predict-able as the rising of the sun. And yet, for all this talent, British teams took a long time to make an impact in Europe.

The first steps into Europe had been as painful as the Common Market negotiations. Though Hibernian entered the European Cup in its inaugural season (1955–56), reached the semi-finals and made £25,000 from the venture (a large sum for a Scottish club at the time), the Football League, in traditionally short-sighted fashion, had 'advised' Chelsea not to enter. It is worth remembering that the League had only just begun to allow floodlit fixtures at this time, and they 'advised' Manchester United the same way the following year. But Matt Busby was more farsighted than his superiors and took no notice.

Revenge was swift. After the Munich crash in 1958 the organizing committee invited United to enter the European Cup the following year along with the League Champions, Wolves. A joint committee of the League and FA finally refused permission on the grounds that it was against the competition's rules (those already waived by the organizers). It was the shabbiest paragraph in a truly parochial chapter.

Europe was a tremendous catalyst for the British. Not only did Football and Scottish League clubs come to adopt entry into European competition as a major goal, but it changed the face of the game in these somewhat isolated Isles. It was not long before club sides realized that the good old-fashioned tackle from behind and charge on the goalkeeper were not going to be tolerated by crowds, opponents or referees in European matches. The less physical game gradually crossed the Channel and its advantages led to a growing rejection of the intimidating behaviour so characteristic of the 1950s. By 1971 the charge on the goalkeeper was no more than a memory and the Football Association felt strongly enough to try and cut out the equally contentious tackle from behind.

So Britain finally came to accept the discipline of Europe, just as she came to accept a new concept in tactics and coaching and the widespread influx of supposedly 'continental' systems. The combination of an emphasis on sheer physical fitness, leading to the 'perpetual motion' players of whom Alan Ball was probably the best example, and the rejection of the more strictly positional 'stopper' or '3–2–5' formation, with its familiar full-backs, inside-forwards and wingers, led to considerable confusion on the terraces in the 1960s.

That a man could wear a number seven shirt and *not* patrol the right touchline seemed quite revolutionary to many used to watching Matthews and Finney. Dick Graham achieved some early success with an all-purpose Crystal Palace side— once threatening to number his players in alphabetical order as he claimed numbers did not count any more (which assumes that they once did of course)—and Matt Gillies and Bert Johnson took Leicester to the Cup Finals of 1961 and 1963 with similarly revolutionary concepts on how the game should be played.

But while Alf Ramsey achieved the most obvious success with methodical rather than inspired football—neither his Ipswich side of 1962 nor the England of 1966 will ever be categorized among the world's great entertainers—a more appealingly influential figure in the English game of the period was Ron Greenwood, manager of West Ham from 1961. This, in part, was a result of his willingness to allow journalists a view of the inner workings of the football world and his propensity to sit and discuss the game for hours with those who could take his views outside the dressing-room.

Greenwood himself has often suggested that the real credit for the new ideas that gained so much currency in the 1960s should go to Walter Winterbottom. The Football Association's Chief Coach from 1946 to 1963, Winterbottom spent most of that period doubling-up as manager of England's various teams, roles whose compatability was not always obvious. While he is widely remembered for a relatively unspectacular spell as team manager, his work on the coaching side at Lilleshall is known only to those inside the game. His tactical appreciation, his encouragement of personal skills and his insistence on a team's corporate knowledge of its objectives are factors that no one who has taken an FA course could ignore. It was at Lilleshall, not Wembley, that the foundations of the 1966 World Cup win

were laid. Winterbottom saw the way ahead for football.

Attitudes were changing. It was not that whether Wolves or Manchester United won the League became less significant, more that the most important consequence was that success gained entry to the European Cup. Whereas a climax used to occur every season—around the time of the Cup Final—it now seemed to occur only once every four years, at the time of the World Cup.

Before 1950 the British regarded the World Cup as an event competed for by foreigners. But the dispute with FIFA having been healed, the four home countries finally agreed to enter and FIFA accepted the Home International Championship as a qualifying competition. The first and second countries were to go through to the final rounds—virtually carte blanche for England and Scotland.

In the event, it provided the Scots with a fine opportunity to display that shortsighted foolishness which has often made

Top *Euphoria on the bench as Geoff Hurst scores England's fourth goal in the 1966 World Cup Final against West Germany. The only man still seated? Alf Ramsey.*
Above *Bobby Charlton practises his skills under the watchful eye of Harold Shepherdson during an England training session at Lilleshall. It was here, not Wembley, where the foundations of success were laid.*

The most controversial goal scored in the history of British, and possibly World, football was England's third in the 1966 World Cup final against West Germany. Geoff Hurst turned on an Alan Ball pass, thumped the ball past defender Willi Schulz and onto the crossbar. The ball bounced down and out so fast that no one could tell whether it

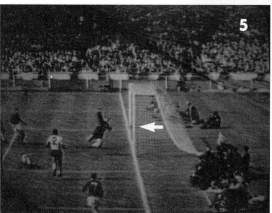 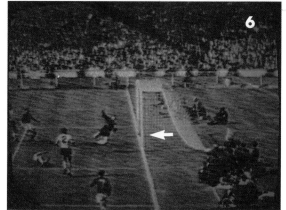

was over the line or not. The body of keeper Hans Tilkowski obscured the line of vision of the television cameras while other cameras, there for the film Goal!, were placed along the penalty line at an inconclusive angle. There was, however, another motor camera present which was almost exactly on the goal-line and the pictures above are taken from

the English FA appear prophetic visionaries by comparison. England beat Scotland 1–0 at Hampden in the deciding match and the losers, coming only second in the Championship, refused to go to Brazil for the World Cup.

So England went alone and came back even lonelier. At Belo Horizonte they suffered a footballing humiliation not surpassed before or since, although the 0–0 draw with Morocco in the 1986 World Cup runs it close. That 1950 game against the USA was expected to be a canter. That vast country had never adopted the world's most popular version of football, preferring instead its own brutal perversion. The American coach—irony of ironies—was a Scotsman, Bill Jeffrey, and the night before the game his team were up until the early hours at a party; the only unanswered question was the size of the defeat.

Instead they won 1–0; one British press agency assumed the score was a mistake and printed the result as 10–1. To be fair to England, it was one of those days that every team sometimes has—nothing would go right. Looking back, paradoxically, the outcome was more of a disappointment to the Americans than the English. The latter lost 1–0 to Spain in the next game and went home having got nowhere. But the Americans sincerely believed that their victory was going to be the spark that ignited the game across the Atlantic. They could not have been more wrong.

In England the result was not treated seriously—in fact it was dismissed as the fluke it undoubtedly was and the tower of English self-confidence survived, if only for another three years. The main reason for that pride was 80 years of internationals in which England had never lost at home to foreign opposition.

True, Eire had won a poor game 2–0 at Everton in 1949, but as nine of their side were regular Football League players they can hardly be regarded as aliens. That record was threatened in November 1951 when England drew 2–2 with Austria thanks to an Alf Ramsey penalty. In October 1953

they were 4–3 down to a FIFA side in a full international with only one minute left. Mortensen collided with an opponent and England were awarded a penalty ('although it was still two months to Christmas' as a reporter put it). Ramsey scored again and England's record was safe—but for just four weeks.

The moment of truth arrived on the afternoon of 25 November 1953. Ramsey later said that the game against Hungary had a profound effect on him; it could hardly have had any other. While the game against the USA could be dismissed as a freak the defeat by Hungary was without excuse. A far better team had shown England that reputation was no longer enough.

Eighteen years later that same England side were gathered at a function also attended by Ferenc Puskas. Ramsey greeted his full-back partner that day, the late Bill Eckersley, rather quizically; 'Hello, it is Bill isn't it?' and Puskas was heard to remark: 'It was like that when they played us—the team hardly seemed to know each other's names.'

England lost 6–3. Far worse, they had made no plans when, six months later, they played a return in Budapest. That one was lost 7–1. England were totally exposed by a side that shamed them in ability, fitness and, above all, in tactical awareness.

English football had entered a period in the doldrums from which it was not to emerge for a dozen years. In the 1954 World Cup the Uruguayan side that had defeated Scotland 7–0 also put out England 4–2. In 1958 England failed even to reach the quarter-finals, losing to the USSR in a group play-off. England's style was summed up by Vittorio Pozzo when he described a goal by Kevan as being scored with the 'outside of his head', implying that England were still not one of the world's more thoughtful soccer nations. That year, at least, Northern Ireland and Wales reached the quarter-finals.

In 1962 England went out 3–1 to Brazil, again in the quarter-finals; Scotland, Wales and Ireland failed to qualify.

whole *ball could ever have been over the line. The time sequence can be judged by the position of Tilkowski's falling body. Hurst's last minute goal, giving him a hat-trick and England a 4–2 success, helped still the uncertainty but the eventual result might have been very different had Dienst given the benefit of doubt to the defending side.*

its frames. Referee Dienst asked his linesman, Bakhramov, to decide and the Russian said it was a goal. Judged by the sequence above, the linesman was wrong. Even allowing for the very slight angle, the ball is always in vision to the field side of the near post (arrows indicate the ball's position) and it is inconceivable that, at any point, the

That was the end of Walter Winterbottom's reign as team manager. Alf Ramsey took over what ought to have been one of the best teams in the world. The first game after his appointment was against France, who declined in the 1960s to the Third Division of European football. England lost that game 5–2, Ramsey declared that they would win the World Cup anyway and the rest is history.

The World Cup victory is not to be denigrated—but what really stands out from 1966 is how sceptical about England's abilities (after previous World Cups) supporters had become and how little chance England were given of winning. Look at the facts. England played six games, all of them at Wembley. In nearly 60 years of internationals against foreign opposition, England had lost only four times at home—to Eire in 1949, to Hungary in 1953, to Sweden in 1959 and to Austria in 1965. Not even Brazil had managed to win at Wembley. Of the 40 full international games England had played against her six opponents, Uruguay, Mexico, France, Argentina, Portugal and West Germany, she had lost only eight. Not a single one of those had been at home and none of those six countries had managed even a draw at Wembley.

In fact the Germans, the other finalists, had never beaten England anywhere, managing just one draw back in Berlin in 1930. Quite simply each of those six matches should have been won and had they been ordinary mid-week 'friendlies' no one would have expected anything but the eventual results. But it is easy to be wise after the event. At the time there was always Brazil, seeking a hat-trick of victories, a rampant Hungarian attack, Eusebio in startling form and the ever-present threat of West Germany, Russia and Italy.

Ramsey's strength was in his free hand. At long last the FA had realized that the system devised by Stanley Rous during the Second World War—whereby he did everything—was the most effective available. Thus, although there was still an international committee technically in existence, Ramsey was the only man who did any selecting. When asked by one of

this committee at a cocktail party exactly what its official duties were, Ramsey is reputed to have replied: 'To come to cocktail parties.'

Being a defender himself, it is not surprising that Ramsey, like a successful First World War general, believed that defence was the key to victory. For the 1966 World Cup final England ended up with just two fulltime forwards, Hurst and Hunt, five defenders (Stiles, at 'half-back', playing an auxiliary defensive role wherever he was needed), the goalkeeper and three providers.

The formation was substantially the same for the traumatic game in Leon four years later—except that now both Peters and Ball were required to be preoccupied in midfield—when it was proved beyond dispute that the best laid schemes of men, mice and Alf Ramsey can be thwarted by individual error.

Peter Bonetti, deputizing in goal for Banks, was adjudged to have been at fault for the first German goal and was possibly not blameless for the other two. It is sad that one display—albeit the most important of his career—will always be remembered before so many excellent ones elsewhere. Banks later speculated that he might even have been deliberately poisoned but the truth on the field was a little harder to take—it had been an excellent game but, in a sense, just one of those days. Though Bonetti might have saved Beckenbauer's goal, Seeler's back header was surely nothing more than a fluke and Ramsey was horribly unlucky.

The years 1953 and 1966 must be considered the landmarks of the post-War era for English soccer. The former had the effect of an earthquake—it overthrew all the misconceptions English football had about itself, though it took ten years for all the lessons to filter through. The second date was notable for an atmosphere more akin to VE-day, but it was a moment that was to be misunderstood. It did conclude a great era, but it did not shepherd in another. Twenty years later, one pines for the days of innocence.

CHAPTER SIX

THE FOOTBALL LEAGUE CUP

There are some who say that Oxford United won the Milk Cup in 1986, there are some who say Oxford United won the Littlewoods Cup in 1986; there are some who say it should have been the Thames Valley Royals winning the Football League Cup in 1986; there are many who do not care one way or the other.

In its first quarter century of existence, the Football League/Milk/Littlewoods Cup has had three names, sixteen winners, a limited number of devotees and a clear lack of ability to convince. Even now, it is very difficult to put forward a justification for its existence other than as a means of making more money for a number of clubs and helping promote a random selection of sponsors. And even these two arguments are debatable. It is difficult to see quite what the Milk Marketing Board got from its four-year association with football at such a difficult time. Presumably most people know milk exists; presumably they will drink it or not depending on their attitude to such matters, not whether or not its name is on a football trophy.

There is also a convincing argument to be made out that the introduction of the League Cup hastened the decline of attendances at regular League matches. Unless the tie was a very attractive one, large numbers of otherwise regular attenders decided that this supposedly first-class fixture could be given a miss. And once they had got used to the idea of missing League Cup ties, it was not so difficult to decide to skip Birmingham on Saturday, or Coventry next Wednesday in the League. The very existence of the League Cup (a name almost chosen to create confusion anyway) inevitably devalued the FA Cup, even if it left the League largely untouched. In retrospect, it is clear English football needed fewer, better matches, not more of random quality and appeal. Why, one should ask, do American football teams play just 16 matches in a regular season?

At the start, there were many who were thoroughly cynical about adding a largely meaningless trophy to an already overcrowded fixture list. The Cup, voted in at the annual meeting of the League in 1960 by a majority of only 15, was a very sickly infant, and the reception it received in some quarters was, to put it kindly, lukewarm. British managers, players and crowds were just beginning to adjust to the thought of European competition and here was another tournament, created to help the smaller sides and not particularly lucrative, to clog up the fixture list still further. It was not right to expect footballers to play 60 times a season.

Five clubs, including those who had finished second, third, fourth and fifth in the First Division the previous season, refused to enter, thus devaluing the competiton before it had even started. The following year the number of absentees swelled to 10, including seven of the top ten. Shades of the Full Members Cup 25 years later.

The early, two-legged finals were hardly affairs to shake the football world and in 1962, when it was played out between a Second and a Fourth Division side, the two games pulled in barely 30,000 spectators. So, as the big clubs continued to view it with contempt and the smaller ones

entered almost as a matter of form, as the press and the public looked on with detachment, the League Cup stuttered on.

Alan Hardaker, the Football League secretary, remained the most ardent of its few committed supporters. He had always been obsessed with what was essentially his idea though, as he points out, he could not and did not implement it. 'It's been called Hardaker's baby and even Hardaker's folly,' he explained, 'but I did not take the decision to introduce it. Like everything else done by the League it was a matter for the clubs to vote on.'

Hardaker's early optimism was based on comparisons with the competition's much older sister, the FA Cup. 'Every worthwhile development in football has faced initial problems and criticism, and the League Cup was no exception. The early history of the FA Cup shows that it too had to face a variety of problems for several years, not least lack of interest. It was strongly criticized on its inception because it introduced a competitive element into amateur football, namely the winning of a trophy. There were 15 entries. After ten seasons there were 73.'

But the FA Cup was the first national competition. It was the natural result of the enthusiasm and aspirations of an emerging sport. The League Cup, by contrast, was anything but; money was its motivating force. It had to be created, and then it took several severe changes—with more commercial carrots being dangled—to drag it from a struggling child into a promising adolescent. They came in 1966.

The previous season the eight absent clubs had included seven from the top eight in the First Division—among them League Champions Manchester United, FA Cup holders Liverpool and, most indicative of all, Chelsea, the holders of the League Cup itself. Tommy Docherty apparently thought the Fairs Cup a good deal more important. Attendances, though slightly improved, remained mediore.

There were two major changes. First, the awkward home

Albion's opponents were QPR, then running away with the Third Division championship. Rangers had started as they meant to go on with a 5–0 win over Colchester, but they had only one game against a First Division club on the way, beating Leicester 4–2. The match at Wembley, in danger of being a one-sided anti-climax, proved to be the opposite. Lowly QPR, down two goals by an ex-player of their's, Clive Clark, were faced with an apparently impossible task against a club separated from them by about 30 places in the League. But they did do it, with goals from Roger Morgan, Rodney Marsh (a splendid effort which, with the help of television, made him a household name by the Monday morning) and Mark Lazarus.

Had the League Cup come of age? From some quarters came an honest conversion, from others came grudging acknowledgement. Cynics pointed out the fact that no Third Division club had reached the FA Cup Final in the 47 years

Far left *Alan Hudson, John Dempsey and Paddy Mulligan can only watch helplessly as Terry Conroy heads Stoke in front against Chelsea in the 1972 League Cup Final—both clubs' second appearance in the final.*
Above centre *Jimmy Greenhoff celebrates after Conroy's goal. George Eastham went on to score Stoke's second to complete a 2–1 win—Stoke's 12th game of the competition and their first major success in a 109-year history.*
Right *Arsenal's Bobby Gould (10) equalizes in the 1969 League Cup Final. But Swindon's Don Rogers scored twice in extra-time and the Third Division club, like Queen's Park Rangers in 1967, had beaten First Division opposition in the final.*

and away final was abolished in favour of a more romantic (and lucrative) climax at Wembley. Second, the Fairs Cup committee decided to accept the winners as entrants for its competition the following year—provided they were a First Division side. (Though an obvious incentive this move never actually promoted an entrant: in 1967 and 1969 the winners, Queen's Park Rangers and Swindon, were both Third Division sides, in 1968 Leeds—who were to win the Fairs Cup later that season—qualified by coming fourth in the League, and in 1970 Manchester City went on to win the Cup Winners Cup, thus defending that trophy the following year. Spurs, in 1971, were the first club able to take up the offer, and by then the actual Fairs Cup was no more.)

The changes completely revitalized a flagging League Cup. All but League Champions Liverpool and Cup winners Everton now entered, and the converts included four sides who had remained aloof from the start—Arsenal, Sheffield Wednesday, Spurs and Wolves. Perhaps there was a certain justice in the fact that all four of them went out to sides of lesser standing in the League, and not one of them reached the last 16—that is, won more than one game.

In fact West Ham, who had seen something in the League Cup from the start, were responsible for the elimination of the two North London sides who had just joined the fold. They then beat Leeds (7–0) and Blackpool but were stopped short of Wembley by WBA—in a repeat of the previous year's two-legged final—after crashing 4–0 at The Hawthorns.

that section had been in existence, let alone won it, and said that the big sides were still loath to take it at all seriously. But 98,000 at Wembley and millions more in their armchairs thought differently.

The moves had apparently done the trick. Though some clubs committed in Europe continued to opt out—notably Manchester United—the competition grew in stature over the next few years and the average attendance (all for mid-week games except the final) soared from just over 11,000 in 1965–66 to over 19,000 in 1971–72.

In 1968 Leeds at last won a domestic honour, with a laboured 1–0 victory over a re-emerging Arsenal on a dreadful Wembley pitch. The following year Arsenal were back (this time on an even worse Wembley surface, thanks to the Horse of the Year Show) to face Swindon, who had played 11 matches to reach the final.

Swindon were trying to repeat Queen's Park Rangers' double of League Cup and promotion to the Second Division, and they succeeded. Brilliant goalkeeping from Peter Downsborough and two goals from Don Rogers helped them to a 3–1 win, though the effects of a recent 'flu epidemic at Highbury took its toll of the Arsenal players during extra time. Nine of the Arsenal squad appeared in both 1968 and 1969, among them Frank McLintock, who thus finished on the losing side at Wembley for the fourth time.

Extra time was again required in 1970, this time for Manchester City's 2–1 win over West Bromwich Albion. The

115

tie of the comptition, however, was the semi-final between the Manchester giants. City—promoted in 1966, League Champions in 1968, FA Cup winners in 1969, and now on their way to a European triumph—had been severely challenging the supremacy of a Manchester United side desperately trying to maintain the status achieved by the European Cup win over Benfica at Wembley in 1968, and a side competing in the League Cup for the first time since 1960–61.

For the first time, perhaps, a League Cup match apart from the final took on a significance outside the competition. The edited versions of both games were televised, and millions saw City confirm their suspicions with a 2–1 win at Maine Road and a 2–2 draw at Old Trafford, the second leg being played in front of 63,418—a record for the League Cup away from Wembley. 'Perhaps now they'll bloody well believe us,' said City wing-half Mick Doyle after the tie. The final, a dull, grinding affair, was a disappointment.

For those who thought the age of the lower clubs was over in the League Cup the 1970–71 competition was something of a revelation. Aston Villa, like QPR and Swindon chasing escape from the Third Division, reached Wembley. They were fortunate in meeting only one First Division side in their first five ties—a struggling Burnley in the second round—but when they did meet opponents of renown and calibre in Manchester United they proved nothing was missing. First they secured a 1–1 draw at Old Trafford and then, in front of 62,500, beat United 2–1 at Villa Park. But Wembley, Tottenham and Martin Chivers proved to be more difficult. Villa held Spurs for 80 minutes, but then two goals from the England man kept the League Cup firmly in the First Division.

There it was to stay in 1972, when Stoke beat Chelsea at Wembley in the final of what had been the first competition it had been compulsory for all 92 clubs to enter—a rather late and empty gesture at the 1971 annual general meeting. But, like the previous two seasons, it was the semi-final stage that stole the headlines.

While Chelsea and Spurs were battling out their tie, West Ham were trying to make the final an all-London affair by beating Stoke. They got off to a good start with a 2–1 win at the Victoria Ground, but John Ritchie pulled a goal back at Upton Park in the return and, in the dying minutes of extra time Gordon Banks (who had been beaten by a Geoff Hurst penalty in the first leg) made a brilliant save to stop his England colleague repeating the feat. A fine replay at Hillsborough produced no goals, and then in the second replay at Old Trafford there was the strange sight of Bobby Moore donning the goalkeeper's jersey while the injured Ferguson was off the field.

Stoke beat him once, with Bernard following up a penalty kick Moore had managed to save first time; then, with Ferguson restored, West Ham took the lead through Bonds and Brooking; Dobing pulled Stoke level before half-time and, as the two sides approached seven hours of battle, Conroy scored the winner.

The final didn't stand a chance. Three of the Stoke–West Ham clashes and both Chelsea–Spurs games had been covered by television and, though the pre-match publicity was as great as for any FA Cup Final, the match was almost inevitably a come-down. Stoke, by no means standing on ceremony or overawed by Wembley, absorbed all Chelsea's subtle pressure and took their chances well to win 2–1. After 12 matches in the tournament that year they deserved some reward.

Following on the heels of Stoke's belated success, Norwich City reached the 1973 final (their first Wembley appearance) despite not having won any of their previous 12 League

matches. After the final it was to be another eight before they recorded a success. Just ten days before Wembley they had sold their star forward Jim Bone, and their resulting contest with Spurs produced a dreadful match. The only romance came from Ralph Coates, who scored the game's only goal after coming on as subsitute.

That final began a remarkable hat-trick for Ron Saunders, then the manager of Norwich. Twelve months later he led out Manchester City, his new club, to meet Wolverhampton Wanderers in the 1974 Final. Again he was loser. Yet remarkably 1975 saw Saunders in charge of a third League Cup finalist, Second Division Aston Villa—and this time he was a winner, ironically over Norwich City.

It was also ironic that the League Cup should gain in popularity just as the fixture list was becoming congested, with an increasing number of clubs entering Europe and the emergence of peripheral competitions: the Watney Cup, the Texaco Cup and the Anglo-Italian Tournament.

It may be that the League Cup provided the incentive; that officials and administrators saw the financial rewards to be reaped from competitive matches outside the two established folds. Certainly for a club stuck in the middle of the Third or Fourth Division and eliminated from the first round of the FA Cup in November, a run to the last eight or four can provide

the only financial and psychological release during a mundane season.

In 1977 and 1978 both Wembley finals produced goalless draws which were eventually resolved at Old Trafford. Aston Villa beat Everton in the second replay of the 1977 final to win the Cup for a record time and in 1978 Nottingham Forest achieved a remarkable win over Liverpool—whom they were to depose in the first round of the 1978–79 European Cup.

These were early days in the strange relationship between Liverpool and Forest. In fact, in the three seasons after Forest's promotion in 1977 the two clubs met 13 times in first-class matches. Liverpool won three, six were drawn and Forest won four. The League Cup final was the first of their major clashes and it followed the soon-to-become familiar pattern. Liverpool attacked a Forest side short of five regulars, and with teenage reserve Chris Woods in goal, for 120 minutes and didn't score. In the replay at Old Trafford, Phil Thompson brought John O'Hare down outside the penalty area, referee Pat Partridge gave a spot-kick which John Robertson converted and Forest won 1–0.

It was an incident which led to one of football's most humorous interviews, when Peter Taylor, hugging the trophy (Forest's first under the Clough/Taylor management), was told that it certainly wasn't a penalty and Forest should therefore not have won. He rhetorically replied: 'Oh, who's got the Cup then?' and made off down the corridor with it.

Forest were back the next year, 1979, beating Southampton 3–2 in the final with two goals from Garry Birtles. In 1980 they made it a hat-trick of appearances, becoming the first club ever to appear in three consecutive Wembley finals. They had gone a record 25 games and 17 ties without defeat in the competition between September 1976 and March 1980. There the records ended after an absurd defensive mix-up between Peter Shilton and David Needham let in Andy Gray to score the only goal of the game and give Wolves a 1–0 victory.

Liverpool beat London opposition in the next two finals—West Ham after a replay in 1981 and Spurs 3–1 after extra-time in 1982. Spurs had led until three minutes from time and the defeat was their first in nine domestic cup finals, their first in nine games at Wembley and also broke an unbeaten run of 25 cup games.

The week before the Spurs v Liverpool final the competition had been renamed the Milk Cup. This was not a move calculated to enhance the stature of either the competition or milk, even though Liverpool gratefully accepted the award of

not one but two trophies. In actual fact, the competition was slipping back into the 1960s again, being seen as something of an irrelevance compared with other fixtures in a crowded list and having lost some of its romance—the minor sides no longer progressed so far as the financial demands of the bigger clubs insisted that they did not slip up.

In retrospect, the competition had reached its peak with those excellent semi-finals involving Chelsea and Stoke in 1972. At that time the Wembley finals were still a rare treat. In the decade that followed, the fact of having *two* finals a year at Wembley, plus a large number of replays (six in the two competitions) helped to devalue both events.

For Liverpool, however, 1983 and 1984 were red-letter years. Beating Manchester United 2–1 in the 1983 final, they became the first club to win three consecutive Wembley finals and only the fifth to achieve a hat-trick in any domestic competition (Wanderers and Blackburn in the FA Cup, and Huddersfield and Arsenal in the League being the others), an achievement reinforced by their League hat-trick in 1984.

In 1984 they earned a niche all of their own by becoming the first club to win four consecutive finals when they beat neighbours and rivals Everton 1–0. This was yet another final which went to a replay after a 0–0 draw at Wembley and it heralded some other notable firsts besides Liverpool's remarkable achievement. The Wembley final was the first to be played on a Sunday, the first to be televised live, the first to carry shirt advertising and it was also Joe Fagan's first major trophy as Liverpool manager. There was a bonus too. Liverpool were allowed to keep the Milk Cup trophy in recognition of their hat-trick.

Liverpool's run was, of course, commendable and praise-worthy, though it became a little tedious for the rest of the country and the competition was lucky in that they met probably the best three clubs available in successive finals—Spurs, Manchester United and Everton. Certainly the Everton game, the first sign that Howard Kendall possessed a team to be reckoned with in the mid-1980s, was a point of national interest and it was to be repeated (with similar results) in the 1986 FA Cup final.

Liverpool were finally beaten 1–0 in 1985 by Spurs at White Hart Lane. It was their first defeat in a single tie (they had lost games in the two-legged semi-finals) since 1980.

The 1985 final broke a record or two, generally the wrong ones. Norwich won it 1–0 when an Asa Hartford shot was deflected. It was Norwich's fourth League Cup final appearance, while opponents Sunderland had seen little of Wembley in recent years excepting their dramatic 1973 FA Cup final win. Sunderland had arrived there after the controversy of the semi-final against Chelsea, and there were further upsets ahead of them when Clive Walker put a first half penalty against the foot of the post. It was the first penalty ever to be missed in a Wembley final, and only the second in any major English final (Charlie Wallace of Aston Villa missed a penalty in the 1913 FA Cup final.)

Norwich capitalized on the error to win with the only goal. The real talking point came later, however, when both clubs were relegated from the First Division.

It was unusual for any Cup finalist to be relegated but no winner had ever suffered that way and it was quite unprecedented for both clubs to fall through the trapdoor at once. Norwich, it must be said, were unlucky. Coventry won all their last three games to pip them by a point.

After the era of domination by the big guns of Forest and Liverpool, it seemed that the competition had slipped back into a sort of rural, homely repechage for the also-rans. In 1986 lowly QPR and Oxford arrived at Wembley with some surprise and before a few empty seats. This was a familiar

Left above *Asa Hartford of Norwich about to shoot in the 1985 League (Milk) Cup Final. The ball was deflected off Sunderland's Gordon Chisholm (5) into the net for the only goal of the match. It was Norwich's second League Cup.*

experience for QPR—their FA Cup final replay of 1982 and their League Cup final of 1967 were the two previous Wembley finals for which tickets were still available at kick-off time. Oxford were not too worried about that. The year the League Cup came into being, 1960, was the year they entered the League (they were still called Headington United at the time) and they had never been near a final before. Despite QPR being favourites, Oxford won easily by three goals, from Hebberd, Houghton and Charles.

Oxford's win was no doubt good for the competition. It confirmed its place as something extra that the little guys might just, with some skill and a fair dollop of luck, steal from under the noses of their betters. If the competition, whatever its title, had any justification, then it was surely to encourage the also-rans in an era when they could no longer dream of Europe.

In 1987, however, the pattern was changed, when giants Liverpool, leading the First Division, were back against Arsenal, who had led for much of the season in their Centenary Year. Arsenal had won an exciting three-match encounter with Spurs, coming from behind at White Hart Lane, having lost at Highbury. The final was an excellent game, the Gunners coming from behind again with two Charlie Nicholas goals to take the trophy for the first time.

FOOTBALL LEAGUE AND MILK CUP FINALS 1960–87

1960–61 ASTON VILLA
First leg: Rotherham 22 August 1961 Attendance 12,226
Rotherham United **2** — Aston Villa **0**
Webster, Kirkman
Second leg: Villa Park 5 September 1961 Attendance 27,000
Aston Villa **3** — Rotherham United **0**
O'Neill, Burrows, McParland

1961–62 NORWICH CITY
First leg: Rochdale 26 April 1962 Attendance 11,123
Rochdale **0** — Norwich City **3**
Lythgoe 2, Punton
Second leg: Norwich 1 May 1962 Attendance 19,708
Norwich City **1** — Rochdale **0**
Hill

1962–63 BIRMINGHAM CITY
First leg: St Andrew's 23 May 1963 Attendance 31,850
Birmingham City **3** — Aston Villa **1**
Leek 2, Bloomfield — Thomson
Second leg: Villa Park 27 May 1963 Attendance 37,921
Aston Villa **0** — Birmingham City **0**

1963–64 LEICESTER CITY
First leg: Stoke 15 April 1964 Attendance 22,309
Stoke City **1** — Leicester City **1**
Bebbington — Gibson
Second leg: Leicester 22 April 1964 Attendance 25,372
Leicester City **3** — Stoke City **2**
Stringfellow, Gibson, Riley — Viollet, Kinnell

1964–65 CHELSEA
First leg: Stamford Bridge 15 March 1965 Attendance 20,690
Chelsea **3** — Leicester City **2**
Tambling, Venables (pen). McCreadie — Appleton, Goodfellow
Second leg: Leicester 5 April 1965 Attendance 26,957
Leicester **0** — Chelsea **0**

1965–66 WEST BROMWICH ALBION
First leg: Upton Park 9 March 1966 Attendance 28,341
West Ham United **2** — West Bromwich Albion **1**
Moore, Byrne — Astle
Second leg: The Hawthorns 23 March 1966 Attendance 31,925
West Bromwich Albion **4** — West Ham United **1**
Kaye, Brown, Clark, Williams — Peters

1966–67 QUEEN'S PARK RANGERS
Final: Wembley 4 March 1967 Attendance 97,952
Queen's Park Rangers **3** — West Bromwich Albion **2**
Morgan (R), Marsh, Lazarus — Clark 2

1967–68 LEEDS UNITED
Final: Wembley 2 March 1968 Attendance 97,887
Leeds United **1** — Arsenal **0**
Cooper

1968–69 SWINDON TOWN
Final: Wembley 15 March 1969 Attendance 98,189
Swindon Town **3** — Arsenal **1**
Smart, Rogers 2 — Gould

1969–70 MANCHESTER CITY
Final: Wembley 7 March 1970 Attendance 97,963
Manchester City **2** — West Bromwich Albion **1**
Doyle, Pardoe — Astle

1970–71 TOTTENHAM HOTSPUR
Final: Wembley 27 February 1971 Attendance 98,096
Tottenham Hotspur **2** — Aston Villa **0**
Chivers 2

1971–72 STOKE CITY
Final: Wembley 4 March 1972 Attendance 99,998
Stoke City **2** — Chelsea **1**
Conroy, Eastham — Osgood

1972–3 TOTTENHAM HOTSPUR
Final: Wembley 3 March 1973 Attendance 100,000
Tottenham Hotspur **1** — Norwich City **0**
Coates

1973–74 WOLVERHAMPTON WANDERERS
Final: Wembley 2 March 1974 Attendance 100,000
Wolverhampton W. **2** — Manchester City **1**
Hibbitt, Richards — Bell

1974–75 ASTON VILLA
Final: Wembley 1 March 1975 Attendance 100,000
Aston Villa **1** — Norwich City **0**
Graydon

1976–76 MANCHESTER CITY
Final: Wembley 28 February 1976 Attendance 100,000
Manchester City **2** — Newcastle United **1**
Barnes, Tueart — Gowling

1976–77 ASTON VILLA
Final: Wembley 12 March 1977 Attendance 100,000
Aston Villa **0** — Everton **0**
Hillsborough 16 March 1977 Attendance 55,000
Aston Villa **1** — Everton **1**
Kenyon (og) — Latchford
Old Trafford 13 April 1977 Attendance 54,749
Aston Villa **3** — Everton **2**
Nicholl, Little 2 — Latchford, Lyons

1977–78 NOTTINGHAM FOREST
Final: Wembley 18 March 1978 Attendance 100,000
Nottingham Forest **0** — Liverpool **0**
Old Trafford 22 March 1978 Attendance 54,350
Nottingham Forest **1** — Liverpool **0**
Robertson (pen)

1978–79 NOTTINGHAM FOREST
Final: Wembley 17 March 1979 Attendance 100,000
Nottingham Forest **3** — Southampton **2**
Birtles 2, Woodcock — Peach, Holmes

1979–80 WOLVERHAMPTON WANDERERS
Final: Wembley 15 March 1980 Attendance 100,000
Wolverhampton W. **1** — Nottingham Forest **0**
Gray

1980–81 LIVERPOOL
Final: Wembley 14 March 1981 Attendance 100,000
Liverpool **1** — West Ham United **1**
A. Kennedy — Stewart (pen)
Villa Park 1 April 1981 Attendance 36,693
Liverpool **2** — West Ham United **1**
Dalglish, Hansen — Goddard

1981–82 LIVERPOOL
Final: Wembley 13 March 1982 Attendance 100,000
Liverpool **3** — Tottenham Hotspur **1**
Whelan 2, Rush — Archibald

1982–83 LIVERPOOL
Final: Wembley 25 March 1983 Attendance 100,000
Liverpool **2** — Manchester United **1**
A. Kennedy, Whelan — Whiteside

1983–84 LIVERPOOL
Final: Wembley 25 March 1984 Attendance 100,000
Liverpool **0** — Everton **0**
Maine Road 28 March 1984 Attendance 52,089
Liverpool **1** — Everton **0**
Souness

1984–85 NORWICH CITY
Final: Wembley 24 March 1985 Attendance 100,000
Norwich City **1** — Sunderland **0**
Chisholm own goal

1985–86 OXFORD UNITED
Final: Wembley 20 April 1986 Attendance 90,396
Oxford United **3** — Queens Park Rangers **0**
Hebberd, Houghton, Charles

1986–87 ARSENAL
Final: Wembley 5 April 1987 Attendance 96,000
Arsenal **2** — Liverpool **1**
Nicholas 2 — Rush

CHAPTER SEVEN

THE DECADES OF DOUBT
-the 1970s and 1980s

In 1970 Chelsea and Leeds contested one of the most memorable finals of the post-war era. Their games at Wembley and Old Trafford, the famous match that the better team lost, were watched by the biggest television audiences in British history, and they remain fresher in the memory than virtually all major domestic matches since. Nearly twenty years later, no-one was likely to be watching Chelsea or Leeds on a television set anywhere, despite far more hours of transmission time and far more available channels. And that is not just because neither club is likely to reach the Cup final.

Towards the end of 1986 there were hardly any games to be seen at all, and those that did appear were a grudging concession by the television moguls. In November 1986 the ITV companies decided to show the Juventus (hence Platini) versus Napoli (hence Maradona) top of the table Italian League clash live one Sunday. Great entertainment, good for the sport, one would have thought. 'Oh no, we cannot allow that,' said the FA, in effect. 'Aldershot and Stockport have decided to play at home that day. We can't risk damaging their attendances can we? And, anyway, we will not let the television companies show foreign games when they will not show enough of ours, no matter how interesting they might be.' And this from a sport which, under Robert Maxwell's chairmanship, had argued just two years before that televised football was severely damaging attendances, and if they were going to tolerate it, then they wanted a lot more money. In any case, went the argument, television definitely needed football far more than football needed television. The FA, more particularly the League, continued to act on that erroneous belief until long after the horse had bolted.

Twenty-four months is obviously a long time in football. With English fans denied any sight of European teams in competitive fixtures, the FA was now intent on denying any televised access to the best as well. Ostriches were positively clear sighted compared with the football authorities of the late 1980s. Where would they go from here, pray? Playing games on Tuesday afternoons? Asking spectators to take blood tests before they pass through the turnstiles? Anything seemed possible in the administrative quest to alienate the public.

Perhaps, with Juventus versus Napoli as an example, it is hardly surprising that snooker, a game of rightfully zero significance or public interest when Chelsea played Leeds, can now attract eight-digit viewing figures for hour after tedious hour. Or why American Football can draw as many ratings as a live League game on a Sunday. Or why otherwise intelligent people apparently regard nonsense like darts, the *Superstars* series and utterly artifical city centre cycle races as valid 'entertainment'. With pap like this for competition, football should be able to wipe the floor with the television companies and anyone else standing in its way. But all it does is continually shoot itself in its remaining good foot. How had the world changed, so quickly, so comprehensively, in such a

short time since Chelsea and Leeds drew 2–2 and Alf Ramsey's England set off for the very real excitement of the 1970 Mexico World Cup?

The first half of the 1970s was a depressing time for England and the rest of the home countries, though Scotland were to enjoy a pocket of consolation in qualifying for, and doing themselves some justice, at last, in the finals of the 1974 World Cup. For England, however, there was no consolation—failing in the latter stages of the 1970 World Cup, eliminated in the quarter-finals of the 1972 European Championship and failing to qualify for the 1974 World Cup finals—and, on 1 May 1974, Sir Alf Ramsey paid the traditional price for failure when he was sacked by the Football Association. Joe Mercer became England's caretaker

Frank McLintock with the FA Cup which signalled Arsenal's Double in 1970–71. Arsenal came late to overhaul Leeds in the League, and again in the Cup Final, beating Liverpool 2–1 after extra time.

manager through the 1974 home internationals and a summer tour during which England provided opposition for more fortunate nations warming up for the 1974 World Cup finals.

The Football Association then announced that Don Revie, fresh from Leeds' magnificent twenty-nine game unbeaten run at the beginning of the 1973–74 season, would be the new England team manager.

Yet Revie was to experience much the same difficulties as his predecessor. England failed to qualify for the quarter-finals of the 1976 European Championship and in the following post mortem there were some familiar points made: the length and toughness of the English season led to injuries and exhausted players, there was too much football, not enough co-operation between the League and the FA, and not enough time for preparation. Yet, with the wisdom of hindsight, Revie's policy also carried one major flaw. He continually altered his line-up and team work suffered badly. The only unchanged side he ever fielded was his last, against Uruguay in Montevideo. In July 1977, shortly after that match, Revie gave an exclusive interview to the *Daily Mail* in which he announced that he had resigned as England's manager. This was the first the FA knew about it. It provided an unsavoury end to his three-year term in succession to Ramsey, and with England on the brink of failing to qualify for the second successive World Cup, he had been rather less than successful.

Yet, with England football at its lowest ebb for years, with Don Revie's resignation and England's sorry goal-scoring attempts against Finland and Luxembourg, there was Liverpool. Marching magnificently through Europe and England, they were to become only the third English team to reach a European Cup final. Four months later, Ron Greenwood, the new England team manager, included seven Liverpool

players in the side to play Switzerland—yet England could manage no more than a goalless draw. More significantly his side, still based on Liverpool, failed to reduce the World Cup deficit with a meagre 2–0 victory in Luxembourg. England then had to achieve an expansive win over Italy to qualify, but they could do no more than reverse the Rome scoreline— Scotland were once again to be Britain's only representatives in the World Cup finals.

In domestic football, Arsenal had become the fourth side in the history of the game to complete the League and Cup double. Their triumph in 1971 perhaps has more merit than the previous doubles of Preston, Aston Villa and Tottenham Hotspur. Their unceasing hounding of Leeds United in the League race and the character they showed in coming from behind to win the FA Cup in extra-time (after even more of a tightrope performance against Stoke in the semi-final) some-how compensated for the steamrollering style which was often more effective than pretty.

Stoke City added a little glitter to the League Cup when they beat Chelsea in the 1972 final. Appropriately enough for a team which has always recognized the value of age and experience, 35-year-old George Eastham shot the winning goal (his first for three years) and another veteran, Gordon Banks, won his first club medal.

But even Stoke's feat was eclipsed 14 months later by Stokoe's. As manager of Second Division Sunderland, Bob Stokoe was the key figure in the most dramatic of FA Cup finals. A solidly struck goal by midfield player Ian Porterfield created the biggest upset of the century by beating Leeds United, the odds-on favourites.

For Leeds, it was another of the bewildering occasions

Gerd Muller completes West Germany's remarkable comeback in the World Cup quarter-final at Leon in Mexico. England had been 2–0 ahead but conceded fluke goals to Beckenbauer and Seeler. In extra-time Grabowski centred, Labone and Bonetti were left helpless and Muller made it 3–2.

when they failed at the last hurdle. In four FA Cup finals under Don Revie, they had only once won. Five times they had been runners-up in the First Division; winners again only once.

Leeds United were the microcosm of the problems of the early 1970s. Their gradual evolution into a strong team was based on physical play with an emphasis on defence. They were also roundly accused of overstepping the mark in terms of what is called professionalism, of setting a bad example from the top. Their disciplinary record was appalling, and at the start of the 1972–73 season their ground was closed because of the behaviour of the crowd (not for the last time either).

Yet there was a significant change at the start of the following campaign. Their players, under the threat of the FA, behaved; not only did they win but they became a free scoring side. They extended a League record by going through their first 29 games of the season unbeaten. Then their character was put to a considerable test when they lost four matches in quick succession and a nine-point advantage over Liverpool had been whittled away. Yet, faced by the threat (and their supporters' expectation) of once again coming second, Revie's squad mustered a final effort and deservedly won their second Championship. It was to be the last success of an ageing side which had still to face the mortification of losing the 1975 European Cup final to Bayern Munich after dominating the game's opening half and having a seemingly good goal disallowed.

While Leeds were trying to rebuild under Jimmy Armfield in 1976, many of the side must have felt slightly better about their defeat by Sunderland when Second Division South-

ampton put paid to Manchester United in the 1976 Cup final.

It was United's first season back in the First Division after being relegated in 1974—ravaged by the retirements and declines of Charlton, Law, Best, Crerand and company. Tommy Docherty fielded a team of talented but very young players who for most of the season had chased the elusive League and Cup double—the League title going to Liverpool.

Queen's Park Rangers and Derby County had also challenged for the 1976 Championship, but Liverpool's swarming, supremely efficient teamwork proved too much. Their style and success had characterized both the 1960s and 1970s, but Bob Paisley's success in taking them to that record ninth Championship was generally regretted outside Merseyside. The other three contenders—QPR, Manchester United and Derby—had all contributed rather more originality.

County under Brian Clough had discarded the garb of Second Division also-rans for the cloak of League Champions in 1972. But in 1973 it was Clough himself who was discarded after an undignified boardroom feud.

Clough by this time had established a national reputation as a controversially outspoken pundit. When he and Derby County parted company the story led the front pages as well as the back. Derby's players, bemused and hurt by the incident, threatened a strike, which thankfully did not materialize. Dave Mackay, a former player, was brought back from Nottingham Forest in a successful attempt to quell the storm.

Ironically, both Clough and his assistant Peter Taylor were in charge of Nottingham Forest when Mackay himself was dismissed from County 18 months after his Derby side had achieved a second Championship of the decade. By that time the tide in the East Midlands was flowing rapidly back to Nottingham and Clough.

In both England and Scotland, by the end of the 1970s two of the reasons most often mentioned for the decline in attendances at first-class football matches were televised games and hooliganism. By 1976, even mighty Leeds were only covering three-quarters of their £800,000 outgoings from gate receipts. In fact, only a handful of League clubs were actually operating in the black, something which once again reinforced doubts that the accepted League structure could survive—though legislation the following year allowed the use of lucrative lotteries to boost the ailing coffers. A more serious threat to football as a whole, however, came from violence on the terraces and around League grounds. Whilst accepting that a mindless minority were culprits, the spread of hooliganism—given impetus by its coverage in the media—grew in its intensity and regularity. Fences around grounds, strict segregation of fans and the actual banning of visiting supporters from Manchester United and Chelsea (two notable clubs whose reputations had been particularly scarred by the violent conduct of their so-called followers) helped a little to curb the disturbances within the stadia.

The loan of Birmingham and England forward Trevor Francis to Philadelphia of the North American Soccer League for the summer of 1978 highlighted a more direct threat to the quality of the game. Coinciding with the passing of the retain-and-transfer system (after years of negotiation, the clubs finally forfeited their rights to keep players once the period of an individual contract had elapsed), the lure of Europe and the United States took on an added glow. With the British tax system vastly penalising stars in all areas, who could blame the country's best footballers from following in the steps of businessmen, golfers and pop-stars?

Ten years earlier the NASL had been a rest-home for ageing professionals, a chance for one final pay-day. All that seemed to have changed when Pele joined New York Cosmos;

Manchester United were the first of the major clubs to erect barriers round their pitch as a result of the bad behaviour of their fans. At this match in 1974 the policemen watch the crowd rather than the match, a sad reflection on changing times—football duty was once a pleasurable bonus for policemen.

no longer could players scoff at the standards. Pele became the catalyst who injected the League with excitement as well as credibility; the big-business that was attracted to invest ensured that the North American clubs could and would bid for the likes of Trevor Francis, at the height of their careers, and no longer for those who were fading into oblivion. With a supply of coaches like Gordon Jago, Freddie Goodwin, Eddie McCreadie and Ken Furphy they were certainly not short of contacts through whom to make the deals.

Clubs like Luton, whose creditors gave them just one month to live in 1975, were more than happy to off-load players to the States for the summer in order to ease inflated wage bills, even though these players would always miss pre-season preparation and often the opening League games. But, in fact, as League clubs became keener to loan, the American

game declined. By 1983 only twelve of the 24 teams of seven years before survived in North America and the problem had become peripheral. The NASL had been a graveyard of hopes for more than a few British players and entrepreneurs. One of the most intriguing financial stories in British football during the decade was that of Coventry City's involvement with the game in America. Jimmy Hill, once the Sky Blue manager, had become chairman of the club and proved himself an excellent financial director. His policy of clearing the club's debts while transfer fees were still high and creating an all-seater stadium was widely applauded. His successes were not repeated across the Atlantic. The failure of the franchises in Detroit and Washington (despite the presence of Cruyff and Francis) left both the Hill family and Coventry City heavy losers. In the end, it cost him his role at Highfield Road, though he was to come back with even more controversial stadium schemes as a director of Charlton.

By August 1977 Brian Clough had been out of the First Division for nearly three years (following his sacking by Leeds United after a tempestuous reign of 42 days as their manager). Now his Nottingham Forest side had just sneaked into the third promotion spot of the Second Division, a point ahead of Bolton Wanderers and Blackpool.

Although Clough had been reunited with his assistant Peter Taylor, who had not been at Leeds with him, Forest were generally tipped for a rapid return from whence they came rather than honours. But Forest became a revelation. Clough strengthened the side for the new season by paying £270,000 for goalkeeper Peter Shilton, by bringing his former Derby midfield lynch-pin Archie Gemmill into the camp and by signing centre half Dave Needham from Queen's Park Rangers. For three years Forest ruled the roost. But as they strutted on a European stage, three decades of ostrich-like behaviour were, at long last, beginning to catch up with the rest of the Football League. Bristol City were the earliest, and still the best, example.

On a sunny Saturday in September 1979 City defeated Wolves 2–0 before 18,835 people at Ashton Gate and moved into sixth place in the First Division of the Football League. It

was the highest position they had achieved since the First World War. Exactly three years later, in September 1982, they took the field against York City. By this time they had lost nearly nine-tenths of their supporters and Bristol City, effectively bankrupt, were 92nd in the Football League, bottom of the Fourth Division. It was the fastest descent in history and City's troubles were a microcosm of those facing the whole business. Opponents Wolves of 1979 had nothing to be sanguine about either. Just seven years later the famous old gold and black was struggling to stay afloat in the bottom half of the Fourth Division, six years after beating Forest at Wembley in the League Cup final.

It was in 1981 that the realities of the new decade began to come home to the Football League. The signs had been there for some time, but not until the shakings rather than stirrings of recession were felt did matters accelerate. A string of clubs suddenly found bank managers more stony faced than before, and there was a rash of what would have been, in any other business, bankruptcies.

Bristol City, Hereford and Hull declared themselves as good as finished in their present form, Halifax and Derby were clearly on the edge, while Wolves, £2½ million in debt with no apparent means of clearing it and possessing a massive white elephant of a stand, all but went over the brink twice, in 1982 and 1986.

All of these clubs, and others whose plights were less publicized, were saved in some way or another but, after the 1982 World Cup, matters took a dramatic turn for the worse. The problem was in large part outside football, a direct result of the appalling recession. The heartlands of British football—Glasgow, the North East, Lancashire and the West Midlands were all suffering 15 per cent unemployment rates and football was no longer at the top of most families' shopping lists.

The most obvious effect was on attendances. Suddenly they dropped by a consistent 10 per cent. When Everton played Arsenal in a Milk Cup tie in November 1982, 13,089 were prepared to turn out and see it. Given that Everton had around 8,000 season ticket holders, it presumably meant no

more than 6,000 had bothered to pay at the gate. Interestingly, 20,000 Evertonians turned out the same season for the Youth Cup final against Norwich. Two weeks earlier, West Brom, second in the League, had attracted just 6,000 for another Milk Cup tie against Nottingham Forest. And there was now a clutch of First Division clubs—Notts County, Birmingham, Coventry, Luton, Brighton—who could not expect to get as many as 10,000 for a run-of-the-mill match. Thirty years before many Third Division clubs would have turned their noses up at such a figure.

One result was the creation of a new industry—working parties on football's future. They seemed to appear everywhere. The most prestigious was, ironically, chaired by Norman Chester, who had prepared a similar, eminently sensible, report nearly 20 years before and seen all of his proposals rejected with barely a hearing.

There was no lack of reasons being put forward for the slump in gates—but a singular dearth of solutions acceptable to most people in it. And most of the arguments were sadly familiar.

Most significant, but least offered, was the simplest; that the world had changed. When football attendances were at their height, in the 1940s and early 1950s, the options facing the working man were remarkably limited by present day standards. He had money to spend perhaps, but little to spend it on. Even that simplest, now taken for granted, option of sitting in front of a television set was unavailable—there was no Saturday afternoon viewing. The opportunities, particularly with the gradual disappearance of Saturday morning work, have now increased remarkably. It would, in fact, be a more pertinent question to ask how football has ever managed to retain half the attendances of the peak years of the 1940s, rather than why it has lost the rest.

The recession, beginning in 1979 and getting dramatically worse through to 1987 (and with few prepared to guess where the economy would be in 1990), was another major element. For a father with two sons, a Saturday football match was not likely to cost much less than £25, no small proportion of the average after-tax take-home pay of around £140 per week, and that was before considering the plethora of mid-week matches. By 1982 the more perceptive observers were beginning to note an age gap on the terraces. Life-long supporters, perhaps retired, or not so pressed for money later in life, still came along, as did teenagers and the unmarried with some disposable income. But those in their late 20s and 30s, with perhaps a mortgage and family, were dropping away. In hard times the money could be better spent elsewhere, and how, then, would *their* children develop the viewing habit?

Hooliganism was another reason for families to stay away from football grounds. Chanting had led to fighting, to forced segregation, violent pitch invasions and, eventually, deaths. Fatalities after fights outside grounds (and obviously totally outside the control of clubs) occurred in Cardiff, Coventry, Millwall, Middlesbrough and London. Interestingly, the real level of violence inside grounds had fallen away dramatically, partially because of segregation, partially because of an apparent decline in passions.

When Manchester United played Anderlecht in a European match, the Belgian club's chant was heard for the first time on television and, within a season, every club in the land was being 'encouraged' (or depressed) by the local equivalent of 'United, United, we are the Champions', even if they were 22nd in the League. Was there ever any reason why Third Division clubs should have had supporters who '... hate Nottingham Forest, we hate Liverpool too', or why the players of teams from Aberdeen to Plymouth should be reassured to know that they would never walk alone? The ultimate in television propagation was (hopefully) to be heard in 1981 when chants were increasingly taken from television advertising (e.g. 'We'll take more care of you...' a British Airways theme from a national institution at that time sicker financially than even football) and passed on down the League's kops by television again for a second time.

Television was no less guilty in spreading tactical ideas quickly (and perhaps inaccurately) and destroying the magic of the major personalities. A visit from Arsenal in the 1930s, or from Stanley Matthews in the 1950s, was a moment to be savoured. It came round once a year and it was worth going to see. By 1982 a resident of Penzance could be reasonably sure of seeing Liverpool or Spurs at least once a fortnight on television, which was as often as the season ticket holder in Ormskirk or Enfield. It has to be stressed that television presenters themselves were in no way responsible for these developments; rather it was the way the medium itself tends to allow the viewer a simplified view of everything. Excellent presenters on both television networks worked hard to explain the game and to ensure that the viewer did not take away false impressions, while Jimmy Hill's tactical analyses added a new depth to the public's awareness of the sport.

The influence of the media has been the most debated and most emotional of all of the 'problems' facing the game in the mid-1980s, more so even than hooliganism. Much of the criticism, if not downright false, has tended to miss the point. It is foolish to ignore the fact that television has brought football to a wider audience and has placed the game more centrally on the national stage (just as it is foolish to forget that millions enjoy *playing* the game each weekend). It is obvious nonsense to suggest that television must damage live interest in a sport. American football games are televised three times a week, live in their entirety, during the season and yet virtually every match is a sell out (the critical points here probably being that there are a limited number of teams playing only 16 games a season and that the event is shown complete). Baseball attendances have risen fast at a time when it is possible in many American cities to watch the local team, live, at least three nights a week, and it is surely the case that televised one-day cricket has encouraged crowds and interest in a sport which was dying on its feet.

The real problems of football as a televised product are complex but revolve around three points—the loss of 'the magic', highlights and frequency. The familiarity with the legends of the game that television makes possible has been a crucial influence. It has not, in fact, greatly damaged the Tottenhams and Liverpools of this world, but it has dealt a major blow not only to Third and Fourth Division sides but also to the less celebrated clubs in the First. A child's vision of football must now largely be determined by what he sees on television. That is his or her first experience of the game. It is the Ian Rushs and Glenn Hoddles that he associates with, whether he lives in Newcastle or Norwich, Tottenham or Torquay. They are far more real than the players at his local club, who advertise a poorer brand of the same product and, because they don't appear on television, are not to be taken too seriously.

One of the more depressing aspects of watching children play football in, say, West London has been their enthusiasms—in the late 1960s boys who had never been north

of St Albans swore undying allegiance to Leeds United, ten years later their younger brothers could not be persuaded that they did not have an inate, unbreakable link with Liverpool or even Nottingham Forest. Television has tended to damage, if not destroy, the essential provincialism of the game, the association of club and town, which was its source and has been its strength for so many decades. Highlights and frequency are more technical matters and were the basis of intense debates in April and May 1983. In an attempt to limit the damage television could do to crowds, the League and FA insisted around 1960 that games should not be shown in entirety, or live, but cut down to approximately 30 minutes at most and shown late in the evenings. This proved a perfect illustration of Brady's Law—that legislation tends to generate the exact opposite effect to that which was intended. Rather than making televised football less exciting or interesting, showing just highlights (particularly when action replays from two angles became the norm in the 1970s) proved rather more appealing than the real thing—particularly when it could be experienced from your own fireside. A child reared on televised football will inevitably find the real thing dull when he visits his local ground and has to watch all the parts that the TV scissors cut out—even if the atmosphere can make up for it a little.

Frequency is another side of the same coin. In 1983 it was

Modern marketing, Highbury 1980s' style. The players look unconvinced, perhaps wondering which ball to keep their eye on. Arsenal, one of the game's richest clubs, celebrated their centenary season in 1986–87, and looked for a while as if they might recapture some of the 1930s glory.

125

usually possible to watch highlights of three matches on a Saturday night, two on a Sunday afternoon, the goals from up to ten more on Saturday lunchtime, plus perhaps four European or international games on a Wednesday evening. Major clubs, such as Manchester United, would almost certainly appear on television 20 times a year.

Why it took so long for this large penny to drop is one of life's mysteries. There had been one brief experiment of live League football in 1960, but it was chopped after one goal-less match—hardly a serious appraisal. The authorities seemed concerned, reasonably, that fans would not go to games if they knew they were being televised, but the problem seemed less that fans won't turn up to watch a televised Liverpool v Everton, rather that they won't watch Brentford v Lincoln at the same time. It was a complex problem, but one that the FA and League had to tackle. They did so in 1985 by agreeing to ten live matches a season, plus a very limited number of midweek highlights (the League wanted more, television less). It should also be said that, if football and television are to pursue a symbiotic relationship, then football might extract more cash for its product. While the example of American football is not necessarily a good guide to what might happen elsewhere, in the early 1980s the 28 major clubs (roughly the equivalent of the First Division) negotiated a package that gave them each $20 million per season in TV rights. That figure is approximately ten times the annual gate receipts of a successful First Division club today.

It is very easy, of course, for football to point to external problems and to ignore facts closer to home. As well as there being too much televised football in the early 1980s, there was clearly too much football full stop. The major clubs had long been playing far too many games—somewhere between 60 and 70 a season if they were in Europe—and destroying their chances as result. Spurs, for instance, in pursuit of League, Cup and Cup Winners Cup, had to play 23 matches between 20 March and 27 May 1982.

While club European football at least could still bring in the crowds if the opposition was right, at a national level it suffered one disastrous experience at the beginning of the decade. In keeping with the previous two World Cups, blanket television coverage was to be the norm for the 1980 European Championship, held in Italy. The tournament proved to be extremely tedious, the worse for football because the games were shown live. England's performances were uninspired (eventually a 1–0 defeat by Italy eliminated her), none of the other home countries had qualified, the crowds were tiny when Italy was not playing and the final was poor—a typically hard, last-minute winner performance from the Germans. As a curtain raiser to the decade it was a long-term disaster. The expanded 24-team World Cup in Spain two years later was better, but had its faults. Primarily it went on too long—for a month—and there were too many mediocre games. Scotland were eliminated on goal difference for the third time running, and while Northern Ireland's performances were interesting, if not overwhelming, England deflation at the end left a sense of intense disappointment. Not

Two of England's leading midfield players of the 1980s. Bryan Robson of Manchester United (left), the England skipper, was very unlucky with injuries, which continued to hamper him even during the World Cup finals of 1986. Nottingham Forest's Neil Webb (right) was spoken of as a future England midfield star.

to score in either of the second series games and, worse, not to look like scoring, was a poor end after a promising beginning. At the finish the fact that the bad guys won (Italy and West Germany) and the good guys were eliminated (Algeria, Cameroons, Brazil, France) was not a great advertisement for football either. It showed that, at the highest level, cynicism, illegalities and 'professionalism' could pay off and we couldn't always rely on the Brazilian cavalry for rescue.

'Cynical' and 'professional' were adjectives that were increasingly applied to many players in the domestic game as well—though more off the field than on it. Kevin Keegan's move from Southampton to Newcastle, coinciding with a court case over a contract with an agent, was not greeted with the interest (away from the banks of the Tyne) that his earlier perambulations had generated. While an authentic hero, and the only British player to be voted European Footballer of the Year in two consecutive polls, Keegan might arguably be judged by history as having failed at the critical moment—specifically with an easy header in front of the Spanish goal 21 minutes from the end of England's World Cup. When salaries and promotional incentives of between £100,000 and £200,000 a year were being bandied around by the press at a time of 15 per cent unemployment, it was difficult to feel too much sympathy for Keegan's need for 'a new challenge'.

Eventually economic reality and the depression took effect. Clubs began to sell players, or just lay them off, simply to save the wages. Bristol City cancelled the contracts of eight of their most highly paid players, arguing that the alternative was going out of business. Transfer fees collapsed at the same time. Steve Daley, for whom Manchester City's Malcolm Allison had paid £1,450,000, went at a loss of £1 million a year later. Garry Birtles went from Nottingham Forest to Manchester United for over £1 million, didn't score for nearly a whole season, ended with just 11 goals and returned for a million pounds less. Justin Fashanu, who had cost Brian Clough another £1 million in 1981, could barely attract one-tenth of that sum a year later. Clubs would sell who they could where they could, just to obtain cash. The brightest and the best went abroad, where the wages were higher and the transfer fees were limited by the European Community (to a generally accepted limit of around £500,000). Manchester City were in such dire straits that they had to sell the jewel in their crown, Trevor Francis, to Sampdoria of Genoa for £400,000 less than they had paid a year before. Forest, in their turn, had sold Francis because his contract had only a year to run and, at the end of it, he would be a free agent and they would then receive so much less for him.

Individual players saw their colleagues move, receive £25,000, and sometimes more, as 'signing-on fees' and told themselves: 'My career's short, I might break a leg next week—why shouldn't I move for £25,000? What do I owe this club?' The public eventually became cynical. The true heroes, the great players of yesteryear who were seen to be honest, decent, loyal men, the Billy Wrights and Jimmy Dickinsons, were few and far between. Those that could be identified—like Steve Perryman or Joe Corrigan—began to be appre-

Two of London's most combative battlers clash at Stamford Bridge in 1984. Billy Bonds (left), the West Ham veteran, attempts to stop the progress of Chelsea's Scottish international David Speedie.

Two England newcomers of the mid-1980s in opposition, Trevor Steven (left, on the ball) of Everton, and Steve Hodge of Aston Villa. Both became regulars in the side during the 1986 World Cup finals. Hodge was later transferred to Tottenham Hotspur.

ciated more for it, but the mood on the terraces and in the pubs was less enthusiastic, and attendances suffered because of it.

But, at the end of the day, the single most important reason why people were deciding not to go to football matches was that they were losing interest in the game. This was simply related to what happened on the field, the development of tactics since, say, the heyday of the great Spurs Double side in the early 1960s, the fall in the number of goals scored and the increasing primacy of easily coached defence over attack.

It is mere survival that troubles most clubs as the 1990s approach. Even if they transfer their highest paid players, they are still faced with the biggest financial headache—interest payments to the bank. They are not unlike the Mexicos and Argentinas of the world—they have borrowed too much to be able to repay their debts from what is now actually coming in. The loans which had been advanced against the collateral of the value of the ground, or the transferability of the team (always a tenuous security when the only purchasers were other football clubs), were less safe at a time when property values were collapsing and no one was buying even the best players. By 1987 Chelsea were still fighting what seemed a losing battle to stop the property developers moving in at Stamford Bridge, and both Charlton and Derby went beyond the 11th hour before being rescued from the jaws of closure. In both cases it was the tax man rather than the bank manager who was turning the screw. In Tory Britain the hunt was on even for the lame ducks of football, and, eventually, there would not be a last-minute saviour for a famous name.

Where this leaves the Football League is anything but clear. There is no doubt that, given the will, the problems can be solved—but not for 92 clubs. On the other hand, if there are no changes, and if the recession continues through the 1990s, there seems only one way for many clubs—to simply disappear from public view. Norman Chester presented his report in March 1983. It had few surprises and the formula of a smaller First Division and regionalised lower divisions had been rejected before. The idea that home clubs should keep all their receipts was quickly branded as a means of the rich becoming richer, but the big clubs bluffed with threats of a Super League, prompted by their justified fears about a massive drop in revenue without Europe, and eventually won the argument. Now the home club kept home receipts, the pool from the League Cup and television was distributed much

more in the First Division's favour, and the League Management Committee was restructured to give the game's giants effective control.

Ultimately there was probably not much wrong with this. If America's NFL was to be a role model, it certainly made sense. It really could not be said to matter what Halifax did any more, except by the 1,000 people who occasionally watched them. But no one had ever suggested that football was an overly logical business, as was seen in the 81–6 vote on whether Luton could ban away support for their League Cup matches. Simon Barnes, in *The Times*, summed up the public reaction to this after going to Luton for a League game: 'True, it doesn't seem like a proper football match without hundreds of sulky, contemptuous coppers herding hundreds of nasty, showing-off boys through the town. But what is amazing is that it has become accepted that every time 22 men plan to kick a bladder about a full-scale military operation is required.

'Is it worth it? Yes, yes, yes, scream the clubs, whose survival plan is to squeeze the last drop of admission money from the hooligans in any pointless and spurious Cup competition they can think of. And while most clubs have continued with this policy, it has reached the stage where the normal business of (a town like Luton) cannot continue on a (Saturday afternoon).'

Many football officials would dispute this view, and many, such as Ken Friar at Arsenal, Irving Scholar at Spurs, Brian Clough at Forest and the whole management at Watford and Luton have done much to try to ensure that these problems do not afflict their own clubs. What counted now was that the *public* believed this to be the case, as did the government, and much of the media. And, for that reason among others, prospective supporters continued to vote with their feet. The attendance figures, viewed in hindsight, are extremely interesting. It was obvious at the time that a peak of 40 million in the late 1940s was artificial, but even as late as 1979–80 nearly 25 million were paying each year (and even then there were moans about falling attendances). The real break came the following season, when over $2\frac{1}{2}$ million were lost, and the annual total has fallen ever since. In 1985–86 it was less than $16\frac{1}{2}$ million.

Why 1979–80 should have been the break year is difficult to determine. Certainly alternative ways of spending time had been growing apace, and perhaps the declining birthrate of the late 1950s played a part (there being fewer teenagers around), but more interesting is the possibility that the football itself was simply less appealing. After the joys of 1966 came the period of Leeds domination highlighted by the two or three seasons of conflict between the cynical Yorkshiremen and London's Arsenal and Chelsea. The famous 1970 Cup final, first drawn 2–2 at Wembley and then won with David Webb's 'Golden Shoulder' at Old Trafford, was in many ways the domestic highlight of the period. It actually attracted the largest domestic television audience (30 million) of any programme before or since. In 1972–73, the effect of Leeds' tactics, the inevitable comparisons between the Arsenal and Spurs Doubles (Spurs scored 115 League goals in 1961, Arsenal 71 in 1971), had taken their toll, as had England's elimination from the World Cup quarter-finals in 1970, and there was an understandable feeling that the mood had passed and the product had deteriorated. Over three million spectators were lost this season.

For the next decade there was breast-beating a plenty, but no-one with the power to force through solutions until the

game fell off a cliff in 1985. Attendances dropped by 1.36 million between 1984–85 and in 1985–86. The points of interest at this stage were Manchester United's decline (and the dismissal of Ron Atkinson), whether David Pleat could revive a Spurs which threatened much and achieved little, and whether anyone (particularly Brian Clough's delightful young Forest, with Johnny Metgod behind them, perhaps the best player in the League) could do anything about tedious old Liverpool. The Liverpudlians' championship in 1985–86 was

Above *Two teams who went 'plastic' in the 1980s in opposition. Peter Nicholas of Luton Town being tackled by Mike Fillery of Queen's Park Rangers at Rangers' Loftus Road ground. QPR were the first club to instal an artificial pitch—in 1986 they and Luton were the only First Division sides not to play on grass at home.*
Left *Two great teams who had some ups and downs in the 1980s, both on and off the pitch. Each had spectator problems, and Chelsea severe ground problems, with Stamford Bridge under threat of development. Bryan Robson rises above Joe McLaughlin to get in a header, while Colin Pates and Peter Davenport watch.*

their ninth in fourteen seasons. Perhaps the loss of Ian Rush to Juventus would at long last portend the end of an era. Sportswriters had been looking for, and predicting, this event for as long as Arthur searched for the Holy Grail.

But perhaps the most interesting story of 1986 concerned that South London trio of little supported and unsung also runs Wimbledon, Crystal Palace and Charlton Athletic. They had won only one trophy among the three of them—Charlton having taken the Cup in 1947—and it was unlikely the three together would attract more than a dozen five figure attendances in the whole season. But interest they did provide in abundance and it centred on the infectious, delightful and highly unusual character of Ron Noades. A London builder, Noades had bought tiny Southern League Wimbledon back in the mid-1970s. By virtue of some good Cup results against Leeds and Burnley (when they knocked Burnley out of the Cup at Turf Moor in 1975 they became the first non-League club to defeat a First Division side on their own ground since the formation of the Third Division in 1921, though Altrincham later did the same to Birmingham in 1986) they soon became favourites to enter the Football League. In 1978 they managed it, taking Workington's place.

The next few years were equally record-strewn. For no less than six consecutive seasons (1978–79 to 1983–84) they were either promoted or relegated, a feat previously (not surprisingly) unknown in League history. In 1983 they were Fourth Division Champions and in 1984 went straight through to the Second Division. There they paused a while, but only for one

season, until, in 1985–86, they surprised everyone by surging through in the third promotion place to reach the unlikely sanctuary of the First Division. Well, said the world, if Wimbledon can do it (before 1986 they had never even had a player capped), anyone can.

By this stage Ron Noades had left, moving on to supposedly greener pastures with the nearby big boys, Crystal Palace. Noades even tried to take his extrovert and quite remarkable young manager Dave Bassett with him, but Bassett stayed at Selhurst Park for just one day before going back to Plough Lane and establishing yet another record, this time for the shortest managerial career in history.

Further east another South London club with little contemporary support, Charlton Athletic, were desperately trying to extricate themselves from the contemporary mire. Having paid a fortune for Allan Simonsen and seen him play just a dozen indifferent games, the board had collapsed in total disarray when the owners of the ground (and previous controllers of the club) decided they would rather build houses on it and preferred the club to leave. The club could not afford to buy the ground (shades of the problem both Fulham and Chelsea were preparing to face in the late 1980s) and were virtually forced to move out. The owners, incidentally, saw their plans stymied in 1986 when the controversy caused the local council to refuse permission for redevelopment anyway. The Valley, as their ground was known, was something of a monument, being the biggest left in British football and the only one never to have been filled to capacity.

130

So Charlton were groundless and struggling. They had effectively gone bankrupt in 1984–85, were saved at the last minute, and now had nowhere to play. Ron Noades offered Selhurst Park on alternate weeks and Charlton accepted. It was the first of the long overdue ground-sharing schemes (Bristol Rovers moved to Bath soon afterwards and there were many more on the cards—Chelsea/Fulham, Forest/County, Walsall/Wolves/Birmingham).

And then, lo and behold, peculiar miracles happened. Charlton, with a team as anonymous as Wimbledon's but under a very shrewd and little-known manager in Lenny Lawrence, fought to the last day of the 1985–86 season and found themselves accompanying Wimbledon up to the First Division. It did not end there. In September 1986, Wimbledon came to Selhurst Park for a First Division derby and won 1–0. That did not mean a lot in itself. It was a poor game, played before well under 10,000 fans. What was peculiar, indeed utterly unprecedented and broadly incomprehensible, was that it was a win which took Wimbledon to the top of the First Division. There must have been some moral in all this for the Football League, though it was well concealed if there was. Ron Noades, a member of the League management committee, an imaginative, innovative and far-sighted man, was thus able to sit in his grandstand and watch two clubs—the one he had brought into the Fourth Division a decade before and the one he had invited to share his home—fight out a game which determined the leadership of the First Division. And Crystal Palace? Well, they were in the top half of the Second and there they looked likely to stay.

It was all something of a fantasy, reflecting two things. Outside the top three of four clubs, the First Division was an open race and the other teams could apparently beat each other almost at random (perhaps a strong argument for

Another ground which 20 years earlier was light-years away from First Division football was Plough Lane, Wimbledon. The rise of the local team from non-Leaguers to First Division leaders is one of football's more astonishing stories. Brian Gayle and Nigel Winterburn chase Southampton's Colin Clarke.

Arsenal found a mix of veteran international defenders and young attackers a winning combination in 1986–87. Niall Quinn, a tall centre-forward, was one of their discoveries. Here he gets in front of Gary Mabbutt of Spurs. Arsenal and Spurs fought out a tremendous League Cup semi-final, which Arsenal won with two late goals in the third match.

reducing its establishment). Equally, and despite Liverpool, Everton and United, the power had gradually bled away from the north to the south. In 1987 sides like Wimbledon, Norwich, Charlton, Oxford, Watford, Luton and Southampton were steady First Division members, by no means the worst in the League. Twenty years before, in 1967–68, only Southampton were in the First Division while Oxford and Watford were in the Third, Luton were in the Fourth and Wimbledon were nowhere at all.

Old stagers like Bolton, Sheffield United, Blackpool, Wolves, Preston, Burnley, Stoke and Blackburn had ceased to be names in the land by the same inexorable forces that had economically depressed the north and brought what limited wealth there was to London and the southern satellites.

Wimbledon's freakish arrival may have delighted democrats and students of the obscure, but it did not exactly please the purists. Rarely has any club, team or side gathered so many bad reviews so quickly. One in *The Times*, by Nicholas Harling, on 10 November 1986, is typical, and relates to a game against Luton: 'Three things spoiled this match. One was the football itself, which was dreadful; the second was the decision by the Luton goalkeeper, Les Sealey, not to do with the replacement ball what he had done with the original, which was to boot it out of the ground; third was the smoke which drifted across the ground towards the end and did not totally obliterate it. Fresh ... from a win at Spurs (where two men were sent off) Wimbledon went back to basics, their own unedifying basics, in a game which was a masquerade of a First Division fixture.'

At least reporters, and the few thousand fans who turned up regularly to watch Wimbledon, had something to talk about. Wimbledon had followed Watford and Sheffield Wednesday into playing a hard-running style of long balls over the defence and cutting out the midfield. By allowing keeper Dave Beasant to take all of the free-kicks anywhere in his own half, they even introduced tactical originality. The theory was that the more often the ball got into the opposing penalty area the more likely they were to score. Wimbledon combined this with a competitiveness worthy of Leeds—for five consecutive seasons they had been summoned before the FA to explain their poor disciplinary record.

Against all that, there was undeniably something romantic in Wimbledon's rise and surely there was a place for the toing and froing that South London was experiencing, though apparently not enjoying overmuch. The sadness was that only about 6,000 thought it worthwhile turning out each week to see it all in the flesh.

So the 1980s were to draw to their close with a number of key questions unanswered. When, if ever, would English clubs get back into Europe? How, if at all, could hooliganism be curbed? And could the English national team ever, ever hope to travel abroad again with anticipation centred on the field rather than off it? Would the FA and League ever come to a satisfactory and stable agreement with the television companies on how to cover the 'national sport' (and hence reduce the hundreds of letters to newspapers asking: 'How come last weekend the BBC and ITV showed seven hours of snooker, six hours of bowls, five hours of canoeing, four hours of American Football, three hours of darts, two hours of tiddlywinks and one hour of underwater ludo and not a single minute or our 'national game'?')? Would attendances ever stop falling or England again reach a World Cup semi-final?

It was a game in flux. It was not impossible that it might fall so far as to lose any claim to being 'the national game'. It needed its saviour, either the sanity or disappearance of the hooligan minority, and the charm and style of times gone by to bring the fathers and sons back to the paddock.

CHAPTER EIGHT

RESURGENT SCOTLAND
-whither Wales and Ireland?

For most of the last century the great truism of Scottish football was that it was the history of three clubs, a series of internationals against England and a stream of talent flowing south across the border.

In 1980 that would still have been valid, but, a mere eight years later, it seemed a statement from another age. The resurgence in the Scottish domestic game was the result of a peculiar set of largely unconnected factors. The first, and ultimately most important, was the rise, on the one hand, of the eastern clubs Aberdeen, Dundee United and Hearts, and the relative decline of Rangers and Celtic. This gave the championship division (reduced to 10 clubs in 1975) a breadth it had not experienced for thirty years. The reasons for the rise of the east are not easy to trace. In Aberdeen's case it was clearly associated with North Sea oil and the economic boom which followed. The influx of money into the North East spilled over onto the football field, and Aberdeen were able to retain the highest paid manager in Britain (Alex Ferguson until he departed for Old Trafford late in 1986), and buy and keep many players who would have gone elsewhere ten years before.

Dundee United's elevation was less straightforward, but it owed a lot to another outstanding manager, Jim McLean, and a very well run club. Hearts, bouncing back in the mid-1980s, were again well financed and well managed by Alex MacDonald. In 1986 they almost clinched their dramtic recovery with the championship, only to lose it on goal difference to Celtic on the very last day with a 2–0 defeat by Dundee. Celtic won 5–0. A four-goal advantage in goal difference in favour of Hearts was changed to a three-goal advantage for Celtic. To Midlothian fans it must have brought back memories of that awful day in May 1965 when Hearts contrived to do the very same thing at home to Kilmarnock. It was the last day of the season, Hearts were at home. Hearts were two points clear of Kilmarnock and needed only to draw to take the Championship. They lost 2–0. If they had lost 2–1 or 1–0 they would still have been champions. They were not a game or a victory away, they were literally one goal away. It is surprising any Hearts fans survived the replay a full 21 years later.

It was the eastern clubs which have provided Scotland's European excitement of the 1980s, and Aberdeen's victory in the 1983 Cup Winners Cup final against Real Madrid is Scotland's sole European final appearance since 1972. Dundee United came closest to matching that feat in 1985 when they reached the semi-final of the European Cup, winning 2–0 at home but going down, unluckily, 0–3 to Roma. Rangers and Celtic, by comparison, have had a poor spell abroad.

In the three domestic competitions, the 1980s have been far more equally shared than in the past. Ten of the first twenty-one trophies that decade did not go to Rangers and Celtic, a poor reflection of alternative strength in other countries, maybe, but in Scotland a literal revolution. Aberdeen even

managed the unheard of feat of winning a hat-trick of Scottish Cups in 1982, 1983 and 1984—in all three cases against the old firm. And if the English care to mock the Scots' tendency to divide up trophies among a small number of clubs, they might care to note that, in the same period, Liverpool, Everton and Manchester United won no less than 14 of the equivalent 21 trophies in England, with Liverpool alone taking 10.

The second, and totally unpredictable, factor which boosted the Scottish game in the 1980s was simply the misfortune of the English. The ban on English clubs in Europe in 1985 was a dramatic blow in its own right—and one quickly made flesh in the rapid disappearance of Ian Rush, Mark Hughes and Gary Lineker. But it also gave an unexpected boost to the Scottish game. The Scots (as well as the Welsh and Irish) were still in Europe. Each of the big four (Rangers, Celtic, Aberdeen, Dundee United) was virtually guaranteed an annual European place (Hearts became a competitor in 1986), and this added great spice to their regular fare. One result was the increased interest in Scottish football in England and, more tangibly, the fact that English players were now willing to change the patterns of a century and move north.

The arrival of Graeme Souness at Ibrox in 1986 was the

Willie Miller of Aberdeen gets up higher than Celtic attackers in the 1984 Scottish Cup Final, which Aberdeen won 2–1 after extra time. After 11 years of Celtic-Rangers victories, Aberdeen won four times in five years.

catalyst for this. A tremendous coup for Rangers, Souness became player–manager on his departure from Sampdoria and quickly persuaded England internationals Terry Butcher and Chris Woods to join him. The lure of Europe was a major part of the appeal, but so was money. Rangers, regularly able to fill their 44,000 capacity ground (probably already the best in Britain), were able to match the highest wages going. And for Butcher and Woods, used to East Anglian crowds in the 10–15,000 region, the appeal of medals, a packed ground and a winning team was undeniable. In the first three months of the 1986–87 season Rangers averaged over 25,000, second only to Manchester United in the United Kingdom.

The appeal of Europe was more subtle, and less noticeable, in the way it kept players at home as well. Suddenly England was much less attractive, they were no longer on the world stage, and Pittodrie and Dens Park took on a new appeal. Some players even came back—notably Mo Johnston from Watford to Celtic and Ally McCoist from Sunderland to Rangers.

The new balance of power was best illustrated by the brief debate about a 'British Cup' late in 1986. The English had approached the Scots about an idea often mooted but rarely taken seriously south of the border. There was no disguising the fact that the English were trying to find attractive fixtures for a Europe-less First Division, but the Scots, given a long awaited opportunity, were predictably cool. The Scottish FA barely even discussed the idea, putting it into abeyance for at least two years. They had good reasons. The first was that they had increased the Premier Division to twelve clubs for seasons 1986–87 and 1987–88, meaning that each side had 44 League fixtures as well as the two cups, and European games for the big four. The second concern was that acknowledgement of a British Cup might strengthen the case of those in FIFA who wanted to reduce the United Kingdom's World Cup entries from four to one, as well as the UK representation on the international board, the law-making body. And the third, slightly tongue in cheek, response, from a Scottish League

official, was concern about English hooligans travelling north. This was a sweet response after the years of restrictions on Scots fans travelling to Wembley for the annual international.

So the English went back to lick their wounds and contest nonsense like the Full Members Cup, which attracted 967 fans to Millwall the night Celtic drew 50,000 for a European Cup match. As David Lacey said in *The Guardian*: 'The Full Members Cup is a begging bowl of a tournament which surely falls foul of the Vagrancy Act'. Just as surely it was not the solution to England's problems.

The Scots, for all their new found confidence, were not without their problems either. Two stories, both dated 28 October 1986, sum up the continuing peculiarities of the Scottish game. On the previous Sunday Celtic had lost the Scottish League Cup (temporarily named Skol) final 2–1 to Rangers. The last few minutes had developed into something of a riot after Rangers had been awarded a penalty. Mo Johnston was sent off, and the referee appeared to send off another Celtic player, Tony Shepherd, only to change his mind. David Hay, the Celtic manager, in a somewhat intemperate interview after the match, declared that '... if it was up to me, I'd have my application for the English League in tomorrow.' But, rather more interesting, was a comment from a Celtic director, Tom Grant, who said that Maurice Johnston would be dealt with for blessing himself as he was ordered off. The Celtic staff had apparently been warned against such actions after Tommy Burns blessed himself on scoring the winning goal against Motherwell in the semi-final.

This rather unfootballing item was reinforced by another story the same day. A former Dundee captain, John McCormack, had been fined £100 after being found guilty of inciting Rangers supporters at Dens Park. Rangers supporters had said that McCormack had made the sign of the cross to fans in the enclosure, and had spat and thrown gravel at them after Dundee had been awarded a penalty. Fans were quoted as expressing the fear that: 'If McCormack goes on

Paul Hegarty of Dundee United gets in a header towards Celtic's goal in the Scottish Cup Final on 1985. The Celtic players are McStay (2), O'Leary (12), McAdam (5) and McGrain. Celtic won 2–1, but Dundee United were enjoying the best period in their history in the mid-1980s.

like that, we're going to have a riot on our hands.'

Just two incidents, but both so symbolic of the strange force still underlying Scottish football—the religious divide between the Protestants of Rangers and the Catholics of Celtic. When Graeme Souness took over as Rangers manager in 1986, he became understandably annoyed at his first press conference to be continually asked whether he would sign a Catholic. As far as Souness was concerned he'd sign anyone who was good enough but the fact remained that Rangers had never, in their 113-year history, knowingly signed a Catholic. They are even known to have rejected players simply on the strength of their name—when Danny McGrain was approached by a Rangers scout and gave his name, the scout immediately decided he wasn't interested, assuming (wrongly) that Daniel implied a Catholic background.

As far as both Rangers and Celtic (who have never had such a restriction—Jock Stein was a Protestant) are officially concerned, there is no such prejudice and, indeed, they will now go out of their way to say so, but as far as the fans are concerned this surely remains a foundation of their support. Needless to say, it has been exacerbated by the Ulster troubles of the past two decades, the Ulster Protestants being the descendants of lowland Scots who moved across the Irish Sea after the Battle of the Boyne (in 1689) finally confirmed the United Kingdom as a Protestant country.

When the initiated ask why Rangers and Celtic have been so dominant, when, after all, there are other big clubs, the answer is easy. After all, Aberdeen, the two Dundee Clubs, Hearts and Hibs are also 'big city' clubs, so why have they never (until the 1980s) enjoyed a protracted run of success? And since there were six First Division teams in Glasgow—none of them, theoretically at least, enjoying a proportionate population advantage over the others—why have Patrick Thistle, Clyde, Queen's Park and Third Lanark (now sadly defunct) not even taken a minor share of the 'Old Firm's' success?

The answer—in a word—can only be religion. Rangers and Celtic very quickly became more than just football clubs. They were causes—to be fought for, defended, devoted to and, if the need arose, died for. And, but for the dedicated medical staff who man the casualty departments of Glasgow's infirmaries, the supreme sacrifice—martyrdom—would, over the years, have taken its toll of the city's population on many a drunken Saturday night.

Exactly when the religious rift between the two clubs occurred is strangely obscure. Certainly Celtic, founded in 1887 by Brother Walfrid, of the Catholic teaching order of Marist Brothers, had religious influences from the very first. Celtic Football and Atheltic Club was formed principally to raise money for food for needy children in the missions of St Mary's, Sacred Heart and St Michael's in the impoverished east end of the city.

Rangers have no such deep-rooted affinity with Protestantism, although Ibrox Park, their wide-open stadium just south of the Clyde, has come to mean to Glasgow's Protestants almost what the Vatican means to the world's Catholics.

Rangers were founded by a group of enthusiastic rowers who used to 'kick the ball' after their strenuous work-outs on the Clyde. In fact, Rangers' first ground was at Glasgow Green, to this day the centre for rowing enthusiasts in the city. A Catholic is known to have played for Rangers in the 1920s, and although they had since made 'mistakes' and signed one or two others (who were quickly released) it was only in 1976 that the religious discrimination—against 'left-footers' to use the Glasgow vernacular—was actually formally admitted and abolished.

Celtic, for their part, judge a man solely by his ability.

With English clubs banned from Europe, 100 years of traffic which had seen Scottish players move south was suddenly reversed in the mid-1980s. Rangers signing of Graeme Souness as player-manager was a big coup which accelerated the trend.

Many of the greatest players in the club's history—John Thomson, Bobby Evans, Bobby Collins, Willie Fernie, and as many as four of the European Cup winning team of 1967 were Protestants. In fact Ronnie Simpson, the goalkeeper in the 1967 side, is the son of an ex-Rangers centre-half, Jimmy Simpson.

But for all that, Celtic's supporters are 99 per cent Catholic. Much more to the point, they are Irish Catholic—or of Irish extraction. Those 'needy children' for whom the club was founded were largely the offspring of the droves of Irish workers who came to Glasgow at the end of the last century looking for work and enough to live on.

With a background like that Rangers and Celtic seem to be guaranteed the undying allegiance of tens of thousands. So has any provincial outfit a hope of competing with these two over the long term? Until the early 1980s, it seemed extremely unlikely, and even now, outside Aberdeen and Dundee, other clubs cannot get the money through the turnstiles.

So every player in the country outside Ibrox and Parkhead is available for transfer. Players don't have to ask away. If somebody comes along to buy a provincial player, he'll be allowed to go if the price is right; those clubs just can't afford to turn down big money.

Nor can they afford to offer a youngster with potential star quality the same kind of money as Rangers or Celtic. So, as a direct result of the bitter rivalry between two clubs and their

FULL INTERNATIONALS PLAYED BY SCOTLAND 1870–MAY 1987

Date		Venue	Opponents	Score
*19 November	1870	Kennington Oval	England	0–1
*28 February	1871	Kennington Oval	England	1–1
*18 November	1871	Kennington Oval	England	1–2
*24 February	1872	Kennington Oval	England	0–1
30 November	1872	Glasgow	England	0–0
8 March	1873	London	England	2–4
7 March	1874	Glasgow	England	2–1
6 March	1875	London	England	2–2
4 March	1876	Glasgow	England	3–0
25 March	1876	Glasgow	Wales	4–0
3 March	1877	London	England	3–1
15 March	1877	Wrexham	Wales	2–0
2 March	1878	Glasgow	England	7–2
23 March	1878	Glasgow	Wales	9–0
5 April	1879	London	England	4–5
7 April	1879	Wrexham	Wales	3–0
13 March	1880	Glasgow	England	5–4
27 March	1880	Glasgow	Wales	5–1
12 March	1881	London	England	6–1
14 March	1881	Wrexham	Wales	5–1
11 March	1882	Glasgow	England	5–1
25 March	1882	Glasgow	Wales	5–0
10 March	1883	Sheffield	England	3–2
12 March	1883	Wrexham	Wales	3–0
15 March	1884	Glasgow	England	1–0
26 March	1884	Belfast	Ireland	5–0
29 March	1884	Glasgow	Wales	4–1
14 March	1885	Glasgow	Ireland	8–2
21 March	1885	London	England	1–1
23 March	1885	Wrexham	Wales	8–1
20 March	1886	Belfast	Ireland	7–2
27 March	1886	Glasgow	England	1–1
10 April	1886	Glasgow	Wales	4–1
19 February	1887	Glasgow	Ireland	4–1
19 March	1887	Blackburn	England	3–2
21 March	1887	Wrexham	Wales	2–0
10 March	1888	Edinburgh	Wales	5–1
17 March	1888	Glasgow	England	0–5
24 March	1888	Belfast	Ireland	10–2
9 March	1889	Glasgow	Ireland	7–0
13 April	1889	London	England	3–2
15 April	1889	Wrexham	Wales	0–0
22 March	1890	Paisley	Wales	5–0
29 March	1890	Belfast	Ireland	4–1
5 April	1890	Glasgow	England	1–1
21 March	1891	Wrexham	Wales	4–3
28 March	1891	Glasgow	Ireland	2–1
4 April	1891	Blackburn	England	1–2
19 March	1892	Belfast	Ireland	3–2
26 March	1892	Edinburgh	Wales	6–1
2 April	1892	Glasgow	England	1–4
18 March	1893	Wrexham	Wales	8–0
25 March	1893	Glasgow	Ireland	6–1
1 April	1893	London	England	2–5
24 March	1894	Kilmarnock	Wales	5–2
31 March	1894	Belfast	Ireland	2–1
7 April	1894	Glasgow	England	2–2
23 March	1895	Wrexham	Wales	2–2
30 March	1895	Glasgow	Ireland	3–1
6 April	1895	Liverpool	England	0–3
21 March	1896	Dundee	Wales	4–0
28 March	1896	Belfast	Ireland	3–3
4 April	1896	Glasgow	England	2–1
20 March	1897	Wrexham	Wales	2–2
27 March	1897	Glasgow	Ireland	5–1
3 April	1897	London	England	2–1
19 March	1898	Motherwell	Wales	5–2
26 March	1898	Belfast	Ireland	3–0
2 April	1898	Glasgow	England	1–3
18 March	1899	Wrexham	Wales	6–0
25 March	1899	Glasgow	Ireland	9–1
8 April	1899	Birmingham	England	1–2
3 February	1900	Aberdeen	Wales	5–2
3 March	1900	Belfast	Ireland	3–0
7 April	1900	Glasgow	England	4–1
23 February	1901	Glasgow	Ireland	11–0
2 March	1901	Wrexham	Wales	1–1
30 March	1901	London	England	2–2
1 March	1902	Belfast	Ireland	5–1
15 March	1902	Greenock	Wales	5–1
15 April	1902	Glasgow	England	1–1
3 May	1902	Birmingham	England	2–2
9 March	1903	Cardiff	Wales	1–0
21 March	1903	Glasgow	Ireland	0–2
4 April	1903	Sheffield	England	2–1
12 March	1904	Dundee	Wales	1–1
26 March	1904	Dublin	Ireland	1–1
9 April	1904	Glasgow	England	0–1
6 March	1905	Wrexham	Wales	1–3
18 March	1905	Glasgow	Ireland	4–0
1 April	1905	London	England	0–1
3 March	1906	Edinburgh	Wales	0–2
17 March	1906	Dublin	Ireland	1–0
7 April	1906	Glasgow	England	2–1
4 March	1907	Wrexham	Wales	0–1
16 March	1907	Glasgow	Ireland	3–0
6 April	1907	Newcastle	England	1–1
7 March	1908	Dundee	Wales	2–1
14 March	1908	Dublin	Ireland	5–0
4 April	1908	Glasgow	England	1–1
1 March	1909	Wrexham	Wales	2–3
27 March	1909	Glasgow	Ireland	5–0
3 April	1909	London	England	0–2
5 March	1910	Kilmarnock	Wales	1–0
19 March	1910	Belfast	Ireland	0–1
2 April	1910	Glasgow	England	2–0
6 March	1911	Cardiff	Wales	2–2
18 March	1911	Glasgow	Ireland	2–0
1 April	1911	Liverpool	England	1–1
2 March	1912	Edinburgh	Wales	1–0
16 March	1912	Belfast	Ireland	4–1
23 March	1912	Glasgow	England	1–1
3 March	1913	Wrexham	Wales	0–0
15 March	1913	Dublin	Ireland	2–1
5 April	1913	London	England	0–1
28 February	1914	Glasgow	Wales	0–0
14 March	1914	Belfast	Ireland	1–1
4 April	1914	Glasgow	England	3–1
V26 April	1919	Everton	England	2–2
V 3 May	1919	Glasgow	England	3–4
26 February	1920	Cardiff	Wales	1–1
13 March	1920	Glasgow	Ireland	3–0
10 April	1920	Sheffield	England	4–5
12 February	1921	Aberdeen	Wales	2–1
26 February	1921	Belfast	Ireland	2–0
9 April	1921	Glasgow	England	3–0
4 February	1922	Wrexham	Wales	1–2
4 March	1922	Glasgow	Ireland	2–1
8 April	1922	Birmingham	England	1–0
3 March	1923	Belfast	Ireland	1–0
17 March	1923	Paisley	Wales	2–0
14 April	1923	Glasgow	England	2–2
16 February	1924	Cardiff	Wales	0–2
1 March	1924	Glasgow	N Ireland	2–0
12 April	1924	Wembley	England	1–1
14 February	1925	Edinburgh	Wales	3–1
28 February	1925	Belfast	N Ireland	3–0
4 April	1925	Glasgow	England	2–0
31 October	1925	Cardiff	Wales	3–0
27 February	1926	Glasgow	N Ireland	4–0
17 April	1926	Manchester	England	1–0
30 October	1926	Glasgow	Wales	3–0
26 February	1927	Belfast	N Ireland	2–0
2 April	1927	Glasgow	England	1–2
29 October	1927	Wrexham	Wales	2–2
25 February	1928	Glasgow	N Ireland	0–1
31 March	1928	Wembley	England	5–1
27 October	1928	Glasgow	Wales	4–2
23 February	1929	Belfast	N Ireland	7–3
13 April	1929	Glasgow	England	1–0
1 June	1929	Berlin	Germany	1–1
4 June	1929	Amsterdam	Netherlands	2–0
26 October	1929	Cardiff	Wales	4–2
22 February	1930	Glasgow	N Ireland	3–1
5 April	1930	Wembley	England	2–5
18 May	1930	Paris	France	2–0
25 October	1930	Glasgow	Wales	1–1
21 February	1931	Belfast	N Ireland	0–0
28 March	1931	Glasgow	England	2–0
16 May	1931	Vienna	Austria	0–5
20 May	1931	Rome	Italy	0–3
24 May	1931	Geneva	Switzerland	3–2
19 September	1931	Glasgow	N Ireland	3–1
31 October	1931	Wrexham	Wales	3–2
9 April	1932	Wembley	England	0–3
8 May	1932	Paris	France	3–1
17 September	1932	Belfast	N Ireland	4–0
26 October	1932	Edinburgh	Wales	2–5
1 April	1933	Glasgow	England	2–1
16 September	1933	Glasgow	N Ireland	1–2
4 October	1933	Cardiff	Wales	2–3
29 November	1933	Glasgow	Austria	2–2
14 April	1934	Wembley	England	0–3
20 October	1934	Belfast	N Ireland	1–2
21 November	1934	Aberdeen	Wales	3–2
6 April	1935	Glasgow	England	2–0
J21 August	1935	Glasgow	England	4–2
5 October	1935	Cardiff	Wales	1–1
13 November	1935	Edinburgh	N Ireland	2–1
4 April	1936	Wembley	England	1–1
14 October	1936	Glasgow	Germany	2–0
31 October	1936	Belfast	N Ireland	3–1
2 December	1936	Dundee	Wales	1–2
17 April	1937	Glasgow	England	3–1
9 May	1937	Vienna	Austria	1–1
15 May	1937	Prague	Czechoslovakia	3–1
30 October	1937	Cardiff	Wales	1–2
10 November	1937	Aberdeen	N Ireland	1–1
8 December	1937	Glasgow	Czechoslovakia	5–0
9 April	1938	Wembley	England	1–0
21 May	1938	Amsterdam	Netherlands	3–1
8 October	1938	Belfast	N Ireland	2–0
9 November	1938	Edinburgh	Wales	3–2
7 December	1938	Glasgow	Hungary	3–1
15 April	1939	Glasgow	England	1–2
WT 2 December	1939	Newcastle	England	1–2
WT11 May	1940	Glasgow	England	1–1
WT 8 February	1941	Newcastle	England	3–2
WT 3 May	1941	Glasgow	England	1–3
WT 4 October	1941	Wembley	England	0–2
WT17 January	1942	Wembley	England	0–3
WT18 April	1942	Glasgow	England	5–4
WT10 October	1942	Wembley	England	0–0
WT17 April	1943	Glasgow	England	0–4
WT16 October	1943	Manchester	England	0–8
WT19 February	1944	Wembley	England	2–6
WT22 April	1944	Glasgow	England	2–3
WT14 October	1944	Wembley	England	2–6
WT 3 February	1945	Villa Park	England	3–2
WT14 April	1945	Glasgow	England	1–6
V13 April	1946	Glasgow	England	1–0
23 January	1946	Glasgow	Belgium	2–2
15 May	1946	Glasgow	Switzerland	3–1
19 October	1946	Wrexham	Wales	1–3
27 November	1946	Glasgow	N Ireland	0–0
12 April	1947	Wembley	England	1–1
18 May	1947	Brussels	Belgium	1–2
24 May	1947	Luxembourg	Luxembourg	6–0
4 October	1947	Belfast	N Ireland	0–2
12 November	1947	Glasgow	Wales	1–2
10 April	1948	Glasgow	England	0–2
28 April	1948	Glasgow	Belgium	2–0
17 May	1948	Berne	Switzerland	1–2
23 May	1948	Paris	France	0–3
23 October	1948	Cardiff	Wales	3–1
17 November	1948	Glasgow	N Ireland	3–2
9 April	1949	Wembley	England	3–1
27 April	1949	Glasgow	France	2–0
WC 1 October	1949	Belfast	N Ireland	8–2
WC 9 November	1949	Glasgow	Wales	2–0
WC15 April	1950	Glasgow	England	0–1
26 April	1950	Glasgow	Switzerland	3–1
21 May	1950	Lisbon	Portugal	2–2
27 May	1950	Paris	France	1–0
21 October	1950	Cardiff	Wales	3–1
1 November	1950	Glasgow	N Ireland	6–1
13 December	1950	Glasgow	Austria	0–1
14 April	1951	Wembley	England	3–2
12 May	1951	Glasgow	Denmark	3–1
16 May	1951	Glasgow	France	1–0
20 May	1951	Brussels	Belgium	5–0
27 May	1951	Vienna	Austria	0–4
6 October	1951	Belfast	N Ireland	3–0
14 November	1951	Glasgow	Wales	0–1
5 April	1952	Glasgow	England	1–2
30 April	1952	Glasgow	USA	6–0
25 May	1952	Copenhagen	Denmark	2–1
30 May	1952	Stockholm	Sweden	1–3
18 October	1952	Cardiff	Wales	2–1
5 November	1952	Glasgow	N Ireland	1–1
18 April	1952	Wembley	England	2–2
6 May	1953	Glasgow	Sweden	1–2
WC 3 October	1953	Belfast	N Ireland	3–1
WC 4 November	1953	Glasgow	Wales	3–3
WC 3 April	1954	Glasgow	England	2–4
5 May	1954	Glasgow	Norway	1–0
19 May	1954	Oslo	Norway	1–1
25 May	1954	Helsinki	Finland	2–1
WC16 June	1954	Zurich	Austria	0–1
WC19 June	1954	Basle	Uruguay	0–7
16 October	1954	Cardiff	Wales	1–0
3 November	1954	Glasgow	N Ireland	2–2
8 December	1954	Glasgow	Hungary	2–4
2 April	1955	Wembley	England	2–7

fans, Glasgow is generally able to skim the cream of the talent.

In 1975 the Scottish League split into three divisions in an attempt to bring more competitiveness into the competition. The Premier League was restricted to the top ten clubs who played each other four times during the season. The First and Second Divisions each contained 14 clubs (with Meadowbank Thistle making up the even numbers). After an attempt to increase fixtures for the First and Second Division clubs by the introduction of a Spring Cup had failed, the clubs met each other three times in 1976–77 season. This new structure, very much on trial, was not helped by the results of its first season. Rangers became the first Premier Division winners—six clear points ahead of who else but Celtic, themselves five points above Hibernian. Even under a new system the old order prevailed with Rangers going on to complete the treble.

It wasn't always like that—until about 1960 the game was thriving in Scotland. It wasn't uncommon for crowds of 30,000 to turn up for a Third Lanark versus Hibs match at Cathkin Park. And, of course, in the years following the last War, the problem for most clubs was simply how quickly they could get people through the turnstiles. Yet Rangers and Celtic still managed to monopolize the top of the heap.

Joint runners-up in the League Championship stakes to the big two are Aberdeen, Hearts and Hibs, with four wins apiece. But two of Hearts' victories were gained in the 1890s, and the

Date		Venue	Opponents	Score
4 May	1955	Glasgow	Portugal	3–0
15 May	1955	Belgrade	Yugoslavia	2–2
19 May	1955	Vienna	Austria	4–1
29 May	1955	Budapest	Hungary	1–3
8 October	1955	Belfast	N Ireland	1–2
9 November	1955	Glasgow	Wales	2–0
14 April	1956	Glasgow	England	1–1
2 May	1956	Glasgow	Austria	1–1
20 October	1956	Cardiff	Wales	2–2
7 November	1956	Glasgow	N Ireland	1–0
21 November	1956	Glasgow	Yugoslavia	2–0
6 April	1957	Wembley	England	1–2
WC 8 May	1957	Glasgow	Spain	4–2
WC19 May	1957	Basle	Switzerland	2–1
22 May	1957	Stuttgart	West Germany	3–1
WC26 May	1957	Madrid	Spain	1–4
5 October	1957	Belfast	N Ireland	1–1
WC 6 November	1957	Glasgow	Switzerland	3–2
13 November	1957	Glasgow	Wales	1–1
19 April	1958	Glasgow	England	0–4
7 May	1958	Glasgow	Hungary	1–1
1 June	1958	Warsaw	Poland	2–1
WC 8 June	1958	Vasteras	Yugoslavia	1–1
WC11 June	1958	Norrkoping	Paraquay	2–3
WC15 June	1958	Orebro	France	1–2
18 October	1958	Cardiff	Wales	3–0
5 November	1958	Glasgow	N Ireland	2–2
11 April	1959	Wembley	England	0–1
6 May	1959	Glasgow	West Germany	3–2
27 May	1959	Amsterdam	Netherlands	2–1
3 June	1959	Lisbon	Portugal	0–1
3 October	1959	Belfast	N Ireland	4–0
4 November	1959	Glasgow	Wales	1–1
9 April	1960	Glasgow	England	1–1
4 May	1960	Glasgow	Poland	2–3
29 May	1960	Vienna	Austria	1–4
5 June	1960	Budapest	Hungary	3–3
8 June	1960	Ankara	Turkey	2–4
22 October	1960	Cardiff	Wales	0–2
9 November	1960	Glasgow	N Ireland	5–2
15 April	1961	Wembley	England	3–9
WC 3 May	1961	Glasgow	Eire	4–1
WC 7 May	1961	Dublin	Eire	3–0
WC14 May	1961	Bratislava	Czechoslovakia	0–4
WC26 September	1961	Glasgow	Czechoslovakia	3–2
7 October	1961	Belfast	N Ireland	6–1
8 November	1961	Glasgow	Wales	2–0
WC29 November	1961	Brussels	Czechoslovakia	2–4
14 April	1962	Glasgow	England	2–0
2 May	1962	Glasgow	Uruguay	2–3
20 October	1962	Cardiff	Wales	3–2
7 November	1962	Glasgow	N Ireland	5–1
6 April	1963	Wembley	England	2–1
‡ 8 May	1963	Glasgow	Austria	4–1
4 June	1963	Bergen	Norway	3–4
9 June	1963	Dublin	Eire	0–1
13 June	1963	Madrid	Spain	6–2
12 October	1963	Belfast	N Ireland	1–2
7 November	1963	Glasgow	Norway	6–1
20 November	1963	Glasgow	Wales	2–1
11 April	1964	Glasgow	England	1–0
12 May	1964	Hanover	West Germany	2–2
3 October	1964	Cardiff	Wales	2–3
WC21 October	1964	Glasgow	Finland	3–1
25 November	1964	Glasgow	N Ireland	3–2
10 April	1965	Wembley	England	2–2
8 May	1965	Glasgow	Spain	0–0
WC23 May	1965	Chorzow	Poland	1–1
WC27 May	1965	Helsinki	Finland	2–1
2 October	1965	Belfast	N Ireland	2–3
WC13 October	1965	Glasgow	Poland	1–2
WC 9 November	1965	Glasgow	Italy	1–0
24 November	1965	Glasgow	Wales	4–1
WC 7 December	1965	Naples	Iraly	0–3
2 April	1966	Glasgow	England	3–4
11 May	1966	Glasgow	Holland	0–3
18 June	1966	Glasgow	Portugal	0–1
25 Juhne	1966	Glasgow	Brazil	1–1
22 October	1966	Cardiff	Wales	1–1
16 November	1966	Glasgow	N Ireland	2–1
15 April	1967	Wembley	England	3–2
10 May	1967	Glasgow	Russia	0–2
21 October	1967	Belfast	N Ireland	0–1
22 November	1967	Glasgow	Wales	3–2
24 February	1968	Glasgow	England	1–1
30 May	1968	Amsterdam	Holland	0–0
16 October	1968	Copenhagen	Denmark	1–0
WC 6 November	1968	Glasgow	Austria	2–1

Date		Venue	Opponents	Score
WC11 December	1968	Nicosia	Cyprus	5–0
WC16 April	1969	Glasgow	West Germany	1–1
3 May	1969	Wrexham	Wales	5–3
6 May	1969	Glasgow	N Ireland	1–1
10 May	1969	Wembley	England	1–4
WC12 May	1969	Glasgow	Cyprus	8–0
21 September	1969	Dublin	Eire	1–1
WC22 October	1969	Hamburg	West Germany	2–3
WC 5 November	1969	Vienna	Austria	0–2
18 April	1970	Belfast	N Ireland	1–0
22 April	1970	Glasgow	Wales	0–0
25 April	1970	Glasgow	England	0–0
EC11 November	1970	Glasgow	Denmark	1–0
EC 3 February	1971	Liege	Belgium	0–3
EC21 April	1971	Lisbon	Portugal	0–2
15 May	1971	Cardiff	Wales	0–0
18 May	1971	Glasgow	N Ireland	0–1
22 May	1971	Wembley	England	1–3
EC 9 June	1971	Copenhagen	Denmark	0–1
14 June	1971	Moscow	Russia	0–1
EC13 October	1971	Glasgow	Portugal	2–1
EC10 November	1971	Glasgow	Belgium	1–0
1 December	1971	Rotterdam	Holland	1–2
26 April	1972	Glasgow	Peru	2–0
20 May	1972	Glasgow	N Ireland	2–0
24 May	1972	Glasgow	Wales	1–0
28 May	1972	Glasgow	England	0–1
28 June	1972	Belo Horizonte	Yugoslavia	2–2
2 July	1972	Porto Alegre	Czechoslovakia	0–0
5 July	1972	Rio de Janeiro	Brazil	0–1
WC18 October	1972	Copenhagen	Denmark	4–1
WC15 November	1973	Glasgow	Denmark	2–0
14 February	1973	Glasgow	England	0–5
12 May	1973	Wrexham	Wales	2–0
16 May	1973	Glasgow	N Ireland	1–2
19 May	1973	Wembley	England	0–1
22 June	1973	Berne	Switzerland	0–1
30 June	1973	Glasgow	Brazil	0–1
WC26 September	1973	Glasgow	Czechoslovakia	2–1
WC17 October	1973	Bratislava	Czechoslovakia	0–1
14 November	1973	Glasgow	West Germany	1–1
27 March	1974	Frankfurt	West Germany	1–2
27 May	1974	Glasgow	N Ireland	0–1
14 May	1974	Glasgow	Wales	2–0
18 May	1974	Glasgow	England	2–0
1 June	1974	Bruges	Belgium	1–2
6 June	1974	Oslo	Norway	2–1
WC14 June	1974	Dortmund	Zaire	2–0
WC18 June	1974	Frankfurt	Brazil	0–0
WC22 June	1974	Frankfurt	Yugoslavia	1–1
30 October	1974	Glasgow	East Germany	3–0
EC20 November	1974	Glasgow	Spain	1–2
EC 5 February	1975	Valencia	Spain	1–1
16 April	1975	Gothenburg	Sweden	1–1
13 May	1975	Glasgow	Portugal	1–0
17 May	1975	Cardiff	Wales	2–2
20 May	1975	Glasgow	N Ireland	3–0
24 May	1975	Wembley	England	1–5
EC 1 June	1975	Bucharest	Rumania	1–1
EC 3 September	1975	Copenhagen	Denmark	1–0
EC29 October	1975	Glasgow	Denmark	3–1
EC17 December	1975	Glasgow	Rumania	1–1
7 April	1976	Glasgow	Switzerland	1–0
6 May	1976	Glasgow	Wales	3–1
8 May	1976	Glasgow	N Ireland	3–0
15 May	1976	Glasgow	England	2–1
8 September	1976	Glasgow	Finland	6–0
WC13 October	1976	Prague	Czechoslovakia	0–2
WC17 November	1976	Glasgow	Wales	1–0
27 April	1977	Glasgow	Sweden	3–1
28 May	1977	Wrexham	Wales	0–0
1 June	1977	Glasgow	N Ireland	3–0
4 June	1977	Wembley	England	2–1
15 June	1977	Santiago	Chile	4–2
18 June	1977	Buenos Aires	Argentina	1–1
23 June	1977	Rio de Janeiro	Brazil	0–2
7 September	1977	East Berlin	East Germany	0–1
WC21 September	1977	Glasgow	Czechoslovakia	3–1
WC12 October	1977	Liverpool	Wales	2–0
22 February	1978	Glasgow	Bulgaria	2–1
13 May	1978	Glasgow	N Ireland	1–1
17 May	1978	Glasgow	Wales	1–1
20 May	1978	Glasgow	England	0–1
WC 3 June	1978	Cordoba	Peru	1–3
WC 7 June	1978	Cordoba	Iran	1–1
WC11 June	1978	Mendoza	Holland	3–2
EC20 September	1978	Vienna	Austria	2–3
25 October	1978	Glasgow	Norway	3–2

Date		Venue	Opponents	Score
EC29 November	1978	Lisbon	Portugal	0–1
19 May	1979	Cardiff	Wales	0–3
22 May	1979	Glasgow	N Ireland	1–0
26 May	1979	Wembley	England	1–3
2 June	1979	Glasgow	Argentina	1–3
EC 7 June	1979	Oslo	Norway	4–0
12 September	1979	Glasgow	Peru	1–1
EC17 October	1979	Glasgow	Austria	1–1
EC21 November	1979	Brussels	Belgium	0–2
EC19 December	1979	Glasgow	Belgium	1–3
EC26 March	1980	Glasgow	Portugal	4–1
16 May	1980	Belfast	N Ireland	0–1
21 May	1980	Glasgow	Wales	1–0
24 May	1980	Glasgow	England	0–2
28 May	1980	Poznan	Poland	0–1
31 May	1980	Budapest	Hungary	1–3
WC10 September	1980	Stockholm	Sweden	1–0
WC15 October	1980	Glasgow	Portugal	0–0
WC25 February	1981	Tel Aviv	Israel	1–0
WC25 March	1981	Glasgow	N Ireland	1–1
WC28 April	1981	Glasgow	Israel	3–1
16 May	1981	Swansea	Wales	0–2
19 May	1981	Glasgow	N Ireland	2–0
23 May	1981	Wembley	England	1–0
WC 9 September	1981	Glasgow	Sweden	2–0
WC14 October	1981	Belfast	N Ireland	0–0
WC18 November	1981	Lisbon	Portugal	1–2
24 February	1982	Valencia	Spain	0–3
23 March	1982	Glasgow	Holland	2–1
28 April	1982	Belfast	N Ireland	1–1
24 May	1982	Glasgow	Wales	1–0
29 May	1982	Glasgow	England	0–1
WC15 June	1982	Malaga	New Zealand	5–2
WC18 June	1982	Seville	Brazil	1–4
WC22 June	1982	Malaga	Soviet Union	2–2
EC13 October	1982	Glasgow	E. Germany	2–0
EC17 November	1982	Bern	Switzerland	0–2
EC15 December	1982	Brussels	Belgium	2–3
EC30 March	1983	Glasgow	Switzerland	2–2
24 May	1983	Glasgow	N Ireland	0–0
28 May	1983	Cardiff	Wales	2–0
1 June	1983	Wembley	England	0–2
12 June	1983	Vancouver	Canada	2–0
16 June	1983	Edmonton	Canada	3–0
20 June	1983	Toronto	Canada	2–0
21 September	1983	Glasgow	Uruguay	2–0
EC12 October	1983	Glasgow	Gelgium	1–1
EC16 November	1983	Halle	East Germany	1–2
13 December	1983	Belfast	N Ireland	0–2
28 February	1984	Glasgow	Wales	2–1
26 May	1984	Glasgow	England	1–1
1 June	1984	Marseilles	France	0–2
12 September	1984	Glasgow	Yugoslavia	6–1
WC17 October	1984	Glasgow	Iceland	3–0
WC14 November	1984	Glasgow	Spain	3–1
WC27 February	1985	Seville	Spain	0–1
WC27 March	1985	Glasgow	Wales	0–1
25 May	1985	Glasgow	England	1–0
WC28 May	1985	Reykjavik	Iceland	1–0
WC10 September	1985	Cardiff	Wales	1–1
16 October	1985	Glasgow	East Germany	0–0
WC20 November	1985	Glasgow	Australia	2–0
WC 4 December	1985	Sydney	Australia	0–0
28 January	1986	Tel-aviv	Israel	1–0
26 March	1986	Glasgow	Rumania	3–0
23 April	1986	Wembley	England	1–2
29 April	1986	Eindhoven	Holland	0–0
WC 4 June	1986	Nezahualcoyotl	Denmark	0–1
WC 8 June	1986	Corregidora	West Germany	1–2
WC13 June	1986	Nezahualcoyotl	Uruguay	0–0
EC10 September	1986	Glasgow	Bulgaria	0–0
EC15 October	1986	Dublin	Eire	0–0
EC12 November	1986	Glasgow	Luxembourg	3–0
EC18 February	1987	Glasgow	Eire	0–1
EC 1 April	1987	Brussels	Belgium	1–4
RC23 May	1987	Glasgow	England	0–0*
RC26 May	1987	Glasgow	Brazil	0–2

*These matches were played by a team of Scots resident in London. They are not regarded as official.
†This match was abandoned after a disaster at the ground. It is not regarded as official.
‡Abandoned after 79 minutes. V—Victory games. J—Jubilee game. WT—War-time game. WC—World Cup. EC—European Championship. RC – Rous Cup

Hearts enjoyed an excellent season in 1985–86—or perhaps enjoyed is not the word, as they were pipped for both League and Cup honours. Hearts players surround Stewart McKimmie of Aberdeen in the Cup Final, which Aberdeen won 3–0.

other two in 1958 and 1960. Hibs won the League in 1902–3, and then three times in their halcyon days between 1948 and 1952. By 1987 Aberdeen and Hibs were still the only clubs outside Rangers and Celtic to win the title in successive years. Until Aberdeen in the 1980s the two great Edinburgh teams of the early and late 1950s were the nearest anybody ever came to sustaining a serious threat to the Glasgow stranglehold. But even they didn't last long.

Hearts, for instance, with the near-legendary Dave Mackay at wing-half and the formidable inside trio of Conn, Bauld and Wardhaugh up front, looked invincible in their heyday. But sandwiched between their two League titles was one by Rangers, who were only mediocre by comparison. The Old Firm refused to surrender.

Hearts did win a Scottish Cup and two League Cups as well as their League Championships, but never completed the big double in one season. So it was with Hibs. They won three League Championships in five years, with what many Scots still regard as the finest forward line in history (Smith, Johnston, Reilly, Turnbull and Ormond), but never won a cup. Indeed, in the 40 years since the Scottish League Cup became a major competition, only two seasons have gone by when the Old Firm failed to land one of the major trophies. They were 1951–52, when Hibs won the League, Motherwell the Scottish Cup, and Dundee the League Cup, and 1954–55 when Aberdeen won the League, Clyde the Scottish Cup and Hearts the League Cup.

The hopelessness of the provincials was put in a nutshell by the late Tom Preston, chairman of Airdrie. Tom, a great talker who played in Airdrie's Scottish Cup winning team of 1924, rarely thought, never mind spoke, about anything but football. A distinguished Scottish journalist recalls a walk through Airdrie with Preston: 'Two little boys about ten years old skipped past us. They were wearing Celtic scarves and wollen ski hats. Tom spread his hands and said, "See that? That's what we've got to compete with." He was, of course, referring to the fact that here were two local boys who, even at their age, were leaving the town to follow Celtic.' In the 1960s

and 1970s it was a situation found all over the country.

Considered from a detached viewpoint, Scottish football has often adopted the features of a farce. For instance, between the years 1904 and 1948, only once (1931–32) did a team outside the duo manage to win the Scottish First Division. The Motherwell of the 1930s were generally regarded as the finest team in the country. Yet at the end of their purple patch that solitary League Championship was all they had to show. Rangers saw to that with an incredible eight wins in nine years. Motherwell were runners-up four times. It is almost as if the Scottish League had a rule prohibiting provincial clubs from even challenging Glasgow.

At the other end of the scale, for most First and Second Division sides surviving economically is the name of their game.

The secret of keeping heads above water, as practised so successfully by the Stranraers, the Brechins, the Stenhousemuirs, lies in these clubs' realistic attitude to life. They realize only too well that a town of 10,000 inhabitants—which is about average among the 'rabbits'—just could not support an ambitious football club.

Others, with even bigger populations, have tried to live with the Celtics and in the end all have failed spectacularly. Dunfermline Athletic are the latest and perhaps greatest example.

In the middle of the 1950s, the Fife club were determined to put themselves on the soccer map. By the end of the first decade they had made it to the First Division.

In 1961, under the management of Jock Stein, they won the Scottish Cup, beating Celtic in the final. There was no turning back now. By 1968, when they again won the Scottish Cup, they had proved themselves one of the most progressive— and one of the most feared—provincial clubs in the country.

But the strain of having to maintain their status inevitably proved too much. By season 1971–72 they were reduced to calling for public aid, saying they needed an immediate £50,000 to save the club from extinction. At the end of the same season they were relegated to the Second Division whence they had come. They await further honours.

Football had flourished in Scotland just as much as it had in England. The Scots did not, however, get together to try to create a single set of rules, a fact which perhaps reflected the different influences at work. It was most popular not through the public schools, as it was in the south of England, but through the young artisans and professional classes who recognized the game for the simple, enjoyable pastime that it was. It had its greatest following in the industrial areas of the central lowlands (in Edinburgh, the South and the Borders rugby union remains the number one game even today), and in Glasgow the keenest players eventually gravitated, in the mid-1860s, to one of the city's three public parks—Queen's Park.

On 9 July 1867, together with YMCA members and caber-tossing Highlanders who also used the park for recreation, they met to form the 'Queen's Park Football Club', thus officially establishing the game in Scotland and founding a tradition in Glasgow which, for single-minded fanaticism, would be difficult to parallel anywhere but in Rio de Janeiro.

The early history of Queen's Park is one of virtually undiluted success. Between their formation in 1867 and 1872 not a single goal was scored against them; they did not lose a single match until February 1876, when they were beaten by London's Wanderers, and only in December of the same year, by which time Scottish competition had become extremely fierce, did they go down at home.

In the very early years, Queen's Park were so dominant that not only did they attract the best results—they also laid down the rules, which were obediently followed by early local opponents such as Thistle, Hamilton Gymnasium and Airdrie (all of whom, incidentally, played their football in the summer months).

In 1870, however, Queen's Park's reputation ensured the acceptance of Scottish football on the national map. Charles Alcock, the recently elected Secretary of the FA, wrote a letter to the *Glasgow Herald* announcing that teams of English and Scottish players were to meet at Kennington Oval. He invited nominations from Scotland with a stirring call to arms: 'In Scotland, once essentially the land of football, there should still be a spark left of the old fire, and I confidently appeal to Scotsmen ... etc. etc.'

It was a stroke of genius on Alcock's part. No one, least of all a gentleman footballer, could resist a provocative challenge like that. Queen's Park nominated one Robert Smith, a member of a famous Queen's Park family now based in London, as their player, and the teams met on 19 November 1870, England winning 1–0.

This was not, as yet, international football, or anything like it. The Scottish team was in reality composed of a lot of well-heeled young men who owed family name and background to Scotland, but who were all living in or near, London, and had time on their hands. One of their number was an Old Rugbeian, who had presumably learnt his football in the handling tradition; another was the son of the Prime Minister W E Gladstone, and was himself an MP at the time of the match; yet another was Quintin Hogg, the grandfather of a later Lord Chancellor

And, most illustrious of all, the Old Etonian Arthur Fitzgerald Kinnaird, aristocrat, football patriarch, successful banker, later Lord High Commissioner of the Church of Scotland—and a football fanatic, who played whenever he possibly could, and whose personality swayed the Football Association for five decades. His influence on the game is incalculable; that it came unscathed through the early troubled years of professionalism into the heyday of popularity in the years before the First World War is in considerable

part due to this remarkable Scot and his 33 years as President of the Football Association.

This first encounter between 'England' and 'London Scottish', was followed by repeat performances on roughly the same lines, twice in 1871 (a 1–1 draw and 2–1 win to 'England') and once in February 1872 (1–0 to 'England').

It was the Queen's Park visit to London for the semi-final of the first FA Cup competition that really formalized international football. Donating a guinea (one sixth of that year's income) toward the purchase of the Cup, Queen's Park drew with Wanderers but could not afford to return for a replay. Nevertheless their style impressed everyone present and also made them aware that the 400 mile journey was not only feasible but might even be worthwhile. The result was the very first football international, played in 1872.

Alcock and Kinnaird probably had most to do with arranging the trip north—Alcock was originally chosen to play for England and Kinnaird for Scotland though neither actually performed—but, looking back, the most interesting

Chris Woods playing for Norwich in the Milk Cup Final at Wembley in 1985. Two seasons later he was playing brilliantly for Rangers in Scotland, keeping a succession of clean sheets as his team went to the top of a Championship they had not won for eight years.

SCOTTISH FA CUP FINALS

Year	Venue	Winners		Runners-up	
1874	Hampden Park	Queen's Park	2	Clydesdale	0
1875	Hampden Park	Queen's Park	3	Renton	0
1876	Hampden Park	Queen's Park	1:2	Third Lanark	1:0
1877	Hampden Park	Vale of Leven	0:1:3	Rangers	0:1:2
1878	Hampden Park	Vale of Leven	1	Third Lanark	0
1879[1]	Hampden Park	Vale of Leven	1	Rangers	1
1880	Cathkin Park	Queen's Park	3	Thornliebank	0
1881	Kinning Park	Queen's Park	3	Dumbarton	1
1882	Cathkin Park	Queen's Park	2:4	Dumbarton	2:1
1883	Hampden Park	Dumbarton	2:2	Vale of Leven	2:1
1884[2]	Hampden Park	Queen's Park		Vale of Leven	
1885	Hampden Park	Renton	0:3	Vale of Leven	0:1
1886	Cathkin Park	Queen's Park	3	Renton	1
1887	Hampden Park	Hibernian	2	Dumbarton	1
1888	Hampden Park	Renton	6	Cambuslang	1
1889	Hampden Park	Third Lanark	2	Celtic	1
1890	Ibrox Park	Queen's Park	1:2	Vale of Leven	1:1
1891	Hampden Park	Hearts	1	Dumbarton	0
1892[3]	Ibrox Park	Celtic	5	Queen's Park	1
1893	Ibrox Park	Queen's Park	2	Celtic	1
1894	Hampden Park	Rangers	3	Celtic	1
1895	Ibrox Park	St Bernard's	2	Renton	1
1896	Logie Green	Hearts	3	Hibernian	1
1897	Hampden Park	Rangers	5	Dumbarton	1
1898	Hampden Park	Rangers	2	Kilmarnock	0
1899	Hampden Park	Celtic	2	Rangers	0
1900	Ibrox Park	Celtic	4	Queen's Park	3
1901	Ibrox Park	Hearts	4	Celtic	3
1902	Celtic Park	Hibernian	1	Celtic	0
1903	Celtic Park	Rangers	1:0:2	Hearts	1:0:0
1904	Hampden Park	Celtic	3	Rangers	2
1905	Hampden Park	Third Lanark	0:3	Rangers	0:1
1906	Ibrox Park	Hearts	1	Third Lanark	0
1907	Hampden Park	Celtic	3	Hearts	0
1908	Hampden Park	Celtic	5	St Mirren	1
1909[4]					
1910	Ibrox Park	Dundee	2:0:2	Clyde	2:0:1
1911	Ibrox Park	Celtic	0:2	Hamilton Acad	0:0
1912	Ibrox Park	Celtic	2	Clyde	0
1913	Celtic Park	Falkirk	2	Raith Rovers	0
1914	Ibrox Park	Celtic	0:4	Hibernian	0:1
1915–19	No competition				
1920	Hampden Park	Kilmarnock	3	Albion Rovers	2
1921	Celtic Park	Partick Thistle	1	Rangers	0
1922	Hampden Park	Morton	1	Rangers	0
1923	Hampden Park	Celtic	1	Hibernian	0
1924	Ibrox Park	Airdrieonians	2	Hibernian	0
1925	Hampden Park	Celtic	2	Dundee	1
1926	Hampden Park	St Mirren	2	Celtic	0
1927	Hampden Park	Celtic	3	East Fife	1
1928	Hampden Park	Rangers	4	Celtic	0
1929	Hampden Park	Kilmarnock	2	Rangers	0
1930	Hampden Park	Rangers	0:2	Partick Thistle	0:1
1931	Hampden Park	Celtic	2:4	Motherwell	2:2
1932	Hampden Park	Rangers	1:3	Kilmarnock	1:0
1933	Hampden Park	Celtic	1	Motherwell	0
1934	Hampden Park	Rangers	5	St Mirren	0
1935	Hampden Park	Rangers	2	Hamilton Acad	1
1936	Hampden Park	Rangers	1	Third Lanark	0
1937	Hampden Park	Celtic	2	Aberdeen	1
1938	Hampden Park	East Fife	1:4	Kilmarnock	1:2
1939	Hampden Park	Clyde	4	Motherwell	0
1940–46	No competition				
1947	Hampden Park	Aberdeen	2	Hibernian	1
1948	Hampden Park	Rangers	1:1	Morton	1:0
1949	Hampden Park	Rangers	4	Clyde	1
1950	Hampden Park	Rangers	3	East Fife	0
1951	Hampden Park	Celtic	1	Motherwell	0
1952	Hampden Park	Motherwell	4	Dundee	0
1953	Hampden Park	Rangers	1:1	Aberdeen	1:0
1954	Hampden Park	Celtic	2	Aberdeen	1
1955	Hampden Park	Clyde	1:1	Celtic	1:0
1956	Hampden Park	Hearts	3	Celtic	1
1957*	Hampden Park	Falkirk	1:2	Kilmarnock	1:1
1958	Hampden Park	Clyde	1	Hibernian	0
1959	Hampden Park	St Mirren	3	Aberdeen	1
1960	Hampden Park	Rangers	2	Kilmarnock	0
1961	Hampden Park	Dunfermline Ath	0:2	Celtic	0:0
1962	Hampden Park	Rangers	2	St Mirren	0
1963	Hampden Park	Rangers	1:3	Celtic	1:0
1964	Hampden Park	Rangers	3	Dundee	1
1965	Hampden Park	Celtic	3	Dunfermline Ath	2
1966	Hampden Park	Rangers	0:1	Celtic	0:0
1967	Hampden Park	Celtic	2	Aberdeen	0
1968	Hampden Park	Dunfermline Ath	3	Hearts	1
1969	Hampden Park	Celtic	4	Rangers	0
1970	Hampden Park	Aberdeen	3	Celtic	1
1971	Hampden Park	Celtic	1:2	Rangers	1:1
1972	Hampden Park	Celtic	6	Hibernian	1
1973	Hampden Park	Rangers	3	Celtic	2
1974	Hampden Park	Celtic	3	Dundee Utd	0
1975	Hampden Park	Celtic	3	Airdrieonians	1
1976	Hampden Park	Rangers	3	Hearts	1
1977	Hampden Park	Celtic	1	Rangers	0
1978	Hampden Park	Rangers	2	Aberdeen	1
1979	Hampden Park	Rangers	0:0:3	Hibernian	0:0:2
1980	Hampden Park	Celtic	1	Rangers	0
1981	Hampden Park	Rangers	0:4	Dundee Utd	0:1
1982	Hampden Park	Aberdeen	4	Rangers	1
1983	Hampden Park	Aberdeen	1	Rangers	0
1984	Hampden Park	Aberdeen	2	Celtic	1
1985	Hampden Park	Celtic	2	Dundee Utd	1
1986	Hampden Park	Aberdeen	3	Hearts	0
1987	Hampden Park	†St Mirren	1	Dundee United	0

[1] Vale of Leven awarded the Cup after Rangers failed to attend the replay.
[2] Queen's Park awarded the Cup after Vale of Leven failed to attend the final.
[3] After Queen's Park protested at the first game, which Celtic won 1–0.
[4] Owing to riots the Cup was withheld after two drawn games (2–2, 1–1) at Hampden.

SCOTTISH LEAGUE CHAMPIONSHIP

Season	First	Pts	Second	Pts
1890–91	†Dumbarton	29	†Rangers	29
1891–92	Dumbarton	37	Celtic	35
1892–93	Celtic	29	Rangers	27
1893–94	Celtic	29	Hearts	26
1894–95	Hearts	31	Celtic	26
1895–96	Celtic	30	Rangers	26
1896–97	Hearts	28	Hibernian	26
1897–98	Celtic	33	Rangers	29
1898–99	Rangers	36	Hearts	26
1899–1900	Rangers	32	Celtic	25
1900–01	Rangers	35	Celtic	29
1901–02	Rangers	28	Celtic	26
1902–03	Hibernian	37	Dundee	31
1903–04	Third Lanark	43	Hearts	39
1904–05	‡Celtic	41	Rangers	41

Opposite *The programme for an 1875 friendly between Queen's Park and the Wanderers. As players did not wear numbers, they were identified by the colour of their caps or stockings. Queen's Park, despite their strange 2-2-3-3 formation, had still not lost a game since their formation eight years earlier.*

feature was the patronizing attitude of the Londoners—that England were going north to show the Scots how to play the game.

Nothing could have been further from reality. Sadly lacking is a photograph of the teams—the players would not promise to buy prints so the official photographer refused to take any frames. At Kennington the following year there was more trouble over photographs—on that occasion they never materialized because the England players insisted on pulling faces.

The match was played at the West of Scotland Cricket Club's ground in Partick. The Scots included nine Queen's Park men (and two more, the brothers Smith, who had played for the club before moving to London a couple of seasons earlier). This provided an understanding between players that the scratch English team could not match, but skilfully though the Scotsmen played, neither side could score—and so the first England–Scotland match ended in a goalless draw. (It happened only twice more in the next century—in 1942 and in 1970.)

The success of the encounter—4,000 spectators turned up, 'including many ladies'—led Queen's Park to search for a suitable ground to play further fixtures. The following season Glasgow Town Council agreed to let 'Hampden Park, Mount

Florida' to the club. Ten years later railway construction forced them to move to another site in Hampden Park. The present stadium was completed on yet another site in 1903.

In the spring of 1873, Scotland travelled south to take on the English giants at Kennington. Again the majority of their side was composed of Queen's Park men and again the crowd was enormous by contemporary standards, 3,000 of them at a shilling a head. They saw a splendidly contested match, with England's powerful dribbling earning them a 2–0 lead, which Scotland equalized only to allow England to score twice more in the closing stages.

The following year, 1874, was a great one for Scottish football. In the first place, Scotland now had its own Football Association, formed in 1873 not specifically to run football north of the border (Queen's Park were doing that very effectively at that time without help from outside), but to institute their own cup competition for the 1873–74 season. Of the original eight SFA members, only Queen's Park now survives (the others were Clydesdale, Dumbreck, Easter, Granville, Rovers, Vale of Leven and Third Lanark, the last to fade away as late as 1967). There were 16 entrants for the first Scottish Cup, which in 1874 was duly won by Queen's Park, as it was in the two following seasons as well.

And, on 7 March 1874, the Scots defeated England. There

Season	First	Pts	Second	Pts
1905–06	Celtic	49	Hearts	43
1906–07	Celtic	55	Dundee	48
1907–08	Celtic	55	Falkirk	51
1908–09	Celtic	51	Dundee	50
1909–10	Celtic	54	Falkirk	52
1910–11	Rangers	52	Aberdeen	48
1911–12	Rangers	51	Celtic	45
1912–13	Rangers	53	Celtic	49
1913–14	Celtic	65	Rangers	59
1914–15	Celtic	65	Hearts	61
1915–16	Celtic	67	Rangers	56
1916–17	Celtic	64	Morton	54
1917–18	Rangers	56	Celtic	55
1918–19	Celtic	58	Rangers	57
1919–20	Rangers	71	Celtic	68
1920–21	Rangers	76	Celtic	66
1921–22	Celtic	67	Rangers	66
1922–23	Rangers	55	Airdrieonians	50
1923–24	Rangers	59	Airdrieonians	50
1924–25	Rangers	60	Airdrieonians	57
1925–26	Celtic	58	Airdrieonians	50
1926–27	Rangers	56	Motherwell	51
1927–28	Rangers	60	*Celtic	55
1928–29	Rangers	67	Celtic	51
1929–30	Rangers	60	Motherwell	55
1930–31	Rangers	60	Celtic	58
1931–32	Motherwell	66	Rangers	61
1932–33	Rangers	62	Motherwell	59
1933–34	Rangers	66	Motherwell	62
1934–35	Rangers	55	Celtic	52
1935–36	Celtic	66	*Rangers	61
1936–37	Rangers	61	Aberdeen	54
1937–38	Celtic	61	Hearts	58
1938–39	Rangers	59	Celtic	48
1939–46	No competition			
1946–47	Rangers	46	Hibernian	44
1947–48	Hibernian	48	Rangers	46
1948–49	Rangers	46	Dundee	45
1949–50	Rangers	50	Hibernian	49
1950–51	Hibernian	48	Rangers	38
1951–52	Hibernian	45	Rangers	41
1952–53	*Rangers	43	Hibernian	43
1953–54	Celtic	43	Hearts	38
1954–55	Aberdeen	49	Celtic	46
1955–56	Rangers	52	Aberdeen	46
1956–57	Rangers	55	Hearts	53
1957–58	Hearts	62	Rangers	49
1958–59	Rangers	50	Hearts	48
1959–60	Hearts	54	Kilmarnock	50
1960–61	Rangers	51	Kilmarnock	50
1961–62	Dundee	54	Rangers	51
1962–63	Rangers	57	Kilmarnock	48
1963–64	Rangers	55	Kilmarnock	49
1964–65	*Kilmarnock	50	Hearts	50
1965–66	Celtic	57	Rangers	55
1966–67	Celtic	58	Rangers	55
1967–68	Celtic	63	Rangers	61
1968–69	Celtic	54	Rangers	49
1969–70	Celtic	57	Rangers	45
1970–71	Celtic	56	Aberdeen	54
1971–72	Celtic	60	Aberdeen	50
1972–73	Celtic	57	Rangers	56
1973–74	Celtic	53	Hibernian	49
1974–75	Rangers	56	Hibernian	49
1975–76	Rangers	54	Celtic	48
1976–77	Celtic	55	Rangers	46
1977–78	Rangers	55	Aberdeen	53
1978–79	Celtic	48	Rangers	45
1979–80	Aberdeen	48	Celtic	47
1980–81	Celtic	56	Aberdeen	49
1981–82	Celtic	55	Aberdeen	53
1982–83	Dundee Utd	56	Celtic	55
1983–84	Aberdeen	57	Celtic	39

Season	First	Pts	Second	Pts
1984–85	Aberdeen	59	Celtic	52
1985–86	*Celtic	50	Hearts	50
1986–87	Rangers	69	Celtic	63

†Shared after indecisive play off (2–2). ‡Celtic won play off. *Goal average.

SCOTTISH LEAGUE CUP FINALS

Year	Venue	Winners		Runners-up	
1945–46	Hampden Park	Aberdeen	3	Rangers	2
1946–47	Hampden Park	Rangers	4	Aberdeen	0
1947–48	Hampden Park	East Fife	1:4	Falkirk	1:1
1948–49	Hampden Park	Rangers	2	Raith Rovers	0
1949–50	Hampden Park	East Fife	3	Dunfermline Ath	0
1950–51	Hampden Park	Motherwell	3	Hibernian	0
1951–52	Hampden Park	Dundee	3	Rangers	2
1952–53	Hampden Park	Dundee	2	Kilmarnock	0
1953–54	Hampden Park	East Fife	3	Partick Thistle	2
1954–55	Hampden Park	Hearts	4	Motherwell	2
1955–56	Hampden Park	Aberdeen	2	St Mirren	1
1956–57	Hampden Park	Celtic	0:3	Partick Thistle	0:0
1957–58	Hampden Park	Celtic	7	Rangers	1
1958–59	Hampden Park	Hearts	5	Partick Thistle	1
1959–60	Hampden Park	Hearts	2	Third Lanark	1
1960–61	Hampden Park	Rangers	2	Kilmarnock	0
1961–62	Hampden Park	Rangers	1:3	Hearts	1:1
1962–63	Hampden Park	Hearts	1	Kilmarnock	0
1963–64	Hampden Park	Rangers	5	Morton	0
1964–65	Hampden Park	Rangers	2	Celtic	1
1965–66	Hampden Park	Celtic	2	Rangers	1
1966–67	Hampden Park	Celtic	1	Rangers	0
1967–68	Hampden Park	Celtic	5	Dundee	3
1968–69	Hampden Park	Celtic	6	Hibernian	2
1969–70	Hampden Park	Celtic	1	St Johnstone	0
1970–71	Hampden Park	Rangers	1	Celtic	0
1971–72	Hampden Park	Partick Thistle	4	Celtic	1
1972–73	Hampden Park	Hibernian	2	Celtic	1
1973–74	Hampden Park	Dundee	1	Celtic	0
1974–75	Hampden Park	Celtic	6	Hibernian	3
1975–76	Hampden Park	Rangers	1	Celtic	0
1976–77	Hampden Park	Aberdeen	2	Celtic	1
1977–78	Hampden Park	Rangers	2	Celtic	1
1978–79	Hampden Park	Rangers	2	Aberdeen	1
1979–80	Hampden/Dens	Dundee Utd	0:3	Aberdeen	0:0
1980–81	Dens Park	Dundee Utd	3	Dundee	0
1981–82	Hampden Park	Rangers	2	Dundee Utd	1
1982–83	Hampden Park	Celtic	2	Rangers	1
1983–84	Hampden Park	†Rangers	3	Celtic	2
1984–85	Hampden Park	Rangers	1	Dundee Utd	0
1985–86	Hampden Park	Aberdeen	3	Hibernian	0
1986–87	Hampden Park	Rangers	2	Celtic	1

*Won title on goal average. †After extra time.

were 7,000 spectators to watch the 2–1 triumph, and a game which, by all accounts, was notable for its 'beautiful and scientific play'. The English, as usual, excelled in individual brilliance. The Scots, also as usual, knew each other's play (seven men from Queen's Park), and bewildered their opponents with their accurate, defence-splitting passes. The home side's winning goal was described as '... a scene which can never be forgotten as long as internationals are played'; Harry McNeil, the midfield wizard, was carried shoulder-high to the pavilion; and the first of Scottish football's 'finest hours' was complete.

The pattern was to be prepared in the coming years, all too often for the self respect of the English clubs. The two countries drew in 1875, Scotland won 3–0 in 1876, beat England in England for the first time in 1877, and thrashed them 7–2 at Hampden in 1878. Of the first eleven matches, from 1872 to 1882, England won two and Scotland seven; on four occasions Scotland scored five or more goals. There was no doubt about it, the Scots had taken on England at their own game and made them look silly.

Both sides were still, of course, amateur but Scotland were playing like professionals. There will always be a dispute about who first developed the passing game—the great Royal Engineers club, which had many successful seasons in

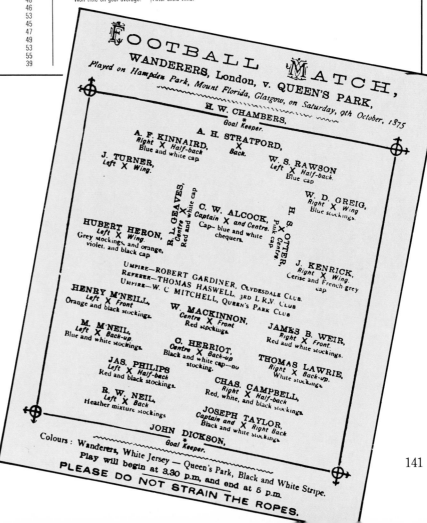

London football in the 1870s and 1880s, claim some credit for 'the combination game', and Sheffield were also early to discover the weaknesses of the individualistic dribbling method, with eight forwards, one half-back, one back and one goalkeeper.

But it is traditionally held that Queen's Park were the first club to perfect football as a *team* game, rather than a game played by a group of individuals. And while the English gentlemen footballers of the 1870s and 1880s were still vainly dribbling solo at the opposing defenders—just as they had done at school—their undoubted skills were quite impotent when faced with the understanding and team work built up by the Glaswegians.

And this skilled passing game was not only effective, it was attractive too for it increased the scope of the game and the speed of the attacks, and it led to more goals. No wonder they were packing 12,000 into Hampden Park for the internationals as early as 1880.

The popularity of football in Scotland at the start of the 1880s and the skill of the young footballers who flocked to the new clubs—long-forgotten names like Renton and Oxford Glasgow, still-familiar ones like Kilmarnock and Dum-

FULL INTERNATIONALS PLAYED BY WALES MARCH 1876–MAY 1987

Date		Venue	Opponents	Score
25 March	1876	Glasgow	Scotland	0–4
15 March	1877	Wrexham	Scotland	0–2
23 March	1878	Glasgow	Scotland	0–9
18 January	1879	London	England	1–2
7 April	1879	Wrexham	Scotland	0–3
15 March	1880	Wrexham	England	2–3
27 March	1880	Glasgow	Scotland	1–5
26 February	1881	Blackburn	England	1–0
14 March	1881	Wrexham	Scotland	1–5
25 February	1882	Wrexham	Ireland	7–1
13 March	1882	Wrexham	England	5–3
25 March	1882	Glasgow	Scotland	0–5
3 February	1883	London	England	0–5
12 March	1883	Wrexham	Scotland	0–3
17 March	1883	Belfast	Ireland	1–1
9 February	1884	Wrexham	Ireland	6–0
17 March	1884	Wrexham	England	0–4
29 March	1884	Glasgow	Scotland	1–4
14 March	1885	Blackburn	England	1–1
23 March	1885	Wrexham	Scotland	1–8
11 April	1885	Belfast	Ireland	8–2
27 February	1886	Wrexham	Ireland	5–0
29 March	1886	Wrexham	England	1–3
10 April	1886	Glasgow	Scotland	1–4
26 February	1887	London	England	0–4
12 March	1887	Belfast	Ireland	1–4
21 March	1887	Wrexham	Scotland	0–2
4 February	1888	Crewe	England	1–5
3 March	1888	Wrexham	Ireland	11–0
10 March	1888	Edinburgh	Scotland	1–5
23 February	1889	Stoke	England	1–4
15 April	1889	Wrexham	Scotland	0–0
27 April	1889	Belfast	Ireland	3–1
8 February	1890	Shrewsbury	Ireland	5–2
15 March	1890	Wrexham	England	1–3
22 March	1890	Paisley	Scotland	0–5
7 February	1891	Belfast	Ireland	2–7
7 March	1891	Sunderland	England	1–4
21 March	1891	Wrexham	Scotland	3–4
27 February	1892	Bangor (Wales)	Ireland	1–1
5 March	1892	Wrexham	England	0–2
26 March	1892	Edinburgh	Scotland	1–6
13 March	1893	Stoke	England	0–6
18 March	1893	Wrexham	Scotland	0–8
8 April	1893	Belfast	Ireland	3–4
24 February	1894	Swansea	Ireland	4–1
12 March	1894	Wrexham	England	1–5
24 March	1894	Kilmarnock	Scotland	2–5
16 March	1895	Belfast	Ireland	2–2
18 March	1895	London	England	1–1
23 March	1895	Wrexham	Scotland	2–2
29 February	1896	Wrexham	Ireland	6–1
16 March	1896	Cardiff	England	1–9
21 March	1896	Dundee	Scotland	0–4
6 March	1897	Belfast	Ireland	3–4
20 March	1897	Wrexham	England	2–2
29 March	1897	Sheffield	England	0–4
19 February	1898	Llandudno	Ireland	0–1
19 March	1898	Motherwell	Scotland	2–5
28 March	1989	Wrexham	England	0–3
4 March	1899	Belfast	Ireland	0–1
18 March	1899	Wrexham	Scotland	0–6
20 March	1899	Bristol	England	1–4
3 February	1900	Aberdeen	Scotland	2–5
24 February	1900	Llandudno	Ireland	2–0
26 March	1900	Cardiff	England	1–1
2 March	1901	Wrexham	Scotland	1–1
18 March	1901	Newcastle	England	0–6
23 March	1901	Llandudno	Ireland	1–0
3 March	1902	Wrexham	England	0–0
15 March	1902	Greenock	Scotland	1–5
22 March	1902	Cardiff	Ireland	0–3
2 March	1903	Portsmouth	England	1–2
9 March	1903	Cardiff	Scotland	0–1
28 March	1903	Belfast	Ireland	0–2
29 February	1904	Wrexham	England	2–2
12 March	1904	Dundee	Scotland	1–1
21 March	1904	Bangor (Wales)	Ireland	0–1
6 March	1905	Wrexham	Scotland	3–1
27 March	1905	Liverpool	England	1–3
8 April	1905	Belfast	Ireland	2–2
3 March	1906	Edinburgh	Scotland	2–0
19 March	1906	Cardiff	England	0–1
2 April	1906	Wrexham	Ireland	4–4
23 February	1907	Belfast	Ireland	3–2
4 March	1907	Wrexham	Scotland	1–0
18 March	1907	London	England	1–1
7 March	1908	Dundee	Scotland	1–2
16 March	1908	Wrexham	England	1–7
11 April	1908	Aberdare	Ireland	0–1
1 March	1909	Wrexham	Scotland	3–2
15 March	1909	Nottingham	England	0–2
20 March	1909	Belfast	Ireland	3–2
5 March	1910	Kilmarnock	Scotland	0–1
11 March	1910	Wrexham	Ireland	4–1
14 March	1910	Cardiff	England	0–1
6 March	1911	Cardiff	Scotland	2–2
13 March	1911	London	England	0–3
28 March	1911	Belfast	Ireland	2–1
2 March	1912	Edinburgh	Scotland	0–1
11 March	1912	Wrexham	England	0–2
13 April	1912	Cardiff	Ireland	2–3
18 January	1913	Belfast	Ireland	1–0
3 March	1913	Wrexham	Scotland	0–0
17 March	1913	Bristol	England	3–4
19 January	1914	Wrexham	Ireland	1–2
28 February	1914	Glasgow	Scotland	0–0
16 March	1914	Cardiff	England	0–2
V11 October	1919	Cardiff	England	2–1
V18 October	1919	Stoke	England	0–2
14 February	1920	Belfast	Ireland	2–2
26 February	1920	Cardiff	Scotland	1–1
15 March	1920	London	England	2–1
12 February	1921	Aberdeen	Scotland	1–2
14 March	1921	Cardiff	England	0–0
9 April	1921	Swansea	Ireland	2–1
4 February	1922	Wrexham	Scotland	2–1
13 March	1922	Liverpool	England	1–1
1 April	1922	Belfast	Ireland	1–1
5 March	1923	Paisley	Scotland	0–2
17 March	1923	Cardiff	England	2–2
14 April	1923	Wrexham	Ireland	0–3
16 February	1924	Cardiff	Scotland	2–0
3 March	1924	Blackburn	England	2–1
15 March	1924	Belfast	N Ireland	1–0
14 February	1925	Edinburgh	Scotland	1–3
28 February	1925	Swansea	England	1–2
18 April	1925	Wrexham	N Ireland	0–0
31 October	1925	Cardiff	England	0–3
13 January	1926	Belfast	N Ireland	0–3
1 March	1926	London	England	3–1
30 October	1926	Glasgow	Scotland	0–3
12 February	1927	Wrexham	England	3–3
9 April	1927	Cardiff	N Ireland	2–2
29 October	1927	Wrexham	Scotland	2–2
28 November	1927	Burnley	England	2–1
4 February	1928	Belfast	N Ireland	2–1
27 October	1928	Glasgow	Scotland	2–4
17 November	1928	Swansea	England	2–3
2 February	1929	Wrexham	N Ireland	2–2
26 October	1929	Cardiff	Scotland	2–4
20 November	1929	London	England	0–6
1 February	1930	Belfast	N Ireland	0–7
25 October	1930	Glasgow	Scotland	1–1
22 November	1930	Wrexham	England	0–4
22 April	1931	Wrexham	N Ireland	3–2
31 October	1931	Wrexham	Scotland	2–3
18 November	1931	Liverpool	England	1–3
5 December	1931	Belfast	N Ireland	0–4
26 October	1932	Edinburgh	Scotland	5–2
16 November	1932	Wrexham	England	0–0
7 December	1932	Wrexham	N Ireland	4–1
25 May	1933	Paris	France	1–1
4 October	1933	Cardiff	Scotland	3–2
4 November	1933	Belfast	N Ireland	1–1
15 November	1933	Newcastle	England	2–1
29 September	1934	Cardiff	England	0–4
21 November	1934	Aberdeen	Scotland	2–3
27 March	1935	Wrexham	N Ireland	3–1
5 October	1935	Cardiff	Scotland	1–1
5 February	1936	Wolverhampton	England	2–1
11 March	1936	Belfast	N Ireland	2–3
17 October	1936	Cardiff	England	2–1
2 December	1936	Dundee	Scotland	2–1
17 March	1937	Wrexham	N Ireland	4–1
30 October	1937	Cardiff	Scotland	2–1
17 November	1937	Middlesbrough	England	1–2
16 March	1938	Belfast	N Ireland	0–1
22 October	1938	Cardiff	England	4–2
9 November	1938	Edinburgh	Scotland	2–3
15 March	1939	Wrexham	N Ireland	3–1
20 May	1939	Paris	France	1–2
WT11 November	1939	Cardiff	England	1–1
WT18 November	1939	Wrexham	England	2–3
WT13 April	1940	Wembley	England	1–0
WT26 April	1941	Nottingham	England	1–4
WT 7 June	1941	Cardiff	England	2–3
WT25 October	1941	Birmingham	England	1–2
WT 9 May	1942	Cardiff	England	1–0
WT24 October	1942	Wolverhampton	England	2–1
WT27 February	1943	Wembley	England	3–5
WT 8 May	1943	Cardiff	England	1–1
WT25 September	1943	Wembley	England	3–8
WT 6 May	1944	Cardiff	England	0–2
WT16 September	1944	Liverpool	England	2–2
WT 5 May	1945	Cardiff	England	2–3
V20 October	1945	West Bromwich	England	1–0
19 October	1946	Wrexham	Scotland	3–1
13 November	1946	Manchester	England	0–3
16 April	1947	Belfast	N Ireland	1–2
18 October	1947	Cardiff	England	0–3
12 November	1947	Glasgow	Scotland	2–1
10 March	1948	Wrexham	N Ireland	2–0
23 October	1948	Cardiff	Scotland	1–3
10 November	1948	Birmingham	England	0–1
9 March	1949	Belfast	N Ireland	2–0
15 May	1949	Lisbon	Portugal	2–3
22 May	1949	Liege	Belgium	1–3
26 May	1949	Berne	Switzerland	0–4
WC15 October	1949	Cardiff	England	1–4
WC 9 November	1949	Glasgow	Scotland	0–2
23 November	1949	Cardiff	Belgium	5–1
WC 8 March	1950	Wrexham	N Ireland	0–0
21 October	1950	Cardiff	Scotland	1–3
15 November	1950	Sunderland	England	2–4
7 March	1951	Belfast	N Ireland	2–1
12 May	1951	Cardiff	Portugal	2–1
16 May	1951	Wrexham	Switzerland	3–2
20 October	1951	Cardiff	England	1–1
14 November	1951	Glasgow	Scotland	1–0
19 March	1952	Swansea	N Ireland	3–0
18 October	1952	Cardiff	Scotland	1–2
12 November	1952	Wembley	England	2–5
15 April	1953	Belfast	N Ireland	2–4
14 May	1953	Paris	France	1–6
21 May	1953	Belgrade	Yugoslavia	2–5
WC10 October	1953	Cardiff	England	1–4
WC 4 November	1953	Glasgow	Scotland	3–3
WC31 March	1954	Wrexham	N Ireland	1–2

barton—transformed the game. The non-London clubs were demanding universal laws. Rules for goal-kicks and corners were regularized into the form they have today; handling the ball was reserved for the goalkeeper alone; free-kicks for infrigements were accepted. After a series of squabbles between English and Scottish clubs, the Scottish throw-in was adopted all over the country.

The rules were settled more or less amicably. The dispute over professionalism was not. The rumblings began at the end of the 1870s: rumours started over the alleged payment of players by some of the northern English clubs, and by the early 1880s a full-scale row was brewing. Teams with unashamed working-class origins were making themselves felt, especially as in many parts of the country factories and offices were beginning to close after noon on Saturday, allowing the working man a full half-day's leisure every week. And the teams emerging in the North of England—Darwen and Preston, Blackburn and Accrington—often fielded more Scots than Englishmen.

At first, perhaps, the chance of a job in the prosperous factories of Lancashire was as much a lure as the prospect of a weekly shilling or two for playing football, but soon the northern clubs were competing for the services of the Scottish football names and talent scouts were scouring the parks of Glasgow for a likely catch.

In 1885 England accepted professionalism, under strict supervision. Scotland held out against it for another eight years. It was a bad time for Scottish football. On the one hand their strong ideological principles forced them to reject the idea of paying sportsmen money; on the other, they saw quite clearly that the English clubs were ready to snap up those footballers whose principles were less rigid, and Scottish football could only suffer in consequence.

It is surprising, in fact, and a tribute to the deep wells of talent to be tapped in the Scottish Lowlands in those days, that the effect was not worse. The professionalism crisis soured the FA Cup, and the Scottish clubs who still competed. In 1886, the professionals of the fast-rising Preston North End thrashed the amateur Queen's Park 3–0 in Glasgow, and in a game of brutal tackling and foul temper. The next year (after a club called Rangers had reached the semi-finals of the FA Cup before going down to Aston Villa), the Scottish Association decreed that '... clubs belonging to this association shall not be members of any other national association.' Scotland

Opposite *A ticket for the first international football match at Partick in 1872. The Scots included nine Queen's Park men but could only draw 0–0.*

Date		Venue	Opponents	Score
9 May	1954	Vienna	Austria	0–2
22 September	1954	Cardiff	Yugoslavia	1–3
16 October	1954	Cardiff	Scotland	0–1
10 November	1954	Wembley	England	2–3
20 April	1955	Belfast	N Ireland	3–2
22 October	1955	Cardiff	England	2–1
9 November	1955	Glasgow	Scotland	0–2
23 November	1955	Wrexham	Austria	1–2
11 April	1956	Cardiff	N Ireland	1–1
20 October	1956	Cardiff	Scotland	2–2
14 November	1956	Wembley	England	1–3
10 April	1957	Belfast	N Ireland	0–0
WC 1 May	1957	Cardiff	Czechoslovakia	1–0
WC19 May	1957	Leipzig	East Germany	1–2
WC26 May	1957	Prague	Czechoslovakia	0–2
WC25 September	1957	Cardiff	East Germany	4–1
19 October	1957	Cardiff	England	0–4
13 November	1957	Glasgow	Scotland	1–1
WC15 January	1958	Tel-Aviv	Israel	2–0
WC 5 February	1958	Cardiff	Israel	2–0
16 April	1958	Cardiff	N Ireland	1–1
WC 8 June	1958	Sandviken	Hungary	1–1
WC11 June	1958	Stockholm	Mexico	1–1
WC15 June	1958	Stockholm	Sweden	0–0
WC17 June	1958	Stockholm	Hungary	2–1
WC19 June	1958	Gottenburg	Brazil	0–1
18 October	1958	Cardiff	Scotland	0–3
26 November	1958	Birmingham	England	2–2
22 April	1959	Belfast	N Ireland	1–4
17 October	1959	Cardiff	England	1–1
4 November	1959	Glasgow	Scotland	1–1
6 April	1960	Wrexham	N Ireland	3–2
28 September	1960	Dublin	Eire	3–2
22 October	1960	Cardiff	Scotland	2–0
23 November	1960	Wembley	England	1–5
12 April	1961	Belfast	N Ireland	5–1
WC19 April	1961	Cardiff	Spain	1–2
WC18 May	1961	Madrid	Spain	1–1
28 May	1961	Budapest	Hungary	2–3
14 October	1961	Cardiff	England	1–1
8 November	1961	Glasgow	Scotland	0–2
11 April	1962	Cardiff	N Ireland	4–0
12 May	1962	Rio de Janiero	Brazil	1–3
16 May	1962	Sao Paulo	Brazil	1–3
22 May	1962	Mexico City	Mexico	1–2
22 October	1962	Cardiff	Scotland	2–3
ENC 7 November	1962	Budapest	Hungary	1–3
21 November	1962	Wembley	England	0–4
ENC20 March	1963	Cardiff	Hungary	1–1
3 April	1963	Belfast	N Ireland	4–1
12 October	1963	Cardiff	England	0–4
20 November	1963	Glasgow	Scotland	1–2
15 April	1964	Swansea	N Ireland	3–2
3 October	1964	Cardiff	Scotland	3–2
WC21 October	1964	Copenhagen	Denmark	0–1
18 November	1964	Wembley	England	1–2
WC 9 December	1964	Athens	Greece	0–2
WC17 March	1965	Cardiff	Greece	4–1
31 March	1965	Belfast	N Ireland	5–0
1 May	1965	Florence	Italy	1–4
WC30 May	1965	Moscow	Russia	1–2
2 October	1965	Cardiff	England	0–0
WC27 October	1965	Cardiff	Russia	2–1
24 November	1965	Glasgow	Scotland	1–4
WC 1 December	1965	Wrexham	Denmark	4–2
30 March	1966	Cardiff	N Ireland	1–4
14 May	1966	Rio de Janeiro	Brazil	1–3
18 May	1966	Belo Horizonte	Brazil	0–1
22 May	1966	Santiago	Chile	0–2
22 October	1966	Glasgow	Scotland	1–1
16 November	1966	Wembley	England	1–5
12 April	1967	Belfast	N Ireland	0–0
21 October	1967	Cardiff	England	0–3
22 November	1967	Glasgow	Scotland	2–3
28 February	1968	Wrexham	N Ireland	2–0
8 May	1968	Cardiff	West Germany	1–1
WC23 October	1968	Cardiff	Italy	0–1
26 March	1969	Frankfurt	West Germany	1–1
WC16 April	1969	Dresden	East Germany	1–2
3 May	1969	Wrexham	Scotland	3–5
7 May	1969	Wembley	England	1–2
10 May	1969	Belfast	N Ireland	0–0
28 July	1969	Cardiff	Rest of Britain	0–0
WC22 October	1969	Cardiff	East Germany	1–3
WC 4 November	1969	Rome	Italy	1–4
18 April	1970	Cardiff	England	1–1
22 April	1970	Glasgow	Scotland	0–0
25 April	1970	Swansea	N Ireland	1–0
EC11 November	1970	Cardiff	Rumania	0–0
EC21 April	1971	Swansea	Czechoslovakia	1–3
15 May	1971	Cardiff	Scotland	0–0
18 May	1971	Wembley	England	0–0
22 May	1971	Belfast	N Ireland	0–1
EC26 May	1971	Helsinki	Finland	1–0
EC13 October	1971	Swansea	Finland	3–0
EC27 October	1971	Prague	Czechoslovakia	0–1
EC24 November	1971	Bucharest	Rumania	0–2
20 May	1972	Cardiff	England	0–3
24 May	1972	Glasgow	Scotland	0–1
28 May	1972	Wrexham	N Ireland	0–0
WC15 November	1972	Cardiff	England	0–1
WC24 January	1973	Wembley	England	1–1
WC28 March	1973	Cardiff	Poland	2–0
12 May	1973	Wrexham	Scotland	0–2
15 May	1973	Wembley	England	0–3
19 May	1973	Everton	N Ireland	0–1
WC26 September	1973	Katowice	Poland	0–3
11 May	1974	Cardiff	England	0–2
14 May	1974	Glasgow	Scotland	0–2
18 May	1974	Wrexham	N Ireland	1–0
EC 4 September	1974	Vienna	Austria	1–2
EC30 October	1974	Cardiff	Hungary	2–0
EC20 November	1974	Swansea	Luxembourg	5–0
EC16 April	1975	Budapest	Hungary	2–1
EC 1 May	1975	Luxembourg	Luxembourg	3–1
17 May	1975	Cardiff	Scotland	2–2
21 May	1975	Wembley	England	2–2
23 May	1975	Belfast	N Ireland	0–1
EC19 November	1975	Wrexham	Austria	1–0
24 March	1976	Wrexham	England	1–2
EC24 April	1976	Zagreb	Yugoslavia	0–2
6 May	1976	Glasgow	Scotland	1–3
8 May	1976	Cardiff	England	0–1
14 May	1976	Swansea	N Ireland	1–0
EC22 May	1976	Cardiff	Yugoslavia	1–1
6 October	1976	Cardiff	West Germany	0–2
WC17 November	1976	Glasgow	Scotland	0–1
WC30 March	1977	Wrexham	Czechoslovakia	3–0
28 May	1977	Wrexham	Scotland	0–0
31 May	1977	Wembley	England	1–0
3 June	1977	Belfast	N Ireland	1–1
6 September	1977	Wrexham	Kuwait	0–0
20 September	1977	Kuwait	Kuwait	0–0
WC12 October	1977	Liverpool	Scotland	0–2
WC17 November	1977	Prague	Czechoslovakia	0–1
14 December	1977	Dortmund	West Germany	1–1
18 April	1978	Teheran	Iran	1–0
13 May	1978	Cardiff	England	1–3
17 May	1978	Glasgow	Scotland	1–1
19 May	1978	Wrexham	N Ireland	1–0
EC25 October	1978	Wrexham	Malta	7–0
EC29 November	1978	Wrexham	Turkey	1–0
EC 2 May	1979	Wrexham	West Germany	0–2
19 May	1979	Cardiff	Scotland	3–0
23 May	1979	Wembley	England	0–0
25 May	1979	Belfast	N Ireland	1–1
EC 2 June	1979	Valetta	Malta	2–0
11 September	1979	Swansea	Eire	2–1
EC17 October	1979	Cologne	West Germany	1–5
EC21 November	1979	Izmir	Turkey	0–1
17 May	1980	Wrexham	England	4–1
21 May	1980	Hampden	Scotland	0–1
23 May	1980	Cardiff	N Ireland	0–4
WC 2 June	1980	Reykjavik	Iceland	4–0
WC15 October	1980	Cardiff	Turkey	4–0
WC19 November	1980	Cardiff	Czechoslovakia	1–0
24 February	1981	Dublin	Eire	3–1
WC25 March	1981	Ankara	Turkey	1–0
16 May	1981	Swansea	Scotland	2–0
20 May	1981	Wembley	England	0–0
WC30 May	1981	Wrexham	Soviet Union	0–0
WC 9 September	1981	Prague	Czechoslovakia	0–2
WC14 October	1981	Swansea	Iceland	2–2
WC18 November	1981	Tbilisi	Soviet Union	0–3
24 March	1982	Valencia	Spain	1–1
27 April	1982	Cardiff	England	0–1
24 May	1982	Hampden	Scotland	0–1
27 May	1982	Wrexham	N Ireland	3–0
2 June	1982	Toulouse	France	1–0
EC22 September	1982	Swansea	Norway	1–0
EC15 December	1982	Titograd	Yugoslavia	4–4
23 February	1983	Wembley	England	1–2
EC27 April	1983	Wrexham	Bulgaria	1–0
28 May	1983	Cardiff	Scotland	0–2
31 May	1983	Belfast	N Ireland	1–0
12 June	1983	Cardiff	Brazil	1–1
EC21 September	1983	Oslo	Norway	0–0
12 October	1983	Wrexham	Rumania	5–0
EC16 November	1983	Sofia	Bulgaria	0–1
EC14 December	1983	Cardiff	Yugoslavia	1–1
28 February	1984	Glasgow	Scotland	1–2
2 May	1984	Wrexham	England	1–0
22 May	1984	Swansea	N Ireland	1–1
6 June	1984	Trondheim	Norway	0–1
10 June	1984	Tel-Aviv	Israel	0–0
WC12 September	1984	Reykjavik	Iceland	0–1
WC17 October	1984	Seville	Spain	0–3
WC14 November	1984	Cardiff	Iceland	2–1
26 February	1985	Wrexham	Norway	1–1
WC27 March	1985	Glasgow	Scotland	1–0
WC30 April	1985	Wrexham	Spain	3–0
5 June	1985	Bergen	Norway	2–4
WC10 September	1985	Cardiff	Scotland	1–1
16 October	1985	Cardiff	Hungary	0–3
25 February	1986	Dhahran	Saudi Arabia	2–1
26 March	1986	Dublin	Eire	1–0
21 April	1986	Cardiff	Uruguay	0–0
10 May	1986	Toronto	Canada	0–2
20 May	1986	Vancouver	Canada	3–0
EC10 September	1986	Helsinki	Finland	1–1
18 February	1987	Swansea	Soviet Union	0–0
EC 1 April	1987	Wrexham	Finland	4–0
EC29 April	1987	Wrexham	Czechoslovakia	1–1

WC—World Cup games.
EC—European Championship games.
V—Victory International. WT—War time International.
ENC—European Nations Cup games.

One of the problems (and one of the strengths) of football in Glasgow is the antipathy, not to say hatred, which exists between some Rangers and Celtic supporters. The game goes on above, even though there seems to be more action on the terraces.

aristocrats. In 1896, the first year in which the 'Anglos' (the Scottish professionals playing in the English League) were allowed to be selected for Scotland, Queen's Park, for the first time, provided only one member of Scotland's team. But the balance was restored, Scotland's sorry run ended, and they started winning again. And there were 50,000 supporters there to see it.

For Queen's Park it had been a glorious run. In the years between their formation in 1867 and the coming of professionalism, they had, virtually alone, run Scottish football. Losing in two consecutive Finals, they had come closer than any Scottish team to taking the coveted FA Cup out of England; they had, again virtually alone, provided international terms to humble England; they had won the Scottish Cup nine times.

They had provided Scottish crowds with an attractive and fast-moving game which was supported with all the fervour of a new religion. What is more, it grew unopposed. Cricket had never really thrived in Scotland, and rugby was even more haughtily upper-class in Edinburgh and the Borders than it was in southern England. And against all odds and all predictions Queen's Park have remained both amateur and, relatively, talented. In the 1890s, with the advent of professionalism, Celtic and Rangers took over the commanding heights of Scottish football and, sadly perhaps, have shared the battle for supremacy ever since.

Maybe that was not so clear ninety years ago. 'You might as well attempt to stop the flow of Niagara with a kitchen chair as to endeavour to stem the tide of professionalism,' said the leading voice of one of the factions at the 1893 AGM of the Scottish Football Association. The speaker was J H

had broken away, just as it seemed that the still-amateur South of England might be proposing to form a British League.

The decision of the Scottish clubs to form a Scottish League in 1891 (and so grant two seasons of glory to Dumbarton, who won the first two Championships) heralded the end of the first chapter in Scottish football. Although professionalism was still banned (until 1893, when the SFA bowed to the inevitable), payments to League players were made quite openly; Queen's Park, still fiercely amateur, refused to join the league until 1900, and the relentless advance of the hard, working-class clubs finally overshadowed these Scottish

FULL INTERNATIONALS PLAYED BY EIRE MAY 1924–MAY 1987

Date		Venue	Opponents	Score	Date		Venue	Opponents	Score	Date		Venue	Opponents	Score
28 May	1924	Paris	Bulgaria	1–0	16 November	1952	Dublin	France	1–1	30 October	1968	Katowice	Poland	0–1
2 June	1924	Paris	Netherlands	1–2	25 March	1953	Dublin	Austria	4–0	10 November	1968	Dublin	Austria	2–2
3 June	1924	Paris	Estonia	3–1	WC 4 October	1953	Dublin	France	3–5	4 December	1968	Dublin	Denmark	1–1
16 June	1925	Dublin	USA	3–1	WC28 October	1953	Dublin	Luxembourg	4–0	WC 4 May	1969	Dublin	Czechoslovakia	1–2
21 March	1926	Turin	Italy	0–3	WC25 November	1953	Paris	France	0–1	WC27 May	1969	Copenhagen	Denmark	2–0
23 April	1927	Dublin	Italy	1–2	WC 7 March	1954	Luxembourg	Luxembourg	1–0	21 September	1969	Dublin	Scotland	1–1
12 February	1928	Liege	Belgium	4–2	8 November	1954	Dublin	Norway	2–1	WC 7 October	1969	Prague	Czechoslovakia	0–3
20 April	1929	Dublin	Belgium	4–0	1 May	1955	Dublin	Netherlands	1–0	6 May	1970	Dublin	Poland	1–2
11 May	1930	Brussels	Belgium	3–1	25 May	1955	Oslo	Norway	3–1	9 May	1970	Berlin	West Germany	1–2
26 April	1931	Barcelona	Spain	1–1	28 May	1955	Hamburg	West Germany	1–2	23 September	1970	Dublin	Poland	0–2
13 December	1931	Dublin	Spain	0–5	19 September	1955	Dublin	Yugoslavia	1–4	EC14 October	1970	Dublin	Sweden	1–1
8 May	1932	Amsterdam	Netherlands	2–0	27 November	1955	Dublin	Spain	2–2	EC28 October	1970	Malmo	Sweden	0–1
WC25 February	1934	Dublin	Belgium	4–4	10 May	1956	Rotterdam	Netherlands	4–1	EC 8 December	1970	Rome	Italy	0–3
WC 8 April	1934	Amsterdam	Netherlands	2–5	WC 3 October	1956	Dublin	Denmark	2–1	EC10 May	1971	Dublin	Italy	1–2
15 December	1934	Dublin	Hungary	2–4	25 November	1956	Dublin	West Germany	3–0	EC30 May	1971	Dublin	Austria	1–4
5 May	1935	Basle	Switzerland	0–1	WC 8 May	1957	Wembley	England	1–5	EC10 October	1971	Linz	Austria	0–6
8 May	1935	Dortmund	Germany	1–3	WC19 May	1957	Dublin	England	1–1	11 June	1972	Recife	Iran	2–1
8 December	1935	Dublin	Netherlands	3–5	WC 2 October	1957	Copenhagen	Denmark	2–0	18 June	1972	Natal (Brazil)	Equador	3–2
17 March	1936	Dublin	Switzerland	1–0	11 May	1958	Katowice	Poland	2–2	21 June	1972	Recife	Chile	1–2
3 May	1936	Budapest	Hungary	3–3	14 May	1958	Vienna	Austria	1–3	25 June	1972	Recife	Portugal	1–2
9 May	1936	Luxembourg	Luxembourg	5–1	5 October	1958	Dublin	Poland	2–2	WC18 October	1972	Dublin	Russia	1–2
17 October	1936	Dublin	Germany	5–2	ENC 5 May	1959	Dublin	Czechoslovakia	2–0	WC15 November	1972	Dublin	France	2–1
6 December	1936	Dublin	Hungary	2–3	ENC10 May	1959	Bratislava	Czechoslovakia	0–4	WC13 May	1973	Moscow	USSR	0–1
17 May	1937	Berne	Switzerland	1–0	1 November	1959	Dublin	Sweden	3–2	16 May	1973	Wroclaw	Poland	0–2
23 May	1937	Paris	France	2–0	30 March	1960	Dublin	Chile	2–0	WC19 May	1973	Paris	France	1–1
WC10 October	1937	Oslo	Norway	2–3	11 May	1960	Dusseldorf	West Germany	1–0	6 June	1973	Oslo	Norway	1–1
WC 7 November	1937	Dublin	Norway	3–3	18 May	1960	Malmo	Sweden	1–4	21 October	1973	Dublin	Poland	1–0
18 May	1938	Prague	Czechoslovakia	2–2	28 September	1960	Dublin	Wales	2–3	5 May	1974	Rio de Janeiro	Brazil	1–2
22 May	1938	Warsaw	Poland	0–6	6 November	1960	Dublin	Norway	3–2	8 May	1974	Montevideo	Uruguay	0–2
18 September	1938	Dublin	Switzerland	4–0	WC 3 May	1961	Glasgow	Scotland	1–4	EC12 May	1974	Santiago	Chile	2–1
13 November	1938	Dublin	Poland	3–2	WC 7 May	1961	Dublin	Scotland	0–3	30 October	1974	Dublin	USSR	3–0
19 March	1939	Cork	Hungary	2–2	WC 8 October	1961	Dublin	Czechoslovakia	1–3	EC20 November	1974	Izmin	Turkey	1–1
18 May	1939	Budapest	Hungary	2–2	WC29 October	1961	Prague	Czechoslovakia	1–7	EC10 May	1975	Dublin	Switzerland	2–1
23 May	1939	Bremen	Germany	1–1	8 April	1962	Dublin	Austria	2–3	EC18 May	1975	Kiev	USSR	1–2
16 June	1946	Lisbon	Portugal	1–3	ENC12 August	1962	Dublin	Iceland	4–2	EC21 May	1975	Berne	Switzerland	0–1
23 June	1946	Madrid	Spain	1–0	ENC 2 September	1962	Reykjavik	Iceland	1–1	EC29 October	1975	Dublin	Turkey	4–0
30 September	1946	Dublin	England	0–1	9 June	1963	Dublin	Scotland	1–0	24 March	1976	Dublin	Norway	3–0
2 March	1947	Dublin	Spain	3–2	25 September	1963	Vienna	Austria	0–0	26 May	1976	Poznan	Poland	2–0
4 May	1947	Dublin	Portugal	0–2	13 October	1963	Dublin	Austria	3–2	8 September	1976	Wembley	England	1–1
23 May	1948	Lisbon	Portugal	0–2	11 March	1964	Seville	Spain	1–5	13 October	1976	Ankara	Turkey	3–3
30 May	1948	Barcelona	Spain	1–2	8 April	1964	Dublin	Spain	0–2	WC17 November	1976	Paris	France	0–2
5 December	1948	Dublin	Switzerland	0–1	10 May	1964	Cracow	Poland	1–3	9 February	1977	Dublin	Spain	0–1
24 April	1949	Dublin	Belgium	0–2	13 May	1964	Oslo	Norway	4–1	WC30 March	1977	Dublin	France	1–0
22 May	1949	Dublin	Portugal	1–0	24 May	1964	Dublin	England	1–3	24 April	1977	Dublin	Poland	0–0
WC 2 June	1949	Stockholm	Sweden	1–3	25 October	1964	Dublin	Poland	3–2	WC 1 June	1977	Sofia	Bulgaria	1–2
12 June	1949	Dublin	Spain	1–4	24 March	1965	Dublin	Belgium	0–2	WC12 October	1977	Dublin	Bulgaria	0–0
WC 8 September	1949	Dublin	Finland	3–0	WC 5 May	1965	Dublin	Spain	1–0	5 April	1978	Dublin	Turkey	4–2
21 September	1949	Everton	England	2–0	WC21 October	1965	Seville	Spain	1–4	12 April	1978	Lodz	Poland	0–3
WC 9 October	1949	Helsinki	Finland	1–1	WC10 November	1965	Paris	Spain	0–1	21 May	1978	Oslo	Norway	0–0
WC13 November	1949	Dublin	Sweden	1–3	4 May	1966	Dublin	West Germany	0–4	EC24 May	1978	Copenhagen	Denmark	3–3
10 May	1950	Brussels	Belgium	1–5	22 May	1966	Vienna	Austria	0–1	EC20 September	1978	Dublin	N Ireland	0–0
26 November	1950	Dublin	Norway	2–2	25 May	1966	Liege	Belgium	3–2	EC25 September	1978	Dublin	England	1–1
13 May	1951	Dublin	Argentina	0–1	ENC23 October	1966	Dublin	Spain	0–0	EC 2 May	1979	Dublin	Denmark	2–0
30 May	1951	Oslo	Norway	3–1	16 November	1966	Dublin	Turkey	2–1	EC19 May	1979	Sofia	Bulgaria	0–1
17 October	1951	Dublin	West Germany	3–2	ENC 7 December	1966	Valencia	Spain	0–2	22 May	1979	Dublin	West Germany	1–3
4 May	1952	Cologne	West Germany	0–3	22 February	1967	Ankara	Turkey	1–2	29 May	1979	Dublin	Argentina	0–0
7 May	1952	Vienna	Austria	0–6	21 May	1967	Dublin	Czechoslovakia	0–2	11 September	1979	Swansea	Wales	1–2
1 June	1952	Madrid	Spain	0–6	22 November	1967	Prague	Czechoslovakia	2–1	26 September	1979	Prague	Czechoslovakia	1–4

McLaughlin of Celtic, a prime advocate of the issue at question, the legalization of professionalism in Scotland.

And from that meeting—the third inside a year when the question of allowing professionalism was the main item on the agenda—the motion was finally carried. And from that day in May, the story of Scottish football has virtually become the story of Rangers and Celtic. Indeed, of the next 80 Scottish First Division championships contested, only seven different clubs on only 14 occasions took the title away from Glasgow's 'Old Firm'.

Looking back on the first day of 1980, a casual observer would have seen that from 1893 Rangers and Celtic had been champions 64 times—Rangers 36, Celtic 28; their records in the Scottish Cup would be hardly less impressive—45 times they had lifted the trophy out of a possible 72.

Those figures reflect a situation that was prophesied as far back as 1890 by the almost clairvoyant members of the club which is now the last bastion of amateurism in the senior British game, Queen's Park.

Queen's Park, nonetheless, remained in the upper reaches of the Scottish League because they had plenty of friends who voted to keep them there. Until 1922, entry to the Scottish First Division was by election only, a fact which upset many clubs in Fife and Stirling. After the First World War, they organized a breakaway Central League, which so worried the Scottish League that the Second Division was formally recognized with the usual promotion and relegation formalities.

The League retained, with minor adjustments, this format for over 50 years, until 1975 when a new three-division format was introduced which allowed the top ten clubs to play each other four times a season.

On the international rather than domestic field of play, the record of the Scots is, at best, unimpressive. They have yet to get beyond the first round of the finals of any major international competition. Despite reaching four consecutive World Cup final series (1974 in West Germany, 1978 in Argentina, 1982 in Spain and 1986 in Mexico) they have not once progressed to the second round. Their main claim to fame has been the remarkable record of being eliminated on goal difference in three consecutive finals—1974, 1978 and 1982. In 1986 their chances seemed better; they played the last 89 minutes of their final group game against 10 Uruguayans (one having been sent off in the first minute) and needed just a goal to go through. They barely managed a shot and left the competition with just one goal scored, and that by midfielder Strachan. It was a great disappointment to everyone, but perhaps it should not have been such a surprise.

To a rather depressing extent, the Scots almost seem to define themselves by their antipathy to, differences from, and contests with the English. For 100 years these were the highlights of each Scottish season. When the Scots were knocked out of the 1954 World Cup, one selector immortalized himself by saying to the players: 'Never mind lads, just so long as we beat the English next April.' And many Scots seemed to believe that a reasonable statement, though the English had long relegated the game to a rather meaningless friendly. It was not until the 1980s that some sort of reality began to take hold, when the game was placed in the context of all the other decisions facing football.

Kenny Dalglish (left) stretched his record number of Scottish caps to 89 when he played against Belgium on 15 December 1982. He ruled himself out of the World Cup finals of 1986 (by which time he was Liverpool's player-manager), but had by then become the first Scot to reach 100 caps.

Date		Venue	Opponents	Score
EC17 October	1979	Dublin	Bulgaria	3–0
29 October	1979	Dublin	United States	3–2
EC21 November	1979	Belfast	N Ireland	0–1
EC 6 February	1980	Wembley	England	0–2
WC26 March	1980	Nicosia	Cyprus	3–2
30 April	1980	Dublin	Switzerland	2–0
16 May	1980	Dublin	Argentina	0–1
WC10 September	1980	Dublin	Holland	2–1
WC15 October	1980	Dublin	Belgium	1–1
WC28 October	1980	Paris	France	0–2
WC19 November	1980	Dublin	Cyprus	6–0
24 February	1981	Dublin	Wales	1–3
WC25 March	1981	Brussels	Belgium	0–1
WC 9 September	1981	Amsterdam	Holland	2–2
WC14 October	1981	Dublin	France	3–2
28 April	1982	Algiers	Algeria	0–2
22 May	1982	Santiago	Chile	0–1
27 May	1982	Uberlandia	Brazil	0–7
EC22 September	1982	Rotterdam	Holland	1–0
EC13 October	1982	Dublin	Iceland	2–0
EC17 November	1982	Dublin	Spain	3–3
EC30 March	1983	Valletta	Malta	1–0
EC27 April	1983	Zaragosa	Spain	0–2
EC21 September	1983	Reykjavik	Iceland	3–0
EC12 October	1983	Dublin	Holland	2–3
EC16 November	1983	Dublin	Malta	8–0
4 April	1984	Tel-Aviv	Israel	0–3
23 May	1984	Dublin	Poland	0–0
WC12 September	1984	Dublin	USSR	1–0
WC17 October	1984	Oslo	Norway	0–1
WC14 November	1984	Copenhagen	Denmark	0–3
5 February	1985	Dublin	Italy	1–2
WC 1 May	1985	Dublin	Norway	0–0
11 September	1985	Berne	Switzerland	0–0
WC16 October	1985	Moscow	USSR	0–2
WC13 November	1985	Dublin	Denmark	1–4
26 March	1986	Dublin	Wales	0–1
23 April	1986	Dublin	Uruguay	1–1
EC15 October	1986	Dublin	Scotland	0–0
12 November	1986	Warsaw	Poland	0–1
EC18 February	1987	Glasgow	Scotland	1–0
EC 1 April	1987	Sofia	Bulgaria	1–2
24 May	1987	Dublin	Brazil	1–0
28 May	1987	Luxembourg	Luxembourg	2–0

ENC—European Nations Cup games WC—World Cup games
EC—European Championship games

FULL INTERNATIONALS PLAYED BY IRELAND AND NORTHERN IRELAND

Date		Venue	Opponents	Score
18 February	1882	Belfast	England	0–13
25 February	1882	Wrexham	Wales	1–7
24 February	1883	Liverpool	England	0–7
17 March	1883	Belfast	Wales	1–1
9 February	1884	Wrexham	Wales	0–6
23 February	1884	Belfast	England	1–8
26 March	1884	Belfast	Scotland	0–5
28 February	1885	Manchester	England	0–4
14 March	1885	Glasgow	Scotland	2–8
11 April	1885	Belfast	Wales	2–8
27 February	1886	Wrexham	Wales	0–5
13 March	1886	Belfast	England	1–6
20 March	1886	Belfast	Scotland	2–7
5 February	1887	Sheffield	England	0–7
19 February	1887	Glasgow	Scotland	1–4
12 March	1887	Belfast	Wales	4–1
3 March	1888	Wrexham	Wales	0–11
24 March	1888	Belfast	Scotland	2–10
31 March	1888	Belfast	England	1–5
2 March	1889	Liverpool	England	1–6
9 March	1889	Glasgow	Scotland	0–7
27 April	1889	Belfast	Wales	1–3
8 February	1890	Shrewsbury	Wales	2–5
15 March	1890	Belfast	England	1–9
29 March	1890	Belfast	Scotland	1–4
7 February	1891	Belfast	Wales	7–2
7 March	1891	Wolverhampton	England	1–6
28 March	1891	Glasgow	Scotland	1–2
27 February	1892	Bangor (Wales)	Wales	1–1
5 March	1892	Belfast	England	0–2
19 March	1892	Belfast	Scotland	2–3
25 February	1893	Birmingham	England	1–6
25 March	1893	Glasgow	Scotland	1–6
8 April	1893	Belfast	Wales	4–3
24 February	1894	Swansea	Wales	1–4
3 March	1894	Belfast	England	2–2
31 March	1894	Belfast	Scotland	1–2
9 March	1895	Derby	England	0–9
16 March	1895	Belfast	Wales	2–2
30 March	1895	Glasgow	Scotland	1–3
29 February	1895	Wrexham	Wales	1–6
7 March	1896	Belfast	England	0–2
28 March	1896	Belfast	Scotland	3–3
20 February	1897	Nottingham	England	0–6
6 March	1897	Belfast	Wales	4–3
27 March	1897	Glasgow	Scotland	1–5
19 February	1898	Llandudno	Wales	1–0
5 March	1898	Belfast	England	2–3
26 March	1898	Belfast	Scotland	0–3
18 February	1899	Sunderland	England	2–13
4 March	1899	Belfast	Wales	1–0
25 March	1899	Glasgow	Scotland	1–9
24 February	1900	Llandudno	Wales	0–2
3 March	1900	Belfast	Scotland	0–3
17 March	1900	Dublin	England	0–2
23 February	1901	Glasgow	Scotland	0–11
9 March	1901	Southampton	England	0–3
23 March	1901	Llandudno	Wales	0–1
1 March	1902	Belfast	Scotland	1–5
22 March	1902	Belfast	England	0–1
22 March	1902	Cardiff	Wales	3–0
14 February	1903	Wolverhampton	England	0–4
21 March	1903	Glasgow	Scotland	2–0
28 March	1903	Belfast	Wales	2–0
12 March	1904	Belfast	England	1–3
21 March	1904	Bangor (Wales)	Wales	1–0
26 March	1904	Dublin	Scotland	1–1
25 February	1905	Middlesbrough	England	1–1
18 March	1905	Glasgow	Scotland	0–4

Date		Venue	Opponents	Score
8 April	1905	Belfast	Wales	2–2
17 February	1906	Belfast	England	0–5
17 March	1906	Dublin	Scotland	0–1
2 April	1907	Wrexham	Wales	4–4
16 February	1907	Liverpool	England	0–1
23 February	1908	Belfast	Wales	2–3
16 March	1908	Glasgow	Scotland	0–3
15 February	1908	Belfast	England	1–3
14 March	1908	Dublin	Scotland	0–5
11 April	1908	Aberdare	Wales	1–0
13 February	1909	Bradford	England	0–4
20 March	1909	Belfast	Wales	2–3
27 March	1909	Glasgow	Scotland	0–5
12 February	1910	Belfast	England	1–1
11 March	1910	Wrexham	Wales	1–4
19 March	1910	Belfast	Scotland	1–0
11 February	1911	Derby	England	1–2
18 March	1911	Glasgow	Scotland	0–2
28 March	1911	Belfast	Wales	1–2
10 February	1912	Dublin	England	1–6
16 March	1912	Belfast	Scotland	1–4
16 March	1912	Belfast	Scotland	1–4
13 April	1912	Cardiff	Wales	3–2
18 January	1913	Belfast	Wales	0–1
15 February	1913	Belfast	England	2–1
15 March	1913	Dublin	Scotland	1–2
19 January	1914	Wrexham	Wales	2–1
14 February	1914	Middlesbrough	England	3–0
14 March	1914	Belfast	Scotland	1–1
25 October	1919	Belfast	England	1–1
14 February	1920	Belfast	Wales	2–2
13 March	1920	Glasgow	Scotland	0–3
23 October	1920	Sunderland	England	0–2
26 February	1921	Belfast	Scotland	0–2
9 April	1921	Swansea	Wales	1–2
22 October	1921	Belfast	England	1–1
4 March	1922	Glasgow	Scotland	1–2
1 April	1922	Belfast	Wales	1–1
21 October	1922	West Bromwich	England	0–2
3 March	1923	Belfast	Scotland	0–1
14 April	1923	Wrexham	Wales	3–0
20 October	1923	Belfast	England	2–1
1 March	1924	Glasgow	Scotland	0–2
15 March	1924	Belfast	Wales	0–1
22 October	1924	Liverpool	England	1–3
28 February	1925	Belfast	Scotland	0–3
18 April	1925	Wrexham	Wales	0–0
24 October	1925	Belfast	England	0–0
13 January	1926	Belfast	Wales	3–0
27 February	1926	Glasgow	Scotland	0–4
20 October	1926	Liverpool	England	3–3
26 February	1927	Belfast	Scotland	0–2
9 April	1927	Cardiff	Wales	2–2
22 October	1927	Belfast	England	2–0
4 February	1928	Belfast	Wales	1–2
25 February	1928	Glasgow	Scotland	1–0
22 October	1928	Liverpool	England	1–2
2 February	1929	Wrexham	Wales	2–2
23 February	1929	Belfast	Scotland	3–7
19 October	1929	Belfast	England	0–3
1 February	1930	Belfast	Wales	7–0
22 February	1930	Glasgow	Scotland	1–3
20 October	1930	Sheffield	England	1–5
21 February	1931	Belfast	Scotland	0–0
22 April	1931	Wrexham	Wales	2–3
19 September	1931	Glasgow	Scotland	1–3
17 October	1931	Belfast	England	2–6
5 December	1931	Belfast	Wales	4–0
17 September	1932	Belfast	Scotland	0–4

Date		Venue	Opponents	Score
17 October	1932	Blackpool	England	0–1
7 December	1932	Wrexham	Wales	1–4
16 September	1933	Glasgow	Scotland	2–1
14 October	1933	Belfast	England	0–3
4 November	1933	Belfast	Wales	1–1
20 October	1934	Belfast	Scotland	2–1
6 February	1935	Liverpool	England	1–2
27 March	1935	Wrexham	Wales	1–3
19 October	1935	Belfast	England	1–3
13 November	1935	Edinburgh	Scotland	1–2
11 March	1936	Belfast	Wales	3–2
31 October	1936	Belfast	Scotland	1–3
18 November	1936	Stoke	England	1–3
17 March	1937	Wrexham	Wales	1–4
23 October	1937	Belfast	England	1–5
10 November	1937	Aberdeen	Scotland	1–1
16 March	1938	Belfast	Wales	1–0
8 October	1938	Belfast	Scotland	0–2
16 November	1938	Manchester	England	0–7
15 March	1939	Wrexham	Wales	1–3
V15 September	1945	Belfast	England	0–1
28 September	1946	Belfast	England	2–7
27 November	1946	Glasgow	Scotland	0–0
16 April	1947	Belfast	Wales	2–1
4 October	1947	Belfast	Scotland	2–0
5 November	1947	Liverpool	England	2–2
10 March	1948	Wrexham	Wales	0–2
5 November	1947	Liverpool	England	2–2
10 March	1948	Wrexham	Wales	0–2
9 October	1948	Belfast	England	2–6
17 November	1948	Glasgow	Scotland	2–3
9 March	1949	Belfast	Wales	0–2
WC 1 October	1949	Belfast	Scotland	2–8
WC16 November	1949	Manchester	England	2–9
WC 8 March	1950	Wrexham	Wales	0–0
7 October	1950	Belfast	England	1–4
1 November	1950	Glasgow	Scotland	1–6
7 March	1951	Belfast	Wales	1–2
12 May	1951	Belfast	France	2–2
6 October	1951	Belfast	Scotland	0–3
14 November	1951	Birmingham	England	0–2
19 March	1952	Swansea	Wales	0–3
4 October	1952	Belfast	England	2–2
5 November	1952	Glasgow	Scotland	1–1
11 November	1952	Paris	France	1–3
15 April	1953	Belfast	Wales	2–3
WC 3 October	1953	Belfast	Scotland	1–3
WC11 November	1953	Liverpool	England	1–3
WC31 March	1954	Wrexham	Wales	2–1
2 October	1954	Belfast	England	0–2
3 November	1954	Glasgow	Scotland	2–2
20 April	1955	Belfast	Wales	2–3
8 October	1955	Belfast	Scotland	2–1
2 November	1955	Wembley	England	0–3
11 April	1956	Cardiff	Wales	1–1
6 October	1956	Belfast	England	1–1
7 November	1956	Glasgow	Scotland	0–1
WC16 January	1957	Lisbon	Portugal	1–1
10 April	1957	Belfast	Wales	0–0
WC25 April	1957	Rome	Italy	0–1
WC 1 May	1957	Belfast	Portugal	3–0
5 October	1957	Belfast	Scotland	1–1
6 November	1957	Wembley	England	3–2
4 December	1957	Belfast	Italy	2–2
WC15 January	1958	Belfast	Italy	2–1
16 April	1958	Cardiff	Wales	1–1
WC 8 June	1958	Halmstad	Czechoslovakia	1–0
WC11 June	1958	Halmstad	Argentina	1–3
WC15 June	1958	Malmo	West Germany	2–2

Matches were switched from Wembley to Hampden by a government tired of the tartan army's invasion, and a string of poor, televised plods reinforced the public image of a rather meaningless spectacle. In 1986 even the game's attendance was reflecting reality—just over 60,000 at a game which had been a sell-out for three generations and which, with the exception of the very biggest games in the Maracana, had created most of the world's soccer attendance records.

The ending of the Home International Championship (towards the end of its life called officially, though never by the public, the British Championship) in 1984 also reduced the game's significance. That was a step prompted by both the English and the Scots, neither of whom felt it was particularly helpful trying to find space for games against a mixture of English First and Second Division players who were on the field by virtue of some (often obscure) Welsh or Irish connection.

For the latter two countries, however, it was not a question of an irritation, more a matter of life and death. Their very survival as independent soccer powers (a survival increasingly being called into question by third world and Latin American FIFA members) depended to a large extent on the money they gained from the annual fixtures against England and Scotland.

The very existence of Northern Ireland and Wales as international powers is a historical accident which, to an outsider, seems to become quirkier and quirkier. This was never better illustrated than in 1982. As that year began, Northern Ireland found herself in the company of 23 other countries in the World Cup draw. In itself this was remarkable, for her qualification group performance had been by far the worst of all the countries present (and the worst of the five teams in the British Isles), with just six goals scored and nine points from eight matches. By contrast, Wales and the Republic of Ireland had managed 10 points each, had played in much tougher groups and apparently had, by any international standards, far better squads.

For both these countries, however, the World Cup had been something of a tragedy. Both failed to proceed on goal difference—Eire largely because of two very debatable penalty decisions that went against her, Wales because, absurdly, she had failed to beat Iceland in Swansea.

On 27 May 1982, Billy Bingham brought his World Cup qualifiers to Wrexham for a Home International Championship match and drew a crowd of 2,315, the lowest for any home international this century. Ireland played badly and lost 3–0. And yet, two months later, the Irish were contesting what was effectively a World Cup quarter-final tie with France and,

Date		Venue	Opponents	Score
WC17 June	1958	Malmo	Czechoslovakia	2–1
WC19 June	1958	Norrkoping	France	0–4
4 October	1958	Belfast	England	3–3
15 October	1958	Madrid	Spain	2–6
5 November	1958	Glasgow	Scotland	2–2
22 April	1959	Belfast	Wales	4–1
3 October	1959	Belfast	Scotland	0–4
18 November	1959	Wembley	England	1–2
6 April	1960	Wrexham	Wales	2–3
8 October	1960	Belfast	England	2–5
WC26 October	1960	Belfast	West Germany	3–4
9 November	1960	Glasgow	Scotland	2–5
12 April	1961	Belfast	Wales	1–5
25 April	1961	Bologna	Italy	2–3
WC 3 May	1961	Athens	Greece	1–2
WC10 May	1961	West Berlin	West Germany	1–2
7 October	1961	Belfast	Scotland	1–6
WC17 October	1961	Belfast	Greece	2–0
22 November	1961	Wembley	England	1–1
11 April	1962	Cardiff	Wales	0–4
9 May	1962	Rotterdam	Netherlands	0–4
ENC10 October	1962	Katowice	Poland	2–0
20 October	1962	Belfast	England	1–3
7 November	1962	Glasgow	Scotland	1–5
ENC28 November	1962	Belfast	Poland	2–0
3 April	1963	Belfast	Wales	1–4
30 May	1963	Bilbao	Spain	1–1
12 October	1963	Belfast	Scotland	2–1
30 October	1963	Belfast	Spain	0–1
20 November	1963	Wembley	England	3–8
15 April	1964	Swansea	Wales	3–2
29 April	1964	Belfast	Uruguay	3–0
3 October	1964	Belfast	England	3–4
WC14 October	1964	Belfast	Switzerland	1–0
WC14 November	1964	Lausanne	Switzerland	1–2
25 November	1964	Glasgow	Scotland	2–3
WC17 March	1965	Belfast	Holland	2–1
31 March	1965	Belfast	Wales	0–5
WC 7 April	1965	Rotterdam	Holland	0–0
WC 7 May	1965	Belfast	Albania	4–1
2 October	1965	Belfast	Scotland	3–2
10 November	1965	Wembley	England	1–2
WC24 November	1965	Tirana	Albania	1–1
30 March	1966	Cardiff	Wales	4–1
7 May	1966	Belfast	West Germany	0–2
22 June	1966	Belfast	Mexico	4–1
22 October	1966	Belfast	England	0–2
16 November	1966	Glasgow	Scotland	1–2
12 April	1967	Belfast	Wales	0–0
21 October	1967	Belfast	Scotland	1–0
22 November	1967	Wembley	England	0–2
28 February	1968	Wrexham	Wales	0–2
10 September	1968	Jaffa	Israel	3–2
WC23 October	1968	Belfast	Turkey	4–1
WC11 December	1968	Istanbul	Turkey	3–0
3 May	1969	Belfast	England	1–3
6 Ma6	1969	Glasgow	Scotland	1–1
10 May	1969	Belfast	Wales	0–0
WC10 September	1969	Belfast	Russia	0–0
WC22 October	1969	Moscow	Russia	0–2
18 April	1970	Belfast	Scotland	0–1
21 April	1970	Wembley	England	1–3
25 April	1970	Swansea	Wales	0–1
EC11 November	1970	Seville	Spain	0–3
EC 3 February	1971	Nicosia	Cyprus	3–0
EC21 April	1971	Belfast	Cyprus	5–0
15 May	1971	Belfast	England	0–1
18 May	1971	Glasgow	Scotland	1–0
22 May	1971	Belfast	Wales	1–0

Date		Venue	Opponents	Score
EC22 September	1971	Moscow	Russia	0–1
EC13 October	1971	Belfast	Russia	1–1
EC16 February	1972	Hull	Spain	1–1
20 May	1972	Glasgow	Scotland	0–2
24 May	1972	Wembley	England	1–0
27 May	1972	Wrexham	Wales	0–0
WC18 October	1972	Sofia	Bulgaria	0–3
WC14 February	1973	Nicosia	Cyprus	0–1
WC28 March	1973	Coventry	Portugal	1–1
WC 8 May	1973	Fulham	Cyprus	3–0
12 May	1973	Everton	Englnad	1–2
16 May	1973	Glasgow	Scotland	2–1
19 May	1973	Everton	Wales	1–0
WC26 September	1973	Sheffield	Bulgaria	0–0
WC14 November	1973	Lisbon	Portugal	1–1
11 May	1974	Glasgow	Scotland	1–0
15 May	1974	Wembley	England	0–1
18 May	1974	Wrexham	Wales	0–1
EC 4 September	1974	Oslo	Norway	1–2
EC30 October	1974	Solna	Sweden	2–0
EC16 March	1975	Belfast	Yugoslavia	1–0
17 May	1975	Belfast	England	0–0
20 May	1975	Glasgow	Scotland	0–3
23 May	1975	Belfast	Wales	1–0
EC 3 September	1975	Belfast	Sweden	1–2
EC29 October	1975	Belfast	Norway	3–0
EC19 November	1975	Belgrade	Yugoslavia	0–1
3 March	1976	Tel Aviv	Israel	1–1
8 May	1976	Glasgow	Scotland	0–3
11 May	1976	Wembley	England	0–4
14 May	1976	Swansea	Wales	0–1
WC13 October	1976	Rotterdam	Holland	2–2
WC10 November	1976	Liege	Belgium	0–2
27 April	1977	Cologne	West Germany	0–5
28 May	1977	Belfast	England	1–2
1 June	1977	Glasgow	Scotland	0–3
3 June	1977	Belfast	Wales	1–1
WC11 June	1977	Reykjavik	Iceland	0–1
WC29 September	1977	Belfast	Iceland	2–0
WC12 October	1977	Belfast	Holland	0–1
WC16 November	1977	Belfast	Belgium	3–0
13 May	1978	Glasgow	Scotland	1–1
16 May	1978	Wembley	England	0–1
19 May	1978	Wrexham	Wales	0–1
EC20 September	1978	Dublin	Eire	0–0
EC25 October	1978	Belfast	Denmark	2–1
EC29 November	1978	Sofia	Bulgaria	2–0
EC 7 February	1979	Wembley	England	0–4
EC 2 May	1979	Belfast	Bulgaria	2–0
19 May	1979	Belfast	England	0–2
22 May	1979	Hampden	Scotland	0–1
25 May	1979	Belfast	Wales	1–1
EC 6 June	1979	Copenhagen	Denmark	0–4
EC17 October	1979	Belfast	England	1–5
EC21 November	1979	Belfast	Eire	1–0
WC26 March	1980	Tel Aviv	Israel	0–0
16 May	1980	Belfast	Scotland	1–0
20 May	1980	Wembley	England	1–1
23 May	1980	Cardiff	Wales	1–0
11 June	1980	Sydney	Australia	2–1
15 June	1980	Melbourne	Australia	1–1
18 June	1980	Adelaide	Australia	2–1
WC15 October	1980	Belfast	Sweden	3–0
WC19 November	1980	Lisbon	Portugal	0–1
WC25 March	1981	Glasgow	Scotland	1–1
WC29 April	1981	Belfast	Portugal	1–0
19 May	1981	Glasgow	Scotland	0–2
WC 3 June	1981	Stockholm	Sweden	0–1
WC14 October	1981	Belfast	Scotland	0–0

Date		Venue	Opponents	Score
WC18 November	1981	Belfast	Israel	1–0
23 February	1982	Wembley	England	0–4
24 March	1982	Paris	France	0–4
28 April	1982	Belfast	Scotland	1–1
27 May	1982	Wrexham	Wales	0–3
WC17 June	1982	Zaragoza	Yugoslavia	0–0
WC21 June	1982	Zaragoza	Honduras	1–1
WC25 June	1982	Valencia	Spain	1–0
WC 1 July	1982	Madrid	Austria	2–2
WC 4 July	1982	Madrid	France	1–4
EC13 October	1982	Vienna	Austria	0–2
EC17 November	1982	Belfast	W. Germany	1–0
EC15 December	1982	Tirana	Albania	0–0
EC30 March	1983	Belfast	Turkey	2–1
EC27 April	1983	Belfast	Albania	1–0
24 May	1983	Glasgow	Scotland	0–0
28 May	1983	Belfast	England	0–0
31 May	1983	Belfast	Wales	0–1
EC21 September	1983	Belfast	Austria	3–1
EC12 October	1983	Ankara	Turkey	0–1
EC16 November	1983	Hamburg	West Germany	1–0
13 December	1983	Glasgow	Scotland	2–0
4 April	1984	Wembley	England	0–1
22 May	1984	Swansea	Wales	1–1
WC27 May	1984	Pori	Finland	0–1
WC12 September	1984	Belfast	Rumania	3–2
16 October	1984	Belfast	Israle	3–0
WC 14 November	1984	Belfast	Finland	2–1
WC27 February	1985	Belfast	England	0–1
27 March	1985	Palma	Spain	0–0
WC 1 May	1985	Belfast	Turkey	2–0
WC11 September	1985	Izmir	Turkey	0–0
WC16 October	1985	Bucharest	Rumania	1–0
WC13 November	1985	Wembley	England	0–0
26 February	1986	Paris	France	0–0
26 March	1986	Belfast	Denmark	1–1
23 April	1986	Belfast	Morroco	2–1
WC 3 June	1986	Guadalajara	Algeria	1–1
WC 7 June	1986	Guadalajara	Spain	1–2
WC12 June	1986	Guadalajara	Brazil	0–3
EC15 October	1986	Wembley	England	0–3
EC12 November	1986	Izmir	Turkey	0–0
18 February	1987	Tel-Aviv	Israel	1–1
EC 1 April	1987	Belfast	England	0–2

ENC—European Nations Cup games   WC—World Cup games
EC—European Championship games   V—Victory International

had a perfectly good early goal by Martin O'Neill not been disallowed by an incompetent linesman, the Irish might have gone further. In the first qualifying group the Irish had drawn with Yugoslavia and then gone on to beat the hosts, Spain, in Valencia for the best international result in Irish history.

The world's—and Britain's—press wrote of the magnificent reception the players would surely get when they returned to Belfast, missing another critical point about the Irish. Alone of the qualifiers, they were not going home to the country they represented. Of the whole squad of 22, no more than half-a-dozen lived there. Many, by their own admission, never went there other than for international matches.

It was very easy to understand the annoyance of many other soccer nations that the British Isles have somehow managed to maintain five international teams, despite the fact that virtually all their players compete in just one League competition. After the declining attendances at home international matches in recent years, it was also very difficult to argue that there was any obsessive domestic desire for all of these international teams. At Wrexham, the excuse for that 2,000 attendance was that the FA Cup final replay was on television; a threadbare one to be sure—why should a public that cared about Wales prefer to stay in and watch a Cup final between two sides from London?

The fact was that international football had lost much of its appeal over a fifteen year period in which the number of matches played had more than doubled and the inability of the Welsh and Irish to call on squads of genuinely first-class players had become increasingly obvious. Notwithstanding Ireland's amazing performance in Spain (which was surely the exception tending to prove the rule) an Ireland v Wales game was no better and no worse than an English Second Division match. Even when England and Scotland are the opposition, the power of the Irish and Welsh has tended to be that of frustrating their bigger brothers, that determined defence which has become so much less appealing to crowds in recent decades.

This is not to say that the two Irelands and Wales have not had their successes in recent years. In 1980 Northern Ireland won the Home International Championship outright for only the second time in her history (the first was in 1914), appropriately in the Irish FA's Centenary year. That being said, it was not an entirely glorious campaign—1–0 defeats of Scotland and Wales and a 1–1 draw at Wembley.

It was essentially the same squad that did so well in Spain, a team that had been denied any immediate opportunity of repeating its 1980 success when both England and Wales refused to travel to Belfast the following year at the height of

the Maze hunger strikes. Rather than rearrange the matches elsewhere, the fixtures were dropped, giving rise to understandable suspicions that both managers were not entirely unhappy to lose one game from an extremely crowded club and country fixture list. For the first time in peacetime since it had been instituted in 1883–84 the Championship was left unfinished—a conclusion that drew forth surprisingly little comment.

That was indeed the thin end of the wedge for the Irish and Welsh. Two years later the HIC came to an end and, in the manner of these things, the Irish won the final tournament for only the third time in their history. The results of Ireland's games—2–0 versus Scotland, 0–1 versus England and 1–1 versus Wales—summed up precisely why the competition had come stumbling to its necessary end.

Whether Northern Ireland and Wales survive as independ-

Above Mike England (left) at the heart of the Welsh defence against his namesake country in the early 1970s. A decade later he was the Welsh manager and took his side to the very fringes of the 1982 World Cup finals. In the end, they failed to qualify because of a 2–2 draw with Iceland in Swansea but the Welsh still obtained one more point than did England and Northern Ireland.

Right Port Vale's Sammy Morgan scores Northern Ireland's equalizing goal against Spain at Hull City's Boothferry Park in February 1972. A large number of Irish internationals in the 1970s had to be transferred from Belfast because of the security situation, a trend that reached a peak in 1981 when both England and Wales refused to play Home International Championship matches there and the tournament was left incomplete. In the World Cup finals of 1982 Northern Ireland again beat Spain—in Spain—perhaps their greatest performance.

ent soccer powers is open to question. They have both, plus the Republic of Ireland, taken advantage in recent years of the new eligibility rules governing a player's choice of country. Because of the peculiarity of the British situation, with numerous colonies, thousands of Britons being born abroad to British civil servants and members of the armed forces in the 1960s, and there being four home countries plus Eire, some strange situations regularly occur. A player born in one of the old colonies such as a West Indian island or an African state who is now resident in the United Kingdom and carrying a British passport can elect to play for any of the four home countries (where he lives doesn't matter). Everton's Pat van den Hauwe, who gave up his Belgian nationality, was in just this position. He chose to play for Wales, though he was no more Welsh than any other Belgian, largely because his teammates Neville Southall and Kevin Ratcliffe were Welsh.

In the sense that this is rather distant from the traditional view of what a national team should be, this was probably another factor in the noticeable decline of interest in the performances of the home countries, except at the highest level. When Northern Ireland were beaten 3–0 by England at Wembley in a European Championship match in October 1986 the crowd only just struggled over 30,000. A far cry from twenty years before, and it did not seem at all fanciful to imagine England playing to 10,000 and 15,000 in the foreseeable future.

In the late 1980s whether the independent home associations would survive the century was a genuine question. Northern Ireland's displays in Spain had probably stemmed the tide (though they were little better than makeweights in Mexico) but there was bound to be a revival of the subtle campaign to decrease the United Kingdom's numerical chances in major competitions. Paradoxically, it was a suggestion most people in the British Isles would probably welcome—ever since the days of Manchester United being able to win the European Cup with a squad containing George Best, Denis Law and Bobby Charlton, only to see them head off for different international sides, it had been clear that the United Kingdom's international chances were reduced rather than enhanced by the maintenance of this outdated system.

The Scots would fight any such proposal to the death, and they have a proud history and a credible League, but the banning of English sides from Europe and the disenchantment with things British suggests the tide of history is against them. Perhaps bidding for the World Cup in 1998 might be Scotland's answer. Otherwise, who knows whether the year 2000 will still see four international teams from the British Isles preparing to contest the 2002 World Cup.

CHAPTER NINE

AGONY ABROAD
-two decades of paradox

English football reached its international peak in Leon, Mexico in 1970. In one of the best, and most dramatic, games ever played by an English side abroad, West Germany were to triumph 3–2 after being 2–0 down twenty minutes from time. But England were still the better side, probably the only one capable of running the Brazilians close (Brazil had just squeezed a group game, famed for the 'Astle Miss' which was to enter the language, 1–0) and the German result was a fluke, dependent as much as anything on Gordon Banks' illness and Peter Bonetti's uncertainties.

But, from this peak onwards, England, like the other home countries, have never looked like winning, nor even getting a sniff, of a major title. And here lies the paradox; for in those two decades British club sides have been the dominant force in European soccer, and in particular in the flagship European Champions Cup. From 1970 to the Heysel tragedy in Brussels in 1985, British clubs won seven of the sixteen European Cups, four of the Cup Winners Cups and seven of the UEFA Cups, nearly 40% of all of the trophies available. No other European nation can begin to compare. So why did the Italians reach the 1970 World Cup final and win the trophy in 1982? And how did the Germans reach the finals of 1974, 1982 and 1986? And why did the Dutch reach two consecutive finals in 1974 and 1978?

And how, by comparison, did Liverpool, Nottingham Forest, Celtic and, in their way, Spurs become such powerful forces in Europe when their teams consisted of English and Scots players?

The question is a complex one, not yielding any simple answers. There is no reason to suppose that the English club system is inherently superior to that of the Germans or the Italians, nor to assume that English club players are somehow better (because, if they are, why don't they show it at international level?) Indeed the strains put on English clubs by the tough 42-game (up to 1987) League programme plus FA Cup plus League Cup plus Europe is a strong reason to argue they should have performed rather more poorly than they did. The cry was always too much football—but the club sides did well enough anyway.

The paradox, then, would seem to relate more to the international rather than the club game. After Leon, England went into a rapid decline. In 1972 hopes of reaching the European Championship finals fell apart in West Germany's 3–1 win at Wembley, known now as Netzer's game. For the return, in Berlin, Ramsey was at his most cynical—a blatantly defensive side achieved a goalless draw but it was impossible to see where Ramsey thought the two goals he needed were coming from.

Eighteen months later came the Polish interlude—the 'clown' Tomaszewski, the giant Gorgon ('Joe Bugner in boots' said Clough) and a 1–1 draw which consigned England to the World Cup sidelines for the very first time since she originally entered the tournament after the Second World War.

The 1976 European Championship was little better—the Czechs headed England's group after a 2–1 win in Bratislava, though England had beaten them 3–0 at Wembley. Then 1978 saw another World Cup failure, a home win against Italy not being enough to compensate for insufficient goals against Luxembourg. So the 1970s saw four consecutive failures to qualify in the four major international competitions. A poor record, perhaps, but what is easily forgotten is that West Germany and Czechoslovakia went on to win the European Championships of 1972 and 1976, Poland came a surprise third in the World Cup of 1974 and Italy came fourth in Agentina in 1978. There was certainly a case for arguing that England suffered from the luck of the draw. Or perhaps a defeat of England inspired these countries to greater things. In the 1980s the situation was reversed, the Scots in particular being quick to point out how easy England's World Cup groups always seemed to be.

The 1980s and Ron Greenwood certainly saw an improvement. The 1980 European Championship was the first final series of any sort England had reached for a decade, though a 1–0 defeat by Tardelli and the home side in Turin, earlier accompanied by some of the worst crowd riots of the period, put paid to further hopes. England were less successful in 1984, going out to emergent Denmark, everyone's favourites

The two principal rivals for the title of midfield terror in the early 1970s clash at Hampden during the England v Scotland match on 27 May 1972. The conflicts between Billy Bremner (centre) of Scotland and Leeds and Peter Storey (right) of Arsenal and England were as real at club as at international level, their two sides being the main protagonists of the period. The Scots had an unhappy time against England in the 1970s, winning only three of the eleven clashes while England won seven, including the 1972 game 1–0.

FULL INTERNATIONALS PLAYED BY ENGLAND NOVEMBER 1870–MAY 1987

Date		Venue	Opponents	Score
*19 November	1870	Kennington Oval	Scotland	1–0
*28 February	1871	Kennington Oval	Scotland	1–1
*18 November	1871	Kennington Oval	Scotland	2–1
*24 February	1872	Kennington Oval	Scotland	1–0
30 November	1872	Glasgow	Scotland	0–0
8 March	1873	Kennington Oval	Scotland	4–2
7 March	1874	Glasgow	Scotland	1–2
6 March	1875	Kennington Oval	Scotland	2–2
4 March	1876	Glasgow	Scotland	0–3
3 March	1877	Kennington Oval	Scotland	1–3
2 March	1878	Glasgow	Scotland	2–7
18 January	1879	Kennington Oval	Wales	2–1
5 April	1879	Kennington Oval	Scotland	5–4
13 March	1880	Glasgow	Scotland	4–5
15 March	1880	Wrexham	Wales	3–2
26 February	1881	Blackburn	Wales	0–1
12 March	1881	Kennington Oval	Scotland	1–6
18 February	1882	Belfast	Ireland	13–0
11 March	1882	Glasgow	Scotland	1–5
13 March	1882	Wrexham	Wales	3–5
3 February	1883	Kennington Oval	Wales	5–0
24 February	1883	Liverpool	Ireland	7–0
10 March	1883	Sheffield	Scotland	2–3
23 February	1884	Belfast	Ireland	8–1
15 March	1884	Glasgow	Scotland	0–1
17 March	1884	Wrexham	Wales	4–0
28 February	1885	Manchester	Ireland	4–0
14 March	1885	Blackburn	Wales	1–1
21 March	1885	Kennington Oval	Scotland	1–1
13 March	1886	Belfast	Ireland	6–1
29 March	1886	Wrexham	Wales	3–1
31 March	1886	Glasgow	Scotland	1–1
5 February	1887	Sheffield	Ireland	7–0
26 February	1887	Kennington Oval	Wales	4–0
19 March	1887	Blackburn	Scotland	2–3
4 February	1888	Crewe	Wales	5–1
17 March	1888	Glasgow	Scotland	5–0
31 March	1888	Belfast	Ireland	5–1
23 February	1889	Stoke-on-Trent	Wales	4–1
2 March	1889	Everton	Ireland	6–1
13 April	1889	Kennington Oval	Scotland	2–3
†15 March	1890	Belfast	Ireland	9–1
†15 March	1890	Wrexham	Wales	3–1
5 April	1890	Glasgow	Scotland	1–1
† 7 March	1891	Sunderland	Wales	4–1
† 7 March	1891	Wolverhampton	Ireland	6–1
6 April	1891	Blackburn	Scotland	2–1
† 5 March	1892	Wrexham	Wales	2–0
† 5 March	1892	Belfast	Ireland	2–0
2 April	1892	Glasgow	Scotland	4–1
25 February	1893	Birmingham	Ireland	6–1
13 March	1893	Stoke-on-Trent	Wales	6–0
1 April	1893	Richmond	Scotland	5–2
3 March	1894	Belfast	Ireland	2–2
12 March	1894	Wrexham	Wales	5–1
7 April	1894	Glasgow	Scotland	2–2
9 March	1895	Derby	Ireland	9–0
18 March	1895	Queen's Club, Kensington	Wales	1–1
6 April	1895	Everton	Scotland	3–0
7 March	1896	Belfast	Ireland	2–0
16 March	1896	Cardiff	Wales	9–1
4 April	1896	Glasgow	Scotland	1–2
20 February	1897	Nottingham	Ireland	6–0
29 March	1897	Sheffield	Wales	4–0
3 April	1897	Crystal Palace	Scotland	1–2
5 March	1898	Belfast	Ireland	3–2
28 March	1898	Wrexham	Wales	3–0
2 April	1898	Glasgow	Scotland	3–1
18 February	1899	Sunderland	Ireland	13–2
20 March	1899	Bristol	Wales	4–1
8 April	1899	Birmingham	Scotland	2–1
17 March	1900	Dublin	Ireland	2–0
26 March	1900	Cardiff	Wales	1–1
7 April	1900	Glasgow	Scotland	1–4
9 March	1901	Southampton	Ireland	3–0
18 March	1901	Newcastle	Wales	6–0
30 March	1901	Crystal Palace	Scotland	2–2
3 March	1902	Wrexham	Wales	0–0
22 March	1902	Belfast	Ireland	1–0
‡ 5 April	1902	Glasgow	Scotland	1–1
3 May	1902	Birmingham	Scotland	2–2
14 February	1903	Wolverhampton	Ireland	4–0
2 March	1903	Portsmouth	Wales	2–1
4 April	1903	Sheffield	Scotland	1–2
29 February	1904	Wrexham	Wales	2–2
12 March	1904	Belfast	Ireland	3–1
9 April	1904	Glasgow	Scotland	1–0
25 February	1905	Middlesborough	Ireland	1–1
27 March	1905	Liverpool	Wales	3–1
1 April	1905	Crystal Palace	Scotland	1–0
17 February	1906	Belfast	Ireland	5–0
19 March	1906	Cardiff	Wales	1–0
7 April	1906	Glasgow	Scotland	1–2
16 February	1907	Everton	Ireland	1–0
18 March	1907	Fulham	Wales	1–1
6 April	1907	Newcastle	Scotland	1–1
15 February	1908	Belfast	Ireland	3–1
16 March	1908	Wrexham	Wales	7–1
4 April	1908	Glasgow	Scotland	1–1
6 June	1908	Vienna	Austria	6–1
8 June	1908	Vienna	Austria	11–1
10 June	1908	Budapest	Hungary	7–0
13 June	1908	Prague	Bohemia	4–0
13 February	1909	Bradford	Ireland	4–0
15 March	1909	Nottingham	Wales	2–0
3 April	1909	Crystal Palace	Scotland	2–0
29 May	1909	Budapest	Hungary	4–2
31 May	1909	Budapest	Hungary	8–2
1 June	1909	Vienna	Austria	8–1
12 February	1910	Belfast	Ireland	1–1
14 March	1910	Cardiff	Wales	1–0
2 April	1910	Glasgow	Scotland	0–2
C29 June	1910	Durban	South Africa	3–0
C23 July	1910	Johannesburg	South Africa	6–2
C30 July	1910	Capetown	South Africa	6–3
11 February	1911	Derby	Ireland	2–1
13 March	1911	Millwall	Wales	3–0
1 April	1911	Everton	Scotland	1–1
10 February	1912	Dublin	Ireland	6–1
11 March	1912	Wrexham	Wales	2–0
23 March	1912	Glasgow	Scotland	1–1
15 February	1913	Belfast	Ireland	1–2
17 March	1913	Bristol	Wales	4–3
5 April	1913	Stamford Bridge	Scotland	1–0
14 February	1914	Middlesbrough	Ireland	0–3
16 March	1914	Cardiff	Wales	2–0
4 April	1914	Glasgow	Scotland	1–3
V26 April	1919	Everton	Scotland	2–2
V 3 May	1919	Glasgow	Scotland	4–3
V11 October	1919	Cardiff	Wales	1–2
V18 October	1919	Stoke-on-Trent	Wales	2–0
25 October	1919	Belfast	Ireland	1–1
15 March	1920	Highbury	Wales	1–2
10 April	1920	Sheffield	Scotland	5–4
23 October	1920	Sunderland	Ireland	2–0
C26 June	1920	Durban	South Africa	3–1
C17 July	1920	Johannesburg	South Africa	3–1
C19 July	1920	Capetown	South Africa	9–1
14 March	1921	Cardiff	Wales	0–0
9 April	1921	Glasgow	Scotland	0–3
21 May	1921	Brussels	Belgium	2–0
22 October	1921	Belfast	N Ireland	1–1
13 March	1922	Liverpool	Wales	1–0
8 April	1922	Villa Park	Scotland	0–1
21 October	1922	West Bromwich	N Ireland	2–0
5 March	1923	Cardiff	Wales	2–2
19 March	1923	Highbury	Belgium	6–1
14 April	1923	Glasgow	Scotland	2–2
10 May	1923	Paris	France	4–1
21 May	1923	Stockholm	Sweden	4–2
24 May	1923	Stockholm	Sweden	3–1
20 October	1923	Belfast	N Ireland	1–2
1 November	1923	Antwerp	Belgium	2–2
3 March	1924	Blackburn	Wales	1–2
12 April	1924	Wembley	Scotland	1–1
17 May	1924	Paris	France	3–1
22 October	1924	Everton	N Ireland	3–1
8 December	1924	West Bromwich	Belgium	4–0
28 February	1925	Swansea	Wales	2–1
4 April	1925	Glasgow	Scotland	0–2
21 May	1925	Paris	France	3–2
C27 June	1925	Brisbane	Australia	5–1
C 4 July	1925	Sydney	Australia	2–1
C11 July	1925	Maitland	Australia	8–2
C18 July	1925	Sydney	Australia	5–0
C25 July	1925	Melbourne	Australia	2–0
24 October	1925	Belfast	N Ireland	0–0
1 March	1926	Crystal Palace	Wales	1–3
17 April	1926	Manchester	Scotland	1–0
24 May	1926	Antwerp	Belgium	5–3
20 October	1926	Liverpool	N Ireland	3–3
12 February	1927	Wrexham	Wales	3–3
2 April	1927	Glasgow	Scotland	2–1
11 May	1927	Brussels	Belgium	9–1
21 May	1927	Luxembourg	Luxembourg	5–2
26 May	1927	Paris	France	6–0
22 October	1927	Belfast	N Ireland	0–2
28 November	1927	Burnley	Wales	1–2
31 March	1928	Wembley	Scotland	1–5
17 May	1928	Paris	France	5–1
19 May	1928	Antwerp	Belgium	3–1
22 October	1928	Everton	N Ireland	2–1
17 November	1928	Swansea	Wales	3–2
13 April	1929	Glasgow	Scotland	0–1
9 May	1929	Paris	France	4–1
11 May	1929	Brussels	Belgium	5–1
15 May	1929	Madrid	Spain	3–4
C15 June	1929	Durban	South Africa	3–2
C13 July	1929	Johannesburg	South Africa	2–1
C17 July	1929	Capetown	South Africa	3–1
19 October	1929	Belfast	N Ireland	3–0
20 November	1929	Stamford Bridge	Wales	6–0
5 April	1930	Wembley	Scotland	5–2
10 May	1930	Berlin	Germany	3–3
14 May	1930	Vienna	Austria	0–0
20 October	1930	Sheffield	N Ireland	5–1
22 November	1930	Wrexham	Wales	4–0
28 March	1931	Glasgow	Scotland	0–2
14 May	1931	Paris	France	2–5
16 May	1931	Brussels	Belgium	4–1
17 October	1931	Belfast	Ireland	6–2
18 November	1931	Liverpool	Wales	3–1
9 December	1931	Highbury	Spain	7–1
9 April	1932	Wembley	Scotland	3–0
17 October	1932	Blackpool	N Ireland	1–0
16 November	1932	Wrexham	Wales	0–0
7 December	1932	Stamford Bridge	Austria	4–3
1 April	1933	Glasgow	Scotland	1–2
13 May	1933	Rome	Italy	1–1
20 May	1933	Berne	Switzerland	4–0
14 October	1933	Belfast	N Ireland	3–0
15 November	1933	Newcastle	Wales	1–2
6 December	1933	Tottenham	France	4–1
14 April	1934	Wembley	Scotland	3–0
10 May	1934	Budapest	Hungary	1–2
16 May	1934	Prague	Czechoslovakia	1–2
29 September	1934	Cardiff	Wales	4–0
14 November	1934	Highbury	Italy	3–2
6 February	1935	Everton	N Ireland	2–1
6 April	1935	Glasgow	Scotland	0–2
18 May	1935	Amsterdam	Netherlands	1–0
J21 August	1935	Glasgow	Scotland	2–4
19 October	1935	Belfast	N Ireland	3–1
4 December	1935	Tottenham	Germany	3–0
5 February	1936	Wolverhampton	Wales	1–2
4 April	1936	Wembley	Scotland	1–1
6 May	1936	Vienna	Austria	1–2
9 May	1936	Brussels	Belgium	2–3
17 October	1936	Cardiff	Wales	1–2
18 November	1936	Stoke-on-Trent	N Ireland	3–1
2 December	1936	Highbury	Hungary	6–2
17 April	1937	Glasgow	Scotland	1–3
14 May	1937	Oslo	Norway	6–0
17 May	1937	Stockholm	Sweden	4–0
20 May	1937	Helsinki	Finland	8–0
23 October	1937	Belfast	N Ireland	5–1
17 November	1937	Middlesbrough	Wales	2–1
1 December	1937	Tottenham	Czechoslovakia	5–4
9 April	1938	Wembley	Scotland	0–1
14 May	1938	Berlin	Germany	6–3
21 May	1938	Zurich	Switzerland	1–2
26 May	1938	Paris	France	4–2
22 October	1938	Cardiff	Wales	2–4
26 October	1938	Highbury	FIFA	3–0
9 November	1938	Newcastle	Norway	4–0
16 November	1938	Manchester	N Ireland	7–0
15 April	1939	Glasgow	Scotland	2–1
13 May	1939	Milan	Italy	2–2
18 May	1939	Belgrade	Yugoslavia	1–2
24 May	1939	Bucharest	Rumania	2–0
C17 June	1939	Johannesburg	South Africa	3–0
C24 June	1939	Durban	South Africa	8–2
C 1 July	1939	Johannesburg	South Africa	2–1
WT11 November	1939	Cardiff	Wales	1–1
WT18 November	1939	Wrexham	Wales	3–2
WT 2 December	1939	Newcastle	Scotland	2–1
WT12 April	1940	Wembley	Wales	0–1
WT11 May	1940	Glasgow	Scotland	1–1
WT 8 February	1941	Newcastle	Scotland	2–3
WT26 April	1941	Nottingham	Wales	4–1
WT 3 May	1941	Glasgow	Scotland	3–1
WT 7 June	1941	Cardiff	Wales	3–2
WT 4 October	1941	Wembley	Scotland	2–0
WT25 October	1941	Birmingham	Wales	2–1
WT17 January	1942	Wembley	Scotland	3–0
WT18 April	1942	Glasgow	Scotland	4–5
WT 9 May	1942	Cardiff	Wales	0–1
WT10 October	1942	Wembley	Scotland	0–0
WT24 October	1942	Wolverhampton	Wales	1–2
WT27 February	1943	Wembley	Wales	5–3
WT17 April	1943	Glasgow	Scotland	4–0
WT 8 May	1943	Cardiff	Wales	1–1
WT29 May	1943	Wembley	Wales	8–3
WT16 October	1943	Manchester	Scotland	8–0
WT19 February	1944	Wembley	Scotland	6–2
WT22 April	1944	Glasgow	Scotland	3–2
WT 6 May	1944	Cardiff	Wales	2–0
WT16 September	1944	Liverpool	Wales	2–2
WT14 October	1944	Wembley	Scotland	6–2
WT13 February	1945	Birmingham	Scotland	3–2
WT14 April	1945	Glasgow	Scotland	6–1
WT 5 May	1945	Cardiff	Wales	3–2
WT26 May	1945	Wembley	France	2–2
V15 September	1945	Belfast	N Ireland	1–0
V20 October	1945	West Bromwich	Wales	0–1
V19 January	1946	Wembley	Belgium	2–0
V13 April	1946	Glasgow	Scotland	0–1
V11 May	1946	Stamford Bridge	Switzerland	4–1
28 September	1946	Belfast	N Ireland	7–2
30 September	1946	Dublin	Eire	1–0
13 November	1946	Manchester	Wales	3–0
27 November	1946	Huddersfield	Netherlands	8–2
12 April	1947	Wembley	Scotland	1–1
3 May	1947	Highbury	France	3–0
18 May	1947	Zurich	Switzerland	0–1
25 May	1947	Lisbon	Portugal	10–0
21 September	1947	Brussels	Belgium	5–2
18 October	1947	Cardiff	Wales	3–0
5 November	1947	Everton	N Ireland	2–2
19 October	1947	Highbury	Sweden	4–2
10 April	1948	Glasgow	Scotland	2–0
16 May	1948	Turin	Italy	4–0
26 September	1948	Copenhagen	Denmark	0–0
9 October	1948	Belfast	N Ireland	6–2
10 November	1948	Birmingham	Wales	1–0
2 December	1948	Highbury	Switzerland	6–0
9 April	1949	Wembley	Scotland	1–3
13 May	1949	Stockholm	Sweden	1–3
18 May	1949	Oslo	Norway	4–1
22 May	1949	Paris	France	3–1
21 September	1949	Everton	Eire	0–2
WC15 October	1949	Cardiff	Wales	4–1
WC16 November	1949	Manchester	N Ireland	9–2
30 November	1949	Tottenham	Italy	2–0
WC15 April	1950	Glasgow	Scotland	1–0
14 May	1950	Lisbon	Portugal	5–3
18 May	1950	Brussels	Belgium	4–1
WC25 June	1950	Rio de Janeiro	Chile	2–0
WC29 June	1950	Belo Horizonte	USA	0–1
WC 2 July	1950	Rio de Janeiro	Spain	0–1
7 October	1950	Belfast	N Ireland	4–1
15 November	1950	Sunderland	Wales	4–2
22 November	1950	Highbury	Yugoslavia	2–2
14 April	1951	Wembley	Scotland	2–3
9 May	1951	Wembley	Argentina	2–1
19 May	1951	Everton	Portugal	5–2
C26 May	1951	Sydney	Australia	4–1
C30 June	1951	Sydney	Australia	17–0
C 7 July	1951	Brisbane	Australia	4–1
C14 July	1951	Sydney	Australia	6–1
C21 July	1951	Newcastle NSW	Australia	5–0
3 October	1951	Highbury	France	2–2
20 October	1951	Cardiff	Wales	1–1
14 November	1951	Birmingham	N Ireland	2–0
28 November	1951	Wembley	Austria	2–2
5 April	1952	Glasgow	Scotland	2–1
18 May	1952	Florence	Italy	1–1
25 May	1952	Vienna	Austria	3–2
28 May	1952	Zurich	Switzerland	3–0
4 October	1952	Belfast	N Ireland	2–2
12 November	1952	Wembley	Wales	5–2
26 November	1952	Wembley	Belgium	5–0
18 April	1953	Wembley	Scotland	2–2
A17 May	1953	Buenos Aires	Argentina	0–0
24 May	1953	Santiago	Chile	2–1
31 May	1953	Montevideo	Uruguay	1–2
8 June	1953	New York	USA	6–3
WC10 October	1953	Cardiff	Wales	4–1
21 October	1953	Wembley	FIFA	4–4
WC11 November	1953	Liverpool	N Ireland	3–1
25 November	1953	Wembley	Hungary	3–6
WC 3 April	1954	Glasgow	Scotland	4–2
16 May	1954	Belgrade	Yugoslavia	0–1
23 May	1954	Budapest	Hungary	1–7
WC17 June	1954	Basle	Belgium	4–4
WC20 June	1954	Berne	Switzerland	2–0

Date		Venue	Opponents	Score
WC26 June	1954	Basle	Uruguay	2–4
2 October	1954	Belfast	N Ireland	2–0
10 November	1954	Wembley	Wales	3–2
1 December	1954	Wembley	West Germany	3–1
2 April	1955	Wembley	Scotland	7–2
15 May	1955	Paris	France	0–1
18 May	1955	Madrid	Spain	1–1
22 May	1955	Oporto	Portugal	1–3
2 October	1955	Copenhagen	Denmark	5–1
22 October	1955	Cardiff	Wales	1–2
2 November	1955	Wembley	N Ireland	3–0
30 November	1955	Wembley	Spain	4–1
14 April	1956	Glasgow	Scotland	1–1
9 May	1956	Wembley	Brazil	4–2
16 May	1956	Stockholm	Sweden	0–1
20 May	1956	Helsinki	Finland	5–1
26 May	1956	Berlin	West Germany	3–1
6 October	1956	Belfast	N Ireland	1–1
14 November	1956	Wembley	Wales	3–1
28 November	1956	Wembley	Yugoslavia	3–0
WC 5 December	1956	Wolverhampton	Denmark	5–2
6 April	1957	Wembley	Scotland	2–1
WC 8 May	1957	Wembley	Eire	5–1
WC15 May	1957	Copenhagen	Denmark	4–1
WC19 May	1957	Dublin	Eire	1–1
19 October	1957	Cardiff	Wales	4–0
6 November	1957	Wembley	N Ireland	2–3
27 November	1957	Wembley	France	4–0
19 April	1958	Glasgow	Scotland	4–0
7 May	1958	Wembley	Portugal	2–1
11 May	1958	Belgrade	Yugoslavia	0–5
18 May	1958	Moscow	USSR	1–1
WC 8 June	1958	Gothenburg	USSR	2–2
WC11 June	1958	Gothenburg	Brazil	0–0
WC15 June	1958	Boras	Austria	2–2
WC17 June	1958	Gothenburg	USSR	0–1
4 October	1958	Belfast	N Ireland	3–3
22 October	1958	Wembley	USSR	5–0
26 November	1958	Birmingham	Wales	2–2
11 April	1959	Wembley	Scotland	1–0
6 May	1959	Wembley	Italy	2–2
13 May	1959	Rio de Janeiro	Brazil	0–2
17 May	1959	Lima	Peru	1–4
24 May	1959	Mexico City	Mexico	1–2
28 May	1959	Los Angeles	USA	8–1
17 October	1959	Cardiff	Wales	1–1
28 October	1959	Wembley	Sweden	2–3
18 November	1959	Wembley	N Ireland	2–1
9 April	1960	Glasgow	Scotland	1–1
11 May	1960	Wembley	Yugoslavia	3–3
15 May	1960	Madrid	Spain	0–3
22 May	1960	Budapest	Hungary	0–2
8 October	1960	Belfast	N Ireland	5–2
WC19 October	1960	Luxembourg	Luxembourg	9–0
26 October	1960	Wembley	Spain	4–2
23 November	1960	Wembley	Wales	5–1
15 April	1961	Wembley	Scotland	9–3
10 May	1961	Wembley	Mexico	8–0
WC21 May	1961	Lisbon	Portugal	1–1
24 May	1961	Rome	Italy	3–2
27 May	1961	Vienna	Austria	1–3
WC28 September	1961	Highbury	Luxembourg	4–1
14 October	1961	Cardiff	Wales	1–1
WC25 October	1961	Wembley	Portugal	2–0
22 November	1961	Wembley	N Ireland	1–1
4 April	1962	Wembley	Austria	3–1
14 April	1962	Glasgow	Scotland	0–2
9 May	1962	Wembley	Switzerland	3–1
20 May	1962	Lima	Peru	4–0
WC31 May	1962	Rancagua	Hungary	1–2
WC 2 June	1962	Rancagua	Argentina	3–1
WC 7 June	1962	Rancagua	Bulgaria	0–0
WC10 June	1962	Vina del Mar	Brazil	1–3
ENC 3 October	1962	Sheffield	France	1–1
20 October	1962	Belfast	N Ireland	3–1
21 November	1962	Wembley	Wales	4–0
ENC27 February	1962	Paris	France	2–5
6 April	1963	Wembley	Scotland	1–2
8 May	1963	Wembley	Brazil	1–1
29 May	1963	Bratislava	Czechoslovakia	4–2
2 June	1963	Leipzig	East Germany	2–1
5 June	1963	Basle	Switzerland	8–1
12 October	1963	Cardiff	Wales	4–0
23 October	1963	Wembley	FIFA	2–1
20 November	1963	Wembley	N Ireland	8–3
11 April	1964	Glasgow	Scotland	0–1
6 May	1964	Wembley	Uruguay	2–1
17 May	1964	Lisbon	Portugal	4–3
24 May	1964	Dublin	Eire	3–1
27 May	1964	New York	USA	10–0
30 May	1964	Rio de Janeiro	Brazil	1–5
4 June	1964	Sao Paulo	Portugal	1–1
6 June	1964	Rio de Janeiro	Argentina	0–1
3 October	1964	Belfast	N Ireland	4–3
21 October	1964	Wembley	Belgium	2–2
18 November	1964	Wembley	Wales	2–1
9 December	1964	Amsterdam	Netherlands	1–1
10 April	1965	Wembley	Scotland	2–2
5 May	1965	Wembley	Hungary	1–0
9 May	1965	Belgrade	Yugoslavia	1–1
12 May	1965	Nurnburg	West Germany	1–0
16 May	1965	Gothenburg	Sweden	2–1
2 October	1965	Cardiff	Wales	0–0
20 October	1965	Wembley	Austria	2–3
10 November	1965	Wembley	N Ireland	2–1
8 December	1965	Madrid	Spain	2–0
5 January	1966	Everton	Poland	1–1
23 February	1966	Wembley	West Germany	1–0
2 April	1966	Glasgow	Scotland	4–3
4 May	1966	Wembley	Yugoslavia	2–0
26 June	1966	Helsinki	Finland	3–0
29 June	1966	Oslo	Norway	6–1
3 July	1966	Copenhagen	Denmark	2–0
5 July	1966	Chorzow	Poland	1–0
WC11 July	1966	Wembley	Uruguay	0–0
WC16 July	1966	Wembley	Mexico	2–0
WC20 July	1966	Wembley	France	2–0
WC23 July	1966	Wembley	Argentina	1–0
WC26 July	1966	Wembley	Portugal	2–1

Date		Venue	Opponents	Score
WC30 July	1966	Wembley	West Germany	4–2
EC22 October	1966	Belfast	N Ireland	2–0
2 November	1966	Wembley	Czechoslovakia	0–0
EC16 November	1966	Wembley	Wales	5–1
EC15 April	1967	Wembley	Scotland	2–3
24 May	1967	Wembley	Spain	2–0
27 May	1967	Vienna	Austria	1–0
EC21 October	1967	Cardiff	Wales	3–0
EC22 November	1967	Wembley	N Ireland	2–0
6 December	1967	Wembley	USSR	2–2
EC24 February	1968	Glasgow	Scotland	1–1
3 April	1968	Wembley	Spain	1–0
8 May	1968	Madrid	Spain	2–1
22 May	1968	Wembley	Sweden	3–1
1 June	1968	Hanover	West Germany	0–1
EC 5 June	1968	Florence	Yugoslavia	0–1
EC 8 June	1968	Rome	USSR	2–0
6 November	1968	Bucharest	Rumania	0–0
11 December	1968	Wembley	Bulgaria	1–1
15 January	1969	Wembley	Rumania	1–1
12 March	1969	Wembley	France	5–0
3 May	1969	Belfast	N Ireland	3–1
7 May	1969	Wembley	Wales	2–1
10 May	1969	Wembley	Scotland	4–1
1 June	1969	Mexico City	Mexico	0–0
8 June	1969	Montevideo	Uruguay	2–1
12 June	1969	Rio de Janeiro	Brazil	1–2
5 November	1969	Amsterdam	Netherlands	1–0
10 December	1969	Wembley	Portugal	1–0
14 January	1970	Wembley	Netherlands	0–0
25 February	1970	Brussels	Belgium	3–1
18 April	1970	Cardiff	Wales	1–1
21 April	1970	Wembley	N Ireland	3–1
25 April	1970	Glasgow	Scotland	0–0
24 May	1970	Quito	Equador	2–0
WC 2 June	1970	Guadalajara	Rumania	1–0
WC 7 June	1970	Guadalajara	Brazil	0–1
WC11 June	1970	Guadalajara	Czechoslovakia	1–0
WC14 June	1970	Leon	West Germany	2–3
25 November	1970	Wembley	East Germany	3–1
EC 3 February	1971	Valetta	Malta	1–0
EC21 April	1971	Wembley	Greece	3–0
EC12 May	1971	Wembley	Malta	5–0
15 May	1971	Belfast	N Ireland	1–0
19 May	1971	Wembley	Wales	0–0
22 May	1971	Wembley	Scotland	3–1
EC13 October	1971	Basle	Switzerland	3–2
EC10 November	1971	Wembley	Switzerland	1–1
EC 1 December	1971	Athens	Greece	2–0
EC29 April	1972	Wembley	West Germany	1–3
EC13 May	1972	Berlin	West Germany	0–0
20 May	1972	Cardiff	Wales	3–0
23 May	1972	Wembley	N Ireland	0–1
27 May	1972	Glasgow	Scotland	1–0
11 October	1972	Wembley	Yugoslavia	1–1
WC15 November	1972	Cardiff	Wales	1–0
WC24 January	1973	Wembley	Wales	1–1
14 February	1973	Glasgow	Scotland	5–0
12 May	1973	Everton	N Ireland	2–1
15 May	1973	Wembley	Wales	3–0
19 May	1973	Wembley	Scotland	1–0
27 May	1973	Prague	Czechoslovakia	1–1
WC 6 June	1973	Katowice	Poland	0–2
10 June	1973	Moscow	USSR	2–1
14 June	1973	Turin	Italy	0–2
26 September	1973	Wembley	Austria	7–0
WC17 October	1973	Wembley	Poland	1–1
14 November	1973	Wembley	Italy	0–1
3 April	1974	Lisbon	Portugal	0–0
11 May	1974	Cardiff	Wales	2–0
15 May	1974	Wembley	N Ireland	1–0
18 May	1974	Glasgow	Scotland	0–2
22 May	1974	Wembley	Argentina	2–2
29 May	1974	Leipzig	East Germany	1–1
1 June	1974	Sofia	Bulgaria	1–0
5 June	1974	Belgrade	Yugoslavia	2–2
EC30 October	1974	Wembley	Czechoslovakia	3–0
EC20 November	1974	Wembley	Portugal	0–0
12 March	1975	Wembley	West Germany	2–0
EC16 April	1975	Wembley	Cyprus	5–0
EC11 May	1975	Limassol	Cyprus	1–0
17 May	1975	Belfast	N Ireland	0–0
21 May	1975	Wembley	Wales	2–2
24 May	1975	Wembley	Scotland	5–1
3 September	1975	Basle	Switzerland	2–1
EC30 October	1975	Bratislava	Czechoslovakia	1–2
EC19 November	1975	Lisbon	Portugal	1–1
24 March	1976	Wrexham	Wales	2–1
8 May	1976	Cardiff	Wales	1–0
11 May	1976	Wembley	N Ireland	4–0
14 May	1976	Glasgow	Scotland	1–2
23 May	1976	Los Angeles	Brazil	0–1
28 May	1976	New York	Italy	3–2
WC13 June	1976	Helsinki	Finland	4–1
8 September	1976	Wembley	Eire	1–1
WC13 October	1976	Wembley	Finland	2–1
WC17 November	1976	Rome	Italy	0–2
9 February	1977	Wembley	Holland	0–2
WC30 March	1977	Wembley	Luxembourg	5–0
28 May	1977	Belfast	N Ireland	2–1
31 May	1977	Wembley	Wales	0–1
4 June	1977	Wembley	Scotland	1–2
8 June	1977	Rio de Janeiro	Brazil	0–0
12 June	1977	Buenos Aires	Argentina	1–1
15 June	1977	Montevideo	Uruguay	0–0
7 September	1977	Wembley	Switzerland	0–0
WC12 October	1977	Luxembourg	Luxembourg	2–0
WC16 November	1977	Wembley	Italy	2–0
22 February	1978	Munich	West Germany	1–2
19 April	1978	Wembley	Brazil	1–1
13 May	1978	Cardiff	Wales	3–1
16 May	1978	Wembley	N Ireland	1–0
20 May	1978	Glasgow	Scotland	1–0
24 May	1978	Wembley	Hungary	4–1
EC20 September	1978	Copenhagen	Denmark	4–3
EC25 October	1978	Dublin	Eire	1–1
29 November	1978	Wembley	Czechoslovakia	1–0
EC 7 February	1979	Wembley	N Ireland	4–0
19 May	1979	Belfast	N Ireland	2–0

Date		Venue	Opponents	Score
23 May	1979	Wembley	Wales	0–0
26 May	1979	Wembley	Scotland	3–1
EC 6 June	1979	Sofia	Bulgaria	3–0
10 June	1979	Stockholm	Sweden	0–0
13 June	1979	Vienna	Austria	3–4
EC 9 September	1979	Wembley	Denmark	1–0
EC17 October	1979	Belfast	N Ireland	5–1
EC22 November	1979	Wembley	Bulgaria	2–0
EC 6 February	1980	Wembley	Eire	2–0
26 March	1980	Barcelona	Spain	2–0
13 May	1980	Wembley	Argentina	3–1
17 May	1980	Wrexham	Wales	1–4
20 May	1980	Wembley	N Ireland	1–1
24 May	1980	Glasgow	Scotland	2–0
31 May	1980	Sydney	Australia	2–1
EC12 June	1980	Turin	Belgium	1–1
EC15 June	1980	Turin	Italy	0–1
EC18 June	1980	Naples	Spain	2–1
WC10 September	1980	Wembley	Norway	4–0
WC15 October	1980	Bucharest	Rumania	1–2
WC19 November	1980	Wembley	Switzerland	2–1
25 March	1981	Wembley	Spain	1–2
WC29 April	1981	Wembley	Rumania	0–0
12 May	1981	Wembley	Brazil	0–1
20 May	1981	Wembley	Wales	0–0
23 May	1981	Wembley	Scotland	0–1
WC30 May	1981	Basle	Switzerland	1–2
WC 6 June	1981	Budapest	Hungary	3–1
WC 9 September	1981	Oslo	Norway	1–2
WC18 November	1981	Wembley	Hungary	1–0
23 February	1982	Wembley	N Ireland	4–0
27 April	1982	Cardiff	Wales	1–0
25 May	1982	Wembley	Holland	2–0
29 May	1982	Glasgow	Scotland	1–0
2 June	1982	Reykjavik	Iceland	1–1
3 June	1982	Helsinki	Finland	4–1
WC16 June	1982	Bilbao	France	3–1
WC20 June	1982	Bilbao	Czechoslovakia	2–0
WC25 June	1982	Bilbao	Kuwait	1–0
WC29 June	1982	Madrid	West Germany	0–0
WC 5 July	1982	Madrid	Spain	0–0
EC22 September	1982	Copenhagen	Denmark	2–2
13 October	1982	Wembley	West Germany	1–2
EC17 November	1982	Salonika	Greece	3–0
EC15 December	1982	Wembley	Luxembourg	9–0
23 February	1983	Wembley	Wales	2–1
EC30 March	1983	Wembley	Greece	0–0
EC27 April	1983	Wembley	Hungary	2–0
28 May	1983	Belfast	N Ireland	0–0
1 June	1983	Wembley	Scotland	2–0
12 June	1983	Sydney	Australia	0–0
15 June	1983	Brisbane	Australia	1–0
19 June	1983	Melbourne	Australia	1–1
EC21 September	1983	Wembley	Denmark	0–1
EC12 October	1983	Budapest	Hungary	3–0
EC16 November	1983	Luxembourg	Luxembourg	4–0
28 February	1984	Paris	France	0–2
4 April	1984	Wembley	N Ireland	1–0
2 May	1984	Wrexham	Wales	0–1
26 May	1984	Glasgow	Scotland	1–1
2 June	1984	Wembley	USSR	0–2
10 June	1984	Rio de Janeiro	Brazil	2–0
13 June	1984	Montevideo	Uruguay	0–2
17 June	1984	Santiago	Chile	0–0
12 September	1984	Wembley	East Germany	1–0
WC17 October	1984	Wembley	Finland	5–0
WC14 November	1984	Istanbul	Turkey	8–0
WC26 February	1985	Belfast	N Ireland	1–0
26 March	1985	Wembley	Eire	2–1
WC 1 May	1985	Bucharest	Rumania	0–0
WC22 May	1985	Helsinki	Finland	1–1
25 May	1985	Glasgow	Scotland	0–1
6 June	1985	Mexico City	Italy	1–2
9 June	1985	Mexico City	Mexico	0–1
12 June	1985	Mexico City	West Germany	3–0
16 June	1985	Los Angeles	USA	5–0
WC11 September	1985	Wembley	Rumania	1–1
WC16 October	1985	Wembley	Turkey	5–0
WC13 November	1985	Wembley	N Ireland	0–0
29 January	1986	Cairo	Egypt	4–0
26 February	1986	Tel-Aviv	Israel	2–1
26 March	1986	Tbilisi	USSR	1–0
23 April	1986	Wembley	Scotland	2–1
17 May	1986	Los Angeles	Mexico	3–0
24 May	1986	Vancouver	Canada	1–0
WC 3 June	1986	Monterry	Portugal	0–1
WC 6 June	1986	Monterry	Morroco	0–0
WC11 June	1986	Monterry	Poland	3–0
WC18 June	1986	Mexico City	Paraguay	3–0
WC21 June	1986	Mexico City	Argentina	1–2
10 September	1986	Stockholm	Sweden	0–1
EC15 October	1986	Wembley	N Ireland	3–0
EC12 November	1986	Wembley	Yugoslavia	2–0
18 February	1987	Madrid	Spain	4–2
EC 2 April	1987	Belfast	N Ireland	2–0
EC29 April	1987	Izmir	Turkey	0–0
RC19 May	1987	Wembley	Brazil	1–1
RC23 May	1987	Glasgow	Scotland	0–0

*These four games were all between an England XI and a team of Scots resident in England. The FA does not regard them as official matches

†On each of these days England played two internationals. The FA asked the Corinthian Casuals to provide the teams against Wales, while they themselves selected the sides to play Ireland. Corinthians are the only club side to have represented England in toto

‡This match was abandoned owing to a disaster at the ground. The FA does not regard it as an official match

V—Victory internationals (not regarded as official)

J—Jubilee game (not regarded as official)

WT—War-time internationals (not regarded as official)

WC—World Cup games

ENC—European Nations Cup games

EC—European Championship games

RC—Rous Cup

C—Commonwealth tour games. Though billed as 'England' these teams were usually FA Touring XIs. One cap was awarded to each of the players who went on the tour but individual games are not regarded as official internationals

A—Abandoned after 20 minutes owing to torrential rain

of both 1984 and 1986, via a penalty and a 1–0 defeat at Wembley.

The two World Cups could certainly not be called failures, as were their equivalents in the 1970s. In both 1982 and 1986 England found herself one game away from a place in the semi-finals, though clearly failing on both occasions. Nonetheless, it was a respectable position to reach, even if they ulitmately lacked a depth of conviction that they could go further in either tournament.

The other home counties have far poorer records of course. With the single exception of Northern Ireland's magnificent display in Spain in 1982, none of them has done anything of note since the 1950s. Not once have Scotland, Ireland or Wales reached the final stages of the European Championship and, with the exception of 1982, none has gone beyond the group stage in the World Cup either. Scotland have a startlingly poor record in finals. In 1974, 1978 and 1982 they were eliminated only on goal difference, and 1978 should really have been their year. A group containing Peru, Iran and the Dutch (whom they beat 3–2 in perhaps their best ever World Cup display) was surely not beyond their capabilities. But Masson's penalty miss against Peru, Willie Johnston's despatch home following a drug test after the same game, and Ally MacLeod's peverse style of team management and selection condemned them to almost hysterical abuse back home.

So one comes back to the same question—why have the club sides done so outstandingly well when the national squads have done so badly?

To a large extent it comes down to the clubs in question. The real moment of truth came in 1973, at just the time the English national team was sliding to obscurity. The actual dates can even be identified. Liverpool, already well on the way to becoming the strongest of the British club sides, were contesting the European Cup. On 24 October 1973 they went to Belgrade to play Red Star and lost 2–1. At home on 6 November they lost again 2–1. Full-back Chris Lawler scored both Liverpool goals. The result itself was humbling, but on the pitch it was a humiliation, far worse than the scores suggest. Liverpool seemed to have stepped right out of the stone-age. Red Star, not even one of Europe's outstanding sides and easily beaten by Atletico Madrid in the next round,

were from another league.

The styles were so obviously different. Red Star, and the other European sides, built from the back. They played on the ground; they did not rely on fast wingers and big lumbering battleship centre-forwards; they knocked the one-twos around the box and darted into the spaces. They used a sweeper to close down attackers unfamiliar with the tactic in the English domestic game. Above all, they could all play, full-backs and centre-backs included (Spurs were one of the few British sides to try to copy this, which they did successfully in the late 1970s and early 1980s). There were no passengers.

Shankly, Paisley, Fagan, Moran and the rest decided that patience and ball skills were essential, but the stamina and strength of the English game should not be abandoned. As a combination exemplified by Liverpool it was to prove irresistible. By 1977 they were European champions, winning one of the best European finals in Rome against an excellent Borussia Moenchengladbach, and for nearly a decade they were clearly the best on the continent. They may still be so, but what a deeply ironic tragedy that their ability to prove this point has been taken from them, possibly for ever, by fans whom, back in 1973, were a byword for good behaviour. That was one problem the late Bill Shankly never had to worry about.

It was Nottingham Forest, under the remarkable and almost incomprehensible duo of Brian Clough and Peter Taylor who briefly took over Liverpool's mantle for a time and did so with an even deeper understanding of the prevailing realities. The Forest side was, physically, one of the oddest great teams ever. And, despite their being remembered for the skills of successive England forwards in the shape of Withe, Woodcock, Birtles (even in the late 1980s still a truly great touch footballer) Francis, Hodge and Davenport, they were essentially a defensive team. Their whole game was built on getting behind the ball and closing down space. They depended massively on their one great provider, winger John Robertson.

Villa had a peculiar, though probably well deserved, European Cup win in 1982, but it was as if time had stood still. They rose without trace, and fell as inconspicuously. One somehow feels they caught Europe asleep and stole away in the night with an unexpected fortune discovered under the

bed. Certainly they left no profound tactical trace, or memory (apart from their semi-final goal at Anderlecht with a 'fan' on the pitch); none of the players went on to greater things.

The same could certainly not be said for the Spurs Double team, perhaps the most exciting English club side (in terms of League football) of the post-war era. They were the first, not surprisingly, to breach finally the walls of Europe, after the British had watched in frustration through eight years of Iberian domination. Going back to 1963, when Tottenham beat Atletico Madrid 5–1 in Rotterdam in the Cup Winners' Cup final, perhaps we can look for the reasons for club success abroad, and debate why it has not been duplicated at national level since Ramsey, an old Spurs player, and the mid-1960s.

Spurs' victory was significant for two reasons. The 1961 Double winners, who had run Benfica so close in the semi-finals of the Champions' Cup the previous season, achieved their historic win without Dave Mackay, one of the men who so typified their storming, glory glory style. But, perhaps more importantly, Spurs were the first British club to use a real first team squad. They had two goalkeepers in Brown and Hollowbread, three full backs in Baker, Henry and Hopkins, four defenders in Norman, Marchi, Mackay and Blanchflower, and seven forwards: Jones, White, Smith, Greaves, Dyson, Medwin and Allen. It was to set a pattern from which other British clubs would profit.

In 1965 it was West Ham's turn to lift the Cup Winners' Cup with a 2–0 win over TSV Munich 1860 in what was the middle leg of three successive cup-winning Wembley appearances for skipper Bobby Moore.

In the year of England's World Cup win, Liverpool were the beaten Cup Winners' Cup finalists and the following year, Leeds made the first of eight successive Fairs and UEFA Cup final appearances by English clubs. They lost the 1967 final against Dynamo Zagreb but returned to triumph the following year when they beat Ferencvaros over two legs thanks to a solitary goal scored by Mick Jones. Newcastle, Arsenal, Leeds again and then Tottenham and Liverpool in the new-style UEFA competition all won their respective finals before Spurs faltered in the 1974 final against Feijenoord.

The tide that was sweeping clubs to victory in the lesser European competitions finally breached the walls of the premier event in 1967. It may be significant in this context that as clubs like six-times winners Real Madrid and double winners Benfica built up reputations of invincibility, it was often the clubs who beat them who became the new masters of Europe. Benfica succeeded Real Madrid after beating them in the 1962 final, then it was the turn of Milan clubs AC and Inter to inherit the crown. Celtic's one victory in 1967 proved an exception, but they were worthy victors nonetheless. The only British club ever to make a clean sweep of domestic and European honours, Celtic achieved that distinction through a mixture of vitality and good luck. Inter Milan were without their Spanish inside-left Luis Suarez, who had a leg injury, and without his midfield organization they lacked the heart and stamina to keep up with a younger, fitter Celtic side. The Italians admitted as much when they were forced to switch Facchetti to mark Jimmy Johnstone because international right back Burgnich didn't have the legs to keep up with the mesmerising ball play of the little winger.

Inter went ahead with a sixth minute penalty by Mazzola—and that was probably their undoing. Had they scored a little later, Celtic might not have had time to find a way through the defensive cordon Inter threw around their goal in the hope of holding out. Gemmell struck a ferocious second half equalizer and Chalmers added Celtic's winner.

If Celtic's victory was a hit-and-run affair, the next British win in the European Cup was the result of a crusade which had its roots in the tragedy of Munich ten years earlier. Manchester United, who had gone against the insular wishes of the FA by entering the 1957 competition, where they reached the semifinals, were once again within sight of the final the following year when they were struck down by the air crash which claimed the lives of eight first team players. Having overcome Red Star Belgrade in the quarter-finals, the traumatized United side again went out in the semi-finals, to AC Milan.

By 1968 Matt Busby had reassembled a United side capable of sustaining a challenge in Europe. But once again the semi-finals looked like proving the stumbling block. United's slender 1–0 win in the first leg against Real Madrid seemed insufficient when the home side went 3–1 up in the return. But goals by Sadler and Foulkes sealed an unlikely United victory which brought them back to Wembley for what was virtually a home game against Benfica. That advantage was partially cancelled out by the absence of Denis Law, who missed the final with a knee injury. The teams forsook their traditional red colours, United playing in all-blue and Benfica in white, for a final which was the most emotional in British club history. With the score standing at 1–1, United goalkeeper Stepney produced a magnificent save from Eusebio in the closing minutes and so snatched them from the jaws of almost certain defeat. Extra time goals from Best, Charlton, and Kidd brought a 4–1 win and England's first European Cup victory. It also brought Busby, the game's best-loved figure, a knighthood.

Following West Ham's 1965 Cup Winners' Cup win, Liverpool and Rangers kept up the British presence in the finals the following two years while the Fairs Cup went on a four-year round-trip of England. Celtic should have added to their 1967 European Cup triumph three years later but inexplicably lost the final to an uninspiring Feyenoord. Another five years passed before Leeds became the next British club to reach the final but on this occasion it was the cream of West Germany's World Cup winners who were their opponents. Bayern Munich won 2–0 to complete the second of their three successive victories.

As Manchester City, Chelsea and Rangers scored consecutive successes in the Cup Winners' Cup in the early seventies and Leeds became the fourth British club in a row to reach the final, Liverpool were making inroads on the UEFA trophy which were to have remarkable sequels a few years later.

In the 1973 final, they beat Borussia Moenchengladbach 3–2 on aggregate with two goals from Keegan and one from Lloyd. It was the beginning of an era in which the English club were to dominate first the domestic game and then Europe too. Three years later Bill Shankly's team were back in another UEFA Final this time against Bruges. Kennedy, Case and Keegan staged a remarkable second recovery in the first Anfield leg after Bruges had taken a 2–0 lead. A more resilient Liverpool performance in the return saw Keegan score in a 1–1 draw and the trophy return to Merseyside.

The significance of the victories over Borussia Moenchengladbach and Bruges became apparent in the run-up to the 1977 and 1978 European Cup Finals. Shankly had retired after Liverpool's 1974 FA Cup win but the continuity which has underpinned the greatest success machine in British soccer history was maintained with the elevation of Bob Paisley from coach to the manager's chair.

Nothing changed except the side's accomplishment in winning more cups for their new boss than they had for their old. Formalities out of the way with a 7–0 aggregate win over Crusaders, Liverpool got down to the real business with a victory over Turkish side Trabzonspor, overturning a 1–0 away defeat 3–0 in the return. Liverpool had to overcome another 1–0 first leg deficit against French champions Saint Etienne and after winning 3–1 at Anfield, they'd done the hard part of reaching the final. Swiss side Zurich were swept aside in the semi-final 6–1 on aggregate for Liverpool to find themselves up against a team over whom they held a considerable psychological advantage, their UEFA Cup victims Borussia Moenchengladbach.

Bonhof gave them a fright when he hit a post from 25 yards with the score 0–0 but a goal after 27 minutes by McDermott put Liverpool deservedly in front. Simonsen—a player whose regular presence in European finals was a tribute in itself—sent another ripple of anxiety through the Liverpool camp with a 60th minute equalizer after a rare mistake by Case. Clemence staved off further cracks appearing in the Liverpool defence with fine saves from Simonsen and Heynkes before

EUROPEAN CHAMPION CLUBS' CUP

1955–56
REAL MADRID
Paris   12 June 1956   Attendance 38,329
Real Madrid (2) **4**   **Reims** (2) 3
di Stefano, Rial 2,   Leblond, Templin,
Marquitos   Hidalgo
Real: Alonso, Atienza, Lesmes, Munoz, Marquitos, Zaggara, Joseito, Marchal, di Stefano, Rial, Gento
Reims: Jacquet, Zimny, Giraudo, Leblond, Jonquet, Siatka, Hidalgo, Glovacki, Kopa, Bliard, Templin

1956–57
REAL MADRID
Madrid   30 May 1957   Attendance 125,000
Real Madrid (0) **2**   **Fiorentina** (0) 0
di Stefano, Gento
Real: Alonso, Torres, Lesmes, Munoz, Marquitos, Zaggara, Kopa, Mateos, di Stefano, Rial, Gento
Fiorentina: Sarti, Magnini, Cervato, Scaramucci, Orzan, Segato, Julinho, Gratton, Virgili, Montuori, Bizzarri

1957–58
REAL MADRID
Brussels   29 May 1958   Attendance 67,000
Real Madrid (0) (2) **3**   **AC Milan** (0) (2) 2
di Stefano, Rial, Gento   Schiaffino, Grillo
Real: Alonso, Atienza, Lesmes, Santisteban, Santamaria, Zaggara, Kopa, Joseito, di Stefano, Rial, Gento
AC Milan: Soldan, Fontana, Beraldo, Bergamaschi, Maldini, Radice, Danova, Liedholm, Schiaffino, Grillo, Cucchiaroni

1958–59
REAL MADRID
Stuttgart   3 June 1959   Attendance 80,000
Real Madrid (1) **2**   **Reims** (0) 0
Mateos, di Stefano
Real: Dominguez, Marquitos, Zaggara, Santisteban, Santamaria, Ruiz, Kopa, Mateos, di Stefano, Rial, Gento
Reims: Colonna, Rodzik, Giraudo, Penverne, Jonquet, Leblond, Lamartine, Bliard, Fontaine, Piantoni, Vincent

1959–60
REAL MADRID
Glasgow   18 May 1960   Attendance 127,621
Real Madrid (3) **7**   **Eintracht Frankfurt** (1) 3
di Stefano 3, Puskas 4   Kress, Stein 2
Real: Dominguez, Marquitos, Pachin, Vidal, Santamaria, Zaggara, Canario, Del Sol, di Stefano, Puskas, Gento
Eintracht: Loy, Lutz, Hoefer, Weilbacher, Eigenbrodt, Stinka, Kress, Lindner, Stein, Pfaff, Meier

1960–61
BENFICA
Berne   31 May 1961   Attendance 33,000
Benfica (2) **3**   **Barcelona** (1) 2
Aguas, Ramallets (og), Coluna   Kocsis, Czibor
Benfica: Costa Pereira, Joao, Angelo, Neto, Germano, Cruz, Augusto, Santana, Aguas, Coluna, Cavem
Barcelona: Ramallets, Foncho, Gracia, Verges, Gensana, Garay, Kubala, Kocsis, Evaristo, Suarez, Czibor

1961–62
BENFICA
Amsterdam   2 May 1962   Attendance 68,000
Benfica (2) **5**   **Real Madrid** (3) 3
Aguas, Caven, Coluna,   Puskas 3
Eusebio 2 (1 pen)
Benfica: Costa Pereira, Joao, Angelo, Cavem, Germano, Cruz, Augusto, Eusebio, Aguas, Coluna, Simoes
Real: Araquistain, Casado, Miera, Felo, Santamaria, Pachin, Tejada, Del Sol, di Stefano, Puskas, Gento

1962–63
AC MILAN
Wembley   22 May 1963   Attendance 45,000
AC Milan (0) **2**   **Benfica** (1) 1
Altafini 2   Eusebio
Milan: Ghezzi, David, Trebbi, Benitez, Maldini, Trapattoni, Pivatelli, Dino Sani, Altafini, Rivera, Mora
Benfica: Costa Pereira, Cavem, Cruz, Humberto, Raul, Coluna, Augusto, Santana, Torres, Eusebio, Simoes

1963–64
INTER MILAN
Vienna   27 May 1964   Attendance 72,000
Inter Milan (1) **3**   **Real Madrid** (0) 1
Mazzola 2, Milani   Felo
Inter: Sarti, Burgnich, Facchetti, Tagnin, Guarneri, Picchi, Jair, Mazzola, Milani, Suarez, Corso
Real: Vicente, Isidro, Pachin, Zoco, Santamaria, Muller, Amancio, Felo, di Stefano, Puskas, Gento

1964–65
INTER MILAN
Milan   27 May 1965   Attendance 80,000
Inter Milan (1) **1**   **Benfica** (0) 0
Jair
Inter: Sarti, Burgnich, Facchetti, Bendin, Guarneri, Pichi, Jair, Mazzola, Peiro, Suarez, Corso
Benfica: Costa Pereira, Cavem, Cruz, Neto, Germano, Paul, Augusto Eusebio, Torres Coluna, Simoes

1965–66
REAL MADRID
Brussels   11 May 1966   Attendance 38,714
Real Madrid (0) **2**   **Partizan Belgrade** (0) 1
Amancio, Serena   Vasovic
Real: Araquistain, Pachin, Sanchis, Pirri, De Felipe, Zoco, Serena, Amancio, Grosso, Velasquez, Gento
Partizan: Soskic, Jusufi, Migailovic, Becejac, Rasovic, Vasovic, Bajic, Kovacevic, Hasanagic, Galic, Pirmajer

1966–67
CELTIC
Lisbon   25 May 1967   Attendance 45,000
Celtic (0) **2**   **Inter Milan** (1) 1
Gemmell, Chalmers   Mazzola (pen)
Celtic: Simpson, Craig, Gemmell, Murdoch, McNeill, Clark, Johnstone, Wallace, Chalmers, Auld, Lennox
Inter: Sarti, Burgnich, Facchetti, Bedin, Guarneri, Picchi, Domenghini, Mazzola, Cappellini, Biccli, Corso

1967–68
MANCHESTER UNITED
Wembley   29 May 1968   Attendance 100,000
Manchester United (0) (1) **4**   **Benfica** (0) (1) 1
Charlton 2, Best, Kidd   Graca
United: Stepney, Brennan, Dunne, Crerand, Foulkes, Stiles, Best, Kidd, Charlton, Sadler, Aston
Benfica: Henrique, Adolfo, Cruz, Graca, Humberto, Jacinto, Augusto, Eusebio, Torres, Coluna, Simoes

1968–69
AC MILAN
Madrid   28 May 1969   Attendance 50,000
AC Milan (2) **4**   **Ajax Amsterdam** (0) 1
Prati 3, Sormani   Vasovic
Milan: Cudicini, Anquiletti, Schnellinger, Maldera, Rosato, Trapattoni, Hamrin, Lodetti, Sormani, Rivera, Prati
Ajax: Bals, Suurbier (sub Muller), Van Duivenbode, Pronk, Hulsoff, Vasovic, Swart, Cruyff, Danielson Groot (sub Nuninga), Keizer

1969–70
FEYENOORD
Milan   6 May 1970   Attendance 50,000
Feyenoord (1) (1) **2**   **Celtic** (1) (1) 1
Israel, Kindvall   Gemmell
Feyenoord: Graafland, Romeyns, Laseroms, Israel, Van Duivenbode, Hasil, Jansen, Van Hanegem, Wery, Kindvall, Mouljin (sub Haak)
Celtic: Williams, Hay, Gemmell, Murdoch, McNeill, Brogan, Johnstone, Lennox, Wallace, Auld (sub Connolly), Hughes

1970–71
AJAX AMSTERDAM
Wembley   2 June 1971   Attendance 90,000
Ajax Amsterdam (1) **2**   **Panathinaikos** (0) 0
Van Dijk, Haan
Ajax: Stuy, Vasovic, Suurbier, Hulsoff, Rijinders (sub Haan), Neeskens, Swart (sub Blankenburg), Muhren, Keizer, Van Dijk, Cruyff
Panathinaikos: Economopoulos, Tomaras, Vlahos, Elefetrakis, Kamaras, Sourpis, Grammos, Filokouris, Antoniadis, Domazos, Kapsis

1971–72
AJAX AMSTERDAM
Rotterdam   31 May 1972   Attendance 67,000
Ajax Amsterdam (0) **2**   **Inter Milan** (0) 0
Cruyff 2
Ajax: Stuy, Suurbier, Blankenburg, Hulshoff, Krol, Neeskens, Haan, Muhren, Swart, Cruyff, Keizer
Inter: Bordon, Burgnich, Bellugi, Oriali, Facchetti, Bedin, Mazzola, Giubertoni (sub Bertini), Jair, Pellicarro, Boninsegna, Frustalupi

1972–73
AJAX AMSTERDAM
Belgrade   30 May 1973   Attendance 93,500
Ajax Amsterdam (0) **1**   **Juventus** (0) 0
Rep
Ajax: Stuy, Suurbier, Blankenburg, Hulshoff, Krol, Neeskens, Haan, G. Muhren, Rep, Cruyff, Keizer
Juventus: Zoff, Longobucco, Marchetti, Furino, Morini, Salvadore, Altafini, Causio (sub Cuccureddu), Anastasi, Capello, Bettega (sub Haller)

154

Tommy Smith wrote his own Anfield epitaph with a glorious header.

Keegan, who had been locked in battle with his marker Vogts all evening, eventually set the seal on Liverpool's victory by earning a penalty when he went down tackled from behind by the blond West German. A photograph of the incident casts doubt on the correctness of the referee's decision since Vogts can clearly be seen playing the ball. Phil Neal converted the penalty and Liverpool became the second English club to lift the European crown.

The final was also Keegan's farewell for Liverpool, a £500,000 move to SV Hamburg having already been negotiated. In his place Paisley signed Celtic's Kenny Dalglish who became an instant hero at Anfield with his brilliant ball control and breathtaking goals. Liverpool went into the 1978 European Cup as both holders and League champions again. A bye in the first round was followed by an overwhelming 6–3 aggregate win over Dynamo Dresden. Liverpool hit another six in beating Benfica in the quarter-finals before coming up against Borussia Moenchengladbach for a third

time. The Germans won their home leg 2–1 but were imperiously brushed aside at Anfield 3–0. History was repeating itself in an uncanny way, for Liverpool's opponents for this final were FC Bruges—a second repeat final for the Merseysiders.

With a Wembley venue, Liverpool were odds-on favourites to retain the trophy but the game was not the pushover many expected. Indeed it marked the start of a series of tense but extremely dull finals involving British clubs. Bruges, suffering from a spate of injuries, shut up shop and Liverpool won thanks to a solitary goal by Dalglish.

The following season saw the champions of Europe paired in the first round with the new champions of England, Nottingham Forest. It was a pity one had to go out so early in the competition and there were many who had their suspicions about how the pairing came about. Forest won the home leg 2–0 and deposed the holders by keeping them to a goalless draw at Anfield. As Liverpool had become the team to beat, now Forest were en route to becoming the new kings of Europe.

1973–74   **BAYERN MUNICH**
Brussels   15 May 1974   Attendance 65,000

| Bayern Munich | (0) (0) 1 | Atletico Madrid | (0) (0) 1 |
Schwarzenbeck   Luis

Brussels   17 May 1974   Attendance 65,000

| Bayern Munich | (1) 4 | Atletico Madrid | (0) 0 |
Muller 2, Hoeness 2

Bayern Munich: Maier, Hansen, Breitner, Schwarzenbeck, Beckenbauer, Roth, Torstensson (sub Durnberger first match), Zobel, Muller, Hoeness, Kappelmann
Atletico Madrid: Reina, Melo, Capon, Adelardo (sub Benegas second march), Heredia, Eusebio, Luis, Garate, Salcedo (sub Alberto in first match), Ufarte (sub Becerra in both matches), Alberto (Irureta played in first match)

1974–75   **BAYERN MUNICH**
Paris   28 May 1975   Attendance 50,000

| Bayern Munich | (0) 2 | Leeds United | (0) 0 |
Roth, Muller

Bayern Munich: Maier, Durnberger, Andersson (sub Weiss), Schwarzenbeck, Beckenbauer, Roth, Torstensson, Zobel, Muller, Hoeness (sub Wunder), Kappelmann
Leeds United: Stewart, Raeney, F. Gray, Bremner, Madeley, Hunter, Lorimer, Clarke, Jordan, Giles, Yorath (sub E. Gray)

1975–76   **BAYERN MUNICH**
Glasgow   12 May 1976   Attendance 54,864

| Bayern Munich | (0) 1 | St. Etienne | (0) 0 |
Roth

Bayern Munich: Maier, Hansen, Schwarzenbeck, Beckenbauer, Horsmann, Roth, Durnberger, Kappelmann, Rummenigge, Muller, Hoeness
St Etienne: Curkovic, Repellini, Piazza, Lopez, Janvion, Bathenay, Santini, Larque, P. Revelli, H. Revelli, Sarramanga.(sub Rocheteau)

1976–77   **LIVERPOOL**
Final: Rome   25 May 1977   Attendance 57,000

| Liverpool | (1) 3 | Borussia Monchengladbach | (0) 1 |
McDermott, Smith, Neal (pen), Simonsen

Liverpool: Clemence, Neal, Jones, Smith, Kennedy, Hughes, Keegan, Case, Heighway, Callaghan, McDermott.
Borussia Monchengladbach: Kneib, Vogts, Klinkhammer, Wittkamp, Schaffer, Wohlers (sub Hannes), Bonhoff, Wimmer (sub Kulik), Stielike, Simonsen, Heynckes.

1977–78   **LIVERPOOL**
Wembley   10 May 1978   Attendance 92,000

| Liverpool | (0) 1 | FC Bruges | (0) 0 |
Dalglish

Liverpool: Clemence, Neal, Thompson, Hansen, Hughes, McDermott, Kennedy, Souness, Case (sub Heighway), Fairclough, Dalglish
FC Bruges: Jensen, Bastijns, Krieger, Leekens, Maes (sub Volders), Cools, De Cubber, Vandereycken, Ku (sub Sanders), Simoen, Sorensen

1978–79   **NOTTINGHAM FOREST**
Munich   30 May 1979   Attendance 57,500

| Nottingham Forest | (1) 1 | Malmo | (0) 0 |
Francis

Nottm Forest: Shilton, Anderson, Lloyd, Burns, Clark, Francis, McGovern, Bowyer, Robertson, Woodcock, Birtles
Malmo: Moller, Roland Andersson, Jonsson, Magnus Andersson, Erlandsson, Tapper (sub Malmberg), Ljungberg, Prytz, Kinnvall, Hansson (sub Tommy Andersson), Cervin

1979–80   **NOTTINGHAM FOREST**
Madrid   28 May 1980   Attendance 50,000

| Nottingham Forest | (1) 1 | SV Hamburg | (0) 0 |
Robertson

Nottm Forest: Shilton, Anderson, Gray (sub Gunn), McGovern, Lloyd, Burns, O'Neill, Bowyer, Birtles, Mills (sub O'Hare), Robertson
SV Hamburg: Kargus, Kaltz, Nogly, Jakobs, Buljan, Hieronymus (sub Hrubesch), Keegan, Memering, Milewski, Magath, Reimann

1980–81   **LIVERPOOL**
Paris   27 May 1981   Attendance 48,360

| Liverpool | (0) 1 | Real Madrid | (0) 0 |
A. Kennedy

Liverpool: Clemence, Neal, A. Kennedy, Thompson, R. Kennedy, Hansen, Dalglish (sub Case), Lee, Johnson, McDermott, Souness
Real Madrid: Rodriguez, Garcia Cortes, Camacho, Stielike, Sabido (sub Pineda), Del Bosque, Juanito, De Los Santos, Santillana, Navajas, Cunningham

1981–82   **ASTON VILLA**
Rotterdam   26 May 1982   Attendance 46,000

| Aston Villa | (0) 1 | Bayern Munich | (0) 0 |
Withe

Aston Villa: Rimmer (sub Spink), Swain, Williams, Evans, McNaught, Mortimer, Bremner, Shaw, Withe, Cowans, Morley
Bayern Munich: Muller, Dremmler, Horsmann, Weiner, Augenthaler, Kraus (sub Niedermayer), Durnberger, Breitner, Hoeness, Mathy (sub Guttler), Rummenigge

1982–83   **SV HAMBURG**
Athens   25 May 1983   Attendance 80,000

| SV Hamburg | (1) 1 | Juventus | (0) 0 |
Magath

SV Hamburg: Stein, Kaltz, Wehmeyer, Jakobs, Heironymus, Rolff, Milewski, Groh, Hrubesch, Magath, Bastrup
Juventus: Zoff, Gentile, Cabrini, Bonini, Brio, Scirea, Bettaga, Tardelli, Rossi (sub Marocchino), Platini, Boniek

1983–84   **LIVERPOOL**
Rome   30 May 1984   Attendance 69,693

| Liverpool | (1) 1 | Roma | (1) 1 aet |
Neal   Pruzzo
(Liverpool win 4–2 on penalties)

Liverpool: Grobbelaar, Neal, Kennedy, Lawrenson, Whelan, Hansen, Dalglish (sub Robinson), Lee, Rush, Johnston (sub Nicol), Souness
Roma: Tancredi, Nappi, Bonetti, Righetti, Nela, Di Bartolomei, Falcao, Cerezo (sub Strkelj), Conti, Pruzzo (sub Chierico), Graziani

1984–85   **JUVENTUS**
Brussels   29 May 1985   Attendance 58,000

| Juventus | (0) 1 | Liverpool | (0) 0 |
Platini (pen)

Juventus: Tacconi, Favero, Cabrini, Bonini, Brio, Scirea, Briaschi, Tardelli, Rossi, Platini, Boniek
Liverpool: Grobbelaar, Neal, Beglin, Lawrenson (sub Gillespie), Nicol, Hansen, Dalglish, Whelan, Rush, Walsh (sub Johnston), Wark

1985–86   **STEAUA BUCHAREST**
Seville   7 May 1986   Attendance 70,000

| Steaua Bucharest | (0) 0 | Barcelona | (0) 0 aet |
(Steaua win 2–0 on penalties)

Steaua Bucharest: Ducadam, Belodedici, Iovan, Bombescu, Barbulescu, Balint, Balan (sub Ionescu), Boloni, Majearu, Lacatus, Piturca (sub Radu)
Barcelona: Urruti, Gerrardo, Migueli, Alesanco, Julio Alberto, Victor, Marcos, Schuster (sub Moratalla), Pedraza, Archibald (sub Pichi Alonso), Carrasco

1986–87   **FC PORTO**
Vienna   27 May 1987   Attendance 59,000

| FC Porto | (0) 2 | Bayern Munich | (1) 1 |
Madjer, Juary   Kogl

FC Porto: Mlynarczyk, Pinto, Inacio, Eduardo Luis, Celso, Quim (sub Juary), Magalhaes, Madjer, Sousa, Futre, Andre
Bayern Munich: Pfaff, Winklhofer, Pflugler, Eder, Nachtweih, Brehme, Flick, Matthaus, Hoeness, M. Rummenigge, Kogl

1960–61   **FIORENTINA**
First Leg: Glasgow 17 May 1961 Attendance 80,000
Rangers (0) 0   Fiorentina (1) 2
   Milan 2
Second Leg: Florence 27 May 1961 Attendance 50,000
Fiorentina (1) 2   Rangers (1) 1
Milan, Hamrin   Scott
Rangers: Ritchie, Shearer, Caldow, Davis, Paterson, Baxter, Wilson, McMillan, Scott, Brand, Hume (Millar in second leg)

1961–62   **ATLETICO MADRID**
Final: Glasgow 10 May 1962 Attendance 27,389
Atletico Madrid (1) 1   Fiorentina (1) 1
Peiro   Hamrin
Replay: Stuttgart 5 September 1962 Attendance 45,000
Atletico Madric (2) 3   Fiorentina (0) 0
Jones, Mendoca, Peiro

1962–63   **TOTTENHAM HOTSPUR**
Final: Rotterdam 15 May 1963 Attendance 25,000
Tottenham Hotspur (2) 5   Atletico Madrid (0) 1
Greaves 2, White, Dyson 2   Collar (pen)
Tottenham Hotspur: Brown, Baker, Henry, Blanchflower, Norman, Marchi, Jones, White, Smith, Greaves, Dyson

1963–64   **SPORTING LISBON**
Final: Brussels 13 May 1964 Attendance 9,000
Sporting Lisbon (1) (3) 3   MTK Budapest (1) (3) 3
Figueiredo 2, Dansky (og)   Sandor 2, Kuti
Replay: Antwerp 15 May 1964 Attendance 18,000
Sporting Lisbon (1) 1   MTK Budapest (0) 0
Morais

1964–65   **WEST HAM UNITED**
Final: Wembley 19 May 1965 Attendance 100,000
West Ham United (0) 2   TSV Munich 1860 (0) 0
Sealey 2
West Ham United: Standen, Kirkup, Burkett, Peters, Brown Moore, Sealey, Boyce, Hurst, Dear, Sissons

1965–66   **BORUSSIA DORTMUND**
Final: Glasgow 5 May 1966 Attendance 41,657
Borussia Dortmund (0) (1) 2   Liverpool (0) (1) 1
Held, Yeasts (og)   Hunt
Liverpool: Lawrence, Lawler, Byrne, Milne, Yeats, Stevenson, Callaghan, Hunt, St John, Smith, Thompson

1966–67   **BAYERN MUNICH**
Final: Nuremberg 31 May 1967 Attendance 69,480
Bayern Munich (0) (0) 1   Rangers (0) (0) 0
Roth
Rangers: Martin, Johansen, Provan, Jardine, McKinnon, Greig, Henderson, Smith (A), Hynd, Smith (D), Johnston

1967–68   **AC MILAN**
Final: Rotterdam 23 May 1968
AC Milan (2) 2   SV Hamburg (0) 0
Hamrin 2

1968–69   **SLOVAN BRATISLAVA**
Final: Basle 21 May 1969
Slovan Bratislava (3) 3   Barcelona (1) 2
Cvetler, Hrivnak, Jan Capkovic   Zaldua, Rexach

1969–70   **MANCHESTER CITY**
Final: Vienna 29 April 1970 Attendance 10,000
Manchester City (2) 2   Gornik Zabrze (0) 1
Young, Lee penalty   Oslizlo
Manchester City: Corrigan, Book, Pardoe, Doyle (Bowyer), Booth, Oakes, Heslop, Bell, Lee, Young, Towers

1970–71   **CHELSEA**
Final: Athens 19 May 1971 Attendance 42,000
Chelsea (0) (1) 1   Real Madrid (0) (1) 1
Osgood   Zoco
Replay: Athens 21 May 1971 Attendance 24,000
Chelsea (2) 2   Real Madrid (0) 1
Dempsey, Osgood   Fleitas
Chelsea: *Final:* Bonetti, Boyle, Harris, Hollins (Mulligan), Dempsey, Webb, Weller, Cooke, Osgood (Baldwin), Hudson, Houseman
Replay: Bonetti, Boyle, Harris, Cooke, Dempsey, Webb, Weller, Baldwin, Osgood (Smethurst), Hudson, Houseman

1971–72   **RANGERS**
Final: Barcelona 24 May 1972 Attendance 45,000
Rangers (2) 3   Moscow Dynamo (0) 2
Stein, Johnston 2   Eschtrekov, Makiovic
Rangers: McCloy, Jardine, Mathieson, Greig, Johnstone, Smith, McLean, Conn, Stein, Macdonald, Johnston

1972–73   **AC MILAN**
Final: Salonika 16 May 1973 Attendance 45,000
AC Milan (1) 1   Leeds United (0) 0
Chiaguri
Leeds United: Harvey, Rearney, Cherry, Bates, Madeley, Hunter, Lorimer, Jordan, Jones, Gray (F). Yorath (sub McQueen)

1973–74   **FC MAGDEBURG**
Final: Rotterdam 8 May 1974 Attendance 5,000
FC Magdeburg (1) 2   AC Milan (0) 0
Lanzi og, Seguin

1974–75   **DYNAMO KIEV**
Final: Basle 14 May 1975 Attendance 13,000
Dynamo Kiev (2) 3   Ferencvaros (0) 0
Onischenko (2), Blochin

1975–76   **ANDERLECHT**
Final: Brussels 5 May 1976 Attendance 58,000
Anderlecht (1) 4   West Ham United (1) 2
Rensenbrink 2 (1 pen)   Holland, Robson
Van der Elst 2
West Ham United: Day, Coleman, Bond, T. Taylor, Lampard (sub A. Taylor), McDowell, Brooking, Paddon, Holland, Jennings, Robson

1976–77   **HAMBURG**
Final: Amsterdam 11 May 1977 Attendance 65,000
Hamburg (0) 2   Anderlecht (0) 0
Volkert (pen)
Magath

1977–78   **ANDERLECHT**
Final: Paris 3 May 1978 Attendance 48,679
Anderlecht (3) 4   Wien (0) 0
Rensenbrink (2)
Van Binst (2)

1978–79   **BARCELONA**
Final: Basle 16 May 1979 Attendance 50,000
Barcelona (2) (2) 4   Fortuna Dusseldorf (2) (2) 3 aet
Sanchez, Asensi, Rexach,   Klaus Allofs, Seel 2
Krankl

1979–80   **VALENCIA**
Final: Brussels 14 May 1980 Attendance 40,000
Valencia (0) 0   Arsenal (0) 0 aet
Valencia won 5–4 on pens
Arsenal: Jennings, Rice, Nelson, Talbot, O'Leary, Young, Brady, Sunderland, Stapleton, Price (sub Hollins), Rix

1980–81   **DYNAMO TBLISI**
Final: Dusseldorf 13 May 1981 Attendance 9,000
Dynamo Tblisi (0) 2   Carl Zeiss Jena (0) 1
Gutsayev, Daraselia   Hoppe

1981–82   **BARCELONA**
Final: Barcelona 12 May 1982 Attendance 100,000
Barcelona (1) 2   Standard Liege (1) 1
Simonsen, Quini   Vandermissen

1982–83   **ABERDEEN**
Final: Gothenborg 11 May 1983 Attendance 17,804
Aberdeen (1) (1) 2   Real Madrid (1) (1) 1 aet
Black, Hewitt   Juanito (pen)
Aberdeen: Leighton, Rougvie, McMaster, Cooper, McLeish, Miller, Strachan, Simpson, McGhee, Black (sub Hewitt), Weir
Real Madrid: Augustin, Jean Jose, Camacho, (sub San Jose), Metgod, Bonet, Gallego, Juanito, Angel, Santillana, Stielike, Isidoro (sub Salguero)

1983–84   **JUVENTUS**
Final: Basle 16 May 1984 Attendance 60,000
Juventus (2)   Porto (1) 1
Vignola, Boniek   Sousa
Juventus: Tacconi, Gentile, Brio, Scirea, Cabrini, Tardelli, Bonini, Vignola (sub Caricola), Rossi, Platini, Boniek
Porto: Ze Beto, Joao Pinto, Lima Pereira, Eurico, Eduardo Luis (sub Costa), Jaime Megalhaes, (sub Walsh), Frasco, Jaime Pacheco, Sousa, Gomes, Vermelhinho

1984–85   **EVERTON**
Final: Rotterdam 15 May 1985 Attendance 50,000
Everton (0) 3   Papid Vienna (0) 1
Gray, Steven, Sheedy   Krankl
Everton: Southall, Stevens, Van Den Hauwe, Ratcliffe, Mountfield, Reid, Steven, Gray, Sharp, Bracewell, Sheedy
Rapid Vienna: Kohsel, Kienast, Garger, Weber, Lainer, Hristic, Kranjcar, Weinhofer (sub Panenka), Brauneder, Pacult (sub Gross), Krankl

1985–86   **DYNAMO KIEV**
Final: Lyon 2 May 1986 Attendance 39,300
Dynamo Kiev (1) 3   Athletico Madrid (0) 0
Zavarov, Blokhin, Yevtushenko
Dynamo Kiev: Chanov, Baltacha (sub Bal), Bessonov, Kuznetsov, Demianenko, Yaremchuk, Zavarov (sub Yevtushenko), Yakovenko, Rats, Belanov, Blokhin
Athletico Madrid: Fillol, Tomas, Arteche, Ruiz, Clemente, Julio Prieto, Marina, Landaburu (sub Setien), Ramos, Cabrera, Da Silva

1986–87   **AJAX AMSTERDAM**
Final: Athens 14 May 1987 Attendance 35,000
Ajax Amsterdam (1) 1   Lokomotiv Leipzig (0) 0
van Basten
Ajax Amsterdam: Menzos, Silooy, Verlaat, Rijkaard, Boeve, Winter, van't Schip, Wouters, van Basten, Muhren, Witschge
Lokomotiv Leipzig: Muller, Kreek, Baum, Lindner, Zoetzsche, Bredon, Scholz, Liebers, Ebmond, Richter, Marschall

They reached the semi-finals with panache but a 3–3 home draw with Cologne left them with a formidable task. Yet as the return showed, it's never wise to bet against a motivator like Forest manager Brian Clough. Forest won 1–0 in Cologne through an Ian Bowyer goal to earn their first ever place in a European final. For Trevor Francis, transferred from Birmingham the previous winter as Britain's first million pound footballer, the final was his first-ever appearance in Europe. He'd had to sit out earlier rounds in order to qualify.

For Forest, Francis was worth the wait. Seconds before half-time he rose to a superb John Robertson cross to head the only goal of the game. Did that repay a huge slice of Francis's transfer fee, Clough was asked afterwards. No, came the reply, John Robertson was my man of the match and he only cost ten bob.

The following season roles were reversed as Forest entered the competition as holders and Liverpool back in their familiar position of League champions. The two avoided each other in the first round on this occasion but it was of no benefit to Liverpool who fell to the powerful Soviet side Dynamo Tbilisi. Forest ploughed on through a tough series of fixtures, notably against Dynamo Berlin whom they lost against at the City Ground but beat 3–1 away thanks to two goals by Francis, to reach their second consecutive final. But this time there was no Francis. Just as the England player was reaching peak form for the first time in his career, the hard pitches of the English spring caused an achilles tendon injury which kept him out of the game for six months.

Clough told Francis to keep away from the Madrid final for fear that the sight of him on crutches would upset the rest of the squad. The final, which brought Forest up against Kevin Keegan's Hamburg, did little to commend itself to anyone but the most committed Forest fan. An early goal by Robertson, who cut inside Kaltz on the left and scored from 20 yards with his right foot, let Forest sit back on their lead as Keegan became more and more frustrated in his search for an equaliser. After a good first half, he came back looking for the ball and thus hindered rather than helped Hamburg's cause by staying out of the area where he was likely to do most damage. For the third year in succession, the European Cup had been decided by a single goal.

Goals hardly flowed in the Cup Winners' Cup final of 1980 either until Arsenal and Valencia were reduced to a penalty shoot-out. Arsenal had hit the unusually high total of 13 en route but the prospect of a British double in Europe faded when, after a goalless draw, Rix had the unhappy distinction of being the man who missed his spot kick. Arsenal thus gathered the unique record of going through a whole European competition undefeated and still not winning the trophy.

The following year did see the double achieved with Liverpool regaining their European crown from Forest and Ipswich winning the UEFA Cup. This time it was Forest's turn to take a first round knock-out at the hands of CSKA Sofia. But the Bulgarian army side couldn't produce an encore when they met Liverpool in the quarter final, going out 6–1 on aggregate. Liverpool squeezed into their third final thanks to a Ray Kennedy goal in Munich which, with the scores level at 1–1 after a 0–0 draw at Anfield, counted double.

The 1981 final pitted the old masters of Europe against the new. But the Real Madrid vintage of the new decade was poor compared with that of the illustrious fifties. Another dour struggle saw another final decided by one goal, this one coming from Alan Kennedy in the 81st minute. Among the few points of interest was that the opposition again contained an England international though this, like the rest of Laurie Cunningham's Spanish experience, was not the stuff

memories are made from.

Liverpool's victory was accomplished with the help of Sammy Lee's hold on Stielike, who once again found himself on the losing side against them. Lee forced the West German international back into his own half and out of the match. A performance like that would have earned most continental youngsters immediate international recognition. Yet it was not until 18 months later, in November 1982, that Lee received his first England cap. Moreover it was the reluctance shown by Ron Greenwood to select young talent which some critics believe was at the root of the disparity between the performance of British clubs in Europe during the late seventies and early eighties and the faltering progress of the national side.

Bobby Robson, who marked his card as a future England manager by guiding Ipswich to such a high level of consistency culminating in their UEFA Cup win over AZ Alkmaar, would soon be putting the theory to the test. When he took over from Greenwood after the 1982 World Cup, Lee was one among several young additions to the England squad.

But 1982 brought a new name on the European Cup. For the sixth year in succession it was British and again it emphasized the paradox of club supremacy and international mediocrity. Aston Villa's triumph was the more remarkable for two reasons: their inexperience in Europe and the events at Villa Park the previous season which had seen the departure of Ron Saunders, the manager who had guided the club to their first championship win in 71 years.

As Liverpool faltered in the quarter-finals against perennial upsetters CSKA Sofia, Villa's European novices, under the thoughtful guidance of their former coach, Tony Barton, powered on. Their only two previous campaigns had been short-lived. They had lost a first round UEFA tie in 1975 and two years later reached the quarter-finals. The road to

Keith Robson scores for West Ham but the 1976 Cup Winners Cup Final against Anderlecht ended in a 4–2 defeat. It was West Ham's second Cup Winners Final.

Rotterdam took in Valur in Iceland, Dynamo Berlin, Dynamo Kiev and Anderlecht, where crowd disturbances by spectators almost lost Villa a hard-earned place in the final.

Villa arrived in Rotterdam very much the underdogs against a Bayern Munich side containing the most potent constituents of the West German World Cup squad. But every underdog has his day and Bayern, admittedly hampered by having European Footballer of the Year Karl-Heinz Rummenigge less than fully fit (how often Rummenigge seems to have been below par for the big occasions) failed to take advantage of their domination.

Bayern's lapse was the more astonishing for the fact that Villa lost their goalkeeper, Jimmy Rimmer, after ten minutes and played the rest of the game with the goal in the brave but untested hands of a teenager. Nineteen-year-old Nigel Spink rose to the occasion with a series of crucial saves as Bayern turned the screw on the Villa defence. McNaught and Evans dominated the aerial battle with Rummenigge and the game hinged on one moment of brilliance by Villa winger Tony Morley. Scorer of a brilliant solo match-winner against Anderlecht in the semi-final, Morely sliced through the German defence with the speed of forked lightning and sent over the low cross from which Withe miss-hit Villa's winner. The ball went in off the far post in a better turn of luck than the England centre-forward enjoyed on his international debut against Brazil twelve months earlier, when a similar shot rebounded back into play. Jimmy Rimmer, on the subs' bench for Manchester United in 1968, thus won his second European Cup Winners' medal having played only ten minutes out of 180.

That was the end of Villa's moment of glory. They slipped away as rapidly as they had risen, finishing eleventh in the League in their European Cup year, then sixth, tenth and into trouble via a succession of managers and continual boardroom criticism. By 1986–87 they had become one of a clutch of First Division clubs (among them Luton, Coventry, Oxford, Charlton, Wimbledon, QPR and Leicester) for whom 15,000 was an attendance as acceptable as it was exceptional.

The flag kept flying for another three years. On 19 May 1983 Aberdeen won an emotional and enjoyable Cup Winners' Cup final against Real Madrid in Gothenburg. It had rained torrentially for the previous 24 hours and the Swedish port was virutally flooded. The weather never let up and the Spaniards looked ill at ease in this twilight northern summer, clearly playing for penalties virtually from the start. (Alex Ferguson had watched pre-match training sessions and was amazed to note that all they did was practise penalties. It did give him an early clue to Real's tactics, which proved useful.) They got one, from Juanito, but Black and Hewitt, in extra time, ensured justice was done. The game was notable for an excellent performance at left-back by McMaster and a dashing winger's display from Peter Weir. The Scots now had three European trophies under their belts, one each from Celtic, Rangers and Aberdeen. It was an outstanding record for a country of only five million people—countries of comparable size like Sweden, Denmark and Switzerland had little to show for their efforts, though the Portuguese, through Benfica, had cause for pride.

Liverpool were to win their fourth European Cup in Rome in 1984. The game was decided on penalties, only the second time this had occured in a major club final (the first being Arsenal v Valencia in the Cup Winners' Cup in 1980). Phil Neal had put Liverpool ahead, Pruzzo equalizing for Roma, who were playing at home. Liverpool won the shoot-out 4–2, Bartelemei and Graziani both missing and Grobbelaar's antics amusing the watching millions. Alan Kennedy scored the decisive penalty, highlighting Liverpool's unusual penchant for depending on their full-backs for vital goals. Chris Lawler still holds the British record for the most goals scored from open play in a season by a full-back, and Phil Neal scored in both the 1977 European Cup final and the 1984 equivalent. Alan Kennedy scored the winner against Real Madrid in 1981 as well as getting the vital penalty in 1984. To place this in context, it should be noted that the FA Cup was 110 years old before a full-back (Terry Fenwick of QPR) scored a goal from open play in a Cup final. Kennedy also added goals in the 1981 and 1983 League Cup finals—four goals in four cup finals in four years is not a bad record for a full-back.

Liverpool's 1984 win was the first final in which more than

European glory for Aberdeen. Eric Black scores for the Scottish Cup-holders in the European Cup Winners Cup Final of 1983 in Gothenburg. Aberdeen beat Real Madrid 2–1.

1955–58 BARCELONA

First Leg:
Stamford Bridge 5 March 1958 Attendance 45,466

London		(1) 2	Barcelona	(2) 2
Greaves, Langley (pen)			Tajada, Martinez	

Second Leg:
Barcelona 1 May 1958 Attendance 62,000

Barcelona		(3) 6	London	(0) 0
Suarez 2, Evaristo 2, Martinez, Verges				

London:
First Leg: Kelsey (Arsenal); Sillett P. (Chelsea), Langley (Fulham); Blanchflower (Spurs), Norman (Spurs), Coote (Brentford); Groves (Arsenal), Greaves (Chelsea), Smith (Spurs), Hayes (Fulham), Robb (Spurs).
Second Leg: Kelsey (Arsenal); Wright (West Ham), Cantwell (West Ham); Blanchflower (Spurs), Brown (West Ham), Bowen (Arsenal); Medwin (Spurs), Groves (Arsenal), Smith (Spurs), Bloomfield (Arsenal), Lewis (Chelsea).

1958–60 BARCELONA

First Leg:
Birmingham 29 March 1960 Attendance 40,500

Birmingham City		(0) 0	Barcelona	(0) 0

Second Leg:
Barcelona 4 May 1960 Attendance 70,000

Barcelona		(2) 4	Birmingham City	(0) 1
Martinez, Czibor 2, Coll			Hooper	

1960–61 AS ROMA

First Leg:
Birmingham 27 September 1961 Attendance 21,005

Birmingham City		(0) 2	AS Roma	(1) 2
Hellawell, Orritt			Manfredini 2	

Second Leg:
Rome 11 November 1961 Attendance 60,000

AS Roma		(0) 2	Birmingham City	(0) 0
Farmer (og), Pestrin				

1961–62 VALENCIA

First Leg:
Valencia 8 September 1962 Attendance 65,000

Valencia		6	Barcelona	2
Guillot 3, Yosu 2, H Nunez			Kocsis 2	

Second Leg:
Barcelona 12 September 1962 Attendance 60,000

Barcelona		1	Valencia	1
Kocsis			Guillot	

1962–63 VALENCIA

First Leg:
Zagreb 12 June 1963 Attendance 40,000

Dynamo Zagreb		(1) 1	Valencia	(0) 2
Zambata			Waldo, Urtiaga	

Second Leg:
Valencia 26 June 1963 Attendance 55,000

Valencia		2	Dynamo Zagreb	0
Mano, Nunez				

1963–64 REAL ZARAGOZA

Final:
Barcelona 24 June 1964 Attendance 50,000

Real Zaragoza		(1) 2	Valencia	(1) 1
Villa, Marcelino			Urtiaga	

1964–65 FERENCVAROS

Final:
Turin 23 June 1965 Attendance 25,000

Ferencvaros		(1) 1	Juventus	(0) 0
Fenyvesi				

1965–66 BARCELONA

First Leg:
Barcelona 14 September 1966 Attendance 70,000

Barcelona		(0) 0	Real Zaragoza	(1) 1
			Canario	

Second Leg:
Zaragoza 21 Septemper 1966 Attendance 70,000

Real Zaragoza		(1) 2	Barcelona	(1) 4
Marcelino 2			Pujol 3, Zaballa	

1966–67 DYNAMO ZAGREB

First Leg:
Zagreb 30 August 1967 Attendance 40,000

Dynamo Zagreb		(1) 2	Leeds United	(0) 0
Cercer 2				

Second Leg:
Leeds 6 September 1967 Attendance 35,604

Leeds United		(0) 0	Dynamo Zagreb	(0) 0

1967–68 LEEDS UNITED

First Leg:
Leeds 7 August 1968 Attendance 25,368

Leeds United		(1) 1	Ferencvaros	(0) 0
Jones				

Second Leg:
Budapest 11 September 1968 Attendance 70,000

Ferencvaros		(0) 0	Leeds United	(0) 0

Leeds United:
Sprake; Reaney, Cooper, Bremner, Charlton, Hunter, Lorimer, Madeley, Jones (sub Hibbitt), Gray (sub O'Grady)

1968–69 NEWCASTLE UNITED

First Leg:
Newcastle 29 May 1969 Attendance 60,000

Newcastle United		(0) 3	Ujpest Dozsa	(0) 0
Moncur 2, Scott				

Second Leg:
Budapest 11 June 1969 Attendance 37,000

Ujpest Dozsa		(2) 2	Newcastle United	(0) 3
Bene, Gorocs			Moncur, Arentoft, Foggon	

Newcastle United:
McFaul; Craig, Clark, Gibb, Burton, Moncur, Scott, Robson, Davies, Arentoft, Sinclair. (Foggon substituted for Scott in first leg and for Sinclair in second leg).

1969–70 ARSENAL

First Leg:
Brussels 22 April 1970 Attendance 37,000

Anderlecht		(2) 3	Arsenal	(0) 1
Devrindt, Mulder 2			Kennedy	

Second Leg:
London 28 April 1970 Attendance 51,612

Arsenal		(1) 3	Anderlecht	(0) 0
Kelly, Radford, Sammels				

Arsenal:
Wilson; Storey, McNab, Kelly, McLintock, Simpson, Armstrong, Sammels, Radford, George (sub Kennedy in first leg), Graham.

1970–71 LEEDS UNITED

First Leg:
Turin 26 May 1971 Attendance 65,000

Juventus		(0) 0	Leeds United	(0) 0

(game abandoned after 51 minutes)
Turin 28 May 1971 Attendance 65,000

Juventus		(1) 2	Leeds United	(0) 2
Bettega, Capello			Madeley, Bates	

Second Leg:
Leeds 3 June 1971 Attendance 42,483

Leeds United		(1) 1	Juventus	(1) 1
Clarke			Anastasi	

Leeds United:
Sprake; Reaney, Cooper, Bremner, Charlton, Hunter, Lorimer, Clarke, Jones (sub Bates in first leg), Giles. Madeley (sub Bates in second leg).
(Leeds won on the 'away goals count double' rule).

---

one goal was scored since the last time they were in Rome, back in 1977. There had been six consecutive 1–0 results and this dreadful sequence was to continue afterwards. The only goal of the irrelevant 1985 final was a penalty, and in 1986 things got even worse in Seville, with a goalless draw and then a penalty decider. Just nine goals in nine finals is hardly the stuff of which romantic stories are made. The European cup final of 1960 saw more goals in a single game.

Liverpool's win in Rome was also notable as the first by a team on an 'away' ground in a single game final. As UEFA choose their final venues well in advance, it was inevitable that some teams would find themselves in their own city. This had happened on six previous occasions, and though the 'home' side were not necessarily playing on their own pitch, the visitors had never won (though Fiorentina actually beat Rangers 2–0 in Glasgow in the first leg of a two-legged Cup Winners' Cup final in 1961). The advantage to Roma was so clear that UEFA decided to eliminate this element of lottery from 1984 onwards by the simple expedient of not choosing a city which had a represenatative in the relevant competition. One wonders why they had not done it before—though it did mean Glasgow, Brussels (which would hardly be likely to want too many matches nowadays) and Lisbon were unlikely to see too many finals in the foreseeable future. Spurs also won the UEFA Cup in 1984, and like Liverpool they did it on

penalties, against an Anderlecht side which was generally superior and unlucky. Everton won a rather dull season's Cup Winners' Cup in Rotterdam against Austria Vienna in 1985 and the stage was set for Liverpool to become the first city ever to take the two major trophies in one year. It is Everton's everlasting misfortune that not only did Liverpool's disaster obliterate virtually all memory of Everton's success, but that the subsequent ban affected Everton, League champions in 1985, more than anyone else. But after Rome and Rotterdam came Brussels and after that came the deluge. The Scots, Irish and Welsh were still in (Wrexham almost knocking out Real Zaragoza in the 1986–87 Cup Winners' Cup by drawing 0–0 in Spain and 1–1 at home and perhaps justifying the peculiar appearance of Football League Fourth Division clubs on grounds where the likes of Manchester United and Nottingham Forest were firmly banned). The English could look only to their international matches as an unlikely source of solace. The World Cup of 1986 showed some promise, but was to end before 115,000 people in that deeply emotional and symbolic quarter-final against Argentina in the Aztec Stadium. As a game it will always be remembered for the goal that wasn't—Maradona's helping hand which was to guarantee his team their progress to the final.

How different it all was in the far-off days of the first international when, on a cold, wet, windy night in 1872, a

John McGovern holds the European Cup aloft in the first of Nottingham Forest's triumphs in 1979, when they beat Malmo 1–0. McGovern had been with manager Clough at Derby before both went to Forest.

group of officers and gentlemen gathered in the Royal Garrick Hotel in Glasgow. Instead of the frugal glasses of orangeade or coca-cola, and the starchless main meals, they tucked into a gargantuan feast with all the gusto of men who had endured the rigours of a train journey from London.

It had been a journey with nothing of the cushioned plushness of a modern Inter-City line. Limbs ached from the buffeting on the wooden austerity of the seats, and the acrid smell of smoke had the travellers still heavy with catarrh.

The game itself ended in a scoreless draw, a surprising result for the Englishmen, who had arranged the fixture, in the words of the FA minutes, 'In order to further the interests of the Association in Scotland'. There was to be ample opportunity to regret the condescending tone of that statement.

In the next 19 years England were to beat Scotland only twice but at least the significance of those defeats was not lost on 'Pa' Jackson, assistant secretary of the FA, who determined that England should create a team on the Queen's Park pattern. So, in 1882, Jackson formed his Corinthians from former public schools and university men and, in the next seven years, of the 88 players capped by England, 52 were Corinthians. On two occasions when the FA agreed to play Ireland and Wales on the same day, the entire Corinthians side was sent to represent England.

The International Selection Committee, later to hold so much sway, was not formed until 1888. Originally it was composed of seven men but by the fifties this figure had risen to more than 30.

It was not until Alf Ramsey took over in 1963 that the team selection for full and Under-23 internationals was taken out of the hands of a committee.

Players were not so much selected as voted for. A committee enthusiast from, for example, south-east London would report that he had seen a promising player with Millwall. If he could lobby enough support, his discovery would go in to the exclusion of an established star. One interesting result, reflecting the fact that the FA is based in London, is that all the Third Divison players who have ever appeared for England came from Third Division South clubs. Not one ever hailed from the Third Division North.

Ironically enough, there was much more continuity during the War itself when, with so many leading players serving abroad, the pool of stars available for internationals was restricted.

That meant that the same players—Swift, Scott, Hardwick, Denis and Leslie Compton, Soo, Franklin, Mercer, Matthews, Carter, Lawton, Finney—came up for selection time after time. In a sense they were the harbingers of the squad system of the 1960s.

A further important step came later in the War when Sir Stanley Rous, later to become President of FIFA, proposed to the FA, of which he was then secretary, that England should have a team manager.

The choice fell upon Walter Winterbottom, a schoolteacher who had been centre-half for Manchester United. A man of charm and insight, Winterbottom was well qualified, but he was to learn unhappily that he had been given responsibility without power. Winterbottom was asked merely to coach and prepare players, while the actual selection remained firmly in the hands of the selection committee. To have a team manager was one thing, but to allow him the licence to decide who should play for England was quite different.

It was in this pantomime atmosphere that England, grievously under-prepared, embarked on her first World Cup sortie to Brazil in 1950. The inglorious defeat at the hands of the USA was just one in a whole catalogue of disasters. Things had gone wrong from the very start when two of the England players—Matthews and Taylor—both missed the first game because they had been touring with an FA team in Canada when the England party arrived in Brazil.

That, however, was but one of Walter Winterbottom's problems. When the party took a dislike to the Brazilian food, he even found himself entrusted with the task of cooking. That defeat by the USA and Hungary's historic 6–3 win at Wembley three years later taught the FA what the world had long suspected—that the British were no longer the masters of football.

Something drastic should have been done, but the only significant change came during the 1954 World Cup when some of the senior players were invited to advise on team selection.

Preparations were still as chaotic as ever. The England party arrived in Sweden for the 1958 World Cup finals to find that no training camp had been laid on. The harassed Winterbottom, whose experience of World Cups seemed never less than horrific, was left to chase around for accommodation only days before the first game.

Chile was hardly any better. Incredibly, the England party travelled to the tournament without a team doctor, and the result was that Peter Swan fell ill and, after receiving the wrong treatment, almost died.

The man who achieved more than anyone to create a professional and realistic environment within England's international soccer was, of course, Sir Alf Ramsey. As the successful and unequivocal manager of Ipswich, he did not need to seek the England job when Winterbottom lost, as he was bound to do, his vain battle against administrative incompetence and selectorial vanity in 1962.

Although he was said to have been only third choice for the job, Ramsey could take the post on his own terms. He would not countenance the intolerable pressure which had been laid upon his hamstrung predecessor. He would pick the players and, if the selectors *had* to remain in existence, they would do so only as a rubber stamp.

Ten to four-thirty, Monday to Thursday, Ramsey would be in his Lancaster Gate office, and he expected the same discipline and punctuality from everyone else. The awesome combination of Harold Sheperdson and Les Cocker—'as cuddly as a sack of cobblestones' said Max Marquis—were brought in as trainers and strict rules of conduct were laid down for the players.

What Ramsey accomplished for England needs little reiteration. He promised that England would win the World Cup in 1966 and they did. Consciously or otherwise, he succeeded by going back to 'Pa' Jackson's concept of running an international side on the same lines as a club.

His stubborn, unsmiling defence of his players did little in the field of public relations; yet on the field of play those players responded to his fierce loyalty. But for England's amazing quarter-final in Leon—quite out of character for a Ramsey side—the World Cup might have been retained, or at least lost to Brazil in the final.

Finally Ramsey paid the usual managerial price for failure—in his case England's failure to qualify for the 1974 World Cup. His succesor, Don Revie, steeped in the success of Leeds United, faced a similar problem and England did not reach the last eight of the 1976 European Championship.

Eventually as Revie's squad set out along the qualification route for the 1978 World Cup, the Football League grudgingly agreed to postpone League matches to increase preparation time. Temporarily, at least, the massive withdrawals because of club injuries and commitments were ended—in 1972 Ramsey had lost *nine* of his original squad in such circumstances for the international against Yugoslavia. Revie still faced the problem of making the concession be seen to work, but it made that advertisement for 'young men to play in an international' seem that much further away.

Revie would undoubtedly have suffered the same fate as Ramsey had he not jumped off the ship before it went down. Failure to qualify for the 1978 World Cup finals and Revie's hasty departure to the Middle East left morale at international level at an all-time low. Ron Greenwood's appointment brought muted optimism and some fresh ideas. Club managers working in tandem were given responsibility for nurturing the under-21 and England B sides while Greenwood

himself worked in conjunction with Arsenal coach Don Howe. Instead of the big leap into the senior side, there were now a clear series of stepping stones.

After qualification for the 1980 European Championship came the next attempt to get England to her first World Cup finals since 1966. Expansion of the competition to 24 countries made it virtually impossible to fail to qualify.

Even then it took a belated decision by the Football League to agree to postpone some Saturday games before vital qualifying matches to clear what was becoming an increasingly rocky path to Spain. With Greenwood's retirement after fulfilling all that could reasonably have been expected of him—qualification for Spain, a robust if uninspiring performance in the finals and England's longest ever run of first-class victories—England moved nearer the era of the soccer supremo. When Bobby Robson took over, he dispensed with the FA's long-serving director of coaching, Allan Wade, and assumed responsibility for that department himself. England now had a manager whose personal influence reached from the internationals to playing fields across the country.

Early results, however, were as disappointing as they could be. Far from building on England's limited rehabilitation in Spain, Robson found even qualification for the 1984 European championships beyond him. Having gained five points out of a possible six in their opening three games, England dropped a vital home point to Greece, were beaten at Wembley by a superior Danish side and then found they had left the back door open for the deserving Danes to shade them for a place in the finals.

England's performances in Mexico were no less dramatic. They qualified as the only undefeated European side, with four wins and four draws in eight games. They even had the good fortune to draw an easy group—Morocco, Portugal and the weakest of the seeds, Poland. After their best run of results for many years (six consecutive wins, eleven matches without defeat), England had great cause for confidence on arrival in Monterrey. Their first opponents were the Portuguese, in disarray over money and little fancied. It should have been a

Below *The crowning achievement of Irish football history probably came in Valencia during her 1982 World Cup first group game against hosts Spain. Despite a vicious performance from opponents desperate to win the match, appallingly poor refereeing and Mal Donaghy being sent off, the Irish defeated Spain 1–0 with a Gerry Armstrong goal. The Irish spent much of the match in defence—in this picture John McClelland, Gerry Armstrong, Billy Hamilton and Chris Nicholl fend off Jesus Satrustegui at a corner. Both Armstrong and Hamilton, particularly after his two goals against Austria, became internationally recognized personalities and both featured prominently in many of the 'Best Players of the Tournament' polls afterwards.*

formality. Needless to say, it was not. Carlos Manuel scored the only goal with 15 minutes left, after some dreadful defensive ball watching, and England's unbeaten record and confidence had gone. A few days later came even worse news. Little fancied Morocco had drawn with Poland and were to do the same with England despite having every chance of winning. In a disastrous five minutes before half-time captain Bryan Robson's shoulder suffered another dislocation (just as it had against Canada, though Bobby Robson kept this from the press) and vice-captain Ray Wilkins was sent off for throwing the ball towards the referee. England hung on grimly for a goalless draw, her fourth consecutive World Cup finals match without scoring. The Moroccans seemed pleased.

Matters came to a head in the England camp. Bobby Robson had stuck with a team selection he had clearly made several months before, despite his namesake's obvious injury problems. Robson admitted he believed his captain was essential, that England simply could not win anything without him. He had persisted with Wilkins, Waddle (after the Spurs' man's goal which defeated Russia) and Mark Hateley. England were the only team in Mexico still playing to the head of a big centre-forward, and it was not working. Perhaps there, one wondered, was the answer to why England perform poorly as a national team. The outdated ideas magically come alive, the old tactics are always there, ready to be resuscitated as soon as a winger or a centre-forward of any quality appears on the scene.

By all accounts one group of players virtually told Robson what he had to do. Even Bryan Robson concurred. Four across the middle – Peter Reid, Trevor Steven, Steve Hodge and Glenn Hoddle. Two quick runners and ground ball players up front—Peter Beardsley and Gary Lineker. It was a

UEFA CUP WINNERS AND FINALS

1971–72 TOTTENHAM HOTSPUR
First Leg: Wolverhampton 3 May 1972 Attendance 45,000
Wolverhampton Wanderers (0) 1 — Tottenham Hotspur (0) 2
McCalliog — Chivers 2
Second Leg: Tottenham 17 May 1972 Attendance 48,000
Tottenham Hotspur (1) 1 — Wolverhampton Wanderers (0) 1
Mullery — Wagstaffe
Tottenham Hotspur: Jennings, Kinnear, Knowles, Mullery, England, Beal, Coates (sub Pratt in first leg), Perryman, Chivers, Peters, Gilzean.

1972–73 LIVERPOOL
First Leg: Liverpool 10 May 1973 Attendance 41,169
Liverpool (3) 3 — Borussia Monchengladbach (0) 0
Keegan 2, Lloyd
Second Leg: Monchengladbach 23 May 1973 Attendance 35,000
Borussia Monchengladbach (2) 2 — Liverpool (0) 0
Liverpool: Clemence, Lawler, Lindsay, Smith, Lloyd, Hughes, Keegan, Cormack, Toshack, Heighway (sub Hall in first leg, Boersma in second leg), Callaghan.

1973–74 FEYENOORD
First Leg: Tottenham 21 May 1974 Attendance 46,281
Tottenham Hotspur (1) 2 — Feyenoord (1) 2
England, Van Daele og — Van Hanegem, De Jong
Second Leg: Rotterdam 29 May 1974 Attendance 68,000
Feyenoord (1) 2 — Tottenham Hotspur (0) 0
Rijsbergen, Ressel

1974–75 BORUSSIA MONCHENGLADBACH
First Leg: Dusseldorf 7 May 1975 Attendance 45,000
Borussia Monchengladbach (0) 0 — Twente Enschede (0) 0
Second Leg: Enschede 21 May 1975 Attendance 24,500
Twente Enschede (0) 1 — Borussia Monchengladbach (2) 5
Drost — Heynckes 3, Simonsen 2 (1 pen)

1975–76 LIVERPOOL
First Leg: Liverpool 28 April 1976 Attendance 56,000
Liverpool (0) 3 — Bruges (2) 2
Kennedy, Case, Keegan (pen) — Lambert, Cools
Second Leg: Bruges 19 May 1976 Attendance 32,000
Bruges (1) 1 — Liverpool (1) 1
Lambert (pen) — Keegan
Liverpool: Clemence, Smith, Neal, Thompson, Kennedy, Hughes, Keegan, Case (Fairclough played in first leg), Heighway, Toshack (sub Case first leg, sub Fairclough second leg) Callaghan.

1976–77 JUVENTUS
First Leg: Turin 4 May 1977 Attendance 75,000
Juventus (1) 1 — Athletico Bilbao (0) 0
Tardelli
Second Leg: Bilbao 18 May 1977 Attendance 43,000
Athletico Bilbao (1) 2 — Juventus (1) 1
Irureta, Carlos — Bettega

1977–78 PSV EINDHOVEN
First Leg: Corsica 26 April 1978 Attendance 15,000
Bastia (0) 0 — PSV Eindhoven (0) 0
Second Leg: Eindhoven 9 May 1978 Attendance 27,000
PSV Eindhoven (1) 3 — Bastia (0) 0
W. Van der Kerkhof, Deijkers, Van der Kuylen

1978–79 BORUSSIA MONCHENGLADBACH
First leg: Belgrade 9 May 1979 Attendance 87,500
Red Star Belgrade (1) 1 — Borussia Monchengladbach (0) 1
Sestic — Juristic og
Second Leg: Dusseldorf 23 May 1979 Attendance 54,000
Borussia Monchengladbach (1) 1 — Red Star Belgrade (0) 0
Simonson

1979–80 EINTRACHT FRANKFURT
First Leg: Monchengladbach 7 May 1980 Attendance 25,000
Borussia Moenchengladbach (1) 3 — Eintracht (1) 2
Kulik 2, Matthus — Karger, Holzenbein
Second Leg: Frankfurt 21 May 1980 Attendance 60,000
Eintracht (0) 1 — Borussia Monchengladbach (0) 0
Schaub
Eintracht won on away goals

1980–81 IPSWICH TOWN
First Leg: Ipswich 6 May 1981 Attendance 27,532
Ipswich (1) 3 — AZ 67 Alkmaar (0) 0
Wark pen, Thijssen, Mariner
Second Leg: Amsterdam 20 May 1981 Attendance 28,500
AZ 67 Alkmaar (3) 4 — Ipswich (2) 2
Welzl, Metgod, Tol, — Thijssen, Wark
Jonker
Ipswich: Cooper, Mills, McCall, Thijssen, Osman, Butcher, Wark, Muhren, Mariner, Brazil, Gates.

1981–82 IFK GOTHENBURG
First Leg: Gothenburg 5 May 1982 Attendance 42,548
IFK Gothenburg (0) 1 — SV Hamburg (0) 0
Tord Holmgren
Second Leg: Hamburg 19 May 1982 Attendance 60,000
SV Hamburg (0) 0 — IFK Gothenburg (1) 3
Corneliusson, Nilsson, Fredriksson pen

1982–83 ANDERLECHT
First Leg: Brussels 4 May 1983 Attendance 55,000
Anderlecht (1) 1 — Benfica (1) 0
Brylle
Second Leg: Lisbon 18 May 1983 Attendance 80,000
Benfica (1) 1 — Anderlecht (1) 1
Sheu — Lozano

1983–84 TOTTENHAM HOTSPUR
First Leg: Brussels 9 May 1984 Attendance 40,000
Anderlecht (0) 1 — Tottenham Hotspur (0) 1
Olsen — Miller
Second Leg: London 23 May 1984 Attendance 46,205
Tottenham Hotspur (0) (1) 1 — Anderlecht (0) (1) 1 aet
Roberts — Czerniatynski
Tottenham Hotspur win 4–3 on penalties
Tottenham Hotspur: Parks, Thomas, Hughton, Roberts, Miller (sub Ardiles in second leg), Perryman (Mabbutt played in second leg) (sub Dick Replaced Mabbutt in second leg), Stevens (sub Mabbutt replaced Stevens in first leg), Hazard, Archibald, Falco, Galvin.

1984–85 REAL MADRID
First Leg: Szekesfehervar 8 May 1985 Attendance 30,000
Videoton (0) 0 — Real Madrid (1) 3
— Michel, Santillana, Juanito
Second Leg: Madrid 22 May 1985 Attendance 90,000
Real Madrid (0) 0 — Videoton (0) 1
— Majer

1985–86 REAL MADRID
First Leg: Madrid 30 April 1986 Attendance 80,000
Real Madrid (2) 5 — Cologne (1) 1
Sanchez, Gordillo, — K. Allofs
Valdano 2, Santillana
Second Leg: Berlin 6 May 1986 Attendance 15,000
Cologne (1) 2 — Real Madrid (0) 0
Bein, Geilenkirchen

1986–87 IFK GOTHENBURG
First Leg: Gothenburg 6 May 1987 Attendance 50,000
IFK Gothenburg (1) 1 — Dundee United (0) 0
Pettersson
Second Leg: Dundee 20 May 1987 Attendance 20,911
Dundee United (0) 1 — IFK Gothenburg (1) 1
Clark — Nilsson
Dundee United: Thomson, Holt, Malpas, McInally, Hegarty (Clark second leg), Narey, Kirkwood, Bowman (Gallagher second leg), Bannon (Ferguson second leg), Sturrock, Redford

team with an Everton core. There was to be no more pumping balls upfield to Hateley's head, no more chasing after remote chances. It was too hot and there was too little air for that. Against Poland, in the vital third group game, it all worked perfectly. Lineker scored a hat-trick, England's first in the finals since Hurst in 1966, all grabbed from close in with the defence stretched. England sneaked through second in their group to play Paraguay in the last 16. But if Robson had not been forced to change his team and his tactics who knows where England might have been.

Paraguay were also disposed of 3–0, Lineker getting two and Beardsley the other. England looked a good side again, but the real test was about to come. Argentina could only mean the Falklands, revenge, a Maradona at the peak of his powers. In 1982 British television had refused to show the World Cup opening game because Argentina were playing. This time they were not so squeamish, and England even chose (very peculiarly indeed) to play in Argentinian colours—white shirts and light blue shorts.

Argentina were clearly the better side. Until the last 20 minutes, when Argentina sat back on their 2–0 lead, England hardly created a respectable chance. Maradona scored twice, the first with his infamous helping hand (surely the most celebrated goal of the 1980s), secondly with a glorious run from the centre circle past five defenders. The Mexicans were

so impressed with this second goal that they put up a plaque celebrating it in the entrance to the Azteca Stadium. John Barnes got round the back on the left side in the last few minutes to make a headed goal for Lineker (his sixth, making him the first Englishman ever to lead the World Cup scorers), and did the same in the dying seconds. Lineker flung himself bravely at the ball on the far post and seemed certain to score. But the ball deflected fortuitously off the top of an Argentinian head and passed Lineker by. As with Keegan's headed miss against Spain in 1982, the World Cup door could be heard slamming shut at that moment.

So England were out, but not disgraced. Argentina were worthy World Cup winners and England had lost to them by only 2–1, and one of these goals went in off Maradona's hand (the fact that FIFA banned the Tunisian referee from further international matches was cold comfort—it was an absurd decision to put an inexperienced Tunisian in charge of such an emotional event in the first place).

Yet again, England did not seem to have adapted to the modern game in the way that her club sides had. There were still large Tommy Lawton surrogates at centre-forward, still tall centre-backs whose job was to stop a breed of tall centre-forwards long gone from foreign penalty areas. And the skilful, clever midfield was still undermanned when England arrived. A country with that potential could not afford a joker in the pack like Waddle anymore—he didn't do the unexpected well enough often enough. He wasn't a Drajan Djazic. A fourth midfielder was necessary in that particular climate. It may not necessarily be attractive, it may not be what the manager or fans wanted, but it was the right camouflage for the environment of football in the late 1980s.

And so England, Scotland, Wales, Northern Ireland and Eire looked ahead to Italy and the World Cup of 1990. Bobby Robson remained, but Jock Stein had tragically died at the end of Scotland's qualifying draw against Wales in Cardiff. Alex Ferguson did not want the job and Andy Roxburgh was something of a surprise choice. For the English the 1988 European championship and 1990 World Cup had particular significance. They were the only opportunies she was likely to have for international competition of any sort, and would be a test of the ability and willingness of the football authorities (and government) to control their fans and perhaps persuade UEFA to readmit some, if not all, clubs to the three competitions. It would not be an easy task off the field, no easier than that on it. Of the two, it was probably more important to solve the hooligan problem than it was to win the World Cup. The long term future depends far more on that than mere trophies—but in itself that was an interesting commentary on how desperate the problem had become. And without regular European competition, surely the English game would slip back into its old ways, would lose the tactical superiority Liverpool had given it and, perhaps in the 1990s, English clubs would be no more significant in the major tournaments than the English side had been in the 1970s. It was not an entirely cheerful prospect.

Trevor Francis comes in for the less than affectionate attentions of West German sweeper Uli Stielike during the England v West Germany clash in Madrid during the 1982 World Cup finals. After an excellent start, which saw three wins in the first qualifying group and a modern-day record of nine consecutive international victories, England proved a great disappointment in the second groups. Her two games, against the Germans and hosts Spain, did not produce a single goal and England went out of the competition, like the Cameroons, undefeated.

CHAPTER TEN

THE RECORDS

Lee Sinnott of Watford makes a determined challenge on Everton's Trevor Steven in the 1984 FA Cup Final but the England winger got the ball across. Everton went on to win 2–0.

FA CUP 1871-72

FIRST ROUND
Clapham Rovers v Upton Park	3-0
Crystal Palace v Hitchin	0-0*
Maidenhead v Great Marlow	2-0
Barnes v Civil Service	2-0
Wanderers v Harrow Chequers (scratched)	wo
Royal Engineers v Reigate Priory (scratched)	wo
Queen's Park	bye
Donington School	bye
Hampstead Heathens	bye

SECOND ROUND
Wanderers v Clapham Rovers	3-1
Crystal Palace v Maidenhead	3-0
Royal Engineers v Hitchin	3-1
Hampstead Heathens v Barnes	2-0
Queen's Park v Donington School (scratched)	wo

THIRD ROUND
Wanderers v Crystal Palace	†*
Royal Engineers v Hampstead Heathens	2-0
Queen's Park	‡bye

†Drawn game for which no score is available.
‡Queen's Park were granted a bye from the third round into the semi-final because of travelling.

SEMI-FINAL
Royal Engineers v Crystal Palace	3-0
Wanderers v Queen's Park (scratched)††	0-0, wo

††Queen's Park could not afford to travel to London for the replay.

FINAL AT KENNINGTON OVAL
Wanderers v Royal Engineers	1-0

*The progress of Crystal Palace and Hitchin into the second round and Crystal Palace and Wanderers into the semi-final round was covered by Rule 8 of the competition whereby in the case of a draw both clubs could compete in the next round.

FA CUP 1872-73

FIRST ROUND
Oxford University v Crystal Palace	3-2
Royal Engineers v Civil Service	3-0
1st Surrey Rifles v Upton Park	2-0
Maidenhead v Great Marlow	1-0
South Norwood v Barnes	1-0
Windsor Home Park v Reigate Priory	4-2
Clapham Rovers v Hitchin (scratched)	wo
Queen's Park	*bye
Wanderers	†bye

*Queen's Park, Glasgow, because of the travelling involved, were awarded byes to the semi-final round.
†This was the only occasion when the Cup holders were excused from taking part until the Final.

SECOND ROUND
Clapham Rovers v Oxford University	0-3
1st Surrey Rifles v Maidenhead	1-3
South Norwood v Windsor Home Park	0-3
Royal Engineers	bye
Queen's Park	bye
Wanderers	bye

THIRD ROUND
Oxford University v Royal Engineers	1-0
Maidenhead v Windsor Home Park	1-0
Queen's Park	bye
Wanderers	bye

FOURTH ROUND
Oxford University v Maidenhead	4-0
Queen's Park	bye
Wanderers	bye

SEMI-FINAL
Oxford University v Queen's Park (scratched)	*wo
Wanderers	bye

*Queen's Park apparently beat Oxford but could not afford to travel to London for the Final.

FINAL AT LILLIE BRIDGE*
Wanderers v Oxford University	2-0

*Wanderers, as Cup holders, had choice of ground.

FA CUP 1873-74

FIRST ROUND
Oxford University v Upton Park	4-0
Barnes v 1st Surrey Rifles	1-0
Cambridge University v South Norwood	1-0
Pilgrims v Great Marlow	1-0
Royal Engineers v Brondesbury	5-0
Uxbridge v Gitanos	3-0
Swifts v Crystal Palace	1-0
Woodford Wells v Reigate Priory	3-0
Sheffield v Shropshire Wanderers	††
Wanderers v Southall (scratched)	wo
Trojans v Farningham (scratched)	wo
Clapham Rovers v A A C (scratched)	wo
Maidenhead v Civil Service (scratched)	wo
High Wycombe v Old Etonians (scratched)	wo

††After two drawn games Sheffield won on the toss of a coin

SECOND ROUND
Oxford University v Barnes	2-1
Clapham Rovers v Cambridge University	4-1
Sheffield v Pilgrims	1-0
Royal Engineers v Uxbridge	2-1
Maidenhead v High Wycombe	1-0
Swifts v Woodford Wells	2-1
Wanderers v Trojans (scratched)	wo

THIRD ROUND
Oxford University v Wanderers	1-0
Clapham Rovers v Sheffield	2-1
Royal Engineers v Maidenhead	7-0
Swifts	bye

SEMI-FINAL
Oxford University v Clapham Rovers	1-0
Royal Engineers v Swifts	2-0

FINAL AT KENNINGTON OVAL
Oxford University v Royal Engineers	2-0

Top Queen's Park in 1874, still undefeated and the first winners of the Scottish Cup.
Bottom Royal Engineers in 1872, 7-4 on favourites for the FA Cup, but only runners-up.

SCOTTISH FA CUP 1873-74

FIRST ROUND
Queen's Park v Dumbreck	7-0
Clydesdale v Granville	6-0
Western v Blythwood	0-1
Alexandria Athletic v Callander	2-0
Eastern v Rovers	4-0
Renton v Kilmarnock	2-0
Dumbarton v Vale of Leven (scratched)	wo
3rd Lanark Rifle Volunteers v Southern (scratched)	wo

SECOND ROUND
Queen's Park v Eastern	1-0
Alexandria Athletic v Blythwood	0-2
Renton v Dumbarton	0-0, 1-0
Clydesdale v 3rd Lanark Rifle Volunteers	1-1, 0-0, 2-0

SEMI-FINAL
Queen's Park v Renton	2-0
Clydesdale v Blythwood	4-0

FINAL AT HAMPDEN PARK
Queen's Park v Clydesdale	2-0

The first FA Cup competitions were far less organised than those a century later. The first winners, Wanderers, won only one game before defeating Royal Engineers in the Final. They received a walk over in the first round, beat Clapham in the second, went through after only drawing in the third and received a walk-over in the semi-final after Queen's Park had been unable to pay for the long journey to London for a replay.

Wanderers' goal in the Final — the first in an FA Cup Final — was scored by M P Betts, who played under the name of A H Chequer, indicating that he had come from Harrow Chequers, who had scratched to Wanderers in the first round. Queen's Park had the same trouble the next year. After defeating Oxford they were unable to travel to the Final and Oxford took their place — thus being one of only three clubs to have reached a Final after losing an earlier match.

FA CUP 1874-75

FIRST ROUND
Royal Engineers v Great Marlow	3-0
Cambridge University v Crystal Palace	†2-1
Clapham Rovers v Panthers	3-0
Pilgrims v South Norwood	2-1
Oxford University v Brondesbury	6-0
Wanderers v Farningham	16-0
Barnes v Upton Park	3-0
Old Etonians v Swifts	††3-0
Maidenhead v Hitchin	1-0
Woodford Wells v High Wycombe	1-0
Southall v Leyton	†5-0
Windsor Home Park v Uxbridge (scratched)	wo
Shropshire Wanderers v Sheffield (scratched)	wo
Civil Service v Harrow Chequers (scratched)	wo
Reigate Priory	bye

†Drawn game for which no score is available

SECOND ROUND
Royal Engineers v Cambridge University	5-0
Clapham Rovers v Pilgrims	2-0
Wanderers v Barnes	4-0
Maidenhead v Reigate Priory	2-1
Woodford Wells v Southall	3-0
Oxford University v Windsor Home Park (scratched)	wo
Shropshire Wanderers v Civil Service (scratched)	†two
Old Etonians	bye

†Drawn game for which no score is available

THIRD ROUND
Royal Engineers v Clapham Rovers	3-2
Oxford University v Wanderers	2-1
Old Etonians v Maidenhead	1-0
Shropshire Wanderers v Woodford Wells	†2-0

†Drawn game for which no score is available

SEMI-FINAL
Royal Engineers v Oxford University	†1-0
Old Etonians v Shropshire Wanderers	1-0

†Drawn game for which no score is available

FINAL AT KENNINGTON OVAL
Royal Engineers v Old Etonians	1-1, 2-0

SCOTTISH FA CUP 1874-75

FIRST ROUND
Helensburgh v 3rd Edinburgh Rifle Volunteers	3-0
Rangers v Oxford	2-0
West End v Star of Leven	3-0
Kilmarnock v Vale of Leven Rovers	4-0
Dumbreck v Alexandria Athletic	5-1
3rd Lanark Rifle Volunteers v Barrhead	1-0
Dumbarton v Arthurlie	3-0
Queen's Park v Western	1-0
Eastern v 23rd Renfrew Rifle Volunteers	3-0
Renton v Blythwood (scratched)	wo
Clydesdale v Vale of Leven (scratched)	wo
Rovers v Hamilton Academicals (scratched)	wo
Standard	bye

SECOND ROUND
Eastern v Kilmarnock	3-0
Renton v Helensburgh	2-0
3rd Lanark Rifle Volunteers v Standard	2-0
Queen's Park v West End	7-0
Clydesdale v Dumbreck	2-0
Dumbarton v Rangers	1-0
Rovers	bye

THIRD ROUND
Renton v Eastern	1-0
Dumbarton v 3rd Lanark Rifle Volunteers	1-0
Queen's Park v Rovers (scratched)	wo
Clydesdale	bye

SEMI-FINAL
Renton v Dumbarton	0-0, 1-0
Queen's Park v Clydesdale	0-0, 2-2, 1-0

FINAL AT HAMPDEN PARK
Queen's Park v Renton	3-0

FA CUP 1875-76

FIRST ROUND
Wanderers v 1st Surrey Rifles	5-0
Crystal Palace v 105th Regiment	†3-0
Upton Park v Southall	1-0
Swifts v Great Marlow	2-0
Royal Engineers v High Wycombe	15-0
Panthers v Woodford Wells	1-0
Reigate Priory v Barnes	1-0
Oxford University v Forest School	6-0
Hertfordshire Rangers v Rochester	4-0
Old Etonians v Pilgrims	4-1
Maidenhead v Ramblers	2-0
Sheffield v Shropshire Wanderers (scratched)	wo
South Norwood v Clydesdale (scratched)	wo
Cambridge University v Civil Service (scratched)	wo
Clapham Rovers v Hitchin (scratched)	wo
Leyton v Harrow Chequers (scratched)	wo

†Drawn game for which no score is available

SECOND ROUND
Wanderers v Crystal Palace	3-0
Swifts v South Norwood	5-0
Reigate Priory v Cambridge University	0-8
Oxford University v Hertfordshire Rangers	8-2
Old Etonians v Maidenhead	8-0
Clapham Rovers v Leyton	12-0
Sheffield v Upton Park (scratched)	wo
Royal Engineers v Panthers (scratched)	

THIRD ROUND
Wanderers v Sheffield	2-0
Swifts v Royal Engineers	3-1
Cambridge University v Oxford University	0-4
Old Etonians v Clapham Rovers	1-0

SEMI-FINAL
Wanderers v Swifts	2-1
Oxford University v Old Etonians	0-1

FINAL AT KENNINGTON OVAL
Wanderers v Old Etonians	1-1, 3-0

SCOTTISH FA CUP 1875-76

SECOND ROUND
3rd Edinburgh Rifle Volunteers v Edinburgh Thistle	1-0
Levern v Hamilton Academicals	3-0
Drumpellier v Heart of Midlothian	2-0
Vale of Leven v Renton	3-0
Queen's Park v Northern	5-0
3rd Lanark Rifle Volunteers v Rangers	2-1
Helensburgh v 23rd Renfrew Rifle Volunteers	1-0
Clydesdale v Kilmarnock	6-0
Dumbarton v Renton Thistle	2-1
Western v Sandyford	3-0
Dumbreck v St Andrew's	2-0
Rovers v West End	6-0
Partick Thistle v Towerhill	2-0
Mauchline v Kilbirnie (scratched)	wo

THIRD ROUND
Queen's Park v Clydesdale	2-0
Vale of Leven v Mauchline	6-0
3rd Lanark Rifle Volunteers v Levern	3-0
Dumbreck v Partick Thistle	5-0
Rovers v 3rd Edinburgh Rifle Volunteers	4-0
Western v Helensburgh	2-0
Dumbarton v Drumpellier	5-1

FOURTH ROUND
Queen's Park v Dumbreck	2-0
3rd Lanark Rifle Volunteers v Western	5-0
Vale of Leven v Rovers	2-0
Dumbarton	bye

SEMI-FINAL
Queen's Park v Vale of Leven	3-1
3rd Lanark Rifle Volunteers v Dumbarton	3-0

FINAL AT HAMPDEN PARK
Queen's Park v 3rd Lanark Rifle Volunteers	1-1, 2-0

FA CUP 1876-77

FIRST ROUND
Pilgrims v Ramblers	4-1
Panthers v Wood Grange	3-0
Clapham Rovers v Reigate Priory	5-0
Rochester v Union	5-0
Swifts v Reading Hornets	2-0
Royal Engineers v Old Harrovians	2-1
South Norwood v Saxons	4-1
105th Regiment v 1st Surrey Rifles	3-0
Upton Park v Leyton	7-0
Great Marlow v Hertfordshire Rangers	2-1
Forest School v Gresham	4-1
Wanderers v Saffron Walden (scratched)	wo
Southall v Old Wykehamists (scratched)	wo
Cambridge University v High Wycombe (scratched)	wo
Shropshire Wanderers v Druids (scratched)	wo
Sheffield v Trojans (scratched)	wo
Oxford University v Old Salopians (scratched)	wo
Barnes v Old Etonians (scratched)	wo
Queen's Park	bye

SECOND ROUND
Wanderers v Southall	6-1
Pilgrims v Panthers	1-0
Cambridge University v Clapham Rovers	2-1
Rochester v Swifts	1-0
Royal Engineers v Shropshire Wanderers	3-0
Sheffield v South Norwood	7-0
Oxford University v 105th Regiment	6-1
Upton Park v Barnes	1-0
Great Marlow v Forest School	1-0
Queen's Park	bye

THIRD ROUND
Wanderers v Pilgrims	3-0
Cambridge University v Rochester	4-0
Royal Engineers v Sheffield	1-0
Upton Park v Great Marlow	†1-0
Oxford University v Queen's Park (scratched)	wo

†Drawn game for which no score is available.

FOURTH ROUND
Cambridge University v Royal Engineers	1-0
Oxford University v Upton Park	†1-0
Wanderers	bye

†Drawn game for which no score is available

SEMI-FINAL
Wanderers v Cambridge University	1-0
Oxford University	bye

FINAL AT KENNINGTON OVAL
Wanderers v Oxford University	2-1

SCOTTISH FA CUP 1876-77

FOURTH ROUND
Queen's Park v Northern	4-0
Vale of Leven v Busby	4-0
Lennox v Swifts	4-0
Lancefield v Hamilton	2-0
Rangers v Mauchline	3-0
Ayr Thistle v Partick Thistle (disqualified)	wo

FIFTH ROUND
Rangers v Lennox	3-0
Vale of Leven v Queen's Park	2-1
Ayr Thistle v Lancefield	2-2, 1-0

SEMI-FINAL
Vale of Leven v Ayr Thistle	9-0
Rangers	bye

FINAL AT HAMPDEN PARK
Vale of Leven v Rangers	1-1, 0-0, 3-2

Queen's Park conceded their first ever goal in the Scottish Cup semi-final against Vale of Leven early in 1876. They had been in existence for almost nine years. Their first ever defeat in Scotland was also at the hands of Vale of Leven on 30 December 1876. The latter won a fifth round Scottish Cup tie 2-1.

FA CUP 1877-78

FIRST ROUND
Wanderers v Panthers	9-1
High Wycombe v Wood Grange	4-0
Great Marlow v Hendon	2-0
Sheffield v Notts County	3-0
Darwen v Manchester	3-1
Pilgrims v Ramblers	†1-0
Druids v Shropshire Wanderers	1-0
Oxford University v Hertfordshire Rangers	5-2
Clapham Rovers v Grantham	2-0
Swifts v Leyton	8-2
Old Harrovians v 105th Regiment	2-0
1st Surrey Rifles v Forest School	1-0
Cambridge University v Southill Park	3-1
Maidenhead v Reading Hornets	10-0
Upton Park v Rochester	3-0
Reading v South Norwood	2-0
Remnants v St Stephens	4-1
Hawks v Minerva	5-2
Barnes v St Marks (scratched)	wo
Royal Engineers v Union (scratched)	wo
Old Foresters v Old Wykehamists (scratched)	wo
Queen's Park	*bye

†Drawn game for which no score is available
*Queen's Park later withdrew

SECOND ROUND
Wanderers v High Wycombe	9-0
Barnes v Great Marlow	3-1
Sheffield v Darwen	1-0
Royal Engineers v Pilgrims	6-0
Oxford University v Old Foresters	1-0
Clapham Rovers v Swifts	4-0
Old Harrovians v 1st Surrey Rifles	6-0
Cambridge University v Maidenhead	4-2
Upton Park v Reading	1-0
Remnants v Hawks	2-0
Druids	bye

THIRD ROUND
Wanderers v Barnes	4-1
Royal Engineers v Druids	8-0
Oxford University v Clapham Rovers	3-2
Old Harrovians v Cambridge University	2-0
Upton Park v Remnants	3-0
Sheffield	bye

FOURTH ROUND
Wanderers v Sheffield	3-0
Royal Engineers v Oxford University	4-2
Old Harrovians v Upton Park	3-1

SEMI-FINAL
Royal Engineers v Old Harrovians	2-1
Wanderers	bye

FINAL AT KENNINGTON OVAL
Wanderers v Royal Engineers	3-1

SCOTTISH FA CUP 1877-78

FOURTH ROUND
Renton v Rovers	4-0
South Western v Glengowan	5-0
Mauchline v Kilbirnie	2-1
Parkgrove v Drumpellier	3-1
3rd Lanark Rifle Volunteers v Govan	7-0
Vale of Leven v Rangers	5-0
Thornliebank v Hibernian	**
Beith v Dundas St Clement's (scratched)	wo
Partick Thistle v Barrhead (disqualified)	wo
Jordanhill	bye
Renfrew	†bye

**After two draws, both teams went through to the next round
† Renfrew, who had earlier been beaten by Barrhead, were reinstated on the latter's disqualification

FIFTH ROUND
Vale of Leven v Jordanhill	10-0
Parkgrove v Partick Thistle	2-1
South Western v Hibernian	3-1
Renton v Thornliebank	2-1
3rd Lanark Rifle Volunteers v Beith	4-0
Mauchline v Renfrew (scratched)	wo

SIXTH ROUND
Vale of Leven v Parkgrove	5-0
3rd Lanark Rifle Volunteers v South Western	2-1
Renton v Mauchline	3-1

SEMI-FINAL
3rd Lanark Rifle Volunteers v Renton	1-1, 1-0
Vale of Leven	bye

FINAL AT HAMPDEN PARK
Vale of Leven v 3rd Lanark Rifle Volunteers	1-0

SCOTTISH FA CUP 1878-79

FOURTH ROUND
Hibernian v Roy Roy	9-0
3rd Lanark Rifle Volunteers v Renfrew	4-0
Vale of Leven v Govan	11-1
Dumbarton v Portland	6-1
Queen's Park v Mauchline	5-0
Rangers v Alexandria Athletic	3-0
Beith v Kilmarnock Athletic	9-1
Helensburgh v Heart of Midlothian (scratched)	wo
Stonelaw v Thistle (disqualified)	wo
Partick Thistle	bye

FIFTH ROUND
Queen's Park v 3rd Lanark Rifle Volunteers	5-0
Rangers v Partick Thistle	4-0
Helensburgh v Hibernian	2-1
Dumbarton v Stonelaw	9-1
Vale of Leven v Beith	6-1

SIXTH ROUND
Rangers v Queen's Park	1-0
Vale of Leven v Dumbarton	3-1
Helensburgh	bye

SEMI-FINAL
Vale of Leven v Helensburgh	3-0
Rangers	bye

FINAL AT HAMPDEN PARK
Vale of Leven v Rangers	1-1*

*Cup awarded to Vale of Leven. Rangers refused to play the replay within the time allotted by the SFA. Rangers refused to turn up after the SFA had turned down a protest that they had scored a perfectly legitimate second goal in the first game.

FA CUP 1878-79

FIRST ROUND
Old Etonians v Wanderers	7-2
Reading v Hendon	1-0
Grey Friars v Great Marlow	2-1
Pilgrims v Brentwood	3-1
Nottingham Forest v Notts County	†1-0
Sheffield v Grantham	†3-1
Old Harrovians v Southill Park	8-0
Oxford University v Wednesbury Strollers	7-0
Royal Engineers v Old Foresters	3-0
Barnes v Maidenhead	†4-0
Upton Park v Saffron Walden	5-0
Forest School v Rochester	4-2
Cambridge University v Hertfordshire Rangers	2-0
Swifts v Hawks	2-1
Romford v Ramblers	3-1
Minerva v 105th Regiment (scratched)	wo
Darwen v Birch (scratched)	wo
Remnants v Unity (scratched)	wo
Panthers v Runnymede (scratched)	†two
Clapham Rovers v Finchley (scratched)	wo
South Norwood v Leyton (scratched)	wo
Eagley	bye

†Drawn game for which no score is available

SECOND ROUND
Old Etonians v Reading	1-0
Minerva v Grey Friars	3-0
Darwen v Eagley	4-1
Remnants v Pilgrims	6-2
Nottingham Forest v Sheffield	2-0
Old Harrovians v Panthers	3-0
Oxford University v Royal Engineers	4-0
Barnes v Upton Park	3-2
Clapham Rovers v Forest School	10-1
Cambridge University v South Norwood	3-0
Swifts v Romford	3-1

THIRD ROUND
Old Etonians v Minerva	5-2
Darwen v Remnants	3-2
Nottingham Forest v Old Harrovians	2-0
Oxford University v Barnes	2-1
Clapham Rovers v Cambridge University	1-0
Swifts	bye

FOURTH ROUND
Old Etonians v Darwen	5-5, 2-2, 6-2
Nottingham Forest v Oxford University	2-1
Clapham Rovers v Swifts	8-1

SEMI-FINAL
Old Etonians v Nottingham Forest	2-1
Clapham Rovers	bye

FINAL AT KENNINGTON OVAL
Old Etonians v Clapham Rovers	1-0

The first ever Welsh Cup tie was played on Saturday 30 October, 1877, between Druids of Ruabon and Newtown at Newtown. The founder of the Welsh FA, Llewelyn Kenrick, captained Druids that day; they won the game and eventually reached the final to meet Wrexham. Wrexham won 1-0, apparently using a 2-3-5 line up. If that is in fact correct, then it is the first recorded instance of what remained the standard formation for half a century. At the time the Welsh FA had not even purchased a trophy, but when they did it was a magnificent affair which dwarfed the FA Cup.

Because of the dearth of clubs in Wales, the Cup has always been open to English sides. This produced an English winner as early as 1884 when Oswestry defeated Druids 3-2. The situation became a little absurd in 1934, however, with a final replay which is surely unparalleled in any cup competition. The game was between two English clubs — Bristol City and Tranmere Rovers — and was played on an English ground, Chester's Sealand Road. City won 3-0 and it was not until 1948 that the Cup actually returned to a Welsh club.

The Scottish Cup of 1878-79 saw two scenes unfamiliar a century later. Hearts failed to turn up for their tie at Helensburgh and, later, mighty Rangers refused to play a final replay against Vale of Leven in a fit of pique over a disputed goal.

The 1878-79 Cup season was notable for the arrival of the northern teams. Nottingham Forest became the first northern side to reach the semi-finals (and the only one of the present League clubs to have got so far at the first attempt) but Darwen's displays were more newsworthy. In their fourth round tie against Old Etonians at the Oval, Darwen scored four times in the last 15 minutes to draw 5-5. Etonians refused to play extra time and it took a public subscription to bring Darwen back for a 2-2 draw. A third game was decisive, Etonians winning 6-2 and eventually taking the Cup.

Darwen had in their ranks two Scots — James Love and Fergus Suter — who were reputedly the first of the 'professionals' to find money in their boots. They had come down to Darwen as part of a touring Partick Thistle side, played a friendly, and been persuaded to stay. The tide was on the turn and the days of the gentlemen amateurs almost at an end. Wanderers, after a hat-trick of successes in 1876-78, were defeated in the very first round of the 1878-79 competition by Old Etonians, who went on to become their successors as Cup holders.

167

FA CUP 1879-80

SECOND ROUND
Clapham Rovers v South Norwood	4-0
Hendon v Mosquitoes	7-1
Wanderers v Old Carthusians	1-0
West End v Hotspurs	1-0
Oxford University v Birmingham	6-0
Aston Villa v Stafford Road Works	3-1
Maidenhead v Henley	3-1
Royal Engineers v Upton Park	4-1
Grey Friars v Gresham	9-0
Nottingham Forest v Turton	6-0
Blackburn Rovers v Darwen	3-1
Sheffield v Sheffield Providence	3-0
Pilgrims v Hertfordshire Rangers (scratched)	wo
Old Harrovians	bye
Old Etonians	bye

THIRD ROUND
Clapham Rovers v Pilgrims	7-0
Old Etonians v Wanderers	3-1
Royal Engineers v Old Harrovians	2-0
Nottingham Forest v Blackburn Rovers	6-0
Oxford University v Aston Villa (scratched)	wo
Hendon	bye
West End	bye
Maidenhead	bye
Grey Friars	bye
Sheffield	bye

FOURTH ROUND
Clapham Rovers v Hendon	2-0
Old Etonians v West End	5-1
Oxford University v Maidenhead	1-0
Royal Engineers v Grey Friars	1-0
Nottingham Forest v Sheffield	* 2-2

*Sheffield disqualified for refusing to play extra time

FIFTH ROUND
Clapham Rovers v Old Etonians	1-0
Oxford University v Royal Engineers	†1-0
Nottingham Forest	bye

†Drawn game for which no score is available

SEMI-FINAL
Oxford University v Nottingham Forest	1-0
Clapham Rovers	bye

FINAL AT KENNINGTON OVAL
Clapham Rovers v Oxford University	1-0

SCOTTISH FA CUP 1879-80

FOURTH ROUND
South Western v Arbroath	4-0
Pollockshields Athletic v Renfrew	2-1
Dumbarton v Clyde	11-0
Third Lanark v Kirkintilloch	5-1
Rob Roy v Johnstone Athletic	4-2
Thornliebank v Possilpark	13-0
Mauchline v Hamilton Academicals	2-0
Cambuslang v Plains Bluebell	3-0
Queen's Park v Strathblane	10-1
Parkgrove v Hibernian	2-2, 2-2,**
Hurlford v Kilbirnie	1-1, 1-1,**

** After two draws both teams went through to the next round

FIFTH ROUND
South Western v Parkgrove	3-2
Dumbarton v Kilbirnie	6-2
Queen's Park v Hurlford	15-1
Thornliebank v Rob Roy	12-0
Pollockshields Athletic v Cambuslang	4-0
Hibernian v Mauchline	2-0
Third Lanark	bye

SIXTH ROUND
Pollockshields Athletic v South Western	6-1
Dumbarton v Hibernian	6-2
Thornliebank v Third Lanark	2-1
Queen's Park	bye

SEMI-FINAL
Queen's Park v Dumbarton	1-0
Thornliebank v Pollockshields Athletic	2-1

FINAL AT CATHKIN PARK
Queen's Park v Thornliebank	3-0

SCOTTISH FA CUP 1880-81

FOURTH ROUND
Heart of Midlothian v Cambuslang	3-0
Hurlford v Cartside	3-1
Central v Edinburgh University	1-0
Dumbarton v Glasgow University	9-0
Rangers v Clyde	11-0
Queen's Park v Beith	11-2
St Mirren v Cowlairs	1-0
Arthurlie v South Western (disqualified)	wo
Mauchline v Clarkston (disqualified)	wo
Vale of Leven v Arbroath (scratched)	wo
Thistle	bye

FIFTH ROUND
Vale of Leven v Thistle	7-1
Dumbarton v St Mirren	5-1
Arthurlie v Heart of Midlothian	4-0
Queen's Park v Mauchline	2-0
Rangers v Hurlford	3-0
Central	bye

SIXTH ROUND
Queen's Park v Central	10-0
Dumbarton v Rangers	3-1
Vale of Leven v Arthurlie	2-0

SEMI-FINAL
Dumbarton v Vale of Leven	2-0
Queen's Park	bye

FINAL AT KINNING PARK
Queen's Park v Dumbarton	2-1*, 3-1

*Dumbarton's protest about spectators on the pitch during the first game was upheld

---

FA CUP 1880-81

SECOND ROUND
Old Carthusians v Dreadnought	5-1
Royal Engineers v Pilgrims	1-0
Swifts v Reading	1-0
Upton Park v Weybridge	3-0
Darwen v Sheffield	5-1
The Wednesday v Blackburn Rovers	4-0
Turton v Astley Bridge	3-0
Reading Abbey v Acton	2-1
Great Marlow v West End	4-0
Old Etonians v Hendon	2-0
Grey Friars v Maidenhead	1-0
Stafford Road Works v Grantham	†7-1
Aston Villa v Nottingham Forest	2-1
Notts County	bye
Rangers	bye
Clapham Rovers	bye
Romford	bye
Hertfordshire Rangers	bye

†Drawn game for which no score is available

THIRD ROUND
Royal Engineers v Rangers	6-0
Clapham Rovers v Swifts	2-1
The Wednesday v Turton	2-0
Romford v Reading Abbey	2-0
Old Etonians v Hertfordshire Rangers	3-0
Aston Villa v Notts County	3-1
Old Carthusians	bye
Upton Park	bye
Darwen	bye
Great Marlow	bye
Stafford Road Works	bye
Grey Friars	bye

FOURTH ROUND
Old Carthusians v Royal Engineers	2-1
Clapham Rovers v Upton Park	5-4
Darwen v The Wednesday	5-1
Romford v Great Marlow	2-1
Old Etonians v Grey Friars	4-0
Stafford Road Works v Aston Villa	3-2

FIFTH ROUND
Old Carthusians v Clapham Rovers	4-1
Darwen v Romford	15-0
Old Etonians v Stafford Road Works	2-1

SEMI-FINAL
Old Carthusians v Darwen	4-1
Old Etonians	bye

FINAL AT KENNINGTON OVAL
Old Carthusians v Old Etonians	3-0

The two Scottish Cup finals of 1881 between Queen's Park and Dumbarton resulted in quite unprecedented scenes. The game was played at Rangers' home, Kinning Park, and the crowds were so great that many spent most of the game on the pitch. Because of this Dumbarton protested that Queen's second and winning goal was invalid, the pitch having virtually been invaded, and the SFA ordered a replay. Queen's threatened to withdraw from the Association, but eventually turned out and won 3-1. At the second game the gates had to be closed, the first time that this had happened in Scottish history. This was not really surprising for Dumbarton and Queen's were the Rangers and Celtic of pre-1900 Scotland.
The next year, 1882, there was even more trouble when the two met in the final. The crowd was bad-tempered and there were protests over yet another disputed goal – this time to level at 2-2. Queen's Park went on to win the replay, 4-1, before a record 15,000 crowd, but the two games left a remarkably bitter taste. Up to that point there had been a well-attended friendly every year between the clubs, but this was abandoned . and, indeed, never reinstated. Dumbarton finally won the Cup the following year, beating Vale of Leven, after defeating Queen's Park in the sixth round.

Above The reason Blackburn Rovers won the Cup so often? F H Ayres and Company ran this advertisement regularly for ten years, but 1879-80 was a little premature for it. In their first expedition into the Cup, which was that season, Rovers were rudely dismissed 6-0 by Nottingham Forest, who were at the time on the way to a second consecutive semi-final.

Old Carthusians defeat of Old Etonians in the 1881 Cup Final was the first leg of a rare double. In 1894 they also won the first Amateur Cup final by defeating Casuals 2-1. In fact this oft-repeated 'unique' record is not so: Royal Engineers, FA Cup winners in 1875, later went on to win the Amateur Cup in 1908 as Depot Battalion, Royal Engineers.

FA CUP 1881-82

SECOND ROUND
Blackburn Rovers v Bolton Wanderers	6-2
Darwen v Accrington	3-1
Turton v Bootle	4-0
Wednesbury Old Alliance v Small Heath Alliance	6-0
Notts County v Wednesbury Strollers	11-1
Staveley v Grantham	3-1
Heeley v Sheffield	4-1
Upton Park v Hanover United	3-1
Hotspur v Reading Abbey	4-1
Reading Minster v Romford	3-1
Swifts v Old Harrovians	7-1
Maidenhead v Acton	2-1
Great Marlow v St Bartholomew's Hospital	2-0
Reading v West End (scratched)	*wo
Old Foresters v Pilgrims	3-1
Old Carthusians v Barnes	7-1
Aston Villa	bye
The Wednesday	bye
Old Etonians	bye
Dreadnought	bye
Royal Engineers	bye

*West End scratched after a drawn game

THIRD ROUND
Darwen v Turton	4-2
Aston Villa v Notts County	**4-1
The Wednesday v Staveley	**5-1
Hotspur v Reading Minster	2-0
Old Etonians v Swifts	3-0
Great Marlow v Dreadnought	2-1
Royal Engineers v Old Carthusians	2-0
Blackburn Rovers	bye
Wednesbury Old Alliance	bye
Heeley	bye
Upton Park	bye
Maidenhead	bye
Reading	bye
Old Foresters	bye

**two drawn games for which no scores are available

FOURTH ROUND
Blackburn Rovers v Darwen	5-1
Wednesbury Old Alliance v Aston Villa	4-2
The Wednesday v Heeley	3-1
Upton Park v Hotspur	5-0
Old Etonians v Maidenhead	6-3
Great Marlow v Reading (scratched)	wo
Old Foresters v Royal Engineers	2-1

FIFTH ROUND
Blackburn Rovers v Wednesbury Old Alliance	3-1
The Wednesday v Upton Park	6-0
Great Marlow v Old Foresters	*1-0
Old Etonians	bye

*drawn game for which no score is available

SEMI-FINAL
Blackburn Rovers v The Wednesday	0-0, 5-1
Old Etonians v Great Marlow	5-0

FINAL AT KENNINGTON OVAL
Old Etonians v Blackburn Rovers	1-0

The 1882 FA Cup Final was the real bridging point between the old 'gentlemen's' football and the new professionalism. It was the first appearance of a northern club — Blackburn Rovers — and the last time a Southern side was to win for 30 years. After the game Lord Kinnaird, the victorious captain, stood on his head in front of the pavillion. He had appeared in 8 Finals and won 5 winners medals, a record that was to be equalled but never surpassed. He also appeared in the following year's Final, when he collected a ninth medal.

Before a first round FA Cup tie against Everton late in 1881, Bootle discovered that they only had eight players. Three spectators were asked to play and Bootle won the tie. In the second round, with a full team, Bootle lost 4-0 to a team called Turton.

SCOTTISH FA CUP 1881-82

FOURTH ROUND
Falkirk v Milton of Campsie	3-1
Rangers v Thornliebank	2-0
Clyde v Edinburgh University	3-2
Kilmarnock v Our Boys	9-2
Queen's Park v Johnstone	3-2
Cartvale v Glasgow University	5-4
Hibernian v West Benhar	*8-0
Kilmarnock Athletic v Mauchline	3-2
Partick Thistle v Glasgow Athletic	1-0
Arthurlie v Helensburgh	*1-0
West Calder v Stranraer (scratched)	wo
South Western	bye
Dumbarton	bye
Beith	bye
Vale of Teith	bye
Shotts	bye

*after a drawn game

FIFTH ROUND
Arthurlie v Kilmarnock	4-1
West Calder v Falkirk	4-2
Queen's Park v Partick Thistle	10-0
Shotts v Vale of Teith	5-0
Kilmarnock Athletic v Beith	2-1
Cartvale v Clyde	5-4
Rangers v South Western	†6-4
Dumbarton v Hibernian	†4-1

†after a protested game

SIXTH ROUND
Queen's Park v Shotts	15-0
Kilmarnock Athletic v Arthurlie	5-2
Dumbarton v Rangers	†5-1
Cartvale v West Calder	5-3

†after a protested game

SEMI-FINAL
Queen's Park v Kilmarnock Athletic	3-2
Dumbarton v Cartvale	11-2

FINAL AT CATHKIN PARK
Queen's Park v Dumbarton	2-2, 4-1

SCOTTISH FA CUP 1882-83

FOURTH ROUND
Hurlford v Vale of Teith	3-2
Hibernian v Thistle	2-2, 4-1
Arthurlie v Queen of the South Wanderers	3-1
Dumbarton v Thornliebank	3-0
Queen's Park v Cambuslang	5-0
Lugar Boswell v Renton	5-3
Third Lanark v Dunblane	7-1
Kilmarnock Athletic v Abercorn	5-2
Pollockshields Athletic v Johnstone	3-1
Vale of Leven v Edinburgh University	2-0
Partick Thistle v Glasgow University (scratched)	wo

FIFTH ROUND
Vale of Leven v Lugar Boswell	0-0, 5-1
Queen's Park v Hurlford	7-2
Arthurlie v Hibernian	†6-0
Third Lanark	bye
Dumbarton	bye
Kilmarnock Athletic	bye
Partick Thistle	bye
Pollockshields Athletic	bye

†after a protested game

SIXTH ROUND
Vale of Leven v Partick Thistle	4-0
Pollockshields Athletic v Third Lanark	1-1, 5-2
Dumbarton v Queen's Park	3-1
Kilmarnock Athletic v Arthurlie	***1-0

***after three drawn games

SEMI-FINAL
Vale of Leven v Kilmarnock Athletic	1-1, 2-0
Dumbarton v Pollockshields Athletic	0-0, 1-0

*after a drawn game

FINAL AT HAMPDEN PARK
Dumbarton v Vale of Leven	2-2, 2-1

FA CUP 1882-83

SECOND ROUND
Blackburn Olympic v Lower Darwen	9-1
Darwen Ramblers v Haslingden	3-2
Darwen v Blackburn Rovers	1-0
Druids v Northwich Victoria	5-0
Bolton Wanderers v Liverpool Ramblers	3-0
Eagley v Halliwell	3-1
Old Carthusians v Etonian Ramblers	7-0
Royal Engineers v Reading	8-0
Clapham Rovers v Hanover United	7-1
Windsor v United Hospitals	3-1
Old Etonians v Brentwood	2-1
Swifts v Upton Park	*3-2
Hendon v Chatham	2-1
Great Marlow v Reading Minster (scratched)	wo
Phoenix Bessemer v Grimsby	8-1
The Wednesday v Lockwood Brothers	6-0
Nottingham Forest v Heeley	7-2
Aston Villa v Wednesbury Old Alliance	4-1
Aston Unity v Mitchell's St George's	3-0
Walsall Town v Stafford Road Works	4-1
Church	bye
Old Westminsters	bye
Rochester	bye
South Reading	bye
Notts County	bye

*drawn game for which no score is available

THIRD ROUND
Blackburn Olympic v Darwen Ramblers	8-0
Church v Darwen	*2-0
Druids v Bolton Wanderers	**1-0
Old Carthusians v Old Westminsters	3-2
Clapham Rovers v Windsor	3-0
Old Etonians v Rochester	7-0
Hendon v South Reading	11-1
Notts County v Phoenix Bessemer	*3-2
The Wednesday v Nottingham Forest	*3-2
Aston Villa v Aston Unity	3-1
Eagley	bye
Royal Engineers	bye
Swifts	bye
Great Marlow	bye
Walsall Town	bye

*drawn game for which no score is available
**two drawn games for which no scores are available

FOURTH ROUND
Blackburn Olympic v Church	2-0
Druids v Eagley	2-1
Old Carthusians v Royal Engineers	6-2
Old Etonians v Swifts	2-0
Hendon v Great Marlow	3-0
Notts County v The Wednesday	4-1
Aston Villa v Walsall Town	2-1
Clapham Rovers	bye

FIFTH ROUND
Blackburn Olympic v Druids	4-0
Old Carthusians v Clapham Rovers	5-3
Old Etonians v Hendon	4-2
Notts County v Aston Villa	4-3

SEMI-FINAL
Blackburn Olympic v Old Carthusians	4-0
Old Etonians v Notts County	2-1

FINAL AT KENNINGTON OVAL
Blackburn Olympic v Old Etonians	2-1

Blackburn Olympic, the first winners of the Cup to come from the North of England, and the first overtly professional winners, are perhaps the least known of all successful Cup Finalists. Their star rose suddenly and declined just as quickly. After reaching the semi-final the following season they were never heard of again. Olympic even had a manager, one Jack Hunter, whose earlier career had been with a travelling circus. He took his team away to Blackpool before the Final. Of his players, two were weavers, one a spinner, one a plumber, one a metal worker and two were unemployed other than football. A far cry from Old Etonians, last of the English amateur finalists.

169

WEST BROMWICH

Albion Football Club.

SEASON TICKET.

1883-1884.

To Admit to all Matches on the

FOUR ACRES,

SITUATE IN SEAGAR STREET.

PRICE :—THREE SHILLINGS.

Above *A West Bromwich Albion season ticket for 1883-84. For one third of the price of admission to the popular side for a single game in 1974, the Throstles fan could watch a whole season's football in the Midlands.*

Top *The first Blackburn Rovers side to win the FA Cup in 1884. Their opponents were the Scots side Queen's Park. If the latter had won they would have completed a remarkable double, for they had already won the Scottish Cup. In fact they returned to Glasgow extremely bitter at the game's refereeing. Under Scottish rules at the time the offside law only required two defenders between the ball and the goal, but English law required three. Queen's scored two goals that would have been allowed in Scotland and felt thoroughly deprived. They were also upset that Blackburn had four full-time professionals, payment of players still being illegal in Scotland.*

When Blackburn Rovers reached The Oval for the Cup Final in 1882 they had gone 35 consecutive games without defeat, then recognised to be the longest run of first-class

---

FA CUP 1883-84

THIRD ROUND

Blackburn Rovers v Padiham	3-0
Staveley v Lockwood Brothers	1-0
Upton Park v Reading	6-1
Eagley v Preston North End	1-9
Swifts v Clapham Rovers	2-1
Notts County v Grantham	4-1
Bolton Wanderers v Irwell Springs	8-1
Queen's Park v Oswestry	7-1
Aston Villa v Wednesbury Old Alliance	7-4
Wednesbury Town v Derby Midland	1-0
Romford v Brentwood	1-4
Old Foresters	bye
Old Westminsters	bye
Blackburn Olympic	bye
Old Wykehamists	bye
Northwich Victoria	bye

FOURTH ROUND

Blackburn Rovers v Staveley	5-0
Upton Park v Preston North End	1-1, wo*
Swifts v Old Foresters	2-1
Notts County v Bolton Wanderers	2-2, 2-1
Queen's Park v Aston Villa	6-1
Old Westminsters v Wednesbury Town	5-1
Blackburn Olympic v Old Wykehamists	9-1
Brentwood v Northwich Victoria	1-3

*Upton Park protested that Preston paid their players. The FA upheld the protest and disqualified Preston before the replay.

FIFTH ROUND

Blackburn Rovers v Upton Park	3-0
Swifts v Notts County	1-1, 0-1
Queen's Park v Old Westminsters	1-0
Blackburn Olympic v Northwich Victoria	9-1

SEMI-FINAL

Blackburn Rovers v Notts County	1-0
Queen's Park v Blackburn Olympic	4-1

FINAL AT KENNINGTON OVAL

Blackburn Rovers v Queen's Park	2-1

SCOTTISH FA CUP 1883-84

FOURTH ROUND

Mauchline v Royal Albert	4-0
St Bernard's v Thornliebank	2-0
Vale of Leven v Harp	6-0
Pollockshields Athletic v Our Boys	11-0
Dunblane v Rangers	0-6
Kilmarnock Athletic v Cambuslang	2-3
5th KRV v Hibernian	1-8
Partick Thistle v Queen's Park	0-4
Cartvale v Abercorn	4-2
Battlefield v Edinburgh University (scratched)	wo
Arthurlie	bye

FIFTH ROUND

Arthurlie v Vale of Leven	0-0, 1-3
Mauchline v Pollockshields Athletic	2-3
St Bernard's v Rangers	0-3
Queen's Park	bye
Battlefield	bye
Hibernian	bye
Cambuslang	bye
Cartvale	bye

SIXTH ROUND

Cambuslang v Rangers	2-5
Queen's Park v Cartvale	6-1
Vale of Leven v Pollockshields Athletic	4-2
Hibernian v Battlefield	6-1

SEMI-FINAL

Vale of Leven v Rangers	3-0
Hibernian v Queen's Park	1-5

FINAL

Cup awarded to Queen's Park	†

†Vale of Leven wanted to postpone the final because of the illness of two players and the family bereavement of another. But the FA, although sympathetic, decided that was impossible due to other engagements, such as the international against England. Vale did not turn up for the final and the Cup was awarded to Queen's Park.

---

fixtures without setback in English football. Since Darwen defeated them in the first round of the 1880-81 competition. Rovers had won 31 games and drawn four. One of

those victories was against mighty Preston North End in the latter's first ever professional game. Blackburn won reasonably convincingly, 16-0.

FA CUP 1884-85

THIRD ROUND
Blackburn Rovers v Witton	6-1
West Bromwich Albion v Aston Villa	††3-0
Druids v Chirk	4-1
Grimsby Town v Lincoln City	1-0
Chatham v Hanover United	2-0
Lower Darwen v Darwen Old Wanderers	4-2
Church v Southport	10-0
Queen's Park v Leek	3-2
Old Wykehamists v Upton Park	2-1
Notts County v Sheffield	9-0
Walsall Swifts v Mitchell's St George's	3-2
Nottingham Forest v The Wednesday	2-1
Swifts v Old Westminsters	2-1
Romford	bye
Old Carthusians	bye
Darwen	bye
Old Etonians	bye
Middlesbrough	bye

††Two drawn games (scores unavailable)

FOURTH ROUND
Blackburn Rovers v Romford	8-0
West Bromwich Albion v Druids	1-0*
Old Carthusians v Grimsby Town	3-0
Chatham v Lower Darwen	1-0
Church v Darwen	3-0
Queen's Park v Old Wykehamists	7-0
Notts County v Walsall Swifts	4-1
Nottingham Forest v Swifts	1-0
Old Etonians v Middlesbrough	5-2

*Druids arrived with only ten men and refused to take the field. West Bromwich therefore scored within five seconds of the kick-off, whereupon Druids decided to take part. This 'goal' is not normally recorded and West Bromwich scored again to 'officially' win 1-0

FIFTH ROUND
Old Carthusians v Chatham	3-0
Blackburn Rovers	bye
West Bromwich Albion	bye
Church	bye
Queen's Park	bye
Notts County	bye
Nottingham Forest	bye
Old Etonians	bye

SIXTH ROUND
Blackburn Rovers v West Bromwich Albion	2-0
Old Carthusians v Church	1-0
Queen's Park v Notts County	2-2, 2-1
Nottingham Forest v Old Etonians	2-0

SEMI-FINAL
Blackburn Rovers v Old Carthusians	5-0
Queen's Park v Nottingham Forest	1-1, 3-0

FINAL AT KENNINGTON OVAL
Blackburn Rovers v Queen's Park	2-0

Blackburn Rovers defeated Queen's Park in both the 1884 and 1885 FA Cup Finals. These remain the only occasions on which the same clubs have contested consecutive Finals. Queen's Park were also the last amateur club to appear in an English Cup Final.

On the way to the 1885 Cup Final Queen's Park defeated both the Nottingham clubs, then considered second only to Blackburn, after a replay. The second semi-final against Nottingham Forest is the only semi-final ever to be played outside England. It was staged at Merchiston Castle School in Edinburgh and it helped Forest set up their remarkable record of having been drawn to play Cup ties in all four home countries. In the first round of the 1888-89 competition they were drawn to play Linfield in Belfast. In fact by the time they arrived Linfield had withdrawn so the game became a friendly instead. No Scottish club ever reached the final again and three years later, the Scottish Football Association banned its members from entering competitions other than its own.

SCOTTISH FA CUP 1884-85

FOURTH ROUND
Hibernian v Ayr	5-1
Morton v Wishaw Swifts	2-1
Vale of Leven v Arthurlie	2-1
Annbank v Queen of the South Wanderers	5-2
Battlefield v Pollockshields Athletic	3-0
Our Boys v West Benhar	3-3, 3-8
Renton v St Mirren	2-1
Rangers v Arbroath	3-4†, 8-1
Dumbarton v Partick Thistle	6-3
Cambuslang v Thornliebank	2-2, 0-0*

†Rangers protested the result and the SFA ordered a replay
*Both teams went through to the next round

FIFTH ROUND
Hibernian v Morton	4-0
Cambuslang v Dumbarton	4-1
Annbank v West Benhar	5-1
Rangers	bye
Renton	bye
Battlefield	bye
Vale of Leven	bye
Thornliebank	bye

SIXTH ROUND
Hibernian v Annbank	5-0
Vale of Leven v Thornliebank	4-3
Renton v Rangers	5-3
Cambuslang v Battlefield	3-1

SEMI-FINAL
Renton v Hibernian	3-2
Vale of Leven v Cambuslang	0-0, 3-1

FINAL AT HAMPDEN PARK
Renton v Vale of Leven	0-0, 3-1

SCOTTISH FA CUP 1885-86

FOURTH ROUND
Dumbarton v Partick Thistle	3-0
Queen of the South Wanderers v Arthurlie	†
Cambuslang v Wishaw Swifts	9-0
Hibernian v Arbroath	5-3
Renton v Cowlairs	4-0
Queen's Park v Airdrieonians	1-0
Third Lanark v Ayr	3-2*, 3-3, 5-1
Abercorn v Strathmore	7-2
Vale of Leven v Harp	6-0
Port Glasgow Athletic	bye

* replayed after Ayr protested
† Arthurlie won the tie. There is no record of the score

FIFTH ROUND
Renton v Vale of Leven	2-2, 3-0
Third Lanark v Port Glasgow Athletic	1-1, 1-1, 4-1
Arthurlie v Queen's Park	1-2
Abercorn v Cambuslang	0-1
Dumbarton v Hibernian	2-2, 3-4

SIXTH ROUND
Hibernian v Cambuslang	3-2
Third Lanark	bye
Renton	bye
Queen's Park	bye

SEMI-FINAL
Hibernian v Renton	0-2
Third Lanark v Queen's Park	0-3

FINAL AT CATHKIN PARK
Queen's Park v Renton	3-1

Rangers were drawn to play Arbroath in the Fourth Round of the 1884-85 Scottish Cup. Having lost 4-3 they sent home a telegram reading 'beaten on a back green'. Having measured the pitch they found it was only 49 yards 2 ft 1 in wide, 11 inches short of the minimum. They protested, the game was replayed, and Rangers won 8-1.

FA CUP 1885-86

THIRD ROUND
Blackburn Rovers v Darwen Old Wanderers	6-1
Staveley v Nottingham Forest	2-1
South Reading v Clapham Rovers*	wo
Burslem Port Vale v Leek (scratched)	wo
Swifts v Old Harrovians*	wo
Church v Rossendale	5-1
South Shore v Halliwell	6-1
Notts County v Notts Rangers	3-0
Wolverhampton Wanderers v Walsall Swifts	5-1
Old Westminsters v Romford	5-1
Preston North End* v Bolton Wanderers	3-2‡
Small Heath Alliance v Derby County	4-2
Davenham v Crewe Alexandra	2-1
Middlesbrough v Grimsby Town	2-1
Brentwood	bye
West Bromwich Albion	bye
Old Carthusians	bye
Redcar	bye

*disqualified
‡Preston disqualified after a protest

FOURTH ROUND
West Bromwich Albion v Wolverhampton Wanderers	3-1
Brentwood v South Reading	3-0
Blackburn Rovers	bye
Staveley	bye
Burslem Port Vale	bye
Swifts	bye
Church	bye
South Shore	bye
Notts County	bye
Old Carthusians	bye
Old Westminsters	bye
Bolton Wanderers	bye
Small Heath Alliance	bye
Davenham	bye
Redcar	bye
Middlesbrough	bye

FIFTH ROUND
Blackburn Rovers v Staveley	7-1
Brentwood v Burslem Port Vale †	wo
Swifts v Church	6-2
South Shore v Notts County	2-1
West Bromwich Albion v Old Carthusians	1-0
Old Westminsters v Bolton Wanderers*	wo
Small Heath Alliance v Davenham	2-1
Redcar v Middlesbrough	2-1

*disqualified
†Burslem Port Vale scratched after one drawn game

SIXTH ROUND
Blackburn Rovers v Brentwood	3-1
Swifts v South Shore	2-1
West Bromwich Albion v Old Westminsters	6-0
Small Heath Alliance v Redcar	2-0

SEMI-FINAL
Blackburn Rovers v Swifts	2-1
West Bromwich Albion v Small Heath Alliance	4-0

FINAL AT KENNINGTON OVAL
Blackburn Rovers v West Bromwich Albion	0-0, 2-0*

*replay at The Racecourse, Derby

The 1886 Cup Final replay, played at The Racecourse, Derby, was the first Final ever played outside London. In winning the game Blackburn Rovers completed a hat-trick of successes never since repeated and were presented with a special shield — which still hangs in their boardroom — to mark the feat. The match is far more famous however, for the performance of the Blackburn captain Jimmy Brown. In his last ever game for the club, Brown dribbled the length of the pitch to score one of the greatest goals in the history of the Cup. In so doing he became the only man ever to score in three consecutive Cup Finals, and, more surprisingly, was immortalized in Arnold Bennett's 'The Card' for the feat.

171

FA CUP 1886-87†

THIRD ROUND
Aston Villa v Wolverhampton Wanderers	
	2-2, 3-3, 2-0
Horncastle v Grantham	2-0
Darwen v Bolton Wanderers	4-3
Chirk v Goldenhill (disqualified)	wo
Glasgow Rangers v Cowlairs	3-2
Lincoln City v Gainsborough Trinity	2-2, 1-0
Old Westminsters v Old Etonians	3-0
Partick Thistle v Cliftonville	11-1
Mitchell's St George's v Walsall Town	7-2
Lockwood Brothers v Nottingham Forest	2-1
Notts County v Staveley	3-0
Great Marlow v Dulwich	2-0
Preston North End v Renton	2-0
Old Foresters v Chatham	4-1
Old Carthusians v Caledonians (absent)	wo
Leek v Burslem Port Vale	2-2, 1-1, 3-1
Crewe Alexandra	bye
Swifts	bye
West Bromwich Albion	bye

FOURTH ROUND
Leek v Crewe Alexandra	1-0
Old Foresters v Swifts	2-0
West Bromwich Albion v Mitchell's St George's	1-0
Aston Villa	bye
Horncastle	bye
Darwen	bye
Chirk	bye
Glasgow Rangers	bye
Lincoln City	bye
Old Westminsters	bye
Partick Thistle	bye
Lockwood Brothers	bye
Notts County	bye
Great Marlow	bye
Preston North End	bye
Old Carthusians	bye

FIFTH ROUND
Aston Villa v Horncastle	5-0
Darwen v Chirk	3-1
Glasgow Rangers v Lincoln City	3-0
Old Westminsters v Partick Thistle	1-0
West Bromwich Albion v Lockwood Brothers	2-1*
Notts County v Great Marlow	5-2
Preston North End v Old Foresters	3-0
Old Carthusians v Leek	2-0
*after a disputed game	

SIXTH ROUND
Aston Villa v Darwen	3-2
Glasgow Rangers v Old Westminsters	5-1
West Bromwich Albion v Notts County	4-1
Preston North End v Old Carthusians	2-1

SEMI-FINAL
Aston Villa v Glasgow Rangers	3-1
West Bromwich Albion v Preston North End	3-1

FINAL AT KENNINGTON OVAL
Aston Villa v West Bromwich Albion	2-0

†There is some confusion as to the exact specification of the rounds. The *Football Annual for 1887*, edited by the honorary secretary of the Football Association, Charles Alcock, gives seven rounds and a Final. Later historys, such as the official *History of the Cup* give only three rounds and a Final after qualifying matches.

Hibernian's defeat of Dumbarton in the 1887 Scottish Cup final was the first time that an Edinburgh club had won the Scottish Cup. It was also the first and only time that the final was contested at Crosshills. The same year Hibs played and defeated Preston North End at their new ground, Easter Road, in what was billed as the 'Association Football Championship of the World' More remotely Hibernian's success was one of the main promptings for the founding of Celtic in Glasgow.

SCOTTISH FA CUP 1886-87

FIFTH ROUND
Hibernian v Queen of the South Wanderers	7-3
Vale of Leven v Cambuslang Hibernians	2-0
Clyde v Third Lanark	0-0, 2-4
Queen's Park v Cambuslang	1-1, 5-4
Hurlford v Morton	5-1
Kilmarnock v Dunblane	6-0
Port Glasgow Athletic v St Bernard's	6-2
Dumbarton v Harp (scratched)	wo

SIXTH ROUND
Port Glasgow Athletic v Vale of Leven	1-3
Kilmarnock v Queen's Park	0-5
Third Lanark v Hibernian	1-2
Hurlford v Dumbarton	0-0, 2-1*, 1-3
*Hurlford insisted on playing on a frozen pitch; the result was declared null and void by the Scottish FA	

SEMI-FINAL
Hibernian v Vale of Leven	3-1
Queen's Park v Dumbarton	1-2

FINAL AT CROSSHILLS
Hibernian v Dumbarton	2-1

Below The West Bromwich Albion side that won the FA Cup in 1888. It was their third consecutive Final but their first ever success. Billy Bassett is seated, second from the left. After defeating Preston North End at Trent Bridge in the 1887 semi-final, West Bromwich met them again in the actual Final in 1888. To say that Preston were confident is to put it mildly. One of their modest requests was that they might be photographed with the Cup before the game. They explained that they would be dirty afterwards and that this would spoil the picture. The referee, Major Marindin, who controlled eight Finals in all as well as playing in two, suggested that 'Had you not better win it first?' Apparently they had ten good scoring chances to Albion's two, but Albion converted 100% and Preston only 10%. It was called the greatest upset in the history of the Cup, and perhaps remained so until Sunderland defeated Leeds. West Bromwich's inspiration was 5ft 5in Billy Bassett, who went on to win eight consecutive caps against the Scots. Albion went on to beat Aston Villa in a series of three games to become the 'Champions of the Midlands'. Then then went to Scotland to play Scottish Cup winners Renton for the title of 'Champions of the World'. The game was played in a blinding snowstorm and Renton won.

FA CUP 1887-88†

FIFTH ROUND
West Bromwich Albion v Stoke	4-1
Old Carthusians v Bootle	2-0
Derby Junction v Chirk	1-0
Darwen v Blackburn Rovers	0-3
Nottingham Forest v The Wednesday	2-4
Aston Villa v Preston North End	1-3
Middlesbrough v Old Foresters (scratched)	4-0*
Crewe Alexandra v Derby County	1-0

*Old Foresters protested at the state of the pitch and the FA ordered a replay. Meanwhile, Old Foresters scratched and Middlesbrough thus went through without a second game

SIXTH ROUND
West Bromwich Albion v Old Carthusians	4-2
Derby Junction v Blackburn Rovers	2-1
The Wednesday v Preston North End	1-3
Middlesbrough v Crewe Alexandra	0-2

SEMI-FINAL
West Bromwich Albion v Derby Junction	3-0
Preston North End v Crewe Alexandra	4-0

FINAL AT KENNINGTON OVAL
West Bromwich Albion v Preston North End	2-1

†There is confusion about the exact specification of the rounds. The *Football Annual for 1888* gives seven rounds and a Final, as do newspapers for that year.

SCOTTISH FA CUP 1887-88

FIFTH ROUND
Arbroath v Cowlairs	5-1
Cambuslang v Ayr	10-0
Thistle v Vale of Leven Wanderers	2-9
Abercorn v St Bernard's	9-0
Queen's Park v Partick Thistle	2-0
St Mirren v Renton	2-3
Our Boys v Albion Rovers	4-1
Dundee Wanderers v Carfin Shamrock	5-2

SIXTH ROUND
Abercorn v Arbroath	3-1
Renton v Dundee Wanderers	5-1
Cambuslang v Our Boys	6-0
Queen's Park v Vale of Leven Wanderers	7-1

SEMI-FINAL
Renton v Queen's Park	3-1
Abercorn v Cambuslang	1-1, 1-10

FINAL AT HAMPDEN PARK
Renton v Cambuslang	6-1

FA CUP 1888-89

FIRST ROUND
Grimsby Town v Sunderland Albion	3-1
Bootle v Preston North End	0-3
Halliwell v Crewe Alexandra	2-2, 5-1
Birmingham St George's v Long Eaton Rangers	3-2
Chatham v South Shore	2-1
Nottingham Forest v Linfield (scratched)	2-2, wo*
Small Heath v West Bromwich Albion	2-3
Burnley v Old Westminsters	4-3
Wolverhampton Wanderers v Old Carthusians	4-3
Walsall Town Swifts v Sheffield Heeley	5-1
The Wednesday v Notts Rangers	1-1, 3-0
Notts County v Old Brightonians	2-0
Blackburn Rovers v Accrington	1-1, 5-0
Swifts v Wrexham	3-1
Aston Villa v Witton	3-2
Derby County v Derby Junction	1-0

*Nottingham Forest travelled to Belfast for the replay but Linfield had scratched in the interim and the clubs played a friendly instead

SECOND ROUND
Grimsby Town v Preston North End	0-2
Halliwell v Birmingham St George's	2-3
Chatham v Nottingham Forest	1-1, 2-2, 3-2
West Bromwich Albion v Burnley	5-1
Wolverhampton Wanderers v Walsall Town Swifts	6-1
The Wednesday v Notts County	3-2
Blackburn Rovers v Swifts (scratched)	wo
Aston Villa v Derby County	5-3

THIRD ROUND
Preston North End v Birmingham St George's	2-0
Chatham v West Bromwich Albion	1-10
Wolverhampton Wanderers v The Wednesday	5-0
Blackburn Rovers v Aston Villa	8-1

SEMI-FINAL
Preston North End v West Bromwich Albion	1-0
Wolverhampton Wanderers v Blackburn Rovers	1-1, 3-1

FINAL AT KENNINGTON OVAL
Preston North End v Wolverhampton Wanderers	3-0

SCOTTISH FA CUP 1888-89

FIFTH ROUND
Third Lanark v Abercorn	5-4*, 2-2, 2-2, 3-1
Renton v Arbroath	3-3, 4-0
Celtic v Clyde	0-1†, 9-2
Dumbarton v Mossend Swifts	3-1
St Mirren v Queen of the South Wanderers	3-1
Campsie	bye
Dumbarton Athletic	bye
East Stirlingshire	bye

*Abercorn protested about bad light
†Celtic protested about bad light and the state of the pitch

SIXTH ROUND
Third Lanark v Campsie	6-1
Dumbarton v St Mirren	2-2, 2-2, 3-1
Dumbarton Athletic v Renton	1-2
East Stirlingshire v Celtic	1-2

SEMI-FINAL
Dumbarton v Celtic	1-4
Third Lanark v Renton	2-0

FINAL AT HAMPDEN PARK
Third Lanark v Celtic	3-0‡, 2-1

‡The first game was declared unofficial because of a snowstorm. Third Lanark tried to claim the Cup but the SFA ordered a replay.

William Townley scored the first ever Cup Final hat-trick for Blackburn against The Wednesday in the 1890 Final. Rovers won 6-1 to record the highest score in a Final tie. Wednesday arrived for the Final having lost a disputed earlier tie against Notts County.

FOOTBALL LEAGUE 1888-89
		P	W	D	L	F	A	Pts
1	Preston	22	18	4	0	74	15	40
2	Aston Villa	22	12	5	5	61	43	29
3	Wolves	22	12	4	6	50	37	28
4	Blackburn	22	10	6	6	66	45	26
5	Bolton	22	10	2	10	63	59	22
6	WBA	22	10	2	10	40	46	22
7	Accrington	22	6	8	8	48	48	20
8	Everton	22	9	2	11	35	46	20
9	Burnley	22	7	3	12	42	62	17
10	Derby	22	7	2	13	41	60	16
11	Notts County	22	5	2	15	39	73	12
12	Stoke	22	4	4	14	26	51	12

Top William McGregor of Aston Villa, whose open letter of 2 March 1888 led to the formation of the Football League. A meeting was held at Anderton's Hotel on the eve of the Cup Final (23 March 1888) and the idea was approved in principle. The details were finalized on 17 April at the Royal Hotel in Manchester by the twelve member clubs. With only 22 fixture dates available, other hopefuls—including Sheffield Wednesday and Nottingham Forest—had to be turned down. The League had grown in simple response to the need to guarantee fixtures. While there were only Cup competitions fixtures would always be called off at short notice for replays, and friendlies could never be guaranteed. Because of the uncertainty, spectators were increasingly reluctant to commit themselves to turning up to a match that might never be played—and so emerged McGregor's inevitable solution. Preston were the first winners of the League. Their performance in 1888-89 was unique for they remain the only side in England and Scotland to have gone a whole season without a League or or Cup defeat.

FOOTBALL LEAGUE 1889-90
		P	W	D	L	F	A	Pts
1	Preston	22	15	3	4	71	30	33
2	Everton	22	14	3	5	65	40	31
3	Blackburn	22	12	3	7	78	41	27
4	Wolves	22	10	5	7	51	38	25
5	WBA	22	11	3	8	47	50	25
6	Accrington	22	9	6	7	53	56	24
7	Derby	22	9	3	10	43	55	21
8	Aston Villa	22	7	5	10	43	51	19
9	Bolton	22	9	1	12	54	65	19
10	Notts County	22	6	5	11	43	51	17
11	Burnley	22	4	5	13	36	65	13
12	Stoke	22	3	4	15	27	69	10

FA CUP 1889-90

FIRST ROUND
Preston North End v Newton Heath	6-1
Lincoln City v Chester	2-0
Bolton Wanderers v Belfast Distillery	10-1
Sheffield United v Burnley	2-1
The Wednesday v Swifts	6-1
Accrington v West Bromwich Albion	3-1
Notts County v Birmingham St George's	4-4, 6-2
South Shore v Aston Villa	2-4
Bootle v Sunderland Albion*	1-3
Derby Midland v Nottingham Forest	3-0
Blackburn Rovers v Sunderland	4-2
Newcastle West End v Grimsby Town	1-2
Wolverhampton Wanderers v Old Carthusians	2-0
Small Heath v Clapton	3-1
Stoke v Old Westminsters	3-0
Everton v Derby County	11-2

*Sunderland Albion were disqualified

SECOND ROUND
Preston North End v Lincoln City	4-0
Bolton Wanderers v Sheffield United	13-0
The Wednesday v Accrington	2-1
Notts County v Aston Villa	4-1
Bootle v Derby Midland	2-1
Blackburn Rovers v Grimsby Town	3-0
Wolverhampton Wanderers v Small Heath	2-1
Stoke v Everton	4-2

THIRD ROUND
Preston North End v Bolton Wanderers	2-3
The Wednesday v Notts County	5-0*, 2-3*, 2-1
Bootle v Blackburn Rovers	0-7
Wolverhampton Wanderers v Stoke	3-2

*replayed after protest on both occasions

SEMI-FINAL
Bolton Wanderers v The Wednesday	1-2
Blackburn Rovers v Wolverhampton Wanderers	1-0

FINAL AT KENNINGTON OVAL
Blackburn Rovers v The Wednesday	6-1

SCOTTISH FA CUP 1889-90

FOURTH ROUND
Aberdeen v Queen's Park	1-13
Airdrieonians v Abercorn	2-3
Grangemouth v Vale of Leven	1-7
Third Lanark v Linthouse	2-0
Lanemark v St Mirren	2-8
Moffat v Carfin Shamrock	4-2
Ayr v Leith Athletic	1-1, 1-4
Cowdenbeath v Dunblane	6-4
Hibernian v Queen of the South Wanderers	7-3
Kilbirnie v East Stirlingshire	5-2
Heart of Midlothian v Alloa Athletic	9-1
East End v Cambuslang	3-2,* 3-2

*Protested

FIFTH ROUND
Queen's Park v St Mirren	1-0
Cowdenbeath v Abercorn	2-8
Vale of Leven v Heart of Midlothian	3-1
East End v Moffat	2-2, 5-1
Third Lanark	bye
Hibernian	bye
Leith Athletic	bye
Kilbirnie	bye

*East End won the replay

SIXTH ROUND
Queen's Park v Leith Athletic	1-0
Abercorn v Hibernian	6-2
Vale of Leven v East End	4-0
Third Lanark v Kilbirnie	4-1

SEMI-FINAL
Vale of Leven v Third Lanark	3-0
Queen's Park v Abercorn	2-0

FINAL AT IBROX PARK
Queen's Park v Vale of Leven	1-1, 2-1

FA CUP 1890-91

FIRST ROUND
Middlesbrough Ironopolis v Blackburn Rovers	1-2*, 0-3
Chester v Lincoln City	1-0
Accrington v Bolton Wanderers	2-2, 5-1
Long Eaton Rangers v Wolverhampton Wanderers	2-3
Royal Arsenal v Derby County	1-2
The Wednesday v Halliwell	12-0
Crusaders v Birmingham St George's	0-2
West Bromwich Albion v Old Westminsters (scratched)	wo
Darwen v Kidderminster	3-1*, 13-0
Sunderland v Everton	1-0
Clapton v Nottingham Forest	0-14
Sunderland Albion v 93rd Highlanders	2-0
Sheffield United v Notts County	1-9
Burnley v Crewe Alexandra	4-2
Stoke v Preston North End	3-0
Aston Villa v Casuals	13-1

*replayed after protest

SECOND ROUND
Blackburn Rovers v Chester	7-0
Accrington v Wolverhampton Wanderers	2-3
Derby County v The Wednesday	2-3
Birmingham St George's v West Bromwich Albion	0-3
Darwen v Sunderland	0-2
Nottingham Forest v Sunderland Albion	1-1, 0-0, 5-0
Notts County v Burnley	2-1
Stoke v Aston Villa	3-0

THIRD ROUND
Blackburn Rovers v Wolverhampton Wanderers	2-0
The Wednesday v West Bromwich Albion	0-2
Sunderland v Nottingham Forest	4-0
Notts County v Stoke	1-0

SEMI-FINAL
Blackburn Rovers v West Bromwich Albion	3-2
Sunderland v Notts County	3-3, 0-2

FINAL AT KENNINGTON OVAL
Blackburn Rovers v Notts County	3-1

SCOTTISH FA CUP 1890-91

FIFTH ROUND
Dumbarton v 5th KRV	8-0
Heart of Midlothian v Morton	5-1
Royal Albert v Celtic	0-4*, 0-2
St Mirren v Queen's Park	2-3
Abercorn	bye
Third Lanark	bye
East Stirlingshire	bye
Leith Athletic	bye

*Crowd invaded the pitch 10 minutes before time and forced a replay, which was played at Ibrox.

SIXTH ROUND
Dumbarton v Celtic	3-0
Heart of Midlothian v East Stirlingshire	3-1
Third Lanark v Queen's Park	1-1, 2-2, 4-1
Leith Athletic v Abercorn	2-3

SEMI-FINAL
Dumbarton v Abercorn	3-1
Heart of Midlothian v Third Lanark	4-1

FINAL AT HAMPDEN PARK
Heart of Midlothian v Dumbarton	1-0

FOOTBALL LEAGUE 1890-91

		P	W	D	L	F	A	Pts
1	Everton	22	14	1	7	63	29	29
2	Preston	22	12	3	7	44	23	27
3	Notts County	22	11	4	7	52	35	26
4	Wolves	22	12	2	8	39	50	26
5	Bolton	22	12	1	9	47	34	25
6	Blackburn	22	11	2	9	52	43	24
7	Sunderland	22	10	5	7	51	31	23*
8	Burnley	22	9	3	10	52	63	21
9	Aston Villa	22	7	4	11	45	58	18
10	Accrington	22	6	4	12	28	50	16
11	Derby	22	7	1	14	47	81	15
12	WBA	22	5	2	15	34	57	12

*Two points deducted for fielding Ned Doig against WBA on 20 September 1890 before the League had approved his registration from Arbroath.

SCOTTISH LEAGUE 1890-91

		P	W	D	L	F	A	Pts
1=	Dumbarton†	18	13	3	2	61	21	29
1=	Rangers†	18	13	3	2	58	25	29
3	Celtic*	18	11	3	4	48	21	21
4	Cambuslang	18	8	4	6	47	42	20
5	Third Lanark*	18	8	3	7	38	39	15
6	Hearts	18	6	2	10	31	37	14
7	Abercorn	18	5	2	11	36	47	12
8	St Mirren	18	5	1	12	39	62	11
9	Vale of Leven	18	5	1	12	27	65	11
10	Cowlairs*	18	3	4	11	24	50	6

†Dumbarton and Rangers drew 2-2 in a play-off and were declared joint Champions.
*Each had four points deducted for infringements.

FOOTBALL LEAGUE 1891-92

		P	W	D	L	F	A	Pts
1	Sunderland	26	21	0	5	93	36	42
2	Preston	26	18	1	7	61	31	37
3	Bolton	26	17	2	7	51	37	36
4	Aston Villa	26	15	0	11	89	56	30
5	Everton	26	12	4	10	49	49	28
6	Wolves	26	11	4	11	59	46	26
7	Burnley	26	11	4	11	49	45	26
8	Notts County	26	11	4	11	55	51	26
9	Blackburn	26	10	6	10	58	65	26
10	Derby	26	10	4	12	46	52	24
11	Accrington	26	8	4	14	40	78	20
12	WBA	26	6	6	14	51	58	18
13	Stoke	26	5	4	17	38	61	14
14	Darwen	26	4	3	19	38	112	11

SCOTTISH LEAGUE 1891-92

		P	W	D	L	F	A	Pts
1	Dumbarton	22	18	1	3	79	28	37
2	Celtic	22	16	3	3	62	22	35
3	Hearts	22	15	4	3	65	35	34
4	Leith	22	12	1	9	51	41	25
5	Rangers	22	11	2	9	59	46	24
6	Third Lanark	22	9	4	9	44	47	22
7	Renton	22	8	5	10	38	44	21
8	Clyde	22	8	4	10	63	62	20
9	Abercorn	22	6	5	11	47	59	17
10	St Mirren	22	4	5	13	43	60	13
11	Cambuslang	22	2	6	14	22	53	10
12	Vale of Leven	22	0	5	17	24	100	5

FA CUP 1891-92

FIRST ROUND
Old Westminsters v West Bromwich Albion	2-3
Blackburn Rovers v Derby County	4-1
The Wednesday v Bolton Wanderers	4-1
Small Heath v Royal Arsenal	5-1
Sunderland Albion v Birmingham St George's	4-0
Nottingham Forest v Newcastle East End	2-1
Luton v Middlesbrough	0-3
Preston North End v Middlesbrough Ironopolis	2-2, 6-0
Crewe Alexandra v Wolverhampton Wanderers	2-2, 1-4
Blackpool v Sheffield United	0-3
Aston Villa v Heanor Town	4-1
Bootle v Darwen	0-2
Crusaders v Accrington	1-4
Sunderland v Notts County	4-0
Everton v Burnley	1-3
Stoke v Casuals	3-0

SECOND ROUND
West Bromwich Albion v Blackburn Rovers	3-1
The Wednesday v Small Heath	2-0
Sunderland Albion v Nottingham Forest	0-1
Middlesbrough v Preston North End	1-2
Wolverhampton Wanderers v Sheffield United	3-1
Aston Villa v Darwen	2-0
Accrington v Sunderland	1-3
Burnley v Stoke	1-3

THIRD ROUND
West Bromwich Albion v The Wednesday	2-1
Nottingham Forest v Preston North End	2-0
Wolverhampton Wanderers v Aston Villa	1-3
Sunderland v Stoke	2-2, 4-0

SEMI-FINAL
West Bromwich Albion v Nottingham Forest	1-1, 1-1, 6-2
Aston Villa v Sunderland	4-1

FINAL AT KENNINGTON OVAL
West Bromwich Albion v Aston Villa	3-0

SCOTTISH FA CUP 1891-92

SECOND ROUND
Rangers v Kilmarnock	0-0, 1-1, 3-1
Third Lanark v Dumbarton	1-3
Broxburn Shamrock v Heart of Midlothian	4-5
Annbank v Leith Athletic	2-1
Queen's Park v Bathgate Rovers	6-0
Arbroath v Renton	0-3
Celtic v Kilmarnock Athletic	3-0
Cowlairs v Mid-Annandale	11-2

THIRD ROUND
Celtic v Cowlairs	4-1
Rangers v Annbank	2-0
Renton v Heart of Midlothian	4-4, 1-1, 3-2
Dumbarton v Queen's Park	2-2, 1-4

SEMI-FINAL
Renton v Queen's Park	1-1, 0-3
Celtic v Rangers	5-3

FINAL AT IBROX PARK
Celtic v Queen's Park	1-0*, 5-1

*The final had to be replayed, the first game having been disrupted by an unexpectedly large crowd.

In the first round of the FA Cup in 1890–91, Nottingham Forest beat Clapton 14-0 at Clapton. This remains the highest away win in any English first-class fixture. In the same round Darwen scored 13 against Kidderminster, Villa 13 against Casuals and Sheffield Wednesday 12 against Halliwell. Forest's performance was part of a good day for Nottingham – County also won 9-1 away from home.

During the 1890–91 FA Cup quarter-final between Notts County and Stoke at Trent Bridge a shot was punched off the line by County's left-back Hendry with his goalkeeper Toone well beaten. As the laws made no mention of penalties at the time, Stoke had to take a free-kick on the goal-line which Toone smothered easily. County won the match 1-0 and went on to the Final. The incident provoked so much comment that, partially as a result, penalties were introduced by the FA from September 1891. This led to another controversial incident in which Stoke were also the sufferers the next season. During a

League game at Aston Villa, Stoke were losing 1-0 when a penalty was awarded them just two minutes from time. The Villa keeper picked up the ball and booted it out of the ground. By the time it had been found the referee had blown for full time. The law was soon changed to allow referees to add on time for penalties. The penalty law was changed again as late as 1892 when players were banned from touching the ball twice – and hence dribbling into the net.

FIRST DIVISION

		P	W	D	L	F	A	Pts
1	Sunderland	30	22	4	4	100	36	48
2	Preston	30	17	3	10	57	39	37
3	Everton	30	16	4	10	74	51	36
4	Aston Villa	30	16	3	11	73	62	35
5	Bolton	30	13	6	11	56	55	32
6	Burnley	30	13	4	13	51	44	30
7	Stoke	30	12	5	13	58	48	29
8	WBA	30	12	5	13	58	69	29
9	Blackburn	30	8	13	9	47	56	29
10	Nottm Forest	30	10	8	12	48	52	28
11	Wolves	30	12	4	14	47	68	28
12	Wednesday	30	12	3	15	55	65	27
13	Derby	30	9	9	12	52	64	27
14	Notts County	30	10	4	16	53	61	24
15	Accrington	30	6	11	13	57	81	23
16	Newton Heath	30	6	6	18	50	85	18

SCOTTISH FA CUP 1892-93

FIRST ROUND

Celtic v Linthouse	3-1
Airdrieonians v Third Lanark	3-6
Cowlairs v Queen's Park	1-4
Clyde v Dumbarton	1-6*
Motherwell v Campsie	9-2†, 6-4
St Mirren v Aberdeen	6-4
Dunblane v Broxburn Shamrock	0-3
Stenhousemuir v Heart of Midlothian	1-1, 0-8
Northern v Leith Athletic	1-3
Royal Albert v Cambuslang	6-1
Abercorn v Renton	6-0
St Bernard's v Queen of South Wanderers	5-1
Rangers v Annbank	7-0
King's Park v Monkcastle	6-1
5th KVR v Camelon	5-3
Albion Rovers v Kilmarnock	1-2

*The invasion of the pitch by the crowd caused the game to be abandoned with 25 minutes left to play. The SFA awarded the tie to Dumbarton.

† After a protest about the size of the pitch the tie was replayed.

SECOND ROUND

Celtic v 5th KVR	7-0
Leith Athletic v St Mirren	0-2
Abercorn v Third Lanark	4-5
St Bernard's v Royal Albert	5-2
Broxburn Shamrock v King's Park	3-0
Heart of Midlothian v Motherwell	4-2
Dumbarton v Rangers	0-1
Kilmarnock v Queen's Park	0-8

THIRD ROUND

Heart of Midlothian v Queen's Park	1-1, 2-5
Celtic v Third Lanark	5-1
St Bernard's v Rangers	3-2
Broxburn Shamrock v St Mirren	4-3

SEMI-FINAL

Queen's Park v Broxburn Shamrock	4-2
Celtic v St Bernard's	5-0

FINAL AT IBROX PARK

Queen's Park v Celtic	2-1

SECOND DIVISION

		P	W	D	L	F	A	Pts
1	Small Heath	22	17	2	3	90	35	36
2	Sheff United	22	16	3	3	62	19	35
3	Darwen	22	14	2	6	60	36	30
4	Grimsby	22	11	1	10	42	41	23
5	Ardwick	22	9	3	10	45	40	21
6	Burton Swifts	22	9	2	11	47	47	20
7	Northwich Vic	22	9	2	11	42	58	20
8	Bootle	22	8	3	11	49	63	19
9	Lincoln	22	7	3	12	45	51	17
10	Crewe	22	6	3	13	42	69	15
11	Burslem PV	22	6	3	13	30	57	15
12	Walsall TS	22	5	3	14	37	75	13

TEST MATCHES 1892-93

Sheffield United 1 Accrington 0
Darwen 3 Notts County 2
Newton Heath 1 Small Heath 1

Play-off
Newton Heath 5 Small Heath 2

Sheffield United and Darwen promoted
Notts County relegated
Accrington resigned from the League

SCOTTISH LEAGUE

		P	W	D	L	F	A	Pts
1	Celtic	18	14	1	3	54	25	29
2	Rangers	18	12	4	2	41	27	28
3	St Mirren	18	9	2	7	40	39	20
4	Third Lanark	18	9	1	8	54	40	19
5	Hearts	18	8	2	8	40	42	18
6	Leith	18	8	1	9	35	31	17
7	Dumbarton	18	8	1	9	35	35	17
8	Renton	18	5	5	8	31	44	15
9	Abercorn	18	5	1	12	35	52	11
10	Clyde	18	2	2	14	25	55	6

1892-93 Champions Sunderland were the second side to be called 'The Team of all the Talents'. They became the first to score 100 goals or more in a single League season. In fact this total was not surpassed until after the First World War though, by then of course teams were playing far more games. Sunderland's winning margin of 11 points over the second club, Preston North End, has been equalled but never beaten in the division since. Aston Villa equalled it in 1897 as did Manchester United in 1956.

FA CUP 1892-93

FIRST ROUND

Everton v West Bromwich Albion	4-1
Nottingham Forest v Casuals	4-0
The Wednesday v Derby County	3-2*, 0-1†, 4-2
Burnley v Small Heath	2-0
Accrington v Stoke	2-1
Preston North End v Burton Swifts	9-2
Marlow v Middlesbrough Ironopolis	1-3
Notts County v Shankhouse	4-0
Wolverhampton Wanderers v Bolton Wanderers	1-1, 2-1
Newcastle United v Middlesbrough	2-3
Darwen v Aston Villa	5-4
Grimsby Town v Stockton	5-0
Blackburn Rovers v Newton Heath	4-0
Loughborough Town v Northwich Victoria	1-2
Blackpool v Sheffield United	1-3
Sunderland v Woolwich Arsenal	6-0

*Replay after protest
† Replay after second protest

SECOND ROUND

Everton v Nottingham Forest	4-2
The Wednesday v Burnley	1-0
Accrington v Preston North End	1-4
Middlesbrough Ironopolis v Notts County	3-2
Wolverhampton Wanderers v Middlesbrough	2-1
Darwen v Grimsby Town	2-0
Blackburn Rovers v Northwich Victoria	4-1
Sheffield United v Sunderland	1-3

THIRD ROUND

Everton v The Wednesday	3-0
Preston North End v Middlesbrough Ironopolis	2-2, 7-0
Wolverhampton Wanderers v Darwen	5-0
Blackburn Rovers v Sunderland	3-0

SEMI-FINAL

Everton v Preston North End	2-2, 0-0, 2-1
Wolverhampton Wanderers v Blackburn Rovers	2-1

FINAL AT FALLOWFIELD (MANCHESTER)

Wolverhampton Wanderers v Everton	1-0

With the introduction of a Second Division in 1892 – in fact the Football League simply absorbed the Football Alliance – a promotion/relegation system of test matches was instituted. This lasted until 1898 when Stoke and Burnley, realising that if they drew their match they would both be in the First Division, contrived a scoreless draw. Suspicions were aroused and a system of two up/two down was introduced.

Right Wolverhampton's 1893 team which won the only Final ever to be played at Fallowfield, Manchester, and the first to be initially contested outside London. An Everton reserve side had beaten the Wolves first team 4-2 the week before, but the underdogs won the real thing with a long-range headed goal from captain Harry Allen. The crowd, officially 45,000 but probably twice that number, broke down the gates and invaded the pitch and the match was played in near chaos.

On 10 December 1892 Sheffield United defeated Burslem Port Vale 10-0 in a League fixture at Burslem. This remains the biggest away win in any Football League match. A contemporary report commented that: 'The Vale keeper lost his spectacles in the mud.'

FIRST DIVISION

		P	W	D	L	F	A	Pts
1	Aston Villa	30	19	6	5	84	42	44
2	Sunderland	30	17	4	9	72	44	38
3	Derby	30	16	4	10	73	62	36
4	Blackburn	30	16	2	12	69	53	34
5	Burnley	30	15	4	11	61	51	34
6	Everton	30	15	3	12	90	57	33
7	Nottm Forest	30	14	4	12	57	48	32
8	WBA	30	14	4	12	66	59	32
9	Wolves	30	14	3	13	52	63	31
10	Sheff United	30	13	5	12	47	61	31
11	Stoke	30	13	3	14	65	79	29
12	Wednesday	30	9	8	13	48	57	26
13	Bolton	30	10	4	16	38	52	24
14	Preston	30	10	3	17	44	56	23
15	Darwen	30	7	5	18	37	83	19
16	Newton Heath	30	6	2	22	36	72	14

SECOND DIVISION

		P	W	D	L	F	A	Pts
1	Liverpool	28	22	6	0	77	18	50
2	Small Heath	28	21	0	7	103	44	42
3	Notts County	28	18	3	7	70	31	39
4	Newcastle	28	15	6	7	66	39	36
5	Grimsby	28	15	2	11	71	58	32
6	Burton Swifts	28	14	3	11	79	61	31
7	Burslem PV	28	13	4	11	66	64	30
8	Lincoln	28	11	6	11	59	58	28
9	Woolwich A	28	12	4	12	52	55	28
10	Walsall TS	28	10	3	15	51	61	23
11	Md Ironopolis	28	8	4	16	37	72	20
12	Crewe	28	6	7	15	42	73	19
13	Ardwick	28	8	2	18	47	71	18
14	Rotherham Twn	28	6	3	19	44	91	15
15	Northwich Vic	28	3	3	22	30	98	9

TEST MATCHES 1893-94

Preston North End 4 Notts County 0
Small Heath 3 Darwen 1
Liverpool 2 Newton Heath 0

Liverpool and Small Heath promoted
Darwen and Newton Heath relegated

FA CUP 1893-94

FIRST ROUND

Middlesbrough Ironopolis v Luton Town	2-1
Nottingham Forest v Heanor Town	1-0
Notts County v Burnley	1-0
Stockport County v Burton Wanderers	0-1
Leicester Fosse v South Shore	2-1
Derby County v Darwen	2-0
Newton Heath v Middlesbrough	4-0
West Bromwich Albion v Blackburn Rovers	2-3
Newcastle United v Sheffield United	2-0
Small Heath v Bolton Wanderers	3-4
Liverpool v Grimsby Town	3-0
Preston North End v Reading	18-0
Woolwich Arsenal v The Wednesday	1-2
Stoke v Everton	1-0
Sunderland v Accrington	3-0
Aston Villa v Wolverhampton Wanderers	4-2

SECOND ROUND

Middlesbrough Ironopolis v Nottingham Forest	0-2
Notts County v Burton Wanderers	2-1
Leicester Fosse v Derby County	0-0, 0-3
Newton Heath v Blackburn Rovers	0-0, 1-5
Newcastle United v Bolton Wanderers	1-2
Liverpool v Preston North End	3-2
The Wednesday v Stoke	1-0
Sunderland v Aston Villa	2-2, 1-3

THIRD ROUND

Nottingham Forest v Notts County	1-1, 1-4
Derby County v Blackburn Rovers	1-4
Bolton Wanderers v Liverpool	3-0
The Wednesday v Aston Villa	3-2

SEMI-FINAL

Notts County v Blackburn Rovers	1-0
Bolton Wanderers v The Wednesday	2-1

FINAL AT GOODISON PARK

Notts County v Bolton Wanderers	4-1

SCOTTISH FIRST DIVISION

		P	W	D	L	F	A	Pts
1	Celtic	18	14	1	3	53	32	29
2	Hearts	18	11	4	3	46	32	26
3	St Bernard's	18	11	1	6	53	41	23
4	Rangers	18	8	4	6	44	30	20
5	Dumbarton	18	7	5	6	32	35	19
6	St Mirren	18	7	3	8	50	46	17
7	Third Lanark	18	7	3	8	37	45	17
8	Dundee	18	6	3	9	43	58	15
9	Leith	18	4	2	12	36	46	10
10	Renton	18	1	2	15	23	52	4

Below *Notts County, the first Second Division side to win the FA Cup, in 1894.*

SCOTTISH FA CUP 1893-94

FIRST ROUND

Arbroath v Broxburn Shamrock	8-3
St Bernard's v Kilmarnock	3-1
Renton v Grangemouth	7-1
Cambuslang v East Stirlingshire	3-2
Port Glasgow Athletic v Airdrieonians	7-5
Dumbarton v Vale of Leven	2-1
Clyde v King's Park	5-2
Albion Rovers v 2nd Black Watch	6-0
Battlefield v Thistle	3-0
Leith Athletic v Orion	11-2
Queen's Park v Linthouse	5-1
Third Lanark v Inverness Thistle	9-3
Celtic v Hurlford	6-0
Abercorn v 5th KRV	2-1
St Mirren v Heart of Midlothian	1-0
Rangers v Cowlairs	8-0

SECOND ROUND

Abercorn v Battlefield	3-0
Port Glasgow Athletic v Renton	3-1
Queen's Park v Arbroath	3-0
Clyde v Cambuslang	6-0
Rangers v Leith Athletic	2-0
Third Lanark v St Mirren	3-2
Celtic v Albion Rovers	7-0
St Bernard's v Dumbarton	3-1

THIRD ROUND

Third Lanark v Port Glasgow Athletic	2-1
Celtic v St Bernard's	8-1
Clyde v Rangers	0-5
Abercorn v Queen's Park	3-3, 3-3, 0-2

SEMI-FINAL

Third Lanark v Celtic	3-5
Rangers v Queen's Park	1-1, 3-1

FINAL AT HAMPDEN PARK

Rangers v Celtic	3-1

SCOTTISH SECOND DIVISION

		P	W	D	L	F	A	Pts
1	Hibernian	18	13	3	2	83	29	29
2	Cowlairs	18	13	1	4	75	32	27
3	Clyde †	18	11	2	5	51	36	24
4	Motherwell	18	11	1	6	61	46	23
5	Partick	18	10	0	8	56	58	20
6	Port Glasgow	18	9	2	7	52	53	13*
7	Abercorn	18	5	2	11	42	60	12
8	Morton	18	4	1	13	36	62	9
9	Northern	18	3	3	12	29	66	9
10	Thistle	18	2	3	13	31	74	7

*Port Glasgow Athletic had 7 points deducted for fielding an ineligible player
† Clyde promoted to First Division

At the beginning of the 1894-95 season Liverpool completed what remained the longest League run without defeat until Leeds broke it in 1969. They had joined the Second Division in 1893 and remained undefeated in the 28-game season. They then won their Test Match to gain promotion to the First, where they drew the first two games before suffering their first ever League defeat by Aston Villa. This was after a run of 31 games.

Aston Villa turned the tables on Sunderland in Season 1893-94 by taking the League Championship with a margin of 6 points. It was the start of an era in which they became the leading club in the land. Over a period of seven years Villa won five Championships and two FA Cup Finals. They also become only the second club to win the double (after Preston North End) in 1897. Yet as recently as 1891 they had finished fourth from bottom and had had to seek re-election to the League.

When the FA made Goodison the venue for the 1894 Cup Final Notts County protested that it was virtually a home tie for Bolton. They won anyway, with Jimmy Logan (seated centre) scoring a hat-trick to equal William Townley's feat of 1890. Only one man, Stan Mortensen in 1953, has done it since.

During the 1893-94 season Everton scored 22 goals in the space of four matches. Jack Southworth claimed 15 of these, including six on the trot against West Bromwich on 30 December 1893. Everton won 7-1.

COLORSPORT

FIRST DIVISION

		P	W	D	L	F	A	Pts
1	Sunderland	30	21	5	4	80	37	47
2	Everton	30	18	6	6	82	50	42
3	Aston Villa	30	17	5	8	82	43	39
4	Preston	30	15	5	10	62	46	35
5	Blackburn	30	11	10	9	59	49	32
6	Sheff United	30	14	4	12	57	55	32
7	Nottm Forest	30	13	5	12	50	56	31
8	Wednesday	30	12	4	14	50	55	28
9	Burnley	30	11	4	15	44	56	26
10	Bolton	30	9	7	14	61	62	25
11	Wolves	30	9	7	14	43	63	25
12	Small Heath	30	9	7	14	50	74	25
13	WBA	30	10	4	16	51	66	24
14	Stoke	30	9	6	15	50	67	24
15	Derby	30	7	9	14	45	68	23
16	Liverpool	30	7	8	15	51	70	22

SECOND DIVISION

		P	W	D	L	F	A	Pts
1	Bury	30	23	2	5	78	33	48
2	Notts County	30	17	5	8	75	45	39
3	Newton Heath	30	15	8	7	78	44	38
4	Leicester Fosse	30	15	8	7	72	53	38
5	Grimsby	30	18	1	11	79	52	37
6	Darwen	30	16	4	10	74	43	36
7	Burton Wand	30	14	7	9	67	39	35
8	Woolwich A	30	14	6	10	75	58	34
9	Man City	30	14	3	13	82	72	31
10	Newcastle	30	12	3	15	72	84	27
11	Burton Swifts	30	11	3	16	52	74	25
12	Rotherham T	30	11	2	17	55	62	24
13	Lincoln	30	10	0	20	52	92	20
14	Walsall TS	30	10	0	20	47	92	20
15	Burslem PV	30	7	4	19	39	77	18
16	Crewe	30	3	4	23	26	103	10

FA CUP 1894-95

FIRST ROUND

Aston Villa v Derby County	2-1
Newcastle United v Burnley	2-1
Barnsley St Peter's v Liverpool	1-1, 0-4
Southampton St Mary's v Nottingham Forest	1-4
Sunderland v Fairfield	11-1
Luton Town v Preston North End	0-2
Bolton Wanderers v Woolwich Arsenal	1-0
Bury v Leicester Fosse	4-1
Sheffield United v Millwall Athletic	3-1
Small Heath v West Bromwich Albion	1-2
Darwen v Wolverhampton Wanderers	0-0, 0-2
Newton Heath v Stoke	2-3
The Wednesday v Notts County	5-1
Middlesbrough v Chesterfield	4-0
Southport Central v Everton	0-3
Burton Wanderers v Blackburn Rovers	1-2

SECOND ROUND

Aston Villa v Newcastle United	7-1
Liverpool v Nottingham Forest	0-2
Sunderland v Preston North End	2-0
Bolton Wanderers v Bury	1-0
Sheffield United v West Bromwich Albion	1-1, 1-2
Wolverhampton Wanderers v Stoke	2-0
The Wednesday v Middlesbrough	6-1
Everton v Blackburn Rovers	1-1, 3-2

THIRD ROUND

Aston Villa v Nottingham Forest	6-2
Sunderland v Bolton Wanderers	2-1
West Bromwich Albion v Wolverhampton Wanderers	1-0
The Wednesday v Everton	2-0

SEMI-FINAL

Aston Villa v Sunderland	2-1
West Bromwich Albion v The Wednesday	2-0

FINAL AT CRYSTAL PALACE

Aston Villa v West Bromwich Albion	1-0

SCOTTISH FIRST DIVISION

		P	W	D	L	F	A	Pts
1	Hearts	18	15	1	2	50	18	31
2	Celtic	18	11	4	3	50	29	26
3	Rangers	18	10	2	6	41	26	22
4	Third Lanark	18	10	1	7	51	39	21
5	St Mirren	18	9	1	8	34	36	19
6	St Bernard's	18	8	1	9	39	40	17
7	Clyde	18	8	0	10	40	49	16
8	Dundee	18	6	2	10	28	33	14
9	Leith	18	3	1	14	32	64	7
10	Dumbarton	18	3	1	14	27	58	7

SCOTTISH SECOND DIVISION

		P	W	D	L	F	A	Pts
1	Hibernian†	18	14	2	2	92	27	30
2	Motherwell	18	10	2	6	56	39	22
3	Port Glasgow	18	8	4	6	62	56	20
4	Renton*	17	10	0	7	46	44	20
5	Morton	18	9	1	8	59	63	19
6	Airdrieonians	18	8	2	8	68	45	18
7	Partick	18	8	2	8	50	60	18
8	Abercorn	18	7	3	8	48	65	17
9	Dundee Wand*	17	3	1	13	44	86	9*
10	Cowlairs	18	2	3	13	37	77	7

† Hibernian elected to First Division
* Dundee Wanderers and Renton played each other only once. Dundee were awarded two points when Renton failed to turn up for the return fixture.

TEST MATCHES 1894-95

Bury 1 Liverpool 0
Stoke 3 Newton Heath 0
Derby County 2 Notts County 1
Bury promoted. Liverpool relegated.

SCOTTISH FA CUP 1894-95

FIRST ROUND

St Bernard's v Airdrieonians	4-2
Slamannan Rovers v Renton	2-3*, 0-4
Ayr Parkhouse v Polton Vale	5-2
Clyde v Stevenston Thistle	7-2
Rangers v Heart of Midlothian	1-2
Orion v Dundee	1-5
Kilmarnock v East Stirlingshire	5-1
Raith Rovers v 5th KRV	6-3*, 3-4
Celtic v Queen's Park	4-1
Dumbarton v Galston.	2-1
Leith Athletic v Abercorn	5-1*, 1-4
St Mirren v Battlefield	5-0*, 8-1
Annbank v Third Lanark	6-4
Hibernian v Forfar Athletic	6-1
Motherwell v Mossend Swifts	1-2
Lochee United v King's Park	2-5

*These four ties were replayed after various protests. For example the Slamannan crowd was unruly; Raith Rovers failed to provide goal nets.

SECOND ROUND

St Bernard's v Kilmarnock	3-1
Renton v 5th KRV	6-0
Dundee v St Mirren	2-0
Heart of Midlothian v Abercorn	6-1
Clyde v Annbank	4-2
Ayr Parkhouse v Mossend Swifts	3-1
King's Park v Dumbarton	2-1
Hibernian v Celtic	2-0†, 0-2

†Celtic protested that Hibs fielded an ineligible player and a replay was agreed.

THIRD ROUND

St Bernard's v Clyde	2-1
Ayr Parkhouse v Renton	2-3
Dundee v Celtic	1-0
Heart of Midlothian v King's Park	4-2

SEMI-FINAL

Dundee v Renton	1-1, 3-3, 0-3
Heart of Midlothian v St Bernard's	0-0, 0-1

FINAL AT IBROX PARK

St Bernard's v Renton	2-1

The 1895 Cup Final was the first ever to be held at the Crystal Palace, and it got off to a remarkable start. Within 30 seconds a shot from Bob Chatt had ricocheted off John Devey's knee past the helpless West Bromwich goalkeeper Reader and Villa had won the Cup. Because of confusion at the turnstiles—the crowd of 42,000 was then the largest ever seen in London—many spectators missed the game's only goal, which remains the quickest ever scored in a Cup Final. The match was the third Final between Villa and their neighbours in 8 years; Villa had won 2-0 in 1887 and West Brom 3-0 in 1892, so the aggregate was level at three goals each. They remain the only pair of clubs ever to have met each other in three Finals. Yet another oddity to emerge from this game was that both teams, West Bromwich and Aston Villa, lost the Cup. In the winners' case this was the result of its theft, on 11 September, from **below** the window of one William

Shillcock, a boot and shoe manufacturer, who was displaying it to help advertise his wares. The Cup was never recovered and Villa were fined £25, which was used to purchase a replica of the original from Vaughton's of Birmingham. The Monday after the Final, meanwhile, Albion played their last League match needing a five-goal victory to avoid the test matches. They beat Wednesday 6-0; allegations of 'fixing' were never substantiated. In 1958 one Harry Burge, then 83, confessed to having stolen the Cup and having melted it down to make half-crowns. It was probably worth about £20.

HEINEMANN

FIRST DIVISION

	P	W	D	L	F	A	Pts
1 Aston Villa	30	20	5	5	78	45	45
2 Derby	30	17	7	6	68	35	41
3 Everton	30	16	7	7	66	43	39
4 Bolton	30	16	5	9	49	37	37
5 Sunderland	30	15	7	8	52	41	37
6 Stoke	30	15	0	15	56	47	30
7 Wednesday	30	12	5	13	44	53	29
8 Blackburn	30	12	5	13	40	50	29
9 Preston	30	11	6	13	44	48	28
10 Burnley	30	10	7	13	48	44	27
11 Bury	30	12	3	15	50	54	27
12 Sheff United	30	10	6	14	40	50	26
13 Nottm Forest	30	11	3	16	42	57	25
14 Wolves	30	10	1	19	61	65	21
15 Small Heath	30	8	4	18	39	79	20
16 WBA	30	6	7	17	30	59	19

SECOND DIVISION

	P	W	D	L	F	A	Pts
1 Liverpool	30	22	2	6	106	32	46
2 Man City	30	21	4	5	63	38	46
3 Grimsby	30	20	2	8	82	38	42
4 Burton Wand	30	19	4	7	69	40	42
5 Newcastle	30	16	2	12	73	50	34
6 Newton Heath	30	15	3	12	66	57	33
7 Woolwich A	30	14	4	12	59	42	32
8 Leicester Fosse	30	14	4	12	57	44	32
9 Darwen	30	12	6	12	72	67	30
10 Notts County	30	12	2	16	57	54	26
11 Burton Swifts	30	10	4	16	39	69	24
12 Loughborough	30	9	5	16	40	67	23
13 Lincoln	30	9	4	17	53	75	22
14 Burslem PV	30	7	4	19	43	78	18
15 Rotherham Tn	30	7	3	20	34	97	17
16 Crewe	30	5	3	22	30	95	13

SCOTTISH FIRST DIVISION

	P	W	D	L	F	A	Pts
1 Celtic	18	15	0	3	64	25	30
2 Rangers	18	11	4	3	57	39	26
3 Hibernian	18	11	2	5	58	39	24
4 Hearts	18	11	0	7	68	36	22
5 Dundee	18	7	2	9	33	42	16
6 Third Lanark	18	7	1	10	47	51	15
7 St Bernard's	18	7	1	10	36	53	15
8 St Mirren	18	5	3	10	31	51	13
9 Clyde	18	4	3	11	39	59	11
10 Dumbarton	18	4	0	14	36	74	8

SCOTTISH SECOND DIVISION

	P	W	D	L	F	A	Pts
1 Abercorn*	18	12	3	3	55	31	27
2 Leith	18	11	1	6	55	37	23
3 Renton	18	9	3	6	40	28	21
4 Kilmarnock	18	10	1	7	45	45	21
5 Airdrieonians	18	7	4	7	48	44	18
6 Partick	18	8	2	8	44	54	18
7 Port Glasgow	18	6	4	8	40	41	16
8 Motherwell	18	5	3	10	31	47	13
9 Morton	18	4	4	10	32	40	12
10 Linthouse	18	5	1	12	25	48	11

*Abercorn elected to First Division

FA CUP 1895-96

SECOND ROUND

Wolverhampton Wanderers v Liverpool	2-0
Burnley v Stoke	1-1, 1-7
Derby County v Newton Heath	1-1, 5-1
Grimsby Town v West Bromwich Albion	1-1, 0-3
The Wednesday v Sunderland	2-1
Everton v Sheffield United	3-0
Blackpool v Bolton Wanderers	0-2
Newcastle United v Bury	1-3

THIRD ROUND

Wolverhampton Wanderers v Stoke	3-0
Derby County v West Bromwich Albion	1-0
The Wednesday v Everton	4-0
Bolton Wanderers v Bury	2-0

SEMI-FINAL

Wolverhampton Wanderers v Derby County	2-1
The Wednesday v Bolton Wanderers	1-1, 3-1

FINAL AT CRYSTAL PALACE

The Wednesday v Wolverhampton Wanderers	2-1

SCOTTISH FA CUP 1895-96

FIRST ROUND

Blantyre v Heart of Midlothian	1-12
East Stirlingshire v Hibernian	2-3
St Bernard's v Clackmannan	8-1
Renton v Cowdenbeath	1-0
Lochgelly United v Raith Rovers	2-1*, 2-5
Dumbarton v Rangers	1-1, 1-3
Celtic v Queen's Park	2-4
Third Lanark v Leith Athletic	6-0
Annbank v Kilmarnock	3-2
Ayr v Abercorn	3-2
Port Glasgow Athletic v Arthurlie	4-2
St Mirren v Alloa Athletic	7-0
Arbroath v King's Park	5-0
Morton v Dundee	2-3
Clyde v Polton Vale	3-0
St Johnstone v Dundee Wanderers	4-2

*A Lochgelly player, David 'Anderson', was in fact David McLaren of Lochee United and had already appeared for that club in an earlier round. After a protest from Raith the tie was replayed.

SECOND ROUND

Heart of Midlothian v Ayr	5-1
Hibernian v Raith Rovers	6-1
St Bernard's v Annbank	2-0
Renton v Clyde	2-1
Rangers v St Mirren	5-1
Third Lanark v Dundee	4-1
Queen's Park v Port Glasgow Athletic	8-1
Arbroath v St Johnstone	3-1

THIRD ROUND

Heart of Midlothian v Arbroath	4-0
Hibernian v Rangers	3-2
St Bernard's v Queen's Park	3-2
Renton v Third Lanark	3-3, 2-0

SEMI-FINAL

Heart of Midlothian v St Bernard's	1-0
Hibernian v Renton	2-1

FINAL AT LOGIE GREEN, EDINBURGH

Heart of Midlothian v Hibernian	3-1

Below *Fred Spiksley, the Wednesday left-winger who scored both goals in the 2-1 win over Wolverhampton Wanderers which took the FA Cup to Sheffield for the first time. It was also the first time the new Cup, made after the original had been stolen from a Birmingham shop, had been presented.*

TEST MATCHES 1895-96

Man City 1 WBA 1	Liverpool 2 WBA 0
Small Heath 0 Liverpool 0	Liverpool 4 Small Heath 0
WBA 6 Man City 1	Small Heath 8 Man City 0
Man City 3 Small Heath 0	WBA 2 Liverpool 0

	P	W	D	L	F	A	Pts
Liverpool	4	2	1	1	6	2	5
WBA	4	2	1	1	9	4	5
Small Heath	4	1	1	2	8	7	3
Man City	4	1	1	2	5	15	3

Liverpool promoted. Small Heath relegated.

Above left *John Reynolds, who played at half-back in the England team which defeated Scotland 3-0 at Everton in 1895. Reynolds, though born in Blackburn, had played five times for Ireland during a spell with Distillery in 1890 and 1891. He then moved to West Bromwich, with whom he won a cap for England against Scotland. He then moved to Villa, with whom he won another seven caps. Only one other player, R E Evans, has been known to play for two of the home countries.*

League Tables 1896-97

FIRST DIVISION

		P	W	D	L	F	A	Pts
1	Aston Villa	30	21	5	4	73	38	47
2	Sheff United	30	13	10	7	42	29	36
3	Derby	30	16	4	10	70	50	36
4	Preston	30	11	12	7	55	40	34
5	Liverpool	30	12	9	9	46	38	33
6	Wednesday	30	10	11	9	42	37	31
7	Everton	30	14	3	13	62	57	31
8	Bolton	30	12	6	12	40	43	30
9	Bury	30	10	10	10	39	44	30
10	Wolves	30	11	6	13	45	41	28
11	Nottm Forest	30	9	8	13	44	49	26
12	WBA	30	10	6	14	33	56	26
13	Stoke	30	11	3	16	48	59	25
14	Blackburn	30	11	3	16	35	62	25
15	Sunderland	30	7	9	14	34	47	23
16	Burnley	30	6	7	17	43	61	19

SECOND DIVISION

		P	W	D	L	F	A	Pts
1	Notts County	30	19	4	7	92	43	42
2	Newton Heath	30	17	5	8	56	34	39
3	Grimsby	30	17	4	9	66	45	38
4	Small Heath	30	16	5	9	69	47	37
5	Newcastle	30	17	1	12	56	52	35
6	Man City	30	12	8	10	58	50	32
7	Gainsborough	30	12	7	11	50	47	31
8	Blackpool	30	13	5	12	59	56	31
9	Leicester Fosse	30	13	4	13	59	56	30
10	Woolwich A	30	13	4	13	68	70	30
11	Darwen	30	14	0	16	67	61	28
12	Walsall	30	11	4	15	53	69	26
13	Loughborough	30	12	1	17	50	64	25
14	Burton Swifts	30	9	6	15	46	61	24
15	Burton Wand	30	9	2	19	31	67	20
16	Lincoln	30	5	2	23	27	85	12

TEST MATCHES 1896-97

Notts County 1 Sunderland 0
Newton Heath 2 Burnley 0
Burnley 0 Notts County 1
Sunderland 2 Newton Heath 0
Sunderland 0 Notts County 0
Newton Heath 1 Sunderland 1
Burnley 2 Newton Heath 0
Notts County 1 Burnley 1

	P	W	D	L	F	A	Pts
Notts County	4	2	2	0	3	1	6
Sunderland	4	1	2	1	3	2	4
Burnley	4	1	1	2	3	4	3
Newton Heath	4	1	1	2	3	5	3

Notts County promoted
Burnley relegated

FA CUP 1896-97

FIRST ROUND

Aston Villa v Newcastle United	5-0
Small Heath v Notts County	1-2
Preston North End v Manchester City	6-0
Stoke v Glossop North End	5-2
Burnley v Sunderland	0-1
Nottingham Forest v The Wednesday	1-0
Luton Town v West Bromwich Albion	0-1
Liverpool v Burton Swifts	4-3
Everton v Burton Wanderers	5-2
Stockton v Bury	0-0, 1-12
Blackburn Rovers v Sheffield United	2-1
Millwall Athletic v Wolverhampton Wanderers	1-2
Derby County v Barnsley St Peter's	8-1
Bolton Wanderers v Grimsby Town	0-0, 3-3, 3-2
Heanor Town v Southampton St Mary's	1-1, 0-1
Newton Heath v Kettering	5-1

SECOND ROUND

Aston Villa v Notts County	2-1
Preston North End v Stoke	2-1
Sunderland v Nottingham Forest	1-3
West Bromwich Albion v Liverpool	1-2
Everton v Bury	3-0
Blackburn Rovers v Wolverhampton Wanderers	2-1
Derby County v Bolton Wanderers	4-1
Southampton St Mary's v Newton Heath	1-1, 1-3

THIRD ROUND

Aston Villa v Preston North End	1-1, 0-0, 3-2
Nottingham Forest v Liverpool	1-1, 0-1
Everton v Blackburn Rovers	2-0
Derby County v Newton Heath	2-0

SEMI-FINAL

Aston Villa v Liverpool	3-0
Everton v Derby County	3-2

FINAL AT CRYSTAL PALACE

Aston Villa v Everton	3-2

SCOTTISH FA CUP 1896-97

FIRST ROUND

Arthurlie v Celtic	4-2
Third Lanark v Newton Stewart Athletic	8-1
Heart of Midlothian v Clyde	2-0
St Bernard's v Queen's Park	2-1
St Mirren v Renton	5-1
Partick Thistle v Rangers	2-4
Dumbarton v Raith Rovers	2-1
Duncrab Park v Hibernian	1-10
Motherwell v Kilmarnock	3-3, 2-5
Abercorn v Hurlford	4-0
Falkirk v Orion	2-0
Dundee v Inverness Thistle	7-1
Morton v Johnstone	3-1
Blantyre v Bathgate	5-0
Leith Athletic v Dunblane	5-1
Lochgelly United v King's Park	1-2

SECOND ROUND

Arthurlie v Morton	1-5
Kilmarnock v Falkirk	7-3
Third Lanark v Heart of Midlothian	5-2
Dumbarton v Leith Athletic	4-4, 3-3, 3-2
Rangers v Hibernian	3-0
Dundee v King's Park	5-0
St Bernard's v St Mirren	5-0
Abercorn v Blantyre	4-1

THIRD ROUND

Dumbarton v St Bernard's	2-0
Morton v Abercorn	2-2, 3-2
Dundee v Rangers	0-4
Kilmarnock v Third Lanark	3-1

SEMI-FINAL

Morton v Rangers	2-7
Dumbarton v Kilmarnock	4-3

FINAL AT HAMPDEN PARK

Rangers v Dumbarton	5-1

SCOTTISH FIRST DIVISION

		P	W	D	L	F	A	Pts
1	Hearts	18	13	2	3	47	22	28
2	Hibernian	18	12	2	4	50	20	26
3	Rangers	18	11	3	4	64	30	25
4	Celtic	18	10	4	4	42	18	24
5	Dundee	18	10	2	6	38	30	22
6	St Mirren	18	9	1	8	38	29	19
7	St Bernard's	18	7	0	11	32	40	14
8	Third Lanark	18	5	1	12	29	46	11
9	Clyde	18	4	0	14	27	65	8
10	Abercorn	18	1	1	16	21	88	3

SCOTTISH SECOND DIVISION

		P	W	D	L	F	A	Pts
1	Partick †	18	14	3	1	61	28	31
2	Leith	18	13	1	4	54	28	27
3	Kilmarnock	18	10	1	7	44	33	21
4	Airdrieonians	18	10	1	7	48	39	21
5	Morton	18	7	2	9	38	40	16
6	Renton	18	6	2	10	34	40	14
7	Linthouse	18	8	2	8	44	52	14*
8	Port Glasgow	18	4	5	9	39	50	13
9	Motherwell	18	6	1	11	40	55	13
10	Dumbarton	18	2	2	14	27	64	6

*Four points deducted for fielding an ineligible player.
† Partick elected to First Division

Above *Footballs from Lancashire, as used in the 1890s.*

Left *The Aston Villa side that won the double in 1897. Their eleven point margin over the second League club remains a record and the double was not repeated until the Spurs of 64 years later.*

FIRST DIVISION

		P	W	D	L	F	A	Pts
1	Sheff United	30	17	8	5	56	31	42
2	Sunderland	30	16	5	9	43	30	37
3	Wolves	30	14	7	9	57	41	35
4	Everton	30	13	9	8	48	39	35
5	Wednesday	30	15	3	12	51	42	33
6	Aston Villa	30	14	5	11	61	51	33
7	WBA	30	11	10	9	44	45	32
8	Nottm Forest	30	11	9	10	47	49	31
9	Liverpool	30	11	6	13	48	45	28
10	Derby	30	11	6	13	57	61	28
11	Bolton	30	11	4	15	28	41	26
12	Preston NE	30	8	8	14	35	43	24
13	Notts County	30	8	8	14	36	46	24
14	Bury	30	8	8	14	39	51	24
15	Blackburn	30	7	10	13	39	54	24
16	Stoke	30	8	8	14	35	55	24

SECOND DIVISION

		P	W	D	L	F	A	Pts
1	Burnley	30	20	8	2	80	24	48
2	Newcastle	30	21	3	6	64	32	45
3	Man City	30	15	9	6	66	36	39
4	Newton Heath	30	16	6	8	64	35	38
5	Woolwich A	30	16	5	9	69	49	37
6	Small Heath	30	16	4	10	58	50	36
7	Leicester Fosse	30	13	7	10	46	35	33
8	Luton	30	13	4	13	68	50	30
9	Gainsborough	30	12	6	12	50	54	30
10	Walsall	30	12	5	13	58	58	29
11	Blackpool	30	10	5	15	49	61	25
12	Grimsby	30	10	4	16	52	62	24
13	Burton Swifts	30	8	5	17	38	69	21
14	Lincoln	30	6	5	19	43	82	17
15	Darwen	30	6	2	22	31	76	14
16	Loughborough	30	6	2	22	24	87	14

SCOTTISH FIRST DIVISION

		P	W	D	L	F	A	Pts
1	Celtic	18	15	3	0	56	13	33
2	Rangers	18	13	3	2	71	15	29
3	Hibernian	18	10	2	6	48	28	22
4	Hearts	18	8	4	6	54	33	20
5	Third Lanark	18	8	2	8	37	38	18
6	St Mirren	18	8	2	8	30	36	18
7	Dundee*	18	5	3	10	29	36	13
8	Partick*	18	6	1	11	34	64	13
9	St Bernard's	18	4	1	13	35	67	9
10	Clyde	18	1	3	14	20	84	5

*Partick Thistle and Dundee played a test match to decide the bottom three and Dundee won 2-0

SCOTTISH SECOND DIVISION

		P	W	D	L	F	A	Pts
1	Kilmarnock	18	14	1	3	64	29	29
2	Port Glasgow	18	12	1	5	66	35	25
3	Morton	18	9	4	5	47	38	22
4	Leith	18	9	2	7	39	38	20
5	Linthouse	18	6	4	8	37	39	16
6	Ayr	18	7	2	9	36	42	16
7	Abercorn	18	6	4	8	33	41	16
8	Airdrieonians	18	6	2	10	44	56	14
9	Hamilton*	18	5	2	11	28	51	12
10	Motherwell	18	3	4	11	31	56	10

*Took the place of Renton, who resigned

Left Ernest 'Nudger' Needham, who led his club, Sheffield United, to the League Championship, the first honour in their history.

Below Harry Linacre, the Nottingham Forest goalkeeper and an England cap in the early part of the twentieth century. Linacre came from a great footballing family in Aston-on-Trent, near Derby. His two uncles, Frank and Fred Forman, played in all the 1898-99 season internationals for England and remain the only brothers from the same professional club to have played together for England. They were also Forest regulars, like their nephew, and Frank Forman was captain of the Forest team that won the club's first honour with the FA Cup in 1898. Five days before the Final their opponents and local rivals Derby County had thrashed them 5-0 in a League match. But, despite this and a crippling injury to wing-half Wragg, Forest won the Final 3-1.

COLORSPORT

FA CUP 1897-98

FIRST ROUND

Southampton St Mary's v Leicester Fosse	2-1
Preston North End v Newcastle United	1-2
Luton Town v Bolton Wanderers	0-1
Manchester City v Wigan County	2-1
West Bromwich Albion v New Brighton Tower	2-0
Sunderland v The Wednesday	0-1
Nottingham Forest v Grimsby Town	4-0
Long Eaton Rangers v Gainsborough Trinity	0-1
Liverpool v Hucknall St John's	2-0
Newton Heath v Walsall	1-0
Notts County v Wolverhampton Wanderers	0-1
Derby County v Aston Villa	1-0
Burnley v Woolwich Arsenal	3-1
Burslem Port Vale v Sheffield United	1-1, 2-1
Everton v Blackburn Rovers	1-0
Bury v Stoke	1-2

SECOND ROUND

Southampton St Mary's v Newcastle United	1-0
Bolton Wanderers v Manchester City	1-0
West Bromwich Albion v The Wednesday	1-0
Nottingham Forest v Gainsborough Trinity	4-0
Liverpool v Newton Heath	0-0, 2-1
Wolverhampton Wanderers v Derby County	0-1
Burnley v Burslem Port Vale	3-0
Everton v Stoke	0-0, 5-1

THIRD ROUND

Southampton St Mary's v Bolton Wanderers	0-0, 4-0
West Bromwich Albion v Nottingham Forest	2-3
Liverpool v Derby County	1-1, 1-5
Burnley v Everton	1-3

SEMI-FINAL

Southampton St Mary's v Nottingham Forest	1-1, 0-2
Derby County v Everton	3-1

FINAL AT CRYSTAL PALACE

Nottingham Forest v Derby County	3-1

SCOTTISH FA CUP 1897-98

SECOND ROUND

Dundee v St Mirren	2-0
Rangers v Cartvale	12-0
Third Lanark v Celtic	3-2
Kilmarnock v Leith Athletic	9-2
Dundee Wanderers v Ayr Parkhouse	3-6
Hibernian v East Stirlingshire	3-1
Heart of Midlothian v Morton	4-1
St Bernard's v Queen's Park	0-5

THIRD ROUND

Queen's Park v Rangers	1-3
Third Lanark v Hibernian	2-0
Ayr Parkhouse v Kilmarnock	2-7
Dundee v Heart of Midlothian	3-0

SEMI-FINAL

Rangers v Third Lanark	1-1, 2-2, 2-0
Kilmarnock v Dundee	3-2

FINAL AT HAMPDEN PARK

Rangers v Kilmarnock	2-0

TEST MATCHES 1897-98

Newcastle 2 Stoke 1	Blackburn 1 Burnley 3
Burnley 2 Blackburn 0	Stoke 1 Newcastle 0
Newcastle 4 Blackburn 0	Blackburn 4 Newcastle 3
Burnley 0 Stoke 2	Stoke 0 Burnley 0

	P	W	D	L	F	A	Pts
Stoke	4	2	1	1	4	2	5
Burnley	4	2	1	1	5	3	5
Newcastle	4	2	0	2	9	6	4
Blackburn	4	1	0	3	5	12	2

Burnley and Newcastle promoted
No clubs relegated

FIRST DIVISION

		P	W	D	L	F	A	Pts
1	Aston Villa	34	19	7	8	76	40	45
2	Liverpool	34	19	5	10	49	33	43
3	Burnley	34	15	9	10	45	47	39
4	Everton	34	15	8	11	48	41	38
5	Notts County	34	12	13	9	47	51	37
6	Blackburn	34	14	8	12	60	52	36
7	Sunderland	34	15	6	13	41	41	36
8	Wolves	34	14	7	13	54	48	35
9	Derby	34	12	11	11	62	57	35
10	Bury	34	14	7	13	48	49	35
11	Nottm Forest	34	11	11	12	42	42	33
12	Stoke	34	13	7	14	47	52	33
13	Newcastle	34	11	8	15	49	48	30
14	WBA	34	12	6	16	42	57	30
15	Preston	34	10	9	15	44	47	29
16	Sheff United	34	9	11	14	45	51	29
17	Bolton	34	9	7	18	37	51	25
18	Wednesday	34	8	8	18	32	61	24

SECOND DIVISION

		P	W	D	L	F	A	Pts
1	Man City	34	23	5	6	92	35	52
2	Glossop NE	34	20	6	8	76	38	46
3	Leicester Fosse	34	18	9	7	64	42	45
4	Newton Heath	34	19	5	10	67	43	43
5	New Brighton	34	18	7	9	71	52	43
6	Walsall	34	15	12	7	79	36	42
7	Woolwich A	34	18	5	11	72	41	41
8	Small Heath	34	17	7	10	85	50	41
9	Burslem PV	34	17	5	12	56	34	39
10	Grimsby	34	15	5	14	71	60	35
11	Barnsley	34	12	7	15	52	56	31
12	Lincoln	34	12	7	15	51	56	31
13	Burton Swifts	34	10	8	16	51	70	28
14	Gainsborough	34	10	5	19	56	72	25
15	Luton	34	10	3	21	51	95	23
16	Blackpool	34	8	4	22	49	90	20
17	Loughborough	34	6	6	22	38	92	18
18	Darwen	34	2	5	27	22	141	9

SCOTTISH FIRST DIVISION

		P	W	D	L	F	A	Pts
1	Rangers	18	18	0	0	79	18	36
2	Hearts	18	12	2	4	56	30	26
3	Celtic	18	11	2	5	51	33	24
4	Hibernian	18	10	3	5	42	43	23
5	St Mirren	18	8	4	6	46	32	20
6	Third Lanark	18	7	3	8	33	38	17
7	St Bernard's	18	4	4	10	30	37	12
8	Clyde	18	4	4	10	23	48	12
9	Partick	18	2	2	14	19	58	6
10	Dundee	18	1	2	15	23	65	4

SCOTTISH SECOND DIVISION

		P	W	D	L	F	A	Pts
1	Kilmarnock*	18	14	4	0	73	24	32
2	Leith	18	12	3	3	63	38	27
3	Port Glasgow	18	12	1	5	75	51	25
4	Motherwell	18	7	6	5	41	40	20
5	Hamilton	18	7	1	10	48	58	15
6	Airdrieonians	18	6	3	9	35	46	15
7	Morton	18	6	1	11	36	41	13
8	Ayr	18	5	3	10	35	51	13
9	Linthouse	18	5	1	12	29	62	11
10	Abercorn	18	4	1	13	41	65	9

*Kilmarnock elected to First Division

Below *The Aston Villa side which won the First Division Championship in 1899.*

Second Division Darwen are the only side to have suffered three 10-goal defeats in a single season. In 1898-99 they lost 10-0 to Manchester City, Walsall and Loughborough, all in the space of six weeks. Their 141 goals against was also a record.

Season 1898-99 provided one unique record. Glasgow Rangers won every single game they played in the Scottish League, the only time that this feat has been performed by a British club. Their only defeat in 1898-99 in fact was a shock collapse, 2-0, to Glasgow rivals Celtic in the Scottish Cup final. Only four other clubs — Celtic, Kilmarnock, Preston and Liverpool — have gone a League season without defeat.

FA CUP 1898-99

FIRST ROUND

Everton v Jarrow	3-1
Nottingham Forest v Aston Villa	2-1
Sheffield United v Burnley	2-2, 2-1
Preston North End v Grimsby Town	7-0
West Bromwich Albion v South Shore	8-0
Heanor Town v Bury	0-3
Liverpool v Blackburn Rovers	2-0
Glossop North End v Newcastle United	0-1
Notts County v Kettering Town	2-0
New Brompton v Southampton	0-1
Woolwich Arsenal v Derby County	0-6
Bolton Wanderers v Wolverhampton Wanderers	0-0, 0-1
Small Heath v Manchester City	3-2
Stoke v The Wednesday	2-2, 2-0
Newton Heath v Tottenham Hotspur	1-1, 3-5
Bristol City v Sunderland	2-4

SECOND ROUND

Everton v Nottingham Forest	0-1
Sheffield United v Preston North End	2-2, 2-1
West Bromwich Albion v Bury	2-1
Liverpool v Newcastle United	3-1
Notts County v Southampton	0-1
Derby County v Wolverhampton Wanderers	2-1
Small Heath v Stoke	2-2, 1-2
Tottenham Hotspur v Sunderland	2-1

THIRD ROUND

Nottingham Forest v Sheffield United	0-1
West Bromwich Albion v Liverpool	0-2
Southampton v Derby County	1-2
Stoke v Tottenham Hotspur	4-1

SEMI-FINAL

Sheffield United v Liverpool	2-2, 4-4, 0-1*, 1-0
Derby County v Stoke	3-1
*abandoned	

FINAL AT CRYSTAL PALACE

Sheffield United v Derby County	4-1

SCOTTISH FA CUP 1898-99

FIRST ROUND

Queen's Park v Kilsyth Wanderers	4-0
Hibernian v Royal Albert	2-1
6th G R V v Celtic	1-8
St Bernard's v Bo'ness	3-3, 4-2
Port Glasgow Athletic v Renton	3-2
Forfar Athletic v West Calder Swifts	4-5
Irvine v Partick Thistle	0-5
Morton v Annbank	3-1
St Mirren v Leith Athletic	7-1
Third Lanark v Arthurlie	4-1
Orion v Kilmarnock	0-2
East Stirlingshire v Dumbarton	4-1
Rangers v Heart of Midlothian	4-1
Ayr Parkhouse v Dundee	3-1
Clyde v Wishaw Thistle	3-0
Airdrieonians v Arbroath	3-3, 2-3

SECOND ROUND

Queen's Park v Hibernian	5-1
Celtic v St Bernard's	3-0
Port Glasgow Athletic v West Calder Swifts	3-1
Morton v Partick Thistle	2-2, 1-2
Third Lanark v St Mirren	1-2
East Stirlingshire v Kilmarnock	1-1, 0-0, 2-4
Ayr Parkhouse v Rangers	1-4
Clyde v Arbroath	3-1

THIRD ROUND

Celtic v Queen's Park	4-2*, 2-1
Port Glasgow Athletic v Partick Thistle	7-3
Kilmarnock v St Mirren	1-2
Rangers v Clyde	4-0
*abandoned	

SEMI-FINAL

Celtic v Port Glasgow Athletic	4-2
St Mirren v Rangers	1-2

FINAL AT HAMPDEN PARK

Celtic v Rangers	2-0

FIRST DIVISION

		P	W	D	L	F	A	Pts
1	Aston Villa	34	22	6	6	77	35	50
2	Sheff United	34	18	12	4	63	33	48
3	Sunderland	34	19	3	12	50	35	41
4	Wolves	34	15	9	10	48	37	39
5	Newcastle	34	13	10	11	53	43	36
6	Derby	34	14	8	12	45	43	36
7	Man City	34	13	8	13	50	44	34
8	Nottm Forest	34	13	8	13	56	55	34
9	Stoke	34	10	10	14	37	45	34
10	Liverpool	34	14	5	15	49	45	33
11	Everton	34	13	7	14	47	49	33
12	Bury	34	13	6	15	40	44	32
13	WBA	34	11	8	15	43	51	30
14	Blackburn	34	13	4	17	49	61	30
15	Notts County	34	9	11	14	46	60	29
16	Preston	34	12	4	18	38	48	28
17	Burnley	34	11	5	18	34	54	27
18	Glossop NE	34	4	10	20	31	74	18

SECOND DIVISION

		P	W	D	L	F	A	Pts
1	Wednesday	34	25	4	5	84	22	54
2	Bolton	34	22	8	4	79	25	52
3	Small Heath	34	20	6	8	78	38	46
4	Newton Heath	34	20	4	10	63	27	44
5	Leicester Fosse	34	17	9	8	53	36	43
6	Grimsby	34	17	6	11	67	46	40
7	Chesterfield	34	16	6	12	65	60	38
8	Woolwich A	34	16	4	14	61	43	36
9	Lincoln	34	14	8	12	46	43	36
10	New Brighton	34	13	9	12	66	58	35
11	Burslem PV	34	14	6	14	39	49	34
12	Walsall	34	12	8	14	50	55	32
13	Gainsborough	34	9	7	18	47	75	25
14	Middlesbrough	34	8	8	18	39	69	24
15	Burton Swifts	34	9	6	19	43	84	24
16	Barnsley	34	8	7	19	46	79	23
17	Luton	34	5	8	21	40	75	18
18	Loughborough	34	1	6	27	18	100	8

SCOTTISH FIRST DIVISION

		P	W	D	L	F	A	Pts
1	Rangers	18	15	2	1	69	27	32
2	Celtic	18	9	7	2	46	27	25
3	Hibernian	18	9	6	3	43	24	24
4	Hearts	18	10	3	5	41	24	23
5	Kilmarnock	18	6	6	6	30	37	18
6	Dundee	18	4	7	7	36	39	15
7	Third Lanark	18	5	5	8	31	37	15
8	St Mirren	18	3	6	9	30	46	12
9	St Bernard's	18	4	4	10	29	47	12
10	Clyde	18	2	0	16	25	70	4

The Manchester City keeper, C Williams, scored with a goal-kick against Sunderland on 14 April 1900 when his opposite number, Ned Doig, touched the ball on its way into the net. At that time full-backs used to tap goal-kicks into the keeper's hands and he would punt the ball from the 6-yard semi-circle.

SCOTTISH SECOND DIVISION

		P	W	D	L	F	A	Pts
1	Partick*	18	14	1	3	56	26	29
2	Morton*	18	14	0	4	66	25	28
3	Port Glasgow	18	10	0	8	50	41	20
4	Motherwell	18	9	1	8	38	36	19
5	Leith	18	9	1	8	32	37	19
6	Abercorn	18	7	2	9	46	39	16
7	Hamilton	18	7	1	10	33	46	15
8	Ayr	18	6	2	10	39	48	14
9	Airdrieonians	18	4	3	11	27	49	11
10	Linthouse	18	2	5	11	28	68	9

*Partick Thistle and Morton were elected to the First Division.

Below Part of the huge crowd at the 1900 Cup Final at Crystal Palace.

FA CUP 1899-1900

FIRST ROUND

Preston North End v Tottenham Hotspur	1-0
Blackburn Rovers v Portsmouth	0-0, 1-1, 5-0
Nottingham Forest v Grimsby Town	3-0
Sunderland v Derby County	2-2, 3-0
The Wednesday v Bolton Wanderers	1-0
Sheffield United v Leicester Fosse	1-0
Notts County v Chorley	6-0
Burnley v Bury	0-1
Southampton v Everton	3-0
Newcastle United v Reading	2-1
West Bromwich Albion v Walsall	1-1, 6-0
Liverpool v Stoke	0-0, 1-0
Wolverhampton Wanderers v Queen's Park Rangers	1-1, 0-1
Jarrow v Millwall Athletic	0-2
Aston Villa v Manchester City	1-1, 3-1
Bristol City v Stalybridge Rovers	2-1

SECOND ROUND

Preston North End v Blackburn Rovers	1-0
Nottingham Forest v Sunderland	3-0
The Wednesday v Sheffield United	1-1, 0-2
Notts County v Bury	0-0, 0-2
Southampton v Newcastle United	4-1
West Bromwich Albion v Liverpool	1-1, 2-1
Queen's Park Rangers v Millwall Athletic	0-2
Aston Villa v Bristol City	5-1

THIRD ROUND

Preston North End v Nottingham Forest	0-0, 0-1
Sheffield United v Bury	2-2, 0-2
Southampton v West Bromwich Albion	2-1
Millwall Athletic v Aston Villa	1-1, 0-0, 2-1

SEMI-FINAL

Nottingham Forest v Bury	1-1, 2-3
Southampton v Millwall Athletic	0-0, 3-0

FINAL AT CRYSTAL PALACE

Bury v Southampton	4-0

SCOTTISH FA CUP 1899-1900

FIRST ROUND

Rangers v Morton	4-2
Celtic v Bo'ness	7-1
Third Lanark v Raith Rovers	5-1
Heart of Midlothian v St Mirren	0-0, 3-0
Kilmarnock v East Stirlingshire	2-0
Hamilton Academicals v Hibernian	2-3
St Bernard's v Arbroath	1-0
Galston v Partick Thistle	1-2
Forfar Athletic v Motherwell	3-4
Abercorn v Ayr Parkhouse	5-2
Port Glasgow Athletic v Falkirk	7-1
Dundee v Douglas Wanderers	8-0
Maybole v Wishaw Thistle	3-2
Forres Mechanics v Orion	1-1, 1-4
Queen's Park v Leith Athletic	3-0
Airdrieonians v Clyde	0-1

SECOND ROUND

Heart of Midlothian v Hibernian	1-1, 2-1
Dundee v Clyde	3-3, 3-0
Queen's Park v Abercorn	5-1
Rangers v Maybole	12-0
Kilmarnock v Orion	10-0
Partick Thistle v St Bernard's	2-1
Third Lanark v Motherwell	2-1
Port Glasgow Athletic v Celtic	1-5

THIRD ROUND

Rangers v Partick Thistle	6-1
Celtic v Kilmarnock	4-0
Queen's Park v Dundee	1-0
Third Lanark v Heart of Midlothian	1-2

SEMI-FINAL

Rangers v Celtic	1-1, 0-4
Queen's Park v Heart of Midlothian	2-1

FINAL AT IBROX PARK

Celtic v Queen's Park	4-3

FIRST DIVISION

		P	W	D	L	F	A	Pts
1	Liverpool	34	19	7	8	59	35	45
2	Sunderland	34	15	13	6	57	26	43
3	Notts County	34	18	4	12	54	46	40
4	Nottm Forest	34	16	7	11	53	36	39
5	Bury	34	16	7	11	53	37	39
6	Newcastle	34	14	10	10	42	37	38
7	Everton	34	16	5	13	55	42	37
8	Wednesday	34	13	10	11	52	42	36
9	Blackburn	34	12	9	13	39	47	33
10	Bolton	34	13	7	14	39	55	33
11	Man City	34	13	6	15	48	58	32
12	Derby	34	12	7	15	55	42	31
13	Wolves	34	9	13	12	39	55	31
14	Sheff United	34	12	7	15	35	52	31
15	Aston Villa	34	10	10	14	45	51	30
16	Stoke	34	11	5	18	46	57	27
17	Preston	34	9	7	18	49	75	25
18	WBA	34	7	8	19	35	62	22

SECOND DIVISION

		P	W	D	L	F	A	Pts
1	Grimsby	34	20	9	5	60	33	49
2	Small Heath	34	19	10	5	57	24	48
3	Burnley	34	20	4	10	53	29	44
4	New Brighton	34	17	8	9	57	38	42
5	Glossop NE	34	15	8	11	51	33	38
6	Middlesbrough	34	15	7	12	50	40	37
7	Woolwich A	34	15	6	13	39	35	36
8	Lincoln	34	13	7	14	43	39	33
9	Burslem PV	34	11	11	12	45	47	33
10	Newton Heath	34	14	4	16	42	38	32
11	Leicester Fosse	34	11	10	13	39	37	32
12	Blackpool	34	12	7	15	33	58	31
13	Gainsborough	34	10	10	14	45	60	30
14	Chesterfield	34	9	10	15	46	58	28
15	Barnsley	34	11	5	18	47	60	27
16	Walsall	34	7	13	14	40	56	27
17	Stockport	34	11	3	20	38	68	25
18	Burton Swifts	34	8	4	22	34	66	20

SCOTTISH FIRST DIVISION

		P	W	D	L	F	A	Pts
1	Rangers	20	17	1	2	60	25	35
2	Celtic	20	13	3	4	49	28	29
3	Hibernian	20	9	7	4	29	22	25
4	Morton	20	9	3	8	40	40	21
5	Kilmarnock	20	7	4	9	35	47	18
6	Third Lanark	20	6	6	8	20	29	18
7	Dundee	20	6	5	9	36	35	17
8	Queen's Park	20	7	3	10	33	37	17
9	St Mirren	20	5	6	9	33	43	16
10	Hearts	20	5	4	11	22	30	14
11	Partick	20	4	2	14	28	49	10

SCOTTISH SECOND DIVISION

		P	W	D	L	F	A	Pts
1	St Bernard's	18	10	5	3	41	26	25
2	Airdrieonians	18	11	1	6	46	35	23
3	Abercorn	18	9	3	6	37	33	21
4	Clyde	18	9	2	7	43	35	20
5	Port Glasgow	18	9	1	8	45	44	19
6	Ayr	18	9	0	9	32	34	18
7	E Stirlingshire	18	7	4	7	35	39	18
8	Leith	18	5	3	10	23	33	13
9	Hamilton	18	4	4	10	44	51	12
10	Motherwell	18	4	3	11	26	42	11

Below The legendary Fatty Foulke, Sheffield United's goalkeeper, fishes the ball out of the net after one of two goals scored against his team in the 1901 Cup Final by Sandy Brown of Tottenham Hotspur. Brown's goals earned the Londoners a 2-2 draw and won him a place in the record books. For Brown had become the first man to score in every round of the competition and the centre-forward's tally of 15 goals—including the one he got in the replay at Bolton—remains a record. Spurs were then members of the Southern League and are the only non-League club to have won the Cup since 1888.

FA CUP 1900-01

FIRST ROUND
Bolton Wanderers v Derby County	1-0
Reading v Bristol Rovers	2-0
Tottenham Hotspur v Preston North End	1-1, 4-2
The Wednesday v Bury	0-1
Middlesbrough v Newcastle United	3-1
Kettering Town v Chesterfield Town	1-1, 2-1
Woolwich Arsenal v Blackburn Rovers	2-0
West Bromwich Albion v Manchester City	1-0
Notts County v Liverpool	2-0
Wolverhampton Wanderers v New Brighton Tower	5-1
Sunderland v Sheffield United	1-2
Southampton v Everton	1-3
Stoke v Small Heath	1-1, 1-2
Newton Heath v Burnley	0-0, 1-7
Aston Villa v Millwall Athletic	5-0
Nottingham Forest v Leicester Fosse	5-1

SECOND ROUND
Bolton Wanderers v Reading	0-1
Tottenham Hotspur v Bury	2-1
Middlesbrough v Kettering Town	5-0
Woolwich Arsenal v West Bromwich Albion	0-1
Notts County v Wolverhampton Wanderers	2-3
Sheffield United v Everton	2-0
Small Heath v Burnley	1-0
Aston Villa v Nottingham Forest	0-0, 3-1

THIRD ROUND
Reading v Tottenham Hotspur	1-1, 0-3
Middlesbrough v West Bromwich Albion	0-1
Wolverhampton Wanderers v Sheffield United	0-4
Small Heath v Aston Villa	0-0, 0-1

SEMI-FINAL
Tottenham Hotspur v West Bromwich Albion	4-0
Sheffield United v Aston Villa	2-2, 3-0

FINAL AT CRYSTAL PALACE
Tottenham Hotspur v Sheffield United	2-2, 3-1*

*replay at Bolton

SCOTTISH FA CUP 1900-01

FIRST ROUND
Dundee Wanderers v Abercorn	0-3
Celtic v Rangers	1-0
Third Lanark v Douglas Wanderers	5-0
Kilmarnock v Airdrieonians	3-2
St Mirren v Kilwinning Eglinton	10-0
Morton v Bo'ness	10-0
Dundee v Arthurlie	3-1
Stenhousemuir v Queen's Park	1-3
St Bernard's v Partick Thistle	5-0
Heart of Midlothian v Mossend Swifts	7-0
Ayr v Orion	2-2, 3-1
Port Glasgow Athletic v Newton Stewart Athletic	9-1
Hibernian v Dumbarton	7-0
Royal Albert v St Johnstone	1-1, 2-2, 2-0
Forfar Athletic v Leith Athletic	0-4
Clyde v East Stirlingshire	6-0

SECOND ROUND
Clyde v Dundee	3-5
Heart of Midlothian v Queen's Park	2-1
Royal Albert v Hibernian	1-1, 0-1
Ayr v St Mirren	1-3
Celtic v Kilmarnock	6-0
Third Lanark v Abercorn	1-1, 1-0
Morton v St Bernard's	3-1
Leith Athletic v Port Glasgow Athletic	0-3

THIRD ROUND
Dundee v Celtic	0-1
St Mirren v Third Lanark	0-0, 1-1, 3-3, 1-0
Port Glasgow Athletic v Heart of Midlothian	1-5
Hibernian v Morton	2-0

SEMI-FINAL
Heart of Midlothian v Hibernian	1-1, 2-1
St Mirren v Celtic	0-1

FINAL AT IBROX PARK
Heart of Midlothian v Celtic	4-3

FIRST DIVISION

		P	W	D	L	F	A	Pts
1	Sunderland	34	19	6	9	50	35	44
2	Everton	34	17	7	10	53	35	41
3	Newcastle	34	14	9	11	48	34	37
4	Blackburn	34	15	6	13	52	48	36
5	Nottm Forest	34	13	9	12	43	43	35
6	Derby	34	13	9	12	39	41	35
7	Bury	34	13	8	13	44	38	34
8	Aston Villa	34	13	8	13	42	40	34
9	Wednesday	34	13	8	13	48	52	34
10	Sheff United	34	13	7	14	53	48	33
11	Liverpool	34	10	12	12	42	38	32
12	Bolton	34	12	8	14	51	56	32
13	Notts County	34	14	4	16	51	57	32
14	Wolves	34	13	6	15	46	57	32
15	Grimsby	34	13	6	15	44	60	32
16	Stoke	34	11	9	14	45	55	31
17	Small Heath	34	11	8	15	47	45	30
18	Man City	34	11	6	17	42	58	28

SECOND DIVISION

		P	W	D	L	F	A	Pts
1	WBA	34	25	5	4	82	29	55
2	Middlesbrough	34	23	5	6	90	24	51
3	Preston NE	34	18	6	10	71	32	42
4	Woolwich A	34	18	6	10	50	26	42
5	Lincoln	34	14	13	7	45	35	41
6	Bristol City	34	17	6	11	52	35	40
7	Doncaster	34	13	8	13	49	58	34
8	Glossop NE	34	10	12	12	36	40	32
9	Burnley	34	10	10	14	41	45	30
10	Burton United	34	11	8	15	46	54	30
11	Barnsley	34	12	6	16	51	63	30
12	Burslem PV	34	10	9	15	43	59	29
13	Blackpool	34	11	7	16	40	56	29
14	Leicester Fosse	34	12	5	17	38	56	29
15	Newton Heath	34	11	6	17	38	53	28
16	Chesterfield	34	11	6	17	47	68	28
17	Stockport	34	8	7	19	36	72	23
18	Gainsborough	34	4	11	19	30	80	19

SCOTTISH FIRST DIVISION

		P	W	D	L	F	A	Pts
1	Rangers	18	13	2	3	43	29	28
2	Celtic	18	11	4	3	38	28	26
3	Hearts	18	10	2	6	32	21	22
4	Third Lanark	18	7	5	6	30	26	19
5	St Mirren	18	8	3	7	29	28	19
6	Hibernian	18	6	4	8	36	24	16
7	Kilmarnock	18	5	6	7	21	25	16
8	Queen's Park	18	5	4	9	21	32	14
9	Dundee	18	4	5	9	16	31	13
10	Morton	18	1	5	12	18	40	7

SCOTTISH SECOND DIVISION

		P	W	D	L	F	A	Pts
1	Port Glasgow*	22	14	4	4	71	31	32
2	Partick*	22	14	3	5	55	26	31
3	Motherwell	22	12	2	8	50	44	26
4	Airdrieonians	22	10	5	7	40	32	25
5	Hamilton	22	11	3	8	45	40	25
6	St Bernard's	22	10	2	10	30	30	22
7	Leith	22	9	3	10	34	38	21
8	Ayr	22	8	5	9	27	33	21
9	E Stirlingshire	22	8	3	11	36	46	19
10	Arthurlie	22	6	5	11	32	42	17
11	Abercorn	22	4	5	13	27	57	13
12	Clyde	22	5	3	14	22	50	13

*Elected to First Division

On 5 April 1902, England met Scotland in an International Championship match at Ibrox Park, Glasgow. The day produced the worst disaster the game had known.

The ground was full by kick-off time, and latecomers, anxious not to miss too much of the game, made a dash from the packed East terrace to the West terrace. They charged up the staircases to the top, and settled to watch the match. Heavy rain was falling. Suddenly, rows of steel pylons at the back and front of the terrace shook and a yawning gap 70 feet by 14 feet wide appeared. People literally dropped through to the ground below, and others followed and fell

on top of them. Officially, 25 were killed, 24 dangerously injured, 153 injured, and 172 slightly injured. The match ended 1-1, but was deleted from international records, and later replayed at Birmingham.

Top The Aston Villa forwards attack Sunderland's goal in March 1902. Before the start of the following season, the curved line marking the goal area was replaced by the six-yard box.

Bottom 'Fatty' Foulke, Sheffield United's 21-stone goalkeeper, prepares to gather a tentative shot from the old-style lines during the 1902 Cup Final.

FA CUP 1901-02

FIRST ROUND
Tottenham Hotspur v Southampton	1-1, 2-2, 1-2
Liverpool v Everton	2-2, 2-0
Bury v West Bromwich Albion	5-1
Walsall v Burnley	1-0
Glossop North End v Nottingham Forest	1-3
Manchester City v Preston North End	1-1, 0-0, 4-2*
Stoke v Aston Villa	2-2, 2-1
Bristol Rovers v Middlesbrough	1-1, 1-0
Northampton Town v Sheffield United	0-2
Wolverhampton Wanderers v Bolton Wanderers	0-2
Woolwich Arsenal v Newcastle United	0-2
The Wednesday v Sunderland	0-1
Blackburn Rovers v Derby County	0-2
Lincoln City v Oxford City	0-0, 4-0
Portsmouth v Grimsby Town	1-1, 2-0
Notts County v Reading	1-2

*At Preston. Preston won the toss for choice of ground.

SECOND ROUND
Southampton v Liverpool	4-1
Walsall v Bury	0-5
Manchester City v Nottingham Forest	0-2
Bristol Rovers v Stoke	0-1
Sheffield United v Bolton Wanderers	2-1
Newcastle United v Sunderland	1-0
Lincoln City v Derby County	1-3
Reading v Portsmouth	0-1

THIRD ROUND
Bury v Southampton	2-3
Nottingham Forest v Stoke	2-0
Newcastle United v Sheffield United	1-1, 1-2
Derby County v Portsmouth	0-0, 6-3

SEMI-FINAL
Southampton v Nottingham Forest	3-1
Sheffield United v Derby County	1-1, 1-1, 1-0

FINAL AT CRYSTAL PALACE
Sheffield United v Southampton	1-1, 2-1†

†replay at Crystal Palace

SCOTTISH FA CUP 1901-02

FIRST ROUND
Arbroath v Kilwinning Eglinton (scratched)	wo
Third Lanark v Morton	0-0, 3-2
St Mirren v Airdrieonians	1-0
Ayr v Dundee	0-0, 0-2
Arthurlie v Port Glasgow Athletic	1-1, 1-3
Celtic v Thornliebank	3-0
Rangers v Johnstone	6-1
Queen's Park v Maxwelltown Volunteers	7-0
Partick Thistle v Kilmarnock	0-4
Falkirk	bye
Forfar Athletic	bye
Heart of Midlothian	bye
Hibernian	bye
Inverness Caledonian	bye
St Bernard's	bye
Stenhousemuir	bye

SECOND ROUND
Heart of Midlothian v Third Lanark	4-1
St Mirren v Stenhousemuir	6-0
Arbroath v Celtic	2-3
Rangers v Inverness Caledonian	5-1
Kilmarnock v Dundee	2-0
Falkirk v St Bernard's	2-0
Forfar Athletic v Queen's Park	1-4
Port Glasgow Athletic v Hibernian	1-5

THIRD ROUND
Falkirk v St Mirren	0-1
Heart of Midlothian v Celtic	1-1, 1-2
Hibernian v Queen's Park	7-1
Rangers v Kilmarnock	2-0

SEMI-FINAL
Rangers v Hibernian	0-2
St Mirren v Celtic	2-3

FINAL AT CELTIC PARK,
Hibernian v Celtic	1-0

184

FIRST DIVISION

		P	W	D	L	F	A	Pts
1	Wednesday	34	19	4	11	54	36	42
2	Aston Villa	34	19	3	12	61	40	41
3	Sunderland	34	16	9	9	51	36	41
4	Sheff United	34	17	5	12	58	44	39
5	Liverpool	34	17	4	13	68	49	38
6	Stoke	34	15	7	12	46	38	37
7	WBA	34	16	4	14	54	53	36
8	Bury	34	16	3	15	54	43	35
9	Derby	34	16	3	15	50	47	35
10	Nottm Forest	34	14	7	13	49	47	35
11	Wolves	34	14	5	15	48	57	33
12	Everton	34	13	6	15	45	47	32
13	Middlesbrough	34	14	4	16	41	50	32
14	Newcastle	34	14	4	16	41	51	32
15	Notts County	34	12	7	15	41	49	31
16	Blackburn	34	12	5	17	44	63	29
17	Grimsby	34	8	9	17	43	62	25
18	Bolton	34	8	3	23	37	73	19

SECOND DIVISION

		P	W	D	L	F	A	Pts
1	Man City	34	25	4	5	95	29	54
2	Small Heath	34	24	3	7	74	36	51
3	Woolwich A	34	20	8	6	66	30	48
4	Bristol City	34	17	8	9	59	38	42
5	Man United	34	15	8	11	53	38	38
6	Chesterfield	34	14	9	11	67	40	37
7	Preston	34	13	10	11	56	40	36
8	Barnsley	34	13	8	13	55	51	34
9	Burslem PV	34	13	8	13	57	62	34
10	Lincoln	34	12	6	16	46	53	30
11	Glossop NE	34	11	7	16	43	58	29
12	Gainsborough	34	11	7	16	41	59	29
13	Burton United	34	11	7	16	39	59	29
14	Blackpool	34	9	10	15	44	59	28
15	Leicester Fosse	34	10	8	16	41	65	28
16	Doncaster	34	9	7	18	35	72	25
17	Stockport	34	7	6	21	39	74	20
18	Burnley	34	6	8	20	30	77	20

SCOTTISH FIRST DIVISION

		P	W	D	L	F	A	Pts
1	Hibernian	22	16	5	1	48	18	37
2	Dundee	22	13	5	4	31	12	31
3	Rangers	22	12	5	5	56	30	29
4	Hearts	22	11	6	5	46	27	28
5	Celtic	22	8	10	4	36	30	26
6	St Mirren	22	7	8	7	39	40	22
7	Third Lanark	22	8	5	9	34	27	21
8	Partick	22	6	7	9	34	50	19
9	Kilmarnock	22	6	4	12	24	43	16
10	Queen's Park	22	5	5	12	33	48	15
11	Port Glasgow	22	3	5	14	26	49	11
12	Morton	22	2	5	15	22	55	9

SCOTTISH SECOND DIVISION

		P	W	D	L	F	A	Pts
1	Airdrieonians*	22	15	5	2	43	19	35
2	Motherwell*	22	12	4	6	44	35	28
3	Ayr	22	12	3	7	34	24	27
4	Leith	22	11	5	6	43	41	27
5	St Bernard's	22	12	2	8	45	32	26
6	Hamilton	22	11	1	10	44	35	23
7	Falkirk	22	8	7	7	39	37	23
8	E Stirlingshire	22	9	3	10	46	41	21
9	Arthurlie	22	6	8	8	34	46	20
10	Abercorn	22	5	2	15	35	58	12
11	Raith	22	3	5	14	34	55	11
12	Clyde	22	2	7	13	22	40	11

*elected to First Division

FA CUP 1902-03

FIRST ROUND

Tottenham Hotspur v West Bromwich Albion	0-0, 2-0
Bolton Wanderers v Bristol City	0-5
Aston Villa v Sunderland	4-1
Barnsley v Lincoln City	2-0
Woolwich Arsenal v Sheffield United	1-3
Bury v Wolverhampton Wanderers	1-0
Grimsby Town v Newcastle United	2-1
Notts County v Southampton	0-0, 2-2, 2-1
Derby County v Small Heath	2-1
Blackburn Rovers v The Wednesday	0-0, 1-0
Nottingham Forest v Reading	0-0, 6-3
Glossop North End v Stoke	2-3
Millwall Athletic v Luton Town	3-0
Preston North End v Manchester City	3-1
Everton v Portsmouth	5-0
Manchester United v Liverpool	2-1

SECOND ROUND

Tottenham Hotspur v Bristol City	1-0
Aston Villa v Barnsley	4-1
Sheffield United v Bury	0-1
Grimsby Town v Notts County	0-2
Derby County v Blackburn Rovers	2-0
Nottingham Forest v Stoke	0-0, 0-2
Millwall Athletic v Preston North End	4-1
Everton v Manchester United	3-1

THIRD ROUND

Tottenham Hotspur v Aston Villa	2-3
Bury v Notts County	1-0
Derby County v Stoke	3-0
Millwall Athletic v Everton	1-0

SEMI-FINAL

Aston Villa v Bury	0-3
Derby County v Millwall Athletic	3-0

FINAL AT CRYSTAL PALACE

Bury v Derby County	6-0

SCOTTISH FA CUP 1902-03

FIRST ROUND

Celtic v St Mirren	0-0, 1-1, 4-0
St Johnstone v Third Lanark	1-10
Nithsdale Wanderers v Orion	1-0
Queen's Park v Motherwell	1-2
Abercorn v Douglas Wanderers	2-2, 1-3
Vale of Leven v Partick Thistle	0-4
Hamilton Academicals v Airdrieonians	5-0
Arbroath v Kilmarnock	1-3
Leith Athletic v Broxburn United	4-1
St Bernard's v Port Glasgow Athletic	1-2
Rangers v Auchterarder Thistle	7-0
Clyde v Heart of Midlothian	1-2
Hibernian v Morton	7-0
Ayr v Camelon	2-0
Dundee v Barholm Rovers	wo
Stenhousemuir v Inverness Caledonian	wo

SECOND ROUND

Celtic v Port Glasgow Athletic	2-0
Hamilton Academicals v Third Lanark	2-2, 1-3
Stenhousemuir v Douglas Wanderers	6-1
Motherwell v Partick Thistle	0-2
Dundee v Nithsdale Wanderers	7-0
Rangers v Kilmarnock	4-0
Ayr v Heart of Midlothian	2-4
Hibernian v Leith Athletic	4-1

THIRD ROUND

Celtic v Rangers	0-3
Dundee v Hibernian	0-0, 0-0, 1-0
Heart of Midlothian v Third Lanark	2-1
Stenhousemuir v Partick Thistle	3-0

SEMI-FINAL

Stenhousemuir v Rangers	1-4
Dundee v Heart of Midlothian	0-0, 0-1

FINAL AT CELTIC PARK

Rangers v Heart of Midlothian	1-1, 0-0, 2-0

Bury on the attack against Derby County on their way to the record win, 6-0, in an FA Cup Final.

CONWAY PICTURE LIBRARY

185

FIRST DIVISION

	P	W	D	L	F	A	Pts
1 Wednesday	34	20	7	7	48	28	47
2 Man City	34	19	6	9	71	45	44
3 Everton	34	19	5	10	59	32	43
4 Newcastle	34	18	6	10	58	45	42
5 Aston Villa	34	17	7	10	70	48	41
6 Sunderland	34	17	5	12	63	49	39
7 Sheff United	34	15	8	11	62	57	38
8 Wolves	34	14	8	12	44	66	36
9 Nottm Forest	34	11	9	14	57	57	31
10 Middlesbrough	34	9	12	13	46	47	30
11 Small Heath	34	11	8	15	39	52	30
12 Bury	34	7	15	12	40	53	29
13 Notts County	34	12	5	17	37	61	29
14 Derby	34	9	10	15	58	60	28
15 Blackburn	34	11	6	17	48	60	28
16 Stoke	34	10	7	17	54	57	27
17 Liverpool	34	9	8	17	49	62	26
18 WBA	34	7	10	17	36	60	24

SECOND DIVISION

	P	W	D	L	F	A	Pts
1 Preston	34	20	10	4	62	24	50
2 Woolwich A	34	21	7	6	91	22	49
3 Man United	34	20	8	6	65	33	48
4 Bristol City	34	18	6	10	73	41	42
5 Burnley	34	15	9	10	50	55	39
6 Grimsby	34	14	8	12	50	49	36
7 Bolton	34	12	10	12	59	41	34
8 Barnsley	34	11	10	13	38	57	32
9 Gainsborough	34	14	3	17	53	60	31
10 Bradford City	34	12	7	15	45	59	31
11 Chesterfield	34	11	8	15	37	45	30
12 Lincoln	34	11	8	15	41	58	30
13 Burslem PV	34	10	9	15	54	52	29
14 Burton United	34	11	7	16	45	61	29
15 Blackpool	34	11	5	18	40	67	27
16 Stockport	34	8	11	15	40	72	27
17 Glossop NE	34	10	6	18	57	64	26
18 Leicester Fosse	34	6	10	18	42	82	22

SCOTTISH FIRST DIVISION

	P	W	D	L	F	A	Pts
1 Third Lanark	26	20	3	3	61	26	43
2 Hearts	26	18	3	5	62	34	39
3 Celtic	26	18	2	6	68	27	38
4 Rangers	26	16	6	4	80	33	38
5 Dundee	26	13	2	11	54	45	28
6 St Mirren	26	11	5	10	45	38	27
7 Partick	26	10	7	9	46	41	27
8 Queen's Park	26	6	9	11	28	47	21
9 Port Glasgow	26	8	4	14	32	49	20
10 Hibernian	26	7	5	14	29	40	19
11 Morton	26	7	4	15	32	53	18
12 Airdrieonians	26	7	4	15	32	62	18
13 Motherwell	26	6	3	17	26	61	15
14 Kilmarnock	26	4	5	17	24	63	13

SCOTTISH SECOND DIVISION

	P	W	D	L	F	A	Pts
1 Hamilton	22	16	5	1	56	19	37
2 Clyde	22	12	5	5	51	36	29
3 Ayr	22	11	6	5	33	30	28
4 Falkirk	22	11	4	7	50	34	26
5 Raith	22	8	5	9	40	38	21
6 E Stirlingshire	22	8	5	9	35	40	21
7 Leith	22	8	4	10	42	40	20
8 St Bernard's	22	9	2	11	31	43	20
9 Albion*	22	8	5	9	47	37	19
10 Abercorn	22	6	4	12	38	55	16
11 Arthurlie	22	5	5	12	37	50	15
12 Ayr Parkhouse	22	3	4	15	23	61	10

*Two points deducted for fielding an unregistered player.

FA CUP 1903-04

FIRST ROUND
Manchester City v Sunderland	3-2
Woolwich Arsenal v Fulham	1-0
Millwall Athletic v Middlesbrough	0-2
Preston North End v Grimsby Town	1-0
Plymouth Argyle v The Wednesday	2-2, 0-2
Notts County v Manchester United	3-3, 1-2
Everton v Tottenham Hotspur	1-2
Stoke v Aston Villa	2-3
Reading v Bolton Wanderers	1-1, 2-3
Southampton v Burslem Port Vale	3-0
Bristol City v Sheffield United	1-3
Bury v Newcastle United	2-1
Portsmouth v Derby County	2-5
Stockton v Wolverhampton Wanderers	1-4
Blackburn Rovers v Liverpool	3-1
West Bromwich Albion v Nottingham Forest	1-1, 1-3

SECOND ROUND
Woolwich Arsenal v Manchester City	0-2
Preston North End v Middlesbrough	0-3
The Wednesday v Manchester United	6-0
Tottenham Hotspur v Aston Villa	0-1*, 1-0
Bolton Wanderers v Southampton	4-1
Bury v Sheffield United	1-2
Derby County v Wolverhampton Wanderers	2-2, 2-2, 1-0
Blackburn Rovers v Nottingham Forest	3-1

*The Tottenham crowd invaded the pitch when Villa were leading 1-0 and the game was abandoned. Tottenham were fined £350 and the FA ordered the return to be played at Villa Park.

THIRD ROUND
Manchester City v Middlesbrough	0-0, 3-1
Tottenham Hotspur v The Wednesday	1-1, 0-2
Sheffield United v Bolton Wanderers	0-2
Derby County v Blackburn Rovers	2-1

SEMI-FINAL
Manchester City v The Wednesday	3-0
Bolton Wanderers v Derby County	1-0

FINAL AT CRYSTAL PALACE
Manchester City v Bolton Wanderers	1-0

SCOTTISH FA CUP 1903-04

FIRST ROUND
Abercorn v Maxwelltown Volunteers	2-2, 1-1, 2-1
Nithsdale Wanderers v Kilmarnock	2-2, 1-1, 1-2
Clyde v Arbroath	2-2, 0-4
Rangers v Heart of Midlothian	3-2
Dundee v Queen's Park	3-0
Hibernian v Airdrieonians	2-1
Motherwell v Partick Thistle	2-1
Ayr v St Mirren	0-2
St Johnstone v Hearts of Beath	2-0
Albion Rovers v Kilwinning Eglinton	2-1
St Bernard's v West Calder Swifts	1-1, 3-3, 2-1
Port Glasgow Athletic v Leith Athletic	1-2
Alloa Athletic v Aberdour	2-1
Third Lanark v Newton Stewart Athletic (scratched)	wo
Celtic v Stanley (scratched)	wo
Morton v Dalbeattie Star (scratched)	wo

SECOND ROUND
Kilmarnock v Albion Rovers	2-2, 1-0
St Bernard's v Celtic	0-4
Dundee v Abercorn	4-0
Third Lanark v Alloa Athletic	3-1
Hibernian v Rangers	1-2
Leith Athletic v Motherwell	3-1
Morton v Arbroath	2-0
St Mirren v St Johnstone	4-0

THIRD ROUND
Celtic v Dundee	1-1, 0-0, 5-0
Third Lanark v Kilmarnock	3-0
St Mirren v Rangers	0-1
Leith Athletic v Morton	1-3

SEMI-FINAL
Celtic v Third Lanark	2-1
Rangers v Morton	3-0

FINAL AT HAMPDEN PARK
Celtic v Rangers	3-2

Below *The Manchester City side that won the FA Cup in 1903-04. Seated in the centre is the captain and great Welsh right-winger, Billy Meredith of Chirk.*

At Bradford, Sheffield FC, the oldest football club in the world, won their first and only honour when they beat Ealing 3-1 in the 1904 Amateur Cup final.

MANCHESTER CITY FOOTBALL CLUB.

WINNERS OF ENGLISH CUP, 1903-4.

RUNNERS-UP, FOOTBALL LEAGUE, 1903-4. ♦ JOINT HOLDERS MANCHESTER CUP, 1903-4.

FIRST DIVISION

		P	W	D	L	F	A	Pts
1	Newcastle	34	23	2	9	72	33	48
2	Everton	34	21	5	8	63	36	47
3	Man City	34	20	6	8	66	37	46
4	Aston Villa	34	19	4	11	63	43	42
5	Sunderland	34	16	8	10	60	44	40
6	Sheff United	34	19	2	13	64	56	40
7	Small Heath	34	17	5	12	54	38	39
8	Preston	34	13	10	11	42	37	36
9	Wednesday	34	14	5	15	61	57	33
10	Woolwich A	34	12	9	13	36	40	33
11	Derby	34	12	8	14	37	48	32
12	Stoke	34	13	4	17	40	58	30
13	Blackburn	34	11	5	18	40	51	27
14	Wolves	34	11	4	19	47	73	26
15	Middlesbrough	34	9	8	17	36	56	26
16	Nottm Forest	34	9	7	18	40	61	25
17	Bury	34	10	4	20	47	67	24
18	Notts County	34	5	8	21	36	69	18

SECOND DIVISION

		P	W	D	L	F	A	Pts
1	Liverpool	34	27	4	3	93	25	58
2	Bolton	34	27	2	5	87	32	56
3	Man United	34	24	5	5	81	30	53
4	Bristol City	34	19	4	11	66	45	42
5	Chesterfield	34	14	11	9	44	35	39
6	Gainsborough	34	14	8	12	61	58	36
7	Barnsley	34	14	5	15	38	56	33
8	Bradford City	34	12	8	14	45	49	32
9	Lincoln	34	12	7	15	42	40	31
10	WBA	34	13	4	17	56	48	30
11	Burnley	34	12	6	16	43	52	30
12	Glossop NE	34	10	10	14	37	46	30
13	Grimsby	34	11	8	15	33	46	30
14	Leicester Fosse	34	11	7	16	40	55	29
15	Blackpool	34	9	10	15	36	48	28
16	Burslem PV	34	10	7	17	47	72	27
17	Burton United	34	8	4	22	30	84	20
18	Doncaster	34	3	2	29	23	81	8

SCOTTISH FIRST DIVISION

		P	W	D	L	F	A	Pts
1	Celtic*	26	18	5	3	68	31	41
2	Rangers	26	19	3	4	83	28	41
3	Third Lanark	26	14	7	5	60	28	35
4	Airdrieonians	26	11	5	10	38	45	27
5	Hibernian	26	9	8	9	39	39	26
6	Partick	26	12	2	12	36	56	26
7	Dundee	26	10	5	11	38	32	25
8	Hearts	26	11	3	12	46	44	25
9	Kilmarnock	26	9	5	12	29	45	23
10	St Mirren	26	9	4	13	33	36	22
11	Port Glasgow	26	8	5	13	30	51	21
12	Queen's Park	26	6	8	12	28	45	20
13	Morton	26	7	4	15	27	50	18
14	Motherwell	26	6	2	18	28	53	14

*Celtic won a deciding match against Rangers

SCOTTISH SECOND DIVISION

		P	W	D	L	F	A	Pts
1	Clyde	22	13	6	3	38	22	32
2	Falkirk*	22	12	4	6	31	25	28
3	Hamilton	22	12	3	7	40	22	27
4	Leith	22	10	4	8	36	26	24
5	Ayr	22	11	1	10	46	37	23
6	Arthurlie	22	9	5	8	37	42	23
7	Aberdeen*	22	7	7	8	36	26	21
8	Albion	22	8	4	10	38	53	20
9	E Stirlingshire	22	7	5	10	38	38	19
10	Raith	22	9	1	12	30	34	19
11	Abercorn	22	8	1	13	31	45	17
12	St Bernard's	22	3	5	14	23	54	11

*Aberdeen and Falkirk were elected to the First Division

FA CUP 1904-05

FIRST ROUND

Lincoln City v Manchester City	1-2
Bolton Wanderers v Bristol Rovers	1-1, 3-0
Middlesbrough v Tottenham Hotspur	1-1, 0-1
Newcastle United v Plymouth Argyle	1-1, 1-1, 2-0
Woolwich Arsenal v Bristol City	0-0, 0-1
Derby County v Preston North End	0-2
Blackburn Rovers v The Wednesday	1-2
Small Heath v Portsmouth	0-2
Stoke v Grimsby Town	2-0
Liverpool v Everton	1-1, 1-2
Sunderland v Wolverhampton Wanderers	1-1, 0-1
Southampton v Millwall Athletic	3-1
Aston Villa v Leicester Fosse	5-1
Bury v Notts County	1-0
Fulham v Reading	0-0, 0-0, 1-0
Nottingham Forest v Sheffield United	2-0

SECOND ROUND

Manchester City v Bolton Wanderers	1-2
Tottenham Hotspur v Newcastle United	1-1, 0-4
Bristol City v Preston North End	0-0, 0-1
The Wednesday v Portsmouth	2-1
Stoke v Everton	0-4
Wolverhampton Wanderers v Southampton	2-3
Aston Villa v Bury	3-2
Fulham v Nottingham Forest	1-0

THIRD ROUND

Bolton Wanderers v Newcastle United	0-2
Preston North End v The Wednesday	1-1, 0-3
Everton v Southampton	4-0
Aston Villa v Fulham	5-0

SEMI-FINAL

Newcastle United v The Wednesday	1-0
Everton v Aston Villa	1-1, 1-2

FINAL AT CRYSTAL PALACE

Aston Villa v Newcastle United	2-0

SCOTTISH FA CUP 1904-05

FIRST ROUND

Rangers v Ayr	2-1
Dundee v Heart of Midlothian	1-3
Dumfries v Celtic	1-2
Port Glasgow Athletic v Stranraer	3-0
Airdrieonians v St Johnstone	7-0
Aberdeen v Queen's Park	2-1
St Mirren v Clyde	1-0
Third Lanark v Leith Athletic	4-1
Morton v Renton	2-0
Kilmarnock v Beith	2-2, 1-3
Bathgate v Arbroath	2-1
Arthurlie v Motherwell	0-0, 0-1
Hibernian v Partick Thistle	1-1, 2-4
Kirkcaldy United v Crieff Morrisonians	3-1
Cowdenbeath v 6th GRV	6-0
Lochgelly United v Inverness Caledonian	5-1

SECOND ROUND

Celtic v Lochgelly United	3-0
Aberdeen v Bathgate	1-1, 6-1
Kirkcaldy United v Partick Thistle	0-1
Morton v Rangers	0-6
Airdrieonians v Port Glasgow Athletic	3-0
Motherwell v Third Lanark	0-1
St Mirren v Heart of Midlothian	1-0
Beith v Cowdenbeath	4-0

THIRD ROUND

St Mirren v Airdrieonians	0-0, 1-3
Rangers v Beith	5-1
Celtic v Partick Thistle	3-0
Third Lanark v Aberdeen	4-1

SEMI-FINAL

Celtic v Rangers	0-2
Airdrieonians v Third Lanark	1-2

FINAL AT HAMPDEN PARK

Third Lanark v Rangers	0-0, 3-1

Doncaster Rovers had a disastrous spell in the Second Division and were voted out of the League in 1905 after gaining the fewest number of points (8) ever won by a League club in a single season. Not one of those 8 was won away from home. This equalled Loughborough Town's dreadful 1899-1900 season when they also accumulated just 8 points. Loughborough, however, established a record by winning only one of their 34 League games.

Below The only known panoramic view of Crystal Palace during a Cup Final. The event was played there from 1895 to 1914 but, apart from the small stands on the right, there was little accommodation available. The Crystal Palace itself, which had been moved from Hyde Park after the Great Exhibition of the 1850s, was on the hill above the funfair to the right. The 1905 Final attracted over 100,000 spectators, only the second time in history an English football match had drawn a six-figure crowd. Some fans can be seen clinging on to trees on the left as Aston Villa play Newcastle United.

FIRST DIVISION

		P	W	D	L	F	A	Pts
1	Liverpool	38	23	5	10	79	46	51
2	Preston NE	38	17	13	8	54	39	47
3	Wednesday	38	18	8	12	63	52	44
4	Newcastle	38	18	7	13	74	48	43
5	Man City	38	19	5	14	73	54	43
6	Bolton	38	17	7	14	81	67	41
7	Birmingham	38	17	7	14	65	59	41
8	Aston Villa	38	17	6	15	72	56	40
9	Blackburn	38	16	8	14	54	52	40
10	Stoke	38	16	7	15	54	55	39
11	Everton	38	15	7	16	70	66	37
12	Woolwich A	38	15	7	16	62	64	37
13	Sheff United	38	15	6	17	57	62	36
14	Sunderland	38	15	5	18	61	70	35
15	Derby	38	14	7	17	39	58	35
16	Notts County	38	11	12	15	55	71	34
17	Bury	38	11	10	17	57	74	32
18	Middlesbrough	38	10	11	17	56	71	31
19	Nottm Forest	38	13	5	20	58	79	31
20	Wolves	38	8	7	23	58	99	23

SECOND DIVISION

		P	W	D	L	F	A	Pts
1	Bristol City	38	30	6	2	83	28	66
2	Man United	38	28	6	4	90	28	62
3	Chelsea	38	22	9	7	90	37	53
4	WBA	38	22	8	8	79	36	52
5	Hull	38	19	6	13	67	54	44
6	Leeds City	38	17	9	12	59	47	43
7	Leicester Fosse	38	15	12	11	53	48	42
8	Grimsby	38	15	10	13	46	46	40
9	Burnley	38	15	8	15	42	53	38
10	Stockport	38	13	9	16	44	56	35
11	Bradford City	38	13	8	17	46	60	34
12	Barnsley	38	12	9	17	60	62	33
13	Lincoln	38	12	6	20	69	72	30
14	Blackpool	38	10	9	19	37	62	29
15	Gainsborough	38	12	4	22	44	57	28
16	Glossop NE	38	10	8	20	49	71	28
17	Burslem PV	38	12	4	22	49	82	28
18	Chesterfield	38	10	8	20	40	72	28
19	Burton United	38	10	6	22	34	67	26
20	Clapton Orient	38	7	7	24	35	78	21

SCOTTISH FIRST DIVISION

		P	W	D	L	F	A	Pts
1	Celtic	30	24	1	5	76	19	49
2	Hearts	30	18	7	5	64	27	43
3	Airdrieonians	30	15	8	7	53	31	38
4	Rangers	30	15	7	8	58	48	37
5	Partick	30	15	6	9	44	40	36
6	Third Lanark	30	16	2	12	62	39	34
7	Dundee	30	11	12	7	40	33	34
8	St Mirren	30	13	5	12	41	37	31
9	Motherwell	30	9	8	13	50	62	26
10	Morton	30	10	6	14	35	54	26
11	Hibernian	30	10	5	15	35	40	25
12	Aberdeen	30	8	8	14	36	48	24
13	Falkirk	30	9	5	16	52	68	23
14	Kilmarnock	30	8	4	18	46	68	20
15	Port Glasgow	30	6	8	16	38	68	20
16	Queen's Park	30	5	4	21	39	87	14

SCOTTISH SECOND DIVISION

		P	W	D	L	F	A	Pts
1	Leith	22	15	4	3	46	21	34
2	Clyde*	22	11	9	2	37	21	31
3	Albion	22	12	3	7	48	29	27
4	Hamilton*	22	12	2	8	45	34	26
5	St Bernard's	22	9	4	9	42	34	22
6	Arthurlie	22	10	2	10	42	43	22
7	Ayr	22	9	3	10	43	51	21
8	Raith	22	6	7	9	36	42	19
9	Cowdenbeath	22	7	3	12	27	39	17
10	Abercorn	22	6	5	11	29	45	17
11	Vale of Leven	22	6	4	12	34	49	16
12	E Stirlingshire	22	1	10	11	26	47	12

*Elected to First Division

Below *The Everton team that won the club's first ever FA Cup in 1906.*

FA CUP 1905-06

SECOND ROUND
Woolwich Arsenal v Watford	3-0
Sunderland v Gainsborough Trinity	1-1, 3-0
Manchester United v Norwich City	3-0
Aston Villa v Plymouth Argyle	0-0, 5-1
Derby County v Newcastle United	0-0, 1-2
Blackpool v Sheffield United	2-1
Tottenham Hotspur v Reading	3-2
Stoke v Birmingham	0-1
Chesterfield Town v Everton	0-3
Bradford City v Wolverhampton Wanderers	5-0
The Wednesday v Millwall Athletic	1-1, 3-0
Fulham v Nottingham Forest	1-3
Barnsley v Liverpool	0-1
Brentford v Lincoln City	3-0
New Brompton v Southampton	0-0, 0-1
Brighton v Middlesbrough	1-1, 1-1, 1-3

THIRD ROUND
Woolwich Arsenal v Sunderland	5-0
Manchester United v Aston Villa	5-1
Newcastle United v Blackpool	5-0
Tottenham Hotspur v Birmingham	1-1, 0-2
Everton v Bradford City	1-0
The Wednesday v Nottingham Forest	4-1
Liverpool v Brentford	2-0
Southampton v Middlesbrough	6-1

FOURTH ROUND
Manchester United v Woolwich Arsenal	2-3
Birmingham v Newcastle United	2-2, 0-3
Everton v The Wednesday	4-3
Liverpool v Southampton	3-0

SEMI-FINAL
Woolwich Arsenal v Newcastle United	0-2
Everton v Liverpool	2-0

FINAL AT CRYSTAL PALACE
Everton v Newcastle United	1-0

SCOTTISH FA CUP 1905-06

FIRST ROUND
Dundee v Celtic	1-2
Kilmarnock v Clyde	2-1
Beith v Inverness Thistle	2-0
Third Lanark v Galston	5-0
Forfar Athletic v Queen's Park	0-4
Falkirk v Hibernian	1-2
Leith Athletic v Partick Thistle	1-2
Heart of Midlothian v Nithsdale Wanderers	4-1
Motherwell v Hamilton Academicals	2-3
Airdrieonians v Maxwelltown Volunteers	9-2
Aberdeen v Dunfermline Athletic	3-0
Morton v Lochgelly United	4-3
St Mirren v Black Watch	7-2
Arthurlie v Rangers	1-7
Arbroath v Bo'ness	1-4
Port Glasgow Athletic v Dunblane	6-1

SECOND ROUND
Aberdeen v Rangers	2-3
Hibernian v Partick Thistle	1-1, 1-1, 2-1
Beith v Heart of Midlothian	0-3
Celtic v Bo'ness	3-0
Third Lanark v Hamilton Academicals	2-2, 3-1
St Mirren v Morton	3-1
Kilmarnock v Port Glasgow Athletic	2-2, 0-0, 0-0, 0-1
Queen's Park v Airdrieonians	1-2

THIRD ROUND
Celtic v Heart of Midlothian	1-2
Airdrieonians v St Mirren	0-0, 0-2
Port Glasgow Athletic v Rangers	1-0
Hibernian v Third Lanark	1-2

SEMI-FINAL
St Mirren v Third Lanark	1-1, 0-0, 0-1
Port Glasgow Athletic v Heart of Midlothian	0-2

FINAL AT IBROX PARK
Heart of Midlothian v Third Lanark	1-0

COLORSPORT

FIRST DIVISION

		P	W	D	L	F	A	Pts
1	Newcastle	38	22	7	9	74	46	51
2	Bristol City	38	20	8	10	66	47	48
3	Everton	38	20	5	13	70	46	45
4	Sheff United	38	17	11	10	57	55	45
5	Aston Villa	38	19	6	13	78	52	44
6	Bolton	38	18	8	12	59	47	44
7	Woolwich A	38	20	4	14	66	59	44
8	Man United	38	17	8	13	53	56	42
9	Birmingham	38	15	8	15	52	52	38
10	Sunderland	38	14	9	15	65	66	37
11	Middlesbrough	38	15	6	17	56	63	36
12	Blackburn	38	14	7	17	56	59	35
13	Wednesday	38	12	11	15	49	60	35
14	Preston	38	14	7	17	44	57	35
15	Liverpool	38	13	7	18	64	65	33
16	Bury	38	13	6	19	58	68	32
17	Man City	38	10	12	16	53	77	32
18	Notts County	38	8	15	15	46	50	31
19	Derby	38	9	9	20	41	59	27
20	Stoke	38	8	10	20	41	64	26

SECOND DIVISION

		P	W	D	L	F	A	Pts
1	Nottm Forest	38	28	4	6	74	36	60
2	Chelsea	38	26	5	7	80	34	57
3	Leicester Fosse	38	20	8	10	62	39	48
4	WBA	38	21	5	12	83	45	47
5	Bradford City	38	21	5	12	70	53	47
6	Wolves	38	17	14	14	66	53	41
7	Burnley	38	17	6	15	62	47	40
8	Barnsley	38	15	8	15	73	55	38
9	Hull	38	15	7	16	65	57	37
10	Leeds City	38	13	10	15	55	63	36
11	Grimsby	38	16	3	19	57	62	35
12	Stockport	38	12	11	15	42	52	35
13	Blackpool	38	11	11	16	33	51	33
14	Gainsborough	38	14	5	19	45	72	33
15	Glossop NE	38	13	6	19	53	79	32
16	Burslem PV	38	12	7	19	60	83	31
17	Clapton Orient	38	11	8	19	45	67	30
18	Chesterfield	38	11	7	20	50	66	29
19	Lincoln	38	12	4	22	46	73	28
20	Burton United	38	8	7	23	34	68	23

FA CUP 1906-07

SECOND ROUND

Burslem Port Vale v Notts County	2-2, 0-5
Blackburn Rovers v Tottenham Hotspur	1-1, 1-1, 1-2
West Bromwich Albion v Norwich City	1-0
Derby County v Lincoln City	1-0
Fulham v Crystal Palace	0-0, 0-1
Brentford v Middlesbrough	1-0
West Ham United v Everton	1-2
Bolton Wanderers v Aston Villa	2-0
Woolwich Arsenal v Bristol City	2-1
Bristol Rovers v Millwall	3-0
Barnsley v Portsmouth	1-0
Bury v New Brompton	1-0
Oldham Athletic v Liverpool	0-1
Bradford City v Accrington Stanley	1-0
Southampton v The Wednesday	1-1, 1-3
Luton Town v Sunderland	0-0, 0-1

THIRD ROUND

Notts County v Tottenham Hotspur	4-0
West Bromwich Albion v Derby County	2-0
Crystal Palace v Brentford	1-1, 1-0
Everton v Bolton Wanderers	0-0, 3-0
Woolwich Arsenal v Bristol Rovers	1-0
Barnsley v Bury	1-0
Liverpool v Bradford City	1-0
The Wednesday v Sunderland	0-0, 1-0

FOURTH ROUND

West Bromwich Albion v Notts County	3-1
Crystal Palace v Everton	1-1, 0-4
Barnsley v Woolwich Arsenal	1-2
The Wednesday v Liverpool	1-0

SEMI-FINAL

West Bromwich Albion v Everton	1-2
Woolwich Arsenal v The Wednesday	1-3

FINAL AT CRYSTAL PALACE

The Wednesday v Everton	2-1

SCOTTISH FIRST DIVISION

		P	W	D	L	F	A	Pts
1	Celtic	34	23	9	2	80	30	55
2	Dundee	34	18	12	4	53	26	48
3	Rangers	34	19	7	8	69	33	45
4	Airdrieonians	34	18	6	10	59	44	42
5	Falkirk	34	17	7	10	73	58	41
6	Third Lanark	34	15	9	10	57	48	39
7	St Mirren	34	12	13	9	50	44	37
8	Clyde	34	15	6	13	47	52	36
9	Hearts	34	11	13	10	47	43	35
10	Motherwell	34	12	9	13	45	49	33
11	Aberdeen	34	10	10	14	48	55	30
12	Hibernian	34	10	10	14	40	49	30
13	Morton	34	11	6	17	41	50	28
14	Partick Thistle	34	9	8	17	40	60	26
15	Queen's Park	34	9	6	19	51	66	24
16	Hamilton	34	8	5	21	40	64	21
17	Kilmarnock	34	8	5	21	40	72	21
18	Port Glasgow	34	7	7	20	30	67	21

SCOTTISH SECOND DIVISION

		P	W	D	L	F	A	Pts
1	St Bernard's	22	14	4	4	41	24	32
2	Vale of Leven	22	13	1	8	54	35	27
3	Arthurlie	22	12	3	7	50	39	27
4	Dumbarton	22	11	3	8	52	35	25
5	Leith	22	10	4	8	40	35	24
6	Albion	22	10	3	9	43	36	23
7	Cowdenbeath	22	10	5	7	36	39	23※
8	Ayr	22	7	6	9	34	38	20
9	Abercorn	22	5	7	10	29	47	17
10	Raith	22	6	4	12	39	47	16
11	E Stirlingshire	22	6	4	12	37	48	16
12	Ayr Parkhouse	22	5	2	15	32	64	12

※two points deducted for an irregularity

Below A plate produced by The Wednesday to commemorate winning the Cup in 1907.

SCOTTISH FA CUP 1906-07

FIRST ROUND

Third Lanark v St Johnstone	4-1
Falkirk v Rangers	1-2
Heart of Midlothian v Airdrieonians	0-0, 2-0
Dumfries v Port Glasgow Athletic	2-2, 0-2
Maxwelltown Volunteers v Morton	0-3
Ayr v Cowdenbeath	2-0
Raith Rovers v Aberdeen University	5-1
Arbroath v Queen's Park	1-1, 0-4
Renton v St Bernard's	0-0, 1-1, 2-0
Aberdeen v Johnstone	0-0, 1-2
Celtic v Clyde	2-1
Arthurlie v St Mirren	1-2
Partick Thistle v Dundee	2-2, 1-5
Galston v Motherwell	2-1
Kilmarnock v Clachnacuddin	4-0

SECOND ROUND

Queen's Park v Third Lanark	3-1
Raith Rovers v Ayr	4-0
St Mirren v Port Glasgow Athletic	4-1
Morton v Celtic	0-0, 1-1, 1-2
Hibernian v Johnstone	1-1, 5-0
Galston v Rangers	0-4
Kilmarnock v Heart of Midlothian	0-0, 1-2
Renton v Dundee	1-0

THIRD ROUND

Rangers v Celtic	0-3
St Mirren v Hibernian	1-1, 0-2
Queen's Park v Renton	4-1
Heart of Midlothian v Raith Rovers	2-2, 1-0

SEMI-FINAL

Celtic v Hibernian	0-0, 0-0, 3-0
Heart of Midlothian v Queen's Park	1-0

FINAL AT HAMPDEN PARK

Celtic v Heart of Midlothian	3-0

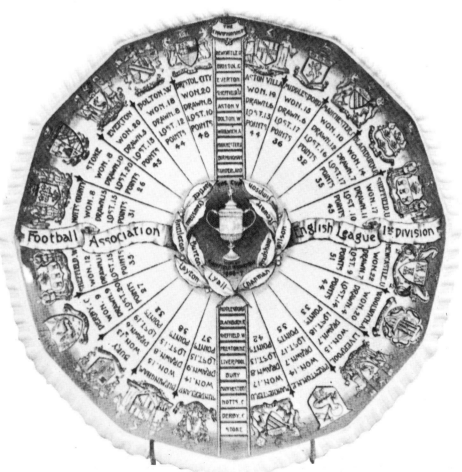

C PROCTOR: COURTESY OF J DANIELS, 20 SILVERTHORNE ROAD, S.W.8

189

FIRST DIVISION

		P	W	D	L	F	A	Pts
1	Man United	38	23	6	9	81	48	52
2	Aston Villa	38	17	9	12	77	59	43
3	Man City	38	16	11	11	62	54	43
4	Newcastle	38	15	12	11	65	54	42
5	Wednesday	38	19	4	15	73	64	42
6	Middlesbrough	38	17	7	14	54	45	41
7	Bury	38	14	11	13	58	61	39
8	Liverpool	38	16	6	16	68	61	38
9	Nottm Forest	38	13	11	14	59	62	37
10	Bristol City	38	12	12	14	58	61	36
11	Everton	38	15	6	17	58	64	36
12	Preston	38	12	12	14	47	53	36
13	Chelsea	38	14	8	16	53	62	36
14	Blackburn*	38	12	12	14	51	63	36
15	Woolwich A*	38	12	12	14	51	63	36
16	Sunderland	38	16	3	19	78	75	35
17	Sheff United	38	12	11	15	52	58	35
18	Notts County	38	13	8	17	39	51	34
19	Bolton	38	14	5	19	52	58	33
20	Birmingham	38	9	12	17	40	60	30

*equal

SECOND DIVISION

		P	W	D	L	F	A	Pts
1	Bradford City	38	24	6	8	90	42	54
2	Leicester Fosse	38	21	10	7	72	47	52
3	Oldham	38	22	6	10	76	42	50
4	Fulham	38	22	5	11	82	49	49
5	WBA	38	19	9	10	61	39	47
6	Derby	38	21	4	13	77	45	46
7	Burnley	38	20	6	12	67	50	46
8	Hull	38	21	4	13	73	62	46
9	Wolves	38	15	7	16	50	45	37
10	Stoke	38	16	5	17	57	52	37
11	Gainsborough	38	14	7	17	47	71	35
12	Leeds City	38	12	8	18	53	65	32
13	Stockport	38	12	8	18	48	67	32
14	Clapton Orient	38	11	10	17	40	65	32
15	Blackpool	38	11	9	18	51	58	31
16	Barnsley	38	12	6	20	54	68	30
17	Glossop NE	38	11	8	19	54	74	30
18	Grimsby	38	11	8	19	43	71	30
19	Chesterfield	38	6	11	21	46	92	23
20	Lincoln	38	9	3	26	46	83	21

SCOTTISH FIRST DIVISION

		P	W	D	L	F	A	Pts
1	Celtic	34	24	7	3	86	27	55
2	Falkirk	34	22	7	5	102	40	51
3	Rangers	34	21	8	5	74	40	50
4	Dundee	34	20	8	6	70	27	48
5	Hibernian	34	17	8	9	55	42	42
6	Airdrieonians	34	18	5	11	58	41	41
7	St Mirren	34	13	10	11	50	59	36
8	Aberdeen	34	13	9	12	45	44	35
9	Third Lanark	34	13	7	14	45	50	33
10	Motherwell	34	12	7	15	61	53	31
11	Hamilton	34	10	8	16	54	65	28
12	Hearts	34	11	6	17	50	62	28
13	Morton	34	9	9	16	43	66	27
14	Kilmarnock	34	6	13	15	38	61	25
15	Partick	34	8	9	17	43	69	25
16	Queen's Park	34	7	8	19	54	84	22
17	Clyde	34	5	8	21	36	75	18
18	Port Glasgow	34	5	7	22	39	98	17

SCOTTISH SECOND DIVISION

		P	W	D	L	F	A	Pts
1	Raith	22	14	2	6	37	23	30
2	Dumbarton	22	12	5	5	49	32	27*
3	Ayr	22	11	5	6	40	33	27
4	Abercorn	22	9	5	8	33	30	23
5	E Stirlingshire	22	9	5	8	30	32	23
6	Ayr Parkhouse	22	11	0	11	38	38	22
7	Leith	22	8	5	9	41	40	21
8	St Bernard's	22	8	5	9	31	32	21
9	Albion	22	7	5	10	36	48	19
10	Vale of Leven	22	5	8	9	25	31	18
11	Arthurlie	22	6	5	11	33	45	17
12	Cowdenbeath	22	5	4	13	26	35	14

*Two points deducted for a registration irregularity

Below *Wednesday goalkeeper Lyell, well backed up by his defence, repulses a Chelsea attack in a First Division match. It was Chelsea's first ever season in the First Division.*

RADIO TIMES HULTON PICTURE LIBRARY

FA CUP 1907-08

SECOND ROUND

Wolverhampton Wanderers v Bury	2-0
Swindon Town v Queen's Park Rangers	2-1
Stoke v Gainsborough Trinity	1-1, 2-2, 3-1
Portsmouth v Leicester Fosse	1-0
Notts County v Bolton Wanderers	1-1, 1-2
Oldham Athletic v Everton	0-0, 1-6
Southampton v West Bromwich Albion	1-0
Bristol Rovers v Chesterfield Town	2-0
Newcastle United v West Ham United	2-0
Liverpool v Brighton	1-1, 3-0
Grimsby Town v Carlisle United	6-2
Plymouth Argyle v Crystal Palace	2-3
Manchester City v New Brompton	1-1, 2-1
Norwich City v Fulham	1-2
Manchester United v Chelsea	1-0
Aston Villa v Hull City	3-0

THIRD ROUND

Wolverhampton Wanderers v Swindon Town	2-0
Portsmouth v Stoke	0-1
Bolton Wanderers v Everton	3-3, 1-3
Southampton v Bristol Rovers	2-0
Newcastle United v Liverpool	3-1
Grimsby Town v Crystal Palace	1-0
Manchester City v Fulham	1-1, 1-3
Aston Villa v Manchester United	0-2

FOURTH ROUND

Stoke v Wolverhampton Wanderers	0-1
Everton v Southampton	0-0, 2-3
Newcastle United v Grimsby Town	5-1
Fulham v Manchester United	2-1

SEMI-FINAL

Wolverhampton Wanderers v Southampton	2-0
Newcastle United v Fulham	6-0

FINAL AT CRYSTAL PALACE

Wolverhampton Wanderers v Newcastle United 3-1

SCOTTISH FA CUP 1907-08

FIRST ROUND

Falkirk v Rangers	2-2, 1-4
Heart of Midlothian v St Johnstone	2-1
Celtic v Peebles Rovers	4-0
Hibernian v Abercorn	5-1
St Bernard's v Queen's Park	1-1, 1-1, 0-1
Aberdeen v Albion Rovers	3-0
Dumfries v Motherwell	0-4
Partick Thistle v Bo'ness	4-0
Port Glasgow Athletic v Ayr Parkhouse	7-1
Dunblane v Elgin City	8-3
Kilmarnock v Hamilton Academicals	2-1
Raith Rovers v Inverness Thistle	2-0
Galston v Uphall	wo
St Mirren v Third Lanark	3-1
Morton v Vale of Atholl	7-1
Airdrieonians v Dundee	0-1

SECOND ROUND

Motherwell v St Mirren	2-2, 0-2
Heart of Midlothian v Port Glasgow Athletic	4-0
Rangers v Celtic	1-2
Partick Thistle v Raith Rovers	1-1, 1-2
Queen's Park v Galston	6-2
Kilmarnock v Dunblane	3-0
Hibernian v Morton	3-0
Aberdeen v Dundee	0-0, 2-2, 3-1

THIRD ROUND

Aberdeen v Queen's Park	3-1
Raith Rovers v Celtic	0-3
Hibernian v Kilmarnock	0-1
St Mirren v Heart of Midlothian	1-0*, 3-1

*abandoned

SEMI-FINAL

Aberdeen v Celtic	0-1
Kilmarnock v St Mirren	0-0, 0-2

FINAL AT HAMPDEN PARK

Celtic v St Mirren 5-1

FIRST DIVISION

		P	W	D	L	F	A	Pts
1	Newcastle	38	24	5	9	65	41	53
2	Everton	38	18	10	10	82	57	46
3	Sunderland	38	21	2	15	78	63	44
4	Blackburn	38	14	13	11	61	50	41
5	Wednesday	38	17	6	15	67	61	40
6	Woolwich A	38	14	10	14	52	49	38
7	Aston Villa	38	14	10	14	58	56	38
8	Bristol City	38	13	12	13	45	58	38
9	Middlesbrough	38	14	9	15	59	53	37
10	Preston	38	13	11	14	48	44	37
11	Chelsea	38	14	9	15	56	61	37
12	Sheff United	38	14	9	15	51	59	37
13	Man United	38	15	7	16	58	68	37
14	Nottm Forest	38	14	8	16	66	57	36
15	Notts County	38	14	8	16	51	48	36
16	Liverpool	38	15	6	17	57	65	36
17	Bury	38	14	8	16	63	77	36
18	Bradford City	38	12	10	16	47	47	34
19	Man City	38	15	4	19	67	69	34
20	Leicester Fosse	38	8	9	21	54	102	25

SECOND DIVISION

		P	W	D	L	F	A	Pts
1	Bolton	38	24	4	10	59	28	52
2	Tottenham	38	20	11	7	67	32	51
3	WBA	38	19	13	6	56	27	51
4	Hull	38	19	6	13	63	39	44
5	Derby	38	16	11	11	55	41	43
6	Oldham	38	17	6	15	55	43	40
7	Wolves	38	14	11	13	56	48	39
8	Glossop NE	38	15	8	15	57	53	38
9	Gainsborough	38	15	8	15	49	70	38
10	Fulham	38	13	11	14	58	48	37
11	Birmingham	38	14	9	15	58	61	37
12	Leeds City	38	14	7	17	43	53	35
13	Grimsby	38	14	7	17	41	54	35
14	Burnley	38	13	7	18	51	58	33
15	Clapton Orient	38	12	9	17	37	49	33
16	Bradford PA	38	13	6	19	51	59	32
17	Barnsley	38	11	10	17	48	57	32
18	Stockport	38	14	3	21	39	71	31
19	Chesterfield	38	11	8	19	37	67	30
20	Blackpool	38	9	11	18	46	68	29

SECOND ROUND

Manchester United v Everton	1-0
Blackburn Rovers v Chelsea	2-1
Tottenham Hotspur v Fulham	1-0
Crystal Palace v Burnley	0-0, 0-9
Newcastle United v Blackpool	2-1
Leeds City v West Ham United	1-1, 1-2
Preston North End v Sunderland	1-2
West Bromwich Albion v Bradford City	1-2
Bristol City v Bury	2-2, 1-0
Liverpool v Norwich City	2-3
Stockport County v Glossop North End	1-1, 0-1
Portsmouth v The Wednesday	2-2, 0-3
Leicester Fosse v Derby County	0-2
Plymouth Argyle v Exeter City	2-0
Nottingham Forest v Brentford	1-0
Woolwich Arsenal v Millwall Athletic	1-1, 0-1

THIRD ROUND

Manchester United v Blackburn Rovers	6-1
Tottenham Hotspur v Burnley	0-0, 1-3
West Ham United v Newcastle United	0-0, 1-2
Bradford City v Sunderland	0-1
Bristol City v Norwich City	2-0
The Wednesday v Glossop North End	0-1
Derby County v Plymouth Argyle	1-0
Nottingham Forest v Millwall Athletic	3-1

FOURTH ROUND

Burnley v Manchester United	1-0*, 2-3
Newcastle United v Sunderland	2-2, 3-0
Glossop North End v Bristol City	0-0, 0-1
Derby County v Nottingham Forest	3-0

*abandoned

SEMI-FINAL

Manchester United v Newcastle United	1-0
Bristol City v Derby County	1-1, 2-1

FINAL AT CRYSTAL PALACE

Manchester United v Bristol City	1-0

SCOTTISH FIRST DIVISION

		P	W	D	L	F	A	Pts
1	Celtic	34	23	5	6	71	24	51
2	Dundee	34	22	6	6	70	32	50
3	Clyde	34	21	6	7	61	37	48
4	Rangers	34	19	7	8	91	38	45
5	Airdrieonians	34	16	9	9	67	46	41
6	Hibernian	34	16	7	11	40	32	39
7	St Mirren	34	15	6	13	53	45	36
8	Aberdeen	34	15	6	13	61	53	36
9	Falkirk	34	13	7	14	58	56	33
10	Kilmarnock	34	13	7	14	47	61	33
11	Third Lanark	34	11	10	13	56	49	32
12	Hearts	34	12	8	14	54	49	32
13	Port Glasgow	34	10	8	16	39	52	28
14	Motherwell	34	11	6	17	47	73	28
15	Queen's Park	34	6	13	15	42	65	25
16	Hamilton	34	6	12	16	42	72	24
17	Morton	34	8	7	19	39	90	23
18	Partick	34	2	4	28	38	102	8

SCOTTISH SECOND DIVISION

		P	W	D	L	F	A	Pts
1	Abercorn	22	13	5	4	40	18	31
2	Raith	22	11	6	5	46	22	28
3	Vale of Leven	22	12	4	6	39	25	28
4	Dumbarton	22	10	5	7	34	34	25
5	Ayr	22	10	3	9	43	36	23
6	Leith	22	10	3	9	37	33	23
7	Ayr Parkhouse	22	8	5	9	29	31	21
8	St Bernard's	22	9	3	10	34	37	21
9	E Stirlingshire	22	9	3	10	28	34	21
10	Albion	22	9	2	11	37	48	20
11	Cowdenbeath	22	4	4	14	19	42	12
12	Arthurlie	22	5	1	16	29	55	11

Below *After a 1-1 draw, 1908 League Champions Manchester United, beat Queen's Park Rangers, the Southern League winners, 4-0 in September to become the first holders of* **inset** *the Charity Shield.*

SECOND ROUND

Third Lanark v Aberdeen	4-1
Clyde v Hibernian	1-0
Airdrieonians v Heart of Midlothian	2-0
St Mirren v Beith	3-0
Dundee v Rangers	0-0, 0-1
Queen's Park v Partick Thistle	3-0
Motherwell v Falkirk	1-3
Celtic v Port Glasgow Athletic	4-0

THIRD ROUND

Celtic v Airdrieonians	3-1
Third Lanark v Falkirk	1-2
Clyde v St Mirren	3-1
Rangers v Queen's Park	1-0

SEMI-FINAL

Falkirk v Rangers	0-1
Celtic v Clyde	0-0, 2-0

FINAL AT HAMPDEN PARK

Rangers v Celtic	2-2, 1-1†

†Some newspapers had suggested that, if the first replay ended level, extra-time would be played. The rules, in fact, stated that extra-time could only be played after a third game. When the players left the field some sections of the crowd obviously felt cheated and started protesting. This led to a full-scale riot with pay-boxes burned and hundreds injured. Rangers and Celtic both refused to play a third game as a result, threatening that one or other would simply scratch, and the Scottish FA agreed that the Cup would be withheld.

RADIO TIMES HULTON PICTURE LIBRARY

In April 1909 Leicester Fosse, already relegated to the Second Division, were beaten 12-0 by neighbours Nottingham Forest in one of the last games of the season. As this was a record Division One score, and as those two points confirmed Forest's place in the First Division, a League Commission inquiry examined the circumstances surrounding the match. Their finding was quite simply that the Leicester Fosse players had been celebrating the wedding of a colleague the day before the game was played.

Broxburn and Beith met five times in a first-round Scottish Cup tie. The last three games were played on three consecutive days, Beith finally winning 4-2 on a Friday. The following day they met St Mirren in the next round, their fourth game in four days. They lost . . .

FIRST DIVISION

	P	W	D	L	F	A	Pts
1 Aston Villa	38	23	7	8	84	42	53
2 Liverpool	38	21	6	11	78	57	48
3 Blackburn	38	18	9	11	73	55	45
4 Newcastle	38	19	7	12	70	56	45
5 Man United	38	19	7	12	69	61	45
6 Sheff United	38	16	10	12	62	41	42
7 Bradford City	38	17	8	13	64	47	42
8 Sunderland	38	18	5	15	66	51	41
9 Notts County	38	15	10	13	67	59	40
10 Everton	38	16	8	14	51	56	40
11 Wednesday	38	15	9	14	60	63	39
12 Preston	38	15	5	18	52	58	35
13 Bury	38	12	9	17	62	66	33
14 Nottm Forest	38	11	11	16	54	72	33
15 Tottenham	38	11	10	17	53	69	32
16 Bristol City	38	12	8	18	45	60	32
17 Middlesbrough	38	11	9	18	56	73	31
18 Woolwich A	38	11	9	18	37	67	31
19 Chelsea	38	11	7	20	47	70	29
20 Bolton	38	9	6	23	44	71	24

SECOND DIVISION

	P	W	D	L	F	A	Pts
1 Man City	38	23	8	7	81	40	54
2 Oldham	38	23	7	8	79	39	53
3 Hull City	38	23	7	8	80	46	53
4 Derby	38	22	9	7	72	47	53
5 Leicester Fosse	38	20	4	14	79	58	44
6 Glossop NE	38	18	7	13	64	57	43
7 Fulham	38	14	13	11	51	43	41
8 Wolves	38	17	6	15	64	63	40
9 Barnsley	38	16	7	15	62	59	39
10 Bradford PA	38	17	4	17	64	59	38
11 WBA	38	16	5	17	58	56	37
12 Blackpool	38	14	8	16	50	52	36
13 Stockport	38	13	8	17	50	47	34
14 Burnley	38	14	6	18	62	61	34
15 Lincoln	38	10	11	17	42	69	31
16 Clapton Orient	38	12	6	20	37	60	30
17 Leeds City	38	10	7	21	46	80	27
18 Gainsborough	38	10	6	22	33	75	26
19 Grimsby	38	9	6	23	50	77	24
20 Birmingham	38	8	7	23	42	78	23

SCOTTISH FIRST DIVISION

	P	W	D	L	F	A	Pts
1 Celtic	34	24	6	4	63	22	54
2 Falkirk	34	22	8	4	71	28	52
3 Rangers	34	20	6	8	70	35	46
4 Aberdeen	34	16	8	10	44	29	40
5 Clyde	34	14	9	11	47	40	37
6 Dundee	34	14	8	12	52	44	36
7 Third Lanark	34	13	8	13	62	44	34
8 Hibernian	34	14	6	14	33	40	34
9 Airdrieonians	34	12	9	13	46	57	33
10 Motherwell	34	12	8	14	59	60	32
11 Kilmarnock	34	12	8	14	53	60	32
12 Hearts	34	12	7	15	59	50	31
13 St Mirren	34	13	5	16	49	58	31
14 Queen's Park	34	12	6	16	54	74	30
15 Hamilton	34	11	6	17	50	67	28
16 Partick	34	8	10	16	47	59	26
17 Morton	34	11	3	20	38	60	25
18 Port Glasgow	34	3	5	26	25	95	11

SCOTTISH SECOND DIVISION

	P	W	D	L	F	A	Pts
1 Leith	22	13	7	2	44	19	33
2 Raith*	22	14	5	3	36	21	33
3 St Bernard's	22	12	3	7	43	31	27
4 Dumbarton	22	9	5	8	44	38	23
5 Abercorn	22	7	8	7	38	40	22
6 Vale of Leven	22	8	5	9	36	38	21
7 Ayr	22	9	3	10	37	40	21
8 E Stirlingshire	22	9	2	11	38	43	20
9 Albion	22	7	5	10	34	39	19
10 Arthurlie	22	6	5	11	34	47	17
11 Cowdenbeath	22	7	3	12	22	34	17
12 Ayr Parkhouse	22	4	3	15	27	43	11

*Elected to First Division

Below *In 1910 Newcastle were the last club to win the second FA Cup. The design had been pirated for a minor competition and the old Cup was presented to Lord Kinnaird.*

FA CUP 1909-10

SECOND ROUND
Newcastle United v Fulham	4-0
Bradford City v Blackburn Rovers	1-2
Leicester Fosse v Bury	3-2
Stockport County v Leyton	0-2
Swindon Town v Burnley	2-0
Chelsea v Tottenham Hotspur	0-1
Southampton v Manchester City	0-5
Aston Villa v Derby County	6-1
Bristol Rovers v Barnsley	0-4
Bristol City v West Bromwich Albion	1-1, 2-4
Southend United v Queen's Park Rangers	0-0, 2-3
Wolverhampton Wanderers v West Ham United	1-5
Everton v Woolwich Arsenal	5-0
Sunderland v Bradford Park Avenue	3-1
Portsmouth v Coventry City	0-1
Northampton Town v Nottingham Forest	0-0, 0-1

THIRD ROUND
Newcastle United v Blackburn Rovers	3-1
Leicester Fosse v Leyton	1-0
Swindon Town v Tottenham Hotspur	3-2
Aston Villa v Manchester City	1-2
Barnsley v West Bromwich Albion	1-0
Queen's Park Rangers v West Ham United	1-1, 1-0
Everton v Sunderland	2-0
Coventry City v Nottingham Forest	3-1

FOURTH ROUND
Newcastle United v Leicester Fosse	3-0
Swindon Town v Manchester City	2-0
Barnsley v Queen's Park Rangers	1-0
Coventry City v Everton	0-2

SEMI-FINAL
Newcastle United v Swindon Town	2-0
Barnsley v Everton	0-0, 3-0

FINAL AT CRYSTAL PALACE
Newcastle United v Barnsley	1-1, 2-0*

*Replay at Goodison Park

SCOTTISH FA CUP 1909-10

FIRST ROUND
Rangers v Inverness Thistle	3-1
Queen's Park v Kirkcaldy United	0-0, 6-0
St Mirren v Elgin City	8-0
Kilmarnock v Third Lanark	0-0, 0-2
Dumbarton v Celtic	1-2
Morton v Partick Thistle	4-3
Airdrieonians v Douglas Wanderers	6-0
Leith Athletic v Clyde	0-1
Motherwell v Forfar Athletic	1-0
Bathgate v Heart of Midlothian	0-4
Hamilton v Hibernian	0-0, 0-2
Falkirk v Port Glasgow Athletic	3-0
Dundee v Beith	1-1, 1-0
Ayr v Alloa Athletic	3-2
Aberdeen v Bo'ness	3-0
East Fife v Hurlford	4-1

SECOND ROUND
Motherwell v Morton	3-0
Dundee v Falkirk	3-0
Clyde v Rangers	2-0
St Mirren v Heart of Midlothian	2-2, 0-0, 0-4
Ayr v Hibernian	0-1
Celtic v Third Lanark	3-1
Aberdeen v Airdrieonians	3-0
East Fife v Queen's Park	2-3

THIRD ROUND
Hibernian v Heart of Midlothian	0-1*, 1-0
Celtic v Aberdeen	2-1
Queen's Park v Clyde	2-2, 2-2, 1-2
Motherwell v Dundee	1-3

*abandoned

SEMI-FINAL
Clyde v Celtic	3-1
Hibernian v Dundee	0-0, 0-0, 0-1

FINAL AT IBROX PARK
Dundee v Clyde	2-2, 0-0, 2-1

FIRST DIVISION

		P	W	D	L	F	A	Pts
1	Man United	38	22	8	8	72	40	52
2	Aston Villa	38	22	7	9	69	41	51
3	Sunderland	38	15	15	8	67	48	45
4	Everton	38	19	7	12	50	36	45
5	Bradford City	38	20	5	13	51	42	45
6	Wednesday	38	17	8	13	47	48	42
7	Oldham	38	16	9	13	44	41	41
8	Newcastle	38	15	10	13	61	43	40
9	Sheff United	38	15	8	15	49	43	38
10	Woolwich A	38	13	12	13	41	49	38
11	Notts County	38	14	10	14	37	45	38
12	Blackburn	38	13	11	14	62	54	37
13	Liverpool	38	15	7	16	53	53	37
14	Preston	38	12	11	15	40	49	35
15	Tottenham	38	13	6	19	52	63	32
16	Middlesbrough	38	11	10	17	49	63	32
17	Man City	38	9	13	16	43	58	31
18	Bury	38	9	11	18	43	71	29
19	Bristol City	38	11	5	22	43	66	27
20	Nottm Forest	38	9	7	22	55	75	25

SECOND DIVISION

		P	W	D	L	F	A	Pts
1	WBA	38	22	9	7	67	41	53
2	Bolton	38	21	9	8	69	40	51
3	Chelsea	38	20	9	9	71	35	49
4	Clapton Orient	38	19	7	12	44	35	45
5	Hull	38	14	16	8	55	39	44
6	Derby	38	17	8	13	73	52	42
7	Blackpool	38	16	10	12	49	38	42
8	Burnley	38	13	15	10	45	45	41
9	Wolves	38	15	8	15	51	52	38
10	Fulham	38	15	7	16	52	48	37
11	Leeds City	38	15	7	16	58	56	37
12	Bradford PA	38	14	9	15	53	55	37
13	Huddersfield	38	13	8	17	57	58	34
14	Glossop NE	38	13	8	17	48	62	34
15	Leicester Fosse	38	14	5	19	52	62	33
16	Birmingham	38	12	8	18	42	64	32
17	Stockport	38	11	8	19	47	79	30
18	Gainsborough	38	9	11	18	37	55	29
19	Barnsley	38	7	14	17	52	62	28
20	Lincoln	38	7	10	21	28	72	24

SCOTTISH FIRST DIVISION

		P	W	D	L	F	A	Pts
1	Rangers	34	23	6	5	90	34	52
2	Aberdeen	34	19	10	5	53	28	48
3	Falkirk	34	17	10	7	65	42	44
4	Partick	34	17	8	9	50	41	42
5	Celtic	34	15	11	8	48	18	41
6	Dundee	34	18	5	11	54	42	41
7	Clyde	34	14	11	9	45	36	39
8	Third Lanark	34	16	7	11	59	53	39
9	Hibernian	34	15	6	13	44	48	36
10	Kilmarnock	34	12	10	12	43	45	34
11	Airdrieonians	34	12	9	13	49	53	33
12	St Mirren	34	12	7	15	46	57	31
13	Morton	34	9	11	14	49	51	29
14	Hearts	34	8	8	18	42	59	24
15	Raith	34	7	10	17	36	56	24
16	Hamilton	34	8	5	21	31	60	21
17	Motherwell	34	8	4	22	37	66	20
18	Queen's Park	34	5	4	25	28	80	14

SCOTTISH SECOND DIVISION

		P	W	D	L	F	A	Pts
1	Dumbarton	22	15	1	6	55	31	31
2	Ayr	22	12	3	7	52	36	27
3	Albion	22	10	5	7	27	21	25
4	Leith	22	9	6	7	42	43	24
5	Cowdenbeath	22	9	5	8	31	27	23
6	St Bernard's	22	10	2	10	36	39	22
7	E Stirlingshire	22	7	6	9	28	35	20
8	Port Glasgow	22	8	3	11	27	32	19
9	Dundee Hibs	22	7	5	10	29	36	19
10	Arthurlie	22	7	5	10	26	33	19
11	Abercorn	22	9	1	12	39	50	19
12	Vale of Leven	22	4	8	10	22	31	16

Below *Bradford City defend in depth as New-castle threaten their goal in the 1911 Cup Final at Crystal Palace. The game, which ended 0-0, was the Tynesiders' fifth appearance at Crystal Palace in seven years.*

FA CUP 1910-11

SECOND ROUND
Bradford City v Norwich City	2-1
Crewe Alexandra v Grimsby Town	1-5
Burnley v Barnsley	2-0
Brighton v Coventry City	0-0, 0-2
Blackburn Rovers v Tottenham Hotspur	0-0, 2-0
Middlesbrough v Leicester Fosse	0-0, 2-1
West Ham United v Preston North End	3-0
Manchester United v Aston Villa	2-1
Newcastle United v Northampton Town	1-1, 1-0†
Hull City v Oldham Athletic	1-0
Derby County v West Bromwich Albion	1-0
Everton v Liverpool	2-1
Chesterfield Town v Chelsea	1-4
Wolverhampton Wanderers v Manchester City	1-0
Swindon Town v Woolwich Arsenal	1-0
Darlington v Bradford Park Avenue	2-1

† Both games played at Newcastle. Northampton sold their rights to a replay at home for £900.

THIRD ROUND
Bradford City v Grimsby Town	1-0
Burnley v Coventry City	5-0
Middlesbrough v Blackburn Rovers	0-3
West Ham United v Manchester United	2-1
Newcastle United v Hull City	3-2
Derby County v Everton	5-0
Wolverhampton Wanderers v Chelsea	0-2
Darlington v Swindon Town	0-3

FOURTH ROUND
Bradford City v Burnley	1-0
West Ham United v Blackburn Rovers	2-3
Newcastle United v Derby County	4-0
Chelsea v Swindon Town	3-1

SEMI-FINAL
Bradford City v Blackburn Rovers	3-0
Newcastle United v Chelsea	3-0

FINAL AT CRYSTAL PALACE
Bradford City v Newcastle United	0-0, 1-0*

*Replay at Old Trafford

SCOTTISH FA CUP 1910-11

FIRST ROUND
Aberdeen v Brechin City	3-0
Airdrieonians v Bo'ness	2-0
Celtic v St Mirren	2-0
Heart of Midlothian v Clyde	1-1, 0-1
Dundee v Hibernian	2-1
Leith Athletic v Falkirk	2-2, 1-4
Forfar Athletic v 5th KOSB	3-0
Galston v Lochgelly United	8-0
Rangers v Kilmarnock	2-1
East Stirlingshire v Morton	1-4
Third Lanark v Hamilton Academicals	0-1
Inverness Thistle v Johnstone	0-1
Motherwell v Annbank	5-0
Nithsdale Wanderers v Inverness Caledonian	3-1
Partick Thistle v St Bernard's	7-2
Stanley v Queen's Park	1-6

SECOND ROUND
Aberdeen v Airdrieonians	1-0
Clyde v Queen's Park	4-1
Partick Thistle v Dundee	0-3
Forfar Athletic v Falkirk	2-0
Celtic v Galston	1-0
Rangers v Morton	3-0
Hamilton Academicals v Johnstone	1-1, 3-1
Nithsdale Wanderers v Motherwell	0-0, 0-1

THIRD ROUND
Aberdeen v Forfar Athletic	6-0
Celtic v Clyde	1-0
Dundee v Rangers	2-1
Hamilton Academicals v Motherwell	2-1

SEMI-FINAL
Celtic v Aberdeen	1-0
Hamilton Academicals v Dundee	3-2

FINAL AT IBROX PARK
Celtic v Hamilton Academicals	0-0, 2-1

FIRST DIVISION

		P	W	D	L	F	A	Pts
1	Blackburn	38	20	9	9	60	43	49
2	Everton	38	20	6	12	46	42	46
3	Newcastle	38	18	8	12	64	50	44
4	Bolton	38	20	3	15	54	43	43
5	Wednesday	38	16	9	13	69	49	41
6	Aston Villa	38	17	7	14	76	63	41
7	Middlesbrough	38	16	8	14	56	45	40
8	Sunderland	38	14	11	13	58	51	39
9	WBA	38	15	9	14	43	47	39
10	Woolwich A	38	15	8	15	55	59	38
11	Bradford City	38	15	8	15	46	50	38
12	Tottenham	38	14	9	15	53	53	37
13	Man United	38	13	11	14	45	60	37
14	Sheff United	38	13	10	15	63	56	36
15	Man City	38	13	9	16	56	58	35
16	Notts County	38	14	7	17	46	63	35
17	Liverpool	38	12	10	16	49	55	34
18	Oldham	38	12	10	16	46	54	34
19	Preston	38	13	7	18	40	57	33
20	Bury	38	6	9	23	32	59	21

SECOND DIVISION

		P	W	D	L	F	A	Pts
1	Derby	38	23	8	7	74	28	54
2	Chelsea	38	24	6	8	64	34	54
3	Burnley	38	22	8	8	77	41	52
4	Clapton Orient	38	21	3	14	61	44	45
5	Wolves	38	16	10	12	57	33	42
6	Barnsley	38	15	12	11	45	42	42
7	Hull	38	17	8	13	54	51	42
8	Fulham	38	16	7	15	66	58	39
9	Grimsby	38	15	9	14	48	55	39
10	Leicester Fosse	38	15	7	16	49	66	37
11	Bradford PA	38	13	9	16	44	45	35
12	Birmingham	38	14	6	18	55	59	34
13	Bristol City	38	14	6	18	41	60	34
14	Blackpool	38	13	8	17	32	52	34
15	Nottm Forest	38	13	7	18	46	48	33
16	Stockport	38	11	11	16	47	54	33
17	Huddersfield	38	13	6	19	50	64	32
18	Glossop NE	38	8	12	18	42	56	28
19	Leeds City	38	10	8	20	50	78	28
20	Gainsborough	38	5	13	20	30	64	23

SCOTTISH FIRST DIVISION

		P	W	D	L	F	A	Pts
1	Rangers	34	24	3	7	86	34	51
2	Celtic	34	17	11	6	58	33	45
3	Clyde	34	19	4	11	56	32	42
4	Hearts	34	16	8	10	54	40	40
5	Partick	34	16	8	10	47	40	40
6	Morton	34	14	9	11	44	44	37
7	Falkirk	34	15	6	13	46	43	36
8	Dundee	34	13	9	12	52	41	35
9	Aberdeen	34	14	7	13	44	44	35
10	Airdrieonians	34	12	8	14	40	41	32
11	Third Lanark	34	12	7	15	40	57	31
12	Hamilton	34	11	8	15	32	44	30
13	Hibernian	34	12	5	17	44	47	29
14	Motherwell	34	11	5	18	34	44	27
15	Raith	34	9	9	16	39	59	27
16	Kilmarnock	34	11	4	19	38	60	26
17	Queen's Park	34	8	9	17	29	53	25
18	St Mirren	34	7	10	17	32	59	24

SCOTTISH SECOND DIVISION

		P	W	D	L	F	A	Pts
1	Ayr	22	16	3	3	54	24	35
2	Abercorn	22	13	4	5	43	22	30
3	Dumbarton	22	13	1	8	47	31	27
4	Cowdenbeath	22	12	2	8	39	31	26
5	St Johnstone	22	10	4	8	29	27	24
6	St Bernard's	22	9	5	8	38	36	23
7	Leith	22	9	4	9	31	34	22
8	Arthurlie	22	7	5	10	26	30	19
9	E Stirlingshire	22	7	3	12	21	31	17
10	Dundee Hibs	22	5	5	12	21	41	15
11	Vale of Leven	22	6	1	15	19	37	13
12	Albion	22	6	1	15	26	50	13

Below *Spurs entertain the Football League champions, Blackburn Rovers, at White Hart Lane. Bob Crompton (right of goalkeeper), Blackburn's captain, watches anxiously as his keeper is challenged by a Tottenham forward.*

FA CUP 1911-12

SECOND ROUND

Coventry City v Manchester United	1-5
Aston Villa v Reading	1-1, 0-1
Derby County v Blackburn Rovers	1-2
Wolverhampton Wanderers v Lincoln City	2-1
Leeds City v West Bromwich Albion	0-1
Crystal Palace v Sunderland	0-0, 0-1
Fulham v Liverpool	3-0
Darlington v Northampton Town	1-1, 0-2
Swindon Town v Notts County	2-0
Middlesbrough v West Ham United	1-1, 1-2
Everton v Bury	1-1, 6-0
Manchester City v Oldham Athletic	0-1
Bradford City v Chelsea	2-0
Bradford Park Avenue v Portsmouth	2-0
Barnsley v Leicester Fosse	1-0
Bolton Wanderers v Blackpool	1-0

THIRD ROUND

Reading v Manchester United	1-1, 0-3
Blackburn Rovers v Wolverhampton Wanderers	3-2
Sunderland v West Bromwich Albion	1-2
Fulham v Northampton Town	2-1
West Ham United v Swindon Town	1-1, 0-4
Oldham Athletic v Everton	0-2
Bradford Park Avenue v Bradford City	0-1
Bolton Wanderers v Barnsley	1-2

FOURTH ROUND

Manchester United v Blackburn Rovers	1-1, 2-4
West Bromwich Albion v Fulham	3-0
Swindon Town v Everton	2-1
Barnsley v Bradford City	0-0, 0-0, 0-0, 3-2

SEMI-FINAL

Blackburn Rovers v West Bromwich Albion	0-0, 0-1
Swindon Town v Barnsley	0-0, 0-1

FINAL AT CRYSTAL PALACE

Barnsley v West Bromwich Albion	0-0, 1-0*

*Replay at Bramall Lane

SCOTTISH FA CUP 1911-12

FIRST ROUND

St Mirren v Aberdeen	3-3, 0-4
Raith Rovers v Airdrieonians	0-0, 1-3
Armadale v Peterhead	2-1
Broxburn Athletic v Beith	6-0
Celtic v Dunfermline Athletic	1-0
Clyde v Abercorn	2-0
Partick Thistle v Dundee	2-2, 0-3
East Stirlingshire v Dumbarton	3-1
Falkirk v King's Park	2-2, 6-1
Rangers v Stenhousemuir	3-0
Morton v Clachnacuddin	2-0
Hibernian v Heart of Midlothian	1-1, 0-0, 1-2
Kilmarnock v Hamilton Academicals	1-0
Leith v Ayr United	3-0
St Johnstone v Motherwell	0-2
Third Lanark v Renton	5-0

SECOND ROUND

Aberdeen v Armadale	3-0
Celtic v East Stirlingshire	3-0
Clyde v Rangers	3-1
Heart of Midlothian v Dundee	1-0
Leith Athletic v Kilmarnock	0-2
Falkirk v Morton	0-0, 1-3
Motherwell v Airdrieonians	5-1
Third Lanark v Broxburn Athletic	6-1

THIRD ROUND

Aberdeen v Celtic	2-2, 0-2
Kilmarnock v Clyde	1-6
Morton v Heart of Midlothian	0-1
Third Lanark v Motherwell	3-1

SEMI-FINAL

Celtic v Heart of Midlothian	3-0
Clyde v Third Lanark	3-1

FINAL AT IBROX PARK

Celtic v Clyde	2-0

FIRST DIVISION

	P	W	D	L	F	A	Pts
1 Sunderland	38	25	4	9	86	43	54
2 Aston Villa	38	19	12	7	86	52	50
3 Wednesday	38	21	7	10	75	55	49
4 Man United	38	19	8	11	69	43	46
5 Blackburn	38	16	13	9	79	43	45
6 Man City	38	18	8	12	53	37	44
7 Derby	38	17	8	13	69	66	42
8 Bolton	38	16	10	12	62	63	42
9 Oldham	38	14	14	10	50	55	42
10 WBA	38	13	12	13	57	50	38
11 Everton	38	15	7	16	48	54	37
12 Liverpool	38	16	5	17	61	71	37
13 Bradford City	38	12	11	15	50	60	35
14 Newcastle	38	13	8	17	47	47	34
15 Sheff United	38	14	6	18	56	70	34
16 Middlesbrough	38	11	10	17	55	69	32
17 Tottenham	38	12	6	20	45	72	30
18 Chelsea	38	11	6	21	51	73	28
19 Notts County	38	7	9	22	28	56	23
20 Woolwich A	38	3	12	23	26	74	18

SECOND DIVISION

	P	W	D	L	F	A	Pts
1 Preston	38	19	15	4	56	33	53
2 Burnley	38	21	8	9	88	53	50
3 Birmingham	38	18	10	10	59	44	46
4 Barnsley	38	19	7	12	57	47	45
5 Huddersfield	38	17	9	12	66	40	43
6 Leeds City	38	15	10	13	70	64	40
7 Grimsby	38	15	10	13	51	50	40
8 Lincoln	38	15	10	13	50	52	40
9 Fulham	38	17	5	16	65	55	39
10 Wolves	38	14	10	14	56	54	38
11 Bury	38	15	8	15	53	57	38
12 Hull	38	15	6	17	60	56	36
13 Bradford PA	38	14	8	16	60	60	36
14 Clapton Orient	38	10	14	14	34	47	34
15 Leicester Fosse	38	13	7	18	50	65	33
16 Bristol City	38	9	15	14	46	72	33
17 Nottm Forest	38	12	8	18	58	59	32
18 Glossop NE	38	12	8	18	49	68	32
19 Stockport	38	8	10	20	56	78	26
20 Blackpool	38	9	8	21	39	69	26

SCOTTISH FIRST DIVISION

	P	W	D	L	F	A	Pts
1 Rangers	34	24	5	5	76	41	53
2 Celtic	34	22	5	7	53	28	49
3 Hearts	34	17	7	10	71	43	41
4 Airdrieonians	34	15	11	8	64	46	41
5 Falkirk	34	14	12	8	56	38	40
6 Hibernian	34	16	5	13	63	54	37
7 Motherwell	34	12	13	9	47	39	37
8 Aberdeen	34	14	9	11	47	40	37
9 Clyde	34	13	9	12	41	44	35
10 Hamilton	34	12	8	14	44	47	32
11 Kilmarnock	34	10	11	13	37	54	31
12 St Mirren	34	10	10	14	50	60	30
13 Morton	34	11	7	16	50	59	29
14 Dundee	34	8	13	13	33	46	29
15 Third Lanark	34	8	12	14	31	41	28
16 Raith	34	8	10	16	46	60	26
17 Partick	34	10	4	20	40	55	24
18 Queen's Park	34	5	3	26	34	88	13

SCOTTISH SECOND DIVISION

	P	W	D	L	F	A	Pts
1 Ayr*	26	13	8	5	45	19	34
2 Dunfermline	26	13	7	6	45	27	33
3 E Stirlingshire	26	12	8	6	43	27	32
4 Abercorn	26	12	7	7	33	31	31
5 Cowdenbeath	26	12	6	8	36	27	30
6 Dumbarton*	26	12	5	9	39	30	29
7 St Bernard's	26	12	3	11	36	34	27
8 Johnstone	26	9	6	11	31	43	24
9 Albion	26	10	3	13	38	40	23
10 Dundee Hibs	26	6	10	10	34	43	22
11 St Johnstone	26	7	7	12	29	38	21
12 Vale of Leven	26	8	5	13	28	45	21
13 Arthurlie	26	7	5	14	37	49	19
14 Leith	26	5	8	13	26	47	18

*Ayr United and Dumbarton were elected to the First Division. Nevertheless, no clubs were demoted from the First Division.

FA CUP 1912-13

SECOND ROUND
Aston Villa v West Ham United	5-0
Crystal Palace v Bury	2-0
Bradford Park Avenue v Wolverhampton Wanderers	3-0
Chelsea v The Wednesday	1-1, 0-6
Oldham Athletic v Nottingham Forest	5-1
Plymouth Argyle v Manchester United	0-2
Brighton v Everton	0-0, 0-1
Bristol Rovers v Norwich City	1-1, 2-2, 1-0
Sunderland v Manchester City	2-0
Huddersfield Town v Swindon Town	1-2
Hull City v Newcastle United	0-0, 0-3
Woolwich Arsenal v Liverpool	1-4
Burnley v Gainsborough Trinity	4-1
Middlesbrough v Queen's Park Rangers	3-2
Barnsley v Blackburn Rovers	2-3
Reading v Tottenham Hotspur	1-0

THIRD ROUND
Aston Villa v Crystal Palace	5-0
Bradford Park Avenue v The Wednesday	2-1
Oldham Athletic v Manchester United	0-0, 2-1
Bristol Rovers v Everton	0-4
Sunderland v Swindon Town	4-2
Liverpool v Newcastle United	1-1, 0-1
Burnley v Middlesbrough	3-1
Reading v Blackburn Rovers	1-2

FOURTH ROUND
Bradford Park Avenue v Aston Villa	0-5
Everton v Oldham Athletic	0-1
Sunderland v Newcastle United	0-0, 2-2, 3-0
Blackburn Rovers v Burnley	0-1

SEMI-FINAL
Aston Villa v Oldham Athletic	1-0
Sunderland v Burnley	0-0, 3-2

FINAL AT CRYSTAL PALACE
Aston Villa v Sunderland	1-0

SCOTTISH FA CUP 1912-13

SECOND ROUND
Ayr United v Airdrieonians	0-2
Celtic v Arbroath	4-0
East Stirlingshire v Clyde	1-1, 0-0, 0-1
Dumbarton v Aberdeen	2-1
Dundee v Thornhill	5-0
Morton v Falkirk	2-2, 1-3
Hamilton Academicals v Rangers	1-1, 0-2
Heart of Midlothian v Dunfermline Athletic	3-1
Hibernian v Motherwell	0-0, 1-1, 2-1
Kilmarnock v Abercorn	5-1
Partick Thistle v Inverness Caledonian	4-1
Aberdeen University v Peebles Rovers	0-3
Queen's Park v Dundee Hibernians	4-2
Raith Rovers v Broxburn United	5-0
St Johnstone v East Fife	3-0
St Mirren v Third Lanark	0-0, 2-0

THIRD ROUND
Celtic v Peebles Rovers	3-0
Clyde v Queen's Park	1-0
Dumbarton v St Johnstone	1-0
Partick Thistle v Dundee	0-1
Rangers v Falkirk	1-3
Kilmarnock v Heart of Midlothian	0-2
Raith Rovers v Hibernian	2-2, 1-0
St Mirren v Airdrieonians	1-0

FOURTH ROUND
Clyde v Dundee	1-1, 0-0, 2-1
Falkirk v Dumbarton	1-0
Celtic v Heart of Midlothian	0-1
Raith Rovers v St Mirren	2-1

SEMI-FINAL
Falkirk v Heart of Midlothian	1-0
Raith Rovers v Clyde	1-1, 1-0

FINAL AT CELTIC PARK
Falkirk v Raith Rovers	2-0

Above *Aston Villa's one goal victory over Oldham in the semi-final of the FA Cup meant that for the only time in the history of the competition the Finalists — Villa and Sunderland — were also the clubs that finished first and second in the League. Here, a Villa attack against Oldham comes to nothing but Villa did win the Cup, 1-0.*

FIRST DIVISION

		P	W	D	L	F	A	Pts
1	Blackburn	38	20	11	7	78	42	51
2	Aston Villa	38	19	6	13	65	50	44
3	Oldham	38	17	9	12	55	45	43
4	Middlesbrough	38	19	5	14	77	60	43
5	WBA	38	15	13	10	46	42	43
6	Bolton	38	16	10	12	65	52	42
7	Sunderland	38	17	6	15	63	52	40
8	Chelsea	38	16	7	15	46	55	39
9	Bradford City	38	12	14	12	40	40	38
10	Sheff United	38	16	5	17	63	60	37
11	Newcastle	38	13	11	14	39	48	37
12	Burnley	38	12	12	14	61	53	36
13	Man City	38	14	8	16	51	53	36
14	Man United	38	15	6	17	52	62	36
15	Everton	38	12	11	15	46	55	35
16	Liverpool	38	14	7	17	46	62	35
17	Tottenham	38	12	10	16	50	62	34
18	Wednesday	38	13	8	17	53	70	34
19	Preston	38	12	6	20	52	69	30
20	Derby	38	8	11	19	55	71	27

SECOND DIVISION

		P	W	D	L	F	A	Pts
1	Notts County	38	23	7	8	77	36	53
2	Bradford PA	38	23	3	12	71	47	49
3	Arsenal	38	20	9	9	54	38	49
4	Leeds City	38	20	7	11	76	46	47
5	Barnsley	38	19	7	12	51	45	45
6	Clapton Orient	38	16	11	11	47	35	43
7	Hull	38	16	9	13	53	37	41
8	Bristol City	38	16	9	13	52	50	41
9	Wolves	38	18	5	15	51	52	41
10	Bury	38	15	10	13	39	40	40
11	Fulham	38	16	6	16	46	43	38
12	Stockport	38	13	10	15	55	57	36
13	Huddersfield	38	13	8	17	47	53	34
14	Birmingham	38	12	10	16	48	60	34
15	Grimsby	38	13	8	17	42	58	34
16	Blackpool	38	9	14	15	33	44	32
17	Glossop NE	38	11	6	21	51	67	28
18	Leicester Fosse	38	11	4	23	45	61	26
19	Lincoln	38	10	6	22	36	66	26
20	Nottm Forest	38	7	9	22	37	76	23

SCOTTISH FIRST DIVISION

		P	W	D	L	F	A	Pts
1	Celtic	38	30	5	3	81	14	65
2	Rangers	38	27	5	6	79	31	59
3	Hearts	38	23	8	7	70	29	54
4	Morton	38	26	2	10	76	51	54
5	Falkirk	38	20	9	9	69	51	49
6	Airdrieonians	38	18	12	8	72	43	48
7	Dundee	38	19	5	14	64	53	43
8	Third Lanark	38	13	10	15	42	51	36
9	Clyde	38	11	11	16	46	46	33
10	Ayr	38	13	7	18	58	74	33
11	Raith	38	13	6	19	56	57	32
12	Kilmarnock	38	11	9	18	48	68	31
13	Hibernian	38	12	6	20	58	75	30
14	Aberdeen	38	10	10	18	38	55	30
15	Partick	38	10	9	19	37	51	29
16	Queen's Park	38	10	9	19	52	84	29
17	Motherwell	38	11	6	21	49	66	28
18	Hamilton	38	11	6	21	46	65	28
19	Dumbarton	38	10	7	21	45	87	27
20	St Mirren	38	8	6	24	38	73	22

SCOTTISH SECOND DIVISION

		P	W	D	L	F	A	Pts
1	Cowdenbeath	22	13	5	4	34	17	31
2	Albion	22	10	7	5	38	33	27
3	Dunfermline	22	11	4	7	46	28	26
4	Dundee Hibs	22	11	4	7	36	31	26
5	St Johnstone	22	9	5	8	48	38	23
6	Abercorn	22	10	3	9	32	32	23
7	St Bernard's	22	8	6	8	39	31	22
8	E Stirlingshire	22	7	8	7	40	36	22
9	Arthurlie	22	8	4	10	35	37	20
10	Leith	22	5	9	8	31	37	19
11	Vale of Leven	22	5	3	14	23	47	13
12	Johnstone	22	4	4	14	20	55	12

Below *September 1913 and Woolwich Arsenal play Hull at Highbury. It had been a rush removal to what were then the grounds of a theological college, and in Arsenal's first match there, earlier in the month, the players washed in bowls of water, while an injured player was taken away on a milk-cart.*

FA CUP 1913-14

SECOND ROUND
Sheffield United v Bradford Park Avenue	3-1
Millwall Athletic v Bradford City	1-0
Manchester City v Tottenham Hotspur	2-1
Blackburn Rovers v Bury	2-0
Burnley v Derby County	3-2
Bolton Wanderers v Swindon Town	4-2
Sunderland v Plymouth Argyle	2-1
Glossop North End v Preston North End	0-1
Exeter City v Aston Villa	1-2
Leeds City v West Bromwich Albion	0-2
Wolverhampton Wanderers v The Wednesday	1-1, 0-1
Brighton v Clapton Orient	3-1
Liverpool v Gillingham	2-0
West Ham United v Crystal Palace	2-0
Swansea Town v Queen's Park Rangers	1-2
Birmingham v Huddersfield Town	1-0

THIRD ROUND
Millwall Athletic v Sheffield United	0-4
Blackburn Rovers v Manchester City	1-2
Burnley v Bolton Wanderers	3-0
Sunderland v Preston North End	2-0
Aston Villa v West Bromwich Albion	2-1
The Wednesday v Brighton	3-0
West Ham United v Liverpool	1-1, 1-5
Birmingham v Queen's Park Rangers	1-2

FOURTH ROUND
Manchester City v Sheffield United	0-0, 0-0, 0-1
Sunderland v Burnley	0-0, 1-2
The Wednesday v Aston Villa	0-1
Liverpool v Queen's Park Rangers	2-1

SEMI-FINAL
Sheffield United v Burnley	0-0, 0-1
Aston Villa v Liverpool	0-2

FINAL AT CRYSTAL PALACE
Burnley v Liverpool	1-0

SCOTTISH FA CUP 1913-14

SECOND ROUND
Aberdeen v Albion Rovers	4-1
Airdrieonians v Dundee Hibernian	5-0
Broxburn United v Dumfries	5-1
Celtic v Clyde	0-0, 2-0
Morton v Hibernian	1-1, 1-2
East Stirlingshire v Forfar Athletic	1-1, 0-2
Kilmarnock v Hamilton Academicals	3-1
Leith Athletic v Motherwell	1-1, 2-5
Partick Thistle v Nithsdale Wanderers	1-0
Forres Mechanics v Peebles Rovers	0-4
Queen's Park v Arthurlie	1-0
Raith Rovers v Heart of Midlothian	2-0
Rangers v Alloa Athletic	5-0
St Mirren v Dundee	2-1
Kirkcaldy United v Stevenston United	0-4
Third Lanark v Dumbarton	2-0

THIRD ROUND
Forfar Athletic v Celtic	0-5
Hibernian v Rangers	2-1
Broxburn United v Motherwell	0-2
Kilmarnock v Partick Thistle	1-4
Airdrieonians v Queen's Park	1-1, 1-2
Aberdeen v St Mirren	1-2
Stevenston United v Peebles Rovers	3-2
Third Lanark v Raith Rovers	4-1

FOURTH ROUND
Motherwell v Celtic	1-3
Queen's Park v Hibernian	1-3
St Mirren v Partick Thistle	1-0
Third Lanark v Stevenston United	1-1, 0-0, 1-0

SEMI-FINAL
Celtic v Third Lanark	2-0
Hibernian v St Mirren	3-1

FINAL AT IBROX PARK
Celtic v Hibernian	0-0, 4-1

RADIO TIMES HULTON PICTURE LIBRARY

FIRST DIVISION 1914-15

		P	W	D	L	F	A	Pts
1	Everton	38	19	8	11	76	47	46
2	Oldham	38	17	11	10	70	56	45
3	Blackburn	38	18	7	13	83	61	43
4	Burnley	38	18	7	13	61	47	43
5	Man City	38	15	13	10	49	39	43
6	Sheff United	38	15	13	10	49	41	43
7	Wednesday	38	15	13	10	61	54	43
8	Sunderland	38	18	5	15	81	72	41
9	Bradford PA	38	17	7	14	69	65	41
10	Bradford City	38	13	14	11	55	49	40
11	WBA	38	15	10	13	49	43	40
12	Middlesbrough	38	13	12	13	62	74	38
13	Aston Villa	38	13	11	14	62	72	37
14	Liverpool*	38	14	9	15	65	75	37
15	Newcastle	38	11	10	17	46	48	32
16	Notts County	38	9	13	16	41	57	31
17	Bolton	38	11	8	19	68	84	30
18	Man United*	38	9	12	17	46	62	30
19	Chelsea	38	8	13	17	51	65	29
20	Tottenham	38	8	12	18	57	90	28

*A commission concluded that the Manchester United–Liverpool game on 2 April 1915 had been 'fixed' but the result (2-0) was allowed to stand. No points were deducted.

SCOTTISH DIVISION 'A' 1914-15

		P	W	D	L	F	A	Pts
1	Celtic	38	30	5	3	91	25	65
2	Hearts	38	27	7	4	83	32	61
3	Rangers	38	23	4	11	74	47	50
4	Morton	38	18	12	8	74	48	48
5	Ayr	38	20	8	10	55	40	48
6	Falkirk	38	16	7	15	48	48	39
7	Hamilton	38	16	6	16	60	55	38
8	Partick	38	15	8	15	56	58	38
9	St Mirren	38	14	8	16	56	65	36
10	Airdrieonians	38	14	7	17	54	60	35
11	Hibernian	38	12	11	15	59	66	35
12	Kilmarnock	38	15	4	19	55	59	34
13	Dumbarton	38	13	8	17	51	66	34
14	Aberdeen	38	11	11	16	39	52	33
15	Dundee	38	12	9	17	43	61	33
16	Third Lanark	38	10	12	16	51	57	32
17	Clyde	38	12	6	20	44	59	30
18	Motherwell	38	10	10	18	49	66	30
19	Raith	38	9	10	19	53	68	28
20	Queen's Park	38	4	5	29	27	90	13

SECOND DIVISION 1914-15

		P	W	D	L	F	A	Pts
1	Derby	38	23	7	8	71	33	53
2	Preston	38	20	10	8	61	42	50
3	Barnsley	38	22	3	13	51	51	47
4	Wolves	38	19	7	12	77	52	45
5	Arsenal	38	19	5	14	69	41	43
6	Birmingham	38	17	9	12	62	39	43
7	Hull	38	19	5	14	65	54	43
8	Huddersfield	38	17	8	13	61	42	42
9	Clapton Orient	38	16	9	13	50	48	41
10	Blackpool	38	17	5	16	58	57	39
11	Bury	38	15	8	15	61	56	38
12	Fulham	38	15	7	16	53	47	37
13	Bristol City	38	15	7	16	62	56	37
14	Stockport	38	15	7	16	54	60	37
15	Leeds City	38	14	4	20	65	64	32
16	Lincoln	38	11	9	18	46	65	31
17	Grimsby	38	11	9	18	48	76	31
18	Nottm Forest	38	10	9	19	43	77	29
19	Leicester Fosse	38	10	4	24	47	88	24
20	Glossop NE	38	6	6	26	31	87	18

SCOTTISH DIVISION 'B' 1914-15

		P	W	D	L	F	A	Pts
1	Cowdenbeath	26	16	5	5	49	17	37
2	Leith	26	15	7	4	54	31	37
3	St Bernard's	26	18	1	7	66	34	37
4	E Stirlingshire	26	13	5	8	53	46	31
5	Clydebank	26	13	4	9	68	37	30
6	Dunfermline	26	13	2	11	49	39	28
7	Johnstone	26	11	5	10	41	52	27
8	St Johnstone	26	10	6	10	56	53	26
9	Albion	26	9	7	10	37	42	25
10	Lochgelly	26	9	3	14	44	60	21
11	Dundee Hibs	26	8	3	15	48	61	19
12	Abercorn	26	5	7	14	35	65	17
13	Arthurlie	26	6	4	16	36	66	16
14	Vale of Leven	26	4	5	17	33	66	13

WINNERS 1914-15

Southern League Watford
Central League Huddersfield Town
Irish Cup Linfield
Irish League Belfast Celtic
Welsh Cup Wrexham

FA CUP 1914-15

FIRST ROUND

Blackpool v Sheffield United	1-2
Liverpool v Stockport County	3-0
Bradford Park Avenue v Portsmouth	1-0
Bury v Plymouth Argyle	1-1, 2-1
Croydon Common v Oldham Athletic	0-3
Rochdale v Gillingham	2-0
Birmingham v Crystal Palace	2-2, 3-0
Brighton v Lincoln City	2-1
Bolton Wanderers v Notts County	2-1
Millwall Athletic v Clapton Orient	2-1
Burnley v Huddersfield Town	3-1
Bristol Rovers v Southend United	0-0, 0-3
Hull City v West Bromwich Albion	1-0
Grimsby Town v Northampton Town	0-3
Southampton v Luton Town	3-0
South Shields v Fulham	1-2
Chelsea v Swindon	1-1, 5-2
Arsenal v Merthyr Town	3-0
Preston North End v Manchester City	0-0, 0-3
Aston Villa v Exeter City	2-0
West Ham United v Newcastle United	2-2, 2-3
Swansea Town v Blackburn Rovers	1-0
The Wednesday v Manchester United	1-0
Reading v Wolverhampton Wanderers	0-1
Everton v Barnsley	3-0
Bristol City v Cardiff City	2-0
Queen's Park Rangers v Glossop North End	2-1
Derby County v Leeds City	1-2
Darlington v Bradford City	0-1
Middlesbrough v Goole Town	9-3
Nottingham Forest v Norwich City	1-4
Tottenham Hotspur v Sunderland	2-1

SECOND ROUND

Sheffield United v Liverpool	1-0
Bury v Bradford Park Avenue	0-1
Oldham Athletic v Rochdale	3-0
Brighton v Birmingham	0-0*, 0-3
Bolton Wanderers v Millwall Athletic	0-0*, 2-2*, 4-1
Burnley v Southend United	6-0
Hull City v Northampton Town	2-1
Fulham v Southampton	2-3*
Chelsea v Arsenal	1-0
Manchester City v Aston Villa	1-0
Newcastle United v Swansea Town	1-1*, 2-0
The Wednesday v Wolverhampton Wanderers	2-0
Everton v Bristol City	4-0
Queen's Park Rangers v Leeds City	1-0
Bradford City v Middlesbrough	1-0
Norwich City v Tottenham Hotspur	3-2

THIRD ROUND

Sheffield United v Bradford Park Avenue	1-0*
Birmingham v Oldham Athletic	2-3
Bolton Wanderers v Burnley	2-1*
Southampton v Hull City	2-2*, 0-4
Manchester City v Chelsea	0-1
The Wednesday v Newcastle United	1-2
Queen's Park Rangers v Everton	1-2
Bradford City v Norwich City	1-1*, 0-0*, 2-0

FOURTH ROUND

Oldham Athletic v Sheffield United	0-0*, 0-3
Bolton Wanderers v Hull City	4-2
Chelsea v Newcastle United	1-1*, 1-0
Bradford City v Everton	0-2

SEMI-FINAL

Sheffield United v Bolton Wanderers	2-1
Chelsea v Everton	2-0

FINAL AT OLD TRAFFORD

Sheffield United v Chelsea	3-0

*Extra time played

Left *A heatwave in London during August 1914 prompts this St John's Ambulance man to supply the crowd with drinking water.*

There was such a rush of games at the end of season 1915-16 that Celtic played two League games on 15 April. They beat Raith Rovers 6-0 and, in the evening, Motherwell 3-1.

WINNERS 1915-16

Lancashire Regional Tournament
Manchester City
Lancashire Tournament Northern Division Burnley
Lancashire Tournament Southern Division
Manchester City
Midland Regional Tournament
Nottingham Forest
Midland Tournament Southern Division
Nottingham Forest
Midland Tournament Northern Division
Leeds City
Midland Tournament Midland Division
Grimsby Town
London Combination Chelsea
London Supplementary Tournament 'A' Chelsea
London Supplementary Tournament 'B'
West Ham United
South Western Combination Portsmouth
Irish Cup Linfield

WINNERS 1916-17

Lancashire Regional Tournament Liverpool
Lancashire Subsidiary Tournament Rochdale
Midland Regional Tournament Leeds City
Midland Subsidiary Tournament Bradford PA
London Combination West Ham United
Irish Cup Glentoran
Belfast and District League Glentoran

WINNERS 1917-18

Lancashire Regional Tournament Stoke
Lancashire Subsidiary Tournament Liverpool
Midland Regional Tournament Leeds City
Midland Subsidiary Tournament Grimsby Town
League Championship Play-off Leeds City
London Combination Chelsea
Irish Cup Belfast Celtic
Belfast and District League Linfield

WINNERS 1918-19

Lancashire Regional Tournament Everton
Lancashire Subsidiary Tournament 'A' Blackpool
Lancashire Subsidiary Tournament 'B'
Oldham Athletic
Lancashire Subsidiary Tournament 'C'
Manchester City
Lancashire Subsidiary Tournament 'D' Liverpool
Midland Regional Tournament Nottingham Forest
Midland Subsidiary Tournament 'A'
Sheffield United
Midland Subsidiary Tournament 'B'
Birmingham
Midland Subsidiary Tournament 'C'
Bradford PA
Midland Subsidiary Tournament 'D' Hull City
League Championship Play-off
Nottingham Forest
London Combination Brentford
Irish Cup Linfield

SCOTTISH LEAGUE 1915-16

		P	W	D	L	F	A	Pts
1	Celtic	38	32	3	3	116	23	67
2	Rangers	38	25	6	7	87	39	56
3	Morton*	37	22	7	8	83	35	51
4	Ayr	38	20	8	10	72	45	48
5	Partick	38	19	8	11	65	41	46
6	Hearts*	37	20	6	11	66	45	46
7	Hamilton	38	19	3	16	68	76	41
8	Dundee	38	18	4	16	57	49	40
9	Dumbarton	38	13	11	14	53	64	37
10	Kilmarnock	38	12	11	15	46	49	35
11	Aberdeen	38	11	12	15	51	64	34
12	Falkirk	38	12	9	17	45	61	33
13	St Mirren	38	13	4	21	50	67	30
14	Motherwell	38	11	8	19	55	81	30
15	Airdrieonians	38	11	8	19	44	71	30
16	Clyde	38	11	7	20	49	71	29
17	Third Lanark	38	9	11	18	38	56	29
18	Queen's Park	38	11	6	21	53	100	28
19	Hibernian	38	9	7	22	44	70	25
20	Raith	38	9	5	24	30	65	23

*Morton and Hearts only played each other once.

SCOTTISH LEAGUE 1916-17

		P	W	D	L	F	A	Pts
1	Celtic	38	27	10	1	77	17	64
2	Morton	38	24	6	8	72	39	54
3	Rangers	38	24	5	9	68	32	53
4	Airdrieonians	38	21	8	9	71	38	50
5	Third Lanark	38	19	11	8	53	37	49
6	Kilmarnock	38	18	7	13	69	45	43
7	St Mirren	38	15	10	13	49	43	40
8	Motherwell	38	16	6	16	57	58	38
9	Partick	38	14	7	17	44	43	35
10	Dumbarton	38	12	11	15	56	73	35
11	Hamilton	38	13	9	16	54	73	35
12	Falkirk	38	12	10	16	57	57	34
13	Clyde	38	10	14	14	41	51	34
14	Hearts	38	14	4	20	44	59	32
15	Ayr	38	12	7	19	46	59	31
16	Dundee	38	13	4	21	58	71	30
17	Hibernian	38	10	10	18	57	72	30
18	Queen's Park	38	11	7	20	56	81	29
19	Raith	38	8	7	23	42	91	23
20	Aberdeen	38	7	7	24	36	68	21

SCOTTISH LEAGUE 1917-18

		P	W	D	L	F	A	Pts
1	Rangers	34	25	6	3	66	24	56
2	Celtic	34	24	7	3	66	26	55
3	Kilmarnock	34	19	5	10	69	41	43
4	Morton	34	17	9	8	53	42	43
5	Motherwell	34	16	9	9	70	51	41
6	Partick	34	14	12	8	51	37	40
7	Queen's Park	34	14	6	14	64	63	34
8	Dumbarton	34	13	8	13	48	49	34
9	Clydebank	34	14	5	15	55	56	33
10	Hearts	34	14	4	16	41	58	32
11	St Mirren	34	11	7	16	42	50	29
12	Hamilton	34	11	6	17	52	63	28
13	Third Lanark	34	10	7	17	56	62	27
14	Falkirk	34	9	9	16	38	58	27
15	Airdrieonians	34	10	6	18	46	58	26
16	Hibernian	34	8	9	17	42	57	25
17	Clyde	34	9	2	23	37	72	20
18	Ayr	34	5	9	20	32	61	19

SCOTTISH LEAGUE 1918-19

		P	W	D	L	F	A	Pts
1	Celtic	34	26	6	2	70	22	58
2	Rangers	34	26	5	3	86	16	57
3	Morton	34	18	11	5	76	38	47
4	Partick	34	17	7	10	62	43	41
5	Motherwell	34	14	10	10	51	40	38
6	Hearts	34	14	9	11	59	52	37
7	Ayr	34	14	9	11	57	53	37
8	Queen's Park	34	15	5	14	59	57	35
9	Kilmarnock	34	14	7	13	61	59	35
10	Clydebank	34	12	8	14	52	65	32
11	St Mirren	34	10	12	12	43	55	32
12	Third Lanark	34	11	9	14	60	60	31
13	Airdrieonians	34	9	11	14	45	54	29
14	Hamilton	34	11	5	18	49	75	27
15	Dumbarton	34	7	8	19	31	57	22
16	Falkirk	34	6	8	20	46	72	20
17	Clyde	34	7	6	21	45	75	20
18	Hibernian	34	5	4	25	28	87	14

Right *George Utley leads Sheffield United out for their semi-final FA Cup tie with Bolton Wanderers in 1915. United won 2-1, going on to the only Final this century initially played outside London. That Final, in which they beat Chelsea 3-0, was played at Old Trafford, and has always been known as the 'Khaki Final' because of the large number of soldiers in the crowd.*

The only first-class game in English football played without spectators was the 1915 Bradford City-Norwich second Cup replay. Questions had been raised in the Commons about British-made shells failing to explode in France. The Government decided that the people making the shells were being distracted, and banned football matches during working hours in the vicinity of munitions factories. The game, at Lincoln, was played behind locked doors.

FIRST DIVISION

		P	W	D	L	F	A	Pts
1	WBA	42	28	4	10	104	47	60
2	Burnley	42	21	9	12	65	59	51
3	Chelsea	42	22	5	15	56	51	49
4	Liverpool	42	19	10	13	59	44	48
5	Sunderland	42	22	4	16	72	59	48
6	Bolton	42	19	9	14	72	65	47
7	Man City	42	18	9	15	71	62	45
8	Newcastle	42	17	9	16	44	39	43
9	Aston Villa	42	18	6	18	75	73	42
10	Arsenal	42	15	12	15	56	58	42
11	Bradford PA	42	15	12	15	60	63	42
12	Man United	42	13	14	15	54	50	40
13	Middlesbrough	42	15	10	17	61	65	40
14	Sheff United	42	16	8	18	59	69	40
15	Bradford City	42	14	11	17	54	63	39
16	Everton	42	12	14	16	69	68	38
17	Oldham	42	15	8	19	49	52	38
18	Derby	42	13	12	17	47	57	38
19	Preston	42	14	10	18	57	73	38
20	Blackburn	42	13	11	18	64	77	37
21	Notts County	42	12	12	18	56	74	36
22	Wednesday	42	7	9	26	28	64	23

SECOND DIVISION

		P	W	D	L	F	A	Pts
1	Tottenham	42	32	6	4	102	32	70
2	Huddersfield	42	28	8	6	97	38	64
3	Birmingham	42	24	8	10	85	34	56
4	Blackpool	42	21	10	11	65	47	52
5	Bury	42	20	8	14	60	44	48
6	Fulham	42	19	9	14	61	50	47
7	West Ham	42	19	9	14	47	40	47
8	Bristol City	42	13	17	12	46	43	43
9	South Shields	42	15	12	15	58	48	42
10	Stoke	42	18	6	18	60	54	42
11	Hull	42	18	6	18	78	72	42
12	Barnsley	42	15	10	17	61	55	40
13	Port Vale*	42	16	8	18	59	62	40
14	Leicester	42	15	10	17	41	61	40
15	Clapton Orient	42	16	6	20	51	59	38
16	Stockport	42	14	9	19	52	61	37
17	Rotherham Co	42	13	8	21	51	83	34
18	Nottm Forest	42	11	9	22	43	73	31
19	Wolves	42	10	10	22	55	80	30
20	Coventry	42	9	11	22	35	73	29
21	Lincoln	42	9	9	24	44	101	27
22	Grimsby	42	10	5	27	34	75	25

*Leeds City were expelled from the League on 4 October 1919, when their record was P8 W4 D2 L2 F17 A10 Pts10. Port Vale took over their remaining fixtures

SCOTTISH LEAGUE

		P	W	D	L	F	A	Pts
1	Rangers	42	31	9	2	106	25	71
2	Celtic	42	29	10	3	89	31	68
3	Motherwell	42	23	11	8	73	53	57
4	Dundee	42	22	6	14	79	65	50
5	Clydebank	42	20	8	14	78	54	48
6	Morton	42	16	13	13	71	48	45
7	Airdrieonians	42	17	10	15	57	43	44
8	Third Lanark	42	16	11	15	57	62	43
9	Kilmarnock	42	20	3	19	59	74	43
10	Ayr	42	15	10	17	72	69	40
11	Dumbarton	42	13	13	16	57	65	39
12	Queen's Park	42	14	10	18	67	73	38
13	Partick	42	13	12	17	51	62	38
14	St Mirren	42	15	8	19	63	81	38
15	Hearts	42	14	9	19	57	72	37
16	Clyde	42	14	9	19	64	71	37
17	Aberdeen	42	11	13	18	46	64	35
18	Hibernian	42	13	7	22	60	79	33
19	Raith	42	11	10	21	61	82	32
20	Falkirk	42	10	11	21	45	74	31
21	Hamilton	42	11	7	24	56	86	29
22	Albion	42	10	7	25	42	77	27

SCOTTISH FA CUP 1919-20

FIRST ROUND

Cowdenbeath v Aberdeen	0-1
Albion Rovers v Dykehead	0-0, 2-1
Dunfermline Harp v Alloa Athletic	0-0, 0-1
Armadale v Clyde	1-0
Dundee v Airdrieonians	1-0
East Fife v Arthurlie	4-0
East Stirlingshire v Thornhill	6-0
St Bernard's v Bathgate	2-0
Heart of Midlothian v Nithsdale Wanderers	5-1
Galston v Hibernian	0-0, 1-2
Lochgelly United v Clachnacuddin	2-0
Morton v Forfar Athletic	4-0
Partick Thistle v Motherwell	3-1
Queen's Park v Hamilton Academicals	2-0
Rangers v Dumbarton	0-0, 1-0
Royal Albert v Forres Mechanics	7-0
Stevenston United v St Mirren	1-2
Third Lanark v Inverness Caledonian	4-1

SECOND ROUND

Aberdeen v Gala Fairydean	2-0
Albion Rovers v Huntingtower (scratched)	w o
Armadale v Hibernian	1-0
Ayr United v St Mirren	2-1
Broxburn United v Queen of the South Wanderers	1-0
Dundee v Celtic	1-3
St Bernard's v Bathgate	2-0
Heart of Midlothian v Falkirk	2-0
Alloa Athletic v Kilmarnock	0-2
Lochgelly United v Royal Albert	2-1
St Johnstone v Morton	1-1, 3-5
Partick Thistle v East Fife	5-0
Queen's Park v Vale of Leithen	3-0
Raith Rovers v East Stirlingshire	0-0, 1-1, 0-0, 4-0
Rangers v Arbroath	5-0
Third Lanark v Vale of Leven	2-1

THIRD ROUND

Aberdeen v Heart of Midlothian	1-0
St Bernard's v Albion Rovers	1-1, 1-4
Ayr United v Armadale	1-1, 0-1
Celtic v Partick Thistle	2-0
Kilmarnock v Queen's Park	4-1
Raith Rovers v Morton	2-2, 0-3
Rangers v Broxburn United	3-0
Lochgelly United v Third Lanark	0-3

FOURTH ROUND

Albion Rovers v Aberdeen	2-1
Morton v Third Lanark	3-0
Armadale v Kilmarnock	1-2
Rangers v Celtic	1-0

SEMI-FINAL

Kilmarnock v Morton	3-2
Albion Rovers v Rangers	0-0, 1-1, 2-0

FINAL AT HAMPDEN PARK

Kilmarnock v Albion Rovers	3-2

FA CUP 1919-20

FIRST ROUND

Aston Villa v Queen's Park Rangers	2-1
Port Vale v Manchester United	1-2
Sunderland v Hull City	6-2
Thorneycroft's Wanderers v Burnley	0-0, 0-5
Bristol Rovers v Tottenham Hotspur	1-4
West Stanley v Gillingham	3-1
Southampton v West Ham United	0-0, 1-3
Bury v Stoke	2-0
Bolton Wanderers v Chelsea	0-1
Fulham v Swindon Town	1-2
Newport County v Leicester City	0-0, 0-2
Manchester City v Clapton Orient	4-1
Bradford Park Avenue v Nottingham Forest	3-0
Castleford Town v Hednesford Town	2-0
Notts County v Millwall Athletic	2-0
Middlesbrough v Lincoln City	4-1
Grimsby Town v Bristol City	1-2
Arsenal v Rochdale	4-2
Cardiff City v Oldham Athletic	2-0
Blackburn Rovers v Wolverhampton Wanderers	2-2, 0-1
Bradford City v Portsmouth	2-2*, 2-0
Sheffield United v Southend United	3-0
Preston North End v Stockport County	3-1
Blackpool v Derby County	0-0, 4-1
Huddersfield Town v Brentford	5-1
Newcastle United v Crystal Palace	2-0
Plymouth Argyle v Reading	2-0
West Bromwich Albion v Barnsley	0-1
South Shields v Liverpool	1-1, 0-2
Luton Town v Coventry City	2-2, 1-0
Birmingham v Everton	2-0
Darlington v The Wednesday	0-0, 2-0

*abandoned

SECOND ROUND

Manchester United v Aston Villa	1-2
Burnley v Sunderland	1-1, 0-2
Tottenham Hotspur v West Stanley	4-0
West Ham United v Bury	6-0
Chelsea v Swindon Town	4-0
Leicester City v Manchester City	3-0
Bradford Park Avenue v Castleford Town	3-2
Notts County v Middlesbrough	1-0
Bristol City v Arsenal	1-0
Wolverhampton Wanderers v Cardiff City	1-2
Bradford City v Sheffield United	2-1
Preston North End v Blackpool	2-1
Newcastle United v Huddersfield Town	0-1
Plymouth Argyle v Barnsley	4-1
Luton Town v Liverpool	0-2
Birmingham v Darlington	4-0

THIRD ROUND

Aston Villa v Sunderland	1-0
Tottenham Hotspur v West Ham United	3-0
Chelsea v Leicester City	3-0
Notts County v Bradford Park Avenue	3-4
Bristol City v Cardiff City	2-1
Preston North End v Bradford City	0-3
Huddersfield Town v Plymouth Argyle	3-1
Liverpool v Birmingham	2-0

FOURTH ROUND

Tottenham Hotspur v Aston Villa	0-1
Chelsea v Bradford Park Avenue	4-1
Bristol City v Bradford City	2-0
Huddersfield Town v Liverpool	2-1

SEMI-FINAL

Aston Villa v Chelsea	3-1
Huddersfield Town v Bristol City	2-1

FINAL AT STAMFORD BRIDGE

Aston Villa v Huddersfield Town	1-0

Far left Billy Walker, the Aston Villa forward whose two goals in Villa's 3-1 win over Chelsea in the FA Cup semi-final saved the Football Association an embarrassing situation. If Chelsea had won they would have played the Final on their own ground, Stamford Bridge. This was against the rules of the competition but arrangements were too far advanced to be changed.

199

FIRST DIVISION

		P	W	D	L	F	A	Pts
1	Burnley	42	23	13	6	79	36	59
2	Man City	42	24	6	12	70	50	54
3	Bolton	42	19	14	9	77	53	52
4	Liverpool	42	18	15	9	63	35	51
5	Newcastle	42	20	10	12	66	45	50
6	Tottenham	42	19	9	14	70	48	47
7	Everton	42	17	13	12	66	55	47
8	Middlesbrough	42	17	12	13	53	53	46
9	Arsenal	42	15	14	13	59	63	44
10	Aston Villa	42	18	7	17	63	70	43
11	Blackburn	42	13	15	14	57	59	41
12	Sunderland	42	14	13	15	57	60	41
13	Man United	42	15	10	17	64	68	40
14	WBA	42	13	14	15	54	58	40
15	Bradford City	42	12	15	15	61	63	39
16	Preston	42	15	9	18	61	65	39
17	Huddersfield	42	15	9	18	42	49	39
18	Chelsea	42	13	13	16	48	58	39
19	Oldham	42	9	15	18	49	86	33
20	Sheff United	42	6	18	18	42	68	30
21	Derby	42	5	16	21	32	58	26
22	Bradford PA	42	8	8	26	43	76	24

SECOND DIVISION

		P	W	D	L	F	A	Pts
1	Birmingham	42	24	10	8	79	38	58
2	Cardiff	42	24	10	8	59	32	58
3	Bristol City	42	19	13	10	49	29	51
4	Blackpool	42	20	10	12	54	42	50
5	West Ham	42	19	10	13	51	30	48
6	Notts County	42	18	11	13	55	40	47
7	Clapton Orient	42	16	13	13	43	42	45
8	South Shields	42	17	10	15	61	46	44
9	Fulham	42	16	10	16	43	47	42
10	Wednesday	42	15	11	16	48	48	41
11	Bury	42	15	10	17	45	49	40
12	Leicester	42	12	16	14	39	46	40
13	Hull	42	10	20	12	43	53	40
14	Leeds	42	14	10	18	40	45	38
15	Wolves	42	16	6	20	49	66	38
16	Barnsley	42	10	16	16	48	50	36
17	Port Vale	42	11	14	17	43	49	36
18	Nottm Forest	42	12	12	18	48	55	36
19	Rotherham Co	42	12	12	18	37	53	36
20	Stoke	42	12	11	19	46	56	35
21	Coventry	42	12	11	19	39	70	35
22	Stockport	42	9	12	21	42	75	30

THIRD DIVISION

		P	W	D	L	F	A	Pts
1	Crystal Palace	42	24	11	7	70	34	59
2	Southampton	42	19	16	7	64	28	54
3	QPR	42	22	9	11	61	32	53
4	Swindon	42	21	10	11	73	49	52
5	Swansea	42	18	15	9	56	45	51
6	Watford	42	20	8	14	59	44	48
7	Millwall Ath	42	18	11	13	42	30	47
8	Merthyr Town	42	15	15	12	60	49	45
9	Luton	42	16	12	14	61	56	44
10	Bristol Rovers	42	18	7	17	68	57	43
11	Plymouth	42	11	21	10	35	34	43
12	Portsmouth	42	12	15	15	46	48	39
13	Grimsby	42	15	9	18	49	59	39
14	Northampton	42	15	8	19	59	75	38
15	Newport	42	14	9	19	43	64	37
16	Norwich	42	10	16	16	44	53	36
17	Southend	42	14	8	20	44	61	36
18	Brighton	42	14	8	20	42	61	36
19	Exeter	42	10	15	17	39	54	35
20	Reading	42	12	7	23	42	59	31
21	Brentford	42	9	12	21	42	67	30
22	Gillingham	42	8	12	22	34	74	28

SCOTTISH LEAGUE

		P	W	D	L	F	A	Pts
1	Rangers	42	35	6	1	91	24	76
2	Celtic	42	30	6	6	86	35	66
3	Hearts	42	20	10	12	74	49	50
4	Dundee	42	19	11	12	54	48	49
5	Motherwell	42	19	10	13	75	51	48
6	Partick	42	17	12	13	53	39	46
7	Clyde	42	21	3	18	63	62	45
8	Third Lanark	42	19	6	17	74	61	44
9	Morton	42	15	14	13	66	58	44
10	Airdrieonians	42	17	9	16	71	64	43
11	Aberdeen	42	14	14	14	53	54	42
12	Kilmarnock	42	17	8	17	62	68	42
13	Hibernian	42	16	9	17	58	57	41
14	Ayr	42	14	12	16	62	69	40
15	Hamilton	42	14	12	16	44	57	40
16	Raith	42	16	5	21	54	58	37
17	Albion	42	11	12	19	57	68	34
18	Falkirk	42	11	12	19	54	72	34
19	Queen's Park	42	11	11	20	45	80	33
20	Clydebank	42	7	14	21	47	72	28
21	Dumbarton	42	10	4	28	41	89	24
22	St Mirren	42	7	4	31	43	92	18

FA CUP 1920-21

SECOND ROUND
Southend United v Blackpool	1-0
Tottenham Hotspur v Bradford City	4-0
Notts County v Aston Villa	0-0, 0-1
Bradford Park Avenue v Huddersfield Town	0-1
Crystal Palace v Hull City	0-2
Burnley v Queen's Park Rangers	4-2
South Shields v Luton Town	0-4
Preston North End v Watford	4-1
Everton v The Wednesday	1-1, 1-0
Newcastle United v Liverpool	1-0
Lincoln City v Fulham	0-0, 0-1
Derby County v Wolverhampton Wanderers	1-1, 0-1
Grimsby Town v Southampton	1-3
Brighton v Cardiff City	0-0, 0-1
Swansea Town v Plymouth Argyle	1-2
Swindon Town v Chelsea	0-2

THIRD ROUND
Southend United v Tottenham Hotspur	1-4
Aston Villa v Huddersfield Town	2-0
Hull City v Burnley	3-0
Luton Town v Preston North End	2-3
Everton v Newcastle United	3-0
Fulham v Wolverhampton Wanderers	0-1
Southampton v Cardiff City	0-1
Plymouth Argyle v Chelsea	0-0, 0-0, 1-2

FOURTH ROUND
Tottenham Hotspur v Aston Villa	1-0
Hull City v Preston North End	0-0, 0-1
Everton v Wolverhampton Wanderers	0-1
Cardiff City v Chelsea	1-0

SEMI-FINAL
Tottenham Hotspur v Preston North End	2-1
Wolverhampton Wanderers v Cardiff City	0-0, 3-1

FINAL AT STAMFORD BRIDGE
Tottenham Hotspur v Wolverhampton Wanderers 1-0

SCOTTISH FA CUP 1920-21

SECOND ROUND
Kilmarnock v Aberdeen	1-2
Albion Rovers v Mid-Annandale	3-1
Clydebank v Alloa Athletic	0-0, 1-1, 0-1
Bo'ness v Armadale	0-0, 0-2
Ayr United v Dykehead	4-0
Vale of Leven v Celtic	0-3
Dumbarton v Elgin City	3-0
Dundee v Stenhousemuir	1-0
Stevenston United v East Fife	0-0, 1-2
East Stirlingshire v Solway Star	5-1
Broxburn United v Hamilton Academicals	1-2
Clyde v Heart of Midlothian	0-0, 1-1, 2-3
Motherwell v Renton	3-0
Queen of the South v Nithsdale Wanderers	1-3
Partick Thistle v Hibernian	0-0, 0-0, 1-0
Rangers v Morton	2-0

THIRD ROUND
Armadale v Albion Rovers	0-0, 0-0, 2-2, 0-2
East Fife v Celtic	1-3
Dumbarton v Nithsdale Wanderers	5-0
Aberdeen v Dundee	1-1, 0-0, 0-2
Hamilton Academicals v Heart of Midlothian	0-1
Motherwell v Ayr United	1-1, 1-1, 3-1
East Stirlingshire v Partick Thistle	1-2
Rangers v Alloa Athletic	0-0, 4-1

FOURTH ROUND
Dundee v Albion Rovers	0-2
Celtic v Heart of Midlothian	1-2
Partick Thistle v Motherwell	0-0, 2-2, 2-1
Dumbarton v Rangers	0-3

SEMI-FINAL
Partick v Heart of Midlothian	0-0, 0-0, 2-0
Rangers v Albion Rovers	4-1

FINAL AT CELTIC PARK
Partick Thistle v Rangers 1-0

Burnley's Championship side which went 30 games without defeat in 1920-21.

RADIO TIMES HULTON PICTURE LIBRARY

FIRST DIVISION

		P	W	D	L	F	A	Pts
1	Liverpool	42	22	13	7	63	36	57
2	Tottenham	42	21	9	12	65	39	51
3	Burnley	42	22	5	15	72	54	49
4	Cardiff	42	19	10	13	61	53	48
5	Aston Villa	42	22	3	17	74	55	47
6	Bolton	42	20	7	15	68	59	47
7	Newcastle	42	18	10	14	59	45	46
8	Middlesbrough	42	16	14	12	79	69	46
9	Chelsea	42	17	12	13	40	43	46
10	Man City	42	18	9	15	65	70	45
11	Sheff United	42	15	10	17	59	54	40
12	Sunderland	42	16	8	18	60	62	40
13	WBA	42	15	10	17	51	63	40
14	Huddersfield	42	15	9	18	53	54	39
15	Blackburn	42	13	12	17	54	57	38
16	Preston	42	13	12	17	42	65	38
17	Arsenal	42	15	7	20	47	56	37
18	Birmingham	42	15	7	20	48	60	37
19	Oldham	42	13	11	18	38	50	37
20	Everton	42	12	12	18	57	55	36
21	Bradford City	42	11	10	21	48	72	32
22	Man United	42	8	12	22	41	73	28

SECOND DIVISION

		P	W	D	L	F	A	Pts
1	Nottm Forest	42	22	12	8	51	30	56
2	Stoke	42	18	16	8	60	44	52
3	Barnsley	42	22	8	12	67	52	52
4	West Ham	42	20	8	14	52	39	48
5	Hull	42	19	10	13	51	41	48
6	South Shields	42	17	12	13	43	38	46
7	Fulham	42	18	9	15	57	38	45
8	Leeds	42	16	13	13	48	38	45
9	Leicester	42	14	17	11	39	34	45
10	Wednesday	42	15	14	13	47	50	44
11	Bury	42	15	10	17	54	55	40
12	Derby	42	15	9	18	60	64	39
13	Notts County	42	12	15	15	47	51	39
14	Crystal Palace	42	13	13	16	45	51	39
15	Clapton Orient	42	15	9	18	43	50	39
16	Rotherham Co	42	14	11	17	32	43	39
17	Wolves	42	13	11	18	44	49	37
18	Port Vale	42	14	8	20	43	57	36
19	Blackpool	42	15	5	22	44	57	35
20	Coventry	42	12	10	20	51	60	34
21	Bristol City	42	12	9	21	37	58	33
22	Bradford PA	42	12	9	21	46	62	33

FA CUP 1921-22

SECOND ROUND

Crystal Palace v Millwall Athletic	0-0, 0-2
Southend United v Swansea Town	0-1
Swindon Town v Blackburn Rovers	0-1
Brighton v Huddersfield Town	0-0, 0-2
Aston Villa v Luton Town	1-0
Northampton Town v Stoke	2-2, 0-3
Liverpool v West Bromwich Albion	0-1
Bradford City v Notts County	1-1, 1-1, 0-1
Bradford Park Avenue v Arsenal	2-3
Leicester City v Fulham	2-0
Barnsley v Oldham Athletic	3-1
Preston North End v Newcastle United	3-1
Southampton v Cardiff City	1-1, 0-2
Nottingham Forest v Hull City	3-0
Bolton Wanderers v Manchester City	1-3
Tottenham Hotspur v Watford	1-0

THIRD ROUND

Millwall Athletic v Swansea Town	4-0
Blackburn Rovers v Huddersfield Town	1-1, 0-5
Stoke v Aston Villa	0-0, 0-4
West Bromwich Albion v Notts County	1-1, 0-2
Arsenal v Leicester City	3-0
Barnsley v Preston North End	1-1, 0-3
Cardiff City v Nottingham Forest	4-1
Tottenham Hotspur v Manchester City	2-1

FOURTH ROUND

Huddersfield Town v Millwall Athletic	3-0
Notts County v Aston Villa	2-2, 4-3
Arsenal v Preston North End	1-1, 1-2
Cardiff City v Tottenham Hotspur	1-1, 1-2

SEMI-FINAL

Huddersfield Town v Notts County	3-1
Preston North End v Tottenham Hotspur	2-1

FINAL AT STAMFORD BRIDGE

Huddersfield Town v Preston North End	1-0

THIRD DIVISION (NORTH)

		P	W	D	L	F	A	Pts
1	Stockport	38	24	8	6	60	21	56
2	Darlington	38	22	6	10	81	37	50
3	Grimsby	38	21	8	9	72	47	50
4	Hartlepools	38	17	8	13	52	39	42
5	Accrington	38	19	3	16	73	57	41
6	Crewe	38	18	5	15	60	56	41
7	Stalybridge Cel	38	18	5	15	62	63	41
8	Walsall	38	18	3	17	66	65	39
9	Southport	38	14	10	14	55	44	38
10	Ashington	38	17	4	17	59	66	38
11	Durham City	38	17	3	18	68	67	37
12	Wrexham	38	14	9	15	51	56	37
13	Chesterfield	38	16	3	19	48	67	35
14	Lincoln	38	14	6	18	48	59	34
15	Barrow	38	14	5	19	42	54	33
16	Nelson	38	13	7	18	48	66	33
17	Wigan Borough	38	11	9	18	46	72	31
18	Tranmere	38	9	11	18	51	61	29
19	Halifax	38	10	9	19	56	76	29
20	Rochdale	38	11	4	23	52	77	26

THIRD DIVISION (SOUTH)

		P	W	D	L	F	A	Pts
1	Southampton	42	23	15	4	68	21	61
2	Plymouth	42	25	11	6	63	24	61
3	Portsmouth	42	18	17	7	62	39	53
4	Luton	42	22	8	12	64	35	52
5	QPR	42	18	13	11	53	44	49
6	Swindon	42	16	13	13	72	60	45
7	Watford	42	13	18	11	54	48	44
8	Aberdare Ath	42	17	10	15	57	51	44
9	Brentford	42	16	11	15	52	43	43
10	Swansea	42	13	15	14	50	47	41
11	Merthyr Town	42	17	6	19	45	56	40
12	Millwall Ath	42	10	18	14	38	42	38
13	Reading	42	14	18	10	40	47	38
14	Bristol Rovers	42	14	10	18	52	67	38
15	Norwich	42	12	13	17	50	62	37
16	Charlton	42	13	11	18	43	56	37
17	Northampton	42	13	11	18	47	71	37
18	Gillingham	42	14	8	20	47	60	36
19	Brighton	42	13	9	20	45	51	35
20	Newport	42	11	12	19	44	61	34
21	Exeter	42	11	12	19	38	59	34
22	Southend	42	8	11	23	34	74	27

SCOTTISH FA CUP 1921-22

SECOND ROUND

Aberdeen v Queen's Park	1-1, 2-1
Cowdenbeath v Airdrieonians	0-0, 1-4
Vale of Leven v Alloa Athletic	0-0, 0-1
Bathgate v Falkirk	1-0
Celtic v Third Lanark	1-0
Clyde v Bo'ness	5-1
Royal Albert v Dundee	0-1
East Stirlingshire v Dunfermline Athletic	2-1
Morton v Clydebank	1-1, 3-1
Hamilton Academicals v King's Park	4-1
Broxburn United v Heart of Midlothian	2-2, 2-2, 1-3
Motherwell v Hibernian	3-2
Ayr United v Partick Thistle	0-1
Inverness Citadel v Queen of the South	2-2, 1-2
Albion Rovers v Rangers	1-1, 0-4
Kilmarnock v St Mirren	1-4

THIRD ROUND

Aberdeen v Dundee	3-0
Morton v Clyde	4-1
Celtic v Hamilton Academicals	1-3
Motherwell v Alloa Athletic	1-0
Partick Thistle v Bathgate	3-0
Queen of the South v East Stirlingshire	2-0
Heart of Midlothian v Rangers	0-4
St Mirren v Airdrieonians	3-0

FOURTH ROUND

Hamilton Academicals v Aberdeen	0-0, 0-2
Motherwell v Morton	1-2
Partick Thistle v Queen of the South	1-0
Rangers v St Mirren	1-1, 2-0

SEMI-FINAL

Morton v Aberdeen	3-1
Rangers v Partick Thistle	2-0

FINAL AT HAMPDEN PARK

Morton v Rangers	1-0

SCOTTISH FIRST DIVISION

		P	W	D	L	F	A	Pts
1	Celtic	42	27	13	2	83	20	67
2	Rangers	42	28	10	4	83	26	66
3	Raith	42	19	13	10	66	43	51
4	Dundee	42	19	11	12	57	40	49
5	Falkirk	42	16	17	9	48	38	49
6	Partick	42	20	8	14	57	53	48
7	Hibernian	42	16	14	12	55	44	46
8	St Mirren	42	17	12	13	71	61	46
9	Third Lanark	42	17	12	13	58	52	46
10	Clyde	42	16	12	14	60	51	44
11	Albion	42	17	10	15	55	51	44
12	Morton	42	16	10	16	58	57	42
13	Motherwell	42	16	7	19	63	58	39
14	Ayr	42	13	12	17	55	63	38
15	Aberdeen	42	13	9	20	48	54	35
16	Airdrieonians	42	12	11	19	46	56	35
17	Kilmarnock	42	13	9	20	56	83	35
18	Hamilton	42	9	16	17	51	62	34
19	Hearts	42	11	10	21	50	60	32
20	Dumbarton*	42	10	10	22	46	81	30
21	Queen's Park*	42	9	10	23	38	82	28
22	Clydebank*	42	6	8	28	34	103	20

* Three clubs relegated to Second Division

SCOTTISH SECOND DIVISION

		P	W	D	L	F	A	Pts
1	Alloa*	38	26	8	4	81	32	60
2	Cowdenbeath	38	19	9	10	56	30	47
3	Armadale	38	20	5	13	64	49	45
4	Vale of Leven	38	17	10	11	56	43	44
5	Bathgate	38	16	11	11	56	41	43
6	Bo'ness	38	16	7	15	57	49	39
7	Broxburn	38	14	11	13	43	43	39
8	Dunfermline	38	14	10	14	56	42	38
9	St Bernard's	38	15	8	15	50	49	38
10	Stenhousemuir	38	14	10	14	50	51	38
11	Johnstone	38	14	10	14	46	59	38
12	East Fife	38	15	7	16	55	54	37
13	St Johnstone	38	12	11	15	41	52	35
14	Forfar	38	11	12	15	44	53	34
15	E Stirlingshire	38	12	10	16	43	60	34
16	Arbroath	38	11	11	16	45	56	33
17	King's Park	38	10	12	16	47	65	32
18	Lochgelly Utd	38	11	9	18	46	56	31
19	Dundee Hibs	38	10	8	20	47	65	28
20	Clackmannan	38	10	7	21	41	75	27

* Only Alloa promoted

On Boxing Day 1921, Aston Villa's winning goal in their Division One fixture with Sheffield United was a spectacular 30-yard header. Frank Barson, Villa's centre-half, was the man responsible. Another Villa player, Billy Walker, had also done the unusual in a League match that season. In November, he had scored three penalties against Bradford City—a record for one game.

Jimmy Evans, Southend United's full-back, scored a total of 10 goals in the Third Division South in 1921-22. All were from penalties, and meant that Evans became the first full-back to finish a season as a club's top League scorer.

The Scottish Second Division restarted in 1921-22, with promotion by position.

FIRST DIVISION

		P	W	D	L	F	A	Pts
1	Liverpool	42	26	8	8	70	31	60
2	Sunderland	42	22	10	10	72	54	54
3	Huddersfield	42	21	11	10	60	32	53
4	Newcastle	42	18	12	12	45	37	48
5	Everton	42	20	7	15	63	59	47
6	Aston Villa	42	18	10	14	64	51	46
7	WBA	42	17	11	14	58	49	45
8	Man City	42	17	11	14	50	49	45
9	Cardiff	42	18	7	17	73	59	43
10	Sheff United	42	16	10	16	68	64	42
11	Arsenal	42	16	10	16	61	62	42
12	Tottenham	42	17	7	18	50	50	41
13	Bolton	42	14	12	16	50	58	40
14	Blackburn	42	14	12	16	47	62	40
15	Burnley	42	16	6	20	58	59	38
16	Preston	42	13	11	18	60	64	37
17	Birmingham	42	13	11	18	41	57	37
18	Middlesbrough	42	13	10	19	57	63	36
19	Chelsea	42	9	18	15	45	53	36
20	Nottm Forest	42	13	8	21	41	70	34
21	Stoke	42	10	10	22	47	67	30
22	Oldham	42	10	10	22	35	65	30

SECOND DIVISION

		P	W	D	L	F	A	Pts
1	Notts County	42	23	7	12	46	34	53
2	West Ham	42	20	11	11	63	38	51
3	Leicester	42	21	9	12	65	44	51
4	Man United	42	17	14	11	51	36	48
5	Blackpool	42	18	11	13	60	43	47
6	Bury	42	18	11	13	55	46	47
7	Leeds	42	18	11	13	43	36	47
8	Wednesday	42	17	12	13	54	47	46
9	Barnsley	42	17	11	14	62	51	45
10	Fulham	42	16	12	14	43	32	44
11	Southampton	42	14	14	14	40	40	42
12	Hull	42	14	14	14	43	45	42
13	South Shields	42	15	10	17	35	44	40
14	Derby	42	14	11	17	46	50	39
15	Bradford City	42	12	13	17	41	45	37
16	Crystal Palace	42	13	11	18	54	62	37
17	Port Vale	42	14	9	19	39	51	37
18	Coventry	42	15	7	20	46	63	37
19	Clapton Orient	42	12	12	18	40	50	36
20	Stockport	42	14	8	20	43	58	36
21	Rotherham Co	42	13	9	20	44	63	35
22	Wolves	42	9	9	24	42	77	27

FA CUP 1922-23

SECOND ROUND

Bolton Wanderers v Leeds United	3-1
Millwall Athletic v Huddersfield Town	0-0, 0-3
Charlton Athletic v Preston North End	2-0
West Bromwich Albion v Sunderland	2-1
Middlesbrough v Sheffield United	1-1, 0-3
Wolverhampton Wanderers v Liverpool	0-2
Wigan Borough v Queen's Park Rangers	2-4
South Shields v Blackburn Rovers	0-0, 1-0
Bury v Stoke	3-1
Chelsea v Southampton	0-0, 0-1
Brighton v West Ham United	1-1, 0-1
Plymouth Argyle v Bradford Park Avenue	4-1
Bristol City v Derby County	0-3
The Wednesday v Barnsley	2-1
Tottenham Hotspur v Manchester United	4-0
Leicester City v Cardiff City	0-1

THIRD ROUND

Huddersfield Town v Bolton Wanderers	1-1, 0-1
Charlton Athletic v West Bromwich Albion	1-0
Liverpool v Sheffield United	1-2
Queen's Park Rangers v South Shields	3-0
Bury v Southampton	0-0, 0-1
West Ham United v Plymouth Argyle	2-0
Derby County v The Wednesday	1-0
Cardiff City v Tottenham Hotspur	2-3

FOURTH ROUND

Charlton Athletic v Bolton Wanderers	0-1
Queen's Park Rangers v Sheffield United	0-1
Southampton v West Ham United	1-1, 1-1, 0-1
Tottenham Hotspur v Derby County	0-1

SEMI-FINAL

Bolton Wanderers v Sheffield United	1-0
West Ham United v Derby County	5-2

FINAL

Bolton Wanderers v West Ham United	2-0

THIRD DIVISION (SOUTH)

		P	W	D	L	F	A	Pts
1	Bristol City	42	24	11	7	66	40	59
2	Plymouth	42	23	7	12	61	29	53
3	Swansea	42	22	9	11	78	45	53
4	Brighton	42	20	11	11	52	34	51
5	Luton	42	21	7	14	68	49	49
6	Portsmouth	42	19	8	15	58	52	46
7	Millwall Ath	42	14	18	10	45	40	46
8	Northampton	42	17	11	14	54	44	45
9	Swindon	42	17	11	14	62	56	45
10	Watford	42	17	10	15	57	54	44
11	QPR	42	16	10	16	54	49	42
12	Charlton	42	14	14	14	55	51	42
13	Bristol Rovers	42	13	16	13	35	36	42
14	Brentford	42	13	12	17	41	51	38
15	Southend	42	12	13	17	49	54	37
16	Gillingham	42	15	7	20	51	59	37
17	Merthyr Town	42	11	14	17	39	48	36
18	Norwich	42	13	10	19	51	71	36
19	Reading	42	10	14	18	36	55	34
20	Exeter	42	13	7	22	47	84	33
21	Aberdare Ath	42	9	11	22	42	70	29
22	Newport	42	8	11	23	40	70	27

THIRD DIVISION (NORTH)

		P	W	D	L	F	A	Pts
1	Nelson	38	24	3	11	61	41	51
2	Bradford PA	38	19	9	10	67	38	47
3	Walsall	38	19	8	11	51	44	46
4	Chesterfield	38	19	7	12	68	52	45
5	Wigan Borough	38	18	8	12	64	39	44
6	Crewe	38	17	9	12	48	38	43
7	Halifax	38	17	7	14	53	46	41
8	Accrington	38	17	7	14	59	65	41
9	Darlington	38	15	10	13	59	46	40
10	Wrexham	38	14	10	14	38	48	38
11	Stalybridge Cel	38	15	6	17	42	47	36
12	Rochdale	38	13	10	15	42	53	36
13	Lincoln	38	13	10	15	39	55	36
14	Grimsby	38	14	5	19	55	52	33
15	Hartlepools	38	10	12	16	48	54	32
16	Tranmere	38	12	8	18	49	59	32
17	Southport	38	12	7	19	32	46	31
18	Barrow	38	13	4	21	50	60	30
19	Ashington	38	11	8	19	51	77	30
20	Durham City	38	9	10	19	43	59	28

SCOTTISH FA CUP 1922-23

SECOND ROUND

Airdrieonians v Aberdeen	1-1, 0-2
Ayr United v Rangers	2-0
Bo'ness v Heart of Midlothian	3-2
Celtic v Hurlford	4-0
Dundee v St Bernard's	0-0, 3-2
Dunfermline Athletic v Clydebank	1-0
Hibernian v Peebles Rovers	0-0, 3-0
Kilmarnock v East Fife	1-1, 0-1
Johnstone v Falkirk	0-1
Hamilton Academicals v King's Park	1-0
Motherwell v St Mirren	2-1
Dundee Hibernians v Nithsdale Wanderers	0-1
Peterhead v Galston	1-0
Queen's Park v Bathgate	1-1, 2-0
Raith Rovers v Cowdenbeath	2-0
Vale of Leven v Third Lanark	2-2, 1-2

THIRD ROUND

Aberdeen v Peterhead	13-0
Bo'ness v Nithsdale Wanderers	2-0
Celtic v East Fife	2-1
Dundee v Hamilton Academicals	0-0, 1-0
Hibernian v Queen's Park	2-0
Motherwell v Falkirk	3-0
Dunfermline Athletic v Raith Rovers	0-3
Third Lanark v Ayr United	2-0

FOURTH ROUND

Celtic v Raith Rovers	1-0
Hibernian v Aberdeen	2-0
Motherwell v Bo'ness	4-2
Dundee v Third Lanark	0-0, 1-1, 0-1

SEMI-FINAL

Celtic v Motherwell	2-0
Hibernian v Third Lanark	1-0

FINAL AT HAMPDEN PARK

Celtic v Hibernian	1-0

SCOTTISH FIRST DIVISION

		P	W	D	L	F	A	Pts
1	Rangers	38	23	9	6	67	29	55
2	Airdrieonians	38	20	10	8	58	38	50
3	Celtic	38	19	8	11	52	39	46
4	Falkirk	38	14	17	7	44	32	45
5	Aberdeen	38	15	12	11	46	34	42
6	St Mirren	38	15	12	11	54	44	42
7	Dundee	38	17	7	14	51	45	41
8	Hibernian	38	17	7	14	45	40	41
9	Raith	38	13	13	12	31	43	39
10	Ayr	38	13	12	13	43	44	38
11	Partick	38	14	9	15	51	48	37
12	Hearts	38	11	15	12	51	50	37
13	Motherwell	38	13	10	15	59	60	36
14	Morton	38	12	11	15	44	47	35
15	Kilmarnock	38	14	7	17	57	66	35
16	Clyde	38	12	9	17	36	44	33
17	Third Lanark	38	11	8	19	40	59	30
18	Hamilton	38	11	7	20	43	59	29
19	Albion	38	8	10	20	38	64	26
20	Alloa	38	6	11	21	27	52	23

SCOTTISH SECOND DIVISION

		P	W	D	L	F	A	Pts
1	Queen's Park	38	24	9	5	73	31	57
2	Clydebank	38	21	10	7	69	29	52
3	St Johnstone	38	19	12	7	60	39	48*
4	Dumbarton	38	17	8	13	61	40	42
5	Bathgate	38	16	9	13	67	55	41
6	Armadale	38	15	11	12	63	52	41
7	Bo'ness	38	12	17	9	48	46	41
8	Broxburn	38	14	12	12	40	43	40
9	East Fife	38	16	7	15	48	42	39
10	Lochgelly	38	16	5	17	41	64	37
11	Cowdenbeath	38	16	6	16	56	52	36*
12	King's Park	38	14	6	18	46	60	34
13	Dunfermline	38	11	11	16	47	44	33
14	Stenhousemuir	38	13	7	18	53	67	33
15	Forfar	38	13	7	18	51	73	33
16	Johnstone	38	13	6	19	41	62	32
17	Vale of Leven	38	11	8	19	50	59	30
18	St Bernard's	38	8	15	15	39	50	29*
19	E Stirlingshire	38	10	8	20	48	69	28
20	Arbroath	38	8	12	18	45	69	28

*Two points deducted for fielding an ineligible player.

In Division Two, 1922-23, Southampton had an uneventful season, finishing in the middle of the table. But their final record is something of a curiosity. It reads, P42, W14, D14, L14, F40, A40, Pts42.

Liverpool won the League Championship for the second successive season.

The most goals a player has scored in an FA Cup game and yet finished on the losing side is seven. Billy Minter of St Albans City scored seven times against Dulwich Hamlet in a replayed Fourth Round qualifying tie on 22 November 1922. But despite poor Minter's monumental contribution, his side eventually lost the match 8-7.

FIRST DIVISION

		P	W	D	L	F	A	Pts
1	Huddersfield	42	23	11	8	60	33	57
2	Cardiff	42	22	13	7	61	34	57
3	Sunderland	42	22	9	11	71	54	53
4	Bolton	42	18	14	10	68	34	50
5	Sheff United	42	19	12	11	69	49	50
6	Aston Villa	42	18	13	11	52	37	49
7	Everton	42	18	13	11	62	53	49
8	Blackburn	42	17	11	14	54	50	45
9	Newcastle	42	17	10	15	60	54	44
10	Notts County	42	14	14	14	44	49	42
11	Man City	42	15	12	15	54	71	42
12	Liverpool	42	15	11	16	49	48	41
13	West Ham	42	13	15	14	40	43	41
14	Birmingham	42	13	13	16	41	49	39
15	Tottenham	42	12	14	16	50	56	38
16	WBA	42	12	14	16	51	62	38
17	Burnley	42	12	12	18	55	60	36
18	Preston	42	12	10	20	52	67	34
19	Arsenal	42	12	9	21	40	63	33
20	Nottm Forest	42	10	12	20	42	64	32
21	Chelsea	42	9	14	19	31	53	32
22	Middlesbrough	42	7	8	27	37	60	22

SECOND DIVISION

		P	W	D	L	F	A	Pts
1	Leeds	42	21	12	9	61	35	54
2	Bury	42	21	9	12	63	35	51
3	Derby	42	21	9	12	75	42	51
4	Blackpool	42	18	13	11	72	47	49
5	Southampton	42	17	14	11	52	31	48
6	Stoke	42	14	18	10	44	42	46
7	Oldham	42	14	17	11	45	52	45
8	Wednesday	42	16	12	14	54	51	44
9	South Shields	42	17	10	15	49	50	44
10	Clapton Orient	42	14	15	13	40	36	43
11	Barnsley	42	16	11	15	57	61	43
12	Leicester	42	17	8	17	64	54	42
13	Stockport	42	13	16	13	44	52	42
14	Man United	42	13	14	15	52	44	40
15	Crystal Palace	42	13	13	16	53	65	39
16	Port Vale	42	13	12	17	50	66	38
17	Hull	42	10	17	15	46	51	37
18	Bradford City	42	11	15	16	35	48	37
19	Coventry	42	11	13	18	52	68	35
20	Fulham	42	10	14	18	45	56	34
21	Nelson	42	10	13	19	40	74	33
22	Bristol City	42	7	15	20	32	65	29

THIRD DIVISION (SOUTH)

		P	W	D	L	F	A	Pts
1	Portsmouth	42	24	11	7	87	30	59
2	Plymouth	42	23	9	10	70	34	55
3	Millwall Ath	42	22	10	10	64	38	54
4	Swansea	42	22	8	12	60	48	52
5	Brighton	42	21	9	12	68	37	51
6	Swindon	42	17	13	12	58	44	47
7	Luton	42	16	14	12	50	44	46
8	Northampton	42	17	11	14	64	47	45
9	Bristol Rovers	42	15	13	14	52	46	43
10	Newport	42	17	9	16	56	64	43
11	Norwich	42	16	8	18	60	59	40
12	Aberdare Ath	42	12	14	16	45	58	38
13	Merthyr Town	42	11	16	15	45	65	38
14	Charlton	42	11	15	16	38	45	37
15	Gillingham	42	12	13	17	43	58	37
16	Exeter	42	15	7	20	37	52	37
17	Brentford	42	14	8	20	54	71	36
18	Reading	42	13	9	20	51	57	35
19	Southend	42	12	10	20	53	84	34
20	Watford	42	9	15	18	45	54	33
21	Bournemouth	42	11	11	20	40	65	33
22	QPR	42	11	9	22	37	77	31

THIRD DIVISION (NORTH)

		P	W	D	L	F	A	Pts
1	Wolves	42	24	15	3	76	27	63
2	Rochdale	42	25	12	5	60	26	62
3	Chesterfield	42	22	10	10	70	39	54
4	Rotherham Co	42	23	6	13	70	43	52
5	Bradford PA	42	21	10	11	69	43	52
6	Darlington	42	20	8	14	70	53	48
7	Southport	42	16	14	12	44	42	46
8	Ashington	42	18	8	16	59	61	44
9	Doncaster	42	15	12	15	59	53	42
10	Wigan Borough	42	14	14	14	55	53	42
11	Grimsby	42	14	13	15	49	47	41
12	Tranmere	42	13	15	14	51	60	41
13	Accrington	42	16	8	18	48	61	40
14	Halifax	42	15	10	17	42	59	40
15	Durham City	42	15	9	18	59	60	39
16	Wrexham	42	10	18	14	37	44	38
17	Walsall	42	14	8	20	44	59	36
18	New Brighton	42	11	13	18	40	53	35
19	Lincoln	42	10	12	20	48	59	32
20	Crewe	42	7	13	22	32	58	27
21	Hartlepools	42	7	11	24	33	70	25
22	Barrow	42	8	9	25	35	80	25

SCOTTISH FIRST DIVISION

		P	W	D	L	F	A	Pts
1	Rangers	38	25	9	4	72	22	59
2	Airdrieonians	38	20	10	8	72	46	50
3	Celtic	38	17	12	9	56	33	46
4	Raith	38	18	7	13	56	38	43
5	Dundee	38	15	13	10	70	57	43
6	St Mirren	38	15	12	11	53	45	42
7	Hibernian	38	15	11	12	66	52	41
8	Partick	38	15	9	14	58	55	39
9	Hearts	38	14	10	14	61	50	38
10	Motherwell	38	15	7	16	58	63	37
11	Morton	38	16	5	17	48	54	37
12	Hamilton	38	15	6	17	52	57	36
13	Aberdeen	38	13	10	15	37	41	36
14	Ayr	38	12	10	16	38	60	34
15	Falkirk	38	13	6	19	46	53	32
16	Kilmarnock	38	12	8	18	48	65	32
17	Queen's Park	38	11	9	18	43	60	31
18	Third Lanark	38	11	8	19	54	78	30
19	Clyde	38	10	9	19	40	70	29
20	Clydebank	38	10	5	23	42	71	25

SCOTTISH SECOND DIVISION

		P	W	D	L	F	A	Pts
1	St Johnstone	38	22	12	4	79	33	56
2	Cowdenbeath	38	23	9	6	78	33	55
3	Bathgate	38	16	12	10	58	49	44
4	Stenhousemuir	38	16	11	11	58	45	43
5	Albion	38	15	12	11	67	53	42
6	King's Park	38	16	10	12	67	56	42
7	Dunfermline	38	14	11	13	52	45	39
8	Johnstone	38	16	7	15	60	56	39
9	Dundee United	38	12	15	11	41	41	39
10	Dumbarton	38	17	5	16	55	58	39
11	Armadale	38	16	6	16	56	63	38
12	Bo'ness	38	13	11	14	45	52	37
13	East Fife	38	14	9	15	54	47	37
14	Forfar	38	14	7	17	43	68	35
15	Broxburn	38	13	8	17	50	56	34
16	Alloa	38	14	6	18	44	53	34
17	Arbroath	38	12	8	18	49	51	32
18	St Bernard's	38	11	10	17	49	54	32
19	Vale of Leven	38	11	9	18	41	67	31
20	Lochgelly	38	4	4	30	20	86	12

The first player to have scored two goals for each side in a single Football League game is Sammy Wynne of Oldham. In the Division Two match with Manchester United on 6 October 1923, Wynne scored for his own side with a free-kick and a penalty, but also put two through his own goal. Those four goals probably give poor Wynne the dubious record for the most goals scored by a full-back in one League game.

A Birch, Chesterfield's goalkeeper, set a League goalscoring record for a keeper in 1923-24. Birch, who played in every one of his club's Division Three North fixtures, scored from five penalties.

During the Third Division North match between Crewe and Bradford Park Avenue on 8 March 1924, four penalties were awarded in five minutes, a League record.

FA CUP 1923-24

SECOND ROUND
Derby County v Newcastle United	2-2, 2-2, 2-2, 3-5
Exeter City v Watford	0-0, 0-1
Southampton v Blackpool	3-1
Bolton Wanderers v Liverpool	1-4
Manchester City v Halifax Town	2-2, 0-0, 3-0
Brighton v Everton	5-2
Cardiff City v Arsenal	1-0
The Wednesday v Bristol City	1-1, 0-2
Swansea Town v Aston Villa	0-2
West Ham United v Leeds United	1-1, 0-1
West Bromwich Albion v Corinthians	5-0
Charlton Athletic v Wolverhampton Wanderers	0-0, 0-1
Swindon Town v Oldham Athletic	2-0
Crystal Palace v Notts County	0-0, 0-0, 0-0, 2-1
Burnley v Fulham	0-0, 1-0
Manchester United v Huddersfield Town	0-3

THIRD ROUND
Watford v Newcastle United	0-1
Southampton v Liverpool	0-0, 0-2
Brighton v Manchester City	1-5
Cardiff City v Bristol City	3-0
Aston Villa v Leeds United	3-0
West Bromwich Albion v Wolverhampton Wanderers	1-1, 2-0
Crystal Palace v Swindon Town	1-2
Burnley v Huddersfield Town	1-0

FOURTH ROUND
Newcastle United v Liverpool	1-0
Manchester City v Cardiff City	0-0, 1-0
West Bromwich Albion v Aston Villa	0-2
Swindon Town v Burnley	1-1, 1-3

SEMI-FINAL
Newcastle United v Manchester City	2-0
Aston Villa v Burnley	3-0

FINAL
Newcastle United v Aston Villa	2-0

SCOTTISH FA CUP 1923-24

SECOND ROUND
Airdrieonians v St Johnstone	4-0
Forfar Athletic v Motherwell	1-3
Ayr United v Kilmarnock	1-0
Clydebank v Arbroath	4-0
Falkirk v East Fife	2-0
Queen's Park v Armadale	3-1
Heart of Midlothian v Galston	6-0
Clyde v Vale of Leven	2-0
Cowdenbeath v Aberdeen	0-2
East Stirlingshire v Mid-Annandale	2-0
St Bernard's v Stenhousemuir	0-0, 0-0, 2-0
Dundee v Raith Rovers	0-0, 0-1
Hibernian v Alloa Athletic	1-1, 5-0
St Mirren v Rangers	0-1
Partick Thistle v Bo'ness	3-0
Hamilton Academicals v Queen of the South	2-1

THIRD ROUND
Motherwell v Airdrieonians	0-5
Clydebank v Ayr United	2-3
Falkirk v Queen's Park	0-0, 2-0
Heart of Midlothian v Clyde	3-1
Aberdeen v East Stirlingshire	2-0
Raith Rovers v St Bernard's	0-1
Rangers v Hibernian	1-2
Partick Thistle v Hamilton Academicals	1-1, 2-1

FOURTH ROUND
Airdrieonians v Ayr United	1-1, 0-0, 1-0
Heart of Midlothian v Falkirk	1-2
Aberdeen v St Bernard's	3-0
Hibernian v Partick Thistle	2-2, 1-1, 2-1

SEMI-FINAL
Airdrieonians v Falkirk	2-1
Aberdeen v Hibernian	0-0, 0-0, 0-1

FINAL AT IBROX PARK
Airdrieonians v Hibernian	2-0

203

FIRST DIVISION

		P	W	D	L	F	A	Pts
1	Huddersfield	42	21	16	5	69	28	58
2	WBA	42	23	10	9	58	34	56
3	Bolton	42	22	11	9	76	34	55
4	Liverpool	42	20	10	12	63	55	50
5	Bury	42	17	15	10	54	51	49
6	Newcastle	42	16	16	10	61	42	48
7	Sunderland	42	19	10	13	64	51	48
8	Birmingham	42	17	12	13	49	53	46
9	Notts County	42	16	13	13	42	31	45
10	Man City	42	17	9	16	76	68	43
11	Cardiff	42	16	11	15	56	51	43
12	Tottenham	42	15	12	15	52	43	42
13	West Ham	42	15	12	15	62	60	42
14	Sheff United	42	13	13	16	55	63	39
15	Aston Villa	42	13	13	16	58	71	39
16	Blackburn	42	11	13	18	53	66	35
17	Everton	42	12	11	19	40	60	35
18	Leeds	42	11	12	19	46	59	34
19	Burnley	42	11	12	19	46	75	34
20	Arsenal	42	14	5	23	46	58	33
21	Preston	42	10	6	26	37	74	26
22	Nottm Forest	42	6	12	24	29	65	24

SECOND DIVISION

		P	W	D	L	F	A	Pts
1	Leicester	42	24	11	7	90	32	59
2	Man United	42	23	11	8	57	23	57
3	Derby	42	22	11	9	71	36	55
4	Portsmouth	42	15	18	9	58	50	48
5	Chelsea	42	16	15	11	51	37	47
6	Wolves	42	20	6	16	55	51	46
7	Southampton	42	13	18	11	40	36	44
8	Port Vale	42	17	8	17	48	56	42
9	South Shields	42	12	17	13	42	38	41
10	Hull	42	15	11	16	50	49	41
11	Clapton Orient	42	14	12	16	42	42	40
12	Fulham	42	15	10	17	41	56	40
13	Middlesbrough	42	10	19	13	36	44	39
14	Wednesday	42	15	8	19	50	56	38
15	Barnsley	42	13	12	17	46	59	38
16	Bradford City	42	13	12	17	37	50	38
17	Blackpool	42	14	9	19	65	61	37
18	Oldham	42	13	11	18	35	51	37
19	Stockport	42	13	11	18	37	57	37
20	Stoke	42	12	11	19	34	46	35
21	Crystal Palace	42	12	10	20	38	54	34
22	Coventry	42	11	9	22	45	84	31

THIRD DIVISION (SOUTH)

		P	W	D	L	F	A	Pts
1	Swansea	42	23	11	8	68	35	57
2	Plymouth	42	23	10	9	77	38	56
3	Bristol City	42	22	9	11	60	41	53
4	Swindon	42	20	11	11	66	38	51
5	Millwall Ath	42	18	13	11	58	38	49
6	Newport	42	20	9	13	62	42	49
7	Exeter	42	19	9	14	59	48	47
8	Brighton	42	19	8	15	59	45	46
9	Northampton	42	20	6	16	51	44	46
10	Southend	42	19	5	18	51	61	43
11	Watford	42	17	9	16	38	47	43
12	Norwich	42	14	13	15	53	51	41
13	Gillingham	42	13	14	15	35	44	40
14	Reading	42	14	10	18	37	38	38
15	Charlton	42	13	12	17	46	48	38
16	Luton	42	10	17	15	49	57	37
17	Bristol Rovers	42	12	13	17	42	49	37
18	Aberdare Ath	42	14	9	19	54	67	37
19	QPR	42	14	8	20	42	63	36
20	Bournemouth	42	13	8	21	40	58	34
21	Brentford	42	9	7	26	38	91	25
22	Merthyr Town	42	8	5	29	35	77	21

THIRD DIVISION (NORTH)

		P	W	D	L	F	A	Pts
1	Darlington	42	24	10	8	78	33	58
2	Nelson	42	23	7	12	79	50	53
3	New Brighton	42	23	7	12	75	50	53
4	Southport	42	22	7	13	59	37	51
5	Bradford PA	42	19	12	11	84	42	50
6	Rochdale	42	21	7	14	75	53	49
7	Chesterfield	42	17	11	14	60	44	45
8	Lincoln	42	18	8	16	53	58	44
9	Halifax	42	16	11	15	56	52	43
10	Ashington	42	16	10	16	68	76	42
11	Wigan Borough	42	15	11	16	62	65	41
12	Grimsby	42	15	9	18	60	60	39
13	Durham City	42	13	13	16	50	68	39
14	Barrow	42	16	7	19	51	74	39
15	Crewe	42	13	13	16	53	78	39
16	Wrexham	42	15	8	19	53	61	38
17	Accrington	42	15	8	19	60	72	38
18	Doncaster	42	14	10	18	54	65	38
19	Walsall	42	13	11	18	44	53	37
20	Hartlepools	42	12	11	19	45	63	35
21	Tranmere	42	14	4	24	59	78	32
22	Rotherham Co	42	7	7	28	42	88	21

SCOTTISH FIRST DIVISION

		P	W	D	L	F	A	Pts
1	Rangers	38	25	10	3	77	27	60
2	Airdrieonians	38	25	7	6	85	31	57
3	Hibernian	38	22	8	8	78	43	52
4	Celtic	38	18	8	12	76	43	44
5	Cowdenbeath	38	16	10	12	76	65	42
6	St Mirren	38	18	4	16	65	63	40
7	Partick	38	14	10	14	60	61	38
8	Dundee	38	14	8	16	48	55	36
9	Raith	38	14	8	16	52	60	36
10	Hearts	38	12	11	15	65	69	35
11	St Johnstone	38	12	11	15	56	71	35
12	Kilmarnock	38	12	9	17	53	64	33
13	Hamilton	38	15	3	20	50	63	33
14	Morton	38	12	9	17	46	69	33
15	Aberdeen	38	11	10	17	46	56	32
16	Falkirk	38	12	8	18	44	54	32
17	Queen's Park	38	12	8	18	50	71	32
18	Motherwell	38	10	10	18	55	64	30
19	Ayr	38	11	8	19	43	65	30
20	Third Lanark	38	11	8	19	53	84	30

SCOTTISH SECOND DIVISION

		P	W	D	L	F	A	Pts
1	Dundee United	38	20	10	8	58	44	50
2	Clydebank	38	20	8	10	65	42	48
3	Clyde	38	20	7	11	72	39	47
4	Alloa	38	17	11	10	57	33	45
5	Arbroath	38	16	10	12	47	46	42
6	Bo'ness	38	16	9	13	71	48	41
7	Broxburn	38	16	9	13	48	54	41
8	Dumbarton	38	15	10	13	45	44	40
9	East Fife	38	17	5	16	66	58	39
10	King's Park	38	15	8	15	54	46	38
11	Stenhousemuir	38	15	7	16	51	58	37
12	Arthurlie	38	14	8	16	56	60	36
13	Dunfermline	38	14	7	17	62	57	35
14	Armadale	38	15	5	18	55	62	35
15	Albion	38	15	5	18	46	61	35
16	Bathgate	38	12	10	16	58	74	34
17	St Bernard's	38	14	4	20	52	70	32
18	E Stirlingshire	38	11	8	19	58	72	30
19	Johnstone	38	12	4	22	53	85	28
20	Forfar	38	10	7	21	46	67	27

Merthyr Town, who finished bottom of the Third Division South, suffered 29 defeats in their 42 matches, the greatest number ever lost in a single season in that division.

Manchester United conceded only 23 goals in their 42 Second Division matches. This is the lowest number of goals ever recorded against a club in that division.

Arthur Chandler, of Second Division champions Leicester City, not only led that division's scoring lists with 33 goals, but also established a record by finding the net in sixteen consecutive League games.

Huddersfield, in winning their second consecutive Championship, did not concede more than two goals in any League game.

FA CUP 1924-25

SECOND ROUND
Cardiff City v Fulham	1-0
Notts County v Norwich City	4-0
Hull City v Crystal Palace	3-2
Newcastle United v Leicester City	2-2, 0-1
Bradford Park Avenue v Blackpool	1-1, 1-2
Nottingham Forest v West Ham United	0-2
Tottenham Hotspur v Bolton Wanderers	1-1, 1-0
Blackburn Rovers v Portsmouth	0-0, 0-0, 1-0
Southampton v Brighton	1-0
Barnsley v Bradford City	0-3
Birmingham v Stockport County	1-0
Bristol City v Liverpool	0-1
West Bromwich Albion v Preston North End	2-0
Swansea Town v Aston Villa	1-3
Sunderland v Everton	0-0, 1-2
Sheffield United v The Wednesday	3-2

THIRD ROUND
Notts County v Cardiff City	0-2
Hull City v Leicester City	1-1, 1-3
West Ham United v Blackpool	1-1, 0-3
Tottenham Hotspur v Blackburn Rovers	2-2, 1-3
Southampton v Bradford City	2-0
Liverpool v Birmingham	2-1
West Bromwich Albion v Aston Villa	1-1, 2-1
Sheffield United v Everton	1-0

FOURTH ROUND
Cardiff City v Leicester City	2-1
Blackburn Rovers v Blackpool	1-0
Southampton v Liverpool	1-0
Sheffield United v West Bromwich Albion	2-0

SEMI-FINAL
Cardiff City v Blackburn Rovers	3-1
Sheffield United v Southampton	2-0

FINAL
Sheffield United v Cardiff City	1-0

SCOTTISH FA CUP 1924-25

SECOND ROUND
Celtic v Alloa Athletic	2-1
Vale of Leven v Solway Star	2-2, 3-3, 1-2
St Mirren v Ayr United	1-0
Partick Thistle v Dundee United	5-1
Montrose v Rangers	0-2
Arbroath v Clyde	3-0
Kilmarnock v Heart of Midlothian	2-1
Dykehead v Peebles Rovers	3-1
Dundee v Lochgelly United	2-1
Airdrieonians v Queen's Park	4-0
Royal Albert v Broxburn United	1-3
Falkirk v Dumbarton	2-0
Hamilton Academicals v East Stirlingshire	4-0
Raith Rovers v Bo'ness	0-0, 3-1
Armadale v Aberdeen	1-1, 0-2
Motherwell v Arthurlie	2-0

THIRD ROUND
Celtic v Solway Star	2-0
St Mirren v Partick Thistle	2-0
Rangers v Arbroath	5-3
Kilmarnock v Dykehead	5-3
Dundee v Airdrieonians	3-1
Broxburn United v Falkirk	2-1
Hamilton Academicals v Raith Rovers	1-0
Aberdeen v Motherwell	0-0, 2-1

FOURTH ROUND
St Mirren v Celtic	0-0, 1-1, 0-1
Kilmarnock v Rangers	1-2
Dundee v Broxburn United	1-0
Aberdeen v Hamilton Academicals	0-2

SEMI-FINAL
Celtic v Rangers	5-0
Dundee v Hamilton Academicals	1-1, 2-0

FINAL
Celtic v Dundee	2-1

FIRST DIVISION

		P	W	D	L	F	A	Pts
1	Huddersfield	42	23	11	8	92	60	57
2	Arsenal	42	22	8	12	87	63	52
3	Sunderland	42	21	6	15	96	80	48
4	Bury	42	20	7	15	85	77	47
5	Sheff United	42	19	8	15	102	82	46
6	Aston Villa	42	16	12	14	86	76	44
7	Liverpool	42	14	16	12	70	63	44
8	Bolton	42	17	10	15	75	76	44
9	Man United	42	19	6	17	66	73	44
10	Newcastle	42	16	10	16	84	75	42
11	Everton	42	12	18	12	72	70	42
12	Blackburn	42	15	11	16	91	80	41
13	WBA	42	16	8	18	79	78	40
14	Birmingham	42	16	8	18	66	81	40
15	Tottenham	42	15	9	18	66	79	39
16	Cardiff	42	16	7	19	61	76	39
17	Leicester	42	14	10	18	70	80	38
18	West Ham	42	15	7	20	63	76	37
19	Leeds	42	14	8	20	64	76	36
20	Burnley	42	13	10	19	85	108	36
21	Man City	42	12	11	19	89	100	35
22	Notts County	42	13	7	22	54	74	33

SECOND DIVISION

		P	W	D	L	F	A	Pts
1	Wednesday	42	27	6	9	88	48	60
2	Derby	42	25	7	10	77	42	57
3	Chelsea	42	19	14	9	76	49	52
4	Wolves	42	21	7	14	84	60	49
5	Swansea	42	19	11	12	77	57	49
6	Blackpool	42	17	11	14	76	69	45
7	Oldham	42	18	8	16	74	62	44
8	Port Vale	42	19	6	17	79	69	44
9	South Shields	42	18	8	16	74	65	44
10	Middlesbrough	42	21	2	19	77	68	44
11	Portsmouth	42	17	10	15	79	74	44
12	Preston	42	18	7	17	71	84	43
13	Hull	42	16	9	17	63	61	41
14	Southampton	42	15	8	19	63	63	38
15	Darlington	42	14	10	18	72	77	38
16	Bradford City	42	13	10	19	47	66	36
17	Nottm Forest	42	14	8	20	51	73	36
18	Barnsley	42	12	12	18	58	84	36
19	Fulham	42	11	12	19	46	77	34
20	Clapton Orient	42	12	9	21	50	65	33
21	Stoke	42	12	8	22	54	77	32
22	Stockport	42	8	9	25	51	97	25

THIRD DIVISION (NORTH)

		P	W	D	L	F	A	Pts
1	Grimsby	42	26	9	7	91	40	61
2	Bradford PA	42	26	8	8	101	43	60
3	Rochdale	42	27	5	10	104	58	59
4	Chesterfield	42	25	5	12	100	54	55
5	Halifax	42	17	11	14	53	50	45
6	Hartlepools	42	18	8	16	82	73	44
7	Tranmere	42	19	6	17	73	83	44
8	Nelson	42	16	11	15	89	71	43
9	Ashington	42	16	11	15	70	62	43
10	Doncaster	42	16	11	15	80	72	43
11	Crewe	42	17	9	16	63	61	43
12	New Brighton	42	17	8	17	69	67	42
13	Durham City	42	18	6	18	63	70	42
14	Rotherham	42	17	7	18	69	92	41
15	Lincoln	42	17	5	20	66	82	39
16	Coventry	42	16	6	20	73	82	38
17	Wigan Borough	42	13	11	18	68	74	37
18	Accrington	42	17	3	22	81	105	37
19	Wrexham	42	11	10	21	63	92	32
20	Southport	42	11	10	21	62	92	32
21	Walsall	42	10	6	26	58	107	26
22	Barrow	42	7	4	31	50	98	18

THIRD DIVISION (SOUTH)

		P	W	D	L	F	A	Pts
1	Reading	42	23	11	8	77	52	57
2	Plymouth	42	24	8	10	107	67	56
3	Millwall	42	21	11	10	73	39	53
4	Bristol City	42	21	9	12	72	51	51
5	Brighton	42	19	9	14	84	73	47
6	Swindon	42	20	6	16	69	64	46
7	Luton	42	18	7	17	80	75	43
8	Bournemouth	42	17	9	16	75	91	43
9	Aberdare	42	17	8	17	74	66	42
10	Gillingham	42	17	8	17	53	49	42
11	Southend	42	19	4	19	78	73	42
12	Northampton	42	17	7	18	82	80	41
13	Crystal Palace	42	19	3	20	75	79	41
14	Merthyr Town	42	14	11	17	69	75	39
15	Watford	42	15	9	18	73	89	39
16	Norwich	42	15	9	18	58	73	39
17	Newport	42	14	10	18	64	74	38
18	Brentford	42	16	6	20	69	94	38
19	Bristol Rovers	42	15	6	21	66	69	36
20	Exeter	42	15	5	22	72	70	35
21	Charlton	42	11	13	18	48	68	35
22	QPR	42	6	9	27	37	84	21

SCOTTISH FIRST DIVISION

		P	W	D	L	F	A	Pts
1	Celtic	38	25	8	5	97	40	58
2	Airdrieonians	38	23	4	11	95	54	50
3	Hearts	38	21	8	9	87	56	50
4	St Mirren	38	20	7	11	62	52	47
5	Motherwell	38	19	8	11	67	46	46
6	Rangers	38	19	6	13	79	55	44
7	Cowdenbeath	38	18	6	14	87	68	42
8	Falkirk	38	14	14	10	61	57	42
9	Kilmarnock	38	17	7	14	79	77	41
10	Dundee	38	14	9	15	47	59	37
11	Aberdeen	38	13	10	15	49	54	36
12	Hamilton	38	13	9	16	68	79	35
13	Queen's Park	38	15	4	19	70	81	34
14	Partick	38	10	13	15	64	73	33
15	Morton	38	12	7	19	57	84	31
16	Hibernian	38	12	6	20	72	77	30
17	Dundee United	38	11	6	21	52	74	28
18	St Johnstone	38	9	10	19	43	78	28
19	Raith	38	11	4	23	46	81	26
20	Clydebank	38	7	8	23	55	92	22

SCOTTISH SECOND DIVISION

		P	W	D	L	F	A	Pts
1	Dunfermline	38	26	7	5	109	43	59
2	Clyde	38	24	5	9	87	51	53
3	Ayr	38	20	12	6	77	39	52
4	East Fife	38	20	9	9	98	73	49
5	Stenhousemuir	38	19	10	9	74	52	48
6	Third Lanark	38	19	8	11	72	47	46
7	Arthurlie	38	17	5	16	81	75	39
8	Bo'ness	38	17	5	16	65	70	39
9	Albion	38	16	6	16	78	71	38
10	Arbroath	38	17	4	17	80	73	38
11	Dumbarton	38	14	10	14	54	58	38
12	Nithsdale	38	15	7	16	79	82	37
13	King's Park	38	14	9	15	67	73	37
14	St Bernard's	38	15	5	18	86	82	35
15	Armadale	38	14	5	19	82	101	33
16	Alloa	38	11	8	19	54	63	30
17	Queen of the S	38	10	8	20	64	88	28
18	E Stirlingshire	38	10	7	21	59	89	27
19	Bathgate	38	7	6	25	60	105	20
20	Broxburn	38	4	6	28	55	126	14

FA CUP 1925-26

FOURTH ROUND

Bournemouth v Bolton Wanderers	2-2, 2-6
South Shields v Birmingham	2-1
Nottingham Forest v Swindon Town	2-0
Southend United v Derby County	4-1
Swansea Town v Stoke City	6-3
Bury v Millwall	3-3, 0-2
Arsenal v Blackburn Rovers	3-1
West Bromwich Albion v Aston Villa	1-2
Manchester City v Huddersfield Town	4-0
Crystal Palace v Chelsea	2-1
Clapton Orient v Middlesbrough	4-2
Cardiff City v Newcastle United	0-2
Tottenham Hotspur v Manchester United	2-2, 0-2
Sheffield United v Sunderland	1-2
Fulham v Liverpool	3-1
Notts County v New Brighton	2-0

FIFTH ROUND

Bolton Wanderers v South Shields	3-0
Southend United v Nottingham Forest	0-1
Millwall v Swansea Town	0-1
Aston Villa v Arsenal	1-1, 0-2
Manchester City v Crystal Palace	11-4
Clapton Orient v Newcastle United	2-0
Sunderland v Manchester United	3-3, 1-2
Notts County v Fulham	0-1

SIXTH ROUND

Nottingham Forest v Bolton Wanderers	2-2, 0-0, 0-1
Swansea Town v Arsenal	2-1
Clapton Orient v Manchester City	1-6
Fulham v Manchester United	1-2

SEMI-FINAL

Bolton Wanderers v Swansea Town	3-0
Manchester City v Manchester United	3-0

FINAL

Bolton Wanderers v Manchester City	1-0

SCOTTISH FA CUP 1925-26

SECOND ROUND

Arbroath v St Mirren	0-0, 0-3
Partick Thistle v King's Park	4-1
Hibernian v Airdrieonians	2-3
Bo'ness v Bathgate	1-1, 1-3
Rangers v Stenhousemuir	1-0
Falkirk v Montrose	5-1
Morton v Raith Rovers	3-1
Albion Rovers v Peebles Rovers	1-1, 4-0
Celtic v Hamilton Academicals	4-0
Alloa Athletic v Heart of Midlothian	2-5
Forfar Athletic v Dumbarton	2-2, 1-4
Arthurlie v Clyde	2-2, 0-1
Aberdeen v Dundee	0-0, 3-0
St Johnstone v Queen's Park	7-2
Third Lanark v Leith Athletic	6-1
Solway Star v Brechin City	0-3

THIRD ROUND

St Mirren v Partick Thistle	2-1
Bathgate v Airdrieonians	2-5
Falkirk v Rangers	0-2
Morton v Albion Rovers	1-0
Heart of Midlothian v Celtic	0-4
Dumbarton v Clyde	3-0
Aberdeen v St Johnstone	2-2, 1-0
Third Lanark v Brechin City	4-0

FOURTH ROUND

St Mirren v Airdrieonians	2-0
Morton v Rangers	0-4
Celtic v Dumbarton	6-1
Third Lanark v Aberdeen	1-1, 0-3

SEMI-FINAL

St Mirren v Rangers	1-0
Celtic v Aberdeen	1-0

FINAL

St Mirren v Celtic	2-0

Manchester City had a distressing end to the 1925-26 season. After losing the Cup Final 1-0 to Bolton, City went to Newcastle for their last League game. They missed a penalty, lost 3-2, and were relegated. Had they scored from the penalty they would have remained in the First Division. City thus became the first club to reach the Cup Final and be relegated in the same season.

Huddersfield created a League record by playing 18 consecutive First Division games away from home without defeat. This run lasted from 15 November 1924 to 14 November 1925 and included 12 wins.

Louis Page scored a double hat-trick in his first game as centre-forward for Burnley, against Birmingham, on 10 April 1926.

FIRST DIVISION

		P	W	D	L	F	A	Pts
1	Newcastle	42	25	6	11	96	58	56
2	Huddersfield	42	17	17	8	76	60	51
3	Sunderland	42	21	7	14	98	70	49
4	Bolton	42	19	10	13	84	62	48
5	Burnley	42	19	9	14	91	80	47
6	West Ham	42	19	8	15	86	70	46
7	Leicester	42	17	12	13	85	70	46
8	Sheff United	42	17	10	15	74	86	44
9	Liverpool	42	18	7	17	69	61	43
10	Aston Villa	42	18	7	17	81	83	43
11	Arsenal	42	17	9	16	77	86	43
12	Derby	42	17	7	18	86	73	41
13	Tottenham	42	16	9	17	76	78	41
14	Cardiff	42	16	9	17	55	65	41
15	Man United	42	13	14	15	52	64	40
16	Wednesday	42	15	9	18	75	92	39
17	Birmingham	42	17	4	21	64	73	38
18	Blackburn	42	15	8	19	77	96	38
19	Bury	42	12	12	18	68	77	36
20	Everton	42	12	10	20	64	90	34
21	Leeds	42	11	8	23	69	88	30
22	WBA	42	11	8	23	65	86	30

SECOND DIVISION

		P	W	D	L	F	A	Pts
1	Middlesbrough	42	27	8	7	122	60	62
2	Portsmouth	42	23	8	11	87	49	54
3	Man City	42	22	10	10	108	61	54
4	Chelsea	42	20	12	10	62	52	52
5	Nottm Forest	42	18	14	10	80	55	50
6	Preston	42	20	9	13	63	52	49
7	Hull	42	20	7	15	63	52	47
8	Port Vale	42	16	13	13	88	78	45
9	Blackpool	42	18	8	16	95	80	44
10	Oldham	42	19	6	17	74	84	44
11	Barnsley	42	17	9	16	88	87	43
12	Swansea	42	16	11	15	68	72	43
13	Southampton	42	15	12	15	60	62	42
14	Reading	42	16	8	18	64	72	40
15	Wolves	42	14	7	21	73	75	35
16	Notts County	42	15	5	22	70	96	35
17	Grimsby	42	11	12	19	74	91	34
18	Fulham	42	13	8	21	58	92	34
19	South Shields	42	11	11	20	71	96	33
20	Clapton Orient	42	12	7	23	60	96	31
21	Darlington	42	12	6	24	79	98	30
22	Bradford City	42	7	9	26	50	88	23

FA CUP 1926-27

FOURTH ROUND

Chelsea v Accrington Stanley	7-2
Fulham v Burnley	0-4
Leeds United v Bolton Wanderers	0-0, 0-3
Darlington v Cardiff City	0-2
The Wednesday v South Shields	1-1, 0-1
Barnsley v Swansea Town	1-3
Reading v Portsmouth	3-1
West Ham United v Brentford	1-1, 0-2
Port Vale v Arsenal	2-2, 0-1
Liverpool v Southport	3-1
Wolverhampton Wanderers v Nottingham Forest	2-0
Hull City v Everton	1-1, 2-2, 3-2
Derby County v Millwall	0-2
Preston North End v Middlesbrough	0-3
Southampton v Birmingham	4-1
Corinthians v Newcastle United	1-3

FIFTH ROUND

Chelsea v Burnley	2-1
Bolton Wanderers v Cardiff City	0-2
South Shields v Swansea Town	2-2, 1-2
Reading v Brentford	1-0
Arsenal v Liverpool	2-0
Wolverhampton Wanderers v Hull City	1-0
Millwall v Middlesbrough	3-2
Southampton v Newcastle United	2-1

SIXTH ROUND

Chelsea v Cardiff City	0-0, 2-3
Swansea Town v Reading	1-3
Arsenal v Wolverhampton Wanderers	2-1
Millwall v Southampton	0-0, 0-2

SEMI-FINAL

Cardiff City v Reading	3-0
Arsenal v Southampton	2-1

FINAL

Cardiff City v Arsenal	1-0

THIRD DIVISION (NORTH)

		P	W	D	L	F	A	Pts
1	Stoke	42	27	9	6	92	40	63
2	Rochdale	42	26	6	10	105	65	58
3	Bradford PA	42	24	7	11	101	59	55
4	Halifax	42	21	11	10	70	53	53
5	Nelson	42	22	7	13	104	75	51
6	Stockport	42	22	7	13	93	69	49*
7	Chesterfield	42	21	5	16	92	68	47
8	Doncaster	42	18	11	13	81	65	47
9	Tranmere	42	19	8	15	85	67	46
10	New Brighton	42	18	10	14	79	67	46
11	Lincoln	42	15	12	15	90	78	42
12	Southport	42	15	9	18	80	85	39
13	Wrexham	42	14	10	18	65	73	38
14	Walsall	42	14	10	18	68	81	38
15	Crewe	42	14	9	19	71	81	37
16	Ashington	42	12	12	18	60	90	36
17	Hartlepools	42	14	6	22	66	81	34
18	Wigan Borough	42	11	10	21	66	83	32
19	Rotherham	42	10	12	20	70	92	32
20	Durham City	42	12	6	24	58	105	30
21	Accrington	42	10	7	25	62	98	27
22	Barrow	42	7	8	27	34	117	22

*Two points deducted for fielding Joe Smith without FA permission on 26 March 1927.

THIRD DIVISION (SOUTH)

		P	W	D	L	F	A	Pts
1	Bristol City	42	27	8	7	104	54	62
2	Plymouth	42	25	10	7	95	61	60
3	Millwall	42	23	10	9	89	51	56
4	Brighton	42	21	11	10	79	50	53
5	Swindon	42	21	9	12	100	85	51
6	Crystal Palace	42	18	9	15	84	81	45
7	Bournemouth	42	18	8	16	78	66	44
8	Luton	42	15	14	13	68	66	44
9	Newport	42	19	6	17	57	71	44
10	Bristol Rovers	42	16	9	17	78	80	41
11	Brentford	42	13	14	15	70	61	40
12	Exeter	42	15	10	17	76	73	40
13	Charlton	42	16	8	18	60	61	40
14	QPR	42	15	9	18	65	71	39
15	Coventry	42	15	7	20	71	86	37
16	Norwich	42	12	11	19	59	71	35
17	Merthyr Town	42	13	9	20	63	80	35
18	Northampton	42	15	5	22	59	83	35
19	Southend	42	14	6	22	64	77	34
20	Gillingham	42	11	10	21	54	72	32
21	Watford	42	12	8	22	57	87	32
22	Aberdare Ath	42	9	7	26	62	101	25

SCOTTISH FA CUP 1926-27

SECOND ROUND

Buckie Thistle v Beith	2-0
Bo'ness v Cowdenbeath	2-1
Kilmarnock v Dundee	1-1, 1-5
Brechin City v Celtic	3-6
Falkirk v Queen's Park	6-3
Mid-Annandale v Forfar Athletic	3-0
Rangers v St Mirren	6-0
Hamilton Academicals v Clydebank	5-1
Alloa Athletic v Dumbarton	1-1, 4-0
St Bernard's v Arthurlie	0-3
East Fife v Aberdeen	1-1, 2-1
Dunfermline Athletic v Airdrieonians	2-1
Elgin City v Clyde	2-4
Partick Thistle v King's Park	4-2
Dundee United v Vale of Leven	4-1
Broxburn United v Montrose	2-2, 0-1

THIRD ROUND

Buckie Thistle v Bo'ness	0-3
Dundee v Celtic	2-4
Falkirk v Mid-Annandale	3-0
Rangers v Hamilton Academicals	4-0
Alloa Athletic v Arthurlie	0-0, 0-3
East Fife v Dunfermline Athletic	2-0
Clyde v Partick Thistle	0-1
Dundee United v Montrose	2-2, 3-1

FOURTH ROUND

Bo'ness v Celtic	2-5
Falkirk v Rangers	2-2, 1-0
Arthurlie v East Fife	0-3
Partick Thistle v Dundee United	5-0

SEMI-FINAL

Celtic v Falkirk	1-0
East Fife v Partick Thistle	2-1

FINAL

Celtic v East Fife	3-1

SCOTTISH FIRST DIVISION

		P	W	D	L	F	A	Pts
1	Rangers	38	23	10	5	85	41	56
2	Motherwell	38	23	5	10	81	52	51
3	Celtic	38	21	7	10	101	55	49
4	Airdrieonians	38	18	9	11	97	64	45
5	Dundee	38	17	9	12	77	51	43
6	Falkirk	38	16	10	12	77	60	42
7	Cowdenbeath	38	18	6	14	74	60	42
8	Aberdeen	38	13	14	11	73	72	40
9	Hibernian	38	16	7	15	62	71	39
10	St Mirren	38	16	5	17	78	76	37
11	Partick	38	15	6	17	89	74	36
12	Queen's Park	38	15	6	17	74	84	36
13	Hearts	38	12	11	15	65	64	35
14	St Johnstone	38	13	9	16	55	69	35
15	Hamilton	38	13	9	16	60	85	35
16	Kilmarnock	38	12	8	18	54	71	32
17	Clyde	38	10	9	19	54	85	29
18	Dunfermline	38	10	8	20	53	85	28
19	Morton	38	12	4	22	56	101	28
20	Dundee United	38	7	8	23	56	101	22

SCOTTISH SECOND DIVISION

		P	W	D	L	F	A	Pts
1	Bo'ness	38	23	10	5	86	41	56
2	Raith	38	21	7	10	92	52	49
3	Clydebank	38	18	9	11	94	75	45
4	Third Lanark	38	17	10	11	67	48	44
5	E Stirlingshire	38	18	8	12	93	75	44
6	East Fife	38	19	4	15	103	91	42
7	Arthurlie	38	18	5	15	90	83	41
8	Ayr	38	13	15	10	67	68	41
9	Forfar	38	15	7	16	66	79	37
10	Stenhousemuir	38	12	12	14	69	75	36
11	Queen of the S	38	16	4	18	72	80	36
12	King's Park	38	13	9	16	76	75	35
13	St Bernard's	38	14	6	18	70	77	34
14	Armadale	38	12	10	16	69	78	34
15	Alloa	38	11	11	16	70	78	33
16	Albion	38	11	11	16	74	87	33
17	Bathgate	38	13	7	18	76	98	33
18	Dumbarton	38	13	6	19	69	84	32
19	Arbroath	38	13	6	19	64	82	32
20	Nithsdale	38	7	9	22	59	100	23

Middlesbrough's George Camsell established an individual scoring record with his 59 Second Division goals in 1926-27. William Dean beat it by just one the following season, 1927-28. Camsell also established a record for the number of League hat-tricks in a season with his nine in 1926-27.

The highest number of goals scored by a recognized half-back in a League match is three. T McDonald of Newcastle grabbed a hat-trick against Cardiff on Christmas Day 1926.

FIRST DIVISION

		P	W	D	L	F	A	Pts
1	Everton	42	20	13	9	102	66	53
2	Huddersfield	42	22	7	13	91	68	51
3	Leicester	42	18	12	12	96	72	48
4	Derby	42	17	10	15	96	83	44
5	Bury	42	20	4	18	80	80	44
6	Cardiff	42	17	10	15	70	80	44
7	Bolton	42	16	11	15	81	66	43
8	Aston Villa	42	17	9	16	78	73	43
9	Newcastle	42	15	13	14	79	81	43
10	Arsenal	42	13	15	14	82	86	41
11	Birmingham	42	13	15	14	70	75	41
12	Blackburn	42	16	9	17	66	78	41
13	Sheff United	42	15	10	17	79	86	40
14	Wednesday	42	13	13	16	81	78	39
15	Sunderland	42	15	9	18	74	76	39
16	Liverpool	42	13	13	16	84	87	39
17	West Ham	42	14	11	17	81	88	39
18	Burnley	42	16	7	19	82	98	39
19	Man United	42	16	7	19	72	87	39
20	Portsmouth	42	16	7	19	66	90	39
21	Tottenham	42	15	8	19	74	86	38
22	Middlesbrough	42	11	15	16	81	88	37

SECOND DIVISION

		P	W	D	L	F	A	Pts
1	Man City	42	25	9	8	100	59	59
2	Leeds	42	25	7	10	98	49	57
3	Chelsea	42	23	8	11	75	45	54
4	Preston	42	22	9	11	100	66	53
5	Stoke	42	22	8	12	78	59	52
6	Swansea	42	18	12	12	75	63	48
7	Oldham	42	19	8	15	75	51	46
8	WBA	42	17	12	13	90	70	46
9	Port Vale	42	18	8	16	68	57	44
10	Nottm Forest	42	15	10	17	83	84	40
11	Grimsby	42	14	12	16	69	83	40
12	Bristol City	42	15	9	18	76	79	39
13	Hull	42	12	15	15	41	54	39
14	Barnsley	42	14	11	17	65	85	39
15	Notts County	42	13	12	17	68	74	38
16	Wolves	42	13	10	19	63	91	36
17	Southampton	42	14	7	21	68	77	35
18	Reading	42	11	13	18	53	75	35
19	Blackpool	42	13	8	21	83	101	34
20	Clapton Orient	42	11	12	19	55	85	34
21	Fulham	42	13	7	22	68	89	33
22	South Shields	42	7	9	26	56	111	23

THIRD DIVISION (SOUTH)

		P	W	D	L	F	A	Pts
1	Millwall	42	30	5	7	127	50	65
2	Northampton	42	23	9	10	102	64	55
3	Plymouth	42	23	7	12	85	54	53
4	Brighton	42	19	10	13	81	69	48
5	Crystal Palace	42	18	12	12	79	72	48
6	Swindon	42	19	9	14	90	69	47
7	Southend	42	20	6	16	80	64	46
8	Exeter	42	17	12	13	70	60	46
9	Newport	42	18	9	15	81	84	45
10	QPR	42	17	9	16	72	71	43
11	Charlton	42	15	13	14	60	70	43
12	Brentford	42	16	8	18	76	74	40
13	Luton	42	16	7	19	94	87	39
14	Bournemouth	42	13	12	17	72	79	38
15	Watford	42	14	10	18	68	78	38
16	Gillingham	42	13	11	18	62	81	37
17	Norwich	42	10	16	16	66	70	36
18	Walsall	42	12	9	21	75	101	33
19	Bristol Rovers	42	14	4	24	67	93	32
20	Coventry	42	11	9	22	67	96	31
21	Merthyr Town	42	9	13	20	53	91	31
22	Torquay	42	8	14	20	53	103	30

THIRD DIVISION (NORTH)

		P	W	D	L	F	A	Pts
1	Bradford PA	42	27	9	6	101	45	63
2	Lincoln	42	24	7	11	91	64	55
3	Stockport	42	23	8	11	89	51	54
4	Doncaster	42	23	7	12	80	44	53
5	Tranmere	42	22	9	11	105	72	53
6	Bradford City	42	18	12	12	85	60	48
7	Darlington	42	21	5	16	89	74	47
8	Southport	42	20	5	17	79	70	45
9	Accrington	42	18	8	16	76	67	44
10	New Brighton	42	14	14	14	72	62	42
11	Wrexham	42	18	6	18	64	67	42
12	Halifax	42	13	15	14	73	71	41
13	Rochdale	42	17	7	18	74	77	41
14	Rotherham	42	14	11	17	65	69	39
15	Hartlepools	42	16	6	20	69	81	38
16	Chesterfield	42	13	10	19	71	78	36
17	Crewe	42	12	10	20	77	86	34
18	Ashington	42	11	11	20	77	103	33
19	Barrow	42	10	11	21	54	102	31
20	Wigan Borough	42	10	10	22	56	97	30
21	Durham City	42	11	7	24	53	100	29
22	Nelson	42	10	6	26	76	136	26

SCOTTISH FIRST DIVISION

		P	W	D	L	F	A	Pts
1	Rangers	38	26	8	4	109	36	60
2	Celtic	38	23	9	6	93	39	55
3	Motherwell	38	23	9	6	92	46	55
4	Hearts	38	20	7	11	89	50	47
5	St Mirren	38	18	8	12	77	76	44
6	Partick	38	18	7	13	85	67	43
7	Aberdeen	38	19	5	14	71	61	43
8	Kilmarnock	38	15	10	13	68	78	40
9	Cowdenbeath	38	16	7	15	66	68	39
10	Falkirk	38	16	5	17	76	69	37
11	St Johnstone	38	14	8	16	66	67	36
12	Hibernian	38	13	9	16	73	75	35
13	Airdrieonians	38	12	11	15	59	69	35
14	Dundee	38	14	7	17	65	80	35
15	Clyde	38	10	11	17	46	72	31
16	Queen's Park	38	12	6	20	69	80	30
17	Raith	38	11	7	20	60	89	29
18	Hamilton	38	11	6	21	67	86	28
19	Bo'ness	38	9	8	21	48	86	26
20	Dunfermline	38	4	4	30	41	126	12

SCOTTISH SECOND DIVISION

		P	W	D	L	F	A	Pts
1	Ayr	38	24	6	8	117	60	54
2	Third Lanark	38	18	9	11	99	66	45
3	King's Park	38	16	12	10	84	68	44
4	East Fife	38	18	7	13	87	73	43
5	Forfar	38	18	7	13	83	73	43
6	Dundee United	38	17	9	12	81	73	43
7	Arthurlie	38	18	4	16	84	90	40
8	Albion	38	17	4	17	79	69	38
9	E Stirlingshire	38	14	10	14	84	76	38
10	Arbroath	38	16	4	18	84	86	36
11	Dumbarton	38	16	4	18	66	72	36
12	Queen of the S	38	15	6	17	92	106	36
13	Leith	38	13	9	16	76	71	35
14	Clydebank	38	16	3	19	78	80	35
15	Alloa	38	12	11	15	72	76	35
16	Stenhousemuir	38	15	5	18	75	81	35
17	St Bernard's	38	15	5	18	75	101	35
18	Morton	38	13	8	17	65	82	34
19	Bathgate	38	10	11	17	62	81	31
20	Armadale	38	8	8	22	53	112	24

On 3 March 1928 Ronnie Dix became the youngest person to score in the League. Dix, aged 15 years and 180 days, scored for Bristol Rovers against Norwich in a Division Three South match. Dix had made his League debut just seven days earlier against Charlton.

Dixie Dean's 60 goals in 39 League games for Everton set a League scoring record.

1927-28 saw the keenest relegation struggle in the League's history. Of the last nine clubs in Division One, seven finished the season with 39 points, one had 38, and one 37. Spurs and Middlesbrough were demoted. Spurs' 38 points meant that they were relegated with the highest number of points ever secured by a club removed from either the First or Second Division.

FA CUP 1927-28

FOURTH ROUND

Exeter City v Blackburn Rovers	2-2, 1-3
Port Vale v New Brighton	3-0
Bury v Manchester United	1-1, 0-1
Wrexham v Birmingham	1-3
Arsenal v Everton	4-3
Aston Villa v Crewe Alexandra	3-0
Sunderland v Manchester City	1-2
Stoke City v Bolton Wanderers	4-2
Huddersfield Town v West Ham United	2-1
Southport v Middlesbrough	0-3
Reading v Leicester City	0-1
Tottenham Hotspur v Oldham Athletic	3-0
Sheffield United v Wolverhampton Wanderers	3-1
Swindon Town v The Wednesday	1-2
Derby County v Nottingham Forest	0-0, 0-2
Cardiff City v Liverpool	2-1

FIFTH ROUND

Blackburn Rovers v Port Vale	2-1
Manchester United v Birmingham	1-0
Arsenal v Aston Villa	4-1
Manchester City v Stoke City	0-1
Huddersfield Town v Middlesbrough	4-0
Leicester City v Tottenham Hotspur	0-3
The Wednesday v Sheffield United	1-1, 1-4
Nottingham Forest v Cardiff City	2-1

SIXTH ROUND

Blackburn Rovers v Manchester United	2-0
Arsenal v Stoke City	4-1
Huddersfield Town v Tottenham Hotspur	6-1
Sheffield United v Nottingham Forest	3-0

SEMI-FINAL

Blackburn Rovers v Arsenal	1-0
Huddersfield Town v Sheffield United	2-2, 0-0, 1-0

FINAL

Blackburn Rovers v Huddersfield Town	3-1

SCOTTISH FA CUP 1927-28

SECOND ROUND

Rangers v Cowdenbeath	4-2
Armadale v King's Park	2-4
Brechin City v Albion Rovers	1-4
Airdrieonians v Hamilton Academicals	2-1
Third Lanark v Hibernian	0-2
Ayr United v Falkirk	2-4
Dunfermline Athletic v Leith Amateurs	3-1
Dundee United v Dundee	3-3, 0-1
Keith v Celtic	1-6
Stenhousemuir v Alloa Athletic	1-2
Motherwell v Raith Rovers	2-2, 2-1
Heart of Midlothian v Forres Mechanics	7-0
Queen's Park v Morton	4-1
Forfar Athletic v Kilmarnock	1-2
Partick Thistle v Nithsdale Wanderers	4-0
St Mirren v Vale of Atholl	5-1

THIRD ROUND

Rangers v King's Park	3-1
Albion Rovers v Airdrieonians	3-1
Hibernian v Falkirk	0-0, 1-0
Dundee v Dunfermline Athletic	1-2
Celtic v Alloa Athletic	2-0
Heart of Midlothian v Motherwell	1-2
Kilmarnock v Queen's Park	4-4, 0-1
St Mirren v Partick Thistle	0-5

FOURTH ROUND

Albion Rovers v Rangers	0-1
Dunfermline Athletic v Hibernian	0-4
Motherwell v Celtic	0-2
Queen's Park v Partick Thistle	1-0

SEMI-FINAL

Rangers v Hibernian	3-0
Celtic v Queen's Park	2-1

FINAL

Rangers v Celtic	4-0

FIRST DIVISION

		P	W	D	L	F	A	Pts
1	Wednesday	42	21	10	11	86	62	52
2	Leicester	42	21	9	12	96	67	51
3	Aston Villa	42	23	4	15	98	81	50
4	Sunderland	42	20	7	15	93	75	47
5	Liverpool	42	17	12	13	90	64	46
6	Derby	42	18	10	14	86	71	46
7	Blackburn	42	17	11	14	72	63	45
8	Man City	42	18	9	15	95	86	45
9	Arsenal	42	16	13	13	77	72	45
10	Newcastle	42	19	6	17	70	72	44
11	Sheff United	42	15	11	16	86	85	41
12	Man United	42	14	13	15	66	76	41
13	Leeds	42	16	9	17	71	84	41
14	Bolton	42	14	12	16	73	80	40
15	Birmingham	42	15	10	17	68	77	40
16	Huddersfield	42	14	11	17	70	61	39
17	West Ham	42	15	9	18	86	96	39
18	Everton	42	17	4	21	63	75	38
19	Burnley	42	15	8	19	81	103	38
20	Portsmouth	42	15	6	21	56	80	36
21	Bury	42	12	7	23	62	99	31
22	Cardiff	42	8	13	21	43	59	29

SECOND DIVISION

		P	W	D	L	F	A	Pts
1	Middlesbrough	42	22	11	9	92	57	55
2	Grimsby	42	24	5	13	82	61	53
3	Bradford PA	42	22	4	16	88	70	48
4	Southampton	42	17	14	11	74	60	48
5	Notts County	42	19	9	14	78	65	47
6	Stoke	42	17	12	13	74	51	46
7	WBA	42	19	8	15	80	79	46
8	Blackpool	42	19	7	16	92	76	45
9	Chelsea	42	17	10	15	64	65	44
10	Tottenham	42	17	9	16	75	81	43
11	Nottm Forest	42	15	12	15	71	70	42
12	Hull	42	13	14	15	58	63	40
13	Preston	42	15	9	18	78	79	39
14	Millwall	42	16	7	19	71	86	39
15	Reading	42	15	9	18	63	86	39
16	Barnsley	42	16	6	20	69	66	38
17	Wolves	42	15	7	20	77	81	37
18	Oldham	42	16	5	21	54	75	37
19	Swansea	42	13	10	19	62	75	36
20	Bristol City	42	13	10	19	58	72	36
21	Port Vale	42	15	4	23	71	86	34
22	Clapton Orient	42	12	8	22	45	72	32

THIRD DIVISION (SOUTH)

		P	W	D	L	F	A	Pts
1	Charlton	42	23	8	11	86	60	54
2	Crystal Palace	42	23	8	11	81	67	54
3	Northampton	42	20	12	10	96	57	52
4	Plymouth	42	20	12	10	83	51	52
5	Fulham	42	21	10	11	101	71	52
6	QPR	42	19	14	9	82	61	52
7	Luton	42	19	11	12	89	73	49
8	Watford	42	19	10	13	79	74	48
9	Bournemouth	42	19	9	14	84	77	47
10	Swindon	42	15	13	14	75	72	43
11	Coventry	42	14	14	14	62	57	42
12	Southend	42	15	11	16	80	75	41
13	Brentford	42	14	10	18	56	60	38
14	Walsall	42	13	12	17	73	79	38
15	Brighton	42	16	6	20	58	76	38
16	Newport	42	13	9	20	69	86	35
17	Norwich	42	14	6	22	69	81	34
18	Torquay	42	14	6	22	66	84	34
19	Bristol Rovers	42	13	7	22	60	79	33
20	Merthyr Town	42	11	8	23	55	103	30
21	Exeter	42	9	11	22	67	88	29
22	Gillingham	42	10	9	23	43	83	29

THIRD DIVISION (NORTH)

		P	W	D	L	F	A	Pts
1	Bradford City	42	27	9	6	128	43	63
2	Stockport	42	28	6	8	111	58	62
3	Wrexham	42	21	10	11	91	69	52
4	Wigan Borough	42	21	9	12	82	49	51
5	Doncaster	42	20	10	12	76	66	50
6	Lincoln	42	21	6	15	91	67	48
7	Tranmere	42	22	3	17	79	77	47
8	Carlisle	42	19	8	15	86	77	46
9	Crewe	42	18	8	16	80	68	44
10	South Shields	42	18	8	16	83	74	44
11	Chesterfield	42	18	5	19	71	77	41
12	Southport	42	16	8	18	75	85	40
13	Halifax	42	13	13	16	63	62	39
14	New Brighton	42	15	9	18	64	71	39
15	Nelson	42	17	5	20	77	90	39
16	Rotherham	42	15	9	18	60	77	39
17	Rochdale	42	13	10	19	79	96	36
18	Accrington	42	13	8	21	68	82	34
19	Darlington	42	13	7	22	64	88	33
20	Barrow	42	10	8	24	64	93	28
21	Hartlepools	42	10	6	26	59	112	26
22	Ashington	42	8	7	27	45	115	23

SCOTTISH FIRST DIVISION

		P	W	D	L	F	A	Pts
1	Rangers	38	30	7	1	107	32	67
2	Celtic	38	22	7	9	67	44	51
3	Motherwell	38	20	10	8	85	66	50
4	Hearts	38	19	9	10	91	57	47
5	Queen's Park	38	18	7	13	100	69	43
6	Partick Thistle	38	17	7	14	91	70	41
7	Aberdeen	38	16	8	14	81	69	40
8	St Mirren	38	16	8	14	78	74	40
9	St Johnstone	38	14	10	14	57	70	38
10	Kilmarnock	38	14	8	16	79	74	36
11	Falkirk	38	14	8	16	68	86	36
12	Hamilton	38	13	9	16	58	83	35
13	Cowdenbeath	38	14	5	19	55	69	33
14	Hibernian	38	13	6	19	54	62	32
15	Airdrieonians	38	12	7	19	56	65	31
16	Ayr	38	12	7	19	65	84	31
17	Clyde	38	12	6	20	47	71	30
18	Dundee	38	9	11	18	58	68	29
19	Third Lanark	38	10	6	22	71	102	26
20	Raith	38	9	6	23	52	105	24

SCOTTISH SECOND DIVISION

		P	W	D	L	F	A	Pts
1	Dundee United	36	24	3	9	99	55	51
2	Morton	36	21	8	7	85	49	50
3	Arbroath	36	19	9	8	90	60	47
4	Albion	36	18	8	10	95	67	44
5	Leith	36	18	7	11	78	56	43
6	St Bernard's	36	16	9	11	77	55	41
7	Forfar	35	14	10	11	69	75	38
8	East Fife	35	15	6	14	88	77	36
9	Queen of the S	36	16	4	16	86	79	36
10	Bo'ness	35	15	5	15	62	62	35
11	Dunfermline	36	13	7	16	66	72	33
12	E Stirlingshire	36	14	4	18	71	75	32
13	Alloa	36	12	7	17	64	77	31
14	Dumbarton	36	11	9	16	59	78	31
15	King's Park	36	8	13	15	60	84	29
16	Clydebank	36	11	5	20	70	86	27
17	Arthurlie *	32	9	7	16	51	73	25
18	Stenhousemuir	35	9	6	20	52	90	24
19	Armadale	36	8	7	21	47	99	23

*Arthurlie resigned towards the end of the season—but their record was allowed to stand.

The worst kind of record

During the 1928-29 season, Rotherham United became only the second side to have had at least 10 goals scored against them in more than one Football League game in the same season. Rotherham, of Division Three North, first lost 11-1 at Bradford City on 25 August 1928, and then 10-1 away to South Shields on 16 March 1929.

The Scottish team in the Football League

In the First Division, the record for fielding a side containing the most Scotsmen belongs to Newcastle United. In the Newcastle side that faced Leeds United on 6 October 1928, only Wood, the centre-half, came from outside Scotland. In 1955-56 Accrington went one better by fielding a team of 11 Scots in several Third Division North fixtures.

FA CUP 1928-29

FOURTH ROUND
Blackburn Rovers v Derby County	1-1, 3-0
Manchester United v Bury	0-1
Leicester City v Swansea Town	1-0
Liverpool v Bolton Wanderers	0-0, 2-5
West Bromwich Albion v Middlesbrough	1-0
Plymouth Argyle v Bradford Park Avenue	0-1
Huddersfield Town v Leeds United	3-0
Millwall v Crystal Palace	0-0, 3-5
Chelsea v Birmingham	1-0
Portsmouth v Bradford City	2-0
Bournemouth v Watford	6-4
West Ham United v Corinthians	3-0
Reading v The Wednesday	1-0
Aston Villa v Clapton Orient	0-0, 8-0
Burnley v Swindon Town	3-3, 2-3
Arsenal v Mansfield Town	2-0

FIFTH ROUND
Blackburn Rovers v Bury	1-0
Leicester City v Bolton Wanderers	1-2
West Bromwich Albion v Bradford Park Avenue	6-0
Huddersfield Town v Crystal Palace	5-2
Chelsea v Portsmouth	1-1, 0-1
Bournemouth v West Ham United	1-1, 1-3
Reading v Aston Villa	1-3
Swindon Town v Arsenal	0-0, 0-1

SIXTH ROUND
Blackburn Rovers v Bolton Wanderers	1-1, 1-2
West Bromwich Albion v Huddersfield Town	1-1, 1-2
Portsmouth v West Ham United	3-2
Aston Villa v Arsenal	1-0

SEMI-FINAL
Bolton Wanderers v Huddersfield Town	3-1
Portsmouth v Aston Villa	1-0

FINAL
Bolton Wanderers v Portsmouth	2-0

SCOTTISH FA CUP 1928-29

SECOND ROUND
Celtic v East Stirlingshire	3-0
Murrayfield Amateurs v Arbroath	1-1, 2-5
Cowdenbeath v Airdrieonians	0-0, 2-3
St Johnstone v Motherwell	2-3
Bathgate v Raith Rovers	1-1, 2-5
Fraserburgh v Dumbarton	0-3
Albion Rovers v Clackmannan	8-1
Kilmarnock v Bo'ness	3-2
Rangers v Partick Thistle	5-1
Clyde v Hamilton Academicals	1-1, 2-1
Dundee v Brechin City	6-1
Stenhousemuir v Dundee United	1-1, 0-2
Aberdeen v Queen's Park	4-0
Queen of the South v Falkirk	1-2
Ayr United v Armadale	5-1
Third Lanark v St Mirren	0-1

THIRD ROUND
Celtic v Arbroath	4-1
Airdrieonians v Motherwell	1-1, 1-3
Raith Rovers v Dumbarton	3-2
Albion Rovers v Kilmarnock	0-1
Clyde v Rangers	0-2
Dundee v Dundee United	1-1, 0-1
Falkirk v Aberdeen	3-5
Ayr United v St Mirren	0-2

FOURTH ROUND
Celtic v Motherwell	0-0, 2-1
Raith Rovers v Kilmarnock	2-3
Rangers v Dundee United	3-1
St Mirren v Aberdeen	4-3

SEMI-FINAL
Celtic v Kilmarnock	0-1
Rangers v St Mirren	3-2

FINAL
Kilmarnock v Rangers	2-0

FIRST DIVISION

	P	W	D	L	F	A	Pts
1 Sheff Wed	42	26	8	8	105	57	60
2 Derby	42	21	8	13	90	82	50
3 Man City	42	19	9	14	91	81	47
4 Aston Villa	42	21	5	16	92	83	47
5 Leeds	42	20	6	16	79	63	46
6 Blackburn	42	19	7	16	99	93	45
7 West Ham	42	19	5	18	86	79	43
8 Leicester	42	17	9	16	86	90	43
9 Sunderland	42	18	7	17	76	80	43
10 Huddersfield	42	17	9	16	63	69	43
11 Birmingham	42	16	9	17	67	62	41
12 Liverpool	42	16	9	17	63	79	41
13 Portsmouth	42	15	19	17	66	62	40
14 Arsenal	42	14	11	17	78	66	39
15 Bolton	45	15	9	18	74	74	39
16 Middlesbrough	42	16	6	20	82	84	38
17 Man United	42	15	8	19	67	88	38
18 Grimsby	42	15	7	20	73	89	37
19 Newcastle	42	15	7	20	71	92	37
20 Sheff United	42	15	6	21	91	96	36
21 Burnley	42	14	8	20	79	97	36
22 Everton	42	12	11	19	80	92	35

SECOND DIVISION

	P	W	D	L	F	A	Pts
1 Blackpool	42	27	4	11	98	67	58
2 Chelsea	42	22	11	9	74	46	55
3 Oldham	42	21	11	10	90	51	53
4 Bradford PA	42	19	12	11	91	70	50
5 Bury	42	22	5	15	78	67	49
6 WBA	42	21	5	16	105	73	47
7 Southampton	42	17	11	14	77	76	45
8 Cardiff	42	18	8	16	61	59	44
9 Wolves	42	16	9	17	77	79	41
10 Nottm Forest	42	13	15	14	55	69	41
11 Stoke	42	16	8	18	74	72	40
12 Tottenham	42	15	9	18	59	61	39
13 Charlton	42	14	11	17	59	63	39
14 Millwall	42	12	15	15	57	73	39
15 Swansea	42	14	9	19	57	61	37
16 Preston	42	13	11	18	65	80	37
17 Barnsley	42	14	8	20	56	71	36
18 Bradford City	42	12	12	18	60	77	36
19 Reading	42	12	11	19	54	67	35
20 Bristol City	42	13	9	20	61	83	35
21 Hull	42	14	7	21	51	78	35
22 Notts County	42	9	15	18	54	70	33

THIRD DIVISION (SOUTH)

	P	W	D	L	F	A	Pts
1 Plymouth	42	30	8	4	98	38	68
2 Brentford	42	28	5	9	94	44	61
3 QPR	42	21	9	12	80	68	51
4 Northampton	42	21	8	13	82	58	50
5 Brighton	42	21	8	13	87	63	50
6 Coventry	42	19	9	14	88	73	47
7 Fulham	42	18	11	13	87	83	47
8 Norwich	42	18	10	14	88	77	46
9 Crystal Palace	42	17	12	13	81	74	46
10 Bournemouth	42	15	13	14	72	61	43
11 Southend	42	15	13	14	69	59	43
12 Clapton Orient	42	14	13	15	55	62	41
13 Luton	42	14	12	16	64	78	40
14 Swindon	42	13	12	17	73	83	38
15 Watford	42	15	8	19	60	73	38
16 Exeter	42	12	11	19	67	73	35
17 Walsall	42	13	8	21	71	78	34
18 Newport	42	12	10	20	74	85	34
19 Torquay	42	10	11	21	64	94	31
20 Bristol Rovers	42	11	8	23	67	93	30
21 Gillingham	42	11	8	23	51	80	30
22 Merthyr Town	42	6	9	27	60	135	21

THIRD DIVISION (NORTH)

	P	W	D	L	F	A	Pts
1 Port Vale	42	30	7	5	103	37	67
2 Stockport	42	28	7	7	106	44	63
3 Darlington	42	22	6	14	108	73	50
4 Chesterfield	42	22	6	14	76	56	50
5 Lincoln	42	17	14	11	83	61	48
6 York	42	15	16	11	77	64	46
7 South Shields	42	18	10	14	77	74	46
8 Hartlepools	42	17	11	14	81	74	45
9 Southport	42	15	13	14	81	74	43
10 Rochdale	42	18	7	17	89	91	43
11 Crewe	42	17	8	17	82	71	42
12 Tranmere	42	16	9	17	83	86	41
13 New Brighton	42	16	8	18	69	79	40
14 Doncaster	42	15	9	18	62	69	39
15 Carlisle	42	16	7	19	90	101	39
16 Accrington	42	14	9	19	84	81	37
17 Wrexham	42	13	8	21	67	88	34
18 Wigan Borough	42	13	7	22	60	88	33
19 Nelson	42	13	7	22	51	80	33
20 Rotherham	42	11	8	23	67	113	30
21 Halifax	42	10	8	24	44	79	28
22 Barrow	42	11	5	26	41	98	27

SCOTTISH FIRST DIVISION

	P	W	D	L	F	A	Pts
1 Rangers	38	28	4	6	94	32	60
2 Motherwell	38	25	5	8	104	48	55
3 Aberdeen	38	23	7	8	85	61	53
4 Celtic	38	22	5	11	88	46	49
5 St Mirren	38	18	5	15	73	56	41
6 Partick	38	16	9	13	72	61	41
7 Falkirk	38	16	9	13	62	64	41
8 Kilmarnock	38	15	9	14	77	73	39
9 Ayr	38	16	6	16	70	92	38
10 Hearts	38	14	9	15	69	69	37
11 Clyde	38	13	11	14	64	69	37
12 Airdrieonians	38	16	4	18	60	66	36
13 Hamilton	38	14	7	17	76	81	35
14 Dundee	38	14	6	18	51	58	34
15 Queen's Park	38	15	4	19	67	80	34
16 Cowdenbeath	38	13	7	18	64	74	33
17 Hibernian	38	9	11	18	45	62	29
18 Morton	38	10	7	21	67	95	27
19 Dundee United	38	7	8	23	56	109	22
20 St Johnstone	38	6	7	25	48	96	19

SCOTTISH SECOND DIVISION

	P	W	D	L	F	A	Pts
1 Leith Athletic	38	23	11	4	92	42	57
2 East Fife	38	26	5	7	114	58	57
3 Albion	38	24	6	8	101	60	54
4 Third Lanark	38	23	6	9	92	53	52
5 Raith	38	18	8	12	94	67	44
6 King's Park	38	17	8	13	109	80	42
7 Queen of the S	38	18	6	14	65	63	42
8 Forfar	38	15	11	12	98	95	41
9 Arbroath	38	16	7	15	83	87	39
10 Dunfermline	38	16	6	16	99	85	38
11 Montrose	38	14	10	14	79	87	38
12 E Stirlingshire	38	16	4	18	83	75	36
13 Bo'ness	38	15	4	19	67	95	34
14 St Bernard's	38	13	6	19	65	65	32
15 Armadale	38	13	5	20	56	91	31
16 Dumbarton	38	14	2	22	77	95	30
17 Stenhousemuir	38	11	5	22	75	108	27
18 Clydebank	38	7	10	21	66	92	24
19 Alloa	38	9	6	23	55	104	24
20 Brechin	38	7	4	27	57	125	18

FA CUP 1929-30

FOURTH ROUND

West Ham United v Leeds United	4-1
Millwall v Doncaster Rovers	4-0
Arsenal v Birmingham	2-2, 1-0
Middlesbrough v Charlton Athletic	1-1, 1-1, 1-0
Hull City v Blackpool	3-1
Swindon Town v Manchester City	1-1, 1-10
Newcastle United v Clapton Orient	3-1
Portsmouth v Brighton	0-1
Aston Villa v Walsall	3-1
Blackburn Rovers v Everton	4-1
Huddersfield Town v Sheffield United	2-1
Wrexham v Bradford City	0-0, 1-2
Nottingham Forest v Fulham	2-1
Sunderland v Cardiff City	2-1
Oldham Athletic v Sheffield Wednesday	3-4
Derby County v Bradford Park Avenue	1-1, 1-2

FIFTH ROUND

West Ham United v Millwall	4-1
Middlesbrough v Arsenal	0-2
Manchester City v Hull City	1-2
Newcastle United v Brighton	3-0
Aston Villa v Blackburn Rovers	4-1
Huddersfield Town v Bradford City	2-1
Sunderland v Nottingham Forest	2-2, 1-3
Sheffield Wednesday v Bradford Park Avenue	5-1

SIXTH ROUND

West Ham United v Arsenal	0-3
Newcastle United v Hull City	1-1, 0-1
Aston Villa v Huddersfield Town	1-2
Nottingham Forest v Sheffield Wednesday	2-2, 1-3

SEMI-FINAL

Arsenal v Hull City	2-2, 1-0
Huddersfield Town v Sheffield Wednesday	2-1

FINAL

Arsenal v Huddersfield Town	2-0

SCOTTISH FA CUP 1929-30

SECOND ROUND

Rangers v Cowdenbeath	2-2, 3-0
Motherwell v Clyde	3-0
Montrose v Citadel	3-1
Albion Rovers v Beith	2-1
Dundee v St Johnstone	4-1
Airdrieonians v Murrayfield Amateurs	8-3
Heart of Midlothian v St Bernard's	0-0, 5-1
Ayr United v Hibernian	1-3
Forfar Athletic v St Mirren	0-0, 0-3
Celtic v Arbroath	5-0
Hamilton Academicals v Kilmarnock	4-2
Vale of Leithen v King's Park	2-7
Falkirk v Queen of the South	1-1, 4-3
Leith Athletic v Clachnacuddin	2-0
Dundee United v Partick Thistle	0-3
Aberdeen v Nithsdale Wanderers	5-1

THIRD ROUND

Motherwell v Rangers	2-5
Albion Rovers v Montrose	2-2, 1-3
Dundee v Airdrieonians	0-0, 0-0, 1-0
Hibernian v Heart of Midlothian	1-3
Celtic v St Mirren	1-3
Hamilton Academicals v King's Park	4-0
Falkirk v Leith Athletic	0-0, 1-1, 1-1, 1-0
Partick Thistle v Aberdeen	3-2

FOURTH ROUND

Rangers v Montrose	3-0
Dundee v Heart of Midlothian	2-2, 0-4
St Mirren v Hamilton Academicals	3-4
Partick Thistle v Falkirk	3-1

SEMI-FINAL

Rangers v Heart of Midlothian	4-1
Partick Thistle v Hamilton Academicals	3-1

FINAL

Rangers v Partick Thistle	0-0, 2-1

Jim Barrett of West Ham United made his international debut for England against Northern Ireland on 19 October 1929. After only eight minutes he was injured and carried off, and as he never played for England again, his became the shortest international career on record.

Sheffield Wednesday won the League Championship for the second successive season.

Albert Geldard of Bradford Park Avenue became the youngest footballer to play in the League when, aged 15 years and 158 days, he played against Millwall in a Division Two match on 16 September 1929.

Joe Bambrick's six goals in Northern Ireland's 7-0 win over Wales in February 1930 made him the highest individual scorer in an international match between Home Countries.

FIRST DIVISION

		P	W	D	L	F	A	Pts
1	Arsenal	42	28	10	4	127	59	66
2	Aston Villa	42	25	9	8	128	78	59
3	Sheff Wed	42	22	8	12	102	75	52
4	Portsmouth	42	18	13	11	84	67	49
5	Huddersfield	42	18	12	12	81	65	48
6	Derby	42	18	10	14	94	79	46
7	Middlesbrough	42	19	8	15	98	90	46
8	Man City	42	18	10	14	75	70	46
9	Liverpool	42	15	12	15	86	85	42
10	Blackburn	42	17	8	17	83	84	42
11	Sunderland	42	16	9	17	89	85	41
12	Chelsea	42	15	10	17	64	67	40
13	Grimsby	42	17	5	20	82	87	39
14	Bolton	42	15	9	18	68	81	39
15	Sheff United	42	14	10	18	78	84	38
16	Leicester	42	16	6	20	80	95	38
17	Newcastle	42	15	6	21	78	87	36
18	West Ham	42	14	8	20	79	94	36
19	Birmingham	42	13	10	19	55	70	36
20	Blackpool	42	11	10	21	71	125	32
21	Leeds	42	12	7	23	68	81	31
22	Man United	42	7	8	27	53	115	22

SECOND DIVISION

		P	W	D	L	F	A	Pts
1	Everton	42	28	5	9	121	66	61
2	WBA	42	22	10	10	83	49	54
3	Tottenham	42	22	7	13	88	55	51
4	Wolves	42	21	5	16	84	67	47
5	Port Vale	42	21	5	16	67	61	47
6	Bradford PA	42	18	10	14	97	66	46
7	Preston	42	17	11	14	83	64	45
8	Burnley	42	17	11	14	81	77	45
9	Southampton	42	19	6	17	74	62	44
10	Bradford City	42	17	10	15	61	63	44
11	Stoke	42	17	10	15	64	71	44
12	Oldham	42	16	10	16	61	72	42
13	Bury	42	19	3	20	75	82	41
14	Millwall	42	16	7	19	71	80	39
15	Charlton	42	15	9	18	59	86	39
16	Bristol City	42	15	8	19	54	82	38
17	Nottm Forest	42	14	9	19	80	85	37
18	Plymouth	42	14	8	20	76	84	36
19	Barnsley	42	13	9	20	59	79	35
20	Swansea	42	12	10	20	51	74	34
21	Reading	42	12	6	24	72	96	30
22	Cardiff	42	8	9	25	47	87	25

THIRD DIVISION (SOUTH)

		P	W	D	L	F	A	Pts
1	Notts County	42	24	11	7	97	46	59
2	Crystal Palace	42	22	7	13	107	71	51
3	Brentford	42	22	6	14	90	64	50
4	Brighton	42	17	15	10	68	53	49
5	Southend	42	22	5	15	76	60	49
6	Northampton	42	18	12	12	77	59	48
7	Luton	42	19	8	15	76	51	46
8	QPR	42	20	3	19	82	75	43
9	Fulham	42	18	7	17	77	75	43
10	Bournemouth	42	15	13	14	72	73	43
11	Torquay	42	17	9	16	80	84	43
12	Swindon	42	18	6	18	89	94	42
13	Exeter	42	17	8	17	84	90	42
14	Coventry	42	16	9	17	75	65	41
15	Bristol Rovers	42	16	8	18	75	92	40
16	Gillingham	42	14	10	18	61	76	38
17	Walsall	42	14	9	19	78	95	37
18	Watford	42	14	7	21	72	75	35
19	Clapton Orient	42	14	7	21	63	91	35
20	Thames	42	13	8	21	54	93	34
21	Norwich	42	10	8	24	47	76	28
22	Newport	42	11	6	25	69	111	28

THIRD DIVISION (NORTH)

		P	W	D	L	F	A	Pts
1	Chesterfield	42	26	6	10	102	57	58
2	Lincoln	42	25	7	10	102	59	57
3	Tranmere	42	24	6	12	111	74	54
4	Wrexham	42	21	12	9	94	62	54
5	Southport	42	22	9	11	88	56	53
6	Hull	42	20	10	12	99	55	50
7	Stockport	42	20	9	13	77	61	49
8	Carlisle	42	20	5	17	98	81	45
9	Gateshead	42	16	13	13	71	73	45
10	Wigan Borough	42	19	5	18	76	86	43
11	Darlington	42	16	10	16	71	59	42
12	York	42	18	6	18	85	82	42
13	Accrington	42	15	9	18	84	108	39
14	Rotherham	42	13	12	17	81	83	38
15	Doncaster	42	13	11	18	65	65	37
16	Barrow	42	15	7	20	68	89	37
17	Halifax	42	13	9	20	55	89	35
18	Crewe	42	14	6	22	66	93	34
19	New Brighton	42	13	7	22	49	76	33
20	Hartlepools	42	12	6	24	67	86	30
21	Rochdale	42	12	6	24	62	107	30
22	Nelson	42	6	7	29	43	113	19

SCOTTISH FIRST DIVISION

		P	W	D	L	F	A	Pts
1	Rangers	38	27	6	5	96	29	60
2	Celtic	38	24	10	4	101	34	58
3	Motherwell	38	24	8	6	102	42	56
4	Partick	38	24	5	9	76	44	53
5	Hearts	38	19	6	13	90	63	44
6	Aberdeen	38	17	7	14	79	63	41
7	Cowdenbeath	38	17	7	14	58	65	41
8	Dundee	38	17	5	16	65	63	39
9	Airdrieonians	38	17	5	16	59	66	39
10	Hamilton	38	16	5	17	59	57	37
11	Kilmarnock	38	15	5	18	59	60	35
12	Clyde	38	15	4	19	60	87	34
13	Queen's Park	38	13	7	18	71	72	33
14	Falkirk	38	14	4	20	77	87	32
15	St Mirren	38	11	8	19	49	72	30
16	Morton	38	11	7	20	58	83	29
17	Leith	38	8	11	19	52	85	27
18	Ayr	38	8	11	19	53	92	27
19	Hibernian	38	9	7	22	49	81	25
20	East Fife	38	8	4	26	45	113	20

SCOTTISH SECOND DIVISION

		P	W	D	L	F	A	Pts
1	Third Lanark	38	27	7	4	107	42	61
2	Dundee United	38	21	8	9	93	54	50
3	Dunfermline	38	20	7	11	83	50	47
4	Raith	38	20	6	12	93	72	46
5	Queen of the S	38	18	6	14	83	66	42
6	St Johnstone	38	18	6	14	76	64	42
7	E Stirlingshire	38	17	7	14	85	74	41
8	Montrose	38	19	3	16	75	90	41
9	Albion	38	14	11	13	80	83	39
10	Dumbarton	38	15	8	15	73	72	38
11	St Bernard's	38	14	9	15	85	66	37
12	Forfar	38	15	6	17	78	83	36
13	Alloa	38	15	5	18	65	87	35
14	King's Park	38	14	6	18	78	70	34
15	Arbroath	38	15	4	19	83	94	34
16	Brechin	38	13	7	18	52	84	33
17	Stenhousemuir	38	13	6	19	78	98	32
18	Armadale	38	13	2	23	74	99	28
19	Clydebank	38	10	2	26	61	108	22
20	Bo'ness	38	9	4	25	54	100	22

FA CUP 1930-31

FOURTH ROUND

Birmingham v Port Vale	2-0
Watford v Brighton	2-0
Chelsea v Arsenal	2-1
Blackburn Rovers v Bristol Rovers	5-1
Bolton Wanderers v Sunderland	1-1, 1-3
Sheffield United v Notts County	4-1
Bury v Exeter City	1-2
Leeds United v Newcastle United	4-1
Crystal Palace v Everton	0-6
Grimsby Town v Manchester United	1-0
Southport v Blackpool	2-1
Bradford Park Avenue v Burnley	2-0
Brentford v Portsmouth	0-1
West Bromwich Albion v Tottenham Hotspur	1-0
Barnsley v Sheffield Wednesday	2-1
Bradford City v Wolverhampton Wanderers	0-0, 2-4

FIFTH ROUND

Birmingham v Watford	3-0
Chelsea v Blackburn Rovers	3-0
Sunderland v Sheffield United	2-1
Exeter City v Leeds United	3-1
Everton v Grimsby Town	5-3
Southport v Bradford Park Avenue	1-0
Portsmouth v West Bromwich Albion	0-1
Barnsley v Wolverhampton Wanderers	1-3

SIXTH ROUND

Birmingham v Chelsea	2-2, 3-0
Sunderland v Exeter City	1-1, 4-2
Everton v Southport	9-1
West Bromwich Albion v Wolverhampton Wanderers	1-1, 2-1

SEMI-FINAL

Birmingham v Sunderland	2-0
Everton v West Bromwich Albion	0-1

FINAL

West Bromwich Albion v Birmingham	2-1

SCOTTISH FA CUP 1930-31

SECOND ROUND

Dundee United v Celtic	2-3
Queen's Park v Morton	0-1
Aberdeen v Partick Thistle	1-1, 3-0
Rangers v Dundee	1-2
Kilmarnock v Heart of Midlothian	3-2
Montrose v Civil Service Strollers	2-0
Bo'ness v Alloa Athletic	4-2
Murrayfield Amateurs v Ayr United	0-1
Motherwell v Albion Rovers	4-1
Hamilton Academicals v Hibernian	2-2, 2-5
Cowdenbeath v St Johnstone	1-1, 4-0
King's Park v St Bernard's	1-1, 0-1
St Mirren v Clyde	3-1
Inverness Caledonian v Falkirk	2-7
Third Lanark v Airdrieonians	1-0
Arbroath v Edinburgh City	1-0

THIRD ROUND

Morton v Celtic	1-4
Dundee v Aberdeen	1-1, 0-2
Montrose v Kilmarnock	0-3
Bo'ness v Ayr United	1-0
Hibernian v Motherwell	0-3
Cowdenbeath v St Bernard's	3-0
St Mirren v Falkirk	2-0
Third Lanark v Arbroath	4-2

FOURTH ROUND

Celtic v Aberdeen	4-0
Bo'ness v Kilmarnock	1-1, 0-5
Cowdenbeath v Motherwell	0-1
Third Lanark v St Mirren	1-1, 0-3

SEMI-FINAL

Celtic v Kilmarnock	3-0
Motherwell v St Mirren	1-0

FINAL

Celtic v Motherwell	2-2, 4-2

The outstanding example of each member of a forward line scoring in a single game was when all five Everton forwards scored against Charlton Athletic at the Valley in an 18 minute spell. The Everton forwards were Stein, Dean, Dunn, Critchley and Johnson. The match, a Division Two League fixture played on 7 February 1931, ended as a convincing 7-0 victory for the Merseysiders, who went on to win the Division Two Championship.

The famous occasion when a referee was 'sent off' occurred in the annual Sheffield versus Glasgow match on 22 September 1930. Sheffield were playing in white shirts and black shorts, and the referee, Mr J Thomson of Burnbank, wore a white shirt without a jacket. When Sheffield's captain, Jimmy Seed, found that he was passing to the referee in error, he asked him to stop the game and put on a jacket. Mr Thomson obliged.

FIRST DIVISION

	P	W	D	L	F	A	Pts
1 Everton	42	26	4	12	116	64	56
2 Arsenal	42	22	10	10	90	48	54
3 Sheff Wed	42	22	6	14	96	82	50
4 Huddersfield	42	19	10	13	80	63	48
5 Aston Villa	42	19	8	15	104	72	46
6 WBA	42	20	6	16	77	55	46
7 Sheff United	42	20	6	16	80	75	46
8 Portsmouth	42	19	7	16	62	62	45
9 Birmingham	42	18	8	16	78	67	44
10 Liverpool	42	19	6	17	81	93	44
11 Newcastle	42	18	6	18	80	87	42
12 Chelsea	42	16	8	18	69	73	40
13 Sunderland	42	15	10	17	67	73	40
14 Man City	42	13	12	17	83	73	38
15 Derby	42	14	10	18	71	75	38
16 Blackburn	42	16	6	20	89	95	38
17 Bolton	42	17	4	21	72	80	38
18 Middlesbrough	42	15	8	19	64	89	38
19 Leicester	42	15	7	20	74	94	37
20 Blackpool	42	12	9	21	65	102	33
21 Grimsby	42	13	6	23	67	98	32
22 West Ham	42	12	7	23	62	107	31

SECOND DIVISION

	P	W	D	L	F	A	Pts
1 Wolves	42	24	8	10	115	49	56
2 Leeds	42	22	10	10	78	54	54
3 Stoke	42	19	14	9	69	48	52
4 Plymouth	42	20	9	13	100	66	49
5 Bury	42	21	7	14	70	58	49
6 Bradford PA	42	21	7	14	72	63	49
7 Bradford City	42	16	13	13	80	61	45
8 Tottenham	42	16	11	15	87	78	43
9 Millwall	42	17	9	16	61	61	43
10 Charlton	42	17	9	16	61	66	43
11 Nottm Forest	42	16	10	16	77	72	42
12 Man United	42	17	8	17	71	72	42
13 Preston	42	16	10	16	75	77	42
14 Southampton	42	17	7	18	66	77	41
15 Swansea	42	16	7	19	73	75	39
16 Notts County	42	13	12	17	75	75	38
17 Chesterfield	42	13	11	18	64	86	37
18 Oldham	42	13	10	19	62	84	36
19 Burnley	42	13	9	20	59	87	35
20 Port Vale	42	13	7	22	58	89	33
21 Barnsley	42	12	9	21	55	91	33
22 Bristol City	42	6	11	25	39	78	23

FA CUP 1931-32

FOURTH ROUND

Huddersfield Town v Queen's Park Rangers	5-0
Preston North End v Wolverhampton Wanderers	2-0
Portsmouth v Aston Villa	1-1, 1-0
Arsenal v Plymouth Argyle	4-2
Bury v Sheffield United	3-1
Sunderland v Stoke City	1-1, 1-1, 1-2
Manchester City v Brentford	6-1
Derby County v Blackburn Rovers	3-2
Chesterfield v Liverpool	2-4
Grimsby Town v Birmingham	2-1
Sheffield Wednesday v Bournemouth	7-0
Chelsea v West Ham United	3-1
Newcastle United v Southport	1-1, 1-1, 9-0
Port Vale v Leicester City	1-2
Watford v Bristol City	2-1
Bradford Park Avenue v Northampton Town	4-2

FIFTH ROUND

Huddersfield Town v Preston North End	4-0
Portsmouth v Arsenal	0-2
Bury v Stoke City	3-0
Manchester City v Derby County	3-0
Liverpool v Grimsby Town	1-0
Sheffield Wednesday v Chelsea	1-1, 0-2
Newcastle United v Leicester City	3-1
Watford v Bradford Park Avenue	1-0

SIXTH ROUND

Huddersfield Town v Arsenal	0-1
Bury v Manchester City	3-4
Liverpool v Chelsea	0-2
Newcastle United v Watford	5-0

SEMI-FINAL

Arsenal v Manchester City	1-0
Chelsea v Newcastle United	1-2

FINAL

Newcastle United v Arsenal	2-1

THIRD DIVISION (SOUTH)

	P	W	D	L	F	A	Pts
1 Fulham	42	24	9	9	111	62	57
2 Reading	42	23	9	10	97	67	55
3 Southend	42	21	11	10	77	53	53
4 Crystal Palace	42	20	11	11	74	63	51
5 Brentford	42	19	10	13	68	52	48
6 Luton	42	20	7	15	95	70	47
7 Exeter	42	20	7	15	77	62	47
8 Brighton	42	17	12	13	73	58	46
9 Cardiff	42	19	8	15	87	73	46
10 Norwich	42	17	12	13	76	67	46
11 Watford	42	19	8	15	81	79	46
12 Coventry	42	18	8	16	108	97	44
13 QPR	42	15	12	15	79	73	42
14 Northampton	42	16	7	19	69	69	39
15 Bournemouth	42	13	12	17	70	78	38
16 Clapton Orient	42	12	11	19	77	90	35
17 Swindon	42	14	6	22	70	84	34
18 Bristol Rovers	42	13	8	21	65	92	34
19 Torquay	42	12	9	21	72	106	33
20 Mansfield	42	11	10	21	75	108	32
21 Gillingham	42	10	8	24	40	82	28
22 Thames	42	7	9	26	53	109	23

THIRD DIVISION (NORTH)

	P	W	D	L	F	A	Pts
1 Lincoln	40	26	5	9	106	47	57
2 Gateshead	40	25	7	8	94	48	57
3 Chester	40	21	8	11	78	60	50
4 Tranmere	40	19	11	10	107	58	49
5 Barrow	40	24	1	15	86	59	49
6 Crewe	40	21	6	13	95	66	48
7 Southport	40	18	10	12	58	53	46
8 Hull	40	20	5	15	82	53	45
9 York	40	18	7	15	76	81	43
10 Wrexham	40	18	7	15	64	69	43
11 Darlington	40	17	4	19	66	69	38
12 Stockport	40	13	11	16	55	53	37
13 Hartlepools	40	16	5	19	78	100	37
14 Accrington	40	15	6	19	75	80	36
15 Doncaster	40	16	4	20	59	80	36
16 Walsall	40	16	3	21	57	85	35
17 Halifax	40	13	8	19	61	87	34
18 Carlisle	40	11	11	18	64	79	33
19 Rotherham	40	14	4	22	63	72	32
20 New Brighton	40	8	8	24	38	76	24
21 Rochdale	40	4	3	33	48	135	11
22 Wigan Borough resigned from the League							

SCOTTISH FA CUP 1931-32

SECOND ROUND

Raith Rovers v Rangers	0-5
Heart of Midlothian v Cowdenbeath	4-1
Queen's Park v Motherwell	0-2
St Johnstone v Celtic	2-4
Hamilton Academicals v Armadale	5-2
Clyde v Arbroath	1-0
Edinburgh City v St Bernard's	2-3
Kilmarnock v Albion Rovers	2-0
Queen of the South v Dundee United	2-2, 1-1, 1-2
Dunfermline Athletic v Dundee	1-0
Airdrieonians v King's Park	2-2, 3-1
Bo'ness v Partick Thistle	2-2, 1-5

THIRD ROUND

Heart of Midlothian v Rangers	0-1
Motherwell v Celtic	2-0
Clyde v St Bernard's	2-0
Dundee United v Kilmarnock	1-1, 0-3
Hamilton Academicals	bye
Dunfermline Athletic	bye
Airdrieonians	bye
Partick Thistle	bye

FOURTH ROUND

Rangers v Motherwell	2-0
Clyde v Hamilton Academicals	0-2
Dunfermline Athletic v Kilmarnock	1-3
Airdrieonians v Partick Thistle	4-1

SEMI-FINAL

Rangers v Hamilton Academicals	5-2
Kilmarnock v Airdrieonians	3-2

FINAL

Rangers v Kilmarnock	1-1, 3-0

SCOTTISH FIRST DIVISION

	P	W	D	L	F	A	Pts
1 Motherwell	38	30	6	2	119	31	66
2 Rangers	38	28	5	5	118	42	61
3 Celtic	38	20	8	10	94	50	48
4 Third Lanark	38	21	4	13	92	81	46
5 St Mirren	38	20	4	14	77	56	44
6 Partick	38	19	4	15	58	59	42
7 Aberdeen	38	16	9	13	57	49	41
8 Hearts	38	17	5	16	63	61	39
9 Kilmarnock	38	16	7	15	68	70	39
10 Hamilton	38	16	6	16	84	65	38
11 Dundee	38	14	10	14	61	72	38
12 Cowdenbeath	38	15	8	15	66	78	38
13 Clyde	38	13	9	16	58	70	35
14 Airdrieonians	38	13	6	19	74	81	32
15 Morton	38	12	7	19	78	87	31
16 Queen's Park	38	13	5	20	59	79	31
17 Ayr	38	11	7	20	70	90	29
18 Falkirk	38	11	5	22	70	76	27
19 Dundee United	38	6	7	25	40	118	19
20 Leith	38	6	4	28	46	137	16

SCOTTISH SECOND DIVISION

	P	W	D	L	F	A	Pts
1 E Stirlingshire	38	26	3	9	111	55	55
2 St Johnstone	38	24	7	7	102	52	55
3 Raith	38	20	6	12	83	65	46
4 Stenhousemuir	38	19	8	11	88	76	46
5 St Bernard's	38	19	7	12	81	62	45
6 Forfar	38	19	7	12	90	79	45
7 Hibernian	38	18	8	12	73	52	44
8 East Fife	38	18	5	15	107	77	41
9 Queen of the S	38	18	5	15	99	91	41
10 Dunfermline	38	17	6	15	78	73	40
11 Arbroath	38	17	5	16	82	78	39
12 Dumbarton	38	14	10	14	70	68	38
13 Alloa	38	14	7	17	73	74	35
14 Bo'ness	38	15	4	19	70	103	34
15 King's Park	38	14	5	19	97	93	33
16 Albion	38	13	2	23	81	104	28
17 Montrose	38	11	6	21	60	96	28
18 Armadale	38	10	5	23	68	102	25
19 Brechin	38	9	7	22	52	97	25
20 Edinburgh City	38	5	7	26	78	146	17

There is thought to have been only one League game without a corner kick. That was a Division One match between Newcastle United and Portsmouth, 5 December 1931, which ended as it began, 0-0.

On 26 October 1931, Wigan Borough became the first League club to resign during a season. Their record was expunged.

Rochdale break all the wrong records

Rochdale had a grim season in Division Three North. They set a League record by losing 17 games in succession: on 7 November 1931, they beat New Brighton 3-2, but then failed to gain another point until their 1-1 draw with the same team on 9 March 1932. Their 33 defeats in 40 matches were also a record for the division.

FIRST DIVISION

		P	W	D	L	F	A	Pts
1	Arsenal	42	25	8	9	118	61	58
2	Aston Villa	42	23	8	11	92	67	54
3	Sheff Wed	42	21	9	12	80	68	51
4	WBA	42	20	9	13	83	70	49
5	Newcastle	42	22	5	15	71	63	49
6	Huddersfield	42	18	11	13	66	53	47
7	Derby	42	15	14	13	76	69	44
8	Leeds	42	15	14	13	59	62	44
9	Portsmouth	42	18	7	17	74	76	43
10	Sheff United	42	17	9	16	74	80	43
11	Everton	42	16	9	17	81	74	41
12	Sunderland	42	15	10	17	63	80	40
13	Birmingham	42	14	11	17	57	57	39
14	Liverpool	42	14	11	17	79	84	39
15	Blackburn	42	14	10	18	76	102	38
16	Man City	42	16	5	21	68	71	37
17	Middlesbrough	42	14	9	19	63	73	37
18	Chelsea	42	14	7	21	63	73	35
19	Leicester	42	11	13	18	75	89	35
20	Wolves	42	13	9	20	80	96	35
21	Bolton	42	12	9	21	78	92	33
22	Blackpool	42	14	5	23	69	85	33

SECOND DIVISION

		P	W	D	L	F	A	Pts
1	Stoke	42	25	6	11	78	39	56
2	Tottenham	42	20	15	7	96	51	55
3	Fulham	42	20	10	12	78	65	50
4	Bury	42	20	9	13	84	59	49
5	Nottm Forest	42	17	15	10	67	59	49
6	Man United	42	15	13	14	71	68	43
7	Millwall	42	16	11	15	59	57	43
8	Bradford PA	42	17	8	17	77	71	42
9	Preston	42	16	10	16	74	70	42
10	Swansea	42	19	4	19	50	54	42
11	Bradford City	42	14	13	15	65	61	41
12	Southampton	42	18	5	19	66	66	41
13	Grimsby	42	14	13	15	79	84	41
14	Plymouth	42	16	9	17	63	67	41
15	Notts County	42	15	10	17	67	78	40
16	Oldham	42	15	8	19	67	80	38
17	Port Vale	42	14	10	18	66	79	38
18	Lincoln	42	12	13	17	72	87	37
19	Burnley	42	11	14	17	67	79	36
20	West Ham	42	13	9	20	75	93	35
21	Chesterfield	42	12	10	20	61	84	34
22	Charlton	42	12	7	23	60	91	31

THIRD DIVISION (SOUTH)

		P	W	D	L	F	A	Pts
1	Brentford	42	26	10	6	90	49	62
2	Exeter	42	24	10	8	88	48	58
3	Norwich	42	22	13	7	88	55	57
4	Reading	42	19	13	10	103	71	51
5	Crystal Palace	42	19	8	15	78	64	46
6	Coventry	42	19	6	17	106	77	44
7	Gillingham	42	18	8	16	72	61	44
8	Northampton	42	18	8	16	76	66	44
9	Bristol Rovers	42	15	14	13	61	56	44
10	Torquay	42	16	12	14	72	67	44
11	Watford	42	16	12	14	66	63	44
12	Brighton	42	17	8	17	66	65	42
13	Southend	42	15	11	16	65	82	41
14	Luton	42	13	13	16	78	78	39
15	Bristol City	42	12	13	17	83	90	37
16	QPR	42	13	11	18	72	87	37
17	Aldershot	42	13	10	19	61	72	36
18	Bournemouth	42	12	12	18	60	81	36
19	Cardiff	42	12	7	23	69	99	31
20	Clapton Orient	42	8	13	21	59	93	29
21	Newport	42	11	7	24	61	105	29
22	Swindon	42	9	11	22	60	105	29

THIRD DIVISION (NORTH)

		P	W	D	L	F	A	Pts
1	Hull	42	26	7	9	100	45	59
2	Wrexham	42	24	9	9	106	51	57
3	Stockport	42	21	12	9	99	58	54
4	Chester	42	22	8	12	94	66	52
5	Walsall	42	19	10	13	75	58	48
6	Doncaster	42	17	14	11	77	79	48
7	Gateshead	42	19	9	14	78	67	47
8	Barnsley	42	19	8	15	92	80	46
9	Barrow	42	18	7	17	60	60	43
10	Crewe	42	20	3	19	80	84	43
11	Tranmere	42	17	8	17	70	66	42
12	Southport	42	17	7	18	70	67	41
13	Accrington	42	15	10	17	78	76	40
14	Hartlepools	42	16	7	19	87	116	39
15	Halifax	42	15	8	19	71	90	38
16	Mansfield	42	14	7	21	84	100	35
17	Rotherham	42	14	6	22	60	84	34
18	Rochdale	42	13	7	22	58	80	33
19	Carlisle	42	13	7	22	51	75	33
20	York	42	13	6	23	72	92	32
21	New Brighton	42	11	10	21	63	88	32
22	Darlington	42	10	8	24	66	109	28

SCOTTISH FIRST DIVISION

		P	W	D	L	F	A	Pts
1	Rangers	38	26	10	2	113	43	62
2	Motherwell	38	27	5	6	114	53	59
3	Hearts	38	21	8	9	84	51	50
4	Celtic	38	20	8	10	75	44	48
5	St Johnstone	38	17	10	11	70	57	44
6	Aberdeen	38	18	6	14	85	58	42
7	St Mirren	38	18	6	14	73	60	42
8	Hamilton	38	18	6	14	92	78	42
9	Queen's Park	38	17	7	14	78	79	41
10	Partick	38	17	6	15	75	55	40
11	Falkirk	38	15	6	17	70	70	36
12	Clyde	38	15	5	18	69	75	35
13	Third Lanark	38	14	7	17	70	80	35
14	Kilmarnock	38	13	9	16	72	86	35
15	Dundee	38	12	9	17	58	74	33
16	Ayr	38	13	4	21	62	96	30
17	Cowdenbeath	38	10	5	23	65	111	25
18	Airdrieonians	38	10	3	25	55	102	23
19	Morton	38	6	9	23	49	97	21
20	E Stirlingshire	38	7	3	28	55	115	17

SCOTTISH SECOND DIVISION

		P	W	D	L	F	A	Pts
1	Hibernian	34	25	4	5	80	29	54
2	Queen of the S	34	20	9	5	93	59	49
3	Dunfermline	34	20	7	7	89	44	47
4	Stenhousemuir	34	18	6	10	67	58	42
5	Albion	34	19	2	13	82	57	40
6	Raith	34	16	4	14	83	67	36
7	East Fife	34	15	4	15	85	71	34
8	King's Park	34	13	8	13	85	80	34
9	Dumbarton	34	14	6	14	69	67	34
10	Arbroath	34	14	5	15	65	62	33
11	Alloa	34	14	5	15	60	58	33
12	St Bernard's	34	13	6	15	67	64	32
13	Dundee United	34	14	4	16	65	67	32
14	Forfar	34	12	4	18	68	87	28
15	Brechin	34	11	4	19	65	95	26
16	Leith	34	10	5	19	43	81	25
17	Montrose	34	8	5	21	63	89	21
18	Edinburgh City	34	4	4	26	39	133	12

The international Rangers

Towards the end of 1932-33, Glasgow Rangers had 13 internationals on their books. They were: Archibald, Brown, Craig, Fleming, Gray, T Hamilton, McPhail, Marshall, Meiklejohn and Morton, all Scotsmen, and English, R Hamilton and McDonald, who were Irish internationals. This considerable array of Scots and Irish talent helped Rangers finish the season at the top of the Scottish First Division, three points clear of Motherwell.

FA CUP 1932-33

FOURTH ROUND

Burnley v Sheffield United	3-1
Darlington v Chesterfield	0-2
Bolton Wanderers v Grimsby Town	2-1
Manchester City v Walsall	2-0
Southend United v Derby County	2-3
Aldershot v Millwall	1-0
Aston Villa v Sunderland	0-3
Blackpool v Huddersfield Town	2-0
Everton v Bury	3-1
Tranmere Rovers v Leeds United	0-0, 0-4
Chester v Halifax Town	0-0, 2-3
Luton Town v Tottenham Hotspur	2-0
Brighton v Bradford Park Avenue	2-1
West Ham United v West Bromwich Albion	2-0
Middlesbrough v Stoke City	4-1
Birmingham v Blackburn Rovers	3-0

FIFTH ROUND

Burnley v Chesterfield	1-0
Bolton Wanderers v Manchester City	2-4
Derby County v Aldershot	2-0
Sunderland v Blackpool	1-0
Everton v Leeds United	2-0
Halifax Town v Luton Town	0-2
Brighton v West Ham United	2-2, 0-1
Middlesbrough v Birmingham	0-0, 0-3

SIXTH ROUND

Burnley v Manchester City	0-1
Derby County v Sunderland	4-4, 1-0
Everton v Luton Town	6-0
West Ham United v Birmingham	4-0

SEMI-FINAL

Manchester City v Derby County	3-2
Everton v West Ham United	2-1

FINAL

Everton v Manchester City	3-0

SCOTTISH FA CUP 1932-33

SECOND ROUND

Celtic v Falkirk	2-0
Partick Thistle v Ayr United	1-1, 2-0
Albion Rovers v Dumbarton	2-1
Heart of Midlothian v Airdrieonians	6-1
St Johnstone v Dundee United	4-3
Hibernian v Aberdeen	1-1, 1-0
Motherwell v Montrose	7-1
Dundee v Bo'ness	4-0
Kilmarnock v St Mirren	1-0
Rangers v Queen's Park	1-1, 1-1, 3-1
Clyde v Leith Athletic	1-1, 5-0
Stenhousemuir v Third Lanark	2-0

THIRD ROUND

Celtic v Partick Thistle	2-1
Heart of Midlothian v St Johnstone	2-0
Motherwell v Dundee	5-0
Kilmarnock v Rangers	1-0
Albion Rovers	bye
Hibernian	bye
Clyde	bye
Stenhousemuir	bye

FOURTH ROUND

Celtic v Albion Rovers	1-1, 3-1
Heart of Midlothian v Hibernian	2-0
Motherwell v Kilmarnock	3-3, 8-3
Clyde v Stenhousemuir	3-2

SEMI-FINAL

Celtic v Heart of Midlothian	0-0, 2-1
Motherwell v Clyde	2-0

FINAL

Celtic v Motherwell	1-0

Reduced to ten men after 10 minutes, Wales did well to beat Scotland 5-2 at Tynecastle, Edinburgh, in October 1932. It was their first win on Scottish soil since 1906.

Everton capped a memorable three seasons by winning the FA Cup. In 1931-32, they were League champions, the season before, they had won the Second Division Championship.

FIRST DIVISION

	P	W	D	L	F	A	Pts
1 Arsenal	42	25	9	8	75	47	59
2 Huddersfield	42	23	10	9	90	61	56
3 Tottenham	42	21	7	14	79	56	49
4 Derby	42	17	11	14	68	54	45
5 Man City	42	17	11	14	65	72	45
6 Sunderland	42	16	12	14	81	56	44
7 WBA	42	17	10	15	78	70	44
8 Blackburn	42	18	7	17	74	81	43
9 Leeds	42	17	8	17	75	66	42
10 Portsmouth	42	15	12	15	52	55	42
11 Sheff Wed	42	16	9	17	62	67	41
12 Stoke	42	15	11	16	58	71	41
13 Aston Villa	42	14	12	16	78	75	40
14 Everton	42	12	16	14	62	63	40
15 Wolves	42	14	12	16	74	86	40
16 Middlesbrough	42	16	7	19	68	80	39
17 Leicester	42	14	11	17	59	74	39
18 Liverpool	42	14	10	18	79	87	38
19 Chelsea	42	14	8	20	67	69	36
20 Birmingham	42	12	12	18	54	56	36
21 Newcastle	42	10	14	18	68	77	34
22 Sheff United	42	12	7	23	58	101	31

SECOND DIVISION

	P	W	D	L	F	A	Pts
1 Grimsby	42	27	5	10	103	59	59
2 Preston	42	23	6	13	71	52	52
3 Bolton	42	21	9	12	79	55	51
4 Brentford	42	22	7	13	85	60	51
5 Bradford PA	42	23	3	16	86	67	49
6 Bradford City	42	20	6	16	73	67	46
7 West Ham	42	17	11	14	78	70	45
8 Port Vale	42	19	7	16	60	55	45
9 Oldham	42	17	10	15	72	60	44
10 Plymouth	42	15	13	14	69	70	43
11 Blackpool	42	15	13	14	62	64	43
12 Bury	42	17	9	16	70	73	43
13 Burnley	42	18	6	18	60	72	42
14 Southampton	42	15	8	19	54	58	38
15 Hull	42	13	12	17	52	68	38
16 Fulham	42	15	7	20	48	67	37
17 Nottm Forest	42	13	9	20	73	74	35
18 Notts County	42	12	11	19	53	62	35
19 Swansea	42	10	15	17	51	60	35
20 Man United	42	14	6	22	59	85	34
21 Millwall	42	11	11	20	39	68	33
22 Lincoln	42	9	8	25	44	75	26

FA CUP 1933-34

THIRD DIVISION (NORTH)

	P	W	D	L	F	A	Pts
1 Barnsley	42	27	8	7	118	61	62
2 Chesterfield	42	27	7	8	86	43	61
3 Stockport	42	24	11	7	115	52	59
4 Walsall	42	23	7	12	97	60	53
5 Doncaster	42	22	9	11	83	61	53
6 Wrexham	42	23	5	14	102	73	51
7 Tranmere	42	20	7	15	84	63	47
8 Barrow	42	19	9	14	116	94	47
9 Halifax	42	20	4	18	80	91	44
10 Chester	42	17	6	19	89	86	40
11 Hartlepools	42	16	7	19	89	93	39
12 York	42	15	8	19	71	74	38
13 Carlisle	42	15	8	19	66	81	38
14 Crewe	42	15	6	21	81	97	36
15 New Brighton	42	14	8	20	62	87	36
16 Darlington	42	13	9	20	70	101	35
17 Mansfield	42	11	12	19	81	88	34
18 Southport	42	8	17	17	63	90	33
19 Gateshead	42	12	9	21	76	110	33
20 Accrington	42	13	7	22	65	101	33
21 Rotherham	42	10	8	24	53	91	28
22 Rochdale	42	9	6	27	53	103	24

THIRD DIVISION (SOUTH)

	P	W	D	L	F	A	Pts
1 Norwich	42	25	11	6	88	49	61
2 Coventry	42	21	12	9	100	54	54
3 Reading	42	21	12	9	82	50	54
4 QPR	42	24	6	12	70	51	54
5 Charlton	42	22	8	12	83	56	52
6 Luton	42	21	10	11	83	61	52
7 Bristol Rovers	42	20	11	11	77	47	51
8 Swindon	42	17	11	14	64	68	45
9 Exeter	42	16	11	15	68	57	43
10 Brighton	42	15	13	14	68	60	43
11 Clapton Orient	42	16	10	16	75	69	42
12 Crystal Palace	42	16	9	17	71	67	41
13 Northampton	42	14	12	16	71	78	40
14 Aldershot	42	13	12	17	52	71	38
15 Watford	42	15	7	20	71	63	37
16 Southend	42	12	10	20	51	74	34
17 Gillingham	42	11	11	20	75	96	33
18 Newport	42	8	17	17	49	70	33
19 Bristol City	42	10	13	19	58	85	33
20 Torquay	42	13	7	22	53	93	33
21 Bournemouth	42	9	9	24	60	102	27
22 Cardiff	42	9	6	27	57	105	24

SCOTTISH FA CUP 1933-34

SCOTTISH FIRST DIVISION

	P	W	D	L	F	A	Pts
1 Rangers	38	30	6	2	118	41	66
2 Motherwell	38	29	4	5	97	45	62
3 Celtic	38	18	11	9	78	53	47
4 Queen of the S	38	21	3	14	75	78	45
5 Aberdeen	38	18	8	12	90	57	44
6 Hearts	38	17	10	11	86	59	44
7 Kilmarnock	38	17	9	12	73	64	43
8 Ayr	38	16	10	12	87	92	42
9 St Johnstone	38	17	6	15	74	53	40
10 Falkirk	38	16	6	16	73	68	38
11 Hamilton	38	15	8	15	65	79	38
12 Dundee	38	15	6	17	68	64	36
13 Partick	38	14	5	19	73	78	33
14 Clyde	38	10	11	17	56	70	31
15 Queen's Park	38	13	5	20	65	85	31
16 Hibernian	38	12	3	23	51	69	27
17 St Mirren	38	9	9	20	46	75	27
18 Airdrieonians	38	10	6	22	59	103	26
19 Third Lanark	38	8	9	21	62	103	25
20 Cowdenbeath	38	5	5	28	58	118	15

SCOTTISH SECOND DIVISION

	P	W	D	L	F	A	Pts
1 Albion	34	20	5	9	74	47	45
2 Dunfermline	34	20	4	10	90	52	44
3 Arbroath	34	20	4	10	83	53	44
4 Stenhousemuir	34	18	4	12	70	73	40
5 Morton	34	17	5	12	67	64	39
6 Dumbarton	34	17	3	14	67	68	37
7 King's Park	34	14	8	12	78	70	36
8 Raith	34	15	5	14	71	55	35
9 E Stirlingshire	34	14	7	13	65	74	35
10 St Bernard's	34	15	4	15	75	56	34
11 Forfar	34	13	7	14	77	71	33
12 Leith	34	12	8	14	63	60	32
13 East Fife	34	12	8	14	71	76	32
14 Brechin	34	13	5	16	60	70	31
15 Alloa	34	11	9	14	55	68	31
16 Montrose	34	11	4	19	53	81	26
17 Dundee United	34	10	4	20	81	88	24
18 Edinburgh City	34	4	6	24	37	111	14

The record number of goals scored by a conventional half-back in a Football League game is three. The record was set in 1926 by a Newcastle player, T McDonald, and equalled against Wolves on 21 April 1934 by another Newcastle player, W Imrie.

In June 1934, Stanley Rous was appointed secretary of the Football Association.

S Milton had surely one of the unhappiest Football League debuts on record. A goalkeeper, Milton was picked to play in that position for Halifax Town against Stockport County in a Third Division North League match on 6 January 1934. Milton was faced with a Stockport attack in fine fettle, and he had to retrieve the ball from his net 13 times, an unenviable record. The score—13-0—also set a record, for the highest score in a League match.

213

FIRST DIVISION

	P	W	D	L	F	A	Pts
1 Arsenal	42	23	12	7	115	46	58
2 Sunderland	42	19	16	7	90	51	54
3 Sheff Wed	42	18	13	11	70	64	49
4 Man City	42	20	8	14	82	67	48
5 Grimsby	42	17	11	14	78	60	45
6 Derby	42	18	9	15	81	66	45
7 Liverpool	42	19	7	16	85	88	45
8 Everton	42	16	12	14	89	88	44
9 WBA	42	17	10	15	83	83	44
10 Stoke	42	18	6	18	71	70	42
11 Preston	42	15	12	15	62	67	42
12 Chelsea	42	16	9	17	73	82	41
13 Aston Villa	42	14	13	15	74	88	41
14 Portsmouth	42	15	10	17	71	72	40
15 Blackburn	42	14	11	17	66	78	39
16 Huddersfield	42	14	10	18	76	71	38
17 Wolves	42	15	8	19	88	94	38
18 Leeds	42	13	12	17	75	92	38
19 Birmingham	42	13	10	19	63	81	36
20 Middlesbrough	42	10	14	18	70	91	34
21 Leicester	42	12	9	21	61	86	33
22 Tottenham	42	10	10	22	54	93	30

SECOND DIVISION

	P	W	D	L	F	A	Pts
1 Brentford	42	26	9	7	93	48	61
2 Bolton	42	26	4	12	96	48	56
3 West Ham	42	26	4	12	80	63	56
4 Blackpool	42	21	11	10	79	57	53
5 Man United	42	23	4	15	76	55	50
6 Newcastle	42	22	4	16	89	68	48
7 Fulham	42	17	12	13	76	56	46
8 Plymouth	42	19	8	15	75	64	46
9 Nottm Forest	42	17	8	17	76	70	42
10 Bury	42	19	4	19	62	73	42
11 Sheff United	42	16	9	17	79	70	41
12 Burnley	42	16	9	17	63	73	41
13 Hull	42	16	8	18	63	74	40
14 Norwich	42	14	11	17	71	61	39
15 Bradford PA	42	11	16	15	55	63	38
16 Barnsley	42	13	12	17	60	83	38
17 Swansea	42	14	8	20	56	67	36
18 Port Vale	42	11	12	19	55	74	34
19 Southampton	42	11	12	19	46	75	34
20 Bradford City	42	12	8	22	50	68	32
21 Oldham	42	10	6	26	56	95	26
22 Notts County	42	9	7	26	46	97	25

THIRD DIVISION (SOUTH)

	P	W	D	L	F	A	Pts
1 Charlton	42	27	7	8	103	52	61
2 Reading	42	21	11	10	89	65	53
3 Coventry	42	21	9	12	86	50	51
4 Luton	42	19	12	11	92	60	50
5 Crystal Palace	42	19	10	13	86	64	48
6 Watford	42	19	9	14	76	49	47
7 Northampton	42	19	8	15	65	67	46
8 Bristol Rovers	42	17	10	15	73	77	44
9 Brighton	42	17	9	16	69	62	43
10 Torquay	42	18	6	18	81	75	42
11 Exeter	42	16	9	17	70	75	41
12 Millwall	42	17	7	18	57	62	41
13 QPR	42	16	9	17	63	72	41
14 Clapton Orient	42	15	10	17	65	65	40
15 Bristol City	42	15	9	18	52	68	39
16 Swindon	42	13	12	17	67	78	38
17 Bournemouth	42	15	7	20	54	71	37
18 Aldershot	42	13	10	19	50	75	36
19 Cardiff	42	13	9	20	62	82	35
20 Gillingham	42	11	13	18	55	75	35
21 Southend	42	11	9	22	65	78	31
22 Newport	42	10	5	27	54	112	25

THIRD DIVISION (NORTH)

	P	W	D	L	F	A	Pts
1 Doncaster	42	26	5	11	87	44	57
2 Halifax	42	25	5	12	76	67	55
3 Chester	42	20	14	8	91	58	54
4 Lincoln	42	22	7	13	87	58	51
5 Darlington	42	21	9	12	80	59	51
6 Tranmere	42	20	11	11	74	55	51
7 Stockport	42	22	3	17	90	72	47
8 Mansfield	42	19	9	14	75	62	47
9 Rotherham	42	19	7	16	86	73	45
10 Chesterfield	42	17	10	15	71	52	44
11 Wrexham	42	16	11	15	76	69	43
12 Hartlepools	42	17	7	18	80	78	41
13 Crewe	42	14	11	17	66	86	39
14 Walsall	42	13	10	19	81	72	36
15 York	42	15	6	21	76	82	36
16 New Brighton	42	14	8	20	59	76	36
17 Barrow	42	13	9	20	58	87	35
18 Accrington	42	12	10	20	63	89	34
19 Gateshead	42	13	8	21	58	96	34
20 Rochdale	42	11	11	20	53	71	33
21 Southport	42	10	12	20	55	85	32
22 Carlisle	42	8	7	27	51	102	23

SCOTTISH FIRST DIVISION

	P	W	D	L	F	A	Pts
1 Rangers	38	25	5	8	96	46	55
2 Celtic	38	24	4	10	92	45	52
3 Hearts	38	20	10	8	87	51	50
4 Hamilton	38	19	10	9	87	67	48
5 St Johnstone	38	18	10	10	66	46	46
6 Aberdeen	38	17	10	11	68	54	44
7 Motherwell	38	15	10	13	83	64	40
8 Dundee	38	16	8	14	63	63	40
9 Kilmarnock	38	16	6	16	76	68	38
10 Clyde	38	14	10	14	71	69	38
11 Hibernian	38	14	8	16	59	70	36
12 Queen's Park	38	13	10	15	61	80	36
13 Partick	38	15	5	18	61	68	35
14 Airdrieonians	38	13	7	18	64	72	33
15 Dunfermline	38	13	5	20	56	96	31
16 Albion	38	10	9	19	62	77	29
17 Queen of the S	38	11	7	20	52	72	29
18 Ayr	38	12	5	21	61	112	29
19 St Mirren	38	11	5	22	49	70	27
20 Falkirk	38	9	6	23	58	82	24

SCOTTISH SECOND DIVISION

	P	W	D	L	F	A	Pts
1 Third Lanark	34	23	6	5	94	43	52
2 Arbroath	34	23	4	7	78	42	50
3 St Bernard's	34	20	7	7	103	47	47
4 Dundee United	34	18	6	10	105	65	42
5 Stenhousemuir	34	17	5	12	86	80	39
6 Morton	34	17	4	13	88	64	38
7 King's Park	34	18	2	14	86	71	38
8 Leith	34	16	5	13	69	71	37
9 East Fife	34	16	3	15	79	73	35
10 Alloa	34	12	10	12	68	61	34
11 Forfar	34	13	8	13	77	73	34
12 Cowdenbeath	34	13	6	15	84	75	32
13 Raith	34	13	3	18	68	73	29
14 E Stirlingshire	34	11	7	16	57	76	29
15 Brechin	34	10	6	18	51	98	26
16 Dumbarton	34	9	4	21	60	105	22
17 Montrose	34	7	6	21	58	105	20
18 Edinburgh City	34	3	2	29	45	134	8

FA CUP 1934-35

FOURTH ROUND

Wolverhampton Wanderers v Sheffield Wednesday	1-2
Norwich City v Leeds United	3-3, 2-1
Reading v Millwall	1-0
Leicester City v Arsenal	0-1
Southampton v Birmingham	0-3
Blackburn Rovers v Liverpool	1-0
Nottingham Forest v Manchester United	0-0, 3-0
Burnley v Luton Town	3-1
Plymouth Argyle v Bolton Wanderers	1-4
Tottenham Hotspur v Newcastle United	2-0
Derby County v Swansea Town	3-0
Sunderland v Everton	1-1, 4-6
Swindon Town v Preston North End	0-2
Portsmouth v Bristol City	0-0, 0-2
Bradford City v Stockport County	0-0, 2-3
West Bromwich Albion v Sheffield United	7-1

FIFTH ROUND

Norwich City v Sheffield Wednesday	0-1
Reading v Arsenal	0-1
Blackburn Rovers v Birmingham	1-2
Nottingham Forest v Burnley	0-0, 0-3
Tottenham Hotspur v Bolton Wanderers	1-1, 1-1, 0-2
Everton v Derby County	3-1
Bristol City v Preston North End	0-0, 0-5
Stockport County v West Bromwich Albion	0-5

SIXTH ROUND

Sheffield Wednesday v Arsenal	2-1
Burnley v Birmingham	3-2
Everton v Bolton Wanderers	1-2
West Bromwich Albion v Preston North End	1-0

SEMI-FINAL

Sheffield Wednesday v Burnley	3-0
Bolton Wanderers v West Bromwich Albion	1-1, 0-2

FINAL

Sheffield Wednesday v West Bromwich Albion	4-2

SCOTTISH FA CUP 1934-35

SECOND ROUND

Motherwell v Morton	7-1
Rangers v Third Lanark	2-0
St Mirren v Forfar Athletic	3-0
Airdrieonians v Rosyth Dockyard	1-0
Ayr United v King's Park	1-1, 2-2, 4-4, 1-2
Heart of Midlothian v Kilmarnock	2-0
Dundee United v Queen's Park	6-3
Aberdeen v Albion Rovers	4-0
Hibernian v Clachnacuddin	7-1
Celtic v Partick Thistle	1-1, 3-1
Brechin City v Raith Rovers	1-1, 4-2
Clyde v Hamilton Academicals	3-3, 3-6
St Johnstone v Dumbarton	4-0
Buckie Thistle	bye

THIRD ROUND

Rangers v St Mirren	1-0
Airdrieonians v King's Park	6-2
Heart of Midlothian v Dundee United	2-2, 4-2
Aberdeen v Hibernian	0-0, 1-1, 3-2
Brechin City v Hamilton Academicals	2-4
Buckie Thistle v St Johnstone	0-1
Motherwell	bye
Celtic	bye

FOURTH ROUND

Motherwell v Rangers	1-4
Airdrieonians v Heart of Midlothian	2-3
Aberdeen v Celtic	3-1
Hamilton Academicals v St Johnstone	3-0

SEMI-FINAL

Rangers v Heart of Midlothian	1-1, 2-0
Aberdeen v Hamilton Academicals	1-2

FINAL

Rangers v Hamilton Academicals	2-1

The famous occasion when a player headed a goal from a penalty-kick took place on 5 January 1935. Anfield was the setting for a North-South clash between Liverpool and Arsenal. In the course of the game, Arsenal were awarded a penalty which their full-back, Eddie Hapgood, elected to take. Liverpool's goalkeeper, Riley, fisted Hapgood's spot-kick back out, and Hapgood headed home the rebound. Arsenal won the match 2-0.

The record gate for an English League match was broken on 23 February 1935, when 77,582 people paid to see Manchester City play Arsenal at Maine Road, Manchester. Season-ticket holders brought the total number of spectators present to 80,000.

S Raleigh, Gillingham's centre-forward, died from concussion sustained in a match with Brighton, 1 December 1934.

FIRST DIVISION

		P	W	D	L	F	A	Pts
1	Sunderland	42	25	6	11	109	74	56
2	Derby	42	18	12	12	61	52	48
3	Huddersfield	42	18	12	12	59	56	48
4	Stoke	42	20	7	15	57	57	47
5	Brentford	42	17	12	13	81	60	46
6	Arsenal	42	15	15	12	78	48	45
7	Preston	42	18	8	16	67	64	44
8	Chelsea	42	15	13	14	65	72	43
9	Man City	42	17	8	17	68	60	42
10	Portsmouth	42	17	8	17	54	67	42
11	Leeds	42	15	11	16	66	64	41
12	Birmingham	42	15	11	16	61	63	41
13	Bolton	42	14	13	15	67	76	41
14	Middlesbrough	42	15	10	17	84	70	40
15	Wolves	42	15	10	17	77	76	40
16	Everton	42	13	13	16	89	89	39
17	Grimsby	42	17	5	20	65	73	39
18	WBA	42	16	6	20	89	88	38
19	Liverpool	42	13	12	17	60	64	38
20	Sheff Wed	42	13	12	17	63	77	38
21	Aston Villa	42	13	9	20	81	110	35
22	Blackburn	42	12	9	21	55	96	33

SECOND DIVISION

		P	W	D	L	F	A	Pts
1	Man United	42	22	12	8	85	43	56
2	Charlton	42	22	11	9	85	58	55
3	Sheff United	42	20	12	10	79	50	52
4	West Ham	42	22	8	12	90	68	52
5	Tottenham	42	18	13	11	91	55	49
6	Leicester	42	19	10	13	79	57	48
7	Plymouth	42	20	8	14	71	57	48
8	Newcastle	42	20	6	16	88	79	46
9	Fulham	42	15	14	13	76	52	44
10	Blackpool	42	18	7	17	93	72	43
11	Norwich	42	17	9	16	72	65	43
12	Bradford City	42	15	13	14	55	65	43
13	Swansea	42	15	9	18	67	76	39
14	Bury	42	13	12	17	66	84	38
15	Burnley	42	12	13	17	50	59	37
16	Bradford PA	42	14	9	19	62	84	37
17	Southampton	42	14	9	19	47	65	37
18	Doncaster	42	14	9	19	51	71	37
19	Nottm Forest	42	12	11	19	69	76	35
20	Barnsley	42	12	9	21	54	80	33
21	Port Vale	42	12	8	22	56	106	32
22	Hull	42	5	10	27	47	111	20

THIRD DIVISION (SOUTH)

		P	W	D	L	F	A	Pts
1	Coventry	42	24	9	9	102	45	57
2	Luton	42	22	12	8	81	45	56
3	Reading	42	26	2	14	87	62	54
4	QPR	42	22	9	11	84	53	53
5	Watford	42	20	9	13	80	54	49
6	Crystal Palace	42	22	5	15	96	74	49
7	Brighton	42	18	8	16	70	63	44
8	Bournemouth	42	16	11	15	60	56	43
9	Notts County	42	15	12	15	60	57	42
10	Torquay	42	16	9	17	62	62	41
11	Aldershot	42	14	12	16	53	61	40
12	Millwall	42	14	12	16	58	71	40
13	Bristol City	42	15	10	17	48	59	40
14	Clapton Orient	42	16	6	20	55	61	38
15	Northampton	42	15	8	19	62	90	38
16	Gillingham	42	14	9	19	66	77	37
17	Bristol Rovers	42	14	9	19	69	95	37
18	Southend	42	13	10	19	61	62	36
19	Swindon	42	14	8	20	64	73	36
20	Cardiff	42	13	10	19	60	73	36
21	Newport	42	11	9	22	60	111	31
22	Exeter	42	8	11	23	59	93	27

THIRD DIVISION (NORTH)

		P	W	D	L	F	A	Pts
1	Chesterfield	42	24	12	6	92	39	60
2	Chester	42	22	11	9	100	45	55
3	Tranmere	42	22	11	9	93	58	55
4	Lincoln	42	22	10	10	91	51	53
5	Stockport	42	20	8	14	65	49	48
6	Crewe	42	19	9	14	80	76	47
7	Oldham	42	18	9	15	86	73	45
8	Hartlepools	42	15	12	15	57	61	42
9	Accrington	42	17	8	17	63	72	42
10	Walsall	42	16	9	17	79	59	41
11	Rotherham	42	16	9	17	69	66	41
12	Darlington	42	17	6	19	74	79	40
13	Carlisle	42	14	12	16	56	62	40
14	Gateshead	42	13	14	15	56	76	40
15	Barrow	42	13	12	17	58	65	38
16	York	42	13	12	17	62	95	38
17	Halifax	42	15	7	20	57	61	37
18	Wrexham	42	15	7	20	66	75	37
19	Mansfield	42	14	9	19	80	91	37
20	Rochdale	42	10	13	19	58	88	33
21	Southport	42	11	9	22	48	90	31
22	New Brighton	42	9	6	27	43	102	24

SCOTTISH FIRST DIVISION

		P	W	D	L	F	A	Pts
1	Celtic	38	32	2	4	115	33	66
2	Rangers	38	27	7	4	110	43	61
3	Aberdeen	38	26	9	3	96	50	61
4	Motherwell	38	18	12	8	77	58	48
5	Hearts	38	20	7	11	88	55	47
6	Hamilton	38	15	7	16	77	74	37
7	St Johnstone	38	15	7	16	70	81	37
8	Kilmarnock	38	14	7	17	69	64	35
9	Partick	38	12	10	16	64	72	34
10	Dunfermline	38	13	8	17	73	92	34
11	Third Lanark	38	14	5	19	63	71	33
12	Arbroath	38	11	11	16	46	69	33
13	Dundee	38	11	10	17	67	80	32
14	Queen's Park	38	11	10	17	58	75	32
15	Queen of the S	38	11	9	18	54	72	31
16	Albion	38	13	4	21	69	92	30
17	Hibernian	38	11	7	20	56	82	29
18	Clyde	38	10	8	20	63	84	28
19	Airdrieonians	38	9	9	20	68	91	27
20	Ayr	38	11	3	24	53	98	25

SCOTTISH SECOND DIVISION

		P	W	D	L	F	A	Pts
1	Falkirk	34	28	3	3	132	34	59
2	St Mirren	34	25	2	7	114	41	52
3	Morton	34	21	6	7	117	60	48
4	Alloa	34	19	6	9	65	51	44
5	St Bernard's	34	18	4	12	106	78	40
6	East Fife	34	16	6	12	86	79	38
7	Dundee United	34	16	5	13	108	81	37
8	E Stirlingshire	34	13	8	13	70	75	34
9	Leith	34	15	3	16	67	77	33
10	Cowdenbeath	34	13	5	16	76	77	31
11	Stenhousemuir	34	13	3	18	59	78	29
12	Montrose	34	13	3	18	58	82	29
13	Forfar	34	10	7	17	60	81	27
14	King's Park	34	11	5	18	55	109	27
15	Edinburgh City	34	8	9	17	57	83	25
16	Brechin	34	8	6	20	57	96	22
17	Raith	34	9	3	22	60	96	21
18	Dumbarton	34	5	6	23	52	121	16

FA CUP 1935-36

FOURTH ROUND

Liverpool v Arsenal	0-2
Sheffield Wednesday v Newcastle United	1-1, 1-3
Tranmere Rovers v Barnsley	2-4
Stoke City v Manchester United	0-0, 2-0
Port Vale v Grimsby Town	0-4
Manchester City v Luton Town	2-1
Middlesbrough v Clapton Orient	3-0
Leicester City v Watford	6-3
Fulham v Blackpool	5-2
Chelsea v Plymouth Argyle	4-1
Bradford City v Blackburn Rovers	3-1
Derby County v Nottingham Forest	2-0
Preston North End v Sheffield United	0-0, 0-2
Leeds United v Bury	2-1*, 3-2
Tottenham Hotspur v Huddersfield Town	1-0
Bradford Park Avenue v West Bromwich Albion	1-1, 1-1, 2-0

*abandoned

FIFTH ROUND

Newcastle United v Arsenal	3-3, 0-3
Barnsley v Stoke City	2-1
Grimsby Town v Manchester City	3-2
Middlesbrough v Leicester City	2-1
Chelsea v Fulham	0-0, 2-3
Bradford City v Derby County	0-1
Sheffield United v Leeds United	3-1
Bradford Park Avenue v Tottenham Hotspur	0-0, 1-2

SIXTH ROUND

Arsenal v Barnsley	4-1
Grimsby Town v Middlesbrough	3-1
Fulham v Derby County	3-0
Sheffield United v Tottenham Hotspur	3-1

SEMI-FINAL

Arsenal v Grimsby Town	1-0
Fulham v Sheffield United	1-2

FINAL

Arsenal v Sheffield United	1-0

SCOTTISH FA CUP 1935-36

SECOND ROUND

Aberdeen v King's Park	6-0
Celtic v St Johnstone	1-2
Dalbeattie Star v St Mirren	0-1
Albion Rovers v Rangers	1-3
Clyde v Hibernian	4-1
Dundee v Airdrieonians	2-1
Cowdenbeath v Dundee United	5-3
Motherwell v St Bernard's	3-0
Falkirk v Kilmarnock	1-1, 3-1
Dunfermline Athletic v Galston	5-2
Morton v Stenhousemuir	3-0
Elgin City v Queen of the South	0-3
Third Lanark v Leith Athletic	2-0
Dumbarton	bye

THIRD ROUND

Aberdeen v St Johnstone	1-1, 1-0
St Mirren v Rangers	1-2
Clyde v Dundee	1-1, 3-0
Cowdenbeath v Motherwell	1-3
Morton v Queen of the South	2-0
Third Lanark v Dumbarton	8-0
Falkirk	bye
Dunfermline Athletic	bye

FOURTH ROUND

Aberdeen v Rangers	0-1
Clyde v Motherwell	3-2
Falkirk v Dunfermline Athletic	5-0
Morton v Third Lanark	3-5

SEMI-FINAL

Rangers v Clyde	3-0
Falkirk v Third Lanark	1-3

FINAL

Rangers v Third Lanark	1-0

The loneliness of long-distance football
On Good Friday, 10 April 1936, Swansea Town defeated Plymouth by two goals to one in a Second Division match at Home Park, Plymouth. The following day, Swansea met Newcastle at St James' Park, Newcastle, losing 2-0. Between the two games, Swansea travelled 400 miles, a record distance for a League club to travel between games played on consecutive days.

Footballing fatality
James Thorpe, Sunderland's goalkeeper, died a few days after his team had met Chelsea on 1 February 1936. His death was due to diabetes, but a coroner's jury found that the illness had been accelerated by rough usage of the goalkeeper. They criticized the referee (who was not called as a witness), and urged all referees to exercize stricter control. An FA commission later exonerated the referee, adding that he had acted totally in accordance with his instructions.

FIRST DIVISION

		P	W	D	L	F	A	Pts
1	Man City	42	22	13	7	107	61	57
2	Charlton	42	21	12	9	58	49	54
3	Arsenal	42	18	16	8	80	49	52
4	Derby	42	21	7	14	96	90	49
5	Wolves	42	21	5	16	84	67	47
6	Brentford	42	18	10	14	82	78	46
7	Middlesbrough	42	19	8	15	74	71	46
8	Sunderland	42	19	6	17	89	87	44
9	Portsmouth	42	17	10	15	62	66	44
10	Stoke	42	15	12	15	72	57	42
11	Birmingham	42	13	15	14	64	60	41
12	Grimsby	42	17	7	18	86	81	41
13	Chelsea	42	14	13	15	52	55	41
14	Preston	42	14	13	15	56	67	41
15	Huddersfield	42	12	15	15	62	64	39
16	WBA	42	16	6	20	77	98	38
17	Everton	42	14	9	19	81	78	37
18	Liverpool	42	12	11	19	62	84	35
19	Leeds	42	15	4	23	60	80	34
20	Bolton	42	10	14	18	43	66	34
21	Man United	42	10	12	20	55	78	32
22	Sheff Wed	42	9	12	21	53	69	30

SECOND DIVISION

		P	W	D	L	F	A	Pts
1	Leicester	42	24	8	10	89	57	56
2	Blackpool	42	24	7	11	88	53	55
3	Bury	42	22	8	12	74	55	52
4	Newcastle	42	22	5	15	80	56	49
5	Plymouth	42	18	13	11	71	53	49
6	West Ham	42	19	11	12	73	55	49
7	Sheff United	42	18	10	14	66	54	46
8	Coventry	42	17	11	14	66	54	45
9	Aston Villa	42	16	12	14	82	70	44
10	Tottenham	42	17	9	16	88	66	43
11	Fulham	42	15	13	14	71	61	43
12	Blackburn	42	16	10	16	70	62	42
13	Burnley	42	16	10	16	57	61	42
14	Barnsley	42	16	9	17	50	64	41
15	Chesterfield	42	16	8	18	84	89	40
16	Swansea	42	15	7	20	50	65	37
17	Norwich	42	14	8	20	63	71	36
18	Nottm Forest	42	12	10	20	68	90	34
19	Southampton	42	11	12	19	53	77	34
20	Bradford PA	42	12	9	21	52	88	33
21	Bradford City	42	9	12	21	54	94	30
22	Doncaster	42	7	10	25	30	84	24

THIRD DIVISION (NORTH)

		P	W	D	L	F	A	Pts
1	Stockport	42	23	14	5	84	39	60
2	Lincoln	42	25	7	10	103	57	57
3	Chester	42	22	9	11	87	57	53
4	Oldham	42	20	11	11	77	59	51
5	Hull	42	17	12	13	68	69	46
6	Hartlepools	42	19	7	16	75	69	45
7	Halifax	42	18	9	15	68	63	45
8	Wrexham	42	16	12	14	71	57	44
9	Mansfield	42	18	8	16	91	76	44
10	Carlisle	42	18	8	16	65	68	44
11	Port Vale	42	17	10	15	58	64	44
12	York	42	16	11	15	79	70	43
13	Accrington	42	16	9	17	76	69	41
14	Southport	42	12	13	17	73	87	37
15	New Brighton	42	13	11	18	55	70	37
16	Barrow	42	13	10	19	70	86	36
17	Rotherham	42	14	7	21	78	91	35
18	Rochdale	42	13	9	20	69	86	35
19	Tranmere	42	12	9	21	71	88	33
20	Crewe	42	10	12	20	55	83	32
21	Gateshead	42	11	10	21	63	98	32
22	Darlington	42	8	14	20	66	96	30

THIRD DIVISION (SOUTH)

		P	W	D	L	F	A	Pts
1	Luton	42	27	4	11	103	53	58
2	Notts County	42	23	10	9	74	52	56
3	Brighton	42	24	5	13	74	43	53
4	Watford	42	19	11	12	85	60	49
5	Reading	42	19	11	12	76	60	49
6	Bournemouth	42	20	9	13	65	59	49
7	Northampton	42	20	6	16	85	68	46
8	Millwall	42	18	10	14	64	54	46
9	QPR	42	18	9	15	73	52	45
10	Southend	42	17	11	14	78	67	45
11	Gillingham	42	18	8	16	52	66	44
12	Clapton Orient	42	14	15	13	52	52	43
13	Swindon	42	14	11	17	75	73	39
14	Crystal Palace	42	13	12	17	62	61	38
15	Bristol Rovers	42	16	4	22	71	80	36
16	Bristol City	42	15	6	21	58	70	36
17	Walsall	42	13	10	19	62	84	36
18	Cardiff	42	14	7	21	54	87	35
19	Newport	42	12	10	20	67	98	34
20	Torquay	42	11	10	21	57	80	32
21	Exeter	42	10	12	20	59	88	32
22	Aldershot	42	7	9	26	50	89	23

SCOTTISH FIRST DIVISION

		P	W	D	L	F	A	Pts
1	Rangers	38	26	9	3	88	32	61
2	Aberdeen	38	23	8	7	89	44	54
3	Celtic	38	22	8	8	89	58	52
4	Motherwell	38	22	7	9	96	54	51
5	Hearts	38	24	3	11	99	60	51
6	Third Lanark	38	20	6	12	79	61	46
7	Falkirk	38	19	6	13	98	66	44
8	Hamilton	38	18	5	15	91	96	41
9	Dundee	38	12	15	11	58	69	39
10	Clyde	38	16	6	16	59	70	38
11	Kilmarnock	38	14	9	15	60	70	37
12	St Johnstone	38	14	8	16	74	68	36
13	Partick	38	11	12	15	73	68	34
14	Arbroath	38	13	5	20	57	84	31
15	Queen's Park	38	9	12	17	51	77	30
16	St Mirren	38	11	7	20	68	81	29
17	Hibernian	38	6	13	19	54	83	25
18	Queen of the S	38	8	8	22	49	95	24
19	Dunfermline	38	5	11	22	65	98	21
20	Albion	38	5	6	27	53	116	16

SCOTTISH SECOND DIVISION

		P	W	D	L	F	A	Pts
1	Ayr	34	25	4	5	122	49	54
2	Morton	34	23	5	6	110	42	51
3	St Bernard's	34	22	4	8	102	51	48
4	Airdrieonians	34	18	8	8	85	60	44
5	East Fife	34	15	8	11	76	51	38
6	Cowdenbeath	34	14	10	10	75	59	38
7	E Stirlingshire	34	18	2	14	81	78	38
8	Raith	34	16	4	14	72	66	36
9	Alloa	34	13	7	14	64	65	33
10	Stenhousemuir	34	14	4	16	82	86	32
11	Leith	34	13	5	16	62	65	31
12	Forfar	34	11	8	15	73	89	30
13	Montrose	34	11	6	17	65	100	28
14	Dundee United	34	9	9	16	72	97	27
15	Dumbarton	34	11	5	18	57	83	27
16	Brechin	34	8	9	17	64	98	25
17	King's Park	34	11	3	20	61	106	25
18	Edinburgh City	34	2	3	29	42	120	7

Ted Harston of Mansfield Town set a record for goals scored in a season in Division Three North. In the 41 games he played during the season, Harston found the net 55 times.

On 30 January 1937, there was not one away win in all the 35 FA Cup and League matches played.

On 17 April 1937, 149,547 people watched Scotland beat England 3-1 at Hampden Park in the last match of the Home Championship. This was both a British and a world record attendance. The receipts totalled £24,303. Seven days later, at the same ground, 144,303 people paid £11,000 to watch Celtic triumph 2-1 over Aberdeen in the Scottish Cup final. Both the attendance and the receipts broke all previous records for the Scottish Cup final.

FA CUP 1936-37

FOURTH ROUND

Luton Town v Sunderland	2-2, 1-3
Swansea Town v York City	0-0, 3-1
Grimsby Town v Walsall	5-1
Wolverhampton Wanderers v Sheffield United	2-2, 2-1
Millwall v Chelsea	3-0
Derby County v Brentford	3-0
Bolton Wanderers v Norwich City	1-1, 2-1
Manchester City v Accrington Stanley	2-0
Tottenham Hotspur v Plymouth Argyle	1-0
Everton v Sheffield Wednesday	3-0
Preston North End v Stoke City	5-1
Exeter City v Leicester City	3-1
Coventry City v Chester	2-0
West Bromwich Albion v Darlington	3-2
Burnley v Bury	4-1
Arsenal v Manchester United	5-0

FIFTH ROUND

Sunderland v Swansea Town	3-0
Grimsby Town v Wolverhampton Wanderers	1-1, 2-6
Millwall v Derby County	2-1
Bolton Wanderers v Manchester City	0-5
Everton v Tottenham Hotspur	1-1, 3-4
Preston North End v Exeter City	5-3
Coventry City v West Bromwich Albion	2-3
Burnley v Arsenal	1-7

SIXTH ROUND

Wolverhampton Wanderers v Sunderland	1-1, 2-2, 0-4
Millwall v Manchester City	2-0
Tottenham Hotspur v Preston North End	1-3
West Bromwich Albion v Arsenal	3-1

SEMI-FINAL

Sunderland v Millwall	2-1
Preston North End v West Bromwich Albion	4-1

FINAL

Sunderland v Preston North End	3-1

SCOTTISH FA CUP 1936-37

SECOND ROUND

Inverness Caledonian v East Fife	1-6
Albion Rovers v Celtic	2-5
Duns v Dumbarton	2-0
Falkirk v Motherwell	0-3
St Mirren v Brechin City	1-0
Cowdenbeath v Solway Star	9-1
Clyde v St Johnstone	3-1
Dundee v Queen's Park	2-0
Hamilton Academicals v Hibernian	2-1
Heart of Midlothian v King's Park	15-0
Aberdeen v Third Lanark	4-2
Partick Thistle v Arbroath	4-1
Queen of the South v Airdrieonians	2-0
Morton	bye

THIRD ROUND

East Fife v Celtic	0-3
Duns v Motherwell	2-5
St Mirren v Cowdenbeath	1-0
Clyde v Dundee	0-0, 1-0
Hamilton Academicals v Heart of Midlothian	2-1
Morton v Partick Thistle	1-1, 2-1
Aberdeen	bye
Queen of the South	bye

FOURTH ROUND

Celtic v Motherwell	4-4, 2-1
St Mirren v Clyde	0-3
Hamilton Academicals v Aberdeen	1-2
Morton v Queen of the South	4-1

SEMI-FINAL

Celtic v Clyde	2-0
Aberdeen v Morton	2-0

FINAL

Celtic v Aberdeen	2-1

FIRST DIVISION

		P	W	D	L	F	A	Pts
1	Arsenal	42	21	10	11	77	44	52
2	Wolves	42	20	11	11	72	49	51
3	Preston	42	16	17	9	64	44	49
4	Charlton	42	16	14	12	65	51	46
5	Middlesbrough	42	19	8	15	72	65	46
6	Brentford	42	18	9	15	69	59	45
7	Bolton	42	15	15	12	64	60	45
8	Sunderland	42	14	16	12	55	57	44
9	Leeds	42	14	15	13	64	69	43
10	Chelsea	42	14	13	15	65	65	41
11	Liverpool	42	15	11	16	65	71	41
12	Blackpool	42	16	8	18	61	66	40
13	Derby	42	15	10	17	66	87	40
14	Everton	42	16	7	19	79	75	39
15	Huddersfield	42	17	5	20	55	68	39
16	Leicester	42	14	11	17	54	75	39
17	Stoke	42	13	12	17	58	59	38
18	Birmingham	42	10	18	14	58	62	38
19	Portsmouth	42	13	12	17	62	68	38
20	Grimsby	42	13	12	17	51	68	38
21	Man City	42	14	8	20	80	77	36
22	WBA	42	14	8	20	74	91	36

SECOND DIVISION

		P	W	D	L	F	A	Pts
1	Aston Villa	42	25	7	10	73	35	57
2	Man United	42	22	9	11	82	50	53
3	Sheff United	42	22	9	11	73	56	53
4	Coventry	42	20	12	10	66	45	52
5	Tottenham	42	19	6	17	76	54	44
6	Burnley	42	17	10	15	54	54	44
7	Bradford PA	42	17	9	16	69	56	43
8	Fulham	42	16	11	15	61	57	43
9	West Ham	42	14	14	14	53	52	42
10	Bury	42	18	5	19	63	60	41
11	Chesterfield	42	16	9	17	63	63	41
12	Luton	42	15	10	17	89	86	40
13	Plymouth	42	14	12	16	57	65	40
14	Norwich	42	14	11	17	56	75	39
15	Southampton	42	15	9	18	55	77	39
16	Blackburn	42	14	10	18	71	80	38
17	Sheff Wed	42	14	10	18	49	56	38
18	Swansea	42	13	12	17	45	73	38
19	Newcastle	42	14	8	20	51	58	36
20	Nottm Forest	42	14	8	20	47	60	36
21	Barnsley	42	11	14	17	50	64	36
22	Stockport	42	11	9	22	43	70	31

THIRD DIVISION (NORTH)

		P	W	D	L	F	A	Pts
1	Tranmere	42	23	10	9	81	41	56
2	Doncaster	42	21	12	9	74	49	54
3	Hull	42	20	13	9	80	43	53
4	Oldham	42	19	13	10	67	46	51
5	Gateshead	42	20	11	11	84	59	51
6	Rotherham	42	20	10	12	68	56	50
7	Lincoln	42	19	8	15	66	50	46
8	Crewe	42	18	9	15	71	53	45
9	Chester	42	16	12	14	77	72	44
10	Wrexham	42	16	11	15	58	63	43
11	York	42	16	10	16	70	68	42
12	Carlisle	42	15	9	18	57	67	39
13	New Brighton	42	15	8	19	60	61	38
14	Bradford City	42	14	10	18	66	69	38
15	Port Vale	42	12	14	16	65	73	38
16	Southport	42	12	14	16	53	82	38
17	Rochdale	42	13	11	18	67	78	37
18	Halifax	42	12	12	18	44	66	36
19	Darlington	42	11	10	21	54	79	32
20	Hartlepools	42	10	12	20	53	80	32
21	Barrow	42	11	10	21	41	71	32
22	Accrington	42	11	7	24	45	75	29

THIRD DIVISION (SOUTH)

		P	W	D	L	F	A	Pts
1	Millwall	42	23	10	9	83	37	56
2	Bristol City	42	21	13	8	68	40	55
3	QPR	42	22	9	11	80	47	53
4	Watford	42	21	11	10	73	43	53
5	Brighton	42	21	9	12	64	44	51
6	Reading	42	20	11	11	71	63	51
7	Crystal Palace	42	18	12	12	67	47	48
8	Swindon	42	17	10	15	49	49	44
9	Northampton	42	17	9	16	51	57	43
10	Cardiff	42	15	12	15	67	54	42
11	Notts County	42	16	9	17	50	50	41
12	Southend	42	15	10	17	70	68	40
13	Bournemouth	42	14	12	16	56	57	40
14	Mansfield	42	15	9	18	62	67	39
15	Bristol Rovers	42	13	13	16	46	61	39
16	Newport	42	11	16	15	43	52	38
17	Exeter	42	13	12	17	57	70	38
18	Aldershot	42	15	5	22	39	59	35
19	Clapton Orient	42	13	7	22	42	61	33
20	Torquay	42	9	12	21	38	73	30
21	Walsall	42	11	7	24	52	88	29
22	Gillingham	42	10	6	26	36	77	26

SCOTTISH FIRST DIVISION

		P	W	D	L	F	A	Pts
1	Celtic	38	27	7	4	114	42	61
2	Hearts	38	26	6	6	90	50	58
3	Rangers	38	18	13	7	75	49	49
4	Falkirk	38	19	9	10	82	52	47
5	Motherwell	38	17	10	11	78	69	44
6	Aberdeen	38	15	9	14	74	59	39
7	Partick	38	15	9	14	68	70	39
8	St Johnstone	38	16	7	15	78	81	39
9	Third Lanark	38	11	13	14	68	73	35
10	Hibernian	38	11	13	14	57	65	35
11	Arbroath	38	11	13	14	58	79	35
12	Queen's Park	38	11	12	15	59	74	34
13	Hamilton	38	13	7	18	81	76	33
14	St Mirren	38	14	5	19	58	66	33
15	Clyde	38	10	13	15	68	78	33
16	Queen of the S	38	11	11	16	58	71	33
17	Ayr	38	9	15	14	66	85	33
18	Kilmarnock	38	12	9	17	65	91	33
19	Dundee	38	13	6	19	70	74	32
20	Morton	38	6	3	29	64	127	15

SCOTTISH SECOND DIVISION

		P	W	D	L	F	A	Pts
1	Raith	34	27	5	2	142	54	59
2	Albion	34	20	8	6	97	50	48
3	Airdrieonians	34	21	5	8	100	53	47
4	St Bernard's	34	20	5	9	75	49	45
5	East Fife	34	19	5	10	104	61	43
6	Cowdenbeath	34	17	9	8	115	71	43
7	Dumbarton	34	17	5	12	85	66	39
8	Stenhousemuir	34	17	5	12	87	78	39
9	Dunfermline	34	17	5	12	82	76	39
10	Leith	34	16	5	13	71	56	37
11	Alloa	34	11	4	19	78	106	26
12	King's Park	34	11	4	19	64	96	26
13	E Stirlingshire	34	9	7	18	55	95	25
14	Dundee United	34	9	5	20	69	104	23
15	Forfar	34	8	6	20	67	100	22
16	Montrose	34	7	8	19	56	88	22
17	Edinburgh City	34	7	3	24	77	135	17
18	Brechin	34	5	2	27	53	139	12

During the season, Jimmy Richardson, the Millwall inside-right, appeared in all three divisions of the Football League, playing with Huddersfield, Newcastle and Millwall.

Raith Rovers, with 142 goals from 34 games, amassed the highest aggregate of goals in a League season in British League football. On their way to this record, they set another, by losing only two of their League matches, the second fewest in any post-1919 division.

FA CUP 1937-38

FOURTH ROUND

Preston North End v Leicester City	2-0
Wolverhampton Wanderers v Arsenal	1-2
Barnsley v Manchester United	2-2, 0-1
Brentford v Portsmouth	2-1
Manchester City v Bury	3-1
Luton Town v Swindon Town	2-1
Charlton Athletic v Leeds United	2-1
Aston Villa v Blackpool	4-0
Everton v Sunderland	0-1
Bradford Park Avenue v Stoke City	1-1, 2-1
Chesterfield v Burnley	3-2
New Brighton v Tottenham Hotspur	0-0, 2-5
York City v West Bromwich Albion	3-2
Nottingham Forest v Middlesbrough	1-3
Sheffield United v Liverpool	1-1, 0-1
Huddersfield Town v Notts County	1-0

FIFTH ROUND

Arsenal v Preston North End	0-1
Brentford v Manchester United	2-0
Luton Town v Manchester City	1-3
Charlton Athletic v Aston Villa	1-1, 2-2, 1-4
Sunderland v Bradford Park Avenue	1-0
Chesterfield v Tottenham Hotspur	2-2, 1-2
York City v Middlesbrough	1-0
Liverpool v Huddersfield Town	0-1

SIXTH ROUND

Brentford v Preston North End	0-3
Aston Villa v Manchester City	3-2
Tottenham Hotspur v Sunderland	0-1
York City v Huddersfield Town	0-0, 1-2

SEMI-FINAL

Preston North End v Aston Villa	2-1
Sunderland v Huddersfield Town	1-3

FINAL

Preston North End v Huddersfield Town	1-0

SCOTTISH FA CUP 1937-38

SECOND ROUND

Rangers v Queen of the South	3-1
Falkirk v St Mirren	3-2
Ross County v Albion Rovers	2-5
Larbert Amateurs v Morton	2-3
Queen's Park v Ayr United	1-1, 1-2
Celtic v Nithsdale Wanderers	5-0
St Bernard's v King's Park	1-1, 4-3
Stenhousemuir v Motherwell	1-1, 1-6
Hamilton Academicals v Forfar Athletic	5-1
Raith Rovers v Edinburgh City	9-2
Partick Thistle v Cowdenbeath	1-0
Aberdeen v St Johnstone	5-1
East Fife v Dundee United	5-0
Kilmarnock	bye

THIRD ROUND

Falkirk v Albion Rovers	4-0
Morton v Ayr United	1-1, 1-4
Celtic v Kilmarnock	1-2
Motherwell v Hamilton Academicals	2-0
Partick Thistle v Raith Rovers	1-2
East Fife v Aberdeen	1-1, 2-1
Rangers	bye
St Bernard's	bye

FOURTH ROUND

Falkirk v Rangers	1-2
Kilmarnock v Ayr United	1-1, 5-0
St Bernard's v Motherwell	3-1
East Fife v Raith Rovers	2-2, 3-2

SEMI-FINAL

Rangers v Kilmarnock	3-4
St Bernard's v East Fife	1-1, 1-1, 1-2

FINAL

Kilmarnock v East Fife	1-1, 2-4

The only Second Division Scottish club to win the Scottish Cup is East Fife, who achieved this distinction in 1937-38. East Fife, who had two players on loan because of injuries to their regular players, took part in five replays during the course of the competition. This included the final, when after a 1-1 draw, East Fife disposed of Kilmarnock by four goals to two.

217

FIRST DIVISION

		P	W	D	L	F	A	Pts
1	Everton	42	27	5	10	88	52	59
2	Wolves	42	22	11	9	88	39	55
3	Charlton	42	22	6	14	75	59	50
4	Middlesbrough	42	20	9	13	93	74	49
5	Arsenal	42	19	9	14	55	41	47
6	Derby	42	19	8	15	66	55	46
7	Stoke	42	17	12	13	71	68	46
8	Bolton	42	15	15	12	67	58	45
9	Preston	42	16	12	14	63	59	44
10	Grimsby	42	16	11	15	61	69	43
11	Liverpool	42	14	14	14	62	63	42
12	Aston Villa	42	15	11	16	71	60	41
13	Leeds	42	16	9	17	59	67	41
14	Man United	42	11	16	15	57	65	38
15	Blackpool	42	12	14	16	56	68	38
16	Sunderland	42	13	12	17	54	67	38
17	Portsmouth	42	12	13	17	47	70	37
18	Brentford	42	14	8	20	53	74	36
19	Huddersfield	42	12	11	19	58	64	35
20	Chelsea	42	12	9	21	64	80	33
21	Birmingham	42	12	8	22	62	84	32
22	Leicester	42	9	11	22	48	82	29

SECOND DIVISION

		P	W	D	L	F	A	Pts
1	Blackburn	42	25	5	12	94	60	55
2	Sheff United	42	20	14	8	69	41	54
3	Sheff Wed	42	21	11	10	88	59	53
4	Coventry	42	21	8	13	62	45	50
5	Man City	42	21	7	14	96	72	49
6	Chesterfield	42	20	9	13	69	52	49
7	Luton	42	22	5	15	82	66	49
8	Tottenham	42	19	9	14	67	62	47
9	Newcastle	42	18	10	14	61	48	46
10	WBA	42	18	9	15	89	72	45
11	West Ham	42	17	10	15	70	52	44
12	Fulham	42	17	10	15	61	55	44
13	Millwall	42	14	14	14	64	53	42
14	Burnley	42	15	9	18	50	56	39
15	Plymouth	42	15	8	19	49	55	38
16	Bury	42	12	13	17	65	74	37
17	Bradford PA	42	12	11	19	61	82	35
18	Southampton	42	13	9	20	56	82	35
19	Swansea	42	11	12	19	50	83	34
20	Nottm Forest	42	10	11	21	49	82	31
21	Norwich	42	13	5	24	50	91	31
22	Tranmere	42	6	5	31	39	99	17

THIRD DIVISION (SOUTH)

		P	W	D	L	F	A	Pts
1	Newport	42	22	11	9	58	45	55
2	Crystal Palace	42	20	12	10	71	52	52
3	Brighton	42	19	11	12	68	49	49
4	Watford	42	17	12	13	62	51	46
5	Reading	42	16	14	12	69	59	46
6	QPR	42	15	14	13	68	49	44
7	Ipswich	42	16	12	14	62	52	44
8	Bristol City	42	16	12	14	61	63	44
9	Swindon	42	18	8	16	72	77	44
10	Aldershot	42	16	12	14	53	66	44
11	Notts County	42	17	9	16	59	54	43
12	Southend	42	16	9	17	61	64	41
13	Cardiff	42	15	11	16	61	65	41
14	Exeter	42	13	14	15	65	82	40
15	Bournemouth	42	13	13	16	52	58	39
16	Mansfield	42	12	15	15	44	62	39
17	Northampton	42	15	8	19	51	58	38
18	Port Vale	42	14	9	19	52	58	37
19	Torquay	42	14	9	19	54	70	37
20	Clapton Orient	42	11	13	18	53	55	35
21	Walsall	42	11	11	20	68	69	33
22	Bristol Rovers	42	10	13	19	55	61	33

THIRD DIVISION (NORTH)

		P	W	D	L	F	A	Pts
1	Barnsley	42	30	7	5	94	34	67
2	Doncaster	42	21	14	7	87	47	56
3	Bradford City	42	22	8	12	89	56	52
4	Southport	42	20	10	12	75	54	50
5	Oldham	42	22	5	15	76	59	49
6	Chester	42	20	9	13	88	70	49
7	Hull	42	18	10	14	83	74	46
8	Crewe	42	19	6	17	82	70	44
9	Stockport	42	17	9	16	91	77	43
10	Gateshead	42	14	14	14	74	67	42
11	Rotherham	42	17	8	17	64	64	42
12	Halifax	42	13	16	13	52	54	42
13	Barrow	42	16	9	17	66	65	41
14	Wrexham	42	17	7	18	66	79	41
15	Rochdale	42	15	9	18	92	82	39
16	New Brighton	42	15	9	18	68	73	39
17	Lincoln	42	12	9	21	66	92	33
18	Darlington	42	13	7	22	62	92	33
19	Carlisle	42	13	7	22	64	111	33
20	York	42	12	8	22	66	92	32
21	Hartlepools	42	12	7	23	55	94	31
22	Accrington	42	7	6	29	49	103	20

SCOTTISH FIRST DIVISION

		P	W	D	L	F	A	Pts
1	Rangers	38	25	9	4	112	55	59
2	Celtic	38	20	8	10	99	53	48
3	Aberdeen	38	20	6	12	91	61	46
4	Hearts	38	20	5	13	98	70	45
5	Falkirk	38	19	7	12	73	63	45
6	Queen of the S	38	17	9	12	69	64	43
7	Hamilton	38	18	5	15	67	71	41
8	St Johnstone	38	17	6	15	85	82	40
9	Clyde	38	17	5	16	78	70	39
10	Kilmarnock	38	15	9	14	73	86	39
11	Partick Thistle	38	17	4	17	74	87	38
12	Motherwell	38	16	5	17	82	86	37
13	Hibernian	38	14	7	17	68	69	35
14	Ayr	38	13	9	16	76	83	35
15	Third Lanark	38	12	8	18	80	96	32
16	Albion	38	12	6	20	65	90	30
17	Arbroath	38	11	8	19	54	75	30
18	St Mirren	38	11	7	20	57	80	29
19	Queen's Park	38	11	5	22	57	83	27
20	Raith	38	10	2	26	65	99	22

SCOTTISH SECOND DIVISION

		P	W	D	L	F	A	Pts
1	Cowdenbeath	34	28	4	2	120	45	60
2	Alloa	34	22	4	8	91	46	48
3	East Fife	34	21	6	7	99	61	48
4	Airdrieonians	34	21	5	8	85	57	47
5	Dunfermline	34	18	5	11	99	78	41
6	Dundee	34	15	7	12	99	63	37
7	St Bernard's	34	15	6	13	79	79	36
8	Stenhousemuir	34	15	5	14	74	69	35
9	Dundee United	34	15	3	16	78	69	33
10	Brechin	34	11	9	14	82	106	31
11	Dumbarton	34	9	12	13	68	76	30
12	Morton	34	11	6	17	74	88	28
13	King's Park	34	12	2	20	87	92	26
14	Montrose	34	10	5	19	82	96	25
15	Forfar	34	11	3	20	74	138	25
16	Leith	34	10	4	20	57	83	24
17	E Stirlingshire	34	9	4	21	89	130	22
18	Edinburgh	34	6	4	24	58	119	16

Dixie Dean goes West
On 25 January 1939, Dixie Dean, the most prolific goalscorer of the time, left Notts County and English football to join Sligo Rovers in Eire. In April of that year, he played centre-forward for Sligo in the FA of Ireland Cup final against Shelbourne. The game ended in a 1-1 draw, and Sligo lost the replay 1-0.

1938-39 was the last season when players went unidentified. In 1939-40, players wore numbers in League games for the first time.

In Division Two, Tranmere Rovers lost 31 of their 42 League games, a Division Two record. Wolves set a First Division record in 1938-39 by conceding only 39 goals in 42 games, a record under the new offside rule. Barnsley also set a record—in Division Three North—letting in only 34 goals in 42 games.

FA CUP 1938-39

FOURTH ROUND

Portsmouth v West Bromwich Albion	2-0
West Ham United v Tottenham Hotspur	3-3, 1-1, 2-1
Preston North End v Aston Villa	2-0
Cardiff City v Newcastle United	0-0, 1-4
Leeds United v Huddersfield Town	2-4
Notts County v Walsall	0-0, 0-4
Middlesbrough v Sunderland	0-2
Blackburn Rovers v Southend United	4-2
Wolverhampton Wanderers v Leicester City	5-1
Liverpool v Stockport County	5-1
Everton v Doncaster Rovers	8-0
Birmingham v Chelmsford City	6-0
Chelsea v Fulham	3-0
Sheffield Wednesday v Chester	1-1, 1-1, 2-0
Sheffield United v Manchester City	2-0
Millwall v Grimsby Town	2-2, 2-3

FIFTH ROUND

Portsmouth v West Ham United	2-0
Newcastle United v Preston North End	1-2
Huddersfield Town v Walsall	3-0
Sunderland v Blackburn Rovers	1-1, 0-0, 0-1
Wolverhampton Wanderers v Liverpool	4-1
Birmingham v Everton	2-2, 1-2
Chelsea v Sheffield Wednesday	1-1, 0-0, 3-1
Sheffield United v Grimsby Town	0-0, 0-1

SIXTH ROUND

Portsmouth v Preston North End	1-0
Huddersfield Town v Blackburn Rovers	1-1, 2-1
Wolverhampton Wanderers v Everton	2-0
Chelsea v Grimsby Town	0-1

SEMI-FINAL

Portsmouth v Huddersfield Town	2-1
Wolverhampton Wanderers v Grimsby Town	5-0

FINAL

Portsmouth v Wolverhampton Wanderers	4-1

SCOTTISH FA CUP 1938-39

SECOND ROUND

Dundee v Clyde	0-0, 0-1
Rangers v Hamilton Academicals	2-0
Blairgowrie v Buckie Thistle	3-3, 1-4
Third Lanark v Cowdenbeath	3-0
Dunfermline Athletic v Duns	2-0
Hibernian v Kilmarnock	3-1
Falkirk v Airdrieonians	7-0
Aberdeen v Queen's Park	5-1
Queen of the South v Babcock & Wilcox	5-0
Heart of Midlothian v Elgin City	14-1
Montrose v Celtic	1-7
Edinburgh City v St Mirren	1-3
Dundee United v Motherwell	1-5
Alloa Athletic	bye

THIRD ROUND

Rangers v Clyde	1-4
Buckie Thistle v Third Lanark	0-6
Dunfermline Athletic v Alloa Athletic	1-1, 2-3
Falkirk v Aberdeen	2-3
Heart of Midlothian v Celtic	2-2, 1-2
Motherwell v St Mirren	4-2
Hibernian	bye
Queen of the South	bye

FOURTH ROUND

Clyde v Third Lanark	1-0
Hibernian v Alloa Athletic	3-1
Aberdeen v Queen of the South	2-0
Motherwell v Celtic	3-1

SEMI-FINAL

Clyde v Hibernian	1-0
Aberdeen v Motherwell	1-1, 1-3

FINAL

Clyde v Motherwell	4-0

FIRST DIVISION 1939-40

	P	W	D	L	F	A	Pts
Blackpool	3	3	0	0	5	2	6
Sheff United	3	2	1	0	3	1	5
Arsenal	3	2	1	0	8	4	5
Liverpool	3	2	0	1	6	3	4
Everton	3	1	2	0	5	4	4
Bolton	3	2	0	1	6	5	4
Charlton	3	2	0	1	3	4	4
Derby	3	2	0	1	3	3	4
Man United	3	1	1	1	5	3	3
Chelsea	3	1	1	1	4	4	3
Stoke	3	1	1	1	7	4	3
Brentford	3	1	1	1	3	3	3
Leeds	3	1	1	1	2	4	3
Grimsby	3	1	1	1	2	4	3
Sunderland	3	1	0	2	6	7	2
Aston Villa	3	1	0	2	3	3	2
Wolverhampton	3	0	2	1	3	4	2
Huddersfield	3	1	0	2	2	3	2
Preston	3	0	2	1	0	2	2
Portsmouth	3	1	0	2	3	5	2
Blackburn	3	0	1	2	3	5	1
Middlesbrough	3	0	1	2	3	8	1

SECOND DIVISION 1939-40

	P	W	D	L	F	A	Pts
Luton	3	2	1	0	7	1	5
Birmingham	3	2	1	0	5	1	5
West Ham	3	2	0	1	5	4	4
Coventry	3	1	2	0	8	6	4
Leicester	3	2	0	1	6	5	4
Nottm Forest	3	2	0	1	5	5	4
Plymouth	3	2	0	1	4	3	4
Tottenham	3	1	2	0	6	5	4
WBA	3	1	1	1	8	8	3
Bury	3	1	1	1	4	5	3
Newport	3	1	1	1	5	4	3
Millwall	3	1	1	1	5	4	3
Man City	3	1	1	1	6	5	3
Southampton	3	1	0	2	5	6	2
Swansea	3	1	0	2	5	11	2
Barnsley	3	1	0	2	7	8	2
Chesterfield	2	1	0	1	2	2	2
Newcastle	3	1	0	2	8	6	2
Sheff Wed	3	1	0	2	3	5	2
Bradford	3	0	1	2	2	7	1
Fulham	3	0	1	2	3	6	1
Burnley	2	0	1	1	1	3	1

THIRD DIVISION (NORTH) 1939-40

	P	W	D	L	F	A	Pts
Accrington	3	3	0	0	6	1	6
Halifax	3	2	1	0	6	1	5
Darlington	3	2	1	0	5	2	5
Chester	3	2	1	0	5	2	5
Rochdale	3	2	0	1	2	2	4
New Brighton	3	2	0	1	4	5	4
Tranmere	3	1	1	1	6	6	3
Rotherham	3	1	1	1	5	6	3
Wrexham	3	1	1	1	3	2	3
Lincoln	3	1	1	1	6	7	3
Crewe	2	1	1	0	3	0	3
Oldham	3	1	0	2	3	5	2
Doncaster	3	1	0	2	4	5	2
Gateshead	3	1	0	2	6	7	2
Southport	3	0	2	1	4	5	2
Hull	2	0	2	0	3	3	2
Hartlepools	3	0	2	1	1	4	2
Barrow	3	0	2	1	4	5	2
Carlisle	2	1	0	1	3	3	2
York	3	0	1	2	3	5	1
Bradford City	3	0	1	2	3	6	1
Stockport	2	0	0	2	0	5	0

THIRD DIVISION (SOUTH) 1939-40

	P	W	D	L	F	A	Pts
Reading	3	2	1	0	8	2	5
Exeter	3	2	1	0	5	3	5
Cardiff	3	2	0	1	5	4	4
Crystal Palace	3	2	0	1	8	9	4
Brighton	3	1	2	0	5	4	4
Ipswich	3	1	2	0	5	3	4
Notts County	2	2	0	0	6	3	4
Southend	3	1	1	1	3	3	3
Bristol City	3	1	1	1	5	5	3
Clapton Orient	3	0	3	0	3	3	3
Mansfield	3	1	1	1	8	8	3
Norwich	3	1	1	1	4	4	3
Torquay	3	0	3	0	4	4	3
Bournemouth	3	1	1	1	13	4	3
Walsall	3	1	1	1	3	3	3
Northampton	3	1	0	2	2	12	2
QPR	3	0	2	1	4	5	2
Watford	3	0	2	1	4	5	2
Bristol Rovers	3	0	1	2	2	7	1
Port Vale	2	0	1	1	0	1	1
Aldershot	3	0	1	2	3	4	1
Swindon	3	0	1	2	2	4	1

SCOTTISH DIVISION 'A' 1939-40

	P	W	D	L	F	A	Pts
Rangers	5	4	1	0	14	3	9
Falkirk	5	4	0	1	20	10	8
Aberdeen	5	3	0	2	9	9	6
Celtic	5	3	0	2	7	7	6
Hearts	5	2	2	1	13	9	6
Partick Thistle	5	2	2	1	7	7	6
Motherwell	5	2	1	2	14	12	5
Hamilton	5	2	1	1	7	11	5
Third Lanark	5	2	1	2	9	8	5
Queen of the S	5	2	1	2	10	9	5
Albion	5	2	1	2	12	7	5
St Mirren	5	1	3	1	8	8	5
Kilmarnock	5	2	1	2	10	9	5
Hibernian	5	2	0	3	11	13	4
Alloa	5	2	0	3	8	13	4
Arbroath	5	2	0	3	9	9	4
St Johnstone	5	2	0	3	7	8	4
Ayr	5	2	0	3	10	17	4
Clyde	5	1	0	4	10	14	2
Cowdenbeath	5	1	0	4	6	14	2

SCOTTISH DIVISION 'B' 1939-40

	P	W	D	L	F	A	Pts
Dundee	4	3	1	0	13	5	7
Dunfermline	4	2	2	0	10	5	6
King's Park	4	2	2	0	11	7	6
East Fife	4	2	1	1	12	6	5
Queen's Park	4	1	3	0	7	5	5
Stenhousemuir	4	2	1	1	6	5	5
Dundee United	4	2	1	1	8	7	5
Dumbarton	4	2	1	1	9	9	5
E Stirlingshire	4	1	2	1	7	7	4
St Bernard's	4	1	2	1	7	7	4
Airdrieonians	4	2	0	2	7	8	4
Edinburgh	4	1	1	2	9	8	3
Montrose	4	1	1	2	7	8	3
Raith	4	1	1	2	8	12	3
Morton	4	1	1	2	4	7	3
Leith	4	1	0	3	4	7	2
Brechin	4	0	2	2	3	8	2
Forfar	4	0	0	4	7	18	0

WINNERS 1939-40

League Cup West Ham United
Midland League Wolverhampton Wanderers
North East League Huddersfield Town
North West League Bury
South 'A' League Arsenal
South 'B' League Queen's Park Rangers
South 'C' League Tottenham Hotspur
South 'D' League Crystal Palace
West League Stoke City
South West League Plymouth Argyle
East Midland League Chesterfield
Scottish Emergency Cup Rangers
Scottish Regional League West & South Rangers
Scottish Regional League East & North Falkirk
Irish FA Cup Ballymena United
FA of Ireland Cup (Eire) Shamrock Rovers
League of Ireland (Eire) St James' Gate

WINNERS 1940-41

League Cup Preston North End
Football League South Watford
Northern Regional League Preston North End
Southern Regional League Crystal Palace
London Cup Reading
Lancashire Cup Manchester United
Midland Cup Leicester City
Combined Cities Cup Middlesbrough
Western Regional Cup Bristol City
Scottish Southern League Cup Rangers
Scottish Summer Cup Hibernian
Scottish Southern League Rangers
Irish FA Cup Belfast Celtic
FA of Ireland Cup (Eire) Cork United
League of Ireland (Eire) Cork United

WINNERS 1941-42

League Cup Wolverhampton Wanderers
League North Blackpool
League South Leicester City
London Cup Brentford
London League Arsenal
Scottish Southern League Cup Rangers
Scottish Summer Cup Rangers
Scottish Southern League Rangers
Scottish North Eastern League 1st series Rangers
Scottish North Eastern League 2nd series Aberdeen
Irish FA Cup Linfield
FA of Ireland Cup (Eire) Dundalk
League of Ireland (Eire) Cork United

WINNERS 1942-43

League North Cup Blackpool
League North Blackpool
League South Cup Arsenal
League South Arsenal
League West Cup Swansea Town
League West Lovells Athletic
Scottish Southern League Cup Rangers
Scottish Summer Cup St Mirren
Scottish Southern League Rangers
Scottish North Eastern League 1st series Aberdeen
Scottish North Eastern League 2nd series Aberdeen
Irish FA Cup Belfast Celtic
FA of Ireland Cup (Eire) Drumcondra
League of Ireland (Eire) Cork United

WINNERS 1943-44

League North Cup Aston Villa
League North Blackpool
League South Cup Charlton Athletic
League South Tottenham Hotspur
League West Cup Bath City
League West Lovells Athletic
Scottish Southern League Cup Hibernian
Scottish Summer Cup Motherwell
Scottish Southern League Rangers
Scottish North Eastern League 1st series Raith Rovers
Scottish North Eastern League 2nd series Aberdeen
Irish FA Cup Belfast Celtic
FA of Ireland Cup (Eire) Shamrock Rovers
League of Ireland (Eire) Shelbourne

Above *When War broke out, the 1939-40 football season had hardly got under way. The tables above show the state of each division when the League programme was halted. Goal average has not been calculated, as at such an early stage in the season, the figures presented in these hitherto unpublished tables serve as a guide to each team's performance, rather than a means of listing the teams in order.*

The Englishman who played for Wales
Stanley Mortensen made his war-time international debut against his own country. At Wembley, on 25 September 1943, England played Wales. Mortensen was reserve for England, but when the injured Welsh left-half, Ivor Powell, was unable to resume after the interval, it was agreed by both sides that Mortensen should take Powell's place. The game ended in an 8-3 victory for England.

219

WINNERS 1944-45

League North Cup Bolton Wanderers
League North Huddersfield Town
League South Cup Chelsea
League South Tottenham Hotspur
League West Cup Bath City
League West Cardiff City
Scottish Southern League Cup Rangers
Scottish Summer Cup Partick Thistle
Scottish Southern League Rangers
Scottish North Eastern League 1st series Dundee
Scottish North Eastern League 2nd series Aberdeen
Irish FA Cup Linfield
FA of Ireland Cup (Eire) Shamrock Rovers
League of Ireland (Eire) Cork United

WINNERS 1945-46

League North Sheffield United
League South Birmingham City
League Three North Cup Rotherham United
League Three North (West) Accrington Stanley
League Three North (East) Rotherham United
League Three South Cup Bournemouth
League Three South (North) Queen's Park Rangers
League Three South (South) Crystal Palace
Scottish Southern League 'A' Rangers
Scottish Southern League 'B' Dundee
Scottish Victory Cup Rangers
Irish FA Cup Linfield
FA of Ireland Cup (Eire) Drumcondra
League of Ireland (Eire) Cork United

SCOTTISH SOUTHERN LEAGUE CUP 1945-46 (LEAGUE CUP)

SECTION WINNERS

Division A	Division B
1 Heart of Midlothian	1 East Fife
2 Rangers	2 Ayr United
3 Aberdeen	3 Airdrieonians
4 Clyde	4 Dundee

QUARTER-FINAL

Aberdeen v Ayr United	2-0
Airdrieonians v Clyde	1-0
Heart of Midlothian v East Fife	3-0
Rangers v Dundee	3-1

SEMI-FINAL

Aberdeen v Airdrieonians	2-2, 5-3
Rangers v Hearts	2-1

FINAL

Aberdeen v Rangers	3-2

LEADING GOALSCORERS (ENGLAND) 1939-46

Albert Stubbins, Newcastle United	226
Jock Dodds, Blackpool	221
Tommy Lawton, Everton, Tranmere Rovers, Aldershot and Chelsea	212

FA CUP 1945-46

THIRD ROUND (two legs)

Stoke City v Burnley	3-1, 1-2
Huddersfield Town v Sheffield United	1-1, 0-2
Mansfield Town v Sheffield Wednesday	0-0, 0-5
Chesterfield v York City	1-1, 2-3
Bolton Wanderers v Blackburn Rovers	1-0, 3-1
Chester v Liverpool	0-2, 1-2
Wrexham v Blackpool	1-4, 1-4
Leeds United v Middlesbrough	4-4, 2-7
Accrington Stanley v Manchester United	2-2, 1-5
Preston North End v Everton	2-1, 2-2
Charlton Athletic v Fulham	3-1, 1-2
Lovells Athletic v Wolverhampton Wanderers	2-4, 1-8
Southampton v Newport County	4-3, 2-1
Queen's Park Rangers v Crystal Palace	0-0, 0-0*, 1-0
Bristol City v Swansea Town	5-1, 2-2
Tottenham Hotspur v Brentford	2-2, 0-2
Chelsea v Leicester City	1-1, 2-0
West Ham United v Arsenal	6-0, 0-1
Northampton Town v Millwall	2-2, 0-3
Coventry City v Aston Villa	2-1, 0-2
Norwich City v Brighton	1-2, 1-4
Aldershot v Plymouth Argyle	2-0, 1-0
Luton Town v Derby County	0-6, 0-3
Cardiff City v West Bromwich Albion	1-1, 0-4
Newcastle United v Barnsley	4-2, 0-3
Rotherham United v Gateshead	2-2, 2-0
Bradford Park Avenue v Port Vale	2-1, 1-1
Manchester City v Barrow	6-2, 2-2
Grimsby Town v Sunderland	1-3, 1-2
Bury v Rochdale	3-3, 4-2
Birmingham City v Portsmouth	1-0, 0-0
Nottingham Forest v Watford	1-1, 1-1*, 0-1

*abandoned

FOURTH ROUND (two legs)

Stoke City v Sheffield United	2-0, 2-3
Sheffield Wednesday v York City	5-1, 6-1
Bolton Wanderers v Liverpool	5-0, 0-2
Blackpool v Middlesbrough	3-2, 2-3, 0-1
Manchester United v Preston North End	1-0, 1-3
Charlton Athletic v Wolverhampton Wanderers	5-2, 1-1
Southampton v Queen's Park Rangers	0-1, 3-4
Bristol City v Brentford	2-1, 0-5
Chelsea v West Ham United	2-0, 0-1
Millwall v Aston Villa	2-4, 1-9
Brighton v Aldershot	3-0, 4-1
Derby County v West Bromwich Albion	1-0, 3-1
Barnsley v Rotherham United	3-0, 1-2
Bradford Park Avenue v Manchester City	1-3, 8-2
Sunderland v Bury	3-1, 4-5
Birmingham City v Watford	5-0, 1-1

FIFTH ROUND (two legs)

Stoke City v Sheffield Wednesday	2-0, 0-0
Bolton Wanderers v Middlesbrough	1-0, 1-1
Preston North End v Charlton Athletic	1-1, 0-6
Queen's Park Rangers v Brentford	1-3, 0-0
Chelsea v Aston Villa	0-1, 0-1
Brighton v Derby County	1-4, 0-6
Barnsley v Bradford Park Avenue	0-1, 1-1
Sunderland v Birmingham City	1-0, 1-3

SIXTH ROUND (two legs)

Stoke City v Bolton Wanderers	0-2, 0-0
Charlton Athletic v Brentford	6-3, 3-1
Aston Villa v Derby County	3-4, 1-1
Bradford Park Avenue v Birmingham City	2-2, 0-6

SEMI-FINAL

Bolton Wanderers v Charlton Athletic	0-2
Derby County v Birmingham City	1-1, 4-0

FINAL

Derby County v Charlton Athletic	4-1

TOPIX

TOPIX

Top In 1945 Jack Tinn, manager of Portsmouth, proudly shows Field Marshal Montgomery the FA Cup won by Portsmouth six years earlier. There was no FA Cup competition during the War, so Pompey held the Cup until the competition restarted in 1945-46.

Above A shot by Duncan, deflected by Charlton's Bert Turner, enters the net for Derby's first goal in the 1946 Cup Final. During this game, the ball burst. Oddly enough, the chances of this happening were discussed in a BBC broadcast shortly before the game, and the referee, Mr E D Smith of Cumberland, remarked that it was a million-to-one chance. Even more curiously, the ball also burst when Derby played Charlton in a League match just five days after their Wembley meeting.

FIRST DIVISION

		P	W	D	L	F	A	Pts
1	Liverpool	42	25	7	10	84	52	57
2	Man United	42	22	12	8	95	54	56
3	Wolves	42	25	6	11	98	56	56
4	Stoke	42	24	7	11	90	53	55
5	Blackpool	42	22	6	14	71	70	50
6	Sheff United	42	21	7	14	89	75	49
7	Preston	42	18	11	13	76	74	47
8	Aston Villa	42	18	9	15	67	53	45
9	Sunderland	42	18	8	16	65	66	44
10	Everton	42	17	9	16	62	67	43
11	Middlesbrough	42	17	8	17	73	68	42
12	Portsmouth	42	16	9	17	66	60	41
13	Arsenal	42	16	9	17	72	70	41
14	Derby	42	18	5	19	73	79	41
15	Chelsea	42	16	7	19	69	84	39
16	Grimsby	42	13	12	17	61	82	38
17	Blackburn	42	14	8	20	45	53	36
18	Bolton	42	13	8	21	57	69	34
19	Charlton	42	11	12	19	57	71	34
20	Huddersfield	42	13	7	22	53	79	33
21	Brentford	42	9	7	26	45	88	25
22	Leeds	42	6	6	30	45	90	18

SECOND DIVISION

		P	W	D	L	F	A	Pts
1	Man City	42	26	10	6	78	35	62
2	Burnley	42	22	14	6	65	29	58
3	Birmingham	42	25	5	12	74	33	55
4	Chesterfield	42	18	14	10	58	44	50
5	Newcastle	42	19	10	13	95	62	48
6	Tottenham	42	17	14	11	65	53	48
7	WBA	42	20	8	14	88	75	48
8	Coventry	42	16	13	13	66	59	45
9	Leicester	42	18	7	17	69	64	43
10	Barnsley	42	17	8	17	84	86	42
11	Nottm Forest	42	15	10	17	69	74	40
12	West Ham	42	16	8	18	70	76	40
13	Luton	42	16	7	19	71	73	39
14	Southampton	42	15	9	18	69	76	39
15	Fulham	42	15	9	18	63	74	39
16	Bradford PA	42	14	11	17	65	77	39
17	Bury	42	12	12	18	80	78	36
18	Millwall	42	14	8	20	56	79	36
19	Plymouth	42	14	5	23	79	96	33
20	Sheff Wed	42	12	8	22	67	88	32
21	Swansea	42	11	7	24	55	83	29
22	Newport	42	10	3	29	61	133	23

THIRD DIVISION (NORTH)

		P	W	D	L	F	A	Pts
1	Doncaster	42	33	6	3	123	40	72
2	Rotherham	42	29	6	7	114	53	64
3	Chester	42	25	6	11	95	51	56
4	Stockport	42	24	2	16	78	53	50
5	Bradford City	42	20	10	12	62	47	50
6	Rochdale	42	19	10	13	80	64	48
7	Wrexham	42	17	12	13	65	51	46
8	Crewe	42	17	9	16	70	74	43
9	Barrow	42	17	7	18	54	62	41
10	Tranmere	42	17	7	18	66	77	41
11	Hull	42	16	8	18	49	53	40
12	Lincoln	42	17	5	20	86	87	39
13	Hartlepools	42	15	9	18	64	73	39
14	Gateshead	42	16	6	20	62	72	38
15	York	42	14	9	19	67	81	37
16	Carlisle	42	14	9	19	70	93	37
17	Darlington	42	15	6	21	68	80	36
18	New Brighton	42	14	8	20	57	77	36
19	Oldham	42	12	8	22	55	80	32
20	Accrington	42	14	4	24	56	92	32
21	Southport	42	7	11	24	53	85	25
22	Halifax	42	8	6	28	43	92	22

THIRD DIVISION (SOUTH)

		P	W	D	L	F	A	Pts
1	Cardiff	42	30	6	6	93	30	66
2	QPR	42	23	11	8	74	40	57
3	Bristol City	42	20	11	11	94	56	51
4	Swindon	42	19	11	12	84	73	49
5	Walsall	42	17	12	13	74	59	46
6	Ipswich	42	16	14	12	61	53	46
7	Bournemouth	42	18	8	16	72	54	44
8	Southend	42	17	10	15	71	60	44
9	Reading	42	16	11	15	83	74	43
10	Port Vale	42	17	9	16	68	63	43
11	Torquay	42	15	12	15	52	61	42
12	Notts County	42	15	10	17	63	63	40
13	Northampton	42	15	10	17	72	75	40
14	Bristol Rovers	42	16	8	18	59	69	40
15	Exeter	42	15	9	18	60	69	39
16	Watford	42	17	5	20	61	76	39
17	Brighton	42	13	12	17	54	72	38
18	Crystal Palace	42	13	11	18	49	62	37
19	Leyton Orient	42	12	8	22	54	75	32
20	Aldershot	42	10	12	20	48	78	32
21	Norwich	42	10	8	24	64	100	28
22	Mansfield	42	9	10	23	48	96	28

SCOTTISH DIVISION 'A'

		P	W	D	L	F	A	Pts
1	Rangers	30	21	4	5	76	26	46
2	Hibernian	30	19	6	5	69	33	44
3	Aberdeen	30	16	7	7	58	41	39
4	Hearts	30	16	6	8	52	43	38
5	Partick Thistle	30	16	3	11	74	59	35
6	Morton	30	12	10	8	58	45	34
7	Celtic	30	13	6	11	53	55	32
8	Motherwell	30	12	5	13	58	54	29
9	Third Lanark	30	11	6	13	56	64	28
10	Clyde	30	9	9	12	55	65	27
11	Falkirk	30	8	10	12	62	61	26
12	Queen of the S	30	9	8	13	44	69	26
13	Queen's Park	30	8	6	16	47	60	22
14	St Mirren	30	9	4	17	47	65	22
15	Kilmarnock	30	6	9	15	44	66	21
16	Hamilton	30	2	7	21	38	85	11

SCOTTISH DIVISION 'B'

		P	W	D	L	F	A	Pts
1	Dundee	26	21	3	2	113	30	45
2	Airdrieonians	26	19	4	3	78	38	42
3	East Fife	26	12	7	7	58	39	31
4	Albion	26	10	7	9	50	54	27
5	Alloa	26	11	5	10	51	57	27
6	Raith	26	10	6	10	45	52	26
7	Stenhousemuir	26	8	7	11	43	53	23
8	Dunfermline	26	10	3	13	50	72	23
9	St Johnstone	26	9	4	13	45	47	22
10	Dundee United	26	9	4	13	53	60	22
11	Ayr	26	9	2	15	56	73	20
12	Arbroath	26	7	6	13	42	63	20
13	Dumbarton	26	7	4	15	41	54	18
14	Cowdenbeath	26	6	6	14	44	77	18

When Italy beat Hungary 3-2 on 11 May 1947, a record ten members of the victorious Italian team came from Torino.

Hull City used 42 players in the Third Division North, 1946-47. This was only the third time in the history of the League that such a large pool of players had been used in one season by a single club.

Cardiff equalled a Division Three South record by winning 30 of their 42 matches. By contrast, Leeds set a First Division record by losing 30 of their 42 matches.

Doncaster Rovers enjoyed an enormously successful season in winning the Third Division North championship in 1946-47. They set four League records during the course of the season. Their points total (72) was the highest number of points ever won by a club in any division of the League; that total included 37 points won away from home, also a League record. By winning 18 of their 21 away games, Doncaster established a third League record, for the most games won away from home and, in all, Doncaster Rovers won 33 of their 42 Division Three North games to set another League record. They also equalled the record for the division by losing just three matches during the season.

FA CUP 1946-47

FOURTH ROUND

West Bromwich Albion v Charlton Athletic	1-2
Blackburn Rovers v Port Vale	2-0
Preston North End v Barnsley	6-0
Sheffield Wednesday v Everton	2-1
Newcastle United v Southampton	3-1
Brentford v Leicester City	0-0, 0-0, 1-4
Wolverhampton Wanderers v Sheffield United	0-0, 0-2
Chester v Stoke City	0-0, 2-3
Burnley v Coventry City	2-0
Luton Town v Swansea Town	2-0
Middlesbrough v Chesterfield	2-1
Manchester United v Nottingham Forest	0-2
Liverpool v Grimsby Town	2-0
Chelsea v Derby County	2-2, 0-1
Birmingham City v Portsmouth	1-0
Bolton Wanderers v Manchester City	3-3, 0-1

FIFTH ROUND

Charlton Athletic v Blackburn Rovers	1-0
Sheffield Wednesday v Preston North End	0-2
Newcastle United v Leicester City	1-1, 2-1
Stoke City v Sheffield United	0-1
Luton Town v Burnley	0-0, 0-3
Nottingham Forest v Middlesbrough	2-2, 2-6
Liverpool v Derby County	1-0
Birmingham City v Manchester City	5-0

SIXTH ROUND

Charlton Athletic v Preston North End	2-1
Sheffield United v Newcastle United	0-2
Middlesbrough v Burnley	1-1, 0-1
Liverpool v Birmingham City	4-1

SEMI-FINAL

Charlton Athletic v Newcastle United	4-0
Burnley v Liverpool	0-0, 1-0

FINAL

Charlton Athletic v Burnley	1-0

SCOTTISH FA CUP 1946-47

SECOND ROUND

Aberdeen v Ayr United	8-0
East Fife v East Stirlingshire	5-1
Morton	bye
Dundee	bye
Albion Rovers	bye
Arbroath	bye
Raith Rovers	bye
Heart of Midlothian	bye
Cowdenbeath	bye
Hibernian	bye
Rangers	bye
Dumbarton	bye
Third Lanark	bye
Motherwell	bye
Falkirk	bye
Queen's Park	bye

THIRD ROUND

Morton v Aberdeen	1-1, 1-2
Dundee v Albion Rovers	3-0
Arbroath v Raith Rovers	5-4
Heart of Midlothian v Cowdenbeath	2-0
Rangers v Hibernian	0-0, 0-2
Dumbarton v Third Lanark	2-0
Falkirk v Motherwell	0-0, 0-1
East Fife v Queen's Park	3-1

FOURTH ROUND

Dundee v Aberdeen	1-2
Arbroath v Heart of Midlothian	2-1
Hibernian v Dumbarton	2-0
East Fife v Motherwell	0-2

SEMI-FINAL

Aberdeen v Arbroath	2-0
Hibernian v Motherwell	2-0

FINAL

Aberdeen v Hibernian	2-1

FIRST DIVISION

		P	W	D	L	F	A	Pts
1	Arsenal	42	23	13	6	81	32	59
2	Man United	42	19	14	9	81	48	52
3	Burnley	42	20	12	10	56	43	52
4	Derby	42	19	12	11	77	57	50
5	Wolves	42	19	9	14	83	70	47
6	Aston Villa	42	19	9	14	65	57	47
7	Preston	42	20	7	15	67	68	47
8	Portsmouth	42	19	7	16	68	50	45
9	Blackpool	42	17	10	15	57	41	44
10	Man City	42	15	12	15	52	47	42
11	Liverpool	42	16	10	16	65	61	42
12	Sheff United	42	16	10	16	65	70	42
13	Charlton	42	17	6	19	57	66	40
14	Everton	42	17	6	19	52	66	40
15	Stoke	42	14	10	18	41	55	38
16	Middlesbrough	42	14	9	19	71	73	37
17	Bolton	42	16	5	21	46	58	37
18	Chelsea	42	14	9	19	53	71	37
19	Huddersfield	42	12	12	18	51	60	36
20	Sunderland	42	13	10	19	56	67	36
21	Blackburn	42	11	10	21	54	72	32
22	Grimsby	42	8	6	28	45	111	22

SECOND DIVISION

		P	W	D	L	F	A	Pts
1	Birmingham	42	22	15	5	55	24	59
2	Newcastle	42	24	8	10	72	41	56
3	Southampton	42	21	10	11	71	53	52
4	Sheff Wed	42	20	11	11	66	53	51
5	Cardiff	42	18	11	13	61	58	47
6	West Ham	42	16	14	12	55	53	46
7	WBA	42	18	9	15	63	58	45
8	Tottenham	42	15	14	13	56	43	44
9	Leicester	42	16	11	15	60	57	43
10	Coventry	42	14	13	15	59	52	41
11	Fulham	42	15	10	17	47	46	40
12	Barnsley	42	15	10	17	62	64	40
13	Luton	42	14	12	16	56	59	40
14	Bradford PA	42	16	8	18	68	72	40
15	Brentford	42	13	14	15	44	61	40
16	Chesterfield	42	16	7	19	54	55	39
17	Plymouth	42	9	20	13	40	58	38
18	Leeds	42	14	8	20	62	72	36
19	Nottm Forest	42	12	11	19	54	60	35
20	Bury	42	9	16	17	58	68	34
21	Doncaster	42	9	11	22	40	66	29
22	Millwall	42	9	11	22	44	74	29

THIRD DIVISION (SOUTH)

		P	W	D	L	F	A	Pts
1	QPR	42	26	9	7	74	37	61
2	Bournemouth	42	24	9	9	76	35	57
3	Walsall	42	21	9	12	70	40	51
4	Ipswich	42	23	3	16	67	61	49
5	Swansea	42	18	12	12	70	52	48
6	Notts County	42	19	8	15	68	59	46
7	Bristol City	42	18	7	17	77	65	43
8	Port Vale	42	16	11	15	63	54	43
9	Southend	42	15	13	14	51	58	43
10	Reading	42	15	11	16	56	58	41
11	Exeter	42	15	11	16	55	63	41
12	Newport	42	14	13	15	61	73	41
13	Crystal Palace	42	13	13	16	49	49	39
14	Northampton	42	14	11	17	58	72	39
15	Watford	42	14	10	18	57	79	38
16	Swindon	42	10	16	16	41	46	36
17	Leyton Orient	42	13	10	19	51	73	36
18	Torquay	42	11	13	18	63	62	35
19	Aldershot	42	10	15	17	45	67	35
20	Bristol Rovers	42	13	8	21	71	75	34
21	Norwich	42	13	8	21	61	76	34
22	Brighton	42	11	12	19	43	73	34

THIRD DIVISION (NORTH)

		P	W	D	L	F	A	Pts
1	Lincoln	42	26	8	8	81	40	60
2	Rotherham	42	25	9	8	95	49	59
3	Wrexham	42	21	8	13	74	54	50
4	Gateshead	42	19	11	12	75	57	49
5	Hull	42	18	11	13	59	48	47
6	Accrington	42	20	6	16	62	59	46
7	Barrow	42	16	13	13	49	40	45
8	Mansfield	42	17	11	14	57	51	45
9	Carlisle	42	18	7	17	88	77	43
10	Crewe	42	18	7	17	61	63	43
11	Oldham	42	14	13	15	63	64	41
12	Rochdale	42	15	11	16	48	72	41
13	York	42	13	14	15	65	60	40
14	Bradford City	42	15	10	17	65	66	40
15	Southport	42	14	11	17	60	63	39
16	Darlington	42	13	13	16	54	70	39
17	Stockport	42	13	12	17	63	67	38
18	Tranmere	42	16	4	22	54	72	36
19	Hartlepools	42	14	8	20	51	73	36
20	Chester	42	13	9	20	64	67	35
21	Halifax	42	7	13	22	43	76	27
22	New Brighton	42	8	9	25	38	81	25

SCOTTISH DIVISION 'A'

		P	W	D	L	F	A	Pts
1	Hibernian	30	22	4	4	86	27	48
2	Rangers	30	21	4	5	64	28	46
3	Partick	30	16	4	10	61	42	36
4	Dundee	30	15	3	12	67	51	33
5	St Mirren	30	13	5	12	54	58	31
6	Clyde	30	12	7	11	52	57	31
7	Falkirk	30	10	10	10	55	48	30
8	Motherwell	30	13	3	14	45	47	29
9	Hearts	30	10	8	12	37	42	28
10	Aberdeen	30	10	7	13	45	45	27
11	Third Lanark	30	10	6	14	56	73	26
12	Celtic	30	10	5	15	41	56	25
13	Queen of the S	30	10	5	15	49	74	25
14	Morton	30	9	6	15	47	43	24
15	Airdrieonians	30	7	7	16	39	78	21
16	Queen's Park	30	9	2	19	45	75	20

SCOTTISH DIVISION 'B'

		P	W	D	L	F	A	Pts
1	East Fife	30	25	3	2	103	36	53
2	Albion	30	19	4	7	58	49	42
3	Hamilton	30	17	6	7	75	45	40
4	Raith	30	14	6	10	83	66	34
5	Cowdenbeath	30	12	8	10	56	53	32
6	Kilmarnock	30	13	4	13	72	62	30
7	Dunfermline	30	13	3	14	72	71	29
8	Stirling	30	11	6	13	85	66	28
9	St Johnstone	30	11	5	14	69	63	27
10	Ayr	30	9	9	12	59	61	27
11	Dumbarton	30	9	7	14	66	79	25
12	Alloa	30	10	6	14	53	77	24*
13	Arbroath	30	10	3	17	55	62	23
14	Stenhousemuir	30	6	11	13	53	83	23
15	Dundee United	30	10	2	18	58	88	22
16	Leith	30	6	7	17	45	84	19

*Two points deducted for fielding unregistered players.

In the 1947-48 FA Cup, Manchester United were drawn in turn against six Division One clubs. This was the first instance of this happening to any club. The teams United met were, in order, Aston Villa, Liverpool, Charlton Athletic, Preston North End, and Blackpool, whom they beat 4-2 in the Final.

Quick off the mark
William Sharp, of Partick Thistle, scored against Queen of the South just seven seconds after the Scottish Division 'A' match had kicked off on 20 December 1947.

Tommy Lawton became the first Third Division player since World War Two to represent England in the International Championship. Lawton, of Notts County, played at centre-forward in England's 2-0 win over Scotland at Hampden Park on 10 April 1948.

In January 1948, 83,260 people watched Manchester United play Arsenal in a First Division match at Maine Road, Manchester. This was a record for a League match.

FIRST DIVISION

		P	W	D	L	F	A	Pts
1	Portsmouth	42	25	8	9	84	42	58
2	Man United	42	21	11	10	77	44	53
3	Derby	42	22	9	11	74	55	53
4	Newcastle	42	20	12	10	70	56	52
5	Arsenal	42	18	13	11	74	44	49
6	Wolves	42	17	12	13	79	66	46
7	Man City	42	15	15	12	47	51	45
8	Sunderland	42	13	17	12	49	58	43
9	Charlton	42	15	12	15	63	67	42
10	Aston Villa	42	16	10	16	60	76	42
11	Stoke	42	16	9	17	66	68	41
12	Liverpool	42	13	14	15	53	43	40
13	Chelsea	42	12	14	16	69	68	38
14	Bolton	42	14	10	18	59	68	38
15	Burnley	42	12	14	16	43	50	38
16	Blackpool	42	11	16	15	54	67	38
17	Birmingham	42	11	15	16	36	38	37
18	Everton	42	13	11	18	41	63	37
19	Middlesbrough	42	11	12	19	46	57	34
20	Huddersfield	42	12	10	20	40	69	34
21	Preston	42	11	11	20	62	75	33
22	Sheff United	42	11	11	20	57	78	33

SECOND DIVISION

		P	W	D	L	F	A	Pts
1	Fulham	42	24	9	9	77	37	57
2	WBA	42	24	8	10	69	39	56
3	Southampton	42	23	9	10	69	36	55
4	Cardiff	42	19	13	10	62	47	51
5	Tottenham	42	17	16	9	72	44	50
6	Chesterfield	42	15	17	10	51	45	47
7	West Ham	42	18	10	14	56	58	46
8	Sheff Wed	42	15	13	14	63	56	43
9	Barnsley	42	14	12	16	62	61	40
10	Luton	42	14	12	16	55	57	40
11	Grimsby	42	15	10	17	72	76	40
12	Bury	42	17	6	19	67	76	40
13	QPR	42	14	11	17	44	62	39
14	Blackburn	42	15	8	19	53	63	38
15	Leeds	42	12	13	17	55	63	37
16	Coventry	42	15	7	20	55	64	37
17	Bradford PA	42	13	11	18	65	78	37
18	Brentford	42	11	14	17	42	53	36
19	Leicester	42	10	16	16	62	79	36
20	Plymouth	42	12	12	18	49	64	36
21	Nottm Forest	42	14	7	21	50	54	35
22	Lincoln	42	8	12	22	53	91	28

FA CUP 1948-49

FOURTH ROUND

Manchester United v Bradford Park Avenue	1-1, 1-1, 5-0
Yeovil Town v Sunderland	2-1
Hull City v Grimsby Town	3-2
Stoke City v Blackpool	1-1, 1-0
Wolverhampton Wanderers v Sheffield United	3-0
Liverpool v Notts County	1-0
West Bromwich Albion v Gateshead	3-1
Chelsea v Everton	2-0
Leicester City v Preston North End	2-0
Luton Town v Walsall	4-0
Brentford v Torquay United	1-0
Burnley v Rotherham United	1-0
Portsmouth v Sheffield Wednesday	2-1
Newport County v Huddersfield Town	3-3, 3-1
Derby County v Arsenal	1-0
Cardiff City v Aston Villa	2-1

FIFTH ROUND

Manchester United v Yeovil Town	8-0
Hull City v Stoke City	2-0
Wolverhampton Wanderers v Liverpool	3-1
West Bromwich Albion v Chelsea	3-0
Leicester City v Luton Town	5-5 5-3
Brentford v Burnley	4-2
Portsmouth v Newport County	3-2
Derby County v Cardiff City	2-1

SIXTH ROUND

Hull City v Manchester United	0-1
Wolverhampton Wanderers v West Bromwich Albion	1-0
Leicester City v Brentford	2-0
Portsmouth v Derby County	2-1

SEMI-FINAL

Manchester United v Wolverhampton Wanderers	1-1, 0-1
Leicester City v Portsmouth	3-1

FINAL

Wolverhampton Wanderers v Leicester City	3-1

THIRD DIVISION (SOUTH)

		P	W	D	L	F	A	Pts
1	Swansea	42	27	8	7	87	34	62
2	Reading	42	25	5	12	77	50	55
3	Bournemouth	42	22	8	12	69	48	52
4	Swindon	42	18	15	9	64	56	51
5	Bristol Rovers	42	19	10	13	61	51	48
6	Brighton	42	15	18	9	55	55	48
7	Ipswich	42	18	9	15	78	77	45
8	Millwall	42	17	11	14	63	64	45
9	Torquay	42	17	11	14	65	70	45
10	Norwich	42	16	12	14	67	49	44
11	Notts County	42	19	5	18	102	68	43
12	Exeter	42	15	10	17	63	76	40
13	Port Vale	42	14	11	17	51	54	39
14	Walsall	42	15	8	19	56	64	38
15	Newport	42	14	9	19	68	92	37
16	Bristol City	42	11	14	17	44	62	36
17	Watford	42	10	15	17	41	54	35
18	Southend	42	9	16	17	41	46	34
19	Leyton Orient	42	11	12	19	58	80	34
20	Northampton	42	12	9	21	51	62	33
21	Aldershot	42	11	11	20	48	59	33
22	Crystal Palace	42	8	11	23	38	76	27

THIRD DIVISION (NORTH)

		P	W	D	L	F	A	Pts
1	Hull	42	27	11	4	93	28	65
2	Rotherham	42	28	6	8	90	46	62
3	Doncaster	42	20	10	12	53	40	50
4	Darlington	42	20	6	16	83	74	46
5	Gateshead	42	16	13	13	69	58	45
6	Oldham	42	18	9	15	75	67	45
7	Rochdale	42	18	9	15	55	53	45
8	Stockport	42	16	11	15	61	56	43
9	Wrexham	42	17	9	16	56	62	43
10	Mansfield	42	14	14	14	52	48	42
11	Tranmere	42	13	15	14	46	57	41
12	Crewe	42	16	9	17	52	74	41
13	Barrow	42	14	12	16	41	48	40
14	York	42	15	9	18	74	74	39
15	Carlisle	42	14	11	17	60	77	39
16	Hartlepools	42	14	10	18	45	58	38
17	New Brighton	42	14	8	20	46	58	36
18	Chester	42	11	13	18	57	56	35
19	Halifax	42	12	11	19	45	62	35
20	Accrington	42	12	10	20	55	64	34
21	Southport	42	11	9	22	45	64	31
22	Bradford City	42	10	9	23	48	77	29

SCOTTISH DIVISION 'A'

		P	W	D	L	F	A	Pts
1	Rangers	30	20	6	4	63	32	46
2	Dundee	30	20	5	5	71	48	45
3	Hibernian	30	17	5	8	75	52	39
4	East Fife	30	16	3	11	64	46	35
5	Falkirk	30	12	8	10	70	54	32
6	Celtic	30	12	7	11	48	40	31
7	Third Lanark	30	13	5	12	56	52	31
8	Hearts	30	12	6	12	64	54	30
9	St Mirren	30	13	4	13	51	47	30
10	Queen of the S	30	11	8	11	47	53	30
11	Partick	30	9	9	12	50	63	27
12	Motherwell	30	10	5	15	44	49	25
13	Aberdeen	30	7	11	12	39	48	25
14	Clyde	30	9	6	15	50	67	24
15	Morton	30	7	8	15	39	51	22
16	Albion	30	3	2	25	30	105	8

SCOTTISH DIVISION 'B'

		P	W	D	L	F	A	Pts
1	Raith	30	20	2	8	80	44	42
2	Stirling	30	20	2	8	71	47	42
3	Airdrieonians	30	16	9	5	76	42	41
4	Dunfermline	30	16	9	5	80	58	41
5	Queen's Park	30	14	7	9	66	49	35
6	St Johnstone	30	14	4	12	58	51	32
7	Arbroath	30	12	8	10	62	56	32
8	Dundee United	30	10	7	13	60	67	27
9	Ayr	30	10	7	13	51	70	27
10	Hamilton	30	9	8	13	48	57	26
11	Kilmarnock	30	9	7	14	58	61	25
12	Stenhousemuir	30	8	8	14	50	54	24
13	Cowdenbeath	30	9	5	16	53	58	23
14	Alloa	30	10	3	17	42	85	23
15	Dumbarton	30	8	6	16	52	79	22
16	E Stirlingshire	30	6	6	18	38	67	18

SCOTTISH FA CUP 1948-49

SECOND ROUND

Motherwell v Rangers	0-3
Partick Thistle v Queen of the South	3-0
Cowdenbeath v East Fife	1-2
Hibernian v Raith Rovers	1-1, 4-3
Clyde v Alloa Athletic	3-1
Ayr United v Morton	0-2
Stenhousemuir v Albion Rovers	5-1
Dundee v St Mirren	0-0, 2-1
Heart of Midlothian v Third Lanark	3-1
Dumbarton v Dundee United	1-1, 3-1

THIRD ROUND

Clyde v Morton	2-0
Heart of Midlothian v Dumbarton	3-0
Rangers	bye
Partick Thistle	bye
East Fife	bye
Hibernian	bye
Stenhousemuir	bye
Dundee	bye

FOURTH ROUND

Rangers v Partick Thistle	4-0
Hibernian v East Fife	0-2
Stenhousemuir v Clyde	0-1
Heart of Midlothian v Dundee	2-4

SEMI-FINAL

Rangers v East Fife	3-0
Clyde v Dundee	2-2, 2-1

FINAL

Rangers v Clyde	4-1

On Saturday 18 September 1948, there were 9 drawn games in Division One of the Football League, a record for any division of the League in a single day.

In both Divisions One and Two, the tally of goals scored during the season was 1303.

Portsmouth, 1948-49 League champions, and Swansea, who finished top of Division Three South, both completed the season without a home defeat. At Fratton Park, Portsmouth won 18 games and drew 3, while Swansea won 20 and drew one at Vetch Field.

Three honours for Bromley

Bromley won the FA Amateur Cup by beating Romford 1-0 at Wembley; they also won the Kent Amateur Cup with the highest score recorded in the final: 9-1. Bromley completed a magnificent season by capturing the Athenian League championship. George Brown, their centre-forward, scored 100 goals during the season. These included a 7, a 6, two 5's, three 4's and five hat-tricks.

In Scotland, Rangers became the first side to achieve the treble, winning the League, the Scottish Cup and the League Cup.

FIRST DIVISION

		P	W	D	L	F	A	Pts
1	Portsmouth	42	22	9	11	74	38	53
2	Wolves	42	20	13	9	76	49	53
3	Sunderland	42	21	10	11	83	62	52
4	Man United	42	18	14	10	69	44	50
5	Newcastle	42	19	12	11	77	55	50
6	Arsenal	42	19	11	12	79	55	49
7	Blackpool	42	17	15	10	46	35	49
8	Liverpool	42	17	14	11	64	54	48
9	Middlesbrough	42	20	7	15	59	48	47
10	Burnley	42	16	13	13	40	40	45
11	Derby	42	17	10	15	69	61	44
12	Aston Villa	42	15	12	15	61	61	42
13	Chelsea	42	12	16	14	58	65	40
14	WBA	42	14	12	16	47	53	40
15	Huddersfield	42	14	9	19	52	73	37
16	Bolton	42	10	14	18	45	59	34
17	Fulham	42	10	14	18	41	54	34
18	Everton	42	10	14	18	42	66	34
19	Stoke	42	11	12	19	45	75	34
20	Charlton	42	13	6	23	53	65	32
21	Man City	42	8	13	21	36	68	29
22	Birmingham	42	7	14	21	31	67	28

SECOND DIVISION

		P	W	D	L	F	A	Pts
1	Tottenham	42	27	7	8	81	35	61
2	Sheff Wed	42	18	16	8	67	48	52
3	Sheff United	42	19	14	9	68	49	52
4	Southampton	42	19	14	9	64	48	52
5	Leeds	42	17	13	12	54	45	47
6	Preston	42	18	9	15	60	49	45
7	Hull	42	17	11	14	64	72	45
8	Swansea	42	17	9	16	53	49	43
9	Brentford	42	15	13	14	44	49	43
10	Cardiff	42	16	10	16	41	44	42
11	Grimsby	42	16	8	18	74	73	40
12	Coventry	42	13	13	16	55	55	39
13	Barnsley	42	13	13	16	64	67	39
14	Chesterfield	42	15	9	18	43	47	39
15	Leicester	42	12	15	15	55	65	39
16	Blackburn	42	14	10	18	55	60	38
17	Luton	42	10	18	14	41	51	38
18	Bury	42	14	9	19	60	65	37
19	West Ham	42	12	12	18	53	61	36
20	QPR	42	11	12	19	40	57	34
21	Plymouth	42	8	16	18	44	65	32
22	Bradford PA	42	10	11	21	51	77	31

THIRD DIVISION (SOUTH)

		P	W	D	L	F	A	Pts
1	Notts County	42	25	8	9	95	50	58
2	Northampton	42	20	11	11	72	50	51
3	Southend	42	19	13	10	66	48	51
4	Nottm Forest	42	20	9	13	67	39	49
5	Torquay	42	19	10	13	66	63	48
6	Watford	42	16	13	13	45	35	45
7	Crystal Palace	42	15	14	13	55	54	44
8	Brighton	42	16	12	14	57	69	44
9	Bristol Rovers	42	19	5	18	51	51	43
10	Reading	42	17	8	17	70	64	42
11	Norwich	42	16	10	16	65	63	42
12	Bournemouth	42	16	10	16	57	56	42
13	Port Vale	42	15	11	16	47	42	41
14	Swindon	42	15	11	16	59	62	41
15	Bristol City	42	15	10	17	60	61	40
16	Exeter	42	14	11	17	63	75	39
17	Ipswich	42	12	11	19	57	86	35
18	Leyton Orient	42	12	11	19	53	85	35
19	Walsall	42	9	16	17	61	62	34
20	Aldershot	42	13	8	21	48	60	34
21	Newport	42	13	8	21	67	98	34
22	Millwall	42	14	4	24	55	63	32

THIRD DIVISION (NORTH)

		P	W	D	L	F	A	Pts
1	Doncaster	42	19	17	6	66	38	55
2	Gateshead	42	23	7	12	87	54	53
3	Rochdale	42	21	9	12	68	41	51
4	Lincoln	42	21	9	12	60	39	51
5	Tranmere	42	19	11	12	51	48	49
6	Rotherham	42	19	10	13	80	59	48
7	Crewe	42	17	14	11	68	55	48
8	Mansfield	42	18	12	12	66	54	48
9	Carlisle	42	16	15	11	68	51	47
10	Stockport	42	19	7	16	55	52	45
11	Oldham	42	16	11	15	58	63	43
12	Chester	42	17	6	19	70	79	40
13	Accrington	42	16	7	19	57	62	39
14	New Brighton	42	14	10	18	45	63	38
15	Barrow	42	14	9	19	47	53	37
16	Southport	42	12	13	17	51	71	37
17	Darlington	42	11	13	18	56	69	35
18	Hartlepools	42	14	5	23	52	79	33
19	Bradford City	42	12	8	22	61	76	32
20	Wrexham	42	10	12	20	39	54	32
21	Halifax	42	12	8	22	58	85	32
22	York	42	9	13	20	52	70	31

SCOTTISH DIVISION 'A'

		P	W	D	L	F	A	Pts
1	Rangers	30	22	6	2	58	26	50
2	Hibernian	30	22	5	3	86	34	49
3	Hearts	30	20	3	7	86	40	43
4	East Fife	30	15	7	8	58	43	37
5	Celtic	30	14	7	9	51	50	35
6	Dundee	30	12	7	11	49	46	31
7	Partick Thistle	30	13	3	14	55	45	29
8	Aberdeen	30	11	4	15	48	56	26
9	Raith	30	9	8	13	45	54	26
10	Motherwell	30	10	5	15	53	58	25
11	St Mirren	30	8	9	13	42	49	25
12	Third Lanark	30	11	3	16	44	62	25
13	Clyde	30	10	4	16	56	73	24
14	Falkirk	30	7	10	13	48	72	24
15	Queen of the S	30	5	6	19	31	63	16
16	Stirling	30	6	3	21	38	77	15

SCOTTISH DIVISION 'B'

		P	W	D	L	F	A	Pts
1	Morton	30	20	7	3	77	33	47
2	Airdrieonians	30	19	6	5	79	40	44
3	Dunfermline	30	16	4	10	71	57	36
4	St Johnstone	30	15	6	9	64	56	36
5	Cowdenbeath	30	16	3	11	63	56	35
6	Hamilton	30	14	6	10	57	44	34
7	Kilmarnock	30	14	5	11	50	43	33
8	Dundee United	30	14	5	11	74	56	33
9	Queen's Park	30	12	7	11	63	59	31
10	Forfar	30	11	8	11	53	56	30
11	Albion	30	10	7	13	49	61	27
12	Stenhousemuir	30	8	8	14	54	72	24
13	Ayr	30	8	6	16	53	80	22
14	Arbroath	30	5	9	16	47	69	19
15	Dumbarton	30	6	4	20	39	62	16
16	Alloa	30	5	3	22	47	96	13

FA CUP 1949-50

FOURTH ROUND

Arsenal v Swansea Town	2-1
Burnley v Port Vale	2-1
Leeds United v Bolton Wanderers	1-1, 3-2
Charlton Athletic v Cardiff City	1-1, 0-2
Chelsea v Newcastle United	3-0
Chesterfield v Middlesbrough	3-2
Watford v Manchester United	0-1
Portsmouth v Grimsby Town	5-0
Liverpool v Exeter City	3-1
Stockport County v Hull City	0-0, 2-0
Blackpool v Doncaster Rovers	2-1
Wolverhampton Wanderers v Sheffield United	
	0-0, 4-3
West Ham United v Everton	1-2
Tottenham Hotspur v Sunderland	5-1
Bury v Derby County	2-2, 2-5
Bournemouth v Northampton Town	1-1, 1-2

FIFTH ROUND

Arsenal v Burnley	2-0
Leeds United v Cardiff City	3-1
Chesterfield v Chelsea	1-1, 0-3
Manchester United v Portsmouth	3-3, 3-1
Stockport County v Liverpool	1-2
Wolverhampton Wanderers v Blackpool	0-0, 0-1
Everton v Tottenham Hotspur	1-0
Derby County v Northampton Town	4-2

SIXTH ROUND

Arsenal v Leeds United	1-0
Chelsea v Manchester United	2-0
Liverpool v Blackpool	2-1
Derby County v Everton	1-2

SEMI-FINAL

Arsenal v Chelsea	2-2, 1-0
Liverpool v Everton	2-0

FINAL

Arsenal v Liverpool	2-0

SCOTTISH FA CUP 1949-50

SECOND ROUND

Rangers v Cowdenbeath	8-0
Raith Rovers v Clyde	3-2
Queen of the South v Morton	1-1, 3-0
Aberdeen v Heart of Midlothian	3-1
Celtic v Third Lanark	1-1, 4-1
Partick Thistle v Dundee United	5-0
Stirling Albion v Dumbarton	2-2, 1-1, 6-2
Stenhousemuir v St Johnstone	2-2, 4-2
Dunfermline Athletic v Albion Rovers	2-1
Falkirk v East Fife	2-3

THIRD ROUND

Celtic v Aberdeen	0-1
Dunfermline Athletic v Stenhousemuir	1-4
Rangers	bye
Raith Rovers	bye
Queen of the South	bye
Partick Thistle	bye
Stirling Albion	bye
East Fife	bye

FOURTH ROUND

Rangers v Raith Rovers	1-1, 1-1, 2-0
Queen of the South v Aberdeen	3-3, 2-1
Partick Thistle v Stirling Albion	5-1
Stenhousemuir v East Fife	0-3

SEMI-FINAL

Rangers v Queen of the South	1-1, 3-0
Partick Thistle v East Fife	1-2

FINAL

Rangers v East Fife	3-0

Charlie Mortimore scored 15 goals for Aldershot in Division Three South during 1949-50. These made Mortimore the club's top scorer for the season, and meant that he became the second amateur to head a League club's scoring list since the First World War.

England lose to America
On 28 June 1950, an amazing scoreline came out of Brazil. For at Belo Horizonte, the United States had beaten England 1-0.

On 16 July 1950, 199,854 people watched the World Cup Final in Rio de Janeiro, the official record crowd for any football match.

The Third Division was extended from 44 to 48 clubs as a result of the clamour by minor professional clubs for first-class status. The League management committee proposed the enlargement of each section of the Third Division by two clubs, and this proposal was adopted at the 1950 AGM.

John Charles, Leeds United's centre-half, became Wales' youngest ever international when, on 8 March 1950, at the age of 18 years and 71 days, he played against Northern Ireland.

FIRST DIVISION

	P	W	D	L	F	A	Pts
1 Tottenham	42	25	10	7	82	44	60
2 Man United	42	24	8	10	74	40	56
3 Blackpool	42	20	10	12	79	53	50
4 Newcastle	42	18	13	11	62	53	49
5 Arsenal	42	19	9	14	73	56	47
6 Middlesbrough	42	18	11	13	76	65	47
7 Portsmouth	42	16	15	11	71	68	47
8 Bolton	42	19	7	16	64	61	45
9 Liverpool	42	16	11	15	53	59	43
10 Burnley	42	14	14	14	48	43	42
11 Derby	42	16	8	18	81	75	40
12 Sunderland	42	12	16	14	63	73	40
13 Stoke	42	13	14	15	50	59	40
14 Wolves	42	15	8	19	74	61	38
15 Aston Villa	42	12	13	17	66	68	37
16 WBA	42	13	11	18	53	61	37
17 Charlton	42	14	9	19	63	80	37
18 Fulham	42	13	11	18	52	68	37
19 Huddersfield	42	15	6	21	64	92	36
20 Chelsea	42	12	8	22	53	65	32
21 Sheff Wed	42	12	8	22	64	83	32
22 Everton	42	12	8	22	48	86	32

SECOND DIVISION

	P	W	D	L	F	A	Pts
1 Preston	42	26	5	11	91	49	57
2 Man City	42	19	14	9	89	61	52
3 Cardiff	42	17	16	9	53	45	50
4 Birmingham	42	20	9	13	64	53	49
5 Leeds	42	20	8	14	63	55	48
6 Blackburn	42	19	8	15	65	66	46
7 Coventry	42	19	7	16	75	59	45
8 Sheff United	42	16	12	14	72	62	44
9 Brentford	42	18	8	16	75	74	44
10 Hull	42	16	11	15	74	70	43
11 Doncaster	42	15	13	14	64	68	43
12 Southampton	42	15	13	14	66	73	43
13 West Ham	42	16	10	16	68	69	42
14 Leicester	42	15	11	16	68	58	41
15 Barnsley	42	15	10	17	74	68	40
16 QPR	42	15	10	17	71	82	40
17 Notts County	42	13	13	16	61	60	39
18 Swansea	42	16	4	22	54	77	36
19 Luton	42	9	14	19	57	70	32
20 Bury	42	12	8	22	60	86	32
21 Chesterfield	42	9	12	21	44	69	30
22 Grimsby	42	8	12	22	61	95	28

THIRD DIVISION (NORTH)

	P	W	D	L	F	A	Pts
1 Rotherham	46	31	9	6	103	41	71
2 Mansfield	46	26	12	8	78	48	64
3 Carlisle	46	25	12	9	79	50	62
4 Tranmere	46	24	11	11	83	62	59
5 Lincoln	46	25	8	13	89	58	58
6 Bradford PA	46	23	8	15	90	72	54
7 Bradford City	46	21	10	15	90	63	52
8 Gateshead	46	21	8	17	84	62	50
9 Crewe	46	19	10	17	61	60	48
10 Stockport	46	20	8	18	63	63	48
11 Rochdale	46	17	11	18	69	62	45
12 Scunthorpe	46	13	18	15	58	57	44
13 Chester	46	17	9	20	62	64	43
14 Wrexham	46	15	12	19	55	71	42
15 Oldham	46	16	8	22	73	73	40
16 Hartlepools	46	16	7	23	64	66	39
17 York	46	12	15	19	66	77	39
18 Darlington	46	13	13	20	59	77	39
19 Barrow	46	16	6	24	51	76	38
20 Shrewsbury	46	15	7	24	43	74	37
21 Southport	46	13	10	23	56	72	36
22 Halifax	46	11	12	23	50	69	34
23 Accrington	46	11	10	25	42	101	32
24 New Brighton	46	11	8	27	40	90	30

THIRD DIVISION (SOUTH)

	P	W	D	L	F	A	Pts
1 Nottm Forest	46	30	10	6	110	40	70
2 Norwich	46	25	14	7	82	45	64
3 Reading	46	21	15	10	88	53	57
4 Plymouth	46	24	9	13	85	55	57
5 Millwall	46	23	10	13	80	57	56
6 Bristol Rovers	46	20	15	11	64	42	55
7 Southend	46	21	10	15	92	69	52
8 Ipswich	46	23	6	17	69	58	52
9 Bournemouth	46	22	7	17	65	57	51
10 Bristol City	46	20	11	15	64	59	51
11 Newport	46	19	9	18	77	70	47
12 Port Vale	46	16	13	17	60	65	45
13 Brighton	46	13	17	16	71	79	43
14 Exeter	46	18	6	22	62	85	42
15 Walsall	46	15	10	21	52	62	40
16 Colchester	46	14	12	20	63	76	40
17 Swindon	46	18	4	24	55	67	40
18 Aldershot	46	15	10	21	56	88	40
19 Leyton Orient	46	15	8	23	53	75	38
20 Torquay	46	14	9	23	64	81	37
21 Northampton	46	10	16	20	55	67	36
22 Gillingham	46	13	9	24	69	101	35
23 Watford	46	9	11	26	54	88	29
24 Crystal Palace	46	8	11	27	33	84	27

SCOTTISH DIVISION 'A'

	P	W	D	L	F	A	Pts
1 Hibernian	30	22	4	4	78	26	48
2 Rangers	30	17	4	9	64	37	38
3 Dundee	30	15	8	7	47	30	38
4 Hearts	30	16	5	9	72	45	37
5 Aberdeen	30	15	5	10	61	50	35
6 Partick Thistle	30	13	7	10	57	48	33
7 Celtic	30	12	5	13	48	46	29
8 Raith	30	13	2	15	52	52	28
9 Motherwell	30	11	6	13	58	65	28
10 East Fife	30	10	8	12	48	66	28
11 St Mirren	30	9	7	14	35	51	25
12 Morton	30	10	4	16	47	59	24
13 Third Lanark	30	11	2	17	40	51	24
14 Airdrieonians	30	10	4	16	52	67	24
15 Clyde	30	8	7	15	37	57	23
16 Falkirk	30	7	4	19	35	81	18

SCOTTISH DIVISION 'B'

	P	W	D	L	F	A	Pts
1 Queen of the S	30	21	3	6	69	35	45
2 Stirling	30	21	3	6	78	44	45
3 Ayr	30	15	6	9	64	40	36
4 Dundee United	30	16	4	10	78	58	36
5 St Johnstone	30	14	5	11	68	53	33
6 Queen's Park	30	13	7	10	56	53	33
7 Hamilton	30	12	8	10	65	49	32
8 Albion	30	14	4	12	56	51	32
9 Dumbarton	30	12	5	13	52	53	29
10 Dunfermline	30	12	4	14	58	73	28
11 Cowdenbeath	30	12	3	15	61	57	27
12 Kilmarnock	30	8	8	14	44	49	24
13 Arbroath	30	8	5	17	46	78	21
14 Forfar	30	9	3	18	43	76	21
15 Stenhousemuir	30	9	2	19	51	80	20
16 Alloa	30	7	4	19	58	98	18

In their first season in the Football League, Scunthorpe United conceded only nine goals in their 23 home matches in Division Three North. In their 23 away games in the same division, Hartlepools United scored only nine times, failing to break a duck in their last 11 fixtures.

Nottingham Forest won the Third Division South championship with a record points total for that division—70.

Billingham Synthonia did not concede a single goal at home in their Northern League programme, though they scored 44.

On 15 November 1950, Leslie Compton, the Arsenal centre-half, played in that position for England against Wales. It was Compton's first international appearance, and at 38 years and 2 months, he is credited with making the oldest international debut in the Home Championship.

FA CUP 1950-51

FOURTH ROUND

Newcastle United v Bolton Wanderers	3-2
Stoke City v West Ham United	1-0
Luton Town v Bristol Rovers	1-2
Hull City v Rotherham United	2-0
Wolverhampton Wanderers v Aston Villa	3-1
Preston North End v Huddersfield Town	0-2
Sunderland v Southampton	2-0
Newport County v Norwich City	0-2
Blackpool v Stockport County	2-1
Sheffield United v Mansfield Town	0-0, 1-2
Exeter City v Chelsea	1-1, 0-2
Millwall v Fulham	0-1
Derby County v Birmingham City	1-3
Bristol City v Brighton	1-0
Manchester United v Leeds United	4-0
Arsenal v Northampton Town	3-2

FIFTH ROUND

Stoke City v Newcastle United	2-4
Bristol Rovers v Hull City	3-0
Wolverhampton Wanderers v Huddersfield Town	2-0
Sunderland v Norwich City	3-1
Blackpool v Mansfield Town	2-0
Chelsea v Fulham	1-1, 0-3
Birmingham City v Bristol City	2-0
Manchester United v Arsenal	1-0

SIXTH ROUND

Newcastle United v Bristol Rovers	0-0, 3-1
Sunderland v Wolverhampton Wanderers	1-1, 1-3
Blackpool v Fulham	1-0
Birmingham City v Manchester United	1-0

SEMI-FINAL

Newcastle United v Wolverhampton Wanderers	0-0, 2-1
Blackpool v Birmingham City	0-0, 2-1

FINAL

Blackpool v Newcastle United	0-2

SCOTTISH FA CUP 1950-51

SECOND ROUND

Celtic v Duns	4-0
East Stirlingshire v Heart of Midlothian	1-5
Aberdeen v Third Lanark	4-0
St Johnstone v Dundee	1-3
Raith Rovers v Brechin City	5-2
Morton v Airdrieonians	3-3, 1-2
Albion Rovers v Clyde	0-2
Rangers v Hibernian	2-3
Queen's Park v Ayr United	1-3
Motherwell v Hamilton Academicals	4-1

THIRD ROUND

Heart of Midlothian v Celtic	1-2
Airdrieonians v Clyde	4-0
Aberdeen	bye
Dundee	bye
Raith Rovers	bye
Hibernian	bye
Ayr United	bye
Motherwell	bye

FOURTH ROUND

Celtic v Aberdeen	3-0
Dundee v Raith Rovers	1-2
Airdrieonians v Hibernian	0-3
Ayr United v Motherwell	2-2, 1-2

SEMI-FINAL

Celtic v Raith Rovers	3-2
Hibernian v Motherwell	2-3

FINAL

Celtic v Motherwell	1-0

FIRST DIVISION

		P	W	D	L	F	A	Pts
1	Man United	42	23	11	8	95	52	57
2	Tottenham	42	22	9	11	76	51	53
3	Arsenal	42	21	11	10	80	61	53
4	Portsmouth	42	20	8	14	68	58	48
5	Bolton	42	19	10	13	65	61	48
6	Aston Villa	42	19	9	14	79	70	47
7	Preston	42	17	12	13	74	54	46
8	Newcastle	42	18	9	15	98	73	45
9	Blackpool	42	18	9	15	64	64	45
10	Charlton	42	17	10	15	68	63	44
11	Liverpool	42	12	19	11	57	61	43
12	Sunderland	42	15	12	15	70	61	42
13	WBA	42	14	13	15	74	77	41
14	Burnley	42	15	10	17	56	63	40
15	Man City	42	13	13	16	58	61	39
16	Wolves	42	12	14	16	73	73	38
17	Derby	42	15	7	20	63	80	37
18	Middlesbrough	42	15	6	21	64	88	36
19	Chelsea	42	14	8	20	52	72	36
20	Stoke	42	12	7	23	49	88	31
21	Huddersfield	42	10	8	24	49	82	28
22	Fulham	42	8	11	23	58	77	27

SECOND DIVISION

		P	W	D	L	F	A	Pts
1	Sheff Wed	42	21	11	10	100	66	53
2	Cardiff	42	20	11	11	72	54	51
3	Birmingham	42	21	9	12	67	56	51
4	Nottm Forest	42	18	13	11	77	62	49
5	Leicester	42	19	9	14	78	64	47
6	Leeds	42	18	11	13	59	57	47
7	Everton	42	17	10	15	64	58	44
8	Luton	42	16	12	14	77	78	44
9	Rotherham	42	17	8	17	73	71	42
10	Brentford	42	15	12	15	54	55	42
11	Sheff United	42	18	5	19	90	76	41
12	West Ham	42	15	11	16	67	77	41
13	Southampton	42	15	11	16	61	73	41
14	Blackburn	42	17	6	19	54	63	40
15	Notts County	42	16	7	19	71	68	39
16	Doncaster	42	13	12	17	55	60	38
17	Bury	42	15	7	20	67	69	37
18	Hull	42	13	11	18	60	70	37
19	Swansea	42	12	12	18	72	76	36
20	Barnsley	42	11	14	17	59	72	36
21	Coventry	42	14	6	22	59	82	34
22	QPR	42	11	12	19	52	81	34

THIRD DIVISION (SOUTH)

		P	W	D	L	F	A	Pts
1	Plymouth	46	29	8	9	107	53	66
2	Reading	46	29	3	14	112	60	61
3	Norwich	46	26	9	11	89	50	61
4	Millwall	46	23	12	11	74	53	58
5	Brighton	46	24	10	12	87	63	58
6	Newport	46	21	12	13	77	76	54
7	Bristol Rovers	46	20	12	14	89	53	52
8	Northampton	46	22	5	19	93	74	49
9	Southend	46	19	10	17	75	66	48
10	Colchester	46	17	12	17	56	77	46
11	Torquay	46	17	10	19	86	98	44
12	Aldershot	46	18	8	20	78	89	44
13	Port Vale	46	14	15	17	50	66	43
14	Bournemouth	46	16	10	20	69	75	42
15	Bristol City	46	15	12	19	58	69	42
16	Swindon	46	14	14	18	51	68	42
17	Ipswich	46	16	9	21	63	74	41
18	Leyton Orient	46	16	9	21	55	68	41
19	Crystal Palace	46	15	9	22	61	80	39
20	Shrewsbury	46	13	10	23	62	86	36
21	Watford	46	13	10	23	57	81	36
22	Gillingham	46	11	13	22	71	81	35
23	Exeter	46	13	9	24	65	86	35
24	Walsall	46	13	5	28	55	94	31

THIRD DIVISION (NORTH)

		P	W	D	L	F	A	Pts
1	Lincoln	46	30	9	7	121	52	69
2	Grimsby	46	29	8	9	96	45	66
3	Stockport	46	23	13	10	74	40	59
4	Oldham	46	24	9	13	90	61	57
5	Gateshead	46	21	11	14	66	49	53
6	Mansfield	46	22	8	16	73	60	52
7	Carlisle	46	19	13	14	62	57	51
8	Bradford PA	46	19	12	15	74	64	50
9	Hartlepools	46	21	8	17	71	65	50
10	York	46	18	13	15	73	52	49
11	Tranmere	46	21	6	19	76	71	48
12	Barrow	46	17	12	17	57	61	46
13	Chesterfield	46	17	11	18	65	66	45
14	Scunthorpe	46	14	16	16	65	74	44
15	Bradford City	46	16	10	20	61	68	42
16	Crewe	46	17	8	21	63	82	42
17	Southport	46	15	11	20	53	71	41
18	Wrexham	46	15	9	22	63	73	39
19	Chester	46	15	9	22	72	85	39
20	Halifax	46	14	7	25	61	97	35
21	Rochdale	46	11	13	22	47	79	35
22	Accrington	46	10	12	24	61	92	32
23	Darlington	46	11	9	26	64	103	31
24	Workington	46	11	7	28	50	91	29

SCOTTISH DIVISION 'A'

		P	W	D	L	F	A	Pts
1	Hibernian	30	20	5	5	92	36	45
2	Rangers	30	16	9	5	61	31	41
3	East Fife	30	17	3	10	71	49	37
4	Hearts	30	14	7	9	69	53	35
5	Raith	30	14	5	11	43	42	33
6	Partick	30	12	7	11	48	51	31
7	Motherwell	30	12	7	11	51	57	31
8	Dundee	30	11	6	13	53	52	28
9	Celtic	30	10	8	12	52	55	28
10	Queen of the S	30	10	8	12	50	60	28
11	Aberdeen	30	10	7	13	65	58	27
12	Third Lanark	30	9	8	13	51	62	26
13	Airdrieonians	30	11	4	15	54	69	26
14	St Mirren	30	10	5	15	43	58	25
15	Morton	30	9	6	15	49	56	24
16	Stirling	30	5	5	20	36	99	15

SCOTTISH DIVISION 'B'

		P	W	D	L	F	A	Pts
1	Clyde	30	19	6	5	100	45	44
2	Falkirk	30	18	7	5	80	34	43
3	Ayr	30	17	5	8	55	45	39
4	Dundee United	30	16	5	9	75	60	37
5	Kilmarnock	30	16	2	12	62	48	34
6	Dunfermline	30	15	2	13	74	65	32
7	Alloa	30	13	6	11	55	49	32
8	Cowdenbeath	30	12	8	10	66	67	32
9	Hamilton	30	12	6	12	47	51	30
10	Dumbarton	30	10	8	12	51	57	28
11	St Johnstone	30	9	7	14	62	68	25
12	Forfar	30	10	4	16	59	97	24
13	Stenhousemuir	30	8	6	16	57	74	22
14	Albion	30	6	10	14	39	57	22
15	Queen's Park	30	8	4	18	40	62	20
16	Arbroath	30	6	4	20	40	83	16

FA CUP 1951-52

FOURTH ROUND

Tottenham Hotspur v Newcastle United	0-3
Swansea Town v Rotherham United	3-0
Notts County v Portsmouth	1-3
Middlesbrough v Doncaster Rovers	1-4
Blackburn Rovers v Hull City	2-0
Gateshead v West Bromwich Albion	0-2
Burnley v Coventry City	2-0
Liverpool v Wolverhampton Wanderers	2-1
Arsenal v Barnsley	4-0
Birmingham City v Leyton Orient	0-1
Luton Town v Brentford	2-2, 0-0, 3-2
Swindon Town v Stoke City	1-1, 1-0
Chelsea v Tranmere Rovers	4-0
Leeds United v Bradford Park Avenue	2-0
West Ham United v Sheffield United	0-0, 2-4
Southend United v Bristol Rovers	2-1

FIFTH ROUND

Swansea Town v Newcastle United	0-1
Portsmouth v Doncaster Rovers	4-0
Blackburn Rovers v West Bromwich Albion	1-0
Burnley v Liverpool	2-0
Leyton Orient v Arsenal	0-3
Luton Town v Swindon Town	3-1
Leeds United v Chelsea	1-1, 1-1, 1-5
Southend United v Sheffield United	1-2

SIXTH ROUND

Portsmouth v Newcastle United	2-4
Blackburn Rovers v Burnley	3-1
Luton Town v Arsenal	2-3
Sheffield United v Chelsea	0-1

SEMI-FINAL

Newcastle United v Blackburn Rovers	0-0, 2-1
Arsenal v Chelsea	1-1, 3-0

FINAL

Newcastle United v Arsenal	1-0

SCOTTISH FA CUP 1951-52

SECOND ROUND

St Mirren v Motherwell	2-3
Clyde v Dunfermline Athletic	3-4
Rangers v Elgin City	6-1
Cowdenbeath v Arbroath	1-4
Heart of Midlothian v Raith Rovers	1-0
St Johnstone v Queen of the South	2-2, 1-3
Airdrieonians v East Fife	2-1
Clachnacuddin v Morton	1-2
Wigtown & Bladnoch v Dundee	1-7
Alloa Athletic v Berwick Rangers	0-0, 1-4
Aberdeen v Kilmarnock	2-1
Leith Athletic v Dundee United	1-4
Hamilton Academicals v Third Lanark	1-1, 0-4
Albion Rovers v Stranraer	1-1, 4-3
Falkirk v Stirling Albion	3-3, 2-1
Dumbarton v Queen's Park	1-0

THIRD ROUND

Dunfermline Athletic v Motherwell	1-1, 0-4
Arbroath v Rangers	0-2
Queen of the South v Heart of Midlothian	1-3
Airdrieonians v Morton	4-0
Dundee v Berwick Rangers	1-0
Dundee United v Aberdeen	2-2, 2-3
Albion Rovers v Third Lanark	1-3
Dumbarton v Falkirk	1-3

FOURTH ROUND

Rangers v Motherwell	1-1, 1-2
Airdrieonians v Heart of Midlothian	2-2, 4-6
Dundee v Aberdeen	4-0
Third Lanark v Falkirk	1-0

SEMI-FINAL

Motherwell v Heart of Midlothian	1-1, 1-1, 3-1
Dundee v Third Lanark	2-0

FINAL

Motherwell v Dundee	4-0

An Englishman from Wales

The first player to appear in an England representative side while not attached to an English club was Charlie Rutter, Cardiff City's right-back. Rutter played for the England 'B' side against the Netherlands 'B' side in Amsterdam, March 1952. England won the match—a kind of forerunner to the Under-23 international games—1-0.

Freddie Steele's move from Mansfield to Port Vale on 28 December 1951 was the first case of a player-manager being transferred from one Football League club to another.

Billy Foulkes of Newcastle United scored with his first kick in his first international appearance for Wales, against England at Cardiff in October 1951.

FIRST DIVISION

	P	W	D	L	F	A	Pts
1 Arsenal	42	21	12	9	97	64	54
2 Preston	42	21	12	9	85	60	54
3 Wolves	42	19	13	10	86	63	51
4 WBA	42	21	8	13	66	60	50
5 Charlton	42	19	11	12	77	63	49
6 Burnley	42	18	12	12	67	52	48
7 Blackpool	42	19	9	14	71	70	47
8 Man United	42	18	10	14	69	72	46
9 Sunderland	42	15	13	14	68	82	43
10 Tottenham	42	15	11	16	78	69	41
11 Aston Villa	42	14	13	15	63	61	41
12 Cardiff	42	14	12	16	54	46	40
13 Middlesbrough	42	14	11	17	70	77	39
14 Bolton	42	15	9	18	61	69	39
15 Portsmouth	42	14	10	18	74	83	38
16 Newcastle	42	14	9	19	59	70	37
17 Liverpool	42	14	8	20	61	82	36
18 Sheff Wed	42	12	11	19	62	72	35
19 Chelsea	42	12	11	19	56	66	35
20 Man City	42	14	7	21	72	87	35
21 Stoke	42	12	10	20	53	66	34
22 Derby	42	11	10	21	59	74	32

SECOND DIVISION

	P	W	D	L	F	A	Pts
1 Sheff United	42	25	10	7	97	55	60
2 Huddersfield	42	24	10	8	84	33	58
3 Luton	42	22	8	12	84	49	52
4 Plymouth	42	20	9	13	65	60	49
5 Leicester	42	18	12	12	89	74	48
6 Birmingham	42	19	10	13	71	66	48
7 Nottm Forest	42	18	8	16	77	67	44
8 Fulham	42	17	10	15	81	71	44
9 Blackburn	42	18	8	16	68	65	44
10 Leeds	42	14	15	13	71	63	43
11 Swansea	42	15	12	15	78	81	42
12 Rotherham	42	16	9	17	75	74	41
13 Doncaster	42	12	16	14	58	64	40
14 West Ham	42	13	13	16	58	60	39
15 Lincoln	42	11	17	14	64	71	39
16 Everton	42	12	14	16	71	75	38
17 Brentford	42	13	11	18	59	76	37
18 Hull	42	14	8	20	57	69	36
19 Notts County	42	14	8	20	60	88	36
20 Bury	42	13	9	20	53	81	35
21 Southampton	42	10	13	19	68	85	33
22 Barnsley	42	5	8	29	47	108	18

FA CUP 1952-53

THIRD DIVISION (NORTH)

	P	W	D	L	F	A	Pts
1 Oldham	46	22	15	9	77	45	59
2 Port Vale	46	20	18	8	67	35	58
3 Wrexham	46	24	8	14	86	66	56
4 York	46	20	13	13	60	45	53
5 Grimsby	46	21	10	15	75	59	52
6 Southport	46	20	11	15	63	60	51
7 Bradford PA	46	19	12	15	75	61	50
8 Gateshead	46	17	15	14	76	60	49
9 Carlisle	46	18	13	15	82	68	49
10 Crewe	46	20	8	18	70	68	48
11 Stockport	46	17	13	16	82	69	47
12 Chesterfield*	46	18	11	17	65	63	47
13 Tranmere*	46	21	5	20	65	63	47
14 Halifax	46	16	15	15	68	68	47
15 Scunthorpe	46	16	14	16	62	56	46
16 Bradford City	46	14	18	14	75	80	46
17 Hartlepools	46	16	14	16	57	61	46
18 Mansfield	46	16	14	16	55	62	46
19 Barrow	46	16	12	18	66	71	44
20 Chester	46	11	15	20	64	85	37
21 Darlington	46	14	6	26	58	96	34
22 Rochdale	46	14	5	27	62	83	33
23 Workington	46	11	10	25	55	91	32
24 Accrington	46	8	11	27	39	89	27

*Equal

THIRD DIVISION (SOUTH)

	P	W	D	L	F	A	Pts
1 Bristol Rovers	46	26	12	8	92	46	64
2 Millwall	46	24	14	8	82	44	62
3 Northampton	46	26	10	10	109	70	62
4 Norwich	26	25	10	11	99	55	60
5 Bristol City	46	22	15	9	95	61	59
6 Coventry	46	19	12	15	77	62	50
7 Brighton	46	19	12	15	81	75	50
8 Southend	46	18	13	15	69	74	49
9 Bournemouth	46	19	9	18	74	69	47
10 Watford	46	15	17	14	62	63	47
11 Reading	46	19	8	19	69	64	46
12 Torquay	46	18	9	19	87	88	45
13 Crystal Palace	46	15	13	18	66	82	43
14 Leyton Orient	46	16	10	20	68	73	42
15 Newport	46	16	10	20	70	82	42
16 Ipswich	46	13	15	18	60	69	41
17 Exeter	46	13	14	19	61	71	40
18 Swindon	46	14	12	20	64	79	40
19 Aldershot	46	12	15	19	61	77	39
20 Gillingham	46	12	15	19	55	74	39
21 QPR	46	12	15	19	61	82	39
22 Colchester	46	12	14	20	59	76	38
23 Shrewsbury	46	12	12	22	68	91	36
24 Walsall	46	7	10	29	56	118	24

SCOTTISH FA CUP 1952-53

SCOTTISH DIVISION 'A'

	P	W	D	L	F	A	Pts
1 Rangers	30	18	7	5	80	39	43
2 Hibernian	30	19	5	6	93	51	43
3 East Fife	30	16	7	7	72	48	39
4 Hearts	30	12	6	12	59	50	30
5 Clyde	30	13	4	13	78	78	30
6 St Mirren	30	11	8	11	52	58	30
7 Dundee	30	9	11	8	44	37	29
8 Celtic	30	11	7	12	51	54	29
9 Partick	30	10	9	11	55	63	29
10 Queen of the S	30	10	8	12	43	61	28
11 Aberdeen	30	11	5	14	64	68	27
12 Raith Rovers	30	9	8	13	47	53	26
13 Falkirk	30	11	4	15	53	63	26
14 Airdrieonians	30	10	6	14	53	75	26
15 Motherwell	30	10	5	15	57	80	25
16 Third Lanark	30	8	4	18	52	75	20

SCOTTISH DIVISION 'B'

	P	W	D	L	F	A	Pts
1 Stirling	30	20	4	6	64	43	44
2 Hamilton	30	20	3	7	72	40	43
3 Queen's Park	30	15	7	8	70	46	37
4 Kilmarnock	30	17	2	11	74	48	36
5 Ayr	30	17	2	11	76	56	36
6 Morton	30	15	3	12	79	57	33
7 Arbroath	30	13	7	10	52	57	33
8 Dundee United	30	12	5	13	52	56	29
9 Alloa	30	12	5	13	63	68	29
10 Dumbarton	30	11	6	13	58	67	28
11 Dunfermline	30	9	9	12	51	58	27
12 Stenhousemuir	30	10	6	14	56	65	26
13 Cowdenbeath	30	8	7	15	37	54	23
14 St Johnstone	30	8	6	16	41	63	22
15 Forfar	30	8	4	18	54	88	20
16 Albion	30	5	4	21	44	77	14

A Division One match between Aston Villa and Sunderland in September 1952 produced a remarkable goal. It was scored by Peter Aldis, the Aston Villa full-back, who headed the ball into Sunderland's net from 35 yards. This goal, Aldis's first in the League, is reckoned to give Aldis the distance record for a headed goal in League football.

The footballing parson
The only post-War Football League professional who was also a parson was the Reverend Norman Hallam. A Methodist minister, Hallam was right-half for Port Vale in 1952-53. He later played for Barnsley and then Halifax before joining the Midland League club, Goole Town.

FIRST DIVISION

		P	W	D	L	F	A	Pts
1	Wolves	42	25	7	10	96	56	57
2	WBA	42	22	9	11	86	63	53
3	Huddersfield	42	20	11	11	78	61	51
4	Man United	42	18	12	12	73	58	48
5	Bolton	42	18	12	12	75	60	48
6	Blackpool	42	19	10	13	80	69	48
7	Burnley	42	21	4	17	78	67	46
8	Chelsea	42	16	12	14	74	68	44
9	Charlton	42	19	6	17	75	77	44
10	Cardiff	42	18	8	16	51	71	44
11	Preston	42	19	5	18	87	58	43
12	Arsenal	42	15	13	14	75	73	43
13	Aston Villa	42	16	9	17	70	68	41
14	Portsmouth	42	14	11	17	81	89	39
15	Newcastle	42	14	10	18	72	77	38
16	Tottenham	42	16	5	21	65	76	37
17	Man City	42	14	9	19	62	77	37
18	Sunderland	42	14	8	20	81	89	36
19	Sheff Wed	42	15	6	21	70	91	36
20	Sheff United	42	11	11	20	69	90	33
21	Middlesbrough	42	10	10	22	60	91	30
22	Liverpool	42	9	10	23	68	97	28

SECOND DIVISION

		P	W	D	L	F	A	Pts
1	Leicester	42	23	10	9	97	60	56
2	Everton	42	20	16	6	92	58	56
3	Blackburn	42	23	9	10	86	50	55
4	Nottm Forest	42	20	12	10	86	59	52
5	Rotherham	42	21	7	14	80	67	49
6	Luton	42	18	12	12	64	59	48
7	Birmingham	42	18	11	13	78	58	47
8	Fulham	42	17	10	15	98	85	44
9	Bristol Rovers	42	14	16	12	64	58	44
10	Leeds	42	15	13	14	89	81	43
11	Stoke	42	12	17	13	71	60	41
12	Doncaster	42	16	9	17	59	63	41
13	West Ham	42	15	9	18	67	69	39
14	Notts County	42	13	13	16	54	74	39
15	Hull	42	16	6	20	64	66	38
16	Lincoln	42	14	9	19	65	83	37
17	Bury	42	11	14	17	54	72	36
18	Derby	42	12	11	19	64	82	35
19	Plymouth	42	9	16	17	65	82	34
20	Swansea	42	13	8	21	58	82	34
21	Brentford	42	10	11	21	40	78	31
22	Oldham	42	8	9	25	40	89	25

FA CUP 1953-54

FOURTH ROUND

West Bromwich Albion v Rotherham United	4-0
Burnley v Newcastle United	1-1, 0-1
Blackburn Rovers v Hull City	2-2, 1-2
Manchester City v Tottenham Hotspur	0-1
Leyton Orient v Fulham	2-1
Plymouth Argyle v Doncaster Rovers	0-2
Cardiff City v Port Vale	0-2
West Ham United v Blackpool	1-1, 1-3
Sheffield Wednesday v Chesterfield	0-0, 4-2
Everton v Swansea Town	3-0
Headington United v Bolton Wanderers	2-4
Scunthorpe United v Portsmouth	1-1, 2-2, 0-4
Arsenal v Norwich City	1-2
Stoke City v Leicester City	0-0, 1-3
Lincoln City v Preston North End	0-2
Ipswich Town v Birmingham City	1-0

FIFTH ROUND

West Bromwich Albion v Newcastle United	3-2
Hull City v Tottenham Hotspur	1-1, 0-2
Leyton Orient v Doncaster Rovers	3-1
Port Vale v Blackpool	2-0
Sheffield Wednesday v Everton	3-1
Bolton Wanderers v Portsmouth	0-0, 2-1
Norwich City v Leicester City	1-2
Preston North End v Ipswich Town	6-1

SIXTH ROUND

West Bromwich Albion v Tottenham Hotspur	3-0
Leyton Orient v Port Vale	0-1
Sheffield Wednesday v Bolton Wanderers	1-1, 2-0
Leicester City v Preston North End	1-1, 2-2, 1-3

SEMI-FINAL

West Bromwich Albion v Port Vale	2-1
Sheffield Wednesday v Preston North End	0-2

FINAL

West Bromwich Albion v Preston North End	3-2

THIRD DIVISION (SOUTH)

		P	W	D	L	F	A	Pts
1	Ipswich	46	27	10	9	82	51	64
2	Brighton	46	26	9	11	86	61	61
3	Bristol City	46	25	6	15	88	66	56
4	Watford	46	21	10	15	85	69	52
5	Northampton	46	20	11	15	82	55	51
6	Southampton	46	22	7	17	76	63	51
7	Norwich	46	20	11	15	73	66	51
8	Reading	46	20	9	17	86	73	49
9	Exeter	46	20	8	18	68	58	48
10	Gillingham	46	19	10	17	61	66	48
11	Leyton Orient	46	18	11	17	79	73	47
12	Millwall	46	19	9	18	74	77	47
13	Torquay	46	17	12	17	81	88	46
14	Coventry	46	18	9	19	61	56	45
15	Newport	46	19	6	21	61	81	44
16	Southend	46	18	7	21	69	71	43
17	Aldershot	46	17	9	20	74	86	43
18	QPR	46	16	10	20	60	68	42
19	Bournemouth	46	16	8	22	67	70	40
20	Swindon	46	15	10	21	67	70	40
21	Shrewsbury	46	14	12	20	65	76	40
22	Crystal Palace	46	14	12	20	60	86	40
23	Colchester	46	10	10	26	50	78	30
24	Walsall	46	9	8	29	40	87	26

THIRD DIVISION (NORTH)

		P	W	D	L	F	A	Pts
1	Port Vale	46	26	17	3	74	21	69
2	Barnsley	46	24	10	12	77	57	58
3	Scunthorpe	46	21	15	10	77	56	57
4	Gateshead	46	21	13	12	74	55	55
5	Bradford City	46	22	9	15	60	55	53
6	Chesterfield	46	19	14	13	76	64	52
7	Mansfield	46	20	11	15	88	67	51
8	Wrexham	46	21	9	16	81	68	51
9	Bradford PA	46	18	14	14	77	68	50
10	Stockport	46	18	11	17	77	67	47
11	Southport	46	17	12	17	63	60	46
12	Barrow	46	16	12	18	72	71	44
13	Carlisle	46	14	15	17	83	71	43
14	Tranmere	46	18	7	21	59	70	43
15	Accrington	46	16	10	20	66	74	42
16	Crewe	46	14	13	19	49	67	41
17	Grimsby	46	16	9	21	51	77	41
18	Hartlepools	46	13	14	19	59	65	40
19	Rochdale	46	15	10	21	59	77	40
20	Workington	46	13	14	19	59	80	40
21	Darlington	46	12	14	20	50	71	38
22	York	46	12	13	21	64	86	37
23	Halifax	46	12	10	24	44	73	34
24	Chester	46	11	10	25	48	67	32

SCOTTISH FA CUP 1953-54

SECOND ROUND

Falkirk v Celtic	1-2
Stirling Albion v Arbroath	0-0, 3-1
Brechin City v Hamilton Academicals	2-3
Morton v Cowdenbeath	4-0
Tarff Rovers v Partick Thistle	1-9
Peebles Rovers v Buckie Thistle	1-1, 2-7
Motherwell v Dunfermline Athletic	5-2
Coldstream v Raith Rovers	1-10
Third Lanark v Deveronvale	7-2
Rangers v Kilmarnock	2-2, 3-1
Berwick Rangers v Ayr United	5-1
Albion Rovers v Dundee	1-1, 0-4
Queen of the South v Forfar Athletic	3-0
Fraserburgh v Heart of Midlothian	0-3
Hibernian v Clyde	7-0
Duns v Aberdeen	0-8

THIRD ROUND

Stirling Albion v Celtic	3-4
Hamilton Academicals v Morton	2-0
Partick Thistle v Buckie Thistle	5-3
Motherwell v Raith Rovers	4-1
Third Lanark v Rangers	0-0, 4-4, 2-3
Berwick Rangers v Dundee	3-0
Queen of the South v Heart of Midlothian	1-2
Hibernian v Aberdeen	1-3

FOURTH ROUND

Hamilton Academicals v Celtic	1-2
Partick Thistle v Motherwell	1-1, 1-2
Rangers v Berwick Rangers	4-0
Aberdeen v Heart of Midlothian	3-0

SEMI-FINAL

Celtic v Motherwell	2-2, 3-1
Rangers v Aberdeen	0-6

FINAL

Aberdeen v Celtic	1-2

SCOTTISH DIVISION 'A'

		P	W	D	L	F	A	Pts
1	Celtic	30	20	3	7	72	29	43
2	Hearts	30	16	6	8	70	45	38
3	Partick	30	17	1	12	76	54	35
4	Rangers	30	13	8	9	56	35	34
5	Hibernian	30	15	4	11	72	51	34
6	East Fife	30	13	8	9	55	45	34
7	Dundee	30	14	6	10	46	47	34
8	Clyde	30	15	4	11	64	67	34
9	Aberdeen	30	15	3	12	66	51	33
10	Queen of the S	30	14	4	12	72	58	32
11	St Mirren	30	12	4	14	44	54	28
12	Raith	30	10	6	14	56	60	26
13	Falkirk	30	9	7	14	47	61	25
14	Stirling	30	10	4	16	39	62	24
15	Airdrieonians	30	5	5	20	41	92	15
16	Hamilton	30	4	3	23	29	94	11

SCOTTISH DIVISION 'B'

		P	W	D	L	F	A	Pts
1	Motherwell	30	21	3	6	109	43	45
2	Kilmarnock	30	19	4	7	71	39	42
3	Third Lanark	30	13	10	7	78	48	36
4	Stenhousemuir	30	14	8	8	66	58	36
5	Morton	30	15	3	12	85	65	33
6	St Johnstone	30	14	3	13	80	71	31
7	Albion	30	12	7	11	55	63	31
8	Dunfermline	30	11	9	10	48	57	31
9	Ayr	30	11	8	11	50	56	30
10	Queen's Park	30	9	9	12	56	51	27
11	Alloa	30	7	10	13	50	72	24
12	Forfar	30	10	4	16	38	69	24
13	Cowdenbeath	30	9	5	16	67	81	23
14	Arbroath	30	8	7	15	53	67	23
15	Dundee United	30	8	6	16	54	79	22
16	Dumbarton	30	7	8	15	51	92	22

Since the offside rule was changed in 1925, the record number of League games which a club has played in any one season without conceding a goal is 30. Port Vale, with their unpopular yet effective brand of defensive football, set this record in Division Three North, 1953-54. That season, Vale lost but three games, also a record for that division, conceding just 21 goals, a League record.

Stalemate

On 9 January 1954, 15 of the 32 Third Round FA Cup ties played that day ended as draws, a record for the FA Cup competition.

A post-war record Scottish FA Cup win away from home was set on 13 February 1954. Then, in the Second Round, Raith Rovers crumpled Coldstream 10-1.

FIRST DIVISION

		P	W	D	L	F	A	Pts
1	Chelsea	42	20	12	10	81	57	52
2	Wolves	42	19	10	13	89	70	48
3	Portsmouth	42	18	12	12	74	62	48
4	Sunderland	42	15	18	9	64	54	48
5	Man United	42	20	7	15	84	74	47
6	Aston Villa	42	20	7	15	72	73	47
7	Man City	42	18	10	14	76	69	46
8	Newcastle	42	17	9	16	89	77	43
9	Arsenal	42	17	9	16	69	63	43
10	Burnley	42	17	9	16	51	48	43
11	Everton	42	16	10	16	62	68	42
12	Huddersfield	42	14	13	15	63	68	41
13	Sheff United	42	17	7	18	70	86	41
14	Preston	42	16	8	18	83	64	40
15	Charlton	42	15	10	17	76	75	40
16	Tottenham	42	16	8	18	72	73	40
17	WBA	42	16	8	18	76	96	40
18	Bolton	42	13	13	16	62	69	39
19	Blackpool	42	14	10	18	60	64	38
20	Cardiff	42	13	11	18	62	76	37
21	Leicester	42	12	11	19	74	86	35
22	Sheff Wed	42	8	10	24	63	100	26

SECOND DIVISION

		P	W	D	L	F	A	Pts
1	Birmingham	42	22	10	10	92	47	54
2	Luton	42	23	8	11	88	53	54
3	Rotherham	42	25	4	13	94	64	54
4	Leeds	42	23	7	12	70	53	53
5	Stoke	42	21	10	11	69	46	52
6	Blackburn	42	22	6	14	114	79	50
7	Notts County	42	21	6	15	74	71	48
8	West Ham	42	18	10	14	74	70	46
9	Bristol Rovers	42	19	7	16	75	70	45
10	Swansea	42	17	9	16	86	83	43
11	Liverpool	42	16	10	16	92	96	42
12	Middlesbrough	42	18	6	18	73	82	42
13	Bury	42	15	11	16	77	72	41
14	Fulham	42	14	11	17	76	79	39
15	Nottm Forest	42	16	7	19	58	62	39
16	Lincoln	42	13	10	19	68	79	36
17	Port Vale	42	12	11	19	48	71	35
18	Doncaster	42	14	7	21	58	95	35
19	Hull	42	12	10	20	44	69	34
20	Plymouth	42	12	7	23	57	82	31
21	Ipswich	42	11	6	25	57	92	28
22	Derby	42	7	9	26	53	82	23

THIRD DIVISION (SOUTH)

		P	W	D	L	F	A	Pts
1	Bristol City	46	30	10	6	101	47	70
2	Leyton Orient	46	26	9	11	89	47	61
3	Southampton	46	24	11	11	75	51	59
4	Gillingham	46	20	15	11	77	66	55
5	Millwall	46	20	11	15	72	68	51
6	Brighton	46	20	10	16	76	63	50
7	Watford	46	18	14	14	71	62	50
8	Torquay	46	18	12	16	82	82	48
9	Coventry	46	18	11	17	67	59	47
10	Southend	46	17	12	17	83	80	46
11	Brentford	46	16	14	16	82	82	46
12	Norwich	46	18	10	18	60	60	46
13	Northampton	46	19	8	19	73	81	46
14	Aldershot	46	16	13	17	75	71	45
15	QPR	46	15	14	17	69	75	44
16	Shrewsbury	46	16	10	20	70	78	42
17	Bournemouth	46	12	18	16	57	65	42
18	Reading	46	13	15	18	65	73	41
19	Newport	46	11	16	19	60	73	38
20	Crystal Palace	46	11	16	19	52	80	38
21	Swindon	46	11	15	20	46	64	37
22	Exeter	46	11	15	20	47	73	37
23	Walsall	46	10	14	22	75	86	34
24	Colchester	46	9	13	24	53	91	31

THIRD DIVISION (NORTH)

		P	W	D	L	F	A	Pts
1	Barnsley	46	30	5	11	86	46	65
2	Accrington	46	25	11	10	96	67	61
3	Scunthorpe	46	23	12	11	81	53	58
4	York	46	24	10	12	92	63	58
5	Hartlepools	46	25	5	16	64	49	55
6	Chesterfield	46	24	6	16	81	70	54
7	Gateshead	46	20	12	14	65	69	52
8	Workington	46	18	14	14	68	55	50
9	Stockport	46	18	12	16	84	70	48
10	Oldham	46	19	10	17	74	68	48
11	Southport	46	16	16	14	47	44	48
12	Rochdale	46	17	14	15	69	66	48
13	Mansfield	46	18	9	19	65	71	45
14	Halifax	46	15	13	18	63	67	43
15	Darlington	46	14	14	18	62	73	42
16	Bradford PA	46	15	11	20	56	70	41
17	Barrow	46	17	6	23	70	89	40
18	Wrexham	46	13	12	21	65	77	38
19	Tranmere	46	13	11	22	55	70	37
20	Carlisle	46	15	6	25	78	89	36
21	Bradford City	46	13	10	23	47	55	36
22	Crewe	46	10	14	22	68	91	34
23	Grimsby	46	13	8	25	47	78	34
24	Chester	46	12	9	25	44	77	33

SCOTTISH DIVISION 'A'

		P	W	D	L	F	A	Pts
1	Aberdeen	30	24	1	5	73	26	49
2	Celtic	30	19	8	3	76	37	46
3	Rangers	30	19	3	8	67	33	41
4	Hearts	30	16	7	7	74	45	39
5	Hibernian	30	15	4	11	64	54	34
6	St Mirren	30	12	8	10	55	54	32
7	Clyde	30	11	9	10	59	50	31
8	Dundee	30	13	4	13	48	48	30
9	Partick Thistle	30	11	7	12	49	61	29
10	Kilmarnock	30	10	6	14	46	58	26
11	East Fife	30	9	6	15	51	62	24
12	Falkirk	30	8	8	14	42	54	24
13	Queen of the S	30	9	6	15	38	56	24
14	Raith	30	10	3	17	49	57	23
15	Motherwell	30	9	4	17	42	62	22
16	Stirling	30	2	2	26	29	105	6

SCOTTISH DIVISION 'B'

		P	W	D	L	F	A	Pts
1	Airdrieonians	30	18	10	2	103	61	46
2	Dunfermline	30	19	4	7	72	40	42
3	Hamilton	30	17	5	8	74	51	39
4	Queen's Park	30	15	5	10	65	36	35
5	Third Lanark	30	13	7	10	63	49	33
6	Stenhousemuir	30	12	8	10	70	51	32
7	St Johnstone	30	15	2	13	60	51	32
8	Ayr	30	14	4	12	61	73	32
9	Morton	30	12	5	13	58	69	29
10	Forfar	30	11	6	13	63	80	28
11	Albion	30	8	10	12	50	69	26
12	Arbroath	30	8	8	14	55	72	24
13	Dundee United	30	8	6	16	55	70	22
14	Cowdenbeath	30	8	5	17	55	72	21
15	Alloa	30	7	6	17	51	75	20
16	Brechin	30	8	3	19	53	89	19

FA CUP 1954-55

FOURTH ROUND

Everton v Liverpool	0-4
Torquay United v Huddersfield Town	0-1
Hartlepools United v Nottingham Forest	1-1, 1-2
Newcastle United v Brentford	3-2
Sheffield Wednesday v Notts County	1-1, 0-1
Bristol Rovers v Chelsea	1-3
Bishop Auckland v York City	1-3
Tottenham Hotspur v Port Vale	4-2
Swansea Town v Stoke City	3-1
Preston North End v Sunderland	3-3, 0-2
Wolverhampton Wanderers v Arsenal	1-0
West Bromwich Albion v Charlton Athletic	2-4
Birmingham City v Bolton Wanderers	2-1
Doncaster Rovers v Aston Villa	0-0, 2-2, 1-1, 0-0, 3-1
Rotherham United v Luton Town	1-5
Manchester City v Manchester United	2-0

FIFTH ROUND

Liverpool v Huddersfield Town	0-2
Nottingham Forest v Newcastle United	1-1, 2-2, 1-2
Notts County v Chelsea	1-0
York City v Tottenham Hotspur	3-1
Swansea Town v Sunderland	2-2, 0-1
Wolverhampton Wanderers v Charlton Athletic	4-1
Birmingham City v Doncaster Rovers	2-1
Luton Town v Manchester City	0-2

SIXTH ROUND

Huddersfield Town v Newcastle United	1-1, 0-2
Notts County v York City	0-1
Sunderland v Wolverhampton Wanderers	2-0
Birmingham City v Manchester City	0-1

SEMI-FINAL

Newcastle United v York City	1-1, 2-0
Sunderland v Manchester City	0-1

FINAL

Newcastle United v Manchester City	3-1

SCOTTISH FA CUP 1954-55

FIFTH ROUND

Clyde v Albion Rovers	3-0
Morton v Raith Rovers	1-3
Ayr United v Inverness Caledonian	1-1, 2-4
Heart of Midlothian v Hibernian	5-0
Stirling Albion v Aberdeen	0-6
Dundee v Rangers	0-0, 0-1
Airdrieonians v Forfar Athletic	4-3
Dunfermline Athletic v Partick Thistle	4-2
Third Lanark v Queen of the South	2-1
Forres Mechanics v Motherwell	3-4
East Fife v Kilmarnock	1-2
Alloa Athletic v Celtic	2-4
Arbroath v St Johnstone	0-4
Hamilton Academicals v St Mirren	2-1
Falkirk v Stenhousemuir	4-0
Buckie Thistle v Inverness Thistle	2-0

SIXTH ROUND

Clyde v Raith Rovers	3-1
Inverness Caledonian v Falkirk	0-7
Buckie Thistle v Heart of Midlothian	0-6
Aberdeen v Rangers	2-1
Airdrieonians v Dunfermline Athletic	7-0
Third Lanark v Motherwell	1-3
Celtic v Kilmarnock	1-1, 1-0
St Johnstone v Hamilton Academicals	0-1

SEVENTH ROUND

Clyde v Falkirk	5-0
Aberdeen v Heart of Midlothian	1-1, 2-0
Airdrieonians v Motherwell	4-1
Celtic v Hamilton Academicals	2-1

SEMI-FINAL

Aberdeen v Clyde	2-2, 0-1
Airdrieonians v Celtic	2-2, 0-2

FINAL

Celtic v Clyde	1-1, 0-1

A combined effort

Stan Milburn and Jack Froggatt, both Leicester City defenders, are officially recorded as 'sharing one own goal' on 18 December 1954. In the Division One game with Chelsea at Stamford Bridge, Froggatt and Milburn were involved in a misunderstanding in front of goal, and simultaneously booted the ball into the Leicester net, thus sharing the blame. Chelsea won the game by three goals to one.

Stoke City and Bury created an endurance record for an FA Cup match when they met five times in the Third Round in January 1955. Altogether they played for 9 hours and 22 minutes before Stoke won 3-2 at Old Trafford.

On 2 April 1955, Duncan Edwards of Manchester United became the youngest ever England international when, aged 18 years six months, he played against Scotland.

FIRST DIVISION

		P	W	D	L	F	A	Pts
1	Man United	42	25	10	7	83	51	60
2	Blackpool	42	20	9	13	86	62	49
3	Wolves	42	20	9	13	89	65	49
4	Man City	42	18	10	14	82	69	46
5	Arsenal	42	18	10	14	60	61	46
6	Birmingham	42	18	9	15	75	57	45
7	Burnley	42	18	8	16	64	54	44
8	Bolton	42	18	7	17	71	58	43
9	Sunderland	42	17	9	16	80	95	43
10	Luton	42	17	8	17	66	64	42
11	Newcastle	42	17	7	18	85	70	41
12	Portsmouth	42	16	9	17	78	85	41
13	WBA	42	18	5	19	58	70	41
14	Charlton	42	17	6	19	75	81	40
15	Everton	42	15	10	17	55	69	40
16	Chelsea	42	14	11	17	64	77	39
17	Cardiff	42	15	9	18	55	69	39
18	Tottenham	42	15	7	20	61	71	37
19	Preston	42	14	8	20	73	72	36
20	Aston Villa	42	11	13	18	52	69	35
21	Huddersfield	42	14	7	21	54	83	35
22	Sheff United	42	12	9	21	63	77	33

SECOND DIVISION

		P	W	D	L	F	A	Pts
1	Sheff Wed	42	21	13	8	101	62	55
2	Leeds	42	23	6	13	80	60	52
3	Liverpool	42	21	6	15	85	63	48
4	Blackburn	42	21	6	15	84	65	48
5	Leicester	42	21	6	15	94	78	48
6	Bristol Rovers	42	21	6	15	84	70	48
7	Nottm Forest	42	19	9	14	68	63	47
8	Lincoln	42	18	10	14	79	65	46
9	Fulham	42	20	6	16	89	79	46
10	Swansea	42	20	6	16	83	81	46
11	Bristol City	42	19	7	16	80	64	45
12	Port Vale	42	16	13	13	60	58	45
13	Stoke	42	20	4	18	71	62	44
14	Middlesbrough	42	16	8	18	76	78	40
15	Bury	42	16	8	18	86	90	40
16	West Ham	42	14	11	17	74	69	39
17	Doncaster	42	12	11	19	69	96	35
18	Barnsley	42	11	12	19	47	84	34
19	Rotherham	42	12	9	21	56	75	33
20	Notts County	42	11	9	22	55	82	31
21	Plymouth	42	10	8	24	54	87	28
22	Hull	42	10	6	26	53	97	26

THIRD DIVISION (NORTH)

		P	W	D	L	F	A	Pts
1	Grimsby	46	31	6	9	76	29	68
2	Derby	46	28	7	11	110	55	63
3	Accrington	46	25	9	12	92	57	59
4	Hartlepools	46	26	5	15	81	60	57
5	Southport	46	23	11	12	66	53	57
6	Chesterfield	46	25	4	17	94	66	54
7	Stockport	46	21	9	16	90	61	51
8	Bradford City	46	18	13	15	78	64	49
9	Scunthorpe	46	20	8	18	75	63	48
10	Workington	46	19	9	18	75	63	47
11	York	46	19	9	18	85	72	47
12	Rochdale	46	17	13	16	66	84	47
13	Gateshead	46	17	11	18	77	84	45
14	Wrexham	46	16	10	20	66	73	42
15	Darlington	46	16	9	21	60	73	41
16	Tranmere	46	16	9	21	59	84	41
17	Chester	46	13	14	19	52	82	40
18	Mansfield	46	14	11	21	84	81	39
19	Halifax	46	14	11	21	66	76	39
20	Oldham	46	10	18	18	76	86	38
21	Carlisle	46	15	8	23	71	95	38
22	Barrow	46	12	9	25	61	83	33
23	Bradford PA	46	13	7	26	61	122	33
24	Crewe	46	9	10	27	50	105	28

THIRD DIVISION (SOUTH)

		P	W	D	L	F	A	Pts
1	Leyton Orient	46	29	8	9	106	49	66
2	Brighton	46	29	7	10	112	50	65
3	Ipswich	46	25	14	7	106	60	64
4	Southend	46	21	11	14	88	80	53
5	Torquay	46	20	12	14	86	63	52
6	Brentford	46	19	14	13	69	66	52
7	Norwich	46	19	13	14	86	82	51
8	Coventry	46	20	9	17	73	60	49
9	Bournemouth	46	19	10	17	63	51	48
10	Gillingham	46	19	10	17	69	71	48
11	Northampton	46	20	7	19	67	71	47
12	Colchester	46	18	11	17	76	81	47
13	Shrewsbury	46	17	12	17	69	66	46
14	Southampton	46	18	8	20	91	81	44
15	Aldershot	46	12	16	18	70	90	40
16	Exeter	46	15	10	21	58	77	40
17	Reading	46	15	9	22	70	79	39
18	QPR	46	14	11	21	64	86	39
19	Newport	46	15	9	22	58	79	39
20	Walsall	46	15	8	23	68	84	38
21	Watford	46	13	11	22	52	85	37
22	Millwall	46	15	6	25	83	100	36
23	Crystal Palace	46	12	10	24	54	83	34
24	Swindon	46	8	14	24	34	78	30

SCOTTISH LEAGUE 'A'

		P	W	D	L	F	A	Pts
1	Rangers	34	22	8	4	85	27	52
2	Aberdeen	34	18	10	6	87	50	46
3	Hearts	34	19	7	8	99	47	45
4	Hibernian	34	19	7	8	86	50	45
5	Celtic	34	16	9	9	55	39	41
6	Queen of the S	34	16	5	13	69	73	37
7	Airdrieonians	34	14	8	12	85	96	36
8	Kilmarnock	34	12	10	12	52	45	34
9	Partick Thistle	34	13	7	14	62	60	33
10	Motherwell	34	11	11	12	53	59	33
11	Raith	34	12	9	13	58	75	33
12	East Fife	34	13	5	16	61	69	31
13	Dundee	34	12	6	16	56	65	30
14	Falkirk	34	11	6	17	58	75	28
15	St Mirren	34	10	7	17	57	70	27
16	Dunfermline	34	10	6	18	42	82	26
17	Clyde	34	8	6	20	50	74	22
18	Stirling	34	4	5	25	23	82	13

SCOTTISH LEAGUE 'B'

		P	W	D	L	F	A	Pts
1	Queen's Park	36	23	8	5	78	28	54
2	Ayr	36	24	3	9	103	55	51
3	St Johnstone	36	21	7	8	86	45	49
4	Dumbarton	36	21	9	10	83	62	47
5	Stenhousemuir	36	20	4	12	82	54	44
6	Brechin	36	18	6	12	60	56	42
7	Cowdenbeath	36	16	7	13	80	85	39
8	Dundee United	36	12	14	10	78	65	38
9	Morton	36	15	6	15	71	69	36
10	Third Lanark	36	16	3	17	80	64	35
11	Hamilton	36	13	7	16	86	84	33
12	Stranraer	36	14	5	17	77	92	33
13	Alloa	36	12	7	17	67	73	31
14	Berwick	36	11	9	16	52	77	31
15	Forfar	36	10	9	17	62	75	29
16	E Stirlingshire	36	9	10	17	66	94	28
17	Albion	36	8	11	17	58	82	27
18	Arbroath	36	10	6	20	47	67	26
19	Montrose	36	4	3	29	44	133	11

FA CUP 1955-56

FOURTH ROUND
Leyton Orient v Birmingham City	0-4
West Bromwich Albion v Portsmouth	2-0
Charlton Athletic v Swindon Town	2-1
Arsenal v Aston Villa	4-1
Fulham v Newcastle United	4-5
Leicester City v Stoke City	3-3, 1-2
Bolton Wanderers v Sheffield United	1-2
York City v Sunderland	0-0, 1-2
Bristol Rovers v Doncaster Rovers	1-1, 0-1
Tottenham Hotspur v Middlesbrough	3-1
West Ham United v Cardiff City	2-1
Barnsley v Blackburn Rovers	0-1
Port Vale v Everton	2-3
Burnley v Chelsea	1-1, 1-1, 2-2, 0-0, 0-2
Liverpool v Scunthorpe United	3-3, 2-1
Southend United v Manchester City	0-1

FIFTH ROUND
West Bromwich Albion v Birmingham City	0-1
Charlton Athletic v Arsenal	0-2
Newcastle United v Stoke City	2-1
Sheffield United v Sunderland	0-0, 0-1
Doncaster Rovers v Tottenham Hotspur	0-2
West Ham United v Blackburn Rovers	0-0, 3-2
Everton v Chelsea	1-0
Manchester City v Liverpool	0-0, 2-1

SIXTH ROUND
Arsenal v Birmingham City	1-3
Newcastle United v Sunderland	0-2
Tottenham Hotspur v West Ham United	3-3, 2-1
Manchester City v Everton	2-1

SEMI-FINAL
Birmingham City v Sunderland	3-0
Tottenham Hotspur v Manchester City	0-1

FINAL
Manchester City v Birmingham City	3-1

SCOTTISH FA CUP 1955-56

FIFTH ROUND
Heart of Midlothian v Forfar Athletic	3-0
Stirling Albion v St Johnstone	2-1
Rangers v Aberdeen	2-1
Dundee v Dundee United	2-2, 3-0
Hibernian v Raith Rovers	1-1, 1-3
Motherwell v Queen's Park	0-2
Partick Thistle v Alloa Athletic	2-0
Brechin City v Arbroath	1-1, 3-2
Falkirk v Kilmarnock	0-3
Queen of the South v Cowdenbeath	3-1
East Fife v Stenhousemuir	1-3
Clyde v Dunfermline Athletic	5-0
St Mirren v Third Lanark	6-0
Airdrieonians v Hamilton Academicals	7-1
Ayr United v Berwick Rangers	5-2
Morton v Celtic	0-2

SIXTH ROUND
Heart of Midlothian v Stirling Albion	5-0
Dundee v Rangers	0-1
Raith Rovers v Queen's Park	2-2, 2-1
Partick Thistle v Brechin City	3-1
Kilmarnock v Queen of the South	2-2, 0-2
Stenhousemuir v Clyde	0-1
St Mirren v Airdrieonians	4-4, 1-3
Ayr United v Celtic	0-3

SEVENTH ROUND
Heart of Midlothian v Rangers	4-0
Raith Rovers v Partick Thistle	2-1
Queen of the South v Clyde	2-4
Celtic v Airdrieonians	2-1

SEMI-FINAL
Heart of Midlothian v Raith Rovers	0-0, 3-0
Celtic v Clyde	2-0

FINAL
Heart of Midlothian v Celtic	3-1

Accrington Stanley set a League record early in the 1955-56 season by fielding a side composed entirely of Scottish-born players. During the season, this team appeared several times. Indeed, all but four of the first-team squad of 19 players the club used that season in the Third Division North were born in Scotland.

On 3 September 1955, Wolves beat Cardiff 9-1 away from home to equal the Division One record away win. Curiously, later in the season, Cardiff won 2-0 at Wolves.

All four countries in the Home Championship finished level with three points, the first time this had ever happened.

FIRST DIVISION

		P	W	D	L	F	A	Pts
1	Man United	42	28	8	6	103	54	64
2	Tottenham	42	22	12	8	104	56	56
3	Preston	42	23	10	9	84	56	56
4	Blackpool	42	22	9	11	93	65	53
5	Arsenal	42	21	8	13	85	69	50
6	Wolves	42	20	8	14	94	70	48
7	Burnley	42	18	10	14	56	50	46
8	Leeds	42	15	14	13	72	63	44
9	Bolton	42	16	12	14	65	65	44
10	Aston Villa	42	14	15	13	65	55	43
11	WBA	42	14	14	14	59	61	42
12	Birmingham*	42	15	9	18	69	69	39
13	Chelsea*	42	13	13	16	73	73	39
14	Sheff Wed	42	16	6	20	82	88	38
15	Everton	42	14	10	18	61	79	38
16	Luton	42	14	9	19	58	76	37
17	Newcastle	42	14	8	20	67	87	36
18	Man City	42	13	9	20	78	88	35
19	Portsmouth	42	10	13	19	62	92	33
20	Sunderland	42	12	8	22	67	88	32
21	Cardiff	42	10	9	23	53	88	29
22	Charlton	42	9	4	29	62	120	22

*Equal

SECOND DIVISION

		P	W	D	L	F	A	Pts
1	Leicester	42	25	11	6	109	67	61
2	Nottm Forest	42	22	10	10	94	55	54
3	Liverpool	42	21	11	10	82	54	53
4	Blackburn	42	21	10	11	83	75	52
5	Stoke	42	20	8	14	83	58	48
6	Middlesbrough	42	19	10	13	84	60	48
7	Sheff United	42	19	8	15	87	76	46
8	West Ham	42	19	8	15	59	63	46
9	Bristol Rovers	42	18	9	15	81	67	45
10	Swansea	42	19	7	16	90	90	45
11	Fulham	42	19	4	19	84	76	42
12	Huddersfield	42	18	6	18	68	74	42
13	Bristol City	42	16	9	17	74	79	41
14	Doncaster	42	15	10	17	77	77	40
15	Leyton Orient	42	15	10	17	66	84	40
16	Grimsby	42	17	5	20	61	62	39
17	Rotherham	42	13	11	18	74	75	37
18	Lincoln	42	14	6	22	54	80	34
19	Barnsley	42	12	10	20	59	89	34
20	Notts County	42	9	12	21	58	86	30
21	Bury	42	8	9	25	60	96	25
22	Port Vale	42	8	6	28	57	101	22

THIRD DIVISION (SOUTH)

		P	W	D	L	F	A	Pts
1	Ipswich	46	25	9	12	101	54	59
2	Torquay	46	24	11	11	89	64	59
3	Colchester	46	22	14	10	84	56	58
4	Southampton	46	22	10	14	76	52	54
5	Bournemouth	46	19	14	13	88	62	52
6	Brighton	46	19	14	13	86	65	52
7	Southend	46	18	12	16	73	65	48
8	Brentford	46	16	16	14	78	76	48
9	Shrewsbury	46	15	18	13	72	79	48
10	QPR	46	18	11	17	61	60	47
11	Watford	46	18	10	18	72	75	46
12	Newport	46	16	13	17	65	62	45
13	Reading	46	18	9	19	80	81	45
14	Northampton	46	18	9	19	66	73	45
15	Walsall	46	16	12	18	80	74	44
16	Coventry	46	16	12	18	74	84	44
17	Millwall	46	16	12	18	64	84	44
18	Plymouth	46	16	11	19	68	73	43
19	Aldershot	46	15	12	19	79	92	42
20	Crystal Palace	46	11	18	17	62	75	40
21	Exeter	46	12	13	21	61	79	37
22	Gillingham	46	12	13	21	54	85	37
23	Swindon	46	15	6	25	66	96	36
24	Norwich	46	8	15	23	61	94	31

THIRD DIVISION (NORTH)

		P	W	D	L	F	A	Pts
1	Derby	46	26	11	9	111	53	63
2	Hartlepools	46	25	9	12	90	63	59
3	Accrington	46	25	8	13	95	64	58
4	Workington	46	24	10	12	93	63	58
5	Stockport	46	23	8	15	91	75	54
6	Chesterfield	46	22	9	15	96	79	53
7	York	46	21	10	15	75	61	52
8	Hull	46	21	10	15	84	69	52
9	Bradford City	46	22	8	16	78	68	52
10	Barrow	46	21	9	16	76	62	51
11	Halifax	46	21	7	18	65	70	49
12	Wrexham	46	19	10	17	97	74	48
13	Rochdale	46	18	12	16	65	65	48
14	Scunthorpe	46	15	15	16	71	69	45
15	Carlisle	46	16	13	17	76	85	45
16	Mansfield	46	17	10	19	91	90	44
17	Gateshead	46	17	10	19	72	90	44
18	Darlington	46	17	8	21	82	95	42
19	Oldham	46	12	15	19	66	74	39
20	Bradford PA	46	16	3	27	66	93	35
21	Chester	46	10	13	23	55	84	33
22	Southport	46	10	12	24	52	94	32
23	Tranmere	46	7	13	26	51	91	27
24	Crewe	46	6	9	31	43	110	21

SCOTTISH FIRST DIVISION

		P	W	D	L	F	A	Pts
1	Rangers	34	26	3	5	96	48	55
2	Hearts	34	24	5	5	81	48	53
3	Kilmarnock	34	16	10	8	57	39	42
4	Raith	34	16	7	11	84	58	39
5	Celtic	34	15	8	11	58	43	38
6	Aberdeen	34	18	2	14	79	59	38
7	Motherwell	34	16	5	13	72	66	37
8	Partick Thistle	34	13	8	13	53	51	34
9	Hibernian	34	12	9	13	69	56	33
10	Dundee	34	13	6	15	55	61	32
11	Airdrieonians	34	13	4	17	77	89	30
12	St Mirren	34	12	6	16	58	72	30
13	Queen's Park	34	11	7	16	55	59	29
14	Falkirk	34	10	8	16	51	70	28
15	East Fife	34	10	6	18	59	82	26
16	Queen of the S	34	10	5	19	54	96	25
17	Dunfermline	34	9	6	19	54	74	24
18	Ayr	34	7	5	22	48	89	19

SCOTTISH SECOND DIVISION

		P	W	D	L	F	A	Pts
1	Clyde	36	29	6	1	122	39	64
2	Third Lanark	36	24	3	9	105	51	51
3	Cowdenbeath	36	20	5	11	87	65	45
4	Morton	36	18	7	11	81	70	43
5	Albion	36	18	6	12	98	80	42
6	Brechin	36	15	10	11	72	68	40
7	Stranraer	36	15	10	11	79	77	40
8	Stirling	36	17	5	14	81	64	39
9	Dumbarton	36	17	4	15	101	70	38
10	Arbroath	36	17	4	15	79	57	38
11	Hamilton	36	14	8	14	69	68	36
12	St Johnstone	36	14	6	16	79	80	34
13	Dundee United	36	14	6	16	75	80	34
14	Stenhousemuir	36	13	6	17	71	81	32
15	Alloa	36	11	5	20	66	99	27
16	Forfar	36	9	5	22	75	100	23
17	Montrose	36	7	7	22	54	124	21
18	Berwick	36	7	6	23	58	114	20
19	E Stirlingshire	36	5	7	24	56	121	17

FA CUP 1956-57

FOURTH ROUND

Middlesbrough v Aston Villa	2-3
Bristol City v Rhyl	3-0
Burnley v New Brighton	9-0
Huddersfield Town v Peterborough United	3-1
Newport County v Arsenal	0-2
Bristol Rovers v Preston North End	1-4
Blackpool v Fulham	6-2
West Bromwich Albion v Sunderland	4-2
Wrexham v Manchester United	0-5
Everton v West Ham United	2-1
Wolverhampton Wanderers v Bournemouth	0-1
Tottenham Hotspur v Chelsea	4-0
Southend United v Birmingham City	1-6
Millwall v Newcastle United	2-1
Cardiff City v Barnsley	0-1
Portsmouth v Nottingham Forest	1-3

FIFTH ROUND

Aston Villa v Bristol City	2-1
Huddersfield Town v Burnley	1-2
Preston North End v Arsenal	3-3, 1-2
Blackpool v West Bromwich Albion	0-0, 1-2
Manchester United v Everton	1-0
Bournemouth v Tottenham Hotspur	3-1
Millwall v Birmingham City	1-4
Barnsley v Nottingham Forest	1-2

SIXTH ROUND

Burnley v Aston Villa	1-1, 0-2
West Bromwich Albion v Arsenal	2-2, 2-1
Bournemouth v Manchester United	1-2
Birmingham City v Nottingham Forest	0-0, 1-0

SEMI-FINAL

Aston Villa v West Bromwich Albion	2-2, 1-0
Manchester United v Birmingham City	2-0

FINAL

Aston Villa v Manchester United	2-1

SCOTTISH FA CUP 1956-57

FIFTH ROUND

Berwick Rangers v Falkirk	1-2
Hibernian v Aberdeen	3-4
Dundee v Clyde	0-0, 1-2
Queen's Park v Brechin City	3-0
Inverness Caledonian v Raith Rovers	2-3
Stenhousemuir v Dundee United	1-1, 0-4
Queen of the South v Dumbarton	2-2, 2-4
Stirling Albion v Motherwell	1-2
Dunfermline Athletic v Morton	3-0
St Mirren v Partick Thistle	1-1, 2-2, 5-1
Heart of Midlothian v Rangers	0-4
Forres Mechanics v Celtic	0-5
Hamilton Academicals v Alloa Athletic	2-2, 5-3
Stranraer v Airdrieonians	1-2
East Fife v St Johnstone	4-0
Kilmarnock v Ayr United	1-0

SIXTH ROUND

Falkirk v Aberdeen	3-1
Queen's Park v Clyde	1-1, 0-2
Raith Rovers v Dundee United	7-0
Motherwell v Dumbarton	1-3
St Mirren v Dunfermline Athletic	1-0
Celtic v Rangers	4-4, 2-0
Hamilton Academicals v Airdrieonians	1-2
East Fife v Kilmarnock	0-0, 0-2

SEVENTH ROUND

Falkirk v Clyde	2-1
Dumbarton v Raith Rovers	0-4
Celtic v St Mirren	2-1
Kilmarnock v Airdrieonians	3-1

SEMI-FINAL

Falkirk v Raith Rovers	2-2, 2-0
Celtic v Kilmarnock	1-1, 1-3

FINAL

Falkirk v Kilmarnock	1-1, 2-1

New man in charge

On 1 January 1957, Alan Hardaker became secretary to the Football League. Hardaker, once an amateur footballer with Hull City, had been assistant secretary since 1951.

After beating Scunthorpe United 2-1, on 19 September 1956, Crewe Alexandra of the Third Division North did not win again until they beat Bradford City 1-0 on 13 April 1957, a League record of 30 games without a win.

231

FIRST DIVISION

		P	W	D	L	F	A	Pts
1	Wolves	42	28	8	6	103	47	64
2	Preston	42	26	7	9	100	51	59
3	Tottenham	42	21	9	12	93	77	51
4	WBA	42	18	14	10	92	70	50
5	Man City	42	22	5	15	104	100	49
6	Burnley	42	21	5	16	80	74	47
7	Blackpool	42	19	6	17	80	67	44
8	Luton	42	19	6	17	69	63	44
9	Man United	42	16	11	15	85	75	43
10	Nottm Forest	42	16	10	16	69	63	42
11	Chelsea	42	15	12	15	83	79	42
12	Arsenal	42	16	7	19	73	85	39
13	Birmingham	42	14	11	17	76	89	39
14	Aston Villa	42	16	7	19	73	86	39
15	Bolton	42	14	10	18	65	87	38
16	Everton	42	13	11	18	65	75	37
17	Leeds	42	14	9	19	51	63	37
18	Leicester	42	14	5	23	91	112	33
19	Newcastle	42	12	8	22	73	81	32
20	Portsmouth	42	12	8	22	73	88	32
21	Sunderland	42	10	12	20	54	97	32
22	Sheff Wed	42	12	7	23	69	92	31

SECOND DIVISION

		P	W	D	L	F	A	Pts
1	West Ham	42	23	11	8	101	54	57
2	Blackburn	42	22	12	8	93	57	56
3	Charlton	42	24	7	11	107	69	55
4	Liverpool	42	22	10	10	79	54	54
5	Fulham	42	20	12	10	97	59	52
6	Sheff United	42	21	10	11	75	50	52
7	Middlesbrough	42	19	7	16	83	74	45
8	Ipswich	42	16	12	14	68	69	44
9	Huddersfield	42	14	16	12	63	66	44
10	Bristol Rovers	42	17	8	17	85	80	42
11	Stoke	42	18	6	18	75	73	42
12	Leyton Orient	42	18	5	19	77	79	41
13	Grimsby	42	17	6	19	86	83	40
14	Barnsley	42	14	12	16	70	74	40
15	Cardiff	42	14	9	19	63	77	37
16	Derby	42	14	8	20	60	81	36
17	Bristol City	42	13	9	20	63	88	35
18	Rotherham	42	14	5	23	65	101	33
19	Swansea	42	11	9	22	72	99	31
20	Lincoln	42	11	9	22	55	82	31
21	Notts County	42	12	6	24	44	80	30
22	Doncaster	42	8	11	23	56	88	27

THIRD DIVISION (NORTH)

		P	W	D	L	F	A	Pts
1	Scunthorpe	46	29	8	9	88	50	66
2	Accrington	46	25	9	12	83	61	59
3	Bradford City	46	21	15	10	73	49	57
4	Bury	46	23	10	13	94	62	56
5	Hull	46	19	15	12	78	67	53
6	Mansfield	46	22	8	16	100	92	52
7	Halifax	46	20	11	15	83	69	51
8	Chesterfield	46	18	15	13	71	69	51
9	Stockport	46	18	11	17	74	67	47
10	Rochdale	46	19	8	19	79	67	46
11	Tranmere	46	18	10	18	82	76	46
12	Wrexham	46	17	12	17	61	63	46
13	York	46	17	12	17	68	76	46
14	Gateshead	46	15	15	16	68	76	45
15	Oldham	46	14	17	15	72	84	45
16	Carlisle	46	19	6	21	80	78	44
17	Hartlepools	46	16	12	18	73	76	44
18	Barrow	46	13	15	18	66	74	41
19	Workington	46	14	13	19	72	81	41
20	Darlington	46	17	7	22	78	89	41
21	Chester	46	13	13	20	73	81	39
22	Bradford PA	46	13	11	22	68	95	37
23	Southport	46	11	6	29	52	88	28
24	Crewe	46	8	7	31	47	93	23

THIRD DIVISION (SOUTH)

		P	W	D	L	F	A	Pts
1	Brighton	46	24	12	10	88	64	60
2	Brentford	46	24	10	12	82	56	58
3	Plymouth	46	25	8	13	67	48	58
4	Swindon	46	21	15	10	79	50	57
5	Reading	46	21	13	12	79	51	55
6	Southampton	46	22	10	14	112	72	54
7	Southend	46	21	12	13	90	58	54
8	Norwich	46	19	15	12	75	70	53
9	Bournemouth	46	21	9	16	81	74	51
10	QPR	46	18	14	14	64	65	50
11	Newport	46	17	14	15	73	67	48
12	Colchester	46	17	13	16	77	79	47
13	Northampton	46	19	6	21	87	79	44
14	Crystal Palace	46	15	13	18	70	72	43
15	Port Vale	46	16	10	20	67	58	42
16	Watford	46	13	16	17	59	77	42
17	Shrewsbury	46	15	10	21	49	71	40
18	Aldershot	46	12	16	18	59	89	40
19	Coventry	46	13	13	20	61	81	39
20	Walsall	46	14	9	23	61	75	37
21	Torquay	46	11	13	22	49	74	35
22	Gillingham	46	13	9	24	52	81	35
23	Millwall	46	11	9	26	63	91	31
24	Exeter	46	11	9	26	57	99	31

SCOTTISH FIRST DIVISION

		P	W	D	L	F	A	Pts
1	Hearts	34	29	4	1	132	29	62
2	Rangers	34	22	5	7	89	49	49
3	Celtic	34	19	8	7	84	47	46
4	Clyde	34	18	6	10	84	61	42
5	Kilmarnock	34	14	9	11	60	55	37
6	Partick Thistle	34	17	3	14	69	71	37
7	Raith Rovers	34	14	7	13	66	56	35
8	Motherwell	34	12	8	14	68	67	32
9	Hibernian	34	13	5	16	59	60	31
10	Falkirk	34	11	9	14	64	82	31
11	Dundee	34	13	5	16	49	65	31
12	Aberdeen	34	14	2	18	68	76	30
13	St Mirren	34	11	8	15	59	66	30
14	Third Lanark	34	13	4	17	69	88	30
15	Queen of the S	34	12	5	17	61	72	29
16	Airdrieonians	34	13	2	19	71	92	28
17	East Fife	34	10	3	21	45	88	23
18	Queen's Park	34	4	1	29	41	114	9

SCOTTISH SECOND DIVISION

		P	W	D	L	F	A	Pts
1	Stirling Albion	36	25	5	6	105	48	55
2	Dunfermline	36	24	5	7	120	42	53
3	Arbroath	36	21	5	10	89	72	47
4	Dumbarton	36	20	4	12	92	57	44
5	Ayr	36	18	6	12	98	81	42
6	Cowdenbeath	36	17	8	11	100	85	42
7	Brechin	36	16	8	12	80	81	40
8	Alloa	36	15	9	12	88	78	39
9	Dundee United	36	12	9	15	81	77	33
10	Hamilton	36	12	9	15	70	79	33
11	St Johnstone	36	12	9	15	67	85	33
12	Forfar	36	13	6	17	70	71	32
13	Morton	36	12	8	16	77	83	32
14	Montrose	36	13	6	17	55	72	32
15	E Stirlingshire	36	12	5	19	55	79	29
16	Stenhousemuir	36	12	5	19	68	98	29
17	Albion	36	12	5	19	53	79	29
18	Stranraer	36	9	7	20	54	83	25
19	Berwick	36	5	5	26	37	109	15

FA CUP 1957-58

FOURTH ROUND
Everton v Blackburn Rovers	1-2
Cardiff City v Leyton Orient	4-1
Liverpool v Northampton Town	3-1
Newcastle United v Scunthorpe United	1-3
Wolverhampton Wanderers v Portsmouth	5-1
Chelsea v Darlington	3-3, 1-4
Stoke City v Middlesbrough	3-1
York City v Bolton Wanderers	0-0, 0-3
Manchester United v Ipswich Town	2-0
Sheffield Wednesday v Hull City	4-3
West Bromwich Albion v Nottingham Forest	3-3, 5-1
Tottenham Hotspur v Sheffield United	0-3
Bristol Rovers v Burnley	2-2, 3-2
Notts County v Bristol City	1-2
West Ham United v Stockport County	3-2
Fulham v Charlton Athletic	1-1, 2-0

FIFTH ROUND
Cardiff City v Blackburn Rovers	0-0, 1-2
Scunthorpe United v Liverpool	0-1
Wolverhampton Wanderers v Darlington	6-1
Bolton Wanderers v Stoke City	3-1
Manchester United v Sheffield Wednesday	3-0
Sheffield United v West Bromwich Albion	1-1, 1-4
Bristol City v Bristol Rovers	3-4
West Ham United v Fulham	2-3

SIXTH ROUND
Blackburn Rovers v Liverpool	2-1
Bolton Wanderers v Wolverhampton Wanderers	2-1
West Bromwich Albion v Manchester United	2-2, 0-1
Fulham v Bristol Rovers	3-1

SEMI-FINAL
Blackburn Rovers v Bolton Wanderers	1-2
Manchester United v Fulham	2-2, 5-3

FINAL
Bolton Wanderers v Manchester United	2-0

SCOTTISH FA CUP 1957-58

SECOND ROUND
Celtic v Stirling Albion	7-2
Clyde v Arbroath	4-0
Falkirk v St Johnstone	6-3
Montrose v Buckie Thistle	2-2, 1-4
Motherwell v Partick Thistle	2-2, 4-0
Inverness Caledonian v Stenhousemuir	5-2
Morton v Aberdeen	0-1
Raith Rovers v Dundee	0-1
Forfar Athletic v Rangers	1-9
St Mirren v Dunfermline Athletic	1-4
Queen of the South v Stranraer	7-0
Kilmarnock v Vale of Leithen	7-0
Dundee United v Hibernian	0-0, 0-2
Heart of Midlothian v Albion Rovers	4-1
Third Lanark v Lossiemouth	6-1
Queen's Park v Fraserburgh	7-2

THIRD ROUND
Clyde v Celtic	2-0
Buckie Thistle v Falkirk	1-2
Inverness Caledonian v Motherwell	0-7
Dundee v Aberdeen	1-3
Dunfermline Athletic v Rangers	1-2
Kilmarnock v Queen of the South	2-2, 0-3
Heart of Midlothian v Hibernian	3-4
Third Lanark v Queen's Park	5-3

FOURTH ROUND
Clyde v Falkirk	2-1
Motherwell v Aberdeen	2-1
Queen of the South v Rangers	3-4
Hibernian v Third Lanark	3-2

SEMI-FINAL
Clyde v Motherwell	3-2
Rangers v Hibernian	2-2, 1-2

FINAL
Clyde v Hibernian	1-0

In Moscow on 18 May 1958, England played the USSR for the first time ever.

Before the start of the 1957-58 season, it was decided that four Divisions would be introduced in 1958-59. So at the end of the season, the top halves of both Third Divisions formed the new Division Three, and the rest of the teams made up Division Four.

Have boots, will travel
Tony McNamara, a right-winger, played in all four divisions of the Football League inside twelve months. On 12 October 1957, he played his last game for Everton in Division One, and on 27 September 1958 he made his debut for Bury in Division Three. In between, he played in Division Two for Liverpool, and in the Fourth Division for Crewe.

FIRST DIVISION

		P	W	D	L	F	A	Pts
1	Wolves	42	28	5	9	110	49	61
2	Man United	42	24	7	11	103	66	55
3	Arsenal	42	21	8	13	88	68	50
4	Bolton	42	20	10	12	79	66	50
5	WBA	42	18	13	11	88	68	49
6	West Ham	42	21	6	15	85	70	48
7	Burnley	42	19	10	13	81	70	48
8	Blackpool	42	18	11	13	66	49	47
9	Birmingham	42	20	6	16	84	68	46
10	Blackburn	42	17	10	15	76	70	44
11	Newcastle	42	17	7	18	80	80	41
12	Preston	42	17	7	18	70	77	41
13	Nottm Forest	42	17	6	19	71	74	40
14	Chelsea	42	18	4	20	77	98	40
15	Leeds	42	15	9	18	57	74	39
16	Everton	42	17	4	21	71	87	38
17	Luton	42	12	13	17	68	71	37
18	Tottenham	42	13	10	19	85	95	36
19	Leicester	42	11	10	21	67	98	32
20	Man City	42	11	9	22	64	95	31
21	Aston Villa	42	11	8	23	58	87	30
22	Portsmouth	42	6	9	27	64	112	21

SECOND DIVISION

		P	W	D	L	F	A	Pts
1	Sheff Wed	42	28	6	8	106	48	62
2	Fulham	42	27	6	9	96	61	60
3	Sheff United	42	23	7	12	82	48	53
4	Liverpool	42	24	5	13	87	62	53
5	Stoke	42	21	7	14	72	58	49
6	Bristol Rovers	42	18	12	12	80	64	48
7	Derby	42	20	8	14	74	71	48
8	Charlton	42	18	7	17	92	90	43
9	Cardiff	42	18	7	17	65	65	43
10	Bristol City	42	17	7	18	74	70	41
11	Swansea	42	16	9	17	79	81	41
12	Brighton	42	15	11	16	74	90	41
13	Middlesbrough	42	15	10	17	87	71	40
14	Huddersfield	42	16	8	18	62	55	40
15	Sunderland	42	16	8	18	64	75	40
16	Ipswich	42	17	6	19	62	77	40
17	Leyton Orient	42	14	8	20	71	78	36
18	Scunthorpe	42	12	9	21	55	84	33
19	Lincoln	42	11	7	24	63	93	29
20	Rotherham	42	10	9	23	42	82	29
21	Grimsby	42	9	10	23	62	90	28
22	Barnsley	42	10	7	25	55	91	27

FA CUP 1958-59

FOURTH ROUND

Nottingham Forest v Grimsby Town	4-1
Birmingham City v Fulham	1-1, 3-2
Wolverhampton W v Bolton W	1-2
Preston North End v Bradford City	3-2
Charlton Athletic v Everton	2-2, 1-4
Chelsea v Aston Villa	1-2
Blackburn Rovers v Burnley	1-2
Accrington Stanley v Portsmouth	0-0, 1-4
Colchester United v Arsenal	2-2, 0-4
Worcester City v Sheffield United	0-2
Tottenham Hotspur v Newport County	4-1
Norwich City v Cardiff City	3-2
Bristol City v Blackpool	1-1, 0-1
West Bromwich Albion v Brentford	2-0
Stoke City v Ipswich Town	0-1
Leicester City v Luton Town	1-1, 1-4

FIFTH ROUND

Birmingham City v Nottm Forest	1-1, 1-1, 0-5
Bolton W v Preston North End	2-2, 1-1, 1-0
Everton v Aston Villa	1-4
Burnley v Portsmouth	1-0
Arsenal v Sheffield United	2-2, 0-3
Tottenham Hotspur v Norwich City	1-1, 0-1
Blackpool v West Bromwich Albion	3-1
Ipswich Town v Luton Town	2-5

SIXTH ROUND

Nottingham Forest v Bolton Wanderers	2-1
Aston Villa v Burnley	0-0, 2-0
Sheffield United v Norwich City	1-1, 2-3
Blackpool v Luton Town	1-1, 0-1

SEMI-FINAL

Nottingham Forest v Aston Villa	1-0
Norwich City v Luton Town	1-1, 0-1

FINAL

Nottingham Forest v Luton Town	2-1

THIRD DIVISION

		P	W	D	L	F	A	Pts
1	Plymouth	46	23	16	7	89	59	62
2	Hull	46	26	9	11	90	55	61
3	Brentford	46	21	15	10	76	49	57
4	Norwich	46	22	13	11	89	62	57
5	Colchester	46	21	10	15	71	67	52
6	Reading	46	21	8	17	78	63	50
7	Tranmere	46	21	8	17	82	67	50
8	Southend	46	21	8	17	85	80	50
9	Halifax	46	21	8	17	80	77	50
10	Bury	46	17	14	15	69	58	48
11	Bradford City	46	18	11	17	84	76	47
12	Bournemouth	46	17	12	17	69	69	46
13	QPR	46	19	8	19	74	77	46
14	Southampton	46	17	11	18	88	80	45
15	Swindon	46	16	13	17	59	57	45
16	Chesterfield	46	17	10	19	67	64	44
17	Newport	46	17	9	20	69	68	43
18	Wrexham	46	14	14	18	63	77	42
19	Accrington	46	15	12	19	71	87	42
20	Mansfield	46	14	13	19	73	98	41
21	Stockport	46	13	10	23	65	78	36
22	Doncaster	46	14	5	27	50	90	33
23	Notts County	46	8	13	25	55	96	29
24	Rochdale	46	8	12	26	37	79	28

FOURTH DIVISION

		P	W	D	L	F	A	Pts
1	Port Vale	46	26	12	8	110	58	64
2	Coventry	46	24	12	10	84	47	60
3	York	46	21	18	7	73	52	60
4	Shrewsbury	46	24	10	12	101	63	58
5	Exeter	46	23	11	12	87	61	57
6	Walsall	46	21	10	15	95	64	52
7	Crystal Palace	46	20	12	14	90	71	52
8	Northampton	46	21	9	16	85	78	51
9	Millwall	46	20	10	16	76	69	50
10	Carlisle	46	19	12	15	62	65	50
11	Gillingham	46	20	9	17	82	77	49
12	Torquay	46	16	12	18	78	77	44
13	Chester	46	16	12	18	72	84	44
14	Bradford PA	46	18	7	21	75	77	43
15	Watford	46	16	10	20	81	79	42
16	Darlington	46	13	16	17	66	68	42
17	Workington	46	12	17	17	63	78	41
18	Crewe	46	15	10	21	70	82	40
19	Hartlepools	46	15	10	21	74	88	40
20	Gateshead	46	16	8	22	56	85	40
21	Oldham	46	16	4	26	59	84	36
22	Aldershot	46	14	7	25	63	97	35
23	Barrow	46	9	10	27	51	104	28
24	Southport	46	7	12	27	41	86	26

SCOTTISH FA CUP 1958-59

SECOND ROUND

St Mirren v Peebles Rovers	10-0
Airdrieonians v Motherwell	2-7
Montrose v Dunfermline Athletic	0-1
Ayr United v Stranraer	3-0
Fraserburgh v Stirling Albion	3-4
Babcock & Wilcox v Morton	0-5
Celtic v Clyde	1-1, 4-3
Rangers v Heart of Midlothian	3-2
Dundee United v Third Lanark	0-4
Brechin City v Alloa Athletic	3-3, 1-3
Hibernian v Falkirk	3-1
Stenhousemuir v Partick Thistle	1-3
St Johnstone v Queen's Park	3-1
Aberdeen v Arbroath	3-0
Coldstream v Hamilton Academicals	0-4
Dumbarton v Kilmarnock	2-8

THIRD ROUND

St Mirren v Motherwell	3-2
Dunfermline Athletic v Ayr United	2-1
Stirling Albion v Morton	3-1
Celtic v Rangers	2-1
Third Lanark v Alloa Athletic	3-2
Hibernian v Partick Thistle	4-1
St Johnstone v Aberdeen	1-2
Hamilton Academicals v Kilmarnock	0-5

FOURTH ROUND

St Mirren v Dunfermline Athletic	2-1
Stirling Albion v Celtic	1-3
Third Lanark v Hibernian	2-1
Aberdeen v Kilmarnock	3-1

SEMI-FINAL

St Mirren v Celtic	4-0
Third Lanark v Aberdeen	1-1, 0-1

FINAL

St Mirren v Aberdeen	3-1

SCOTTISH FIRST DIVISION

		P	W	D	L	F	A	Pts
1	Rangers	34	21	8	5	92	51	50
2	Hearts	34	21	6	7	92	51	48
3	Motherwell	34	18	8	8	83	50	44
4	Dundee	34	16	9	9	61	51	41
5	Airdrie	34	15	7	12	64	62	37
6	Celtic	34	14	8	12	70	53	36
7	St Mirren	34	14	7	13	71	74	35
8	Kilmarnock	34	13	8	13	58	51	34
9	Partick Thistle	34	14	6	14	59	66	34
10	Hibernian	34	13	6	15	68	70	32
11	Third Lanark	34	11	10	13	74	83	32
12	Stirling	34	11	8	15	54	64	30
13	Aberdeen	34	12	5	17	63	66	29
14	Raith	34	10	9	15	60	70	29
15	Clyde	34	12	4	18	62	66	28
16	Dunfermline	34	10	8	16	68	87	28
17	Falkirk	34	10	7	17	58	79	27
18	Queen of the S	34	6	6	22	38	101	18

SCOTTISH SECOND DIVISION

		P	W	D	L	F	A	Pts
1	Ayr United	36	28	4	4	115	48	60
2	Arbroath	36	23	5	8	86	59	51
3	Stenhousemuir	36	20	6	10	87	68	46
4	Dumbarton	36	19	7	10	94	61	45
5	Brechin	36	16	10	10	79	65	42
6	St Johnstone	36	15	10	11	54	44	40
7	Hamilton	36	15	8	13	76	62	38
8	East Fife	36	15	8	13	83	81	38
9	Berwick	36	16	6	14	63	66	38
10	Albion	36	14	7	15	84	79	35
11	Morton	36	13	8	15	68	85	34
12	Forfar	36	12	9	15	73	87	33
13	Alloa	36	12	7	17	76	81	31
14	Cowdenbeath	36	13	5	18	67	79	31
15	E Stirlingshire	36	10	8	18	50	77	28
16	Stranraer	36	8	11	17	63	76	27
17	Dundee United	36	9	7	20	62	86	25
18	Queen's Park	36	9	6	21	53	80	24
19	Montrose	36	6	6	24	49	96	18

Beginning with the game against France on 3 October 1951, Billy Wright made a world record 70 consecutive appearances for England, ending on 8 May 1959 with the match against the USA. In the Home Championship, he had a record run of 25 games between April 1951 and April 1959.

Denis Law became Scotland's youngest international, when on 18 October 1958, he played against Wales aged just 18 years and 236 days.

The most away wins in any division of the League on a single day is eight, in Division 3, 27 September 1958.

233

FIRST DIVISION

		P	W	D	L	F	A	Pts
1	Burnley	42	24	7	11	85	61	55
2	Wolves	42	24	6	12	106	67	54
3	Tottenham	42	21	11	10	86	50	53
4	WBA	42	19	11	12	83	57	49
5	Sheff Wed	42	19	11	12	80	59	49
6	Bolton	42	20	8	14	59	51	48
7	Man United	42	19	7	16	102	80	45
8	Newcastle	42	18	8	16	82	78	44
9	Preston	42	16	12	14	79	76	44
10	Fulham	42	17	10	15	73	80	44
11	Blackpool	42	15	10	17	59	71	40
12	Leicester	42	13	13	16	66	75	39
13	Arsenal	42	15	9	18	68	80	39
14	West Ham	42	16	6	20	75	91	38
15	Man City	42	17	3	22	78	84	37
16	Everton	42	13	11	18	73	78	37
17	Blackburn	42	16	5	21	60	70	37
18	Chelsea	42	14	9	19	76	91	37
19	Birmingham	42	13	10	19	63	80	36
20	Nottm Forest	42	13	9	20	50	74	35
21	Leeds	42	12	10	20	65	92	34
22	Luton	42	9	12	21	50	73	30

SECOND DIVISION

		P	W	D	L	F	A	Pts
1	Aston Villa	42	25	9	8	89	43	59
2	Cardiff	42	23	12	7	90	62	58
3	Liverpool	42	20	10	12	90	66	50
4	Sheff United	42	19	12	11	68	51	50
5	Middlesbrough	42	19	10	13	90	64	48
6	Huddersfield	42	19	9	14	73	52	47
7	Charlton	42	17	13	12	90	87	47
8	Rotherham	42	17	13	12	61	60	47
9	Bristol Rovers	42	18	11	13	72	78	47
10	Leyton Orient	42	15	14	13	76	61	44
11	Ipswich	42	19	6	17	78	68	44
12	Swansea	42	15	10	17	82	84	40
13	Lincoln	42	16	7	19	75	78	39
14	Brighton	42	13	12	17	67	76	38
15	Scunthorpe	42	13	10	19	57	71	36
16	Sunderland	42	12	12	18	52	65	36
17	Stoke	42	14	7	21	66	83	35
18	Derby	42	14	7	21	61	77	35
19	Plymouth	42	13	9	20	61	89	35
20	Portsmouth	42	10	12	20	59	77	32
21	Hull	42	10	10	22	48	76	30
22	Bristol City	42	11	5	26	60	97	27

THIRD DIVISION

		P	W	D	L	F	A	Pts
1	Southampton	46	26	9	11	106	75	61
2	Norwich	46	24	11	11	82	54	59
3	Shrewsbury	46	18	16	12	97	75	52
4	Coventry	46	21	10	15	78	63	52
5	Grimsby	46	18	16	12	87	70	52
6	Brentford	46	21	9	16	78	61	51
7	Bury	46	21	9	16	64	51	51
8	QPR	46	18	13	15	73	54	49
9	Colchester	46	18	11	17	83	74	47
10	Bournemouth	46	17	13	16	72	72	47
11	Reading	46	18	10	18	84	77	46
12	Southend	46	19	8	19	76	74	46
13	Newport	46	20	6	20	80	79	46
14	Port Vale	46	19	8	19	80	79	46
15	Halifax	46	18	10	18	70	72	46
16	Swindon	46	19	8	19	69	78	46
17	Barnsley	46	15	14	17	65	66	44
18	Chesterfield	46	18	7	21	71	84	43
19	Bradford City	46	15	12	19	66	74	42
20	Tranmere	46	14	13	19	72	75	41
21	York	46	13	12	21	57	73	38
22	Mansfield	46	15	6	25	81	112	36
23	Wrexham	46	14	8	24	68	101	36
24	Accrington	46	11	5	30	57	123	27

FOURTH DIVISION

		P	W	D	L	F	A	Pts
1	Walsall	46	28	9	9	102	60	65
2	Notts County	46	26	8	12	107	69	60
3	Torquay	46	26	8	12	84	58	60
4	Watford	46	24	9	13	92	67	57
5	Millwall	46	18	17	11	84	61	53
6	Northampton	46	22	9	15	85	63	53
7	Gillingham	46	21	10	15	74	69	52
8	Crystal Palace	46	19	12	15	84	64	50
9	Exeter	46	19	11	16	80	70	49
10	Stockport	46	19	11	16	58	54	49
11	Bradford PA	46	17	15	14	70	68	49
12	Rochdale	46	18	10	18	65	60	46
13	Aldershot	46	18	9	19	77	74	45
14	Crewe	46	18	9	19	79	88	45
15	Darlington	46	17	9	20	63	73	43
16	Workington	46	14	14	18	68	60	42
17	Doncaster	46	16	10	20	69	76	42
18	Barrow	46	15	11	20	77	87	41
19	Carlisle	46	15	11	20	51	66	41
20	Chester	46	14	12	20	59	77	40
21	Southport	46	10	14	22	48	92	34
22	Gateshead	46	12	9	25	58	86	33
23	Oldham	46	8	12	26	41	83	28
24	Hartlepools	46	10	7	29	59	109	27

SCOTTISH FIRST DIVISION

		P	W	D	L	F	A	Pts
1	Hearts	34	23	8	3	102	51	54
2	Kilmarnock	34	24	2	8	67	45	50
3	Rangers	34	17	8	9	72	38	42
4	Dundee	34	16	10	8	70	49	42
5	Motherwell	34	16	8	10	71	61	40
6	Clyde	34	15	9	10	77	69	39
7	Hibernian	34	14	7	13	106	85	35
8	Ayr	34	14	6	14	65	73	34
9	Celtic	34	12	9	13	73	59	33
10	Partick Thistle	34	14	4	16	54	78	32
11	Raith Rovers	34	14	3	17	64	62	31
12	Third Lanark	34	13	4	17	75	83	30
13	Dunfermline	34	10	9	15	72	80	29
14	St Mirren	34	11	6	17	78	86	28
15	Aberdeen	34	11	6	17	54	72	28
16	Airdrieonians	34	11	6	17	56	80	28
17	Stirling Albion	34	7	8	19	55	72	22
18	Arbroath	34	4	7	23	38	106	15

SCOTTISH SECOND DIVISION

		P	W	D	L	F	A	Pts
1	St Johnstone	36	24	5	7	87	47	53
2	Dundee United	36	22	6	8	90	45	50
3	Queen of the S	36	21	7	8	94	52	49
4	Hamilton	36	21	6	9	91	62	48
5	Stenhousemuir	36	20	4	12	86	67	44
6	Dumbarton	36	18	7	11	67	53	43
7	Montrose	36	19	5	12	60	52	43
8	Falkirk	36	15	9	12	77	43	39
9	Berwick	36	16	5	15	62	55	37
10	Albion	36	14	8	14	71	78	36
11	Queen's Park	36	17	2	17	65	79	36
12	Brechin	36	14	6	16	66	66	34
13	Alloa	36	13	5	18	70	85	31
14	Morton	36	10	8	18	67	79	28
15	E Stirlingshire	36	10	8	18	68	82	28
16	Forfar	36	10	8	18	53	84	28
17	Stranraer	36	10	3	23	53	79	23
18	East Fife	36	7	6	23	50	87	20
19	Cowdenbeath	36	6	2	28	42	124	14

An expensive agreement

In July 1959, the Football League established the copyright on their fixture lists. As a result, the Pools Promoters agreed to pay the League a minimum of £245,000 each year for 10 years. In return, the Pools firms were to be allowed to reprint the fixtures on their coupons.

Cliff Holton of Watford, the 1959-60 Football League leading goalscorer, became the only player since the War to notch two hat-tricks in League matches in successive days. On Good Friday, 15 April 1960, Holton scored three times against Chester. A day later, he hit three more against Gateshead.

FA CUP 1959-60

FOURTH ROUND

Wolverhampton v Charlton Athletic	2-1
Huddersfield Town v Luton Town	0-1
Leicester City v Fulham	2-1
West Bromwich Albion v Bolton Wanderers	2-0
Bristol Rovers v Preston North End	3-3, 1-5
Rotherham United v Brighton	1-1, 1-1, 0-6
Scunthorpe United v Port Vale	0-1
Chelsea v Aston Villa	1-2
Sheffield United v Nottingham Forest	3-0
Southampton v Watford	2-2, 0-1
Liverpool v Manchester United	1-3
Sheffield Wednesday v Peterborough United	2-0
Bradford City v Bournemouth	3-1
Swansea Town v Burnley	0-0, 1-2
Crewe Alexandra v Tottenham Hotspur	2-2, 2-13
Blackburn Rovers v Blackpool	1-1, 3-0

FIFTH ROUND

Luton Town v Wolverhampton	1-4
Leicester City v West Bromwich Albion	2-1
Preston North End v Brighton	2-1
Port Vale v Aston Villa	1-2
Sheffield United v Watford	3-2
Manchester United v Sheffield Wednesday	0-1
Bradford City v Burnley	2-2, 0-5
Tottenham Hotspur v Blackburn Rovers	1-3

SIXTH ROUND

Leicester City v Wolverhampton Wanderers	1-2
Aston Villa v Preston North End	2-0
Sheffield United v Sheffield Wednesday	0-2
Burnley v Blackburn Rovers	3-3, 0-2

SEMI-FINAL

Wolverhampton Wanderers v Aston Villa	1-0
Sheffield Wednesday v Blackburn Rovers	1-2

FINAL

Wolverhampton Wanderers v Blackburn Rovers 3-0

SCOTTISH FA CUP 1959-60

SECOND ROUND

Rangers v Arbroath	2-0
Dunfermline Athletic v Stenhousemuir	2-3
E Stirlingshire v Inverness Caledonian	2-2, 4-1
Hibernian v Dundee	3-0
Elgin City v Forfar Athletic	5-1
St Mirren v Celtic	1-1, 4-4, 2-5
Dundee United v Partick Thistle	2-2, 1-4
Stirling Albion v Queen of the South	3-3, 1-5
Peebles Rovers v Ayr United	1-6
Alloa Athletic v Airdrieonians	1-5
Aberdeen v Clyde	0-2
Montrose v Queen's Park	2-2, 1-1, 1-2
Eyemouth United v Albion Rovers	1-0
Cowdenbeath v Falkirk	1-0
Motherwell v Keith	6-0
Heart of Midlothian v Kilmarnock	1-1, 1-2

THIRD ROUND

Stenhousemuir v Rangers	0-3
East Stirlingshire v Hibernian	0-3
Elgin City v Celtic	1-2
Partick Thistle v Queen of the South	3-2
Ayr United v Airdrieonians	4-2
Clyde v Queen's Park	6-0
Eyemouth United v Cowdenbeath	3-0
Kilmarnock v Motherwell	2-0

FOURTH ROUND

Rangers v Hibernian	3-2
Celtic v Partick Thistle	2-0
Ayr United v Clyde	0-2
Eyemouth United v Kilmarnock	1-2

SEMI-FINAL

Rangers v Celtic	1-1, 4-1
Clyde v Kilmarnock	0-2

FINAL

Rangers v Kilmarnock 2-0

FIRST DIVISION

		P	W	D	L	F	A	Pts
1	Tottenham	42	31	4	7	115	55	66
2	Sheff Wed	42	23	12	7	78	47	58
3	Wolves	42	25	7	10	103	75	57
4	Burnley	42	22	7	13	102	77	51
5	Everton	42	22	6	14	87	69	50
6	Leicester	42	18	9	15	87	70	45
7	Man United	42	18	9	15	88	76	45
8	Blackburn	42	15	13	14	77	76	43
9	Aston Villa	42	17	9	16	78	77	43
10	WBA	42	18	5	19	67	71	41
11	Arsenal	42	15	11	16	77	85	41
12	Chelsea	42	15	7	20	98	100	37
13	Man City	42	13	11	18	79	90	37
14	Nottm Forest	42	14	9	19	62	78	37
15	Cardiff	42	13	11	18	60	85	37
16	West Ham	42	13	10	19	77	88	36
17	Fulham	42	14	8	20	72	95	36
18	Bolton	42	12	11	19	58	73	35
19	Birmingham	42	14	6	22	62	84	34
20	Blackpool	42	12	9	21	68	73	33
21	Newcastle	42	11	10	21	86	109	32
22	Preston	42	10	10	22	43	71	30

SECOND DIVISION

		P	W	D	L	F	A	Pts
1	Ipswich	42	26	7	9	100	55	59
2	Sheff United	42	26	6	10	81	51	58
3	Liverpool	42	21	10	11	87	58	52
4	Norwich	42	20	9	13	70	53	49
5	Middlesbrough	42	18	12	12	83	74	48
6	Sunderland	42	17	13	12	75	60	47
7	Swansea	42	18	11	13	77	73	47
8	Southampton	42	18	8	16	84	81	44
9	Scunthorpe	42	14	15	13	69	64	43
10	Charlton	42	16	11	15	97	91	43
11	Plymouth	42	17	8	17	81	82	42
12	Derby	42	15	10	17	80	80	40
13	Luton	42	15	9	18	71	70	39
14	Leeds	42	14	10	18	75	83	38
15	Rotherham	42	12	13	17	65	64	37
16	Brighton	42	14	9	19	61	75	37
17	Bristol Rovers	42	15	7	20	73	92	37
18	Stoke	42	12	12	18	51	59	36
19	Leyton Orient	42	14	8	20	55	78	36
20	Huddersfield	42	13	9	20	62	71	35
21	Portsmouth	42	11	11	20	64	91	33
22	Lincoln	42	8	8	26	48	95	24

THIRD DIVISION

		P	W	D	L	F	A	Pts
1	Bury	46	30	8	8	108	45	68
2	Walsall	46	28	6	12	98	60	62
3	QPR	46	25	10	11	93	60	60
4	Watford	46	20	12	14	85	72	52
5	Notts County	46	21	9	16	82	77	51
6	Grimsby	46	20	10	16	77	69	50
7	Port Vale	46	17	15	14	96	79	49
8	Barnsley	46	21	7	18	83	80	49
9	Halifax	46	16	17	13	71	78	49
10	Shrewsbury	46	15	16	15	83	75	46
11	Hull	46	17	12	17	73	73	46
12	Torquay	46	14	17	15	75	83	45
13	Newport	46	17	11	18	81	90	45
14	Bristol City	46	17	10	19	70	68	44
15	Coventry	46	16	12	18	80	83	44
16	Swindon	46	14	15	17	62	55	43
17	Brentford	46	13	17	16	56	70	43
18	Reading	46	14	12	20	72	83	40
19	Bournemouth	46	15	10	21	58	76	40
20	Southend	46	14	11	21	60	76	39
21	Tranmere	46	15	8	23	79	115	38
22	Bradford City	46	11	14	21	65	87	36
23	Colchester	46	11	11	24	68	101	33
24	Chesterfield	46	10	12	24	67	87	32

FOURTH DIVISION

		P	W	D	L	F	A	Pts
1	Peterborough	46	28	10	8	134	65	66
2	Crystal Palace	46	29	6	11	110	69	64
3	Northampton	46	25	10	11	90	62	60
4	Bradford PA	46	26	8	12	84	74	60
5	York	46	21	9	16	80	60	51
6	Millwall	46	21	8	17	97	86	50
7	Darlington	46	18	13	15	78	70	49
8	Workington	46	21	7	18	74	76	49
9	Crewe	46	20	9	17	61	67	49
10	Aldershot	46	18	9	19	79	69	45
11	Doncaster	46	19	7	20	76	78	45
12	Oldham	46	19	7	20	79	88	45
13	Stockport	46	18	9	19	57	66	45
14	Southport	46	19	6	21	69	67	44
15	Gillingham	46	15	13	18	64	66	43
16	Wrexham	46	17	8	21	62	56	42
17	Rochdale	46	17	8	21	60	66	42
18	Accrington	46	16	8	22	74	88	40
19	Carlisle	46	13	13	20	61	79	39
20	Mansfield	46	16	6	24	71	78	38
21	Exeter	46	14	10	22	66	94	38
22	Barrow	46	13	11	22	52	79	37
23	Hartlepools	46	12	8	26	71	103	32
24	Chester	46	11	9	26	61	104	31

SCOTTISH FIRST DIVISION

		P	W	D	L	F	A	Pts
1	Rangers	34	23	5	6	88	46	51
2	Kilmarnock	34	21	8	5	77	45	50
3	Third Lanark	34	20	2	12	100	80	42
4	Celtic	34	15	9	10	64	46	39
5	Motherwell	34	15	8	11	70	57	38
6	Aberdeen	34	14	8	12	72	72	36
7	Hibernian	34	15	4	15	66	69	34
8	Hearts	34	13	8	13	51	53	34
9	Dundee United	34	13	7	14	60	58	33
10	Dundee	34	13	6	15	61	53	32
11	Partick Thistle	34	13	6	15	59	69	32
12	Dunfermline	34	12	7	15	65	81	31
13	Airdrieonians	34	10	10	14	61	71	30
14	St Mirren	34	11	7	16	53	58	29
15	St Johnstone	34	10	9	15	47	63	29
16	Raith Rovers	34	10	7	17	46	67	27
17	Clyde	34	6	11	17	55	77	23
18	Ayr	34	5	12	17	51	81	22

SCOTTISH SECOND DIVISION

		P	W	D	L	F	A	Pts
1	Stirling Albion	36	24	7	5	89	37	55
2	Falkirk	36	24	6	6	100	40	54
3	Stenhousemuir	36	24	2	10	99	69	50
4	Stranraer	36	19	6	11	83	55	44
5	Queen of the S	36	20	3	13	77	52	43
6	Hamilton	36	17	7	12	84	80	41
7	Montrose	36	19	2	15	75	65	40
8	Cowdenbeath	36	17	6	13	71	65	40
9	Berwick	36	14	9	13	62	69	37
10	Dumbarton	36	15	5	16	78	82	35
11	Alloa	36	13	7	16	78	68	33
12	Arbroath	36	13	7	16	56	76	33
13	East Fife	36	14	4	18	70	80	32
14	Brechin	36	9	9	18	60	78	27
15	Queen's Park	36	10	6	20	61	87	26
16	E Stirlingshire	36	9	7	20	59	100	25
17	Albion	36	9	6	21	60	89	24
18	Forfar	36	10	4	22	65	98	24
19	Morton	36	5	11	20	56	93	21

FA CUP 1960-61

FOURTH ROUND

Leicester City v Bristol City	5-1
Birmingham City v Rotherham United	4-0
Huddersfield Town v Barnsley	1-1, 0-1
Luton Town v Manchester City	3-1
Newcastle United v Stockport County	4-0
Stoke City v Aldershot	0-0, 0-0, 3-0
Sheffield United v Lincoln City	3-1
Bolton Wanderers v Blackburn Rovers	3-3, 0-4
Southampton v Leyton Orient	0-1
Sheffield Wednesday v Manchester United	1-1, 7-2
Brighton v Burnley	3-3, 0-2
Swansea Town v Preston North End	2-1
Scunthorpe United v Norwich City	1-4
Liverpool v Sunderland	0-2
Peterborough United v Aston Villa	1-1, 1-2
Tottenham Hotspur v Crewe Alexandra	5-1

FIFTH ROUND

Birmingham City v Leicester City	1-1, 1-2
Barnsley v Luton Town	1-0
Newcastle United v Stoke City	3-1
Sheffield United v Blackburn Rovers	2-1
Leyton Orient v Sheffield Wednesday	0-2
Burnley v Swansea Town	4-0
Norwich City v Sunderland	0-1
Aston Villa v Tottenham Hotspur	0-2

SIXTH ROUND

Leicester City v Barnsley	0-0, 2-1
Newcastle United v Sheffield United	1-3
Sheffield Wednesday v Burnley	0-0, 0-2
Sunderland v Tottenham Hotspur	1-1, 0-5

SEMI-FINAL

Leicester City v Sheffield United	0-0, 0-0, 2-0
Burnley v Tottenham Hotspur	0-3

FINAL

Leicester City v Tottenham Hotspur	0-2

SCOTTISH FA CUP 1960-61

SECOND ROUND

Buckie Thistle v Raith Rovers	0-2
Celtic v Montrose	6-0
Queen of the South v Hamilton Academicals	0-2
Hibernian v Peebles Rovers	15-1
Brechin City v Duns	5-3
Ayr United v Airdrieonians	0-0, 1-3
Cowdenbeath v Motherwell	1-4
Dundee v Rangers	1-5
East Fife v Partick Thistle	1-3
Kilmarnock v Heart of Midlothian	1-2
Dundee United v St Mirren	0-1
Third Lanark v Arbroath	5-2
Aberdeen v Deveronvale	4-2
Stranraer v Dunfermline Athletic	1-3
Alloa Athletic v Dumbarton	2-0
Forfar Athletic v Morton	2-0

THIRD ROUND

Raith Rovers v Celtic	1-4
Hamilton Academicals v Hibernian	0-4
Brechin City v Airdrieonians	0-3
Motherwell v Rangers	2-2, 5-2
Partick Thistle v Heart of Midlothian	1-2
St Mirren v Third Lanark	3-3, 8-0
Aberdeen v Dunfermline Athletic	3-6
Alloa Athletic v Forfar Athletic	2-1

FOURTH ROUND

Celtic v Hibernian	1-1, 1-0
Motherwell v Airdrieonians	0-1
Heart of Midlothian v St Mirren	0-1
Dunfermline Athletic v Alloa Athletic	4-0

SEMI-FINAL

Celtic v Airdrieonians	4-0
Dunfermline Athletic v St Mirren	0-0, 1-0

FINAL

Celtic v Dunfermline Athletic	0-0, 0-2

Tottenham began the season with 11 consecutive wins, a record, and ended it having won 31 of their 42 games, a First Division record. Spurs' 16 away wins—including an unequalled 8 in a row—was another First Division record. Spurs also equalled Arsenal's Division One record points total of 66.

Burnley were fined £1000 by the Football League for fielding ten reserves in a League match against Chelsea.

The maximum wage restrictions were removed and Johnny Haynes of Fulham became the first British footballer to earn £100 a week.

235

FIRST DIVISION

		P	W	D	L	F	A	Pts
1	Ipswich	42	24	8	10	93	67	56
2	Burnley	42	21	11	10	101	67	53
3	Tottenham	42	21	10	11	88	69	52
4	Everton	42	20	11	11	88	54	51
5	Sheff United	42	19	9	14	61	69	47
6	Sheff Wed	42	20	6	16	72	58	46
7	Aston Villa	42	18	8	16	65	56	44
8	West Ham	42	17	10	15	76	82	44
9	WBA	42	15	13	14	83	67	43
10	Arsenal	42	16	11	15	71	72	43
11	Bolton	42	16	10	16	62	66	42
12	Man City	42	17	7	18	78	81	41
13	Blackpool	42	15	11	16	70	75	41
14	Leicester	42	17	6	19	72	71	40
15	Man United	42	15	9	18	72	75	39
16	Blackburn	42	14	11	17	50	58	39
17	Birmingham	42	14	10	18	65	81	38
18	Wolves	42	13	10	19	73	86	36
19	Nottm Forest	42	13	10	19	63	79	36
20	Fulham	42	13	7	22	66	74	33
21	Cardiff	42	9	14	19	50	81	32
22	Chelsea	42	9	10	23	63	94	28

SECOND DIVISION

		P	W	D	L	F	A	Pts
1	Liverpool	42	27	8	7	99	43	62
2	Leyton Orient	42	22	10	10	69	40	54
3	Sunderland	42	22	9	11	85	50	53
4	Scunthorpe	42	21	7	14	86	71	49
5	Plymouth	42	19	8	15	75	75	46
6	Southampton	42	18	9	15	77	62	45
7	Huddersfield	42	16	12	14	67	59	44
8	Stoke	42	17	8	17	55	57	42
9	Rotherham	42	16	9	17	70	76	41
10	Preston	42	15	10	17	55	57	40
11	Newcastle	42	15	9	18	64	58	39
12	Middlesbrough	42	16	7	19	76	72	39
13	Luton	42	17	5	20	69	71	39
14	Walsall	42	14	11	17	70	75	39
15	Charlton	42	15	9	18	69	75	39
16	Derby	42	14	11	17	68	75	39
17	Norwich	42	14	11	17	61	70	39
18	Bury	42	17	5	20	52	76	39
19	Leeds	42	12	12	18	50	61	36
20	Swansea	42	12	12	18	61	83	36
21	Bristol Rovers	42	13	7	22	53	81	33
22	Brighton	42	10	11	21	42	86	31

FA CUP 1961-62

FOURTH ROUND

Burnley v Leyton Orient	1-1, 1-0
Everton v Manchester City	2-0
Peterborough United v Sheffield United	1-3
Norwich City v Ipswich Town	1-1, 2-1
Fulham v Walsall	2-2, 2-0
Sunderland v Port Vale	0-0, 1-3
Stoke City v Blackburn Rovers	0-1
Shrewsbury Town v Middlesbrough	2-2, 1-5
Oldham Athletic v Liverpool	1-2
Preston North End v Weymouth	2-0
Manchester United v Arsenal	1-0
Nottingham Forest v Sheffield Wednesday	0-2
Aston Villa v Huddersfield Town	2-1
Charlton Athletic v Derby County	2-1
Wolverhampton Wanderers v West Bromwich Albion	1-2
Plymouth Argyle v Tottenham Hotspur	1-5

FIFTH ROUND

Burnley v Everton	3-1
Sheffield United v Norwich City	3-1
Fulham v Port Vale	1-0
Blackburn Rovers v Middlesbrough	2-1
Liverpool v Preston North End	0-0, 0-0, 0-1
Manchester United v Sheffield Wednesday	0-0, 2-0
Aston Villa v Charlton Athletic	2-1
West Bromwich Albion v Tottenham Hotspur	2-4

SIXTH ROUND

Sheffield United v Burnley	0-1
Fulham v Blackburn Rovers	2-2, 1-0
Preston North End v Manchester United	0-0, 1-2
Tottenham Hotspur v Aston Villa	2-0

SEMI-FINAL

Burnley v Fulham	1-1, 2-1
Manchester United v Tottenham Hotspur	1-3

FINAL

Burnley v Tottenham Hotspur	1-3

THIRD DIVISION

		P	W	D	L	F	A	Pts
1	Portsmouth	46	27	11	8	87	47	65
2	Grimsby	46	28	6	12	80	56	62
3	Bournemouth	46	21	17	8	69	45	59
4	QPR	46	24	11	11	111	73	59
5	Peterborough	46	26	6	14	107	82	58
6	Bristol City	46	23	8	15	94	72	54
7	Reading	46	22	9	15	77	66	53
8	Northampton	46	20	11	15	85	57	51
9	Swindon	46	17	15	14	78	71	49
10	Hull	46	20	8	18	67	54	48
11	Bradford PA	46	20	7	19	80	78	47
12	Port Vale	46	17	11	18	65	58	45
13	Notts County	46	17	9	20	67	74	43
14	Coventry	46	16	11	19	64	71	43
15	Crystal Palace	46	14	14	18	83	80	42
16	Southend	46	13	16	17	57	69	42
17	Watford	46	14	13	19	63	74	41
18	Halifax	46	15	10	21	62	84	40
19	Shrewsbury	46	13	12	21	73	84	38
20	Barnsley	46	13	12	21	71	95	38
21	Torquay	46	15	6	25	76	100	36
22	Lincoln	46	9	17	20	57	87	35
23	Brentford	46	13	8	25	53	93	34
24	Newport	46	7	8	31	46	102	22

FOURTH DIVISION

		P	W	D	L	F	A	Pts
1	Millwall	44	23	10	11	87	62	56
2	Colchester	44	23	9	12	104	71	55
3	Wrexham	44	22	9	13	96	56	53
4	Carlisle	44	22	8	14	64	63	52
5	Bradford City	44	21	9	14	94	86	51
6	York	44	20	10	14	84	53	50
7	Aldershot	44	22	5	17	81	60	49
8	Workington	44	19	11	14	69	70	49
9	Barrow	44	17	14	13	74	58	48
10	Crewe	44	20	6	18	79	70	46
11	Oldham	44	17	12	15	77	70	46
12	Rochdale	44	19	7	18	71	71	45
13	Darlington	44	18	9	17	61	73	45
14	Mansfield	44	19	6	19	77	66	44
15	Tranmere	44	20	4	20	70	81	44
16	Stockport	44	17	9	18	70	69	43
17	Southport	44	17	9	18	61	71	43
18	Exeter	44	13	11	20	62	77	37
19	Chesterfield	44	14	9	21	70	87	37
20	Gillingham	44	13	11	20	73	94	37
21	Doncaster	44	11	7	26	60	85	29
22	Hartlepools	44	8	11	25	52	101	27
23	Chester	44	7	12	25	54	96	26
24	Accrington Stanley resigned from the League							

SCOTTISH FA CUP 1961-62

SECOND ROUND

Rangers v Arbroath	6-0
Clyde v Aberdeen	2-2, 3-10
Brechin City v Kilmarnock	1-6
Dumbarton v Ross County	2-3
Stirling Albion v Partick Thistle	3-1
East Fife v Albion Rovers	1-0
Stranraer v Montrose	0-0, 1-0
Motherwell v St Johnstone	4-0
Vale of Leithen v Heart of Midlothian	0-5
Morton v Celtic	1-3
Hamilton Academicals v Third Lanark	0-2
Inverness Caledonian v East Stirlingshire	3-0
Dunfermline Athletic v Wigtown	9-0
Queen of the South v Stenhousemuir	0-2
Alloa Athletic v Raith Rovers	1-2
Dundee v St Mirren	0-1

THIRD ROUND

Aberdeen v Rangers	2-2, 5-1
Kilmarnock v Ross County	7-0
Stirling Albion v East Fife	4-1
Stranraer v Motherwell	1-3
Heart of Midlothian v Celtic	3-4
Third Lanark v Inverness Caledonian	6-1
Dunfermline Athletic v Stenhousemuir	0-0, 3-0
Raith Rovers v St Mirren	1-1, 0-4

FOURTH ROUND

Kilmarnock v Rangers	2-4
Stirling Albion v Motherwell	0-6
Celtic v Third Lanark	4-4, 4-0
Dunfermline Athletic v St Mirren	0-1

SEMI-FINAL

Rangers v Motherwell	3-1
Celtic v St Mirren	1-3

FINAL

Rangers v St Mirren	2-0

SCOTTISH FIRST DIVISION

		P	W	D	L	F	A	Pts
1	Dundee	34	25	4	5	80	46	54
2	Rangers	34	22	7	5	84	31	51
3	Celtic	34	19	8	7	81	37	46
4	Dunfermline	34	19	5	10	77	46	43
5	Kilmarnock	34	16	10	8	74	58	42
6	Hearts	34	16	6	12	54	49	38
7	Partick Thistle	34	16	3	15	60	55	35
8	Hibernian	34	14	5	15	58	72	33
9	Motherwell	34	13	6	15	65	62	32
10	Dundee United	34	13	6	15	70	71	32
11	Third Lanark	34	13	5	16	59	60	31
12	Aberdeen	34	10	9	15	60	73	29
13	Raith Rovers	34	10	7	17	51	73	27
14	Falkirk	34	11	4	19	45	68	26
15	Airdrieonians	34	9	7	18	57	78	25
16	St Mirren	34	10	5	19	52	80	25
17	St Johnstone	34	9	7	18	35	61	25
18	Stirling Albion	34	6	6	22	34	76	18

SCOTTISH SECOND DIVISION

		P	W	D	L	F	A	Pts
1	Clyde	36	15	4	7	108	47	54
2	Queen of the S	36	24	5	7	78	33	53
3	Morton	36	19	6	11	78	64	44
4	Alloa	36	17	8	11	92	78	42
5	Montrose	36	15	11	10	63	50	41
6	Arbroath	36	17	7	12	66	59	41
7	Stranraer	36	14	11	11	61	62	39
8	Berwick	36	16	6	14	83	76	38
9	Ayr	36	15	8	13	71	63	38
10	East Fife	36	15	7	14	60	59	37
11	E Stirlingshire	36	15	4	17	70	81	34
12	Queen's Park	36	12	9	15	64	62	33
13	Hamilton	36	14	5	17	78	79	33
14	Cowdenbeath	36	11	9	16	65	77	31
15	Stenhousemuir	36	13	5	18	69	86	31
16	Forfar	36	11	8	17	68	76	30
17	Dumbarton	36	9	10	17	49	66	28
18	Albion	36	10	5	21	42	74	25
19	Brechin	36	5	2	29	44	123	12

Triple success

Only once since the War have three players hit hat-tricks for one side in the same League match. Ron Barnes, Roy Ambler and Wyn Davies did this in Wrexham's 10-1 thrashing of Hartlepools in a Fourth Division game on 3 March 1962.

The England player from the Third Division

Johnny Byrne, the Crystal Palace inside-right, became only the third footballer from the Third Division, to appear for England (v Ireland, 22 November 1961) in the Home Championship since the War.

FIRST DIVISION

		P	W	D	L	F	A	Pts
1	Everton	42	25	11	6	84	42	61
2	Tottenham	42	23	9	10	111	62	55
3	Burnley	42	22	10	10	78	57	54
4	Leicester	42	20	12	10	79	53	52
5	Wolves	42	20	10	12	93	65	50
6	Sheff Wed	42	19	10	13	77	63	48
7	Arsenal	42	18	10	14	86	77	46
8	Liverpool	42	17	10	15	71	59	44
9	Nottm Forest	42	17	10	15	67	69	44
10	Sheff United	42	16	12	14	58	60	44
11	Blackburn	42	15	12	15	79	71	42
12	West Ham	42	14	12	16	73	69	40
13	Blackpool	42	13	14	15	58	64	40
14	WBA	42	16	7	19	71	79	39
15	Aston Villa	42	15	8	19	62	68	38
16	Fulham	42	14	10	18	50	71	38
17	Ipswich	42	12	11	19	59	78	35
18	Bolton	42	15	5	22	55	75	35
19	Man United	42	12	10	20	67	81	34
20	Birmingham	42	10	13	19	63	90	33
21	Man City	42	10	11	21	58	102	31
22	Leyton Orient	42	6	9	27	37	81	21

SECOND DIVISION

		P	W	D	L	F	A	Pts
1	Stoke	42	20	13	9	73	50	53
2	Chelsea	42	24	4	14	81	42	52
3	Sunderland	42	20	12	10	84	55	52
4	Middlesbrough	42	20	9	13	86	85	49
5	Leeds	42	19	10	13	79	53	48
6	Huddersfield	42	17	14	11	63	50	48
7	Newcastle	42	18	11	13	79	59	47
8	Bury	42	18	11	13	51	47	47
9	Scunthorpe	42	16	12	14	57	59	44
10	Cardiff	42	18	7	17	83	73	43
11	Southampton	42	17	8	17	72	67	42
12	Plymouth	42	15	12	15	76	73	42
13	Norwich	42	17	8	17	80	79	42
14	Rotherham	42	17	6	19	67	74	40
15	Swansea	42	15	9	18	51	72	39
16	Portsmouth	42	13	11	18	63	79	37
17	Preston	42	13	11	18	59	74	37
18	Derby	42	12	12	18	61	72	36
19	Grimsby	42	11	13	18	55	66	35
20	Charlton	42	13	5	24	62	94	31
21	Walsall	42	11	9	22	53	89	31
22	Luton	42	11	7	24	61	84	29

THIRD DIVISION

		P	W	D	L	F	A	Pts
1	Northampton	46	26	10	10	109	60	62
2	Swindon	46	22	14	10	87	56	58
3	Port Vale	46	23	8	15	72	58	54
4	Coventry	46	18	17	11	83	69	53
5	Bournemouth	46	18	16	12	63	46	52
6	Peterborough	46	20	11	15	93	75	51
7	Notts County	46	19	13	14	73	74	51
8	Southend	46	19	12	15	75	77	50
9	Wrexham	46	20	9	17	84	83	49
10	Hull	46	19	10	17	74	69	48
11	Crystal Palace	46	17	13	16	68	58	47
12	Colchester	46	18	11	17	73	93	47
13	QPR	46	17	11	18	85	76	45
14	Bristol City	46	16	13	17	100	92	45
15	Shrewsbury	46	16	12	18	83	81	44
16	Millwall	46	15	13	18	82	87	43
17	Watford	46	17	8	21	82	85	42
18	Barnsley	46	15	11	20	63	74	41
19	Bristol Rovers	46	15	11	20	70	88	41
20	Reading	46	16	8	22	74	78	40
21	Bradford PA	46	14	12	20	79	97	40
22	Brighton	46	12	12	22	58	84	36
23	Carlisle	46	13	9	24	61	89	35
24	Halifax	46	9	12	25	64	106	30

FOURTH DIVISION

		P	W	D	L	F	A	Pts
1	Brentford	46	27	8	11	98	64	62
2	Oldham	46	24	11	11	95	60	59
3	Crewe	46	24	11	11	86	58	59
4	Mansfield	46	24	9	13	108	69	57
5	Gillingham	46	22	13	11	71	49	57
6	Torquay	46	20	16	10	75	56	56
7	Rochdale	46	20	11	15	67	59	51
8	Tranmere	46	20	10	16	81	67	50
9	Barrow	46	19	12	15	82	80	50
10	Workington	46	17	13	16	76	68	47
11	Aldershot	46	15	17	14	73	69	47
12	Darlington	46	19	6	21	72	87	44
13	Southport	46	15	14	17	72	106	44
14	York	46	16	11	19	67	62	43
15	Chesterfield	46	13	16	17	70	64	42
16	Doncaster	46	14	14	18	64	77	42
17	Exeter	46	16	10	20	57	77	42
18	Oxford	46	13	15	18	70	71	41
19	Stockport	46	15	11	20	56	70	41
20	Newport	46	14	11	21	76	90	39
21	Chester	46	15	9	22	51	66	39
22	Lincoln	46	13	9	24	68	89	35
23	Bradford City	46	11	10	25	64	93	32
24	Hartlepools	46	7	11	28	56	104	25

SCOTTISH FIRST DIVISION

		P	W	D	L	F	A	Pts
1	Rangers	34	25	7	2	94	28	57
2	Kilmarnock	34	20	8	6	92	40	48
3	Partick Thistle	34	20	6	8	66	44	46
4	Celtic	34	19	6	9	76	44	44
5	Hearts	34	17	9	8	85	59	43
6	Aberdeen	34	17	7	10	70	47	41
7	Dundee United	34	15	11	8	67	52	41
8	Dunfermline	34	13	8	13	50	47	34
9	Dundee	34	12	9	13	60	49	33
10	Motherwell	34	10	11	13	60	63	31
11	Airdrieonians	34	14	2	18	52	76	30
12	St Mirren	34	10	8	16	52	72	28
13	Falkirk	34	12	3	19	54	69	27
14	Third Lanark	34	9	8	17	56	68	26
15	Queen of the S	34	10	6	18	36	75	26
16	Hibernian	34	8	9	17	47	67	25
17	Clyde	34	9	5	20	49	83	23
18	Raith	34	2	5	27	35	118	9

SCOTTISH SECOND DIVISION

		P	W	D	L	F	A	Pts
1	St Johnstone	36	25	5	6	83	37	55
2	E Stirlingshire	36	20	9	7	80	50	49
3	Morton	36	23	2	11	100	49	48
4	Hamilton	36	18	8	10	69	56	44
5	Stranraer	36	16	10	10	81	70	42
6	Arbroath	36	18	4	14	74	51	40
7	Albion	36	18	2	16	72	79	38
8	Cowdenbeath	36	15	7	14	72	61	37
9	Alloa	36	15	6	15	57	56	36
10	Stirling	36	16	4	16	74	75	36
11	East Fife	36	15	6	15	60	69	36
12	Dumbarton	36	15	4	17	64	64	34
13	Ayr	36	13	8	15	68	77	34
14	Queen's Park	36	13	6	17	66	72	32
15	Montrose	36	13	5	18	57	70	31
16	Stenhousemuir	36	13	5	18	54	75	31
17	Berwick	36	11	7	18	57	77	29
18	Forfar	36	9	5	22	73	99	23
19	Brechin	36	3	3	30	39	113	9

FA CUP 1962-63

FOURTH ROUND

Leicester City v Ipswich Town	3-1
Leyton Orient v Derby County	3-0
Manchester City v Bury	1-0
Norwich City v Newcastle United	5-0
Arsenal v Sheffield Wednesday	2-0
Burnley v Liverpool	1-1, 1-2
West Ham United v Swansea Town	1-0
Swindon Town v Everton	1-5
West Bromwich Albion v Nottingham Forest	0-0, 1-2
Middlesbrough v Leeds United	0-2
Southampton v Watford	3-1
Port Vale v Sheffield United	1-2
Portsmouth v Coventry City	1-1, 2-2, 1-2
Gravesend v Sunderland	1-1, 2-5
Charlton Athletic v Chelsea	0-3
Manchester United v Aston Villa	1-0

FIFTH ROUND

Leicester City v Leyton Orient	1-0
Manchester City v Norwich City	1-2
Arsenal v Liverpool	1-2
West Ham United v Everton	1-0
Nottingham Forest v Leeds United	3-0
Southampton v Sheffield United	1-0
Coventry City v Sunderland	2-1
Manchester United v Chelsea	2-1

SIXTH ROUND

Norwich City v Leicester City	0-2
Liverpool v West Ham United	1-0
Nottingham Forest v Southampton	1-1, 3-3, 0-5
Coventry City v Manchester United	1-3

SEMI-FINAL

Leicester City v Liverpool	1-0
Southampton v Manchester United	0-1

FINAL

Leicester City v Manchester United	1-3

SCOTTISH FA CUP 1962-63

SECOND ROUND

Airdrieonians v Rangers	0-6
East Stirlingshire v Motherwell	1-0
Dundee v Montrose	8-0
Brechin City v Hibernian	0-2
Queen's Park v Alloa Athletic	5-1
Ayr United v Dundee United	1-2
Kilmarnock v Queen of the South	0-0, 0-1
Hamilton Academicals v Nairn County	1-1, 2-1
East Fife v Third Lanark	1-1, 0-2
Raith Rovers v Clyde	3-2
St Johnstone v Aberdeen	1-2
Cowdenbeath v Dunfermline Athletic	2-3
Berwick Rangers v St Mirren	1-3
Partick Thistle v Arbroath	1-1, 2-2, 3-2
Gala Fairydean v Duns	1-1, 2-1
Celtic v Heart of Midlothian	3-1

THIRD ROUND

Rangers v East Stirlingshire	7-2
Dundee v Hibernian	1-0
Queen's Park v Dundee United	1-1, 1-3
Queen of the South v Hamilton Academicals	3-0
Third Lanark v Raith Rovers	0-1
Aberdeen v Dunfermline Athletic	4-0
St Mirren v Partick Thistle	1-1, 1-0
Celtic v Gala Fairydean	6-0

FOURTH ROUND

Dundee v Rangers	1-1, 2-3
Dundee United v Queen of the South	1-1, 1-1, 4-0
Raith Rovers v Aberdeen	2-1
St Mirren v Celtic	0-1

SEMI-FINAL

Rangers v Dundee United	5-2
Raith Rovers v Celtic	2-5

FINAL

Rangers v Celtic	1-1, 3-0

Terrible winter disrupts the football programme

The winter of 1962-63 broke all previous records for postponements and abandoned matches due to bad weather. For six weeks, the football programme was wrecked by impossible playing conditions and over 400 League and Cup games were postponed or abandoned in England, Wales and Scotland. The worst-hit day—in fact the worst-hit ever, except for the War years—in England and Scotland was 9 February. Then, 57 games were called off through snow and ice, and only seven were completed. As a result of the severe winter, the football season was extended.

FIRST DIVISION

		P	W	D	L	F	A	Pts
1	Liverpool	42	26	5	11	92	45	57
2	Man United	42	23	7	12	90	62	53
3	Everton	42	21	10	11	84	64	52
4	Tottenham	42	22	7	13	97	81	51
5	Chelsea	42	20	10	12	72	56	50
6	Sheff Wed	42	19	11	12	84	67	49
7	Blackburn	42	18	10	14	89	65	46
8	Arsenal	42	17	11	14	90	82	45
9	Burnley	42	17	10	15	71	64	44
10	WBA	42	16	11	15	70	61	43
11	Leicester	42	16	11	15	61	58	43
12	Sheff United	42	16	11	15	61	64	43
13	Nottm Forest	42	16	9	17	64	68	41
14	West Ham	42	14	12	16	69	74	40
15	Fulham	42	13	13	16	58	65	39
16	Wolves	42	12	15	15	70	80	39
17	Stoke	42	14	10	18	77	78	38
18	Blackpool	42	13	9	20	52	73	35
19	Aston Villa	42	11	12	19	62	71	34
20	Birmingham	42	11	7	24	54	92	29
21	Bolton	42	10	8	24	48	80	28
22	Ipswich	42	9	7	26	56	121	25

SECOND DIVISION

		P	W	D	L	F	A	Pts
1	Leeds	42	24	15	3	71	34	63
2	Sunderland	42	25	11	6	81	37	61
3	Preston	42	23	10	9	79	54	56
4	Charlton	42	19	10	13	76	70	48
5	Southampton	42	19	9	14	100	73	47
6	Man City	42	18	10	14	84	66	46
7	Rotherham	42	19	7	16	90	78	45
8	Newcastle	42	20	5	17	74	69	45
9	Portsmouth	42	16	11	15	79	70	43
10	Middlesbrough	42	15	11	16	67	52	41
11	Northampton	42	16	9	17	58	60	41
12	Huddersfield	42	15	10	17	57	64	40
13	Derby	42	14	11	17	56	67	39
14	Swindon	42	14	10	18	57	69	38
15	Cardiff	42	14	10	18	56	81	38
16	Leyton Orient	42	13	10	19	54	72	36
17	Norwich	42	11	13	18	64	80	35
18	Bury	42	13	9	20	57	73	35
19	Swansea	42	12	9	21	63	74	33
20	Plymouth	42	8	16	18	45	67	32
21	Grimsby	42	9	14	19	47	75	32
22	Scunthorpe	42	10	10	22	52	82	30

FA CUP 1963-64

FOURTH ROUND

West Ham United v Leyton Orient	1-1, 3-0
Aldershot v Swindon Town	1-2
Burnley v Newport County	2-1
Chelsea v Huddersfield Town	1-2
Sunderland v Bristol City	6-1
Leeds United v Everton	1-1, 0-2
Barnsley v Bury	2-1
Manchester United v Bristol Rovers	4-1
Ipswich Town v Stoke City	1-1, 0-1
Sheffield United v Swansea Town	1-1, 0-4
West Bromwich Albion v Arsenal	3-3, 0-2
Liverpool v Port Vale	0-0, 2-1
Oxford United v Brentford	2-2, 2-1
Blackburn Rovers v Fulham	2-0
Bedford Town v Carlisle United	0-3
Bolton Wanderers v Preston North End	2-2, 1-2

FIFTH ROUND

West Ham United v Swindon Town	3-1
Burnley v Huddersfield Town	3-0
Sunderland v Everton	3-1
Barnsley v Manchester United	0-4
Stoke City v Swansea Town	2-2, 0-2
Arsenal v Liverpool	0-1
Oxford United v Blackburn Rovers	3-1
Carlisle United v Preston North End	0-1

SIXTH ROUND

West Ham United v Burnley	3-2
Manchester United v Sunderland	3-3, 2-2, 5-1
Liverpool v Swansea Town	1-2
Oxford United v Preston North End	1-2

SEMI-FINAL

West Ham United v Manchester United	3-1
Swansea Town v Preston North End	1-2

FINAL

West Ham United v Preston North End	3-2

THIRD DIVISION

		P	W	D	L	F	A	Pts
1	Coventry	46	22	16	8	98	61	60
2	Crystal Palace	46	23	14	9	73	51	60
3	Watford	46	23	12	11	79	59	58
4	Bournemouth	46	24	8	14	79	58	56
5	Bristol City	46	20	15	11	84	64	55
6	Reading	46	21	10	15	79	62	52
7	Mansfield	46	20	11	15	76	62	51
8	Hull	46	16	17	13	73	68	49
9	Oldham	46	20	8	18	73	70	48
10	Peterborough	46	18	11	17	75	70	47
11	Shrewsbury	46	18	11	17	73	80	47
12	Bristol Rovers	46	19	8	19	91	79	46
13	Port Vale	46	16	14	16	53	49	46
14	Southend	46	15	15	16	77	78	45
15	QPR	46	18	9	19	76	78	45
16	Brentford	46	15	14	17	87	80	44
17	Colchester	46	12	19	15	70	68	43
18	Luton	46	16	10	20	64	80	42
19	Walsall	46	13	14	19	59	76	40
20	Barnsley	46	12	15	19	68	94	39
21	Millwall	46	14	10	22	53	67	38
22	Crewe	46	11	12	23	50	77	34
23	Wrexham	46	13	6	27	75	107	32
24	Notts County	46	9	9	28	45	92	27

FOURTH DIVISION

		P	W	D	L	F	A	Pts
1	Gillingham	46	23	14	9	59	30	60
2	Carlisle	46	25	10	11	113	58	60
3	Workington	46	24	11	11	76	52	59
4	Exeter	46	20	18	8	62	37	58
5	Bradford City	46	25	6	15	76	62	56
6	Torquay	46	20	11	15	80	54	51
7	Tranmere	46	20	11	15	85	73	51
8	Brighton	46	19	12	15	71	52	50
9	Aldershot	46	19	10	17	83	78	48
10	Halifax	46	17	14	15	77	77	48
11	Lincoln	46	19	9	18	67	75	47
12	Chester	46	19	8	19	65	60	46
13	Bradford PA	46	18	9	19	75	81	45
14	Doncaster	46	15	12	19	70	75	42
15	Newport	46	17	8	21	64	73	42
16	Chesterfield	46	15	12	19	57	71	42
17	Stockport	46	15	12	19	50	68	42
18	Oxford	46	14	13	19	59	63	41
19	Darlington	46	14	12	20	66	93	40
20	Rochdale	46	12	15	19	56	59	39
21	Southport	46	15	9	22	63	88	39
22	York	46	14	7	25	52	66	35
23	Hartlepools	46	12	9	25	54	93	33
24	Barrow	46	6	18	22	51	93	30

SCOTTISH FA CUP 1963-64

SECOND ROUND

Rangers v Duns	9-0
Partick Thistle v St Johnstone	2-0
Morton v Celtic	1-3
Alloa Athletic v Airdrieonians	1-3
East Fife v East Stirlingshire	0-1
Dunfermline Athletic v Fraserburgh	7-0
Aberdeen v Queen's Park	1-1, 2-1
Buckie Thistle v Ayr United	1-3
Hamilton Academicals v Kilmarnock	1-3
Albion Rovers v Arbroath	4-3
St Mirren v Stranraer	2-0
Falkirk v Berwick Rangers	2-2, 5-1
Motherwell v Dumbarton	4-1
Queen of the South v Heart of Midlothian	0-3
Clyde v Forfar Athletic	2-2, 2-3
Brechin City v Dundee	2-9

THIRD ROUND

Rangers v Partick Thistle	3-0
Celtic v Airdrieonians	4-1
East Stirlingshire v Dunfermline Athletic	1-6
Aberdeen v Ayr United	1-2
Kilmarnock v Albion Rovers	2-0
St Mirren v Falkirk	0-1
Motherwell v Heart of Midlothian	3-3, 2-1
Dundee v Forfar Athletic	6-1

FOURTH ROUND

Rangers v Celtic	2-0
Dunfermline Athletic v Ayr United	7-0
Kilmarnock v Falkirk	2-1
Dundee v Motherwell	1-1, 4-2

SEMI-FINAL

Rangers v Dunfermline Athletic	1-0
Kilmarnock v Dundee	0-4

FINAL

Rangers v Dundee	3-1

SCOTTISH FIRST DIVISION

		P	W	D	L	F	A	Pts
1	Rangers	34	25	5	4	85	31	55
2	Kilmarnock	34	22	5	7	77	40	49
3	Celtic	34	19	9	6	89	34	47
4	Hearts	34	19	9	6	74	40	47
5	Dunfermline	34	18	9	7	64	33	45
6	Dundee	34	20	5	9	94	50	45
7	Partick Thistle	34	15	5	14	55	54	35
8	Dundee United	34	13	8	13	65	49	34
9	Aberdeen	34	12	8	14	53	53	32
10	Hibernian	34	12	6	16	59	66	30
11	Motherwell	34	9	11	14	51	62	29
12	St Mirren	34	12	5	17	44	74	29
13	St Johnstone	34	11	6	17	54	70	28
14	Falkirk	34	11	6	17	54	84	28
15	Airdrieonians	34	11	4	19	52	97	26
16	Third Lanark	34	9	7	18	47	74	25
17	Queen of the S	34	5	6	23	40	92	16
18	E Stirlingshire	34	5	2	27	37	91	12

SCOTTISH SECOND DIVISION

		P	W	D	L	F	A	Pts
1	Morton	36	32	3	1	135	37	67
2	Clyde	36	22	9	5	81	44	53
3	Arbroath	36	20	6	10	79	46	46
4	East Fife	36	16	13	7	92	57	45
5	Montrose	36	19	6	11	79	57	44
6	Dumbarton	36	16	6	14	67	59	38
7	Queen's Park	36	17	4	15	57	54	38
8	Stranraer	36	16	6	14	71	73	38
9	Albion	36	12	12	12	67	71	36
10	Raith	36	15	5	16	70	61	35
11	Stenhousemuir	36	15	5	16	83	75	35
12	Berwick	36	10	10	16	68	84	30
13	Hamilton	36	12	6	18	65	81	30
14	Ayr	36	12	5	19	58	83	29
15	Brechin	36	10	8	18	61	98	28
16	Alloa	36	11	5	20	64	92	27
17	Cowdenbeath	36	7	11	18	46	72	25
18	Forfar	36	6	8	22	57	104	20
19	Stirling	36	6	8	22	47	99	20

On 12 October 1963, Tottenham Hotspur had seven players on international duty in the Home Championship, a record. Norman, Greaves and Smith were in the England side that met Wales. The Welsh team included Spurs' brilliant winger, Cliff Jones. Scotland paraded Brown, Mackay and White against Ireland.

Quick off the mark

The fastest goal in first-class football was scored by Jim Fryatt of Bradford Park Avenue on 25 April 1964. Just four seconds after the kick-off, Tranmere Rovers found themselves a goal down. Though a fantastic time, referee R. J. Simon's stop-watch confirmed it.

FIRST DIVISION

	P	W	D	L	F	A	Pts
1 Man United	42	26	9	7	89	39	61
2 Leeds	42	26	9	7	83	52	61
3 Chelsea	42	24	8	10	89	54	56
4 Everton	42	17	15	10	69	60	49
5 Nottm Forest	42	17	13	12	71	67	47
6 Tottenham	42	19	7	16	87	71	45
7 Liverpool	42	17	10	15	67	73	44
8 Sheff Wed	42	16	11	15	57	55	43
9 West Ham	42	19	4	19	82	71	42
10 Blackburn	42	16	10	16	83	79	42
11 Stoke	42	16	10	16	67	66	42
12 Burnley	42	16	10	16	70	70	42
13 Arsenal	42	17	7	18	69	75	41
14 WBA	42	13	13	16	70	65	39
15 Sunderland	42	14	9	19	64	74	37
16 Aston Villa	42	16	5	21	57	82	37
17 Blackpool	42	12	11	19	67	78	35
18 Leicester	42	11	13	18	69	85	35
19 Sheff United	42	12	11	19	50	64	35
20 Fulham	42	11	12	19	60	78	34
21 Wolves	42	13	4	25	59	89	30
22 Birmingham	42	8	11	23	64	96	27

SECOND DIVISION

	P	W	D	L	F	A	Pts
1 Newcastle	42	24	9	9	81	45	57
2 Northampton	42	20	16	6	66	50	56
3 Bolton	42	20	10	12	80	58	50
4 Southampton	42	17	14	11	83	63	48
5 Ipswich	42	15	17	10	74	67	47
6 Norwich	42	20	7	15	61	57	47
7 Crystal Palace	42	16	13	13	55	51	45
8 Huddersfield	42	17	10	15	53	51	44
9 Derby	42	16	11	15	84	79	43
10 Coventry	42	17	9	16	72	70	43
11 Man City	42	16	9	17	63	62	41
12 Preston	42	14	13	15	76	81	41
13 Cardiff	42	13	14	15	64	57	40
14 Rotherham	42	14	12	16	70	69	40
15 Plymouth	42	16	8	18	63	79	40
16 Bury	42	14	10	18	60	66	38
17 Middlesbrough	42	13	9	20	70	76	35
18 Charlton	42	13	9	20	64	75	35
19 Leyton Orient	42	12	11	19	50	72	35
20 Portsmouth	42	12	10	20	56	77	34
21 Swindon	42	14	5	23	63	81	33
22 Swansea	42	11	10	21	62	84	32

THIRD DIVISION

	P	W	D	L	F	A	Pts
1 Carlisle	46	25	10	11	76	53	60
2 Bristol City	46	24	11	11	92	55	59
3 Mansfield	46	24	11	11	95	61	59
4 Hull	46	23	12	11	91	57	58
5 Brentford	46	24	9	13	83	55	57
6 Bristol Rovers	46	20	15	11	82	58	55
7 Gillingham	46	23	9	14	70	50	55
8 Peterborough	46	22	7	17	85	74	51
9 Watford	46	17	16	13	71	64	50
10 Grimsby	46	16	17	13	68	67	49
11 Bournemouth	46	18	11	17	72	63	47
12 Southend	46	19	8	19	78	71	46
13 Reading	46	16	14	16	70	70	46
14 QPR	46	17	12	17	72	80	46
15 Workington	46	17	12	17	58	69	46
16 Shrewsbury	46	15	12	19	76	84	42
17 Exeter	46	12	17	17	51	52	41
18 Scunthorpe	46	14	12	20	65	72	40
19 Walsall	46	15	7	24	55	80	37
20 Oldham	46	13	10	23	61	83	36
21 Luton	46	11	11	24	51	94	33
22 Port Vale	46	9	14	23	41	76	32
23 Colchester	46	10	10	26	50	89	30
24 Barnsley	46	9	11	26	54	90	29

FOURTH DIVISION

	P	W	D	L	F	A	Pts
1 Brighton	46	26	11	9	102	57	63
2 Millwall	46	23	16	7	78	45	62
3 York	46	28	6	12	91	56	62
4 Oxford	46	23	15	8	87	44	61
5 Tranmere	46	27	6	13	99	56	60
6 Rochdale	46	22	14	10	74	53	58
7 Bradford PA	46	20	17	9	86	62	57
8 Chester	46	25	6	15	119	81	56
9 Doncaster	46	20	11	15	84	72	51
10 Crewe	46	18	13	15	90	81	49
11 Torquay	46	21	7	18	70	70	49
12 Chesterfield	46	20	8	18	58	70	48
13 Notts County	46	15	14	17	61	73	44
14 Wrexham	46	17	9	20	84	92	43
15 Hartlepools	46	15	13	18	61	85	43
16 Newport	46	17	8	21	85	81	42
17 Darlington	46	18	6	22	84	87	42
18 Aldershot	46	15	7	24	64	84	37
19 Bradford City	46	12	8	26	70	88	32
20 Southport	46	8	16	22	58	89	32
21 Barrow	46	12	6	28	59	105	30
22 Lincoln	46	11	6	29	58	99	28
23 Halifax	46	11	6	29	54	103	28
24 Stockport	46	10	7	29	44	87	27

SCOTTISH FIRST DIVISION

	P	W	D	L	F	A	Pts
1 Kilmarnock	34	22	6	6	62	33	50
2 Hearts	34	22	6	6	90	49	50
3 Dunfermline	34	22	5	7	83	36	49
4 Hibernian	34	21	4	9	75	47	46
5 Rangers	34	18	8	8	78	35	44
6 Dundee	34	15	10	9	86	63	40
7 Clyde	34	17	6	11	64	58	40
8 Celtic	34	16	5	13	76	57	37
9 Dundee United	34	15	6	13	59	51	36
10 Morton	34	13	7	14	54	54	33
11 Partick Thistle	34	11	10	13	57	58	32
12 Aberdeen	34	12	8	14	59	75	32
13 St Johnstone	34	9	11	14	57	62	29
14 Motherwell	34	10	8	16	45	54	28
15 St Mirren	34	9	6	19	38	70	24
16 Falkirk	34	7	7	20	43	85	21
17 Airdrieonians	34	5	4	25	48	110	14
18 Third Lanark	34	3	1	30	22	99	7

SCOTTISH SECOND DIVISION

	P	W	D	L	F	A	Pts
1 Stirling Albion	36	26	7	3	84	31	59
2 Hamilton	36	21	8	7	86	53	50
3 Queen of the S	36	16	13	7	84	50	45
4 Queen's Park	36	17	9	10	57	41	43
5 ES Clydebank	36	15	10	11	64	50	40
6 Stranraer	36	17	6	13	74	64	40
7 Arbroath	36	13	13	10	56	51	39
8 Berwick	36	15	9	12	73	70	39
9 East Fife	36	15	7	14	78	77	37
10 Alloa	36	14	8	14	71	81	36
11 Albion	36	14	5	17	56	60	33
12 Cowdenbeath	36	11	10	15	55	62	32
13 Raith	36	9	14	13	54	61	32
14 Dumbarton	36	13	6	17	55	67	32
15 Stenhousemuir	36	11	8	17	49	74	30
16 Montrose	36	10	9	17	80	91	29
17 Forfar	36	9	7	20	63	89	25
18 Ayr	36	9	6	21	49	67	24
19 Brechin	36	6	7	23	53	102	19

FA CUP 1964-65

FOURTH ROUND

Liverpool v Stockport County	1-1, 2-0
Preston North End v Bolton Wanderers	1-2
Leicester City v Plymouth Argyle	5-0
Charlton Athletic v Middlesbrough	1-1, 1-2
West Ham United v Chelsea	0-1
Tottenham Hotspur v Ipswich Town	5-0
Peterborough United v Arsenal	2-1
Swansea Town v Huddersfield Town	1-0
Wolverhampton Wanderers v Rotherham United	2-2, 3-0
Sheffield United v Aston Villa	0-2
Stoke City v Manchester United	0-0, 0-1
Reading v Burnley	1-1, 0-1
Southampton v Crystal Palace	1-2
Sunderland v Nottingham Forest	1-3
Millwall v Shrewsbury Town	1-2
Leeds United v Everton	1-1, 2-1

FIFTH ROUND

Bolton Wanderers v Liverpool	0-1
Middlesbrough v Leicester City	0-3
Chelsea v Tottenham Hotspur	1-0
Peterborough United v Swansea Town	0-0, 2-0
Aston Villa v Wolverhampton Wanderers	1-1, 0-0, 1-3
Manchester United v Burnley	2-1
Crystal Palace v Nottingham Forest	3-1
Leeds United v Shrewsbury Town	2-0

SIXTH ROUND

Leicester City v Liverpool	0-0, 0-1
Chelsea v Peterborough United	5-1
Wolverhampton Wanderers v Manchester United	3-5
Crystal Palace v Leeds United	0-3

SEMI-FINAL

Liverpool v Chelsea	2-0
Manchester United v Leeds United	0-0, 0-1

FINAL

Leeds United v Liverpool	1-2

SCOTTISH FA CUP 1964-65

FIRST ROUND

St Mirren v Celtic	0-3
Dumbarton v Queen's Park	0-0, 1-2
Aberdeen v East Fife	0-0, 0-1
Kilmarnock v Cowdenbeath	5-0
Motherwell v Stenhousemuir	3-2
St Johnstone v Dundee	1-0
Clyde v Morton	0-4
Falkirk v Heart of Midlothian	0-3
Hibernian v E S Clydebank	1-1, 2-0
Ayr United v Partick Thistle	1-1, 1-7
Forfar Athletic v Dundee United	0-3
Rangers v Hamilton Academicals	3-0
Stirling Albion v Arbroath	2-1
Airdrieonians v Montrose	7-3
Inverness Caledonian v Third Lanark	1-5
Queen of the South v Dunfermline Athletic	0-2

SECOND ROUND

Queen's Park v Celtic	0-1
East Fife v Kilmarnock	0-0, 0-3
Motherwell v St Johnstone	1-0
Morton v Heart of Midlothian	3-3, 0-2
Hibernian v Partick Thistle	5-1
Dundee United v Rangers	0-2
Stirling Albion v Airdrieonians	1-1, 2-0
Third Lanark v Dunfermline Athletic	1-1, 2-2, 2-4

THIRD ROUND

Celtic v Kilmarnock	3-2
Motherwell v Heart of Midlothian	1-0
Hibernian v Rangers	2-1
Dunfermline Athletic v Stirling Albion	2-0

SEMI-FINAL

Celtic v Motherwell	2-2, 3-0
Hibernian v Dunfermline Athletic	0-2

FINAL

Celtic v Dunfermline Athletic	3-2

Gillingham set a record for an undefeated run of home matches including Cup and League Cup games. From 9 April 1963, Gillingham had gone 52 games—48 of them in the League—at their Priestfield Stadium without a defeat, before losing 1-0 to Exeter on 10 April 1965.

Stan Lynn, Birmingham City's full-back, scored 10 goals (8 from penalties) and ended the 1964-65 season as his club's top League goal-scorer. Only one other full-back—Jimmy Evans of Southend United in 1921-2—has achieved this distinction among Football League clubs.

239

FIRST DIVISION

	P	W	D	L	F	A	Pts
1 Liverpool	42	26	9	7	79	34	61
2 Leeds	42	23	9	10	79	38	55
3 Burnley	42	24	7	11	79	47	55
4 Man United	42	18	15	9	84	59	51
5 Chelsea	42	22	7	13	65	53	51
6 WBA	42	19	12	11	91	69	50
7 Leicester	42	21	7	14	80	65	49
8 Tottenham	42	16	12	14	75	66	44
9 Sheff United	42	16	11	15	56	59	43
10 Stoke	42	15	12	15	65	64	42
11 Everton	42	15	11	16	56	62	41
12 West Ham	42	15	9	18	70	83	39
13 Blackpool	42	14	9	19	55	65	37
14 Arsenal	42	12	13	17	62	75	37
15 Newcastle	42	14	9	19	50	63	37
16 Aston Villa	42	15	6	21	69	80	36
17 Sheff Wed	42	14	8	20	56	66	36
18 Nottm Forest	42	14	8	20	56	72	36
19 Sunderland	42	14	8	20	51	72	36
20 Fulham	42	14	7	21	67	85	35
21 Northampton	42	10	13	19	55	92	33
22 Blackburn	42	8	4	30	57	88	20

SECOND DIVISION

	P	W	D	L	F	A	Pts
1 Man City	42	22	15	5	76	44	59
2 Southampton	42	22	10	10	85	56	54
3 Coventry	42	20	13	9	73	53	53
4 Huddersfield	42	19	13	10	62	36	51
5 Bristol City	42	17	17	8	63	48	51
6 Wolves	42	20	10	12	87	61	50
7 Rotherham	42	16	14	12	75	74	46
8 Derby	42	16	11	15	71	68	43
9 Bolton	42	16	9	17	62	59	41
10 Birmingham	42	16	9	17	70	75	41
11 Crystal Palace	42	14	13	15	47	52	41
12 Portsmouth	42	16	8	18	74	78	40
13 Norwich	42	12	15	15	52	52	39
14 Carlisle	42	17	5	20	60	63	39
15 Ipswich	42	15	9	18	58	66	39
16 Charlton	42	12	14	16	61	70	38
17 Preston	42	11	15	16	62	70	37
18 Plymouth	42	12	13	17	54	63	37
19 Bury	42	14	7	21	62	76	35
20 Cardiff	42	12	10	20	71	91	34
21 Middlesbrough	42	10	13	19	58	86	33
22 Leyton Orient	42	5	13	24	38	80	23

THIRD DIVISION

	P	W	D	L	F	A	Pts
1 Hull	46	31	7	8	109	62	69
2 Millwall	46	27	11	8	76	43	65
3 QPR	46	24	9	13	95	65	57
4 Scunthorpe	46	21	11	14	80	67	53
5 Workington	46	19	14	13	67	57	52
6 Gillingham	46	22	8	16	62	54	52
7 Swindon	46	19	13	14	74	48	51
8 Reading	46	19	13	14	70	63	51
9 Walsall	46	20	10	16	77	64	50
10 Shrewsbury	46	19	11	16	73	64	49
11 Grimsby	46	17	13	16	68	62	47
12 Watford	46	17	13	16	55	51	47
13 Peterborough	46	17	12	17	80	66	46
14 Oxford	46	19	8	19	70	74	46
15 Brighton	46	16	11	19	67	65	43
16 Bristol Rovers	46	14	14	18	64	64	42
17 Swansea	46	15	11	20	81	96	41
18 Bournemouth	46	13	12	21	38	56	38
19 Mansfield	46	15	8	23	59	89	38
20 Oldham	46	12	13	21	55	81	37
21 Southend	46	16	4	26	54	83	36
22 Exeter	46	12	11	23	53	79	35
23 Brentford	46	10	12	24	48	69	32
24 York	46	9	9	28	53	106	27

FOURTH DIVISION

	P	W	D	L	F	A	Pts
1 Doncaster	46	24	11	11	85	54	59
2 Darlington	46	25	9	12	72	53	59
3 Torquay	46	24	10	12	72	49	58
4 Colchester	46	23	10	13	70	47	56
5 Tranmere	46	24	8	14	93	66	56
6 Luton	46	24	8	14	90	70	56
7 Chester	46	20	12	14	79	70	52
8 Notts County	46	19	12	15	61	53	50
9 Newport	46	18	12	16	75	75	48
10 Southport	46	18	12	16	68	69	48
11 Bradford PA	46	21	5	20	102	92	47
12 Barrow	46	16	15	15	72	76	47
13 Stockport	46	18	6	22	71	70	42
14 Crewe	46	16	9	21	61	63	41
15 Halifax	46	15	11	20	67	75	41
16 Barnsley	46	15	10	21	74	78	40
17 Aldershot	46	15	10	21	75	84	40
18 Hartlepools	46	16	8	22	63	75	40
19 Port Vale	46	15	9	22	48	59	39
20 Chesterfield	46	13	13	20	62	78	39
21 Rochdale	46	16	5	25	71	87	37
22 Lincoln	46	13	11	22	57	82	37
23 Bradford City	46	12	13	21	63	94	37
24 Wrexham	46	13	9	24	72	104	35

SCOTTISH FIRST DIVISION

	P	W	D	L	F	A	Pts
1 Celtic	34	27	3	4	106	30	57
2 Rangers	34	25	5	4	91	29	55
3 Kilmarnock	34	20	5	9	73	46	45
4 Dunfermline	34	19	6	9	94	55	44
5 Dundee United	34	19	5	10	79	51	43
6 Hibernian	34	16	6	12	81	55	38
7 Hearts	34	13	12	9	56	48	38
8 Aberdeen	34	15	6	13	61	54	36
9 Dundee	34	14	6	14	61	61	34
10 Falkirk	34	15	1	18	48	72	31
11 Clyde	34	13	4	17	62	64	30
12 Partick Thistle	34	10	10	14	55	64	30
13 Motherwell	34	12	4	18	52	69	28
14 St Johnstone	34	9	8	17	58	81	26
15 Stirling Albion	34	9	8	17	40	68	26
16 St Mirren	34	9	4	21	44	82	22
17 Morton	34	8	5	21	42	84	21
18 Hamilton	34	3	2	29	27	117	8

SCOTTISH SECOND DIVISION

	P	W	D	L	F	A	Pts
1 Ayr	36	22	9	5	78	37	53
2 Airdrieonians	36	22	6	8	107	56	50
3 Queen of the S	36	18	11	7	83	53	47
4 East Fife	36	20	4	12	72	55	44
5 Raith	36	16	11	9	71	43	43
6 Arbroath	36	15	13	8	72	52	43
7 Albion	36	18	7	11	58	54	43
8 Alloa	36	14	10	12	65	65	38
9 Montrose	36	15	7	14	67	63	37
10 Cowdenbeath	36	15	7	14	69	68	37
11 Berwick	36	12	11	13	69	58	35
12 Dumbarton	36	14	7	15	63	61	35
13 Queen's Park	36	13	7	16	62	65	33
14 Third Lanark	36	12	8	16	55	65	32
15 Stranraer	36	9	10	17	64	83	28
16 Brechin	36	10	7	19	52	92	27
17 E Stirlingshire	36	9	5	22	59	91	23
18 Stenhousemuir	36	6	7	23	47	93	19
19 Forfar	36	7	3	26	61	120	17

FA CUP 1965-66

FOURTH ROUND

Bedford Town v Everton	0-3
Crewe Alexandra v Coventry City	1-1, 1-4
Manchester City v Grimsby Town	2-0
Birmingham City v Leicester City	1-2
Manchester United v Rotherham United	0-0, 1-0
Wolverhampton Wanderers v Sheffield United	3-0
Bolton Wanderers v Preston North End	1-1, 2-3
Tottenham Hotspur v Burnley	4-3
Chelsea v Leeds United	1-0
Shrewsbury Town v Carlisle United	0-0, 1-1, 4-3
Hull City v Nottingham Forest	2-0
Southport v Cardiff City	2-0
Norwich City v Walsall	3-2
West Ham United v Blackburn Rovers	3-3, 1-4
Plymouth Argyle v Huddersfield Town	0-2
Newcastle United v Sheffield Wednesday	1-2

FIFTH ROUND

Everton v Coventry City	3-0
Manchester City v Leicester City	2-2, 1-0
Wolverhampton Wanderers v Manchester United	2-4
Preston North End v Tottenham Hotspur	2-1
Chelsea v Shrewsbury Town	3-2
Hull City v Southport	2-0
Norwich City v Blackburn Rovers	2-2, 2-3
Huddersfield Town v Sheffield Wednesday	1-2

SIXTH ROUND

Manchester City v Everton	0-0, 0-0, 0-2
Preston North End v Manchester United	1-1, 1-3
Chelsea v Hull City	2-2, 3-1
Blackburn Rovers v Sheffield Wednesday	1-2

SEMI-FINAL

Everton v Manchester United	1-0
Chelsea v Sheffield Wednesday	0-2

FINAL

Everton v Sheffield Wednesday	3-2

SCOTTISH FA CUP 1965-66

FIRST ROUND

Celtic v Stranraer	4-0
Dundee v East Fife	9-1
Heart of Midlothian v Clyde	2-1
Hibernian v Third Lanark	4-3
Stirling Albion v Queen's Park	3-1
Dunfermline Athletic v Partick Thistle	3-1
Morton v Kilmarnock	1-1, 0-3
East Stirlingshire v Motherwell	0-0, 1-4
Dumbarton v Montrose	2-1
Queen of the South v Albion Rovers	3-0
Hamilton Academicals v Aberdeen	1-3
Dundee United v Falkirk	0-0, 2-1
Cowdenbeath v St Mirren	1-0
Ayr United v St Johnstone	1-1, 0-1
Alloa Athletic v Ross County	3-5
Rangers v Airdrieonians	5-1

SECOND ROUND

Dundee v Celtic	0-2
Heart of Midlothian v Hibernian	2-1
Stirling Albion v Dunfermline Athletic	0-0, 1-4
Kilmarnock v Motherwell	5-0
Dumbarton v Queen of the South	1-0
Aberdeen v Dundee United	5-0
Cowdenbeath v St Johnstone	3-3, 0-3
Ross County v Rangers	0-2

THIRD ROUND

Celtic v Heart of Midlothian	3-3, 3-1
Dunfermline Athletic v Kilmarnock	2-1
Dumbarton v Aberdeen	0-3
Rangers v St Johnstone	2-0

SEMI-FINAL

Celtic v Dunfermline Athletic	2-0
Aberdeen v Rangers	0-0, 1-2

FINAL

Celtic v Rangers	0-0, 0-1

On 1 January 1966, while they were beating Aldershot 3-2 in a Division Four game, Chester lost both their full-backs, Ray Jones and Bryn Jones, with broken legs.

The World Cup final receipts—£204,805— were a world record for a football match.

At the start of the season, Manchester United had 15 internationals on their staff. They were: Pat Dunne, Harry Gregg, Shay Brennan, Noel Cantwell, Pat Crerand, Bill Foulkes, Denis Law, Nobby Stiles, Tony Dunne, George Best, David Herd, John Connelly, Bobby Charlton, Graham Moore, and David Sadler, then an amateur cap.

FIRST DIVISION

		P	W	D	L	F	A	Pts
1	Man United	42	24	12	6	84	45	60
2	Nottm Forest	42	23	10	9	64	41	56
3	Tottenham	42	24	8	10	71	48	56
4	Leeds	42	22	11	9	62	42	55
5	Liverpool	42	19	13	10	64	47	51
6	Everton	42	19	10	13	65	46	48
7	Arsenal	42	16	14	12	58	47	46
8	Leicester	42	18	8	16	78	71	44
9	Chelsea	42	15	14	13	67	62	44
10	Sheff United	42	16	10	16	52	59	42
11	Sheff Wed	42	14	13	15	56	47	41
12	Stoke	42	17	7	18	63	58	41
13	WBA	42	16	7	19	77	73	39
14	Burnley	42	15	9	18	66	76	39
15	Man City	42	12	15	15	43	52	39
16	West Ham	42	14	8	20	80	84	36
17	Sunderland	42	14	8	20	58	72	36
18	Fulham	42	11	12	19	71	83	34
19	Southampton	42	14	6	22	74	92	34
20	Newcastle	42	12	9	21	39	81	33
21	Aston Villa	42	11	7	24	54	85	29
22	Blackpool	42	6	9	27	41	76	21

SECOND DIVISION

		P	W	D	L	F	A	Pts
1	Coventry	42	23	13	6	74	43	59
2	Wolves	42	25	8	9	88	48	58
3	Carlisle	42	23	6	13	71	54	52
4	Blackburn	42	19	13	10	56	46	51
5	Ipswich	42	17	16	9	70	54	50
6	Huddersfield	42	20	9	13	58	46	49
7	Crystal Palace	42	19	10	13	61	55	48
8	Millwall	42	18	9	15	49	58	45
9	Bolton	42	14	14	14	64	58	42
10	Birmingham	42	16	8	18	70	66	40
11	Norwich	42	13	14	15	49	55	40
12	Hull	42	16	7	19	77	72	39
13	Preston	42	16	7	19	65	67	39
14	Portsmouth	42	13	13	16	59	70	39
15	Bristol City	42	12	14	16	56	62	38
16	Plymouth	42	14	9	19	59	58	37
17	Derby	42	12	12	18	68	72	36
18	Rotherham	42	13	10	19	61	70	36
19	Charlton	42	13	9	20	49	53	35
20	Cardiff	42	12	9	21	61	87	33
21	Northampton	42	12	6	24	47	84	30
22	Bury	42	11	6	25	49	83	28

THIRD DIVISION

		P	W	D	L	F	A	Pts
1	QPR	46	26	15	5	103	38	67
2	Middlesbrough	46	23	9	14	87	64	55
3	Watford	46	20	14	12	61	46	54
4	Reading	46	22	9	15	76	57	53
5	Bristol Rovers	46	20	13	13	76	67	53
6	Shrewsbury	46	20	12	14	77	62	52
7	Torquay	46	21	9	16	73	54	51
8	Swindon	46	20	10	16	81	59	50
9	Mansfield	46	20	9	17	84	79	49
10	Oldham	46	19	10	17	80	63	48
11	Gillingham	46	15	16	15	58	62	46
12	Walsall	46	18	10	18	65	72	46
13	Colchester	46	17	10	19	76	73	44
14	Leyton Orient	46	13	18	15	58	68	44
15	Peterborough	46	14	15	17	66	71	43
16	Oxford	46	15	13	18	61	66	43
17	Grimsby	46	17	9	20	61	68	43
18	Scunthorpe	46	17	8	21	58	73	42
19	Brighton	46	13	15	18	61	71	41
20	Bournemouth	46	12	17	17	39	57	41
21	Swansea	46	12	15	19	85	89	39
22	Darlington	46	13	11	22	47	81	37
23	Doncaster	46	12	8	26	58	117	32
24	Workington	46	12	7	27	55	89	31

FOURTH DIVISION

		P	W	D	L	F	A	Pts
1	Stockport	46	26	12	8	69	42	64
2	Southport	46	23	13	10	69	42	59
3	Barrow	46	24	11	11	76	54	59
4	Tranmere	46	22	14	10	66	43	58
5	Crewe	46	21	12	13	70	55	54
6	Southend	46	22	9	15	70	49	53
7	Wrexham	46	16	20	10	76	62	52
8	Hartlepools	46	22	7	17	66	64	51
9	Brentford	46	18	13	15	58	56	49
10	Aldershot	46	18	12	16	72	57	48
11	Bradford City	46	19	10	17	74	62	48
12	Halifax	46	15	14	17	59	68	44
13	Port Vale	46	14	15	17	55	58	43
14	Exeter	46	14	15	17	50	60	43
15	Chesterfield	46	17	8	21	60	63	42
16	Barnsley	46	13	15	18	60	64	41
17	Luton	46	16	9	21	59	73	41
18	Newport	46	12	16	18	56	63	40
19	Chester	46	15	10	21	54	78	40
20	Notts County	46	13	11	22	53	72	37
21	Rochdale	46	13	11	22	53	75	37
22	York	46	12	11	23	65	79	35
23	Bradford PA	46	11	13	22	52	79	35
24	Lincoln	46	9	13	24	58	82	31

SCOTTISH FIRST DIVISION

		P	W	D	L	F	A	Pts
1	Celtic	34	26	6	2	111	33	58
2	Rangers	34	24	7	3	92	31	55
3	Clyde	34	20	6	8	64	48	46
4	Aberdeen	34	17	8	9	72	38	42
5	Hibernian	34	19	4	11	72	49	42
6	Dundee	34	16	9	9	74	51	41
7	Kilmarnock	34	16	8	10	59	46	40
8	Dunfermline	34	14	10	10	72	52	38
9	Dundee United	34	14	9	11	68	62	37
10	Motherwell	34	10	11	13	59	60	31
11	Hearts	34	11	8	15	39	48	30
12	Partick Thistle	34	9	12	13	49	68	30
13	Airdrieonians	34	11	6	17	41	53	28
14	Falkirk	34	11	4	19	33	70	26
15	St Johnstone	34	10	5	19	53	73	25
16	Stirling	34	5	9	20	31	85	19
17	St Mirren	34	4	7	23	25	81	15
18	Ayr	34	1	7	26	20	86	9

SCOTTISH SECOND DIVISION

		P	W	D	L	F	A	Pts
1	Morton	38	33	3	2	113	20	69
2	Raith	38	27	4	7	95	44	58
3	Arbroath	38	25	7	6	75	32	57
4	Hamilton	38	18	8	12	74	60	44
5	East Fife	38	19	4	15	70	63	42
6	Cowdenbeath	38	16	8	14	70	55	40
7	Queen's Park	38	15	10	13	78	68	40
8	Albion	38	17	6	15	66	62	40
9	Queen of the S	38	15	9	14	84	76	39
10	Berwick	38	16	6	16	63	55	38
11	Third Lanark	38	13	8	17	67	78	34
12	Montrose	38	13	8	17	63	77	34
13	Alloa	38	15	4	19	55	74	34
14	Dumbarton	38	12	9	17	56	64	33
15	Stranraer	38	13	7	18	57	73	33
16	Forfar	38	12	3	23	74	106	27
17	Stenhousemuir	38	9	9	20	62	104	27
18	Clydebank	38	8	8	22	59	92	24
19	E Stirlingshire	38	7	10	21	44	87	24
20	Brechin	38	8	7	23	58	93	23

FA CUP 1966-67

FOURTH ROUND

Brighton & Hove Albion v Chelsea	1-1, 0-4
Fulham v Sheffield United	1-1, 1-3
Manchester United v Norwich City	1-2
Sheffield Wednesday v Mansfield Town	4-0
Sunderland v Peterborough United	7-1
Leeds United v West Bromwich Albion	5-0
Cardiff City v Manchester City	1-1, 1-3
Ipswich Town v Carlisle United	2-0
Rotherham United v Birmingham City	0-0, 1-2
Bolton Wanderers v Arsenal	0-0, 0-3
Tottenham Hotspur v Portsmouth	3-1
Bristol City v Southampton	1-0
Nottingham Forest v Newcastle United	3-0
Swindon Town v Bury	2-1
Wolverhampton Wanderers v Everton	1-1, 1-3
Liverpool v Aston Villa	1-0

FIFTH ROUND

Chelsea v Sheffield United	2-0
Norwich City v Sheffield Wednesday	1-3
Sunderland v Leeds United	1-1, 1-1, 1-2
Manchester City v Ipswich Town	1-1, 3-0
Birmingham City v Arsenal	1-0
Tottenham Hotspur v Bristol City	2-0
Nottingham Forest v Swindon Town	0-0, 1-1, 3-0
Everton v Liverpool	1-0

SIXTH ROUND

Chelsea v Sheffield Wednesday	1-0
Leeds United v Manchester City	1-0
Birmingham City v Tottenham Hotspur	0-0, 0-6
Nottingham Forest v Everton	3-2

SEMI-FINAL

Chelsea v Leeds United	1-0
Tottenham Hotspur v Nottingham Forest	2-1

FINAL

Chelsea v Tottenham Hotspur	1-2

SCOTTISH FA CUP 1966-67

FIRST ROUND

Celtic v Arbroath	4-0
Elgin City v Ayr United	2-0
Queen's Park v Raith Rovers	3-2
Stirling Albion v Airdrieonians	1-2
Morton v Clyde	0-1
Motherwell v East Fife	0-1
St Mirren v Cowdenbeath	1-1, 2-0
Inverness Caledonian v Hamilton Academicals	1-3
Heart of Midlothian v Dundee United	0-3
Falkirk v Alloa Athletic	3-1
Partick Thistle v Dumbarton	3-0
Kilmarnock v Dunfermline Athletic	2-2, 0-1
Hibernian v Brechin City	2-0
Berwick Rangers v Rangers	1-0
St Johnstone v Queen of the South	4-0
Aberdeen v Dundee	5-0

SECOND ROUND

Celtic v Elgin City	7-0
Queen's Park v Airdrieonians	1-1, 2-1
Clyde v East Fife	4-1
St Mirren v Hamilton Academicals	0-1
Dundee United v Falkirk	1-0
Partick Thistle v Dunfermline Athletic	1-1, 1-5
Hibernian v Berwick Rangers	1-0
St Johnstone v Aberdeen	0-5

THIRD ROUND

Celtic v Queen's Park	5-3
Clyde v Hamilton Academicals	0-0, 5-1
Dundee United v Dunfermline Athletic	1-0
Hibernian v Aberdeen	1-1, 0-3

SEMI-FINAL

Celtic v Clyde	0-0, 2-0
Dundee United v Aberdeen	0-1

FINAL

Celtic v Aberdeen	2-0

A great year for Celtic

Celtic won the Scottish League, Cup and League Cup, the Glasgow Cup, and became the first British club to win the European Cup, thus completing a remarkable grand slam.

More directors than players

When Workington increased their board of directors by the addition of a 13th member in October 1966, they found themselves with more directors than full-time players.

241

FIRST DIVISION

		P	W	D	L	F	A	Pts
1	Man City	42	26	6	10	86	43	58
2	Man United	42	24	8	10	89	55	56
3	Liverpool	42	22	11	9	71	40	55
4	Leeds	42	22	9	11	71	41	53
5	Everton	42	23	6	13	67	40	52
6	Chelsea	42	18	12	12	62	68	48
7	Tottenham	42	19	9	14	70	59	47
8	WBA	42	17	12	13	75	62	46
9	Arsenal	42	17	10	15	60	56	44
10	Newcastle	42	13	15	14	54	67	41
11	Nottm Forest	42	14	11	17	52	64	39
12	West Ham	42	14	10	18	73	69	38
13	Leicester	42	13	12	17	64	69	38
14	Burnley	42	14	10	18	64	71	38
15	Sunderland	42	13	11	18	51	61	37
16	Southampton	42	13	11	18	66	83	37
17	Wolves	42	14	8	20	66	75	36
18	Stoke	42	14	7	21	50	73	35
19	Sheff Wed	42	11	12	19	51	63	34
20	Coventry	42	9	15	18	51	71	33
21	Sheff United	42	11	10	21	49	70	32
22	Fulham	42	10	7	25	56	98	27

SECOND DIVISION

		P	W	D	L	F	A	Pts
1	Ipswich	42	22	15	5	79	44	59
2	QPR	42	25	8	9	67	36	58
3	Blackpool	42	24	10	8	71	43	58
4	Birmingham	42	19	14	9	83	51	52
5	Portsmouth	42	18	13	11	68	55	49
6	Middlesbrough	42	17	12	13	60	54	46
7	Millwall	42	14	17	11	62	50	45
8	Blackburn	42	16	11	15	56	49	43
9	Norwich	42	16	11	15	60	65	43
10	Carlisle	42	14	13	15	58	52	41
11	Crystal Palace	42	14	11	17	56	56	39
12	Bolton	42	13	13	16	60	63	39
13	Cardiff	42	13	12	17	60	66	38
14	Huddersfield	42	13	12	17	46	61	38
15	Charlton	42	12	13	17	63	68	37
16	Aston Villa	42	15	7	20	54	64	37
17	Hull	42	12	13	17	58	73	37
18	Derby	42	13	10	19	71	78	36
19	Bristol City	42	13	10	19	48	62	36
20	Preston	42	12	11	19	43	65	35
21	Rotherham	42	10	11	21	42	76	31
22	Plymouth	42	9	9	24	38	72	27

THIRD DIVISION

		P	W	D	L	F	A	Pts
1	Oxford	46	22	13	11	69	47	57
2	Bury	46	24	8	14	91	66	56
3	Shrewsbury	46	20	15	11	61	49	55
4	Torquay	46	21	11	14	60	56	53
5	Reading	46	21	9	16	70	60	51
6	Watford	46	21	8	17	74	50	50
7	Walsall	46	19	12	15	74	61	50
8	Barrow	46	21	8	17	65	54	50
9	Swindon	46	16	17	13	74	51	49
10	Brighton	46	16	16	14	57	55	48
11	Gillingham	46	18	12	16	59	63	48
12	Bournemouth	46	16	15	15	56	51	47
13	Stockport	46	19	9	18	70	75	47
14	Southport	46	17	12	17	65	65	46
15	Bristol Rovers	46	17	9	20	72	78	43
16	Oldham	46	18	7	21	60	65	43
17	Northampton	46	14	13	19	58	72	41
18	Leyton Orient	46	12	17	17	46	62	41
19	Tranmere	46	14	12	20	62	74	40
20	Mansfield	46	12	13	21	51	67	37
21	Grimsby	46	14	9	23	52	69	37
22	Colchester	46	9	15	22	50	87	33
23	Scunthorpe	46	10	12	24	56	87	32
24	Peterborough	46	20	10	16	79	67	31†

†Peterborough had 19 points deducted for offering irregular bonuses to their players. They were automatically demoted to the Fourth Division.

FOURTH DIVISION

		P	W	D	L	F	A	Pts
1	Luton	46	27	12	7	87	44	66
2	Barnsley	46	24	13	9	68	46	61
3	Hartlepools	46	25	10	11	60	46	60
4	Crewe	46	20	18	8	74	49	58
5	Bradford City	46	23	11	12	72	51	57
6	Southend	46	20	14	12	77	58	54
7	Chesterfield	46	21	11	14	71	50	53
8	Wrexham	46	20	13	13	72	53	53
9	Aldershot	46	18	17	11	70	55	53
10	Doncaster	46	18	15	13	66	56	51
11	Halifax	46	15	16	15	52	49	46
12	Newport	46	16	13	17	58	63	45
13	Lincoln	46	17	9	20	71	68	43
14	Brentford	46	18	7	21	61	64	43
15	Swansea	46	16	10	20	63	77	42
16	Darlington	46	12	17	17	47	53	41
17	Notts County	46	15	11	20	53	79	41
18	Port Vale	46	12	15	19	61	72	39†
19	Rochdale	46	12	14	20	51	72	38
20	Exeter	46	11	16	19	45	65	38
21	York	46	11	14	21	65	68	36
22	Chester	46	9	14	23	57	78	32
23	Workington	46	10	11	25	54	87	31
24	Bradford PA	46	4	15	27	30	82	23

†Port Vale were expelled from the League at the end of the season for making unauthorised payments. They were re-elected immediately.

SCOTTISH FIRST DIVISION

		P	W	D	L	F	A	Pts
1	Celtic	34	30	3	1	106	24	63
2	Rangers	34	28	5	1	93	34	61
3	Hibernian	34	20	5	9	67	49	45
4	Dunfermline	34	17	5	12	64	41	39
5	Aberdeen	34	16	5	13	63	48	37
6	Morton	34	15	6	13	57	53	36
7	Kilmarnock	34	13	8	13	59	57	34
8	Clyde	34	15	4	15	55	55	34
9	Dundee	34	13	7	14	62	59	33
10	Partick Thistle	34	12	7	15	51	67	31
11	Dundee United	34	10	11	13	53	72	31
12	Hearts	34	13	4	17	56	61	30
13	Airdrieonians	34	10	9	15	45	58	29
14	St Johnstone	34	10	7	17	43	52	27
15	Falkirk	34	7	12	15	36	50	26
16	Raith Rovers	34	9	7	18	58	86	25
17	Motherwell	34	6	7	21	40	66	19
18	Stirling Albion	34	4	4	26	29	105	12

SCOTTISH SECOND DIVISION

		P	W	D	L	F	A	Pts
1	St Mirren	36	27	8	1	100	23	62
2	Arbroath	36	24	5	7	87	34	53
3	East Fife	36	21	7	8	71	47	49
4	Queen's Park	36	20	8	8	76	47	48
5	Ayr	36	18	6	12	69	48	42
6	Queen of the S	36	16	6	14	73	57	38
7	Forfar	36	14	10	12	57	63	38
8	Albion	36	14	9	13	62	55	37
9	Clydebank	36	13	8	15	62	73	34
10	Dumbarton	36	11	11	14	63	74	33
11	Hamilton	36	13	7	16	49	58	33
12	Cowdenbeath	36	12	8	16	57	62	32
13	Montrose	36	10	11	15	54	64	31
14	Berwick	36	13	4	19	34	54	30
15	E Stirlingshire	36	9	10	17	61	74	28
16	Brechin	36	8	12	16	45	62	28
17	Alloa	36	11	6	19	42	69	28
18	Stenhousemuir	36	7	6	23	34	93	20
19	Stranraer	36	8	4	24	41	80	20

FA CUP 1967–68

FOURTH ROUND

Carlisle United v Everton	0-2
Coventry City v Tranmere Rovers	1-1, 0-2
Aston Villa v Rotherham United	0-1
Manchester City v Leicester City	0-0, 3-4
Leeds United v Nottingham Forest	2-1
Middlesbrough v Bristol City	1-1, 1-2
Stoke City v West Ham United	0-3
Sheffield United v Blackpool	2-1
Swansea Town v Arsenal	0-1
Birmingham City v Leyton Orient	3-0
Sheffield Wednesday v Swindon Town	2-1
Chelsea v Norwich City	1-0
Fulham v Portsmouth	0-0, 0-1
West Bromwich Albion v Southampton	1-1, 3-2
Tottenham Hotspur v Preston North End	3-1
Walsall v Liverpool	0-0, 2-5

FIFTH ROUND

Everton v Tranmere Rovers	2-0
Rotherham United v Leicester City	1-1, 0-2
Leeds United v Bristol City	2-0
West Ham United v Sheffield United	1-2
Arsenal v Birmingham City	1-1, 1-2
Sheffield Wednesday v Chelsea	2-2, 0-2
Portsmouth v West Bromwich Albion	1-2
Tottenham Hotspur v Liverpool	1-1, 1-2

SIXTH ROUND

Everton v Leicester City	3-1
Leeds United v Sheffield United	1-0
Birmingham City v Chelsea	1-0
West Bromwich Albion v Liverpool	0-0, 1-1, 2-1

SEMI-FINAL

Everton v Leeds United	1-0
West Bromwich Albion v Birmingham City	2-0

FINAL

Everton v West Bromwich Albion	0-1

SCOTTISH FA CUP 1967–68

FIRST ROUND

Rangers v Hamilton Academicals	3-1
Cowdenbeath v Dundee	0-1
Dundee United v St. Mirren	3-1
Heart of Midlothian v Brechin City	4-1
East Fife v Alloa Athletic	3-0
Morton v Falkirk	4-0
Elgin City v Forfar Athletic	3-1
Ayr United v Arbroath	0-2
Celtic v Dunfermline Athletic	0-2
Aberdeen v Raith Rovers	1-1, 1-0
Partick Thistle v Kilmarnock	0-0, 2-1
Clyde v Berwick Rangers	2-0
Motherwell v Airdrieonians	1-1, 0-1
East Stirlingshire v Hibernian	3-5
St Johnstone v Hawick Royal Albert	3-0
Queen of the South v Stirling Albion	1-1, 3-1

SECOND ROUND

Dundee v Rangers	1-1, 1-4
Dundee United v Heart of Midlothian	5-6
East Fife v Morton	0-0, 2-5
Elgin City v Arbroath	2-0
Dunfermline Athletic v Aberdeen	2-1
Partick Thistle v Clyde	3-2
Airdrieonians v Hibernian	1-0
St Johnstone v Queen of the South	5-2

THIRD ROUND

Rangers v Heart of Midlothian	1-1, 0-1
Morton v Elgin City	2-1
Dunfermline Athletic v Partick Thistle	1-0
St Johnstone v Airdrieonians	2-1

SEMI-FINAL

Heart of Midlothian v Morton	1-1, 2-1
Dunfermline Athletic v St Johnstone	1-1, 2-1

FINAL

Dunfermline Athletic v Heart of Midlothian	3-1

FIRST DIVISION

		P	W	D	L	F	A	Pts
1	Leeds	42	27	13	2	66	26	67
2	Liverpool	42	25	11	6	63	24	61
3	Everton	42	21	15	6	77	36	57
4	Arsenal	42	22	12	8	56	27	56
5	Chelsea	42	20	10	12	73	53	50
6	Tottenham	42	14	17	11	61	51	45
7	Southampton	42	16	13	13	57	48	45
8	West Ham	42	13	18	11	66	50	44
9	Newcastle	42	15	14	13	61	55	44
10	WBA	42	16	11	15	64	67	43
11	Man United	42	15	12	15	57	53	42
12	Ipswich	42	15	11	16	59	60	41
13	Man City	42	15	10	17	64	55	40
14	Burnley	42	15	9	18	55	82	39
15	Sheff Wed	42	10	16	16	41	54	36
16	Wolves	42	10	15	17	41	58	35
17	Sunderland	42	11	12	19	43	67	34
18	Nottm Forest	42	10	13	19	45	57	33
19	Stoke	42	9	15	18	40	63	33
20	Coventry	42	10	11	21	46	64	31
21	Leicester	42	9	12	21	39	68	30
22	QPR	42	4	10	28	39	95	18

SECOND DIVISION

		P	W	D	L	F	A	Pts
1	Derby	42	26	11	5	65	32	63
2	Crystal Palace	42	22	12	8	70	47	56
3	Charlton	42	18	14	10	61	52	50
4	Middlesbrough	42	19	11	12	58	49	49
5	Cardiff	42	20	7	15	67	54	47
6	Huddersfield	42	17	12	13	53	46	46
7	Birmingham	42	18	8	16	73	59	44
8	Blackpool	42	14	15	13	51	41	43
9	Sheff United	42	16	11	15	61	50	43
10	Millwall	42	17	9	16	57	49	43
11	Hull	42	13	16	13	59	52	42
12	Carlisle	42	16	10	16	46	49	42
13	Norwich	42	15	10	17	53	56	40
14	Preston	42	12	15	15	38	44	39
15	Portsmouth	42	12	14	16	58	58	38
16	Bristol City	42	11	16	15	46	53	38
17	Bolton	42	12	14	16	55	67	38
18	Aston Villa	42	12	14	16	37	48	38
19	Blackburn	42	13	11	18	52	63	37
20	Oxford	42	12	9	21	34	55	33
21	Bury	42	11	8	23	51	80	30
22	Fulham	42	7	11	24	40	81	25

THIRD DIVISION

		P	W	D	L	F	A	Pts
1	Watford	46	27	10	9	74	34	64
2	Swindon	46	27	10	9	71	35	64
3	Luton	46	25	11	10	74	38	61
4	Bournemouth	46	21	9	16	60	45	51
5	Plymouth	46	17	15	14	53	49	49
6	Torquay	46	18	12	16	54	46	48
7	Tranmere	46	19	10	17	70	68	48
8	Southport	46	17	13	16	71	64	47
9	Stockport	46	16	14	16	67	68	46
10	Barnsley	46	16	14	16	58	63	46
11	Rotherham	46	16	13	17	56	50	45
12	Brighton	46	16	13	17	72	65	45
13	Walsall	46	14	16	16	50	49	44
14	Reading	46	15	13	18	67	66	43
15	Mansfield	46	16	11	19	58	62	43
16	Bristol Rovers	46	16	11	19	63	71	43
17	Shrewsbury	46	16	11	19	51	67	43
18	Orient	46	14	14	18	51	58	42
19	Barrow	46	17	8	21	56	75	42
20	Gillingham	46	13	15	18	54	63	41
21	Northampton	46	14	12	20	54	61	40
22	Hartlepool	46	10	19	17	40	70	39
23	Crewe	46	13	9	24	52	76	35
24	Oldham	46	13	9	24	50	83	35

FOURTH DIVISION

		P	W	D	L	F	A	Pts
1	Doncaster	46	21	17	8	65	38	59
2	Halifax	46	20	17	9	53	37	57
3	Rochdale	46	18	20	8	68	35	56
4	Bradford City	46	18	20	8	65	46	56
5	Darlington	46	17	18	11	62	45	52
6	Colchester	46	20	12	14	57	53	52
7	Southend	46	19	13	14	78	61	51
8	Lincoln	46	17	17	12	54	52	51
9	Wrexham	46	18	14	14	61	52	50
10	Swansea	46	19	11	16	58	54	49
11	Brentford	46	18	12	16	64	65	48
12	Workington	46	15	17	14	40	43	47
13	Port Vale	46	16	14	16	46	46	46
14	Chester	46	16	13	17	76	66	45
15	Aldershot	46	19	7	20	66	66	45
16	Scunthorpe	46	18	8	20	61	60	44
17	Exeter	46	16	11	19	66	65	43
18	Peterborough	46	13	16	17	60	57	42
19	Notts County	46	12	18	16	48	57	42
20	Chesterfield	46	13	15	18	43	50	41
21	York	46	14	11	21	53	75	39
22	Newport	46	11	14	21	49	74	36
23	Grimsby	46	9	15	22	47	69	33
24	Bradford PA	46	5	10	31	32	106	20

SCOTTISH FIRST DIVISION

		P	W	D	L	F	A	Pts
1	Celtic	34	23	8	3	89	32	54
2	Rangers	34	21	7	6	81	32	49
3	Dunfermline	34	19	7	8	63	45	45
4	Kilmarnock	34	15	14	5	50	32	44
5	Dundee United	34	17	9	8	61	49	43
6	St Johnstone	34	16	5	13	66	59	37
7	Airdrieonians	34	13	11	10	46	44	37
8	Hearts	34	14	8	12	52	54	36
9	Dundee	34	10	12	12	47	48	32
10	Morton	34	12	8	14	58	68	32
11	St Mirren	34	11	10	13	40	54	32
12	Hibernian	34	12	7	15	60	59	31
13	Clyde	34	9	13	12	35	50	31
14	Partick Thistle	34	9	10	15	39	53	28
15	Aberdeen	34	9	8	17	50	59	26
16	Raith	34	8	5	21	45	67	21
17	Falkirk	34	5	8	21	33	69	18
18	Arbroath	34	5	6	23	41	82	16

SCOTTISH SECOND DIVISION

		P	W	D	L	F	A	Pts
1	Motherwell	36	30	4	2	112	23	64
2	Ayr	36	23	7	6	82	31	53
3	East Fife	36	21	6	9	82	45	48
4	Stirling	36	21	6	9	67	40	48
5	Queen of the S	36	20	7	9	75	41	47
6	Forfar	36	18	7	11	71	56	47
7	Albion	36	19	5	12	60	56	43
8	Stranraer	36	17	7	12	57	45	41
9	E Stirlingshire	36	17	5	14	70	62	39
10	Montrose	36	15	4	17	59	71	34
11	Queen's Park	36	13	7	16	50	59	33
12	Cowdenbeath	36	12	5	19	54	67	29
13	Clydebank	36	6	15	15	52	67	27
14	Dumbarton	36	11	5	20	46	69	27
15	Hamilton	36	8	8	20	37	72	24
16	Berwick	36	7	9	20	42	70	23
17	Brechin	36	8	6	22	40	78	22
18	Alloa	36	7	7	22	45	79	21
19	Stenhousemuir	36	6	6	24	55	125	18

On 6 May 1969 only 7,843 people were at Hampden Park to see Northern Ireland play Scotland, then the smallest ever crowd at a full home international. There were on average more people at each of Fourth Division Lincoln City's games during the same season.

On 24 August 1968 the main stand at Nottingham Forest's ground caught fire during the game with Leeds and was completely destroyed. Police evacuated the 34,000 crowd and Forest played out the year on neighbouring Notts County's pitch, three hundred yards away.

FA CUP 1968-69

FOURTH ROUND
Newcastle United v Manchester City	0-0, 0-2
Blackburn Rovers v Portsmouth	4-0
Tottenham Hotspur v Wolverhampton Wanderers	2-1
Southampton v Aston Villa	2-2, 1-2
Sheffield Wednesday v Birmingham City	2-2, 1-2
Manchester United v Watford	1-1, 2-0
Bolton Wanderers v Bristol Rovers	1-2
Coventry City v Everton	0-2
West Bromwich Albion v Fulham	2-1
Arsenal v Charlton Athletic	2-0
Preston North End v Chelsea	0-0, 1-2
Stoke City v Halifax Town	1-1, 3-0
Mansfield Town v Southend United	2-1
Huddersfield v West Ham United	0-2
Liverpool v Burnley	2-1
Millwall v Leicester City	0-1

FIFTH ROUND
Manchester City v Blackburn Rovers	4-1
Tottenham Hotspur v Aston Villa	3-2
Birmingham City v Manchester United	2-2, 2-6
Bristol Rovers v Everton	0-1
West Bromwich Albion v Arsenal	1-0
Chelsea v Stoke City	3-2
Mansfield Town v West Ham United	3-0
Liverpool v Leicester City	0-0, 0-1

SIXTH ROUND
Manchester City v Tottenham Hotspur	1-0
Manchester United v Everton	0-1
Chelsea v West Bromwich Albion	1-2
Mansfield Town v Leicester City	0-1

SEMI-FINAL
Manchester City v Everton	1-0
West Bromwich Albion v Leicester City	0-1

FINAL
Leicester City v Manchester City	0-1

SCOTTISH FA CUP 1968-69

FIRST ROUND
Rangers v Hibernian	1-0
Dundee v Hearts	1-2
Dumbarton v St Mirren	0-1
Stenhousemuir v Airdrieonians	0-3
Aberdeen v Berwick Rangers	3-0
Raith Rovers v Dunfermline Athletic	0-2
Montrose v Cowdenbeath	1-0
Kilmarnock v Glasgow University	6-0
Dundee United v Queen's Park	2-1
Ayr United v Queen of the South	1-0
Stranraer v East Fife	3-1
Falkirk v Morton	1-2
East Stirlingshire v Stirling Albion	2-0
St Johnstone v Arbroath	3-2
Motherwell v Clyde	1-1, 1-2
Partick Thistle v Celtic	3-3, 1-8

SECOND ROUND
Rangers v Hearts	2-0
St Mirren v Airdrieonians	1-1, 1-3
Aberdeen v Dunfermline Athletic	2-2, 2-0
Montrose v Kilmarnock	1-1, 1-4
Dundee United v Ayr United	6-2
Stranraer v Morton	1-3
East Stirlingshire v St Johnstone	1-1, 0-3
Clyde v Celtic	0-0, 0-3

THIRD ROUND
Rangers v Airdrieonians	1-0
Aberdeen v Kilmarnock	0-0, 3-0
Dundee United v Morton	2-3
Celtic v St Johnstone	3-2

SEMI-FINAL
Rangers v Aberdeen	6-1
Morton v Celtic	1-4

FINAL
Celtic v Rangers	4-0

243

FIRST DIVISION

		P	W	D	L	F	A	Pts
1	Everton	42	29	8	5	72	34	66
2	Leeds	42	21	15	6	84	49	57
3	Chelsea	42	21	13	8	70	50	55
4	Derby	42	22	9	11	64	37	53
5	Liverpool	42	20	11	11	65	42	51
6	Coventry	42	19	11	12	58	48	49
7	Newcastle	42	17	13	12	57	35	47
8	Man United	42	14	17	11	66	61	45
9	Stoke	42	15	15	12	56	52	45
10	Man City	42	16	11	15	55	48	43
11	Tottenham	42	17	9	16	54	55	43
12	Arsenal	42	12	18	12	51	49	42
13	Wolves	42	12	16	14	55	57	40
14	Burnley	42	12	15	15	56	61	39
15	Nottm Forest	42	10	18	14	50	71	38
16	WBA	42	14	9	19	58	66	37
17	West Ham	42	12	12	18	51	60	36
18	Ipswich	42	10	11	21	40	63	31
19	Southampton	42	6	17	19	46	67	29
20	Crystal Palace	42	6	15	21	34	68	27
21	Sunderland	42	6	14	22	30	68	26
22	Sheff Wed	42	8	9	25	40	71	25

SECOND DIVISION

		P	W	D	L	F	A	Pts
1	Huddersfield	42	24	12	6	68	37	60
2	Blackpool	42	20	13	9	56	45	53
3	Leicester	42	19	13	10	64	50	51
4	Middlesbrough	42	20	10	12	55	45	50
5	Swindon	42	17	16	9	57	47	50
6	Sheff United	42	22	5	15	73	38	49
7	Cardiff	42	18	13	11	61	41	49
8	Blackburn	42	20	7	15	54	50	47
9	QPR	42	17	11	14	66	57	45
10	Millwall	42	15	14	13	56	56	44
11	Norwich	42	16	11	15	49	46	43
12	Carlisle	42	14	13	15	58	56	41
13	Hull	42	15	11	16	72	70	41
14	Bristol City	42	13	13	16	54	50	39
15	Oxford	42	12	15	15	35	42	39
16	Bolton	42	12	12	18	54	61	36
17	Portsmouth	42	13	9	20	66	80	35
18	Birmingham	42	11	11	20	51	78	33
19	Watford	42	9	13	20	44	57	31
20	Charlton	42	7	17	18	35	76	31
21	Aston Villa	42	8	13	21	36	62	29
22	Preston	42	8	12	22	43	63	28

FA CUP 1969-70

FOURTH ROUND

Chelsea v Burnley	2-2, 3-1
Tottenham Hotspur v Crystal Palace	0-0, 0-1
Charlton Athletic v Queen's Park Rangers	2-3
Derby County v Sheffield United	3-0
Watford v Stoke City	1-0
Gillingham v Peterborough United	5-1
Liverpool v Wrexham	3-1
Southampton v Leicester City	1-1, 2-4
Tranmere Rovers v Northampton Town	0-0, 1-2
Manchester United v Manchester City	3-0
Carlisle United v Aldershot	2-2, 4-1
Middlesbrough v York City	4-1
Swindon Town v Chester	4-2
Sheffield Wednesday v Scunthorpe United	1-2
Blackpool v Mansfield Town	0-2
Sutton United v Leeds United	0-6

FIFTH ROUND

Chelsea v Crystal Palace	4-1
Queen's Park Rangers v Derby County	1-0
Watford v Gillingham	2-1
Liverpool v Leicester City	0-0, 2-0
Northampton Town v Manchester United	2-8
Carlisle United v Middlesbrough	1-2
Swindon Town v Scunthorpe United	3-1
Mansfield Town v Leeds United	0-2

SIXTH ROUND

Queen's Park Rangers v Chelsea	2-4
Watford v Liverpool	1-0
Manchester United v Middlesbrough	1-1, 2-1
Swindon Town v Leeds United	0-2

SEMI-FINAL

Chelsea v Watford	5-1
Manchester United v Leeds United	0-0, 0-0, 0-1

THIRD PLACE PLAY-OFF

Manchester United v Watford	2-0

FINAL

Chelsea v Leeds United	2-2, 2-1

THIRD DIVISION

		P	W	D	L	F	A	Pts
1	Orient	46	25	12	9	67	36	62
2	Luton	46	23	14	9	77	43	60
3	Bristol Rovers	46	20	16	10	80	59	56
4	Fulham	46	20	15	11	81	55	55
5	Brighton	46	23	9	14	57	43	55
6	Mansfield	46	21	11	14	70	49	53
7	Barnsley	46	19	15	12	68	59	53
8	Reading	46	21	11	14	87	77	53
9	Rochdale	46	18	10	18	69	60	46
10	Bradford City	46	17	12	17	57	50	46
11	Doncaster	46	17	12	17	52	54	46
12	Walsall	46	17	12	17	54	67	46
13	Torquay	46	14	17	15	62	59	45
14	Rotherham	46	15	14	17	62	54	44
15	Shrewsbury	46	13	18	15	62	63	44
16	Tranmere	46	14	16	16	56	72	44
17	Plymouth	46	16	11	19	56	64	43
18	Halifax	46	14	15	17	47	63	43
19	Bury	46	15	11	20	75	80	41
20	Gillingham	46	13	13	20	52	64	39
21	Bournemouth	46	12	15	19	48	71	39
22	Southport	46	14	10	22	48	66	38
23	Barrow	46	8	14	24	46	81	30
24	Stockport	46	6	11	29	27	71	23

FOURTH DIVISION

		P	W	D	L	F	A	Pts
1	Chesterfield	46	27	10	9	77	32	64
2	Wrexham	46	26	9	11	84	49	61
3	Swansea	46	21	18	7	66	45	60
4	Port Vale	46	20	19	7	61	33	59
5	Brentford	46	20	16	10	58	39	56
6	Aldershot	46	20	13	13	78	65	53
7	Notts County	46	22	8	16	73	62	52
8	Lincoln	46	17	16	13	66	52	50
9	Peterborough	46	17	14	15	77	69	48
10	Colchester	46	17	14	15	64	63	48
11	Chester	46	21	6	19	58	66	48
12	Scunthorpe	46	18	10	18	67	65	46
13	York	46	16	14	16	55	62	46
14	Northampton	46	16	12	18	64	55	44
15	Crewe	46	16	12	18	51	51	44
16	Grimsby	46	14	15	17	54	58	43
17	Southend	46	15	10	21	59	85	40
18	Exeter	46	14	11	21	57	59	39
19	Oldham	46	13	13	20	60	65	39
20	Workington	46	12	14	20	46	64	38
21	Newport	46	13	11	22	53	74	37
22	Darlington	46	13	10	23	53	73	36
23	Hartlepool	46	10	10	26	42	82	30
24	Bradford P A	46	6	11	29	41	96	23

SCOTTISH FA CUP 1969-70

FIRST ROUND

Celtic v Dunfermline Athletic	2-1
Dundee United v Ayr United	1-0
Dumbarton v Forfar Athletic	1-2
Rangers v Hibernian	3-1
East Fife v Raith Rovers	3-0
Morton v Queen of the South	2-0
Albion Rovers v Dundee	1-2
Airdrieonians v Hamilton Academicals	5-0
Motherwell v St Johnstone	2-1
Stranraer v Inverness Caledonian	2-5
Kilmarnock v Partick Thistle	3-0
Montrose v Heart of Midlothian	1-1, 0-1
Falkirk v Tarff Rovers	3-0
St Mirren v Stirling Albion	2-0
Arbroath v Clydebank	1-2
Clyde v Aberdeen	0-4

SECOND ROUND

Celtic v Dundee United	4-0
Forfar Athletic v Rangers	0-7
East Fife v Morton	1-0
Dundee v Airdrieonians	3-0
Motherwell v Inverness Caledonian	3-1
Kilmarnock v Heart of Midlothian	2-0
Falkirk v St Mirren	2-1
Aberdeen v Clydebank	2-1

THIRD ROUND

Celtic v Rangers	3-1
East Fife v Dundee	0-1
Motherwell v Kilmarnock	0-1
Falkirk v Aberdeen	0-1

SEMI-FINAL

Celtic v Dundee	2-1
Kilmarnock v Aberdeen	0-1

FINAL

Celtic v Aberdeen	1-3

SCOTTISH FIRST DIVISION

		P	W	D	L	F	A	Pts
1	Celtic	34	27	3	4	96	33	57
2	Rangers	34	19	7	8	67	40	45
3	Hibernian	34	19	6	9	65	40	44
4	Hearts	34	13	12	9	50	36	38
5	Dundee United	34	16	6	12	62	64	38
6	Dundee	34	15	6	13	49	44	36
7	Kilmarnock	34	13	10	11	62	57	36
8	Aberdeen	34	14	7	13	55	45	35
9	Dunfermline	34	15	5	14	45	45	35
10	Morton	34	13	9	12	52	52	35
11	Motherwell	34	11	10	13	49	51	32
12	Airdrieonians	34	12	8	14	59	64	32
13	St Johnstone	34	11	9	14	50	62	31
14	Ayr	34	12	6	16	37	52	30
15	St Mirren	34	8	9	17	39	54	25
16	Clyde	34	9	7	18	34	56	25
17	Raith	34	5	11	18	32	67	21
18	Partick Thistle	34	5	7	22	41	82	17

SCOTTISH SECOND DIVISION

		P	W	D	L	F	A	Pts
1	Falkirk	36	25	6	5	94	34	56
2	Cowdenbeath	36	24	7	5	81	35	55
3	Queen of the S	36	22	6	8	72	49	50
4	Stirling	36	18	10	8	70	40	46
5	Arbroath	36	20	4	12	76	39	44
6	Alloa	36	19	5	12	62	41	43
7	Dumbarton	36	17	6	13	55	46	40
8	Montrose	36	15	7	14	57	55	37
9	Berwick	36	15	5	16	67	55	35
10	East Fife	36	15	4	17	59	63	34
11	Albion	36	14	5	17	53	64	33
12	E Stirlingshire	36	14	5	17	58	75	33
13	Clydebank	36	10	10	16	47	65	30
14	Brechin	36	11	6	19	47	74	28
15	Queen's Park	36	10	6	20	38	62	26
16	Stenhousemuir	36	10	6	20	47	89	26
17	Stranraer	36	9	7	20	56	75	25
18	Forfar	36	11	1	24	55	83	23
19	Hamilton	36	8	4	24	42	92	20

Leeds go marching on

Leeds United established a new First Division record for the number of consecutive League games played without a defeat. They completed a run of 34 home and away matches without losing a single game. Their unbeaten run finally ended on 30 August 1969 when they lost 3-2 to Everton, the club that was to take the League title from them.

Six of the Best

George Best scored a record number of goals in a Cup tie, notching six for Manchester United in their 8-2 win over Fourth Division Northampton Town in the fifth round of the FA Cup. Best's team-mate Denis Law, when with Manchester City, once scored six goals in a fourth round tie at Luton, but the match was abandoned and Luton won the replay.

FIRST DIVISION

		P	W	D	L	F	A	Pts
1	Arsenal	42	29	7	6	71	29	65
2	Leeds	42	27	10	5	72	30	64
3	Tottenham	42	19	14	9	54	33	52
4	Wolves	42	22	8	12	64	54	52
5	Liverpool	42	17	17	8	42	24	51
6	Chelsea	42	18	15	9	52	42	51
7	Southampton	42	17	12	13	56	44	46
8	Man United	42	16	11	15	65	66	43
9	Derby	42	16	10	16	56	54	42
10	Coventry	42	16	10	16	37	38	42
11	Man City	42	12	17	13	47	42	41
12	Newcastle	42	14	13	15	44	46	41
13	Stoke	42	12	13	17	44	48	37
14	Everton	42	12	13	17	54	60	37
15	Huddersfield	42	11	14	17	40	49	36
16	Nottm Forest	42	14	8	20	42	61	36
17	WBA	42	10	15	17	58	75	35
18	Crystal Palace	42	12	11	19	39	57	35
19	Ipswich	42	12	10	20	42	48	34
20	West Ham	42	10	14	18	47	60	34
21	Burnley	42	7	13	22	29	63	27
22	Blackpool	42	4	15	23	34	66	23

SECOND DIVISION

		P	W	D	L	F	A	Pts
1	Leicester	42	23	13	6	57	30	59
2	Sheff United	42	21	14	7	73	39	56
3	Cardiff	42	20	13	9	64	41	53
4	Carlisle	42	20	13	9	65	43	53
5	Hull	42	19	13	10	54	41	51
6	Luton	42	18	13	11	62	43	49
7	Middlesbrough	42	17	14	11	60	43	48
8	Millwall	42	19	9	14	59	42	47
9	Birmingham	42	17	12	13	58	48	46
10	Norwich	42	15	14	13	54	52	44
11	QPR	42	16	11	15	58	53	43
12	Swindon	42	15	12	15	61	51	42
13	Sunderland	42	15	12	15	52	54	42
14	Oxford	42	14	14	14	41	48	42
15	Sheff Wed	42	12	12	18	51	69	36
16	Portsmouth	42	10	14	18	46	61	34
17	Orient	42	9	16	17	29	51	34
18	Watford	42	10	13	19	38	60	33
19	Bristol City	42	10	11	21	46	64	31
20	Charlton	42	8	14	20	41	65	30
21	Blackburn	42	6	15	21	37	69	27
22	Bolton	42	7	10	25	35	74	24

FA CUP 1970–71

FOURTH ROUND

Liverpool v Swansea City	3-0
York City v Southampton	3-3, 2-3
Carlisle United v Tottenham Hotspur	2-3
Nottingham Forest v Orient	1-1, 1-0
Everton v Middlesbrough	3-0
Derby County v Wolverhampton Wanderers	2-1
Rochdale v Colchester United	3-3, 0-5
Leeds United v Swindon Town	4-0
Hull City v Blackpool	2-0
Cardiff City v Brentford	0-2
Stoke City v Huddersfield Town	3-3, 0-0, 1-0
West Bromwich Albion v Ipswich Town	1-1, 0-3
Leicester City v Torquay United	3-0
Oxford United v Watford	1-1, 2-1
Chelsea v Manchester City	0-3
Portsmouth v Arsenal	1-1, 2-3

FIFTH ROUND

Liverpool v Southampton	1-0
Tottenham Hotspur v Nottingham Forest	2-1
Everton v Derby County	1-0
Colchester United v Leeds United	3-2
Hull City v Brentford	2-1
Stoke City v Ipswich Town	0-0, 1-0
Leicester City v Oxford United	1-1, 3-1
Manchester City v Arsenal	1-2

SIXTH ROUND

Liverpool v Tottenham Hotspur	0-0, 1-0
Everton v Colchester United	5-0
Hull City v Stoke City	2-3
Leicester City v Arsenal	0-0, 0-1

SEMI-FINAL

Liverpool v Everton	2-1
Stoke City v Arsenal	2-2, 0-2

THIRD PLACE PLAY-OFF

Stoke City v Everton	3-2

FINAL

Liverpool v Arsenal	1-2

THIRD DIVISION

		P	W	D	L	F	A	Pts
1	Preston	46	22	17	7	63	39	61
2	Fulham	46	24	12	10	68	41	60
3	Halifax	46	22	12	12	74	55	56
4	Aston Villa	46	19	15	12	54	46	53
5	Chesterfield	46	17	17	12	66	38	51
6	Bristol Rovers	46	19	13	14	69	50	51
7	Mansfield	46	18	15	13	64	62	51
8	Rotherham	46	17	16	13	64	60	50
9	Wrexham	46	18	13	15	72	65	49
10	Torquay	46	19	11	16	54	57	49
11	Swansea	46	15	16	15	59	56	46
12	Barnsley	46	17	11	18	49	52	45
13	Shrewsbury	46	16	13	17	58	62	45
14	Brighton	46	14	16	16	50	47	44
15	Plymouth	46	12	19	15	63	63	43
16	Rochdale	46	14	15	17	61	68	43
17	Port Vale	46	15	12	19	52	59	42
18	Tranmere	46	10	22	14	45	55	42
19	Bradford City	46	13	14	19	49	62	40
20	Walsall	46	14	11	21	51	57	39
21	Reading	46	14	11	21	48	85	39
22	Bury	46	12	13	21	52	60	37
23	Doncaster	46	13	9	24	45	66	35
24	Gillingham	46	10	13	23	42	67	33

FOURTH DIVISION

		P	W	D	L	F	A	Pts
1	Notts County	46	30	9	7	89	36	69
2	Bournemouth	46	24	12	10	81	46	60
3	Oldham	46	24	11	11	88	63	59
4	York	46	23	10	13	78	54	56
5	Chester	46	24	7	15	69	55	55
6	Colchester	46	21	12	13	70	54	54
7	Northampton	46	19	13	14	63	59	51
8	Southport	46	21	6	19	63	57	48
9	Exeter	46	17	14	15	67	68	48
10	Workington	46	18	12	16	48	49	48
11	Stockport	46	16	14	16	49	65	46
12	Darlington	46	17	11	18	58	57	45
13	Aldershot	46	14	17	15	66	71	45
14	Brentford	46	18	8	20	66	62	44
15	Crewe	46	18	8	20	75	76	44
16	Peterborough	46	18	7	21	70	71	43
17	Scunthorpe	46	15	13	18	56	61	43
18	Southend	46	14	15	17	53	66	43
19	Grimsby	46	18	7	21	57	71	43
20	Cambridge	46	15	13	18	51	66	43
21	Lincoln	46	13	13	20	70	71	39
22	Newport	46	10	8	28	55	85	28
23	Hartlepool	46	8	12	26	34	74	28
24	Barrow	46	7	8	31	51	90	22

SCOTTISH FA CUP 1970–71

THIRD ROUND

Celtic v Queen of the South	5-1
Hibernian v Forfar Athletic	8-1
East Fife v St Mirren	1-1, 1-1, 1-3
St Johnstone v Raith Rovers	2-2, 3-4
Clyde v Brechin City	1-1, 2-0
Airdrieonians v Alloa Athletic	1-1, 2-0
Rangers v Falkirk	3-0
Aberdeen v Elgin City	5-0
Dundee v Partick Thistle	1-0
Clachnacuddin v Cowdenbeath	0-3
Clydebank v Dundee United	0-0, 1-5
Stirling Albion v Motherwell	3-1
Dunfermline v Arbroath	3-1
Morton v Ayr United	2-0
Queen's Park v Kilmarnock	0-1
Heart of Midlothian v Stranraer	3-0

FOURTH ROUND

Dundee United v Aberdeen	1-1, 0-2
Raith Rovers v Clyde	1-1, 2-0
Morton v Kilmarnock	1-2
Cowdenbeath v Airdrieonians	0-4
St Mirren v Rangers	1-3
Dundee v Stirling Albion	2-0
Celtic v Dunfermline	1-1, 1-0
Heart of Midlothian v Hibernian	1-2

FIFTH ROUND

Rangers v Aberdeen	1-0
Hibernian v Dundee	1-0
Celtic v Raith Rovers	7-1
Kilmarnock v Airdrieonians	2-3

SEMI-FINAL

Hibernian v Rangers	0-0, 1-2
Celtic v Airdrieonians	3-3, 2-0

FINAL

Rangers v Celtic	1-1, 1-2

SCOTTISH FIRST DIVISION

		P	W	D	L	F	A	Pts
1	Celtic	34	25	6	3	89	23	56
2	Aberdeen	34	24	6	4	68	18	54
3	St Johnstone	34	19	6	9	59	44	44
4	Rangers	34	16	9	9	58	34	41
5	Dundee	34	14	10	10	53	45	38
6	Dundee United	34	14	8	12	53	54	36
7	Falkirk	34	13	9	12	46	53	35
8	Morton	34	13	8	13	44	44	34
9	Motherwell	34	13	8	13	43	47	34
10	Airdrieonians	34	13	8	13	60	65	34
11	Hearts	34	13	7	14	41	40	33
12	Hibernian	34	10	10	14	47	53	30
13	Kilmarnock	34	10	8	16	43	67	28
14	Ayr	34	9	8	17	37	54	26
15	Clyde	34	8	10	16	33	59	26
16	Dunfermline	34	6	11	17	44	56	23
17	St Mirren	34	7	9	18	38	56	23
18	Cowdenbeath	34	7	3	24	33	77	17

SCOTTISH SECOND DIVISION

		P	W	D	L	F	A	Pts
1	Partick Thistle	36	23	10	3	78	26	56
2	East Fife	36	22	7	7	86	44	51
3	Arbroath	36	19	8	9	80	52	46
4	Dumbarton	36	19	6	11	87	46	44
5	Clydebank	36	17	8	11	57	43	42
6	Montrose	36	17	7	12	78	64	41
7	Albion	36	15	9	12	53	52	39
8	Raith	36	15	9	12	62	62	39
9	Stranraer	36	14	8	14	54	52	36
10	Stenhousemuir	36	14	8	14	64	70	36
11	Queen of the S	36	13	9	14	50	56	35
12	Stirling	36	12	8	16	61	61	32
13	Berwick	36	10	10	16	42	60	30
14	Queen's Park	36	13	4	19	51	72	30
15	Forfar	36	9	11	16	63	75	29
16	Alloa	36	9	11	16	56	86	29
17	E Stirlingshire	36	9	9	18	57	86	27
18	Hamilton	36	8	7	21	50	79	23
19	Brechin	36	6	7	23	30	73	19

The unnecessary goalkeeper

One of the strangest events in all football annals happened on 12 May 1971. In the course of the England–Malta game the ball did not cross the England goal-line once and the England goalkeeper, Gordon Banks, did not receive the ball direct from a Maltese player at any time during the game.

A pools punter's best friend

In the 1970-71 season, Tranmere Rovers of the Third Division broke Plymouth Argyle's 50-year-old record by drawing 22 of their 46 League matches, the most ever tied in a single season. In actual fact, Plymouth's drawn percentage was higher as they played 42 and tied 21 games in the 1920-21 season.

FIRST DIVISION

		P	W	D	L	F	A	Pts
1	Derby	42	24	10	8	69	33	58
2	Leeds	42	24	9	9	73	31	57
3	Liverpool	42	24	9	9	64	30	57
4	Man City	42	23	11	8	77	45	57
5	Arsenal	42	22	8	12	58	40	52
6	Tottenham	42	19	13	10	63	42	51
7	Chelsea	42	18	12	12	58	49	48
8	Man United	42	19	10	13	69	61	48
9	Wolves	42	18	11	13	65	57	47
10	Sheff United	42	17	12	13	61	60	46
11	Newcastle	42	15	11	16	49	52	41
12	Leicester	42	13	13	16	41	46	39
13	Ipswich	42	11	16	15	39	53	38
14	West Ham	42	12	12	18	47	51	36
15	Everton	42	9	18	15	37	48	36
16	WBA	42	12	11	19	42	54	35
17	Stoke	42	10	15	17	39	56	35
18	Coventry	42	9	15	18	44	67	33
19	Southampton	42	12	7	23	52	80	31
20	Crystal Palace	42	8	13	21	39	65	29
21	Nottm Forest	42	8	9	25	47	81	25
22	Huddersfield	42	6	13	23	27	59	25

SECOND DIVISION

		P	W	D	L	F	A	Pts
1	Norwich	42	21	15	6	60	36	57
2	Birmingham	42	19	18	5	60	31	56
3	Millwall	42	19	17	6	64	46	55
4	QPR	42	20	14	8	57	28	54
5	Sunderland	42	17	16	9	67	57	50
6	Blackpool	42	20	7	15	70	50	47
7	Burnley	42	20	6	16	70	55	46
8	Bristol City	42	18	10	14	61	49	46
9	Middlesbrough	42	19	8	15	50	48	46
10	Carlisle	42	17	9	16	61	57	43
11	Swindon	42	15	12	15	47	47	42
12	Hull	42	14	10	18	49	53	38
13	Luton	42	10	18	14	43	48	38
14	Sheff Wed	42	13	12	17	51	58	38
15	Oxford	42	12	14	16	43	55	38
16	Portsmouth	42	12	13	17	59	68	37
17	Orient	42	14	9	19	50	61	37
18	Preston	42	12	12	18	52	58	36
19	Cardiff	42	10	14	18	56	69	34
20	Fulham	42	12	10	20	45	68	34
21	Charlton	42	12	9	21	55	77	33
22	Watford	42	5	9	28	24	75	19

FA CUP 1971-72

FOURTH ROUND

Liverpool v Leeds United	0-0, 0-2
Cardiff City v Sunderland	1-1, 1-1, 3-1
Everton v Walsall	2-1
Tottenham Hotspur v Rotherham United	2-0
Birmingham City v Ipswich Town	1-0
Portsmouth v Swansea City	2-0
Huddersfield Town v Fulham	3-0
Hereford United v West Ham United	0-0, 1-3
Preston North End v Manchester United	0-2
Millwall v Middlesbrough	2-2, 1-2
Tranmere Rovers v Stoke City	2-2, 0-2
Coventry City v Hull City	0-1
Leicester City v Orient	0-2
Chelsea v Bolton Wanderers	3-0
Derby County v Notts County	6-0
Reading v Arsenal	1-2

FIFTH ROUND

Cardiff City v Leeds United	0-2
Everton v Tottenham Hotspur	0-2
Birmingham City v Portsmouth	3-1
Huddersfield Town v West Ham United	4-2
Manchester United v Middlesbrough	0-0, 3-0
Stoke City v Hull City	4-1
Orient v Chelsea	3-2
Derby County v Arsenal	2-2, 0-0, 0-1

SIXTH ROUND

Leeds United v Tottenham Hotspur	2-1
Birmingham City v Huddersfield Town	3-1
Manchester United v Stoke City	1-1, 1-2
Orient v Arsenal	0-1

SEMI-FINAL

Leeds United v Birmingham City	3-0
Arsenal v Stoke City	1-1, 2-1

FINAL

Leeds United v Arsenal	1-0

THIRD DIVISION

		P	W	D	L	F	A	Pts
1	Aston Villa	46	32	6	8	85	32	70
2	Brighton	46	27	11	8	82	47	65
3	Bournemouth	46	23	16	7	73	37	62
4	Notts County	46	25	12	9	74	44	62
5	Rotherham	46	20	15	11	69	52	55
6	Bristol Rovers	46	21	12	13	75	56	54
7	Bolton	46	17	16	13	51	41	50
8	Plymouth	46	20	10	16	74	64	50
9	Walsall	46	15	18	13	62	57	48
10	Blackburn	46	19	9	18	54	57	47
11	Oldham	46	17	11	18	59	63	45
12	Shrewsbury	46	17	10	19	73	65	44
13	Chesterfield	46	18	8	20	57	57	44
14	Swansea	46	17	10	19	46	59	44
15	Port Vale	46	13	15	18	43	59	41
16	Wrexham	46	16	8	22	59	63	40
17	Halifax	46	13	12	21	48	61	38
18	Rochdale	46	12	13	21	57	83	37
19	York	46	12	12	22	57	66	36
20	Tranmere	46	10	16	20	50	71	36
21	Mansfield	46	8	20	18	41	63	36
22	Barnsley	46	9	18	19	32	64	36
23	Torquay	46	10	12	24	41	69	32
24	Bradford City	46	11	10	25	45	77	32

FOURTH DIVISION

		P	W	D	L	F	A	Pts
1	Grimsby	46	28	7	11	88	56	63
2	Southend	46	24	12	10	81	55	60
3	Brentford	46	24	11	11	76	44	59
4	Scunthorpe	46	22	13	11	56	37	57
5	Lincoln	46	21	14	11	77	59	56
6	Workington	46	16	19	11	50	34	51
7	Southport	46	18	14	14	66	46	50
8	Peterborough	46	17	16	13	82	64	50
9	Bury	46	19	12	15	73	59	50
10	Cambridge	46	17	14	15	62	60	48
11	Colchester	46	19	10	17	70	69	48
12	Doncaster	46	16	14	16	56	63	46
13	Gillingham	46	16	13	17	61	67	45
14	Newport	46	18	8	20	60	72	44
15	Exeter	46	16	11	19	61	68	43
16	Reading	46	17	8	21	56	76	42
17	Aldershot	46	9	22	15	48	54	40
18	Hartlepool	46	17	6	23	58	69	40
19	Darlington	46	14	11	21	64	82	39
20	Chester	46	10	18	18	47	56	38
21	Northampton	46	12	13	21	66	79	37
22	Barrow	46	13	11	22	40	71	37
23	Stockport	46	9	14	23	55	87	32
24	Crewe	46	10	9	27	43	69	29

SCOTTISH FA CUP 1971-72

THIRD ROUND

Celtic v Albion Rovers	5-0
Dundee v Queen of the South	3-0
Heart of Midlothian v St Johnstone	2-0
Clydebank v East Fife	1-1, 1-0
Dumbarton v Hamilton Academicals	3-1
Raith Rovers v Dunfermline Athletic	2-0
Elgin City v Inverness Caledonian	3-1
Kilmarnock v Alloa Athletic	5-1
Clyde v Ayr United	0-1
Motherwell v Montrose	2-0
Forfar Athletic v St Mirren	0-1
Falkirk v Rangers	2-2, 0-2
Dundee United v Aberdeen	0-4
Morton v Cowdenbeath	1-0
Arbroath v Airdrieonians	1-3
Partick Thistle v Hibernian	0-2

FOURTH ROUND

Celtic v Dundee	4-0
Heart of Midlothian v Clydebank	4-0
Dumbarton v Raith Rovers	0-3
Elgin City v Kilmarnock	1-4
Ayr United v Motherwell	0-0, 1-2
St Mirren v Rangers	1-4
Aberdeen v Morton	1-0
Hibernian v Airdrieonians	2-0

FIFTH ROUND

Celtic v Heart of Midlothian	1-1, 1-0
Raith Rovers v Kilmarnock	1-3
Motherwell v Rangers	2-2, 2-4
Hibernian v Aberdeen	2-0

SEMI-FINAL

Celtic v Kilmarnock	3-1
Rangers v Hibernian	1-1, 0-2

FINAL

Celtic v Hibernian	6-1

SCOTTISH FIRST DIVISION

		P	W	D	L	F	A	Pts
1	Celtic	34	28	4	2	96	28	60
2	Aberdeen	34	21	8	5	80	26	50
3	Rangers	34	21	2	11	71	38	44
4	Hibernian	34	19	6	9	62	34	44
5	Dundee	34	14	13	7	59	38	41
6	Hearts	34	13	13	8	53	49	39
7	Partick	34	12	10	12	53	54	34
8	St Johnstone	34	12	8	14	52	58	32
9	Dundee United	34	12	7	15	55	70	31
10	Motherwell	34	11	7	16	49	69	29
11	Kilmarnock	34	11	6	17	49	64	28
12	Ayr	34	9	10	15	40	58	28
13	Morton	34	10	7	17	46	52	27
14	Falkirk	34	10	7	17	44	60	27
15	Airdrieonians	34	7	12	15	44	76	26
16	East Fife	34	5	15	14	34	61	25
17	Clyde	34	7	10	17	33	66	24
18	Dunfermline	34	7	9	18	31	50	23

SCOTTISH SECOND DIVISION

		P	W	D	L	F	A	Pts
1	Dumbarton	36	24	4	8	89	51	52
2	Arbroath	36	22	8	6	71	41	52
3	Stirling	36	21	8	7	75	37	50
4	St Mirren	36	24	2	10	84	47	50
5	Cowdenbeath	36	19	10	7	69	28	48
6	Stranraer	36	18	8	10	70	62	44
7	Queen of the S	36	17	9	10	56	38	43
8	E Stirlingshire	36	17	7	12	60	58	41
9	Clydebank	36	14	11	11	60	52	39
10	Montrose	36	15	6	15	73	54	36
11	Raith	36	13	8	15	56	56	34
12	Queen's Park	36	12	9	15	47	61	33
13	Berwick	36	14	4	18	53	50	32
14	Stenhousemuir	36	10	8	18	41	58	28
15	Brechin	36	8	7	21	41	79	23
16	Alloa	36	9	4	23	41	75	22
17	Forfar	36	6	9	21	32	84	21
18	Albion	36	7	6	23	36	61	20
19	Hamilton	36	4	8	24	31	93	16

Mansfield Town did not score a League goal at home until the 23rd minute of their game against Plymouth Argyle on 18 December 1971. This unrewarded period of 833 minutes of Third Division football at Field Mill is thought to constitute a record-breaking start to any Football League club's season. Mansfield still lost the game 3-2.

Aldershot drew 22 of their Fourth Division fixtures to equal Tranmere Rovers' record of the 1970-71 season. Both Tranmere and Aldershot, however, played 46 games that season and their achievement does not, therefore, compare in percentage terms with Plymouth's feat of 1920-21. That year Argyle drew 21 of their 42 League games.

FIRST DIVISION

		P	W	D	L	F	A	Pts
1	Liverpool	42	25	10	6	72	42	60
2	Arsenal	42	23	11	8	57	43	57
3	Leeds	42	21	11	10	77	45	53
4	Ipswich	42	17	14	11	55	45	48
5	Wolves	42	18	11	13	66	54	47
6	West Ham	42	17	12	13	67	53	46
7	Derby	42	19	8	15	56	54	46
8	Tottenham	42	16	13	13	58	48	45
9	Newcastle	42	16	13	13	60	51	45
10	Birmingham	42	15	12	15	53	54	42
11	Man City	42	15	11	16	57	60	41
12	Chelsea	42	13	14	15	49	51	40
13	Southampton	42	11	18	13	47	52	40
14	Sheff United	42	15	10	17	51	59	40
15	Stoke	42	14	10	18	61	56	38
16	Leicester	42	10	17	15	40	46	37
17	Everton	42	13	11	18	41	49	37
18	Man United	42	12	13	17	44	60	37
19	Coventry	42	13	9	20	40	55	35
20	Norwich	42	11	10	21	36	63	32
21	Crystal Palace	42	9	12	21	41	58	30
22	WBA	42	9	10	23	38	62	28

SECOND DIVISION

		P	W	D	L	F	A	Pts
1	Burnley	42	24	14	4	72	35	62
2	QPR	42	24	13	5	81	37	61
3	Aston Villa	42	18	14	10	51	47	50
4	Middlesbrough	42	17	13	12	46	43	47
5	Bristol City	42	17	12	13	63	51	46
6	Sunderland	42	17	12	13	59	49	46
7	Blackpool	42	18	10	14	56	51	46
8	Oxford	42	19	7	16	52	43	45
9	Fulham	42	16	12	14	58	49	44
10	Sheff Wed	42	17	10	15	59	55	44
11	Millwall	42	16	10	16	55	47	42
12	Luton	42	15	11	16	44	53	41
13	Hull	42	14	12	16	64	59	40
14	Nottm Forest	42	14	12	16	47	52	40
15	Orient	42	12	12	18	49	53	36
16	Swindon	42	10	16	16	46	60	36
17	Portsmouth	42	12	11	19	42	59	35
18	Carlisle	42	11	12	19	50	52	34
19	Preston	42	11	12	19	37	64	34
20	Cardiff	42	11	11	20	43	58	33
21	Huddersfield	42	8	17	17	36	56	33
22	Brighton	42	8	13	21	46	83	29

FA CUP 1972-73

FOURTH ROUND

Arsenal v Bradford City	2-0
Bolton Wanderers v Cardiff City	2-2, 1-1, 1-0
Carlisle United v Sheffield United	2-1
Chelsea v Ipswich Town	2-0
Coventry City v Grimsby Town	1-0
Derby County v Tottenham Hotspur	1-1, 5-3
Everton v Millwall	0-2
Hull City v West Ham United	1-0
Leeds United v Plymouth Argyle	2-1
Liverpool v Manchester City	0-0, 0-2
Newcastle United v Luton Town	0-2
Oxford United v Queen's Park Rangers	1-2
Sheffield Wednesday v Crystal Palace	1-1, 1-1, 3-2
Sunderland v Reading	1-1, 3-1
West Bromwich Albion v Swindon Town	2-0
Wolverhampton Wanderers v Bristol City	1-0

FIFTH ROUND

Bolton Wanderers v Luton Town	0-1
Carlisle United v Arsenal	1-2
Coventry City v Hull City	3-0
Derby County v Queen's Park Rangers	4-2
Leeds United v West Bromwich Albion	2-0
Manchester City v Sunderland	2-2, 1-3
Sheffield Wednesday v Chelsea	1-2
Wolverhampton Wanderers v Millwall	1-0

SIXTH ROUND

Chelsea v Arsenal	2-2, 1-2
Derby County v Leeds United	0-1
Sunderland v Luton Town	2-0
Wolverhampton Wanderers v Coventry City	2-0

SEMI-FINAL

Arsenal v Sunderland	1-2
Leeds United v Wolverhampton Wanderers	1-0

FINAL

Leeds United v Sunderland	0-1

THIRD DIVISION

		P	W	D	L	F	A	Pts
1	Bolton	46	25	11	10	73	39	61
2	Notts County	46	23	11	12	67	47	57
3	Blackburn	46	20	15	11	57	47	55
4	Oldham	46	19	16	11	72	54	54
5	Bristol Rovers	46	20	13	13	77	56	53
6	Port Vale	46	21	11	14	56	69	53
7	Bournemouth	46	17	16	13	66	44	50
8	Plymouth	46	20	10	16	74	66	50
9	Grimsby	46	20	8	18	67	61	48
10	Tranmere	46	15	16	15	56	52	46
11	Charlton	46	17	11	18	69	67	45
12	Wrexham	46	14	17	15	55	54	45
13	Rochdale	46	14	17	15	48	54	45
14	Southend	46	17	10	19	61	54	44
15	Shrewsbury	46	15	14	17	46	54	44
16	Chesterfield	46	17	9	20	57	61	43
17	Walsall	46	18	7	21	56	66	43
18	York	46	13	15	18	42	46	41
19	Watford	46	12	17	17	43	48	41
20	Halifax	46	13	15	18	43	53	41
21	Rotherham	46	17	7	22	51	65	41
22	Brentford	46	15	7	24	51	69	37
23	Swansea	46	14	9	23	51	73	37
24	Scunthorpe	46	10	10	26	33	72	30

FOURTH DIVISION

		P	W	D	L	F	A	Pts
1	Southport	46	26	10	10	71	48	62
2	Hereford	46	23	12	11	56	38	58
3	Cambridge	46	20	17	9	67	57	57
4	Aldershot	46	22	12	12	60	38	56
5	Newport	46	22	12	12	64	44	56
6	Mansfield	46	20	14	12	78	51	54
7	Reading	46	17	18	11	51	38	52
8	Exeter	46	18	14	14	57	51	50
9	Gillingham	46	19	11	16	63	58	49
10	Lincoln	46	16	16	14	64	57	48
11	Stockport	46	18	12	16	53	53	48
12	Bury	46	14	18	14	58	51	46
13	Workington	46	17	12	17	59	61	46
14	Barnsley	46	14	16	16	58	60	44
15	Chester	46	14	15	17	61	52	43
16	Bradford	46	16	11	19	61	65	43
17	Doncaster	46	15	12	19	49	58	42
18	Torquay	46	12	17	17	44	47	41
19	Peterborough	46	14	13	19	71	76	41
20	Hartlepool	46	12	17	17	34	49	41
21	Crewe	46	9	18	19	38	61	36
22	Colchester	46	10	11	25	48	76	31
23	Northampton	46	10	11	25	40	73	31
24	Darlington	46	7	15	24	42	85	29

SCOTTISH FA CUP 1972-73

THIRD ROUND

Ayr United v Inverness Thistle	3-0
Berwick Rovers v Falkirk	1-3
Brechin City v Aberdeen	2-4
Celtic v East Fife	4-1
Clyde v Montrose	1-1, 2-4
Dumbarton v Cowdenbeath	4-1
Dunfermline Athletic v Dundee	0-3
Elgin City v Hamilton Academicals	0-1
Heart of Midlothian v Airdrieonians	0-0, 1-3
Hibernian v Morton	2-0
Kilmarnock v Queen of the South	2-1
Motherwell v Raith Rovers	2-1
Rangers v Dundee United	1-0
St Mirren v Partick Thistle	0-1
Stirling Albion v Arbroath	3-3, 1-0
Stranraer v St Johnstone	1-1, 2-1

FOURTH ROUND

Ayr United v Stirling Albion	2-1
Dumbarton v Partick Thistle	2-2, 1-3
Kilmarnock v Airdrieonians	0-1
Montrose v Hamilton Academicals	2-2, 1-0
Motherwell v Celtic	0-4
Rangers v Hibernian	1-1, 2-1
Stranraer v Dundee	2-9
Aberdeen v Falkirk	3-1

FIFTH ROUND

Celtic v Aberdeen	0-0, 1-0
Montrose v Dundee	1-4
Partick Thistle v Ayr United	1-5
Rangers v Airdrieonians	2-0

SEMI-FINAL

Ayr United v Rangers	0-2
Celtic v Dundee	0-0, 3-0

FINAL

Celtic v Rangers	2-3

SCOTTISH FIRST DIVISION

		P	W	D	L	F	A	Pts
1	Celtic	34	26	5	3	93	28	57
2	Rangers	34	26	4	4	74	30	56
3	Hibernian	34	19	7	8	74	33	45
4	Aberdeen	34	16	11	7	61	34	43
5	Dundee	34	17	9	8	68	43	43
6	Ayr	34	16	8	10	50	51	40
7	Dundee United	34	17	5	12	56	51	39
8	Motherwell	34	11	9	14	38	48	31
9	East Fife	34	11	8	15	46	54	30
10	Hearts	34	12	6	16	39	50	30
11	St Johnstone	34	10	9	15	52	67	29
12	Morton	34	10	8	16	47	53	28
13	Partick	34	10	8	16	40	53	28
14	Falkirk	34	7	12	15	38	56	26
15	Arbroath	34	9	8	17	39	63	26
16	Dumbarton	34	6	11	17	43	72	23
17	Kilmarnock	34	7	8	19	40	71	22
18	Airdrieonians	34	4	8	22	34	75	16

SCOTTISH SECOND DIVISION

		P	W	D	L	F	A	Pts
1	Clyde	36	23	10	3	68	28	56
2	Dunfermline	36	23	6	7	95	32	52
3	Raith	36	19	9	8	73	42	47
4	Stirling	36	19	9	8	70	39	47
5	St Mirren	36	19	7	10	79	50	45
6	Montrose	36	18	8	10	82	58	44
7	Cowdenbeath	36	14	10	12	57	53	38
8	Hamilton	36	16	6	14	67	63	38
9	Berwick	36	16	5	15	45	54	37
10	Stenhousemuir	36	14	8	14	44	41	36
11	Queen of the S	36	13	8	15	45	52	34
12	Alloa	36	11	11	14	45	49	33
13	E Stirlingshire	36	12	8	16	52	69	32
14	Queen's Park	36	9	12	15	44	61	30
15	Stranraer	36	13	4	19	56	78	30
16	Forfar	36	10	9	17	38	66	29
17	Clydebank	36	9	6	21	48	72	21
18	Albion	36	5	8	23	35	83	18
19	Brechin	36	5	4	27	46	99	14

Arsenal's defeat in the semi-final at Hillsborough prevented them from becoming the first club this century to appear in three consecutive Cup Finals. It also prevented the first 'repeat' Cup Final of the twentieth century as Leeds were their 1972 opponents.

Sunderland, by defeating Leeds 1-0 in the 1973 Cup Final became only the fifth Second Division side to win the FA Cup. On the way they defeated three of the previous holders – Manchester City, Arsenal and Leeds for a remarkably memorable win.

247

FIRST DIVISION

		P	W	D	L	F	A	Pts
1	Leeds	42	24	14	4	66	31	62
2	Liverpool	42	22	13	7	52	31	57
3	Derby	42	17	14	11	52	42	48
4	Ipswich	42	18	11	13	67	58	47
5	Stoke	42	15	16	11	54	42	46
6	Burnley	42	16	14	12	56	53	46
7	Everton	42	16	12	14	50	48	44
8	QPR	42	13	17	12	56	52	43
9	Leicester	42	13	16	13	51	41	42
10	Arsenal	42	14	14	14	49	51	42
11	Tottenham	42	14	14	14	45	50	42
12	Wolves	42	13	15	14	49	49	41
13	Sheff United	42	14	12	16	44	49	40
14	Man City†	42	14	12	16	39	46	40
15	Newcastle	42	13	12	17	49	48	38
16	Coventry	42	14	10	18	43	54	38
17	Chelsea	42	12	13	17	56	60	37
18	West Ham	42	11	15	16	55	60	37
19	Birmingham	42	12	13	17	52	64	37
20	Southampton*	42	11	14	17	47	68	36
21	Man United*†	42	10	12	20	38	48	32
22	Norwich*	42	7	15	20	37	62	29

* Three clubs relegated.
† Game at Old Trafford abandoned after 86 minutes. Manchester City, who were leading 1-0, awarded both points.

SECOND DIVISION

		P	W	D	L	F	A	Pts
1	Middlesbrough*	42	27	11	4	77	30	65
2	Luton*	42	19	12	11	64	51	50
3	Carlisle*	42	20	9	13	61	48	49
4	Orient	42	15	18	9	55	42	48
5	Blackpool	42	17	13	12	57	40	47
6	Sunderland	42	19	9	14	58	44	47
7	Nottm Forest	42	15	15	12	57	43	45
8	WBA	42	14	16	12	48	45	44
9	Hull	42	13	17	12	46	47	43
10	Notts County	42	15	13	14	55	60	43
11	Bolton	42	15	12	15	44	40	42
12	Millwall	42	14	14	14	51	51	42
13	Fulham	42	16	10	16	39	43	42
14	Aston Villa	42	13	15	14	48	45	41
15	Portsmouth	42	14	12	16	45	62	40
16	Bristol City	42	14	10	18	47	54	38
17	Cardiff	42	10	16	16	49	62	36
18	Oxford	42	10	16	16	35	46	36
19	Sheff Wed	42	12	11	19	51	63	35
20	Crystal Palace‡	42	11	12	19	43	56	34
21	Preston‡§	42	9	14	19	40	62	31
22	Swindon‡	42	7	11	24	36	72	25

* Three clubs promoted.
‡ Three clubs relegated.
§ Preston had one point deducted for fielding an ineligible player.

THIRD DIVISION

		P	W	D	L	F	A	Pts
1	Oldham‡	46	25	12	9	83	47	62
2	Bristol Rovers‡	46	22	17	7	65	33	61
3	York‡	46	21	19	6	67	38	61
4	Wrexham	46	22	12	12	63	43	56
5	Chesterfield	46	21	14	11	55	42	56
6	Grimsby	46	18	15	13	67	50	51
7	Watford	46	19	12	15	64	56	50
8	Aldershot	46	19	11	16	65	52	49
9	Halifax	46	14	21	11	48	51	49
10	Huddersfield	46	17	13	16	56	55	47
11	Bournemouth	46	16	15	15	54	58	47
12	Southend	46	16	14	16	62	62	46
13	Blackburn	46	18	10	18	62	64	46
14	Charlton	46	19	8	19	66	73	46
15	Walsall	46	16	13	17	57	48	45
16	Tranmere	46	15	15	16	50	44	45
17	Plymouth	46	17	10	19	59	54	44
18	Hereford	46	14	15	17	53	57	43
19	Brighton	46	16	11	19	52	58	43
20	Port Vale	46	14	14	18	52	58	42
21	Cambridge*	46	13	9	24	48	81	35
22	Shrewsbury*	46	10	11	25	41	62	31
23	Southport*	46	6	16	24	35	82	28
24	Rochdale*	46	2	17	27	38	94	21

‡ Three clubs promoted.
* Four clubs relegated.

FOURTH DIVISION

		P	W	D	L	F	A	Pts
1	Peterborough*	46	27	11	8	75	38	65
2	Gillingham*	46	25	12	9	90	49	62
3	Colchester*	46	24	12	10	73	36	60
4	Bury*	46	24	11	11	81	49	59
5	Northampton	46	20	13	13	63	48	53
6	Reading	46	16	19	11	58	37	51
7	Chester	46	17	15	14	54	55	49
8	Bradford	46	17	14	15	58	52	48
9	Newport‡	46	16	14	16	56	65	45
10	Exeter†	45	18	8	19	58	55	44
11	Hartlepool	46	16	12	18	48	47	44
12	Lincoln	46	16	12	18	63	67	44
13	Barnsley	46	17	10	19	58	64	44
14	Swansea	46	16	11	19	45	46	43
15	Rotherham	46	15	13	18	56	58	43
16	Torquay	46	13	17	16	52	57	43
17	Mansfield	46	13	17	16	62	69	43
18	Scunthorpe†	45	14	12	19	47	64	42
19	Brentford	46	12	16	18	48	50	40
20	Darlington	46	13	13	20	40	62	39
21	Crewe	46	14	10	22	43	71	38
22	Doncaster	46	12	11	23	47	80	35
23	Workington	46	11	13	22	43	74	35
24	Stockport	46	7	20	19	44	69	34

† Exeter failed to turn up for their fixture at Scunthorpe and the latter were awarded both points.
‡ Newport had one point deducted for fielding an ineligible player.
* Four clubs promoted.

SCOTTISH FIRST DIVISION

		P	W	D	L	F	A	Pts
1	Celtic	34	23	7	4	82	27	53
2	Hibernian	34	20	9	5	75	42	49
3	Rangers	34	21	6	7	67	34	48
4	Aberdeen	34	13	16	5	46	26	42
5	Dundee	34	16	7	11	67	48	39
6	Hearts	34	14	10	10	54	43	38
7	Ayr	34	15	8	11	44	40	38
8	Dundee United	34	15	7	12	55	51	37
9	Motherwell	34	14	7	13	45	40	35
10	Dumbarton	34	11	7	16	43	58	29
11	Partick	34	9	10	15	33	46	28
12	St Johnstone	34	9	10	15	41	60	28
13	Arbroath	34	10	7	17	52	69	27
14	Morton	34	8	10	16	37	49	26
15	Clyde	34	8	9	17	29	65	25
16	Dunfermline	34	8	8	18	43	65	24
17	East Fife	34	9	6	19	26	51	24
18	Falkirk	34	4	14	16	33	58	22

SCOTTISH SECOND DIVISION

		P	W	D	L	F	A	Pts
1	Airdrieonians	36	28	4	4	102	25	60
2	Kilmarnock	36	26	6	4	96	44	58
3	Hamilton	36	24	7	5	68	38	55
4	Queen of the S	36	20	7	9	73	41	47
5	Raith	36	18	9	9	69	48	45
6	Berwick	36	16	13	7	53	35	45
7	Stirling	36	17	6	13	76	50	40
8	Montrose	36	15	7	14	71	64	37
9	Stranraer	36	14	8	14	64	70	36
10	Clydebank	36	13	8	15	47	48	34
11	St Mirren	36	12	10	14	62	66	34
12	Alloa	36	15	4	17	47	58	34
13	Cowdenbeath	36	11	9	16	59	85	31
14	Queen's Park	36	12	4	20	42	64	28
15	Stenhousemuir	36	11	5	20	44	59	27
16	E Stirlingshire	36	9	5	22	47	73	23
17	Albion	36	7	6	23	38	72	20
18	Forfar	36	5	6	25	42	94	16
19	Brechin	36	5	4	27	33	99	14

FA CUP 1973-74

FOURTH ROUND

Arsenal v Aston Villa	1-1, 0-2
Coventry City v Derby County	0-0, 1-0
Everton v West Bromwich Albion	0-0, 0-1
Fulham v Leicester City	1-1, 1-2
Hereford United v Bristol City	0-1
Liverpool v Carlisle United	0-0, 2-0
Luton Town v Bradford City	3-0
Manchester United v Ipswich Town	0-1
Newcastle United v Scunthorpe United	1-1, 3-0
Nottingham Forest v Manchester City	4-1
Oldham Athletic v Burnley	1-4
Peterborough United v Leeds United	1-4
Portsmouth v Orient	0-0, 1-1, 2-0
Queen's Park Rangers v Birmingham City	2-0
Southampton v Bolton Wanderers	3-3, 2-0
Wrexham v Middlesbrough	1-0

FIFTH ROUND

Bristol City v Leeds United	1-1, 1-0
Burnley v Aston Villa	1-0
Coventry City v Queen's Park Rangers	0-0, 2-3
Liverpool v Ipswich Town	2-0
Luton Town v Leicester City	0-4
Nottingham Forest v Portsmouth	1-0
Southampton v Wrexham	0-1
West Bromwich Albion v Newcastle United	0-3

SIXTH ROUND

Bristol City v Liverpool	0-1
Burnley v Wrexham	1-0
Newcastle United v Nottingham Forest	4-3*, 0-0, 1-0
Queen's Park Rangers v Leicester City	0-2

*FA ordered replay because of crowd invasion. Second and third games both played at Goodison Park.

SEMI-FINAL

Burnley v Newcastle United	0-2
Leicester City v Liverpool	0-0, 1-3

FINAL

Liverpool v Newcastle United	3-0

SCOTTISH FA CUP 1973-74

THIRD ROUND

Aberdeen v Dundee	0-2
Arbroath v Dumbarton	1-0
Celtic v Clydebank	6-1
Cowdenbeath v Ayr United	0-5
Dundee United v Airdrieonians	4-1
Falkirk v Dunfermline Athletic	2-2, 0-1
Forfar Athletic v St Johnstone	1-6
Heart of Midlothian v Clyde	3-1
Hibernian v Kilmarnock	5-2
Montrose v Stirling Albion	1-1, 1-3
Motherwell v Brechin City	2-0
Partick Thistle v Ferranti Thistle	6-1
Queen of the South v East Fife	1-0
Raith Rovers v Morton	2-2, 0-0, 0-1
Rangers v Queen's Park	8-0
Stranraer v St Mirren	1-1, 1-1, 3-2

FOURTH ROUND

Arbroath v Motherwell	1-3
Celtic v Stirling Albion	6-1
Dundee United v Morton	1-0
Dunfermline Athletic v Queen of the South	1-0
Heart of Midlothian v Partick Thistle	1-1, 4-1
Rangers v Dundee	0-3
St Johnstone v Hibernian	1-3
Stranraer v Ayr United	1-7

FIFTH ROUND

Celtic v Motherwell	2-2, 1-0
Dunfermline Athletic v Dundee United	1-1, 0-4
Heart of Midlothian v Ayr United	1-1, 2-1
Hibernian v Dundee	3-3, 0-3

SEMI-FINAL

Celtic v Dundee	1-0
Heart of Midlothian v Dundee United	1-1, 2-4

FINAL

Celtic v Dundee United	3-0

FIRST DIVISION

		P	W	D	L	F	A	Pts
1	Derby	42	21	11	10	67	49	53
2	Liverpool	42	20	11	11	60	39	51
3	Ipswich	42	23	5	14	66	44	51
4	Everton	42	16	18	8	56	42	50
5	Stoke	42	17	15	10	64	48	49
6	Sheff United	42	18	13	11	58	51	49
7	Middlesbrough	42	18	12	12	54	40	48
8	Man City	42	18	10	14	54	54	46
9	Leeds	42	16	13	13	57	49	45
10	Burnley	42	17	11	14	68	67	45
11	QPR	42	16	10	16	54	54	42
12	Wolverhampton	42	14	11	17	57	54	39
13	West Ham	42	13	13	16	58	59	39
14	Coventry	42	12	15	15	51	62	39
15	Newcastle	42	15	9	18	59	72	39
16	Arsenal	42	13	11	18	47	49	37
17	Birmingham	42	14	9	19	53	61	37
18	Leicester	42	12	12	18	46	60	36
19	Tottenham	42	13	8	21	52	63	34
20	Luton	42	11	11	20	47	65	33
21	Chelsea	42	9	15	18	42	72	33
22	Carlisle	42	12	5	25	43	59	29

SECOND DIVISION

		P	W	D	L	F	A	Pts
1	Man United	42	26	9	7	66	30	61
2	Aston Villa	42	25	8	9	69	32	58
3	Norwich	42	20	13	9	58	37	53
4	Sunderland	42	19	13	10	65	35	51
5	Bristol City	42	21	8	13	47	33	50
6	WBA	42	18	9	15	54	42	45
7	Blackpool	42	14	17	11	38	33	45
8	Hull	42	15	14	13	40	53	44
9	Fulham	42	13	16	13	44	39	42
10	Bolton	42	15	12	15	45	41	42
11	Oxford	42	15	12	15	41	51	42
12	Orient	42	11	20	11	28	39	42
13	Southampton	42	15	11	16	53	54	41
14	Notts County	42	12	16	14	49	59	40
15	York	42	14	10	18	51	55	38
16	Nottm Forest	42	12	14	16	43	55	38
17	Portsmouth	42	12	13	17	44	54	37
18	Oldham	42	10	15	17	40	48	35
19	Bristol Rovers	42	12	11	19	42	64	35
20	Millwall	42	10	12	20	44	56	32
21	Cardiff	42	9	14	19	36	62	32
22	Sheff Wed	42	5	11	26	29	64	21

THIRD DIVISION

		P	W	D	L	F	A	Pts
1	Blackburn	46	22	16	8	68	45	60
2	Plymouth	46	24	11	11	79	58	59
3	Charlton Ath	46	22	11	13	76	61	55
4	Swindon	46	21	11	14	64	58	53
5	Crystal Palace	46	18	15	13	66	57	51
6	Port Vale	46	18	15	13	61	54	51
7	Peterborough	46	19	12	15	47	53	50
8	Walsall	46	18	13	15	67	52	49
9	Preston NE	46	19	11	16	63	56	49
10	Gillingham	46	17	14	15	65	60	48
11	Colchester	46	17	13	16	70	63	47
12	Hereford	46	16	14	16	64	66	46
13	Wrexham	46	15	15	16	65	55	45
14	Bury	46	16	12	18	53	56	44
15	Chesterfield	46	16	12	18	62	66	44
16	Grimsby	46	15	13	18	55	64	43
17	Halifax	46	13	17	16	49	65	43
18	Southend	46	13	16	17	46	51	42
19	Brighton	46	16	10	20	56	64	42
20	Aldershot	46	14	11	21	53	63	38*
21	Bournemouth	46	13	12	21	44	58	38
22	Tranmere	46	14	9	23	55	57	37
23	Watford	46	10	17	19	52	75	37
24	Huddersfield	46	11	10	25	47	76	32

*One point deducted for playing unregistered player.

FOURTH DIVISION

		P	W	D	L	F	A	Pts
1	Mansfield	46	28	12	6	90	40	68
2	Shrewsbury	46	26	10	10	80	43	62
3	Rotherham	46	22	15	9	71	41	59
4	Chester	46	23	11	12	64	38	57
5	Lincoln	46	21	15	10	79	48	57
6	Cambridge	46	20	14	12	62	44	54
7	Reading	46	21	10	15	63	47	52
8	Brentford	46	18	13	15	53	45	49
9	Exeter	46	19	11	16	60	63	49
10	Bradford	46	17	13	16	56	51	47
11	Southport	46	15	17	14	56	56	47
12	Newport	46	19	9	18	68	75	47
13	Hartlepool	46	16	11	19	52	62	43
14	Torquay	46	14	14	18	46	61	42
15	Barnsley	46	15	11	20	62	65	41
16	Northampton	46	15	11	20	67	73	41
17	Doncaster	46	14	12	20	65	79	40
18	Crewe	46	11	18	17	34	47	40
19	Rochdale	46	13	13	20	59	75	39
20	Stockport	46	12	14	20	43	70	38
21	Darlington	46	13	10	23	54	67	36
22	Swansea	46	15	6	25	26	73	36
23	Workington	46	10	11	25	46	66	31
24	Scunthorpe	46	7	15	24	41	78	29

SCOTTISH FIRST DIVISION

		P	W	D	L	F	A	Pts
1	Rangers	34	25	6	3	86	33	56
2	Hibernian	34	20	9	5	69	37	49
3	Celtic	34	20	5	9	81	41	45
4	Dundee United	34	19	7	8	72	43	41
5	Aberdeen	34	16	9	9	66	43	38
6	Dundee	34	16	6	12	48	42	36
7	Ayr	34	14	8	12	50	61	35
8	Hearts	34	11	13	10	47	52	34
9	St Johnstone	34	11	12	11	41	44	33
10	Motherwell	34	14	5	15	52	57	31
11	Airdrie	34	11	9	14	43	55	31
12	Kilmarnock	34	8	15	11	52	68	31
13	Partick	34	10	10	14	48	62	30
14	Dumbarton	34	7	10	17	44	55	24
15	Dumfermline	34	7	9	18	46	66	23
16	Clyde	34	6	10	18	40	63	22
17	Morton	34	6	10	18	31	62	22
18	Arbroath	34	5	7	22	34	66	17

SCOTTISH SECOND DIVISION

		P	W	D	L	F	A	Pts
1	Falkirk	38	26	2	10	76	29	54
2	Queen of the S	38	23	7	8	77	33	53
3	Montrose	38	23	7	8	70	37	53
4	Hamilton	38	21	7	10	69	30	49
5	East Fife	38	20	9	11	57	42	47
6	St Mirren	38	19	8	11	74	52	46
7	Clydebank	38	18	8	12	50	40	44
8	Stirling	38	17	9	12	67	55	43
9	Berwick	38	17	6	15	53	49	40
10	E. Stirlingshire	38	16	8	14	56	52	40
11	Stenhousemuir	38	14	11	13	52	42	39
12	Albion	38	16	7	15	72	64	39
13	Raith	38	14	9	15	48	44	37
14	Stranraer	38	12	11	15	47	69	35
15	Alloa	38	11	11	16	49	56	33
16	Queen's Park	38	10	10	18	41	54	30
17	Brechin	38	9	7	22	44	85	25
18	Meadowbank	38	9	5	24	26	87	23
19	Cowdenbeath	38	5	12	22	39	78	21
20	Forfar	38	1	7	30	27	102	9

FA CUP 1974-75

FOURTH ROUND

Queens Park Rangers v Notts County	3-0
Aston Villa v Sheffield United	4-1
Bury v Mansfield Town	1-2
Carlisle United v West Bromwich Albion	3-2
Chelsea v Birmingham City	0-1
Coventry City v Arsenal	1-1, 3-0
Ipswich Town v Liverpool	1-0
Leatherhead v Leicester City	2-3
Leeds United v Wimbledon	0-0, 1-0
Middlesbrough v Sunderland	3-1
Plymouth Argyle v Everton	1-3
Stafford Rangers v Peterborough United	1-2
Walsall v Newcastle United	1-0
West Ham United v Swindon Town	1-1, 2-1
Derby County v Bristol Rovers	2-0
Fulham v Nottingham Forest	0-0, 1-1, 1-1, 2-1

FIFTH ROUND

Arsenal v Leicester City	0-0, 1-0
Birmingham City v Walsall	2-1
Everton v Fulham	1-2
Ipswich Town v Aston Villa	3-2
Mansfield Town v Carlisle United	0-1
Peterborough United v Middlesbrough	1-1, 2-0
West Ham United v Queen's Park Rangers	2-1
Derby County v Leeds United	0-1

SIXTH ROUND

Arsenal v West Ham United	0-2
Birmingham City v Middlesbrough	1-0
Carlisle United v Fulham	0-1
Ipswich Town v Leeds United	0-0, 1-1, 0-0, 3-2

SEMI-FINAL

Fulham v Birmingham City	1-1, 1-0
West Ham United v Ipswich Town	0-0, 2-1

FINAL

Fulham v West Ham United	0-2

SCOTTISH FA CUP 1974-75

THIRD ROUND

Aberdeen v Rangers	1-1, 2-1
Arbroath v East Stirling	1-0
Ayr United v Queen's Park	1-2
Clyde v Dundee	0-1
Hibernian v Celtic	0-2
Inverness Caledonian v Albion Rovers	0-1
Motherwell v Partick Thistle	0-0, 1-0
Queen of the South v Raith Rovers	2-0
Montrose v Hamilton Academicals	0-0, 0-3
Airdrieonians v Morton	0-0, 3-0
Clydebank v Dunfermline Athletic	2-1
Dumbarton v Inverness Clachnacuddin	2-1
Heart of Midlothian v Kilmarnock	2-0
St. Johnstone v East Fife	1-0
Ross County v Falkirk	1-5
Dundee United v Berwick Rangers	1-1, 1-0

FOURTH ROUND

Airdrieonians v Falkirk	2-0
Arbroath v Albion Rovers	2-0
Celtic v Clydebank	4-1
Hamilton Academicals v Dumbarton	0-1
Motherwell v Queen's Park	4-0
Queen of the South v Heart of Midlothian	0-2
St. Johnstone v Dundee	0-1
Dundee United v Aberdeen	0-1

FIFTH ROUND

Aberdeen v Motherwell	0-1
Arbroath v Airdrieonians	2-2, 0-3
Dumbarton v Celtic	1-2
Heart of Midlothian v Dundee	1-1, 2-3

SEMI-FINAL

Celtic v Dundee	1-0
Airdrieonians v Motherwell	1-1, 1-0

FINAL

Airdrieonians v Celtic	1-3

249

FIRST DIVISION

		P	W	D	L	F	A	Pts
1	Liverpool	42	23	14	5	66	31	60
2	QPR	42	24	11	7	67	33	59
3	Man United	42	23	10	10	68	42	56
4	Derby	42	21	11	10	75	58	53
5	Leeds	42	21	9	12	65	46	51
6	Ipswich	42	16	14	12	54	48	46
7	Leicester	42	13	19	10	48	51	45
8	Man City	42	16	12	15	64	46	43
9	Tottenham	42	14	15	13	63	63	43
10	Norwich	42	16	10	16	58	58	42
11	Everton	42	15	12	15	60	66	42
12	Stoke	42	15	11	16	48	50	41
13	Middlesbrough	42	15	10	17	46	45	40
14	Coventry	42	13	14	15	47	57	40
15	Newcastle	42	15	9	18	71	62	39
16	Aston Villa	42	11	17	14	51	59	39
17	Arsenal	42	13	10	19	47	53	36
18	West Ham	42	13	10	19	48	71	36
19	Birmingham	42	13	7	22	57	75	33
20	Wolverhampton	42	10	10	22	51	68	30
21	Burnley	42	9	10	23	43	66	28
22	Sheff United	42	6	10	26	33	82	22

SECOND DIVISION

		P	W	D	L	F	A	Pts
1	Sunderland	42	24	8	10	67	36	56
2	Bristol City	42	19	15	8	59	35	53
3	WBA	42	20	13	9	50	33	53
4	Bolton	42	20	12	10	64	38	52
5	Notts County	42	19	11	12	60	41	49
6	Southampton	42	21	7	14	66	50	49
7	Luton	42	19	10	13	61	51	48
8	Nottm Forest	42	17	12	13	55	40	46
9	Charlton	42	15	12	15	61	72	42
10	Blackpool	42	14	14	14	40	49	42
11	Chelsea	42	12	16	14	53	54	40
12	Fulham	42	13	14	15	45	47	40
13	Orient	42	13	14	15	37	39	40
14	Hull	42	14	11	17	45	49	39
15	Blackburn	42	12	14	16	45	50	38
16	Plymouth	42	13	12	17	48	54	38
17	Oldham	42	13	12	17	57	68	38
18	Bristol Rovers	42	11	16	15	38	50	38
19	Carlisle	42	12	13	17	45	59	37
20	Oxford	42	11	11	20	39	59	33
21	York	42	10	8	24	39	71	28
22	Portsmouth	42	9	7	26	32	61	25

FA CUP 1975-76

FOURTH ROUND

Bradford City v Tooting & Mitcham United	3-1
Charlton Athletic v Portsmouth	1-1, 3-0
Coventry City v Newcastle United	1-1, 0-5
Derby County v Liverpool	1-0
Huddersfield Town v Bolton Wanderers	0-1
Ipswich Town v Wolverhampton Wanderers	0-0, 0-1
Leeds United v Crystal Palace	0-1
Leicester City v Bury	1-0
Manchester United v Peterborough United	3-1
Norwich City v Luton Town	2-0
Southampton v Blackpool	3-1
Southend United v Cardiff City	2-1
Stoke City v Manchester City	1-0
Sunderland v Hull City	1-0
West Bromwich Albion v Lincoln City	3-2
York City v Chelsea	0-2

FIFTH ROUND

Bolton Wanderers v Newcastle United	3-3, 0-0, 1-2
Chelsea v Crystal Palace	2-3
Derby County v Southend United	1-0
Leicester City v Manchester United	1-2
Norwich City v Bradford City	1-2
Stoke City v Sunderland	0-0, 1-2
West Bromwich Albion v Southampton	1-1, 0-4
Wolverhampton Wanderers v Charlton Athletic	3-0

SIXTH ROUND

Bradford City v Southampton	0-1
Derby County v Newcastle United	4-2
Manchester Utd v Wolverhampton Wanderers	1-1, 3-2
Sunderland v Crystal Palace	0-1

SEMI-FINAL

Manchester United v Derby County	2-0
Southampton v Crystal Palace	2-0

FINAL

Southampton v Manchester United	1-0

THIRD DIVISION

		P	W	D	L	F	A	Pts
1	Hereford	46	26	11	9	86	55	63
2	Cardiff	46	22	13	11	69	48	57
3	Millwall	46	20	16	10	54	43	56
4	Brighton	46	22	9	15	78	53	53
5	Crystal Palace	46	18	17	11	61	46	53
6	Wrexham	46	20	12	14	66	55	52
7	Walsall	46	18	14	14	74	61	50
8	Preston	46	19	10	17	62	57	48
9	Shrewsbury	46	19	10	17	61	59	48
10	Peterborough	46	15	18	13	63	63	48
11	Mansfield	46	16	15	15	58	52	47
12	Port Vale	46	15	16	15	55	54	46
13	Bury	46	14	16	16	51	46	44
14	Chesterfield	46	17	9	20	69	69	43
15	Gillingham	46	12	19	15	58	68	43
16	Rotherham	46	15	12	19	54	65	42
17	Chester	46	15	12	19	53	62	42
18	Grimsby	46	15	10	21	62	74	40
19	Swindon	46	16	8	22	62	75	40
20	Sheff Wed	46	12	16	18	48	59	40
21	Aldershot	46	13	13	20	59	75	39
22	Colchester	46	12	14	20	41	65	38
23	Southend	46	12	13	21	65	75	37
24	Halifax	46	11	13	22	41	61	35

SCOTTISH PREMIER DIVISION

		P	W	D	L	F	A	Pts
1	Rangers	36	23	8	5	59	24	54
2	Celtic	36	21	6	9	71	42	48
3	Hibernian	36	20	7	9	58	40	43
4	Motherwell	36	16	8	12	57	49	40
5	Hearts	36	13	9	14	39	44	35
6	Ayr	36	14	5	17	46	59	33
7	Aberdeen	36	11	10	15	49	50	32
8	Dundee United	36	12	8	16	46	48	32
9	Dundee	36	11	10	15	49	62	32
10	St Johnstone	36	3	5	28	29	79	11

SCOTTISH FA CUP 1975-76

THIRD ROUND

Albion Rovers v Partick Thistle	1-2
Alloa Athletic v Aberdeen	0-4
Ayr United v Airdrieonians	4-2
Cowdenbeath v St Mirren	3-0
Dumbarton v Keith	2-0
Dundee v Falkirk	1-2
Dundee United v Hamilton Academicals	4-0
Heart of Midlothian v Clyde	2-2, 1-0
Hibernian v Dunfermline Athletic	3-2
Motherwell v Celtic	3-2
Morton v Montrose	1-3
Queen of the South v St Johnstone	3-2
Raith Rovers v Arbroath	1-0
Rangers v East Fife	3-0
Stenhousemuir v Kilmarnock	1-1, 0-1
Stirling Albion v Forfar Athletic	2-1

FOURTH ROUND

Ayr United v Queen of the South	2-2, 4-5
Cowdenbeath v Motherwell	0-2
Heart of Midlothian v Stirling Albion	3-0
Hibernian v Dundee United	1-1, 2-0
Kilmarnock v Falkirk	3-1
Montrose v Raith Rovers	2-1
Partick Thistle v Dumbarton	0-0, 0-1
Rangers v Aberdeen	4-1

FIFTH ROUND

Dumbarton v Kilmarnock	2-1
Montrose v Heart of Midlothian	2-2, 2-2, 1-2
Motherwell v Hibernian	2-2, 1-1, 2-1
Queen of the South v Rangers	0-3

SEMI-FINAL

Motherwell v Rangers	2-3
Dumbarton v Heart of Midlothian	0-0, 0-3

FINAL

Heart of Midlothian v Rangers	1-3

SCOTTISH FIRST DIVISION

		P	W	D	L	F	A	Pts
1	Partick Thistle	26	17	7	2	47	19	40
2	Kilmarnock	26	16	3	7	44	29	40
3	Montrose	26	12	6	8	53	43	35
4	Dumbarton	26	12	4	10	53	46	29
5	Arbroath	26	11	4	11	41	39	29
6	St Mirren	26	9	8	9	37	37	25
7	Airdrieonians	26	7	11	8	44	41	25
8	Falkirk	26	10	5	11	38	35	24
9	Hamilton	26	7	10	9	37	37	24
10	Queen of the S	26	9	6	11	41	47	23
11	Morton	26	7	9	14	31	40	19
12	East Fife	26	8	7	11	39	53	18
13	Dunfermline	26	5	10	11	30	51	17
14	Clyde	26	5	4	17	34	52	16

FOURTH DIVISION

		P	W	D	L	F	A	Pts
1	Lincoln	46	32	10	4	111	39	74
2	Northampton	46	29	10	7	87	40	68
3	Reading	46	24	12	10	70	51	60
4	Tranmere	46	24	10	12	89	55	58
5	Huddersfield	46	21	14	11	55	41	56
6	Bournemouth	46	20	12	14	57	48	52
7	Exeter	46	18	14	14	56	47	50
8	Watford	46	22	6	18	62	62	50
9	Torquay	46	18	14	14	55	63	50
10	Doncaster	46	19	11	16	75	69	49
11	Swansea	46	16	15	15	66	57	47
12	Barnsley	46	14	16	16	52	48	44
13	Cambridge	46	14	15	17	58	62	43
14	Hartlepool	46	16	10	20	62	78	42
15	Rochdale	46	12	18	16	40	54	42
16	Crewe	46	13	15	18	58	57	41
17	Bradford	46	12	17	17	63	65	41
18	Brentford	46	14	13	19	56	60	41
19	Scunthorpe	46	14	10	22	50	59	38
20	Darlington	46	14	10	22	48	57	38
21	Stockport	46	13	12	21	43	76	38
22	Newport	46	13	9	24	57	90	35
23	Southport	46	8	10	28	41	77	26
24	Workington	46	7	7	32	30	87	27

SCOTTISH SECOND DIVISION

		P	W	D	L	F	A	Pts
1	Clydebank	26	17	6	3	44	13	40
2	Raith	26	15	10	1	45	22	40
3	Alloa	26	14	7	5	44	28	35
4	Queen's Park	26	10	9	7	41	33	29
5	Cowdenbeath	26	11	7	8	44	43	29
6	Stirling Albion	26	9	7	10	39	32	25
7	Stranraer	26	11	3	12	49	43	25
8	East Stirling	26	8	8	10	33	33	24
9	Albion	26	7	10	9	35	38	24
10	Stenhousemuir	26	9	5	12	39	44	23
11	Berwick	26	7	5	14	32	44	19
12	Forfar	26	4	10	12	28	48	18
13	Brechin	26	6	5	15	28	51	17
14	Meadowbank T	26	5	6	15	24	53	16

FIRST DIVISION

		P	W	D	L	F	A	Pts
1	Liverpool	42	23	11	8	62	33	57
2	Man City	42	21	14	7	60	34	56
3	Ipswich	42	22	8	12	66	39	56
4	Aston Villa	42	22	7	13	76	50	51
5	Newcastle	42	18	13	11	64	49	49
6	Man United	42	18	11	13	71	62	47
7	WBA	42	16	13	13	62	56	45
8	Arsenal	42	16	11	15	64	59	43
9	Everton	42	14	14	14	62	64	42
10	Leeds	42	15	12	15	48	51	42
11	Leicester	42	12	18	12	47	60	42
12	Middlesbrough	42	14	13	15	40	45	41
13	Birmingham	42	13	12	17	63	61	38
14	QPR	42	13	12	17	47	52	38
15	Derby	42	9	19	14	50	55	37
16	Norwich	42	14	9	19	47	64	37
17	West Ham	42	11	14	17	46	65	36
18	Bristol City	42	11	13	18	38	48	35
19	Coventry	42	10	15	14	48	59	35
20	Sunderland	42	11	12	19	46	54	34
21	Stoke	42	10	14	18	28	51	34
22	Tottenham	42	12	9	21	48	72	33

SECOND DIVISION

		P	W	D	L	F	A	Pts
1	Wolves	42	22	13	7	84	45	57
2	Chelsea	42	21	13	8	73	53	55
3	Nottm Forest	42	21	10	11	77	43	52
4	Bolton	42	20	11	11	74	54	51
5	Blackpool	42	17	17	8	58	42	51
6	Luton	42	23	6	15	67	48	48
7	Charlton	42	16	16	10	71	58	48
8	Notts County	42	19	10	13	65	60	48
9	Southampton	42	17	10	15	72	67	44
10	Millwall	42	17	13	14	57	53	43
11	Sheff United	42	14	12	16	54	63	40
12	Blackburn	42	15	9	18	42	54	39
13	Oldham	42	14	10	18	52	64	38
14	Hull	42	10	17	15	45	53	37
15	Bristol Rovers	42	12	13	17	53	68	37
16	Burnley	42	11	14	17	46	64	36
17	Fulham	42	11	13	18	44	61	35
18	Cardiff	42	12	10	20	56	67	34
19	Orient	42	9	16	17	37	55	34
20	Carlisle	42	11	12	19	49	75	34
21	Plymouth	42	8	16	18	46	65	32
22	Hereford	42	8	15	19	57	78	31

THIRD DIVISION

		P	W	D	L	F	A	Pts
1	Mansfield	46	28	8	10	78	33	64
2	Brighton	46	25	11	10	83	39	61
3	Crystal Palace	46	23	13	10	68	40	59
4	Rotherham	46	22	15	9	69	44	59
5	Wrexham	46	24	10	12	80	54	58
6	Preston	46	21	12	13	64	43	54
7	Bury	46	23	8	15	64	59	54
8	Sheff Wed	46	22	9	15	65	55	53
9	Lincoln	46	25	14	13	77	70	52
10	Shrewsbury	46	18	11	17	65	59	47
11	Swindon	46	15	15	16	68	75	45
12	Gillingham	46	14	12	18	55	64	44
13	Chester	46	18	8	20	48	58	44
14	Tranmere	46	13	17	16	51	53	43
15	Walsall	46	13	15	18	57	65	41
16	Peterborough	46	13	15	18	55	65	41
17	Oxford	46	12	15	19	55	65	39
18	Chesterfield	46	14	10	22	56	64	38
19	Port Vale	46	11	16	19	47	71	38
20	Portsmouth	46	11	14	21	43	70	35
21	Reading	46	13	9	24	49	73	35
22	Northampton	46	13	8	25	60	75	34
23	Grimsby	46	12	9	25	45	69	33
24	York	46	10	12	24	50	89	32

FOURTH DIVISION

		P	W	D	L	F	A	Pts
1	Cambridge	46	26	13	7	87	40	65
2	Exeter	46	25	12	9	70	46	62
3	Colchester	46	25	9	12	77	43	59
4	Bradford	46	23	13	10	71	51	59
5	Swansea	46	25	8	13	82	68	58
6	Barnsley	46	23	9	14	62	39	55
7	Watford	46	18	15	13	67	55	51
8	Doncaster	46	21	9	16	61	65	51
9	Huddersfield	46	19	12	15	60	49	50
10	Southend	46	15	19	12	52	45	49
11	Darlington	46	18	13	15	59	64	49
12	Crewe	46	19	11	16	47	60	49
13	Bournemouth	46	15	18	13	55	44	48
14	Stockport	46	13	19	14	53	57	45
15	Brentford	46	18	7	21	77	76	43
16	Torquay	46	17	9	20	59	67	43
17	Aldershot	46	16	11	19	45	59	43
18	Rochdale	46	13	12	21	50	59	38
19	Newport	46	14	10	22	42	58	38
20	Scunthorpe	46	13	11	22	49	73	37
21	Halifax	46	11	14	21	47	58	36
22	Hartlepool	46	10	12	24	47	73	32
23	Southport	46	3	19	24	53	77	25
24	Workington	46	4	11	31	41	102	19

SCOTTISH PREMIER DIVISION

		P	W	D	L	F	A	Pts
1	Celtic	36	23	9	4	79	39	55
2	Rangers	36	18	10	8	62	37	46
3	Aberdeen	36	16	11	9	56	42	43
4	Dundee United	36	16	9	11	54	45	41
5	Partick Thistle	36	11	13	12	40	44	35
6	Hibernian	36	8	18	10	34	35	34
7	Motherwell	36	10	11	14	57	50	32
8	Ayr	36	11	8	17	44	68	30
9	Hearts	36	7	13	16	49	66	27
10	Kilmarnock	36	4	9	23	32	71	17

SCOTTISH FIRST DIVISION

		P	W	D	L	F	A	Pts
1	St Mirren	39	25	12	2	91	38	62
2	Clydebank	39	24	10	5	89	38	58
3	Dundee	39	21	9	9	90	55	51
4	Morton	39	20	10	9	77	52	50
5	Montrose	39	16	9	14	61	62	41
6	Airdrieonians	39	13	12	14	63	58	38
7	Dumbarton	39	14	9	16	63	68	37
8	Arbroath	39	17	3	19	46	62	37
9	Queen of the S	39	11	13	15	58	65	35
10	Hamilton	39	11	14	18	44	55	32
11	St Johnstone	39	8	13	18	44	64	29
12	East Fife	39	8	13	18	40	71	29
13	Raith	39	8	11	20	45	68	27
14	Falkirk	39	6	8	25	36	85	20

SCOTTISH SECOND DIVISION

		P	W	D	L	F	A	Pts
1	Stirling	39	22	11	6	59	29	55
2	Alloa	39	19	13	7	73	45	51
3	Dunfermline	39	20	10	11	52	36	50
4	Stranraer	39	20	6	13	74	53	46
5	Queens Park	39	17	11	11	65	51	45
6	Albion	39	15	12	12	74	60	42
7	Clyde	39	15	11	13	68	65	41
8	Berwick	39	13	10	16	37	51	36
9	Stenhousemuir	39	15	5	19	38	49	35
10	E Stirlingshire	39	12	8	19	47	63	32
11	Meadowbank	39	8	16	15	41	57	32
12	Cowdenbeath	39	13	5	21	45	64	31
13	Brechin	39	7	12	20	57	77	26
14	Forfar	39	7	10	22	43	68	24

FA CUP 1976-77

FOURTH ROUND

Arsenal v Coventry	3-1
Aston Villa v West Ham	3-0
Birmingham v Leeds	1-2
Blackburn v Orient	3-0
Cardiff v Wrexham	3-2
Chester v Luton	1-0
Colchester v Derby	1-1, 0-1
Ipswich v Wolverhampton Wanderers	2-2, 0-1
Liverpool v Carlisle	3-0
Manchester United v Queen's Park Rangers	1-0
Middlesbrough v Hereford	4-0
Northwich Victoria v Oldham	1-3*
Port Vale v Burnley	2-1
Swindon v Everton	2-2, 1-2
Nottingham Forest v Southampton	3-3, 1-2
Newcastle v Manchester City	1-3

FIFTH ROUND

Aston Villa v Port Vale	3-0
Cardiff v Everton	1-2
Derby v Blackburn	3-1
Leeds v Manchester City	1-0
Liverpool v Oldham	3-1
Middlesbrough v Arsenal	4-1
Southampton v Manchester United	2-2, 1-2
Wolverhampton Wanderers v Chester	1-0

SIXTH ROUND

Everton v Derby	2-0
Liverpool v Middlesbrough	2-0
Manchester United v Aston Villa	2-1
Wolverhampton Wanderers v Leeds	0-1

SEMI-FINALS

Everton v Liverpool	2-2, 0-3
(both games at Maine Rd)	
Leeds v Manchester United	1-2
(at Hillsborough)	

FINAL

Liverpool v Manchester United	1-2

*played at Maine Rd.

SCOTTISH FA CUP 1976-77

THIRD ROUND

Airdrie v Celtic	1-1, 0-5
Arbroath v Brechin	1-0
Dunfermline v Aberdeen	0-1
East Fife v Clyde	2-1
East Stirling v Albion	0-3
Heart of Midlothian v Dumbarton	1-1, 1-0
Morton v Ayr United	0-1
Motherwell v Kilmarnock	3-0
Queen's Park v Alloa	0-0, 0-1
Queen of the South v Montrose	3-2
Rangers v Falkirk	3-1
St Mirren v Dundee	4-1
Stirling Albion v Elgin City	1-1, 2-3
St Johnstone v Dundee	1-1, 2-4
Hamilton v Clydebank	0-0, 0-3
Hibernian v Partick Thistle	3-0

FOURTH ROUND

Arbroath v Hibernian	1-1, 2-1
Dundee v Aberdeen	0-0, 2-1
East Fife v Albion	2-1
Heart of Midlothian v Clydebank	1-0
Motherwell v St Mirren	2-1
Queen of the South v Alloa	2-1
Rangers v Elgin City	3-0
Celtic v Ayr United	1-1, 3-1

FIFTH ROUND

Celtic v Queen of the South	5-1
Heart of Midlothian v East Fife	0-0, 3-1
Rangers v Motherwell	2-0
Arbroath v Dundee	1-3

SEMI-FINALS

Celtic v Dundee	2-0
Rangers v Heart of Midlothian	2-0

FINAL

Celtic v Rangers	1-0

FIRST DIVISION

		P	W	D	L	F	A	Pts
1	Nottm Forest	42	25	14	3	69	24	64
2	Liverpool	42	24	9	9	65	34	57
3	Everton	42	22	11	9	76	45	55
4	Man City	42	20	12	10	74	51	52
5	Arsenal	42	21	10	11	60	37	52
6	WBA	42	18	14	10	62	53	50
7	Coventry	42	18	12	12	75	62	48
8	Aston Villa	42	18	10	14	57	42	46
9	Leeds	42	18	10	14	63	53	46
10	Man United	42	16	10	16	67	63	42
11	Birmingham	42	16	9	17	55	60	41
12	Derby	42	14	13	15	54	59	41
13	Norwich	42	11	18	13	52	66	40
14	Middlesbrough	42	12	15	15	42	54	39
15	Wolves	42	12	12	18	51	64	36
16	Chelsea	42	11	14	17	46	69	36
17	Bristol City	42	11	13	18	49	53	35
18	Ipswich	42	11	13	18	47	61	35
19	QPR	42	9	15	18	47	64	33
20	West Ham	42	12	8	22	52	69	32
21	Newcastle	42	6	10	26	42	78	22
22	Leicester	42	5	12	25	26	70	22

SECOND DIVISION

		P	W	D	L	F	A	Pts
1	Bolton	42	24	10	8	63	33	58
2	Southampton	42	22	13	7	70	39	57
3	Tottenham	42	20	16	6	83	49	56
4	Brighton	42	22	12	8	63	38	56
5	Blackburn	42	16	13	13	56	60	45
6	Sunderland	42	14	16	12	67	59	44
7	Stoke	42	16	10	16	53	49	42
8	Oldham	42	13	16	13	54	58	42
9	Crystal Palace	42	13	15	14	50	47	41
10	Fulham	42	14	13	15	49	49	41
11	Burnley	42	15	10	17	56	64	40
12	Sheff United	42	16	8	18	62	73	40
13	Luton	42	14	10	18	54	52	38
14	Orient	42	10	18	14	43	49	38
15	Notts County	42	11	16	15	54	62	38
16	Millwall	42	12	14	16	49	57	38
17	Charlton	42	13	12	17	55	68	38
18	Bristol Rovers	42	13	12	17	61	77	38
19	Cardiff	42	13	12	17	51	71	38
20	Blackpool	42	12	13	17	59	60	37
21	Mansfield	42	10	11	21	49	69	31
22	Hull	42	8	12	22	34	52	28

THIRD DIVISION

		P	W	D	L	F	A	Pts
1	Wrexham	46	23	15	8	78	45	61
2	Cambridge	46	23	12	11	72	51	58
3	Preston	46	20	16	10	63	38	56
4	Peterborough	46	20	16	10	47	33	56
5	Chester	46	16	22	8	59	56	54
6	Walsall	46	18	17	11	61	50	53
7	Gillingham	46	15	20	11	67	60	50
8	Colchester	46	15	18	13	55	44	48
9	Chesterfield	46	17	14	15	58	49	48
10	Swindon	46	16	16	14	67	60	48
11	Shrewsbury	46	16	15	15	63	57	47
12	Tranmere	46	16	15	15	57	52	47
13	Carlisle	46	14	19	13	59	59	47
14	Sheff Wed	46	15	16	15	50	52	46
15	Bury	46	13	19	14	62	56	45
16	Lincoln	46	15	15	16	53	61	45
17	Exeter	46	15	14	17	49	59	44
18	Oxford	46	13	14	19	64	67	40
19	Plymouth	46	11	17	18	61	68	39
20	Rotherham	46	13	13	20	51	68	39
21	Port Vale	46	8	20	18	46	67	36
22	Bradford	46	12	10	24	56	86	34
23	Hereford	46	9	14	23	34	60	32
24	Portsmouth	46	7	17	22	31	75	31

FOURTH DIVISION

		P	W	D	L	F	A	Pts
1	Watford	46	30	11	5	85	38	71
2	Southend	46	25	10	11	66	39	60
3	Swansea	46	23	10	13	87	47	56
4	Brentford	46	21	14	11	86	54	56
5	Aldershot	46	19	16	11	67	47	54
6	Grimsby	46	21	11	14	57	51	53
7	Barnsley	46	18	14	14	61	49	50
8	Reading	46	18	14	14	55	52	50
9	Torquay	46	16	15	15	57	56	47
10	Northampton	46	17	13	16	63	68	47
11	Huddersfield	46	15	15	16	63	55	45
12	Doncaster	46	14	17	15	52	65	45
13	Wimbledon	46	14	16	16	66	67	44
14	Scunthorpe	46	14	16	16	50	55	44
15	Crewe	46	15	14	17	50	69	44
16	Newport	46	16	11	19	65	73	43
17	Bournemouth	46	14	15	17	41	51	43
18	Stockport	46	16	10	20	56	56	42
19	Darlington	46	14	13	19	52	59	41
20	Halifax	46	10	21	15	52	62	41
21	Hartlepool	46	15	7	24	51	84	37
22	York	46	12	12	22	50	69	36
23	Southport	46	6	19	21	52	76	31
24	Rochdale	46	8	8	30	43	85	24

SCOTTISH PREMIER DIVISION

		P	W	D	L	F	A	Pts
1	Rangers	36	24	7	5	76	39	55
2	Aberdeen	36	22	9	5	68	29	53
3	Dundee United	36	16	8	12	42	32	40
4	Hibernian	36	15	7	14	51	43	37
5	Celtic	36	15	6	15	63	54	36
6	Motherwell	36	13	7	16	45	52	33
7	Partick	36	14	5	17	52	64	33
8	St Mirren	36	11	8	17	52	63	30
9	Ayr	36	9	6	21	36	68	24
10	Clydebank	36	6	7	23	23	64	19

SCOTTISH FIRST DIVISION

		P	W	D	L	F	A	Pts
1	Morton	39	25	8	6	85	42	58
2	Hearts	39	24	10	5	77	42	58
3	Dundee	39	25	7	7	91	44	57
4	Dumbarton	39	16	17	6	65	48	49
5	Stirling	39	15	12	12	60	52	42
6	Kilmarnock	39	14	12	13	52	46	40
7	Hamilton	39	12	12	15	54	56	36
8	St Johnstone	39	15	6	18	52	64	36
9	Arbroath	39	11	13	15	42	55	35
10	Airdrieonians	39	12	10	17	50	64	34
11	Montrose	39	10	9	20	55	71	29
12	Queen of the S	39	8	13	18	44	68	29
13	Alloa	39	8	8	23	44	84	24
14	East Fife	39	4	11	24	39	74	19

SCOTTISH SECOND DIVISION

		P	W	D	L	F	A	Pts
1	Clyde	39	21	11	7	71	32	53
2	Raith	39	19	15	5	63	38	53
3	Dunfermline	39	18	12	9	64	41	48
4	Berwick	39	16	16	7	68	51	48
5	Falkirk	39	15	14	10	51	46	44
6	Forfar	39	17	8	14	61	55	42
7	Queen's Park	39	13	15	11	52	51	41
8	Albion	39	16	8	15	68	68	40
9	East Stirling	39	15	8	16	55	65	38
10	Cowdenbeath	39	13	8	18	75	78	34
11	Stranraer	39	13	7	19	54	59	33
12	Stenhousemuir	39	10	10	19	43	67	30
13	Meadowbank	39	6	10	23	43	89	22
14	Brechin	39	7	6	26	45	73	20

FA CUP 1977-78

FOURTH ROUND

Arsenal v Wolverhampton Wanderers	2-1
Bolton Wanderers v Mansfield Town	1-0
Brighton & Hove Albion v Notts County	1-2
Bristol Rovers v Southampton	2-0
Chelsea v Burnley	6-2
Derby County v Birmingham City	2-1
Ipswich v Hartlepool	4-1
Manchester United v West Bromwich Albion	1-1, 2-3
Middlesbrough v Everton	3-2
Millwall v Luton Town	4-0
Newcastle United v Wrexham	2-2, 1-4
Nottingham Forest v Manchester City	2-1
Orient v Blackburn Rovers	3-1
Stoke City v Blyth Spartans	2-3
Walsall v Leicester City	1-0
West Ham United v Queen's Park Rangers	1-1, 1-6

FIFTH ROUND

Arsenal v Walsall	4-1
Bristol Rovers v Ipswich	2-2, 0-3
Derby County v West Bromwich Albion	2-3
Orient v Chelsea	0-0, 2-1
Middlesbrough v Bolton Wanderers	2-0
Millwall v Notts County	2-1
Queen's Park Rangers v Nottingham Forest	1-1, 1-3
Wrexham v Blyth Spartans	1-1, 2-1

SIXTH ROUND

Middlesbrough v Orient	0-0, 1-2
Millwall v Ipswich	1-6
West Bromwich Albion v Nottingham Forest	2-0
Wrexham v Arsenal	2-3

SEMI-FINALS

Arsenal v Orient	3-0
Ipswich v West Bromwich Albion	3-1

FINAL

Arsenal v Ipswich	0-1

SCOTTISH FA CUP 1977-78

THIRD ROUND

Aberdeen v Ayr United	2-0
Albion Rovers v Morton	0-1
Airdrieonians v Heart of Midlothian	2-3
Arbroath v Motherwell	0-4
Berwick Rangers v Rangers	2-4
Celtic v Dundee	2-1
Dumbarton v Alloa Athletic	2-1
Hamilton Academicals v Dundee United	1-4
Hibernian v East Fife	4-0
Meadowbank v Inverness Caledonia	2-1
Partick Thistle v Cowdenbeath	1-1, 1-0
Queen of the South v Montrose	2-2, 3-1
St Johnstone v Brechin City	1-0
St Mirren v Kilmarnock	1-2
Stirling Albion v Clydebank	0-0 (abandoned), 3-0
Vale of Leithen v Queen's Park	0-1

FOURTH ROUND

Aberdeen v St Johnstone	3-0
Celtic v Kilmarnock	1-1, 0-1
Dumbarton v Heart of Midlothian	1-0
Dundee United v Queen of the South	3-0
Morton v Meadowbank	3-0
Motherwell v Queen's Park	1-3
Rangers v Stirling Albion	1-0
Hibernian v Partick Thistle	0-0, 1-2

FIFTH ROUND

Aberdeen v Morton	2-2, 2-1
Dundee United v Queen's Park	2-0
Partick Thistle v Dumbarton	2-1
Rangers v Kilmarnock	4-1

SEMI-FINALS

Aberdeen v Partick Thistle	4-2
Rangers v Dundee United	2-0

FINAL

Rangers v Aberdeen	2-1

FIRST DIVISION

		P	W	D	L	F	A	Pts
1	Liverpool	42	30	8	4	85	16	68
2	Nottm Forest	42	21	18	3	61	26	60
3	WBA	42	24	11	7	72	35	59
4	Everton	42	17	17	8	52	40	51
5	Leeds	42	18	14	10	70	52	50
6	Ipswich	42	20	9	13	63	49	49
7	Arsenal	42	17	14	11	61	48	48
8	Aston Villa	42	15	16	11	59	49	46
9	Man United	42	15	15	12	60	63	45
10	Coventry	42	14	16	12	58	68	44
11	Tottenham	42	13	15	14	48	61	41
12	Middlesbrough	42	15	10	17	57	50	40
13	Bristol City	42	15	10	17	47	51	40
14	Southampton	42	12	16	14	47	53	40
15	Man City	42	13	13	16	58	56	39
16	Norwich	42	7	23	12	51	57	37
17	Bolton	42	12	11	19	54	75	35
18	Wolves	42	13	8	21	44	68	34
19	Derby	42	10	11	21	44	71	31
20	QPR	42	6	13	23	45	73	25
21	Birmingham	42	6	10	26	37	64	22
22	Chelsea	42	5	10	27	44	92	20

SECOND DIVISION

		P	W	D	L	F	A	Pts
1	Crystal Palace	42	19	19	4	51	24	57
2	Brighton	42	23	10	9	72	39	56
3	Stoke	42	20	16	6	58	31	56
4	Sunderland	42	22	11	9	70	44	55
5	West Ham	42	18	14	10	70	39	50
6	Notts County	42	14	16	12	48	60	44
7	Preston	42	12	18	12	59	57	42
8	Newcastle	42	17	8	17	51	55	42
9	Cardiff	42	16	10	16	56	70	42
10	Fulham	42	13	15	14	50	47	41
11	Orient	42	15	10	17	51	51	40
12	Cambridge	42	12	16	14	44	52	40
13	Burnley	42	14	12	16	51	62	40
14	Oldham	42	13	13	16	52	61	39
15	Wrexham	42	12	14	16	45	42	38
16	Bristol Rovers	42	14	10	18	48	60	38
17	Leicester	42	10	17	15	43	52	37
18	Luton	42	13	10	19	60	57	36
19	Charlton	42	11	13	18	60	69	35
20	Sheff United	42	11	12	19	52	69	34
21	Millwall	42	11	10	21	42	61	32
22	Blackburn	42	10	10	22	41	72	30

THIRD DIVISION

		P	W	D	L	F	A	Pts
1	Shrewsbury	46	21	19	6	61	41	61
2	Watford	46	24	12	10	83	52	60
3	Swansea	46	24	12	10	83	61	60
4	Gillingham	46	21	17	8	65	42	59
5	Swindon	46	25	7	14	74	52	57
6	Carlisle	46	15	22	9	53	42	52
7	Colchester	46	17	17	12	60	55	51
8	Hull	46	19	11	16	66	61	49
9	Exeter	46	17	15	14	61	56	49
10	Brentford	46	19	9	18	53	49	47
11	Oxford	46	14	18	14	44	50	46
12	Blackpool	46	18	9	19	61	59	45
13	Southend	46	15	15	16	51	49	45
14	Sheff Wed	46	13	19	14	53	53	45
15	Plymouth	46	15	14	17	67	68	44
16	Chester	46	14	16	16	57	61	44
17	Rotherham	46	17	10	19	49	55	44
18	Mansfield	46	12	19	15	51	52	43
19	Bury	46	11	20	15	59	65	42
20	Chesterfield	46	13	14	19	51	65	40
21	Peterborough	46	11	14	21	44	63	36
22	Walsall	46	10	12	24	56	71	32
23	Tranmere	46	6	16	24	45	78	28
24	Lincoln	46	7	11	28	41	88	25

FOURTH DIVISION

		P	W	D	L	F	A	Pts
1	Reading	46	26	13	7	76	35	65
2	Grimsby	46	26	9	11	82	49	61
3	Wimbledon	46	25	11	10	78	46	61
4	Barnsley	46	24	13	9	73	42	61
5	Aldershot	46	20	17	9	63	47	57
6	Wigan	46	21	13	12	63	48	55
7	Portsmouth	46	20	12	14	62	48	52
8	Newport	46	21	10	15	66	55	52
9	Huddersfield	46	18	11	17	57	53	47
10	York	46	18	11	17	51	55	47
11	Torquay	46	19	8	19	58	65	46
12	Scunthorpe	46	17	11	18	54	60	45
13	Hartlepool	46	13	18	15	57	66	44
14	Hereford	46	15	13	18	53	53	43
15	Bradford C.	46	17	9	20	62	68	43
16	Port Vale	46	14	14	18	57	70	42
17	Stockport	46	14	12	20	58	60	40
18	Bournemouth	46	14	11	21	47	48	39
19	Northampton	46	15	9	22	64	76	39
20	Rochdale	46	15	9	22	47	64	39
21	Darlington	46	11	15	20	49	66	37
22	Doncaster	46	13	11	22	50	73	37
23	Halifax	46	9	8	29	39	72	26
24	Crewe	46	6	14	26	43	90	26

SCOTTISH PREMIER DIVISION

		P	W	D	L	F	A	Pts
1	Celtic	36	21	6	9	61	37	48
2	Rangers	36	18	9	9	52	35	45
3	Dundee United	36	18	8	10	56	37	44
4	Aberdeen	36	13	14	9	59	36	40
5	Hibernian	36	12	13	11	44	48	37
6	St Mirren	36	15	6	15	45	41	36
7	Morton	36	12	12	12	52	53	36
8	Partick	36	13	8	15	42	39	34
9	Hearts	36	8	7	21	49	71	23
10	Motherwell	36	5	7	24	33	86	17

SCOTTISH FIRST DIVISION

		P	W	D	L	F	A	Pts
1	Dundee	39	24	7	8	68	36	55
2	Kilmarnock	39	22	10	7	72	35	54
3	Clydebank	39	24	6	9	78	50	54
4	Ayr	39	21	5	13	71	52	47
5	Hamilton	39	17	9	13	62	60	43
6	Airdrieonians	39	16	8	15	72	61	40
7	Dumbarton	39	14	11	14	58	49	39
8	Stirling A.	39	13	9	17	43	55	35
9	Clyde	39	13	8	18	54	65	34
10	Arbroath	39	11	11	17	50	61	33
11	Raith	39	12	8	19	47	55	32
12	St Johnstone	39	10	11	18	57	66	31
13	Montrose	39	8	9	22	55	92	25
14	Queen of the S	39	8	8	23	43	93	24

SCOTTISH SECOND DIVISION

		P	W	D	L	F	A	Pts
1	Berwick	39	22	10	7	82	44	54
2	Dunfermline	39	19	14	6	66	40	52
3	Falkirk	39	19	12	8	66	37	50
4	East Fife	39	17	9	13	64	53	43
5	Cowdenbeath	39	16	10	13	63	58	42
6	Alloa	39	16	9	14	57	62	41
7	Albion	39	15	10	14	57	56	40
8	Forfar	39	13	12	14	55	52	38
9	Stranraer	39	18	2	19	52	66	38
10	Stenhousemuir	39	12	8	19	54	58	32
11	Brechin	39	9	14	16	49	65	32
12	E Stirlingshire	39	12	8	19	61	87	32
13	Queen's Park	39	8	12	19	46	57	28
14	Meadowbank	39	8	8	23	37	74	24

FA CUP 1978-79

FOURTH ROUND

Arsenal v Notts County	2-0
Ipswich v Orient	0-0, 2-0
Newcastle v Wolverhampton W	1-1, 0-1
Nottingham Forest v York City	3-1
Shrewsbury v Manchester City	2-0
Crystal Palace v Bristol City	3-0
Aldershot v Swindon	2-1
Liverpool v Blackburn	1-0
Newport v Colchester	0-0, 0-1
Fulham v Manchester United	1-1, 0-1
Bristol Rovers v Charlton Athletic	1-0
Preston v Southampton	0-1
Tottenham v Wrexham	3-3, 3-2
Burnley v Sunderland	1-1, 3-0
West Bromwich Albion v Leeds	3-3, 2-0
Oldham v Leicester	3-1

FIFTH ROUND

Nottingham Forest v Arsenal	0-1
West Bromwich Albion v Southampton	1-1, 1-2
Aldershot v Shrewsbury	2-2, 1-3
Crystal Palace v Wolverhampton W	0-1
Liverpool v Burnley	3-0
Ipswich Town v Bristol Rovers	6-1
Oldham v Tottenham	0-1
Colchester United v Manchester United	0-1

QUARTER-FINALS

Southampton v Arsenal	1-1, 0-2
Wolverhampton W v Shrewsbury	1-1, 3-1
Ipswich v Liverpool	0-1
Tottenham v Manchester United	1-1, 0-2

SEMI-FINALS

Arsenal v Wolverhampton W	2-0
Manchester United v Liverpool	2-2, 1-0

FINAL

Arsenal v Manchester United	3-2

SCOTTISH FA CUP 1978-79

THIRD ROUND

Arbroath v Airdrieonians	0-1
East Fife v Berwick Rangers	0-1
Hamilton v Aberdeen	0-2
Raith Rovers v Heart of Midlothian	0-2
Dunfermline Athletic v Hibernian	1-1, 0-2
Clyde v Kilmarnock	1-5
Clydebank v Queen's Park	3-3, 1-0
Meadowbank v Spartans	2-1
Montrose v Celtic	2-4
Ayr United v Queen of the South	4-0
Rangers v Motherwell	3-1
Dumbarton v Alloa	1-0
Morton v St Johnstone	1-1, 4-2
Stirling Albion v Partick Thistle	0-2
Dundee v Falkirk	1-0
Dundee United v St Mirren	0-2

FOURTH ROUND

Aberdeen v Ayr United	6-2
Meadowbank v Hibernian	0-6
Rangers v Kilmarnock	1-1, 1-0
Dumbarton v Clydebank	3-1
Partick Thistle v Airdrieonians	3-0
Celtic v Berwick	3-0
Dundee v St Mirren	4-1
Heart of Midlothian v Morton	1-1, 1-0

QUARTER-FINALS

Rangers v Dundee	6-3
Dumbarton v Partick Thistle	0-1
Aberdeen v Celtic	1-1, 2-1
Hibernian v Heart of Midlothian	2-1

SEMI-FINALS

Partick Thistle v Rangers	0-0, 0-1
Aberdeen v Hibernian	1-2

FINAL

Rangers v Hibernian	0-0, 0-0, 3-2

FIRST DIVISION

		P	W	D	L	F	A	Pts
1	Liverpool	42	25	10	7	81	30	60
2	Man United	42	24	10	8	65	35	58
3	Ipswich	42	22	9	11	68	39	53
4	Arsenal	42	18	16	8	52	36	52
5	Nottm Forest	42	20	8	14	63	43	48
6	Wolves	42	19	9	14	58	47	47
7	Aston Villa	42	16	14	12	51	50	46
8	Southampton	42	18	9	15	65	53	45
9	Middlesbrough	42	16	12	14	50	44	44
10	WBA	42	11	19	12	54	50	41
11	Leeds	42	13	14	15	46	50	40
12	Norwich	42	13	14	15	58	66	40
13	Crystal Palace	42	12	16	14	41	50	40
14	Tottenham	42	15	10	17	52	62	40
15	Coventry	42	16	7	19	56	66	39
16	Brighton	42	11	15	16	47	57	37
17	Man City	42	12	13	17	43	66	37
18	Stoke	42	13	10	19	44	58	36
19	Everton	42	9	17	16	43	51	35
20	Bristol City	42	9	13	20	37	66	31
21	Derby	42	11	8	23	47	67	30
22	Bolton	42	5	15	22	38	73	25

SECOND DIVISION

		P	W	D	L	F	A	Pts
1	Leicester	42	21	13	8	58	38	55
2	Sunderland	42	21	12	9	69	42	54
3	Birmingham	42	21	11	10	58	38	53
4	Chelsea	42	23	7	12	66	52	53
5	QPR	42	18	13	11	75	53	49
6	Luton	42	16	17	9	66	45	49
7	West Ham	42	20	7	15	54	43	47
8	Cambridge	42	14	16	12	61	53	44
9	Newcastle	42	15	14	13	53	49	44
10	Preston	42	12	19	11	56	52	43
11	Oldham	42	16	11	15	49	53	43
12	Swansea	42	17	9	16	48	53	43
13	Shrewsbury	42	18	5	19	60	53	41
14	Orient	42	12	17	13	48	54	41
15	Cardiff	42	16	8	18	41	48	40
16	Wrexham	42	16	6	20	40	49	38
17	Notts County	42	11	15	16	51	52	37
18	Watford	42	12	13	17	39	46	37
19	Bristol Rovers	42	11	13	18	50	64	35
20	Fulham	42	11	7	24	42	74	29
21	Burnley	42	6	15	21	39	73	27
22	Charlton	42	6	10	26	39	78	22

THIRD DIVISION

		P	W	D	L	F	A	Pts
1	Grimsby	46	26	10	10	73	42	62
2	Blackburn	46	25	9	12	58	36	59
3	Sheff Wed	46	21	16	9	81	47	58
4	Chesterfield	46	23	11	12	71	46	57
5	Colchester	46	20	12	14	64	56	52
6	Carlisle	46	18	12	16	66	56	48
7	Reading	46	16	16	14	66	65	48
8	Exeter	46	19	10	17	60	68	48
9	Chester	46	17	13	16	49	57	47
10	Swindon	46	19	8	19	71	63	46
11	Barnsley	46	16	14	16	53	56	46
12	Sheff United	46	18	10	18	60	66	46
13	Rotherham	46	18	10	18	58	66	46
14	Millwall	46	16	13	17	65	59	45
15	Plymouth	46	16	12	18	59	55	44
16	Gillingham	46	14	14	18	49	51	42
17	Oxford	46	14	13	19	57	62	41
18	Blackpool	46	15	11	20	62	74	41
19	Brentford	46	15	11	20	59	73	41
20	Hull	46	12	16	18	51	69	40
21	Bury	46	16	7	23	45	59	39
22	Southend	46	14	10	22	47	58	38
23	Mansfield	46	10	16	20	47	58	36
24	Wimbledon	46	10	14	22	52	81	34

FOURTH DIVISION

		P	W	D	L	F	A	Pts
1	Huddersfield	46	27	12	7	101	48	66
2	Walsall	46	23	18	5	75	47	64
3	Newport	46	27	7	12	83	50	61
4	Portsmouth	46	24	12	10	91	49	60
5	Bradford	46	24	12	10	77	50	60
6	Wigan	46	21	13	12	76	61	55
7	Lincoln	46	18	17	11	64	42	53
8	Peterborough	46	21	10	15	58	47	52
9	Torquay	46	15	17	14	70	69	47
10	Aldershot	46	16	13	17	62	53	45
11	Bournemouth	46	13	18	15	52	51	44
12	Doncaster	46	15	14	17	62	63	44
13	Northampton	46	16	12	18	51	66	44
14	Scunthorpe	46	14	15	17	58	75	43
15	Tranmere	46	14	13	19	50	56	41
16	Stockport	46	14	12	20	48	72	40
17	York	46	14	11	21	65	82	39
18	Halifax	46	13	13	20	46	72	39
19	Hartlepool	46	14	10	22	59	64	38
20	Port Vale	46	12	12	22	56	70	36
21	Hereford	46	11	14	21	38	52	36
22	Darlington	46	9	17	20	50	74	35
23	Crewe	46	11	13	22	35	68	35
24	Rochdale	46	7	13	26	33	79	27

SCOTTISH PREMIER DIVISION

		P	W	D	L	F	A	Pts
1	Aberdeen	36	19	10	7	68	36	48
2	Celtic	36	18	11	7	61	38	47
3	St Mirren	36	15	12	9	56	49	42
4	Dundee United	36	12	13	11	43	30	37
5	Rangers	36	15	7	14	50	46	37
6	Morton	36	14	8	14	51	46	36
7	Partick	36	11	14	11	43	47	36
8	Kilmarnock	36	11	11	14	36	52	33
9	Dundee	36	10	6	20	47	73	26
10	Hibernian	36	6	6	24	29	67	18

SCOTTISH FIRST DIVISION

		P	W	D	L	F	A	Pts
1	Hearts	39	20	13	6	58	39	53
2	Airdrie	39	21	9	9	78	47	51
3	Ayr	39	16	12	11	64	51	44
4	Dumbarton	39	19	6	14	59	51	44
5	Raith	39	14	15	10	59	46	43
6	Motherwell	39	16	11	12	59	48	43
7	Hamilton	39	15	10	14	60	59	40
8	Stirling	39	13	13	13	40	40	39
9	Clydebank	39	14	8	17	58	57	36
10	Dunfermline	39	11	13	15	39	57	35
11	St Johnstone	39	12	10	17	57	74	34
12	Berwick	39	8	15	16	57	64	31
13	Arbroath	39	9	10	20	50	79	28
14	Clyde	39	6	13	20	43	69	25

SCOTTISH SECOND DIVISION

		P	W	D	L	F	A	Pts
1	Falkirk	39	19	12	8	65	35	50
2	E Stirlingshire	39	21	7	11	55	40	49
3	Forfar	39	19	8	12	63	51	46
4	Albion	39	16	12	11	73	56	44
5	Queen's Park	39	16	9	14	59	47	41
6	Stenhousemuir	39	16	9	14	56	51	41
7	Brechin	39	15	10	14	61	59	40
8	Cowdenbeath	39	14	12	13	54	52	40
9	Montrose	39	14	10	15	60	63	38
10	East Fife	39	12	9	18	45	57	33
11	Stranraer	39	12	8	19	51	65	32
12	Meadowbank	39	12	8	19	42	70	32
13	Queen of the S	39	11	9	19	51	69	31
14	Alloa	39	11	7	21	44	64	29

FA CUP 1979-80

FOURTH ROUND

Arsenal v Brighton	2-0
Birmingham v Middlesbrough	2-1
Blackburn v Coventry	1-0
Bolton v Halifax	2-0
Bradford v Ipswich	1-2
Bury v Burnley	1-0
Cambridge v Aston Villa	1-1, 1-4
Carlisle v Wrexham	0-0, 1-3
Chester v Millwall	2-0
Everton v Wigan	3-0
Nottingham Forest v Liverpool	0-2
Orient v West Ham	2-3
Swansea v Reading	4-1
Swindon v Tottenham Hotspur	0-0, 1-2
Watford v Harlow	4-3
Wolverhampton W v Norwich	1-1, 3-2

FIFTH ROUND

West Ham v Swansea	2-0
Blackburn v Aston Villa	1-1, 0-1
Ipswich v Chester	2-1
Everton v Wrexham	5-2
Liverpool v Bury	2-0
Tottenham Hotspur v Birmingham	3-1
Wolverhampton W v Watford	0-3
Bolton v Arsenal	1-1, 0-3

QUARTER-FINALS

West Ham v Aston Villa	1-0
Everton v Ipswich	2-1
Tottenham Hotspur v Liverpool	0-1
Watford v Arsenal	1-2

SEMI-FINALS

West Ham v Everton	1-1, 2-1
Arsenal v Liverpool	0-0, 1-1, 1-1, 1-0

FINAL

West Ham v Arsenal	1-0

SCOTTISH FA CUP 1979-80

THIRD ROUND

Arbroath v Aberdeen	1-1, 0-5
Berwick v Peterhead	3-1
Celtic v Raith Rovers	2-1
Clyde v Rangers	2-2, 0-2
Clydebank v Stirling Albion	1-1, 1-1, 0-1
Dumbarton v Ayr United	1-2
Hamilton v Keith	2-3
Meadowbank v Hibernian	0-1
Morton v Cowdenbeath	1-0
Queen of the South v Motherwell	2-0
St Mirren v Brechin City	3-1
Airdrieonians v St Johnstone	3-1
Alloa v Heart of Midlothian	0-1
Dundee United v Dundee	5-1
Dunfermline v Buckie Thistle	2-0
Kilmarnock v Partick Thistle	0-1

FOURTH ROUND

Aberdeen v Airdrieonians	8-0
Celtic v St Mirren	1-1, 3-2
Heart of Midlothian v Stirling Albion	2-0
Keith v Berwick	1-2
Morton v Dunfermline	5-0
Queen of the South v Partick Thistle	1-3
Rangers v Dundee United	1-0
Hibernian v Ayr United	2-0

QUARTER-FINALS

Celtic v Morton	2-0
Berwick Rangers v Hibernian	0-0, 0-1
Partick Thistle v Aberdeen	1-2
Rangers v Heart of Midlothian	6-1

SEMI-FINALS

Celtic v Hibernian	5-0
Aberdeen v Rangers	0-1

FINAL

Celtic v Rangers	1-0

FIRST DIVISION

		P	W	D	L	F	A	Pts
1	Aston Villa	42	26	8	8	72	40	60
2	Ipswich	42	23	10	9	77	43	56
3	Arsenal	42	19	15	8	61	45	53
4	WBA	42	20	12	10	60	42	52
5	Liverpool	42	17	17	8	62	46	51
6	Southampton	42	20	10	12	76	56	50
7	Nottm Forest	42	19	12	11	62	45	50
8	Man United	42	15	18	9	51	36	48
9	Leeds	42	17	10	15	39	47	44
10	Tottenham	42	14	15	13	70	68	43
11	Stoke	42	12	18	12	51	60	42
12	Man City	42	14	11	17	56	59	39
13	Birmingham	42	13	12	17	50	61	38
14	Middlesbrough	42	16	5	21	53	51	37
15	Everton	42	13	10	19	55	58	36
16	Coventry	42	13	10	19	48	68	36
17	Sunderland	42	14	7	21	58	53	35
18	Wolves	42	13	9	20	47	55	35
19	Brighton	42	14	7	21	54	67	35
20	Norwich	42	13	7	22	49	73	33
21	Leicester	42	13	6	23	40	67	32
22	Crystal Palace	42	6	7	29	47	83	19

SECOND DIVISION

		P	W	D	L	F	A	Pts
1	West Ham	42	28	10	4	79	29	66
2	Notts County	42	18	17	7	49	38	53
3	Swansea	42	18	14	10	64	44	50
4	Blackburn	42	16	18	8	42	29	50
5	Luton	42	18	12	12	61	46	48
6	Derby	42	15	15	12	57	52	45
7	Grimsby	42	15	15	12	44	42	45
8	QPR	42	15	13	14	56	46	43
9	Watford	42	16	11	15	50	45	43
10	Sheff Wed	42	17	8	17	53	51	42
11	Newcastle	42	14	14	14	30	45	42
12	Chelsea	42	14	12	16	46	41	40
13	Cambridge	42	17	6	17	53	65	40
14	Shrewsbury	42	11	17	14	46	47	39
15	Oldham	42	12	15	15	39	48	39
16	Wrexham	42	12	14	16	43	45	38
17	Orient	42	13	12	17	52	56	38
18	Bolton	42	14	10	18	61	66	38
19	Cardiff	42	12	12	18	44	60	36
20	Preston	42	11	14	17	41	62	36
21	Bristol City	42	7	16	19	29	51	30
22	Bristol Rovers	42	5	13	24	34	65	23

THIRD DIVISION

		P	W	D	L	F	A	Pts
1	Rotherham	46	24	13	9	62	32	61
2	Barnsley	46	21	17	8	72	45	59
3	Charlton	46	25	9	12	63	44	59
4	Huddersfield	46	21	14	11	71	40	56
5	Chesterfield	46	23	10	13	72	48	56
6	Portsmouth	46	22	9	15	55	47	53
7	Plymouth	46	19	14	13	56	44	52
8	Burnley	46	18	14	14	60	48	50
9	Brentford	46	14	19	13	52	49	47
10	Reading	46	18	10	18	62	62	46
11	Exeter	46	16	13	17	62	66	45
12	Newport	46	15	13	18	64	61	43
13	Fulham	46	15	13	18	57	64	43
14	Oxford	46	13	17	16	39	47	43
15	Gillingham	46	12	18	16	48	58	42
16	Millwall	46	14	14	18	43	60	42
17	Swindon	46	13	15	18	51	56	41
18	Chester	46	15	11	20	41	48	41
19	Carlisle	46	14	13	19	57	70	41
20	Walsall	46	13	15	18	59	74	41
21	Sheff United	46	14	13	19	65	62	40
22	Colchester	46	14	11	21	45	65	39
23	Blackpool	46	9	14	23	45	75	32
24	Hull	46	8	16	22	40	71	32

FOURTH DIVISION

		P	W	D	L	F	A	Pts
1	Southend	46	30	7	9	79	31	67
2	Lincoln	46	25	15	6	66	25	65
3	Doncaster	46	22	12	12	59	49	56
4	Wimbledon	46	23	9	14	64	46	55
5	Peterborough	46	17	18	11	68	54	52
6	Aldershot	46	18	14	14	43	41	50
7	Mansfield	46	20	9	17	58	44	49
8	Darlington	46	19	11	16	65	59	49
9	Hartlepool	46	20	9	17	64	61	49
10	Northampton	46	18	13	15	65	67	49
11	Wigan	46	18	11	17	51	55	47
12	Bury	46	17	11	18	70	62	45
13	Bournemouth	46	16	13	17	47	48	45
14	Bradford	46	14	16	16	53	60	44
15	Rochdale	46	14	15	17	60	70	43
16	Scunthorpe	46	11	20	15	60	69	42
17	Torquay	46	18	5	23	55	63	41
18	Crewe	46	13	14	19	48	61	40
19	Port Vale	46	12	15	19	57	68	39
20	Stockport	46	16	7	23	44	57	39
21	Tranmere	46	13	10	23	59	73	36
22	Hereford	46	11	13	22	38	62	35
23	Halifax	46	11	12	23	44	71	34
24	York	46	12	9	25	47	66	33

SCOTTISH PREMIER DIVISION

		P	W	D	L	F	A	Pts
1	Celtic	36	26	4	6	84	37	56
2	Aberdeen	36	19	11	6	61	26	49
3	Rangers	36	16	12	8	60	32	44
4	St Mirren	36	18	8	10	56	47	44
5	Dundee United	36	17	9	10	66	42	43
6	Partick	36	10	10	16	32	48	30
7	Airdrieonians	36	10	9	17	36	55	29
8	Morton	36	10	8	18	36	58	28
9	Kilmarnock	36	5	9	22	23	65	19
10	Hearts	36	6	6	24	27	71	18

SCOTTISH FIRST DIVISION

		P	W	D	L	F	A	Pts
1	Hibernian	39	24	9	6	67	24	57
2	Dundee	39	22	8	9	64	40	52
3	St Johnstone	39	20	11	8	64	45	51
4	Raith	39	20	10	9	49	32	50
5	Motherwell	39	19	11	9	65	51	49
6	Ayr	39	17	11	11	59	42	45
7	Hamilton	39	15	7	17	61	57	37
8	Dumbarton	39	13	11	15	49	50	37
9	Falkirk	39	13	8	18	39	52	34
10	Clydebank	39	10	13	16	48	59	33
11	E Stirlingshire	39	6	17	16	41	56	29
12	Dunfermline	39	10	7	22	41	58	27
13	Stirling	39	6	11	22	18	48	23
14	Berwick	39	5	12	22	31	82	22

SCOTTISH SECOND DIVISION

		P	W	D	L	F	A	Pts
1	Queen's Park	39	16	18	5	62	43	50
2	Queen of the S	39	16	14	9	66	53	46
3	Cowdenbeath	39	18	9	12	63	48	45
4	Brechin	39	15	14	10	52	46	44
5	Forfar	39	17	9	13	63	57	43
6	Alloa	39	15	12	12	61	54	42
7	Montrose	39	16	8	15	66	55	40
8	Clyde	39	14	12	13	68	63	40
9	Arbroath	39	13	12	14	58	54	38
10	Stenhousemuir	39	13	11	15	63	58	37
11	East Fife	39	10	15	14	44	53	35
12	Albion	39	13	9	17	59	72	34
13	Meadowbank	39	11	7	21	42	64	29
14	Stranraer	39	7	8	24	36	83	22

FA CUP 1980-81

FOURTH ROUND

Barnsley v Enfield	1-1, 3-0
Carlisle v Bristol City	1-1, 0-5
Coventry v Birmingham	3-2
Everton v Liverpool	2-1
Fulham v Charlton	1-2
Leicester v Exeter	1-1, 1-3
Manchester City v Norwich	6-0
Middlesbrough v West Bromwich Albion	1-0
Newcastle v Luton	2-1
Nottingham Forest v Manchester United	1-0
Notts County v Peterborough	0-1
Shrewsbury v Ipswich	0-0, 0-3
Tottenham v Hull	2-0
Watford v Wolverhampton W	1-1, 1-2
Wrexham v Wimbledon	2-1
Southampton v Bristol Rovers	3-1

FIFTH ROUND

Ipswich v Charlton	2-0
Middlesbrough v Barnsley	2-1
Newcastle v Exeter	1-1, 0-4
Nottingham Forest v Bristol City	2-1
Peterborough v Manchester City	0-1
Southampton v Everton	0-0, 1-2
Tottenham v Coventry	3-1
Wolverhampton W v Wrexham	3-1

QUARTER-FINALS

Tottenham Hotspur v Exeter	2-0
Middlesbrough v Wolverhampton W	1-1, 1-3
Nottingham Forest v Ipswich	3-3, 0-1
Everton v Manchester City	2-2, 1-3

SEMI-FINALS

Tottenham Hotspur v Wolverhampton W	2-2, 3-0
Ipswich v Manchester City	0-1

FINAL

Tottenham Hotspur v Manchester City	1-1, 3-2

SCOTTISH FA CUP 1980-81

THIRD ROUND

Airdrieonians v Rangers	0-5
Arbroath v Cowdenbeath	1-1, 0-4
Berwick v Celtic	0-2
Brechin v Dundee United	1-2
Buckie Thistle v Stirling Albion	1-3
East Fife v Clydebank	0-0, 4-5
East Stirling v Inverness Thistle	4-1
Falkirk v Dundee	1-0
Hamilton v St Johnstone	0-3
Hibernian v Dunfermline	1-1, 2-1
Kilmarnock v Ayr United	2-1
Morton v Heart of Midlothian	0-0, 3-1
Partick Thistle v Clyde	2-2, 4-2
Raith Rovers v Aberdeen	1-2
St Mirren v Dumbarton	0-2
Stenhousemuir v Motherwell	1-1, 1-2

FOURTH ROUND

Celtic v Stirling Albion	3-0
Cowdenbeath v East Stirlingshire	1-2
Dundee United v Partick Thistle	1-0
Hibernian v Falkirk	1-0
Kilmarnock v Clydebank	0-0, 1-1, 0-1
Morton v Aberdeen	1-0
Motherwell v Dumbarton	2-1
St Johnstone v Rangers	3-3, 1-3

QUARTER-FINALS

Dundee United v Motherwell	6-1
Rangers v Hibernian	3-1
Celtic v East Stirlingshire	2-0
Morton v Clydebank	0-0, 6-0

SEMI-FINALS

Morton v Rangers	1-2
Celtic v Dundee United	0-0, 2-3

FINAL

Rangers v Dundee United	0-0, 4-1

255

FIRST DIVISION

		P	W	D	L	F	A	Pts
1	Liverpool	42	26	9	7	80	32	87
2	Ipswich	42	26	5	11	75	53	83
3	Man United	42	22	12	8	59	29	78
4	Tottenham	42	20	11	11	67	48	71
5	Arsenal	42	20	11	11	48	37	71
6	Swansea	42	21	6	15	58	51	69
7	Southampton	42	19	9	14	72	67	66
8	Everton	42	17	13	12	56	50	64
9	West Ham	42	14	16	12	66	57	58
10	Man City	42	15	13	14	49	50	58
11	Aston Villa	42	15	12	15	55	53	57
12	Nottm Forest	42	15	12	15	42	48	57
13	Brighton	42	13	13	16	43	52	52
14	Coventry	42	13	11	18	56	62	50
15	Notts County	42	13	8	21	45	69	47
16	Birmingham	42	10	14	18	53	61	44
17	WBA	42	11	11	20	46	57	44
18	Stoke	42	12	8	22	44	63	44
19	Sunderland	42	11	11	20	38	58	44
20	Leeds	42	10	12	20	39	61	42
21	Wolves	42	10	10	22	32	63	40
22	Middlesbrough	42	8	15	19	34	52	39

SECOND DIVISION

		P	W	D	L	F	A	Pts
1	Luton	42	25	13	4	86	46	88
2	Watford	42	23	11	8	76	42	80
3	Norwich	42	22	5	15	64	50	71
4	Sheff Wed	42	20	10	12	55	51	70
5	QPR	42	21	6	15	65	43	69
6	Barnsley	42	19	10	13	59	41	67
7	Rotherham	42	20	7	15	66	54	67
8	Leicester	42	18	12	12	56	48	66
9	Newcastle	42	18	8	16	52	50	62
10	Blackburn	42	16	11	15	47	43	59
11	Oldham	42	15	14	13	50	51	59
12	Chelsea	42	15	12	15	60	60	57
13	Charlton	42	13	12	17	50	65	51
14	Cambridge	42	13	9	20	48	53	48
15	Crystal Palace	42	13	9	20	34	45	48
16	Derby	42	12	12	18	53	68	48
17	Grimsby	42	11	13	18	53	65	46
18	Shrewsbury	42	11	3	18	37	57	46
19	Bolton	42	13	7	22	39	61	46
20	Cardiff	42	12	8	22	45	61	44
21	Wrexham	42	11	11	20	40	56	44
22	Orient	42	10	9	23	39	61	39

THIRD DIVISION

		P	W	D	L	F	A	Pts
1	Burnley	46	21	17	8	66	49	80
2	Carlisle	46	23	11	12	65	50	80
3	Fulham	46	21	15	10	77	51	78
4	Lincoln	46	21	14	11	66	40	77
5	Oxford	46	19	14	13	63	49	71
6	Gillingham	46	20	11	15	64	56	71
7	Southend	46	18	15	13	63	51	69
8	Brentford	46	19	11	16	56	47	68
9	Millwall	46	18	13	15	62	62	67
10	Plymouth	46	18	11	17	64	56	65
11	Chesterfield	46	18	10	18	67	58	64
12	Reading	46	17	11	18	67	75	62
13	Portsmouth	46	14	19	13	56	51	61
14	Preston	46	16	13	17	50	56	61
15	Bristol Rovers*	46	18	9	19	58	65	61
16	Newport	46	14	16	16	54	54	58
17	Huddersfield	46	15	12	19	64	59	57
18	Exeter	46	16	9	21	71	84	57
19	Doncaster	46	13	17	16	55	68	56
20	Walsall	46	13	14	19	51	55	53
21	Wimbledon	46	14	11	21	61	75	53
22	Swindon	46	13	13	20	55	71	52
23	Bristol City	46	11	13	22	40	65	46
24	Chester	46	7	11	28	36	78	32

* Two points deducted by League.

FOURTH DIVISION

		P	W	D	L	F	A	Pts
1	Sheff United	46	27	15	4	94	41	96
2	Bradford	46	26	13	7	88	45	91
3	Wigan	46	26	13	7	80	46	91
4	Bournemouth	46	23	19	4	62	30	88
5	Peterborough	46	24	10	12	71	57	82
6	Colchester	46	20	12	14	82	57	72
7	Port Vale	46	18	16	12	56	49	70
8	Hull	46	19	12	15	70	61	69
9	Bury	46	17	17	12	80	59	68
10	Hereford	46	16	19	11	64	58	67
11	Tranmere	46	14	18	14	51	56	60
12	Blackpool	46	15	13	18	66	60	58
13	Darlington	46	15	13	18	61	62	58
14	Hartlepool	46	13	16	17	73	84	55
15	Torquay	46	14	13	19	47	59	55
16	Aldershot	46	13	15	18	57	68	54
17	York	46	14	8	24	69	91	50
18	Stockport	46	12	13	21	48	67	49
19	Halifax	46	9	22	15	51	72	49
20	Mansfield*	46	13	10	23	63	81	47
21	Rochdale	46	10	16	20	50	62	46
22	Northampton	46	11	9	26	57	84	42
23	Scunthorpe	46	9	15	22	43	79	42
24	Crewe	46	6	9	31	29	84	27

* Two points deducted by League.

SCOTTISH PREMIER DIVISION

		P	W	D	L	F	A	Pts
1	Celtic	36	24	7	5	79	33	55
2	Aberdeen	36	23	7	6	71	29	53
3	Rangers	36	16	11	9	57	45	43
4	Dundee United	36	15	10	11	61	38	40
5	St Mirren	36	14	9	13	49	52	37
6	Hibernian	36	11	14	11	48	40	36
7	Morton	36	9	12	15	31	54	30
8	Dundee	36	11	4	21	46	72	26
9	Partick	36	6	10	20	35	59	22
10	Airdrieonians	36	5	8	23	31	76	18

SCOTTISH FIRST DIVISION

		P	W	D	L	F	A	Pts
1	Motherwell	39	26	9	4	92	36	61
2	Kilmarnock	39	17	17	5	60	29	51
3	Hearts	39	21	8	10	65	37	50
4	Clydebank	39	19	8	12	61	53	46
5	St Johnstone	39	17	8	14	69	60	42
6	Ayr	39	15	12	12	56	50	42
7	Hamilton	39	16	8	15	52	49	40
8	Queen's Park	39	13	10	16	41	41	36
9	Falkirk	39	11	14	14	49	52	36
10	Dunfermline	39	11	14	14	46	56	36
11	Dumbarton	39	13	9	17	49	61	35
12	Raith	39	11	7	21	31	59	29
13	E Stirlingshire	39	7	10	22	38	77	24
14	Queen of the S	39	4	10	25	44	93	18

SCOTTISH SECOND DIVISION

		P	W	D	L	F	A	Pts
1	Clyde	39	24	11	4	79	38	59
2	Alloa	39	19	12	8	66	42	50
3	Arbroath	39	20	10	9	62	50	50
4	Berwick	39	20	8	11	66	38	48
5	Brechin	39	18	10	11	61	43	46
6	Forfar	39	15	15	9	59	35	45
7	East Fife	39	14	9	16	48	51	37
8	Stirling	39	12	11	16	39	44	35
9	Cowdenbeath	39	11	13	15	51	57	35
10	Montrose	39	12	8	19	49	74	32
11	Albion	39	13	5	21	52	74	31
12	Meadowbank	39	10	10	19	49	62	30
13	Stenhousemuir	39	11	6	22	41	65	28
14	Stranraer	39	7	6	26	36	85	20

FA CUP 1981-82

FOURTH ROUND

Tottenham Hotspur v Leeds United	1-0
Bristol City v Aston Villa	0-1
Chelsea v Wrexham	0-0, 1-1, 2-1
Sunderland v Liverpool	0-3
Hereford v Leicester	0-1
Watford v West Ham	2-0
Shrewbury v Burnley	1-0
Luton v Ipswich	0-3
Gillingham v West Bromwich Albion	0-1
Norwich v Doncaster Rovers	2-1
Manchester City v Coventry	1-3
Brighton v Oxford United	0-3
Crystal Palace v Bolton	1-0
Huddersfield v Orient	1-1, 0-2
Newcastle v Grimsby	1-2
Blackpool v Queen's Park Rangers	0-0, 1-5

FIFTH ROUND

Tottenham Hotspur v Aston Villa	1-0
Chelsea v Liverpool	2-0
Leicester v Watford	2-0
Shrewsbury v Ipswich	2-1
West Bromwich Albion v Norwich	1-0
Coventry v Oxford United	4-0
Crystal Palace v Orient	0-0, 1-0
Queen's Park Rangers v Grimsby	3-1

QUARTER-FINALS

Chelsea v Tottenham Hotspur	2-3
Leicester v Shrewsbury	5-2
West Bromwich Albion v Coventry	2-0
Queen's Park Rangers v Crystal Palace	1-0

SEMI-FINALS

Tottenham Hotspur v Leicester	2-0
West Bromwich Albion v Queen's Park Rangers	0-1

FINAL

Tottenham Hotspur v Queen's Park Rangers	1-1, 1-0

SCOTTISH FA CUP 1981-82

THIRD ROUND

Motherwell v Aberdeen	0-1
Celtic v Queen of the South	4-0
Kilmarnock v Montrose	1-0
Gala Fairydean v St Johnstone	1-2
Clydebank v Dunfermline	2-1
St Mirren v Morton	2-1
Brechin v Dundee United	2-4
Hibernian v Falkirk	2-0
Airdrieonians v Queen's Park	1-2
Alloa Athletic v Ayr United	2-1
East Stirlingshire v Heart of Midlothian	1-4
Hamilton v Forfar Athletic	0-0, 2-3
Dundee v Raith Rovers	1-0
Clyde v Meadowbank	2-2, 2-4
Partick Thistle v Dumbarton	1-2
Rangers v Albion Rovers	6-2

FOURTH ROUND

Aberdeen v Celtic	1-0
Kilmarnock v St Johnstone	3-1
Clydebank v St Mirren	0-2
Dundee United v Hibernian	1-1, 1-1, 3-0
Queen's Park v Alloa Athletic	2-0
Heart of Midlothian v Forfar Athletic	0-1
Dundee v Meadowbank	3-0
Rangers v Dumbarton	4-0

QUARTER-FINALS

Aberdeen v Kilmarnock	4-2
St Mirren v Dundee United	1-0
Queen's Park v Forfar Athletic	1-2
Rangers v Dundee	2-0

SEMI-FINALS

Aberdeen v St Mirren	1-1, 3-2
Forfar Athletic v Rangers	0-0, 2-3

FINAL

Aberdeen v Rangers	4-1

FIRST DIVISION

		P	W	D	L	F	A	Pts
1	Liverpool	42	24	10	8	87	37	82
2	Watford	42	22	5	15	74	57	71
3	Man United	42	19	13	8	56	38	70
4	Tottenham	42	20	9	13	65	50	69
5	Nottm Forest	42	20	9	13	62	50	69
6	Aston Villa	42	21	5	16	62	50	68
7	Everton	42	18	10	14	66	48	64
8	West Ham	42	20	4	18	68	62	64
9	Ipswich	42	15	13	14	64	50	58
10	Arsenal	42	16	10	16	58	56	58
11	WBA	42	15	12	15	51	49	57
12	Southampton	42	15	12	15	54	58	57
13	Stoke	42	16	9	17	53	64	57
14	Norwich	42	14	12	16	52	58	54
15	Notts County	42	15	7	21	55	71	52
16	Sunderland	42	12	14	16	48	61	50
17	Birmingham	42	12	15	16	40	55	50
18	Luton	42	12	13	17	65	84	49
19	Coventry	42	13	9	20	48	59	48
20	Man City	42	13	8	21	47	70	47
21	Swansea	42	10	11	21	51	69	41
22	Brighton	42	9	13	20	38	67	40

SECOND DIVISION

		P	W	D	L	F	A	Pts
1	QPR	42	26	7	9	77	36	85
2	Wolves	42	20	15	7	68	44	75
3	Leicester	42	20	10	12	72	44	70
4	Fulham	42	20	9	13	64	47	69*
5	Newcastle	42	18	13	11	75	53	67
6	Sheff Wed	42	16	15	11	60	47	63
7	Oldham	42	14	19	9	64	47	61
8	Leeds	42	13	21	8	51	46	60
9	Shrewsbury	42	15	14	13	48	48	59
10	Barnsley	42	14	15	13	57	55	57
11	Blackburn	42	15	12	15	58	58	57
12	Cambridge	42	13	12	17	42	60	51
13	Derby	42	10	19	13	49	58	49*
14	Carlisle	42	12	12	18	68	70	48
15	Crystal Palace	42	12	12	18	43	52	48
16	Middlesbrough	42	11	15	16	46	67	48
17	Charlton	42	13	9	20	63	86	48
18	Chelsea	42	11	14	17	51	61	47
19	Grimsby	42	12	11	19	45	70	47
20	Rotherham	42	10	15	17	45	68	45
21	Burnley	42	12	8	22	56	66	44
22	Bolton	42	11	11	20	42	61	44

*Game between Derby and Fulham abandoned after 88 minutes but result allowed to stand at 1-0.

THIRD DIVISION

		P	W	D	L	F	A	Pts
1	Portsmouth	46	27	10	9	74	41	91
2	Cardiff	46	25	11	10	76	50	86
3	Huddersfield	46	23	13	10	84	49	82
4	Newport	46	23	9	14	76	54	78
5	Oxford	46	22	12	12	71	53	78
6	Lincoln	46	23	7	16	77	51	76
8	Bristol Rovers	46	22	9	15	84	57	75
8	Plymouth	46	19	8	19	61	66	65
9	Brentford	46	18	10	18	88	77	64
10	Walsall	46	17	13	16	64	63	64
11	Sheff United	46	19	7	20	62	64	64
12	Bradford City	46	16	13	17	68	69	61
13	Gillingham	46	16	13	17	58	59	61
14	Bournemouth	46	16	13	17	59	68	61
15	Southend	46	15	14	17	66	65	59
16	Preston	46	15	13	18	60	69	58
17	Millwall	46	14	13	19	64	78	55
18	Wigan	46	15	9	22	60	72	54
19	Exeter	46	14	12	20	81	104	54
20	Orient	46	15	9	22	64	88	54
21	Reading	46	12	17	17	63	80	53
22	Wrexham	46	12	15	19	57	76	51
23	Doncaster	46	9	11	26	57	97	38
24	Chesterfield	46	8	13	25	44	68	37

FOURTH DIVISION

		P	W	D	L	F	A	Pts
1	Wimbledon	46	29	11	6	96	45	98
2	Hull	46	25	15	6	75	34	90
3	Port Vale	46	26	10	10	67	34	88
4	Scunthorpe	46	23	14	9	71	42	83
5	Bury	46	24	12	11	76	44	81
6	Colchester	46	24	9	13	75	55	81
7	York	46	22	13	11	88	58	79
8	Swindon	46	19	11	16	61	54	68
9	Peterborough	46	17	13	16	58	52	64
10	Mansfield	46	16	13	17	61	70	61
11	Halifax	46	16	12	18	59	66	60
12	Torquay	46	17	7	22	56	65	58
13	Chester	46	15	11	20	55	60	56
14	Bristol City	46	13	17	16	59	70	56
15	Northampton	46	14	12	20	67	75	54
16	Stockport	46	14	12	20	60	79	54
17	Darlington	46	13	13	20	61	71	52
18	Aldershot	46	12	15	19	61	82	51
19	Tranmere	46	13	11	22	49	71	50
20	Rochdale	46	11	16	19	55	73	49
21	Blackpool	46	13	12	21	55	74	49
22	Hartlepool	46	13	9	24	46	76	48
23	Crewe	46	11	8	27	53	71	41
24	Hereford	46	11	8	27	43	79	41

SCOTTISH PREMIER DIVISION

		P	W	D	L	F	A	Pts
1	Dundee United	36	24	8	4	90	35	56
2	Celtic	36	25	5	6	90	36	55
3	Aberdeen	36	25	5	6	76	24	55
4	Rangers	36	13	12	11	52	41	38
5	St Mirren	36	11	12	13	47	51	34
6	Dundee	36	9	11	16	42	53	29
7	Hibernian	36	11	7	18	35	51	29
8	Motherwell	36	11	5	20	39	73	27
9	Morton	36	6	8	22	30	74	20
10	Kilmarnock	36	3	11	22	28	91	17

SCOTTISH FIRST DIVISION

		P	W	D	L	F	A	Pts
1	St Johnstone	39	25	5	9	59	37	55
2	Hearts	39	22	10	7	79	38	54
3	Clydebank	39	20	10	9	72	49	50
4	Partick	39	20	9	10	66	45	49
5	Airdrie	39	16	7	16	62	46	39
6	Alloa	39	14	11	14	52	52	39
7	Falkirk	39	15	6	18	45	55	36
8	Dumbarton	39	13	10	16	50	59	36
9	Hamilton	39	11	12	16	54	66	34
10	Raith	39	13	8	18	64	63	34
11	Clyde	39	14	6	19	55	66	34
12	Ayr	39	12	8	19	45	61	32
13	Dunfermline	39	7	17	15	39	69	31
14	Queen's Park	39	16	11	22	44	80	23

SCOTTISH SECOND DIVISION

		P	W	D	L	F	A	Pts
1	Brechin	39	21	3	5	77	38	55
2	Meadowbank	39	23	8	8	64	45	54
3	Arbroath	39	21	7	11	78	51	49
4	Forfar	39	18	12	9	58	37	48
5	Stirling A	39	18	10	11	57	41	46
6	East Fife	39	16	11	12	68	43	43
7	Queen of the S	39	17	7	15	75	56	42
8	Cowdenbeath	39	13	12	14	55	53	38
9	Berwick	39	13	10	16	47	60	36
10	Albion	39	14	6	19	55	66	34
11	Stenhousemuir	39	7	14	18	43	66	29
12	Stranraer	39	10	6	23	46	79	27
13	E Stirling	39	7	9	23	43	79	23
14	Montrose	39	8	6	25	37	86	22

FA CUP 1982-83

FOURTH ROUND

Luton Town v Manchester United	0-2
Derby County v Chelsea	2-1
Tottenham Hotspur v WBA	2-1
Everton v Shrewsbury Town	2-1
Aston Villa v Wolverhampton Wanderers	1-0
Watford v Fulham	1-1, 2-1
Middlesbrough v Notts County	2-0
Arsenal v Leeds United	1-1, 1-1, 2-1
Torquay United v Sheffield Wednesday	2-3
Cambridge United v Barnsley	1-0
Crystal Palace v Birmingham	1-0
Burnley v Swindon Town	3-1
Coventry City v Norwich City	2-2, 1-2
Ipswich Town v Grimsby Town	2-0
Liverpool v Stoke City	2-0
Brighton v Manchester City	4-0

FIFTH ROUND

Derby County v Manchester United	0-1
Everton v Tottenham Hotspur	2-0
Aston Villa v Watford	4-1
Middlesbrough v Arsenal	1-1, 1-2
Cambridge United v Sheffield Wednesday	1-2
Crystal Palace v Burnley	0-0, 0-1
Norwich City v Ipswich Town	1-0
Liverpool v Brighton	1-2

QUARTER-FINALS

Manchester United v Everton	1-0
Arsenal v Aston Villa	2-0
Burnley v Sheffield Wednesday	1-1, 0-5
Brighton v Norwich City	1-0

SEMI-FINALS

Manchester United v Arsenal	2-1
Brighton v Sheffield Wednesday	2-1

FINAL

Manchester United v Brighton	2-2, 4-0

SCOTTISH FA CUP 1982-83

THIRD ROUND

Alloa v Morton	1-2
Ayr v Albion Rovers	1-2
Clyde v Motherwell	0-0, 4-3
Clydebank v Celtic	0-3
Dumbarton v Airdrie	0-1
Dundee v Brora Rangers	2-1
Dunfermline v Elgin City	5-0
East Fife v Raith Rovers	1-0
Falkirk v Rangers	0-2
Forfar v Berwick	2-1
Hibernian v Aberdeen	1-4
Partick v Kilmarnock	1-1, 0-0, 2-2, 1-0
St Mirren v Dundee Utd	1-0
Queen's Park v Stenhousemuir	4-1
Queen of the South v Hearts	1-1, 0-1
Hamilton v St Johnstone	0-1

FOURTH ROUND

Aberdeen v Dundee	1-0
Albion Rovers v Airdrie	0-3
Celtic v Dunfermline	3-0
Hearts v East Fife	2-1
Morton v St Mirren	0-2
Partick Thistle v Clyde	2-2, 1-1, 6-0
Queen's Park v St Johnstone	1-0
Rangers v Forfar	2-1

*abandoned in 13th minute of extra time.

QUARTER-FINALS

Aidrie v St Mirren	0-5
Celtic v Hearts	4-1
Partick Thistle v Aberdeen	1-2
Queen's Park v Rangers	1-2

SEMI-FINALS

Aberdeen v Celtic	1-0
Rangers v St Mirren	1-1, 1-0

FINAL

Aberdeen v Rangers	1-0

FIRST DIVISION

		P	W	D	L	F	A	Pts
1	Liverpool	42	22	14	6	73	32	80
2	Southampton	42	22	11	9	66	38	77
3	Nottm Forest	42	22	8	12	76	45	74
4	Man United	42	20	14	8	71	41	74
5	QPR	42	22	7	13	67	37	73
6	Arsenal	42	18	9	15	74	60	63
7	Everton	42	16	14	12	44	42	62
8	Tottenham	42	17	10	15	64	65	61
9	West Ham	42	17	9	16	60	55	60
10	Aston Villa	42	17	9	16	59	61	60
11	Watford	42	16	9	17	68	77	57
12	Ipswich	42	15	8	19	55	57	53
13	Sunderland	42	13	13	16	42	53	52
14	Norwich	42	12	15	15	48	49	51
15	Leicester	42	13	12	17	65	68	51
16	Luton	42	14	9	19	53	66	51
17	WBA	42	14	9	19	48	62	51
18	Stoke	42	13	11	18	44	63	50
19	Coventry	42	13	11	18	57	77	50
20	Birmingham	42	12	12	18	39	50	48
21	Notts County	42	10	11	21	50	72	41
22	Wolves	42	6	11	25	27	80	29

SECOND DIVISION

		P	W	D	L	F	A	Pts
1	Chelsea	42	25	13	4	90	40	89
2	Sheff Wed	42	26	10	6	72	34	89
3	Newcastle	42	24	8	10	85	53	80
4	Man City	42	20	10	12	66	48	70
5	Grimsby	42	19	13	10	60	47	70
6	Blackburn	42	17	16	9	57	46	67
7	Carlisle	42	16	16	10	48	41	64
8	Shrewsbury	42	17	10	15	49	53	61
9	Brighton	42	17	9	16	69	60	60
10	Leeds	42	16	12	14	55	56	60
11	Fulham	42	15	12	15	60	53	57
12	Huddersfield	42	14	15	13	56	49	57
13	Charlton	42	16	9	17	53	64	57
14	Barnsley	42	15	7	20	57	53	52
15	Cardiff	42	15	6	21	53	66	51
16	Portsmouth	42	14	7	21	73	64	49
17	Middlesbrough	42	12	13	17	41	47	49
18	Crystal Palace	42	12	11	19	42	52	47
19	Oldham	42	13	8	21	47	73	47
20	Derby	42	11	9	22	36	72	42
21	Swansea	42	7	8	27	36	85	29
22	Cambridge	42	4	12	26	28	77	24

THIRD DIVISION

		P	W	D	L	F	A	Pts
1	Oxford	46	28	11	7	91	50	95
2	Wimbledon	46	26	9	11	97	76	87
3	Sheff United	46	24	11	11	86	53	83
4	Hull	46	23	14	9	71	38	83
5	Bristol Rovers	46	22	13	11	68	54	79
6	Walsall	46	22	9	15	68	61	75
7	Bradford	46	20	11	15	73	65	71
8	Gillingham	46	20	10	16	74	69	70
9	Millwall	46	18	13	15	71	65	67
10	Bolton	46	18	10	18	56	60	64
11	Orient	46	18	9	19	71	81	63
12	Burnley	46	16	14	16	76	61	62
13	Newport	46	16	14	16	58	75	62
14	Lincoln	46	16	13	17	59	62	61
15	Wigan	46	16	13	17	46	56	61
16	Preston	46	15	11	20	66	66	56
17	Bournemouth	46	16	7	23	63	73	55
18	Rotherham	46	15	9	22	57	64	54
19	Plymouth	46	13	12	21	56	62	51
20	Brentford	46	11	16	19	69	79	49
21	Scunthorpe	46	9	19	18	54	73	46
22	Southend	46	10	14	22	55	76	44
23	Port Vale	46	11	10	25	51	83	43
24	Exeter	46	6	15	25	50	84	33

FOURTH DIVISION

		P	W	D	L	F	A	Pts
1	York	46	31	8	7	96	39	101
2	Doncaster	46	24	13	9	82	54	85
3	Reading	46	22	16	8	84	56	82
4	Bristol City	46	24	10	12	70	44	82
5	Aldershot	46	22	9	15	76	69	75
6	Blackpool	46	21	9	16	70	52	72
7	Peterborough	46	18	14	14	72	48	68
8	Colchester	46	17	16	13	69	53	67
9	Torquay	46	18	13	15	59	64	67
10	Tranmere	46	17	15	14	53	53	66
11	Hereford	46	16	15	15	54	53	63
12	Stockport	46	17	11	18	60	64	62
13	Chesterfield	46	15	15	16	59	61	60
14	Darlington	46	17	8	21	49	50	59
15	Bury	46	15	14	17	61	64	59
16	Crewe	46	16	11	19	56	67	59
17	Swindon	46	15	13	18	58	56	58
18	Northampton	46	13	14	19	53	78	53
19	Mansfield	46	13	13	20	66	70	52
20	Wrexham	46	11	15	20	59	74	48
21	Halifax	46	12	12	22	55	89	48
22	Rochdale	46	11	13	22	52	80	46
23	Hartlepool	46	10	10	26	47	85	40
24	Chester	46	7	13	26	45	82	34

SCOTTISH PREMIER DIVISION

		P	W	D	L	F	A	Pts
1	Aberdeen	36	25	7	4	78	21	57
2	Celtic	36	21	8	7	80	41	50
3	Dundee United	36	18	11	7	67	39	47
4	Rangers	36	15	12	9	53	41	42
5	Hearts	36	10	16	10	38	47	36
6	St Mirren	36	9	14	13	55	59	32
7	Hibernian	36	12	7	17	45	55	31
8	Dundee	36	11	5	20	50	74	27
9	St Johnstone	36	10	3	23	36	81	23
10	Motherwell	36	4	7	25	31	75	15

SCOTTISH FIRST DIVISION

		P	W	D	L	F	A	Pts
1	Morton	39	21	12	6	75	46	54
2	Dumbarton	39	20	11	8	66	44	51
3	Partick	39	19	8	12	67	50	46
4	Clydebank	39	16	13	10	62	50	45
5	Brechin	39	14	14	11	56	58	42
6	Kilmarnock	39	16	6	17	57	53	38
7	Falkirk	39	16	6	17	46	54	38
8	Clyde	39	12	13	14	53	50	37
9	Hamilton	39	11	14	14	43	46	36
10	Airdrie	39	13	10	16	45	53	36
11	Meadowbank	39	12	10	17	49	69	34
12	Ayr	39	10	12	17	56	70	32
13	Raith	39	10	11	19	53	62	31
14	Alloa	39	8	10	21	41	64	26

SCOTTISH SECOND DIVISION

		P	W	D	L	F	A	Pts
1	Forfar	39	27	9	3	73	31	63
2	East Fife	39	20	7	12	57	42	47
3	Berwick	39	16	11	12	60	38	43
4	Stirling	39	14	14	11	51	42	42
5	Arbroath	39	18	6	15	51	46	42
6	Queen of the S	39	16	10	13	51	46	42
7	Stenhousemuir	39	14	11	14	47	57	39
8	Stranraer	39	13	12	14	47	47	38
9	Dunfirmline	39	13	10	16	44	45	36
10	Queen's Park	39	14	8	17	58	63	36
11	E Stirling	39	10	11	19	51	66	31
12	Montrose	39	12	7	20	36	59	31
13	Cowdenbeath	39	10	9	20	44	58	29
14	Albion R.	39	8	11	20	46	76	27

FA CUP 1983-84

FOURTH ROUND

Brighton v Liverpool	2-0
Charlton v Watford	0-2
C. Palace v West Ham	1-1, 0-2
Derby v Telford	3-2
Everton v Gillingham	0-0, 0-0, 3-0
Huddersfield v Notts County	1-2
Middlesbrough v Bournemouth	2-0
Oxford United v Blackpool	2-1
Plymouth v Darlington	2-1
Portsmouth v Southampton	0-1
Sheffield Wednesday v Coventry	3-2
Shrewsbury v Ipswich	2-0
Sunderland v Birmingham	1-2
Swindon v Blackburn	1-2
Tottenham v Norwich	0-0, 1-2
WBA v Scunthorpe	1-0

FIFTH ROUND

Birmingham v West Ham	3-0
Blackburn v Southampton	0-1
Derby v Norwich	2-1
Everton v Shrewsbury	3-0
Notts County v Middlesbrough	1-0
Oxford United v Sheffield Wednesday	0-3
Watford v Brighton	3-1
West Bromwich v Plymouth	0-1

QUARTER-FINALS

Birmingham v Watford	1-3
Notts County v Everton	1-2
Plymouth v Derby	0-0, 1-0
Sheffield Wednesday v Southampton	0-0, 1-5

SEMI-FINALS

Everton v Southampton	1-0
Watford v Plymouth	1-0

FINAL

Everton v Watford	2-0

SCOTTISH FA CUP 1983-84

THIRD ROUND

Aberdeen v Kilmarnock	1-1, 3-1
Airdrie v St Johnstone	1-0
Berwick v Celtic	0-4
Clydebank v Brechin	0-0, 3-0
Cowdenbeath v Dundee	0-2
Dundee United v Ayr	1-0
Falkirk v Clyde	1-2
Hibernian v East Fife	0-0, 0-2
Hamilton v Alloa	3-1
Hearts v Partick	2-0
Inverness Cal v Stirling A	0-0, 2-1
Meadowbank v St Mirren	0-0, 2-2, 1-2
Morton v East Stirling	2-0
Motherwell v Queen's Park	3-0
Raith v Dumbarton	1-4
Rangers v Dunfermline	2-1

FOURTH ROUND

Clyde v Aberdeen	0-2
Dundee United v Hearts	2-1
East Fife v Celtic	0-6
Inverness Cal v Rangers	0-6
Motherwell v Clydebank	3-1
Morton v Dumbarton	2-1
St Mirren v Hamilton	2-1
Dundee v Airdrie	2-1

QUARTER-FINALS

Aberdeen v Dundee United	0-0, 1-0
Motherwell v Celtic	0-6
Dundee v Rangers	2-2, 3-2
St Mirren v Morton	4-3

SEMI-FINALS

Aberdeen v Dundee	2-0
St Mirren v Celtic	1-2

FINAL

Aberdeen v Celtic	2-1

FIRST DIVISION

		P	W	D	L	F	A	Pts
1	Everton	42	28	6	8	88	43	90
2	Liverpool	42	22	11	9	78	35	77
3	Tottenham	42	23	8	11	78	51	77
4	Man United	42	22	10	10	77	47	76
5	Southampton	42	19	11	12	56	47	68
6	Chelsea	42	18	12	12	63	48	66
7	Arsenal	42	19	9	14	61	49	66
8	Sheffield Wed	42	17	14	11	58	45	65
9	Nottm Forest	42	19	7	16	56	48	64
10	Aston Villa	42	15	11	16	60	60	56
11	Watford	42	14	13	15	81	71	55
12	West Brom	42	16	7	19	58	62	55
13	Luton	42	15	9	18	57	61	54
14	Newcastle	42	13	13	16	55	70	52
15	Leicester	42	15	6	21	65	73	51
16	West Ham	42	13	12	17	51	68	51
17	Ipswich	42	13	11	18	46	57	50
18	Coventry	42	15	5	22	47	64	50
19	QPR	42	13	11	18	53	72	50
20	Norwich	42	13	10	19	46	64	49
21	Sunderland	42	10	10	22	40	62	40
22	Stoke	42	3	8	31	24	91	17

SECOND DIVISION

		P	W	D	L	F	A	Pts
1	Oxford	42	25	9	8	84	36	84
2	Birmingham	42	25	7	10	59	33	82
3	Man City	42	21	11	10	66	40	74
4	Portsmouth	42	20	14	8	69	50	74
5	Blackburn	42	21	10	11	66	41	73
6	Brighton	42	20	12	10	58	34	72
7	Leeds	42	19	12	11	66	43	69
8	Shrewsbury	42	18	11	13	66	53	65
9	Fulham	42	19	8	15	68	64	65
10	Grimsby	42	18	8	16	72	64	62
11	Barnsley	42	14	16	12	42	42	58
12	Wimbledon	42	16	10	16	71	75	58
13	Huddersfield	42	15	10	17	52	64	55
14	Oldham Ath	42	15	8	19	49	67	53
15	Crystal Palace	42	12	12	18	46	65	48
16	Carlisle	42	13	8	21	50	67	47
17	Charlton	42	11	12	19	51	63	45
18	Sheffield Utd	42	10	14	18	54	66	44
19	Middlesborough	42	10	10	22	41	57	40
20	Notts Co	42	10	7	25	45	73	37
21	Cardiff	42	9	8	25	47	79	35
22	Wolves	42	8	9	25	37	79	33

THIRD DIVISION

		P	W	D	L	F	A	Pts
1	Bradford	46	28	10	8	77	45	94
2	Millwall	46	26	12	8	83	42	90
3	Hull City	46	25	12	9	88	49	87
4	Gillingham	46	25	8	13	80	62	83
5	Bristol City	46	24	9	13	74	47	81
6	Bristol Rovers	46	21	12	13	66	48	75
7	Derby	46	19	13	14	65	54	70
8	York	46	20	9	17	70	57	69
9	Reading	46	19	12	15	68	62	69
10	Bournemouth	46	19	11	16	57	46	68
11	Walsall	46	18	13	15	58	52	67
12	Rotherham	46	18	11	17	55	55	65
13	Brentford	46	16	14	16	62	64	62
14	Doncaster	46	17	8	21	72	74	59
15	Plymouth	46	15	14	17	62	65	59
16	Wigan	46	15	14	17	60	64	59
17	Bolton	46	16	6	24	69	75	54
18	Newport	46	13	13	20	55	67	52
19	Lincoln	46	11	18	17	50	51	51
20	Swansea	46	12	11	23	53	80	47
21	Burnley	46	11	13	22	60	73	46
22	Orient	46	11	13	22	51	76	46
23	Preston	46	13	7	26	51	100	46
24	Cambridge	46	4	9	33	37	95	21

FOURTH DIVISION

		P	W	D	L	F	A	Pts
1	Chesterfield	46	26	13	7	64	35	91
2	Blackpool	46	24	14	8	73	39	86
3	Darlington	46	24	13	9	66	49	85
4	Bury	46	24	12	10	76	50	84
5	Hereford	46	22	11	13	65	47	77
6	Tranmere	46	24	3	19	83	66	75
7	Colchester	46	20	14	12	87	65	74
8	Swindon	46	21	9	16	62	58	72
9	Scunthorpe	46	19	14	13	83	62	71
10	Crewe	46	18	12	16	65	69	66
11	Peterborough	46	16	14	16	54	53	62
12	Port Vale	46	14	18	14	61	59	60
13	Aldershot	46	17	8	21	56	63	59
14	Mansfield	46	13	18	15	41	38	57
15	Wrexham	46	15	9	22	67	70	54
16	Chester	46	15	9	22	60	72	54
17	Rochdale	46	13	14	19	55	69	53
18	Exeter	46	13	14	19	57	79	53
19	Hartlepool	46	14	10	22	54	67	52
20	Southend	46	13	11	22	58	83	50
21	Halifax	46	14	5	26	42	69	50
22	Stockport	46	13	8	25	58	79	47
23	Northampton	46	14	5	27	53	74	47
24	Torquay	46	9	14	23	38	63	41

SCOTTISH PREMIER DIVISION

		P	W	D	L	F	A	Pts
1	Aberdeen	36	27	5	4	89	26	59
2	Celtic	36	22	8	6	77	30	52
3	Dundee United	36	20	7	9	67	33	47
4	Rangers	36	13	12	11	47	38	38
5	St Mirren	36	17	4	15	51	56	38
6	Dundee	36	15	7	14	48	50	37
7	Hearts	36	13	5	18	47	64	31
8	Hibernian	36	10	7	19	38	61	27
9	Dumbarton	36	6	7	23	29	64	19
10	Morton	36	5	2	29	29	100	12

SCOTTISH FIRST DIVISION

		P	W	D	L	F	A	Pts
1	Motherwell	39	21	8	10	62	36	50
2	Clydebank	39	17	14	8	57	37	48
3	Falkirk	39	19	7	13	65	54	45
4	Hamilton	39	16	11	12	48	49	43
5	Airdrie	39	17	8	14	70	59	42
6	Forfar	39	14	13	12	54	49	41
7	Ayr	39	15	9	15	57	52	39
8	Clyde	39	14	11	14	47	48	39
9	Brechin	39	14	9	16	49	57	37
10	East Fife	39	12	12	15	55	56	36
11	Partick	39	13	9	17	50	55	35
12	Kilmarnock	39	12	10	17	42	61	34
13	Meadowbank	39	11	10	18	50	66	32
14	St Johnstone	39	10	5	24	51	78	25

SCOTTISH SECOND DIVISION

		P	W	D	L	F	A	Pts
1	Montrose	39	22	9	8	57	40	53
2	Alloa	39	20	10	9	58	40	50
3	Dunfermline	39	17	15	7	61	36	49
4	Cowdenbeath	39	18	11	10	68	39	47
5	Stenhousemuir	39	14	15	9	45	43	45
6	Stirling	39	15	13	11	62	47	43
7	Raith	39	18	6	15	69	57	42
8	Queen of the S	39	10	14	15	42	56	34
9	Albion	39	13	8	18	49	72	34
10	Queens Park	39	12	9	18	48	55	33
11	Stranraer	39	13	6	20	52	67	32
12	East Stirling	39	8	15	16	38	53	31
13	Berwick	39	8	12	19	36	49	28
14	Arbroath	39	9	7	23	35	66	25

FA CUP 1984-85

FOURTH ROUND

Barnsley v Brighton	2-1
Chelsea v Millwall	2-3
Darlington v Telford United	1-1, 0-3
Everton v Doncaster Rovers	2-0
Grimsby Town v Watford	1-3
Ipswich Town v Gillingham	3-2
Leicester City v Carlisle United	1-0
Luton Town v Huddersfield Town	2-0
Manchester United v Coventry City	2-1
Nottingham Forest v Wimbledon	0-0, 0-1
Orient v Southampton	0-2
Oxford United v Blackburn Rovers	0-1
Sheffield Wednesday v Oldham Athletic	5-1
York City v Arsenal	1-0
Liverpool v Tottenham Hotspur	1-0
West Ham United v Norwich City	2-1

FIFTH ROUND

Blackburn Rovers v Manchester United	0-2
Everton v Telford United	3-0
Ipswich v Sheffield Wednesday	3-2
Luton Town v Watford	0-0, 2-2, 1-0
Millwall v Leicester City	2-0
Southampton v Barnsley	1-2
Wimbledon v West Ham United	1-1, 1-5
York City v Liverpool	1-1, 0-7

QUARTER-FINALS

Barnsley v Liverpool	0-4
Everton v Ipswich Town	2-2, 1-0
Luton Town v Millwall	1-0
Manchester United v West Ham United	4-2

SEMI-FINALS

Luton Town v Everton	1-2
Manchester United v Liverpool	2-2, 2-1

FINAL

Everton v Manchester United	0-1

SCOTTISH FA CUP 1984-85

FOURTH ROUND

Ayr v St Mirren	0-1
Brechin City v Hearts	1-1, 0-1
Celtic v Inverness Thistle	6-0
Forfar Athletic v Falkirk	2-1
Meadowbank Thistle v Motherwell	0-2
Queen of the South v Dundee United	0-3
Raith Rovers v Aberdeen	1-2
Rangers v Dundee	0-1

QUARTER-FINALS

Dundee v Celtic	1-1, 1-2
Hearts v Aberdeen	1-1, 0-1
Motherwell v Forfar Athletic	4-1
St Mirren v Dundee United	1-4

SEMI-FINALS

Dundee United v Aberdeen	0-0, 2-1
Motherwell v Celtic	1-1, 0-3

FINAL

Dundee United v Celtic	1-2

FIRST DIVISION

		P	W	D	L	F	A	Pts
1	Liverpool	42	26	10	6	89	37	88
2	Everton	42	26	8	8	87	41	86
3	West Ham	42	26	6	10	74	40	84
4	Man United	42	22	10	10	70	36	76
5	Sheffield Wed	42	21	10	11	63	54	73
6	Chelsea	42	20	11	11	57	56	71
7	Arsenal	42	20	9	13	49	47	69
8	Nottm Forest	42	19	11	12	69	53	68
9	Luton	42	18	12	12	61	44	66
10	Tottenham	42	19	8	15	74	52	65
11	Newcastle	42	17	12	13	67	72	63
12	Watford	42	16	11	15	69	62	59
13	QPR	42	15	7	20	53	64	52
14	Southampton	42	12	10	20	51	62	46
15	Man City	42	11	12	19	43	57	45
16	Aston Villa	42	10	14	18	51	67	44
17	Coventry	42	11	10	21	48	71	43
18	Oxford	42	10	12	20	62	80	42
19	Leicester	42	10	12	20	54	76	42
20	Ipswich	42	11	8	23	32	55	41
21	Birmingham	42	8	5	29	30	73	29
22	West Brom	42	4	12	26	35	89	24

SECOND DIVISION

		P	W	D	L	F	A	Pts
1	Norwich	42	25	9	8	84	39	84
2	Charlton	42	22	11	9	78	45	77
3	Wimbledon	42	21	13	8	58	37	76
4	Portsmouth	42	22	7	13	69	41	73
5	Crystal Palace	42	19	9	14	57	52	66
6	Hull	42	17	13	12	65	55	64
7	Sheffield United	42	17	11	14	64	63	62
8	Oldham	42	17	9	16	62	61	60
9	Millwall	42	17	8	17	64	65	59
10	Stoke	42	14	15	13	48	50	57
11	Brighton	42	16	8	18	64	64	56
12	Barnsley	42	14	14	14	47	50	56
13	Bradford	42	16	6	20	51	63	54
14	Leeds	42	15	8	19	56	72	53
15	Grimsby	42	14	10	18	58	62	52
16	Huddersfield	42	14	10	18	51	67	52
17	Shrewsbury	42	14	9	19	52	64	51
18	Sunderland	42	13	11	18	47	61	50
19	Blackburn	42	12	13	17	53	62	49
20	Carlisle	42	13	7	22	47	71	46
21	Middlesborough	42	12	9	21	44	53	45
22	Fulham	42	10	6	26	45	69	36

THIRD DIVISION

		P	W	D	L	F	A	Pts
1	Reading	46	29	7	10	67	50	94
2	Plymouth	46	26	9	11	88	53	87
3	Derby	46	23	15	8	80	41	84
4	Wigan	46	23	14	9	82	48	83
5	Gillingham	46	22	13	11	81	54	79
6	Walsall	46	22	9	15	90	64	75
7	York	46	20	11	15	77	58	71
8	Notts County	46	19	14	13	71	60	71
9	Bristol City	46	18	14	14	69	60	68
10	Brentford	46	18	12	16	58	61	66
11	Doncaster	46	16	16	14	45	52	64
12	Blackpool	46	17	12	17	66	55	63
13	Darlington	46	15	13	18	61	78	58
14	Rotherham	46	15	12	19	61	59	57
15	Bournemouth	46	15	9	22	65	72	54
16	Bristol Rovers	46	14	12	20	51	75	54
17	Chesterfield	46	13	14	19	61	64	53
18	Bolton	46	15	8	23	54	68	53
19	Newport	46	11	18	17	52	65	51
20	Bury	46	12	13	21	63	65	49
21	Lincoln	46	10	16	20	55	77	46
22	Cardiff	46	12	9	25	53	83	45
23	Wolves	46	11	10	25	57	98	43
24	Swansea	46	11	10	25	43	87	43

FOURTH DIVISION

		P	W	D	L	F	A	Pts
1	Swindon	46	32	6	8	82	43	102
2	Chester	46	23	15	8	83	50	84
3	Mansfield	46	23	12	11	74	47	81
4	Port Vale	46	21	16	9	67	37	79
5	Orient	46	20	12	14	79	64	72
6	Colchester	46	19	13	14	88	63	70
7	Hartlepool	46	20	10	16	68	67	70
8	Northampton	46	18	10	18	79	58	64
9	Southend	46	18	10	18	69	67	64
10	Hereford	46	18	10	18	74	73	64
11	Stockport	46	17	13	16	63	71	64
12	Crewe	46	18	9	19	54	61	63
13	Wrexham	46	17	9	20	68	80	60
14	Burnley	46	16	11	19	60	65	59
15	Scunthorpe	46	15	14	19	50	55	59
16	Aldershot	46	17	7	22	66	74	58
17	Peterborough	46	13	17	16	52	64	56
18	Rochdale	46	14	13	19	57	77	55
19	Tranmere	46	15	9	22	74	73	54
20	Halifax	46	14	12	20	60	71	54
21	Exeter	46	13	15	18	47	59	54
22	Cambridge	46	15	9	22	65	80	54
23	Preston	46	11	10	25	54	89	43
24	Torquay	46	9	10	27	43	88	37

SCOTTISH PREMIER DIVISION

		P	W	D	L	F	A	Pts
1	Celtic	36	20	10	6	67	38	50
2	Hearts	36	20	10	6	59	33	50
3	Dundee United	36	18	11	7	59	31	47
4	Aberdeen	36	16	12	8	62	31	44
5	Rangers	36	13	9	14	53	45	35
6	Dundee	36	14	7	15	45	51	35
7	St Mirren	36	13	5	18	42	63	31
8	Hibernian	36	11	6	19	49	63	28
9	Motherwell	36	7	6	23	33	66	20
10	Clydebank	36	6	8	22	29	77	20

SCOTTISH FIRST DIVISION

		P	W	D	L	F	A	Pts
1	Hamilton	39	24	8	7	77	44	56
2	Falkirk	39	17	11	11	57	39	45
3	Kilmarnock	39	18	8	13	62	49	44
4	Forfar	39	17	10	12	51	43	44
5	East Fife	39	14	15	10	54	46	43
6	Dumbarton	39	16	11	12	59	52	43
7	Morton	39	14	11	14	57	63	39
8	Partick	39	10	16	13	53	64	36
9	Airdrie	39	12	11	16	51	50	35
10	Brechin	39	13	9	17	58	64	35
11	Clyde	39	9	17	13	49	59	35
12	Montrose	39	10	14	15	43	54	34
13	Ayr	39	10	11	18	41	60	31
14	Alloa	39	6	14	19	49	74	26

SCOTTISH SECOND DIVISION

		P	W	D	L	F	A	Pts
1	Dunfermline	39	23	11	5	91	47	57
2	Queen of the S	39	23	9	7	71	36	55
3	Meadowbank	39	19	11	9	68	45	49
4	Queens Park	39	19	8	12	61	39	46
5	Stirling	39	18	8	13	57	43	44
6	St Johnstone	39	18	6	15	63	59	42
7	Stenhousemuir	39	16	8	15	55	63	40
8	Arbroath	39	15	9	15	56	50	39
9	Raith	39	15	7	17	67	65	37
10	Cowdenbeath	39	14	9	16	52	53	37
11	East Stirling	39	11	6	22	49	69	28
12	Berwick	39	7	11	21	45	80	25
13	Albion	39	8	8	23	38	86	24
14	Stranraer	39	9	5	25	41	83	23

FA CUP 1985-86

FOURTH ROUND

Arsenal v Rotherham United	5-1
Aston VIlla v Millwall	1-1, 0-1
Chelsea v Liverpool	1-2
Everton v Blackburn Rovers	3-1
Hull City v Brighton	2-3
Luton Town v Bristol Rovers	4-0
Manchester City v Watford	1-1, 0-0, 1-3
Notts County v Tottenham Hotspur	1-1, 0-5
Peterborough v Carlisle	1-0
Reading v Bury	1-1, 0-3
Sheffield United v Derby	0-1
Sheffield Wednesday v Orient	5-0
Sunderland v Manchester United	0-0, 0-3
Southampton v Wigan Athletic	3-0
West Ham United v Ipswich	0-0, 1-1, 1-0
York City v Altrincham	2-0

FIFTH ROUND

Derby v Sheffield Wednesday	1-1, 0-2
Luton Town v Arsenal	2-2, 0-0, 3-0
Peterborough v Brighton	2-2, 0-1
Southampton v Millwall	0-0, 1-0
Tottenham Hotspur v Everton	1-2
Watford v Bury	1-1, 3-0
West Ham United v Manchester United	1-1, 2-0
York City v Liverpool	1-1, 1-3

QUARTER-FINALS

Brighton v Southampton	0-2
Liverpool v Watford	0-0, 2-1
Luton Town v Everton	2-2, 0-1
Sheffield Wednesday v West Ham United	2-1

SEMI-FINALS

Everton v Sheffield Wednesday	2-1
Liverpool v Southampton	2-0

FINAL

Everton v Liverpool	1-3

SCOTTISH FA CUP 1985-86

FOURTH ROUND

Alloa v Motherwell	1-2
Arbroath v Aberdeen	0-1
Celtic v Queens Park	2-1
Dundee v Airdrieonians	2-0
Dundee United v Kilmarnock	1-1, 1-0
Hamilton v Hearts	1-2
Hibernian v Ayr United	1-0
St Mirren v Falkirk	1-1, 3-0

QUARTER-FINALS

Dundee v Aberdeen	2-2, 1-2
Hearts v St Mirren	4-1
Hibernian v Celtic	4-3
Motherwell v Dundee United	0-1

SEMI-FINALS

Dundee United v Hearts	0-1
Hibernian v Aberdeen	0-3

FINAL

Hearts v Aberdeen	0-3

FIRST DIVISION

		P	W	D	L	F	A	Pts
1	Everton	42	26	8	8	76	31	86
2	Liverpool	42	23	8	11	72	42	77
3	Tottenham	42	21	8	13	68	43	71
4	Arsenal	42	20	10	12	58	35	70
5	Norwich	42	17	17	8	53	51	68
6	Wimbledon	42	19	9	14	57	50	66
7	Luton	42	18	12	12	47	45	66
8	Nottm Forest	42	18	11	13	64	51	65
9	Watford	42	18	9	15	67	54	63
10	Coventry	42	17	12	13	50	45	63
11	Man United	42	14	14	14	52	45	56
12	Southampton	42	14	10	18	69	68	52
13	Sheffield Wed	42	13	13	16	58	59	52
14	Chelsea	42	13	13	16	53	64	52
15	West Ham	42	14	10	18	52	67	52
16	QPR	42	13	11	18	48	64	50
17	Newcastle	42	12	11	19	47	65	47
18	Oxford	42	11	13	18	44	69	46
19	Charlton	42	11	11	20	45	55	44
20	Leicester	42	11	9	22	54	76	42
21	Man City	42	8	15	19	36	57	39
22	Aston Villa	42	8	12	22	45	79	36

SECOND DIVISION

		P	W	D	L	F	A	Pts
1	Derby Co	42	25	9	8	64	38	84
2	Portsmouth	42	23	9	10	53	28	78
3	Oldham	42	22	9	11	65	44	75
4	Leeds	42	19	11	12	58	44	68
5	Ipswich	42	17	13	12	59	43	64
6	Crystal Palace	42	19	5	18	51	53	62
7	Plymouth	42	16	13	13	62	57	61
8	Stoke	42	16	10	16	63	53	58
9	Sheffield Utd	42	15	13	14	50	49	58
10	Bradford	42	15	10	17	62	62	55
11	Barnsley	42	14	13	15	49	52	55
12	Blackburn	42	15	10	17	45	55	55
13	Reading	42	14	11	17	52	59	53
14	Hull	42	13	14	15	41	55	53
15	West Brom	42	13	12	17	51	49	51
16	Millwall	42	14	9	19	39	45	51
17	Huddersfield	42	13	12	17	54	61	51
18	Shrewsbury	42	15	6	21	41	53	51
19	Birmingham	42	11	17	14	47	59	50
20	Sunderland	42	12	12	18	49	59	48
21	Grimsby	42	10	14	18	39	59	44
22	Brighton	42	9	12	21	37	54	39

THIRD DIVISION

		P	W	D	L	F	A	Pts
1	Bournemouth	46	29	10	7	76	40	97
2	Middlesborough	46	28	10	8	67	30	94
3	Swindon	46	25	12	9	77	47	87
4	Wigan	46	25	10	11	83	60	85
5	Gillingham	46	23	9	14	65	48	78
6	Bristol City	46	21	14	11	63	36	77
7	Notts County	46	21	13	12	77	56	76
8	Walsall	46	22	9	15	80	67	75
9	Blackpool	46	16	16	14	74	59	64
10	Mansfield	46	15	16	15	52	55	61
11	Brentford	46	15	15	16	64	66	60
12	Port Vale	46	15	12	19	76	70	57
13	Doncaster	46	14	15	17	56	62	57
14	Rotherham	46	15	12	19	48	57	57
15	Chester	46	13	17	16	61	59	56
16	Bury	46	14	13	19	54	60	55
17	Chesterfield	46	13	15	18	56	69	54
18	Fulham	46	12	17	17	59	77	53
19	Bristol Rovers	46	13	12	21	49	75	51
20	York	46	12	13	21	55	79	49
21	Bolton	46	10	15	21	46	58	45
22	Carlisle	46	10	8	28	39	78	38
23	Darlington	46	7	16	23	45	77	37
24	Newport	46	8	13	25	49	86	37

FOURTH DIVISION

		P	W	D	L	F	A	Pts
1	Northampton	46	30	9	7	103	53	99
2	Preston	46	26	12	8	72	47	90
3	Southend	46	25	5	16	68	55	80
4	Wolves	46	24	7	15	69	50	79
5	Colchester	46	21	7	18	64	56	70
6	Aldershot	46	20	10	16	64	57	70
7	Orient	46	20	9	17	64	61	69
8	Scunthorpe	46	18	12	16	73	57	66
9	Wrexham	46	15	20	11	70	51	65
10	Peterborough	46	17	14	15	57	50	65
11	Cambridge	46	17	11	18	60	62	62
12	Swansea	46	17	11	18	56	61	62
13	Cardiff	46	15	16	15	48	50	61
14	Exeter	46	11	23	12	53	49	56
15	Halifax	46	15	10	21	59	74	55
16	Hereford	46	14	11	21	60	61	53
17	Crewe	46	13	14	19	70	72	53
18	Hartlepool	46	11	18	17	44	65	51
19	Stockport	46	13	12	21	40	69	51
20	Tranmere	46	11	17	18	54	72	50
21	Rochdale	46	11	17	18	54	73	50
22	Burnley	46	12	13	21	53	74	49
23	Torquay	46	10	18	18	56	72	48
24	Lincoln	46	12	12	22	45	65	48

PLAY-OFFS

In order to reduce the number of First Division clubs to 20 over two seasons, a system of play-offs was used to determine some promotion and relegation issues

Leeds	1	Oldham	0	
Oldham	2	Leeds	1	(aet)
Ipswich	0	Charlton	0	
Charlton	2	Ipswich	1	
Charlton	1	Leeds	0	
Leeds	1	Charlton	0	
Charlton	2	Leeds	1	(aet)

(at St Andrews)
Charlton remain in First Division

Gillingham	3	Sunderland	2	
Sunderland	4	Gillingham	3	(aet)
Wigan	2	Swindon	3	
Swindon	0	Wigan	0	
Gillingham	1	Swindon	0	
Swindon	2	Gillingham	1	(aet)
Swindon	2	Gillingham	0	

(at Selhurst Park)
Swindon promoted to Second Division;
Sunderland relegated to Third Division

Aldershot	1	Bolton	0	
Bolton	2	Aldershot	2	(aet)
Colchester	0	Wolves	2	
Wolves	0	Colchester	0	
Aldershot	2	Wolves	0	
Wolves	0	Aldershot	1	

Aldershot promoted to Third Division;
Bolton Wanderers relegated to Fourth Division

FA CUP 1986-87

FIFTH ROUND

Aston Villa v Barnsley	2-0
Leeds v QPR	2-1
Sheffield Wed v West Ham United	1-1, 2-0
Stoke v Coventry	0-1
Tottenham Hotspur v Newcastle	1-0
Walsall v Watford	1-1, 4-4, 0-1
Wigan v Hull	3-0
Wimbledon v Everton	3-1

QUARTER-FINALS

Arsenal v Watford	1-3
Sheffield Wednesday v Coventry	1-3
Wigan v Leeds	0-2
Wimbledon v Tottenham Hotspur	0-2

SEMI-FINALS

Tottenham Hotspur v Watford	4-1
Coventry v Leeds	3-2

FINAL

Coventry v Tottenham Hotspur	3-2

SCOTTISH PREMIER DIVISION

		P	W	D	L	F	A	Pts
1	Rangers	44	31	7	6	85	23	69
2	Celtic	44	27	9	8	90	41	63
3	Dundee United	44	24	12	8	66	37	60
4	Aberdeen	44	21	16	7	63	29	58
5	Hearts	44	21	14	9	64	43	56
6	Dundee	44	18	12	14	74	57	48
7	St Mirren	44	12	12	20	36	51	36
8	Motherwell	44	11	12	21	43	64	34
9	Hibernian	44	10	13	21	44	70	33
10	Falkirk	44	8	10	26	31	70	26
11	Clydebank	44	6	12	26	35	93	24
12	Hamilton	44	6	9	29	39	93	21

SCOTTISH FIRST DIVISION

		P	W	D	L	F	A	Pts
1	Morton	44	24	9	11	88	56	57
2	Dunfermline	44	23	10	11	61	41	56
3	Dumbarton	44	23	7	14	67	52	53
4	East Fife	44	15	21	8	68	55	51
5	Airdrie	44	20	11	13	58	46	51
6	Kilmarnock	44	17	11	16	62	53	45
7	Forfar	44	14	15	15	61	63	43
8	Partick	44	12	15	17	49	54	39
9	Clyde	44	11	16	17	48	56	38
10	Queen of the S	44	11	12	21	50	71	34
11	Brechin	44	11	10	23	44	72	32
12	Montrose	44	9	11	24	37	74	29

SCOTTISH SECOND DIVISION

		P	W	D	L	F	A	Pts
1	Meadowbank	39	23	9	7	69	38	55
2	Raith Rovers	39	16	20	3	73	44	52
3	Stirling A	39	20	12	7	55	33	52
4	Ayr United	39	22	8	9	70	49	52
5	St Johnstone	39	16	13	10	59	49	45
6	Alloa	39	17	7	15	48	50	41
7	Cowdenbeath	39	16	8	15	59	55	40
8	Albion R	39	15	9	15	48	51	39
9	Queen's Park	39	9	19	11	48	49	37
10	Stranraer	39	9	11	19	41	59	29
11	Arbroath	39	11	7	21	46	66	29
12	Stenhousemuir	39	10	9	20	37	58	29
13	East Stirling	39	6	11	22	33	56	23
14	Berwick	39	8	7	24	40	69	23

SCOTTISH FA CUP 1986-87

FOURTH ROUND

Brechin v Dundee United	0-1
Clydebank v Hibernian	1-0
Dundee v Meadowbank	1-1, 1-1, 2-0
Hamilton v Motherwell	1-2
Hearts v Celtic	1-0
Morton v St Mirren	2-3
Raith v Peterhead	2-2, 3-3, 3-0
St Johnstone v Forfar	1-2

QUARTER-FINALS

Clydebank v Dundee	0-4
Dundee United v Forfar	2-2, 2-0
Hearts v Motherwell	1-1, 1-0
Raith v St Mirren	0-2

SEMI-FINALS

Dundee v Dundee United	2-3
Hearts v St Mirren	1-2

FINAL

St Mirren v Dundee United	1-0